An Atlas of Freshwater and Marine CATFISHES

A Preliminary Survey of the Siluriformes

by Dr. Warren E. Burgess

Distributed in the UNITED STATES by T.F.H. Publications, Inc., One T.F.H. Plaza, Neptune City, NJ 07753; in CANADA to the Pet Trade by H & L Pet Supplies Inc., 27 Kingston Crescent, Kitchener, Ontario N2B 2T6; Rolf C. Hagen Ltd., 3225 Sartelon Street, Montreal 382 Quebec; in CANADA to the Book Trade by Macmillan of Canada (A Division of Canada Publishing Corporation), 164 Commander Boulevard, Agincourt, Ontario M1S 3C7; in ENGLAND by T.F.H. Publications Limited, Cliveden House/Priors Way/Bray, Maidenhead, Berkshire SL6 2HP, England; in AUSTRALIA AND THE SOUTH PACIFIC by T.F.H. (Australia) Pty. Ltd., Box 149, Brookvale 2100 N.S.W., Australia; in NEW ZEALAND by Ross Haines & Son, Ltd., 18 Monmouth Street, Grey Lynn, Auckland 2, New Zealand; in the PHILIPPINES by Bio-Research, 5 Lippay Street, San Lorenzo Village, Makati Rizal; in SOUTH AFRICA by Multipet Pty. Ltd., 30 Turners Avenue, Durban 4001. Published by T.F.H. Publications, Inc. Manufactured in the United States of America by T.F.H. Publications, Inc.

DEDICATION

This book is dedicated to those aquarists who have brought the catfishes out of the realm of mere "scavengers" to the status of "real" fishes that are kept for their own characteristics and personalities, and to those ichthyologists who are delving into the often difficult amd perplexing systematics of members of the Siluriformes.

TABLE OF CONTENTS

PREFACE

This book was born in part from frustration and in part from the urging of Dr. Herbert R. Axelrod. The frustration was due to the almost constant need to refer to a single reliable source dealing with catfishes instead of trying to glean information from a thousand different and often conflicting references. These references were largely scattered and many times hard to find as well as commonly erroneous and often misleading. To bring together as much of the pertinent information as possible on the catfishes into a single volume seemed desirous if not absolutely necessary. It was during one of these exasperating periods while I was searching for scraps of information that the urging of Dr. Axelrod propelled me into a study of these fishes that led to the writing of this book.

This book is by no stretch of the imagination meant to be a revision of the catfishes. This I gladly leave to my scientific colleagues who are currently endeavoring to unravel the mysteries of catfish systematics and biology. It is instead designed to provide a quick reference to the catfishes and hopefully to start someone in the right direction if they want to pursue the investigation of these fishes any further. It is also mainly designed with the aquarist in mind, for it is the aquarist who has the greatest need for such a book and will possibly be able to return information manyfold to the aquaristic and scientific communities once he has received basic information on catfish systematics and biology. It is also the aquarist who must at this time deal with many of these fishes on the basis of a common name or, worse yet, an incorrect name, leading to a great deal of confusion when trying to communicate his findings to others or frustration and failure when searching for information about his fishes.

The text of this book is presented in as simple and straightforward a manner as possible. An introduction is presented dealing with the catfishes in general, giving some background information on their anatomy and biology so that the layman can better understand the data and descriptions given in later chapters. These later chapters are restricted to a discussion of the families of catfishes, each chapter dealing with a single family as it is now understood. These family chapters include the basic characteristics of the family, a review of the genera included in the family (with descriptions and keys wherever possible), pertinent information about the catfishes of the family as concerns their natural history and biology, and any information available on the keeping of any of the species of the family in an aquarium and how to breed them.

Obviously, the information available on each family is dependent upon the amount of research and aquarium keeping that has been accomplished on members of that family. The treatment of each family will differ, therefore, as to its completeness, with some thoroughly covered and others just barely touched upon. Even within a family the available information may differ greatly, with perhaps one genus or species very well known as far as its systematics and biology are concerned, and the next genus or species virtually unknown. Sometimes information is available on a catfish or catfish group only through the scientific literature, whereas sometimes it may only be available through the efforts and popular articles of aquarists (all too often overlooked or not easily available to scientists).

I would like to request that any readers of this book who are able to expand on some of the knowledge included on these pages or who wish to correct any misinformation therein (no source is infallible) please contact me. In the event there is another edition of this book, I will try to incorporate the information from such communications.

It is always the hope of an author that his work will benefit someone in some way and perhaps spur some people on to investigate further into the subject matter of the book. It is therefore my hope that this book is not the end of something, but a beginning. . . .

This volume contains the greatest assemblage of color photographs of catfishes ever brought together under a single cover. Only three of the 32 families are not represented here (Cranoglanididae, Olyridae, and Scoloplacidae), two of these having only a single described species each, and there are many photos of rare species and of species rarely photographed. An example of the last-mentioned is *Diplomystes papillosus* from Chile.

The quality of the photos normally ranges from good to excellent, but occasionally there is a poorer one of a species that could otherwise not be included. I hope you will agree that even a poor photo (rather than none at all) will impart information that might be helpful to the reader. Such photos are kept to an absolute minimum. If replacement photos should become available they will certainly be used in any subsequent editions.

At times there are several photos of the same species. In most cases the different photos depict variations in the species either from differing localities or from the same population. Only by knowing the limits of a species's variation can one really begin to understand the species. It is not uncommon that individuals of a single species studied from different locations are subsequently described as separate subspecies or even separate species.

Identifications given for the species are the best possible at the moment, but with the new surge of interest in catfishes almost every issue of a systematic journal includes new information, even revisions, of catfish genera or species. Experts working on various families were contacted whenever possible to help with the identifications, but even they could not succeed at times without being able to see certain diagnostic characters or knowing the geographic origin of the individual photographed. For example, many species (and even genera) are distinguished by the presence or shape of tooth patches on the roof of the mouth, characters not readily visible in normal photos. Sometimes even a "best guess" is not possible, and the genus name followed by "sp." or such indications as "Unidentified loricariid" are the only identifications that can be made. Hopefully additional and more accurate names can be placed on these fishes in subsequent editions. Photos of museum specimens are included because accurate identifications could be made of preserved material, and some of these photos are of species that otherwise could not be included. It is also of interest to compare a museum specimen with a photo of a living individual to see how different they appear. You can then begin to understand what are some of the obstacles an ichthyologist encounters. Following the scientific name under a photo there is a geographic locality or range. If the exact locality where a specimen was captured is known it is indicated after the scientific name without parentheses; if the exact locality is not known the **smallest** range known is given in parens. This may be a river system, a country, several countries, or even a continent for broad-ranging species.

The photos for the most part are in the same systematic order as the families in the text portion of this book, i.e., Diplomystidae first and Astroblepidae last. Whenever possible, members of the same genus are grouped on one plate or at least on neighboring plates. This will help in the comparison of closely related species. Several spawning sequences and habitat photos are included as well. Of particular interest, perhaps, are the photos from the Teotonio rapids where such species as *Merodontotus tigrinus* and *Brachyplatystoma* spp. are captured.

INTRODUCTION

Catfishes in General

Catfishes are an extremely large group of diverse fishes generally regarded as a single order, the Siluriformes (sometimes also called the Nematognathi), or as a suborder, Siluroidei, of the order Cypriniformes. In most modern classifications, including the most followed one of Greenwood, Weitzman, Rosen, and Myers (1966), the catfishes are considered an order, the Siluriformes, and that is the classification that will be followed in this book as well.

The order Siluriformes is divided into approximately 31 families by Greenwood, et al. (1966) (Table 1), with the small family Scoloplacidae added later. With the work currently in progress by various researchers, it would not be surprising to find that this number will more than likely change in the near future. It is my opinion that the number of families will decrease rather than increase as research continues.

Table 1. List of the families of catfishes (order Siluriformes) as accepted by Greenwood, Rosen, Weitzman, and Myers (1966).

Diplomystidae	Mochokidae
Ictaluridae	Ariidae
Bagridae	Doradidae
Cranoglanididae	Auchenipteridae
Siluridae	Aspredinidae
Schilbeidae	Plotosidae
Pangasiidae	Pimelodidae
Amblycipitidae	Ageneiosidae
Amphiliidae	Hypophthalmidae
Akysidae	Helogeneidae
Sisoridae	Cetopsidae
Clariidae	Trichomycteridae
Heteropneustidae	Callichthyidae
Chacidae	Loricariidae
Olyridae	Astroblepidae
Malapteruridae	

Estimates of approximately 2,211 species in some 400 genera of catfishes have been made for the entire order, of which some 1,300 inhabit the waters of the New World (Nelson, 1984). The remainder are scattered over the other continents of the world, with the heaviest concentrations in the tropical regions of Africa and Asia. The distribution of the catfishes seems to be limited somewhat by temperature, for few or no species extend into the extreme southern portions of South America or the northern areas of North America and Eurasia. The most primitive catfishes are said to exist as relicts in South America (Gosline, 1975).

The vast majority of catfishes inhabit fresh waters, but two families, the Plotosidae and the Ariidae, have considerable representation in fully marine environments as well as some brackish and coastal freshwater species. A number of species of various other families have invaded, to some extent, brackish waters. It has been noted that some of the marine catfishes are still tied to fresh water for they migrate up rivers to spawn.

Air Breathing Adaptations

Catfishes are quite varied also in their mode of living, occupying vastly differing environments. Some species inhabit the cool, rapidly flowing waters of mountain streams, whereas others may be found in the sluggish or still waters of lakes and ponds. Many prefer or even require clean, clear, highly oxygenated waters, while others can exist in stagnant, silt-laden, or even polluted waters of swamps where oxygen is present at extremely low levels. Some species even have the ability to survive when their water supply temporarily disappears due to drought or other problems and may even leave the drying-out ditch to travel overland to search for a more suitable place to live. These feats are made possible in part by special respiratory organs or

Representations of the 32 catfish families.

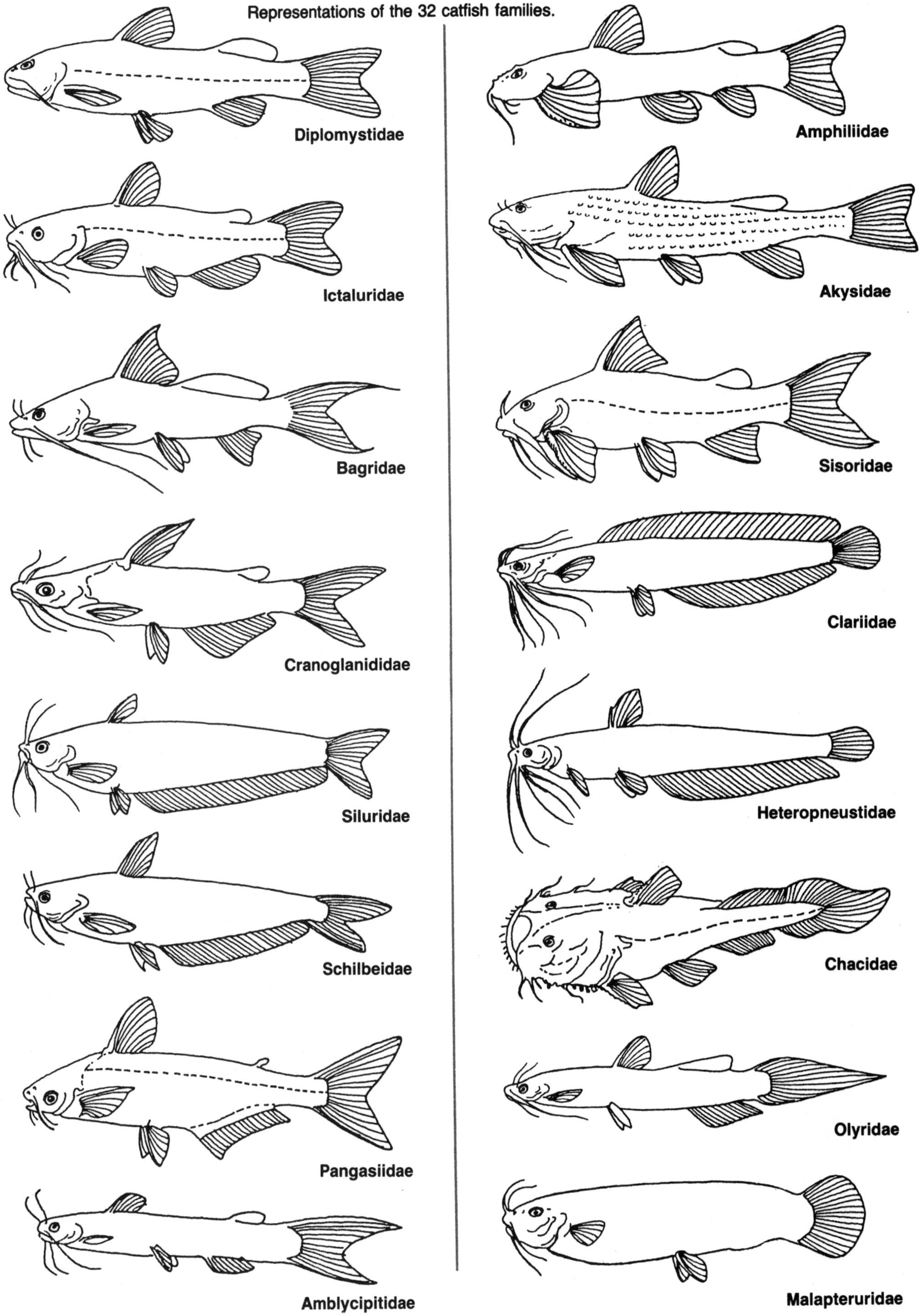

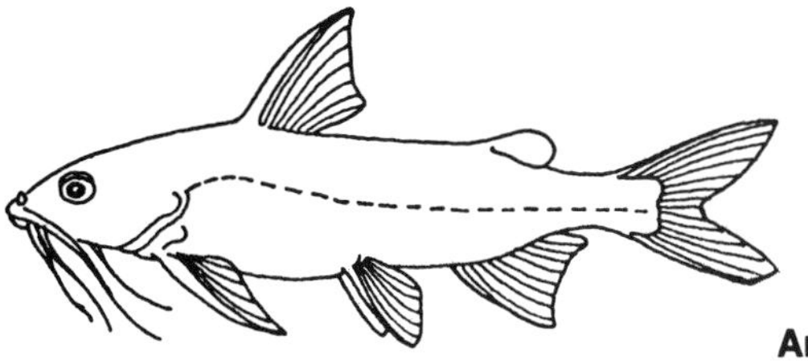
Ariidae

Plotosidae

Mochokidae

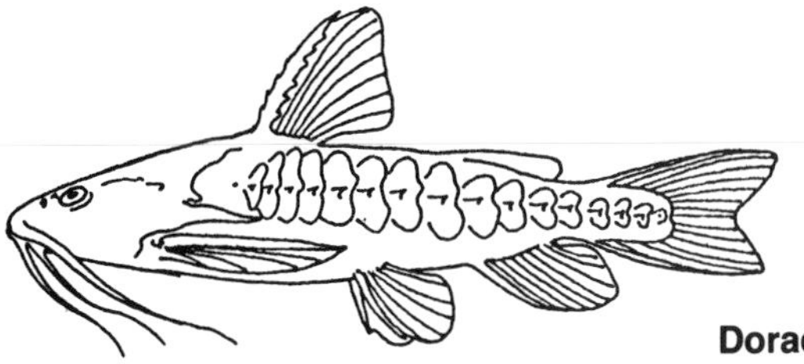
Doradidae

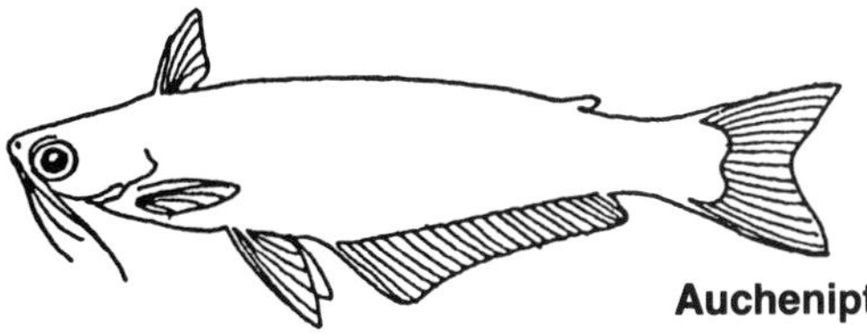
Auchenipteridae

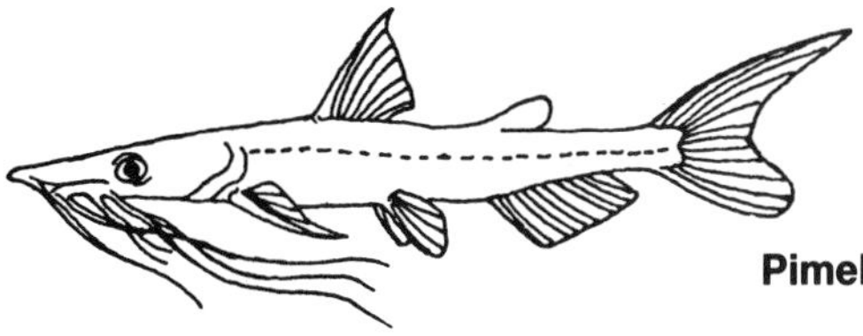
Pimelodidae

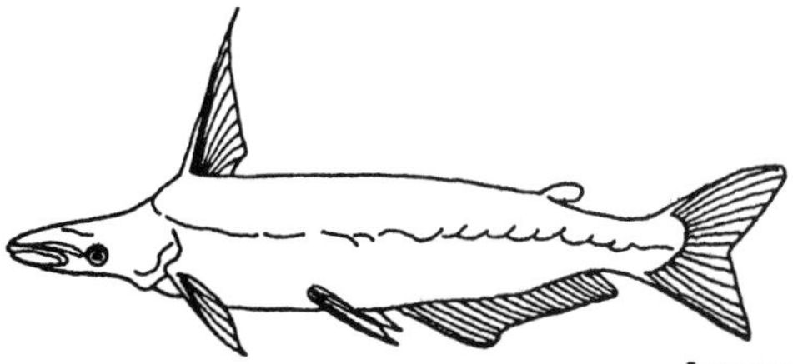
Ageneiosidae

Helogenidae

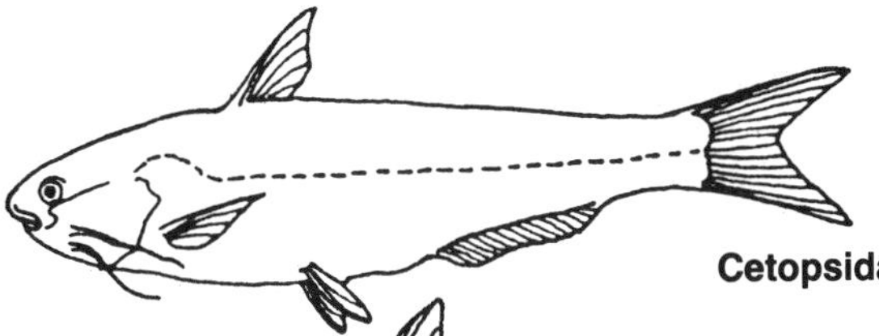
Cetopsidae

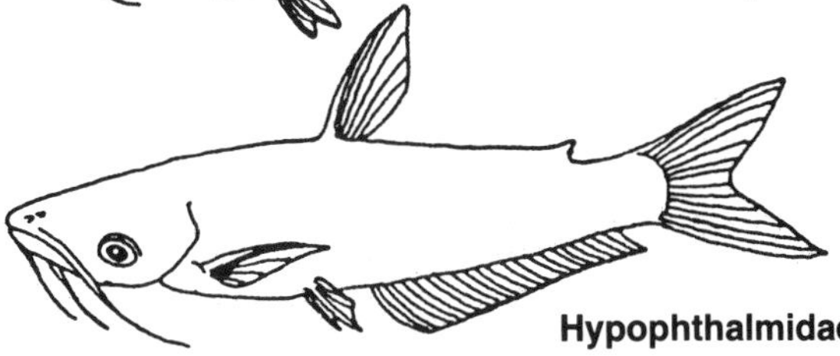
Hypophthalmidae

Aspredinidae

Trichomycteridae

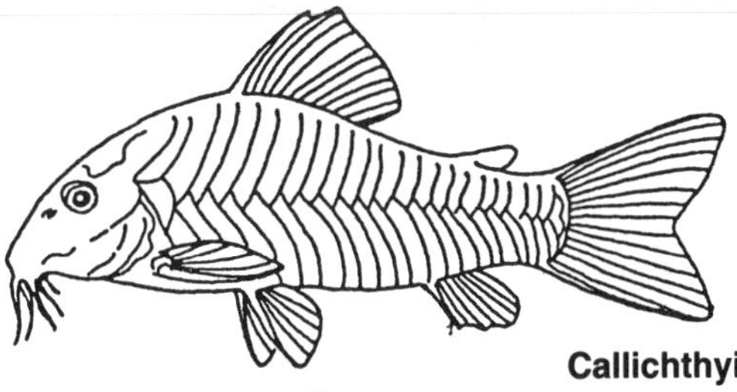
Callichthyidae

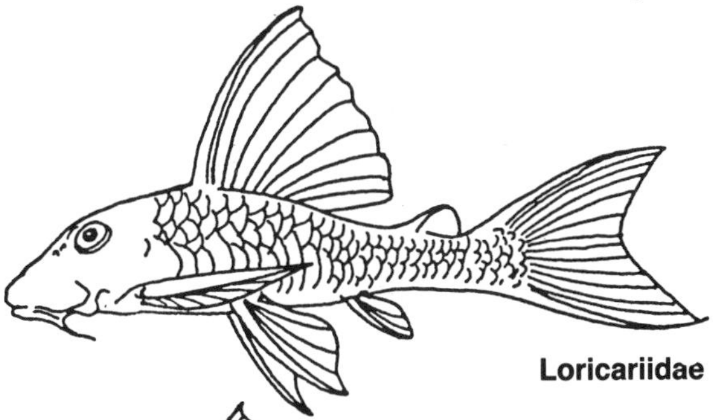
Loricariidae

Astroblepidae

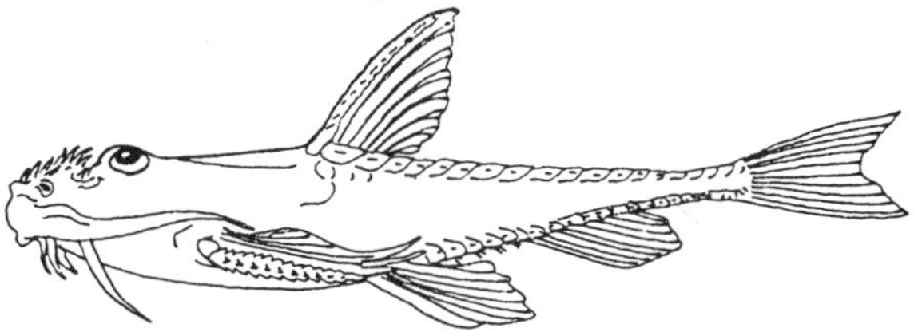
Scoloplacidae

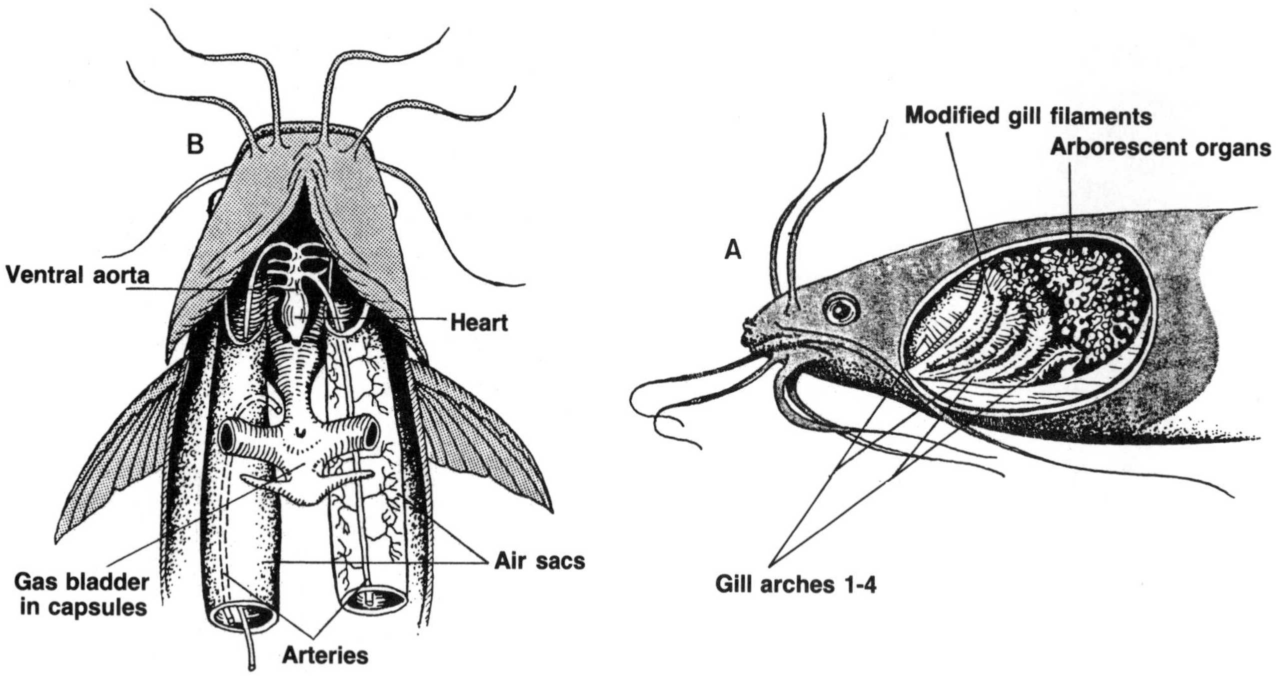

Two types of air-breathing adaptations in the Siluriformes: (A) *Clarias*, a labyrinthic catfish; (B) *Heteropneustes*, an airsac catfish. The swim bladder and intestines may be involved in air-breathing in other catfishes. (After Lagler, et al., 1962.)

other means of extracting the meager supplies of oxygen available from their environment or utilizing atmospheric oxygen in some way.

Loricariids and callichthyids, for example, sometimes use the intestine for respiration by swallowing a certain amount of air from the water's surface that is passed down to the intestine where special thin-walled capillaries lining the intestinal walls extract the oxygen, the remaining gases being voided through the vent. *Pangasius sutchi*, on the other hand, has been found to be an obligate air breather with the accessory respiratory organ being the swim bladder (Browman & Kramer, 1985). Many aquarists have observed their catfishes making quick darts to the surface like the air-breathing anabantoids. *Heterobranchus* has elaborate tree-like structures growing from the upper ends of the gill arches and extending into a pair of specialized air chambers situated above the gills. *Heteropneustes* has somewhat similar organs but the air chambers bear a marked resemblance to lungs, extending back as far as the tail as long tubular sacs growing out from the branchial cavity between the second and third gill arches and situated close to the backbone. The epithelial lining of the cavities in these fishes and the "trees" in *Heterobranchus* have a fine structure similar to that of gill filaments. *Clarias* has the opening between the second and third gill arches leading to two sacs with highly vascularized bush-like or shrub-like arborescent structures called "trees." Bullheads (*Ictalurus*), which often live in stagnant waters, are relatively unaffected by changes in carbon dioxide levels. It has even been reported that in some algae-eating catfishes the oxygen available in the algae is utilized by the catfish when it reaches the highly vascularized digestive tract.

The Problems of Attaching to Rocks

The catfishes that attach themselves by their mouth to the substrate also have problems in breathing, for if they do not retain the suction created by their mouth they are apt to lose their hold on the surface of the substrate and be swept away in the current. Some of these catfishes, such as the loach-like hillstream catfishes of Asia (families Sisoridae

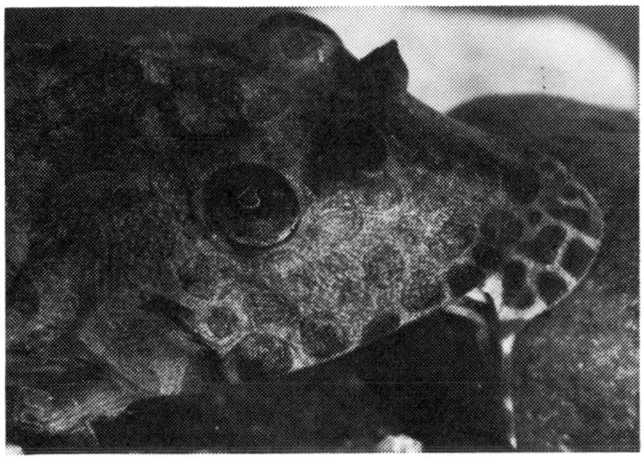

Mouthparts are often adapted for maintaining an attachment to the substrate as in this loricariid. Photo by Harald Schultz.

and Akysidae), have solved this problem by either suspending their breathing for a short time or by possessing modifications of the mouth and gill regions allowing them to accomplish both feats simultaneously, such as grooves protected by the barbels that allow the fish to take in water with a minimal reduction in the suction. Water is pumped in and out solely by the force of opercular movements. In other catfishes (for example, *Astroblepus* of South America) the gill cover is modified so that there are inhalent and exhalent slits or openings that allow respiration to go on as usual while the mouth is occupied with keeping the fish attached to the substrate.

In the fast-flowing mountain streams, then, the main device for holding the fish in position on the substrate is a ventral suctorial mouth in which the thickened, fleshy protrusible lips make very efficient suctorial devices or holdfast organs. These may be seen in such catfishes as some loricariids and some sisorids (*Glyptosternon*). In addition, streamlining has occurred in many of these same groups in the form of a depressed body. There are also extreme variations in the ventral fins, which, with the flattened ventral surface of the catfish, acts as an additional suction disc in some species of *Glyptosternon*.

This *Pseudecheneis sulcatus* has its chest area modified into a washboard-like structure which aids in its attachment to the substrate. (After Nikolsky, 1962.)

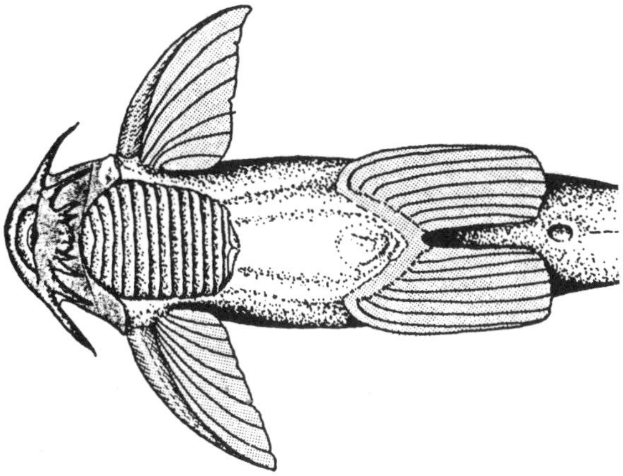

Size

The diversity in the sizes of catfishes is very great, with some of the largest species rivaling even the famous osteoglossid *Arapaima gigas* in dimensions. *Silurus glanis*, the European Wels, for example, is reported to attain lengths of approximately 3.3 meters and weights of 256 kg., exceptionally 5 meters and 330 kg., although most individuals do not approach these lengths. It can be said that *S. glanis*, which also occurs in brackish waters as well as inland seas that are quite saline, is the longest fish that lives primarily in fresh water, whereas *Arapaima gigas* is the longest fish that is *confined* to fresh water. The giant South American catfish *Paulicea lutkeni* (known as the Manguruyu) has been said to approach and even surpass these sizes, but there is no confirmation. *Pangasianodon gigas* of the Mekong River is reported to reach a length of at least 2½ meters and perhaps grows even larger. In contrast to these giants, there are catfishes that fully mature at lengths of no more than 35 mm, such as *Corydoras pygmaeus*.

Activity

Some species of catfishes are fairly accomplished and active swimmers and have taken up a midwater existence. These are types that do best in small schools, such as the glass catfishes, *Schilbe*, the so-called grass-cutters, and the iridescent sharks. They are likely to become nervous wrecks if kept alone (without members of their own species) in an aquar-

Many species of mochokids, particularly of the genus *Synodontis*, swim in an upside-down position as shown here. Photo by D. Palmer.

ium. Most of the catfishes, however, are relatively slow or sluggish swimmers and live on or very near the substrate. In the family Mochokidae, many of the species have adopted an unusual mode of living—that of swimming upside down! This behavior has been known for many, many years. In fact, *Synodontis batensoda* (also called *Brachysynodontis batensoda*) of the Nile was known as early as ancient Egyptian times and was frequently depicted in the upside-down position in sculpture and wall paintings. Unlike "normally" colored fishes that are dark above and light below, many upside-down catfishes have reversed countershaded coloration with the darker colors situated ventrally and the lighter shades dorsally. *S. batensoda* also has a ventrally displaced swim bladder that aids the fish in maintaining this unusual swimming position.

Defense

Many catfishes protect themselves by means of very sharp and sometimes poisonous spines at the leading edges of their dorsal and pectoral fins, the latter spines perhaps being the more potent. Most of the damage to humans is done when the catfishes are inadvertently stepped on or carelessly handled. Spines are believed to have developed as defensive weapons against predator pressure rather than as offensive ones, i.e., they are passive stingers. Yet there are some species that are very aggressive and will actually attack any enemy, even humans. Such an example is *Heteropneustes fossilis* of India, which has a painful and potentially deadly sting. Stings from pimelodids are not too dangerous for there is only little venom involved, but stings from certain plotosids are so bad they might possibly result in the death of the victim. Fishermen soon learn the ways of dealing with catfishes caught in their nets. In many cases as soon as the netted catfishes are brought near, the dangerous spines are broken off or cut off so that they are rendered harmless. The poison involved is generally produced by special glands at the base of the spine or by special glandular cells in the epidermal tissue covering the spines. The glands may open through pores at the base of the spines, and the poison is injected by the spine. The effect on man is a stinging to burning sensation that may intensify to excruciating pain depending upon the species involved. Occasionally there is a numbing sensation that is followed by swelling or even by local paralysis. Although most stings are very painful, they rarely are fatal. In *Noturus*,

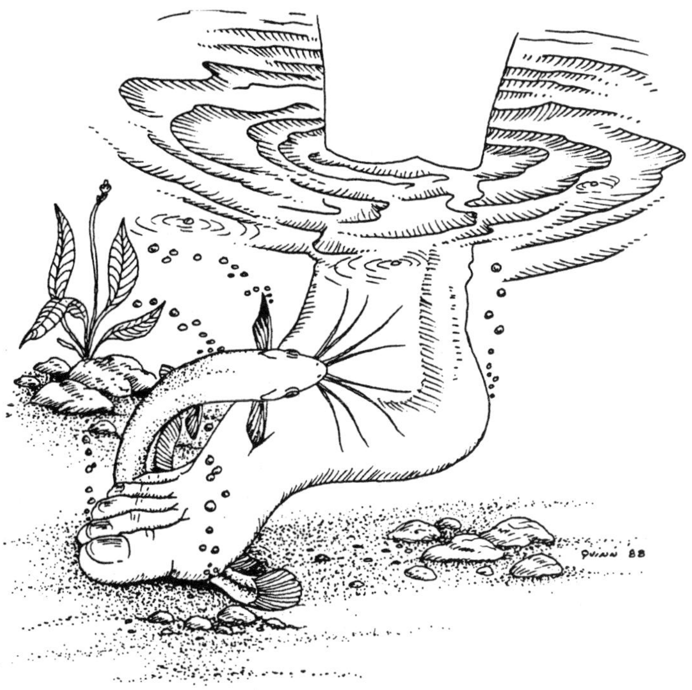

Although most catfishes will not attack, they will defend themselves. This *Heteropneustes fossilis* effectively uses its pectoral spine when stepped on. (After Halstead, 1970.)

Schilbeidae, *Heteropneustes, Galeichthys, Ictalurus, Clarias*, and *Plotosus*, among others, there seems to be more poisonous capabilities involved with the pectoral spines than with the dorsal spine.

Catfish spines, whether venomous or not, cause predaceous fishes and other fish predators (crocodilians, snakes, etc.) problems when they try to swallow the catfishes. In times of stress the catfishes will hold all their fins rigidly out, and the spines themselves are usually provided with a locking mechanism to automatically prevent them from being folded back involuntarily. A fish swallowing such a catfish finds itself in trouble and may even die as a result of punctures through various parts of its digestive tract, if, indeed, it is able to swallow the catfish at all.

Although catfishes are technically naked (without scales), in some the skin is thick and leathery while in others there is dermal armor. The armored catfishes (Loricariidae, Callichthyidae, Doradidae, Akysidae, Aspredinidae, etc.) have sacrificed their speed and agility for this defensive armor. The amount of armor ranges from plates almost completely encasing the fish to scattered plates along the midside. In the callichthyids, for example, there is a double row of scutes along the side, one pair for each muscle segment or vertebra (metameric), whereas in the loricariids there are several rows of bony shields along the sides and back with the chest and abdomen naked or with only small plates. The lateral plates may be provided with sharp keels or small spinules set in sockets. These spinules are similar in structure to the teeth and dermal denticles of sharks and rays, i.e., dentine capped with enamel and, in the case of the shark's teeth, bony bases. The metameric arrangement is essential for flexibility. It is very interesting to note that the astroblepids, which are considered closely related to the loricariids, are without the armor—perhaps as a result of a decrease in the number of predators in its mountain stream habitat?

The row of sharp spines associated with the lateral scutes as well as the serrated pectoral spines of this doradid can clearly be seen in this photo of *Platydoras* by Harald Schultz.

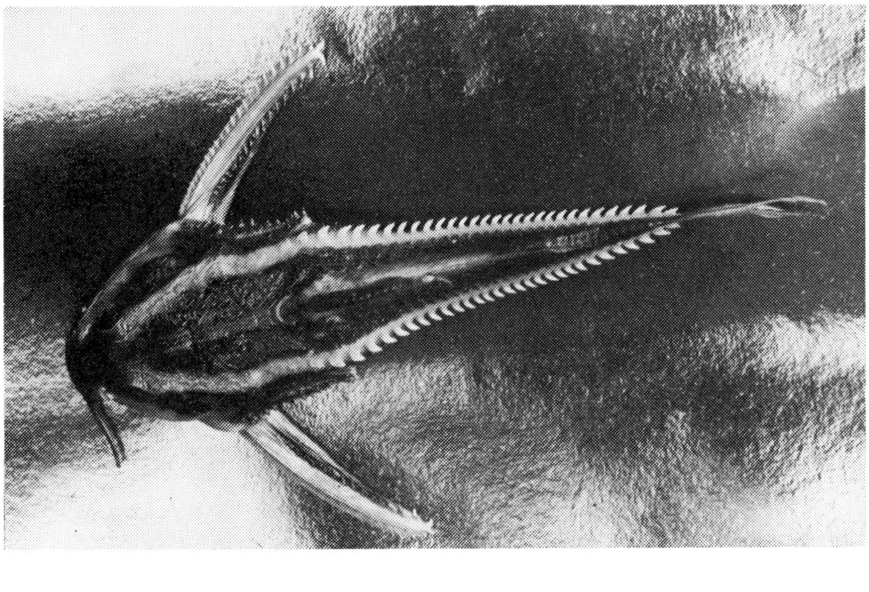

Still other defensive, and possibly also offensive, systems have been developed by catfishes. In the family Malapteruridae, the electric catfishes are able to generate an electrical charge or shock that can deter enemies or perhaps stun potential food organisms. Discharges have been measured between 100 and 450 volts, enough to give a person a jolt that could literally knock him off his feet. The electrical organ is a subcutaneous jacket covering the body; it is semitransparent and thick and flabby in appearance. More will be said about the electric catfishes under their family heading.

Finally, some catfishes have a rugose or rough texture enabling them to blend in with their background so well that they are virtually invisible. Some of the banjo catfishes (Aspredinidae) kept in the confines of home aquaria may be just as camouflaged and therefore difficult to distinguish when the aquarist searches for his pet. To enhance the strategy, in the natural environment these catfishes will lie motionless among the stones, roots, or other debris that they resemble so that movement will not attract attention and give them away. It is interesting that live catfishes of certain marketable species are avoided in Calcutta because their skin is covered with small rounded patches from mid-February to mid-April; it is believed that these catfishes spread small pox at this time. At other times of the year, when the catfishes have a "cleaner" appearance, they are more readily accepted.

Feeding and Sensory Systems

The food habits of catfishes are quite varied. Their diets range from algae obtained by scraping or rasping teeth or other structures to fishes or even higher vertebrates that they actively hunt as predators. At least one family

Two different genera of pimelodids exhibiting the extremely long maxillary barbels common to this family. These barbels are used in a sensory capacity, being provided with high concentrations of taste buds. Photo by Gerhard Marcuse.

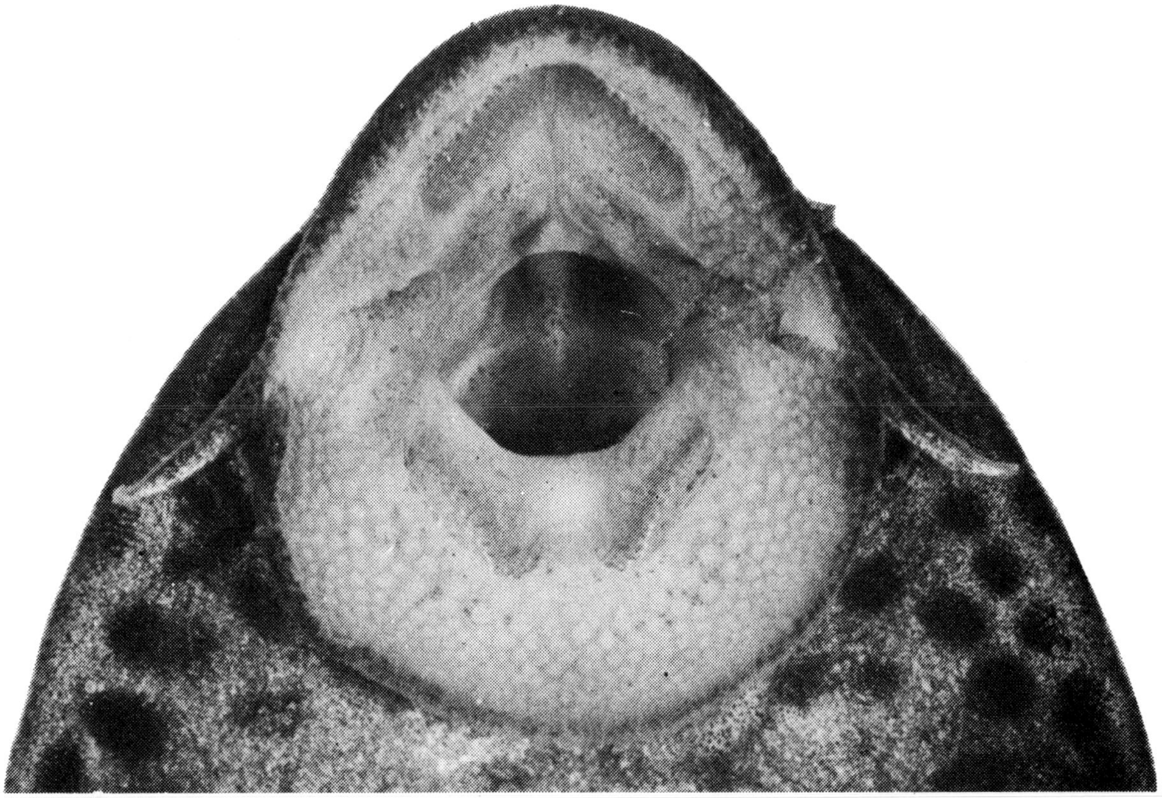

Many catfishes, like this loricariid, have teeth adapted for rasping. The sucker mouth keeps the catfish in position as the teeth go to work on the substrate. Photo by Harald Schultz.

(Trichomycteridae) contains fishes that might be regarded as true parasites. They ordinarily feed on gill tissue and blood of larger fishes. The most famous of these is the small Candiru of South America that has the ability to penetrate and become lodged, by virtue of their spines and barbs, in the urethras of people. In the true herbivores the intestine is elongated and greatly convoluted or arranged in many coils, as in the loricariids. Catfishes that suck in mud from which they extract edible organisms may at times take in a goodly amount of non-edible material. Some are able to extract the food items from the sediments and get rid of the wastes easily, while others (for example Schilbeidae, Siluridae) cannot and therefore must swallow both. This extraneous material is often found in the digestive tract along with the high concentrations of bottom organisms. Some catfishes (for example Clariidae, Schilbeidae) have been found to contain more fat in their bodies than other fishes in the same region, probably due to the specific feeding habits and their ability to better utilize certain foods that are abundant there. Finally, there are catfishes that, like some cichlids and other fishes, feed by snatching scales from the bodies of other fishes (lepidophagy). Scales constitute the bulk of the diet of some of the Indian species of the family Schilbeidae.

Catfishes detect food mainly by taste and smell, rarely by sight. They have high concentrations of taste buds on their barbels; the more and bigger the barbels, the more cells are present. Some of the pimelodids possess exceedingly long barbels. In *Platysilurus*, for example, these are longer than the entire body. Barbels are also the chief aid in locating food items in muddy waters or, in the nocturnal species, during the evening hours, and as such they have additional taste buds. In these species there are extra taste buds covering many parts of the body. More than 100,000 taste buds have been estimated to cover the body of a species of bullhead (*Ictalurus*).

Incidentally, the barbels have added functions. Like a cat's whiskers, the barbels can be used to detect the dimensions of crevices and narrow passageways. The generally smaller mandibular and mental barbels, located on the underside of the jaw, not only help detect objects but also help investigate it regarding its suitability as food. In certain species they are said to participate in straining the food before it is taken into the mouth.

Smell also plays an important part of the sensory makeup of catfishes. While they are breathing, a stream of water is pumped through the nasal sac by the movement of adjacent head bones. When the nostrils of bullheads are plugged they cannot find their food, indicating that they locate food mainly through their sense of smell. The sense of smell in ictalurids also has social implications, for the specific odor of the slime or mucus of a particular fish contributes to the recognition of individuals in their social hierarchy. Ictalurids have also been shown to be responsive to weak electrical stimulation, this sensitivity being centered in the small pit organs of the lateral line system.

Some catfishes, such as some silurids, seem to be sensitive to touch and aquarists are advised to keep handling of these species to a minimum.

Sounds

Many catfishes produce sounds, and in the aquarium hobby mention of the "talking" catfishes or "squeakers" elicits no surprise from advanced hobbyists. Some catfishes simply produce sounds by stridulation of the spines in their bases. Others have more elaborate methods involving the swim bladder. Doradids, for example, are called "croaking" catfishes; they make noise by using the swim bladder to amplify the sounds made by grinding the spines in their sockets. In a number of catfishes an apparatus known as the "elastic spring mechanism" causes the walls of the swim bladder to vibrate. In this structure two strong muscles run from the posterior part of the skull to especially modified portions of the fourth vertebra. These "springs," as they are called, have expanded ends that are attached to the front part of the swim bladder. When the muscles contract, a rumbling noise is produced by the rapidly vibrating walls of the swim bladder. The sound is perhaps intensified by the construction of the swim bladder. The swim bladder is frequently divided into two or more chambers by internal partitions. These chambers communicate freely with each other, and the gases moving across the free edges of the partitions cause them to vibrate and intensify the sound.

Weberian Apparatus

In the Siluriformes the connection between the swim bladder and the inner ear is elaborate and is formed by a set of small paired bones or ossicles. This is called the Weberian apparatus and serves to transmit changes of volume of the swim bladder to the inner ear. These ossicles are formed by modifications of the apophyses of the first four vertebrae immediately behind the skull. They constitute the *tripus* (hindmost), which actually touches the anterior wall of the swim bladder and is connected by a ligament to the second ossicle, the *intercalare*, or, if this bone is missing, to the *scaphium*, which is attached to the *claustrum*. The claustrum is quite small and touches, on each side, a membranous window of the *sinus impar*. The sinus impar is an extension of the perilymph system surrounding the inner ear and lies in the basioccipital bone of the head. Volume changes in the swim bladder activate the Weberian apparatus, which transmits the pressure changes to the perilymph and from there to the sensory cells of the labyrinth (the seat of sound reception). The function then is probably connected with alterations in pressure, thus serving to accentuate sound waves, and acts as an accessory hearing organ. In many catfishes the swim bladder is more or less encased in a capsule of bone or protective connective tissue. This has a reverse effect, lessening the pressure rather than amplifying the pressure on the perilymph. In sisorids, for example, only the anterior chamber of the swim bladder remains. This may be encapsulated but displaced so that it comes in contact with the fish's skin through a lateral window in the capsule.

The Weberian apparatus in the catfishes and cypriniform fishes seems to impart to these fishes a better sound discrimination and range of perception than in fishes that are without such modifications.

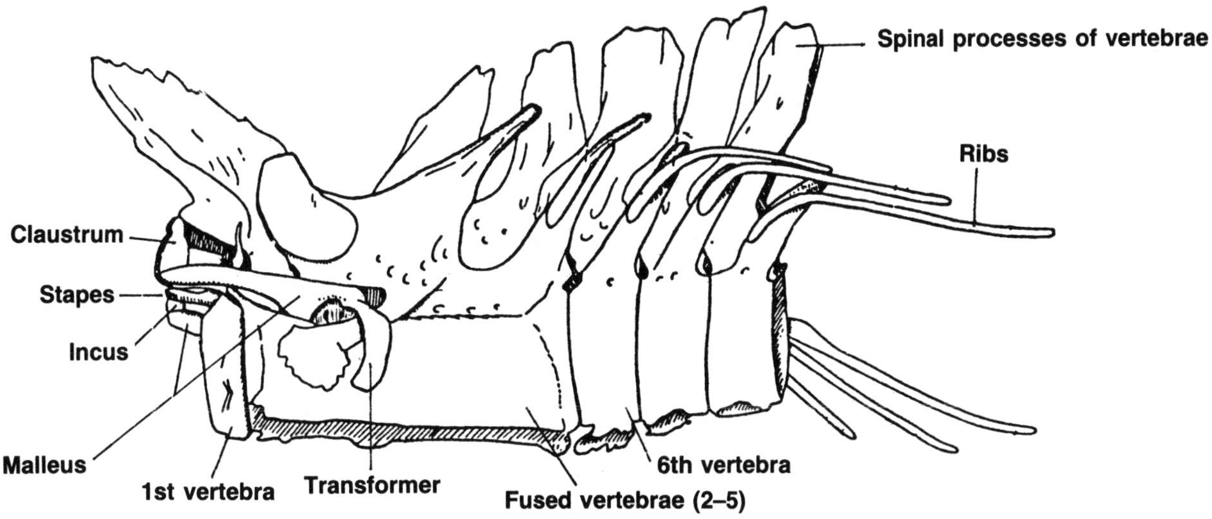

Lateral view of the Weberian ossicles and first six vertebrae of *Silurus glanis*. (From Chranilow, 1929.)

Diagramatic representation of the Weberian ossicles involved in two types of pressure transmission, indirect (A) and direct (B). Dotted lines indicate respective movement of the parts. (From Chranilow, 1929.)

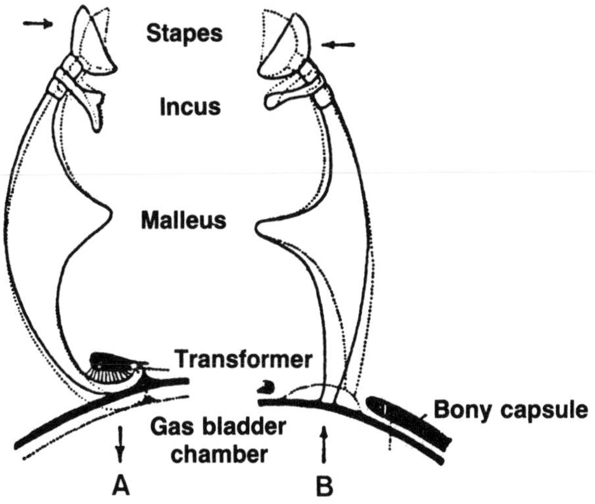

Breeding

Breeding in catfishes is no less varied than any of the other features they possess. Some species scatter eggs on the substrate like so many other fishes. Nest building is practiced in others, with the nest guarded or not by one or both parents. A few utilize mouthbrooding, and in some aspredinids the eggs are attached to the belly of the mother. Many ictalurids will excavate a crude nest in the mud bottom. Both parents share this arduous work, which may last two to three days. More secretive forms build their nests in sheltered spots such as beneath logs, in holes in the river banks, or even in some "foreign" hiding places such as rusty cans or other man-made material lying on the river bottom. The sea catfishes (Ariidae) are mostly mouthbrooders, the male doing the honors of caring for the brood. The eggs are usually very large, up to 20 mm in diameter, so that very few are produced at one time, usually 10 to 30. The fry hatch out and start to forage for themselves but are allowed for a short while the protection of their parent's mouth. Additional modes of reproduction will be covered under the individual species accounts.

Definition of the Group

With such a varied group, to actually define a "catfish" is a rather difficult proposition. The first obvious distinction from most other fishes is that they possess barbels. But, unfortunately, so do a fairly large number of other fishes so this cannot be used to exclu-

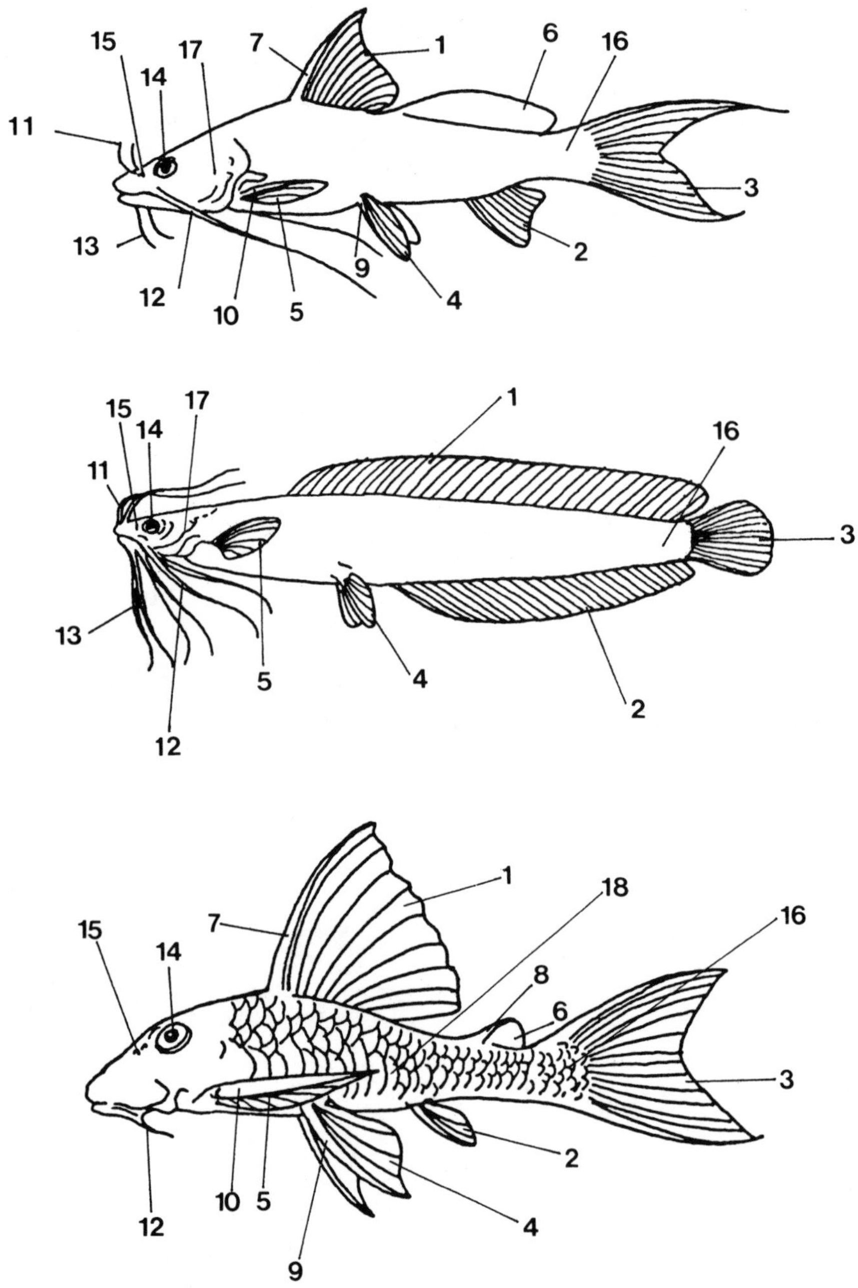

Schematic representation of three different types of catfishes showing different anatomical features.

1. Dorsal fin
2. Anal fin
3. Caudal fin
4. Ventral fins
5. Pectoral fins.
6. Adipose fin
7. Dorsal fin spine
8. Preadipose fin spine
9. Ventral fin spine
10. Pectoral fin spine
11. Nasal barbels
12. Maxillary barbels
13. Mental or mandibular barbels
14. Eye
15. Nostril
16. Caudal peduncle
17. Operculum
18. Lateral scutes

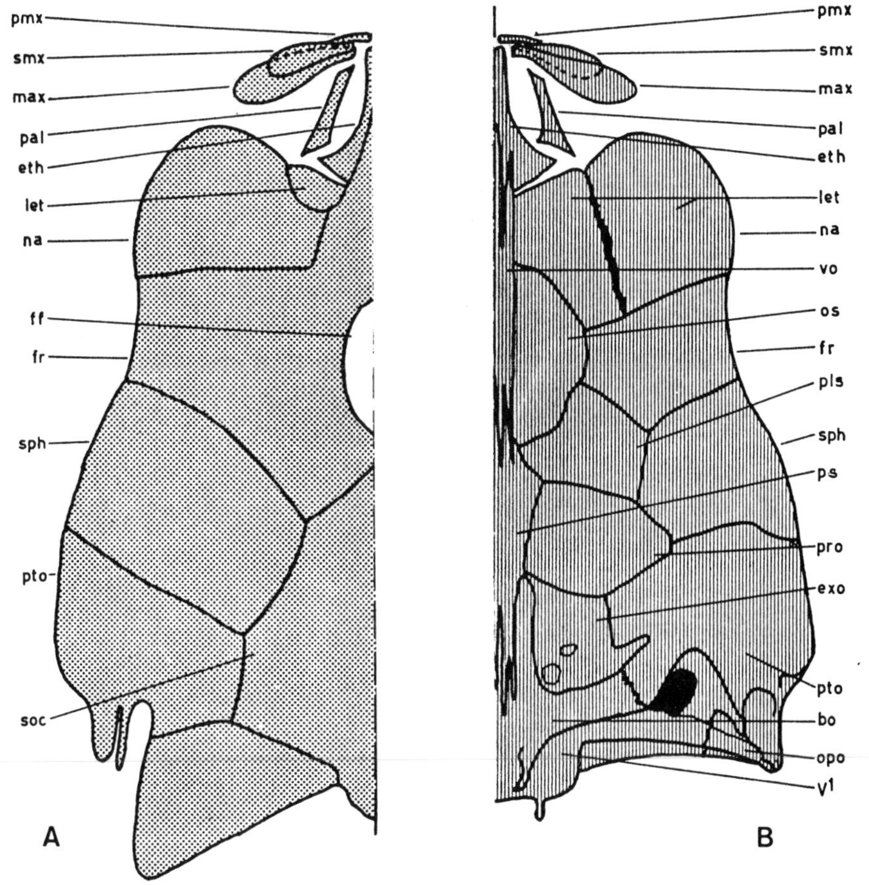

Dorsal (A) and ventral (B) views of the skull of *Callichthys callichthys* showing major bones. (From Hoedeman, 1960.)

pmx = premaxillary	let = lateral ethmoid	ps = parasphenoid
smx = supramaxillary	max = maxillary	pto = pterotic
bo = basioccipital	opo = opisthotic	smx = supramaxillary
eth = ethmoid	os = orbitosphenoid	soc = supraoccipital
exo = exoccipital	pal = palatine	sph = sphenotic
ff = frontal fontanelle	pls = pleurosphenoid	vo = vomer
fr = frontal bone	pro = prootic	V^1 first vertebra

Schematic views of a typical catfish showing some features used in descriptions.

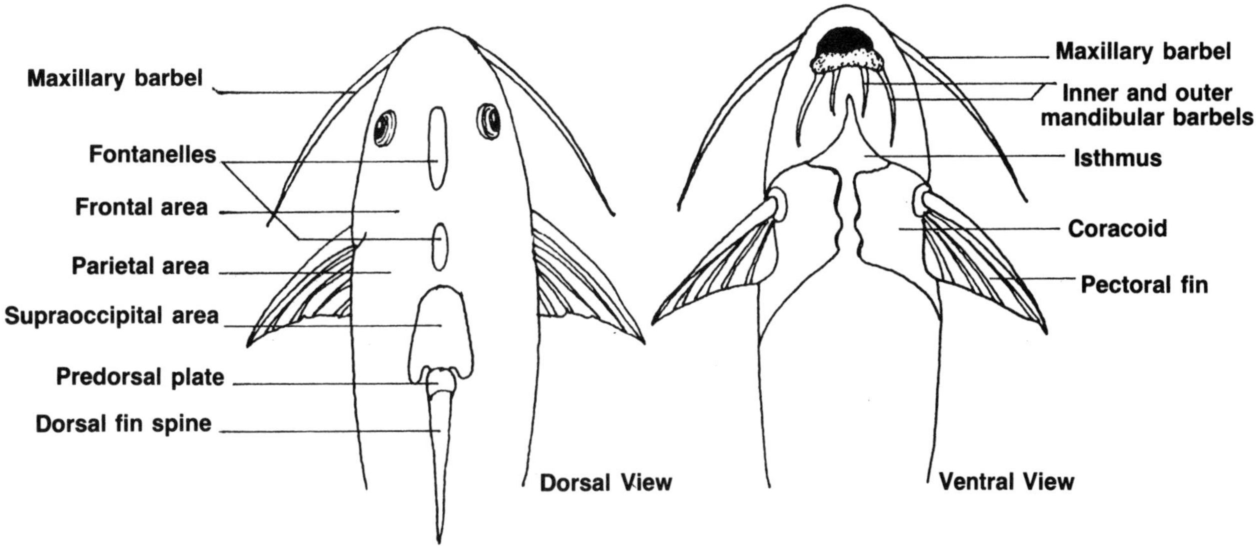

sively delineate the catfishes. They have a group of small paired bones or ossicles that connect the inner ear with the swim bladder called the Weberian apparatus, which narrows the choice considerably. There is commonly, but not always, an adipose fin. This is a flap of fatty tissue covered with skin and located on the back between the dorsal fin and the tail. It may be miniscule or quite large depending upon the species, and there may be a few soft rays supporting it or there may be a stiff spine preceding it. Catfishes are also naked (without true scales) although in some families there are bony plates present (see discussion of armor above), some of which take the form of a row of scattered plates along the sides (for example Doradidae) while others may be nearly completely covered by the plates (Loricariidae). The head of most catfishes is well ossified, with a cephalic shield in which the dermal bones may be rugose or sculptured. This shield may be prolonged by the presence of dorsal or humeral processes. The jaws are not protrusible (able to project forward) although the lips often are. The mouth is bordered by the dentaries and premaxillaries (rarely also the maxillaries), which are generally supplied with villiform teeth set in bands. The maxillaries are short, generally toothless, and serve as a base for the maxillary barbels. The vomer is near the front part of the roof of the mouth and is usually also toothed. There may be tooth plates below the palatines, the branchials usually have small conical or villiform teeth, and the pterygoids may be toothed. The parietals, intercalar, symplectic, subopercular, epineurals, and epipleurals are absent.

Catfish spines are technically not true spines as they differ in developmental history from those of the acanthopterygian fishes. They are best called "spinous rays" and are usually present in the dorsal, pectoral, and sometimes adipose fins. Catfishes are unique in the development of spinous rays in the pectoral fins. These can be quite stout and sawtoothed along one or both margins and attached to the body via an elaborate joint. *Noturus* and *Schilbeides* are provided with special poison glands at the base of these spines, and some catfishes use these spines for traveling overland (for example *Clarias*). The spinous ray of the dorsal fin is similarly formed as a modification of one soft ray and is often serrated on one or both edges, the serrations being at times quite formidable. Additionally there is a small dorsally ossified inverted V-shaped ray at the base of the dorsal spine. Catfishes are unique and easily defined by their possession of locking devices for all spines. In some instances the spinous rays are present but hidden under a layer of thick skin.

The pectoral and ventral fins are almost always distant from one another and the pectorals are inserted quite low on the body. The dorsal and adipose fins are rarely absent, but the adipose fin may disappear when the dorsal and caudal fins are combined into one continuous fin (e.g., some clariids, *Phreatobius*); the anal fin may also be combined with the caudal fin (e.g., many plotosids, some clariids). The ventral fins are abdominal in position. The principal caudal fin rays are fewer than 18, most species having 17. The hypural plates vary from six separate elements to complete fusion.

The lateral line may be ramified and may have short tubular ossicles enclosing the line. The eyes may be quite large, but usually they are small, sometimes even covered by skin or adipose tissue. There are several cave-dwelling species in which the eyes have degenerated or are even absent. The barbels have commonly taken up the function of locating food. Air breathing accessory organs (as in Clariidae and Heteropneustidae) or means of utilizing available oxygen from the water (as in Callichthyidae) are sometimes present. At least one family has developed an electricity-producing organ from body musculature. A swim bladder with a duct to the gut is generally present and may be simple or bilobed or sometimes enclosed in a bony capsule.

Chapter 1

Family — Plate 1

DIPLOMYSTIDAE

(Patagonian Catfishes)

The family Diplomystidae is small, containing only a single genus and two nominal species, although geographic variation suggests that more may exist. It is restricted to the freshwater rivers of South America, in Chile and Argentina. The species are therefore cooler water fishes and rarely, if ever, are seen in the aquarium trade. The species from Chile attains a length of 25 to 27.5 cm; fishermen there refer to it as *pollo de agua dulce*, or freshwater chicken. They are apparently rare now in Chile, perhaps as a result of predation by introduced trout.

The genus *Diplomystes* apparently is the only modern member of the Siluriformes with a toothed maxillary. This feature combined with a number of other characteristics, some of which are primitive and others seemingly specialized, has caused taxonomists not only to separate the diplomystids as a separate family but to also consider them quite distinct from the main evolutionary stem of the catfishes.

Why does *Diplomystes* retain a toothed maxillary of the generalized lower teleostean type when all the other living catfishes do not? Certainly, since this structure is involved with food and feeding, at least part of the answer lies in differences in the feeding adaptations between *Diplomystes* and the other catfishes. In non-diplomystid siluriforms the maxillary is part of a complex barbel apparatus that is able to move somewhat independently of the jaws proper. In *Diplomystes*, however, the maxillary is part of the jaw apparatus itself. The process of locating food seems to involve a combination of the maxillary barbels and the upper lip. Cranial nerve rami extend into the fleshy upper lip, which is directed downward in front of the mouth, and are apparently associated with taste. This sensory system could come into play if the upper lip is pressed against the bottom when feeding. As the maxillary is moved forward, the barbel is brought downward and forward as in cyprinids as opposed to moving laterally as in the case of the other catfishes. In the other catfishes the mental barbels could possibly be brought into play as bottom sensors. The lack of mental barbels in *Diplomystes* may be compensated for by the presence of chin pores.

The dentition of *Diplomystes* is of a specialized type that may be used for scraping. The teeth on the maxillary extend downward and inward, not directly downward as they do in characins. They are mostly long, depressible, incurved somewhat, and flat-tipped, like those found on the premaxillary and dentary. The vomerine teeth are also depressible and flat-tipped but are stouter and more widely spaced. They start as two ovate patches in the young and coalesce into a much larger subcircular patch as the fish matures. *Diplomystes*, incidentally, is one of the few catfishes that have larger teeth on the vomer than in the jaws. This can also be seen in the bagrid genus *Rita* and the marine plotosids. So, although the presence of teeth on the maxillary of *Diplomystes* is a primitive characteristic among catfishes, the type of teeth (depressible and flat-tipped) found there and elsewhere in the mouth appears to be a highly specialized condition.

A description of *Diplomystes*, based on the type species of the genus, *D. papillosus*, has the body slender, rounded in cross-section anteriorly but compressed toward the tail. The head is short, blunt (more pointed in the young), and covered with a layer of muscle and soft skin, the occipital process not being visible externally. The surface of the bones of the head is irregular and rugose, and there are two nearly parallel postorbital median ridges. The fontanel is located between these ridges and extends from in front of the eyes to the base of the occipital process, but with a rather broad interruption behind the eyes. The occipital process is a short but deep crest. The eyes are small, circular, and included about 7½ times in the head length. The nostrils are close together and surrounded by a figure-eight-shaped membrane, that portion between the nasal openings highest.

There are no mental barbels. The maxillary barbels are flat, broad-based, and scarcely reach the pectoral fin base. The snout is usually rounded and projects beyond the lower jaw, while the lips are thick, fleshy, and strongly papillose. The maxillary bone forms the sides of the mouth and bears a very narrow band of teeth. The premaxillaries have a crescent-shaped patch of teeth, the outer four or five series compressed and incisor-like, the inner series being much smaller and not incisor-like. The vomer is provided with two oval patches of large conical teeth, although the patches may coalesce with age.

Diplomystes papillosus; (B) ventral side of head. (After Eigenmann, 1927.)

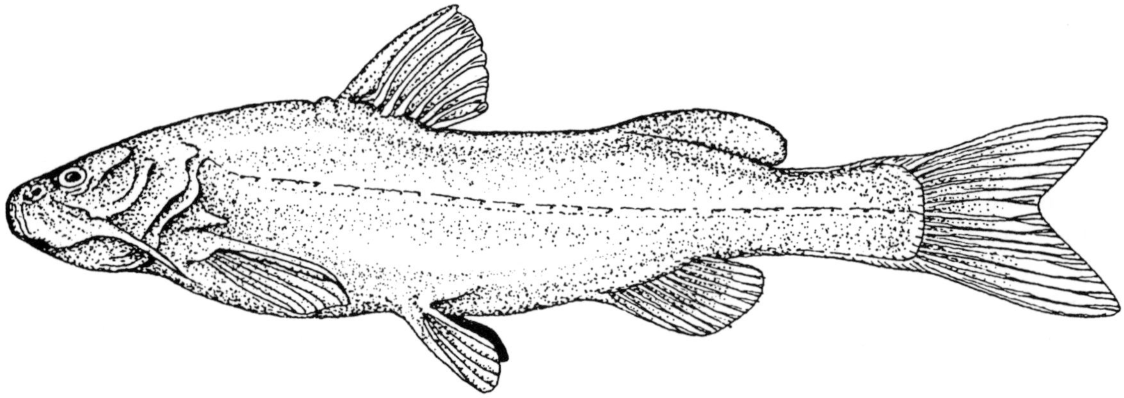

B

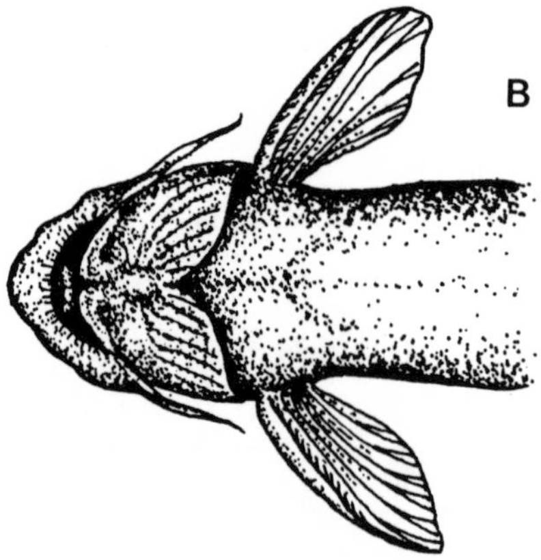

The teeth of the lower jaw are compressed, incisor-like, the band broadest in the middle and tapering quickly toward the rictus.

The dorsal fin is located in the anterior half of the body and is short-based, with a short, smooth spine and 7 or 8 rays. The adipose fin is elongate, about as long as or longer than the anal fin, its distance behind the dorsal fin about equal to its length or up to half again longer. The ventral fins are 6-rayed and inserted under the last dorsal fin ray. The pectoral fins have a strong spine that has a smooth outer edge, but the inner edge has strong recurved teeth along the entire length; a leathery prolongation continues the spine. The anal fin is rather short, with 9 to 12 rays, while the caudal fin is emarginate to forked and has numerous short accessory basal rays.

The skin of the head and body is covered with minute cirri or papillae. This is especially noticeable anteriorly, the posterior portion being smoother. The gill membranes are usually separate to about below the eye and are entirely free from the isthmus. The gill openings are wide and subcontinuous. There are 5 + 8 gill rakers. The pseudobranchiae are well-developed, not covered by a membrane. The swim bladder is relatively large, heart-shaped, and not enclosed in a bony capsule. The color is generally brownish above, lighter below.

Diplomystids are of some economic importance as food fishes in Chile.

Checklist of the species of the family Diplomystidae and their type localities:

Diplomystes Bleeker, 1863 (on *Diplomyste* Dumeril, 1856). Type species *Arius papillosus* Valenciennes, 1840.

- *Diplomystes papillosus* (Valenciennes, 1840). Valparaiso; San Jago (Central Chile).
- *D. viedmensis* (Macdonagh, 1931). Rio Negro, Patagonia, Argentina.

Chapter 2

Family ICTALURIDAE (Bullhead Catfishes)

Plates 1 & 2

The family Ictaluridae is a moderately small family of catfishes restricted in distribution to the fresh waters of North America and Central America from Hudson Bay and the Saint Lawrence drainages of Canada to the Usumacinta River in Guatemala along the eastern seaboard. They also, however, occur in some streams in Mexico that flow westward into the Pacific Ocean. Previous accounts of records from China have been discounted. Some of the larger species of *Ictalurus* and *Pylodictis* are of economic importance, both as food fishes and as sport fishes. Commercial fisheries, including fish farms, have developed this resource. Several of the economically important species have been introduced into temperate waters in several regions of the world.

Ictalurids, as is the case with many catfishes, are nocturnal, being most active at night or on dark, cloudy days, or living much of the time in roiled, murky waters where the light level is quite low. The madtoms and stonecats are especially nocturnal and are rarely seen during the daytime, making them that much more difficult to capture. At night they appear to be relatively common, swarming over an area where they appeared to be uncommon or absent during the day. They prefer areas where the flow of water is not too great, such as quiet lakes and ponds or sluggish rivers or streams, although some *Noturus* are found in flowing streams. They feed primarily from the bottom, seeking out arthropod larvae, tadpoles, fry of other fishes, and even dead material. Spawning occurs in the spring and early summer in a nest in the sand or mud. One or both parents usually guard the eggs.

This family contains a number of interesting and unusual catfishes, some of which seem to adapt easily to aquarium conditions. Among them are albino or semi-albino individuals as well as cave species that are blind. Some are peaceful, but many cannot be trusted with any but larger species that are able to defend themselves. Most are efficient scavengers that are tolerant of a wide variety of water conditions, including a broad temperature range, and once they have become acclimated to aquarium conditions they are hard to kill, even by inexperienced aquarists. Among the "tall tales" associated with members of this family are reports that in lakes that have become frozen over these catfishes will accumulate in large numbers just under the ice. There they swim in circles, wearing a hole in ice that may be as much as a foot thick. Some wags claim that some larger individuals are shipped alive but frozen in blocks of ice to be thawed out at their destination, apparently without any ill effects. On the other end of the spectrum, these catfishes are said to be able to exist in temperatures in excess of 28°C. They not only can survive in areas of low oxygen but are also able to weather periods of drought wherein their ponds dry up by digging into the bottom mud and taking in air through holes. As long as the mud doesn't completely dry out, the fish can hold out for several weeks.

They eat practically anything, locating the food primarily by smell and taste for their eyes are very poor. When food is dropped into the tank when they are quiet, it will not be long before they become active and start to search the bottom. If the food actually touches them as it falls, they will usually react immediately and find the morsel very quickly. They will accept a wide variety of foods from live minnows and pellet food to decaying plants and animals, but it should be available during the evening hours when the light level is very low. It is at night that they are able to capture small live fishes, taking whatever species are available even up to half their own size. A growth rate of 3.7 cm per month is not unusual if food is plentiful and the aquarium is large enough.

It has been suggested that locally collected individuals be quarantined for a month or more in case of possible contamination of a community tank with parasites or diseases. Along with good aeration and filtration, the addition of some malachite green or methylene blue combined with an antibiotic will help, because naked catfishes are susceptible to fungus, especially in soft acid water. (*Warning*: Use caution when adding malachite green (and other chemicals) to tanks containing catfishes. Naked skinned fishes often suffer severe side effects or even death when treated with doses of malachite green that are harmless to scaled fishes.) Newly collected catfishes should not be subject to sudden temperature changes, such as placing them in a heated tank after taking them from their native stream that has a temperature in the fifties (°F). The gradual increase in temperature can be easily accomplished in the quarantine tank along with the adjustment to the chemistry of your tank water.

The springtime is probably the best time of the year to make your collection, and the change in temperature (gradual of course) might even precipitate spawning if there is a pair ready. Later, in the summer, the fishes are generally weaker if their oxygen supply is reduced by the higher temperatures, and they are more difficult to acclimate. Most species spawn by making nests, whether it be in the bottom mud, among weeds, or in shelters such as caves or even tin cans. The eggs are guarded by one or both parents until hatching and they may continue to guard the fry for a time afterward. The young generally school, forming a dense, dark cloud in the water. This behavior was also observed in captivity and seems to continue until they reach a size of about 5 to 7.5 cm. This might be a protective habit, for it was observed that gar would pick off stragglers from the school but would not attack the school directly.

The body of ictalurids is moderately elongated and covered with smooth, thick skin. The posterior nostrils are relatively far from the anterior nostrils and bear the nasal barbels. There are four pairs of long barbels around the mouth: a maxillary pair, two mandibular or mental pairs*, and the nasal barbels. The jaws are provided with villiform teeth (except *Trogloglanis*) and the palate is edentulous. Villiform teeth are present on the upper and lower rear pharyngeal arches. The entopterygoid bones are reduced or absent and the ectopterygoid is broad or reduced. The dorsal fin is placed anteriorly and usually provided with a stout spine (except in *Prietella*) and about six segmented rays. A fleshy adipose fin of variable length is present. The pectoral fins have a stout spine (flexible in *Prietella*) and 5-12 soft rays, while the ventral fins have 8-10 rays. Gill rakers are present anteriorly on all five gill arches but posteriorly only on the third and fourth. The branchiostegal membranes fold across the isthmus. The swim bladder is present (except in *Satan* and *Trogloglanis*) but never encased in bone.

Young *Ictalurus* and members of the genus *Noturus* are reported to be able to inject a venom with their sharp spines. A poison gland, located just below the skin at the spine base, opens directly to the surface by a pore. In the larger *Ictalurus* this opening is reduced or absent, having become smaller and smaller with age, although it remains open in the species of *Noturus*. The madtoms' sting is many times worse than that of the bullheads.

---

* Barbel terminology in catfishes is hopelessly confused. Although all authors agree on the meaning of nasal and maxillary barbels, the barbels on the lower jaw of a catfish are variously called mental (i.e., chin) barbels or mandibular (i.e., lower jaw) barbels; additionally, some authors refer to inner and outer mental or mandibular barbels, the position determined relative to the midline. No effort is made here to standardize usage.

The family Ictaluridae includes six genera, three that are relatively wide-ranging and three that are known only from localized underground waters, with about 50 species. It is interesting to note that each genus from the underground waters is paired with one of the wide-ranging surface genera in Taylor's revision (1969). These natural groups according to him are the *Ictalurus*-group, with *Ictalurus* and *Trogloglanis*; the *Noturus*-group, with *Noturus* and *Prietella*; and the *Pylodictis*-group, with *Pylodictis* and *Satan*. Lundberg (1982) places *Pylodictis* as the sister group of *Satan*, considers *Noturus* as monophyletic and the sister group of *Prietella*, and the subgenus *Amiurus* (bullheads) as monophyletic and the sister group of *Noturus* + *Prietella* + *Pylodictis* + *Satan*. Although he retains *Amiurus* as a subgenus of *Ictalurus*, he says this is probably incorrect and with further study it may again be considered as a full genus. *Trogloglanis* is considered the sister group of the *Amiurus* + *Noturus* + *Prietella* + *Pylodictus* + *Satan* lineage, and the subgenus *Ictalurus* is in turn the sister group of all other living ictalurids and is itself monophyletic.

The six genera can be distinguished by the following key:

1a. Eyes present; variously pigmented (some albinos present); caudal fin various 2
1b. Eyes absent; normally unpigmented; caudal fin slightly emarginate................. 4
2a. Adipose fin long, low to moderately high, adnate to the back and variously connected to or only slightly separated from the caudal fin; caudal fin truncate to rounded to pointed............. *Noturus*
2b. Adipose fin large or small, but remote from the caudal fin; caudal fin rounded to deeply forked............................ 3
3a. Adipose fin small, a high flap with free posterior end; caudal fin rounded to deeply forked....................... *Ictalurus*
3b. Adipose fin large, a high rounded flap with posterior end free from back; caudal fin emarginate to rounded....... *Pylodictis*
4a. Gill rakers 10-14 on first arch; swim bladder present...................... *Prietella*
4b. Gill rakers 17-19 on first arch; swim bladder absent 5
5a. Jaw teeth well developed; jaws strong, lower jaw normal and slightly shorter than upper; mouth not inverted; ventral fin with 8 (rarely 9) rays............ *Satan*
5b. Jaw teeth absent; jaws paper thin, lower jaw much shortened and turned into mouth; 9 or more rays in ventral fin.... .... *Trogloglanis*

The genus *Ictalurus*, which presently also contains the bullheads (subgenus *Amiurus*), have in general ten preoperculomandibular pores, eight ventral fin rays, forked or square tails, and a short, high adipose fin that is free from the back posteriorly and with its base ending at some distance from the caudal fin.

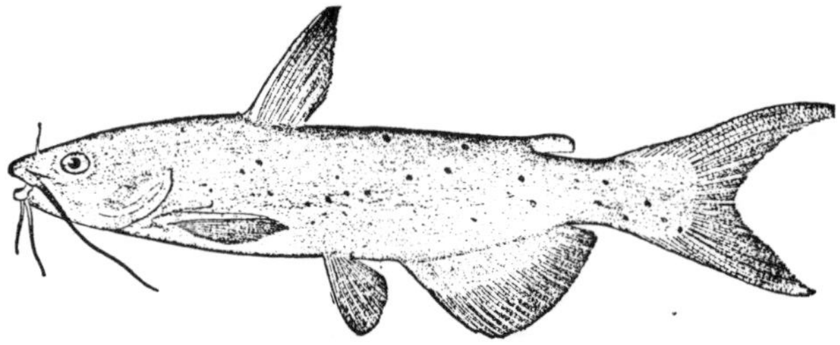

***Ictalurus punctatus*. (From Jordan, 1905.)**

The young are variously mottled, spotted, brown, or blackish above and light below, or light grayish blue with dark borders to the vertical fins. As they grow and attain sexual maturity, they turn an almost uniformly dark color, especially on the back and sides. The shape of the head and caudal fin also changes. The head becomes broader and more flattened, while the caudal fin varies from rounded to deeply forked, the depth of the fork becoming more and more reduced with growth.

Bullheads have highly developed senses of taste and smell. The body of a bullhead is literally covered with taste buds, which are especially dense on the barbels. They can find food by tracking a chemical gradient right to its source. They can also recognize members of their own species, even individuals, by the sense of smell. This is important, for they commonly establish territories (both in nature and in aquaria). A hierarchy is established in a tank in which several individuals are housed and it can be clearly seen, with the lower ranking members having to settle for smaller and more exposed territories. Clashes between individuals may range from mild threat displays to violent battles. In the same community the action is generally restricted to ritualistic displays, and disputes are more or less quietly settled. If a stranger is introduced, however, there may be violent fights, even to the death. If such a stranger is added to a set up aquarium with several bullheads, the subdominant individuals will take refuge in the territory of the dominant individual. Once the stranger is evicted, the smaller subdominants are no longer welcome and get chased out as well.

Species of bullheads have been introduced into many areas outside their natural range, sometimes deliberately, sometimes accidentally. They were carried by settlers from the East who traveled over the Rocky Mountains (they are not native west of the Rockies) and possibly carried from one pond to another as adhesive eggs attached to the feet of wading birds (never actually documented). Of course, fishermen who use bullheads as bait also help their dispersal if the bait bucket is upset and the catfishes escape. They may also multiply in ponds beyond the food capacity of the pond, resulting in stunted fish with oversized heads and shrunken bodies.

Small individuals are suitable for home aquaria. They are very hardy and not very demanding as regards water conditions. A large tank that is provided with hiding places constructed of driftwood and/or rocks and stones is recommended. The bottom substrate can be sandy, possibly mixed with gravelly areas. Plants are optional. There should be moderate aeration and good filtration. Since these fishes are native North Americans, room temperature will be sufficient, and many species will stand considerable cooling without any ill effects. All *Ictalurus* species must be considered predatory, feeding on small invertebrates and small fishes (including their eggs and fry if available). In an aquarium live foods are definitely preferred, but normal aquarium fare can be worked into the diet very quickly.

Ictalurus nebulosus, the Brown Bullhead, is probably the most common species of the genus. It has been artificially established in many regions, including western North America, New Zealand, and much of Europe (France, Germany, Holland, Italy, and as far eastward as Russia) since its introduction there at the turn of the century. It prefers slow-flowing (canals, slow-flowing rivers, etc.) or still (ponds, lakes, etc.) waters where it can be found mostly over muddy bottoms. It survives well under adverse conditions such as the drying up of their pond (it can live in the wet mud). This 0.5 meter species is said to be a voracious feeder on the common invertebrates of the area, including crustaceans, molluscs, insect larvae, and even young fishes. It may also feed on such items as seeds and submerged plant parts. Spawning occurs in the spring after the turnover, when they emerge from the bottom mud where they passed much of the cold winter months. The spawning pair move into shallow areas that are warmed by the sun, where one or both parents-to-be prepare a rough "nest." The nest is usually a saucer-shaped depression fanned out of the mud. Some pairs, however, will spawn in a more secure spot such as along an overhanging bank. The eggs, up to about 10,000 in number and cream-colored, are deposited in the nests in sticky balls that adhere to the bottom. One or both parents stand guard, the male usually guarding the

Ictalurus nebulosus guarding its saucer-shaped nest among the water plants. (From Gill, 1906.)

periphery of the nest area while the female fans the eggs with her fins or even "inhales" them as a mass like a vacuum cleaner, turning them around in her mouth like she was using a mouthwash, and then expelling them. The black, tadpole-like young hatch out in from 5 to 8 days and for the first few days at least are still tended to by one or both parents. The fry may also be inhaled by a parent, but sometimes they may forget to exhale, possibly out of hunger. By the seventh day the fry are free-swimming, and when they leave the nest they do so in a dense school resembling a subsurface black cloud, usually still protected by the parents who actively attack any potential predators. *I. nebulosus* is generally dark brown, but with proper lighting they have a bronzy color with violet or greenish iridescence. They can hear sounds, for experiments have shown that they respond to loud whistling, bells, flute notes, and others. Perhaps this is tied in with their exceptionally large swim bladder.

Ictalurus furcatus, the Blue Catfish, is the largest member of the genus, commonly attaining a length of 1.5 meters and a weight of 36.3 kilos, although records of up to 68 kilos or more exist, but these are mostly from the last century and it is doubted whether such monsters still exist. This is an important commercial species and it is actively fished for with long lines near the bottom using dead fishes as bait. *Ictalurus furcatus* is most common in the deeper waters of the south.

Ictalurus punctatus, the Channel Catfish, is another common species, preferring clear, even flowing waters, although it is more typically found in the still waters of lakes and ponds. It is a top sport fish that may grow to a length of 1.3 meters and weigh in at upwards of 13.6 kilos. This species is actively farmed (it is good eating) and is one of the species used in the "pay as you fish" ponds. It is not finicky about what bait it will accept and has even been caught on bare hooks. But the best baits are the "stink" baits, which may include such tasty items as chicken entrails, a variety of cheeses, "soured" clams, or coagulated blood in doughball mixtures that are allowed to mellow a bit until the odor becomes quite potent and attractive to the catfish. *I. punctatus* starts spawning in the early spring in the southern parts of its range, the season being later further north. It spawns in caves or under rocks where the nest is fairly protected. The male guards the nest and fans the eggs. Like most other *Ictalurus* species, this one does well in captivity, eating almost any type of food offered. An albino form occurs in nature and is sought after by many aquarists.

The genus *Trogloglanis* is one of the underground genera with no external eyes and unpigmented skin. It resembles those species of *Ictalurus* that have high, arched skulls, a relatively shortened head, numerous gill rakers, and a long occipital process. The single species attains a length of about 8.7 cm in standard length. *Trogloglanis* can be described as having a gently convex predorsal profile, a relatively long and shallow caudal peduncle, and a very wide, non-depressed head. There are four pairs of barbels, a maxillary pair, two mental pairs, and a nasal pair which is an extension of the anterior rim of the posterior nostril. The rim of the anterior nostril is expanded to form a cup-like or flattened disc around the nasal aperture. The mouth is situated ventrally, below an overhanging snout. It is an unusual, funnel-like mouth with the upper and lower lips expanded to form fleshy pads provided with transverse plicae. The lips

***Trogloglanis pattersoni*; (b) ventral view of head.**

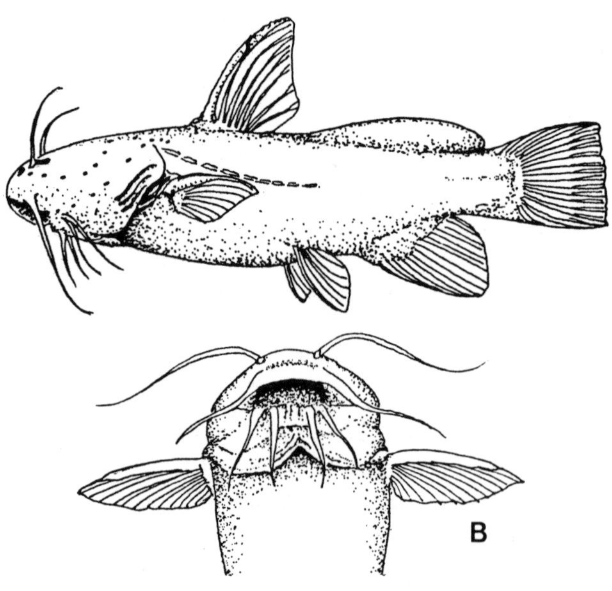

are continuous with the integument of the head except at the mouth angle, where there is a vertical fold. The jaws are without teeth and permanently open. The gape is wide, and prominent oral valves can be seen just inside the lips. The dorsal fin is high, with a straight margin, a long, robust, smooth-edged spine, and 6 or 7 rays. The adipose fin is long and high, rounded posteriorly, and adnate to the back as well as narrowly attached to the upper part of the caudal fin by a ridge of rayless integument. The anal fin is rounded and the caudal fin is slightly emarginate. The pectoral fins have 9 (sometimes 8) soft rays and a long, sharp spine that has a smooth anterior edge and a posterior edge armed with a series of teeth. The ventral fins are rounded with 8 (sometimes 9) soft rays. There is no axillary pore. The branchial membranes are fused to one another across the midline, and there are 18-19 gill rakers on the first arch. The swim bladder is absent. A single species, *T. pattersoni*, has been described.

The mouth is quite similar to catfishes that use such an apparatus as a suction device, such as loricariids, some sisorids (*Glyptosternum, Exostoma, Oreoglanis*), and some mochokids (*Chiloglanis, Euchilichthys*), but similar usage has not yet been demonstrated in *Trogloglanis*. The food probably consists of minute particles taken from substrate detritus and has been reported to include subterranean fungus.

The genus *Prietella* has many features in common with *Noturus*, including infraorbital and preoperculomandibular canals with widely separated anterior ends, the lower jaw being included and almost subterminal, a short lateral line, the patch of premaxillary teeth short but very wide and without visible posterior extensions, and a truncate or slightly emarginate caudal fin. Instead of a dorsal fin spine the first ray is distally segmented and flexible, although the segments are absent or not distinct basally. There is no plate-like spine embedded at the anterior end of the dorsal fin, but pterygiophores are present and they have broad distal ends. On the other hand, a pectoral fin spine is present, although it is short and relatively flexible and with smooth edges. This generic pair differs from the other genera by a combination of

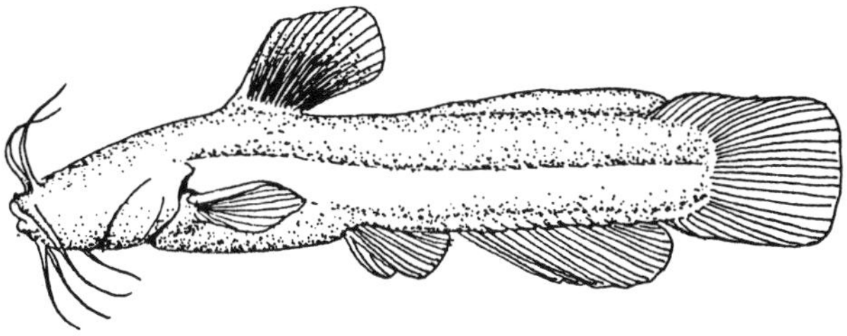

Prietella phreatophila. (Rendering from written description.)

several characters. The occipital process is reduced, the swim bladder is short (not longer than wide), the posttemporal bones are obsolete and the ectopterygoid is slightly reduced, the anterior ends of the preoperculomandibular canals are somewhat widely separated and the infraorbital canals are similarly shaped, there is a long adipose fin, a similar head and body shape, relatively few vertebrae, and a divergence from the usual number of 15 branched caudal fin rays. They differ from each other, however, in several aspects. *Prietella*, being a subterranean form, has no eyes and its skin is unpigmented. It lacks the ossification of the first dorsal fin ray and the ossified tissue at the anterior base of the dorsal fin has degenerated, and the infraorbital and preoperculomandibular canals are interrupted. *Prietella* is known from a single locality in the Rio Grande drainage of Mexico, whereas the genus *Noturus* extends no further south than the Nueces River in Texas. *Prietella* includes the single species *Prietella phreatophila*.

The genus *Noturus* (including *Schilbeodes*), the madtoms, contains 25 described species and several others known but undescribed. The species are generally small (most less than 12.5 cm in length) with a very long adipose fin that is continuous with the truncate or rounded caudal fin. The eyes are subcutaneous and the pectoral fin spines are relatively

Noturus flavus. (From Jordan & Evermann, 1934.)

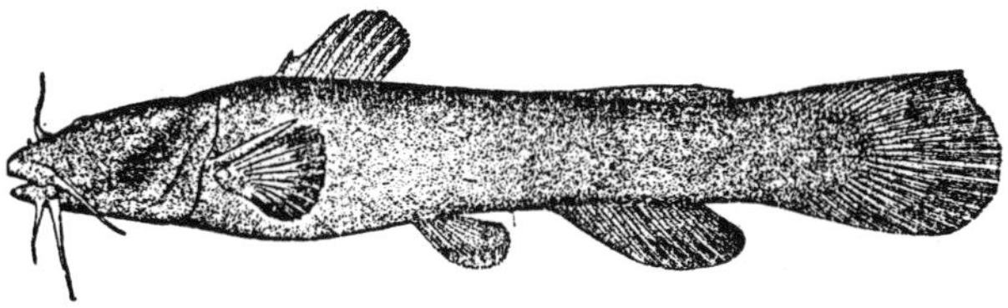

short. Venom glands of species-specific toxicity are associated with both the dorsal and pectoral fin spines. If one is stuck by one of the spines, the effects are said to be comparable to a bee sting, with the pain lasting from a few minutes to an hour. However, like the bee sting, there are people who are allergic to the venom, and the sting can be much worse for them, the pain lasting for several hours and being accompanied by some swelling.

All of the species of *Noturus* are crepuscular or nocturnal, hiding in dark areas beneath various objects during the day. A great majority of the species are associated with high quality clear waters of moderate to high gradient rivers or streams, living in the rapids or riffles, as well as slow-moving streams and the still waters of lakes and ponds. They are usually found over gravel or rubble and occasionally sand in the moderately shallow pools and riffles, but some are found in turbid waters over mud, sand, or debris. They occur at various depths from very shallow (in pools and riffles) to fairly deep (2-3.3 meters in deep, clean pools).

Most species of *Noturus* are found buried in the gravel, under vegetation, in bottles or cans, or under debris piles made of sticks, leaves, logs, gravel, shells, or anything imaginable that creates a low-light situation during the day. Given their cryptic coloration, madtoms can be very difficult to locate among this gravel and debris. During the night madtoms can be seen swimming about just above the bottom searching for food items with their very sensitive barbels.

Madtoms usually mature during their third summer (second year). In the spring (March-May), mature females preparatory to spawning start to develop enlarged yellowish orange oocytes. In males, the muscles on their backs and heads begin to develop, possibly for the tasks of excavating their nests and eventually for guarding them. By the early summer males can be seen in what will eventually be the nesting cavities, which are located near the heads of riffles or in pools, and the females are quite obvious, for the large mature eggs make their abdomens quite distended. The eggs are quite large, ranging from 1.5 to 4.5 mm in diameter, depending on the species. In addition to the hollowed-out nests, holes in the banks, in rooted vegetation, or under logs or stones may be used as nesting sites. Here the male cleans out an area where the eggs will eventually be deposited. Recently, however, madtoms have begun to make use of other structures in their stream environment that can hardly be considered natural, but seem to be quite acceptable to the catfishes. These include the ever-present beer and soda cans, bottles, tires, boards, and other trash items. Cans are particularly acceptable as they provide better shelter for the nest than most of the other objects or the open hollows. Once inside the can, males typically turn to face outward and, with their swollen head muscles, are able to block off the entire opening of a pop-top can.

Spawning is believed to occur in the early morning or late evening hours. An actual spawning has been observed and was described by Mayden (1983) as follows. The pair initiated the spawning act with many tactile gestures while swimming in circles. They then entered a beer can, lined up side-by-side in a head-to-head position, and while vibrating vigorously released a string of eggs on the bottom of the can. The eggs were later grouped into clusters by the male using his mouth. Each year the female madtom apparently lays only about half of her eggs in a male's nest and then moves to a different male's nest to deposit the remaining half. The eggs are yellowish orange and usually clustered in a roundish mass of 5 to 6 eggs. They usually are not attached to anything in the nest cavity and are always to be found in the deepest part of the nest. The number of eggs produced depends a great deal on the size, weight, and age of the female, with older females tending to produce more eggs than younger ones. Egg production is known to range from a minimum of 14-15 (*N. leptacanthus*) to 100-300 (*N. flavipinnis*) to about 1,000 in *N. flavus*, the Stonecat.

Care of the eggs is apparently solely the responsibility of the male. Only occasionally has a female been found in a nest, apparently just after spawning, for the embryos were still in the early stages of development. The embryos take between one and two weeks to develop. During this time, including a few extra days after hatching, the males do not feed. They keep the eggs well aerated by rolling them around the nest cavity with their large heads or by grabbing them in their mouths and shaking vigorously. Once they have hatched, the fry remain in the nest cavity for several days (perhaps three or four or more), presumably learning the art of swimming. This may actually start earlier than hatching because just before hatching the larvae thrash about inside the eggs for several hours, some violent spasms lasting as much as a minute. Upon hatching they are clumsy swimmers, especially hampered by their large yolk sacs, but they soon become more accomplished. Within the first day, however, the fry form a school and start to move about, apparently preferring areas that are dark or where the light level is quite low, and remaining near the bottom. After about a week to ten days, the larvae appear much like miniature adults except for certain characteristic pigment patterns that develop later. The young catfish in the wild feed on microcrustaceans such as copepods, ostracods, and cladocerans, as well as small fly larvae such as chironomids. In captivity they can be fed newly hatched brine shrimp or crushed catfish chow. As they grow, and with the changing seasons, their diet will change in the wild, depending upon what invertebrates are available at that time. Immature aquatic insects and small aquatic crustaceans are a large part of the diet all the time. On occasion, a small minnow or darter may find its way into their stomach.

Because they are nocturnal, feeding occurs mostly by taste. Since they have taste receptors covering their barbels and much of their body, it is by this means that they usually locate their food. Foraging is most intense after dusk and before dawn. Such nocturnal feeding is possibly a means of avoiding predators, for most of the North American predators of freshwater fishes are mainly sight feeders plying their trade during the day.

In an aquarium madtoms readily accept a variety of foods, including brine shrimp, tubificid worms, raw liver, and even flake foods. Once food is introduced into the tank it is only a matter of seconds before the madtoms are active, swimming about frantically following the minute gradient of odors given off by the food.

The fry grow quickly, usually rapidly at first and then at a decreasing rate throughout their life, which may be from two to nine years, depending upon the species. Once the fish attains sexual maturity (about two years) the growth rate declines considerably as the energy is diverted to other priorities.

Madtoms are subject to the normal run of parasites. Most frequently encountered internal parasites include such animals as encysted nematodes (*Spinitectus*) in the outside wall of the stomach and acanthocephalans (*Leptorhynchoides*) and flukes (*Crepidostomum*) in the stomach and intestines. Gill parasites are occasionally encountered but external parasites are not common, although the copepod *Lernaea* and an occasional leech may be seen.

The final pair of genera (*Satan* and *Pylodictis*) is also morphologically similar and is considered a pair of sister groups by Lundberg. Again, one (*Satan*) is eyeless and without pigment. It also differs from *Pylodictis* by lacking a swim bladder, lacking backward extensions of the premaxillary tooth band, by possessing an excessively elongate adipose fin, and by a divergence of the sensory canal system—there are 12 preoperculomandibular pores in the genus *Pylodictis* and 11 to 12 in *Satan*. The two genera, however, have a very similar body form, with a greatly depressed head and a slender body. In both the mouth is wide and transverse, and, although in *Satan* the lower jaw is slightly included and in *Pylodictis* it projects beyond the upper jaw, *Satan* approaches *Pylodictis* in this character more than the other ictalurids do. *Pylodictis* contains but a single species, *P. olivaris*, as does *Satan* (*S. eurystomus*).

Pylodictis olivaris is a species of large lowland rivers, bayous, and lakes of the Mississippi valley. The head and anterior part of the

Pylodictis olivaris. (From Jordan & Evermann, 1902.)

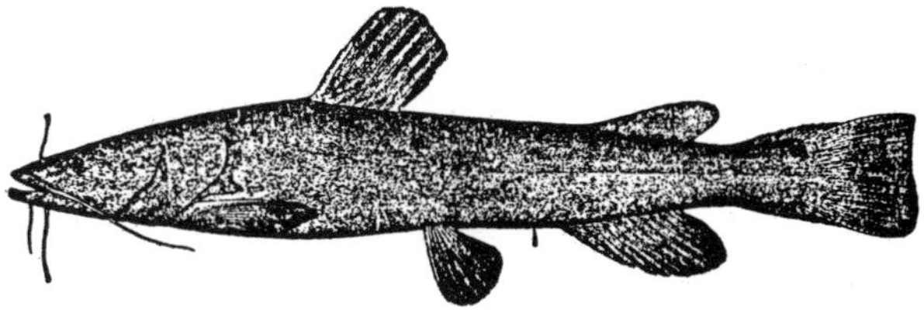

body are flattened, the tail is square-cut, and the lower jaw is projecting. It is a highly aggressive, predatory species feeding heavily on sunfishes and shad. It grows quite large, weights in excess of 45.4 kilos and a length of over 1.5 m having been recorded, although the more usual weight is more like 18 kilos. In Illinois it spawns in May, earlier further south. The young are often cannibalistic because they are very aggressive feeders and rapidly eat all other available food. This is one of the species cultured for food in the southern U.S.

Satan eurystomus was discovered in San Antonio, Texas, where it was taken from an artesian well 1,250 feet deep. Being blind, the lateral line canals and pores of the head have become excessively developed, apparently taking up the slack left by the absence of the eyes. The nostrils are minute. There is a well-developed patch of villiform teeth on the premaxillaries but without backward projections. The palate is edentulous. The dorsal fin is short-based, with a rather weak spine and 7 branched rays, and rather pointed. The anal fin is long and low with 20 rays (14 of which are branched). The pectoral fins have a spine (smooth anterior edges and serrated posterior edges) and 10 branched rays, whereas the ventral fins have 10 rays (9 of which are branched, the first ray being simple and bearing spinules like those on the front of the anal fin). The swim bladder is absent.

***Satan eurystomus*; (b) ventral view of head. (After Hubbs & Bailey, 1947.)**

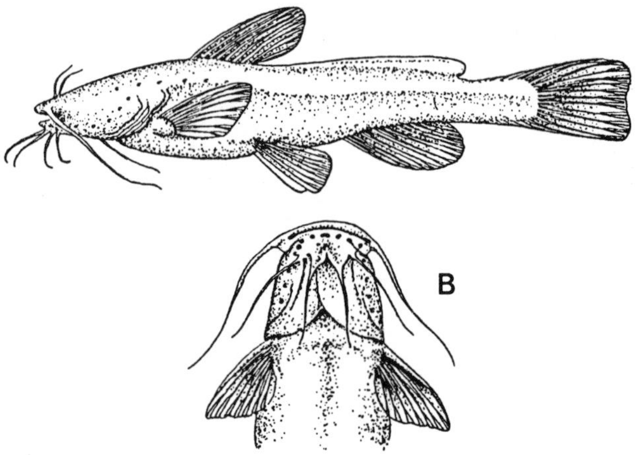

Checklist of the species of the family Ictaluridae and their type localities:

Noturus Rafinesque, 1818. Type species *Noturus flavus* Rafinesque.

- *Noturus albater* Taylor, 1969. White River, Missouri.
- *N. baileyi* Taylor, 1969. Great Smoky Mountains National Park, Tennessee.
- *N. elegans* Taylor, 1969. Fallen Timber Creek, Kentucky.
- *N. eleutherus* Jordan, 1877. French Broad River, Tennessee.
- *N. exilis* Nelson, 1876. McLean Co., Illinois.
- *N. flavater* Taylor, 1969. Flat Creek, Missouri.
- *N. flavipinnis* Taylor, 1969. Hines Creek, Tennessee.
- *N. flavus* Rafinesque, 1818. Falls of Ohio River, Ohio.
- *N. funebris* Gilbert & Swain, 1891. North River tributary, Alabama.
- *N. furiosus* Jordan & Meek, 1889. Neuse River, North Carolina.
- *N. gilberti* Jordan & Evermann, 1889. Roanoke River, Virginia.
- *N. gyrinus* (Mitchill, 1817). Wallkill River, New York.
- *N. hildebrandi* (Bailey & Taylor, 1950). Brushy Creek, Mississippi.
  - *h. lautus* Taylor, 1969. Obion River, Tennessee.
- *N. insignis* (Richardson, 1836). ("Locality not known.")
- *N. lachneri* Taylor, 1969. Middle Fork of the Saline River, Arkansas.
- *N. leptacanthus* Jordan, 1877. Silver Creek, Georgia.
- *N. miurus* Jordan, 1877. White River, Indiana.
- *N. munitus* Suttkus & Taylor, 1965. Pearl River, Mississippi.
- *N. nocturnus* Jordan & Gilbert, 1886. Saline River, Arkansas.
- *N. phaeus* Taylor, 1969. North fork of the Obion River, Tennessee.
- *N. placidus* Taylor, 1969. Neosho River, Kansas.
- *N. stanauli* Etnier & Jenkins, 1980. Tennessee River system, Tennessee.
- *N. stigmosus* Taylor, 1969. Huron River, Michigan.

N. taylori Douglas, 1972. Caddo River, Arkansas.

N. trautmani Taylor, 1969. Big Darby Creek, Ohio.

Ictalurus Rafinesque, 1820. Type species *Silurus punctatus* Rafinesque.

Ictalurus balsanus (Jordan & Snyder, 1900). Rio Ixtla, Puente de Ixtla, Morelos, Mexico.

I. brunneus (Jordan, 1877). South Fork of Ocmulgee River, Georgia.

I. catus (Linnaeus, 1758). Northern part of America.

I. dugesi (Bean, 1898). Rio Turbio, Guanajuato, Mexico.

I. furcatus (Lesueur, 1840). New Orleans, Louisiana.

I. lupus (Girard, 1858). Pecos River, Texas.

I. melas (Rafinesque, 1820). "Ohio River".

I. meridionalis (Günther, 1864). Rio Usumacinta, Guatemala. (= *I. furcatus*)

I. natalis (Lesueur, 1819). "North America" (No locality mentioned, later restricted to Lake Ontario).

n. erebennus (Jordan, 1877), St. Johns River, Florida.

I. nebulosus (Lesueur, 1819). Delaware River at Philadelphia, Pennsylvania.

n. catulus (Girard, 1858). Fort Smith, Arkansas.

n. marmoratus (Holbrook, 1855). South Carolina.

I. platycephalus (Girard, 1860). Near Anderson, South Carolina.

I. pricei (Rutter, 1896). San Bernardino Creek, just south of international border, Sonora, Mexico.

I. punctatus (Rafinesque, 1818). Ohio River.

I. serracanthus Yerger & Relyea, 1968. Shore of Lake Talquin, Florida.

Trogloglanis Eigenmann. 1919. Type species *Trogloglanis pattersoni* Eigenmann.

Trogloglanis pattersoni Eigenmann, 1919. Near San Antonio, Texas.

Pylodictis Rafinesque, 1819. Type species *Silurus olivaris* Rafinesque.

Pylodictis olivaris (Rafinesque, 1818). "Ohio River".

Satan Hubbs & Bailey, 1947. Type species *S. eurystomus* Hubbs & Bailey.

Satan eurystomus Hubbs & Bailey, 1947. Near San Antonio from artesian well 1250 feet deep.

Prietella Carranza, 1954. Type species *P. phreatophila* Carranza.

Prietella phreatophila Carranza, 1954. Coahuila, Mexico.

Chapter 3

Family — Plates 3–18

BAGRIDAE

(Bagrid Catfishes)

The family Bagridae is a fairly large family of fresh and brackish water catfishes whose range extends from Africa and Syria through Pakistan, India, Bangladesh, Sri Lanka, Burma, Thailand, Cambodia, Laos, Vietnam, and Malaya to the East Indies, China, Taiwan, Korea, and Japan. Bagrids are apparently absent from the Arabian peninsula. They reside mostly in rivers, pools, and lakes and are mostly crepuscular or nocturnal in habit but will be active during the daytime if they are living in waters that are so clouded with silt or other material that the light level is very low. Bagrids, especially members of the subfamily Claroteinae, do not swim very much (some may even be referred to as being sedentary) and are clearly adapted to a bottom-living existence. Although not armored like the South American callichthyids or loricariids, they are "heavy" fishes with a considerable expanse of head shield. Bagrids are also quite shy, seeking refuge in such places as caves, among rock crevices, or in holes, almost never appearing in the open over flat sandy or muddy areas during the day, although they may wander over these areas at night as they search for food. Most species are voracious predators, feeding on or near the bottom on such items as fishes and crustaceans. In Lake Tanganyika, at least, bagrids can live at considerable depths as their oxygen requirements are relatively low.

The family Bagridae is said to be the Old World equivalent of the South American family Pimelodidae. More importantly, the bagrids have often been cited as being the basic ancestral catfish family, and other families have undoubtedly been derived from it. Bleeker (1863) was one of the first workers to divide the siluroid complex and erected Bagriformes to accommodate ten stirpes. The Bagrini included the bagrids plus some other, unrelated genera. Boulenger (1904) raised the bagrids to a subfamily, and a few years later Regan (1911) elevated them to full family status. He divided the family Bagridae into two subfamilies, the Chrysichthyinae and the Bagrinae. Jayaram (1966) expanded on Regan's classification and added three subfamilies to the family, the Ritinae, Bagroidinae, and Auchenoglanidinae. Bailey & Stewart (1984) corrected the names Chrysichthyinae to Claroteinae and Bagroidinae to Bagrichthyinae by reason of priority.

Many species grow quite large (the genus *Chrysichthys* is said to include the heaviest freshwater fishes in Africa) and are very important local food fishes, whereas others are quite small and well-suited for the domestic aquarium. Some of the young of certain colorful large species are also kept in home aquaria, but they soon outgrow all but the largest tanks, causing problems for the aquarist. Because of their shyness, bagrids do best in a fairly large aquarium where the light is relatively subdued and there are numerous hiding places such as rock caves, driftwood, and thickets of plants. The bottom should be a mixture of sand and gravel. Water chemistry usually is not a concern for the aquarist, and a temperature in the normal range of 20° to 26°C suits them just fine. Their diet should be varied (happily they will eat almost anything, although they prefer live foods of all kinds), and the amount should be substantial (they are usually voracious feeders). Feeding should be done when the light level is low, usually at night just after "lights out" when they come out to search for food. Some bagrids are said to rest in an inverted position—which may not be that unusual considering some of the antics of other catfish families.

Bagrids generally have a body that is moderately elongate, subterete in cross-section anteriorly, but compressed posteriorly. The head is generally depressed and may or may not be osseus, may be rugose with bare head shields or granulations, or may be covered with thick or thin skin. The nape is sometimes protected by a strong occipital buckler. The snout can be bluntly pointed, rounded, or even spatulate. The eyes range from small to quite large and are covered with skin or have free orbital rims. The nostrils are set far apart (except in *Rita*, where the anterior nostrils are almost contiguous with the posterior nostrils) above the angle of the mouth. The anterior nostrils are tubular and situated on the tip of the snout, whereas the posterior nostrils are nearer the eye than the tip of the snout and may or may not be provided with a nasal barbel. There are three to four pairs of well developed barbels (when only three pairs are present it is usually the nasals that are absent), including a maxillary pair (usually very long), the nasal pair, and two pairs of mandibular barbels. The mouth is terminal to subterminal, transverse, crescentric, with the jaws about equal or the upper jaw the longer. The teeth are arranged in bands in the jaws and are usually villiform, although they may be mixed with molariform teeth in the lower jaw. Villiform or molariform vomero-palatine teeth are usually present and arranged in a single oval patch or in a continuous or interrupted semilunar band.

The dorsal fin is normally in advance of or partly above the ventral fins and is short-based with a spine (strong or weak and smooth or serrated on the posterior edge) and normally 6-7 soft rays (exceptions are *Bagrus* with 8-11 rays, *Notoglanidium* with 14-15, and *Liauchenoglanis* with 19 to 20). An adipose fin is present; it may be small or quite large (in some nearly half of the standard length) and is not confluent with the rayed dorsal or caudal fins. The anal fin is short to slightly elongate (9-28 rays). The caudal fin is lunate to deeply emarginate to forked. The pectoral fins are horizontal and set low on the body, and each one has a strong to moderate, usually serrated spine. The ventral fins are also

A bagrid catfish showing the normal complement of barbels (including a well-developed nasal barbel). Photo by Dr. Herbert R. Axelrod.

placed low, sometimes are horizontally oriented, and have 6 to 8 rays.

A generally complete lateral line is present. The gill membranes are free from or united with the isthmus and each other, and the gill openings are moderate to wide and extend to above the bases of the pectoral fins. The swim bladder is large, moderately thick-walled, and free in the abdominal cavity, i.e., not enclosed in bone.

There are about 32 genera included in the subfamilies proposed by Jayaram and modified by Bailey & Stewart (1984) as follows: (1) Ritinae with a single genus; (2) Claroteinae with 17 genera; (3) Bagrinae with seven genera; (4) Bagrichthyinae with two genera; and (5) Auchenoglanidinae with four genera. *Platyglanis* is the thirty-second genus but the subfamily is not known. These five subfamilies can be distinguished as follows:

1a. Pterygoid rudimentary, loosely connected to mesopterygoid; mesopterygoid loosely connected to palatoquadrate bar; parapophysis of fourth vertebra deeply cleft, divisions not fused at base........ 2
1b. Pterygoid fused with metopterygoid or absent; mesopterygoid firmly connected to palatoquadrate bar; parapophysis of fourth vertebra not deeply cleft, divisions slightly fused to fully fused at base 3
2a. Palatines edentate, not connected to palatoquadrate bar; maxillaries reduced; vomer large, lobed, and dentigerous .... Ritinae
2b. Palatines toothed, loosely connected to palatoquadrate bar; maxillaries slightly enlarged; vomer small, semilunar, with or without teeth .... Claroteinae
3a. Lateral ethmoid facet for articulation of palatines more ventral than lateral; palatines may be dentigerous, broadly connected to palatoquadrate bar; maxillaries rudimentary........................ Bagrinae
3b. Lateral ethmoid facet for articulation of palatines strictly ventral, seen only from below; palatines edentate, firmly connected to palatoquadrate bar; maxillaries large or reduced........................ 4
4a. Maxillaries large; vomer reduced, longitudinally disposed, may have teeth....... .... Auchenoglanidinae
4b. Maxillaries reduced; vomer large, single lobed, with teeth .... Bagrichthyinae

The subfamily Ritinae is distinguishable mainly on the basis of osteological characters. It can be diagnosed by having reduced maxillaries, a large, lobed, dentigerous vomer, the palatines edentate and not connected to the palatoquadrate bar, the lateral ethmoid facet for the articulation of the palatines more ventral than lateral, the pterygoid rudimentary and loosely connected to the mesopterygoid, the mesopterygoid loosely connected to the palatoquadrate bar, and the parapophyses of the fourth vertebra deeply cleft, with the divisions not fused at the base. In addition, there are 34 to 38 vertebrae and 6 to 8 ventral fin rays. A single genus, *Rita*, is included.

Rita contains about four species distributed in the region of India, Pakistan, Bangladesh, Nepal, Burma, and China (Yunnan). The body is generally short and compressed, the

Rita rita; (b) tooth patch arrangement; (c) dorsal view of head. (After Hamilton-Buchanan, 1822; b & c after Jayaram, 1977.)

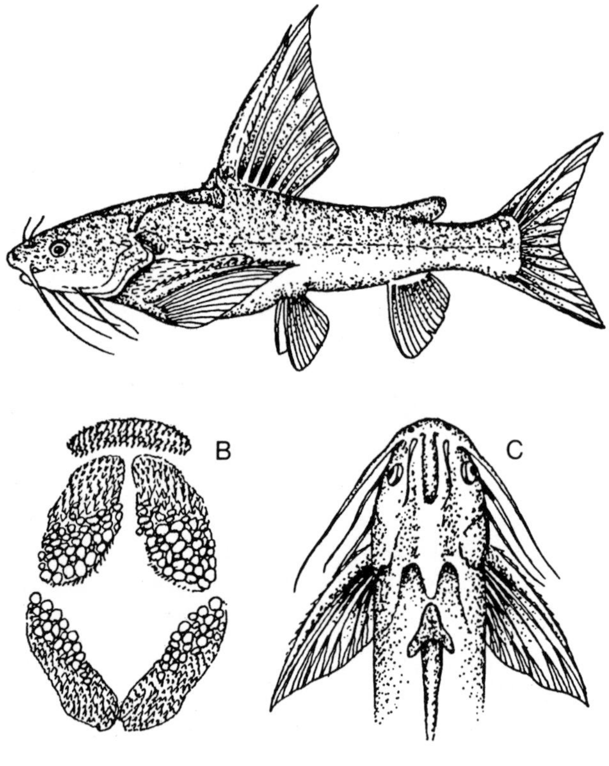

abdomen rounded, and the head is large and depressed, both being covered with smooth skin. The occipital region is bony and roughened, and the occipital process extends to the basal bone of the dorsal fin. The upper surface of the head, the humerocubital with its elongated process, and the scapular regions are also roughened. The snout is obtuse and depressed, while the mouth is subterminal, transverse, moderately wide, with the upper jaw the longer or the jaws subequal. There are villiform teeth in both jaws, or those in the lower jaw are mixed with molariform teeth. The palatal teeth are molariform and in a single patch or may be divided into two patches. The nostrils are contiguous, although the pairs are relatively distant from each other. The eyes are moderate in size and dorsolateral, not visible from below, and they are covered with skin. The lips are thin and occasionally are fimbriate. Three pairs of barbels are present: a maxillary pair, a mandibular pair, and a nasal pair, the last-mentioned small or minute with a valve-like base and located in front of the posterior nostril. The dorsal fin, inserted above the posterior half of the pectoral fins, is short-based, with 6-7 rays and a very strong spine that is serrated on both edges or smooth. The adipose fin is short and low. The anal fin is short, with 8-13 rays. The pectoral fins are set low and horizontal and have a strong spine serrated along both of the edges and 7-10 rays. The ventral fins are also low and horizontally oriented and have 7 or 8 rays. The caudal fin is forked. The lateral line has well developed scutes anteriorly, a character easily distinguishable in all species. The gill openings are broad, and the gill membranes are free from the isthmus. The swim bladder may or may not have a posterior prolongation and is not enclosed in bone. There are 8 branchiostegal rays.

Rita rita is reported to lay adhesive demersal eggs about 7 mm in diameter. The eggs hatch in about 20 hours at a temperature of 28°C.

The subfamily Bagrichthyinae is also distinguishable mainly by osteological characters. The maxillaries are reduced; the vomer is large, single-lobed, and dentigerous; the palatines are edentate and firmly connected to the palatoquadrate bar; the lateral ethmoid facet for the articulation of the palatines is strictly ventral and can be seen only from below; the pterygoid is fused with the mesoptergoid, which is firmly connected to the palatoquadrate bar; and the parapophyses of the fourth vertebra are not deeply cleft and the divisions are fused at the base. There are 39 to 42 vertebrae and 6 ventral fin rays. The subfamily includes only two genera, *Bagroides* and *Bagrichthys*, distributed in Borneo, China, Sumatra, and Thailand. They can be distinguished by the following key:

1a. Dorsal fin spine short, the teeth on the posterior margin pointing downward; inner mandibular barbels never branched; labial teeth absent .... *Bagroides*

1b. Dorsal fin spine long, the teeth on the posterior margin pointing upward; inner mandibular barbels occasionally branched; labial teeth may be present ......*Bagrichthys*

The genus *Bagroides* is a small genus containing only two species, *Bagroides melapterus* from Borneo, Sumatra, and Thailand, and *B. hirsutus* from China. The body is short, compressed, and the dorsal profile is strongly arched. The head is small and compressed with a conical but not produced snout. There is a small subterminal mouth with subequal jaws. The lips are thick and papillated and the teeth in the jaws are villiform and in bands, the mandibular band with rounded ends. The prevomer possesses molariform teeth. The supraoccipital is covered with skin, and the mental pores are quite conspicuous. The eyes are large and superior in position. There are four pairs of barbels: a maxillary pair, two mandibular pairs, and a pair of nasal barbels. The dorsal fin is short-based,

Bagroides melapterus. (From Weber & de Beaufort, 1913.)

with a strong spine that has about a dozen downwardly pointing teeth on its posterior edge and about 7 rays. The adipose fin is rather long, moderately high, and has the posterior end free or occasionally adnate. The anal fin possesses 13-18 rays and the caudal fin is forked. The pectoral fins have a strong spine that is toothed on the posterior margin. The ventral fins are inserted below the last ray of the dorsal fin. The lateral line is straight and may have a row of white fibrils. The gill membranes are united with each other, but they are free from the isthmus. There are 7 to 8 branchiostegal rays. (Jayaram, 1968.)

The second genus of the subfamily is *Bagrichthys* (including *Pseudobagrichthys*), a genus of about three species distributed from Sumatra, Borneo, and Java to Thailand. The body is somewhat elongate, quite compressed, and with the dorsal profile strongly arched. The small, compressed head has a blunt snout, and the narrow mouth is subterminal with subequal jaws. The lips are thick and papillated, and the teeth on the jaws and prevomer are villiform and arranged in bands. Some enlarged labial teeth may also be present on the mandible, with the band laterally produced. Four pairs of barbels are present: a maxillary pair, two mandibular pairs, and a nasal pair; the mandibular barbels are sometimes branched in adults. The supraoccipital is covered with skin. The lateral line is simple. The eyes are large and superior in position. The dorsal fin is short-based, with a strong, long spine that has upwardly pointing teeth on the posterior edge, and 7 rays. The adipose fin is long and quite high, and it is posteriorly adnate to the back. The anal fin has 13-15 rays. The caudal fin is forked. The pectoral fins have a strong spine with antrorse teeth on the posterior margins. The ventral fins are inserted below the last ray of the dorsal fin. The gill membranes are united with each other but are free from the isthmus. There are 7 or 8 branchiostegal rays.

The Black Lancer, currently going under the name *Bagrichthys hypselopterus*, is to hobbyists perhaps the best known species of the entire subfamily. There is still a bit of controversy surrounding this fish in that one report maintains it is hardy while another indicates

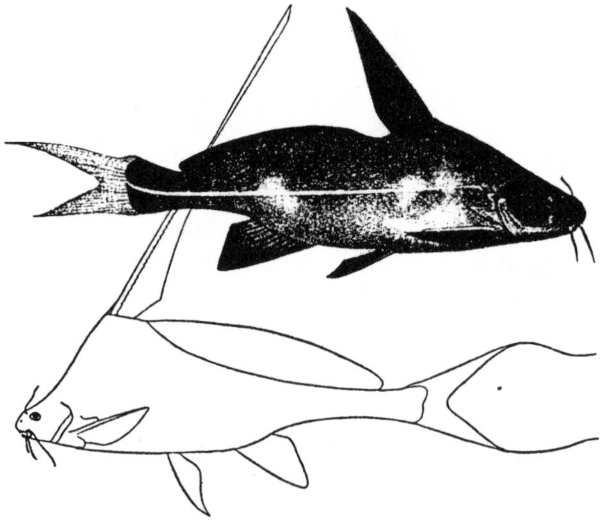

***Bagrichthys hypselopterus*; outline represents full-grown spec. (From Weber & de Beaufort, 1913.)**

that it is rather difficult to keep even after successfully maintaining it for several months. Perhaps this is a case of mistaken identity, for the other two species of the genus may also be sold under the name of Black Lancer even though one of them lacks the characteristic white midlateral stripe. Jayaram (1968) reports that both *B. hypselopterus* and *B. macracanthus* show a white (or bluish) lateral stripe. To distinguish these two he indicates that the maxillary barbels of *hypselopterus* extend back to the operculum, whereas those of *macracanthus* reach only to the posterior margins of the eyes. In addition, *hypselopterus* generally has a longer adipose fin than *macracanthus*. *B. macropterus* is not reported to show a white lateral stripe, but it does have a whitish caudal fin. The most commonly available Black Lancer in the hobby (supposedly *B. hypselopterus*) is described as going through some color changes with age. Smaller individuals less than 5 cm in length have a velvety black (described by one owner as like crushed velour) body and several vertical white bands. As it grows from 5 cm to about 15 cm the white bands fade and the typical white stripe paralleling the lateral line appears. The shape of the fish also changes: the body becomes deeper, the back strongly arched, and the dorsal spine becomes very elongate (to three-fourths of the body length according to one report). It is this very long dorsal spine that led to the fish being called a "lancer." At about a length of 25 to 30 cm the white bands appear again and the upper and lower rays of the caudal fin elongate into filaments. The ventral fins are rounded and have been described as having a shape similar to ping-pong paddles. These are sculled back and forth.

The Black Lancer is a nocturnal fish and will normally seek a dark hiding place during the day. When the lights are put out and some earthworms are placed in the tank, the Black Lancer will often rush out to finish as many of them as it can. It must be remembered that its mouth is fairly small, so the food particles should be of reasonably small size. It will eat a variety of foods, but live earthworms, tubifex, and other worms are definitely favorites. Chopped shrimp and other crustaceans, along with a variety of frozen and freeze-dried foods, are all accepted. Small live fishes may be eaten if they are found asleep at night during the nocturnal wanderings of the Black Lancer, so tankmates must be selected with this in mind. For the luckier hobbyists, Black Lancers can be weaned onto flake food and cichlid pellets. Since the skin is naked it is easily scratched, leading to a possible infection of the wound, so care must be exercised whenever handling this fish. Even if the infection is successfully cured, the scratch remains clearly visible against the velvety black color of the body, thus detracting from the beauty of the fish.

Due to the relative uncommonness of the Black Lancer and the size it attains, there have been no reports on spawning methods, although one hobbyist noticed that some of his specimens had thin white genital papilla-like structures that were rigid and slightly curved located anterior to the urogenital opening but not part of the anal fin. He suspected that these were males but was unable to confirm this opinion.

The third subfamily, the Auchenoglanidinae, contains four genera distributed in tropical Africa. In this subfamily the maxillaries are large; the vomer is reduced in size, longitudinally disposed, and may be dentigerous; the palatines are edentulous and firmly connected to the palatoquadrate bar; the lateral ethmoid facet for the articulation of the palatines is strictly ventral and can be seen only from below; the pterygoid is absent; the mesopterygoid is firmly connected to the palatoquadrate bar; and the parapophyses of the fourth vertebra are not deeply cleft and the divisions are fused at the base. There are 43 to 48 vertebrae and 6 ventral fin rays. The nostrils are modified in that the posterior pair are slit-like. The swim bladder is moderately large and fairly thick-walled, with the lateral or posterior caecum absent. The four genera can be distinguished by the following key:

1a. Dorsal fin rays 6 or 7; adipose fin high, its origin distant from the caudal fin base 2
1b. Dorsal fin rays 12 to 20; adipose fin low, its origin nearer caudal fin base 3
2a. Teeth of jaws in well-formed bands; lips plain, thin .... *Parauchenoglanis*
2b. Teeth of jaws in rudimentary patches; lips papillated, thin .... *Auchenoglanis*
3a. Dorsal fin rays 12 to 15; ventral fins inserted opposite last fourth of dorsal fin. .... *Notoglanidium*
3b. Dorsal fin rays 19 or 20; ventral fins inserted opposite anterior fourth of dorsal fin .... *Liauchenoglanis*

The genus *Notoglanidium* is a small genus of only three species. The body is moderately long, weakly compressed, and the dorsal profile is slightly arched. The large, depressed head has a broadly rounded snout.

***Notoglanidium walkeri*; (b) ventral view of head. (From Boulenger, 1911.)**

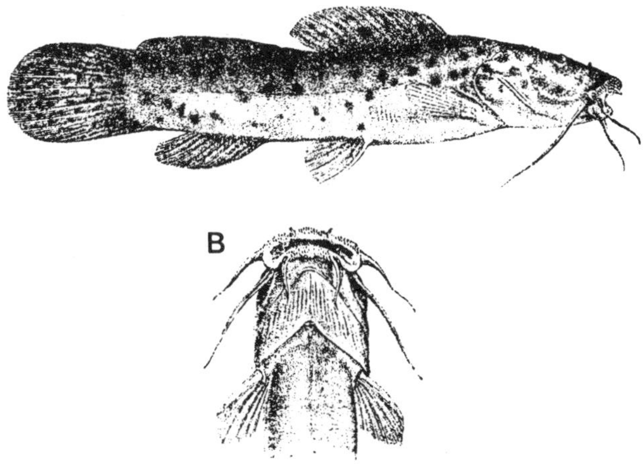

The moderately wide mouth is subterminal, and the jaws are subequal. The lips are thick and papillated, and the jaw teeth are villiform and arranged in bands; there are no teeth on the palate. The supraoccipital bone lacks a backwardly extending process and is covered with skin. The eyes are small and superior in position, and the lateral line is simple. There are only three pairs of barbels, a maxillary pair and two mandibular pairs, the nasal barbels being absent. The dorsal fin has a spine and 12 to 15 soft rays. The adipose fin is long, very low, and adnate to the back posteriorly. It is separated from the fleshy upper margin of the caudal fin by at most an incomplete notch. The anal fin is relatively short-based, with 9 to 12 rays. The ventral fins are inserted opposite the last fourth of the dorsal fin. The gill membranes are free along their posterolateral borders and only narrowly attached to the isthmus.

The genus *Liauchenoglanis* is a monotypic genus from Sierra Leone. It is very closely related to *Notoglanidium*, and some authors believe that the differences between these two genera are not great enough to merit separate generic status. *Liauchenoglanis*, in contrast to *Notoglanidium*, is said to have an obtusely rounded snout (broadly rounded in *Notoglanidium*); comparatively thin and plain lips

Liauchenoglanis maculatus. (From Boulenger, 1911.)

(thick and papillated in *Notoglanidium*); comparatively smaller eyes; 19 to 20 rays in the dorsal fin (12 to 15 in *Notoglanidium*); ventral rays inserted below the anterior fourth of the dorsal fin (opposite the last fourth of the dorsal fin in *Notoglanidium*); and the upper jaw teeth in a rounded or cardiform patch (in bands in *Notoglanidium*).

The genus *Auchenoglanis* is a larger genus of 15 to 20 species with a range extending from West Africa to Lake Tanganyika. Most species feed primarily on insect larvae, worms, and various crustaceans. They are said to be of minor commercial value. The body is short to medium in length and weakly compressed, with the dorsal profile moderately arched. The head is large, moderately compressed, with a narrow, conical (but not produced) snout. The surface of the cranium is rugose and the supraoccipital is not covered with skin. The jaw teeth are villiform and arranged in rudimentary patches; there are no teeth on the palate. The eyes are large, superior in position, and have free borders. The nostrils are well separated. There are three pairs of barbels, a maxillary pair and two mandibular pairs, the nasal barbels being absent. The dorsal fin is short-based, with a spine and 6 or 7 soft rays. The adipose fin is

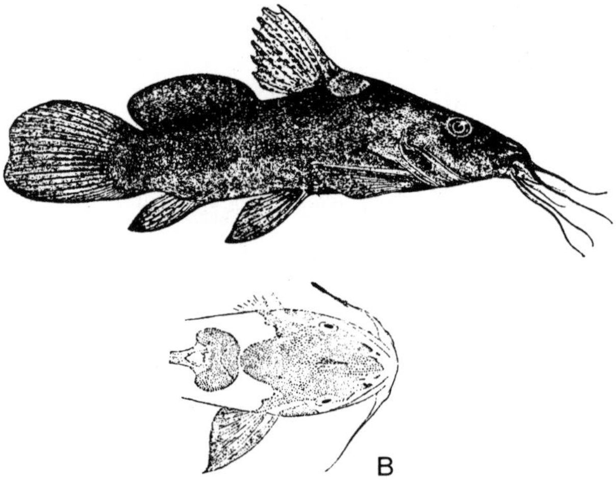

B

Auchenoglanis biscutatus; (b) dorsal view of head. (From Boulenger, 1911.)

long and high, posteriorly free from the back, and not much separated from the dorsal fin. The anal fin has anywhere from 7 to 16 rays. The caudal fin is emarginate. The ventral fins are inserted opposite the last ray of the dorsal fin or slightly ahead of that point. The gill membranes are free only along their lateral borders, but they are completely free from the isthmus. There are 10 to 12 branchiostegal rays.

The most commonly available species of the genus in the aquarium hobby is *Auchenoglanis occidentalis*. Although commonly re-

One of the species of *Auchenoglanis* commonly seen in the aquarium trade is this *A. occidentalis*. Unfortunately it attains a large size and needs plenty of room. Note the snout and mouth modification for sifting through mud and silt. Photo by Klaus Paysan.

ferred to as a subspecies of *A. biscutatus*, the two taxa are now considered to be distinct species. They may be distinguished by the following characters (after Jayaram, 1968, who considered them subspecies):

1a. Adipose fin falcate in outline; snout length 1.54 to 1.60 in head length; maxillary barbels 4.83 to 6.52 in standard length................................*biscutatus*

1b. Adipose fin semilunar in outline; snout length 1.49 to 1.69 in head length; maxillary barbels 3.20 to 9.89 in standard length ....*occidentalis*

Although *A. occidentalis* has been imported for the aquarium trade since 1909, it has never become very popular, possibly because it attains a very large size (to 1 meter) and only young specimens are suitable for home aquaria. It is fairly widely distributed from West Africa to Sudan and Egypt, as well as western equatorial Africa to Kenya and Lake Tanganyika. *A. biscutatus* seems to be restricted to a portion of the Nile River and parts of Sudan. The adults are more common in the swamps in the flood plains of the rivers. It is in these areas that they are said to spawn during the floods following heavy rains. Those seen in lakes are usually not very far from the shoreline and do not descend more than about 20 meters of depth. The young are more apt to be found in the shallows of lakes and rivers. This species is omnivorous, its long snout being used to sift through the mud and silt for food, which may include such items as animal and vegetable detritus, insect larvae and nymphs, sponges, small crustaceans, and at certain times of the year molluscs. Large individuals are not beyond feeding on small fishes. In aquaria, *A. occidentalis* has been referred to as a "living vacuum cleaner," for with their very long and depressed snout surrounded by thick barbels that are said to resemble tree roots they constantly sift through the bottom gravel for food items, rearranging the landscape as they go.

Like many other catfishes, this species does best in a dimly lit tank with plenty of hiding places and a sandy bottom. They will accept live foods of all kinds and are voracious feeders. It is best to keep them isolated in a very large tank to allow for normal growth. The recommended temperature range is 24-28°C. Other than for the aquarium trade, this species does not seem to have much commercial value. In fact, in some areas fishermen refuse to eat this fish because they consider the flesh to be poisonous.

Another species of *Auchenoglanis, A. ngamensis*, is sometimes imported, for the young are attractively marked with numerous large irregular spots. It makes grunting noises when removed from the water, a common occurrence when dealing with catfishes.

The genus *Parauchenoglanis* contains 4 closely related species distributed from Nigeria to Zaire. It is very closely related to *Auchenoglanis* and shares many characters with that genus. It differs from *Auchenoglanis*, however, by having the head comparatively more depressed, the snout rounded, the supraoccipital covered with skin, the eyes small and located in the anterior part of the head, the lips thin and plain, and the jaw teeth in well-formed bands. The three most familiar species are distinguished by Jayaram (1968) as follows:

1a. Eye included 11 times in head length; ventral fins reaching anal fin...*P. ansorgii*

1b. Eye included fewer than 11 times in head length; ventral fins not reaching anal fin.. 2

2a. Maxillary barbels reaching middle of pectoral spine; body depth 3.98 to 6.22 in S.L. .... *P. guttatus*

2b. Maxillary barbels extending beyond tip of pectoral fin spine; body depth 4.5 in S.L. .... *P. macrostoma*

Species of *Parauchenoglanis* normally feed on a wide variety of foods, including such things as fish fry and eggs, crustaceans, insect larvae, and plant material. They are generally imported for the aquarium trade at a size of about 7.5 to 10.0 cm, but will grow to a length of about 30 cm.

Parauchenoglanis macrostoma is the species most commonly seen in the shops and has been imported since 1925. It attains a length of over 24 cm and hails from the Congo and Ogowe Rivers. A second species, *P. guttatus*, is also occasionally imported. These two species are commonly confused by aquarists for they are quite similar in general appearance. In color pattern, *P. guttatus* is said to be brown above, lighter on the sides with 9 vertical rows of round black spots, and pale below; *P. macrostoma* is brown above, yellow below, and with small dark spots and 5 vertical series of more or less confluent black spots. *P. ansorgii* is brown above with small dark spots, has 7 transverse series of round black spots on the side, and is whitish ventrally. Young *P. guttatus* are said to have some yellowish crossbars in addition to the dark spots. Aquarists have dubbed *P. macrostoma* the Spotted African Catfish and *P. guttatus* the Flathead Spotted African Catfish.

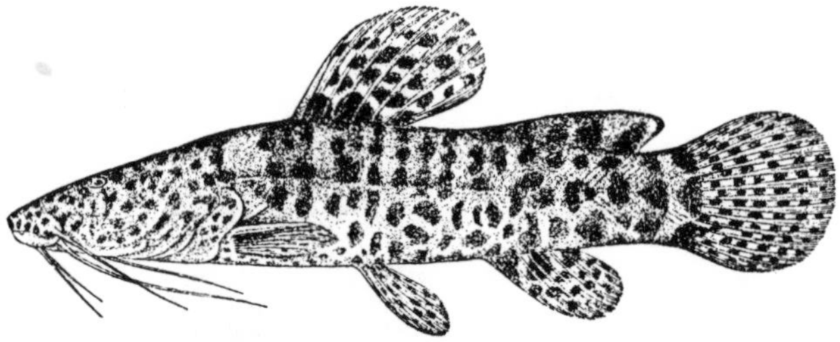

***Parauchenoglanis guttatus*. (From Boulenger, 1911.)**

Both species require a fairly large tank that contains adequate hiding places for they are nocturnal in disposition. Since they are fond of digging, a deep layer of gravel or sand is highly recommended. Although they can tolerate a wide range of temperatures (18° to 30°C), between 21° and 27°C is best. Hardness and pH extremes are to be avoided even though the species of *Parauchenoglanis* can tolerate a wide range of both parameters. Like many catfishes they are nocturnal and crepuscular, preferring to withdraw to various hiding places such as those provided by rock caves, driftwood, or plant thickets during the day. Some specimens tend to become territorial, chasing intruders out of their favorite spots. In nature they prey upon insect larvae, crustaceans, and small fishes. In the aquarium they are ravenous feeders that must be supplied with plenty of food. They will eat almost anything, and aquarists may vary their diet with such things as ground beef heart, chopped and frozen fish, earthworms, rolled oats, and even dog and cat foods. Since they are nocturnal it is best to add the food soon after "lights out." Excess food, if any, can be siphoned out early the next monring. Do not keep fishes much smaller than the *Parauchenoglanis* species with them, for they will often disappear overnight. One last word of caution—the spines of these catfishes can cause nasty wounds, especially the strongly serrated spines of *P. guttatus*.

The subfamily Bagrinae is distinguishable from the other subfamilies of the family Bagridae by the following osteological characters. The maxillaries are rudimentary; the vomer is small, semilunar in shape, and dentigerous; the palatines are broadly connected to the palatoquadrate bar and may be dentigerous; the lateral ethmoid facet for the articulation of the palatines is more ventral than lateral; the mesopterygoid is firmly connected to the palatoquadrate bar; the pterygoid is fused with the mesopterygoid; and the parapophyses of the fourth vertebra are not deeply cleft, the divisions slightly fused at the base. There are 45 to 57 vertebrae and 6 ventral fin rays. In addition, the nostrils are simple, the posterior pair bearing the nasal barbels. The swim bladder is moderately large and moderately thick-walled. Secondary transverse septa may be present in each lateral compartment, but no lateral or posterior cecum is present. Seven genera, *Bagrus, Mystus, Aorichthys, Batasio, Chandramara, Leiocassis,* and *Heterobagrus,* usually are included in this subfamily. They can be distinguished by the following key:

1a. Eyes inferiorly placed, large, visible from below; pectoral rays 5 or 6; branchiostegal rays 6 .... *Chandramara*
1b. Eyes supralateral in position, large or small, not visible from below; pectoral rays 6 to 10; branchiostegal rays 6 to 13 2
2a. Adipose fin high, long..................... 3
2b. Adipose fin low, of varying length..... 4
3a. Dorsal I,7-11; anal rays 9-15; branchiostegal rays 13; African species ..... *Bagrus*
3b. Dorsal I,6 or 7; anal rays 8-10; branchiostegal rays 10-12; Southeast Asia species .... *Heterobagrus*
4a. Eyes small; 8-10 branchiostegal rays..... .... *Leiocassis*
4b. Eyes moderate to large; 6-13 branchiostegal rays 5
5a. Maxillary barbels reach beyond dorsal fin; no pores on ventral surface or sides of head; teeth on lower jaw in a laterally prolonged, deeply curved band, separated in middle............................ 6
5b. Maxillary barbels not reaching beyond pectoral fin base; pores present on ventral surface and sides of head; teeth on lower jaw laterally prolonged, but only slightly, band not separated in middle; 6 branchiostegal rays................ *Batasio*
6a. Interneural shield absent between basal bone of dorsal fin and occipital process; 6-13 branchiostegal rays........... *Mystus*
6b. Interneural shield present between basal bone of dorsal fin and occipital process; 12 branchiostegal rays.......... *Aorichthys*

The genus *Heterobagrus* includes a single species from Thailand, *H. bocourti*. The body is long and compressed, with an arched dorsal profile, and the head is small and compressed

***Heterobagrus bocourti*. (After Thiemmedh, 1966.)**

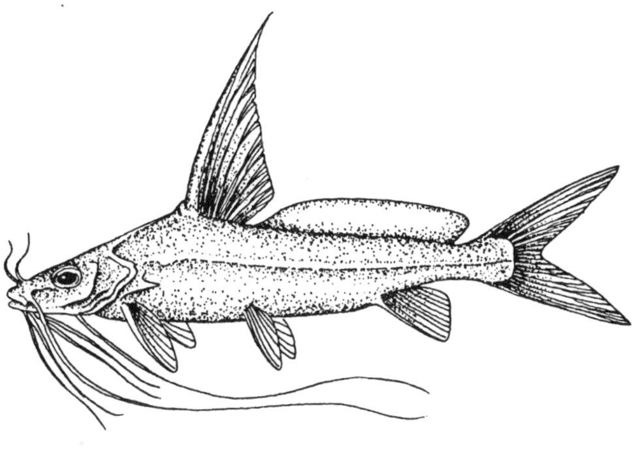

with an obtusely rounded snout. The mouth is subterminal and moderately narrow with subequal jaws, and the lips are thin and plain. Villiform teeth are present on the prevomer and/or the palatines and the mandibles, and are disposed in bands. The eyes are large, superior in position, and the supraoccipital is covered with skin. There are four pairs of barbels: a maxillary pair, two mandibular pairs, and a pair of nasal barbels. The dorsal fin is short-based and inserted above the midpoint of the pectoral fin; it has a very long simple spine and 6 or 7 soft rays. The adipose fin is long, high, and free posteriorly from the back. The ventral fins are inserted below the last ray of the dorsal fin. The pectoral fins are provided with a strong spine possessing 17 to 20 strong, antrorse teeth along its posterior edge. The anal fin has 8 to 10 rays. The caudal fin is forked. The gill membranes are free from each other and also from the isthmus. There are 10 to 12 branchiostegal rays. The lateral line is simple. (Jayaram, 1968.)

Heterobagrus bocourti is superficially very similar to species of the genus *Bagrichthys*, particularly with regard to the extremely elongate dorsal fin spine. The spine in *H. bocourti* is very slender and non-denticulated, and when depressed it may extend beyond the posterior edge of the long adipose fin. The maxillary barbels are also extremely long, reaching to beyond the base of the caudal fin. The caudal fin is deeply forked, with the upper lobe always longer than the lower and often filamentous. In color, *H. bocourti* is dark brown above and on the sides, lighter below. The spines and bony plates are tinged with green.

The genus *Chandramara* is a monotypic genus containing only the species *Chandramara chandramara* from India. The body is short and compressed, with a rounded abdomen. The head is small and compressed, with pores along the sides and ventral surfaces; the snout is obtusely rounded. The moderately wide mouth is subterminal in position. The eyes are large, inferior in position, and plainly visible from the ventral surface of the head. There are four pairs of barbels (a maxillary pair, two mandibular pairs, and a nasal pair), all of which are shorter than the head. The short-based dorsal fin has a spine and 7 rays and is inserted above the end of the cleithral process. The adipose fin is short-based and free posteriorly. The pectoral fin has a spine and 5 or 6 rays, the outermost ray extending to the level of the ventral fin base; the spine is strong, serrated with antrorse teeth along the inner edge. The ventral fins have 6 rays. The anal fin is short, with 13 to 17 rays. The caudal fin is forked, with the lobes equal.

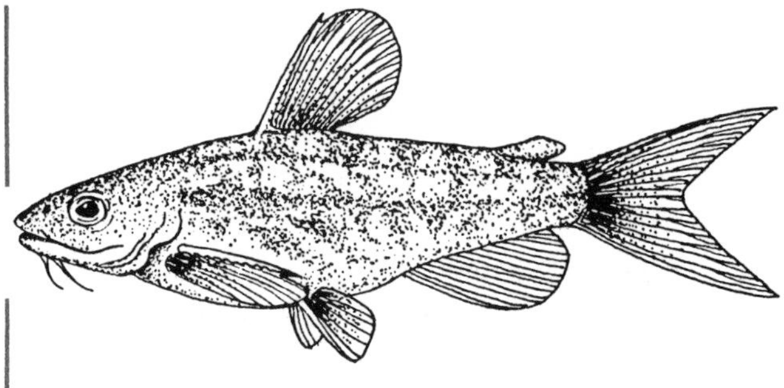

***Chandramara chandramara*. (After Jayaram, 1971.)**

The genus *Batasio* includes three species distributed in India, Bangladesh, Burma, Thailand, and Malaysia. The body is fairly deep, short, and moderately compressed with a rounded abdomen. The head is small, conical, compressed, broadly or bluntly pointed, and covered with skin. The snout is conical, broadly to bluntly pointed, and the mouth is inferior, crescentic, horizontal, and not wide.

***Batasio* ; (b) ventral view of head. (After Misra, 1976.)**

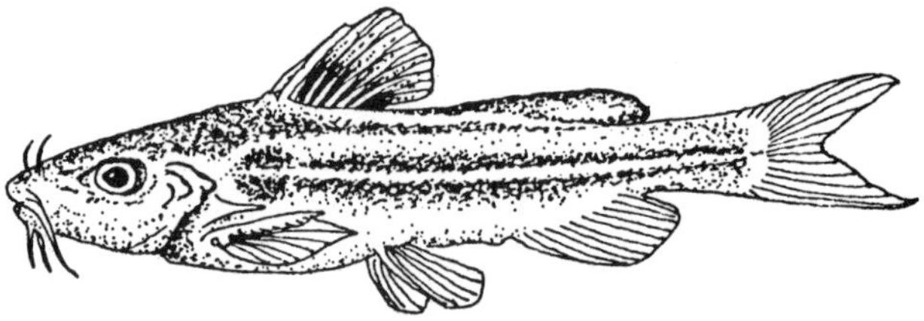

B

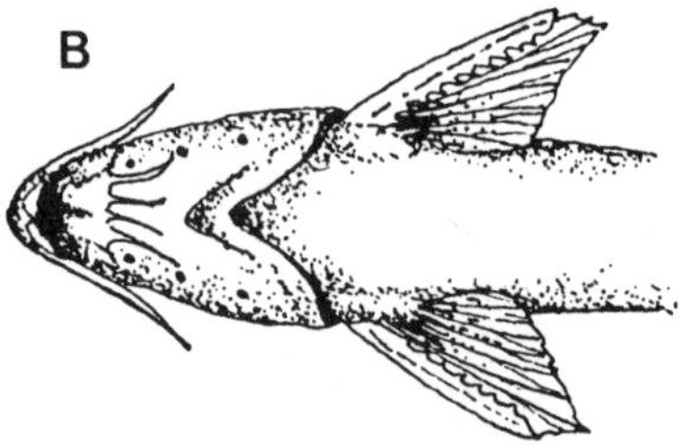

The jaws are subequal or slightly overhanging, and the teeth are small, villiform, and arranged in bands in the jaws and the palate, the band on the lower jaw continuous. The lips are thick, fleshy, and fimbriated. Behind the lower lip there are 4 to 5 oval, slit-like apertures on each side, followed by 4 to 6 pores running obliquely between the outer mandibular base to the gill opening or between the angles of the mouth and gill opening with or without additional pores between. There is a median longitudinal groove present on the head, and the occipital process may or may not reach the basal bone of the dorsal. The humerocubital process is not well developed. The subcutaneous eyes are moderate in size and dorsolateral in position. They are in the middle part of the head and are not visible from below. The nostrils are far apart, the posterior with nasal barbels. There are four pairs of barbels: a maxillary pair, two mandibular pairs, and the nasal pair. The dorsal fin is short-based with a weak or strong spine that is smooth or serrated and 7 or 8 rays. The adipose fin is low and of varying length. The pectoral fins are located above the level of the ventral fins and have 5 to 9 rays and a strong spine that is smooth externally and serrated internally with antrorse teeth. The ventral fins are horizontally oriented and have 6 rays. The anal fin is short, with 12 to 15 rays. The caudal fin is deeply emarginate to forked. The gill openings are wide and the gill membranes are notched and anteriorly confluent with the isthmus. The lateral line is complete, with some sensory pores anteriorly. The swim bladder has two rounded portions enclosed in bone. There are only 6 branchiostegals.

Batasio is one of those genera that seems to move around from family to family, depending upon to which genus the type species, *Pimelodus batasio*, was assigned. Day, who did not have any specimens to study, placed it in *Gagata*, a genus currently in the family Sisoridae. Subsequently it was moved to the genus *Bagrus* by Cuvier & Valenciennes, then to its own genus, *Batasio*, by Blyth, and then to *Macrones* (= *Mystus*) by Günther. Shaw & Shebbeare (1938) decided it should be placed back in *Batasio* and that it should be placed in the family Bagridae. This has been accepted by Jayaram (1981) but not by Misra (1976). Since for the most part I am following Jayaram, who is currently working on a revision of the family, it is here placed in the Bagridae as a full genus.

Batasio tengana has a range from the eastern Himalayas through Burma to the Malay Peninsula. Its pattern varies a bit over its range, with those from Perak described as having a conspicuous black blotch on the lateral line above the anal fin and an anterior blotch marking the spot against which the swim bladder comes to the surface directly in contact with the skin as a sort of pseudotympanum. An oblique horseshoe shaped band present just before the dorsal fin may break up into a pair of oblique lateral bars and dorsal blotch. Submarginal bands on the dorsal and the tips of the caudal fin are dusky.

The genus *Leiocassis* includes about two dozen nominal species inhabiting the waters of Thailand, Malaya, and Indonesia, with a single species extending to Hong Kong, China, and up to Korea. They can be described as having a moderately long, compressed body with an arched dorsal profile. The head is large and compressed anteriorly, with a slightly produced, angular snout. The mouth is inferior or subterminal and moderately wide, and the jaws are subequal. The lips may be thick and papillated or thin and plain, and there are villiform teeth on the premaxillaries, prevomer, and/or palatines. The supraoccipital may or may not be covered with skin. The eyes are small and superior in position. Four pairs of barbels are present: a maxillary pair, two mandibular pairs, and a nasal pair. The dorsal fin is short-based, with a spine and 6 to 7 rays, and is inserted above the tip of the pectoral fin. The adipose fin is long, low, and posteriorly free from the back.

***Leiocassis siamensis*. (From Smith, 1945.)**

Leiocassis siamensis is a strikingly patterned species that is called the bumblebee catfish by aquarists. Note the dark spots on the caudal fin lobes. Photo by Gunter Senfft.

The ventral fins are inserted posterior to the last ray of the dorsal fin. The pectoral fins are provided with strong spines. The anal fin usually has 12 to 16 (normally 15) soft rays. The gill membranes are free from each other and from the isthmus. There are 8 to 10 branchiostegal rays. (Jayaram, 1968.)

Two subgenera have been proposed by Jayaram as distinguished by the following key:

1a. Snout angular and produced beyond the inferior mouth; snout length greater than interorbital width..........*Leiocassis*
1b. Snout rounded or obtuse, not produced beyond the subterminal mouth; snout length equal to or less than interorbital width..........................*Pseudomystus*

This genus is recognized by aquarists particularly because of the bumblebee catfish *Leiocassis siamensis*. The species of this genus are mostly nocturnal and should be provided with many hiding places and subdued lighting for best results. Most species are also territorial, leading to a certain amount of squabbling for the choicest spots in large aquaria and more serious encounters if the space is limited. Water conditions are not critical as long as extremes are avoided, though some aquarists suggest the water be a bit on the soft, acid side. Species of *Leiocassis* also seem fairly tolerant of temperature variations, although wide swings or rapid drops in temperature should be avoided. They are omnivorous and voracious feeders on all types of live foods but will also accept a variety of frozen and dried foods as well. Although small specimens seem well suited to community tanks, they grow quickly and, in the evening when they are wandering about searching for food, they will include rasboras, small tetras, and similar fishes in their diet. Some of the species are known to make sounds, especially when removed from the water. Importation of the first specimens of *Leiocassis* into Europe and the United States seems to have occurred in the early 1950's.

The Asian Bumblebee Catfish, *Leiocassis siamensis*, is the most commonly imported and most popular of the species of the genus because of its attractive pattern. It is widely distributed in Thailand and is even occasionally captured far down rivers in brackish water. Its color pattern is probably protective in function for it is difficult to spot when lying on the debris of the bottom in shallow water where light reflections are seen. It is a nocturnal fish, hiding during the day, but with "lights out" specimens start cruising around the tank searching for food. For this reason it is best not to keep it with fishes that are too small or vulnerable as they sleep, for when hungry *L. siamensis* will swallow the smaller fishes whole and will tear the fins off larger fishes as they come upon them in the dark. Although it shows a distinct preference for live foods of all kinds (such as worms, brine shrimp, small fishes, daphnia), it will also accept other fare such as beef heart, frozen foods, and pellet food, and occasionally some plant food will be eaten. Water conditions are not critical, although frequent water changes are recommended and a temperature range of 18°C to 30°C is tolerated. However, it is best to maintain Asian bumblebees at the upper portion of this range. When caught in a net or even sometimes when roaming free in the tank, your bumblebees might be heard making a croaking sound sometimes described as a "kot" sound, repeated several times in succession. Happily, *L. siamensis* is extremely resistant to diseases, and with proper care your specimens could live up to three years or more in captivity.

It is interesting to note that the two species that are commonly confused by aquarists because of their similar color patterns, *L. siamensis* and *L. poecilopterus*, are placed in separate subgenera by Jayaram, *poecilopterus* in *Leiocassis* and *siamensis* in *Pseudomystus*. The two species have been contrasted as follows: *Leiocassis siamensis* is primarily a mainland species that attains a length of 17 cm and has a color pattern that includes a dark spot or bars running across the caudal fin and the presence of a collar band. The body pattern varies depending upon growth stages or environmental conditions. *L. poecilopterus* is an island archipelago species (although there is a record from Thailand) that attains a length of 30 cm and has a color pattern where the caudal has dark bands running close to the edges of the fin's margins (i.e., submarginal) and a collar band is absent. The light body bands are located just in front of the dorsal and adipose fins and in the type specimen light bars can be seen crossing the anal fin. Sexual dimorphism has been reported for *L. poecilopterus* wherein the males have brighter coloration than the females (the body with alternating deep brown vertical bands).

Of the other species of the genus not very much is known. *L. baramensis* was found to feed on decapod crustaceans in the wild, where they inhabit clear waters of small, gravel-bottomed streams. *L. robustus*, which comes from Borneo, was found only in muddy water. Some specimens were caught on hook and line using earthworms as bait during the flood period (local river people maintain that this is the only time they can be caught in this manner). As *L. robustus* grows, it undergoes some interesting changes. The number of serrations on the dorsal fin spine increases, the head length becomes reduced proportionately but it becomes wider, the body depth increases, and there is an increase in the length of the adipose fin.

The genus *Mystus* is a moderately large genus of some three dozen nominal species inhabiting a large geographic area from Syria through Pakistan, India, Nepal, Sri Lanka, Bangladesh, Burma, Thailand, Indochina, Malaya, Singapore, and the East Indies to China. The heaviest concentration of species is in India, whereas elsewhere they are poorly represented. Most are small, around 25 to 35 cm in length, with the largest attaining a length of up to 60 cm or more. They inhabit a variety of bodies of water, including rivers, lakes, canals, etc., and a few species are able to penetrate the brackish waters of estuaries or even more into the sea itself.

The body is short to moderately elongate, compressed, and usually has a rounded abdomen. The head is moderate, also compressed, and is rugose or smooth and covered with thin skin; it possesses a median longitudinal groove. A distinct, separate, interneural shield is absent. The snout is rounded to obtuse and depressed to even spatulate. The mouth is terminal, transverse, and moderately wide, and the jaws are subequal, with the upper one slightly longer than the lower. The cleft of the mouth does not extend to the orbit. The lips are thin. The teeth are uniformly villiform in the jaws and palate and are arranged in bands. The semilunar vomerine band of teeth is continuous in all species except *Mystus horai*, where it is interrupted. The nostrils are small and far apart. The eyes are moderately large, located in the anterior part of the head, and supralateral in position, so that they are not visible from below. They

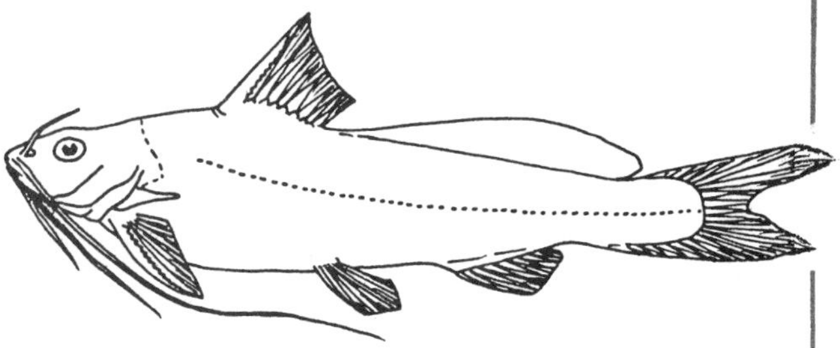

Mystus halepensis. (After Blanc, et al, 1971.)

have free orbital rims. Four pairs of barbels, generally longer than the head, are present: a maxillary pair, two mandibular pairs, and a nasal pair. The short-based dorsal fin is inserted over the last quarter of the pectoral fin and has a strong serrated spine and 7 rays. The adipose fin is low and of varying length depending upon the species. The pectoral fins are placed low on the body and have 6 to 10 rays and a strong spine serrated along the inner edge with a series of antrorse teeth. The ventral fins have their origin below or behind the end of the last dorsal fin rays and possess 6 rays. The anal fin has 9 to 16 rays. The caudal fin is forked. There is a complete, simple lateral line, and an axillary pore is present in most instances. The gill openings are wide, and the gill membranes overlap the isthmus and are free from it. The swim bladder is moderate or large and is attached to the lower surface of the bodies of the anterior vertebrae. There are 6 to 13 branchiostegal rays.

The two species of *Mystus* most commonly seen in the aquarium trade are *M. tengara* and *M. vittatus*. They are often confused but differ in several characters. *Mystus vittatus* has 16 teeth along the inner edge of the pectoral fin spine compared to 8-10 in *M. tengara; M. vittatus* is more deep bodied than *M. tengara*; the median groove in the skull extends as far as the occipital protrusion in *M. tengara* but not in *M. vittatus*; and the maxillary barbels of *M. vittatus* reach the bases of the ventral fins, whereas those of *M. tengara* extend to beyond the anal fin

Mystus tengara attains a maximum size of about 18 cm in the wild, but stays well below this in captivity. It inhabits stagnant or slow-moving waters in India, Bangladesh, and Pakistan. Its diet consists of such things as aquatic insects and their larvae, but it will do well in an aquarium on earthworms, mealworms, tubificid worms, and the like. It is very important that it receive a varied diet, for it is said that growth and vitality are af-

Mystus tengara has a relatively large adipose fin when compared to *M. vittatus* on the opposite page. These fishes are commonly confused because of the similarity in color pattern. Photo by Laurence Perkins.

fected when the diet is monotonous. Even if the proper diet is restored, there is a considerable span of time before it gets back to its original pep and growth rate. This species is most active at night. As it moves about, the barbels are always moving in all directions, searching for morsels of food, or are sometimes pointed straight out in front of the fish (at least until they strike something like the glass side of the tank). Once something edible is located in the dark by this means it is quickly seized and eaten. Water conditions are not critical, and *M. tengara* is often included in community tanks. It can be kept with smaller fishes when it is small itself, but when it gets large it is best not to trust it with the smaller fishes. A large aquarium is best, and there should be plenty of places where it can hide from the light during the day, such as caves, driftwood decorations, or even dense vegetation. It helps if the bottom material is dark-colored and the lighting is subdued. This species is not a digger and it does not attack the plants.

No known sex differences have been reported even though it has been spawned in captivity. After some lively courtship activity, which involves a lot of circling of each other while making "chirping" sounds, the pair spawns in the humus among the plants. The eggs are fairly large and yellowish white in color.

Mystus vittatus is much more widely distributed, occurring in fresh to even brackish waters throughout India, Pakistan, Sri Lanka, Burma, Nepal, Malaya, and Thailand. It attains a length of about 21 cm, although ripe females only about 13 cm long were captured in Thailand. There is apparently a great deal of variation in this species depending upon the location where it was caught and its condition, both in coloration and in proportions. The striping ranges from a steel-blue to blue-black to dark brown or even golden brown on a ground color of white, silver, or pale blue to a bright yellow. The most constant feature is the double stripe arising just behind the head. The belly is a bright white. Some individuals from India are reported to have black spots at the caudal base. The maxillary barbels are quite long and are in constant motion as in *M. tengara*, searching out good things to eat. In the wild these tend to be crustaceans, small fishes, etc., while in captivity they accept a wide variety of items including chopped fish, brine shrimp, earthworms, tubificid worms, beef heart, and even pellet food. They are enthusiastic feeders during the evening hours but usually hide during the day or when the light levels are high. They should have many

***Mystus vittatus*, on the other hand, has a short adipose fin and a more solid central band. Photo by Dr. Herbert R. Axelrod.**

hiding places, not only to be able to avoid the light, but if there are two individuals of the same species in the tank they are needed to provide refuge to the loser of these combats. The number of encounters decreases with a greater number of hiding places and also if there are several specimens in the tank instead of just two. Being active at night causes some problems for the other fishes in the tank. The *Mystus* may develop a habit of "pestering" the other fishes by swimming behind them and nipping at the tail or other fins. Large cichlids and some of the slow, deliberate swimmers are their favorite victims. Although the actual damage usually is not great, this habit can turn the larger fishes into nervous wrecks and/or leave the damaged areas open to fungal and other infections. When the *Mystus* itself is irritated it is said that it holds its barbels out very stiffly and erects the spine-bearing fins while emitting a noise that sounds like the buzzing of a bee. When in this irritable state, they have been known to attack smaller fishes in the aquarium. Although spawning has been reported for this species, there has been some doubt cast as to the identification of the fish spawned (possibly a similarly patterned pimelodid?).

Mystus wyckii from the rivers of Sumatra, Java, and Thailand grows to a length of at least 28 cm (48 cm according to Smith, 1945). In an aquarium it is said to be very aggressive and territorial. It requires sufficient hiding places and, if frightened, is reported to be an excellent jumper, requiring that the tank be covered. There is no problem feeding this species as it accepts a wide variety of different foods, including brine shrimp and other frozen foods, pellet foods, earthworms and other worms, feeder goldfish, and even flake foods.

Mystus nemurus ranges from Indochina and Thailand to Malaya and Java, attaining a length in some cases of nearly 60 cm, although individuals of 25-35 cm are more common. It occurs throughout the lengths of many rivers, from the headwaters down to the mouths, where they may be found in brackish water. There seems to be no evident preference for either clear or muddy environments. They dine on a variety of items, among which are crustaceans (crabs, prawns), aquatic and terrestrial insects, fishes, and vegetation. Among the fishes identified as eaten were species of *Clarias* and *Kryptopterus*. One specimen was reported as having its stomach crammed full of large red ants. Females from 12.3 to 32 cm long contained enlarged ova, the 32 cm specimen with eggs that measured 1 mm in diameter. This species has a thin black lateral stripe at all sizes and a black spot at the end of the adipose fin.

Mystus gulio also has a broad distribution, being found from the East Indies to India and Sri Lanka. It is very common in the lower courses of tidal rivers emptying into the Gulf of Siam. In Sri Lanka they are usually present in brackish water but are capable of ascending the rivers into pure fresh water. In Thailand they are also present in brackish water up to a length of about 25 cm and have the same capability of moving up into fresh water. The smaller fish (6-7 cm) may be seen in immense schools. *M. gulio* is reported to grow to a length of half a meter in the East Indies.

According to Breder & Rosen (1966), this species may carry eggs on the ventral surface on folds of the abdomen. A female with well-developed ova was found to have large and highly vascularized folds, while in unripe fish they were small. In nature *M. gulio* spawns in tidal waters. A report of an aquarium spawning of this species indicated that a great mass of fairly large eggs were hung in plants. Although the spawning was repeated four times, the eggs never hatched.

Mystus cavasius ranges from Java, Sumatra, and Borneo to India. It frequents rivers, canals, and lakes but does not seem to penetrate into brackish or salt waters. The adults are rather plain colored, with a brassy green back and a whitish belly. The dorsal, caudal, and adipose fins are bright green, while the anal and ventral fins are pale salmon with a milky white margin. The young individuals have a dark lateral band bordered on top and bottom by light bands.

Among the other species, *M. leucophasis* from Burma has been referred to as the "topsy-turvy" fish because of its habit of swimming in an inverted position like some of the *Synodontis* species. *M. sabanus* from Borneo is apparently restricted to the large rivers, not having been collected in the estuaries. It feeds primarily on spiders and various insects and insect larvae. *M. gulio* is partly marine (Mirza, 1975).

The genus *Aorichthys* is a small genus containing only two species* of large fishes (they both may attain a length of up to 2 meters) from Bangladesh, India, Pakistan, and Burma. The species are robust, with an elongate, compressed body and a large, slightly depressed head. The dorsal profile is arched to the dorsal fin base and more or less straight thereafter. The upper surface of the head is covered with thin skin, although the occiput and sides may be rugose; the median longitudinal groove is shallow, but reaches to the base of the occipital process. A distinct and

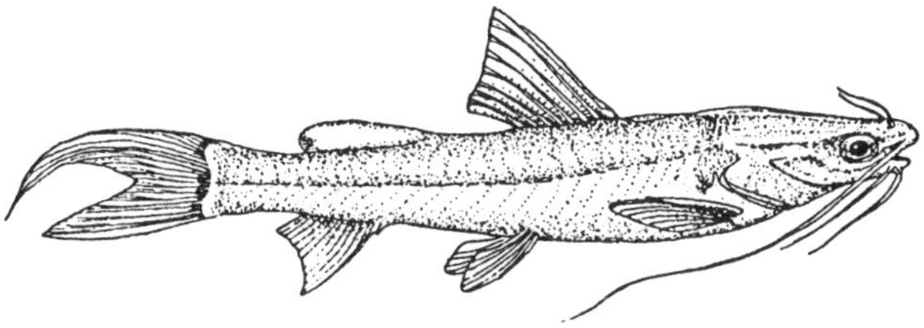

***Aorichthys seenghala*. (After Day, 1877.)**

even prominent interneural shield is present between the basal bone of the dorsal fin and the occipital process. The snout is spatulate and rounded. The mouth is transverse, moderately wide, subterminal with subequal jaws, and has thin lips. The teeth are sharp, villiform, and arranged in bands on the jaws and palate. The bands on the lower jaw are curved along the sides and interrupted in the middle; those on the palate are confined to the vomer and have wing-like lateral processes. The eyes are large, supralateral in position so that they are not visible from below, and located in the middle of the head. The nostrils are far apart, with the anterior nostril tubular and located at the tip of the snout and the posterior bearing the nasal barbel. There are four pairs of barbels: a maxillary pair, two mandibular pairs, and a nasal pair. The dorsal fin is inserted in advance of the ventral fins (about above the last quarter of the pectoral fin) and has a weak, serrated or smooth spine and 7 rays. The adipose fin is smooth, long, low, and its posterior end is free. The paired fins are horizontally inserted, the pectoral with a strong spine provided with antrorse teeth along the inner edge and 9 to 10 rays. The ventral fins have 6 rays. The anal fin is short, with 11 to 13 rays, and the caudal fin is forked. The gill openings are broad and the gill membranes are free from each other and also from the isthmus. A complete lateral line is present. The swim bladder is large, free, and has a posterior elongation. There are 12 branchiostegal rays.

According to Raj (1962), the two species of the genus, *Aorichthys aor* and *A. seenghala*, build nests in small pits in the shallow river bottom. A parent fish with young is commonly found in each nest, but usually no eggs are seen. One of the brooding fish was caught while guarding a nest and reached the local market, where Raj was able to examine it. He was able to determine that it was the male that was brooding and that they had red spongy undersides, including the ventral fins, the anal fin, and the lower part of the caudal fin. The red coloration was due to swollen blood vessels covering numerous tube-like projections that, combined with much folding of the skin itself, gave the characteristic spongy appearance. The fry were seen to be "attached" to the male. When their stomach contents were examined it was found that they were filled with a milky fluid. The males secreted this white fluid, which turned out to be mainly protein in content. Although superficially resembling mammalian milk, it was quite different. If the fry attached to the male were disturbed, they usually scattered but returned in a short while to start picking again at the spongy area. The fry of *A. seenghala* apparently feed solely on this secretion of the male until they reach a length of about 4.5 cm. Although some bunocephalids from South America carry their eggs in a spongy ventral area, it is apparent that the males of the *Aorichthys* species do not do this but leave them in the nest.

Bagrus is a genus of about ten species inhabiting the region from West Africa to Tanganyika. They differ in appearance from other African bagrids and look more like the shovelnose South American catfishes of the

* Misra (1976) considers *Aorichthys* a subgenus of *Mystus* and includes four species, *aor*, *seenghala*, *leucophasis*, and *rufescens*.

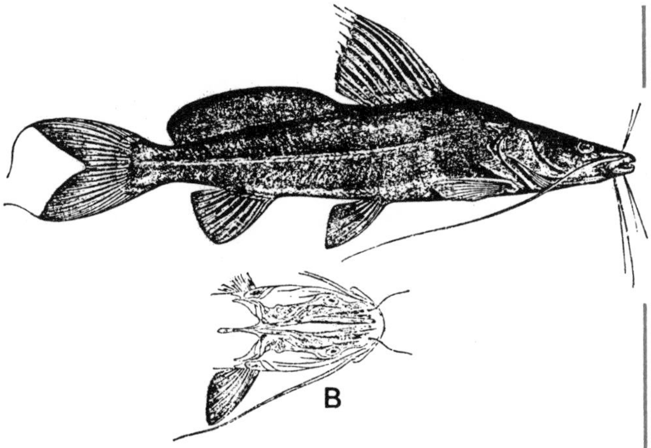

Bagrus bajad; (b) dorsal view of head. (From Boulenger, 1911.)

family Pimelodidae. The body is moderately long and weakly compressed, and the dorsal profile is arched. The head is large and anteriorly depressed, with a flat or obtuse snout. The jaws are subequal, with a wide, subterminal mouth provided with thin, plain lips. Bands of villiform teeth are present on the premaxillaries, mandibles, vomer, and/or palatines. The supraoccipital may or may not be covered with skin, and the large supralateral eyes have free orbital rims. There are four pairs of barbels: a pair of maxillary barbels that extend to the origin of the pectoral fins in most species, two pairs of mandibular barbels, and a pair of nasal barbels. The dorsal fin is short-based, with a spine and 7 to 11 rays, and is inserted above the middle of the pectoral fin. The adipose fin is long, high, and posteriorly free. The ventral fins are inserted below the last ray of the dorsal fin or slightly ahead of that position. The anal fin has 9 to 15 rays. The caudal fin is forked, with filaments (at least on the upper lobe) in many species. There is a simple lateral line. The gill membranes are free from each other and also from the isthmus. There are 13 branchiostegals. Most species feed on fishes and occasional insect larvae and prawns. They are of moderate to high commercial importance.

Bagrus docmak is widely distributed in Nigeria, Ghana, the Nile Basin, and the Great Lakes of Africa. It is quite large, individuals attaining lengths of up to one meter and weighing as much as 22.7 kilos being reliably recorded, although reports of a maximum of 34 kilos are available. It is said to be rare in estuaries and the immediate vicinity and is very littoral and probably fluviatile. Wherever it is common it is generally a valued commercial fish. It is a predatory species that when large feeds mostly on fishes, while the younger individuals find insect larvae and crustaceans more to their liking, along with some vegetable debris. The adults are dark gray, almost black, above and creamy white on the ventral surface. The young are more attractive, with a light smoke gray or olive brown back, a golden ventral surface, and yellowish to dusky fins that occasionally have black spots. Only young individuals are small enough to be kept in home aquaria, and they are not imported very often. Breeding males are reported to be about 76 cm in length and females about 58 cm. The eggs are white and are a little over a millimeter in diameter.

Bagrus bajad also attains a length of about one meter. Like *B. docmak*, adults are mainly piscivores, while the juveniles feed on aquatic insects, crustaceans, and even small fishes. It lives and feeds on or near the bottom, where *Chrysichthys auratus* appears to be the most common prey species.

The fifth and last subfamily, the Claroteinae, is the largest, with 17 genera widely distributed over Africa and Asia. In this subfamily the maxillaries are slightly enlarged; the vomer is small, semilunar, and dentigerous or edentate; the palatines may be dentigerous and loosely connected to the palatoquadrate bar; the lateral ethmoid facet for the articulation of the palatines is more ventral than lateral; the pterygoid is rudimentary and loosely connected to the mesopterygoid; the mesopterygoid is loosely connected to the palatoquadrate bar; and the parapophyses of the fourth vertebra are deeply cleft with the divisions not fused at the base. There are 34 to 56 vertebrae and 6 ventral fin rays. The nostrils are simple, with the posterior pair bearing the nasal barbels. The swim bladder is moderately large and moderately thick-walled; secondary transverse septa may be present in each lateral compartment. There is no lateral or posterior cecum.

Sixteen of the 17 genera (*Austroglanis* is not included due to lack of data) can be distinguished by use of the following key.

1a. Nasal barbels distinct, well-developed; palate always dentigerous, with well-developed teeth 2
1b. Nasal barbels absent or only rudimentary when present; palate edentulous or with rudimentary teeth 6
1c. Nasal barbels absent; only one pair of maxillary and one pair of mandibular barbels present; bands of teeth present on the vomer and dermopalatine......... .... *Bathybagrus*
2a. Anal fin with 9 to 16 rays; base of nasal barbel continued into posterior nostril as a valve 9
2b. Anal fin with 15 to 28 rays; base of nasal barbel not continued into posterior nostril as a valve, but simple 3
3a. Caudal fin forked 4
3b. Caudal fin truncate, rounded, cuneate, or slightly emarginate 5
4a. Eyes inferior, visible when viewed from below .... *Horabagrus*
4b. Eyes superior, not visible when viewed from below .... *Pelteobagrus*
5a. Head width more than 1.2 times in standard length; body long and low, its depth generally more than 5 times in standard length .... *Pseudobagrus*
5b. Head width less than 1.2 times in standard length; body short and deep, its depth generally less than 5 times in standard length .... *Coreobagrus*
6a. Maxillary barbels modified, either flat and strap-like, or fringed on both sides by leaf-like membranes; palate with rudimentary teeth .... *Phyllonemus*
6b. Maxillary barbels simple, not modified, not with leaf-like expansion; palate edentulous 7
7a. Eyes tiny; 6 or 7 branchiostegal rays .... *Zairichthys*
7b. Eyes large; 8 to 10 branchiostegal rays .. 8
8a. Maxillary bone short, immovable and not connected to head by any fold; 6 or 7 dorsal fin rays; 11-17 anal fin rays; adipose fin short, low, not adnate to back . ... *Gephyroglanis*
8b. Maxillary bone long, movable, and connected to head by membranous fold; dorsal rays 5 or 6; anal rays 8-12; adipose long, low, adnate to back ....*Leptoglanis*
9a. Body short, weakly compressed; eyes usually large 10
9b. Body long, strongly depressed; eyes small... 13
9c. Body short, weakly compressed; eyes small, subcutaneous .... *Lophiobagrus*
10a. Otic bones of occipito-auditory region distinct, covered with skin and not fused; lips thin, plain .... *Chrysichthys*
10b. Otic bones of occipito-auditory region not distinct, not covered with skin, and fused together to form a cephalic shield 11
11a. Lower jaw strongly projecting forward; adipose fin fleshy ....*Gnathobagrus*
11b. Lower jaw not projecting; lips thin, plain; adipose fin with rays or a spine and rays.. 12
12a. Head narrow, 25-31% of S.L.; buccal cleft less than 60% of head width; angle of mouth quite distant from level of eyes; eyes supralateral, nearer snout tip than gill openings; adipose fin not as high as first dorsal fin ....*Clarotes*
12b. Head very broad, about 40% of S.L.; width of mouth at least 80% of head width; mouth angle extending to level of eyes; eyes superior, approximately equidistant from tip of snout and gill openings; cranial rugosities hidden by skin; adipose fin about equivalent to height of first dorsal fin .... *Pardiglanis*
13a. Lower jaw strongly protruding; lips thick, papillated ....*Amarginops*
13b. Upper jaw slightly protruding; lips moderately fleshy, non-papillose or with fine papillae...................... *Rheoglanis*

The genus *Pelteobagrus* contains probably fewer than 20 species. They are distributed from the Soviet Far East to southern China, Japan, Hainan, and Hong Kong, and there is one species from Malaya. The body is short and compressed, with the dorsal profile arched. The head is large and slightly compressed, and there is an obtusely rounded snout. The jaws are subequal but may be variable in some species. The mouth is moderately wide, generally subterminal, and usually possesses plain and thin lips. There are villiform teeth on the premaxillaries, prevomer, and mandibles arranged in bands, the band on the mandible produced laterally and separated medially by an edentulous space and the band on the prevomer semilunar in shape and continuous. The eyes are large, superior, and placed in the anterior part of the head. The supraoccipital may or may not be covered with skin but has a posteriorly projecting process. There are four pairs of barbels: a maxillary pair, two mandibular pairs, and a nasal pair. The short-based dorsal fin is inserted above the middle of the pectoral fin and has a spine and 6 or 7 rays. The adipose fin is long, low, and posteriorly free from the back. The ventral fins are inserted below the last ray of the dorsal fin or slightly posterior to that point. The anal fin has 15 to 27 rays. There is a simple lateral line. The gill membranes are free from each other and also from the isthmus. There are 8 to 10 branchiostegal rays. (Jayaram, 1968.)

Pelteobagrus fulvidraco occurs in the Amur River basin, northern China, and southeastern Siberia. It is found mainly in the river channels and lakes and attains a length of about 32 cm. It feeds on the bottom on insects (especially trichopterans and chironomids), molluscs, and occasionally fishes and is a relatively important commercial species where it is common. It tolerates a wide variety of water conditions in its natural habitat, perhaps most important to aquarists being a tolerance of low water temperatures. Spawning of this species occurs in the summer, when shallow nests are excavated in the mud or clay-bottomed river bed. Once the eggs are deposited in the nest, the male, which is the larger of the two parents, guards them and the fry, which hatch out in about two days. The name *"fulvidraco"* means tawny (*fulva*)

Pelteobagrus fulvidraco.

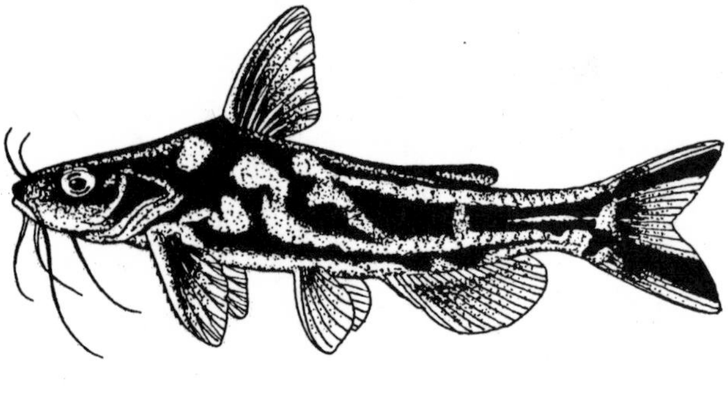

dragon (*draco*). Perhaps the dragon part is connected in some way with the ability of the fish to cause painful puncture wounds by the use of its pectoral spines.

P. fulvidraco is relatively easy to keep. Water conditions are not critical, and a heated tank is not necessary. In fact, it also does well in outdoor ponds. It will eat a wide variety of aquarium foods including earthworms and other worms, beef heart, brine shrimp, and even frozen and freeze-dried foods. One word of caution—small or slow-moving fishes with long flowing fins should not be housed in the same tank as the Tawny Dragon.

A second species that is sometimes seen is *Pelteobagrus brashnikowi*. This is also a good species for aquarists with unheated tanks and outdoor ponds. It also inhabits the Amur River, which freezes over for about six months of the year. Spawning occurs in nature at the beginning of June. The eggs, some 2 to 2.3 mm in diameter, are found among root tangles. Water conditions are not critical, and in captivity this species can be kept at temperatures as low at 10°C, although this is not recommended for they usually become sluggish and hide more than usual. The optimum temperature is said to be between 18° and 20°C. This is a twilight fish that avoids bright lights and must have many hiding places for the daylight hours. If it feels relatively secure and the light level is subdued, you may be able to see them come out during the day. Often individuals can be seen resting on the broad leaves of some of the larger aquatic plants. *Pelteobagrus brashnikowi*, which attains a length of about 13 cm, can be heard producing a gnashing sound when it becomes excited.

The genus *Pseudobagrus* includes approximately two dozen species that range from the Soviet Far East to southern China, Japan, Taiwan, and Hainan Island. The body is moderately long, compressed, and with a nearly straight dorsal profile. The small head is compressed and the snout is obtuse. The jaws are subequal; the mouth is subterminal, moderately wide, and has thin, plain lips. The villiform teeth are arranged in bands on the premaxillaries, prevomer, and mandibles. The supraoccipital is covered with skin, and the eyes are small and superior in position.

There are four pairs of barbels: a maxillary pair, two mandibular pairs, and a nasal pair. The short-based dorsal fin is inserted above the middle of the pectoral fin and possesses a spine and 6 or 7 rays. The adipose fin is long,

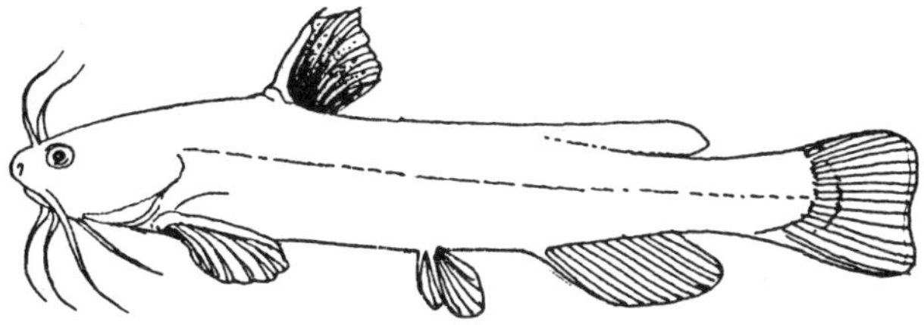

Pseudobagrus aurantiacus. (After Masuda, et al., 1984.)

low, and free posteriorly. The ventral fins are inserted well posterior to the last ray of the dorsal fin. The anal fin has 13 to 24 rays (usually about 18). The lateral line is simple. The gill membranes are free from each other and from the isthmus. There are 8 branchiostegals. (Jayaram, 1968.)

None of the species that are currently included in this genus have become popular in the aquarium trade and they are rarely, if ever, seen. It would be expected that they should receive the same treatment as *Pelteobagrus fulvidraco* and *P. brashnikowi*.

Coreobagrus is a small genus of only three species from Korea and Japan. The body is short and compressed, with an arched dorsal profile. The head is small and depressed, and the snout is blunt and overhangs the mouth slightly. The jaws are subequal, and the mouth is transverse and moderately wide with slightly thick and fleshy lips. The villiform teeth are arranged in bands on the premaxillaries, prevomer, and mandibles, the band on the mandibles being prolonged laterally and interrupted in the center and that on the prevomer semilunar in shape and uninterrupted. The supraoccipital is covered with skin and has a posteriorly prolonged process. The eyes are large, supralateral, and located in the anterior part of the head. There are four pairs of barbels: a maxillary pair, two mandibular pairs, and a nasal pair. The short-based dorsal fin is inserted above the tip of the pectoral fin spine and has a spine and 6 or 7 rays. The adipose fin is moderately long, not very low, and has a free posterior margin. The horizontally oriented pectoral fins have a strong spine. The ventral fins are inserted at a level posterior to the last ray of the dorsal fin. The anal fin has 13 to 20 rays. The caudal fin is emarginate to nearly forked. The gill membranes are free from each other and from the isthmus. There are 8 branchiostegal rays. (Jayaram, 1968.)

Coreobagrus ichikawai. (After Masuda, et al., 1984.)

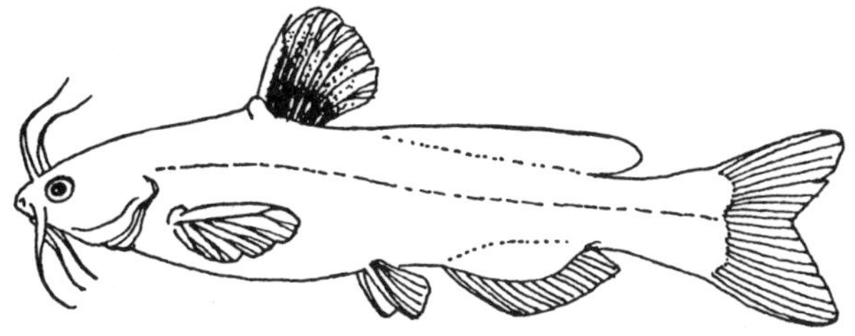

Coreobagrus is close to *Pseudobagrus* but can be distinguished from that genus by the longer and wider head and the shorter body.

The genus *Horabagrus* contains only a single species, *H. brachysoma*, apparently from the backwaters of Kerala State in India (Jayaram, 1981). However, the type locality given for the species by Günther (1864) was Cochin-china (or Cochin according to Trewavas' in-

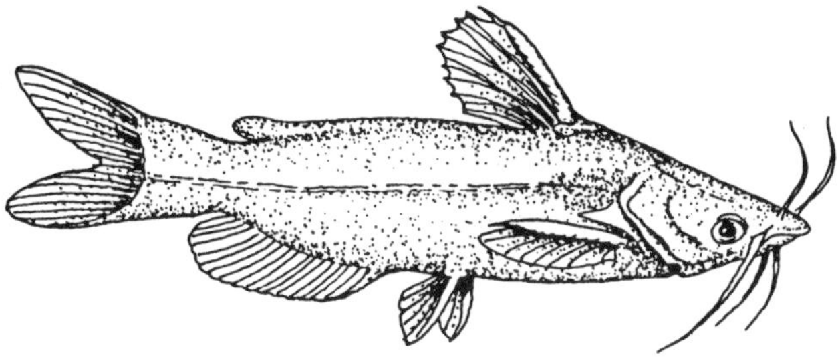

Horabagrus brachysoma. (After Jayaram, 1977.)

terpretation of the label of the type specimen) (Misra, 1976). This discrepancy has not been satisfactorily explained as yet. *Horabagrus* has been considered by some (ex. Misra, 1976) as a synonym of *Pseudobagrus*, along with *Pelteobagrus*, while Jayaram (1981) retains it as a full genus. He describes it as having a moderately elongate body that is compressed but with a rounded abdomen. The head is large and depressed anteriorly with an obtusely rounded snout. The mouth is wide, subterminal, and transverse with thin, plain lips. There are uniformly villiform teeth on the jaws and palate. The eyes are large, inferior, behind the angle of the mouth, and visible when viewed from below. Four pairs of barbels are present: a maxillary pair, two mandibular pairs, and a nasal pair. The short based dorsal fin is inserted above the middle of the pectoral fin and has a spine and 5 to 7 rays. The adipose fin is low, short, and free posteriorly. The pectoral fins have a spine serrated along the inner edge with antrorse teeth and 8 or 9 rays. The anal fin is long, with 23 to 28 rays. The caudal fin is deeply emarginate to forked. The complete lateral line is simple.

The genus *Phyllonemus* contains only two small (less than 10 cm long) species endemic to Lake Tanganyika. The body is compressed and narrow, and the head is long and square-cut. The eye has a free orbital rim. The posterior cleithral process is short and has an acute tip. The palate is dentigerous and the premaxillary tooth band is well developed. The dorsal fin has a spine and 6 rays, the adipose fin is short to moderate sized, and the caudal fin is forked. There are only three pairs of barbels, a maxillary pair and two mandibular (mental) pairs, the nasal barbels being absent.

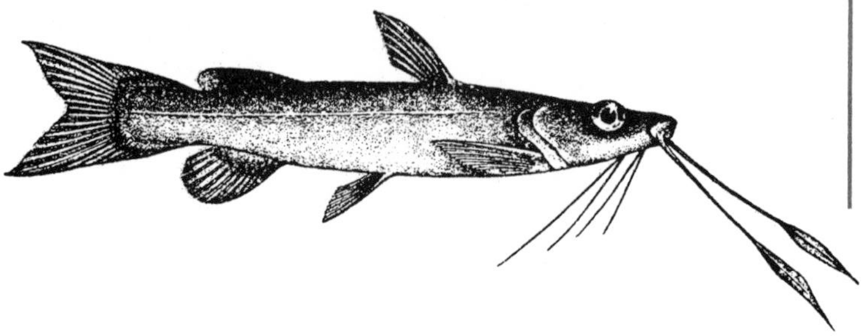

Phyllonemus typus. (From Boulenger, 1911.)

The maxillary barbels are quite long, extending beyond the level of the dorsal fin, and modified in that they are fringed on both edges, particularly at the tips, by a leaf-like or feather-like membrane (*P. typus*), or flattened and strap-like (*P. filinemus*). There are 8 to 12 branchiostegal rays.

Phyllonemus typus occasionally shows up for sale in pet shops. It grows to a length of about 10 cm and comes from Lake Tanganyika, where it is rather uncommon. It has been collected along the coastal areas in depths that do not exceed 20 meters. In the stomachs examined were found shrimps with large pincers, occasionally debris from larval insects, and fish remains that have been identified as clupeids (possibly *Limnothrissa*). Aquarium observations indicate that the fish rests on the bottom with the modified maxillary barbels held so that they form a curve or arc toward the exterior with their membranous tips turned toward the front. This is an interesting species to keep in the home aquarium, but it is relatively rare in the trade.

The genus *Leptoglanis* includes nine species ranging from Zaire and Angola to southern Zimbabwe and the Cameroons. The species are highly adapted to living in the torrents of mountain streams. They inhabit, for example, the high affluents cascading down the mountain slopes into Lake Tanganyika. The fishes are able to maintain their position in the fast-flowing water by means of their short, wide barbels and sucking mouth. The diet consists mostly of aquatic insect larvae. The body is long and weakly compressed, with the dorsal profile nearly straight. The head is small and depressed, and the snout is obtuse but not produced. The jaws are subequal and the mouth is narrow and subterminal, with thin, plain lips. The villiform teeth are arranged in bands on the premaxillaries and mandibles; the palate is edentulous. The supraoccipital is covered with skin, and the eyes are large, superior, and with free orbital margins. There are only three pairs of barbels, a maxillary pair and two mandibular pairs, the nasal barbels being absent. The short-based dorsal fin is inserted above the middle of the pectoral fin and has a spine and 5 or 6 rays. The adipose fin is long, low, posteriorly adnate to the back, and widely separated from the dorsal fin. The ventral fins are inserted below the last ray of the dorsal fin. The anal fin has 8 to 12 rays. The caudal fin is emarginate. There is a simple lateral line. The gill membranes are free from each other and from the isthmus. There are 8 to 10 branchiostegal rays.

This genus was once placed in the family Amphiliidae, but Harry (1953) regarded it as belonging to the family Bagridae because it possesses a large, free swim bladder. In addition, *Leptoglanis* has a strong pectoral spine

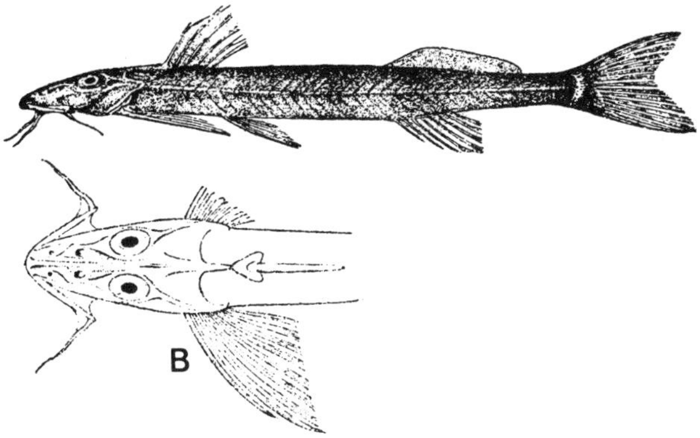

Leptoglanis xenognathus; (b) dorsal view of head. (From Boulenger, 1911.)

(absent in the Amphiliidae), and the dorsal fin is more anteriorly placed than in the amphiliids.

Leptoglanis rotundiceps is perhaps the best known species of this genus. It is one of the smallest catfishes, rarely exceeding 35 mm in length. It occurs almost everywhere in shallow water over sand bottoms in the tributaries of the Zambezi, Sabi, and Lundi Rivers (southern Zimbabwe). *L. brevis* attains a length of about 45 mm. It is a rare species inhabiting the torrential rivers of the western region of Lake Tanganyika, where it feeds on insect larvae.

The genus *Gephyroglanis* as recently restricted has only three species from the area of the Congo. The body is moderately long and weakly compressed, and the dorsal profile is slightly arched. The head is large and moderately depressed with an acuminate snout slightly projecting beyond the upper jaw. The jaws are subequal, and the mouth is subterminal, moderately wide, with thin, plain lips. The villiform teeth are arranged in bands on the premaxillaries and mandibles; the palate is edentulous. The supraoccipital may or may not be covered with skin, and the eyes are large and superior in position. There are three to four pairs of barbels present, a maxillary pair, two mandibular pairs, and a nasal pair (when three pairs are present the nasal barbels are absent). The dorsal fin is short-based, with a spine and 6 or 7 rays, and inserted over about the ¾ point of the pectoral fin. The adipose fin is short, low, and posteriorly free from the back. The ventral fins are inserted below the last ray of the dorsal fin or slightly ahead of that point. The anal fin has 11 to 17 rays, with one to three of the anteriormost rays hardened (calcified) in some places. The lateral line is simple. The gill membranes are free from each other and also from the isthmus. The hard, nearly spinous, anterior rays of the anal fin are generally rather slender but stiffer than the other rays of the fin and tend to break off more easily. This modification may be correlated with age.

Gephyroglanis congicus. (From Boulenger, 1911.)

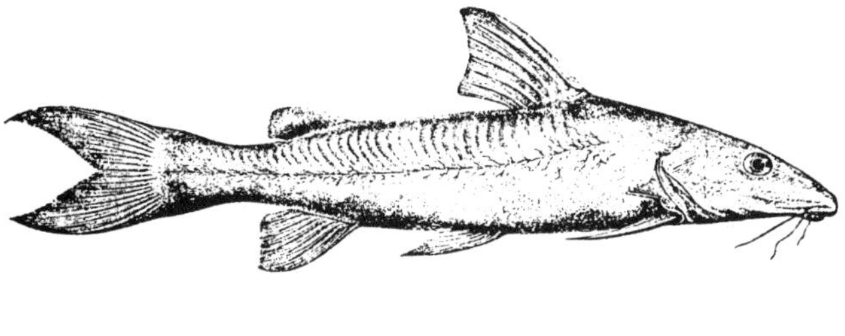

Austroglanis was erected in 1984 with the type species the former *Gephyroglanis sclateri* from the Orange River area of South Africa. Two other South African species, *A. barnardi*,

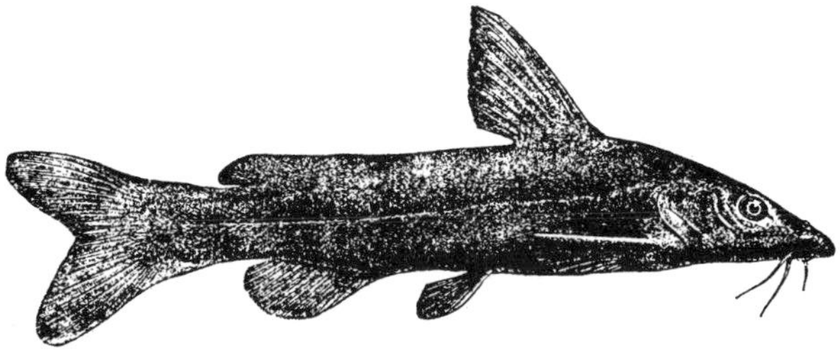

Austroglanis sclateri. (From Boulenger, 1911.)

and *A. gilli*, are also included. The body is moderately elongated and slightly compressed and the head, about one quarter of the body length, is smooth. The snout is obtusely conical and the eyes are relatively small. The occipital process is in contact with the interneural shield. Four pairs of barbels are present, a maxillary pair, an inner and outer mandibular pair, and a short pair of nasal barbels. The dorsal fin is short, with a smooth spine and 6 or 7 rays. The adipose fin is relatively long and situated above the anal fin, which has about 16-18 rays. The pectoral fin has a spine that is serrated on its inner edge. The caudal fin is emarginate to forked.

Both *A. sclateri* and *A. gilli* are said to have individuals with low complete or high ragged dorsal fins. These are supposedly correlated with habitat, the low fins with slow-moving water and muddy bottom and the high with more turbulent water.

Austroglanis sclateri attains a length of about 30 cm, and its preferred habitat is rocky sections of the flowing reaches of rivers, where it feeds mainly on aquatic invertebrates.

Zairichthys was described to hold a single species of minute catfish (which might be the young of an unknown adult) that is adapted to life in rapids. The body is depressed anteriorly and the head is dorsally flattened and laterally broadened. The body is not translucent in the region of the pseudotympanum. The skull bones are covered by skin. The eyes are tiny, with a thick cornea-like covering and a well-developed lens, superior, and located almost directly posterior to the nostrils or slightly lateral to them. The nostrils are close together, the anterior tubular and slightly mesial to the posterior. There are three pairs of barbels, a maxillary pair and two mandibular pairs, both short and simple, and either no nasal barbels or they are reduced to an insignificant flap. The mouth is terminal with a slightly protruding upper jaw, and the lips are moderately fleshy and not united with the barbels or modified into a sucking device. The teeth are well developed, conical, separate, and narrow on the premaxillaries, but absent from the palate. The dorsal fin is short-based, with 2 spines and 6 rays, although the first spine, which is very short and all but invisible, is embedded in the membrane at the base of the fin origin; the second spine is smooth. The anal fin has 9 rays. The pectoral fin has a spine and 8 rays, the anterior edge of the spine smooth, the posterior with small spinelets. The ventral fins have 6 rays. The caudal fin is rounded. The adipose fin is long, low, translucent, originates slightly posterior to the dorsal fin, and extends over several upper procurrent caudal rays. The lateral line is straight and simple. The gill opening is broad and the gill membranes are free from each other and from the isthmus. There are 6 or 7 branchiostegal rays.

Zairichthys zonatus; (b) dorsal view of head. (From Roberts, 1967.)

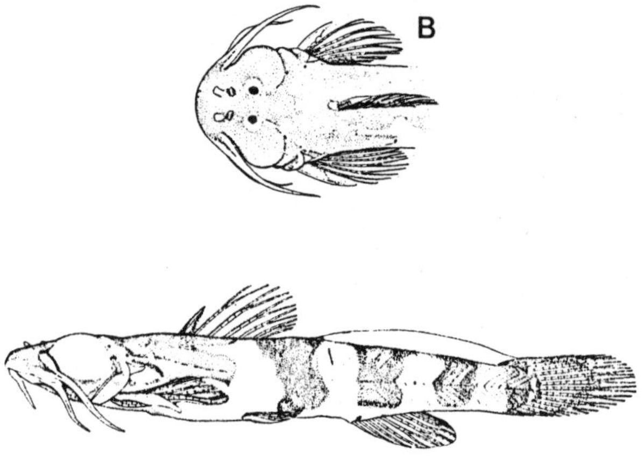

The only species, *Zairichthys zonatus*, was collected in a side channel of the lower rapids of the Congo River just below the Stanley Pool. The substrate was sand or pebbles with cobbles, rocks, and large boulders scattered throughout. Large plants were practically absent, while rheophilic insect larvae were extremely abundant and may form the basis of this fish's diet.

The genus *Amarginops* contains but a single species described from Stanleyville in the Congo (now Kisangani, Zaire). The body is elongate and strongly depressed, being broader than deep except posterior to the anal region, where the caudal peduncle is strongly compressed. The head is small and flattened, and the snout is spatulate. The jaws are unequal, with the lower jaw projecting, thus exposing most of the teeth on that jaw. The mouth is subterminal, wide, the lips thick and papillated. Bands of villiform teeth can be seen on the premaxillaries, vomer, palatines, pterygoids, and mandibles, the crescentic bands on the palate being separated by a narrow space. The body and fins are covered with a thin, lax skin that also extends over the eyes. The eyes are small and superior in position. The nostrils are far apart. There are four pairs of barbels: a maxillary pair, two mandibular pairs, and a nasal pair. The dorsal fin is inserted above the tip of the pectoral fin and has a spine and 6 rays. The adipose fin is short, low, and posteriorly free. The pectoral fins have a spine. The ventral fins are inserted slightly ahead of the last ray of the dorsal fin. The anal fin has 12 rays. The caudal fin is slightly emarginate, almost truncate.

The gill membranes are free from each other and from the isthmus, but deeply notched. There are 10 branchiostegal rays. The lateral line fades beyond the ventral fins (Nichols & Griscom, 1917).

The genus *Amarginops* resembles *Gnathobagrus* in having a strongly depressed head and projecting lower jaw but differs from it (and *Chrysichthys*) in having a strongly depressed body, small eyes, and a subtruncate caudal fin. It differs further from *Chrysichthys* by having the dorsal fin placed in an anterior position; a weak, short dorsal fin spine; thick, papillated lips; and a short occipital process that does not extend to the dorsal plate. The depressed and flattened body, lax skin covering even the eyes, and subtruncate caudal fin may be degenerate characters due to a long residence in muddy river bottoms, which is its typical habitat (Nichols & Griscom, 1917).

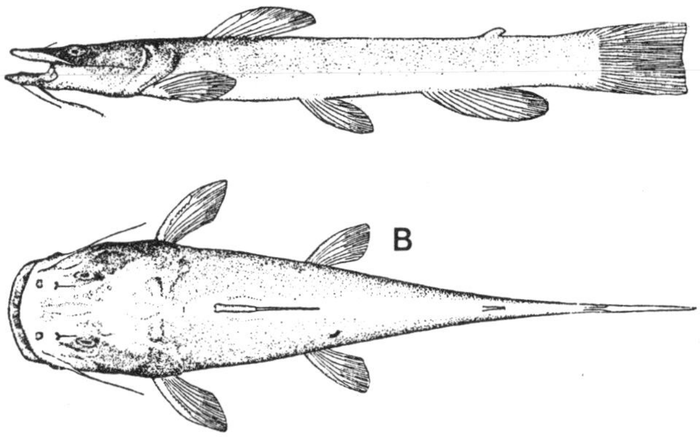

Amarginops platus; (b) dorsal view. (After Nichols & Griscom, 1917.)

The single species, *Amarginops platus*, has the head depressed, almost flat; the nasal barbel about equal to the diameter of the eye; a big fold of skin at each corner of the mouth; the gill rakers long, slender, and closely set; the dorsal fin spine small, blunt, rather stout, not serrated; and the pectoral fin spine small, stout, curved, and strongly serrated on the inner edge (Nichols & Griscom, 1917).

The genus *Gnathobagrus* is yet another genus containing only a single species, *G. depressus*, from Boma, on the Congo River near its delta. The body is cylindrical but is depressed somewhat from the ventral fins forward and compressed posteriorly. The head is strongly depressed, with the upper profile

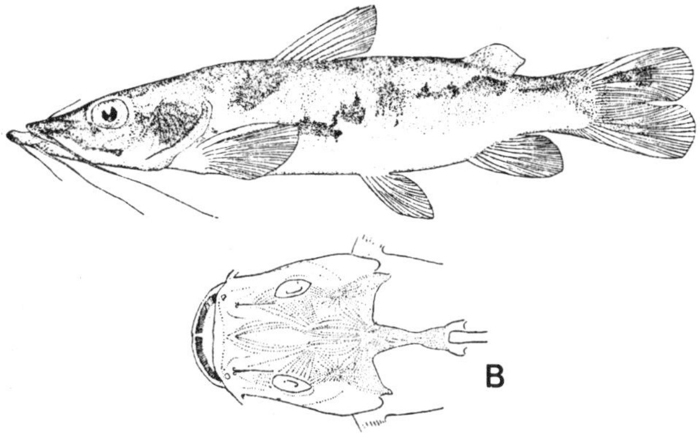

Gnathobagrus depressus; (b) dorsal view of head. (From Nichols & Griscom, 1917.)

concave anterior to the eye. The surface of the head is striated and rugose, and the occipital process is rather narrow and united with the small-sized interneural shield. The snout is broad and very depressed, with the lower jaw strongly projecting so that the teeth are almost all exposed. The width of the mouth is equal to a little more than half the head length. The villiform teeth are arranged in bands, that of the premaxillary almost straight, that of the vomeropterygoid long, narrow, crescentic, and interrupted in the middle. Four pairs of barbels are present: a maxillary pair that is about as long as the head; two mandibular pairs, the outer about twice as long as the inner; and a nasal pair that is very slender and not quite equal to the eye diameter. The eye is large, contained about 5 times in the head length, and there is a free orbital rim. The short-based dorsal fin originates nearer the snout than the caudal base and has 6 rays and a strong spine very weakly serrated on the inner edge and only at the tip of the outer edge. The adipose fin is short, low, and separated from the dorsal fin by about twice its base length. The pectoral fin has a strong spine that is weakly serrated on the outer edge but strongly serrated on the inner edge. The anal fin is short-based, with 11 rays. The caudal fin is deeply forked and has rounded lobes. The gill rakers are short and stout, 12 being counted on the lower limb of the first arch (Nichols & Griscom, 1917).

The genus *Gnathobagrus* is very close to *Chrysichthys* and *Amarginops*. It differs from *Chrysichthys* by having the head remarkably depressed and strongly striated and by having the lower jaw strongly projecting so that almost the entire band of teeth is exposed. *Gnathobagrus* differs from *Amarginops* as noted under *Amarginops* (Nichols & Griscom, 1917).

The genus *Rheoglanis* includes a single species, *R. dendrophorus*, from rapids near the former Leopoldville on the Congo River, adapted to life in fast-flowing waters. The

***Rheoglanis dendrophorus*, Photos by Dr. Tyson R. Roberts.**

head and anterior part of the body are depressed, while the head posterior to the eyes is greatly broadened. The bones of the skull are fully covered with fleshy skin. The snout is bluntly rounded, and the mouth is terminal with the upper jaw slightly protruding. The lips are moderately fleshy and either without papillae or with very fine papillae. They are not broadly united with the barbels and do not form a sucking disc. Dense, broad patches of cardiform teeth are present on the premaxillaries, dentaries, and palate; the premaxillaries are separate (rather than fused) and very broad. The eyes are very small but with well-developed lenses and relatively free borders. They are supralateral, almost superior, and distinctly lateral to the nostrils. The posterior nostril has a flap on either side behind the nasal barbel and is situated close to the tubular anterior nostril and slightly mesial to it. There are four pairs of barbels: a maxillary pair, two mandibular pairs, and a nasal pair, all short, simple, and non-papillose. The dorsal fin is short-based, with two spines embedded in the fleshy skin and therefore not very evident and 6 rays. The pectoral fin has a spine about two-thirds the length of the soft portion of the fin and also embedded in the skin and thus hidden, but it does have small spinelets on the anterior and posterior edges; there are 10 branched rays. The ventral fins have 6 rays. The adipose fin is short, fairly stout, and with a free posterior edge; it is situated well posterior to the dorsal fin. The anal fin has 12 rays, the first two short, slender, and embedded in the skin. The caudal fin is moderately forked, the lobes rounded and of equal length, although the lower lobe is somewhat broader. The gill openings are broad and the gill membranes are free from each other and from the isthmus. There are 8 or 9 branchiostegal rays. The gill rakers (6 + 8) are moderately slender. The swim bladder is small, has tough, not very elastic walls, and there is no pseudotympanum, the body next to the swim bladder being quite thick. The lateral line is straight and simple.

The single species, *Rheoglanis dendrophorus*, was collected over sand and pebbles where there were cobbles, rocks, and even huge boulders scattered everywhere. There were no large plants in the vicinity. Rheophilic insect larvae were abundant, possibly forming a ready food source for the fish.

Rheoglanis differs from *Chrysichthys* in many characters, including having the skull covered with skin (in *Chrysichthys* it is exposed and often rugose in many species), lacking the pseudotympanum (it is well developed and the swim bladder is relatively large in *Chrysichthys*), and having the pectoral spine imbedded and with spinelets on the edges (in *Chrysichthys* the pectoral spine is exposed in most species and the anterior edge is smooth).

Clarotes is a small genus of only 3 species distributed in northern Africa from Senegal to Somalia. It is very closely related to *Chrysichthys*, and some workers prefer to consider it a synonym of that genus. It differs from *Chrysichthys* mainly by the following characters: the ventral surface of the head is more flattened; the bones of the head are firmly interdigitated, forming a casque, and the bony ridges and ornamentation are exposed or show through the skin; and the adipose fin is rayed, some of the anterior rays becoming ossified and spine-like in adults. The modification of the adipose fin into a second rayed dorsal seems to be correlated with age, younger fish having a normal, smooth adipose like most other bagrids.

Clarotes laticeps is a fairly large species attaining a length of about 71 cm and inhabiting the rivers of Central Africa, especially the Niger, Volta, Nile, Chad, and Senegal. It is predominantly a bottom-dwelling species of the rivers and swamps, feeding mainly on fishes, insects, molluscs, and vegetable matter when small but strictly predatory on fishes as an adult. One of the staples in the diet of the adults appears to be *Chrysichthys auratus*. In the Niger River it is reported to breed in July and August when the rivers are at their flood stage. They are moderately important food fishes, being caught in nets, in traps, and on long lines.

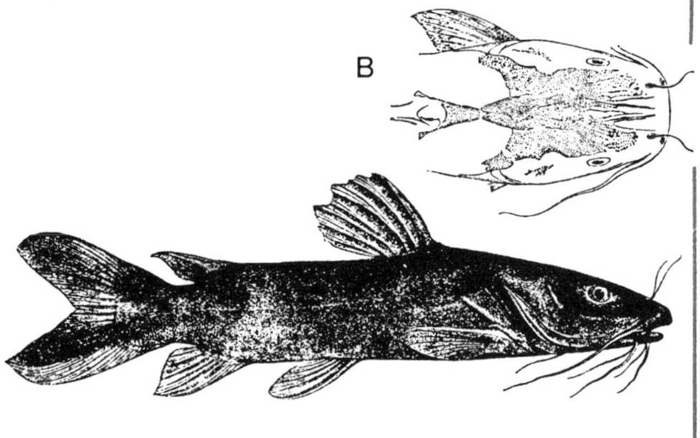

Clarotes laticeps; (b) dorsal view of head. (From Boulenger, 1911.)

The genus *Chrysichthys* is a fairly large genus with approximately 40 species widely distributed in the fresh waters of Africa, especially in the Congo River basin. The body is stout, weakly compressed, and the dorsal profile is slightly arched. The head is large and may be compressed or depressed, with a broadly rounded or acuminate snout. The jaws are subequal, with the lower the longer in some species; the mouth is subterminal, moderately narrow to wide, and has thin, plain lips. Villiform teeth in bands are present on the premaxillaries, mandibles, vomer, palatines, and/or on the pterygoids. The supraoccipital may or may not be covered with skin. The eyes are usually large, supralateral, and with free orbital rims. There are four pairs of barbels: a maxillary pair, two mandibular pairs, and a pair of short (sometimes very small) nasal barbels with valve-like bases. The dorsal fin is inserted over the three-fourths point of the pectoral fin and has a spine and 5 to 7 rays. The adipose fin is short, low, and free posteriorly. The ventral fins are inserted below or slightly ahead of the last ray of the dorsal fin. The anal fin has 9 to 16 rays, and the caudal fin is mostly forked but may be rounded. There is a simple lateral line. The gill membranes are free from each other and from the isthmus. There are 8 to 10 branchiostegal rays.

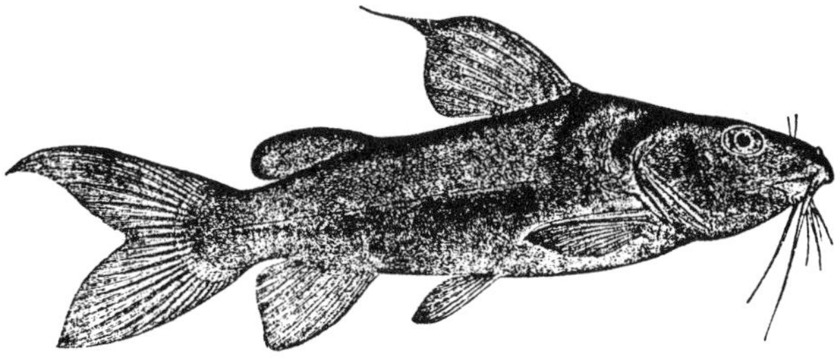

Chrysichthys auratus. (From Boulenger, 1911.)

Species of *Chrysichthys* are among the better food fishes of the Congo basin, and they are fished for by set lines with the hooks baited with manioc or are poisoned. Many are caught in the rapids and stony stretches of the Congo River. They feed on a wide variety of material, from vegetable matter to human excrement. Both *Chrysichthys* and *Auchenoglanis* species can be accommodated in African cichlid tanks, although the catfishes can be very predatory when they reach a large size.

Chrysichthys longipinnis (formerly in *Gephyroglanis*) is a basically silvery and unassuming catfish and has been dubbed the Aluminum Catfish. As it grows, however, it becomes a velvety gray-black. Attaining a length of about 14 cm, the Aluminum Catfish has long maxillary barbels and large eyes. The snout, caudal fin, and dorsal fins outrace the body in growth, giving the adults and juveniles a somewhat different appearance. This species is said to school in large numbers in the Stanley Pool and Upper Congo River. Its diet consists mainly of worms.

Chrysichthys auratus longifilis is very colorful, sporting an intense silvery yellow body color, while adult males possess a very long dusky black dorsal filament that may extend as far posteriorly when depressed as the tip of the caudal fin lobes. It usually is found over soft, slightly muddy bottoms or bottoms with heavy layers of leafy detritus in deep, relatively quiet waters. Insect larvae and small crustaceans form the greater part of its diet, which may be supplemented by dead fish and seeds. During the breeding season some sexual dimorphism can be seen, the most obvious being in the shape of the head. The male's head is narrower and more sculptured than that of the female. *C. auratus longifilis* spawns immediately prior to the flood season in the main river channels. This species is peaceful, easy to feed, and will not hide as readily as some of the other catfishes. It attains a length of about 20 cm and a weight of 200 grams.

Chrysichthys brevibarbis from the Congo attains a length of about 44 cm. The young are said to be very active but are not very good swimmers.

C. ornatus from the middle and upper Congo River and the Ubangi is smaller, attaining a length of about 19 or 20 cm. This is another lively species but may be somewhat shy, especially the smaller ones that are likely to be kept by aquarists, and should be kept in a tank with many hiding places and subdued light.

One of the largest species is *C. grandis*, which attains a length in excess of 2 meters and a weight of 190 kilos. It occurs in Lake Tanganyika.

C. helicophagus, as the name implies, feeds mainly on snails, which it swallows whole. Other species of *Chrysichthys* found in the same area do not seem to utilize the snails as food, or at least not to any noticeable extent.

C. walkeri may be found in brackish waters to the upper parts of rivers where there is pure fresh water. *C. nigrodigitatus* attains a length of over 50 cm and a weight that exceeds 1.5 kilos. Its main food are nymphs of the mayfly *Povillà adusta*. Both *C. walkeri* and *C. nigrodigitatus* excavate caves in the river banks. The eggs are laid in the caves and guarded by the parents until they hatch. The fry are then guarded until they become free-swimming.

C. brachynema is the most common large catfish (to 77 cm) in Lake Tanganyika. This lacustrine species occurs near the coast and does not descend much below 30 meters. It is a voracious omnivore, with crabs forming the largest part of the diet. It also eats snails (*Neothauma*), *Lamprichthys* spp., shrimp, *Trematocara* sp., and other young cichlids.

C. graueri inhabits the muddy bottoms of lakes at depths of at least 30 to 60 meters. It does not seem to approach the shore, nor does it descend to the depths of *C. sianenna*. This is another voracious species, feeding mainly on fishes such as *Lamprologus stappersi*, *L. ornatipinnis*, and *Trematocara* sp., but also small shrimp and similar items in Lake Tanganyika.

C. sianenna attains a length of about 22 to 23 cm and occurs only in Lake Tanganyika. It lives at some distance from the shore on the soft bottom. It is the non-cichlid that reaches the greatest depths habitable in the lake, in this case to 120 meters, although it is more common in less deep water and may even be taken by seine fishermen along the sandy shores. The best fishing seems to be at about 25 to 75 meters. Its diet is varied and consists in part of small fishes (usually *Lamprologus* spp.), ostracods, larvae of dragonflies, and perhaps organic material.

Lophiobagrus is a small genus of only four species from Lake Tanganyika. The body is moderately elongate. The head and body up to the level of the dorsal fin are very depressed, thereafter rapidly becoming laterally compressed. The very large head is rounded anteriorly.

Lophiobagrus cyclurus is a smallish species of about 10 cm maximum length that is endemic to Lake Tanganyika. It is a littoral species inhabiting rocky shores where there are a great number of places in which it can hide. Its lower depth limit seems to be about 4 to 5 meters. This little fish is a voracious predator for its size, feeding on chironomid larvae, beetle larvae, and small crustaceans, with some occasional vegetable material mixed in. It seems to do well in home aquaria that have a sufficient number of hiding places. Most standard aquarium foods, both frozen and freeze-dried, are accepted, although live brine shrimp and daphnia are preferred. Small fishes will also be eaten, whether intended as food or not. Since it comes from Lake Tanganyika, which is hard and alkaline, the water in the tank should be of that type, although this is a very adaptable species and will do al-

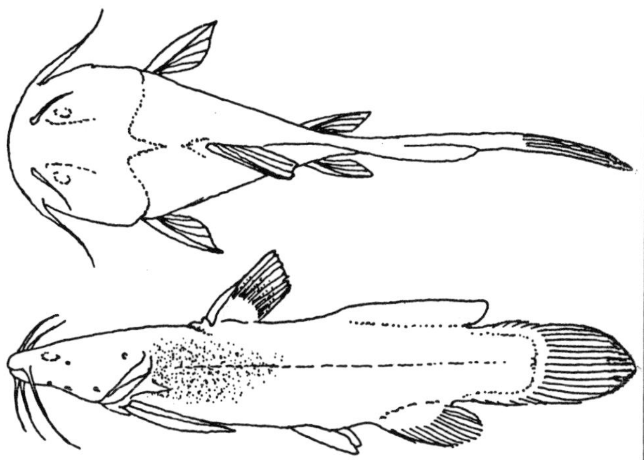

Lophiobagrus cyclurus. (After Poll, 1942.)

most as well in less ideal conditions. It has been stated that when *L. cyclurus* is upset it is able to secrete an easy-flowing sticky, transparent mucus that will mix with water and kill in a very short time other fishes placed with it in a small container (such as an aquarium?). Many individuals have been kept in captivity, but so far there have been no reports of any problems of any kind—yet. In fact, there has been one report of a successful spawning of this species in an aquarium. The eggs were laid in a cave excavated by the parents and hatched in about four to five days. This species resembles a baby bullhead and has a fairly large mouth and quite long nasal barbels. Its most distinctive external character seems to be its rounded tail.

Jayaram (1966), who synonymized the genus *Lophiobagrus* with *Chrysichthys*, suggested that *L. cyclurus* might even be a lacustrine subspecies of the riverine *C. delhezi*.

The genus *Pardiglanis* contains a single large (64 cm) species from southern Somalia. The distinctive head is very broad and flat, as wide as long and about 2.5 times broader than high. The body is only 1.4 times longer than the head and is depressed anteriorly and compressed posteriorly. It is covered with a smooth skin; the lateral line is scarcely evident. The mouth is wide, almost equal to the head width, the angles extending as far as the center of the eyes. The eyes are superior, set apart a distance equal to about half the head width, and contained about 9 times in the head length. The nasal openings are near the edge of the snout and distant from the eyes. The dentition consists mostly of numerous small pointed teeth arranged in bands. There is a long, continuous premaxillary band; a long, curved mandibular band slightly interrupted at the symphysis; and a pair of vomeropterygoid bands. There are four pairs of barbels, all somewhat long. The dorsal fin is higher than long and is composed of a strong non-serrated spine preceded by a small basal bone and followed by 6 branched rays. The adipose fin is high and composed of three spines (the first two short, the third long) and about 8 branched rays. The anal fin is higher than long and has 3 simple rays and 9 branched rays. The caudal is deeply notched,

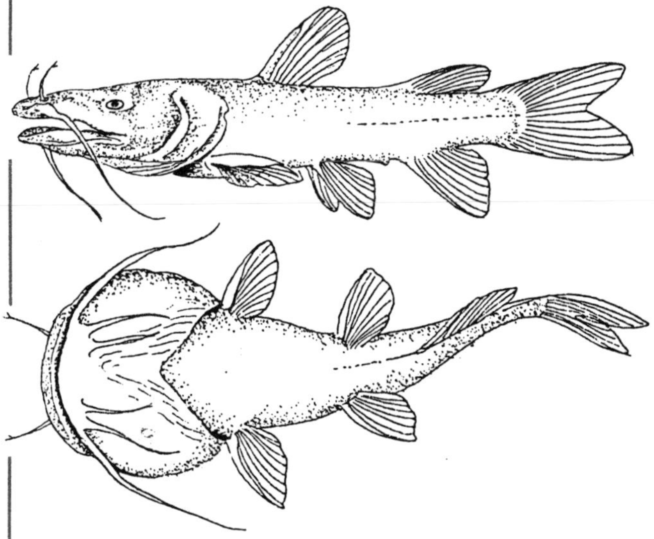

Pardiglanis tarabinii. (After Poll, et al, 1972.)

with the lower lobe a bit longer than the upper. The paired fins are horizontally disposed and relatively short. The pectoral fins each have a strong serrated (interior edge) spine and 8 branched rays. The ventral fins have only a simple ray and five branched rays. There are 10-11 + 11-12 (+3 vestigial) long, slender gill rakers and 9 branchiostegal rays. The gill openings are long and continuous, not connected to the isthmus.

The genus *Bathybagrus* contains a single species, *B. tetranema* from the Zambian waters of Lake Tanganyika. In general aspect this genus resembles *Chrysichthys* having a fairly robust body and slightly depressed head. The eyes are small and without a free

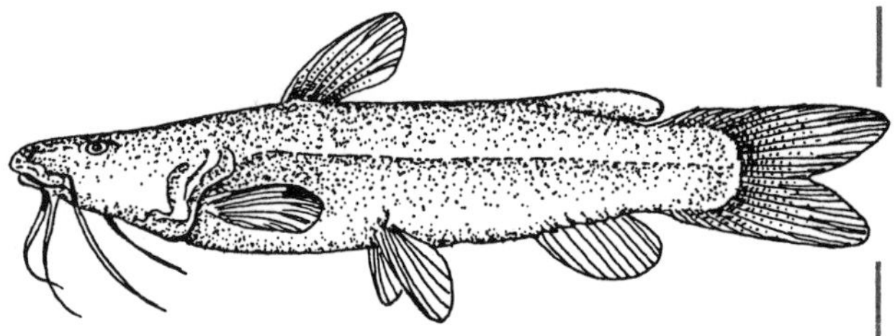

Bathybagrus tetranema. (After Bailey & Stewart, 1984.)

margin. The mouth is subterminal, with the upper jaw longer, and there are narrow bands of teeth on the vomer and dermopalatine. The supraoccipital spine is narrow and does not reach (by a wide gap) the supraneural at the base of the dorsal fin. Only two pairs of threadlike, short barbels are present, a maxillary and a mandibulary pair. All other bagrids (except *Rita*) have three pairs of barbels (two pairs of mandibular and one pair of maxillary barbels) and most (including *Rita*) also have nasal barbels. The dorsal fin is short-based with a short, weak, smooth spine and 6 rays. The anal fin has 13 or 14 rays. The adipose fin is moderate, with a free end. The pectoral fin spine has serrations posteriorly and the fin is provided with 7 rays. The caudal fin is forked. The gill membranes are free from the isthmus and deeply divided.

The specimens were collected in Zambian waters of Lake Tanganyika where they were most abundant at depths between 40 and 80 meters. Those greater than about 12 cm were found to be mature and females examined had relatively few eggs in two size classes. The larger eggs in one female were 3.0-3.5mm long and 34 in number, which is comparable to the numbers seen in mouthbrooding cichlids. It was suggested this might indicate intensive parental care in this species (Bailey & Stewart, 1984).

The genus *Platyglanis* contains a single species from South Cameroon. Its body is elongate and dorsoventrally flattened; the head is flattened as well. The eyes are small, superior, and without a free border. The occipital process is very short and widely separated from the interneural plate. The nares are widely separated, the anterior one being tubular and opening in the upper lip; the posterior is slit-like and located closer to the eyes than to the anterior edge of the snout. The lips are papillose. The jaw teeth are villiform and the palate is toothless. Four pairs of barbels are present, the nasal pair being rudimentary while the maxillary and the inner and outer mandibular pairs are long and filiform. The dorsal fin is very low and composed of a short spine and 9 (-10) soft rays. The long, low adipose fin extends until the caudal fin. The anal fin is long, of about 25-28 rays, and the ventrals, which are inserted under the last ray of the dorsal fin, have 6 rays. The pectoral fin spine is serrated and

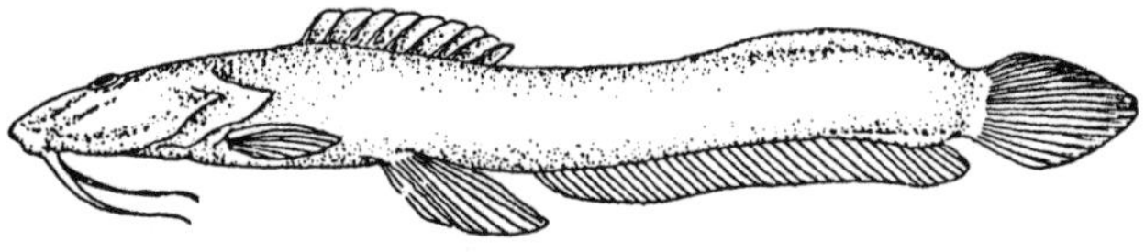

Platyglanis depierrei. (After Daget, 1978.)

the fin has 8 soft rays. The caudal is rounded. The branchiostegal membrane is notched and narrowly attached to the isthmus. There are 9 branchiostegal rays.

This genus is said to be related to *Notoglanidium* but differs in its elongate and dorsoventrally flattened head and body (Daget, 1978).

Checklist of the species of the family Bagridae and their type localities:

Subfamily Ritinae Fowler, 1958 (emend Jayaram, 1966).

Rita Bleeker, 1859. Type species *Pimelodus rita* Hamilton.

- *Rita chrysea* Day, 1877. Orissa (the Mahanaddy).
- *R. gogra* (Sykes, 1838). Beeme River and Mota Mola River at Poona (India).
- *R. kuturnee* (Sykes, 1838). Beeme River at Pairgaon (India).
- *R. rita* (Hamilton, 1822). Estuaries of Bengal.

Subfamily Claroteinae Bleeker, 1862.

Chrysichthys Bleeker, 1858. Type species *Pimelodus auratus* Geoffroy Saint-Hilaire, 1809.

- *Chrysichthys aluuensis* Risch, 1985. Omuehuechi-Aluu, New Calabar River, Nigeria.

C. ansorgii Boulenger, 1910. Quanza River at Dondo and Bengo Rivers.
C. auratus (Geoffroy Saint-Hilaire, 1809). Nile River.
auratus longifilis Pfaff, 1933. "Kabara", Niger River.
auratus tilhoi (Pellegrin, 1909). "Bol" (Lac Tschad).
C. bocagii Boulenger, 1910. Bengo River at Dondo.
C. brachynema Boulenger, 1900. Kalambo, Lake Tanganyika.
C. brevibarbis (Boulenger, 1899). "Boma", Zaire.
C. cranchii (Leach, 1818). Lower Congo River.
C. delhezi Boulenger, 1899. Upper Congo River ("Boma", Zaire).
C. duttoni Boulenger, 1905. Lusambo on the Kasai River.
C. filamentosus Boulenger, 1912. "Luali River at Bucozau".
C. furcatus Günther, 1864. "West Africa" (Niger River).
C. grandis Boulenger, 1917. Kilwa Bay, Lake Tanganyika.
C. graueri Steindachner, 1911. NW shores of Lake Tanganyika.
C. habereri Steindachner, 1912. Dja River ("Dscha River, Congo").
C. helicophagus Roberts & Stewart, 1976. Near Tadi, about 50 km downstream from Luozi, Zaire River.
C. hildae Bell-Cross, 1973. "Buzi River near Dombe", Mozambique.
C. johnelsi Daget, 1959. Bafoulabe, Niokolo-Koba National Park, Senegal.
C. laticeps Pellegrin, 1932. Brazzaville, Congo.
C. longibarbis (Boulenger, 1899). Leopoldville, Congo.
C. longidorsalis Risch & Thys van den Audenaerde, 1981. "Ekongolo", Sanaga River.
l. nyongensis Risch & Thys van den Audenaerde, 1985. "Ebongo, Akonolinga".
C. longipinnis (Boulenger, 1899). "Stanley Pool". (Formerly in *Gephyroglanis*.)
C. mabusi Boulenger, 1905. Lake Bangweulu.
C. macropterus Boulenger, 1920. Stanley Falls.
C. maurus (Valenciennes, 1839). "Senegal".
C. nigrodigitatus (Lacépède, in Buffon, 1803). Senegal.
C. ogooensis (Pellegrin, 1900). "Adouma River", Ogoowe.
C. okae Fowler, 1949. Oka, Congo (Brazzaville).
C. ornatus Boulenger, 1902. Monsembe.
C. persimilis Günther, 1899. Gabon.
C. platycephalus Worthington & Ricardo, 1936. Usumbara.
C. punctatus Boulenger, 1899. "Stanley Pool; Kutu". (Upper Congo River.)
C. rueppelli Boulenger, 1907. Lower Nile River.
C. sharpii Boulenger, 1901. Lake Mweru.
C. sianenna Boulenger, 1906. Niamkozo and Mbete, Lake Tanganyika.
C. stappersi Boulenger, 1917. Kilwa Bay, Lake Tanganyika.
C. thonneri Steindachner, 1912. Dja River.
C. thysi Risch, 1985. "Makoku, Ivindo River; Adouma, Ogowe River; Tchibanga, Nyanga River".
C. uniformis Pellegrin, 1922. "Poko" (ex. Belgian Congo).
C. velifer Norman, 1923. Bandama River.
C. wagenaari Boulenger, 1899. "Upoto", Middle Zaire River.
C. walkeri Günther, 1899. Pra River.

Lophiobagrus Poll, 1942. Type species *L. lestradei* Poll (= *L. cyclurus*).
Lophiobagrus aquilus Bailey & Stewart, 1984. Lake Tanganyika.
L. asperispinis Bailey & Stewart, 1984. Lake Tanganyika.
L. brevispinis Bailey & Stewart, 1984. Lake Tanganyika.
L. cyclurus (Worthington & Ricardo, 1937). Lake Tanganyika.

Clarotes Kner, 1855. Type species *Pimelodus laticeps* Rüppell, 1829.
Clarotes bidorsalis Pellegrin, 1938. "Giloba" (Giuba), Somalia.
C. laticeps (Rüppell, 1829). Nile River ("Cairo").
C. macrocephalus Daget, 1954. "Diafarabe" Niger River.

Gnathobagrus Nichols & Griscom, 1917. Type species *G. depressus* Nichols & Griscom.
Gnathobagrus depressus Nichols & Griscom,

1917. "Boma", Congo River.

Amarginops Nichols & Griscom, 1917. Type species *A. platus* Nichols & Griscom.

Amarginops platus Nichols & Griscom, 1917. Stanleyville (Kisangani), Congo (Zaire).

Rheoglanis Poll, 1966. Type species *R. dendrophorus* Poll.

Rheoglanis dendrophorus Poll, 1966. Congo River near Leopoldville (Kinsuka Rapids, Lower Zaire.

Pardiglanis Poll, Lanza, & Sassi, 1972. Type species *P. tarabinii* Poll, Lanza, & Sassi.

Pardiglanis tarabinii Poll, Lanza, & Sassi, 1972. Gelib, Juba River, southern Somalia.

Zairichthys Roberts, 1967. Type species *Z. zonatus* Roberts.

Zairichthys zonatus Roberts, 1967. Kinsuka Village, just below Stanley Pool, side channel of the Congo River.

Austroglanis Skelton, Risch, & De Vos, 1984. Type species *Gephyroglanis sclateri* Boulenger, 1901.

Austroglanis barnardi (Skelton, 1981). "Noordhoeks River", trib. of Olifants River, Cape Province, South Africa.

A. gilli (Barnard, 1943). Olifants River system.

A. sclateri (Boulenger, 1901). Vaal River, Transvaal.

Gephyroglanis Boulenger, 1899. Type species *G. congicus* Boulenger, 1899.

Gephyroglanis congicus Boulenger, 1899. "Upoto", Congo River (Middle Zaire).

G. gymnorhynchus Pappenheim, 1914. Aruwimi (Congo).

G. habereri Steindachner, 1912. Dja River.

Leptoglanis Boulenger, 1902. Type species *L. xenognathus* Boulenger, 1902.

Leptoglanis bouilloni Poll, 1959. Stanley Pool, Congo.

L. brevis Boulenger, 1915. Lumumbashi River at Elizabethville.

L. brieni Poll, 1959. Stanley Pool, Congo.

L. camerunensis Daget & Stauch, 1963. "Benoué à Lakdo".

L. dorae Poll, 1967. Rapids of the Luachimo, Angola.

L. flavomaculatus Pellegrin, 1928. Kamaiembi, Lulua River.

L. mandevillei Poll, 1959. Stanley Pool, Congo.

L. rotundiceps (Hilgendorf, 1905). Bubu River.

L. xenognathus Boulenger, 1902. Ubangi River.

Phyllonemus Boulenger, 1906. Type species *P. typus* Boulenger, 1906.

Phyllonemus filinemus Worthington & Ricardo, 1936. Kibwezi and Kigoma, Lake Tanganyika.

P. typus Boulenger, 1906. Niamkozo, Lake Tanganyika.

Pelteobagrus Bleeker, 1864. Type species *Silurus calvarius* Basilewski, 1855 (= *P. fulvidraco*).

Pelteobagrus brashnikowi (Berg, 1907). Onon River, Siberia.

P. crassilabris (Günther, 1864). "China".

c. macrops (Nichols, 1926). Near Yenping.

P. crassirostris (Regan, 1913). Kiatiang-Fu.

P. eupogoides (Wu, 1930). Sze-Chwan.

P. eupogon (Boulenger, 1892). Shanghai.

P. fui (Miao, 1934). Chinkiang.

P. fulvidraco (Richardson, 1845). Canton.

P. hoi (Pellegrin & Fang, 1940). Foochow.

P. microps (Rendahl, 1933). Chungking.

P. nitidus (Sauvage & Thiersant, 1874). Yangtze-Kiang.

P. nudiceps (Sauvage, 1883). Biwa Ko, Japan.

?*P. ornatus* (Duncker, 1904).

P. ransonnetii (Steindachner, 1887). Osaka, Japan.

P. tenuifurcatus (Nichols, 1931). Chungan Hsien.

P. vachellii (Richardson, 1845). Canton.

P. virgatus (Oshima, 1926). Kachek River.

P. wangi (Miao, 1934). Chinkiang.

P. wittenbergii (Popta, 1911). Amur River.

P. sp. cf *crassirostris* (Regan, 1913). Foochow.

Pseudobagrus Bleeker, 1860. Type species *Bagrus aurantiacus* Temminck & Schlegel.

Pseudobagrus adiposalis Oshima, 1919. Tamusui River, Taiwan.

P. albomarginatus (Rendahl, 1928). Tsien Tangtu-Hsien, China.

P. analis (Nichols, 1930). Hokow, China.

P. aurantiacus (Temminck & Schlegel, 1846). Sutzuma, Japan.

P. brevianalis Regan, 1908. Lake Candidus, Taiwan.

P. brevicaudatus (Wu, 1930). Chunking.

P. emarginatus (Regan, 1913). Sze-Chwan, China.

P. henryi (Herre, 1932). Canton fish market, China.

P. herzensteini (Berg, 1907). Onon River, Manchuria.

P. hwanghoensis (Mori, 1933). Hwang Ho, China.

P. intermedius Nichols & Pope, 1927. Nodoa, Hainan Island.

P. kaifenensis (Tchang, 1934). Kai-feng, China.

P. lui (Tchang & Shih, 1934). Lower Kialin Kiang, China.

P. medianalis (Regan, 1904). Yunnan Lake, China.

P. omeihensis Nichols, 1941. Omeihsien, China.

P. ondon Shaw, 1930. Shing-Tsong, China.

P. pratti (Günther, 1892). Kiating Fu, China.

P. rendahli (Pellegrin & Fang, 1940). Ou Tchang Ho, China.

P. sinyanensis (Fu, 1935). "Szewangshan" of Sinyang, China.

P. taeniatus (Günther, 1873). Shanghai.

P. taiwanensis Oshima, 1919. Tozen River near Taichu, Taiwan.

P. tenuis (Günther, 1873). Shanghai.

P. truncatus Regan, 1913. Kiating-Fu, China.

P. ussuriensis (Dybowski, 1872). Usuri River, Manchuria.

Horabagrus Jayaram, 1955. Type species *Pseudobagrus brachysoma* Günther. (Possible subgenus of *Pseudobagrus*.)

Horabagrus brachysoma (Günther, 1864). Cochinchina.

Coreobagrus Mori, 1936. Type species *C. brevicorpus* Mori.

Coreobagrus brevicorpus Mori, 1936. Rakuto River at Ei-Yo, Korea.

C. ichikawai Okada & Kubota, 1957. Miya River, Mie Pref., Japan.

C. okadai Jayaram, 1967. Suzuka River, Mie Prefecture, Honshu, Japan.

Bathybagrus Bailey & Stewart, 1984. Type species *B. tetranema* Bailey & Stewart.

Bathybagrus tetranema Bailey & Stewart, 1984. Zambian waters of Lake Tanganyika.

Subfamily Bagrinae Regan, 1911

Bagrus Bosc, 1816. Type species *Silurus bajad* Forsskål, 1775. Called by some authors *Porcus* Geoffroy Saint-Hilaire, 1809, but this name preoccupied.

Bagrus bajad (Forsskål, 1775). Nile River.

B. caeruleus Roberts & Stewart, 1976. Near Inga hydroelectric dam (5° 31.5′S; 13° 17.5′E), near Gombe (or Ngombe), about 20 km downstream from Kinshasa (4° 24′S, 15° 10.5′E), Lower Zaire.

B. degeni Boulenger, 1906. Entebbe, Lake Victoria.

B. docmak (Forsskål, 1775). Lower Nile River, near Deltam.

B. filamentosus Pellegrin, 1924. "Niger at Segou", Mali.

B. lubosicus Lönnberg & Rendahl, 1924. Lubosi River, Lower Zaire.

B. meridionalis Günther, 1893. Upper Shire River.

B. orientalis Boulenger, 1902. Pangani River.

B. ubangensis Boulenger, 1902. Ubangi River at Banzyville.

B. urostigma Vinciguerra, 1895. Gunana, Giuba Rivers, Somalia.

Mystus Scopoli, 1777. Type species, *Silurus pelusius* (Solander) (= *Bagrus halepensis* Valenciennes).

Mystus amemiyae (Kimura, 1934). Howchwan, Szechwan Province.

M. argentivittatus (Regan, 1905) "China".

M. armatus (Day, 1865). Cochin, Malabar.

M. aubentoni Desoutter, 1975. Cambodia.

M. bleekeri (Day, 1877). Sind, Jumna; Upper waters of the Ganges: Burma.

M. cavasius (Hamilton, 1822). Gangetic provinces.

M. chinensis (Steindachner, 1883). Canton, China.

M. colvillii Günther, 1874. (Turkey.) Tigris River, Iraq.

M. elongatus (Günther, 1864). Singapore.

M. gulio (Hamilton, 1822). Higher parts of Gangetic estuaries.

M. halepensis (Valenciennes, 1839). Couiac (Quwayq) River, Syria.

M. havmolleri Smith, 1931. Ronpibun, Thailand.

M. horai (Jayaram, 1954). Kalabagh, Indus R., Pakistan.

M. johorensis Herre, 1940. Seng͂ai Kayu, 16 mi. N of Kota Tinggi, Johore.
M. keletius (Valenciennes, 1839). Pondicherry.
M. leucophasis (Blyth, 1860). Sittang River, Burma.
M. macropterus (Bleeker, 1870). Yang-tse-kiang.
M. malabaricus (Jerdon, 1849). Mountain streams in Malabar.
M. menoda (Hamilton, 1822). Kosi River; Mahananda.
m. trachacanthus (Valenciennes, 1839). Bengal.
M. micracanthus (Bleeker, 1846). Batavia.
M. microphthalmus (Day, 1877). Irrawaddy, Burma.
M. montanus (Jerdon, 1849). Manantoddy, Wynaad.
M. nemurus (Valenciennes, 1839). Java.
M. nigriceps (Valenciennes, 1839). Java.
M. oculatus (Valenciennes, 1839). Malabar.
M. pahangensis Herre, 1942. Pahang.
M. peguensis (Boulenger, 1894). Sittang River, near Toungoo, Burma.
M. planiceps (Valenciennes, 1839). Java.
M. pluriradiatus (Vaillant, 1892). "Tonkin", Indo-China (= Vietnam).
M. pulcher (Chaudhuri, 1911). Bhamo, Burma.
M. punctatus (Jerdon, 1849). Cauvery River, W. Ghats.
M. rufescens (Vinciguerra, 1890). Meetan, Burma.
M. sabanus Inger & Chin, 1959. Kinabatangan River, Deramakot, Kinabatangan District, North Borneo.
M. tengara (Hamilton, 1822). Ponds of India.
M. vittatus (Bloch, 1797). Tranquebar, S. India.
M. wolffii (Bleeker, 1851). Bandjermassing, Borneo.
M. wyckii (Bleeker, 1858). Java.

Aorichthys Wu, 1939. Type species *Bagrus lamarii* Valenciennes [= *Aorichthys seenghala* (Sykes)]. (? = subgenus of *Mystus*.)
Aorichthys aor (Hamilton, 1822). Rivers of Bengal and upper parts of Gangetic provinces.
A. seenghala (Sykes, 1838). Mota Mula (Mutha Mula) River, Poona.

Batasio Blyth, 1860. Type species *Pimelodus batasio* Hamilton.
Batasio batasio (Hamilton, 1822). Tista River System.
B. tengana (Hamilton, 1822). Brahmaputra.
B. travancoria Hora & Law, 1941. The Kolathupuzha, trib. of the Kallada; the Peruntenaruvi at Edakadathy; the Chittar at Palode; the Kallada, 4 miles east of Thenmalai, Travancore.

Chandramara Jayaram, 1972. Type species *Pimelodus chandramara* Hamilton.
Chandramara chandramara (Hamilton, 1822). North Bengal, Assam, India.

Leiocassis Bleeker, 1858. Type species *Bagrus poecilopterus* Valenciennes.
Leiocassis albicollaris Fowler, 1934. Bangkok. (Synonym of *siamensis*?)
L. baramensis Regan, 1906. Baram River, Borneo.
L. bicolor Fowler, 1934. Chiengmai, Thailand.
L. breviceps Regan, 1913. Deli, Sumatra.
L. doriae Regan, 1913. Sarawak.
L. fuscus Popta, 1904. Upper Mahakam River, Borneo.
L. hirsutus Herre, 1934. China.
L. hosii Regan, 1906. Sibu, North Borneo.
L. inornatus Boulenger, 1893. Senah, Sarawak.
L. leiacanthus Weber & de Beaufort, 1912. Kwantan River, Sumatra.
L. longirostris Günther, 1864. North China.
L. macracanthus Bleeker, 1854. Sumatra.
L. mahakamensis Vaillant, 1902. Mahakam River, Borneo.
L. merabensis Regan, 1913. Bongon, Merabeh, North Borneo.
L. micropogon (Bleeker, 1852). Tjirutjup River, Borneo.
L. moeschii Boulenger, 1890. Deli, Sumatra.
L. poecilopterus (Valenciennes, 1839). Hebak River, Java.
L. regani Jayaram, 1965. Sadong, North Borneo.
L. robustus Inger & Chin, 1959. Kinabatangan River at Deramakot, Kinabatangan District, North Borneo.
L. rugosus Regan, 1913. Poeh, Sumatra.
L. saravacensis Boulenger, 1893. Senah, North Borneo.

L. siamensis Regan, 1913. Bangpakong River, Thailand.
L. stenomus (Valenciennes, 1839). Java.
L. vaillanti Regan, 1913. Raoen River, North Borneo.

Heterobagrus Bleeker, 1864. Type species *H. bocourti* Bleeker.
Heterobagrus bocourti Bleeker, 1864. Siam.

Subfamily Bagrichthyinae Bleeker, 1858

Bagroides Bleeker, 1851. Type species *B. melapterus* Bleeker.
Bagroides hirsutus (Herre, 1934). Wuchow, China.
B. melapterus Bleeker, 1851. Bandjermassin River, Borneo.

Bagrichthys Bleeker, 1858. Type species *Bagrus hypselopterus* Bleeker.
Bagrichthys hypselopterus (Bleeker, 1852). Palembang.
B. macracanthus (Bleeker, 1854). Confluence of Enim and Lamatang Rivers.
B. macropterus (Bleeker, 1853). Muara Kompeh, Sumatra.

Subfamily Auchenoglanidinae Jayaram, 1966

Parauchenoglanis Boulenger, 1911. Type species *Pimelodus guttatus* Lönnberg.
Parauchenoglanis ansorgii Boulenger, 1912. N'kutu below Loange Falls. (Possible synonym of *P. guttatus*.)
P. boutchangai Thys, 1965. Rapides de la Ngounié ou de la Louetsi á Lelamba, Gabon.
P. guttatus (Lönnberg, 1895). N'Dian River.
P. macrostoma (Pellegrin, 1909). Ogooue River.

Liauchenoglanis Boulenger, 1916. Type species *L. maculatus* Boulenger.
Liauchenoglanis maculatus Boulenger, 1916. North Sherbo district, Sierra Leone.

Notoglanidium Günther, 1903. Type species *N. walkeri* Günther.
Notoglanidium pallidum Roberts & Stewart, 1976. Near Bulu, about 15 km downstream of Luozi, Zaire River.
N. thomasi Boulenger, 1916. Victoria, Sierra Leone.
N. walkeri Günther, 1903. Ibbi River, Ghana.

Auchenoglanis Günther, 1865. Substitute name for *Auchenaspis* Bleeker, 1858, which is preoccupied. Type species *Pimelodus biscutatus* Geoffroy Saint-Hilaire, 1809.
Auchenoglanis ahli Holly, 1930. "Gebirchsbache von Bakoko, Kamerun".
A. altipinnis Boulenger, 1911. Dja River. "Ja River at Esamesa, Cameroon".
A. balayi (Sauvage, 1879). "Lope", Ogowe River.
A. biscutatus (Geoffroy Saint-Hilaire, 1809). Nile River.
A. buettikoferi Popta, 1913. Warri River, Upper Nigeria.
A. fasciatus Gras, 1960. "Boukoutou" (Rep. Benin).
A. grandis Fowler, 1936. Nola, Central African Republic.
A. guirali (Thominot, 1886). "Riviere San Benito".
A. iturii Steindachner, 1911. Ituri River near Mawambi, Zaire.
A. longiceps Boulenger, 1913. Nyong River at Akonolinga, Cameroons.
A. maculosus Holly, 1927. Not mentioned. (Cameroons?)
A. monkei Keilhack, 1910. 2km south of Logobaba (4°2'N; 9°45'W), Cameroon.
A. ngamensis Boulenger, 1911. Okovango River, near Lake Ngami (Zambesi River system).
A. occidentalis (Valenciennes, 1840). Senegal.
A. pantherinus Pellegrin, 1929. Ntem, Cameroons.
A. pietschmanni Holly, 1926. "Bamfluss", Cameroon.
A. punctatus Boulenger, 1902. Lindi River near Stanley Pool.
A. ubangensis Boulenger, 1902. Ubangi River.

Uncertain as to subfamily:

Platyglanis Daget, 1978. Type species *P. depierrei* Daget, 1978.
Platyglanis depierrei Daget, 1978. "Djim, Cameroon".

Chapter 4

Family CRANOGLANDIDAE (Chinese Catfishes)

The family Cranoglanididae is a small family of Chinese catfishes including but a single genus that in turn includes but a single species, *Cranoglanis bouderius*. The body is rather slender and elongate, but the head is large and the snout depressed. The rough bony plates on top of the head giving it the appearance of being "heavily armored" are actually the uncovered occipital region, the bones being rugose. The head narrows forward to a small mouth, the lower jaw included. There are fine teeth in the jaws but the palate is edentulous. The posterior nostrils bear the nasal barbels and are remote from the anterior nostrils. Four pairs of barbels are present. The eyes are rather large and have a free orbital rim. They are set low so that they are visible when viewed from below. The dorsal fin is short, with a spine and about six branched rays, and there is a short adipose fin that is free behind. The anal fin is rather long, with about 36-41 soft rays, and the caudal fin is deeply forked. There are 12-14 rays in each ventral fin. The gas bladder is

Cranoglanis bouderius.

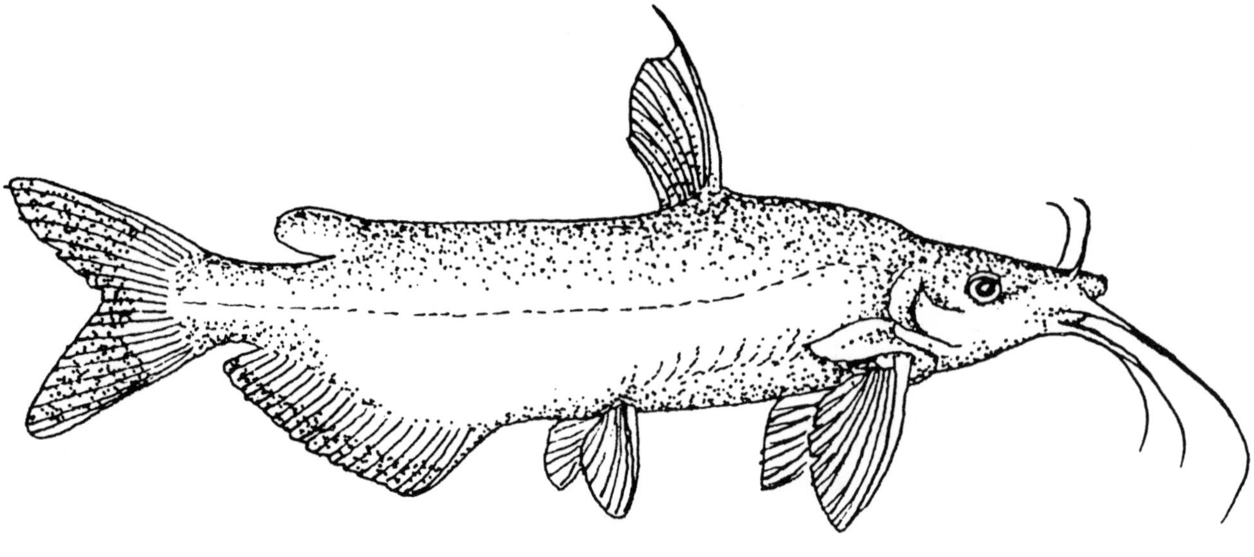

free.

The family Cranoglanididae was defined provisionally by Dr. George S. Myers (1931) and redescribed by K. Jayaram in 1955. It was found that the generic type, *Cranoglanis sinensis*, was synonymous with an earlier described species, *Bagrus bouderius*, and that a subsequently described genus and species, *Pseudeutropichthys multiradiatus*, was also a synonym, leaving the entire family with the single species.

Cranoglanis sinensis (= *C. bouderius*) was described from specimens originally sent from Hong Kong. However, it was later determined that the locality was incorrect and that the specimens in fact came from Wuchow, Kwangsi Province, China. Subsequent collecting proved it to be abundant in the West River and its tributary, the Fu River, at Wuchow. The fish is long and slender, somewhat greenish above and silvery below with dusky fins. It is said to attain a maximum weight of about 2 kilograms.

It has been theorized that the family Cranoglanididae might be allied to the family Ictaluridae, based on the simple resemblance of the tail with that of *Ictalurus furcatus*. This is surely insufficient evidence. It has also been compared with the family Pangasiidae, but *Cranoglanis* appears to be slightly more primitive. Finally, it has been compared with the Bagridae, notably with the Indian genus *Horabagrus*, the similarity being in the form of the fins and the distribution of the barbels. It is very similar in the structure of the anterior vertebrae to *Pseudobagrus*, but these two genera can be distinguished from *Cranoglanis* by certain external features, such as the very inferior position of the eyes, the large number of ventral fin rays, and the great elongation of the anal fin in *Cranoglanis*. The anatomical differences in the Weberian apparatus mentioned by Jayaram appear to be a case of errors of interpretation (Chardon, 1968).

Chardon considers the only important characters for the family Cranoglanididae to be the absence of vomerine teeth and the large number of ventral fin rays. He feels that the recognition of the family rests on flimsy bases and that *Cranoglanis* should best be placed in the family Bagridae, specifically in the subfamily Bagrinae.

It is highly probable that the single species of *Cranoglanis* will not be imported for the aquarium trade.

Checklist of the species of the family Cranoglanididae and its type locality:

Cranoglanis Peters, 1880. Type species *Cranoglanis sinensis* Peters, 1880 (= *Bagrus bouderius* Richardson, 1845).

- *Cranoglanis bouderius* (Richardson, 1845). "Hong Kong" (actually Wuchow, Kwangsi Province, China).

Chapter 5

Family — Plates 19–24

SILURIDAE

(Sheat Catfishes)

The Siluridae is a family of freshwater catfishes with a Eurasian distribution. Actually, there are only two European species, both in the genus *Silurus*, one with a rather limited range (Greece), the other occurring over a large part of Europe and extending eastward to the Aral basin. The Asian species are more numerous (50 to 60), are divided among a number of genera, and range from eastern Siberia and the Amur basin south to the East Indies and the Philippines and west to Asia Minor. They apparently are not found in Africa or the Central Asian Plateau. The size of the species varies from a few centimeters to several meters. They are usually good swimmers, some species even being entirely pelagic, and the prime means of locomotion is by undulations of the anal fin. Most species are nocturnal or active only at twilight, though others are strictly visually oriented. Few species are regularly imported as aquarium fishes.

In the early days the family Siluridae was a catchall family and included most of the known catfishes with the exception of the armored forms. It was C. Tate Regan in 1911 who first broke up this large group of divergent forms, restricting the family Siluridae to the genus *Silurus* and its close relatives. At present, some authors prefer to divide the family further into two subfamilies, the Silurinae and the Kryptopterinae.

The body of the silurid catfishes is elongate, scaleless, and more or less strongly compressed. The head is depressed or compressed (only one genus) and covered with soft skin. The snout is depressed and short or slightly produced. The eyes are lateral and either subcutaneous or with a free orbital margin. The nostrils are remote from each other, with the anterior pair tubular and the posterior pair with a valve. There are two or three pairs of barbels present, one pair of maxillary barbels (usually especially long), and one or two pairs of mandibular barbels (often feebly developed). The mouth is transverse or oblique and provided with widely set, depressible, large (*Belodontichthys*) or villiform teeth in both jaws. The vomerine teeth are depressible, villiform, in either an interrupted (two patches) or an uninterrupted band. The palate is edentulous (except for one genus). The gill openings are wide and the gill membranes are more or less overlapping, free from each other and from the isthmus. There are about 9-21 branchiostegal rays. The lateral line is generally straight, with short ventral branches (dendritic or not) and no dorsal branches. A short (1-7 rays), spineless, dorsal fin is present or absent; when present, it is characteristically set well forward, usually over the ventral fins. There is no adipose fin. The ventral fins may be small, rudimentary, or even entirely absent, but when present usually have about 6-14 rays. The pectoral fins have a spine (articulated for about half its length) and 8-22 rays. The anal fin is very long (50-110 rays) and may be confluent or not with the caudal fin. The caudal fin is elongate and often hypocercal, deeply forked with the lobes rounded or pointed, or it may be truncate. The gas bladder is not enclosed in a bony capsule. The ectopterygoids are lacking.

Approximately nine genera are currently

recognized and can be distinguished by the following key (after Haig, 1950):

1a. Mouth inferior, gape wide but very short; supralabial fold extending below level of eye and at a considerable distance from it; snout truncated; anterior nostrils terminal and close together; posterior nostrils just above and just anterior to eye or above and far behind eye; anal fin very long, with 90 or more rays; dorsal fin absent in known forms....... 2

1b. Mouth terminal, lower jaw projecting, equivalent to or slightly shorter than upper jaw; supralabial fold, if extending below level of eye, very close to it; snout not abruptly truncate; anterior nostrils not terminal, posterior nostrils never behind eye; anal fin with 95 or fewer rays 3

2a. Posterior nostrils above and completely posterior to eye; supralabial fold extending beyond middle of eye; maxillary barbels not osseus and hooked, but sometimes flattened distally into a membrane fringed along one side; anal fin rays 90-95................................ *Hemisilurus*

2b. Posterior nostrils above and just anterior to eye; supralabial fold barely reaching to below middle of eye; maxillary barbels short, heavy, osseus, and hooked; anal fin rays 103-110.........*Ceratoglanis*

3a. Teeth in jaws large, wide-set, arrow-shaped, and in regular rows; head set at an angle of approximately 60° or more from body, the snout tip above the dorsal contour of the fish; head and thorax at pectorals triangular in cross-section, flat below; pectoral fin base long, included about ten times in standard length, pectoral fin itself less than four times in standard length ...*Belodontichthys*

3b. Teeth in jaws small, conical, never arrow-shaped or especially wide-set; head normal, not upturned at an angle; head flat above, neither it nor thorax triangular in cross-section; pectoral fin base shorter, included 14 or more times in standard length, bases of the rays closely approximated; length of pectoral fin included five times or more in standard length 4

4a. Anal fin rays exceedingly long, those at middle of fin equal to or longer than distance from their bases to dorsal contour of fish, the rays covered for more than half their length by integument or muscles; anal fin completely confluent with caudal fin; head very short, included six times or more in standard length; gill rakers rudimentary, reduced to knobs, few in number and set very far apart.... .... *Silurichthys*

4b. Anal fin rays much shorter, those at middle of fin shorter than distance from their bases to dorsal contour of fish; anal fin free from caudal fin or narrowly connected to it, but the two never completely confluent; head longer, 6½ or less in standard length; gill rakers long or short, but never all reduced to knobs, few or many in number......... 5

5a. Caudal fin rounded, truncate, or weakly emarginate, with very bluntly rounded lobes; maxillary barbels heavy, flattened; body compressed but robust anteriorly; anal fin rays covered by integument for more than half their length; pectoral fin spine stout, the fin not extending beyond origin of anal; gape horizontal to somewhat oblique......*Silurus*

5b. Caudal fin distinctly forked or deeply emarginate with pointed lobes; maxillary barbels slender....................... 6

6a. Eye with a free orbital rim and located above level of corner of mouth, not visible from underside of head; gape oblique, wide, and very long, reaching to or beyond anterior border of eye; dorsal fin with five rays; pectoral fin not extending beyond origin of anal fin........ .... *Wallago*

6b. Eye subcutaneous, located opposite corner of mouth or lower border level with it, usually visible from underside of head; gape not extending beyond anterior border of eye; dorsal fin with 1-4 rays or absent 7

7a. Dorsal fin rays 3 or 4; gill rakers 15 or fewer on lower limb of first gill arch and shorter than the branchial filaments; gape straight to sharply oblique; eye opposite corner of mouth or its lower border on a level with it...................... 8

7b. Dorsal fin rays 1 or 2, or dorsal fin absent, the rays, when present, short; gill rakers 15 or more on long limb of first gill arch, long, slender, and curved, usually as long as the branchial filaments; gape straight to somewhat oblique, very short, and not reaching anterior border of eye; eye large, opposite corner of mouth and visible from underside of head .... *Kryptopterus*

8a. Gape horizontal, rather long, but not reaching anterior border of eye; jaws equal or lower jaw slightly shorter; eye opposite corner of mouth, a small portion visible from underside of head; teeth often present on palatines; pectoral fin short and broad, not extending beyond anal fin origin, its spine strongly pectinate on inner margin .... *Hito*

8b. Gape slightly oblique, not extending beyond anterior border of eye; jaws equal or lower prominent; ventral border of eye on level with corner of mouth or below it and usually visible from underside of head; teeth never present on palatines; pectoral fin usually extending beyond anal fin origin, its spine pectinate or smooth .... *Ompok*

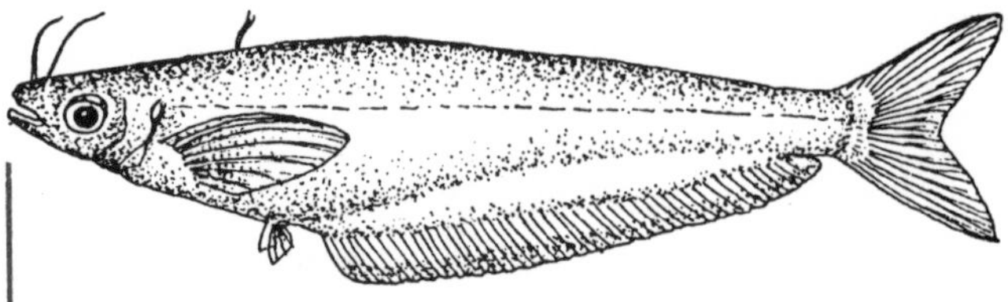

Kryptopterus cryptopterus. (After Bleeker, 1862.)

Species of the genus *Kryptopterus* usually inhabit large rivers (at least in Thailand), some in large enough numbers to have become a significant factor in the food supply of the local peoples. The genus is distributed from Thailand, Vietnam, etc., to the Malay Peninsula, Sumatra, Java, and Borneo. At least one very important aquarium fish is included in this genus, *K. bi cirrhis*. The generic name has often been spelled *Cryptopterus* in the past.

In the genus *Kryptopterus* the body is strongly compressed and the head is depressed. The mouth is straight to oblique and the gape is very short, not reaching the anterior border of the eye. The jaws are equal or either jaw may be slightly longer. The eyes are subcutaneous and positioned opposite the corner of the mouth. They are usually quite large and visible from the underside of the head. The anterior nostrils are tubular, wideset, and located near the anterior edge of the snout. The posterior nostrils are located before the anterior border of the eye or slightly posterior to a vertical drawn through it. There are one or two pairs of barbels, the maxillary pair very slender, of varying length, and the mandibular pair short, rudimentary, or even absent. The teeth in both jaws are short, depressible, and form broad bands. The vomerine teeth are usually in a single patch, more rarely two, and no teeth are present on the palatines. The gill rakers are long, slender, and curved, and usually as long as the gill filaments; they number 15-20 on the long limb of the first gill arch. There are about 8-17 branchiostegal rays. The gill membranes are free from each other and from the isthmus. The dorsal fin is rudimentary or absent; when present, the rays are short, contained about twice in the eye. There is no adipose fin, and the caudal fin is deeply forked, the lower lobe the longer. The ventral fins are small or rudimentary, with about 5-10 rays, and the pectoral fin has a partly osseus spine. The anal fin is free from the caudal fin or it is narrowly connected to it.

There are anywhere from 10 to 20 species currently accepted in the genus *Kryptopterus*, but the number will most surely change when this genus is more closely studied, for although the genus is fairly well defined the species are often very difficult to distinguish. Information on the various species ranges from very sparse to plentiful, depending upon the species under consideration.

Kryptopterus macrocephalus occurs in Sumatra, the Sunda Straits islands, Borneo, and the Malay Peninsula where it attains a length of approximately 20 cm. It inhabits shady spots in running waters and is omnivorous, although larger individuals may prey on smaller fishes. It is often confused with *K. bicirrhis* but is not as translucent as that species and is somewhat yellowish in color. The caudal and anal fins are connected in *K. macrocephalus*, but in *K. bicirrhis* they are separate. *K. bicirrhis* is probably the best known species in the genus. It comes from Java, Sumatra, Borneo, the Malay Peninsula, and Thailand, and attains a maximum length of about 15 cm in the wild but usually no more than 12 cm in captivity. It is this species that is commonly imported for the aquarium trade. In the wild it is generally found in shady spots in running water. Because it is so transparent that the internal organs (or at least the silvery sac that contains them) are quite visible along with the blood vessels, backbone, and other internal features, aquarists have dubbed this species the Glass Catfish. In certain lighting, however, the fish may reflect iridescent hues of virtually any color from yellow to a deep violet; in semi-darkness it has been reported to appear almost a fluorescent blue. No sexual differences are known, although it is said that the males are always smaller and more slender than the females.

In captivity this fish should always be kept in small groups. Single individuals will often exhibit long bouts of rapid swimming back and forth in a tank followed by periods of rest. The fish will eventually languish away and die if kept by itself. The Glass Catfish is a twilight species, preferring to keep in a small group during the day in a darkened, shady spot in the tank, especially where there is a slight current. The group will remain there for hours, but individual fish will constantly change position within the group. Each fish will hold itself at a slight angle, tail lowermost, making undulatory movements with its anal fin and posterior part of its body. It is reported that the Glass Catfish will adopt a blotchy pattern on occasion while resting among the plants (this blotchy pattern resembles the shadows of the leaves and makes the fish difficult to spot) or will at other times exhibit longitudinal, narrow, dark stripes. The proper aquarium for housing Glass Catfish is one that is fairly spacious, not too deep, and with a well planted background. The water chemistry is not critical, although medium hard water seems to be preferred. The pH is best between 6.5 and 7.5, and the water temperature range should be 20° to 26°C. Im-

Most internal structures of the aquarists' glass catfish can be seen quite clearly in these *Kryptopterus bicirrhis*. The soft organs, however, are hidden in a reflective pouch. Photo by G. J. M. Timmerman.

This *Kryptopterus* sp., possibly *K. macrocephalus*, has a mottled pattern, a rudimentary dorsal fin, and only about 50 rays in the anal fin. Photo by G. J. M. Timmerman.

ported specimens are particularly prone to white spot disease at lower temperatures. The Glass Catfish should be fed live animal matter if possible (which should not be too large), and they are especially fond of mosquito larvae. They normally do not grub for food on the bottom like most catfishes, but take it as it floats past them. *K. bicirrhis* is a peaceful, relatively hardy species that poses no threat to plants or other fishes and is therefore well suited for a community aquarium, preferably one housing other peaceful fishes that are not too active or fast swimmers. When transferred from one tank to another, they tend to be shy for a time. They are also shy in a community tank except at feeding time, when they usually are ready to accept their fair share—or even more! Apparently this species has not yet been spawned in captivity.

Kryptopterus limpok grows to a length of about 20 cm, but a ripe female with eggs 1 mm in diameter was discovered in Thailand and it had a length of 15 cm. In that country this species is eaten extensively as a fresh fish or it is preserved by smoking it on spits. It is highly esteemed as a food fish. *Kryptopterus bleekeri* is common in Thailand, according to Smith (1945), living in swamps during high water but frequenting the deeper parts of rivers at other times. *K. bleekeri* is also a good food fish but grows to a length of about 60 cm. It is fished for with mole crickets and is called "red" fish due to its rose, pink, or other reddish shades.

The genus *Ompok* contains perhaps a dozen or so species from India to Korea and south to Sumatra, Borneo, and Java. It is characterized by a strongly compressed body and a depressed head. The mouth is sharply oblique and the gape does not extend beyond the anterior border of the eye. The lower jaw is prominent, and the teeth in the jaws are short, villiform, and in broad bands. The vomerine teeth are in one or two patches of variable size, and there are no teeth on the palatines. The anterior nostrils are wide-set and tubular while the posterior nostrils are provided with valves and are located before the anterior border of the eye. The eyes are subcutaneous, their lower border on a level with the corner of the mouth or even lower, and they are often visible from the underside of the head. There are one or two pairs of barbels, a maxillary pair of variable length and a mandibular pair that is often rudimentary or may be totally absent but when pres-

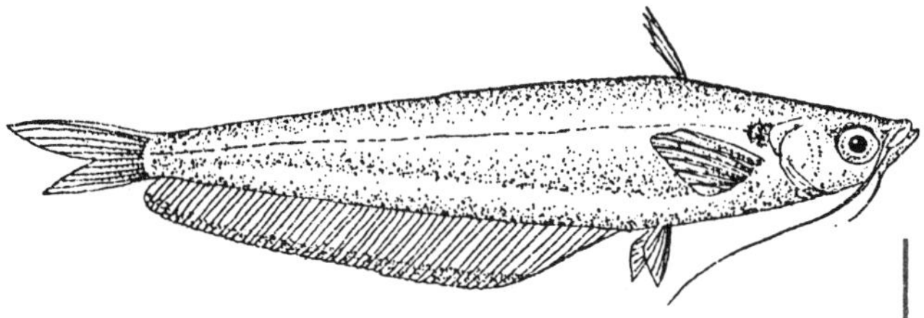

Ompok bimaculatus. (After Day, 1878.)

ent varies in length from shorter than the eye to extending beyond the caudal fin. The dorsal fin is short, with about four rays, or it may be rudimentary or even absent. The adipose fin is absent and the anal fin is either free from the caudal fin or may be narrowly connected to it. The caudal fin is deeply forked. The pectoral fin is provided with a spine that is smooth or denticulate on its inner margin, and the ventral fins have 7-10 rays. The gill rakers are quite short, wide-set, curved, and about 7-11 in number on the lower limb of the first gill arch. The gill opening is wide and the gill membranes are deeply notched and overlapping but free from each other and from the isthmus. There are 9-15 branchiostegals. The gas bladder is small and not enclosed in bone. No auxiliary bone is present.

Only one species, *Ompok bimaculatus*, is generally seen in the aquarium trade. It is widely distributed and abundant in the Malay Peninsula, Thailand, Java, Borneo, Sumatra, Indochina, Burma, India, and Sri Lanka. It attains a maximum length of about 40-46 cm but normally reaches a length of only 18-25 cm (two females of 25 cm captured in Thailand had large ovaries with ripe eggs). The body form of *O. bimaculatus* varies considerably throughout its range, which has led to a great deal of confusion about this species. In some areas it is a relatively important food fish. In appearance it is almost transparent when young, like the Glass Catfish, but older individuals develop a bluish sheen on the back and sides. In captivity it must be kept in a small school, for individuals tend to pine away. This species seems to be more belligerent than *Kryptopterus*, and large individuals, especially, tend to be quarrelsome. The care and tank setup should be similar to that mentioned for the Glass Catfish.

Ompok sabanus grows to a length of about 15 cm and is found mostly in rivers, although some inhabit the mouths of small muddy tributaries and a very few are found in small tur-

Ompok species usually have a better developed, albeit small, dorsal fin. This is probably a young *O. bimaculatus*, so named because of the two dark spots, one above the pectoral fin and the other at the base of the caudal fin. Photo by G. J. M. Timmerman.

bid creeks. None are found in clear water. Investigation of the stomach contents revealed mostly aquatic and terrestrial insects. Some of the females collected (with lengths around 13 cm) contained eggs. Males over 10 cm, on the other hand, possessed 8-14 retrorse hooks on the inside of the pectoral fin spine, possibly a sexual character.

The genus *Hito*, with probably but a single species, is fairly restricted in its distribution, occurring only in the Philippines (Palawan, Busuanga, Culion). The name *Hito* is derived from the Filipino name for certain catfishes, particularly of the genus *Clarias*. The body is strongly compressed and the head is depressed. The mouth is horizontal and the gape quite long, but it does not extend as far as to the anterior border of the eye. The jaws are equal or the lower jaw is slightly shorter, and the teeth are short, distributed in four to five more or less regular rows forming broad bands. The vomerine teeth are usually in a single patch but sometimes are completely divided into two separate patches. A patch of teeth is present on each palatine and may be of different sizes on each palatine, may be present on one side only, rudimentary, with two or three teeth, or the palatine teeth may be completely absent. The anterior nostrils are tubular and wide-set; the posterior nostrils are valved and located in front of the anterior border of the eye. Two or three pairs of barbels are present: a maxillary pair that is long and slender, extending to the origin of the anal fin or perhaps not quite that far, and usually one but sometimes two pairs of mandibular barbels about as long as the head. The eyes are subcutaneous, their lower edge on a level with the angle of the mouth and with a small portion visible from the underside of the head. The anal fin is free from the caudal fin or the last ray is joined to it by a membrane. The pectoral fin has a spine that is strongly denticulate on its inner margin. The caudal fin is forked. There are 14-15 gill rakers on the lower limb of the first gill arch that are slender and about half as long as the gill filaments.

The single species has not been reported as an aquarium fish and nothing is known about its behavior or requirements in captivity.

The genus *Hemisilurus* is a small genus of perhaps only three species, all restricted to the islands of Sumatra and Borneo. The body is strongly compressed and the head is depressed, with a truncate snout. The mouth is inferior and the gape is wide but very short. The supralabial fold extends beyond the middle of the eye and at a considerable distance from it. The anterior nostrils are tubular, close-set, and located toward the front of the snout; the posterior nostrils are farther apart and located above and completely behind the posterior border of the eye. There are conspicuous cavities along the mandible. The teeth on the jaws are short, villiform, and in

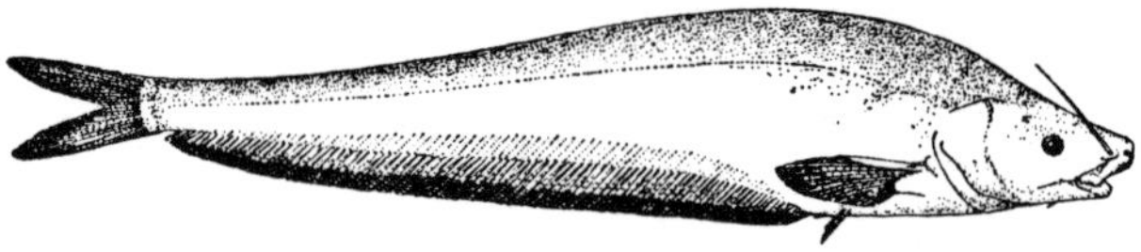

Hemisilurus moolenburghi. (From Weber & de Beaufort, 1913.)

broad bands. The vomerine teeth are in two small patches; there are no teeth on the palatines. The eyes are subcutaneous and located above and behind the corner of the mouth. They are not visible from the underside of the head. There are two pairs of barbels: a pair of maxillary barbels that are flexible, rather short, and in females sometimes longer and flattened distally into a membrane that is fringed along one side, and a single pair of mandibular barbels that are very small or rudimentary and quite distant from the symphysis. There are about 10 to 12 gill rakers on the lower limb of the first gill arch and there are 10-12 branchiostegals. The gill membranes are free from each other and from the isthmus. The dorsal and adipose fins are absent. The anal fin is free from the caudal fin, which is deeply forked, the two lobes being about equal. The pectoral fins have a spine, and the ventral fins have about eight or nine rays.

In *Hemisilurus moolenburghi* of Sumatra and Java the male's maxillary barbels are short and stiff and have been likened to an old fashioned waxed moustache. The maxillary barbels of the female are somewhat different. They are much longer and are distally flattened, with one edge split into three to five thread-like filaments.

Species of this genus have rarely, if ever,

been used as aquarium fishes, therefore little is known about their behavior or requirements in captivity. Considering that the species range from 30 to over 50 cm in length, only young individuals are suitable for the home aquarium.

The genus *Ceratoglanis* contains a single species from Sumatra, Java, and Borneo. It is closely related to the genus *Hemisilurus* but has short, bony, hooked maxillary barbels (versus long, filamentous barbels) and the posterior nostrils are situated anterior to a vertical through the front of the eye (versus on or behind a vertical through the front of the eye). The body is strongly compressed and the head is depressed and with a truncated snout. The mouth is inferior, transverse, and the gape is wide but very short. A supralabial fold extends to below the middle of the eye but at a distance from it. The anterior nostrils are close together at the front of the snout, with short tubes that are directed forward, while the posterior nostrils are barely valved and are located above the anterior border of the eye. The teeth in the jaws

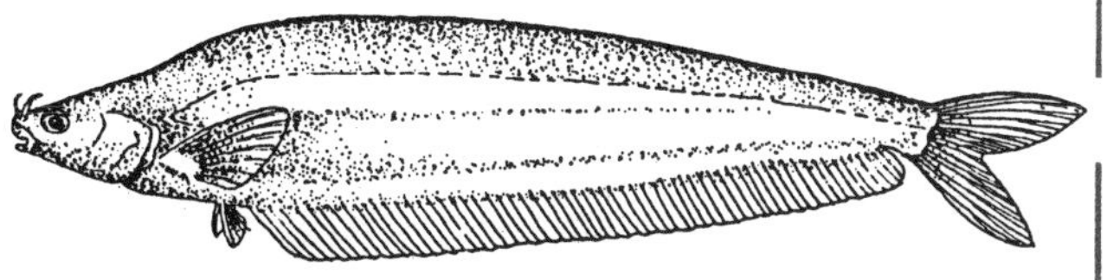

Ceratoglanis scleronema. (After Bleeker, 1862.)

Head of *C. scleronema* showing position of anterior (n) and posterior (n′) nostrils. (From Weber & de Beaufort, 1913.)

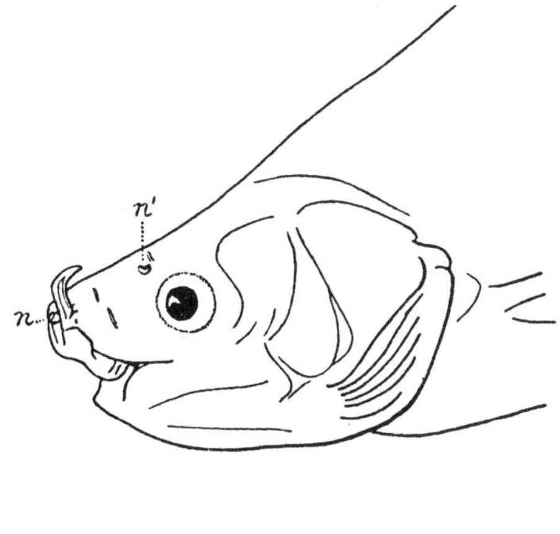

are very small and set in broad bands, whereas those on the vomer are in two small round patches. There are no teeth on the palatines. The eyes are subcutaneous, above and behind the corner of the mouth, and are not visible from the underside of the head. There are two pairs of barbels, a pair of maxillary barbels that are short, hooked, and bony, originating immediately posterior to the anterior pair of nostrils, and a pair of minute mandibular barbels. The gill rakers are short, stiff, and wide-set, numbering about ten on the lower limb of the first gill arch. The anal fin is free from the caudal fin and contains the largest number of rays for any member of the family—110. The dorsal and adipose fins are absent, the pectoral fin spine is smooth, and the caudal fin is deeply forked. The single species in this genus apparently has not been imported as an aquarium fish.

The genus *Belodontichthys* is represented by a single species from Java, Sumatra, Borneo, Thailand, and the Malay Peninsula. The body is strongly compressed and the head is short, compressed, keeled, and depressed only at the tip of the snout. The head and thorax are triangular in cross-section, with one of the flat portions below. The head is also permanently upturned. The gape is long, oblique, and at an angle of about 60-80° from the horizontal. The anterior nostrils are wide-set, tubular, and the posterior nostrils are valved. The eyes are subcutaneous, morphologically above the corner of the mouth but actually low-set, just posterior to the corner, and not visible from the underside of the head. The maxillary bar-

Belodontichthys dinema. (From Weber & de Beaufort, 1913.)

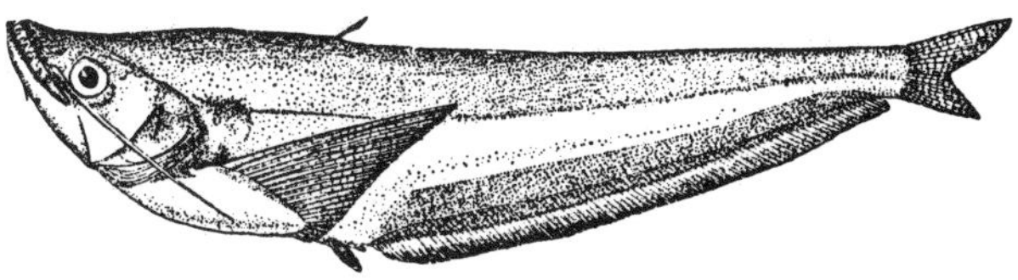

bels are short, extending as far as the ventral fins or even a little bit further, while the mandibular barbels are two in number and shorter than the eye. The teeth in the jaws are very distinct and used, in part, to separate this genus from the others. They are large, wide-set, and arrow-shaped, set in three regular rows in each jaw, those of the outer row shorter and set at a different level outside the mouth. The vomerine teeth are very small and in two small patches, and there are no teeth on the palatines. The gill rakers are short, stiff, elongate-conical, rather widely spaced, and about 30 in number on the lower limb of the first gill arch, while the gill membranes are separated and free from the isthmus. The anal fin is long and free from the caudal fin, which is deeply forked, the upper lobe the longer. The dorsal fin is very short, rudimentary, about equal to the eye. The pectoral fin is long, extending well into the anal and about three to four times in the standard length as compared with six or more in other genera. Its spine is slender and not toothed. The pectoral base is very long, about ten times in the standard length (about 14 or more in the other genera), and the ventral fins are small, of 9-10 rays.

The only species, *Belodontichthys dinema*, is a common and well-known fish in the regions where it occurs, i.e., Sumatra, Borneo, Malacca, Thailand. It prefers the deeper parts of the rivers and is most evident when it is feeding on migrating cyprinoid fishes. Its large pectoral fins, large mouth, and long, sharp teeth make it ideally adapted for rapid swimming and voracious feeding. Although the largest specimen observed was 70 cm, 30- to 40-cm fish are more common. The flesh is good and it is a popular food fish although it dies immediately after being taken from the water and the flesh deteriorates quite fast. As far as known, this species has never been imported for the aquarium trade.

The genus *Silurichthys* is a small genus of perhaps four or five species from Sumatra, Java, Borneo, the Malay Peninsula, and Thailand. The body is compressed and the head is depressed and very short (six and a half to seven and a half in the standard length). The mouth is horizontal or very slightly oblique and the gape is very short, but it reaches to or beyond the anterior border of the eye; the upper jaw is slightly longer than the lower jaw. The anterior nostrils are tubular and wide-set, located above the front border of the snout, while the posterior nostrils are valved and located before the anterior border of the eye. The eyes are subcutaneous, very small, and well above the corner of the mouth.

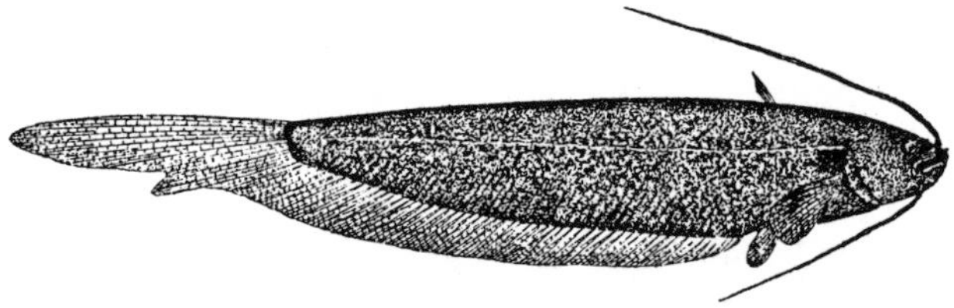

Silurichthys phaiosoma. (From Weber & de Beaufort, 1913.)

There are two pairs of barbels, the maxillary barbels being rather heavy, reaching about to the middle of the anal fin, and the mandibular barbels being longer than the head, sometimes reaching to the anal fin origin or beyond. The teeth are short and in broad bands in the jaws. The vomerine teeth are usually in a single rounded patch but sometimes may be in two slightly separated patches; there are no teeth on the palatines. The gill rakers are rudimentary, sometimes consisting only of small knobs set very far apart and not more than about five on the lower limb of the first gill arch. The gill membranes are free from each other and from the isthmus, but they overlap slightly anteriorly. There are nine branchiostegal rays. The dorsal fin is quite short, with no spine and only four rays, and there is no adipose fin. The anal fin is confluent with the caudal fin and its rays are exceedingly long, those at the middle of the fin as long as or longer than the distance from their bases to the dorsal contour of the fish, the rays covered for more than half their length by integument and muscles. The ventral fins are short, with seven rays, and the pectoral fins have a spine. The caudal fin is obliquely emarginate, the upper lobe the longer.

As far as known, there have been no major importations of any of the species in this genus into the aquarium trade. *Silurichthys phaiosoma* is occasionally imported from Malaya, but only sporadically. It is a small brown catfish that grows only to a length of about 14 cm.

The genus *Silurus* is one of the larger genera of the family, with about 15 species included, among them the well known European Wels, *Silurus glanis*. Species in this genus have a compressed body and a broad, depressed head. The mouth is horizontal or somewhat oblique and the gape is long and wide, sometimes extending beyond the hind border of the eye. The jaws are either equal or either jaw may be longer than the other. The teeth are short and form broad bands in the jaws. The vomerine teeth may be either in a single patch or two patches. The anterior nostrils are tubular and wide-set, while the posterior nostrils are located in front of the anterior border of the eye. The eyes are subcutaneous or with a free orbital rim and set above the corner of the mouth; they are not visible from the underside of the head. There are two or three pairs of barbels, a maxillary pair that are rather heavy, flattened, and vary in length, and one or two pairs of mandibular barbels. The gill rakers are short, about 8-10 of them on the lower limb of the first gill arch, and the gill membranes are deeply notched and free from the isthmus. There are 12 to 15 branchiostegals. The dorsal fin is short and there is no adipose fin. The anal fin

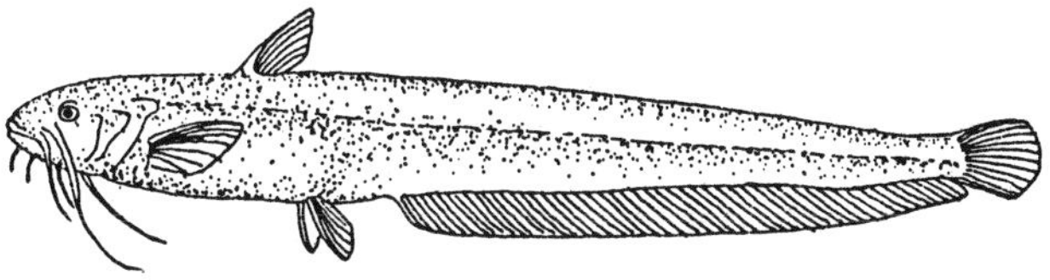

Silurus glanis. (After Wheeler, 1969.)

is free from the caudal or only narrowly attached to it or rather broadly joined to it, the anal rays covered by integument for most of their length. The caudal fin is rounded to weakly emarginate, with bluntly rounded lobes. The ventral fins have 8-10 rays and the pectoral fins have a stout spine that is either denticulate or smooth on its inner margin. The gas bladder is not enclosed in bone.

In the early days just after Linnaeus, most species of catfishes were placed in the genus *Silurus* if they were not armored. Aristotle, Pliny, Aelian, and Atheneus referred to giant catfish as "silurus" and "glanis," and it is quite possible that they were referring to the European Wels. Bleeker was among the first to start breaking up this hodgepodge of species into more natural units. More than half of the genera in the family Siluridae alone are credited to him.

Species of the genus *Silurus* are more or less nocturnal, bottom-living catfishes whose combined distribution covers much of Eurasia. The European Wels, *Silurus glanis*, is probably the most studied species of the family. A record specimen with a length of more than five meters (over 16½ feet) and a weight of 330 kilograms (726 pounds) was captured in the Dnieper River. In Europe, however, this species averages about 150 cm. This large, solitary fish lives in quiet water, usually marshes, lagoons, backwaters, lakes, or the deep reaches of large rivers. The preferred bottom type seems to be mud, although it may also be found over other soft bottoms such as sand. It is nocturnal, keeping close to the bottom during the day and hiding in hollows in the river bed, in holes under the overhanging banks, or under tree roots or other sunken objects. In the Baltic and parts of the Black Sea, the European Wels has a high tolerance to brackish water. It is said to make limited upriver migrations in order to spawn, returning to deep water downriver to spend the cold winters in the northern parts of its range. Because of its large size, in early days individuals were fished for with the aid of oxen. It seems that a team of oxen (or horses) was taken to a favored fishing spot and the fishing line was attached to their yoke. At the other end a sharp hook was baited with the lungs of a wild bull (nothing else seemed to work quite as well). Once the catfish was hooked it was rather a simple matter to use the strong beasts of burden to haul the huge catfish out of the water.

The European Wels is totally carnivorous. While it is young it is content with dining on a variety of bottom-living invertebrates, but when it grows to a large size its menu expands to include a wide range of items including fishes of all sorts, frogs, crayfish, birds (ducklings, etc.), and even small mammals (such as water voles). There are actually few aquatic organisms it cannot tackle.

Silurus glanis breeds in the spring or early summer (mid-May to mid-July) in marshy areas of lakes and on the flood plains of rivers. The eggs are adhesive and stick to the aquatic plants or to the leaf litter of the bottom. No nest is constructed, but the male does guard the eggs. The pale yellow eggs, about 2-3 mm long, hatch in about three weeks. The young have the general appearance of unpigmented tadpoles. They grow very rapidly, attaining an average length of 30 cm in their first year and up to 100 cm by their sixth or seventh year, although the rate of growth is quite variable and depends on a number of factors in their environment. An old female may produce 100,000 or more eggs.

This species is a valuable food fish, and a fishery in eastern Europe and the U.S.S.R. has developed to utilize parts of the fish. The flesh of the young is reported to have good flavor, and the larger specimens yield a type of leather from the skin, glue from the bones and swim bladder, and the eggs are said to be used as a substitute for caviar (or may be used to adulterate true caviar). These are also good fish for the sportsman for they are not particular about the bait and put up a fight that is a test of strength and skill for the angler. In some areas it is even farmed, the major feed being unwanted and unsalable fish species such as the silver bream. The European Wels has been introduced into various regions but does not always seem to have become firmly established every time.

Silurus aristotelis constructs a nest by simply excavating some bottom material. (From Gill, 1906.)

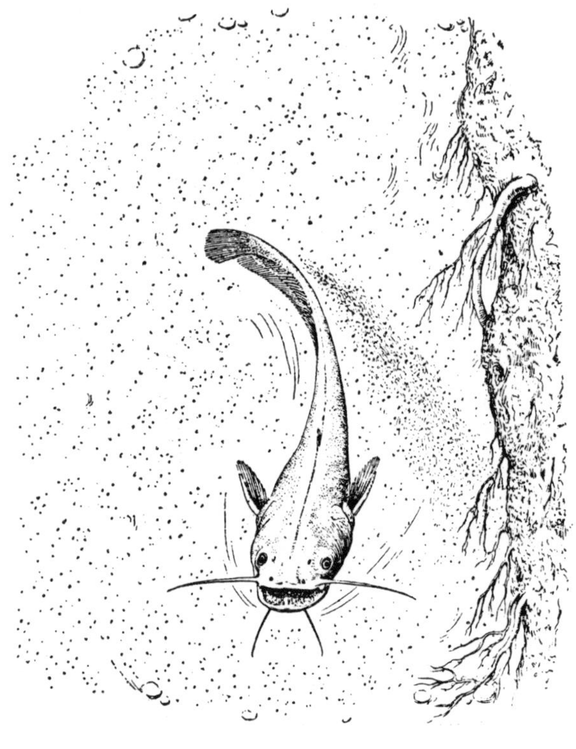

Small Wels do well in unheated aquaria. They are quite hardy, not choosy about their food, and grow rapidly. Large individuals are suitable for exhibition tanks in public aquaria, but they are not quite as hardy as the younger ones. They must be kept by themselves and special care must be exercised in keeping their tank clean. Live fishes are the best food.

Silurus aristotelis from Greece apparently is a nest-builder, but this is just a simple excavation in the bottom. It may also attach its eggs to tree roots, etc., if they are convenient. The male guards the eggs. *S. asotus* from China, Japan, and Korea grows to a length of a mere half meter. It is also a food fish, and the flesh is supposed to be quite firm when the fish comes from cooler waters.

The genus *Wallago* is a small genus of less than a half dozen fairly large species with a distribution from India to Borneo. The name *Wallago* has a complicated taxonomic history involving the names *Belodontichthys* and *Wallagonia*, but this is aptly covered in Haig (1950) and need not be repeated here. In the genus *Wallago* the body is compressed and the snout is depressed. The mouth is oblique and the gape is wide and very long, extending to or beyond the anterior border of the eye. The teeth of the jaws are longer and sharper than in most of the other genera and are set in broad bands. The vomerine teeth are in two patches and there are no teeth on the palatines. The tubular anterior nostrils are set far apart and the posterior nostrils are valved and located before the anterior border of the eye. The eyes have a free orbital rim and are located above the level of the corner of the mouth and are not visible from the underside of the head. There are two pairs of barbels, a long and slender maxillary pair that is variable in length and a mandibulary pair that is shorter than the head, filamentous, and positioned at some distance behind the symphysis of the jaw. There are 9-21 short, stiff, often forked, wide-set gill rakers on the lower limb of the first gill arch. The gill membranes are free from each other and from the isthmus, and there are 15 to 20 branchiostegal rays. The dorsal fin is short-based, consisting of 5 comparatively long rays (about equal to the pectoral fins) and no spine. There is no adipose fin. The anal fin is long and free from the caudal, which is deeply forked to deeply emarginate with pointed lobes. The pectoral fins have a spine, and the ventral fins have 10-11 rays.

Wallago attu is a large, predatory, powerful catfish that attains a length of up to 2 meters. Though huge, it is not particularly heavy, the two-meter fish weighing only about 55 kilos. It is a formidable predator that attacks almost anything, including water birds. The very large, broad, and strongly toothed mouth and the large lateral eyes, plus the powerful tail that permits them to virtually leap on their prey, all combine to make their attacks successful. *W. attu* will pursue small fishes at or near the surface, even jumping entirely out of the water and falling back with a loud splash.

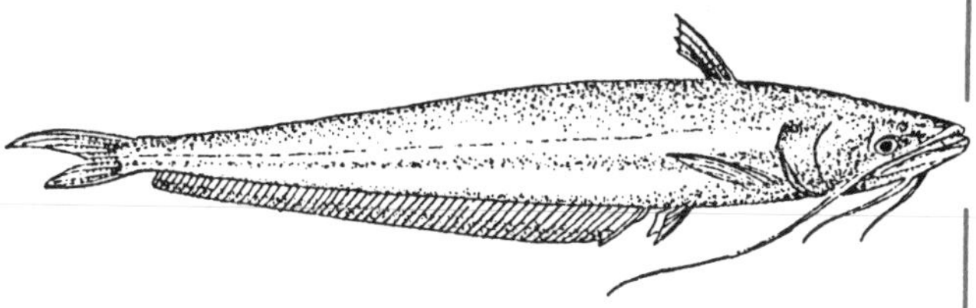

Wallago attu. (After Day, 1878.)

When small cyprinids (pla soi in Thailand) are running upstream, these fish will remain with the schools and gorge themselves. In Bengal, where this species attains a length of 2.4 meters or more, it is called the freshwater shark and some natives are as fearful of it as they are of the crocodile. It is a valued food fish in many parts of its range, although in some areas it is avoided due to its allegedly unclean feeding habits. It is even reported that among the items found in the stomach of this species were parts of human limbs. In some areas where there is a fish culture industry, *W. attu* is considered a pest. Besides being sought after as a food fish, this species is also valued by anglers as a sport fish. It may be caught on a trolled spoon or by use of a stink bait (see the family Ictaluridae for more information on stink baits).

Obviously this is not your typical aquarium fish, although some have been kept when relatively small, perhaps for the novelty. Golf-ball-sized pieces of raw fish or meat tossed into their tank are struck immediately, much to the consternation of anyone who is standing within 2 to 2.5 meters of the tank, for they are showered with water. Some observers report that this fish will swim at an angle of about 30° with the horizontal, much like the position used by the Glass Catfish.

Wallago leerii grows to a length of only a meter and attains a weight of about 50 kilograms. It also has a habit of leaping out of the water in the pursuit of cyprinid fishes. *Wallago maculatus* grows to 75 cm and appears to have no preference for either clear or turbid water. In some of the specimens collected, stomach content analysis revealed insect fragments, a prawn, and a small flower. This is a good food fish that may be caught by hook and line, with a cast net, or by traps.

Checklist of the species of the family Siluridae and their type localities:

Hemisilurus Bleeker, 1858. Type species *Wallago heterorhynchus* Bleeker.
- *Hemisilurus chaperi* (Vaillant, 1891). Knapei, Borneo.
- *H. heterorhynchus* (Bleeker, 1853). Sumatra.
- *H. moolenburghi* Weber & de Beaufort, 1913. Sumatra.

Ceratoglanis Myers, 1938. Type species *Hemisilurus scleronema* Bleeker.
- *Ceratoglanis scleronema* (Bleeker, 1862). Java.

Belodontichthys Bleeker, 1858. Type species *Wallago dinema* Bleeker (= *Belodontichthys macrochir* Bleeker, 1858).
- *Belodontichthys dinema* (Bleeker, 1851). Borneo.

Silurichthys Bleeker, 1858. Type species *Silurus phaiosoma* Bleeker.
- *Silurichthys hasselti* Bleeker, 1858. Java.
- *S. leucopodus* Fowler, 1939. Trang, Thailand.
- *S. phaiosoma* (Bleeker, 1851). Sambas, Borneo.
- *S. schneideri* Volz, 1904. Sumatra.
- *S.* sp. Johore State.

Silurus Linnaeus, 1758. Type species *Silurus glanis* Linnaeus.
- *Silurus aristotelis* (Agassiz, 1856). Greece.
- *S. asotus* Linnaeus, 1758. Asia.
- *S. berdmorei* (Blyth, 1860). Akyab, Tenasserim, India.
  - *b. wynaadensis* (Day, 1873). Wynaad,

Kerala, India.

S. biwaensis (Tomoda, 1961). Lake Biwa-ko.

S. chantrei Sauvage, 1882. Probably Asia Minor (Syria or Tigris Basin).

S. cinereus Dabry, 1872. Yangtze, China.

S. cochinchinensis Valenciennes, 1839. Cochinchina.

S. (?) *furnessi* (Fowler, 1905). Borneo.

S. gangetica (Peters, 1861). India. (Doubtful.)

S. gilberti Hora, 1936. Lunchow, China.

S. glanis Linnaeus, 1758. Eastern and northern Europe and Asia Minor.

S. goae Haig, 1950. India.

S. grahami Regan, 1907. Yunnan, China.

S. lithophilus (Tomoda, 1961). Lake Biwa-ko.

S. mento Regan, 1904. Yunnan, China.

S. microdorsalis (Mori, 1936). Korea.

S. soldatovi Nikolsky & Soin, 1947. Amur River.

Wallago Bleeker, 1851. Type species *Silurus mülleri* Bleeker (= *Silurus attu* Bloch & Schneider, 1801).

Wallago attu (Bloch & Schneider, 1801). Malabar, India.

W. (?) *hexanema* (Kner, 1864-1867). Locality unknown.

W. leerii Bleeker, 1851. Borneo.

W. maculatus Inger & Chin, 1959. Kinabatangan River at Deramakot, North Borneo.

W. tweediei (Hora & Misra, 1941). Kuala Tahan in Pahang, Malay Peninsula. (= *l eerii*)

Hito Herre, 1924. Type species *Hito taytayensis* Herre.

Hito taytayensis Herre, 1924. Palawan, Culion, and Busuanga, Philippines.

Ompok Lacépède, 1803. Type species *Ompok siluroides* Lacépède (= *Silurus bimaculatus* Bloch).

Ompok bimaculatus (Bloch, 1797). Malabar.

O. borneensis (Steindachner, 1901). Borneo. (Doubtful.)

O. miostoma Vaillant, 1902. Tepoe, Borneo.

O. canio (Hamilton, 1822). Northeastern Bengal.

O. eugeneiatus (Vaillant, 1893). Borneo.

O. hypophthalmus (Bleeker, 1846). Batavia, Java.

O. (?) *javanensis* (Hardenberg, 1938). Java.

O. leiacanthus (Bleeker, 1853). Banka.

O. malabaricus (Valenciennes, 1839). India, Mysore. (Doubtful.)

O. pabda (Hamilton, 1822). Bengal.

O. pabo (Hamilton, 1822). Brahmaputra River, Assam, India.

O. sabanus Inger & Chin, 1959. Segama River, Lahad Datu District, North Borneo.

O. sindensis (Day, 1877). Pakistan. (Doubtful.)

O. weberi (Hardenberg, 1937). Borneo.

Kryptopterus Bleeker, 1858. Type species *Kryptopterus micropus* Bleeker (= *Silurus cryptopterus* Bleeker).

Kryptopterus apogon (Bleeker, 1851). Bandjermassing, Borneo.

K. bicirrhis (Valenciennes, 1839). Java.

K. bleekeri Günther, 1864. Thailand.

K. cheveyi Durand, 1940. Cambodia, Indochina.

K. cryptopterus (Bleeker, 1851). Bandjermassing, Borneo.

K. hexapterus (Bleeker, 1851). Bandjermassing, Borneo.

K. lais (Bleeker, 1851). Borneo.

K. limpok (Bleeker, 1852). Palembang, Sumatra.

K. lumholtzi Rendahl, 1922. Borneo.

K. macrocephalus (Bleeker, 1858). "Sumatra?"

K. micronema (Bleeker, 1846). Batavia.

K. mononema (Bleeker, 1847). Java.

K. moorei Smith, 1945. Near Paknampo, Central Thailand.

K. parvanalis Inger & Chin, 1959. Kinabatangan River at Deramakot, North Borneo.

K. schilbeides (Bleeker, 1858). Sumatra, Borneo.

K. sp. Johore State.

Chapter 6

Family SCHILBEIDAE (Glass Catfishes)

Plates 25–28

The family Schilbeidae is an Afro-Asian family of catfishes that generally live in open water. In Africa they are distributed over nearly the entire continent with the exception of the arid regions, while the Asian representatives are mostly distributed in and around India but do extend to the East Indies. The Schilbeidae is often combined with the Pangasiidae into a single family, the Schilbeidae, but I will follow the classification of Nelson (1984) and at least temporarily regard them as separate families. The suggestion to regard them as subfamilies, Schilbeinae being the African group and Pangasiinae the Asian representatives, has not received very much support. The Schilbeidae is therefore most closely related to the Pangasiidae if they are regarded as separate families and to the Siluridae if they are to be combined with the Pangasiidae. They differ from the Siluridae chiefly by having a smaller number of ventral fin rays (with the exception of the schilbeid genus *Irvineia*). Of the variety of species contained within this family, only one or two have found their way into the aquarium trade. These will be discussed under their respective genera.

The body of schilbeid catfishes is sometimes translucent, moderately elongate, compressed, and with the thorax and abdomen keeled or not keeled. The caudal peduncle is generally slightly elongate. The head is conical or blunt and is covered with soft skin or is partially granulated, while the snout is pointed or broadly rounded. The mouth is subterminal to terminal, horizontal to oblique, and either the upper or lower jaw may be the longer of the two. The teeth are villiform and set in bands in both jaws. The vomerine teeth are in two small patches or the vomeropalatine teeth are in two, three, or four separate patches or united into a single continuous band or patch. A median longitudinal groove may be present on the top of the head, and the occipital process may or may not reach to the basal bone of the dorsal. The eyes are large or moderate with narrow or broad adipose eyelids or with free orbital margins. The nostrils may be close together or far apart. There are four pairs of well developed barbels present including a nasal barbel. The gill openings are wide and the gill membranes are free from the isthmus. There are 5-12 branchiostegal rays.

The short-based dorsal fin possesses a slender or strong spine or the dorsal fin may be absent. A small adipose fin may be present or there is no adipose fin. In certain *Clupisoma* an adipose fin is present in the young, but is absent in adults (Mirza, 1975). The pectoral fins have a strong or slender spine; the ventral fins may be absent or present, when present with 6 to 9 rays. The anal fin is moderate or very long, and the caudal fin is deeply forked and slightly hypocercal. The skin is smooth and scaleless. The gas bladder is well developed, moderately developed, or greatly reduced, thin-walled or thick-walled, tubular or non-tubular.

It is more convenient at this time to divide the family into the Asian and African genera and key them out on this geographical basis.

Schilbe mystus.

Key to the Asian genera:

1a. Dorsal fin present; anal fin moderate, 24-54 rays 3
1b. Dorsal fin absent; anal fin long, 59-90 rays 2
2a. Ventral fins present .... *Ailia*
2b. Ventral fins absent ....*Ailiichthys*
3a. Cleft of mouth oblique, extending to front edge or middle or behind hind edge of eye 4
3b. Cleft of mouth not oblique, not extending to front edge of eye.................. 5
4a. Cleft of mouth not extending under eye; vomeropalatine teeth in a crescentric band that is divided or constricted into several parts; gas bladder large, dorsoventrally flattened, free and closely applied to dorsal wall of abdomen.......... ....*Platytropius*
4b. Cleft of mouth extending under eye; vomeropalatine teeth in an uninterrupted crescentric band produced backward at sides; gas bladder small, tubiform, partly enclosed in bone............ .... *Eutropiichthys*
5a. Gas bladder well developed, large; vomeropalatine teeth in two or three separate patches, or sometimes connected by linear series 6
5b. Gas bladder moderate or greatly reduced; vomeropalatine teeth in four distinct patches or in two extensive patches separated in the middle or in one continuous patch................................ 7
6a. Vomeropalatine teeth in two separate patches, sometimes connected by linear series; gas bladder thin-walled............ ....*Pseudeutropius*
6b. Vomeropalatine teeth in three separate patches; gas bladder thick-walled .... *Neotropius*
7a. Vomeropalatine teeth in four distinct patches or in two extensive patches separated in the middle, but not in one continuous patch; gas bladder of moderate size.........................*Proeutropiichthys*
7b. Vomeropalatine teeth in four distinct patches or in two extensive separate patches or in one continuous patch; gas bladder greatly reduced........*Clupisoma*

Key to the African genera:

1a. No rayed dorsal fin; no teeth on palate; maximum length 10 cm........*Parailia*...2
1b. Rayed dorsal fin present; teeth on palate (except in *Siluranodon*, which is wholly toothless); maximum length various... 3
2a. Adipose fin absent.... *Parailia (Parailia)*
2b. Adipose fin present.*Parailia (Physailia)*
3a. Adipose fin absent.......................... 4
3b. Adipose fin present 5
4a. Dorsal fin with spine; teeth on jaws and palate; maximum length 35 cm ....*Schilbe (Schilbe)*
4b. Dorsal fin without spine; no teeth on jaws or on palate; maximum length 18 cm ....*Siluranodon*
5a. Two pairs of mandibular barbels; size greater than 10 cm 6
5b. One pair of mandibular barbels, the internal pair lacking; small size, maximum length 8 cm .... *Eutropiellus (Eutropiellus)*
6a. Ventral fins with 6 rays; gas bladder not extending beyond origin of anal fin.... 7
6b. Ventral fins with 9 rays; gas bladder extending beyond origin of anal fin; maximum length 18 cm................*Irvineia*
7a. Dorsal fin with 6 branched rays (exceptionally 5); 9-10 (rarely 8) gill rakers; maximum length 50 cm.................... ....*Schilbe (Eutropius)*
7b. Dorsal fin with 3-5 branched rays; 8-9 gill rakers; maximum length 10 cm..... ....*Eutropiellus (Pareutropius)*

The genus *Ailia* contains a single species, *A. coila*, from India, Pakistan, Bangladesh, and Nepal. The body is elongate and strongly compressed. The head is covered with skin

Ailia coila. (After Day, 1878.)

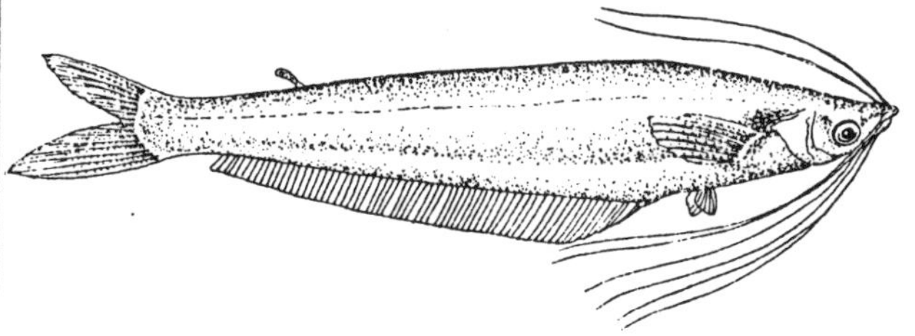

and is as wide as long (less the conical snout). The eyes are provided with adipose lids and are located behind the angle of the mouth and on a level with it. The nostrils are close together, the anterior nostrils at the front of the snout and the posterior nostrils behind the nasal barbels. There are four pairs of barbels, a maxillary pair, two mandibular pairs, and a nasal pair, all long and reaching one-third to one-half the standard length. The mouth is inferior, the cleft extending to mid-orbit. The teeth in the jaws are villiform and set in a band, and there are two very small patches of teeth on the vomer. The dorsal fin is absent but there is a small adipose fin above the posterior part of the very long anal fin. The pectoral fins have a slender spine that is finely serrated on its inner margin, and the ventral fins have 6 rays. The caudal fin is deeply forked, the lower lobe the longer. The gas bladder is tubular, horseshoe-shaped, and greatly reduced.

The genus *Ailiichthys* contains a single species, *A. punctata*, from India and Pakistan. This genus has recently been synonymized with *Ailia*. The body is elongate and strongly compressed and the head width is equal to the post-orbital part of the head. The snout is pointed. The eyes are provided with adipose lids and are located behind the angle of the mouth and on a level with it. The nostrils are close together, one on each side of the nasal barbel. There are four pairs of barbels, one maxillary, two mandibular, and one nasal, extending at least to the anal fin. The mouth is inferior, the cleft extending as far as the middle of the orbit. The teeth in the jaws are villiform and in bands, while the vomerine teeth are in two small patches. The dorsal fin is absent but there is a small adipose fin located above the posterior portion of the very long anal fin. The pectoral fins extend just beyond the origin of the anal fin and are provided with a slender spine that is not serrated on its inner edge. There are no ventral fins. The caudal fin is deeply forked, the lower lobe the longer. The gas bladder is tubular, horseshoe-shaped, and greatly reduced.

Ailiichthys punctata. (After Day, 1878.)

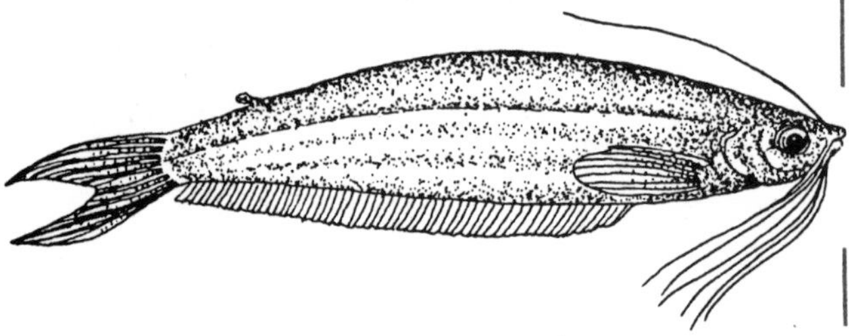

The genus *Clupisoma* includes approximately five species from India, Pakistan, Bangladesh, Nepal, and Burma. The body is elongate and compressed. The thorax and abdomen may or may not be keeled; if keeled, the keel extends as far as the vent or the abdomen may be keeled between the ventrals and the vent. The body has smooth skin and the head is covered with soft skin. The snout is broadly or bluntly pointed and the large eyes are provided with adipose lids. The nostrils are close together, the posterior nostril with a nasal barbel and much longer than the anterior nostril. There are four pairs of barbels, one maxillary pair, two mandibular pairs, and a pair of nasal barbels, the maxillary pair the longest, in some species extending beyond the pectoral base. The mouth is subterminal or inferior, provided with villiform teeth in bands. The vomeropalatine teeth may be in a single continuous band or in two or four separate patches. A median longitudinal groove is present on the head, and the occipital process may or may not reach the basal bone of the dorsal. A dorsal fin is present and provided with a slender spine that is serrated on its inner edge and rugose on its outer edge. There may be no adipose fin or a small one may be present or it may disappear with growth. The pectoral fins have a strong spine with a rough or smooth outer edge and a denticulated inner edge. The

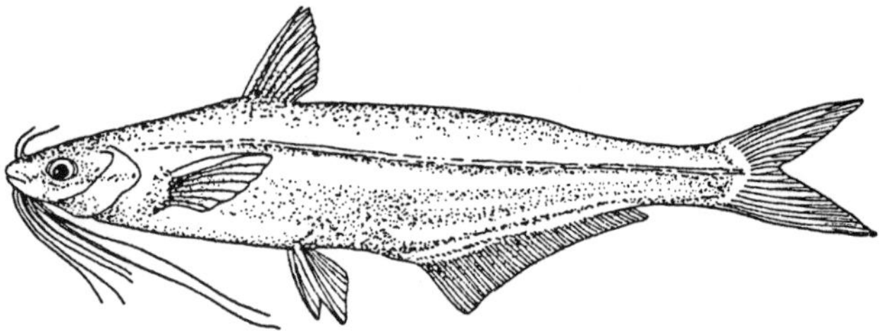

Clupisoma garua. (After Jayaram, 1977.)

ventral fins have 6 rays, the anal fin is long, and the caudal fin is deeply forked, the lobes approximately equal or the lower lobe the longest. The gill openings are wide and the gill membranes are free from the isthmus. The gas bladder is greatly reduced, not tubular, but is thick-walled and flattened.

The genus *Eutropiichthys* contains about three species from India, Pakistan, Bangladesh, Nepal, Burma, and Thailand. The body is elongate and the head and body are compressed and covered with smooth, soft skin. The snout is conical. The eyes are large, lateral, partially on the lower surface of the head, and provided with broad adipose lids. The nostrils are far apart. There are four pairs of barbels, one nasal, one maxillary, and two mandibular pairs, the maxillary pair usually the longest. The cleft of the mouth is oblique, extending to the front or hind border of the eye. The teeth are villiform in the jaws and set in a broad band that is produced backward, while those of the vomeropalatine are set in a pyriform or crescentric band or in separate patches. A median longitudinal groove is present on the head, and the occipital process does not reach the basal bone of the dorsal. The dorsal fin is short, with a slender spine serrated on its inner edge and rugose on its outer edge, and usually has 7 rays. The pectoral fins also have a strong spine that is serrated on its inner edge and rugose on its outer edge. The ventral fins have 6-7 rays. There is a small adipose fin, the anal fin is long, and the caudal fin is deeply forked, the lobes approximately equal. There are 5-11 branchiostegal rays. The gas bladder is greatly reduced and tubular.

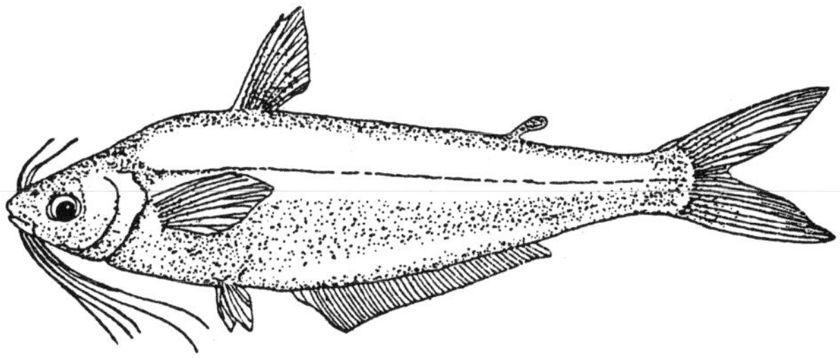

Eutropiichthys vacha. (After Jayaram, 1977.)

The genus *Neotropius* contains a single species, *N. khavalchor*, from the Krishna and Panchaganga Rivers in India. The body is elongate and moderately compressed while the head is short, tapering, and slightly depressed. The eyes are large, lateral, behind and above the angle of the jaw, and without adipose lids. The tubular nostrils are wide apart, the anterior near the anterolateral part of the head. The mouth is inferior, the lips confined to the angle of the jaws, and the upper jaw is overhanging, with denticulations from the tip of the snout to the border of the mouth. The villiform teeth are in bands in the jaws, and there is a crescentric vomerine band and two widely separated patches of vomerine teeth. There are four pairs of barbels, a nasal pair, a maxillary pair extending to the end of the pectoral fins, and two shorter mandibular pairs, the outer one reaching only to the pectoral fin base. A median longitudinal groove is present on the head that extends to the base of the occipital process, which in turn extends as far as the basal bone of the dorsal. The dorsal fin is short-based, with a short serrated spine and 5-6 branched rays. There is a small adipose fin opposite the last quarter of the moderately long anal fin. The pectoral fins are moderately long, not reaching to the ventral fins, and have a strong spine that is serrated on its inner edge. The caudal fin is

Neotropius khavalchor. (After Jayaram, 1977.)

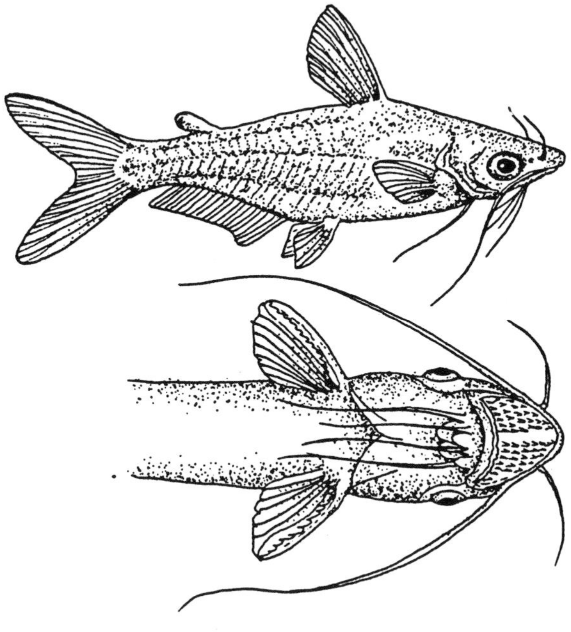

deeply forked, the lobes subequal. The gill openings are wide and the gill membranes overlap each other at the isthmus but are free from the isthmus. There are 9 branchiostegals. The gas bladder is divided into three chambers and is thick-walled.

The rasp-like teeth of the upper snout are used to rip scales from other fishes in its habitat, making this one of the few scale-eating catfishes known.

The genus *Proeutropiichthys* contains a single species, *P. taakree*, from India and Burma. The body is elongate and laterally compressed, as is the head, both being covered with smooth skin. The eyes, located behind the angle of the mouth and partly on the ventral surface of the head, are provided with broad adipose eyelids. The nostrils are close together and the nasal barbel lies between them. There are four pairs of barbels, a nasal pair, two mandibular pairs, and a maxillary

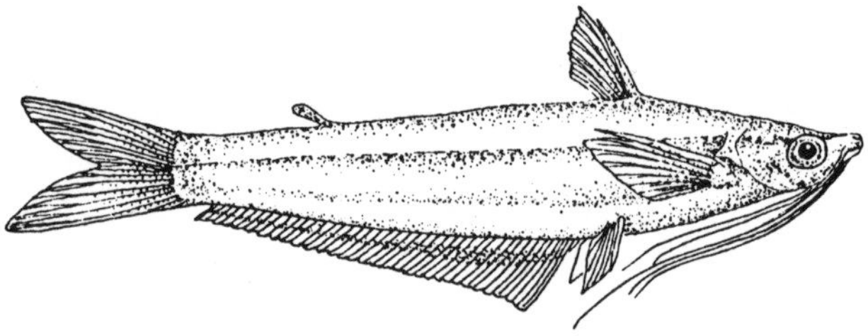

Proeutropiichthys taakree. **(After Day, 1878.)**

pair, which is longest. The mouth is terminal, with the upper jaw overlapping the lower. The jaw teeth are villiform and in a band, while the vomeropalatine teeth are in four patches or the vomerine band is interrupted, each half being subcontinuous with the palatine band. A median longitudinal groove is present on the head, and the occipital process does not reach the basal bone of the dorsal fin. The short dorsal fin is provided with a spine that is serrated on its inner edge and smooth to rugose on its outer edge. A very small adipose fin is present, and the anal fin is very long. The pectoral fins have a strong spine that, like the dorsal spine, is serrated on its inner edge and smooth or rugose on its outer edge. The ventral fins have 6 rays. The caudal fin is deeply forked, with the lobes subequal. The gill openings are broad and the gill membranes are free from the isthmus. The gas bladder is of moderate size.

The genus *Pseudeutropius* is represented by two species from India, Pakistan, and Bangladesh, and two other species from Sumatra and Borneo. The body is elongate and compressed while the head is conical, both covered with smooth skin. The eyes are large, without adipose lids and with a free orbital margin, and located behind the cleft of the mouth on the lower surface of the head. The nostrils are close together and have the nasal barbels between them. There are four pairs of

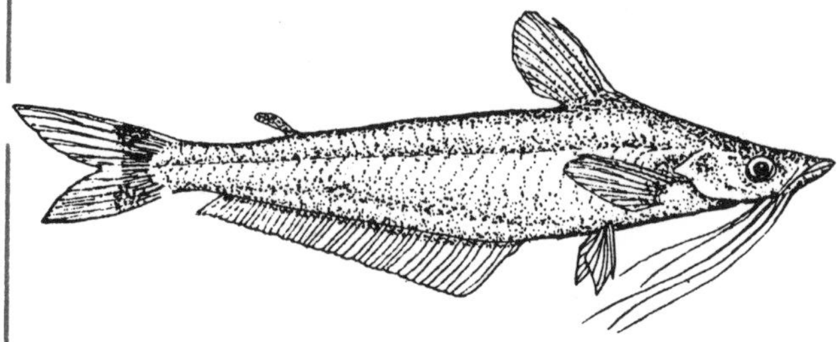

Pseudeutropius atherinoides. **(After Day, 1878.)**

barbels, a nasal pair, two mandibular pairs, and a maxillary pair that reaches to the ventral fins. The mouth is small, terminal, the upper jaw the longer. The jaw teeth are villiform and in bands, and the vomeropalatine teeth are in two separate patches, either broadly oval with a wide space between or transverse or divergent posteriorly with a space between, sometimes medially connected by a linear series. A median longitudinal groove is present on the head, and the occipital process may or may not extend as far as the basal bone of the dorsal. The dorsal fin is short and provided with a strong spine serrated on both edges. A small adipose fin is present. The anal fin is long, with 30-43 rays. The pectoral fins have a strong spine serrated on both edges, the fin extending to or beyond the ventral fins. The ventral fins have 6 rays. The caudal fin is deeply forked, the lobes equal or the upper lobe slightly longer. The gill openings are wide and the gill membranes are free from the isthmus. There are 6-9 branchiostegal rays. The gas bladder is large, somewhat heart-shaped, and forms blister-like areas above the pectoral fins.

The genus *Platytropius* is a small genus

containing a single species from Thailand. It is very close to and shares most of the characteristics of the genus *Pseudeutropius*, which will not be repeated here. *Platytropius* differs from *Pseudeutropius* chiefly in the shape, position, and character of the wall of the gas bladder as well as the continuity or not of the vomeropalatine tooth bands. In *Platytropius* the gas bladder is thick-walled, flattened dorsoventrally, and lies close to the dorsal wall of the abdominal cavity throughout. In *Pseudeutropius* the gas bladder is thin-walled and a portion of it comes in contact with the abdominal parietes at a position above the pectoral fin producing a translucent area. *Platytropius* also has the vomeropalatine teeth arranged in a lunate band that is divided in the middle, each side being composed of two to three patches. *Pseudeutropius*, on the other hand, has the vomeropalatine teeth arranged in a single continuous band. The single species, *P. siamensis*, attains a length of approximately 25 cm.

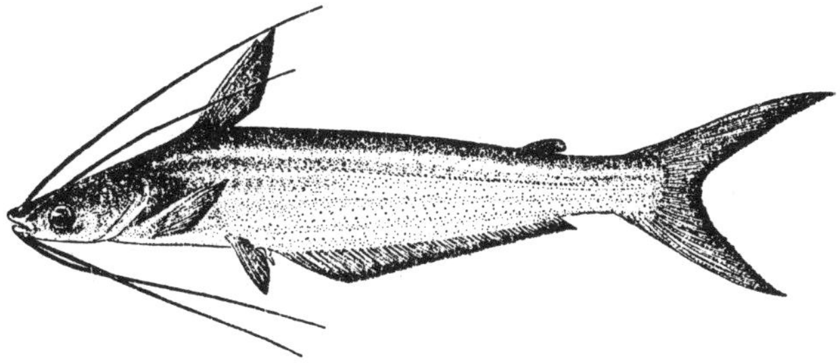

***Platytropius siamensis*. (From H. M. Smith, 1945.)**

The genus *Siluranodon* is a small genus of African catfishes containing a single species, *S. auritus*, from the Nile and Niger River basins. The body is elongate and very compressed. The eye is fairly large and has a free border, the nostrils are close together, and there are no teeth. There are four pairs of barbels, a maxillary pair, two mandibular pairs, and a nasal pair that is as long as or even longer than the head. There is no adipose fin, and the dorsal fin is very small, with only 5 rays and no spine. The anal fin is elongate, with 75-85 rays, and comes very close to the caudal fin but is not confluent with it. The caudal fin is notched, with pointed to rounded lobes, the upper lobe slightly longer than the lower. The pectoral fin has a feeble spine without any serrations, and the ventral fins are rather small and have 6 rays. The gill membranes are deeply notched but free from the isthmus; there are 50-60 long, setiform gill rakers on the lower limb of the first gill arch. The gas bladder is large and free.

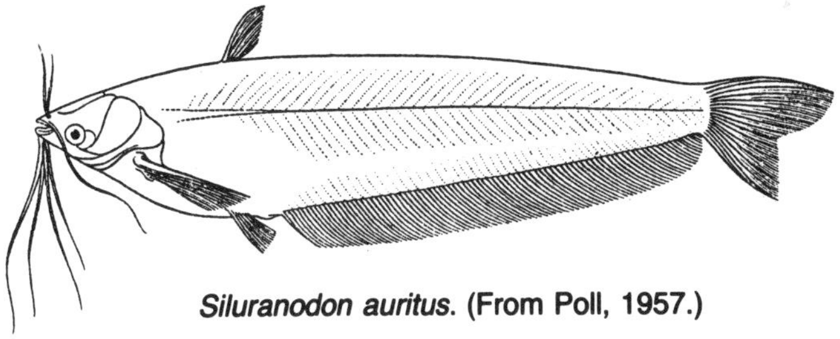

***Siluranodon auritus*. (From Poll, 1957.)**

The genus *Parailia* contains two subgenera, *Parailia* and *Physailia*, distinguishable primarily by the presence (*Physailia*) or absence (*Parailia*) of an adipose fin. Members of the subgenus *Physailia* also have 60-80 anal fin rays compared with 80-92 for subgenus *Parailia*.

The subgenus *Parailia* contains only two species, one from the Congo basin, *P. congica*, and the other, *P. spiniserratus*, from Gambia. The body is elongate and greatly compressed. The eyes are large and have a free orbital rim, and there are teeth in the jaws but not on the palate. The nostrils are close together, and there are four pairs of barbels, a maxillary pair, two mandibular pairs, and a nasal pair, all relatively long. Both dorsal and adipose fins are lacking. The anal fin is very elongate, with 80 to 92 rays, but although it reaches the caudal fin base, the two

***Parailia congica*. (From Poll, 1957.)**

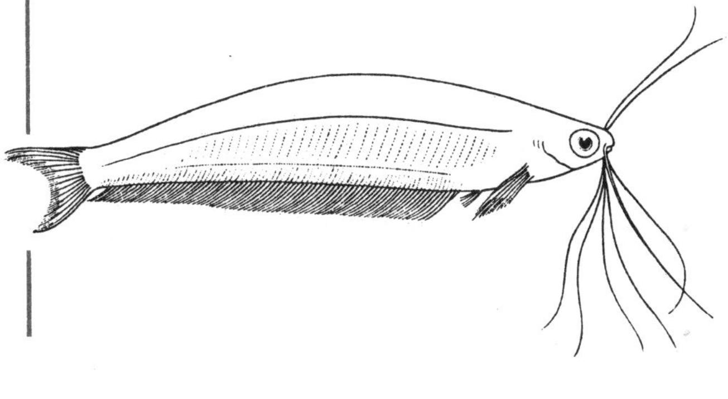

fins are not confluent; the caudal fin is forked. The pectoral fin is provided with a weak or moderately strong spine that is smooth or serrated along the posterior edge. The ventral fins are small, with 6 rays. The gill membranes are deeply notched and free from the isthmus, while the gill rakers are long and slender, about 25 present on the lower limb of the first arch. The gas bladder is small and free.

Parailia (P.) congica, a slender African catfish from the Congo basin, is much like *Parailia (Physailia) pellucida*, the African Glass Catfish, and may be confused with that species by hobbyists, but *P. congica* differs from the African Glass Catfish by having no adipose fin and different coloration. Although quite transparent, *P. congica* has a yellowish tinge and numerous dark pigment spots scattered over the body. The fins are also spotted but the spots are smaller. The upper caudal lobe is also said to have a narrow dark longitudinal stripe. The barbels are quite long and of equal length. This is a crepuscular species that must have a darkened tank provided with many places where it can take refuge when light levels are too high. If hiding places are denied this species and if the lights are too bright, it will exhibit a very interesting behavior: it will lie immobile on the bottom as though it were dead. If the lights are turned off or it begins to get dark, the fish will abandon this habit and start to swim about searching for food. In nature the diet consists mainly of aquatic and small terrestrial insects, but in an aquarium live foods such as *Daphnia*, enchytraeids, midge larvae, etc., are eagerly accepted as substitutes. A temperature of 25-28°C is recommended. *Parailia (P.) spiniserratus* is said to spawn in the Gambian swamps where the river overflows, moving up-river to spawn.

The subgenus *Physailia* contains three species from Somaliland (*P. somalensis*), the Congo (*P. occidentalis*), and the Nile and Niger basins (*P. pellucida*). The body is relatively elongate and strongly compressed. The eyes are fairly large and have a free border, the nostrils are close together, and there is a narrow band of teeth on the jaws but none on the palate. There are four pairs of barbels, a maxillary pair, two mandibular pairs, and a pair of nasal barbels that extends beyond the head (in one species at least they reach the end of the pectoral fin). The dorsal fin is absent but there is a small adipose fin present. The anal fin is long, with approximately 60-80 rays, extending to, but apparently not being confluent with, the caudal fin. The pectoral fin is provided with a spine that is smooth or serrated on its inner edge, while the ventral fins are small and have 6 rays. The gill membranes are deeply notched and free from the isthmus, and the gill rakers are generally long and slender. The gas bladder is small and free.

At least one of the species of *Parailia (Physailia), P. (Ph.) pellucida*, is said to be able to live for years in an aquarium. This species, reaching a length of about 10 cm, has been dubbed by aquarists the African Glass Catfish and comes from the Upper Nile basin. Both the body and fins are as transparent as glass, although there are some black pigment spots in the region of the anal fin and along the upper back. The vertebral column, gas bladder, main blood vessels, and other organs can be clearly seen through the skin and flesh. In the appropriate light (reflected) the body glows with a pale bluish iridescence. For this fish a large, well-planted aquarium is highly recommended. The tank should be in a shaded spot for the African Glass Catfish does not take to direct sunlight and will hide among the plants much of the time in such a situation even though it is not one of the nocturnal or twilight fishes. Once acclimated to tank conditions it is an active fish and will swim about the tank in small schools (it does not do well at all if kept by itself). It rests at an oblique angle with its tail drooping a bit. The minimum temperature should be about 23°C. Feeding is no problem, for the African Glass Catfish will eat almost anything edible, but live foods, especially things like tubificid worms, enchytraeids, and midge larvae, are best. Some vegetable food in the diet is a must. This fish is quite peaceful and will not bother even very small fishes, although it will not pass up a delicacy like newly hatched fry. It has been reported that this fish has spawned in captivity but, unfortunately, the actual spawning was not observed.

The genus *Schilbe* is a moderately large genus of African catfishes that contains 21 species, mostly confined to the more tropical regions. It is divided into two unequal subgenera, *Schilbe* with three species and *Eutropius* with 18 species. The body of *Schilbe (Schilbe)* is moderately elongate and very compressed. The eyes are generally large and with a free orbital rim. The jaws are provided with a band of villiform teeth, and there is an uninterrupted band of vomeropalatine teeth. The nostrils are distant from each other, and there are four pairs of barbels, a maxillary pair, two mandibular or mental pairs, and a nasal pair. The adipose fin is absent, but there is a dorsal fin with a spine and 5 or 6 rays. The anal fin is quite long, with 50-75 rays, and it is not confluent with the forked caudal fin. The pectoral fin has a spine that may be serrated, and the ventral fins have 6 rays. The gill membranes are deeply notched and free from the isthmus, and the gill rakers are moderately long, widely set, with less than 15 on the lower limb of the first arch. The gas bladder is large and free.

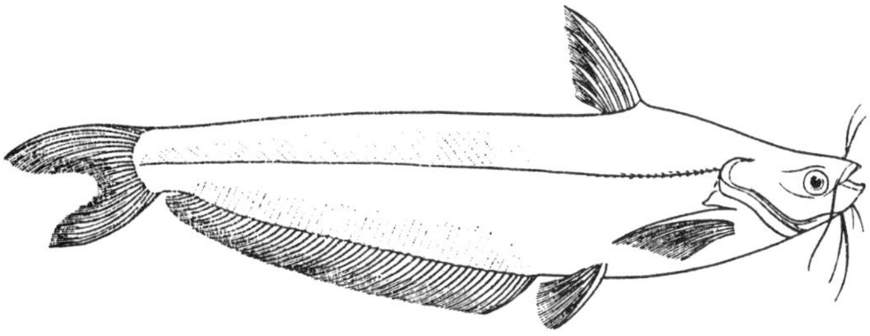

Schilbe mystus. (From Poll, 1957.)

Schilbe (S.) mystus (including *Eutropius depressirostris*) attains a length of approximately 36 cm and is widely distributed in African rivers, including the Nile, the rivers of West Africa, the Congo, and the Zambezi, as well as in the lakes of Africa. It inhabits open shallow waters where it feeds on small fishes and insect larvae and is an active, gregarious species, preferring to be with members of its own kind. The Butter Catfish, as it is often called, spawns in fixed cycles, once a year during the flood season. The flesh is very palatable, and *Schilbe mystus* has some value as a commercial food fish locally. Like *Parailia spiniserratus, Schilbe mystus* is reported to move up-river to spawn. It is silvery gray to olive yellowish in color with a very prominent dark blotch be-

Schilbe mystus is not rare in the aquarium trade. Individuals in captivity are not hard to feed and will even consume small fishes given the chance. Photo by Robert Harris.

hind the gill cover astride the lateral line and a dark band at the base of the anal fin. The young are said to have three longitudinal dark bands on the body. *Schilbe mystus* does get rather large for a home aquarium, but younger individuals are often kept and the species has been in the aquarium trade since the 1930's. Being a lively fish, the tank should be sufficiently large to provide swimming space. The tank should be well planted and contain a number of hiding places, which can be formed from driftwood, rockwork, and similar decorations. The best (but obviously impractical) bottom material is a dark soil, to agree with the bottom in its natural habitat. Freshly imported specimens that are kept in brightly lit aquaria will, like *P. congica*, remain motionless on the bottom until it becomes darker. The recommended temperature range is 22-26°C.

Another species, *S. (S.) marmoratus*, is also seen in the aquarium trade. It can be distinguished from *S. mystus* by color and by the extent of the anal fin (which reaches the caudal fin in *marmoratus*). It is also somewhat smaller, reaching a length of about 16 cm. The color is that of clay or pale gray peppered with brown, and occasionally there are some brownish splotches along the middle of the side. The fins are brownish, some with darkish tips, and the caudal base is dark. The black spot above the pectoral is also present in this species.

The subgenus *Schilbe (Eutropius)* is of moderate size, with 18 species from tropical Africa. The largest species attains a length of about 50 cm. The diets consist mostly of small fishes, insects, and crustaceans. Some species are of moderate commercial importance as food fishes. The body is relatively elongate and strongly compressed. The eyes are relatively large and have a free border. The jaws are provided with a band of villiform teeth and there is a band of vomeropalatine teeth, also villiform. The nostrils are widely separated. There are four pairs of barbels, a maxillary pair, two mental or mandibular pairs, and a nasal pair. The dorsal fin is short-based, with a spine and 5 or 6 rays, and there is a small, often tiny, adipose fin. The anal fin is long, usually with more than 50 rays, and the caudal fin is forked. The pectoral fin has a moderately weak to strong spine that is weakly to strongly serrated on the inner edges. The ventral fins have 6 rays. The gill membranes are deeply notched and free from the isthmus, and the gill rakers are moderately long and widely set, 6 to 12 on the lower limb of the first arch. The gas bladder is large and free.

S. (E.) niloticus, from the Nile, Senegal, Ogowe, and tributaries, has a dark olive to blackish back, delicate fawn-colored to salmon-pink sides with a bronzy or silver iridescence, and a pale pinkish to whitish belly. There is a large dark blotch over the pectoral

Schilbe marmoratus is, as indicated by its specific name, a mottled fish but it also exhibits the black blotch above the pectoral fin. Photo by G. J. M. Timmerman.

fin that has pale greenish edges. The dorsal fin has a dark base and there are dark tips to the caudal fin lobes. The young are said to be translucent. Over its broad range there is a cline in the number of branched anal fin rays as well as number of vertebrae as one travels from west to east. The main items of the diet are small fishes and aquatic insects. *S. (E.) grenfelli* is mostly silvery gray, more brownish above and a paler gray below, and also has the large blotch over the pectoral fin, but in this species the edges are not very sharply defined. The young are said to have a dark longitudinal band along the sides.

S. (E.) mandibularis feeds mostly on terrestrial insects (Hymenoptera, Hemiptera, Coleoptera, etc.) washed into the water and on mayfly larvae. The larvae of chironomids and caddisflies are less utilized as food but do show up, and there is only a little representation of vegetable matter in stomach contents. Once the fish attain a size of 18 to 20 cm SL some fishes start to show up in the diet. The average size of individuals at first spawning varies depending upon the geographic location. In one area (such as Niporie) it may be as small as 8.5 cm, while at another location (such as N'Zi) it might be up to 18.5 cm in the females, the males being a bit smaller. In most individuals spawning occurs at the end of the first year, and the spawning period itself is generally spread out over a four- to five-month period. The female probably spawns only once a year, for the maturing eggs are all approximately the same size, about 0.75 mm in diameter. A female weighing 100 grams (between 17 and 35 cm) may average about 17,600 eggs or roughly 175,800/kilo, although it has been found that some individuals can produce as many as 217,000 eggs/kilo.

The genus *Eutropiellus* (with subgenus *Pareutropius*) is very much like *Schilbe (Eutropius)* and similar characters will not be repeated. *E. (Eutropiellus)* differs from *Eutropius* by having fewer anal fin rays and the anterior lower lip barbels are absent. There are only 2 species in the subgenus, *E. (E.) debauwi* and *E. (E.) buffei*, from the Congo basin and Dahomey respectively. *E. (Eutropiellus) debauwi* is a well-known aquarium species that grows to a moderate length of 8-10 cm. It is translucent

***Eutropiellus debauwi*. (From Poll, 1957.)**

with a silvery throat and belly and three distinct steel blue to blue-black stripes on its sides that become more prominent with age. The Candy-Striped Catfish, as it is sometimes called, is not a predatory fish and does quite well in a community tank as long as the fishes with it are not very much larger than it. *E. debauwi* is also a schooling fish that should never be kept alone, that is, without at least four or five members of its own species. Single individuals will be very sluggish and refuse food, hiding most of the time until they eventually waste away and die. A pair also is not enough, for the two will just follow each other in circles, eventually declining as well. When well adapted to aquarium conditions this fish will be in almost continuous movement, constantly exploring the confines of their aquarium. They swim somewhat at an angle, tail down, the caudal fin continuously moving. Moderate light is best. A temperature range of 18-25°C is suitable, but the temperature should be kept fairly stable for these fish are susceptible to white spot disease. They should be given live foods (small crustaceans, tubificid worms, enchytraeids, etc.) as often as possible, but remember that they will feed to bursting if given the chance. The females are said to have paler stripes and are more robust. They deposit adhesive eggs on plants and apparently do not guard them.

The second species, *E. (E.) buffei*, is very close to *E. debauwi* but has the dark stripe on the back more narrow and not continuing onto the caudal fin. The dark lateral band extends right over the caudal peduncle to the posterior edge of the caudal fin, and a narrow longitudinal band extends from the posterior edge of the gill cover across the belly. In addition, there is a dark, sometimes elongated spot on the upper and lower lobes of the caudal fin. The sexes can be recognized with a little practice by the examination of the genital papilla of the male. It may even not be necessary to capture the fish for examination. In addition the females are a third larger (when of the same age), more robust, and the stripe from the gill cover over the belly is strongly pronounced.

Subgenus *Eutropiellus (Pareutropius)* contains two species and is much like *Eutropiellus (Eutropiellus)* but is distinguished from that subgenus by having only 3 to 5 branched rays in the dorsal fin and only 8 to 9 gill rakers in the lower limb of the first arch. There are two pairs of mandibular barbels (one pair in *Eutropiellus (Eutropiellus)*.

The remaining genus, *Irvineia*, has but two species, *I. voltae* and *I. orientalis*. *Irvineia* is elongate, with a less deep body than the other genera, but still rather compressed. The eye

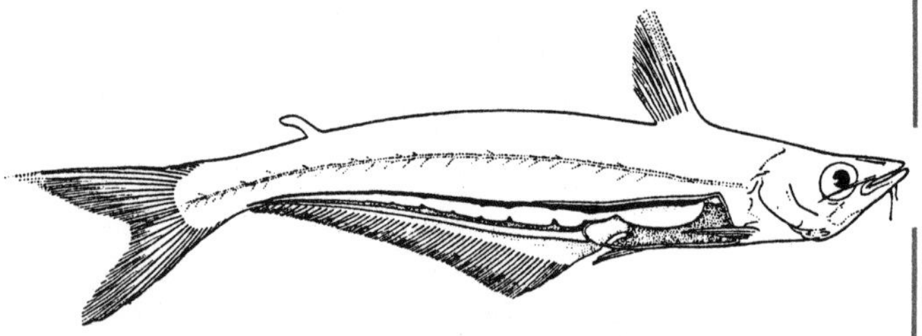

***Irvineia voltae*. (From Poll, 1957.)**

is large and with a free orbital rim, and there are teeth present on the palate. A small adipose fin is present, and there is a dorsal fin with a spine and about 6 rays. Both pectoral and ventral fins are rather small, the pectoral fins with a spine. The anal fin is long and the caudal fin forked. What makes this genus unique are the 9 rays in the ventral fin and the prolongation of the swim bladder almost to the very end of the anal fin base. *Irvineia voltae* comes from the Volta River, West Africa.

Members of the family Schilbeidae are open-water swimmers as opposed to the more common bottom-living existence of catfishes in general, and they are distinctly adapted to this way of life. The head is flattened anteriorly and deep posteriorly, the eyes are lateral in position, and the tail is slightly hypocercal. According to Chardon (1968) other characters link this family with the Bagridae, with the exception of the lack of the ectopterygoid bone. So if one makes allowances for the adaptive characters suited to their pelagic life, the schilbeids would seem to be most closely related to the Bagridae, the resemblance to the family Siluridae being more superficial and possibly due to convergence, being adapted to the same mode of life. This is not necessarily the view accepted by other workers.

Checklist of the species of the family Schilbeidae and their type localities:

Ailia Gray, 1831. Type species *Ailia bengalensis* Gray (= *A. coila*).
- *Ailia coila* (Hamilton, 1822). Freshwater rivers of Bengal, Ganges.

Ailiichthys Day, 1871. Type species *A. punctata* Day. (Currently synonymized with *Ailia*, Jayaram, 1981.)
- *Ailiichthys punctata* Day, 1871. Jumna, below Delhi.

Clupisoma Swainson, 1839. Type species *Clupisoma argentata* Swainson (= *Silurus garua*).
- *Clupisoma bastari* Datta & Karmakar, 1980. Indravati River, Bastar Dist., India.
- *C. garua* (Hamilton, 1822). Freshwater rivers of the Gangetic provinces.
- *C. montana* Hora, 1937. Teesta River below Darjeeling.
- *C. naziri* Mirza & Awan, 1973. Jinnah Barrage (Indus River), Pakistan.
- *C. prateri* Hora, 1937. Mandalay and Bassein, Burma.

Eutropiichthys Bleeker, 1862. Type species *E. vacha* Hamilton, 1822.
- *Euthropiichthys goongwaree* (Sykes, 1838). Mota Mola River, Dekkan.
- *E. murius* (Hamilton, 1822). Mahananda River, India.
- *E. vacha* (Hamilton, 1822). Larger freshwater rivers of the Gangetic provinces.

Neotropius Kulkarni, 1952. Type species *N. khavalchor* Kulkarni.
- *Neotropius khavalchor* Kulkarni, 1952. Krishna and Panchaganga Rivers, India.

Proeutropiichthys Hora, 1937. Type species *Eutropius macrophthalmus* Blyth (= *Proeutropiichthys taakree*).
- *Proeutropiichthys taakree* (Sykes, 1838). Beema River, near Pairgaon, India.

Pseudeutropius Bleeker, 1862. Type species *P. brachypopterus* Bleeker, 1858.
Pseudeutropius atherinoides (Bloch, 1794). Tranquebar.
P. brachypopterus (Bleeker, 1858). Palembang, Sumatra.
P. mitchelli Günther, 1864. Madras Presidency, India.
P. moolenburghae Weber & de Beaufort, 1913. Sumatra.

Platytropius Hora, 1937. Type species *P. siamensis* Sauvage.
Platytropius siamensis (Sauvage, 1883). Menam Chao Phya, Thailand.

Parailia Boulenger, 1899. Type species *P. congica* Boulenger, 1899.
Parailia (Parailia) congica Boulenger, 1899. Ebinga, Zaire.
P. (P.) spiniserratus Svensson, 1933. Gambia, McCarthy Is. area.
P. (Physailia) occidentalis (Pellegrin, 1901). Cape Lopez, Gaboon.
P. (Ph.) pellucida (Boulenger, 1901.) Omdurman, Upper Nile.
P. (Ph.) somalensis (Vinciguerra, 1897). Lugh, Fl. Ganana, Somaliland.

Siluranodon Bleeker, 1858. Type species *Silurus auritus* Geoffroy Sainte-Hilaire, 1827.
Siluranodon auritus (Geoffroy Sainte-Hilaire, 1827). Nile, Egypt.

Eutropiellus Nichols & La Monte, 1933. Type species *Eutropiellus kasai* Nichols & La Monte, 1933 (= *E. debauwi*).
Eutropiellus (Eutropiellus) buffei Gras, 1960. Bas-Oueme, Dahomey.
E. (E.) debauwi (Boulenger, 1900). Uerre, Upper Congo.
E. (Pareutropius) longifilis (Steindachner, 1916). Kiperege, Tanzania.
E. (P.) mandevillei (Poll, 1959). Stanley Pool.

Irvineia Trewavas, 1943. Type species *I. voltae* Trewavas, 1943.
Irvineia orientalis (Trewavas, 1924). Villagio Duca Abruzzi, Uebe Scebeli system.
I. voltae Trewavas, 1943. Volta River, Gold Coast.

Schilbe Oken, 1817. Type species *Silurus mystus* Linnaeus, 1758.
Schilbe (Schilbe) marmoratus Boulenger, 1911. Sankuru River at Kondu, Kasai.
S. (S.) mystus (Linnaeus, 1758). "In Nile."
S. (S.) uranoscopus Rüppell, 1832. Egypt, Nile near Cairo.
S. (Eutropius) ansorgii (Boulenger, 1910). Quanza River at Cunga, Angola.
S. (E.) banguelensis (Boulenger, 1911). Lake Bangwelu.
S. (E.) bocagii (Guimaraes, 1882). Dondo (Quanza) River, Angola.
S. (E.) brevianalis (Pellegrin, 1929). Dehane (Nyong), Cameroons.
S. (E.) congensis (Leach, 1818, in Tuckey). Lower Congo.
S. (E.) djeremi (Thys van den Audenaerde & de Voss, 1982). Djerem River, Cameroons.
S. (E.) durinii (Gianferrari, 1932). Lake Tanganyika.
S. (E.) grenfelli (Boulenger, 1900). Bolobo.
S. (E.) laticeps (Boulenger, 1898). Kutu, Lac Leopold II.
S. (E.) mandibularis (Günther, 1867). Bossumprah River, Gold Coast.
S. (E.) micropogon (Trewavas, 1943). Volta, Gold Coast.
S. (E.) moebiusii (Pfeffer, 1896). Kingani River, East Africa.
S. (E.) multitaeniatus (Pellegrin, 1913). Ngomo (Ogoowe), Cameroon.
S. (E.) niloticus (Rüppell, 1829). Egypt (Nile).
S. (E.) nyongensis (De Voss, 1981). Nyong River, Cameroon.
S. (E.) seraoi (Boulenger, 1910). Bengo and Lucalla Rivers at Lucalla.
S. (E.) tumbanus (Pellegrin, 1926). Tondu, Lac Tumba.
S. (E.) yangambianus (Poll, 1954). Lubulu R., Isalowe R., Boonde R., Zaire Basin.

Chapter 7

Family — Plates 29–32

PANGASIIDAE

(Shark Catfishes)

The family Pangasiidae contains catfishes that are distributed in the fresh waters of Asia. They are very closely related to catfishes of the family Schilbeidae, and many workers consider that there should be only one family, the Schilbeidae, that may or may not be divided into subfamilies (Schilbeinae and Pangasiinae). Chardon (1968) believes that the two groups should be retained as separate families for, among other things, the pangasiids possess ectopterygoids, an elastic spring apparatus, and a posterior cecum in the gas bladder that the schilbeids lack.

Fishes of the family Pangasiidae have elongate, compressed bodies. The mouth is small, subterminal, and the snout is prominent. The teeth are small, villiform, generally arranged in curved bands in the jaws, and may be present or absent on the palatines; when present on the palatines they may or may not be confluent with the vomerine teeth, which are in two patches or a single patch. The head is covered with soft skin. The eyes have a free suborbital margin and are located behind the corner of the mouth and generally partly below the level of the mouth. The anterior nostrils are at the extremity of the snout. There are one to three pairs of barbels, the inner or outer or both mandibular barbels variously missing and the nasal barbel always absent. The dorsal fin is short-based, with 5-7 rays and a pungent spine preceded by a broad but very low rudimentary spine. A small adipose fin is present, located above the posterior part of the anal fin. The anal fin has many rays, but is short when compared to the anal fin of the schilbeid catfishes, and is distant from the forked caudal fin. The pectoral fins have a pungent spine. The ventral fins are well developed, with 6-7 rays, and are situated behind the level of the dorsal fin. The gill membranes are free from the isthmus and more or less united or free from each other; there are 7-11 branchiostegal rays.

The genera of the family Pangasiidae can be distinguished with the aid of the following key:

1a. Two or three pairs of barbels............ 2
1b. One pair of barbels (maxillary); eye below level of angle of mouth; teeth entirely absent; size colossal; Mekong Basin .... *Pangasianodon*
2a. Two pairs of barbels (maxillary and one pair mandibular)............................ 3
2b. Three pairs of barbels (maxillary and two pairs mandibular); vomerine teeth in two separate transverse bands .... *Laides*
3a. Vomerine teeth present, palatine teeth absent; posterior nostril about midway between anterior nostril and eye and in line from anterior nostril to upper edge of eye; eye above a horizontal line through angle of mouth.... *Helicophagus*
3b. Vomerine and palatine teeth present, those in jaws disappearing with age in some species; posterior nostril nearer anterior nostril than eye.................. 4
4a. Abdomen cultrate .... *Pteropangasius*
4b. Abdomen not cultrate but rounded.... 5
5a. Anal fin rays 31-34; gas bladder moderate or large; teeth villiform in jaws...... .... *Pangasius*

5b. Anal rays 40-53; gas bladder greatly reduced .... *Silonia*

The genus *Silonia* includes two species, *S. childreni* and *S. silondia*, from the fresh and tidal waters of India. The body is elongate and compressed, and the head and body are covered with smooth, soft skin. The snout and the nostrils are set close together, the anterior nostrils at the front of the snout, a little more toward the outer edge than the posterior pair. Two pairs of barbels are present, a maxillary pair and a mandibular pair. The eyes are moderate to large, lateral in position, and provided with narrow adipose lids. The mouth is wide, slightly oblique, and the lower jaw is the longer. The jaw teeth are caniniform; in *S. silondia* they are in two series, the outer series projecting beyond the mouth opening, while the villiform vomeropalatine teeth are in a V-shaped or horseshoe-shaped band. There is a median longitudinal groove on the head, and the occipital process does not reach the basal bone of the dorsal. The dorsal fin is short-based with seven rays and a weak spine that is rugose on its outer edge and serrated on the inner edge. A small adipose fin is present opposite the posterior portion of the long (40-50 rays) anal fin. The pectoral fins have a strong spine that is rough on the outer edge and serrated on the inner. The ventral fins are 6-rayed, and the caudal fin is deeply forked. The gas bladder is kidney-shaped, convex anteriorly, and is greatly reduced. The lateral margins are protected by bone. Jayaram (1981) includes this genus in the Schilbeidae.

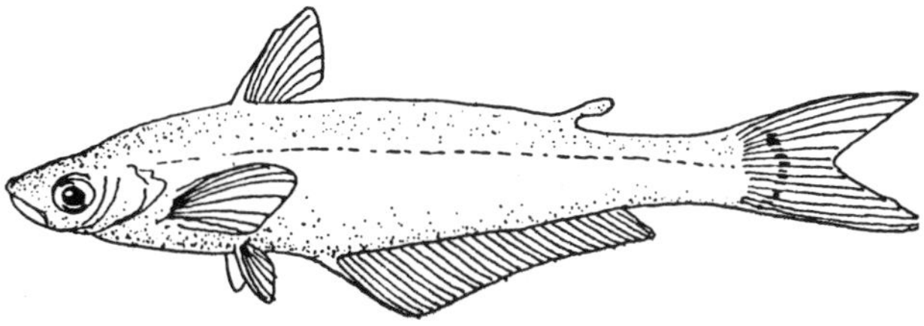

Silonia silondia. (After Misra, 1962.)

Silonia silondia comes mainly from the lower Ganges River in India. It can grow quite large, up to 1.8 meters, but due to heavy fishing pressure few specimens greater than half that size are ever seen. This species is believed to spawn during the rainy season and is said to make an upstream migration to the area of the upper tributaries. Large specimens have abundant curved teeth in their jaws and feed on fishes. The smaller fish, which are common in the swollen rivers and frequently can be found in the flood plain in pools and waterways, feed mainly on invertebrates.

The genus *Pangasius* contains a number of species, including the well known Iridescent Shark of aquarists, *P. sutchi*, from India, Burma, Pakistan, Thailand, and the Malay Peninsula to Java. The body is elongate, compressed, and covered by smooth skin. The head is also covered by skin but there are granulated areas on the upper surface. The nostrils are not too far apart, the anterior nostrils on the upper edge of the snout and the posterior pair, which has an anterior lip, a short distance behind. The eyes have free orbital rims. There are two pairs of barbels, the maxillary and a mandibular. The mouth is small and subterminal and horizontal or slightly oblique. The teeth in the jaws are villiform and arranged in bands, whereas the vomeropalatine teeth are separated into two, three, or four patches or may be in one continuous patch. The short dorsal fin has a strong, serrated spine, sometimes with a filamentous prolongation. There is a small adipose fin opposite the posterior portion of the moderately long to long (28-40 rays) anal fin, and the caudal fin is forked. The pectoral fins have a strong spine that is denticulated on its edges, and the ventral fins are 6-rayed. The gill membranes are united, the hind border, however, deeply notched and free from the

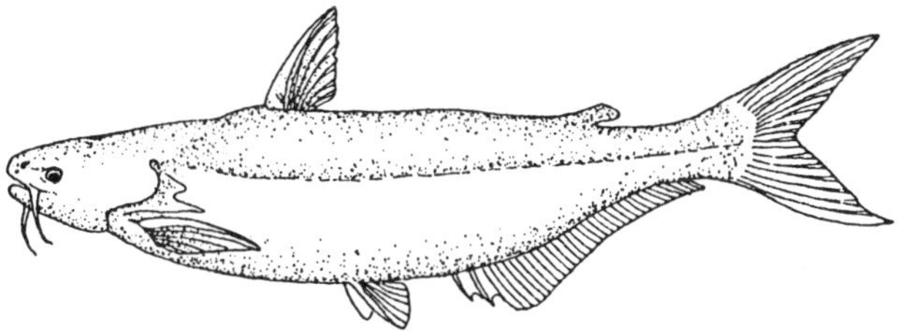

Pangasius sutchi. (After Jayaram, 1977.)

isthmus. There are one or more auxiliary pores and 9-11 branchiostegals. The gas bladder is of moderate to large size with a cecum at the posterior end; it is not enclosed in bone.

Species of the genus *Pangasius* inhabit larger rivers although some are able to live in restricted ponds. Among them are two of the largest catfishes in the world, both exceeding two meters in length. While all species are in part carnivorous, some are able to change their diet to a mostly herbivorous one, primarily fruits or aquatic vegetation, especially those that suffer a loss of their teeth in one way or another and can no longer efficiently capture their prey. It is known that in certain species there is a partial or complete loss of the teeth once the animal has reached a certain age (or size). This is interesting for it is entirely possible that since the genus *Pangasianodon* is largely defined on the basis of a complete absence of teeth, it merely represents an adult or older (senile) form of one of the species of *Pangasius*. Unfortunately no proof has as yet been obtained, and the two genera are at least temporarily kept separate. Some species feed on molluscs and are used as a control against them. This has aided in some instances in lowering or even preventing infestations of the snail-carried diseases such as schistosomiasis. One such snail-eating species is *P. polyuranodon*.

Of all the species in this genus, the only one that has become an established aquarium species is *P. sutchi*, the Iridescent Shark. It has also accumulated many other common names such as Sharkfin Cat, Candy-striped Cat, Silver Cat, etc. One of the reasons that it is so popular is that it is very hardy or "virtually indestructible" as one author called it. Part of this indestructibility is its immunity to most aquarium ailments. It is a large fish, growing to a length of about 46 cm, and is an extremely nervous fish, keeping on the move almost continuously. For these reasons the tank should be large and long (1.8 to 3.6 meters long has been suggested) and they should be kept in groups of at least four or five. (They have been seen in the wild in schools composed of 50 to 60 individuals.) They can be used as community tank fish as long as their tankmates are medium to large fishes and can tolerate such high-strung fish. Feeding is no problem; they have a huge appetite, often stuffing themselves to near bursting if sufficient food is available. The smaller fish are more carnivorous than the adults, which should receive at least some vegetable matter in their diet. *P. sutchi* has the capacity for making sounds, so do not be surprised if

Pangasius sutchi is one of the species that has become well established in the aquarium trade. Because of its reflective tints, general shape, and swimming behavior it has become known as the Iridescent Shark. Photo by Gerhard Marcuse.

when you net them out of the tank you hear them make a sound like the croaking of a frog.

Pangasius larnaudii is regarded as having delicate and extremely nutritious flesh and is rated highly as a food fish. In fact, it is reared in ponds. Young fish are captured in open waters and introduced into the ponds, where they are fattened up until they reach marketable size. Sometimes individuals escape from these ponds and the species becomes established in new regions. They will feed on small fishes and will also eventually eat any kind of fruit or vegetable (they attain a size of about 1.5 meters). They may even become somewhat tame, for it has been reported that some individuals were trained to take bananas from the hand. This species is generally identifiable by the large black humeral spot.

Pangasius sanitwongsei is one of the largest freshwater fishes in the world, with specimens reaching the tremendous size of 2.5 meters and records of up to 3 meters and a maximum thickness of one meter being reported. It is said that this last specimen required the strength of eight men to carry it. It has formidable pectoral fin spines, and when captured the fish is handled with care. One man, while trying to untangle a 2.5-meter individual from a net by diving, received a deep wound from this spine in his side from which he eventually died. This species, as might be expected, may be found in the larger rivers, the larger fish frequenting the deeper sections while the young move into the smaller rivers and tributaries of the larger ones. During the high waters they remain in the deeper holes and are rarely caught at that time. It is said to be a valuable food fish (the market sized fish averaging about 50-60 cm), but in some areas it is less esteemed because it is a scavenger that is said to have a liking for dead dogs and other unsavory refuse that may come floating down the river. Fishermen intent on making a sale will sometimes cut off the fins to mask their identification, although it is said to have a conspicuous white humeral spot. Fishing pressures have mostly decimated the larger (2.5 m plus) specimens.

Pangasius pangasius is another large species, attaining a length of up to 120 cm (a 90-cm fish is said to weigh about 8.2 kilos) and said to inhabit large rivers, their estuaries, and still-water pools in the flood plains. It is said to be a nocturnal fish, scavenging about for food at night. They dine on refuse and bottom-living invertebrates including gastropod molluscs (used in mollusc control), insects, and others, and may even include some fishes in its diet. In some areas it has a reputation for feeding on unsavory items and will not be eaten, but in other areas it is considered an excellent food fish, its very white, well textured sweet flesh being readily salable.

The genus *Pangasianodon* is almost identical to the genus *Pangasius* except for the lack of teeth and mandibular barbels. It is interesting that no specimens of small or even medium-sized *Pangasianodon* have been reported. Since it is well known that in at least some *Pangasius* species the teeth disappear with age, it seems logical to assume that eventually, when the proper sized individuals are caught (or recognized), it can be determined whether or not *Pangasianodon* is a valid genus. The absence of the mandibular barbels may also be associated with age or growth and also must await the examination of a series of individuals from the smallest to the largest. It has been suggested that the jaws became so fat at the extremely large size that these barbels disappear into the flesh.

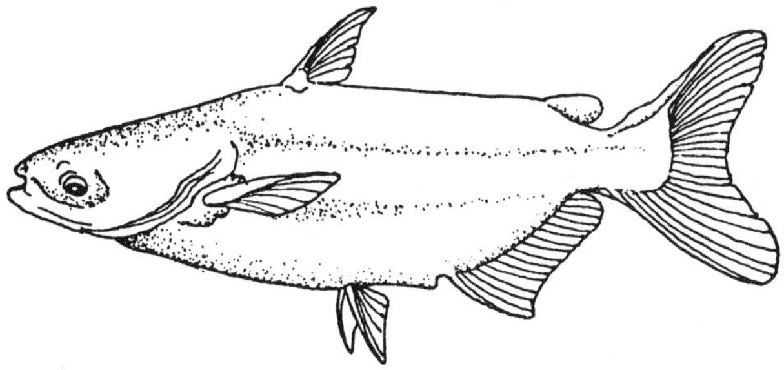

Pangasianodon gigas.

Pangasianodon gigas is confined to the Mekong River system and is thus found in the larger rivers running through Thailand, Laos, Cambodia, and Vietnam, and may even extend into parts of China. It grows to more than 2.1 meters and attains a weight of more than 110 kilos. The adult fish are toothless and are strictly vegetarians, subsisting on soft algae and other soft vegetation cropped from stones, etc., on the bottom. In fact, stones the size of a man's fist have been discovered in the stomachs of this fish, apparently swallowed by accident. This has caused some consternation among the processors who extract oil from this fish. An extremely heavy, waxy fat in the internal organs also may cause problems with the machinery. Spawning migrations of several thousand miles occur. During the flood waters of the rainy season the fish remain in the lower reaches of the rivers in the lower Mekong, but when the flood waters begin to subside they begin their migration upstream. Before this migration their flesh is fatty and not very good. By the time they reach the lakes (such as Lake Tali) and upper reaches of the major tributaries (as far upriver as Yunnan), the fat is mostly lost and the fish become better eating. Thus traps are set by the fishermen to capture the fish as they return downstream. No juveniles have ever been seen. As a valuable food fish, for many years it has been subjected to a great deal of fishing pressure, and the larger specimens have become relatively rare. The giant Mekong catfish is legendary and is celebrated in ethnological and other literature.

The genus *Laides* (formerly *Lais*, a name that was preoccupied) contains but a single species from Thailand, Java, Sumatra, and Borneo. The body is elongate and compressed, and the conical head is covered by thin skin through which the bones are partly visible. The eyes have a broad, circular adipose lid and are situated behind and partly below the mouth. The anterior nostrils are oval and located at the anterior part of the snout while the posterior nostrils are wide transverse slits close to each other on the upper surface of the snout. The mouth is narrow, subterminal, with the upper jaw prominent. The small jaw teeth are set in a rather narrow, curved band, while those on the vomer are in two separate straight bands. There are three pairs of barbels, a pair of long ribbon-like maxillary barbels extending beyond the ventral fins and two pairs of shorter flat mandibular barbels. The dorsal fin is short-based, with a denticulated pungent spine and 7 rays, and there is a minute adipose fin opposite the last third of the fairly elongate (36-39 rays) anal fin. The pectoral fins have a pungent denticulated spine and the ventral fin has 6 rays and is located at a level some distance posterior to the dorsal. The caudal fin is deeply notched. The gill membranes are free from each other and from the isthmus. There are 8-9 branchiostegal rays.

Laides hexanema. (From Weber & de Beaufort, 1913.)

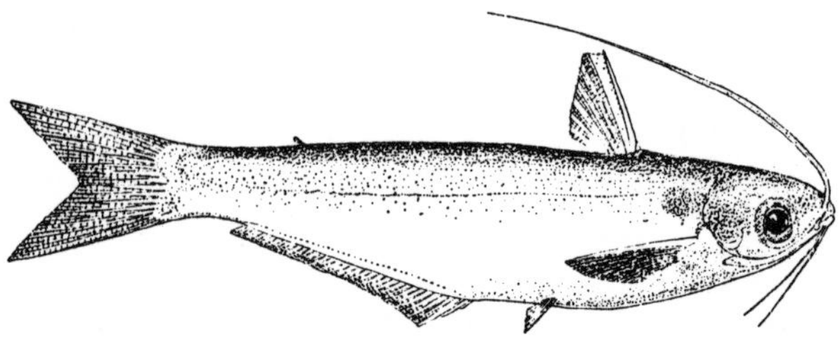

The genus *Helicophagus* contains only a few species that are distributed from Thailand to Sumatra. It is most closely related to the genus *Pangasius* but differs from that genus by always lacking palatine teeth. The name *Helicophagus* indicates that the species are snail-

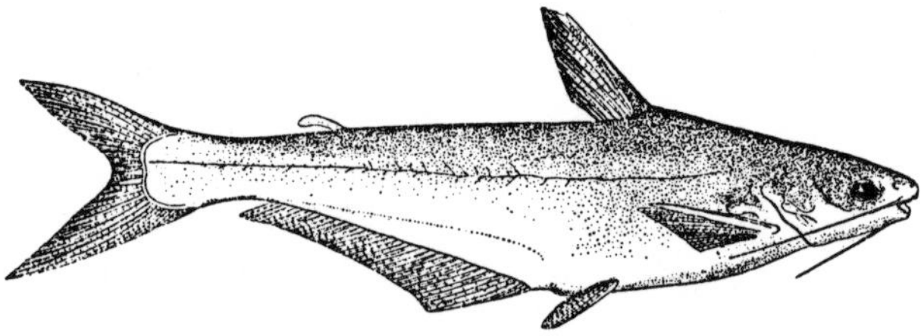

Helicophagus waandersi. (From Weber & de Beaufort, 1913.)

eaters and, indeed, small gastropod molluscs have been found in their stomachs. The body is elongate, compressed, and the conical head with a pointed snout is covered by skin through which some of the head bones are visible. The predorsal area has more or less of a keel formed by the occipital process and interspine. The anterior nostrils are surrounded by an elevated rim and are situated at the front border of the snout and directed forward or upward, whereas the posterior nostrils are provided with an anterior lip and situated midway between the anterior nostrils and the eyes. The eyes have a free orbital margin and are located some distance behind and above the corner of the mouth. There are two pairs of barbels, a maxillary pair and a mandibular pair. The mouth is subterminal, the jaw teeth in a broad band or in the upper jaw in two separate patches. The vomerine teeth are in two separate bands or patches and the palatines are toothless. The dorsal fin is short-based with a strong, flattened, denticulate spine and 6-7 rays, all preceded by a broad, very low, rudimentary spine. The adipose fin is quite small and the anal fin is moderately elongate, with 30 or more rays. The pectoral fins have a strong, flattened, denticulated spine, the ventrals are well developed and have 6 rays, and the caudal fin is forked. The gill membranes are united with each other anteriorly but free from the isthmus. There are 9 branchiostegal rays.

In *Helicophagus hypophthalmus* there are also some changes with growth much like that seen in some of the other genera. The maxillary teeth and vomerine teeth disappear at a size of about one meter. At this same size there is no mandibular barbel and the maxillary barbel is barely 1.5 cm long. This is due mostly to age, for specimens 60 cm in length have the maxillary barbels extending as far as to the edge of the preopercle and the mandibular barbels reach as far as the anterior rim of the orbit. By the time the fish reaches a length of about 75 cm, the maxillary barbels extend as far as the center of the eye and are the same length as the mental barbels, and the vomerine teeth are absent. *Helicophagus waandersi* attains a length of about 34 cm and is said to make a grunting sound when removed from the water.

The final genus, *Pteropangasius*, contains a single species, *P. cultratus*, from Thailand. It is quite distinct in possessing a median keel extending the entire length of the abdomen as well as a greatly compressed body. It has short maxillary barbels and numerous anal fin rays. The snout is short, blunt, and broadly rounded. The eyes are large. The anal fin is long (iv,39), and there is a slender adipose fin. There are two horizontal ovate patches of vomerine teeth along with two oblique patches of palatine teeth forming a crescent in the type specimens of *P. cultratus*, but only two rounded vomerine patches and no palatines in Fowler's later redescription, possibly indicating another genus in which there are changes with age in tooth structure.

Checklist of the species of the family Pangasiidae and their type localities:

Pangasianodon Chevey, 1930. Type species *Pangasianodon gigas* Chevey.
- *Pangasianodon gigas* Chevey, 1930. Mekong basin.

Laides Jordan, 1919. Substitute name for *Lais* Bleeker, 1858. Type species *Pangasius hexanema* Bleeker, 1852.
- *Laides hexanema* (Bleeker, 1852). Palembang, Batavia, Sumatra.

Helicophagus Bleeker, 1858. Type species *Helicophagus typus* Bleeker.
- *Helicophagus hypophthalmus* Sauvage, 1878. Laos, Indo-China.
- *H. typus* Bleeker, 1858. Palembang, Sumatra.
- *H. waandersi* Bleeker, 1858. Palembang, Sumatra.

Pteropangasius Fowler, 1937. Type species *Pangasius cultratus* Smith, 1931.
- *Pteropangasius cultratus* (H.M. Smith, 1931). Tapi River near Bandon, Peninsular Thailand.

Silonia Swainson, 1839. Type species *Pimelodus silondia* Hamilton, 1822.
- *Silonia childreni* (Sykes, 1838). Mota Mola River, Poona.
- *S. silondia* (Hamilton, 1822). Gangetic estuaries, India.

Pangasius Cuvier & Valenciennes, 1840. Type species *Pimelodus pangasius* Hamilton, 1822.
- *Pangasius aequilabialis* Fowler, 1937. Bangkok.
- *P. beani* H.M. Smith, 1931. Lopburi River near Ayuthia, Thailand.
- *P. dezwaani* Weber & de Beaufort, 1912. Taluk, Sumatra.
- *P. fowleri* H.M. Smith, 1931. Lopburi River, Thailand.
- *P. larnaudii* Bocourt, 1866. Siam (= Thailand).
- *P. longibarbis* Fowler, 1934. Mekong at Chiengsen, northern Thailand.
- *P. macronemus* Bleeker, 1851. Bandjermassing, Borneo.
- *P. micronemus* Bleeker, 1847. Java.
- *P. nasutus* (Bleeker, 1863). Borneo.
- *P. nieuwenhuisi* (Popta, 1904). River Bŏ, Borneo.
- *P. pangasius* (Hamilton, 1822). Bengal.

p. godavarii David, 1962. Godavary River, Andhra Pradesh, India.

p. upiensis Srivastava, 1968. Uttar Pradesh, India.

P. pleurotaenius Sauvage, 1878. Laos, Indo-China.

P. polyuranodon Bleeker, 1852. Bandjermassing, Borneo.

P. ponderosus Herre & Myers, 1937. Malaya.

P. sanitwongsei H.M. Smith, 1931. Menam Chao Phya, Thailand.

P. siamensis Steindachner, 1879. Menam Chao Phya at Koh Yai, Thailand.

P. sutchi Fowler, 1937. Bangkok.

P. taeniurus Fowler, 1935. Bangkok.

P. tubbi Inger & Chin, 1959. Confluence of the Deramakot and Kinabatangan Rivers, Kinabatangan District, North Borneo.

Chapter 8

Family — Plates 32–33

AMBLYCIPITIDAE

(Loach Catfishes)

The family Amblycipitidae is a family of small loach-like catfishes inhabiting rivers and streams of India, Burma, China, and Thailand. The species of this family have an elongate, subcylindrical body and a head that is broad, depressed, and covered with smooth skin. The eyes are small, superiorly positioned, and subcutaneous. The wide mouth is terminal and provided with villiform teeth in a band in each jaw; the palate is without teeth. The nostrils are either close together or quite distant, the posterior nostril provided with a nasal barbel. In addition to the nasal barbels, there are three other pairs, one maxillary and two mandibular. A cup-like depression positioned below the opercular flap and above the base of the pectoral spine is present or absent. It is probably associated with some sort of respiratory function. The dorsal fin is short and has a weak, concealed spine. The pectoral fin similarly has a weak, concealed spine. An adipose fin is present, and the caudal fin is forked or truncate. The anal fin is short, with about 9-18 rays, and the pelvic fins have 6-7 rays. The gill openings are wide, and the gill membranes are free from the isthmus. There are 12 branchiostegal rays, and the lateral line is absent. The gas bladder is thick-walled and enclosed in bone.

Two genera are normally referred to this family, *Amblyceps* and *Liobagrus*. They can be distinguished by the following key:

1a. Nostrils close together; cup-like depression below opercular flap present..*Amblyceps*

1b. Nostrils far apart; no cup-like depression below opercular flap.......*Liobagrus*

The genus *Amblyceps* contains only two species and is considered by some workers to be the only genus in the family. It is distributed in India, Pakistan, Bangladesh, Nepal, Burma, and Thailand. The snout is subtruncate or spatulate and the nostrils are close together, the posterior nostril having the nasal barbel. The adipose fin may be confluent or nonconfluent with the caudal fin. This genus is quite notable in possessing a cup-like depression (described by Hora in 1933 as a fold of skin in front of the pectoral fin) that appears to have a special respiratory function for these fishes living in swift currents.

Amblyceps mangois is a small species attaining a length of no more than 13 cm. It inhabits swift-flowing streams or small mountain

Amblyceps mangois. (After Jayaram, 1977.)

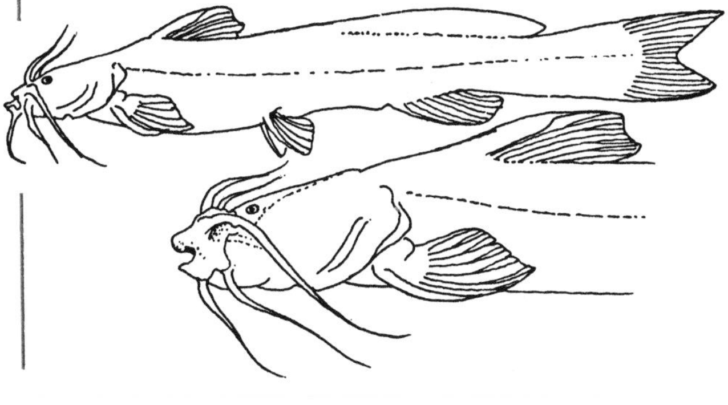

brook tributaries at the base of hills in the Himalayas, northern Burma, and Thailand. The water is usually clear and the bottom type is pebbles with scattered rocks and stones. *A. mangois* lives among these rocks and stones, but when the dry season arrives it buries itself deep into holes on the bottom where there is hidden water or it finds deep pools that do not dry out and remains there until the rains return. It has been reported that *A. mangois* can live out of water for a long time. Observations on living individuals confirm that its respiration is typical of that of other hill-stream fishes, i.e., a series of rapid inhalations followed by a quiet period of anywhere from one to four minutes. This species is said to bite viciously.

Liobagrus is a small genus similar in appearance to *Amblyceps* but with the posterior nostrils remote from the anterior nostrils and without the cup-like depression. The species are not common in their native China, and they are scattered with more or less restricted ranges, usually in hilly country. The adipose fin is long, low and keel-like, and continuous with the rounded or truncate caudal fin.

Liobagrus reini. (After Masuda, et al., 1984.)

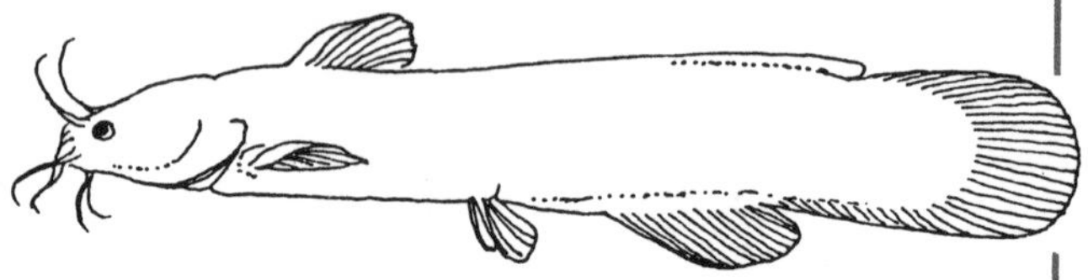

The amblycipitids are closely related to the bagrids but differ in certain features of the skeleton, notably in possessing a lateral extension of the fourth vertebra expanded like an inverted cup to receive the lateral lobes of the swim bladder.

These fishes are rarely, if ever, imported for the aquarium trade, and virtually nothing is known about their requirements. As for other current-loving fishes, the water should be clear and well-aerated. There should also be a number of hiding places provided as well as a current of water (this can be done with a power filter).

Checklist of the species of the family Amblycipitidae and their type localities:

Amblyceps Blyth, 1858. Type species *Amblyceps caecutiens* Blyth (= *A. mangois*).
- *Amblyceps mangois* (Hamilton, 1822). Northern Bihar, India.
- *A. murraystuarti* Chaudhuri, 1919. Upper Burma.

Liobagrus Hilgendorf, 1878. Type species *Liobagrus reini* Hilgendorf.
- *Liobagrus anguillicauda* Nichols, 1926. Northwestern Fukien, China.
- *L. kingi* Tchang, 1935. Yunnan, China.
- *L. marginatus* (Günther, 1892). Szechwan, China.
- ?*L. nantoensis* Oshima, 1919. Taiwan.
- *L. nigricauda* Regan, 1904. Yunnan, China.
- *L. reini* Hilgendorf, 1878. Japan?
- *L. styani* Regan, 1908. South Hupeh, China.

Chapter 9

Family — Plates 33–36

AMPHILIIDAE

(African Hillstream Catfishes)

The amphiliids are small, bottom-dwelling catfishes confined to the fresh waters of Africa, although they are widely distributed throughout that continent. The center of abundance of the amphiliids, however, seems to be the Congo basin, where no less than one-third of the presently accepted species are known to occur. They normally inhabit fast-flowing rivers and rocky streams at high elevations, where they are most often encountered among the rocks. Although they constitute an important part of the mountain stream fauna, some species are not restricted to the montane environment and occur throughout the large river basins.

Most of the species cling to the rocks in the swift-flowing streams and have become adapted to this mode of life in several ways. The lower surfaces of the head and body are flat, while the pectoral and ventral fins are horizontally oriented and placed low on the body as well as being widely spread and expanded. Unlike many other clinging fishes, the mouth is not modified into a sucking organ. Aside from the torrent-loving species, the family Amphiliidae includes some species that are bottom-living sedentary forms.

Most amphiliids are quite small, rarely over 12.5 cm long, the largest species, *Phractura scaphirhynchura*, having some individuals up to 18 cm in length. The head is generally broad and depressed, and around the mouth can be seen three pairs of barbels, a maxillary pair and two mandibular pairs. These barbels are simple and often short. The nostrils are widely separated and the nasal flaps are not prolonged. The eyes are small, without a free orbital rim, and the mouth, which is never developed into a sucking disc, is either terminal or inferior in position. The teeth are numerous, very fine, depressible, and in fine bands in the jaws; there are no teeth on the palate. The body is scaleless, although it is sometimes partially covered with a series of bony scutes. The lateral line is a single slender tube, sometimes with numerous short lateral branches. The fins lack strong spines and contain few rays. The dorsal fin is situated well behind the head and posterior to, or at least over the posterior part of, the pectoral fin. A long, low adipose fin is present and is sometimes preceded by a modified scute resembling a short spine. The paired fins are enlarged, broad, and widely separated, commonly with a greatly thickened outer ray formed of numerous angularly bent segments and produced on the outer side into a fringe imbedded in the thickened skin. The caudal fin is always free from the anal fin and usually free from the adipose fin. The gill membranes are more or less attached to the isthmus, and the gill rakers are slender and short. The gas bladder is reduced and more or less divided into two lateral portions that are enclosed in incomplete bony capsules.

The family Amphiliidae is currently divided into two subfamilies, the Amphiliinae and the Doumeinae, possibly living in entirely different habitats. The Amphiliinae are superficially similar in appearance to the homalopterid loaches, possessing a short, ventrally flattened and moderately compressed body and a depressed head. The caudal peduncle is short and deep, never depressed or elongate. There are no bony plates covering the body. The mouth is subterminal and teeth are present in both jaws. The barbels are long, slender, and smooth, the maxillary barbels being the longest and extending to or beyond the pectoral fin origin. There are no spines in any of the fins, and the adipose fin base is equal to or longer than the head length. The adipose fin may be confluent with the caudal fin or separated from it by a distance equal to the caudal peduncle depth.

The subfamily Amphiliinae contains only two genera, *Amphilius*, with a total of approximately 20 species, and *Paramphilius*, with only three species. They are very closely related and some workers feel that they should be combined into a single genus. This is because the main differentiating character used to separate the two genera, the connection between the adipose fin and the caudal fin, does not seem to hold up. However, there are some other differences between the two genera and they are still considered as being separate.

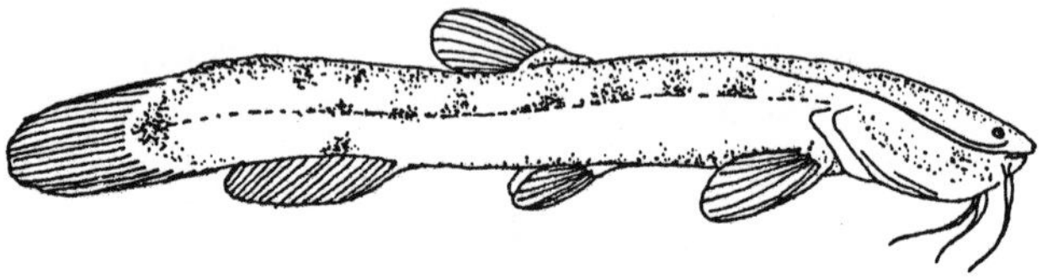

Paramphilius firestonei. **(After Schultz, 1942.)**

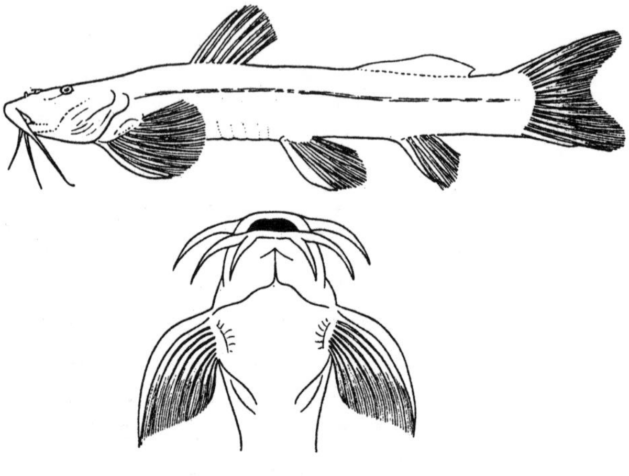

Amphilius platychir. **(From Boulenger, 1911.)**

Key to the genera of the subfamily Amphiliinae:

1a. Pectoral fins extend to vertical from dorsal fin base; posterior nostril always anterior to or midway between tip of snout and eye; 5-6 gill rakers on lower limb of first gill arch...................... *Amphilius*

1b. Pectoral fins not extending to a vertical from dorsal fin base; posterior nostril distinctly nearer eye than tip of snout; only 3 gill rakers on lower limb of first gill arch........................ *Paramphilius*

The Doumeinae are more similar to the Neotropical loricariids in form, having a slender, elongate body that is posteriorly attenuate and generally depressed, an inferior mouth, and specialized development of an external bony armor. The caudal peduncle is long, approximately twice as long as the head length. The barbels are short, thick, and papillose, normally not reaching anywhere near the pectoral fin origin. Nuchal shields are present. Teeth may or may not be present in the jaws and spines may or may not be present in the fins. The adipose fin base is restricted, its length included several times in the length of the head; the adipose fin itself is distinct from the caudal fin. The gill membranes are joined straight across the isthmus, whereas in the Amphiliinae they are deeply incised.

The subfamily Doumeinae contains five or six genera, depending upon which expert is followed. They are *Doumea* with 2 species, *Andersonia* with a single species, *Phractura* with 13 species, *Trachyglanis* with 4 species, and *Belonoglanis* with 2 species. *Paraphractura* is sometimes considered distinct from *Phractura*, a move that would increase the number of genera in the subfamily to six.

Key to the genera of the subfamily Doumeinae:

1a. Body naked, without bony scutes .... *Doumea*

1b. Body provided with bony plates, at least along dorsal and ventral lines........... 2

2a. Some lateral bony scutes on body in front of ventral fins in addition to dorsal and ventral scutes 3

2b. Only dorsal and ventral scutes present.. 4

3a. Pectoral and adipose fins without spines; ventrolateral scutes large; maximum

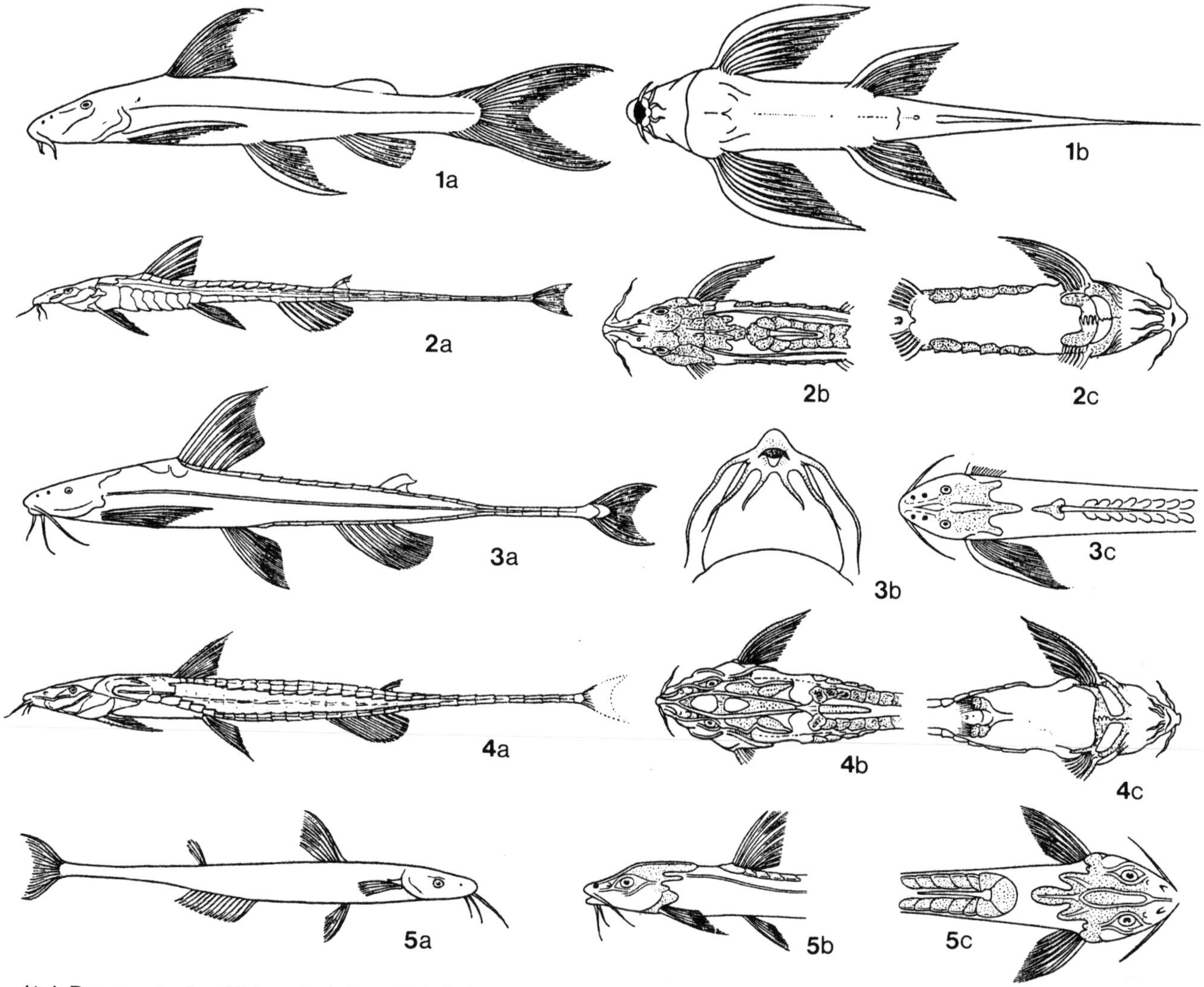

(1a) *Doumea typica*; (1b) ventral view. (2a) *Belonoglanis tenuis*; (2b) dorsal view; (2c) ventral view. (3a) *Phractura bovei*; (3b) ventral view of mouth; (3c) dorsal view. (4a) *Trachyglanis minutus*; (4b) dorsal view; (4c) ventral view. (5a) *Andersonia leptura*; (5b) lateral view; (5c) dorsal view. (From Poll, 1957.)

length 9 cm .... *Belonoglanis*

3b. Dorsal, pectoral, and adipose fins each preceded by a spine; ventrolateral scutes smaller, not much larger than others; maximum length 5 cm...... *Trachyglanis*

4a. Origin of dorsal fin in front of base of ventral fins; no spine preceding pectoral or adipose fins.................... *Phractura*

4b. Origin of dorsal fin above ventrals or a little in front of their base; spine preceding pectoral and adipose fins; maximum length 5 cm............. *Andersonia*

There is not very much information available regarding the members of this family. Most of what is available concerns the members of the genus *Amphilius*. The species of this genus inhabit mountain torrents as well as fast-flowing brooks coming down low hill ridges. To maintain their position in such habitats they rely upon their thick, rubbery pectoral and ventral rays. The horizontal, low pectoral fins embrace the substrate, helping to create a suction. They are said to "walk" on or between the pebbles or coarse sand of the bottom using the pectoral and ventral fins as anchors. Taken out of the water they can wiggle and move forward over short distances.

One of the species occasionally imported for the aquarium trade is *A. platychir*. This is a hill-stream species found at altitudes of 2,000 to 6,000 feet (610-1829 meters) above sea level in the Zambezi River system and

1↑

2↑

3↑

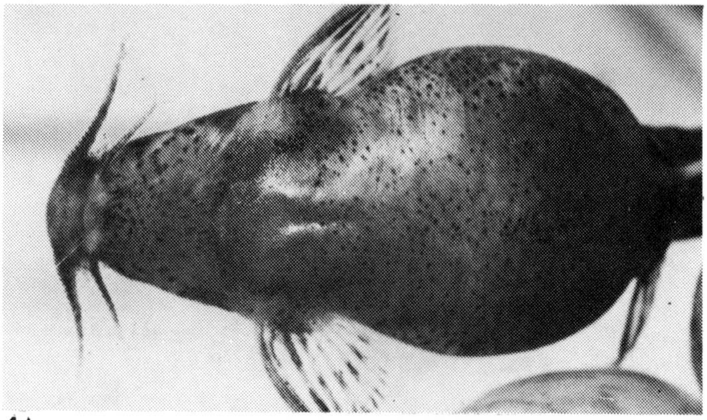

4↑

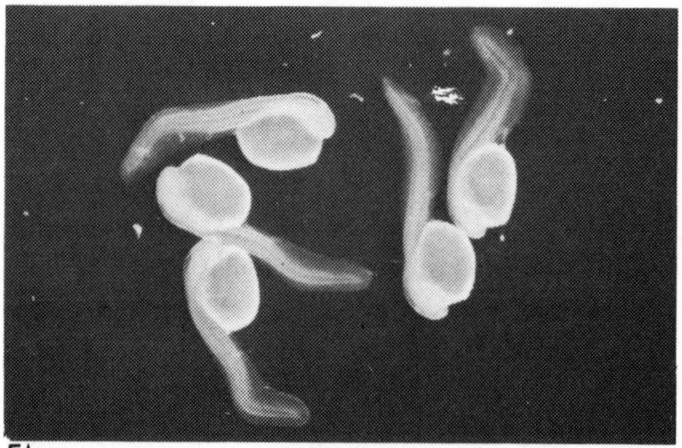

5↑ 7↓

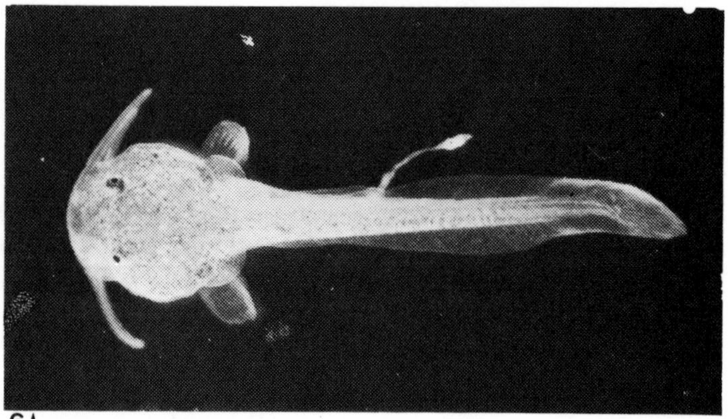

6↑ 8↓

Phractura ansorgii. (1) Male. (2) Female. (3) Ventral view of male. (4) Ventral view of female. (5) Newly hatched fry. (6) Yolk sac has been absorbed and barbels developing but vertical fins still undeveloped. (7) One-month-old fry with fins separated. (8) At about two months of age, about 15 mm in length, the pattern starts to develop. Photos by Dr. W. Foersch.

south to the rivers of Natal. It occurs in rocky streams where it feeds on insect larvae and other invertebrates. It attains a maximum length of about 18 cm. The Mountain Barbel, as it is often called, is said to lay its eggs on the underside of stones; the young resemble tadpoles at first. Another species, *A. grandis*, is commonly found in large numbers in certain streams, where all sizes and age groups are represented. The smaller individuals are the more numerous but a few specimens up to 20 cm have been collected. This is not an angling species because of its size, but it does appear to have some importance as a forage fish in the trout streams, where large introduced trout feed on it. This species also inhabits streams at altitudes up to 1829 meters. It is interesting to note that as the fish grows larger the body becomes deeper.

Phractura species are mostly found on plants, to which they cling by also using their pectoral and pelvic fins, for these plants are located in areas of fast-flowing water where there is a very high oxygen content. They feed from the plant biocover, with tiny insect larvae and microorganisms constituting their main diet. Although living mainly among plants, they are not found in swampy areas where the oxygen content is low. *Phractura longicauda* frequents the torrent areas of shallow rivers, where it can be found among the rocks.

The family Amphiliidae is said to be most closely related to the Bagridae but is distinguished from that family by several characters including the absence of strong spines in the dorsal fin (there is a spine in *Trachyglanis* but it is weakly developed), by the unusual development or modification of the gas bladder (it is normal in the Bagridae), and by the absence of pterygoid and posttemporal bones. Also, the Amphiliidae is strikingly similar to the Asiatic families Akysidae, Sisoridae, and Amblycipitidae. The resemblance to these families is concerned with a common lack of the posttemporal and pterygoid bones as well as the lack of a dorsal fin spine. In addition, they have remarkably similar modifications of the gas bladder and the anterior ankylosed vertebrae. The greatest similarities are to be found between the amphiliids and the akysids and sisorids. *Exostoma* and *Pseudecheneis* are quite similar to the members of the subfamily Amphiliinae, while the sisorid genus *Sisor* and the akysid genus *Breitensteinia* are surprisingly close to the subfamily Doumeinae. Perhaps the family Amphiliidae is intermediate between the Bagridae on the one hand and the three Asiatic families Sisoridae, Akysidae, and Amblycipitidae on the other. It may be possible that the merging of a family or two or three might occur in this area.

Checklist of the species of the family Amphiliidae and their type localities:

Amphilius Günther, 1864. Proposed as a subgenus of the genus *Pimelodus*. Type species *Pimelodus platychir* Günther.

- *Amphilius angustifrons* (Boulenger, 1902). Banzyville.
- *A. atesuensis* Boulenger, 1904. Atesu River, Gold Coast.
- *A. baudoni* Pellegrin, 1928. La Passa River, Ogowe system.
- *A. brevis* Boulenger, 1902. Lindi River, tributary of the Congo.
- *A. cryptobullatus* Skelton, 1986 (1985). Luongo River, Upper Zaire system, Zambia.
- *A. jacksoni* Boulenger, 1912. Hima River, Ruwenzori.
- *A. kakrimensis* Teugels, Skelton & Leveque, 1987. Kakrima River, Guinea.
- *A. kivuensis* Pellegrin, 1933. Kitembo, west of Kivu.
- *A. lamani* Lönnberg & Rendahl, 1920. Kingoyi, Lower Congo.
- *A. lampei* Pietschmann, 1913. Harrar, Abyssinia.
- *A. laticaudatus* Skelton, 1984. Buzi River, Mozambique.
- *A. lentiginosus* Trewavas, 1936. Mt. Moco, Cuvo River system.
- *A. longirostris* (Boulenger, 1901). Batanga, Cameroon.
- *A. maesii* Boulenger, 1917. Oshwe, Zaire River system.
- *A. natalensis* Boulenger, 1917. Krantz Kloof, Natal.
- *A. notatus* Nichols & Griscom, 1917. Faradje, Congo basin.
- *A. opisthophthalmus* Boulenger, 1919. Oshwe, Zaire River.

A. platychir (Günther, 1864). Sierra Leone.
A. pulcher Pellegrin, 1929. Kouilou (Louesse) River.
A. rheophilus Daget, 1959. Mpantie & Banhare, Gambia.
A. uranoscopus (Pfeffer, 1889). Ushonda (Unguu), upper ranges of Wami River.
A. zairensis Skelton, 1986 (1985). Lufu River, about 2 mi. from confluence with Zaire River.

Paramphilius Pellegrin, 1907. Type species *Paramphilius trichomycteroides* Pellegrin, 1907.
Paramphilius firestonei Schultz, 1942. Bromley, Harbel, Liberia.
P. goodei Harry, 1953. Lalodorf, Bikui River, Cameroon.
P. trichomycteroides Pellegrin, 1907. Ditinn (Fouta Djalon), Senegal.

Doumea Sauvage, 1879. Type species *Doumea typica* Sauvage, 1879.
Doumea alula Nichols & Griscom, 1917. Stanleyville, Congo.
D. angolensis Boulenger, 1906. Benguella, Angola.
D. chappuisi Pellegrin, 1933. Danane, Ivory Coast.
D. typica Sauvage, 1879. Doumé, rivière Ogôoué.

Andersonia Boulenger, 1900. Type species *Andersonia leptura* Boulenger, 1900.
Andersonia leptura Boulenger, 1900. A pond near Koshek, Sudan.

Phractura Boulenger, 1900. Type species *Peltura bovei* Perugia, 1891.
Phractura ansorgii Boulenger, 1901. Agberi, Nigeria.
P. bovei (Perugia, 1891). Congo.
P. brevicauda Boulenger, 1911. Ogowe and South Cameroon.
P. clauseni Daget & Stauch, 1963. Haute Comoe a Samago Iri.
P. fasciata Boulenger, 1920. Stanley Falls, Congo.
P. gladysae Pellegrin, 1931. Haute-Louesse, Kouilou River system.
P. intermedia Boulenger, 1911. Ja River at Bitye, Libi River, Nyong River, Kribi River.
P. lindica Boulenger, 1902. Lindi River, tributary of the Congo.
P. longicauda Boulenger, 1903. Kribi River.
P. macrura Poll, 1967. Caungula, Cassange River.
P. scaphirhynchura (Vaillant, 1886). Ogooue a Diele.
P. tenuicauda (Boulenger, 1902). Ubange a Banzyville.

Trachyglanis Boulenger, 1902. Type species *Trachyglanis minutus* Boulenger, 1902.
Trachyglanis ineac (Poll, 1954). Loweo River, Lusambila River.
T. intermedius Pellegrin, 1928. Kasai. Congo basin.
T. minutus Boulenger, 1902. Ubange á Banzyville.
T. sanghensis Pellegrin, 1925. Ouesso (Sangha), Zaire.

Belonoglanis Boulenger, 1902. Type species *Belonoglanis tenuis* Boulenger, 1902.
Belonoglanis brieni Poll, 1959. N'Djili River, Stanley Pool, Congo.
B. tenuis Boulenger, 1902. Ubange á Banzyville.

Chapter 10

Family — Plates 37–38

AKYSIDAE

(Akysid Catfishes)

The Akysidae is a family of small catfishes, including some species that reach sexual maturity when only about 3 cm long, that inhabit the fresh waters of southeastern Asia (Burma, Thailand, Malaya, Sumatra, Borneo, and Java), usually where there is a swift current. They may be described as having an elongate body with the ventral area flattened as far as the pelvic fin base. The skin is covered with tubercles or granules that may be arranged in longitudinal rows. The head is depressed, with or without prominent longitudinal ridges, and covered by soft skin. A median longitudinal fontanel or groove is present, and the eyes are small, superior, and covered by skin. The teeth in the jaws are villiform and in bands; the palate is edentulous. Four pairs of nostrils are present (nasal, maxillary, mandibular, and second mandibular or mental). The anterior nostrils are tubular and remote from the posterior nostrils, which have a circular rim and the broad-based nasal barbel. The dorsal fin is short (of about 5 rays) and preceded by a pungent spine (possibly two) sheathed in thick skin. The adipose fin is present or absent; when present, it is located opposite the short anal fin. The pectoral fins possess a strong, pungent spine covered with thick skin, and these and the six-rayed ventral fins are horizontal. The caudal fin is truncate, emarginate, or deeply emarginate. The gill membranes are united with each other and with the isthmus; the gill opening is narrow to moderate and extends dorsally to the pectoral fin base or even above it. Branchiostegals 6. The gas bladder is thin-walled.

The akysids are probably most closely related to the families Amphiliidae, Sisoridae, and Bagridae. They resemble the Amphiliidae and Sisoridae in the structure of the anterior vertebrae and the swim bladder, but differ in certain characters of the cranium. Like the sisorids, the akysids are adapted to a benthic existence in areas where they are subject to the constant pressures of fast-flowing waters. Compared with the Bagridae, the akysids are less stocky and the fin spines are not as strong. In addition, the akysids have a swim bladder that is reduced to two capsules and the ectopterygoid bone is lacking.

The akysids are said to be close to the Amblycipitidae (Hora, 1926; Regan, 1911) but differ from that family by the remote nostrils (close in some amblycipitids), the strong bony dorsal and pectoral spines (weak and sheathed in skin in the amblycipitids), the skin being granulated or tuberculated (smooth in Amblycipitidae), and a thin-walled swim bladder (thick-walled and enclosed in bone in the amblycipitids).

The family Akysidae contains only four genera, *Acrochordonichthys*, *Akysis*, *Parakysis*, and *Breitensteinia*, which can be distinguished by the following key:

1a. Adipose fin absent; gill openings not extending above base of pectoral fin; two dorsal fin spines............. *Breitensteinia*

1b. Adipose fin present (though may be only a low ridge); gill opening restricted or extending from ventral surface to or slightly above pectoral base; one dorsal fin spine....................................2

2a. Gill membranes separate from each

other; gill openings small, restricted, situated just in front of pectoral fin base .. .. *Parakysis*

2b. Gill membranes united with each other and with isthmus; gill openings extending to ventral surface...................... 3

3a. Gill openings extensive, but restricted to ventral surface and extending dorsally only to pectoral fin bases .... *Acrochordonichthys*

3b. Gill openings extending to ventral surface for considerable distance, though a broad isthmus still separating them, and extending dorsally above pectoral fin bases................................... *Akysis*

The genus *Acrochordonichthys* is a small genus composed of only about five species. The body is elongate and provided with longitudinal rows of tubercles. The head is depressed

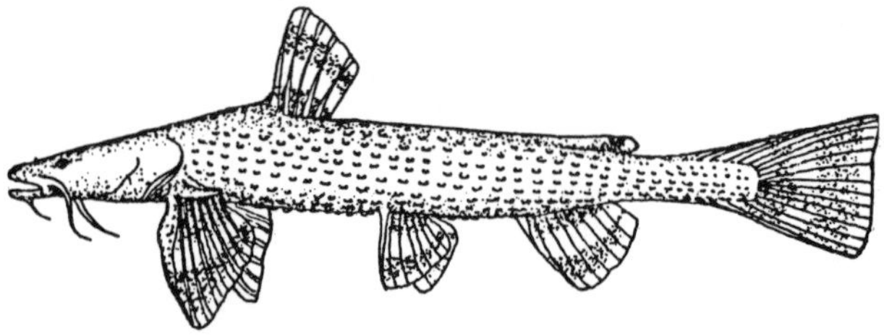

Acrochordonichthys rugosus. **(After Bleeker, 1862.)**

and covered with soft, granular skin. The eyes are small, superior, and subcutaneous. A median fontanel is present on top of the head and is visible when the skin is removed. The posterior nostrils have a circular rim, with the nasal barbel at the front border; the anterior nostrils are tubular and at some distance in front of the posterior nostrils. There is a pair of broad-based maxillary barbels on the upper lip, and at some distance from the angle of the mouth can be seen the slender mandibular barbels; the mental barbels are positioned behind the lower lip. The dorsal fin is short, with five rays and a pungent spine covered by thick skin, the spine's middle hind border being slightly denticulate. A long, low adipose fin is present opposite the short anal fin. The pectoral fin spine is strong, pungent, strongly denticulate behind, and covered with thick skin; the caudal fin is truncate or slightly emarginate. The gill openings are extensive but restricted to the ventral surface and extend dorsally only to the level of the pectoral fin base; the gill membranes are united with each other and with the isthmus (there may be a small ridge-like free fold across the isthmus).

Acrochordonichthys pachyderma from Borneo was collected by use of a hook and line, using earthworms as bait. An individual a little over 10 cm in length caught this way in the muddy flood waters of the Kinabatangan River contained enlarged ova. A 9.5-cm-long female *A. melanogaster* containing ripe ova was taken in the same river by the same method, also during the flood stage. Smaller specimens of this latter species were seined in shallow water on a gravel bar.

The genus *Akysis* contains only about eight species of diminutive catfishes from the freshwater streams of Burma, Thailand, Sumatra, Java, and Borneo. Of the eight species recognized, four of them are known from only a single specimen each. The head is broad, depressed, and covered with skin. The skin of the body is covered with roundish granules or tubercles arranged in horizontal rows. The eyes are small, superior, and subcutaneous. The lips are fleshy and papillated. The median longitudinal groove on the head extends to the base of the occipital process, and the occipital process does not extend as far as the basal bone of the dorsal. The anterior nostrils are tubular and located at some distance from

Akysis variegatus. **(From Weber & de Beaufort, 1913.)**

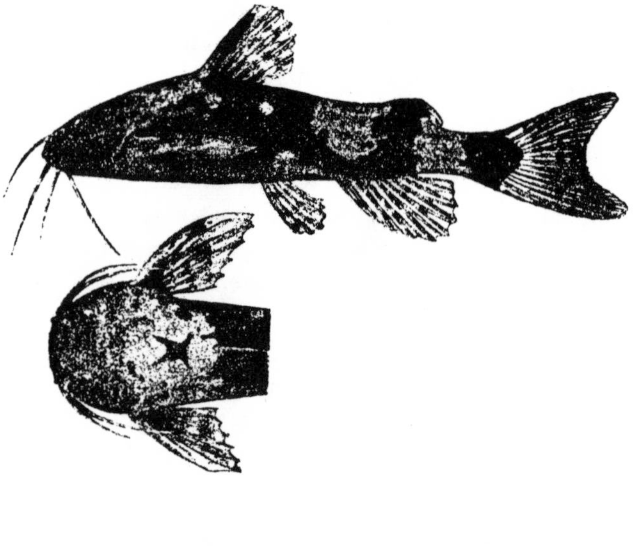

the posterior nostrils; the posterior nostrils are partially surrounded by a rim, from which rises anteriorly a long, broad-based nasal barbel. Long broad-based maxillary barbels originate at the angle of the mouth; the mandibular barbels are close behind the mouth angle, while the mental barbels originate below it. All barbels are long and slender. The dorsal fin is short, with about five rays, and is provided with a pungent spine covered by thick skin. The adipose fin lies opposite the anal fin, and the caudal fin is emarginate. The horizontally oriented pectoral fins are provided with a strong spine that is longitudinally furrowed, may or may not be serrated, and is prolonged by a cartilaginous filament. The spine is covered by thick skin. The pelvic fins are also horizontal, have six rays, and extend as far as the anal fin. The gill openings are moderate, extending dorsally above the level of the pectoral fins; the gill membranes are confluent with the isthmus and with each other. The gas bladder has thin walls.

Akysis hendricksoni was collected in Malaya in a small stagnant backwater not more than a meter deep and about 18 meters downstream from a riffle. The bottom was composed of sandy mud covered with silt, and there was a considerable accumulation of dead leaves. The water was clear and the collecting site was well exposed to the sun. Among the fishes collected with *A. hendricksoni* were some loaches of the genus *Acanthophthalmus*, namely *A. javanicus* (which was very common), *A. kuhli*, and *A. muraeniformis* (which were more or less uncommon). (Alfred, 1966.) *Akysis leucorhynchus* from Thailand, which attains a length of about 4 cm, was reported to be sexually mature at 3 cm, specimens of that size having nearly ripe eggs.

Breitensteinia is a very distinctive genus, its members having an elongate body and tail, the latter becoming more squarish posteriorly. The head is depressed and spatulate, with prominent blunt longitudinal ridges along its upper surface. The eyes are very small, superior, and covered with skin. The skin of the body has longitudinal rows of tubercles that cover the trunk and the anterior part of the tail. The anterior nostril forms a short tubule near the border of the mouth; the posterior nostril is close to the eye and is

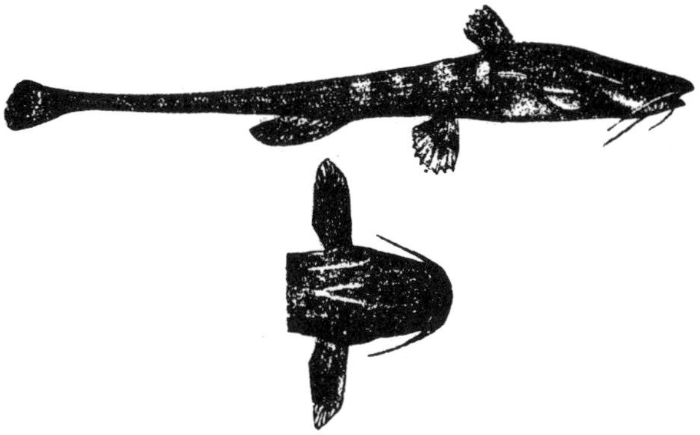

Breitensteinia insignis. (From Weber & de Beaufort, 1913.)

provided with a very short tentacle. The jaw teeth are small, villiform, and arranged in a broad band; the palate is without teeth. A strong barbel is present at the corner of the maxilla, there is a pair of small mental barbels, and there is a pair of larger mandibular barbels some distance behind them. The dorsal fin has two contiguous spines and five rays; the anal fin is also short and is located far behind the anus. There is no adipose fin. The pectoral fins are horizontal, and their spine is strong and denticulate. The ventral fins are behind the dorsal fin, and the caudal fin is truncate. The gill openings do not extend upward above the bases of the pectoral fins; the gill membranes are confluent and united with the isthmus. This genus contains only a single species, *B. insignis*.

The genus *Parakysis* was described by Herre as lacking an adipose fin, but Hora and Gupta, having examined some young specimens 26 to 37 mm in length, came to the conclusion that they indeed possess a long, low,

Parakysis verrucosa. (From Herre, 1940.)

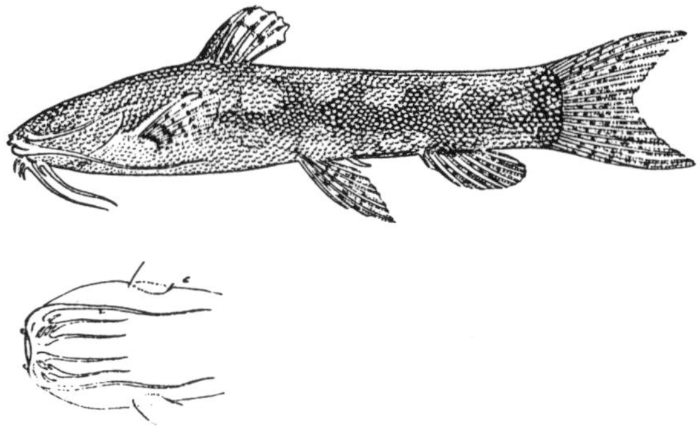

and thick adipose fin. However, it is not very distinct owing to the tubercles on the body and to see it more plainly the specimen must be held up to the light. Herre did notice "a low ridge or keel on the dorsal side of the caudal peduncle" in some specimens, especially those collected in Borneo. There are also short accessory basal barbules at the bases of the mandibular and mental barbels, which seems to be a distinctive feature of this genus. The gill openings are small and extend just around the bases of the pectoral fin spines. They are further reduced functionally, according to Hora and Gupta, because the flow of the exhalent (expiratory) current is restricted by valve-like folds inside the gill openings to the upper portion. There a spout-like structure is formed not unlike that seen in the genus *Amblyceps*. The gill membranes are separated from each other by a considerable distance and therefore the isthmus is very broad. The air bladder is thin-walled and is divided into a pair of small rounded chambers that are enclosed dorsally in bony capsules. (Hora and Gupta, 1941.)

This genus appears to be most closely related to the genus *Akysis*. Its restricted gill openings and the accessory barbules around the mouth are said to be respiratory adaptations that make them better adapted for life in the swift-flowing waters of torrential streams. There is only a single species in *Parakysis, P. verrucosus*.

Members of this family are almost never encountered in the aquarium trade. Occasionally one might be imported as an "oddball" or curiosity or possibly even by accident, but there are never any number of them present at any given time and the chances of obtaining a pair are almost nil. Little or no information about their ability to live in captivity is available. It is expected that they might do very well considering their small size, but because of their natural habitat (fast-flowing waters) it is almost certain that they would do best in clean water with heavy aeration and water changes on a regular basis.

Checklist of the species of the family Akysidae and their type localities:

Acrochordonichthys Bleeker, 1858. Type species *A. platycephalus* Bleeker (= *A. rugosus* Bleeker).
- *Acrochordonichthys ischnosoma* Bleeker, 1858. Java.
- *A. melanogaster* (Bleeker, 1854). Sumatra.
- *A. pachyderma* Vaillant, 1902. Borneo.
- *A. pleurostigma* (Bleeker, 1854). Java.
- *A. rugosus* (Bleeker, 1847). Java, Sumatra.

Akysis Bleeker, 1858. Type species *Pimelodus variegatus* Bleeker.
- *A. armatus* Vaillant, 1902. Borneo.
- *A. hendricksoni* Alfred, 1966. Malaya. (Kuala Brang.)
- *A. leucorhynchus* Fowler, 1934. Chieng Mai, northern Siam.
- *A. macronemus* Bleeker, 1860. Sumatra.
- *A. maculipinnis* Fowler, 1934. Chantaboon, SE Siam.
- *A. pictus* Günther, 1883. Tenasserim, Burma.
- *A. prashadi* Hora, 1936. Myitkyina District, Upper Burma.
- *A. variegatus* (Bleeker, 1846). Java.

Breitensteinia Steindachner, 1881. Type species *B. insignis* Steindachner.
- *Breitensteinia insignis* Steindachner, 1881. Borneo, Sumatra.

Parakysis Herre, 1940. Type species *P. verrucosa* Herre.
- *Parakysis verrucosa* Herre, 1940. Mawai District, Johore.

Chapter 11

Family — Plates 38–45

SISORIDAE

(Asian Hillstream Catfishes)

The family Sisoridae is a moderate-sized family of freshwater catfishes extending over a large geographic area. They are known from Kurdistan in the west to China and Korea in the east, and south to the islands of Sumatra, Java, and Borneo. The sisorids, especially *Conta*, *Pseudecheneis*, and *Glyptothorax*, inhabit rather fast-flowing hill streams and have adapted to this habitat by developing an adhesive apparatus on their ventral surface. This is used for attaching themselves to rocks, boulders, and other objects in order to prevent them from being swept away by the strong current. Some sisorids (for example *Euchiloglanis*, *Myersglanis*, and *Glyptosternon*) occur in the cold mountain streams at altitudes of 1,000 to 1,500 meters. In these habitats they occur mostly over rocky substrates. The species range from very small (20mm in *Erethistes*) to quite large (2 meters in *Bagarius*).

The family Sisoridae contains a rather diverse assemblage of species and is not easy to define properly. The body can be short or elongate, compressed to rounded, although the ventral surfaces of the head and chest are always flattened and either have or lack a thoracic adhesive organ. The head is depressed to conical and is bony, often rugose, and covered with skin. There generally is a large and conspicuous fontanel and considerable flattening of the cranium in the occipital region. The eyes may be small or large and are always subcutaneous. The nostrils are close together or slightly distant, separated by a small membranous lobe or short nasal barbel. There are four pairs of often thick-based barbels (especially the pair at the angle of the mouth): a small nasal pair, a maxillary pair with a stiff base, a mandibular pair, and a mental pair. Teeth may be present or absent; when present, they are villiform. The arrow-shaped vomer has or lacks teeth, and the palate is edentulous. The gill openings are wide and extend ventrally, or they are narrow and are restricted to above the pectoral fin base. The gill membranes are confluent with or free from the isthmus. The dorsal fin is short, with few rays and a spine, and is located in advance of the ventral fins. The adipose fin is present but mostly not well developed. The pectoral and ventral fins are horizontally oriented. The pectoral fin has a strong, flattened spine, the first rays may be thickened and large, or the first ray may be weak with pointed cartilaginous rays along its inner margin for adhesion (usually to take the place of the thoracic adhesive organ if it is absent). The ventral fin has 6 rays. The caudal fin is forked, lunate, or truncate, the upper rays sometimes quite elongate. The skin may be smooth or rough (granular or tuberculate). The air bladder is partially or totally enclosed in bone.

In these torrent-loving catfishes there have been certain modifications of the anatomy of various genera that aid them in maintaining their position in the current, thereby preventing them from being swept away from their preferred habitat into an area with greater predation, less food, or otherwise poorly suited for them. The thoracic adhesive apparatus is primarily involved in this function and consists of a corrugated surface on the flattened thoracic area, the ridges of the corrugations being provided with tiny hooks (for a more detailed account see *Pseudecheneis*). But there are other structures that take over the adhesive function when the thoracic organ is wanting or possibly to complement it when it is there. In forms like *Exostoma, Oreoglanis,* and *Myersglanis* both the lips and the fin rays are equally useful for adhesion. In *Glyptosternon, Coraglanis, Euchiloglanis,* and *Glaridoglanis* the function of adhesion is more or less relegated to the fins and because of this the labial fold is interrupted and the lips are not reflected and spread continuously around the mouth. They live in deeper waters of the main rivers of central Asia where the swiftness of the current does not affect them to the same extent as it would in small, shallow, torrential streams. The segmentation of the pectoral and ventral fin spines makes them pliable to stresses in swift currents, and the pinnate nature affords a greater adhesion to be applied to the substrate along with flexibility.

In specialized hill-stream fishes the inner rays of the paired fins are used to pump out water that leaks onto the ventral side of the fish in order to decrease the pressure there, thus increasing the vacuum and creating a more perfect adhesion to the substrate. In those species wherein the first rays of the pectoral and pelvic fins have developed into a more efficient adhesive organ or where the currents where they live are not so tempestuous, the need for such a pumping apparatus is not as great and therefore the number of such rays remains small (for example, pectorals of *Glyptosternon,* P. i/11; *Coraglanis,* P. i/13; *Glaridoglanis,* P. i/10). In these genera the pectorals do not overlap the pelvic fins and they are separated from each other by a considerable distance. In the genus *Exostoma,* where the function of adhesion is shared by the lips and the first rays of the paired fins, the number of branched rays in the pectoral fins is also less (P. i/10-12). *Oreoglanis* and *Myersglanis* seem to be better adapted for living in swift-flowing waters, for besides possessing adhesive fin rays and adhesive lips, they also possess more branched pectoral fin rays (P. i/16-19).

With the exception of the genus *Glyptosternon,* which is a trans-Himalayan genus of deep, swift, rocky rivers, there is another adaptation in the torrent-loving adhering fishes. The gill openings in all other glyptosternoid sisorids are restricted to the dorsolateral sides and do not extend to the ventral surface of the fish. It is a common occurrence in fishes that adhere to the substrate by their ventral surface that the lower portion of the gill openings becomes non-functional, and in the more extreme forms it eventually disappears. This restriction of the gill openings to a much smaller area does not seem to be a problem for these fishes, probably because the torrential waters are so highly oxygenated.

The family Sisoridae has been divided into three subfamilies, Sisorinae, Glyptosterninae, and Bagarinae. The three subfamilies can be distinguished by the following key:

1a. A series of bony plates extending from dorsal fin to base of caudal; uppermost caudal fin rays very elongate, more than half length of body; adipose fin in the form of a spine; teeth lacking in jaws and on vomer...................... Sisorinae

1b. No series of bony plates extending from dorsal fin to base of caudal; uppermost caudal fin rays not very elongate; adipose fin not in the form of a spine; teeth present in jaws, present or absent on vomer 2

2a. First rays of paired fins soft and weak, ensheathed in thick skin and provided with soft internal pointed cartilaginous rays along anterior margin; thoracic adhesive apparatus of transverse folds of skin present or absent; teeth in jaws only......................... Glyptosterninae

2b. First ray of paired fins strong, without soft internal pointed cartilaginous rays along its anterior margin; thoracic adhesive apparatus of longitudinal plaits of skin present or absent; teeth in jaws present, present or absent on vomer..... .... Bagarinae

The subfamily Sisorinae contains but a single genus, *Sisor. Sisor* is quite distinctive, with an elongate, depressed body and a long, tapering tail. The upper ray of the caudal fin is very elongate, equal in length to the length of the entire fish. The head is depressed, spatulate, and rough and bony on the upper

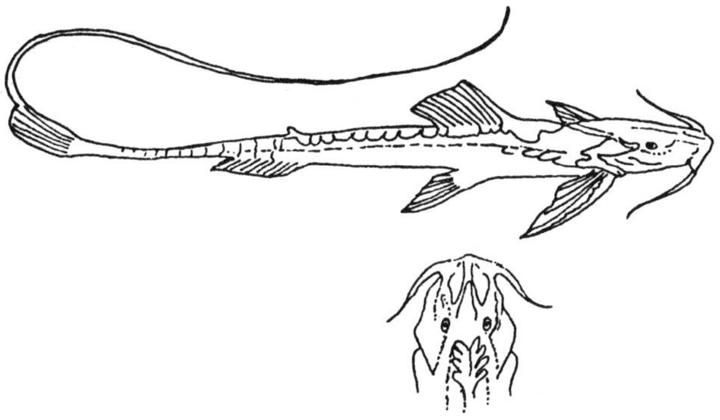

Sisor rhabdophorus. (After Day, 1878.)

surface. A series of bony plates is present, extending from the dorsal fin to the caudal base. The first plate is trilobate and positioned in front of the dorsal. The next five are along the dorsal base, and there are nine from the end of the dorsal to above the anal fin, each with a ridge and the last with a spine (which some consider the adipose spine). Beyond this can be seen 12 bony rings to the base of the tail. The eyes are minute and are provided along the upper edge with an extensible muscular flap. There are six pairs of barbels, a maxillary pair and five mandibular pairs. The nostrils are close together, separated by a small lobe. The mouth is small and inferior in position. The dorsal and anal fins are short and without spines. The pectoral fins are horizontal and provided with a flattened spine serrated on both edges. The lateral line is in the form of a series of small, rough, bony plates. The gill membranes are united with the broad isthmus and the gill openings are narrow. The swim bladder is enclosed by a bony capsule. This genus contains a single species, *Sisor rhabdophorus*, from India and Pakistan.

The subfamily Bagarinae contains 10 genera that may be distinguished by using the following key:

1a. Pectoral spine with outer margin strongly denticulate 2
1b. Pectoral spine not strongly denticulate on outer margin 5
2a. Denticulations on outer edge of pectoral fin spine in the form of divergent spines .... *Erethistes*
2b. Denticulations on outer edge of pectoral spines not in the form of divergent spines 3
3a. Small teeth on outer edge of pectoral spine all directed toward its tip......... 4
3b. Small teeth on outer edge of pectoral spine directed toward base in proximal half and toward tip on distal half........ .... *Erethistoides*
4a. Body elongate; an elongate thoracic adhesive apparatus present, extending to ventrals................................. *Conta*
4b. Body moderately elongate; no thoracic adhesive apparatus .... *Hara*
5a. Head depressed; paired fins horizontal, on the same level 6
5b. Head not depressed; paired fins not horizontal, not on the same level........... 9
6a. Cubitohumeral and scapular processes prominent; thoracic adhesive apparatus well developed or poorly developed.... 7
6b. Cubitohumeral and scapular processes not prominent; a well developed thoracic adhesive apparatus present or absent 8
7a. An elongate, well developed thoracic adhesive apparatus extending to ventrals.. .... *Pseudolaguvia*
7b. A poorly developed thoracic adhesive apparatus not extending to ventrals...... .... *Laguvia*
8a. A well developed thoracic adhesive apparatus present .... *Glyptothorax*
8b. Thoracic adhesive apparatus absent...... .... *Bagarius*
9a. Body robust; head without distinct median groove or bordering ridges; fontanels small; eyes small, more than ten times in head length .... *Sundagagata*
9b. Body slender; head with distinct median groove bordered by prominent longitudinal ridges; fontanels large; eyes large, less than six times in head length........ .... *Gagata*

The genus *Erethistes* contains two species, *E. pusillus* from India and Burma, which attains a length of about 5-6 cm and *E. maesotensis* from the Thai-Burmese border, which attains a length of only about 2 cm. There is a moderately short, flattened body with a triangularly shaped bony head. The eyes are moderate and the nostrils are close together, separated by a flap bearing a short nasal barbel. There are four pairs of short barbels (which in *E. pusillus* are ringed with black and white). There are four to five rows of tubercles on the body, and the top of the head is granulated. A thoracic adhesive apparatus is lacking. The teeth are villiform in the upper jaw and arranged in three to four series, the outer series more elongated; the teeth in the lower jaw are minute and scattered and arranged in a crescent. The dorsal fin is short, with 6 rays and a strong, serrated spine (*pusillus*) or smooth posteriorly (*maesotensis*), and the adipose fin is also short, opposite the short anal fin. The pectoral fins are low, horizontal, non-plaited (a plaited fin has the thickened outer ray or spine ridged or corrugated below), and provided with a strong flattened spine bearing divergent spines (*pusillus*) or outwardly directed denticles (*maesotensis*) on the outer edge and serrations on the inner edge. The 6-rayed ventral fins are non-plaited. The caudal fin is forked. The gill membranes are confluent with the isthmus; the gill openings are narrow. The gas bladder is divided into two globular lateral lobes connected by a transverse tube.

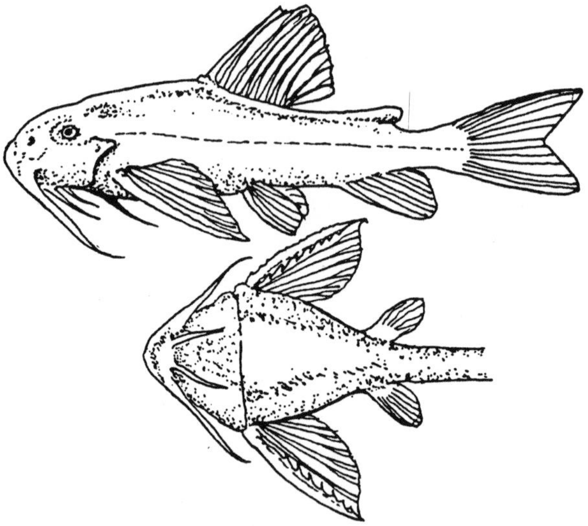

***Erethistes pusillus*. (After Misra, 1976.)**

The genus *Erethistoides* contains only a single species, *E. montana*, generally considered as having two subspecies. The species is distributed in India and attains a length of only about 5 cm. It has a moderately short, flattened body with a depressed, triangular (broader than long) head. The eyes are of moderate size. The nostrils are close together and separated by a barbel-bearing flap. There are four pairs of barbels. The skin is tuberculate or smooth, and the dorsal surface of the head and the cubitohumeral and scapular processes are rough. The teeth are villiform and in bands. No thoracic adhesive apparatus is present. The dorsal fin has a strong spine that has fine serrations on the outer edge and is denticulate on the inner edge. The adipose fin is short and low and opposite the short anal fin. The pectoral fins are low, horizontal, non-plaited, and bear a strong, flattened spine with forwardly directed spinules on the proximal half of the outer edge, backwardly directed spinules on the distal half of the outer edge, and denticulations on the inner edge. The 6-rayed ventral fins are non-plaited. The caudal fin is forked, with the lobes equal or the lower lobe the longest. The gill openings are narrow and the gill membranes are confluent with the isthmus. The

***Erethistoides montana*. (After Misra, 1976.)**

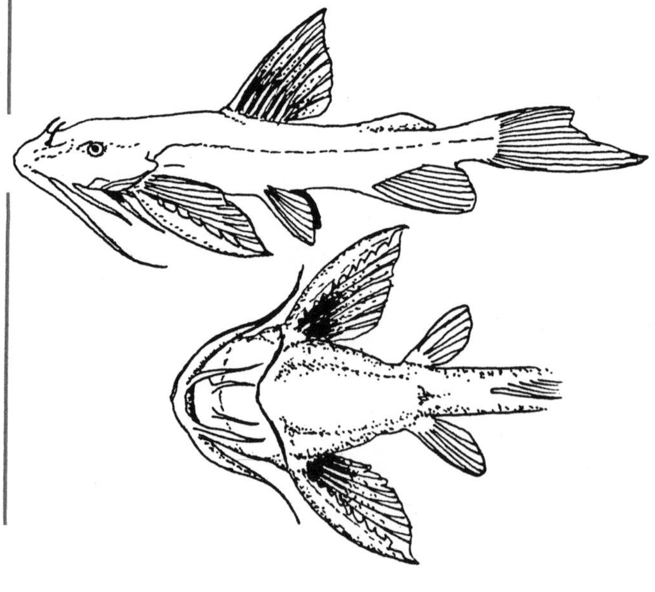

gas bladder is partially or completely enclosed in a bony capsule in two lateral globular lobes.

The genus *Conta* is represented by two species, *C. conta* and *C. elongata*, both from the Indian region, with the largest (*C. elongata*) attaining a length of about 8 cm. This genus has a more elongate body that is subcylindrical and not much flattened ventrally. The head is slightly depressed and flattened ventrally. The eyes are small. The skin is tuberculated and there is an elongate adhesive apparatus that extends from the gill openings to

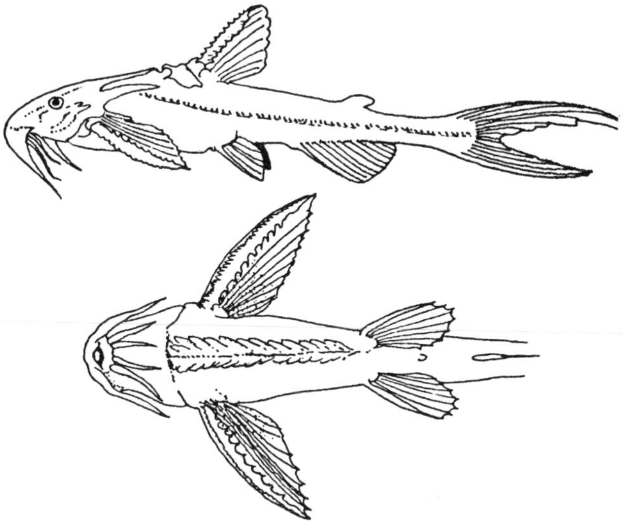

***Conta conta*. (After Jayaram, 1977.)**

the pelvics. The four pairs of barbels are all ringed with black and white. The teeth are villiform in both jaws. The short dorsal fin has a strong spine that is serrated on both edges, and there is a short adipose fin located above the last third of the anal fin with a long interdorsal space. The pectoral fins are low, non-plaited, and provided with a strong flattened spine that is serrated on both edges, the outer serrations pointed backward and the inner serrations pointed forward. The 6-rayed ventral fins are non-plaited. The caudal fin is forked, the upper lobe longer and filamentous. The caudal peduncle is long and narrow, and the lateral line has prominent tubercles. The gill openings are narrow and the gill membranes are confluent with the isthmus. The gas bladder is two-chambered, the chambers connected by horizontal tubes, and covered by bony plates posteriorly.

The genus *Hara* is represented by four species in the Indian region, *H. filamentosus, H. hara, H. jerdoni,* and *H. horai,* the largest attaining a length of about 13.5 cm. The body is moderately elongate and flattened ventrally. The head is depressed, also ventrally flattened, and as broad or broader than long. The eyes are small and there are four pairs of barbels present. The nostrils are set close together and separated by a flap bearing the nasal barbel. The teeth are villiform and set in bands in the jaws. The dorsal fin is short and has a spine that is serrated on its inner edge. There is a short, low adipose fin present opposite the short anal fin. The pectoral fins are low, horizontal, non-plaited, and with a strong spine that is denticulated on the inner

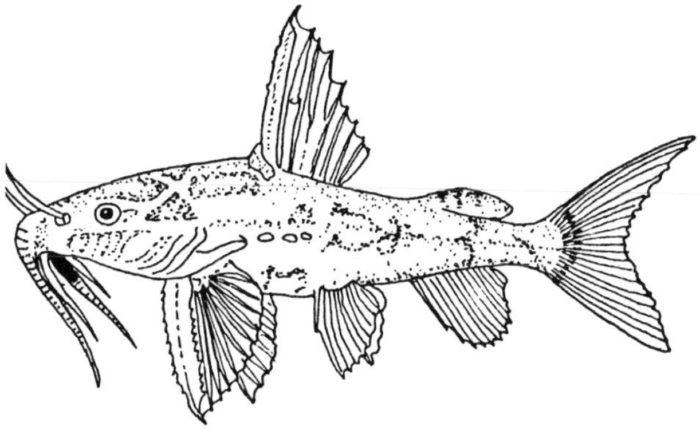

***Hara hara*. (After Jayaram, 1977.)**

edge and serrated on its outer edge; the six-rayed ventral fins are non-plaited. The caudal fin is forked, the upper lobe filamentous or the lower lobe slightly longer. The gill openings are narrow and the gill membranes are confluent with the isthmus. The skin is tuberculate with granular pores on the chest. The gas bladder is two-chambered, lodged in deep pits, and partially enclosed in bone.

Kottelat (1983) had misgivings in accepting *Erethistoides* Hora and *Hara* Blyth as valid genera but without adequate material preferred to use Hora's nomenclature until more investigations were completed.

The genus *Pseudolaguvia* contains but a single species, *P. tuberculatus*, that was found in a hill stream in Burma. As the specific name implies, the body is roughened with minute tubercles. The body is otherwise moderately

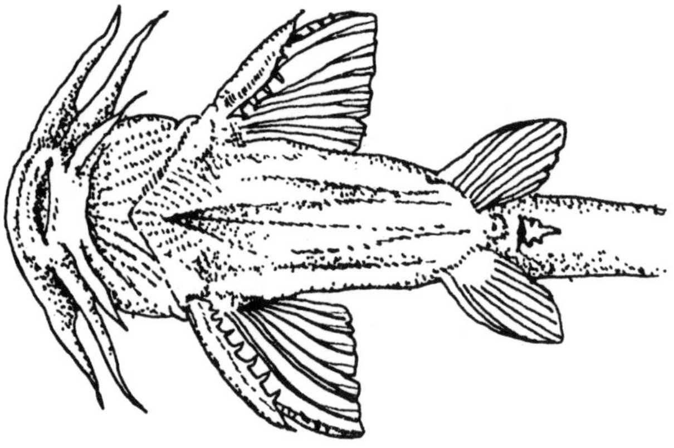

Pseudolaguvia tuberculatus. (After Misra, 1976.)

elongate and subcylindrical, and the head is depressed and longer than broad. The lips are thick, fleshy, and papillated, and the eyes are small. The nostrils are close together, separated by a flap bearing the nasal barbel. There are four pairs of short barbels, the maxillary and mandibular pairs being ringed with black and white. The villiform teeth in the jaws are in bands. There is a well developed adhesive apparatus that is much longer than broad and with an elongate depression medially. The cubitohumeral is conspicuous. The dorsal fin has a strong spine that is serrated on its inner edge. The adipose fin is longer than the dorsal and is continuous with it; a short anal fin lies below the adipose fin. The pectoral fins are situated above the level of the ventral fins, are horizontal, non-plaited, and bear a strong, flat spine that is serrated on its inner edge and roughened on its outer edge. The 6-rayed pelvic fins are non-plaited. The caudal fin is forked. The gill openings are wide and the gill membranes are confluent with the isthmus. The gas bladder is enclosed in bone.

The genus *Laguvia* is a small genus of only three species, *L. asperus*, *L. ribeiroi*, and *L. shawi*, from India, Nepal, Burma, and China. They are small-sized species attaining a length of approximately 3-4.5 cm. The body is moderately elongate and subcylindrical, and the head is slightly depressed. The lips are thick and the nostrils are set close together, separated by a flap bearing the nasal barbel. There are four pairs of short barbels, the maxillary pair being broad-based and ringed with black and white. The eyes are small. The villiform teeth are in bands in the jaws. The chest or thorax is not flattened very much and the poorly developed adhesive apparatus is composed of longitudinal plaits of skin. The cubitohumeral and scapular processes are prominent. The skin is mostly smooth, with the cubitohumeral, scapular, and occipital regions tuberculated. The short dorsal fin has a strong spine that may be serrated or not. A short adipose fin is located

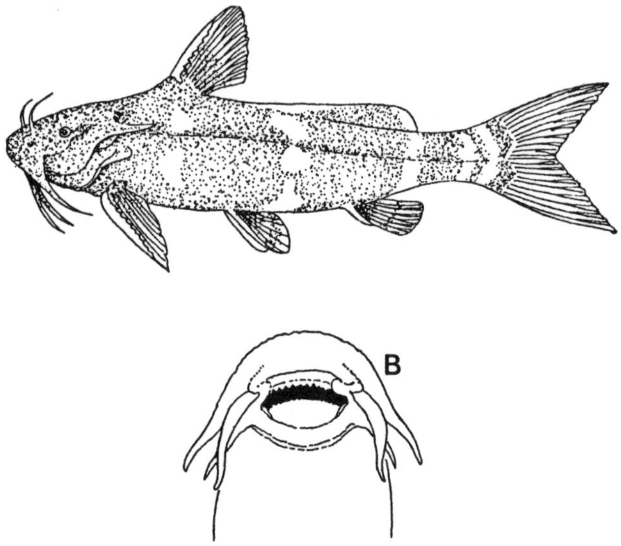

Laguvia asperus; (b) ventral view of mouth. (After Mista, 1976; (b) After Jayaram, 1977.)

above the short anal fin. The pectoral fins are non-plaited, and neither are the 9-10 rayed ventral fins. The caudal fin is forked or semicircular. The gill openings are wide and the gill membranes are confluent with the isthmus. The gas bladder is two-chambered and partially enclosed in bone.

The genus *Glyptothorax* is a larger genus with approximately 35 species ranging in size from about 6.5 cm to 22 cm in length. The genus is wide ranging, extending from Syria in the west to China in the east and extending southward to Sumatra, Java, and Borneo. The species are inhabitants of mountain streams, where they are aided in maintaining themselves against the strong currents by means of an adhesive disc. They have an elongate, subterete body and a greatly depressed, broad head that is covered with soft skin. The mouth has thick, often papillate, lips for adhesion, and the villiform teeth are situated in crescentric bands in the jaws. The eyes are small, superior, and covered by skin; they are not far apart. The nostrils are close, separated by a flap bearing the nasal barbel. There are four pairs of short barbels; the maxillary pair are longer than the others, have a broad base, and do not extend beyond the middle of the pectoral fins. The chest or thorax is flattened, with a "U"- or "V"-shaped adhesive apparatus composed of longitudinal plaits of skin giving it a corrugated appearance. The cubitohumeral and scapular processes are not prominent. The dorsal fin is provided with a weak or a strong spine, and there is a short adipose fin above the anal fin. The pectoral

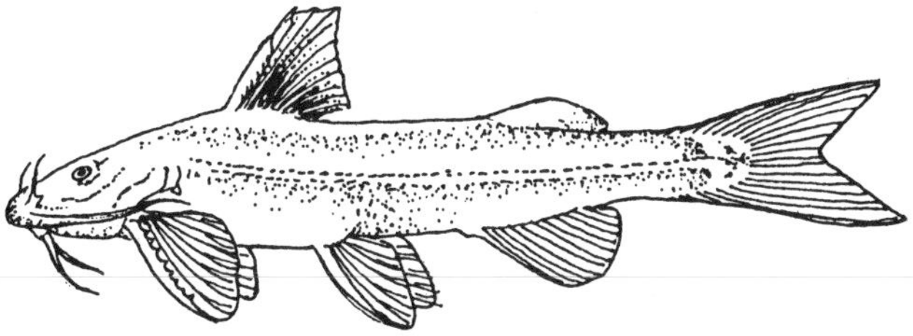

***Glyptothorax trilineatus*. (After Jayaram, 1977.)**

fins are low, plaited or not, horizontal, and have a strong spine that is sharply denticulated on the inner edge. The 6-rayed ventral fins are plaited or not and are located posterior to the dorsal. The caudal fin is forked. An anal papilla may be present or absent. The gill openings are wide and the gill membranes are confluent with the isthmus; the gill rakers are large. The gas bladder is divided into two lateral chambers partially or entirely encased in bone.

Glyptothorax major of Borneo and Thailand inhabits clear streams over rocky bottoms. A female of this species some 6.5 cm long, taken from a waterfall brook, had some well-developed ova. Also, *G. platypogonoides*, which attains a maximum length of some 12 cm, that were collected at Lahat, Sumatra, included a 7.4 cm female that had its belly distended with ripe eggs.

The genus *Bagarius* contains three species: *B. bagarius*, from the Ganges, Chao Phrya, and Mekong basins; *B. yarrelli*, widely distributed in southern and southeastern Asia

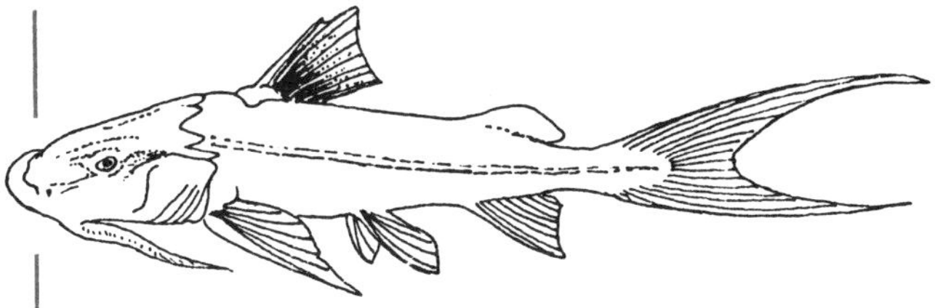

***Bagarius bagarius*. (After Misra, 1976.)**

(Ganges to Java); and *B. suchus*, from the Mekong basin in Laos and Thailand. The body is elongate and flattened ventrally to the ventrals. The broad head is naked, osseus, rugose, and depressed. The eyes are small, and the nostrils are close together, the posterior nostril provided with the nasal barbel. There are four pairs of barbels. The broad mouth is terminal or slightly inferior. The teeth are unequal and located in crescentric bands in the jaws. The skin is scabrous. A thoracic adhesive apparatus is absent and an auxiliary pore is present. The dorsal fin is provided with a relatively smooth spine and there is an adipose fin present. The pectoral fins are low, lateral, and have 9-14 rays and a strong spine that is serrated on the inner edge. The ventral fins are horizontal and have 6 rays. The caudal fin is deeply forked, with the upper lobe the longer. The dorsal and pectoral fins as well as both caudal lobes may have filamentous extensions. The gill openings are wide and the gill membranes are free or narrowly attached to the isthmus. There is a small gas bladder with two lateral chambers enclosed in bone.

Bagarius yarrelli is rather large, reaching a length in excess of 2 meters, with a weight of up to 113 kilograms. It inhabits rapids, where it can be found among the boulders, often in the white water of the rapids, where it apparently is indifferent to the strong current. In Thailand it is said to occur in the larger streams in fresh and tidal waters, but it is not abundant anywhere. It is a voracious predatory fish feeding primarily on prawns, but it will also take small fishes and aquatic insects. In other areas, where it is known as Goonch, it inhabits the same areas as the Mahseer (*Tor* spp.). Fishermen angling for the Mahseer often lose their bait to this fish; it is therefore in great disfavor with them. Even so, it is a locally valuable food fish.

Most references to *Bagarius bagarius*, a smaller species (to 19.2 cm), appear to actually be *B. yarrelli. B. bagarius* feeds mainly on aquatic insects, with occasional small fishes and crustaceans taken. *B. suchus* feeds mainly on fishes.

The genus *Gagata* contains approximately nine species ranging in size from 5 to 30 cm. They are from the fresh and tidal waters of India and Pakistan to Nepal, Burma, and Sumatra. The body is moderately elongate, compressed, and flattened ventrally to the ventral fins. The head is broadly pointed, snub-nosed or conical, with sharp longitudinal ridges and covered by thin smooth skin. The eyes are large or moderate, covered by skin. The skin of the body is also smooth. The mouth is small, transverse, and ventrally positioned. The teeth are small, villiform in the jaws, and the palate is edentulous. The nostrils are far apart in some species and close together in others, the posterior nostril bearing the nasal barbel. There are four pairs of barbels: the nasal barbels are small and thin and are prolongations of the broad flaps that separate the two nostrils on each side; the maxillary barbels have stiff basal portions (osseus proximally) and are provided with membranous flaps along their inner surface. The lips are thick in some species, thin in others, and continuous at the angle of the mouth. They are somewhat fimbriated; the post-labial grooves are restricted around the corners of the mouth. The cubitohumeral process is well-developed or not. The short dorsal fin is provided with a strong spine, and there is a short but prominent adipose fin. The pectoral fins are horizontal, positioned above the level of the ventral fins, and have a strong spine that is denticulate internally. The ventral fins are also horizontal and possess 6 rays. The anal fin is short, and the caudal fin is deeply forked. The gill openings are fairly wide and extend to the ventral surface; the gill membranes are confluent with the isthmus and may be deeply notched. The gas bladder is divided into two rounded portions, partially enclosed in bone, and in direct contact with the outer skin above the pectoral fins. There are 5 to 7 branchiostegal rays.

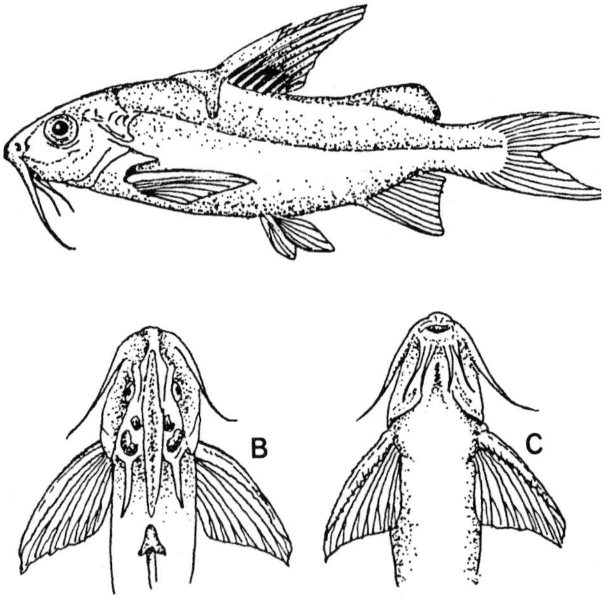

Gagata cenia; dorsal (b) and ventral (c) views of head. (After Jayaram, 1977; b and c after Misra, 1976.)

The species *G. itchkeea, G. nangra, G. robusta*, and *G. viridescens* have the mandibular barbels inserted at different levels and are sometimes referred to *Nangra* Day (*Gagata* in the restricted sense would have the mandibular barbels in a single row). The recently established *Sundagagata* is also very similar to *Gagata*. Its single species, *S. robusta*, occurs well south of the range of other *Gagata* species except the poorly known *G. schmidti*, which may actually belong to *Sundagagata*.

The genus *Sundagagata* contains one or two species, *S. robusta* from Java and (?) *S. schmidti* from Sumatra. The body is relatively robust, rounded in cross-section, but the posterior portion and caudal peduncle are moderately compressed. The head is depressed, with a strongly depressed snout. The head lacks a distinct median groove or bordering ridges, and the fontanels are small (*robusta*) to possibly wanting (*schmidti*). The occipital process extends to the predorsal plate. The predorsal plate is semicircular in outline and without the recurved posterior process. The eyes are small, included more than 10 times in the head length, and the nostrils cover only a small area of the snout. The mouth is rather wide and the teeth are small and villiform;

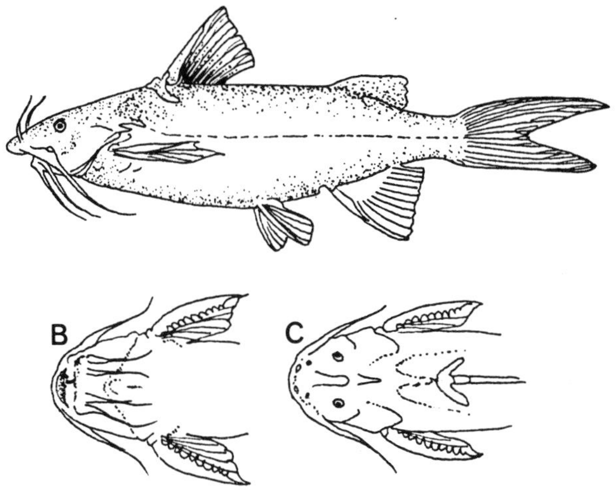

Sundagagata robusta; ventral (b) and dorsal (c) views of head. (After Boeseman, 1966.)

there are no teeth on the palate. Four pairs of barbels are present; the maxillary pair is ossified on the basal portion, the mandibular barbels arranged in a straight transverse line. The dorsal fin has a strong spine and 6 rays, the spine with coarse serrae posteriorly. The adipose fin is rather short and tall, distant from the dorsal. The anal fin has 13-14 rays. The pectoral fins have a strong and curved spine with strong serrae along the interior margin and a few granulations along the outer, and 8-10 rays. The ventral fins are situated well behind the dorsal; the caudal fin is forked. (Boeseman, 1966.)

S. robusta was collected in a stream that, although not a torrential mountain stream, frequently during heavy rainfall does almost appear like one. It is locally rather muddy but with rocks and some vegetation. Boeseman (1966) noted that the aspect of *robusta* was not that of mountain torrent species and that the rocks or vegetation supplied shelter when the stream became torrential.

The subfamily Glyptosterninae contains about eight genera that can be distinguished by the following key:

1a. Thoracic adhesive apparatus consisting of transverse folds of skin present........ .... *Pseudecheneis*
1b. Thoracic adhesive apparatus of transverse folds of skin absent................ 2
2a. Gill openings narrow, restricted to upper parts of head................................ 4
2b. Gill openings broad, restricted to upper parts of head or extending to lower surface of head................................. 3
3a. Gill openings extending to lower surface of head .... *Glyptosternon*
3b. Gill openings restricted to upper parts of head........................ *Glaridoglanis*
4a. Upper jaw teeth in 2 well-separated bands .... *Exostoma*
4b. Upper jaw teeth in a single band....... 5
5a. Teeth in both jaws pointed............... 6
5b. Teeth in both jaws not pointed .... *Oreoglanis*
6a. Postlabial groove continuous; branched pectoral fin rays 16-19........ *Myersglanis*
6b. Postlabial groove interrupted; branched pectoral fin rays 13-17..................... 7
7a. Band of teeth in upper jaw produced backward .... *Coraglanis*
7b. Band of teeth in upper jaw not produced backward .... *Euchiloglanis*

The genus *Pseudecheneis* contains a single species, *P. sulcatus*, from Nepal and northeastern India to northern Burma. It attains a length of approximately 20 cm. The body is elongate and ventrally flattened to the ventral fins, and is covered with smooth skin. The eyes are small; the nostrils are close together, separated by the nasal barbel. There are four

Pseudecheneis sulcatus. (After Jayaram, 1977.)

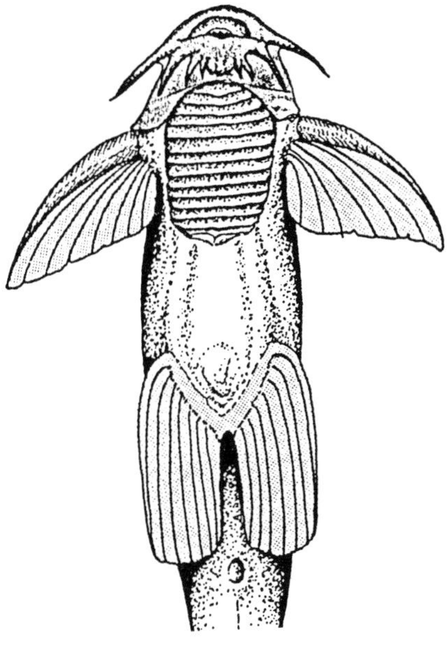

pairs of barbels, all shorter than the head. The teeth in the jaws are villiform and in bands; the lower lip is papillated medially. The dorsal fin is short, with a weak spine that is rough on its inner edge, smooth on its outer edge. An adipose fin is present, and the anal fin is short. The pectoral fins are horizontal, broadly rounded, with the first ray weak and ensheathed in thick skin. They are pectinate ventrally, bearing soft, internally pointed cartilaginous rays along the anterior margin. The ventral fins are similar, with 6 rays. The caudal fin is emarginate. The gill openings are narrow, extending a little below the first pectoral fin ray but not much further; the gill membranes are confluent with the broad isthmus. The gas bladder has rounded lateral portions that are enclosed in bone. There is a sucker-like oval thoracic (between the pectoral fins) adhesive apparatus consisting of about 13 or 14 transverse muscular folds. The epidermis of these ridges is modified, having two spinous layers, two intermediate rows of partly formed spines, and three to four layers of polygonal epithelial cells. The epidermis is normal (without spines) in the grooves, although there may be a few mucous cells and sensory cells scattered there at random. The worn-out spines are shed along with their basal cells, whose caps are detached from the tops of the spines that lie below. This second tier of already formed spines along with their basal cells moves forward to take up their position ready for use. These spines, of course, are used to help hold the fish in place in the strong current.

The genus *Glyptosternon* (also spelled *Glyptosternum*) contains about six species with a broad distribution from eastern Turkistan and Afghanistan through Pakistan and India to eastern Tibet and western China. The species attain lengths of between 15 and 25 cm. They have an elongate body that is flattened ventrally to the base of the ventral fins. The skin is smooth dorsally, but often it is tuberculate ventrally from the head to the ventral base. Other than this there is no thoracic adhesive apparatus. The head is depressed, longer than broad or as long as broad, and is covered by soft skin. The eyes are minute, superior, and subcutaneous. The nostrils are close together, separated only by the flap bearing the nasal barbel. There are four pairs of barbels; the maxillaries are broad-based. The lips are thick and papillated, the lower labial fold interrupted in the middle. The inferior mouth contains pointed teeth that are set in bands; in the upper jaw these are produced backward at the sides. The dorsal fin is

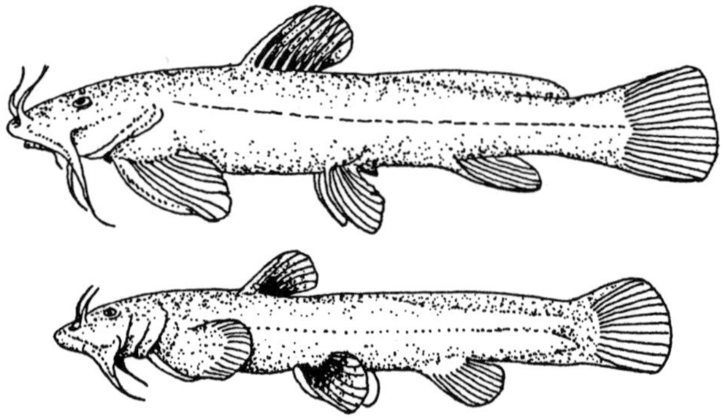

Glyptosternon maculatum (above) and _G. reticulatum_ (below). (After Jayaram, 1977.)

short and without a strong spine. There is a long, low adipose fin that may or may not be continuous with the caudal fin, and an interdorsal space may be present or absent. A short anal fin lies opposite the adipose fin; the caudal fin is truncate. The paired fins are horizontal, broadly rounded, and have the first ray weak and ensheathed in thick skin. It is pectinate ventrally and bears soft internal pointed cartilaginous rays along its inner margin. The ventrals are 6-rayed. The gill openings are wide and extend to the lower surface of the head.

Glyptosternon reticulatum, a species about 25 cm in length, is found only in the mountainous regions of southern Turkistan and northeastern Afghanistan. There they inhabit rivers with swift currents, hiding beneath rocks and adhering to them. They are very adept at this, having a very flattened body to reduce their resistance; the expanded anterior parts of their pectoral fins form a sucker with which to adhere to the rocks. The ventral fins are also swollen and help in the adhesion. *G. reticulatum* feeds mainly on invertebrates, particularly insect larvae. *Glyptosternon pectinopterum* from India is said to spawn several times in a single season.

The genus *Glaridoglanis* contains a single species, *G. andersonii*, from Yunnan and

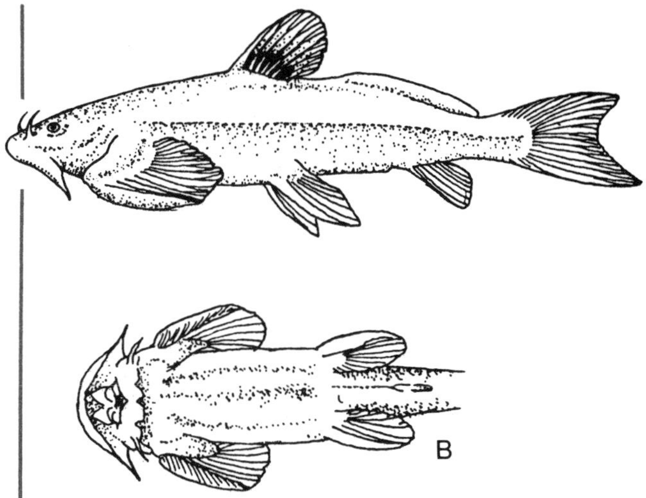

Exostoma stuarti; (b) ventral view of *E. labiatum*. (After Jayaram, 1977.)

Ponsee in China. The head and the anterior part of the body are depressed, while the tail is more or less compressed. The eyes are minute and superior in position. The teeth are very compressed, with broad, truncate, or notched apices. The teeth of the upper jaw are formed into a band that is not produced backward at the sides; those of the lower jaw form two bands that are pointed toward the sides. The mouth is subterminal, and the folds of the lower lip are broadly interrupted. There are four pairs of barbels; the maxillary pair is broad-based and bears striated pads of adhesive skin on the ventral surface of their outer half. The dorsal fin, as well as the other fins, lacks a spine. The first rays of the paired fins are soft and pinnate, with soft, pointed, cartilaginous rays along the anterior margin ensheathed in the fin membrane. The skin of the ventral surface of these fins along the outer rays is produced into pinnate folds as an adhesive device. The gill openings are wide and extend to a point opposite the pectoral fin base, but they do not extend below to the ventral surface.

The genus *Exostoma* contains five species from the area of India, southern China, and Burma. They attain a length of around 5 to 11 cm. The body is elongate and greatly flattened ventrally to the base of the ventral fins, and the tail is compressed. The head is depressed, as long as broad, and covered with soft skin. The skin of the body is soft and sparsely covered with minute papillae ventrally anterior to the ventral fin bases. The eyes are small to minute, superior in position, and subcutaneous. The nostrils are close together, separated by a flap bearing the nasal barbel. There are four pairs of barbels; the maxillaries are broad-based and bear on their ventral surfaces in the outer half striated pads of adhesive skin. The lips are thickly papillated and the fold of the lower lip is continuous. The teeth are small to rather large, movable, oar-shaped, and in two separate bands in each jaw, the outer series flattened distally and directed backward. There is no thoracic adhesive apparatus. The short dorsal fin lacks a strong spine, and the long, low adipose fin may or may not be continuous with the forked, slightly forked, or deeply lunate caudal fin. An interdorsal space is present or absent. The paired fins are horizontal, broadly rounded, the outer ray soft and pinnate, giving off soft, pointed cartilaginqus rays, ensheathed in thick skin, along the anterior margin. A short anal fin lies below the adipose fin. The gill openings are broad to narrow, extending to below the middle of the pectoral fin base or opposite the first ray of the pectoral but do not extend to the ventral surface of the head; the gill membranes are broad and free throughout their length. The gas bladder is partially enclosed in bone.

The genus *Oreoglanis* contains only two species, *O. macropterum* and *O. siamensis*, from Burma and Thailand respectively. The body is elongate and flattened ventrally to the ventral fin base. The head is depressed, as broad as long, and covered by soft skin. The body skin is smooth. The eyes are small, superior in position, and covered with skin. The nostrils are close together, separated by a flap bearing the nasal barbel. There are four pairs of barbels, the maxillaries broad-based. The lips are thick, papillated, and the lower labial fold is continuous. The teeth are pointed in the upper jaw and set in a broad band that is interrupted in the middle. The anterior teeth in the lower jaw are long, with a slender base and an expanded, truncate tip, and the posterior teeth are like those in the upper jaw. There is no thoracic adhesive apparatus. The soft dorsal fin is without a strong spine, and the adipose fin is long and

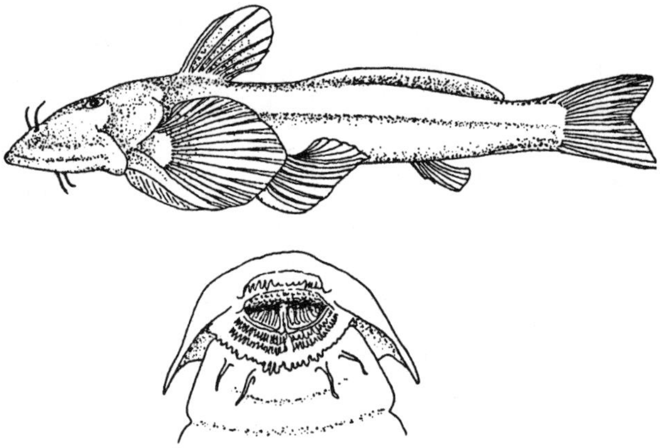

Oreoglanis siamensis. (After H. M. Smith, 1933.)

low. There is an interdorsal space. The paired fins are horizontally positioned, broadly rounded, with the first ray weak and ensheathed in thick skin. It is pectinate ventrally with internal soft, pointed cartilaginous rays along the anterior margin. The short anal fin lies below the adipose fin, and the caudal fin is deeply lunate. The gill openings are narrow, extending to opposite the level of the last pectoral fin ray.

Oreoglanis siamensis comes from fairly cold, clear, swift streams or swift brooks. H. M. Smith made some very interesting observations on this species as follows: "In normal resting attitude, the fish kept its adhesive apparatus in action even in water having no current. It attached itself indifferently to any surface—stone, glass, porcelain, wood basket work or vegetation—and the sucking action of the lower lip was supplemented by corrugations on the front and sides of the head. The respiratory movements of the opercular flaps were rapid but not very marked. As the fish faced the current the long nasal barbels were fully extended vertically and at their base the nostrils were conspicuous as triangular openings, the apex of which reached nearly half the length of the barbels. There was no obvious current of water into the mouth and out of the branchial openings; possibly a feeble current of water to the gills through the branchial openings was induced by the movements of the gill flaps."

The genus *Myersglanis* contains a single species, *M. blythi*, from Nepal. It attains a length of about 7 cm. The body is elongate and flattened ventrally to the base of the ventral fins. The head is depressed and covered with soft skin; the skin of the body is smooth. The eyes are minute, superior in position, and covered by skin. The nostrils are close together, separated by a flap bearing the nasal barbel. There are four pairs of barbels, the maxillaries being broad-based. The lips are thick and papillated, and the lower labial fold is continuous. The teeth are conical and in a band in each jaw, the band of the upper jaw continuous and not produced backward at the sides, the band in the lower jaw being divided in the center and pointed backward toward the sides. There is no thoracic adhesive apparatus. The short dorsal fin is without a strong spine and the long, low adipose fin may or may not be confluent with the caudal fin. The adipose fin is separated by a considerable distance from the dorsal fin. The paired fins are horizontal, flattened, broadly rounded, with the first ray weak; the skin of the ventral surface of this outer ray is corrugated in pinnate folds for adhesion, the ray itself is ensheathed in thick skin pectinate ventrally, and with internal soft, pointed cartilaginous rays along its anterior margin. The short anal fin is located below the adipose fin; the caudal fin may be lunate, truncate, emarginate, or even forked. The gill openings are narrow, extending to below the middle of the base of the first pectoral fin ray; the gill membranes are broad and free. The gas bladder is partially enclosed in bone.

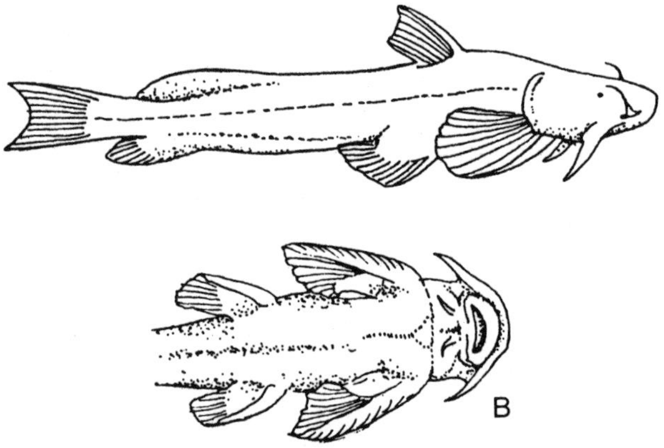

Myersglanis blythi; (b) ventral view. (After Misra, 1976.)

The genus *Coraglanis* contains a single species, *C. kishinouyei,* with a distribution from the eastern Himalayas to China. The length of this species is about 13 cm. The body is elongate and flattened ventrally to the base of the ventral fins. The head is depressed, slightly

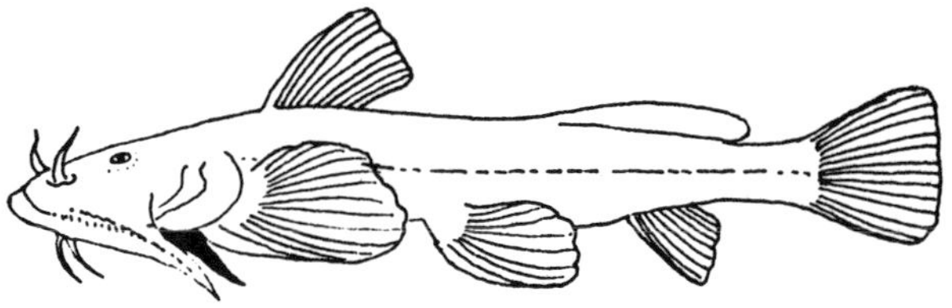

Coraglanis kishinouyei.

longer than broad, and covered with soft skin. The snout is considerably depressed and broad anteriorly, and the eyes are small and superiorly placed. The mouth is subterminal. The teeth are pointed, those in the upper jaw forming a continuous band that is produced backward at the sides, those of the lower jaw in an interrupted band, the ends pointing toward the sides. The thick upper lip is papillated and continuous with the fold of the lower lip at the angles of the mouth; the postlabial groove is broadly interrupted. The nostrils are close together, separated by a flap bearing the nasal barbel. There are four pairs of barbels, the maxillary pair being very broad-based and bearing on the outer half of their ventral surface striated pads of adhesive skin. There is no thoracic adhesive apparatus. The dorsal fin has 6 branched rays and no spine. The adipose fin is long and low and is separated from the caudal fin by a short distance; an interdorsal space is present. The paired fins are horizontal, broad, and rounded, with strong spines. The outer rays of the pectoral and ventral fins are thick, flattened, and pectinate ventrally. The anal fin is short, and the caudal fin is obliquely truncate or somewhat rounded. The gill openings are restricted, not extending below the pectoral base and not extending dorsally beyond just above the base of the pectoral fin spine; the gill membrane is broad and free throughout its length.

The genus *Euchiloglanis* includes approximately seven species distributed in India, Tibet, Nepal, China, and Burma. They are small to medium-sized catfishes that are elongate and greatly flattened ventrally. The head and anterior part of the body are depressed, and the tail is compressed. The skin is soft, and on the ventral surface there are minute papillae. The head is as long as broad or longer than broad. The eyes are minute, subcutaneous, and superior in position, not being visible from the ventral surface. The mouth is inferior and the teeth are pointed, those in the upper jaw in a continuous or partially divided band that is not produced backward at the sides. The nostrils are close together, separated by a flap bearing the nasal barbel. There are four pairs of barbels: nasal, maxillary, and two pairs of mandibular barbels. The maxillary pair are very broad-based and bear striated pads of adhesive skin on the ven-

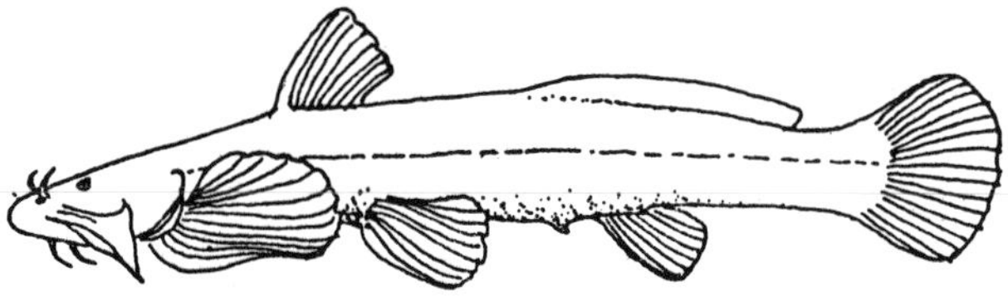

Euchiloglanis davidi.

tral surface of the outer half. The lips are thick and papillated, and the lower labial fold is broadly interrupted in the middle. There is no thoracic adhesive apparatus. The dorsal fin is without a strong spine. The adipose fin is low and moderately long. The paired fins are horizontal, broad, and rounded, the first ray weak, ensheathed in thick skin; the skin on the ventral surface of the first rays of these paired fins is corrugated in pinnate folds. The anal fin is short, and the caudal fin is lunate, obliquely truncate, or somewhat rounded. The gill openings are narrow and restricted to the sides of the head, extending only to opposite the middle of the pectoral spines.

The family Sisoridae is probably most closely related to the family Bagridae, differing mostly by the absence or, when it is present, the slenderness of the dorsal fin spine, and by possessing very broad-based barbels, especially the maxillary barbels. The greatly depressed head and anterior portion of the body, the flattened lower surface (which in some forms is corrugated), and the first rays of the paired fins being large and thickened seem to be adaptations to living in the swift current of mountain streams, a habitat that is preferred by many species in this family. There is also a rather strong affinity with the family Amphiliidae.

Checklist of the species of the family Sisoridae and their type localities:

Sisor Hamilton, 1822. Type species *S. rhabdophorus*.

Sisor rhabdophorus Hamilton, 1822. Northern rivers of Bengal and Bihar.

Erethistes Müller & Troschel, 1849. Type species *E. pusillus* Müller & Troschel.

Erethistes maesotensis Kottelat, 1983. Trib. of Salween River, near Mae Sot, on Thai-Burmese border.

E. pusillus Müller & Troschel, 1849. Assam.

Erethistoides Hora, 1950. Type species *E. montana* Hora.

Erethistoides montana Hora, 1950. Assam, India.

m. pipri Hora, 1950. Rihand River, Pipri, Uttar Pradesh, India.

Conta Hora, 1950. Type species *Pimelodus conta* Hamilton.

Conta conta (Hamilton, 1822). Northeastern Bengal.

C. elongata (Day, 1871). Assam, India.

Hara Blyth, 1860. Type species *Pimelodus hara* Hamilton.

Hara filamentosa Blyth, 1860. Tenasserim, India.

H. hara (Hamilton, 1822). Kosi River, Nepal.

H. horai Misra, 1976. Northern Bengal.

H. jerdoni Day, 1870. Sylhet, Bangladesh.

Pseudolaguvia Misra, 1976. Type species *Glyptothorax tuberculatus* Prashad & Mukerji.

Pseudolaguvia tuberculatus (Prashad & Mukerji, 1929). Upper Burma.

Laguvia Hora, 1921. Type species *Pimelodus asperus* McClellend.

Laguvia asperus (McClellend, 1844). Chusan, China.

L. ribeiroi Hora, 1921. Khoila River, western Bengal.

r. kapuri Tilak & Hussain, 1974. Saharanpur Dist., U.P., India.

L. shawi Hora, 1921. Darjeeling, Himalayas, India.

Glyptothorax Blyth, 1860. Type species *G. trilineatus* Blyth.

Glyptothorax anamaliensis Silas, 1951. Anamalai Hills, Kerala State, India.

G. annandalei Hora, 1923. Bhavani River, India.

G. armeniacum (Berg, 1918). Upper Araks River.

G. baramense (Fowler, 1905). Baram River, Borneo.

G. brevipinnis Hora, 1923. India (exact locality unknown).

b. alaknandi Tilak, 1969. Alaknanda River, U.P., India.

G. buchanani Smith, 1945. Meping River tributary, Thailand.

G. callopterus Smith, 1945. Peninsular Thailand.

G. cavia (Hamilton, 1822). Northern rivers of Bengal.

G. coheni Ganguly, Datta, & Sen, 1972. Bihar, India.

G. conirostre (Steindachner, 1867). Near Simla, northern Bengal.

c. poonaensis Hora, 1942. Mula Mutha River, Poona, India.

G. fuscus Fowler, 1934. Chantabun, Thailand.

G. garhwali Tilak, 1969. Pauri Garhwal, U.P., India.

G. gracilis (Günther, 1864). Nepal.

G. horai Shaw & Shebbeare, 1937. Streams of Terai, western Bengal.

G. housei Herre, 1942. Anamallai Hills, Pollachi District, Kerala, southern India.

G. kashmirensis Hora, 1923. Kashmir Valley, India.

G. kurdistanicus Berg, 1931. Kurdistan.

G. lampris Fowler, 1934. Chiengmai, Thailand.

G. lonah (Sykes, 1838). Deccan, southern India.

G. madraspatanum (Day, 1873). Bhavani River, India.

G. major (Boulenger, 1894). Borneo.

G. naziri Mirza & Naik, 1969. Zhob River, Pakistan.

G. nelsoni Ganguly, Datta, & Sen, 1972. Bihar, India.

G. pectinopterus (McClellend, 1842). Simla, northern Bengal.
G. platypogon (Valenciennes, 1840). Java.
G. platypogonoides (Bleeker, 1855). Sumatra.
G. prashadi Mukerji, 1932. Kyenchang River, lower Burma.
G. punjabensis Mirza & Kashmiri, 1971. Pakistan.
G. saisii (Jenkins, 1910). Bihar, India.
G. sinense (Regan, 1908). Tungting, China.
s. manipurensis Menon, 1954. Manipur Valley, India.
G. steindachneri (Pietschmann, 1913). Eastern Turkey.
G. stocki Mirza & Nijssen, 1978. Swat River, Pakistan.
G. stoliczkae (Steindachner, 1867). Simla, northern Bengal.
G. striatus (McClellend, 1842). Assam, India.
G. silviae Coad, 1981. Southwestern, Iran.
G. telchitta (Hamilton, 1822). Freshwater rivers of Bengal and Bihar, India.
t. sufii Bashir & Mirza, 1975. Sutlej River, Pakistan.
G. trewavasae Hora, 1919. Yenna Valley, India.
G. trilineatus Blyth, 1860. Tenasserim, Burma.

Bagarius Bleeker, 1853. Type species *Pimelodus bagarius* Hamilton.
Bagarius bagarius (Hamilton, 1822). Ganges River and its tributaries.
B. suchus Roberts, 1983. Kemrat, Thailand.
B. yarrelli Sykes, 1841. Mota Mola at Poona, India.

Gagata Bleeker, 1858. Type species *G. typus* Bleeker (= *Pimelodus gagata* Hamilton).
Gagata cenia (Hamilton, 1822). Northern Bengal.
G. gagata (Hamilton, 1822). Bengal.
G. itchkeea (Sykes, 1838). India.
G. nangra (Hamilton, 1822). Kosi River, Nepal.
G. robusta (Mirza & Awan, 1973). Jinnah Barrage (Indus River), Pakistan.
G. schmidti (Volz, 1904). Sumatra (possibly in *Sundagagata*).
G. sexualis Tilak, 1970. Yamuna River, Bihar, India.
G. viridescens (Hamilton, 1822). Northern Bengal.
G. youssoufi Rahman, 1976. Bangladesh.

Sundagagata Boeseman, 1966. Type species *S. robusta* Boeseman.
Sundagagata robusta Boeseman, 1966. River near Buitenzorg, Java

Pseudecheneis Blyth, 1860. Type species *Glyptosternon sulcatus* (McClellend, 1842).
Pseudecheneis sulcatus (McClellend, 1842). Khasi Hills, India.

Glyptosternon McClellend, 1842. Type species *G. reticulatum* McClellend.
Glyptosternon akhtari Silas, 1951. Source of the Kabul River, Afghanistan.
G. fokiensis Rendahl, 1925. Fukien, China.
G. hainanensis Nichols & Pope, 1927. Hainan, China.
G. maculatum (Regan, 1905). Lhasa, Tibet.
G. pallozonum Lin, 1934. Kwangtung, China.
G. reticulatum McClellend, 1842. Source of the Kabul River, Afghanistan (including *G. stoliczkae* (Day)).

Exostoma Blyth, 1860. Type species *Exostoma berdmorei* Blyth, 1860.
Exostoma berdmorei Blyth, 1860. Tenasserim, Burma.
E. labiatum (McClellend, 1842). Mishmee Mountains, Assam, India.
E. stuarti (Hora, 1923). Northern frontier of Burma.
E. vinciguerrae Regan, 1905. Burma.
E. yunnanensis (Tchang, 1935). Yunnan, China.

Oreoglanis Smith, 1933. Type species *O. siamensis* Smith.
Oreoglanis macropterum (Vinciguerra, 1889). Mt. Catein, Burma.
O. siamensis Smith, 1933. Mekang, Thailand.

Myersglanis Hora & Silas, 1952. Type species *Exostoma blythii* Day.
Myersglanis blythi (Day, 1869). Pharping, Nepal.

Coraglanis Hora & Silas, 1952. Type species *Euchiloglanis kishinouyei* Kimura.
Coraglanis kishinouyei (Kimura, 1934). Szechwan, China.

Glaridoglanis Norman, 1925. Type species *Exostoma andersonii* Day.
Glaridoglanis andersoni (Day, 1869). Yun-

nan, China.

Euchiloglanis Regan, 1907. Type species *Chimarrhichthys davidi* Sauvage.

Euchiloglanis davidi (Sauvage, 1874). Tibet.

E. feae (Vinciguerra, 1889). Upper Burma.

E. hodgarti (Hora, 1923). Pharping, Nepal.

E. kamengensis Jayaram, 1979. Arunachal Pradesh, India.

E. macrotrema Norman, 1925. Tonkin, Indo-China (North Vietnam).

E. myzostoma Norman, 1923. Yunnan, China.

E. sinensis Hora & Silas, 1951. Peiping, China.

Chapter 12

Family CLARIIDAE (Labyrinth Catfishes)

Plates 46–48

The family Clariidae is a fairly large family of catfishes inhabiting the fresh waters of much of Africa, through Syria, to southern and southeastern Asia to the Philippines. In addition, they have been introduced deliberately as well as accidentally into many other areas, including such places as Guam, Hawaii, and Florida. They range from quite small to giants well over a meter in length and have little to great commercial value depending upon the species and the area involved. Food items may range from insects to fishes and at times may even include plankton or algae.

The body is naked, elongate, and torpedo-shaped (subcylindrical), with many of the species very eel-like (anguilliform). The head may be depressed and often covered with bony plates forming a casque that covers a diverticulum of the gill cavity; or it may be globular and covered with skin. The eyes may be lateral, with or without free orbital margins, or they may be absent altogether. The nostrils are far apart, with the anterior tubular and the posterior slit-like and located just behind the nasal barbel. There are generally four pairs of barbels, often very long: the nasal pair, the maxillary pair, the mandibular pair, and the mental pair. The mouth is terminal, transverse, with villiform teeth in bands in the jaws. The vomerine teeth are also villiform, disposed in a crescentic band or coalesced with the band of premaxillary teeth. The occipital process does not extend as far as the basal bone of the dorsal, and there may or may not be a median longitudinal groove on the head.

The dorsal fin is usually long and many-rayed, without a spine. It commences a short distance behind the occiput and extends to the caudal region, where it may or may not be united with the caudal fin. A few species have a much shorter dorsal fin, in which case there is always an adipose fin. The anal fin is also long, without a spine, and extends to the caudal, where it may or may not be confluent with the caudal fin. The pectoral fins may be well-developed, with a strong spine serrated on both edges, or they may be small or even vestigial. The ventral fins have 6 rays. The caudal fin is usually rounded.

The swim bladder may be enclosed or not enclosed in a bony capsule. There are 7-11 branchiostegal rays. The gill openings are moderate to wide, and the gill membranes are either free from the isthmus or united with it.

What makes this family quite distinctive is the presence of an accessory breathing apparatus. This involves a much-branched (dendritic) or labyrinthic structure that is generously supplied with minute blood vessels attached to the second, third, and fourth branchial arches within an expanded cavity or pocket in front of the gills or extending backward along the spine from the gill chambers, or is vestigial, as two small bony structures corresponding to the second and fourth branchial arches. The gills themselves are relatively small and seem to be inadequate to be able to keep these fishes alive. In fact, it is said that those individuals that are prevented in some way from reaching the surface will soon suffocate. Many clariids typically inhabit stagnant, foul, or other poorly oxygenated waters, and the auxiliary breathing apparatus is necessary for their survival. Many species also come out of the water onto dry land at night in search of food and can remain out of water for long periods of time as long as they remain sufficiently moist. To aid them in this respect, the skin is relatively thick and provided with numerous mucous pores to keep it lubricated. In the dry season some species are able to bury themselves in the muddy bottom, remaining there quite contentedly until the rains return. Variations in the structure of the accessory breathing apparatus are also useful to scientists in identifying some of the very similar clariids.

As might be expected, clariids are very hardy fishes and survive well in captivity. They are quite undemanding as far as water quality is concerned and are generally long-lived. However, they are very voracious, and many species are aggressive predators that roam about the tank at night looking for food. They thrive on all types of live foods and fleshy morsels, often being so gluttonous that they wind up with a very distended belly. The bottom should be fairly soft and the tank should provide some hiding places such as caves made from rocks or dense planted areas. The recommended temperature range is 20° to 25°C.

The following key can be used to distinguish the genera of the family Clariidae.

1a. Eyes absent; unpigmented species living in caves and other subterranean waters . 2

1b. Eyes present, sometimes very small; generally pigmented (except albinos), usually with at least some dark coloration on back................................ 3

2a. No epibranchial respiratory organ present; epiotics well developed; confined to Africa.............................. *Uegitglanis*

2b. Epibranchial respiratory organ present; epiotics reduced or absent; confined to India............................... *Horaglanis*

3a. Two dorsal fins present, the first rayed, the second an adipose fin................. 4

3b. A single many-rayed dorsal fin......... 5

4a. Adipose fin large; lateral regions of bony cranium protected by bony plates .... *Heterobranchus*

4b. Adipose fin small; lateral regions of bony cranium not protected by bony plates .... *Dinotopterus*

5a. Eyes with a free orbital rim (its marginal border marked by a groove); vertical fins confluent or not....................... 6

5b. Eye without a free border (marginal border not grooved, the limits imprecise); vertical fins always confluent... 10

6a. Bony cranium at surface, with lateral

Species of *Clarias* are hardy aquarium fishes, some of which have interesting patterns. They are also voracious predators so cannot be kept with small fishes. Photo by Gerhard Marcuse.

dermal bone variably developed; vomerine teeth and premaxillary teeth in non-continuous bands 7

6b. Bony cranium not at surface, very narrow and without lateral dermal bone; premaxillary and vomerine teeth forming some continuous bands .... *Tanganikallabes*

7a. Branchial organ present 9

7b. No branchial organ 8

8a. Head length 15-18% of standard length, its width 85-100% of its length; width of median cranial roof at most 30% width of head; lateral dermosphenotic and supraorbital bones very reduced, separated by a space longer than the longer of the two; 59-62 vertebrae .... *Platyclarias*

8b. Head length 20-21% of standard length, its width 75% of its length; median cranial roof broad, at least 50% width of head; lateral dermosphenotic and supraorbital bones large, separated by a moderate space much narrower than the longer of the two; body depth 12.6-15.6% of the standard length; 51-52 vertebrae, 8 pairs of ribs .... *Xenoclarias*

9a. Vertical fins confluent .... *Prophagorus*

9b. Dorsal, anal, and caudal fins separate ... . *Clarias*

10a. Body depth included 15 to 20 times in its length; paired fins present or absent. 11

10b. Body depth included maximum of 10 times in length; pectoral and ventral fins usually present .... *Clariallabes*

11a. Accessory respiratory apparatus present but more or less reduced; body width about equal to its depth or up to only 1-1/4 times greater; head width less than twice its depth and 68-74% of its length; ventral fins reduced or absent; pectorals 1/4 to 2/5 of head, vestigial, or absent .. 12

11b. Accessory respiratory apparatus entirely absent; body width twice or a little less than twice its depth; head width twice or more than twice its depth and 77-93% of its length; ventrals large, 2/5 of head; pectorals 3/5 to 2/3 of head; head grooved longitudinally; median cranial crest not visible, its minimum width 15% of total width of head; 71 vertebrae, 5 pairs of ribs .... *Platyallabes*

12a. Head longitudinally grooved; median cranial crest not visible, its minimum width 20% of total width of head; pectorals 1/4 to 2/5 of head; ventrals small or absent; 89-106 vertebrae; 6 to 10 pairs of ribs 13

12b. Head not longitudinally grooved; median cranial crest visible, its minimum width 36-38% of total width of head; pectoral and ventral fins absent or pectorals vestigial; 102-105 vertebrae; 15-17 pairs of ribs .... *Channallabes*

13a. Body very elongate, about 20 times as long as deep; 106 vertebrae, 6 pairs of ribs; eyes vestigial under the skin or invisible .... *Dolichallabes*

13b. Body less elongate, about 14-15 times as long as deep; 89 vertebrae; 10 pairs of ribs; eyes very small but visible .... *Gymnallabes*

The genus *Clarias* is by far the largest genus of the family, with some 45 species and a range approximating that of the family itself, from Africa to the Philippines. Many of the species are quite common and are commercially important as food fishes in several areas. Some even have a reputation for having wholesome qualities and are commonly fed to invalids and convalescents. Because of their ability to exist out of water for considerable periods of time, these catfishes are regularly offered for sale alive in markets because they can be kept in baskets and tubs with very little water or even no water at all as long as they are kept moist. They are also able to travel across dry land for considerable distances, wriggling along with the help of their fins. They feed mostly on fishes and invertebrates, but some will even take algae. The body is elongate and torpedo-shaped (subcylindrical) to the area of the ventral fins then compressed posteriorly. The head is depressed and covered with bony plates that are superficially rugose. The occipital process does not reach the basal bone of the dorsal, and there is a median longitudinal groove present. The eyes are small, superior in position, and with free orbital margins. The nasal openings are well separated from each other, the anterior nostrils being short and tubular,

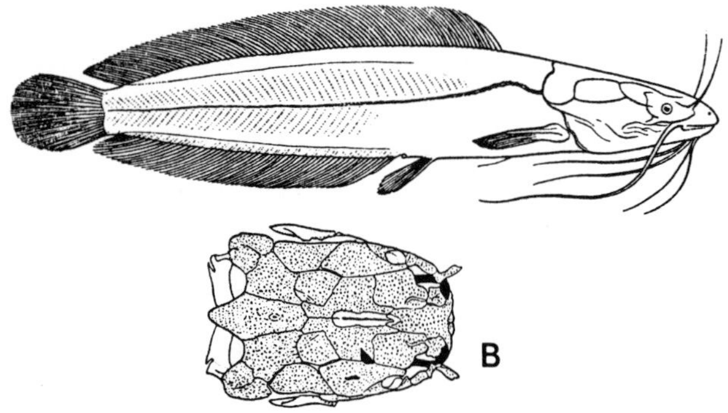

Clarias gariepinus; (b) dorsal view of skull. (From Poll, 1957.)

while the posterior nostrils are slit-like and provided with a barbel at the border. Four pairs of barbels are present: a maxillary pair, a nasal pair, and two mandibular pairs. The mouth is terminal, transverse, with the upper jaw the longer. The teeth are villiform and in bands in the jaws and a crescentic band on the vomer. There is a long-based rayed dorsal fin with no spine that extends to, but is not confluent with, the caudal fin. There is no adipose fin. The anal fin is long-based and, like the dorsal fin, is not confluent with the rounded caudal fin. The pectoral fins are well developed, and the first ray is transformed into a spine. The swim bladder is small and ensheathed in a bony capsule. There are 7 to 9 branchiostegals. The gill openings are wide and the gill membranes are free from the isthmus. There is a well-developed accessory breathing organ attached to the second, third, and fourth branchial arches.

In general *Clarias* will breed in the early months of the summer rainy season. The fish prefer flooded grassy areas, where after a heavy rain the pair ready to spawn can be seen wriggling through the grass in water barely deep enough to cover them. At this time they are quite exposed and very vulnerable to predators. The eggs hatch in a very short time, and the larval time is short as well.

Clarias batrachus is fairly widely distributed in southeastern Asia from India to the Philippines. It has been introduced and has become very successfully established in many other areas around the world. This is the species that received a great deal of publicity in Florida when it escaped from the retaining ponds of tropical fish wholesalers and became established in the canals and natural waterways of the southern part of the state. There was much concern that this new introduction would upset the delicate ecological balance of the Everglades or other similar areas (it did to some extent). Attaining lengths of up to 55 cm, this species inhabits a wide variety of waters both brackish and fresh, including rivers, canals, lakes, and even swamps, and is well established in nature in both its normal dark coloration as well as an albino. The albino is described as pinkish white with a yellowish tinge on the upper surface of the head. Albinos were frequently encountered in northern Thailand (Fowler, 1934). Since this species has an accessory breathing apparatus it can survive in water so foul that other fishes cannot live with it. Even if conditions get so bad it cannot live there itself, it can leave in search of better areas by using wriggling or snake-like movements with the aid of its powerful pectoral fins, which are provided with strong spines. This method of propulsion is capable of moving the eel-like body overland at a respectable rate of speed, somewhat reducing their exposure to potential predators. While this catfish is making the journey, the small gill openings are kept tightly closed to prevent the loss of moisture so that the delicate gills and dendritic organs do not dry out. Attempts at eradication of *Clarias* from certain ponds or other bodies of water have not met with a high degree of success, for the fish when so threatened will simply "get up and walk away!"

Clarias batrachus is known to move into Indian rice fields when they become flooded at the beginning of the rainy season and spawn there. The eggs are generally deposited in nests that may be constructed in submerged bushes and are guarded by the male. The male is more brightly colored and there is a dark blotch at the posterior end of the dorsal fin; the female has no dark markings in the dorsal fin and she is less colorful.

Very young specimens are suitable for large aquaria (though importation is now illegal in many areas), and this species has been known to live in captivity for many years, reaching a length of more than 40 cm. The bottom material should be relatively soft and there should be many hiding places. Only very sturdy plants should be provided if plants are desired for the aquarium. The water conditions seem to be of little importance, and a temperature range of 20° to 25°C suits them just fine although they can withstand a range of between 10° and 32°C if necessary. This species is quite voracious and should not be kept with smaller fishes, which are apt to disappear during the night. It prefers worms or worm-like foods but will greedily accept almost anything offered until its belly becomes quite distended. If this species decides to jump out of the tank and is not noticed for several hours it can usually survive provided it has not become too dried out.

Clarias batrachus has spawned in home aquaria. A number of young were raised in a 1.2-meter tank that was kept at a temperature of 26°C; two gallons of water were changed each day. It was noticed that a male 29 cm long began chasing a 31-cm female around the tank. After a great deal of the back and forth activity the male wrapped his body around the female's head in a "U" shape, an act that was to be repeated often over the next one and a half hours. Both spawners gathered loose material from around the tank into a nest in the center of the tank and nudged each other gently around the genital region. With the dorsal fin flicking as an apparent signal, the back and forth chasing started up again. Finally the male wrapped his body around that of the female and the fish swam in a tight circle over the nest, the male inside the female. After about five minutes a stream of adhesive eggs appeared, and after another minute or two the female started swimming around the tank again. She returned to the male after a couple of laps and the spawning act was repeated. Some half a dozen more spawning acts occurred before one parent patrolled the tank while the other stood guard immediately over the nest. The eggs were described as about 1/2 mm in diameter with a slight gray tint. They hatched in about 24 hours, and the fry were free-swimming in three days.

Clarias gareipinus inhabits a variety of waters in Africa, where it can reach a length of up to 140 cm and a weight of 60 kilos (actually with increased fishing pressure individuals of about 70 cm or less are more common). Although most are encountered in fresh water, individuals may also be found in brackish waters of the upper reaches of estuaries. *C. gareipinus* consumes a wide variety of different foods, but it is particularly fond of small fishes when it has matured. Its flesh is tasty and good eating, therefore it has become a fairly important source of protein in some areas and is the object of aquaculture because of its hardiness, rapid growth, ease of feeding, and ease of handling.

It spawns in small temporary streams that are created during the season when flooding occurs. Large numbers migrate upriver or to lake shores to spawn, usually in early summer once the first heavy rains of the rainy season have started. Spawning itself usually takes place at night in shallow water. After hatching, the young catfish remain in these shallow waters with a lot of plant life for about six months, after which they migrate downstream before the waters start to recede.

In Lake Victoria the spawning fish quickly enter the papyrus swamps after the rains and remain there for about three days. The eggs are about 2 mm in diameter or less, with an adhesive disc, and hatch in about 23 to 30 hours at 22° to 28°C. The eggs appear to remain unguarded. The young are first evident in small groups of half a dozen to a dozen. The males are said to have an elongated sexual organ with a cone-shaped tip; females have a sex organ but there is no cone-shaped tip.

Although *C. gareipinus* is sometimes found in open water it is more common in shallow marginal areas. Like its close relatives, it can survive in poorly oxygenated water and can leave the water at night using its strong pectoral fins and spines in search of land-based food or it can move into the breeding areas through very shallow pathways. In ponds that are drying out they even are able to create pockets in the bottom to retain some of the water longer by thrashing about with their tails; they can survive in the wet mud. This catfish does not, however, have the capacity to exist for long periods in dry mud as do some lungfishes.

Clarias gareipinus is a nocturnal species foraging at night on a wide variety of prey objects. It has been reported to take almost anything that moves, not only the usual things such as insects, fishes, crustaceans, snails, and even plankton, but some unusual items such as fruits, plants, young birds, and rotting flesh.

Clarias buthupogon from the Congo has a fat, fleshy body and is quite prized as a food fish. It inhabits swamps and muddy pools as well as small creeks. They are caught by draining or bailing the pools until the fish can be caught. The diet consists of aquatic and terrestrial insects and crustaceans. This species is pinkish tan mottled with gray and has small white spots all over the body. The ventral area is almost white. It is a nocturnal species with very tiny eyes, but it is quite sensitive to vibrations and the barbels are quite sensitive as well. In captivity only one individual should be placed in a tank unless it is in a very large tank. If several of the same age are introduced into a tank at the same time fighting will occur until a pecking order is established; however, they seem to mellow with age and larger specimens are more compatible with one another. They like to roam around at night in the tank, and it is not unusual for them to leave the tank if it is carelessly left uncovered. If they are found soon enough and they are not completely dried out, they will usually survive. This species is not to be trusted with plants. It tends to rearrange any plants in the tank using its head as a scoop, and will dine on the softer varieties. It will eat almost any aquarium foods and should be given some vegetable matter as well, such as celery tops. For some reason the spelling of this species's name has caused problems, and it is not unusual to see it referred to as *C. bythipogon*, *C. bathypogon*, *C. butupogon*, and other variants.

Clarias cavernicola, which grows to a length of about 15 cm, is a cave-dweller from Aigamas Cave in southwestern Africa. It has very small eyes and lacks most pigmentation. The small size of the fish is said to be possibly due to the cave habitat, as food is not very plentiful. It feeds on the excrement of baboons that frequent the cave and on insects that occasionally are swept in.

Clarias maclareni from the Cameroons has the accessory breathing apparatus reduced in size and has large eyes, usually indications of a deeper water fish.

The Southeast Asian genus *Prophagorus* is basically a *Clarias* in which the dorsal and anal fins have become confluent with the caudal fin. Although this difference appears quite meager, some workers in the group tend to keep the two genera separate, at least for the time being. Tweedie (1952), however, regards *nieuhofi* as a distinct species but should not be included in genus *Clarias*. Only two species, *P. nieuhofi* and *P. cataractus*, are currently considered to belong to this genus.

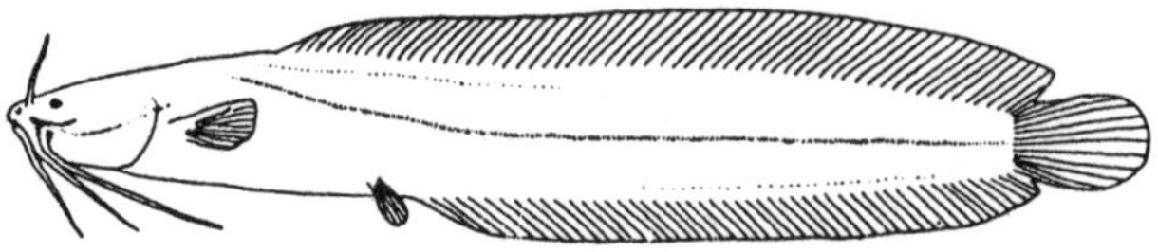

Prophagorus nieuhofi. (After Inger & Chin , 1962.)

The genus *Horaglanis* is a genus of cave-dwelling fish from Kerala, India, that contains but a single species. The body is elongate and subcylindrical. The head is globular and lacks the bony shield, the snout is short and almost square-cut, and the eyes are completely absent. The skin is smooth. The mouth is wide, crescentic, and the villiform teeth are arranged in bands in the jaws, that of the upper jaw in a broad curve, that of the

Horaglanis krishnai. (After Misra, 1976.)

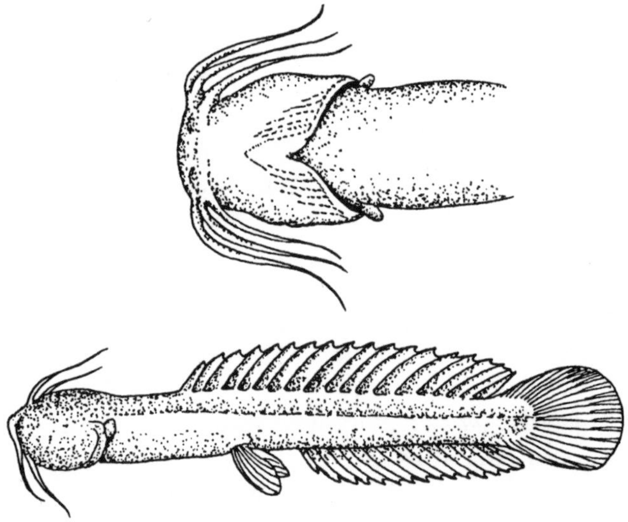

lower jaw as two contiguous patches produced backward. There is no median longitudinal groove on the head. The nostrils are quite small, even minute, with the anterior pair located close to the tip of the snout and the posterior pair behind the nasal barbels and distant from each other as well as from the anterior nostrils. There are four pairs of barbels: the nasal pair, maxillary pair, mandibular pair, and a mental pair. The dorsal fin is long-based, without a spine, and extends to the caudal base but is not confluent with the caudal fin. There is no adipose fin. The long-based anal fin extends to the caudal base but, like the dorsal fin, is not confluent with the rounded caudal fin. The pectoral fins are vestigial, but the ventral fins are well-developed, have 6 rays, and are located somewhat behind the origin of the dorsal fin. The gill openings are broad and extend to above the pectoral fin base. The gill membranes are united with the isthmus. The dendritic accessory breathing organ is vestigial. The swim bladder is bag-like, broader than long, slightly notched anteriorly, and not enclosed in a bony capsule. There are 11 branchiostegal rays.

The single species, *H. krishnai*, is reported to live in wells of Kottayam in Kerala, India.

The genus *Xenoclarias* is a genus of only a single species, *X. eupogon*, from Lake Victoria. It is very similar to the genus *Clarias* but lacks the accessory branchial organ. *X. eupogon* is small and of little commercial importance. It feeds mostly on insects.

The genus *Heterobranchus* is a small genus of five species, including one of the largest freshwater fishes of Africa. The body is elongate, slightly compressed posteriorly. The head is quite depressed and protected by a bony shield dorsally and on the upper sides that generally has a granular surface. A median fontanelle is present. The eyes are small and the mouth wide. The villiform teeth form bands that are crescentic on the vomer and complete or interrupted in the jaws. Four pairs of barbels are present, the nasal barbels sometimes longer than the head. The dorsal fin is short for a clariid, but still has 24-45 rays, and lacks a spine. There is a long based and often high adipose fin. The anal fin is long, of 40-60 rays, and extends to the caudal base, where it may or may not be confluent with the caudal fin. The well developed pectoral fin has a spine that is smooth or weakly serrated on its edges. The ventral fins are well developed and are well back on the ventral surface below the middle of the dorsal fin. About 15-30 short gill rakers are present on the first arch. The accessory breathing apparatus is rather well developed. Four species are African and one is (supposedly) Indonesian.

Heterobranchus longifilis is widely distributed throughout Africa in the Nile, Niger, Congo, and Zambezi basins and their associated lakes. It is one of the largest freshwater fishes in Africa, attaining lengths of over a meter and a half and a weight of over 60 kilograms, although individuals over 25 kilograms are generally unusual. This is an angler's fish, and heavy tackle is required in order to land it. The "Vundu," as it is called, is said to have an uncanny ability to tangle the fisherman's lines. It is eaten, but not nearly as extensively as some of the species of the genus *Clarias*. This species is usually found in creeks and swamps although it has been recorded from some turbulent waters. It prefers the deeper waters in pools or large rivers, moving into shallower waters at night where they are more easily captured (although there is a problem with crocodiles at that time). The Vundu is a powerful predator that will attack most small prey animals, especially fishes and even small birds. It is said to un-

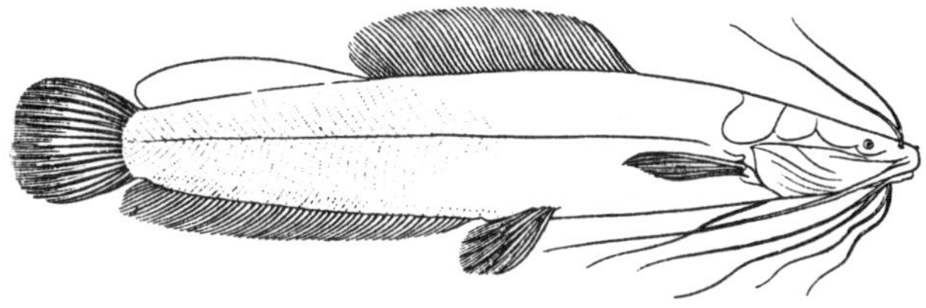

Heterobranchus longifilis. (From Poll, 1957.)

Heterobranchus bidorsalis. (From Boulenger, 1909.)

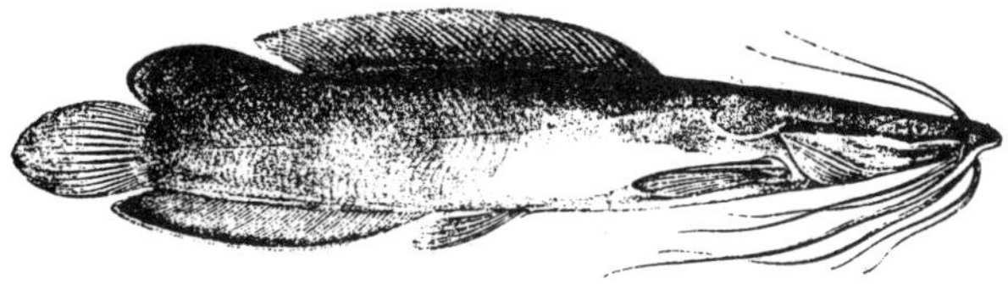

dertake breeding migrations in the summer months. The color is usually brownish gray to brownish olive above and white on the belly, with yellowish fins.

This is a very large and inert sort of fish that is generally not recommended for home aquaria. It will lie motionless on the bottom most of the time, moving only when food is offered. It accepts all kinds of food in large quantities and grows very fast. For example, it was reported that a *H. longifilis* of 30 mm was fed mostly live fishes and hamburger. In six months it had increased its size to 100 mm and by one year to double that. It eventually attained a length of a meter and its ravenous appetite could barely be satisfied.

The African genus *Dinotopterus* is very similar to the preceding genus morphologically but differs sufficiently for it to be considered a separate genus. It has an adipose fin that is quite small and short-based when compared

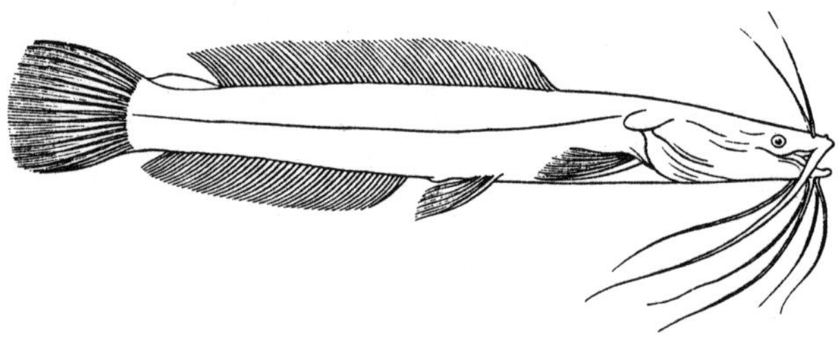

Dinotopterus cunningtoni. (From Poll, 1957.)

with that of *Heterobranchus*. The head shield is also reduced in extent, the bony plates not extending onto the sides of the head. Finally, the accessory branchial apparatus, although present, is very small. There are about a dozen species, mostly from Lakes Malawi and Tanganyika, of medium to very large size, and of moderate commercial importance. Most species feed on fishes.

The genus *Gymnallabes* is one of the genera of "eel-catfishes," so-called because of their long, eel-like bodies. The head is flattened, somewhat globular in shape, and is unprotected by a bony shield laterally; even the postorbital shield is absent. The eyes are very small, with no free borders, or absent. The mouth is wide, the teeth arranged in bands in the jaws, those of the vomer pointed and

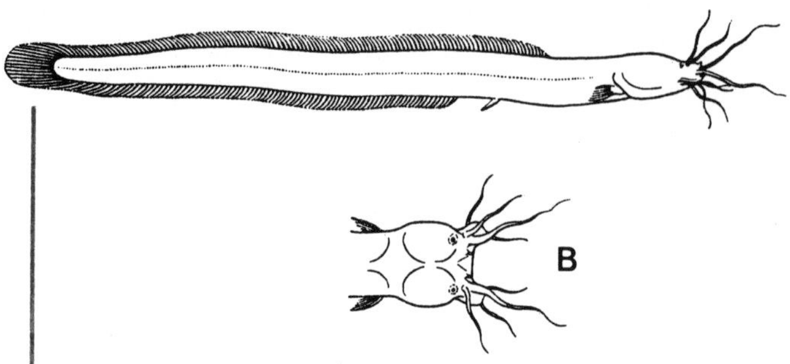

Gymnallabes typus; (b) dorsal view of head. (From Poll, 1957.)

forming a crescentic band. There are four pairs of barbels present: a maxillary pair, two mandibular pairs, and a nasal pair. The dorsal and anal fins are very long (the dorsal ray count may surpass 110 and the anal ray count more than 85) and are confluent with the rounded caudal fin. The pectoral and ventral fins are developed but small, the former with a short smooth spine. The genus contains three species from African waters, one of which is eyeless and depigmented.

The genus *Channallabes* is another genus of "eel catfishes." It contains the single species *C. apus* from Angola and the Congo basin, where it is found in swampy or marshy habitats. The body is extremely elongate, eel-like, and the head is somewat flattened. Two fontanelles are present on top of the head, the anterior larger than the posterior. The eyes are extremely small, all but hidden under the skin in the adult. The teeth are arranged in bands in the jaws, while the pointed vomerine

Channallabes apus; (b) dorsal view of head. (From Poll, 1957.)

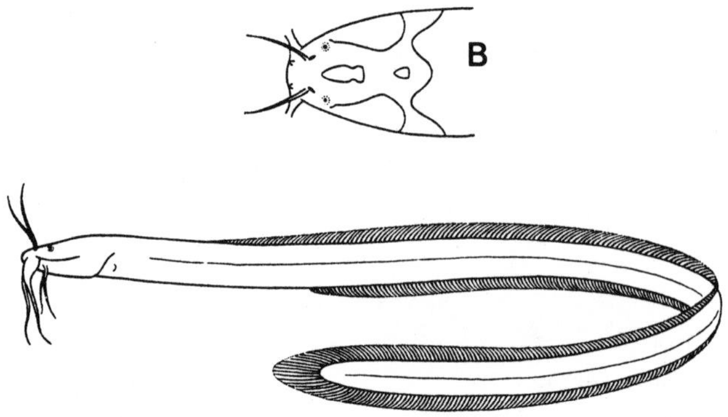

teeth form a crescentic band. There are four pairs of well-developed barbels, the maxillary pair rather broad-based. The dorsal and anal fins are very long (140-150 dorsal rays and 125-130 anal rays) and both are confluent with the caudal fin. The pectoral fins are greatly reduced or absent, without a spine, and there are no ventral fins at all. There are about 9 or 10 moderately long gill rakers on the first arch.

Channallabes apus attains a length of about 30 cm and inhabits swamps and forest streams. It is a nocturnal species that during the day burrows into the soft substrate. It nests along the river banks among the masses of tangled tree roots. *C. apus* is not a difficult species to keep in home aquaria, but it has some drawbacks. Being nocturnal, you may rarely ever see it, for during the day it will be well dug into the sand or other material that is used on the bottom of the tank. Feeding is a little bit of a problem for this species definitely prefers live foods and may shun other items to its own detriment. Tubificid worms, bloodworms, and even earthworms are accepted, and it is said that when food is introduced and the eel catfish is hungry it will burst out of the gravel and swim vigorously back and forth until it has found and eaten its fill. At this time it will return to its sanctuary beneath the gravel or sand. *C. apus* is a social fish and does best when kept with up to a half dozen of its own kind. Other fishes may be kept with this species, but preferably ones not too small and not nocturnal so that there is no competition for food. The tank should be covered, but there is no real danger of having one of these catfish getting out—they seem content with their life at the bottom of the tank. Be sure the gravel has no sharp edges. Like other naked catfishes, this species scratches easily and there is a danger of infection.

The African genus *Clariallabes* contains about 15 species that are very similar to the genus *Clarias*, sharing most of the characters of that genus. *Clariallabes* differs in having some species with the dorsal and anal fins confluent with the caudal fin and the bony shield of the head not protecting the sides of the head. The species are of small size and of little commercial value. The diet consists mainly of insect larvae.

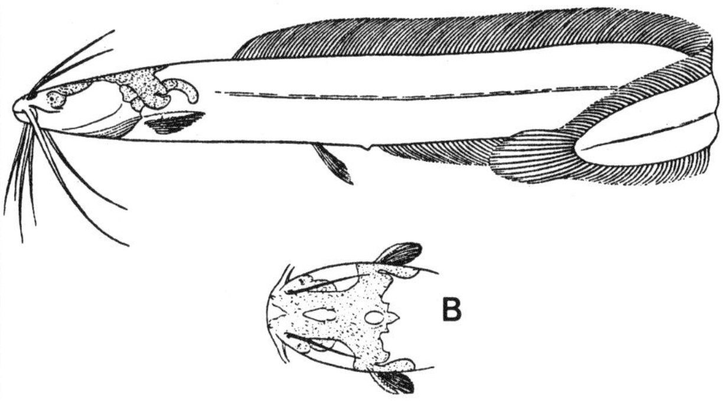

Clariallabes melas; (b) dorsal view of head. (From Poll, 1957.)

The genus *Tanganikallabes* is monotypic, with a single species from Lake Tanganyika. The body is elongate and the head is slightly depressed. The head is not protected by a bony shield but is covered with very thick skin. The eyes are moderately large and somewhat superior in position. There are four pairs of barbels: nasal, maxillary, and two mandibular pairs. A strong median longitudinal groove is present on the head. The dorsal and anal fins are very long, ending at the caudal base, and may be attached to the base of the caudal fin. The pectoral and ventral fins are well-developed, the pectorals provided with spines. According to Brichard, the single species, *T. mortiauxi*, is occasionally found in

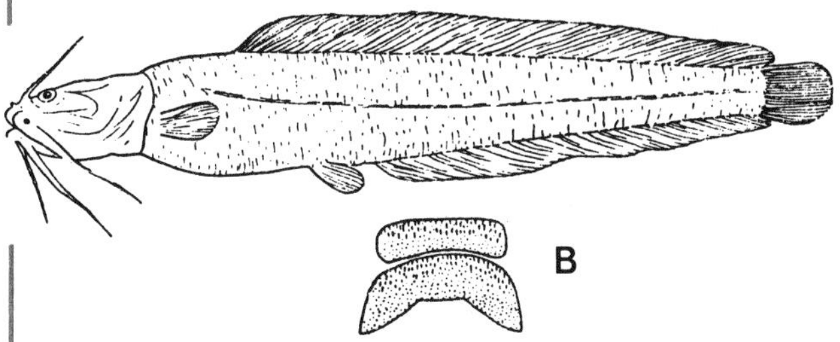

Tanganikallabes mortiauxi; (b) vomerine and premaxillary tooth patches. (From Poll, 1957.)

rock crevices on the rocky slopes. The species is of little commercial importance. (Brichard, 1978.)

The genus *Dolichallabes*, with the single species *D. microphthalmus*, belongs to the "eel catfishes." The body is extremely elongate and the head is depressed but with the temple area inflated. The eyes are minute and without a free border. There are four pairs of bar-

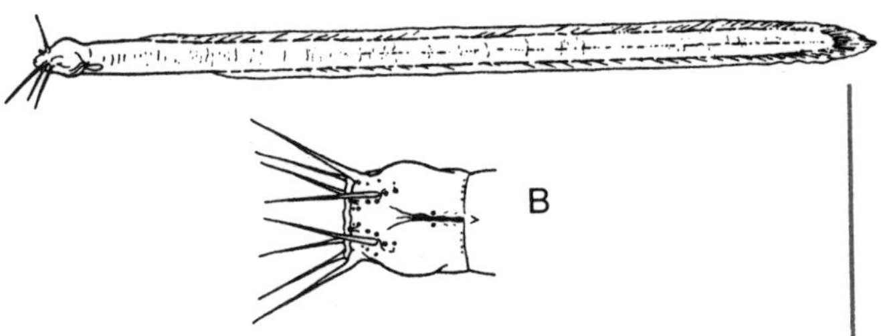

Dolichallabes microphthalmus; (b) dorsal view of head. (After Poll, 1957.)

bels of approximately equal length: nasal, maxillary, and two mandibular pairs. The dorsal and anal fins are extremely long, many-rayed, and completely confluent with the caudal fin, forming a continuous fin around the tail section. Pectoral fins are present, small, and lack spines, while ventral fins are completely absent. The head has a median longitudinal groove. The single species attains a length of about 25 cm and comes from Zaire.

The genus *Platyallabes* contains only a single species, *P. tihoni*, from the Stanley Pool

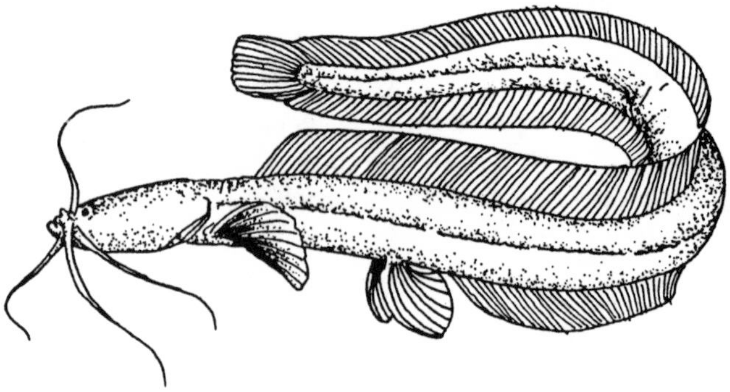

Platyallabes tihoni. (After Poll, 1957.)

region of the Congo. The body is long and very depressed anteriorly, less depressed posteriorly. The distance from the tip of the snout to the anal fin origin (preanal distance) is very short, while the postanal distance is very long, approximately 75% of the standard length. The maximum body depth is much less than its maximum width, being less than half the head length in adults. The head is broad and flat, about as wide as long, subround in shape; the head is included 7-10 times in the standard length. The narrow cranial roof which is logitudinally grooved is covered by skin and not very apparent. The head is not protected laterally by the supraorbital and dermosphenotic bones, but swollen on each side by strong muscular swellings. The eyes are miniscule, superior in position, and without a free border. The dorsal fin originates very near the head, isolated from the occipital process only by a distance about equal to ⅓ of the head. It possesses 130-140 rays. The anal fin has 115-125 rays. The two long, tall, thick vertical fins are confluent with the caudal fin. Large pectoral fins are present and possess a strong, unserrated spine and 10 soft rays. The length of the pectoral is more than half that of the head, and it extends beyond the origin of the dorsal fin. The ventral fins are equally as strong although a little shorter and have 6 rays. There are 8 gill rakers on the lower part of the first arch and about 9 or 10 branchiostegals.

The genus *Platyclarias* contains a single species, *P. machadoi*, from the Upper Congo. The body is elongate and very depressed anteriorly, although compressed posteriorly. The preanal distance is rather long, equalling about 40% of the standard length; the postanal distance is only a little longer than the rest of the body. The maximum depth of the body is much less than the maximum width, measuring less than half the length of the head in adults. The head is broad and very flat, longer than wide, and included 7 (juveniles) to 9 times in the standard length. The rugose cranial roof is not covered by the lateral musculature and is quite apparent. The head is not protected laterally by the supraorbital and dermosphenotic bones, and these wide spaces are not or weakly swollen by the musculature. The eyes are small, superior, and provided with a free border. The dorsal

Platyclarias machadoi. (After Poll, 1977?)

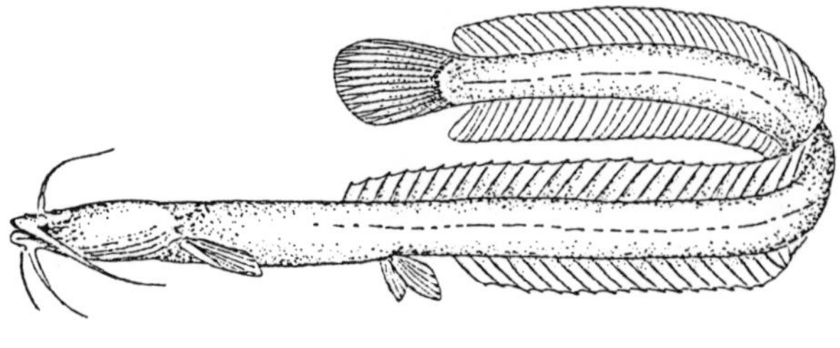

fin originates well behind the head, by a distance equal to or a little shorter than the length of the head. It possesses about 90 rays, the anal fin having about 80. These vertical fins are not confluent, but are contiguous with the caudal fin. Large pectoral fins are present and are provided with a strong unserrated spine and 10 soft rays. The pectorals are equal to ½ (juveniles) to ⅓ the length of the head and do not extend as far as the dorsal origin. The ventral fins are equally strong but measure only about ⅓ the head length. They have 6 rays and are never absent. There are 5 to 6 gill rakers on the lower portion of the first gill arch.

The genus *Uegitglanis* is a small genus containing a single rather small species (maximum length about 12 cm) from Somalia. It is a form that lives in subterranean waters and as such has lost its eyes and the pigmentation of the body. The body is elongate and the head rounded. There are four pairs of barbels: nasal, maxillary, and two mandibular pairs. The dorsal and anal fins are elongate but are not confluent with the caudal fin. Both pectoral and ventral fins are well-developed. The capsules around the swim bladder and the accessory epibranchial organ are missing. It is the lack of these two structures, along with others, that have led Chardon (1968) to propose that this genus is as distinct from the family Clariidae as *Heteropneustes* is, and that like *Heteropneustes* it should merit being placed in a family of its own, the Uegitglanididae. This move has not been received very well, and most classifications still retain *Uegitglanis* within the Clariidae.

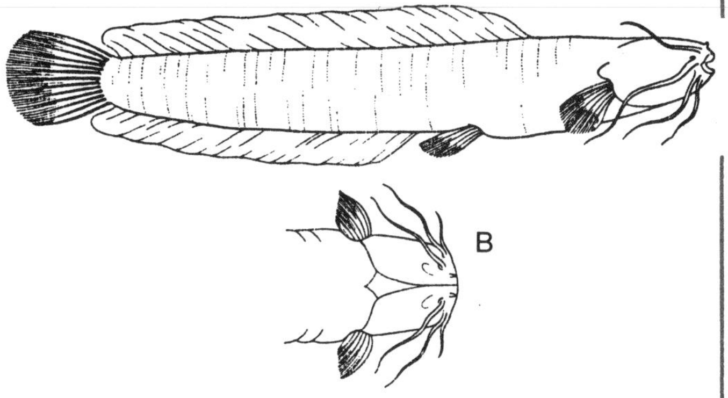

***Uegitglanis zammaranoi*; (b) ventral view of head. (From Poll, 1957.)**

The family Clariidae is said to have the closest affinities with the family Bagridae.

Checklist of the species of the family Clariidae and their type localities:

Channallabes Günther, 1873. Type species *Gymnallabes apus* Günther.
- *Channallabes apus* (Günther, 1873). Ambriz, Angola.

Clariallabes Boulenger, 1900. Type species *Clarias melas* Boulenger, 1887.
- *Clariallabes attemsi* (Holly, 1927). "Kamerun."
- *C. brevibarbis* Pellegrin, 1913. Mgomo, Ogooue.
- *C. centralis* (Poll & Lambert, 1958). Kunungu (Congo).
- *C. dumerili* (David & Poll, 1937). Leopoldville, Belgian Congo.
- *C. heterocephalus* Poll, 1967. Luita River, trib. of Cuilo River, Angola.
- *C. laticeps* (Steindachner, 1911). Mawambi, Ituri River.
- *C. longicauda* (Boulenger, 1902). Ja River, French Congo.
- *C. manyangae* (Boulenger, 1919). Kikenda, Belgian Congo.
- *C. melas* (Boulenger, 1887). Lower Congo.
- *C. petricola* Greenwood, 1956. Nile, about half mile below Owen Falls dam, Jinja, Uganda.
- *C. pietschmanni* (Günther, 1938). Njong River.
- *C. platyprosopus* Jubb, 1965. Upper Zambezi River.
- *C. simeonsi* Poll, 1941. Uele; Mosongolia, Mehokpa, and Matanga Rivers; Ibembo.
- *C. uelensis* (Poll, 1941). Mosongolia, Mehokpa, and Matanga Rivers, Ibembo region, Uele.
- *C. variabilis* Pellegrin, 1926. Belgian Congo.

Clarias Scopoli, 1777. Type species *Silurus batrachus* Linnaeus.
- *Clarias abbreviatus* Valenciennes, 1840. Macao.
- *C. agboyiensis* Sydenham, 1980. Ogun River, Lagos state, Nigeria.
- *C. albopunctatus* Nichols & LaMonte, 1953.

Kotto River, Fr. Equatorial Africa.
C. alluaudi Boulenger, 1906. Kavirondo Bay, Lake Victoria.
C. angolensis Steindachner, 1866. Angola.
C. amplexicauda Boulenger, 1902. Upper Ubanghi.
C. anguillaris (Linnaeus, 1758). Nile.
C. batrachus (Linnaeus, 1758). Asia.
C. buettikoferi Steindachner, 1895. Buluma, Liberia.
C. buthupogon Sauvage, 1879. Ogooue River to Doume, Fr. Congo.
C. brachysoma Günther, 1864. Java; Ceylon.
C. camerunense Lönnberg, 1895. Kamerun.
C. cavernicola Trewavas, 1936. Algamas Cave, N. Otavi, Southwest Africa.
C. dayi Hora, 1936. Wynaad, India.
C. dhonti (Boulenger, 1919). Kabeke, Niemba River, Lake Tanganyika.
C. dumerilii Steindachner, 1866. Old Calabar, Angola.
C. dussumieri Valenciennes, 1840. Pondicherry, Malabar.
C. ebriensis Pellegrin, 1920. Near Bingerville, Ivory Coast.
C. engelseni (Johnsen, 1926). Sudan.
C. fuscus (Lacépède, 1803). China.
C. gabonensis Günther, 1867. Ogowe River, Gaboon.
C. gariepinus (Burchell, 1822). Banks of the Gariep (= Orange) River.
C. hilli Fowler, 1936. Saidis village, Belgian Congo.
C. jaensis Boulenger, 1909. Ja River at Bitye, S. Cameroon.
C. laeviceps Gill, 1863. Probably Liberia.
l. dialonensis Daget, 1962. Bafing near Mamou (Fouta Dialou).
C. lamottei Daget & Planquette, 1967. Aoue Bia, affluent of the Nzi, Bandama basin, near Lamto, Ivory Coast.
C. leiacanthus Bleeker, 1851. Borneo.
C. liocephalus Boulenger, 1898. Kinyamkolo, Lake Tanganyika.
C. longior Boulenger, 1907. Kribi and Lobi Rivers, South Cameroon.
C. maclareni Trewavas, 1962. Lake Barombi-ma-Mbu, NW Cameroon.
C. macrocephalus Günther, 1864. Gambia (erroneous). Distributed from Oueme River in Benin Republic to Niger delta, central Niger and Benue River.
C. meladerma Bleeker, 1846. Batavia.
C. nebulosus Deraniyagala, 1958. Kalu Ganga, Ratnapura, Ceylon.
C. ngamensis Castelnau, 1861. Lake Ngami.
C. nigromarmoratus Poll, 1967. Luita River, Angola.
C. pachynema Boulenger, 1903. Ja River, South Cameroon.
C. platycephalus Boulenger, 1902. Monsembe, Upper Congo.
C. salae Hubricht, 1881. St. Paul River, Liberia.
C. stappersi Boulenger, 1915. Ruisseau affluent of the Lukinda, Congo.
C. submarginatus Peters. 1882. Tooxlong River, W. Africa.
C. teysmanni Bleeker, 1857. Java.
C. theodorae Weber, 1898. Umhloti River, Natal.
C. werneri Boulenger, 1906. Near Gondokoro, Lake Victoria

Dinotopterus Boulenger, 1906. Type species *Dinotopterus cunningtoni* Boulenger, 1906.
Dinotopterus atribranchus Greenwood, 1961. Lake Nyasa.
D. cunningtoni Boulenger, 1906. Lake Tanganyika.
D. euryodon (Jackson, 1959). Nkata Bay, Lake Malawi.
D. filicibarbis (Jackson, 1959). Nkata Bay, Lake Malawi.
D. foveolatus (Jackson, 1955). Lake Malawi.
D. gigas (Jackson, 1959). Lake Malawi.
D. ilesi (Jackson, 1959). Nkata Bay, Lake Malawi.
D. jacksoni, Greenwood, 1961. Nkata Bay.
D. longibarbis (Worthington, 1933). Bar to Nkudzi, Lake Malawi.
D. loweae (Jackson, 1959). Near Nkata Bay, Lake Malawi.
D. nyasensis (Worthington, 1933). Lake Malawi.
D. rotundifrons (Jackson, 1959). Nkata Bay, Lake Malawi.
D. worthington (Jackson, 1959). Nkata Bay, Lake Malawi.

Dolichallabes Poll, 1943. Type species *D. microphthalmus* Poll.
Dolichallabes microphthalmus (Poll, 1942). Kunungu, Zaire.

Gymnallabes Günther, 1867, Type species *G. typus* Günther.

Gymnallabes alvarezi Roman, 1970. Kie River, Rio Muni.

G. nops Roberts & Stewart, 1976. Tadi, Lower Zaire River.

G. typus Günther, 1867. West Africa, probably Old Calabar.

Heterobranchus Geoffroy Saint-Hilaire, 1809. Type species *H. bidorsalis* Geoffroy St.-Hilaire.

Heterobranchus bidorsalis Geoffroy Saint-Hilaire, 1809. Nile.

H. boulengeri Pellegrin, 1922. Lake Moero, Lukonzolwa River.

H. isopterus Bleeker, 1863. Rio Boutry, Guinea.

H. longifilis Valenciennes, 1840. Nile (Egypt).

H. tapeinopterus Bleeker, 1852. Banka; Borneo. (Locality perhaps doubtful.)

Horaglanis Menon, 1950. Type species *H. krishnai* Menon.

Horaglanis krishnai Menon, 1950. Well at Kottayam, Kerala, India.

Prophagorus Smith, 1939. Type species *Clarias nieuhofi* Valenciennes.

Prophagorus cataractus (Fowler, 1939). Trang, Thailand.

P. nieuhofi (Valenciennes, 1840). No locality given.

Platyallabes Poll, 1977. Type species *Gymnallabes tihoni* Poll, 1944.

Platyallabes tihoni (Poll, 1944). Poste de Peche de Kingabwa, Stanley Pool.

Platyclarias Poll, 1977. Type species *P. machadoi* Poll.

Platyclarias machadoi Poll, 1977. Hante Cuango, Cafunfo, Borio River, Angola.

Tanganikallabes Poll, 1943. Type species *T. mortiauxi* Poll.

Tanganikallabes mortiauxi Poll, 1943. Albertville, Lake Tanganyika.

Uegitglanis Gianferrari, 1923. Type species *U. zammaranoi* Gianferrari.

Uegitglanis zammaranoi Gianferrari, 1923. Pozzi de Uegit (El Uegit), Italian Somaliland.

Xenoclarias Greenwood, 1958. Type species *Clarias eupogon* Norman, 1928.

Xenoclarias eupogon (Norman, 1928). Rusinga Channel, Lake Victoria.

Chapter 13

Family — Plate 50

HETEROPNEUSTIDAE

(Airsac Catfishes)

The family Heteropneustidae is a small family of Asiatic catfishes somewhat closely related to the family Clariidae. It contains only a single genus, *Heteropneustes*, and either one or two species depending upon whose classification is being followed. If a single species is accepted it would be *H. fossilis*, whereas if two species are recognized *H. microps* would be the second one.

Heteropneustids are catfishes with an elongate body, subcylindrical to the ventral fin bases and compressed beyond that. The head is depressed and covered on the top and sides with bony plates. The snout is depressed and the nostrils are far apart, the anterior nostrils being tubular and the posterior nostrils, positioned behind the nasal barbels, slit-like. There are four pairs of rather long barbels, the maxillary pair extending as far as the ventral fins and the two pairs of mandibular barbels and the nasal barbels reaching the end of the pectoral fin. The mouth is small and terminal. The jaw teeth are villiform and in bands. The vomerine teeth are villiform also, but are set in two patches; the palate is without teeth. The eyes are relatively small, lateral in position, and with a free orbital rim. The dorsal fin is short, with 6-8 rays and no spine, and there is no adipose fin. The long anal fin (60-80 rays) may be confluent with the rounded caudal fin or free from it. The pectoral fins are provided with a moderately strong spine that may be feebly serrated or strongly serrated on its inner edge and with a few serrations on its outer edge; the ventral fins have 6 rays. The gill openings are wide and the gill membranes are free from the isthmus. There are 7 branchiostegal rays. The gas bladder is enclosed in a bony capsule.

What is quite extraordinary about the heteropneustids is that they possess a pair of long, hollow, cylindrical cavities extending backward on each side of the body from the gill cavity through the muscles of the back. These are accessory breathing organs that serve as primitive lungs enabling the fish to utilize the oxygen of atmospheric air. This appears to be a necessary adaptation for such fishes living habitually in oxygen deficient stagnant pools and swamps as the heteropneustids do. In these same habitats one can find other air-breathers such as *Anabas, Clarias, Trichogaster*, and *Ophiocephalus*. Heteropneustids are also able to withstand severe drought conditions with the aid of this breathing apparatus and a protective mucous secretion that prevents them from drying out. They are not only able to live completely out of water for many hours but, like the clariids, can even cross dry stretches of land in search of better conditions.

The better known of the two species included in this family is *Heteropneustes fossilis*. Its range extends from India, Pakistan, Bangladesh, Nepal, Sri Lanka, and Burma through Thailand to Southeast Asia. It is a fish of ponds, ditches, swamps, and marshes, and sometimes even muddy rivers, all situations in which its accessory breathing organs enable it to survive. *H. fossilis* normally at-

Heteropneustes fossilis is a venomous species and should be handled with care. Any sting, even from a small individual, should be treated promptly. Photo by Gunter Senfft.

tains a length of about 20 cm, although larger individuals of up to 30 cm have been captured in the past. It is reported to be predatory but not necessarily concentrating on fishes. Its flesh is considered quite good to eat and it is sought after in some areas. Because painful (and even deadly) wounds can result from the mishandling of these fish (glands on the pectoral fin spines are poisonous), the fishermen treat them with due respect. In Sri Lanka they are common in ponds and irrigation reservoirs and may even enter brackish water.

Heteropneustes fossilis breeds in India during the rainy season. It moves into the rice fields to spawn when these become flooded, and both male and female set about excavating depressions or hollows in the substrate. The eggs are deposited in these depressions and guarded by both parents. This parental care does not end when the eggs hatch but continues for a considerable length of time afterward. The eggs are of a yellowish to light pea green color.

One unusual aspect of *Heteropneustes* is their reputation for pugnacity. Among workers in Indian rice paddies they are said to actually be aggressive, attacking (and stinging) without apparent provocation. Although this aggressiveness may be exaggerated, it might be wise to remove the fish before reaching into the tank for any reason—this *is* a venomous species.

The venomous nature of stings from *Heteropneustes* should never be underestimated. People have died as a result of stings incurred while handling the fishes or stepping on them in rice fields. Although small, these catfishes are provably deadly. Any sting from the pectoral spines should be given immediate attention. Immersion of the stung hand in hot water (as hot as you can stand without scalding) is the accepted antidote; heat denatures the venom. Consult a doctor for follow-up care and prevention of infection.

As might be expected from the description of the habitat of the heteropneustids, these fishes are very hardy and can withstand the rigors of captivity very well. They are not very demanding as far as water conditions are concerned, but it is recommended that they be supplied with a sufficiently large tank (a 50-gallon aquarium is ideal) with a bottom cover of soft sand or other similar material. There should be ample hiding places constructed of stones or rocks, driftwood, or other such decorations and possibly a few scattered tough plants. Feeding *H. fossilis* is not difficult as they will accept a wide variety of foods, from all types of live foods to pellets commonly fed to pond fishes. The problem with the heteropneustids is that they are gluttonous, eating so much that at times their bellies appear swollen as if they had just swallowed a golf ball. They will also dine on any tankmates if the aquarist is so foolish as to place fishes that are small enough for them to swallow in the tank.

Heteropneustes fossilis has been spawned in captivity. The sex differences are said to be slight, the male being more slender than the female. The spawning is similar to that observed in the wild. Depressions are fanned from the substrate by vigorous action of the fins, and the eggs, in the form of a sticky ball, are deposited therein. The eggs are about the size of millet seeds and yellowish in color. They are guarded by the parents. The young are also tended for a while after they hatch out. The size at spawning seems to range from 20 to 25 cm, and one successful aquarist accomplished the feat in an 86-cm-long tank set up with an undergravel filter. Although the pH and hardness were not recorded, it was suspected that the water was somewhat hard and alkaline. The young were said to grow rapidly and were 8-10 cm long in a few months.

Heteropneustes fossilis was at one time called *Saccobranchus fossilis* and certain references dealing with this species use that name. The corresponding family name Saccobranchidae has also been used.

The closest relatives of the heteropneustids appear to be the clariids; in fact, the genus *Heteropneustes* is often included in the family Clariidae rather than relegating it to its own family. The major differences between the two groups include the short dorsal fin of *Heteropneustes* (in Clariidae it is long and many-rayed) and the replacement of the epibranchial organs of the Clariidae with the two elongate pulmonary sacs. However, the two families share many characters in common, especially in the shape and attachment of several important bones of the skull.

Checklist of species of the family Heteropneustidae and their type localities:

Heteropneustes Müller, 1839. Type species *Silurus fossilis* Bloch.

- *Heteropneustes fossilis* (Bloch, 1794). Tranquebar.
- *H. microps* (Günther, 1864). Ceylon.

Chapter 14

Family CHACIDAE (Frog-mouth Catfishes)

Plates 49–50

The family Chacidae is a small family of curiously shaped catfishes from India, Bangladesh, Nepal, Burma, Malaya, Sumatra, Borneo, and Banka. There is only one genus in the family, *Chaca*, which contains two species. The body is depressed anteriorly, compressed posteriorly, and tapers off rapidly posterior to the ventral fins. The head is very large, very broad (nearly square in shape when viewed from above), and strongly depressed. The skin of the dorsolateral surface of the head and of the body, at least of the more mature individuals, is provided with prominent branched papillae or cirri, sometimes referred to as cutaneous flaps or cutaneous tentacles. The lateral line is marked by a papillated or tuberculated ridge from the upper end of the gill cover to the tail. The skin of the lips, the dorsolateral surfaces of the head and body, and the ventral and median fins have numerous fine granulations. The eyes are very small to minute or rudimentary, widely separated, dorsal in position, and covered by skin. The mouth is very wide and is fringed with short barbel-like appendages. The maxillary bones are entirely included in the gape. The teeth in the jaws are villiform and in bands; the palate is toothless. The anterior nostrils are tubular and located on the anterior border of the mouth; the posterior nostrils are remote from the anterior and may or may not have a short tentacle or barbel on the anterior rim. There are three additional pairs of barbels; a short stub-like pair of maxillary barbels at the corner of the mouth that originate from a broad fold of skin; a pair of mental (or first mandibular) barbels behind the mandibular border; and, some distance behind them, a pair of (second) mandibular barbels. A minute nasal barbel is present in one of the two species. There is a deep median longitudinal groove on the surface of the head, and the occipital process extends to the basal bone of the dorsal.

The dorsal fin is short, of only 3-4 rays, but with a short, strong, weakly serrated spine; the adipose fin is represented by a low ridge and is confluent with the procurrent rays of the caudal fin. The anal fin is short, with about 7-10 rays. The caudal fin is rounded, with the procurrent rays greatly enlarged, 18-25 dorsally and 8-13 ventrally. The pectoral fins are horizontal and have 4-5 rays and a short but strong spine that has 4 to 13 large serrae on its anterior edge (increasing with growth); the posterior margin has a broad flange-like expansion and weak serrae or none at all. The ventral fins are broad, horizontal, with rounded margins and 6 rays. The gill membranes are confluent with the very broad isthmus and the gill openings are somewhat restricted, extending onto the isthmus only a short distance. The gill arches are greatly elongate and enlarged; there are no gill rakers. There are 6 to 8 branchiostegal rays. An axillary pore is present. The swim bladder is large but is not encased in a bony capsule. The species attains lengths to about 23 to 28 cm.

Chaca chaca, the Indian Frog-mouth Cat-

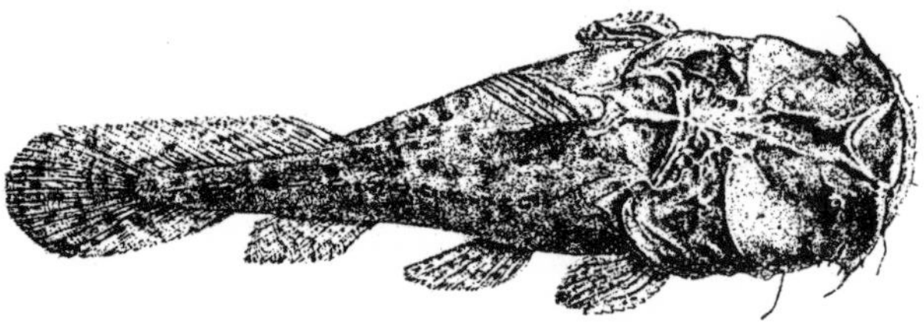

Chaca chaca. (From Day, 1889.)

fish, inhabits lowland streams, rivers, lakes, and pools in the flood plains of its range. It is a strict bottom-dweller, preferring soft substrates where it lies concealed in the "slush" of the river bed. It depends upon this concealment for protection and will not even move when it is touched lightly. Pity the poor unwary fisherman who inadvertently steps upon the upraised dorsal fin spine! At most *Chaca* is a mediocre swimmer and couldn't escape very easily anyway.

Its diet is basically fishes, and it is said that the species of *Chaca* "angle" for their prey. *Chaca* will lie quietly on the bottom until some prey animal approaches. Then it will move its maxillary barbels in a jerky motion, much like the contortions of a small worm. To enhance this effect, in some individuals the distal portions of the barbels may be white in color. As soon as the unwary fish approaches the "worm," the *Chaca* sucks them into its capacious mouth. Prey animals up to half the length of the *Chaca* may be so engulfed, including such fishes as bettas and small cyprinids. *C. bankanensis*, the Malaysian Frog-mouth, was found to eat small cyprinid fishes, *Aplocheilus panchax*, and shrimps. Its dorsal spine is short but can inflict painful wounds, and its flesh is considered poisonous by natives in some parts of Sumatra.

Species of *Chaca* (usually *C. bankanensis*) are only rarely imported for the aquarium trade. Even then, they are welcomed mostly for their unusual appearance, for they have no real beauty and the huge mouth should warn aquarists that they have a large capacity and no small fishes are safe. The tank should be relatively large with plenty of hiding places. The optimal temperature range is roughly 22-24°C. It is interesting to note that when frog-mouth catfishes are taken from the water and placed in a bucket or on the ground, they start to "talk," making a sound very much like their name . . . chaca, chaca, chaca . . . that is repeated rapidly.

The two species of *Chaca* can be distinguished by the following key:

1a. No nasal barbel; 5 pectoral fin rays; a row of cirri on the body above and sometimes below the lateral line; Bangladesh, India, Burma .... *Chaca chaca*

1b. Minute nasal barbel or tentacle present; 4 pectoral fin rays; no row of cirri on body above lateral line; Sumatra, Banka, S. Malay Peninsula .... *C. bankanensis*

According to Chardon (1968) most of the skeletal characters associated with the Chacidae seem to place the family near the Bagridae. Exceptionally, the flexibility of the articulation of the posttemporal bone in regard to the cranium is perhaps a secondary adaptation to the habit of digging. By this feature, along with the reduction of the anterior portion of the saccular, *Chaca* is said to resemble somewhat the South American catfish family Aspredinidae.

Checklist of the species of the family Chacidae and their type localities:

Chaca Gray, 1831. Type species *Chaca hamiltoni* Gray (= *Platystacus chaca* Hamilton).

Chaca bankanensis Bleeker, 1852. "Banka, in fluviis."

C. chaca (Hamilton, 1823). Rivers and pools of northeastern Bengal.

Chapter 15

Family OLYRIDAE (Bannertail Catfishes)

The family Olyridae is a family of small loach-like catfishes distributed from eastern India to Burma. It contains the single genus *Olyra*, which has approximately five species. The size range of the species is from about 5 cm to 11.5 cm. The body is long and slender, somewhat depressed anteriorly but quite compressed toward the tail region. The head is depressed and covered with soft skin. The eyes are small, superior in position, and also covered with skin. The nostrils are distant, the anterior ones tubular and the posterior ones provided with a rim that bears the nasal barbel on its anterior edge. There are four pairs of barbels: the just-mentioned nasal barbels; one pair of maxillary barbels; and two pairs of mandibular barbels. The mouth is small and terminal, with thin and continuous lips and a broadly interrupted labial groove. The jaw teeth are villiform and set in bands, and there is a broad, lunate band of teeth on the palate.

The dorsal fin is short-based, with 7-8 rays and no spine, and the adipose fin is low and short, continuous or not with the caudal fin. The caudal fin is rounded, lanceolate, or forked, and the anal fin is of moderate length (16-23 rays). The pectoral fins are provided with a strong spine serrated on both edges and 4-6 rays. The ventrals are small, horizontal, and with 5-9 rays. The gill openings are restricted, with flaps of skin developed along the lower edges of the gill opening to act as valves for closing the openings. (Hora, 1936.) The gill membranes are united and free from the isthmus. There are 6 to 7 branchiostegal

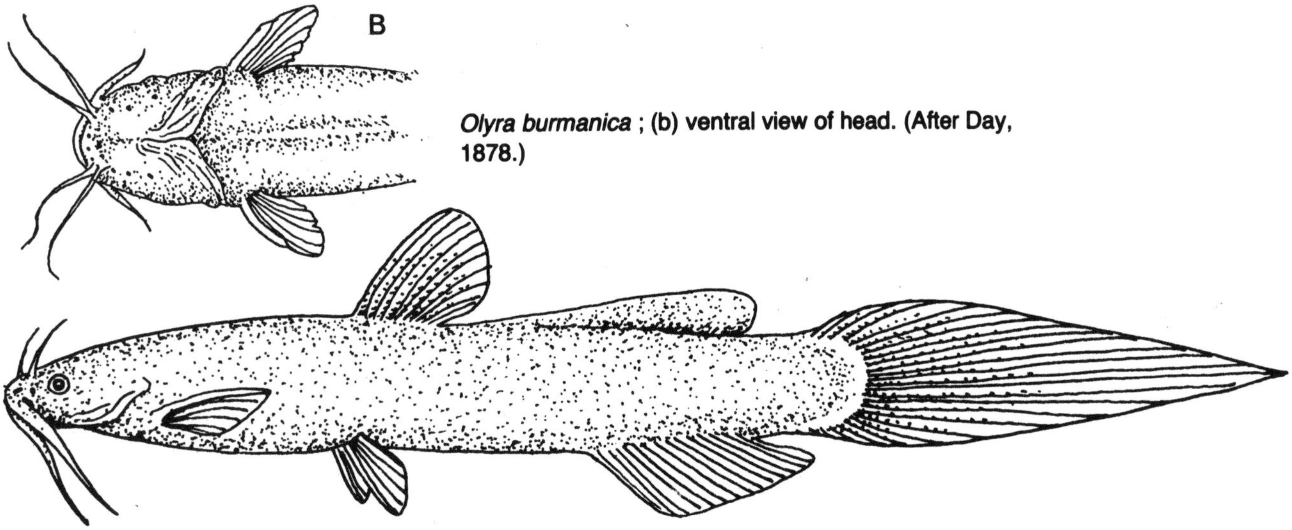

Olyra burmanica ; (b) ventral view of head. (After Day, 1878.)

rays. There is no adhesive apparatus on the chest area. The gas bladder is thick-walled, fairly large, and free in the abdominal cavity, but protected dorsally and laterally by thin wing-like extensions of the transverse processes of compound vertebrae.

The family Olyridae is apparently most closely related to the Bagridae (Regan even placed *Olyra* in the Bagrinae). Little is known about these fishes, and it is doubtful the aquarist will ever get to see one. *Olyra burmanica*, a small (11 cm), slender catfish, is found in the rivers and streams of Burma. It prefers the more rapidly flowing waters, where it is highly secretive, concealed most of the time under rocks.

Checklist of the species of the family Olyridae and their type localities:

Olyra McClellend, 1842. Type species *O. longicaudata* McClellend.

Olyra burmanica Day, 1871. Pegu Yomas, Burma.

O. horai (Prashad & Mukerji, 1929). Shallow parts of Indawgyi Lake, Burma.

O. kempi Chaudhuri, 1912. Mangaldai, Assam. (= *longicaudata* according to Hora, 1936.)

O. laticeps McClellend, 1842. Kasyah Mountains, Assam, India. (Doubtful, probably is a species of *Amblyceps* or even a young *A. mangois* according to Hora, 1936.)

O. longicaudata McClellend, 1842. Khasi Hills, India.

Chapter 16

Family — Plate 50

MALAPTERURIDAE

(Electric Catfishes)

The family Malapteruridae, the electric catfishes, is a small family composed of a single genus and two very closely related species. It is distributed in the tropical fresh waters of Africa from the Nile to the Zambezi River, including most of central and western Africa (it is apparently absent or uncommon in most East African waters). They live mostly in swampy areas but are occasionally found in the quiet parts of streams and rivers such as the reed beds flanking the flowing waters. Pierre Brichard found them in all habitats in Lake Tanganyika. They were common on the rocky slopes and moreso on rocky outcrops that were essentially isolated by sandy areas, the rocks forming the sole cover in the area. In one spot he found a common Electric Catfish (*M. electricus*) approximately 300-1000 mm long every 2 to 3 meters.

Electric catfishes are poor swimmers and remain on or near the bottom most of the time. Their diet consists mainly of small fishes and aquatic invertebrates. They grow fairly large, specimens reaching a length of up to 1.2 meters and a weight of close to 23 kilos having been reported. The average adult size is closer to 75 cm and a weight of about 6-7 kilos according to sources.

Electric catfishes have been known for more than 5,000 years, appearing in heiroglyphics in the tombs of ancient Egyptian kings. The fishes, because of their special properties, may have been used in some sort of ceremonies by the high priest or were considered to have medicinal properties. They are currently used in parts of Africa as a kind of medicine by natives who believe they can cure various ailments. Live specimens are even used to give a kind of electric shock treatment. Although these catfishes are avoided as food fish by natives in some areas in the fear that it will affect their virility, in other areas they are eaten.

Malapterurids are characteristically heavy, flabby, even bloated fish that are moderately elongate and cylindrical in cross-section. They are without scales or armor, the body being covered with smooth, soft skin. They have a terminal mouth with thick lips, and the jaws are provided with very fine teeth. The eyes are small and without a free border. A rayed dorsal fin is absent, but there is a small adipose fin. The anal fin is short and located opposite the adipose fin. The caudal is rounded. The pectoral fins are without spines, and the ventral fins are located in the posterior half of the body. There are three pairs of long, fleshy barbels, one maxillary pair and two mandibular pairs. The nasal openings are far apart, and the gill membranes are broadly attached to the isthmus. It has been reported that medium-sized individuals are often luminescent, while older ones are frequently blind.

The powerful electrical capabilities are of course the most outstanding feature of the

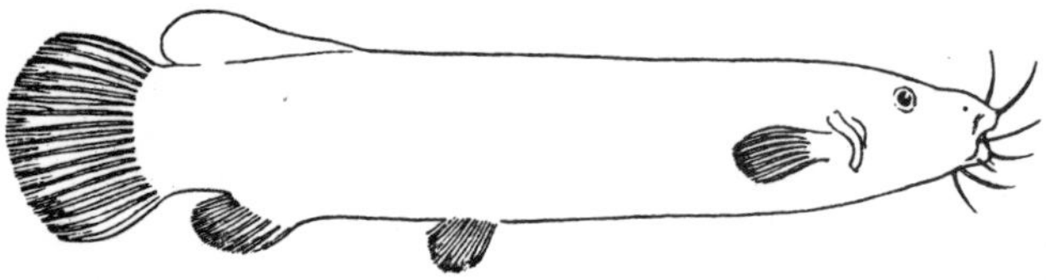

Malapterurus electricus. (From Poll, 1957.)

electric catfishes. Even small individuals have the capacity to inflict a shock when handled. Its shock has been likened to the shock received when a finger is placed across the tracks of a toy electric train. The larger specimens, on the other hand, are far more dangerous, and if stepped on by an unwary fisherman could give him a tremendous jolt, possibly even rendering him unconscious. This shock is said to be equivalent to sticking a finger in an electric outlet, about 110 volts of electricity, although a range of voltage from 100-300 for adult fish has been reported. Individuals in excess of one meter are said to be able to produce an even higher voltage, estimated to be more than 400 volts. Pierre Brichard, on the other hand, says that the jolt from Lake Tanganyika electric catfish seems to be less powerful than equal sized Congo electric catfish. Whether this is due to the conductive properties of the very different types of waters (highly conductive in the hard, alkaline Tanganyika water and much less so in the soft, acid waters of the Congo areas where they are found) or to the catfish themselves (different diets or possibly even different species) is uncertain.

In general, the initial shock is itself short and sharp and is followed by a series of secondary discharges of lesser intensity. The shock is apparently voluntary on the part of the fish, as one can handle an electric catfish for several moments without receiving a shock, only to receive one a few seconds later. In nature this capability is thought to be used for securing food and the repulsion of enemies. It is believed that the electric catfishes stun small fishes before eating them. Just one look at the flabby body of an electric catfish leads one to suspect that this theory is correct, for it does not seem possible for it to pursue and successfully capture the small active fishes that constitute its prey. The electric capabilities are reportedly not used as a sonar device as is the case in certain other fishes with electrical generating properties.

According to Poll (1957) the electric organs are large and are formed by the dermis, which is particularly thick and gives the fish the characteristic flabby appearance. The electric organ includes a large number of electric plates attached in series, giving them a structure much like a "Volta pile" with numerous elements. The difference in potential is very tiny between each element of the pile, but these accumulate in such a way that a very big difference of potential occurs between the two ends of the body. In contrast with the electric eel, which has the positive charge on the head and the negative charge on the tail, the electric catfish has the negative charge on the head and the positive charge near the tail.

Spawning reports are few and far between, and full details are still not available. It is known that in the summer in some areas pairs will spawn in holes that they have dug in the river bank. There are some reports that the electric catfishes are mouthbrooders. In the Gambian drainage spawning is said to occur during the rainy season. The sexes can be distinguished by the configuration of the vent and the generally slim body of the male in contrast to the quite heavy body of the female. In Lake Tanganyika, Brichard was not able to find electric catfish fry. Small individuals of about 30 mm were seen, but they were already living on their own.

For aquarists, an electric catfish must be considered a specialty fish, one for the connoisseur and not for the average aquarist. First of all, it must be kept by itself. Small individuals less than 5 cm in length can sometimes be kept together, but as they grow, fighting among themselves seems to be more and more inevitable. They are also aggressive predators, voracious, and not the kind of species you would want in a community tank. Solitary individuals soon become regular pets and, once settled, do not usually shock their owners. Electric catfishes do well in captivity and are not very particular about pH or hardness, although neutral fresh water is preferred. The tank should be well planted, for

The electric catfish, *Malapterurus electricus*, is for the catfish connoisseur. Who else would love such an ugly beast that can give you a jolt of electricity strong enough to knock you off your feet. Photo by Klaus Paysan.

the fish likes to hide during the day, and the temperature range should be between 20° and 26°C. They generally do well on a high-protein diet, with such items as live earthworms, live fishes, bits of lean meat in strips, tubificid worms, etc. The younger catfish will probably do better on the miscellaneous items, while the adults will probably prefer almost exclusively live fishes. Be careful not to overfeed, for the electric catfish is a veritable glutton and will grow obese, possibly to eventually die of fatty degeneration. It has never been reported as having bred in captivity.

The Malapteruridae is difficult to trace as far as its closest relatives are concerned. It is said that they have several features in common with the Siluridae, but they seem to be more closely related to the Bagridae. They also have a large posterior cecum and an elastic spring apparatus and lack the pterygoids, features found in the Pangasiidae.

Checklist of the species of the family Malapteruridae and their type localities:

Malapterurus Lacépède, 1803. Type species *Silurus electricus* Gmelin, 1789.

Malapterurus electricus (Gmelin, 1789). Rosetta branch of Nile.

M. microstoma Poll & Gosse, 1969. Yangambi, Congo River.

Chapter 17

Family ARIIDAE (Sea Catfishes)

Plates 51–56

The family Ariidae, commonly called the sea or salmon catfishes, is distributed worldwide in tropical and subtropical regions, with a few species straying into temperate areas that are warmer in summer. The species are chiefly coastal, seeming to favor estuaries or coastal lagoons with muddy or sandy bottoms. Many ascend the rivers and streams, some far beyond the influence of the tides, and others are permanently restricted to fresh waters. They are active fishes and are often seen schooling along the shores near the surface; others occur singly. Some grow to a moderately large size and are used for food locally, but most people, although considering them edible, do not prize them highly. Fishermen also tend to avoid them for they are hazardous to handle because of their sharp dorsal and pectoral fin spines, which inflict wounds that are relatively slow to heal. Time is also lost in extricating the spines from nets. Ariids are generally bottom-feeders, omnivorous in their diet, although the majority seem to have carnivorous tendencies.

The many species, particularly of the genus *Arius* (in the broad sense), are quite uniform in shape and difficult to identify. Experts also seem to have considerable trouble with the genera, with many generic names appearing and disappearing from time to time even in the modern literature. Complicating matters is the report that the teeth, which are used commonly in distinguishing the genera and species, in both the jaws and palate tend to change in their arrangement with age.

Ariids are probably most well known as mouthbrooders. All of the marine species and some of the freshwater species are reported to be mouthbrooders, the rather large eggs (few in number) being incubated by one of the parents (usually the male) in its buccal cavity, which becomes greatly distended, until hatching or a little longer. Some species will provide refuge for the young in the parent's mouth even longer, until the fry have completely absorbed their yolk sacs. While the male is incubating the eggs he does not take in any food, this fasting period lasting usually from six to eight weeks. Unfortunately, in some cases the male's appetite is triggered and the eggs or fry wind up as the first food to break his fast. Females of many genera develop "claspers" (thickened pads or hooks on the inner ventral fin rays).

The ariids are medium to large (over a meter) catfishes with an elongate, robust body that is subterete anteriorly and compressed posteriorly. The snout and head are conical to rounded or depressed, the head covered by a strong, bony, granular shield that is more or less visible beneath a thin skin but may also be almost completely obscured by thick skin and muscles in some species. A median longitudinal groove is present on the head. The supraoccipital process or posterior portion of the shield extends posteriorly to touch the predorsal plate. The mouth is terminal to inferior, the upper jaw more or less prominent, wide or narrow, transverse or crescentic. The teeth of the jaws and palate are villiform, conical, granular, or molar-like and arranged in bands and patches, or they may be absent altogether. The nostrils are close together, separated only by a narrow bridge of tissue, the posterior nostril with a valve but no barbel. Usually both maxillary and mandibular barbels are present (two or three pairs total), but in some cases one or the other type of barbel is absent. The eyes of most species have free orbital rims, although in some they are subcutaneous.

The dorsal fin is short-based, with a more or less serrated pungent spine (sometimes preceded by another short spine) and usually 7 rays. An adipose fin shorter than the dorsal fin is present opposite the anal fin. The anal fin is short to moderate, with 14 to 30 rays. The pectoral fins are set very low, close to the ventral profile, and possess a more or less serrated, pungent spine and 8 to 13 rays. The ventral fins have 6 rays. In mature breeding females the ventral fins become modified by hard, protuberant ridges or skin folds that presumably are useful in the spawning process. The caudal fin is forked.

The lateral line is well developed and may have cross-branches. The gill openings are wide or variously restricted. The gill membranes are usually united and attached to the isthmus so as to leave a wide, free fold or free from each other and from isthmus. There are 5 to 9 branchiostegal rays. The swim bladder is enclosed in bone, some species having a posterior chamber. An axillary pore is present. The color is normally grayish blue, dark gray, or dark brownish on the back and sides, possibly with a silvery sheen, and paler to whitish ventrally.

Key to the genera of Ariidae. Several splinter genera of *Arius* are not included.

1a. Mandibular barbels absent 2
1b. Mandibular barbels present.............. 3
2a. Maxillary barbels stiff and bony.......... .... *Osteogeniosus*
2b. Maxillary barbels band-like, of moderate length.................. *Paradiplomystes*
3a. Maxillary barbels absent; one pair of very small mandibular barbels present.. .... *Batrachocephalus*
3b. Maxillary barbels present 4
4a. One pair maxillary barbels and one pair mandibular barbels present; maxillary barbels and filaments of dorsal and pectoral fin spines appearing as long, flattened ribbons.......................... *Bagre*
4b. One pair of maxillary barbels and two pairs of mandibular barbels present ... 5
5a. Teeth present on the palate 6
5b. No teeth present on the palate.......... 8
6a. Gill membranes free from isthmus and from each other; anal fin long, with 28-30 rays; anterior and posterior nostrils separated by distance equal to width of posterior nostril.................. *Doiichthys*
6b. Gill membranes united to each other and to isthmus; anal fin shorter, with 14-26 rays; anterior and posterior nostrils scarcely separated 7
7a. Palatal teeth various, but if in two patches these are attached to skull and not freely movable; Atlantic and Indo-Pacific .... *Arius*
7b. Palatal teeth in two large patches resting on thick fleshy cushion, not attached to skull, freely movable; Brazil... *Genidens*
8a. Mouth opening wide, extending behind eye; a single series of closely set incisor-like teeth in each jaw............. *Ketengus*
8b. Mouth opening small, ending before eye; no incisor-like teeth in jaws....... 9
9a. Minute teeth in 1 or 2 series in jaws; more than 30 large gill rakers; gill membranes totally confluent with skin of isthmus, without free hind margin....... .... *Nedystoma*
9b. Teeth various; gill membranes united, attached to isthmus with only a narrow free hind margin......................... 10
10a. A band of villiform teeth in each jaw; gill rakers short, few or moderate in number....................... *Hemipimelodus*
10b. A narrow patch of conical teeth, few in number, on each side of jaws; 8 short gill rakers......................... *Tetranesodon*

Although most modern workers have adopted the family name Ariidae, the literature is filled with references to family Tachysuridae, a name apparently based on *Tachysurus sinensis* Lacépède, 1803. *T. sinensis* is based on a Chinese painting that, according to modern opinion, does not appear to be satisfactorily identifiable with any of the known catfish species. (Taylor, 1964.)

The genus *Ketengus* has one species distributed in rivers and brackish waters of Java, Sumatra, Borneo, Pinang, Thailand, and the Andaman Islands. The body is elongate, subterete anteriorly and posteriorly compressed,

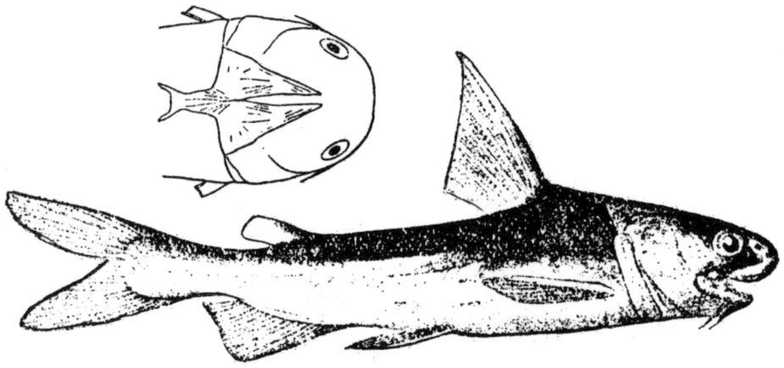

Ketengus typus. (From Weber & de Beaufort, 1913.)

and the large head is very broad, depressed, and with a short, obtuse, prominent snout. The head shield is naked, and the eyes are located in the anterior half of the head and have a free orbital margin. The nostrils are set very close together, the small anterior one possessing a circular rim and separated from the larger posterior nostril by a large valve. The mouth is inferior, with the upper jaw the longer; the mouth opening is large, arcuate, and extends behind the eye. There is a single series of closely set, small, incisor-like teeth that are obtusely tricuspid or subtruncated; the palate is edentulous. Three pairs of barbels are present: a maxillary pair located before the angle of the mouth and two mandibular pairs in a curved line on the chin. The dorsal fin is short-based, with a pungent spine denticulated on both its edges and 7 rays. The adipose fin is short and opposite the anal fin, which has 19 or 20 rays. The ventral fins have 6 rays and extend to the anal, their origin well behind the end of the dorsal fin base. The pectoral fins have a pungent spine with denticulations on both edges. The caudal fin is forked. The gill membranes are confluent, broadly united with the isthmus, and have a free posterior margin without a notch. There are 5 branchiostegal rays.

The single species, *Ketengus typus*, attains a length of about 25 cm and frequents the lower courses of rivers in either fresh or brackish water. It will also venture into coastal waters within the influence of the rivers.

The genus *Tetranesodon* contains a single species from New Guinea. The head is conical, with rugose head shields that are covered with thin skin. The supraoccipital process extends posteriorly to touch the basal bone of the dorsal spine (predorsal plate). The snout is conical, strongly prominent, and overhangs a small, transverse, inferior mouth that has internally swollen lips. A narrow patch of conical teeth is present on each side in the jaws, the teeth few in number; the palate is edentulous. The nostrils are close together, the posterior nostril with a valve. The eyes are of medium size, lateral, and have free

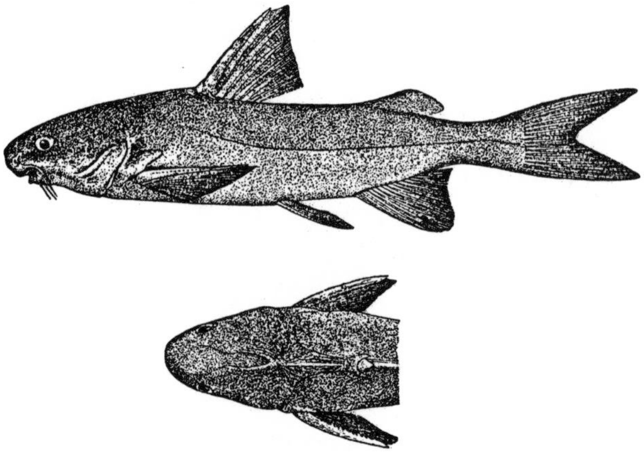

Tetranesodon conorhynchus. (From Weber & de Beaufort, 1913.)

margins. There are three pairs of barbels: a maxillary pair and two pairs of mandibular barbels, all relatively short. The short-based dorsal fin originates approximately midway between the pectoral and ventral fins and possesses a pungent spine and 7 rays. The adipose fin is moderate in size and situated above the anal fin. The ventral fins are 6-rayed. The pectoral fins have a pungent spine. The caudal fin is forked. An axillary pore is present. The gill membranes are united with each other and are connected with the isthmus in the middle, with a free posterior margin. There are 6 branchiostegal rays. The ventral branch of the first gill arch has 8 gill rakers.

The genus *Nedystoma* is another genus containing only a single species. The head is scarcely depressed and but little wider than deep. The median fontanel ends dilated and rounded about in the middle of the rounded occipital shield, which is not covered by skin. The supraoccipital process touches the predorsal plate. The mouth is of moderate size, transverse, with the upper jaw projecting. There are one or two series of feeble, somewhat deciduous teeth in the jaws, and the pal-

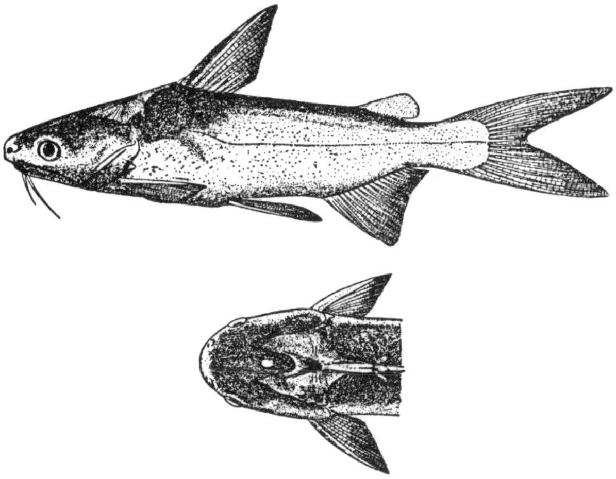

Nedystoma dayi. (From Weber & de Beaufort, 1913.)

ate is edentulous. The nostrils are close together, and the three pairs of barbels (one maxillary pair and two mandibular pairs) are slender and short. The rather large eyes have free rims only anteriorly. The short-based dorsal fin originates midway between the pectoral and ventral fins and has a pungent spine and 7 rays. The adipose fin, located above the anal fin, is rather small. The pectoral fins have a pungent spine. The ventrals are 6-rayed. The caudal fin is deeply forked. There is an axillary pore present. The gill membranes are united, attached to the isthmus along the median line, and confluent with its skin without forming a free margin. There are numerous (23) long, cylindrical gill rakers on the lower limb of the first branchial arch. Six branchiostegal rays are present.

The genus *Hemipimelodus* contains about a dozen species ranging from Southeast Asia to New Guinea. The body is elongate, subterete anteriorly and compressed posteriorly, and the head is more or less depressed. The head-shield is visible and more or less covered by skin, and the supraoccipital process touches the basal bone of the first dorsal fin spine. The mouth is moderate or small, transverse, and the snout is prominent to projecting or gibbous. The jaws are provided with a band of villiform teeth, and the palate is edentulous. The nostrils are close together. There are three pairs of slender, rather long barbels, a maxillary pair and two mandibular pairs. The eyes may or may not have free margins. The short-based dorsal fin originates midway between the ventral and pectoral fins or closer to the pectorals and is provided with 7 rays and a strong spine serrated internally only or on both edges. The adipose fin is short to moderate, originating above or slightly anterior to the anal fin, which has 15 to 20 rays. The pectoral fins have a strong spine. The ventral fins are 6-rayed and located entirely behind the last dorsal fin ray. The caudal fin is deeply forked. An axillary pore is present. The gill membranes are united and are attached to the isthmus along the median line, leaving a narrow margin free. There are 5 or 6 branchiostegal rays and a moderate number of short, more or less conical gill rakers on the lower limb of the first branchial arch. The swim bladder is not enclosed in bone.

Hemipimelodus velutinus. (From Weber & de Beaufort, 1913.)

Species of the genus *Hemipimelodus* inhabit the lower courses of larger rivers. They are oral incubators in which the ovigerous females develop large pads on the inner side of the last ventral fin rays. As the few but large eggs are extruded, the pads apparently serve to hold the eggs until they can be fertilized and taken into the mouth by the male. He then incubates the eggs until they hatch and continues to protect the fry in his mouth until the yolk sacs are completely absorbed. Most of these observations were on *H. borneensis*, which attains a length of about 25 cm but reaches sexual maturity at a size of 15 cm or more. The eggs of this species are large, clear, and amber-colored when ready for extrusion. It also is said to make a grunting noise when caught.

The one or possibly two species of *Osteogeniosus* come from Southeast Asia. The body is elongate and the head strongly depressed and covered with smooth, soft skin. The mouth is anterior, crescentic, with the upper jaw projecting and the lips thin. The jaws are provided with bands of villiform teeth, and there are two separate patches of obtusely conical teeth on the palate. The nostrils are close together, the posterior with a valve, and are situated superiorly near the front border of the snout. There is only one pair of very stiff, bony barbels, the maxillaries. The eye is lateral and has a free orbital rim. The short-based dorsal fin has 7 rays and a pungent spine with serrations on the inner edge and on the outer edge only at the tip. The adipose fin is short and opposite the short anal fin of 19 to 22 rays. The pectoral fin has a strong spine serrated on both edges (stronger than the dorsal fin spine). The ventral fins are 6-rayed. The caudal fin is forked, the lobes rounded. The gill membranes are united, their free hind border deeply emarginate and only anteriorly attached to the isthmus. There are 5 branchiostegal rays.

Osteogeniosus militaris has a range from Java, Sumatra, and Borneo to India. In Thailand it attains a length of about 30 cm and is considered a poor food fish, commanding only a very low price on the market. In India a poor quality of isinglass is made from the

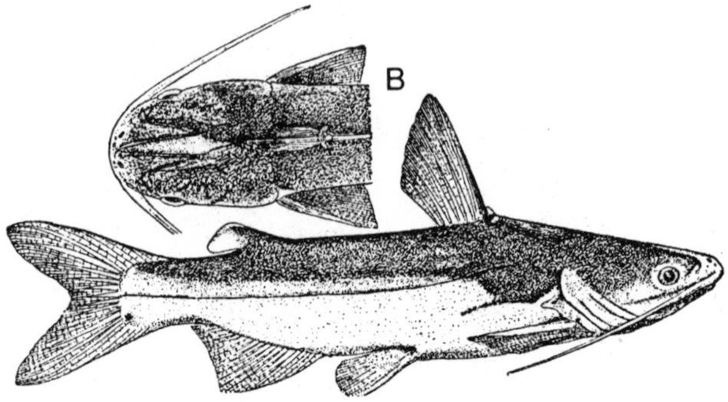

Osteogeniosus militaris; (b) dorsal view of head. (From Weber & de Beaufort, 1913.)

swim bladder. This species is common around the shores of the Gulf of Thailand in the lower courses of rivers and the inner lake of the Tale Sap. Spawning may occur all year long. According to Smith (1945), males 18-23 cm in length collected in fresh water with a strong current were incubating mouthfuls of eggs in various stages of development; females about 25 cm in length had large transparent orange-red eggs that were in a stage nearly ready for extrusion.

The genus *Batrachocephalus* is monotypic. The body is elongate, subterete anteriorly and compressed posteriorly, and the head is large, broad, and depressed, with a very short, obtuse snout. The head shields are naked. The mouth is very wide, with an arcuate gape, and the lower jaw is prominent. The teeth are obtusely conical and arranged in four to five more or less complete series forming a cres-

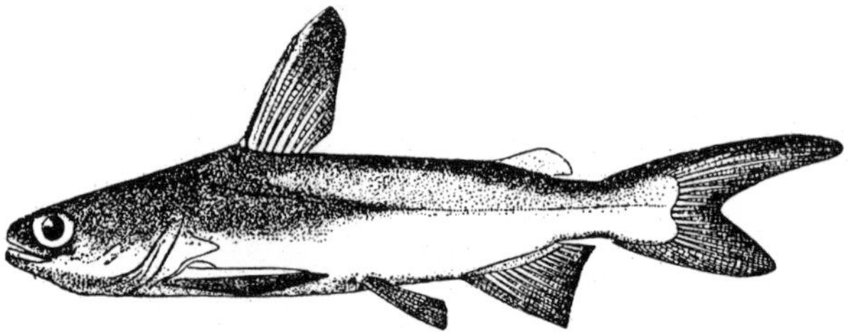

Batrachocephalus mino. (From Weber & de Beaufort, 1913.)

centic band in each jaw. The vomer is without teeth, but the palatines have a longitudinal band of conical teeth. The nostrils are very close together, the posterior separated by a valve from the anterior, which has a circular rim; the nostrils are close to the eyes. The eyes are lateral, with free orbital rims, and they are located in the anterior half of the head, above the angle of the mouth. There is a pair of small mandibular barbels and indications of a second pair on the chin. The short-based dorsal fin has a strong spine denticulated on both edges and 7 rays. The adipose fin is short and opposite the anal fin, which has 21 rays. The pectoral fins have a strong spine denticulated on both edges. The ventral fins are 6-rayed and extend as far as the anal fin or nearly so, their origin well behind the end of the dorsal fin base. The caudal fin is forked. The gill membranes are confluent and united with the isthmus, having a free posterior margin without a notch. There are 5 branchiostegals.

Batrachocephalus mino inhabits the muddy waters of tributaries in fresh water miles above the influence of the tides in Thailand, India, Burma, Java, Sumatra, and Borneo. It is quite distinctive with its two pairs of minute barbels under the chin and very wide mouth running back below the eye. It has been likened in appearance to a frog because of its large eyes placed near the tip of the short blunt snout and the large mouth. When stomachs were examined in Borneo, only plant material was found.

Doiichthys is a monotypic genus that diverges more from the other genera of ariids than do any of the other genera from each other. Some workers in the group have even considered the differences great enough to place it in its own family, the Doiichthyidae. The major characters that distinguish it are given in the key. The head is depressed, as is the snout, which is very broad. The head shields are covered by thin skin, and the occipital process nearly touches the predorsal plate. The mouth is terminal, very wide, and the jaws are equal. There are minute teeth in a single row in the jaws, and there are a few laterally on each side of the palate. The nostrils are separated by a narrow interspace, the anterior at the edge of the snout, the posterior its own width behind it. Three pairs of long, slender barbels are present, a maxillary pair and two mandibular pairs. The small eyes are without free orbital rims and are situated behind the corner of the mouth. The operculum is rhombic in shape and suspended by a membrane, making it very movable. The dorsal fin is short-based, with a strong, pungent spine and 7 rays, and is situated midway between the pectoral and ventral fins. The adipose fin is short and positioned above the anal fin, which has 28-30 rays. The pectoral fins are lateral, low, and provided with a strong, pungent spine that is serrated on both edges.

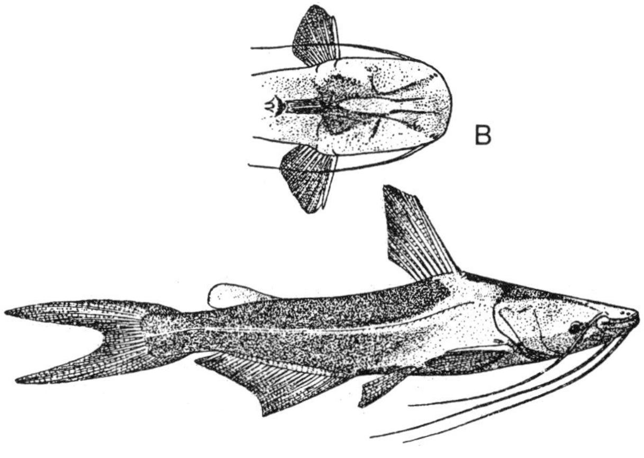

***Doiichthys novaeguineae*; (b) dorsal view of head. (From Weber & de Beaufort, 1913.)**

The ventral fins are 6-rayed. The caudal fin is deeply forked. The gill membranes are narrow, totally free from the isthmus and from each other. There are 6 branchiostegal rays. The gill rakers are long, cylindrical, and numerous.

The genus *Bagre* is a small genus of about five species from tropical American waters. The body is fairly robust, elongate, and little compressed, and the head is broad above and depressed. The nuchal region has a granulated, bony buckler, and the fontanelle is large and placed well forward. The mouth is large, the upper jaw the longer. The teeth are all villiform, those on the vomer and palatine bones forming a more or less crescentic band. The nostrils are close together, the posterior with a valve. Two pairs of barbels are present, a very short mandibular pair and a pair of very long band-like maxillary barbels. The dorsal fin is short-based with a strong spine and 7 rays and is located in front of the ventral fins. The adipose fin is moderate in size and free behind, while the anal fin is moderate in length and emarginate. The pectoral fins have a strong spine. The ventral fins are 6-rayed. The caudal fin is strongly forked. The pectoral and dorsal spines usually end in a long, striated, band-like filament. The gill membranes are somewhat connected.

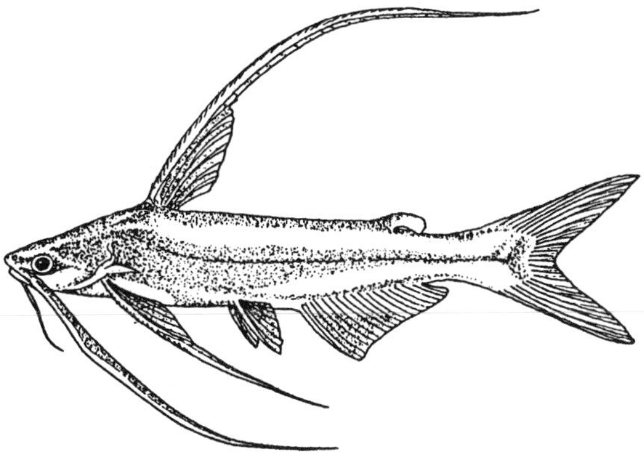

***Bagre bagre*. (After Fischer, 1978.)**

Bagre marinus has a range extending along the eastern and southern Atlantic coasts of the United States, including the Gulf of Mexico. It is fairly common south of Chesapeake Bay, but it occurs most commonly in the coastal and estuarine waters off Florida and in the

Gulf of Mexico. It is basically a solitary species, although it may at times be seen in small groups. Although predominantly marine, it does enter estuaries and moves well upstream into purely fresh water. It is said to be a moderately "noisy" species, vibrations of the swim bladder creating distinctive "yelps" and "sobs" that are clearly audible. The dorsal and pectoral spines are drawn out into long filaments, earning this fish the name of Gafftopsail Catfish. In addition, the maxillary barbels are long, flat, and ribbon-like. This species is said to attain a length of about 60 cm and a weight of some 1.8 kilos. It feeds mainly on fishes and invertebrates such as crabs and shrimps. *Bagre marinus* is one of the species of the family that is used for obtaining skull "crucifixes."

Spawning occurs during the summer months, when males may be found holding up to 55 eggs 15-25 mm in diameter, although the more usual number is 19 or 20. Not too much is known about the actual courtship, although it is said that females probably spawn with more than one male. Both sexes are capable of producing noises, not only those made by the swim bladder, but also sounds created by the manipulating of the pectoral spines as a stridulatory apparatus. These sounds may be involved in the courtship ritual. The male incubates the eggs until they hatch and then continues to provide shelter for the fry for a considerable time, sometimes even until the large yolk sac is absorbed, a total of perhaps 60 to 70 days. It is quite possible that the young may come out of the male's mouth to feed from time to time, but one theory indicates that they might feed within the parent's mouth by filtering out food particles from the sea water taken in by the male.

The genus *Paradiplomystes* is a rather poorly known genus containing but a single species from Brazil. According to Günther's description of Bleeker's genus, the adipose fin is short, the dorsal fin is short and has a pungent spine and 7 rays, and there is a rather short anal fin. Only the maxillary barbels are present, and they are moderate in length and band-like. There are bands of small teeth in the jaws and on the palate. The caudal fin is forked. The brief description of *P. coruscans* in Günther adds that the nuchal shield is keeled, the upper jaw is a little longer than the lower, the cleft of the mouth is wide, the maxillary barbels extend almost to the middle of the body, and the eye is located immediately above the angle of the mouth. Apparently Günther's information was taken directly from Lichtenstein's description of the type.

The genus *Genidens* is another poorly known genus containing a single species from Brazil. The postorbital portion of the head is granular and covered with very thin skin. The occipital process is triangular in shape,

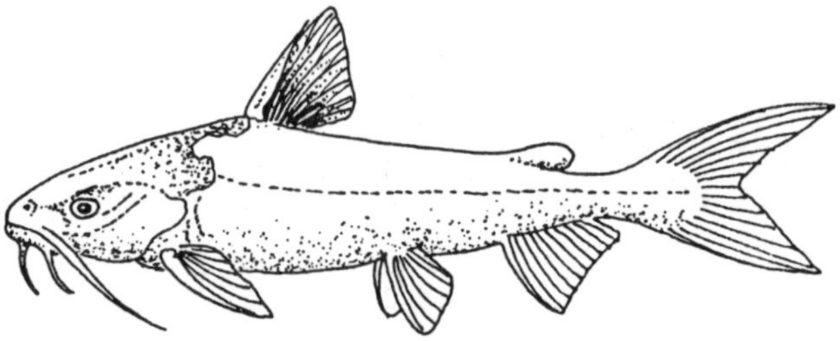

Genidens genidens. (After Fowler, 1951.)

strongly keeled, and articulates with the predorsal plate. The fontanel extends well beyond the level of the eye, continuing beyond the eye as a groove. There are three pairs of barbels, a maxillary pair and two mandibular pairs. The eyes are elliptical in shape and are contained 4 to 5 times in the head length. The upper jaw is projecting and the lips are thick. The jaws contain villiform teeth, those of the upper jaw in a band with a backwardly projecting angle at each end, those of the lower jaw larger, in 5 to 6 regular series, and broadly interrupted in front. The palate has a number of small patches of teeth that are grouped into two large patches, these patches resting on a thick fleshy cushion, not attached to the skull, and freely movable. The short-based dorsal fin has 7 rays and a strong spine that has a few recurved teeth on the inner margin, recurved notches on the upper half, and granules along the basal half of the outer margin. The anal fin has 18 or 19 rays. The caudal fin is deeply forked, the upper lobe narrower and longer than the lower. The pectoral fin spine is strong, depressed, with the outer margin rough and with recurved hooks near the tip in younger individuals (obsolete in adults); the inner margin has a saw-toothed edge in young individuals, the edge becoming somewhat irregular in adults. The gill membranes are united and joined to the isthmus, leaving a narrow free margin. There are 13 gill rakers on the first arch. (Eigenmann & Eigenmann, 1890.)

The genus *Arius* is the largest genus of the family and contains numerous nominal species. It is perhaps the most difficult genus to define, as workers in the group are constantly attempting to split off groups of similar species into separate genera, so far not very successfully. For example, in the tropical western Atlantic Taylor (1978) divided the representatives of the family into five genera, including *Bagre* (discussed above) and the *Arius* group of genera, distinguished by the following key:

1a. Only two pairs of barbels, one of which is mental; maxillary barbels and filaments of dorsal and pectoral fin spines appearing as long, flattened ribbons... *Bagre*

1b. Three pairs of barbels, one maxillary pair and two mandibular pairs, all rounded in cross-section................. 2

2a. A furrow, partially covered by a flap of skin, extending across snout, connecting posterior nostrils..............*Arius* (part)

2b. No fleshy furrow extending between nostrils....................................... 3

3a. No longitudinal fleshy groove in median depression of head and no gill rakers on rear surfaces of first two gill arches...... ....*Arius* (part)

3b. A longitudinal fleshy groove in median depression of head variously developed or absent; gill rakers present on rear surfaces of first two gill arches (minute and few in *Ariopsis*)........................ 4

4a. Teeth on palate small, villiform, arranged into two patches on each side (2 small rounded median patches and two larger obovate lateral patches); gill rakers on rear surfaces of first two arches tiny, usually 3 to 5 in number and confined to upper limb of each arch.................... *Ariopsis*

4b. Teeth on palate molariform in most species, arranged in a small patch on each side; gill rakers well developed and uniformly distributed along rear surfaces of first gill arches.................. *Catharops*

4c. No teeth on palate; gill rakers well developed and uniformly distributed along rear surfaces of first two gill arches...... ....*Potamarius*

In the Pacific *Arius* is no less confusing, with such genera as *Cinetodus, Brustarius, Cochlefelis, Netuma*, and *Hexanematichthys* commonly used. *Brustarius, Netuma*, and *Hexanematichthys* are generally considered synonyms of *Arius*. The other genera may, when regarded as separate from the genus *Arius*, be distinguished by the following key (after Roberts, 1978)—note that the characters used cannot be compared to the characters used in Taylor's key to American genera.

1a. Tooth band of upper jaw entirely exposed when mouth is closed; jaw teeth flattened distally, their tips with sharp lateral margins; inner pair of mental barbels extending farther posteriorly than external pair of mental barbels........... ....*Cochlefelis*

1b. Tooth band of upper jaw partially or entirely hidden when mouth is closed; jaw teeth simply conical, without modified tips; inner pair of mental barbels not extending so far posteriorly as outer pair of mental barbels.......................... 2

2a. Gill membranes broadly united to isthmus, gill openings restricted to sides of head................................*Cinetodus*

2b. Gill membranes free from isthmus, gill openings extending far anteriorly below head ....*Arius*

The genus *Arius* in the broad sense includes species with an elongate body that is compressed posteriorly. The head dorsally has more or less granular or rugose bony shields. The occipital process extends posteriorly to touch the predorsal plate. The eyes are lateral or directed upward slightly and have free orbital rims. The nostrils are close together, the posterior nostril with a valve and situated superiorly near the front border of the snout. Three pairs of barbels are present, a maxillary pair and two mandibular (mental) pairs. The upper jaw is projecting over the moderate to large transverse or arcuate mouth that is provided with thin lips. The teeth in the jaws are arranged in bands, those on the palate (villiform, granular, or conical) arranged in one, two, or three groups on each side; the palatal patches are not freely movable. The dorsal fin is short-based, with a pungent spine and 7 rays, and is situated between the pectoral and ventral fins. The adipose fin is short or moderate in length and located opposite the short anal fin of 14 to 24 rays. The pectoral fin is

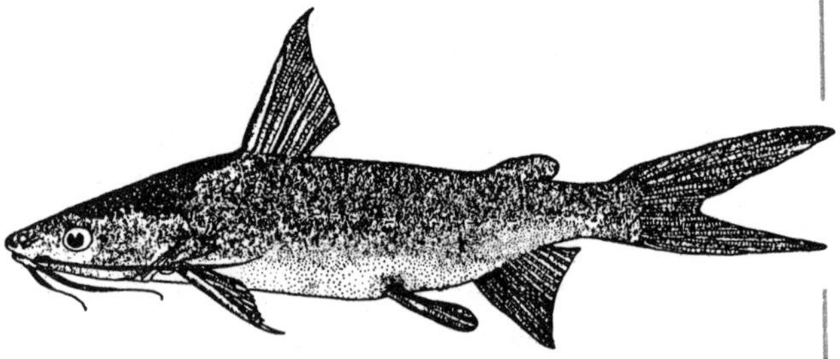

Arius graeffei. (From Allen, 1989.)

provided with a strong, pungent spine. The caudal fin is forked, the lobes rounded or pointed. The gill membranes are united and are connected with the isthmus but with a free posterior margin. There are 5 to 9 branchiostegal rays.

All species of *Arius* are said to orally incubate their eggs. In some cases there are secondary sexually dimorphic characters involving the shape and size of the head, the position and shape of some of the fins, and the development of special appendages on the ventral fins (that is to say, the ventral fins in the female are modified into "claspers" to assist in the retaining of the eggs as they are extruded). The ovaries of the females are said to undergo bilateral development; the eggs attain a very large size (up to 1.5 cm in diameter) before extrusion. Very little space is left in the abdominal cavity, and the other organs shrink or temporarily atrophy. In later stages the intestines are reduced to mere strings and the passage of food is physically impossible. The number of eggs produced is usually less than 100. The male broods the eggs, which may take as long as six to eight weeks to hatch. During this time the male does not feed and he becomes quite emaciated. Some species have males that will retain the young in the mouth for a longer time, at least until the fry have completely absorbed the yolk sac. The species of *Arius* occur in most tropical seas along sandy and muddy shores in bays and estuaries. Although almost all are marine, some are regularly found in pure fresh water. Many species are of economic importance.

Arius felis (also known as *Galeichthys felis* or *Ariopsis felis*) is one of the better known species of the genus. It is an estuarine species with a range from Cape Cod to Panama, and it attains a length of about 30 cm. It inhabits mainly harbors with sandy or muddy bottoms and is said to feed on crabs, shrimp, and occasional fishes. *A. felis* moves in rather large schools that are quite noisy, the noise being produced by vibrations of the swim bladder and clicking of the pectoral fin spines.

One small (6 cm) individual was seen chasing and repeatedly biting the side of a larger striped mullet, in a manner similar to some of the scale-eating cichlids such as *Plecodus*. Examination of stomachs of *A. felis* turned up some isolated fish scales, although most were found in smaller individuals, the larger ones apparently foregoing such habits. Observations were made in aquaria, in which the *A. felis* were attacking larger fishes within one hour of their introduction. The catfish reportedly approached the other fishes from the rear and made their charge against the body somewhere behind the dorsal fin or on the caudal and anal fins. Some recent workers have shown that there is an abundance of essential organic compounds in the mucus of the skin of fishes and that this mucus might provide a valuable food source for the young catfish.

At the onset of the breeding season females show a peculiar enlargement of the inner margins of the ventral fins. A thickened triangular hook-like flap develops on each fin; it is red in color, probably due to its engorgement with blood. These are apparently temporary in nature, occurring in females with ripening eggs and disappearing when the eggs are laid. The functions of these flaps are said to be involved with holding the eggs after extrusion and until the male takes them into his mouth. Spawning itself occurs between May and July, usually at night, and between pairs. The male may incubate more than 50 eggs at a time for a period of about four weeks. An additional two weeks may be spent caring for the young.

This species is of relatively minor economic importance, and in some areas they are considered as pests due to their pungent serrated spines. A school of these fish caught in a net takes many hours to extricate, losing valuable fishing time, and there is the strong possibility of injury from the spines. This is one of the species whose cleaned skull when viewed from the underside often appears to bear a cross. Such skulls are commonly said to be from the "crucifix catfish" and are sold as curios to tourists in many areas of the Caribbean and in some coastal areas of the United States.

A controversy involves spawning behavior in the species *Arius australis*. It has been reported to construct circular nests in the gravel of rapidly flowing streams. The eggs deposited in the nests are buried, so the final result is a mound of gravel. The eggs are said to be much smaller (about 3 mm) than the eggs of oral-incubating species. However, other workers found eggs in the mouths of males. The nesting report is usually assumed to be incorrect.

At least a couple of species are being imported for the aquarium trade. These are called Silver Shark catfishes or Blackfin Shark catfishes and are the young of various species of *Arius*. The one commonly seen in the United States is *A. jordani*, from the coast of Peru. Unfortunately these do grow to a fairly large size and will feed on smaller aquarium inhabitants when the occasion presents itself. The young *Arius* are quite hardy and present no difficulties in captivity. They are highly tolerant of changes in salinity, as one might expect, and are very easy to feed.

Checklist of species of the family Ariidae and their type localities:

Bagre Cuvier, 1817. Type species *Silurus bagre* Linnaeus.
- *Bagre bagre* (Linnaeus, 1766). South America.
- *B. filamentosus* (Swainson, 1839). Estuaries of rivers near Pernambuco, Brazil.
- *B. marinus* (Mitchill, 1814). New York.
- *B. panamensis* (Gill, 1863). Panama. (West coast of Central America.)
- *B. pinnimaculatus* (Steindachner, 1875). Panama, Altata (Sinaloa), and west coast of Costa Rica.

Batrachocephalus Bleeker, 1846. Type species *B. ageniosus* Bleeker (= *B. mino*).
- *Batrachocephalus mino* (Hamilton, 1822). Ganges.

Doiichthys Weber, 1913. Type species *D. novae-guineae* Weber.
- *Doiichthys novaeguineae* Weber, 1913. Tributary of the Lorentz River, New Guinea.

Genidens Castelnau, 1855. Type species *G. cuvieri* Castelnau (= *Bagrus genidens* Valenciennes).
- *Genidens genidens* (Valenciennes, 1839). Rio de Janeiro.

Hemipimelodus Bleeker, 1858. Type species *H. borneensis* Bleeker.
- *Hemipimelodus aaldereni* Hardenberg, 1936. New Guinea (? = *macrorhynchus*).
- *H. bernhardi* Nichols, 1940. Idenburg River, Netherland New Guinea.
- *H. borneensis* (Bleeker, 1851). Sambas, Borneo.
- *H. crassilabrus* Ramsay & Ogilby, 1886. Strickland River, New Guinea.
- *H. intermedius* Vinciguerra, 1880. Sarawak, Borneo.
- *H. macrocephalus* Bleeker, 1858. Borneo, Sumatra.
- *H. macrorhynchus* Weber, 1913. New Guinea.
- *H. manillensis* (Valenciennes, 1840). Manila.
- *H. papillifer* Herre, 1935. Sepik River, New Guinea.
- *H. siamensis* Sauvage, 1878. Laos.
- *H. taylori* Roberts, 1978. Mainstream of Palmer and lower end of small tributary about 1 km up the Palmer from Thompson Junction, New Guinea.
- *H. velutinus* Weber, 1908. New Guinea.

Ketengus Bleeker, 1858. Type species *K. typus* Bleeker.
- *Ketengus typus* Bleeker, 1847. Java.

Nedystoma Ogilby, 1898. Type species *Hemipimelodus dayi* Ramsay & Ogilby, 1886.
- *Nedystoma dayi* (Ramsay & Ogilby, 1886). Strickland and Lorentz Rivers, New Guinea.

Osteogeniosus Bleeker, 1846. Type species *O. macrocephalus* Bleeker (= *O. militaris*).

Osteogeniosus militaris (Linnaeus, 1758). Asia.

Paradiplomystes Bleeker, 1863. Type species *Pimelodus coruscans* Lichtenstein, 1829.

Paradiplomystes coruscans (Lichtenstein, 1829). Brazil.

Tetranesodon Weber, 1913. Type species *T. conorhynchus* Weber.

Tetranesodon conorhynchus Weber, 1913. New Guinea.

Arius Valenciennes, 1840. Type species *Pimelodus arius* Hamilton, 1822.

Arius acrocephalus Weber, 1913. New Guinea.

A. acutirostris Day, 1877. Salwein River at Moulmein, India.

A. africanus Playfair & Günther, 1866. Pangani River, East Africa.

A. agassizi (Eigenmann & Eigenmann, 1888). Rio Grande do Sul.

A. aguadulce (Meek, 1904). Perez, Vera Cruz, Mexico. (*Catharops*).

A. arenatus Valenciennes, 1840. Cayenne. (*Catharops*).

A. argyropleuron Valenciennes, 1840. Java.

A. arius (Hamilton, 1822). Estuaries of Bengal.

A. armiger De Vis, 1884. New Britain.

A. assimilis (Günther, 1864). Lake Yzabel, Guatemala. (*Ariopsis*).

A. ater (Castelnau, 1861). Mers do Cap (Cape of Good Hope). (*Galeichthys*).

?*A. aulometopon* (Eigenmann & Eigenmann, 1876).

?*A. barbus* (Lacépède, 1803). Rio Grande do Sul. (*Netuma*.)

A. berneyi (Whitley, 1941). Rivers flowing into the Gulf of Carpentaria, Queensland.

A. bonillai Miles, 1945. Venezuela. (*Ariopsis*).

A. brevibarbis Boulenger, 1911. Ambohimango, Madagascar. (*Ancharius*).

A. brevirostris Steindachner, 1901. Baram River, Borneo.

A. broadbenti (Ogilby, 1908). North Queensland, Australia.

A. brunelli Zolezzi, 1939. Giuba, Somalia, Yuba River at Giumbo.

A. burmanicus Day, 1869. Moulmein, Burma.

A. caelatus Valenciennes, 1840. Batavia.

A. caerulescens Günther, 1864. Rio Huamuchai, Guatemala.

A. carinatus Weber, 1913. New Guinea.

A. colcloughi (Ogilby, 1910). Crocker Island, Northern Territory, Australia.

A. couma (Valenciennes, 1839). Cayenne.

A. cous Heckel, 1843. Middle East.

A. crossocheilus Bleeker, 1846. Batavia.

A. danielsi Regan, 1908. Fly and Lorentz Rivers, New Guinea. (*Cochlefelis*).

A. digulensis Hardenberg, 1936. New Guinea.

A. dispar Herre, 1926. Paco Market, Manila, Philippines.

A. doriae Vinciguerra, 1880. Sarawak.

A. dowii (Gill, 1863). Panama.

A. dussumieri Valenciennes, 1840. Malabar Coast.

A. feliceps (Valenciennes, 1840). "Environs du Cap". (*Galeichthys*).

A. felis (Linnaeus, 1766). Charleston, S.C. (*Galeichthys* or *Ariopsis*).

A. fissus Valenciennes, 1840. Cayenne. (*Cathorops*) (? = *spixii*).

A. froggatti Ramsay & Ogilby, 1886. Strickland River, New Guinea. (*Cinetodus*).

A. furthi Steindachner, 1876. Panama.

A. fuscus Steindachner, 1881. Tohizona, Madagascar. (*Ancharius*).

A. gagora (Hamilton, 1822). Bengal.

A. gagorides (Valenciennes, 1840). Bengal.

A. gigas Boulenger, 1911. Lokoja, Upper Niger, Nigeria.

A. gilberti Jordan & Williams *in* Jordan, 1895. Mazatlan, Sinaloa, Mexico.

A. goniaspis Bleeker, 1858. Sumatra.

A. graeffei (Kner & Steindachner, 1866). Samoan Islands.

A. grandicassis Valenciennes, 1840. South America (Guyane?).

?*A. grandoculis* (Steindachner, 1876). Rio Doce.

A. guatemalensis (Günther, 1864). Guatemala.

A. harmandi (Sauvage, 1883). Menam.

?*A. henni* Eigenmann, 1822. Colimes, Rio Daule, Ecuador.

A. hertzbergii (Bloch, 1794). Surinam.

A. heudeloti Valenciennes, 1840. Senegal.

A. izabellensis (Hubbs & Miller, 1960). Lago de Izabel, Guatemala. (*Potamarius*).

A. jatius (Hamilton, 1822). Ganges.

A. jella Day, 1877. Vizagapatam, Madras.

A. jordani Jordan & Gilbert, 1882. Mazatlan.

A. kanganamanensis Herre, 1935. New Guinea.

A. laticeps Günther, 1864. Br. Guiana; Trinidad. (*Cathorops*).

A. latirostris Macleay, 1884. Goldie and Lorentz Rivers, New Guinea.

A. latiscutatus Günther, 1864. Fernando Po.

A. leiotetocephalus Bleeker, 1846. Batavia.

A. leptaspis (Bleeker, 1862). Southwestern New Guinea.

A. leptonotacanthus Bleeker, 1849. Madura.

A. liropus (Bristol *in* Gilbert, 1896). San Juan Lagoon, Sonora, Mexico.

A. macracanthus Günther, 1864. Siam.

A. macronotacanthus Bleeker, 1846. Batavia.

?*A. macrocephalus* Bleeker, 1846. Java.

A. maculatus (Thunberg, 1792). Japan.

A. madagascariensis Vaillant, 1894. Moroundave River, Madagascar.

A. magatensis Herre, 1926. Magat River, Nueva Vizcaya Prov., Philippines.

A. malabaricus Day, 1877. Cavara, India (? = *jella*).

?*A. manillensis* Valenciennes, 1840. Manila.

A. mastersi Ogilby, 1898. Northern Australia (Port Darwin?).

A. melanochir Bleeker, 1852. Sumatra; Borneo.

A. melanopus Günther, 1864. Rio Motagua (*Cathorops*).

A. microcephalus Bleeker, 1855. Bandjermasin, Borneo.

A. microstomus Nichols, 1940. Idenburg River, Netherland, New Guinea.

A. multiradiatus Günther, 1864. Rio Bayano, Panama.

A. nella (Valenciennes, 1840). Vizagapatam, India.

A. nelsoni (Evermann & Goldsborough, 1902). Rio Usumacinta, Montecristo, Yucatan [= Tabasco]. (*Potamarius*).

A. nenga (Hamilton, 1822). Estuaries of the Bengal River.

A. nox Herre, 1935. Nyaurangai, Sepik River. (*Brustarius*).

A. nuchalis Günther, 1864. Br. Guiana. (*Cathorops*).

A. nudidens Weber, 1913. Lorentz River, New Guinea.

A. oscula Jordan & Gilbert, 1882. Panama.

A. parkeri (Traill, 1832). Muddy waters of rivers of Guiana. (Cayenne; Surinam).

A. parkii Günther, 1864. Lagos & Niger Rivers.

A. parvipinnis Day, 1877. Coromandel Coast, India.

A. passany (Valenciennes, 1839). Cayenne.

A. phrygiatus Valenciennes, 1839. Cayenne.

A. planiceps Steindachner, 1876. Panama; Altata.

A. platystomus Day, 1877. Canara, India.

A. pleurops Boulenger, 1897. Magoarizinho, Brazil. (*Cathorops*).

A. polystaphylodon Bleeker, 1846. Java; Sumatra.

A. proops (Valenciennes, 1839). Surinam; Puerto Rico.

A. proximus Ogilby, 1898. Port Darwin.

A. quadriscutis Valenciennes, 1840. Cayenne or Mana.

A. rugispinis Valenciennes, 1840. Cayenne.

A. sagor (Hamilton, 1822). Ganges (estuaries of Bengal).

A. satparanus Chaudhuri, 1916. Channel between Satpara and Barnikudai.

A. sciurus H. M. Smith, 1931. Tapi River near Bandon, Thailand.

A. seemani Günther, 1864. Central America.

A. serratus Day, 1877. Sind. (= *thalassinus*).

A. solidus Herre, 1935. Timbunke, Sepik River, New Guinea.

A. sona (Hamilton, 1822). Estuaries of Bengal.

A. spatula Ramsay & Ogilby, 1886. Strickland River, New Guinea.

A. spixii (Agassiz, 1829). Equatorial Brazil.

A. stirlingi Ogilby, 1898. Adelaide River, Northern Territory, Australia.

A. stormi (Bleeker, 1858). Sumatra.

A. subrostratus Valenciennes, 1840. Malabar.

A. sumatranus (Bennett, 1830). Sumatra.

A. taylori Hildebrand, 1926. Rio Lempa, San Marcos, El Salvador.

A. tenuispinis Day, 1877. Bombay.

A. thalassinus (Rüppell, 1835). Massaua, Abyssinia.

A. truncatus Valenciennes, 1840. Java.

A. tuyra Meek & Hildebrand, 1913. Rio

Tuyra, Darien, Panama.
?*A. upsulonophorus* (Eigenmann & Eigenmann, 1889). Rio Grande do Sul.
A. utik Bleeker, 1846. Batavia; Java.
A. variolosus (Valenciennes, 1840). Cayenne. (*Cathorops*).
A. venosus Valenciennes, 1840. Rangoon.

Addenda:

Arius midgley; Kailola & Pierce, 1988. Wickham Gorge, Victoria River, N.T., Australia.

Chapter 18

Family — Plates 57–66

PLOTOSIDAE

(Tandan Catfishes)

The plotosid catfishes, called at times eel-catfishes, coral catfishes, stinging catfishes, and, in Australia, cobblers, are tropical to subtropical catfishes inhabiting coastal waters of the western Pacific and Indian Oceans. A few species inhabit the sea, but most are found in estuaries and brackish and freshwater streams, only occasionally entering the sea outside the rivers. Some push well up the streams, residing permanently in pure fresh water many miles from the sea. At spawning time some species are said to seek river deltas to deposit their eggs in water that is hardly even brackish; others apparently will spawn in fully marine water in rock crevices (concealed spawners); still others are purely freshwater species living far into the interior of Australia and constructing nests of pebbles and gravel on the stream beds, depositing their eggs there and guarding the nest until they hatch. The plotosids and ariids are the only ostariophysan fishes of the freshwaters of Madagascar, Australia, and New Guinea.

Some plotosids grow to a fairly large size. It was reported by William Dampier that in 1684 huge catfishes (presumably plotosids) were said to have prevented Indians from diving for treasure among sunken Spanish shipwrecks (Whitley, 1957). Other plotosids can occur in large schools, their bodies undulating as they move calmly through the water or in the protection of rocks or corals.

Plotosid catfishes generally have elongate, sometimes almost eel-like bodies that are compressed to subcylindrical and taper to pointed tails. The body and head are without scales or bony plates. The head is depressed and covered with skin, while the snout is depressed and bluntly rounded. The eyes are small to moderate, lateral in position, and with free orbital margins. The nostrils are remote from each other, the anterior pair tubular and located in the front border of the upper lip, either directed upward or forward or perforating the upper lip and pointing downward; the posterior nostrils are slit-like and located between the eyes and the upper lip, behind the nasal barbels. Four pairs of barbels are present: a maxillary pair, a nasal pair, and two pairs of mental or mandibular barbels. In some species there is an additional barbel-like filament formed from a labial fold at the corner of the upper lip (angle of the mouth) near the maxillary barbel. The mouth is subterminal and transverse, with thick, often papillate lips. There are conical teeth in the jaws, although they may be absent in some species and may also be mixed with molar-like teeth in the lower jaw in others; the vomer usually has molariform or conical teeth in a patch or band. The lateral line is complete, ends near the caudal fin base, and is well marked by conspicuous pores; an auxiliary humeral pore is present.

There is a short-based anterior dorsal fin usually located close behind the head, above or behind the origin of the pectoral fins, and composed of a strong, pungent spine that is either smooth-edged or serrated on both edges or serrated only along the hind border, and usually 4 or 5 rays (3-7). There is no adipose fin, but there is a long or short so-called second rayed dorsal fin or caudodorsal that is probably a procumbent part of the caudal for it is confluent with the caudal fin and often begins with a fat pad; this caudodorsal is without interneurals, hence the proposal that it is an extension forward of the caudal fin. The anal fin is many-rayed (usually 70-90) and is also confluent with the pointed, bluntly pointed, or rounded caudal fin. The ventral fins have approximately 10-16 rays. The pectoral fins are low, horizontal, and provided with a weak to strong denticulated spine. There are about 7-13 branchiostegal rays.

The swim bladder is large in proportion to the body and free (not enclosed in a bony capsule). The gill openings are wide, extending to above the level of the pectoral fin base; the gill membranes are united or more or less separated from each other, totally or partly united with the isthmus or free from it. The gill rakers are slender and pointed, confined to the first two gill arches, those of the second arch sometimes modified into transverse ridges.

Well-developed dendritic organs (arborescent appendages) between the anus and the anal fin may be present or absent. Dendritic organs are present only in the marine and brackish water species, for none of the known freshwater plotosid genera seem to have them, at least in Australian and New Guinea waters. However, three species in New Guinea, *Plotosus papuensis, Oloplotosus mariae,* and *O. toboro,* apparently have recently entered fresh water and still possess the dendritic organ. The dendritic organ of the marine species is highly vascularized, ventrally located immediately behind the anus, and comprised of numerous papillae with walls several cell layers thick enclosing a lumen that empties to the outside. Ecological, ultrastructural, and physiological studies indicate that the dendritic organ may have a salt-secreting function. The little that is known concerning the ion-regulating abilities of these fishes from a physiological standpoint suggests that the dendritic organ, urinary tract, and possibly the gills may all have a role in the salt balance. The gills of *Plotosus lineatus* are less active in salt secretion than the dendritic organs. It appears that *Plotosus* regulates its internal osmotic environment quite well, even though the gills lack functional chloride cells, due in part to the presence of the salt-secreting dendritic organ. The urinary tract may be involved since bladder urine of *Cnidoglanis* appears to be highly concentrated osmotically.

Plotosus and some of the other plotosids have dorsal and pectoral fin spines that are pungent and venomous and, according to some reports, have caused fatalities. Poison glands emerge at all three spines.

All large species of plotosids are said to be good eating.

The family Plotosidae contains about seven to nine genera depending upon the classification followed. The most commonly accepted genera can be distinguished by the following key (modified from Taylor, 1964).

1a. Anal dendritic organ present; distance between origins of first and second dorsal fins less than head length; chiefly marine, but may contain a few freshwater species 2

1b. Anal dendritic organ absent; distance between origins of first and second dorsal fins usually greater than the head length (except *Anodontoglanis*); only freshwater catfishes 6

2a. Anterior nares near oral border of upper lip and directed downward, surrounded by the papillae extensively covering the lips; gill membranes broadly united, the notch shallow; premaxillary teeth in two triangular or subcircular patches; caudodorsal originates before ventral fins...... .... *Paraplotosus*

2b. Anterior nares on end of snout and directed upward or outward 3

3a. Premaxillary teeth absent; mandible and vomer without molars......... *Oloplotosus*

3b. Premaxillary teeth present 4

4a. Gill membranes free from each other and from isthmus, except anteriorly, forming a deep notch; lips plicate or moderately papillose; band of teeth on premaxillae nearly continuous across midline, about three times as broad as long; caudodorsal originates behind origin of ventral fins.................. *Plotosus*

4b. Gill membranes broadly attached to isthmus, united or free from each other; premaxillary teeth in two small patches;

lips thick and papillose or moderately plicate 5

5a. Gill membranes united to each other and broadly attached to the isthmus, the notch between them shallow; lips papillose or moderately plicate; mandible and vomer with molars .... *Cnidoglanis*

5b. Gill membranes separate, broadly attached to the isthmus; lips thick and papillose; mandible and vomer with molars .... *Euristhmus*

6a. Palate and lower jaw edentulous; premaxilla edentulous or with one or two deciduous teeth on each side; distance between origins of first and second dorsal fins less than head length .... *Anodontoglanis*

6b. Palate, lower jaw, and premaxilla with firmly rooted teeth; distance between origins of first and second dorsal fins equal to or usually greater than head length 7

7a. Anterior nares piercing lower border of thin upper lip and directed downward; spines smoothly rounded or nearly so, without serrae .... *Porochilus*

7b. Anterior nares on end of snout and directed upward or outward; spines, especially pectoral spines, serrate (*Tandanus*) 8

8a. Caudodorsal long, extending well forward on back, above or in front of middle of body almost as far as anal fin; dorsal fin I,6 .... *Tandanus*

8b. Caudodorsal short, extending forward on back nowhere near as far as anal fin; D. I,4 .... *Neosilurus*

Unfortunately, there are several generic names in the literature that may or may not be added to or even replace one or more of the above. *Copidoglanis* is currently considered a synonym of the genus *Tandanus*, and *Neosilurus* has also been combined with that same genus, although some recent authors have been regarding it as a separate genus distinguished as indicated in the key. The question of its validity is also involved with the possibility of its being preoccupied; *Cainosilurus* has been proposed in such an event. *Exilichthys* is currently considered a synonym of *Cnidoglanis*, while *Euristhmus* is considered a separate genus, although it has, at times, also been considered as synonymous with the genus *Cnidoglanis*.

The genus *Paraplotosus* contains species that are elongate and have a tapering tail; the head is depressed. The lips are thick, with papillae and vermiculated folds; the upper lip is very prominent and perforated at its border near the mouth opening by the anterior nostrils. Four pairs of barbels are present: nasal, maxillary, mandibular, and mental. The eyes are not covered by skin. The dorsal fin is short-based, with a strong spine denticulated at both edges and few rays, and located behind the origin of the pectoral fins. The caudodorsal originates before or above the origin of the ventral fins. Both caudodorsal and anal fins are confluent with the caudal fin. The ventral fins have 12-13 rays, and the pectoral fins have a denticulated spine. The maxillary teeth are in two rhombic-shaped patches with the lateral edges rounded; the teeth themselves are conical with rounded tops. The vomerine teeth are molariform and arranged in a crescentic patch. The gill membranes are confluent in the middle, only the anterior portion of their confluent part connected with the isthmus; there are 9-11 branchiostegal rays. There are 22 gill rakers on the entire first arch. A very conspicuous dendritic organ is present between the anus and the anal fin.

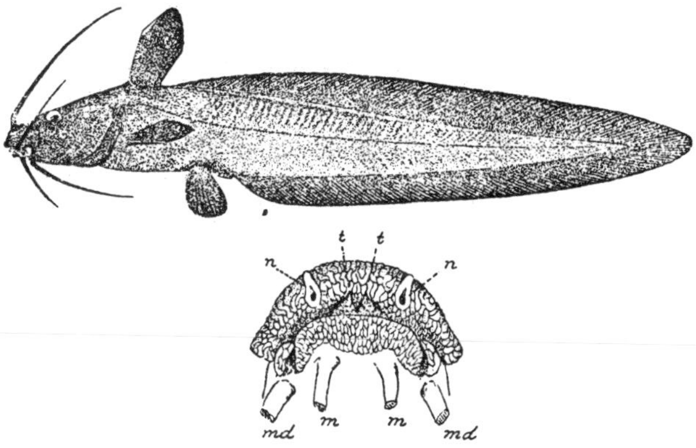

Paraplotosus albilabris; (b) view of mouth and lips, n = nostrils, t = teeth, md = mandibulary barbels, m = mental barbels. (From Weber & de Beaufort, 1913.)

The single species, *Paraplotosus albilabris*, is a marine species with a range that includes Java, Singapore, the Celebes, the Aru Islands, New Guinea, and Australia. It attains a length of about 35 cm. The White-lipped Eel

Catfish can inflict a painful wound with its pectoral fin spines.

The genus *Cnidoglanis* is comprised of species that are elongate with a tapering tail and a compressed head. The eyes are small and covered with skin. There are four pairs of barbels: nasal, maxillary, mandibular, and mental. A lateral fold at the corner of the mouth may also be produced into a short barbel. The lips are thick and papillose and the upper lip is prominent. The anterior nostrils are on the front border of the upper lip. Teeth in the upper jaw are more or less conical; on the lower jaw they are mixed conical and mo-

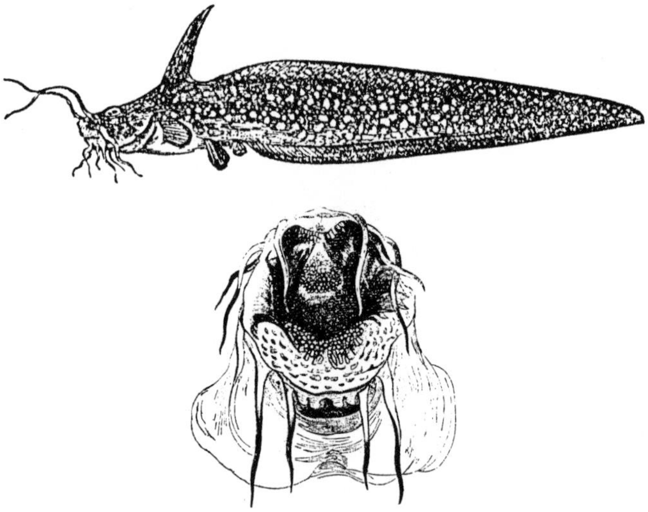

Cnidoglanis microceps; (b) mouth of *C. macrocephalus*. (From Günther, 1880.)

lariform; and on the vomer they are molariform. The origin of the short-based dorsal fin is above or behind the origin of the pectoral fins; both dorsal and pectoral fins have a sharp spine serrated at both borders. The origin of the caudodorsal is above or behind the ventral fins; the caudodorsal and anal fins are confluent with the caudal fin. The ventral fins have 10-12 rays. The lateral line is more or less conspicuous. The gill membranes are united to each other and to a broad isthmus along the median line. The second and third branchial arches have a series of long cartilaginous processes covering the bases of the gill lamellae on the sides facing each other. A conspicuous dendritic organ is present.

Cnidoglanis macrocephalus grows to a length of about 91 cm. It occurs along the coasts of Australia and New Guinea where, at least in some areas, it is quite common. It is basically an estuarine catfish inhabiting shallow bays and sandy inlets near river mouths and occasionally entering fresh water. However, it is found mostly on muddy bottoms in the estuaries. The serrated dorsal and pectoral fin spines can inflict serious and very painful wounds. The conspicuous dendritic organ probably has an osmoregulatory function. The flesh is reported to be good eating.

The genus *Euristhmus* is sometimes regarded as a separate genus and sometimes synonymized with *Cnidoglanis*. It has an elongate body with the tail more than twice as long as the head and trunk; the head is much

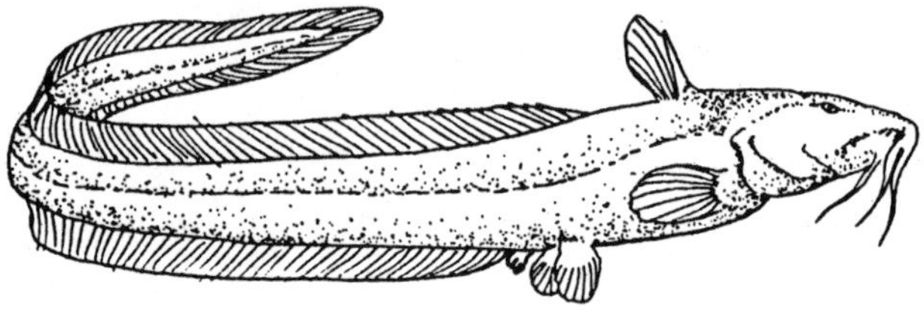

Euristhmus lepturus. (After Grant, 1978.)

broader than long. The eyes are small and without free lids. The occipital region is not osseus and is covered with loose skin. The skin is smooth. The gill membranes are separate (this is the major feature separating *Euristhmus* from *Cnidoglanis*) and broadly united with the isthmus.

E. lepturus, from southern Queensland and New South Wales coastal areas, attains a length of about 40 cm. It appears to form a substantial part of the diet of pied cormorants and shags, at least in southern Queensland estuaries.

The genus *Oloplotosus* is a small genus of three species from New Guinea. The body is elongate and the tail is tapering. The head is

Oloplotosus luteus. (After Roberts, 1978.)

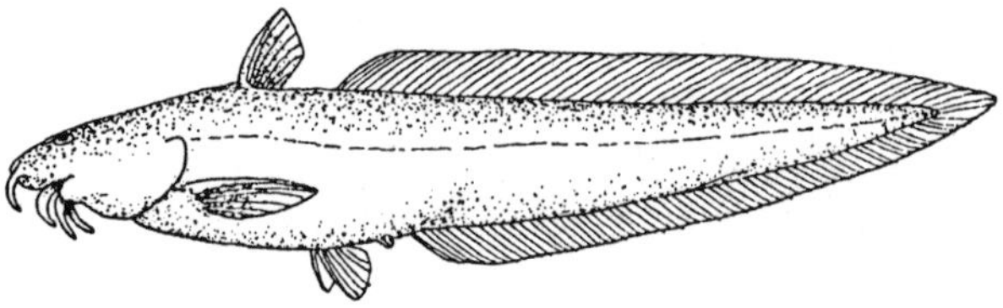

depressed and covered with thick skin; the eyes are also covered with skin. Four pairs of barbels are present: nasal, maxillary, mandibular, and mental. The lips are thick, with lamellated folds, and the upper lip is very prominent and anteriorly perforated by the anterior nostrils that form short rounded tubes. The teeth are conical and arranged in about two rows forming a narrow crescentic band on the lower jaw and vomer; there are no teeth on the upper jaw. The dorsal fin is short, with few rays and a strong spine that is denticulated on both edges, and is located a little behind the origin of the pectoral fins. The caudodorsal begins before the origin of the ventral fins; the caudodorsal and anal fins are confluent with the caudal fin. The pectoral fins have denticulated spines; the ventral fins have 12 or 13 rays. The gill membranes are mesially united with the isthmus along their whole length. There are 10 branchiostegal rays. There are 17 gill rakers on the first gill arch. A conspicuous dendritic organ is present.

One of the species, *O. luteus*, was collected in the area of the upper Fly River highlands where the current was moderate to swift and the bottom was covered with rocks and cobbles. Another, *O. toboro*, was discovered in Lake Kutubu where the bottom was soft and muddy and there was abundant aquatic vegetation.

The genus *Porochilus* contains about three species from Australia and New Guinea. The body is also elongate with a tapering tail. The head is more or less depressed, and the eyes are covered with skin. Four pairs of barbels are present: nasal, maxillary, mandibular, and mental. The lips are rather thin, weakly papillated, the thicker lower lip lamellated and the upper lip slightly prominent. The teeth are conical and are arranged in two to three rows forming two small subtriangular patches in the upper jaw; the vomerine teeth are in a rounded patch anteriorly. The dorsal fin is short-based, with a rather weak spine that has no serrations, and is located conspicuously posterior to the pectoral origin and a little before the ventrals. The caudodorsal is very short, its anterior rays located above the last third of the anal fin and with hardly any fat pad; the anal fin is confluent with the caudal fin. The pectoral fins have 7 or 8 rays and a rather weak spine with a few teeth along its anterior edge; the ventral fins have 11 or 12 rays. The gill membranes are united and free from the isthmus; there are 7 branchiostegal rays and 11 gill rakers. There is no ventrally located dendritic organ.

Porochilus obbesi is distributed in West Irian and the Timor Sea and Gulf drainage systems. It attains a length of about 12 cm. It inhabits slow flowing streams, backwaters, swamps, and lily lagoons, usually among aquatic weeds, such as eel grass. The diet consists mostly of insects and insect larvae, prawns, and molluscs. *P. argenteus* inhabits slow flowing streams over sand or rock bottoms.

The genus *Anodontoglanis* contains a single species from Northern Territory, Australia. It is also elongate with a tapering tail and a depressed head. The snout is relatively elongate. There are four pairs of barbels: nasal, maxillary, and two pairs of mental barbels. The anterior nares are on the end of the snout slightly lateral to the nasal barbel and pointing forward as short projecting tubes. The mouth is transverse, the jaws are equal, and the cleft does not extend as far as the orbit. The lips are finely plicate and the mouth is

Porochilus obbesi. (After Taylor, 1964.)

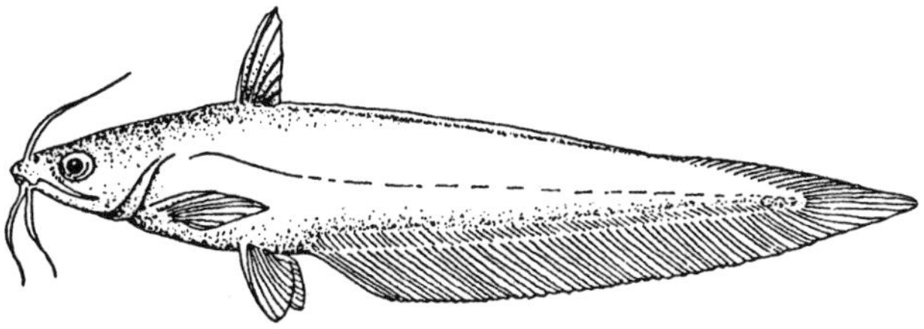

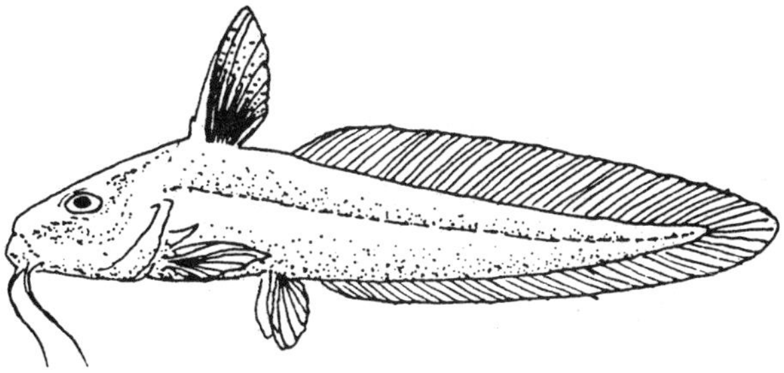

Anodontoglanis dahli. (After Taylor, 1964.)

edentulous except for a small, pointed, movable, probably deciduous tooth on each side of the midline of the premaxilla in larger individuals and two on each side in smaller ones. The pharyngeal teeth are numerous and pointed. The dorsal fin is short, with a spine and 6 rays, and located behind the origin of the pectoral fins; the dorsal fin spine is nearly smooth posteriorly but has hooked step-like processes anteriorly. The second dorsal and anal fins are confluent with the caudal fin, composed of about 175-180 rays, the second dorsal originating anteriorly, above or slightly behind the insertion of the ventral fins. The pectoral fins have 11 rays and spines that are finely serrate anteriorly and have straight, slightly coarser serrae posteriorly, the distal third of the anterior edge with hooked steps. The ventral fins have 12-13 rays. There are about 15-16 moderately long, slender gill rakers on the first arch; those on the second arch are short, rectangular ridges. There is no anal dendritic organ.

The only species in the genus, *Anodontoglanis dahli*, is called the Toothless Catfish in Australia, where it is an endemic species. It is reasonably common in clear, flowing waters of some rivers and attains a length of about 40 cm. Their flesh is somewhat orange in color, and they are reported to be delicious eating. The food consists mainly of aquatic insects, molluscs, prawns, and bottom detritus.

The genus *Tandanus* (including *Neosilurus*) is the largest genus of the family, with about a dozen species described and three to six more awaiting description. The body is elongate with a tapering tail, and the head is more or less depressed. Four pairs of barbels are present: nasal, maxillary, and two pairs of mental barbels. The anterior nostril is a short tube in the front part of the upper lip; the posterior nostril is a narrow slit behind the nasal barbel. The lips are thick and papillated, and the conical teeth in the upper jaw are arranged in two squarish patches. The origin of the dorsal fin is conspicuously posterior to the pectoral fin origin. The dorsal fin is short-based with a serrated spine and few rays. In the group of species sometimes called *Neosilurus* the caudodorsal is not well developed. In *Tandanus* proper the caudodorsal extends forward to varying degrees, never reaching farther than above the origin of the anal fin. The anal fin is confluent with the caudal fin. The pectoral fins have denticulated spines and 8-12 rays; the ventral fins have 11-13 rays. The gill membranes are united, forming a deep notch, and are free from the isthmus. The gill rakers are few in number and stout.

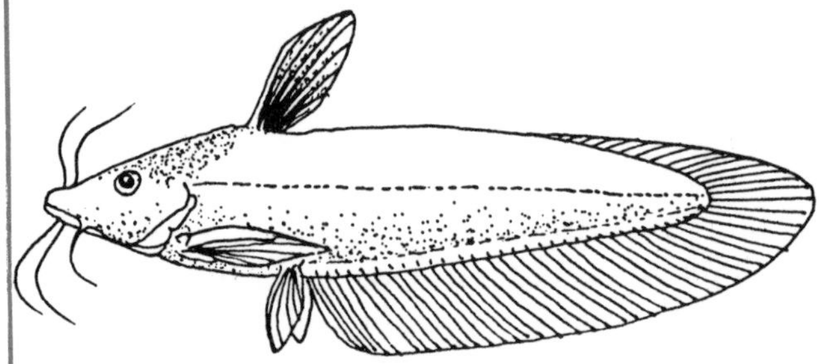

Tandanus ater (often *Neosilurus ater*). (After Taylor, 1964.)

Tandanus is often found in vast schools. They are fast and active fishes, always seeming to be in search of food. There is evidence that some "*Neosilurus*" are egg scatterers over gravel in flowing water; no nests have been described for them. The spawning of *Tandanus tandanus* is described in detail below.

Tandanus tandanus is a species endemic to southern and eastern Australia, where it is found only in fresh water. It inhabits principally muddy or sandy areas of lakes and sluggish rivers, where its main diet includes molluscs and crustaceans. The Tandan or Dewfish, as it is commonly called, grows to a length of 90 cm and attains a weight of 6.5 kilos, and its flesh is reported to be good to eat. Although it has yellow eyes, this species is dark brown and generally unattractive and possesses sharp spines in the dorsal and pectoral fins that can inflict painful wounds.

Tandanus tandanus. (After Grant, 1978.)

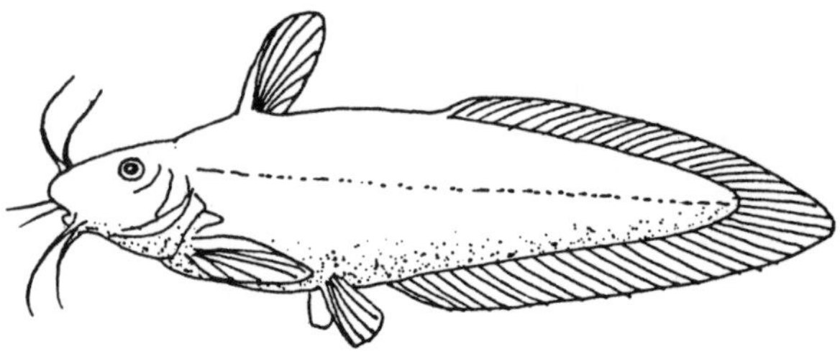

This is one of the better known plotosid catfishes as far as the spawning activities are concerned.

Spawning takes place in late spring to midsummer in Australia, when the temperature reaches to about 24°C. Tandans will spawn quite readily in artificial ponds. The sexes can be distinguished at an age of about one year: the female has a triangular urogenital papilla while in the male it is cylindrical. The male creates a nest in the form of a saucer-like depression up to 200 cm in diameter (larger individuals) on a sandy or muddy bottom in clear water, usually on a gently sloping bank where the water is about a meter deep. The periphery may consist of gravel and rocks. Other nests were described as clear circular openings in weeds with a raised edge of sand. The nest is hollowed out by vigorous fanning movements of the fins, especially the tail, and perhaps, as reported by some observers, excavated by taking away mouthfuls of sand. The nest may be covered with pebbles, small stones, and sticks depending upon what is available in the area. In one report the nest was filled with larger sized stones, some as big as a man's fist. The sticks and stones are carried to the nest in the mouth of the male according to most sources, although others state that the fanning motion of the fins removes only the lighter particles, leaving the heavier material, such as the pebbles, etc., behind.

Once the nest is completed the male sets out looking for a mate. After an interval that varies considerably (from an hour to almost a whole day) the male reappears, driving before him a none-too-willing female. Courtship apparently involves threats and persuasive elements, for at times the male is gentle as he moves her to the nest while at others he attacks with spines erect and forces her into the nest, swimming about her in circles and literally keeping her a prisoner. Eventually he swims up beside her and with quivering movements the eggs are laid in the center of the nest. Once spawning has been completed the female departs. There is also some disagreement concerning this as some observers state two fish continuously swim around the nest after egg-laying, but others report that either parent stays to guard the eggs; most say that it is the male that jealously guards the eggs and nest. In one instance the guarding fish was speared and examined and found to be a 50-cm-long male. The male then continuously swims around and around over the nest, altering this pattern only to chase away any trespassers or to clean house by removing unwanted stones, shells, or debris. If a shell is tossed into the nest by the observer, the male will indignantly pick it up and deposit it away from the nest. The eggs are demersal, non-adhesive, about 3.2 mm in diameter, spherical in shape, and light green in color. Fish of about 39 cm in length and weighing 1.4 kilos yield about 20,000 eggs.

Although the male guards the nest for 16 to 18 days, hatching of the eggs takes place in about seven days (at a temperature of 19-25°C). The newly hatched larvae are approximately 7 mm long and have no barbels or pectoral fins; the barbels make their appearance as tiny buds some three days after hatching and are well-formed a week after hatching, when the larvae are about 1.2 cm long. After two to three weeks the fry have absorbed their yolk sac and have more or less transformed into young catfish. Between 2.5 to 10 cm the young fish feed on zooplankton and small insects, especially chironomids. The adults are bottom-feeding carnivores on molluscs, crustaceans (mostly shrimp), insects, and even some fishes. In an aquarium the young fish do well on chopped earthworms whereas the adults will take whole earthworms, chopped meat, and sometimes dead fishes. They feed by odor more than sight and in their forays will constantly stir up the bottom material of the aquarium.

Tandanus ater inhabits rivers and smaller streams, usually where the currents are relatively swift. Spawning occurs during the wet season. Food items include molluscs, insects, prawns, and earthworms. *T. brevidorsalis* inhabits clear flowing streams and turbid backwaters and lagoons. The diet is mainly insects, prawns, molluscs, and small crayfish.

The genus *Plotosus* contains five species that are principally marine but are often found in estuaries and river mouths, and some even may extend well up into pure fresh water. The body is elongate, compressed, the abdomen is subcylindrical, and the tail is ta-

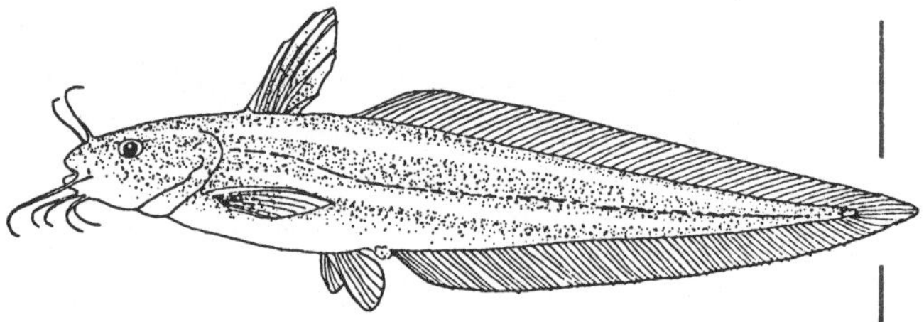

Plotosus lineatus.

pering. The head is short, depressed, and covered with thin skin; the snout is depressed and bluntly rounded. The eyes are moderate, lateral, in the anterior part of the head, and are not covered with skin (with a free orbital margin). The nostrils are far apart, the anterior tubular and on the snout or above the edge of the upper lip; the posterior nostril has a nasal barbel. There are four pairs of barbels, a nasal pair, a maxillary pair, and two mandibular or mental pairs. The mouth is transverse, the upper jaw the longer, and the lips are thick but without barbel-like extensions or mental lobes. The premaxillary teeth are conical, numerous, and arranged in a narrow square band; the teeth of the lower jaw are also conical but they are mixed with molariform teeth and are arranged in 2-5 rows. The vomerine teeth are molariform and arranged in patches or in a crescentic band. The dorsal fin is short, with 4-5 rays and a strong pungent spine denticulated on both edges, and is inserted above or behind the origin of the pectoral fin. The caudodorsal is long, low, and originates between the origin of the ventrals and the anal; both caudodorsal and anal fins are confluent with the caudal fin. The pectoral fins have a weak or strong spine denticulated on both edges; the ventral fins have as many as 11-14 rays. The caudal fin may be rounded to pointed. The lateral line is well-developed and complete. The gill membranes are separate from each other and from the isthmus except for a narrow portion united anteriorly. There are 20-28 gill rakers and 9-12 branchiostegals. The swim bladder is moderate, not enclosed in a bony capsule. Both sexes (even immature individuals) possess arborescent organs just posterior to the genital pore.

In most species of *Plotosus* the spines can inflict painful wounds and should be treated with as much respect as one would the marine scorpionfishes of the genus *Pterois*. J. Pellegrin reports that the *Plotosus* of Madagascar stay on the bottom covered by a light layer of sand or mud and have the dorsal fin raised to present the spine in the manner of the weevers.

Plotosus lineatus is perhaps the widest ranging and best-known of the plotosids. It attains a length of about 30 cm or more and may be found from the Red Sea and eastern Africa to the western Pacific. It is relatively common

Young *Plotosus lineatus* with their characteristic white (sometimes yellowish) stripes are commonly seen in moderate to large schools. Photo by Hilmar Hansen.

throughout its range, where it occurs on reefs and coastal areas, including harbors and estuaries, and is reported to penetrate even into almost pure fresh water in river mouths. Most people are not as familiar with the adult of the species as they are with the more colorful juvenile. Juveniles are striped in black and white (or black and yellow), these stripes fading with age so that the adults are a more uniform grayish brown. The juveniles congregate in schools so dense that they sometimes carpet the bottom. These schools may break up into balls or pods that are spherical groups of often hundreds of blackish individuals and have been observed moving as though a pod were a single creature. Bush children in Australia colorfully refer to these moving schools or pods as "catfish going to church." The young may also occur as solitary individuals in tide pools and under clumps of algae.

Myers prefers to call them "Bumblebee Catfish" and cites several reasons. They are yellow and black striped (although some are white and not yellow and the pattern goes the wrong way), they swarm like bees, and they even buzz like bees when they are removed from the water. On top of all this they can sting like bees. The serrated spines of the dorsal and pectoral fins can inflict a most painful and potentially dangerous wound, early literature even claiming that human deaths have resulted from the stings. The venom apparatus includes the dorsal and pectoral spines and the axillary venom glands. The pectoral spines receive venom from both the axillary gland and the pectoral spine gland. Schools of these fish in shallow water are a constant threat to waders, collectors, and swimmers, and anglers and trawlers must be very careful with their catches if they include any of the plotosids. Herre (1949) reported his experience with a plotosid about 14.5 cm long. It had lain on the bottom of a banka for a good 15 minutes and was assumed to be dead. As soon as he picked it up it fought to be free from his grasp, the result of the fish's movement being a pectoral spine in Herre's thumb. The initial pain was very great but bearable. He continued fishing for another half hour and then returned to care for his catch, bathe, and change. The pain grew worse during this time and the thumb began to swell, followed shortly by the whole hand. The wound was cleaned and bandaged at the hospital, but the pain kept Herre awake all night and the hand, wrist, and forearm all swelled to twice their normal size. Another doctor lanced the wound and put in a drain, giving Herre morphine to combat the pain. The hand was redressed twice a day for a week. After about the first five days the swelling started to slowly go down, but from the third to the sixth days a severe case of diarrhea resulting in a 25-pound weight loss occurred. Even after a month, the wound, although closed, was still painful to the touch, and after two months pressure on the spot where the wound healed still caused pain. It took almost six months for all of the effects of the sting to be dissipated.

In Japan the spawning season of *P. lineatus* occurs during July and August, with the eggs being deposited in cracks and crevices of rocks in very shallow water or in nests constructed by the male under rocks or other large pieces of debris. The eggs are spherical, non-adhesive, demersal, and roughly 3.1-3.5 mm in diameter. Each contains a large bright yellow yolk. The male remains to guard the eggs. The eggs hatch in about seven to ten days. The fry have a fairly large yolk sac, but in about ten days the yolk is absorbed and the fry become free-swimming and start their search for food. They are large enough to accept newly hatched brine shrimp. At a size of about 15 mm they resemble the adults with the exception of their color pattern. Sexual maturity in females is attained in about a year's time, when they are approximately 14 cm long. Most are mature by three years, and the maximum life span is said to be about seven years. At least two large public aquaria in Japan have successfully spawned plotosids.

Although potentially dangerous because of their venomous spines, plotosids are commonly kept in home aquaria (especially the black and white or yellow *P. lineatus*). They are best kept in pure marine water although they can be acclimated to a more brackish system if necessary. They should be kept as a small school, for single specimens usually will not thrive. At least four individuals, although more would be better, are recommended. Hiding places should be provided in the form of coral, rocks, and even PVC tubing. The total population of the tank will probably try and squeeze themselves into a single crevice. In fact, Herre, upon examining a coral head washed up on shore by the surf, poured some formalin into a crack to see what would come out. He heard a "buzzing" sound and several thousand tiny plotosids came out. *P. lineatus* is fairly hardy and will eat almost any decent aquarium food, although they prefer live foods such as small shrimp, fishes, worms, etc. Small individuals will even take flake food. They are usually greedy and grow very quickly, making it necessary to house them in a relatively large tank. A temperature of 22-26°C is recommended. Single specimens, if they survive, are said to be very aggressive.

The Japanese consider them poor quality food, but in Africa they say *P. lineatus* is good eating. In Australia they are preyed upon by shags or cormorants.

According to Chardon (1968) the plotosids resemble the Bagridae but are more depressed and have a much more elongate body and tapering tail. They are nearest the subfamily Bagrinae in the more generalized character of the anterior vertebrae, the swim bladder, and the cranium. The posttemporal, without a dorsal plate although firmly attached, is even more simple than that of the Bagrinae. The plotosids also resemble the Ariidae by their mode of life, i.e., they both are largely marine and euryhaline.

Checklist of the species of the family Plotosidae and their type localities:

Anodontoglanis Rendahl, 1922. Type species *A. dahli* Rendahl.
- *Anodontoglanis dahli* Rendahl, 1922. Glencoe, Northern Territory, Australia.

Paraplotosus Bleeker, 1862. Type species *Plotosus albilabris* Valenciennes.
- *Paraplotosus albilabris* (Valenciennes, 1840). Batavia, Java.

Porochilus Weber, 1913. Type species *Porochilus obbesi* Weber.
- *Porochilus argenteus* (Zietz, 1896), Cooper and Finke Rivers, Central Australia.
- *P. obbesi* Weber, 1913. Lorentz River, New Guinea.
- *P. rendahli* (Whitley, 1928). Glencoe and Hermit Hill, Northern Territory. (Subst. name for *Copidoglanis obscurus* Rendahl, preoccupied).

Cnidoglanis Günther, 1864. Type species *Plotosus megastomus* Richardson (= *Cnidoglanis macrocephalus* (Valenciennes, 1840)).
- *Cnidoglanis macrocephalus* (Valenciennes, 1840). "Timor." (Incorrect designation. Distribution is temperate Australia.)
- *C. microceps* (Richardson, 1845). Northwestern coast of Australia.
- *C. muelleri* Klunzinger, 1879. Port Darwin, Australia.

Euristhmus Ogilby, 1899. Type species *Plotosus elongatus* Castelnau, 1878. (= *E. lepturus* Günther).
- *Euristhmus lepturus* (Günther, 1864). Sydney, New South Wales.
- *E. nudiceps* (Günther, 1880). Arafura Sea.

Oloplotosus Weber, 1913. Type species *Oloplotosus mariae* Weber.
- *Oloplotosus luteus* Gomon & Roberts, 1978. Fly River, New Guinea.
- *O. mariae* Weber, 1913. Sabang and Alkmaar on the Lorentz River, New Guinea.
- *O. toboro* Allen, 1985. Lake Kutubu, New Guinea.

Plotosus Lacépède, 1803. Type species *Platystacus anguillaris* Bloch (= *Silurus anguillaris* Forsskål = *Plotosus lineatus* (Thunberg)).
- *Plotosus canius* Hamilton, 1822. Ganges.
- *P. limbatus* Valenciennes, 1840. Malabar and Pondicherry.
- *P. lineatus* (Thunberg, 1787). East Indian seas.
- *P. nkunga* Gomon & Taylor, 1982. Bashee River, Transkei, South Africa.
- *P. papuensis* Weber, 1910. New Guinea.

Tandanus Mitchell, 1839. Type species *Plotosus (Tandanus) tandanus* Mitchell.
- *Tandanus ater* (Perugia, 1894). Inawi, Papua, New Guinea.
- *T. bartoni* (Regan, 1908). Southern New Guinea.
- *T. bostocki* Whitley, 1944. Southwestern Australia.
- *T. brevidorsalis* (Günther, 1867). New Guinea.
- *T. coatesi* Allen, 1985. Ninar River, Papua, New Guinea.
- *T. equinus* (Weber, 1913). New Guinea.
- *T. gjellerupi* (Weber, 1913). New Guinea.
- *T. glencoensis* (Rendahl, 1922). Daly River

& Glencoe, Northern Territory. (= *T. hyrtlii*.)

T. hyrtlii (Steindachner, 1867). Fitzroy River.

T. meraukensis (Weber, 1913). New Guinea.

T. mortoni (Whitley, 1941). Yam Creek, Northern Territory.

T. novaeguineae (Weber, 1908). New Guinea.

T. perugiae (Ogilby, 1908). New Guinea.

T. tandanus (Mitchell, 1838).

T. spp. Recorded as "barcooensis," "glov-eri," "pseudospinatus," black tandan, mottled tandan, bulloo tandan, white tandan, Cooper's Creek tandan, and Cooper's Creek white tandan. Several of these may prove to be new species.

Chapter 19

Family — Plates 67–94

MOCHOKIDAE

(Upside-Down Catfishes)

The Mochokidae is a family of small to moderate sized (to 72 cm) catfishes that inhabit the fresh waters of Africa, with the exception of some of the desert regions of the northern part of that continent. They normally inhabit the waters of slow-flowing rivers, lakes, and swamps, with some genera being adapted to the swifter-flowing torrents. Most species are bottom-living (usually a hard bottom), exploring the surfaces there with their inferior and more or less adhesive mouths. Many of the species are nocturnal or crepuscular, usually hiding by day under logs, tree roots, in crevices, etc., and becoming more active in the dim twilight hours. In murky or relatively deep water (15 meters or more), where the light level is quite low, they may also be active during the daytime. They generally feed on small invertebrates as well as algae, using their barbels as sensory devices, with some species turning upside down in order to search for food on the undersides of rocks, roots, etc. This habit has become the normal mode of swimming in some species, and the bodies of these fishes have become countershaded, i.e., instead of dark backs and light bellies they have dark bellies and light backs. It is reported that the juveniles start in the normal swimming position and only later adopt the upside-down position. Most species are of little or no commercial value.

The short to moderate length scaleless body is commonly thickset, with the sides only slightly compressed. The head is flattened but covered (encapsulated according to some) with an armor of bony plates with at least one pointed projection that extends to the base of the pectoral fin. The mouth is generally subterminal, except in the case of the torrent-loving genera, which also have their lips spread out and modified into a sucker, and there are three pairs of barbels (the nasals are absent). The mandibular barbels are commonly branched, and occasionally the maxillary barbels will also exhibit some branchlets as well. The dorsal and anal fins are comparatively short-based but of a good size, and the dorsal and pectoral fins may be provided with a strong, sharp spine. There is a well-developed adipose fin, sometimes in the form of a second rayed dorsal, that may be large or even very large. The gill openings are restricted, and the gill membranes are broadly united to the isthmus.

The family Mochokidae (often spelled Mochocidae) is generally said to contain only seven genera, but with the description of a new genus, *Mochokiella*, and the splitting of the genus *Synodontis* into three genera, the number has been increased to ten. The genus *Synodontis* is so large (there are over 100 species) and the other genera so much less publicized that in many aquarists' minds the family Mochokidae is virtually equivalent to the genus *Synodontis*; when they speak of mochokids they actually mean members of the genus *Synodontis*. The ten genera can be distinguished by the following key (modified from Poll, 1957):

1a. Mandibular barbels branched; lips more or less fleshy but not transforming at the mouth into a flattened, rounded sucker. 2

1b. Mandibular barbels simple, not branched; lips flattened and forming a rounded buccal sucker.............................. 8
2a. Eye with a free border 3
2b. Eye lacking a free border; size small.. 6
3a. Pectoral fin spine base simple; adipose fin not rayed................................ 4
3b. Spiny process present above pectoral fin spine base in addition to humeral process; adipose fin weakly rayed; maximum length 5.5 cm*Acanthocleithron*
4a. Operculum not toothed, without free border; mouth small to average; gill rakers 7-33; maximum length 72 cm...*Synodontis*
4b. Opercle toothed or not but with free border; mouth large; gill rakers 39 or more... 5
5a. Operculum not toothed; adipose fin contiguous with the rayed dorsal fin; distal extremity of mandibular barbels membranous; 8-16 mandibular teeth; 59-65 gill rakers...........*Hemisynodontis*
5b. Operculum with a free and many-toothed extremity; adipose fin contiguous with rayed dorsal fin; distal extremity of mandibular barbels not membranous; 33-57 mandibular teeth; 39-42 gill rakers ....*Brachysynodontis*
6a. Second dorsal (adipose) fin provided with branched rays; maximum length 7 cm.................................. *Mochokus*
6b. Second dorsal fin a normal adipose fin, without branched rays 7
7a. Adipose fin long; caudal fin rounded; lower lip well developed; maximum length 10 cm............... *Microsynodontis*
7b. Adipose fin short; caudal fin forked; lower lip weak; maximum length 3.6 cm ....*Mochokiella*
8a. Eye with a free border; teeth (at least in part) truncate............................... 9
8b. Eye without free border; teeth all conical; size small, maximum length 7 cm.. ....*Chiloglanis*
9a. Premaxillary teeth pointed, curved; mandibular teeth truncate or bicuspid; maximum length 40 cm.... *Euchilichthys*
9b. Premaxillary and mandibular teeth truncate; maximum length 10 cm.*Atopochilus*

The genus *Hemisynodontis* is a small genus containing only a single species, *H. membranaceus*, from the basins of the Nile, Tchad, Niger, Senegal, Volta, and Gambia. It is considered by some authors as a synonym of the genus *Synodontis*, while others insist it is a separate genus. The body is short and deep, fairly compressed, with the skin smooth. The head is deeper than long, with the cephalonuchal head shield more or less granulose and the humeral process much shorter than the nuchal process. The operculum has a free

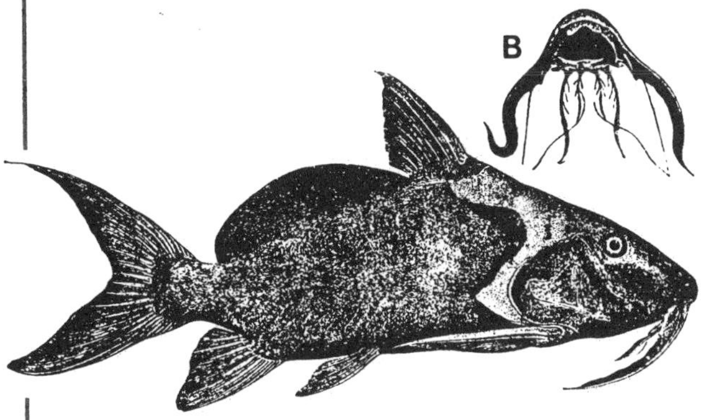

Hemisynodontis membranaceus; (b) ventral view of mouth. (From Boulenger, 1911.)

border but is not denticulate. The mouth is very large and is provided with lips that are non-papillose, membranous, and confluent laterally with very broad mandibular membranes to form a funnel-like arrangement. There are three pairs of barbels, the maxillary pair with a very broad membrane extending as far as their tips; the mandibular pair is branched, although the branches are simple and not very thick, and is also provided with a membrane at the extremity of the barbels. The dentition is weak, the premaxillary teeth vestigial and arranged in a band scarcely as long as the eye, while the mandibular teeth are tiny, curved, in a small patch of 8-16. The dorsal fin is short-based, with a strong spine and 7 rays, and the adipose fin is very large, more or less continuous with the base of the rayed dorsal. The anal fin is short-based and the caudal fin is forked. The pectoral fins have a strong serrated spine, and the ventral fins are located well back on the ventral part of the body beneath the adipose fin. The gill membranes are free from the isthmus except for a narrow attachment less than the eye diameter. The eyes have a free border, and the palate is edentulous. A large peculiar palatine organ is present over the gill openings and there is a gill raker filter formed by rows of gill rakers (about 59-65) provided with lateral barblets on the first gill arch. This structure provides an excellent means for filtering the plankton and surface material that forms the major part of the fish's diet. Like *Brachysynodontis batensoda, Hemisynodontis membranaceus* generally feeds while inverted, often at the surface to obtain the surface microorganisms. It has a countershaded color pattern with a grayish brown back and a blackish belly. The membranes of the barbels are also black.

The genus *Brachysynodontis* is a similarly small genus containing a single species, *B. batensoda*, and is distributed widely in tropical Africa (basins of the Nile, Niger, Tchad, Senegal, and Gambia). Like *Hemisynodontis*, or perhaps even moreso, this genus is not usually accepted as separate from the genus *Synodontis*. The body is short and deep and somewhat compressed, with a smooth skin. The head is deeper than long, with the cephalonuchal shield granulose and with the humeral process much shorter than the nuchal process. The operculum has its lower border free and crenulate and the posterior angle free and denticulate. The eyes have a free border. The mouth is large with moderate, non-papillose lips that are not broadened and not confluent with the unbranched maxillary barbels. There are three pairs of barbels, the mandibular pair being branched and the maxillary pair with a broad base and a broad membrane. The premaxillary teeth are fine, curved, and in a band shorter than the eye diameter; the mandibular teeth, 30-57 in number, are small, curved, compressed, bicuspid, and arranged in a transverse band. There are no teeth on the palate. The dorsal fin is short-based, with a strong spine and 7 rays. The adipose fin is very large and contiguous at the base with the rayed dorsal. The anal fin is short-based and the caudal fin is forked. The pectoral fin is provided with a strong spine that is serrated on the edges, while the ventral fins are located opposite the anterior part of the adipose fin. The gill membranes are free from the isthmus except for an interval about equal to the interorbital space where they are attached. There is no palatine organ but there is a gill raker filter formed by 39-42 elongate gill rakers on the first branchial arch.

Brachysynodontis batensoda; (b) ventral view of mouth. (From Boulenger, 1911.)

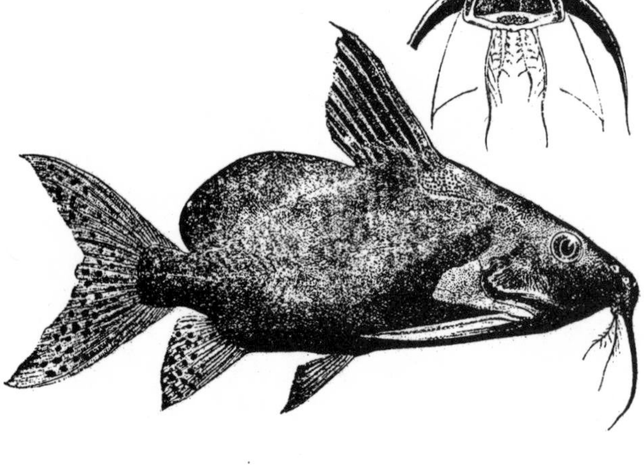

The single species, *Brachysynodontis batensoda*, attains a length of up to 27 cm and is said to be found chiefly in swampy areas, usually in large schools. This is a true upside-down catfish for it spends as much as 90% of the time in the inverted position. It feeds at the surface on various planktonic (animal and vegetable) organisms and may take a few insects as well. There are some reports that it takes in mud, but confirmation of this is yet to be received. In the aquarium it quickly adapts to the available fare. The species is countershaded with a pale brown back and a blackish belly. The young have a pattern of large spots that may be connected to form a marbled pattern. The species is commercially important in Nigeria at least, where it is quite common.

The genus *Synodontis* is by far the largest genus of the family, with better than 100 species included. This also makes it the second largest genus of ostariophysan fishes in Africa, the first of course being the genus *Barbus*. The species of *Synodontis* are widely distributed over much of Africa with the exception of some of the northern desert areas. The greatest diversity of species can be found in the regions of the tropical rain forest. They inhabit a variety of different habitats including torrents but are most likely to be found in lakes and slow-flowing rivers. They are omnivorous, feeding on all stages of aquatic insects, worms, various molluscs, plant material including algae, microorganisms, and will not even pass up pieces of dead fish that are used as bait. A few of the larger species include fishes in their diet. Some of the diets vary from season to season, from habitat to habitat, and from juvenile to adult. It is said that 99% of the species are nocturnal, hiding by day under roots, logs, in crevices, etc., not in the "normal" manner but in unusual head-up or head-down positions. It has been suggested that these daytime positions are but a small step from the more unusual habit of a number of the species of swimming in an inverted position, earning them the common name of upside-down catfishes. Although most species will exhibit this type of swimming at one time or another, very few species actually adopt upside-down swimming as their normal way of swimming, and the common name being applied to the whole genus (and erroneously the whole family) is stretching things a bit. Those species that are more strongly inclined to be more or less permanent upside-down swimmers are generally countershaded, with the back light colored and the belly dark. The size range of members of the genus *Synodontis* is considerable, with small species only 6-7 cm long and fairly large species of over 70 cm.

The characteristics of the genus *Synodontis* sensu stricto (without *Brachysynodontis* and *Hemisynodontis*) are as follows: The body is short to more or less elongate, slightly to moderately compressed, and covered with smooth to villose skin. The head is moderately depressed and the humeral process of the cephalo-nuchal shield is shorter than, equal to, or longer than the nuchal process. The operculum is covered with skin and does not have a denticulate free marginal border. The eyes have a free border and are generally supralateral or sublateral in position. The mouth is of average to small size, and the lips are spread out and papillose, but not sucker-like as in some of the other genera, and the lips are not confluent with the maxillary barbels. The nostrils are far apart. There are three pairs of barbels, the maxillary pair being membranous or not and sometimes branched, while the mandibular barbels are always branched, with the branches often partly enlarged. The premaxillary teeth are

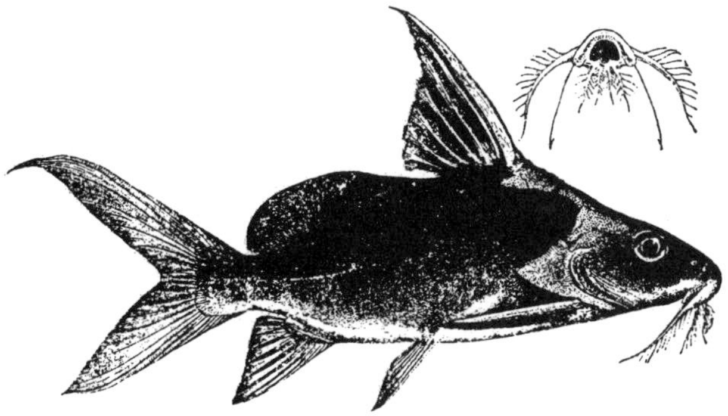

Synodontis clarias. (From Boulenger, 1911.)

conical and arranged in a band that is much longer than the eye diameter and generally exposed (well visible). The mandibular teeth, about 6-90 in number, are arranged in a band or patch, are long or short, curved, compressed, and with a long root implanted in the lower lip. The palate is edentulous. The dorsal fin is short-based, with a strong spine and 6-8 or 9 (usually 7) branched rays. The adipose fin is more or less developed (sometimes very large) and somewhat removed from the base of the rayed dorsal fin. The anal fin is short-based, and the caudal fin is generally forked. The pectoral fins are provided with a stout, serrated spine, and the ventral fins are generally located below the space between the rayed dorsal and adipose fins. The gill membranes are attached to the isthmus from about the level of the pectoral spine base. There is no palatine organ, and the gill raker filter is moderate in size with 7 to 33 gill rakers on the lower limb of the first branchial arch. There are 4-7 branchiostegal rays.

The species of the genus *Synodontis* differ from each other by a number of different characteristics such as the form of the mouth, the number and form of the teeth (especially the mandibular teeth), the number of pectoral fin rays (this varies from 6-10 but within very narrow limits), the number of anal fin rays, the presence or absence of villosities on the skin, the extent of any membrane on the maxillary barbels, the length and branching of the barbels, as well as the proportions of the body and head, the position of the eyes, the color pattern, etc.

Synodontis angelicus is certainly one of the

most beautiful species of the genus and is sought after by any aquarist who can afford its relatively high price. It was first imported into the U.S. in 1955 (into Europe in 1954), when individual specimens were going for $300 and up. The price has decreased somewhat, but it is still one of the highest priced species of *Synodontis* on the market today. Several color variations are said to exist: (1) a jet black to purplish ground color with round white to yellowish spots (some may show very small spots, others have larger and fewer spots); (2) a chocolate brown ground color with light orange spots; and (3) spots intermingled with wavy lines on a dark background (described as a subspecies, *S. a. zonatus*, that was later placed in synonymy). The younger specimens have fewer light spots, and very young specimens may be almost entirely blackish or blackish brown. Older specimens are said to have the ground color graying slightly while the intensity of the fin pattern increases. This species is distributed in the Zaire basin and occupies a variety of habitats (such as Malebo Pool, large and small rivers). Marielle Brichard reported that there are places where *S. angelicus* can be captured in fairly large numbers (50-60) during one collecting session, but this happens infrequently and it might be six months before such collecting can take place again. Many people, including the Brichards and the Japanese, are trying to breed it. Herald observed what might have been courtship in *S. angelicus* at the Steinhart Aquarium. A pair would swim swiftly toward each other from opposite ends of a tank and collide head on. This was repeated at intervals of 30 seconds or so for several minutes. Luckily for aquarists, this is a hardy and long-lived species (the late Braz Walker is said to have had one about 23 years old). It is peaceful, nocturnal, and not a fussy eater. It is omnivorous and fond of chopped earthworms and algae, but it has even accepted flake food, which it takes from the surface in an upside-down position. It swims normally most of the time but will easily invert if there is a reason (such as food on the surface). If the aquarium is kept fairly dim this species may be active during the day. The recommended temperature range is 20° to 28°C. For defense, *S. angelicus* is provided with a strong head shield and sharp dorsal and pectoral spines; the dorsal spine has sharp teeth posteriorly, and the pectoral spines have large, thorny teeth on both edges. This species grows to a length of about 25 cm. According to Brichard, 1978, a female may lay between 3,000 and 4,000 eggs.

Another of the beautiful species of the genus is *Synodontis brichardi*. It is a very slender-bodied species with an exceptionally large tail in proportion to the body. The color is dark brown with thin yellowish to white vertical lines. According to Brichard, wild-caught specimens when first collected show a greenish tint to the vertical lines, and only in captivity do they fade to the yellowish or white color. This may be a dietary consideration. Juveniles tend to have a larger number of stripes and all their fins have distinct blackish spot-bands. As they grow, additional spots (one or two) may be seen in the dorsal fin. *Synodontis brichardi* has a fairly restricted range in the Zaire basin, with some found in the Malebo Pool but the majority of specimens occurring in the rapids to the south of it (a 220-km stretch of rapids, sometimes greater than 30 km long, of the Zaire River). Being from highly oxygenated waters they should not be crowded and there should be heavy aeration. Like many of the other species, *S. brichardi* does best when kept in small groups of their own kind. In a not too brightly lit aquarium it will be seen during the day, provided that there are many hiding places available. In the wild this species will feed on long, flowing green algae and will feed on the algae growing in an aquarium. Although a normal swimmer, if food is present at the surface it will readily invert and feed in an upside-down position. The species attains a length of 19 cm and is long-lived (one individual in a public aquarium was said to be 20 years old).

Synodontis alberti is a species introduced to the U.S. in 1950 from the Zaire basin and Malebo Pool. It is a bluish gray color with some darker spots on the body. Often a distinctive violet cast is seen all over the body in young individuals. The maxillary barbels are unusual in that they are very long, extending the entire length of the body and occasionally even surpassing the end of the caudal fin; the

The barbels of *Synodontis alberti* are unusually long, the maxillary barbels often extending to or beyond the caudal fin. Photo by Dr. Herbert R. Axelrod.

mandibular barbels are also proportionately very long. This is a nocturnal fish that is apparently very light-shy, so the aquarium housing it should be dimly lit and provided with numerous darkened hiding places. It has large eyes, apparently an adaptation for low light levels as are the long maxillary barbels that are used as "feelers." This is a peaceful fish that is suitable for large, well-planted community tanks. The water chemistry is not critical; the proper temperature range is 22°-27°C. *S. alberti* particularly likes tubificid worms as well as other worm foods, aquatic insects and their larvae, and vegetable matter (a vegetable supplement should be provided). It can be seen swimming along the pieces of driftwood or sides of the tank grazing on whatever algae is available, assuming a variety of positions. It is said that it will also dig into the substrate in search of food. Although it attains a length of up to 22 cm in the wild, it generally remains smaller in captivity.

Synodontis nigriventris is one of the species of the genus that habitually swims upside down as a normal position. Its range is restricted to streams of central Zaire where it may be found in large schools consisting of thousands of individuals, and it is suggested that in captivity it be kept with several others of its own kind. Its diet in the wild consists mainly of filamentous algae, diverse vegetable debris, crustaceans, insect larvae, and possibly also terrestrial insects such as ants and beetles. Some of the algae encrusting on the undersides of leaves or cave roofs are grazed with its little rasp-like teeth while in the inverted position, a position also used when taking food from the water's surface. However, it will also hunt for food among bottom debris such as the remains of rotting plants. It is a good scavenger that apparently is not selective about its food but is said to like the bowels of dead fishes very much. *S. nigriventris* is a twilight-active fish with fairly large eyes that prefers to remain in hiding places with subdued light during the day. It is a peaceful fish that will school together in a community tank. It was first imported into the U.S. in 1950 although apparently not in great numbers until late in 1955. *S. nigriventris* is one of the few species of *Synodontis* that has spawned in captivity, although not too many details are available. The females are said to be larger than the males and have more rounded bellies, and the dark markings of the males are said to be more numerous and smaller than those of the females. When spawning time approaches the colors intensify, especially the dark markings. Ceilings of caves formed by rocks or a small flower pot are the preferred sites on which to stick their hundred or so pale yellow eggs. Fortunately, the parents do not have a tendency to eat their eggs. The fry hatch out in about a week, are 5-6 mm long, have small barbels, but are without pigment. Newly hatched brine shrimp can be fed. The young swim normally for about seven weeks, after which they start to swim inverted. The coloration is typically countershaded. The maximum size is a relatively small 25 cm.

Synodontis njassae is a species endemic to Lake Malawi and makes a good companion fish for a lake cichlid community tank for it prefers the hard, alkaline water that is needed to properly keep those fishes. The background color is gray to gray-brown to grayish white, many times with a bronzy caste. The spotting characteristic of the species is quite variable but is said to fall into two fairly distinct patterns: 1) a few large, roundish spots, and 2) scattered smaller and more numerous roundish to slightly irregular black spots. However, Poll was able to examine specimens of both types and came to the conclusion that they both were representatives of the same species, *S. njassae*. This species grows to a length of about 19 cm and feeds primarily on chironomid larvae, ostracods, copepods, fish remains, and *Vallisneria* fragments.

Synodontis acanthomias is one of the larger species (to 60 cm) and comes from the sluggish streams and lagoons of Zaire where there is a rocky bottom. One report said that the body and head were covered with a thick jelly-like coating (slime?) that gave the fish a greenish gray color. This species is suitable for a large, particularly well-planted tank that has many hiding places such as driftwood pieces. It is a twilight species that prefers a dimly lit tank and, once acclimated, will usually swim along the driftwood or sides of the tank in search of algae. It feeds on all sorts of aquatic insects (all stages) as well as algae (a vegetable supplement should be provided). The temperature is not critical (22°-26°C best), and it will tolerate most types of water conditions. This is an aggressive species that tends to be territorial. It not only will fight with its own kind, but tends to become involved in any of the disputes that may arise in the tank (especially between other species of *Synodontis*).

Synodontis schall is another fairly large species (to 56 cm and 1 kg) that is widely distributed from the Nile (where it is the most common *Synodontis* species) to just north of Lake Victoria and west to Gambia and Senegal, where it occurs in rivers, lakes, or streams. This is one of the species depicted in the artwork of the ancient Egyptians. The color pattern is quite variable, and there are naturally occurring albinos reported. Young individuals are marbled with brown and have yellow markings on the head. The diet is quite varied and includes such items as insects and insect larvae, molluscs, algae, and fishes. The young *S. schall* prefer the insect larvae, algae, and molluscs, while adults over 35 cm in length seem to have more fishes in their diet.

Synodontis zambesensis inhabits quiet pools and flood-plain pans in perennial and seasonal rivers. It feeds mostly on seeds, insects, and snails that it finds in the bottom mud, although it will often swim in an inverted position in search of food. When taken from the

Synodontis schall is the most common *Synodontis* species from the Nile River and is one of the species depicted in the artwork of the ancient Egyptians. Photo by Gerhard Marcuse.

water it emits a grunting sound (this is common in the genus, and they have collectively been referred to as "squeakers" in Africa). They are said to be a great nuisance to fishermen who are fishing for their favorite fishes with a worm bait. It is said that once the squeakers have moved into a fishing spot and have started nibbling on the bait, it is time to pack up and leave and try elsewhere. The spines are poisonous and may inflict painful wounds if the fish is handled carelessly. *Synodontis granulosus* is unusual in that its skin is covered with villosities in comparison with the smooth skin of most species of the genus. *S. nigromaculatus* (including *S. melanostictus*) has the mandibular barbels intricately branched.

Synodontis decorus is a moderate-sized species (to over 33 cm) from the larger rivers of the Zaire basin. It is distinctive in having a dorsal filament that may reach to the end of the caudal fin or beyond. The filament, which generally starts to develop when the fish reaches 5-8 cm in length, may be nipped off by tankmates (they must be chosen with this in mind) but will regenerate in time if left alone. This is also one of the species in which the maxillary barbels are branched as well as the usual mandibular barbels. This species feeds on aquatic and terrestrial insects (larvae and adults) that are taken from the bottom along with some vegetable debris. They are heavy eaters in aquaria and grow fast. Although normal swimmers, they will occasionally turn upside down to feed on the surface. The pattern and color are variable, which has led to at least one synonym (*S. vittatus*) from the eastern part of the basin. Because of the filament in the dorsal fin this species is sometimes erroneously referred to as *S. filamentosus*, a valid species from the Nile, Niger, Volta, and Tchad. This species has often been confused with a species called *S. nummifer*, which has even been referred to as the "false *decorus*." Below a length of 8 cm the juveniles of *nummifer* have four to five narrow bands or black spots arranged in a series in each caudal lobe, while similar size *S. decorus* possess only one or two wide black bands on each caudal fin lobe. *S. nummifer* also has a low, long-based adipose fin; in *S. decorus* it is high and short-based. Adding to the confusion are *S. notatus* and *S. congicus*, this latter species sometimes also being erroneously called *S. nummifer*. *S. notatus* grows to a length of about 27 cm and may have zero to three dark spots on each side (all spotted patterns are said to occur in the same population). Younger individuals are not too aggressive but will readily defend a hiding place, while older specimens are more aggressive toward members of their own species, often with fatal results for one of the combatants. The maxillary barbels are the longest of the three species and have no membrane. *S. congicus* has a wide membrane at the base of the maxillary barbel that narrows and finally ends at the middle of the barbel. This species also has one to three spots on the side of the body and may have some small spots on the sides of the head. It is best kept with more peaceful species as it tends to become bullied by the more gregarious species. None of the species are particularly prone to upside-down swimming.

Synodontis contractus is a smaller species attaining a length of only about 10 cm. It comes from the Zaire basin, where it inhabits pools, rivers, and smaller streams over muddy bottoms or among heavy growths of vegetation near the shore. It occurs in large schools in the wild and is best kept in a small group of its own kind. This species prefers to swim upside-down and will feed in this position as it skims along just under the surface sucking in the floating food. The mouth is ventrally located and the teeth are "fused" together into a rasping patch or plate that is used to scrape algae and slime as well as other types of organisms off the surfaces of the plants, stones, driftwood, etc. It is also quite fond of snails. Aquarium fare can include such items as frozen brine shrimp and ground beef heart, but it must also receive a good proportion of vegetable matter. The water quality is not critical as long as sudden changes or extremes are avoided and the temperature is kept in the mid 20's (actually it will tolerate from about 20°C to 28°C). This is also a light-shy species, and many hiding places must be provided or it becomes very upset (at which time it may show a pattern of three ill-defined dark vertical bands, one below the dorsal fin, one below the adipose fin, and one on the caudal peduncle). It is similar to *S. nigriventris* but is chunkier and has a larger head and larger eyes. In the past this species was erroneously known as *S.* "davidi."

Synodontis eupterus is a very sought-after aquarium species because of the extensions to the rays of the dorsal fin that have earned it a common name of "featherfin." It has a fairly wide distribution from the White Nile throughout west Africa. It is very abundant in Lake Tchad over a muddy bottom, but may also be found many times over a rocky substrate in Niger. In flooded areas it will hide around any underwater obstructions such as downed trees. Reaching a length of about 27 cm (10 cm in the first year), it feeds primarily on insect larvae but will also take algae. It will adapt readily to aquarium foods and will even turn upside-down to feed on food floating on the surface. *S. eupterus* is a scrappy fish that can usually hold its own against most fishes, but it is advisable not to keep it with any known fin-nippers. The younger individuals have a yellowish body covered with irregularly winding dark lines. At about 7-8 cm these lines break up into a spotted pattern.

Synodontis multipunctatus from Lake Tanganyika reaches a length of about 30 cm, feeding on snails (*Neothauma*) as well as some insect larvae and shrimp. It has been seen in large schools of 300-400 fish wandering over a bare sand bottom at the foot of rocky slopes some 60-100 meters deep. Here there is a more or less permanent twilight giving the whole scene an eerie appearance. In regard to this fish the Brichards discovered a very interesting occurrence. When some trapped *Ophthalmotilapia nasutus* released their eggs and larvae that they were brooding, they noticed that among them were some *Synodontis* fry about 10 mm long. They raised the fry and discovered that they were *S. multipunctatus*. This phenomenon was not restricted to *Ophthalmotilapia*, but appeared to be somewhat widespread, involving *Tropheus* and *Cyphotilapia* in the wild and has been reported for other mouthbrooding cichlids in aquaria where *S. multipunctatus* spawned. The reasons for this unusual behavior (in some ways similar to a cuckoo laying its eggs in another bird's nest) has not yet been explained although there are several theories available.

Synodontis species do very well in captivity as long as they get reasonable care. Unfortunately, many of them get quite large and a fairly large tank is required, but there are some smaller species, such as *Synodontis contractus*, that are quite comfortable in smaller tanks. Also, many *Synodontis* species are social animals and gather in large schools in the wild. It is best that several individuals of these species be kept together for best results. The bottom material is not of great importance, and its selection depends a great deal upon personal choice. Many aquarists prefer a dark substrate, avoiding any material that has sharp edges that can damage the catfishes' barbels as they search through it for food. These naked catfishes also might get scratched on any sharp objects, which might lead to infections. *Synodontis* tanks should be well-planted and contain a good supply of hiding places. The decorations can be anything from driftwood to flower pots to commercially manufactured rockwork in which there are many caves. These shelters make them feel more "at home" and they are more apt to be seen during the day if light levels are low. Most species are light-shy and will rarely be seen if light levels in the aquarium are kept high. However, in subdued lighting they are more comfortable. It appears that the truly upside-down species are less light-shy than most of the others.

In regard to water chemistry, *Synodontis* species are not very demanding as long as extremes are avoided. The pH can be anywhere between 6.5 and 7.5 for most species, and of course the Rift Lake fishes do best with a pH closer to 8.0 to 8.5. Partial water changes should be made to the extent of about 10% to 20% weekly or biweekly or about 50% a month. Too great a change too often is said to lead to clouding of the eyes. Along with the water changes it is good aquarium practice to stir up the gravel a bit and siphon off as much as possible of the detritus. The new water should be dechlorinated for safety, for there have been reports that *Synodontis* species show an adverse reaction (rubbing on objects) to highly chlorinated water. Normal filtration can be used depending upon personal preference. Aeration is recommended either with a separate air stone or as part of a filtering system. An occasional use of a diatomaceous earth filter may also be beneficial. Temperature is also not critical, and a fairly wide range of 21° to 28°C is tolerated, but as usual, avoid any rapid changes.

Feeding is no problem. Most small live foods are avidly taken, and all sorts of aquarium foods such as beef heart, frozen brine shrimp, and even dry flake foods are accepted. In fact, most species, whether normally upside-down swimmers or not, will invert to feed on the flake food floating on the surface. A regular supplement of vegetable matter is important. If a lot of algae are present in the tank they will graze on it, but most species will soon clean it up and be looking for something more substantial. Lettuce leaves and similar items are excellent substitutes.

Synodontis species are basically peaceful, although some species can cause quite a "ruckus." They do tend to be territorial, and any intrusion by its own kind or even another species is generally resisted. Otherwise they are good community tank fishes. Skitterish tankmates should be avoided as they tend to become quite upset when the catfishes are foraging around the tank in the evening hours and wake them up suddenly by the touch of their barbels. It is best if they are kept with other fishes of comparable size and temperament. It has also been suggested that tankmates should be daytime feeders to prevent a "conflict of interest" at feeding time, but this usually is not necessary. There are several truly aggressive species, among them *S. acanthomias*, *S. nigrita*, and *S. schall* according to most reports. It is suggested that an aquarist should start with eight to ten young fish (7.5 cm or less) in a 76-liter tank. Any new individuals that are to be added later must be of the same size. Any *Synodontis* that is more than 15 cm long is best given its own tank. Be very careful when handling *Synodontis* for a wound from one of their spines can be quite painful as possibly there is a toxin involved. Finally, with proper care expect these catfishes to enjoy a long life. Reports of well over 20 years in captivity have been made for several species of *Synodontis*.

Spawning *Synodontis* species has been quite rare in the past but is now becoming more and more common. Basically, after some preliminary courtship the eggs, which are adhesive, are attached to some solid object, usually in a protected location like the roof of a cave. Apparently neither parent guards eggs or young (although some cichlids may—see the report on *S. multipunctatus* foregoing). The fry hatch out in about a week and become free-swimming some four to five days after that. In the upside-down catfishes the inverted position first manifests itself after about ten weeks, and this position is taken more and more with time until most of the time is spent inverted. It is also about this time that the reverse coloration becomes evident. It is interesting to note that if bottom food is fed to upside-down catfishes they will readily adjust to taking the food from the bottom, much as the bottom-feeding catfishes will invert to feed upside-down on floating foods. Spawning in nature usually occurs in the early part of the rainy season when many areas are flooded, giving the fry a better variety of available foods as well as an increase in sheltered areas. Females are much plumper when filled with eggs, but they also are more rounded in cross-section and generally larger than males of a similar age due, it is said, to a faster growth rate for females. In addition, males have a longer and more or less permanently rigid genital papilla, at least in several species examined. This is not unique for synodontids but has been demonstrated as present in several species of *Mystus*, *Heteropneustes fossilis*, *Schilbe (Eutropius) niloticus*, *Schilbe (Schilbe) mystus*, *Siluranodon auritus*, and *Parailia pellucida* in the Asian and African families, and in *Hoplosternum thoracatum* and certain loricariids in the South American families. One of the more easily sexed species of *Synodontis* using this method is *S. schall*, where in individuals over 30 cm in length the genital papilla is readily observable and there is none to be seen in comparably sized females. Spawning was also observed in this species. It seems the male and female would swim restlessly side by side back and forth over the bottom. They stirred up the bottom mud with their pectoral fins as they released their eggs and sperm. Once the pair was finished they moved off, there being no brood care.

The genus *Acanthocleithron* is a small genus of catfishes containing a single species, some 5.5 cm in length, from the Congo basin. The body is moderately elongate and slightly compressed, and the head is depressed but little longer than broad. The eyes are moderate, with a free border, and the nostrils are remote from each other, each with a valve. A cephalo-nuchal shield is present, and the humeral process is short and rounded. There are three pairs of barbels, a maxillary pair and two

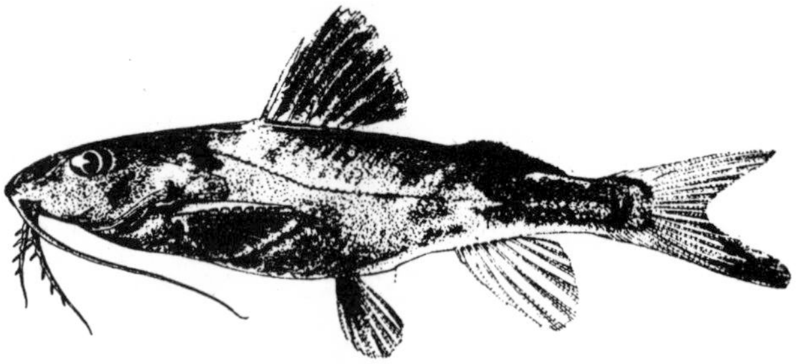

Acanthocleithron chapini. (From Poll, 1963.)

mandibular pairs, the mandibular barbels with slender branches. The mouth is subinferior, rather small and without labial folds, and contains small conical teeth in both jaws; the palate is edentulous. The anterior dorsal fin has a spine and 7 rays, while the second dorsal fin, a modified adipose fin, has very fine rays, their bases hidden by adipose tissue. The pectoral fin is provided with a strong spine, and there is a bony projection or backwardly pointed spine just above and anterior to the pectoral spine base. The gill openings are fairly large, and the gill membrane is narrowly attached to the isthmus.

The genus *Microsynodontis* is a small genus of one to three species depending upon whose classification is followed. The body is elongate, not very compressed, with a relatively short head that is a little longer than broad. The cephalo-nuchal shield is rugose, with rounded or obtuse posterior processes, and the humeral process is long, narrow, and sharply pointed. The eyes are very small, superior to supralateral in position, and without a free orbital rim. The lower lip is well developed, the premaxillary teeth are arranged in a short and broad band, while the mandibular teeth are hook-like and about 20-30 in number. There are three pairs of barbels, a maxillary pair and two mandibular pairs, the latter with thick branches. The dorsal fin is short-based, with a spine and 6 rays, and there is a long, low adipose fin. The anal fin is also short-based and the caudal fin is rounded. The pectoral fins are provided with a strong spine weakly serrated on the outer edge and strongly serrated on the inner. There is a fold across the isthmus but the gill openings are restricted, extending only to the pectoral base.

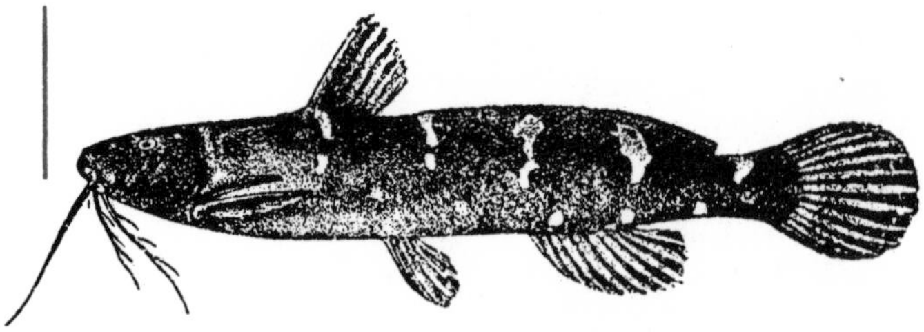

Microsynodontis batesii. (From Boulenger, 1911.)

The genus *Mochokiella* is a small genus from Sierra Leone containing a single dwarf species no more than 3.6 cm standard length. The body is moderately long, slightly compressed, and the head is almost as broad as long. The snout is rounded and the nostrils are distant, the anterior nostrils tubular. The small mouth has a weak lower lip that is de-

Mochokiella paynei. (After Howes, 1980.)

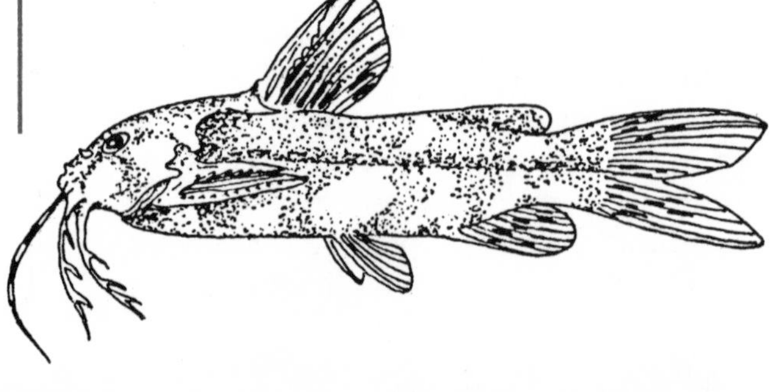

veloped only at the corners and a broad patch of short, conical teeth in the upper jaw as well as a broad semi-crescentric band in the lower. The palate is edentulous. There are three pairs of barbels, a maxillary pair and two mandibular pairs that are branched, the outer mandibular barbels with three branches, the inner mandibular barbels with four. The eyes are moderately small, supralateral in position, and without a free orbital rim. The cephalo-nuchal shield is slightly rugose with three nuchal plates, and the humeral process is elongate and pointed. The dorsal fin is short-based with a strong spine and 6 rays and perhaps a small spine at the front of the base of the large one. The adipose fin is short (compared with *Microsynodontis*) and moderate in depth, and the anal fin is short-based and located about opposite the adipose fin. The pectoral fin spine is strong, serrated on its anterior edge, and has 8-9 strong teeth on its posterior edge. The caudal fin is forked. There are 6 branchiostegal rays and the branchiostegal membrane forms a fold across the ventral surface of the head. The gill opening extends to the pectoral fin spine base.

The single species of the genus, *Mochokiella paynei*, was collected in a forest stream in the Kassewe Forest Reserve by means of a baited trap left overnight. Observations in an aquarium show it to be a light-shy species active at night but retiring to dark hiding places during the day. They seem to be able to orient in any direction sometimes swimming vertically or even upside-down on occasion.

The genus *Mochokus* contains only two small species from the Nile and White Nile Rivers and Lake Rudolf. The body is moderately elongate and slightly compressed, and the head is almost as broad as long and slightly depressed. The cephalo-nuchal shield has short, rounded posterior processes, and the humeral process is long and pointed. The nostrils are remote from each other and provided with a valve, that of the posterior nostril very large. The eyes are moderate and without a free border. The small mouth is subinferior in position and without labial folds. There are small, conical teeth in both jaws and the palate is edentulous. There are three pairs of barbels, a maxillary pair and two branched mandibular pairs. There are two dorsal fins, the adipose fin more or less replaced by a rayed fin. The first dorsal is provided with a spine and 6 to 8 rays, the second with about 9 to 16 rays (which are without endoskeletal supports, interneurals). The anal fin is short-based and opposite the second dorsal fin, and the caudal fin is deeply emarginate to forked. The pectoral fin is provided with a strong spine strongly serrated on the inner edge, weakly on the outer. The gill openings are restricted and the swim bladder is large and free.

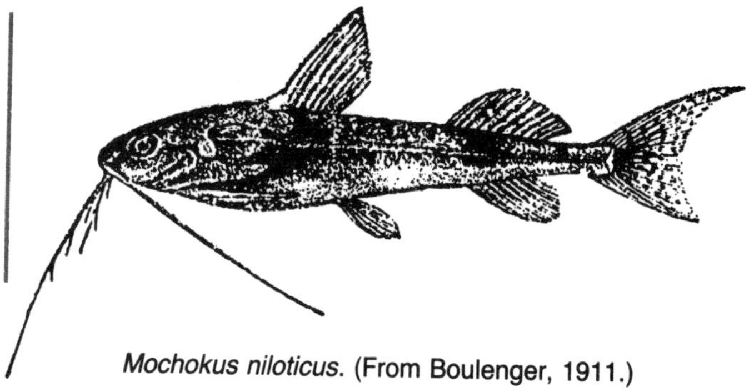

Mochokus niloticus. (From Boulenger, 1911.)

The genus *Chiloglanis* from tropical Africa is a moderate sized genus of about 34 species that are adapted to the fast-flowing torrential waters of mountain streams or rivers. Their lips have become quite modified into a sucking-disc that is so efficient that it is difficult or nearly impossible to pry one of them loose from its purchase without damaging it in some way. They are very efficient algae scrapers and will clean out a tank of algae in a very short time. However, they may be so efficient that once the algae are gone they might starve, for they are not able to adapt to other means of feeding. The body is moderately long, usually depressed anteriorly and weakly compressed posteriorly, while the head is more strongly depressed and a little to somewhat longer than broad. A cephalo-nuchal shield is present. The nostrils are distant from each other and both provided with a valve, that of the anterior tubular. There are three pairs of barbels present, a maxillary pair and two unbranched mandibular pairs. The eyes are moderately small and are without a free border. The mouth is inferior and is surrounded by the highly modified papillose, circular lips forming an efficient sucking disc.

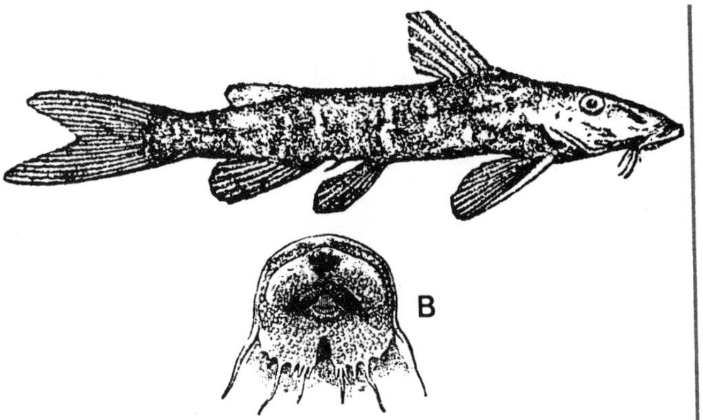

Chiloglanis deckenii; (b) ventral view of mouth. (From Boulenger, 1911.)

The teeth of the upper jaw and vomer are conical, those on the lower jaw slender, curved, and movable, adapted for the algal scraping. The dorsal fin is short-based, with a spine and 5 to 6 branched rays, and there is an adipose fin opposite the anal fin. The pectoral fin has a spine and the ventral fins are located relatively posterior on the ventral side of the body, while the caudal fin is emarginate to forked. The gill openings are restricted to the sides. The swim bladder is small and partially enclosed by the enlarged processes of the anterior vertebrae.

The genus *Euchilichthys* is a relatively small genus of only five species that usually occur in fast-flowing waters such as rapids, clinging to stones with their modified sucker-like mouths. The larger ones are said to clear snail-like trails through the water plants that grow on these stones. The body is relatively elongate and weakly compressed, if at all, while the head is usually quite depressed. A cephalo-nuchal shield is present. The nostrils are close to each other, the posterior nostrils being provided with a valve. The eyes are fairly small, superior to supralateral in position, and with a free border. The mouth is large, inferior in position, and surrounded by the highly modified, circular, papillose lips that form a sucking disc. The premaxillary teeth are curved, pointed, movable, and arranged in a broad band that is entirely in advance of the lower jaw teeth, which are long, slender, with a truncate or notched crown that is hook-like, and also arranged in a band. There are three pairs of barbels, none branched, a maxillary pair and two pairs of mandibular barbels on each side of the lower section of the circular lip. The dorsal fin is short-based, with a spine and 6 rays, and the adipose fin is short and very posteriorly located. The short-based anal fin is opposite the adipose fin; the caudal fin is forked, the lower lobe the larger. The pectoral fins are provided with strong spines, and the ventral fins are located posteriorly, about in the middle of the ventral surface of the body. The gill openings are restricted to the sides. The swim bladder is small, free, and trilocular.

Euchilichthys royauxi; (b) ventral view of mouth. (From Poll, 1957.)

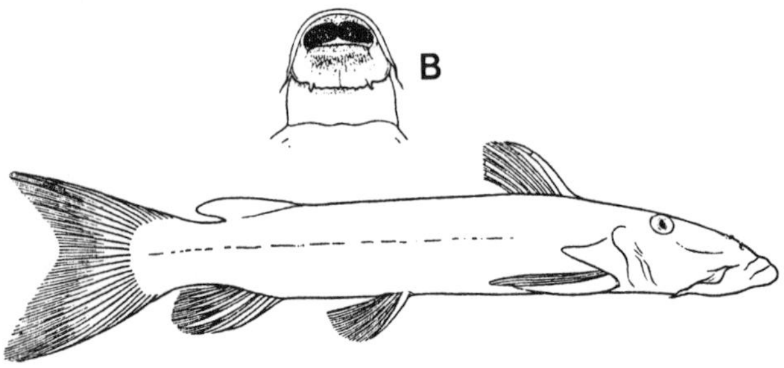

The genus *Atopochilus* contains about seven species, most of which are confined to the Zaire basin, with a single species each in the Ogowe basin and coastal rivers of Tanzania. The largest species attain lengths of more than 50 cm. This genus also contains species that are adapted to the swift-flowing waters of torrents and rapids. The body is moderately elongate and greatly depressed to short and stocky. There is a cephalo-nuchal shield present. The nostrils are close together and the posterior possesses a valve. The eyes are moderate to small, supralateral in position, and with a free border. The mouth is large, inferior in position, and surrounded by an expanded oral disc formed by the lips, which are papillose. The teeth of the upper jaw are in two series, an outer series outside the buccal cavity with spatulate crowns, and an inner series with needle-like crowns opposite the mandibular teeth at the entrance to the buccal cavity. The lower jaw teeth are in a single series with bifid crowns in the young that may remain bifid in adults of some species or may become spatulate in adults of other species. There are three pairs of barbels, a maxillary

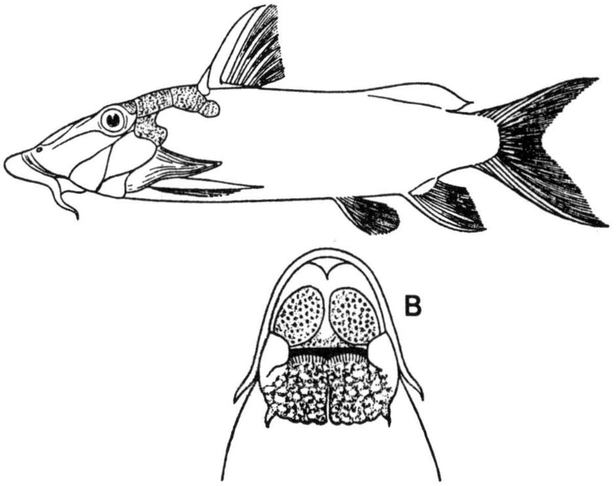

Atopochilus christyi; (b) ventral view of mouth. (From Poll, 1957.)

pair and two mandibular pairs, none of which are branched. The mandibular barbels are on the posterior border of the lower lip. The dorsal fin is short-based, with a spine and 6 rays, and there is a short but well-developed adipose fin. The anal fin is short-based and opposite the adipose fin. The caudal fin is truncate to forked. The pectoral fin has a strong spine, and the ventral fins are located posteriorly on the ventral side of the body. The gill openings are restricted to the sides.

The family Mochokidae is said to be most closely related to the family Bagridae.

Checklist of the species of the family Mochokidae and their type localities:

Hemisynodontis Bleeker, 1862. Type species *Pimelodus membranaceus* Geoffroy-St. Hilaire, 1809. (?= *Synodontis*.)

Hemisynodontis membranaceus (Geoffroy-St. Hilaire, 1809). Nile River, Egypt?.

Brachysynodontis Bleeker, 1862. Type species *Synodontis batensoda* Rüppell, 1832. (? = *Synodontis*.)

Brachysynodontis batensoda (Rüppell, 1832). Nile River near Cairo.

Synodontis Cuvier, 1817. Type species *Silurus clarias* Linnaeus, 1758.

Synodontis acanthomias Boulenger, 1899. Boma, Leopoldville.

S. afrofischeri Hilgendorf, 1888. Nyanza, Lake Victoria.

S. alberti Schilthuis, 1891. Kinshasa, Stanley Pool.

S. albolineatus Pellegrin, 1924. Madjingo, Djoua River, Gabon.

S. angelicus Schilthuis, 1891. Kinshasa, Stanley Pool.

S. annectens Boulenger, 1911. Nianimaru, Gambia and Portuguese Guinea.

S. ansorgii Boulenger, 1911. Bafata, Guba, and Culufi Rivers, Portuguese Guinea.

S. arnoulti Roman, 1966. Kou, affluent of the Black Volta.

S. aterrimus Poll & Roberts, 1968. Bokuma, Zaire basin.

S. bastiani Daget, 1948. Bouafle, Ivory Coast.

S. batesi Boulenger, 1907. Ja River, South Cameroun.

S. brichardi Poll, 1959. Kinsuka, Leopoldville.

S. budgetti Boulenger, 1911. Lokoja, Upper Niger.

S. camelopardalis Poll, 1971. Eala, Ruki River, Zaire.

S. camoensis Daget & Leveque, 1981. Comoe River, National Park of Comoe, Ivory Coast.

S. caudalis Boulenger, 1899. Boma, Leopoldville, Congo.

S. caudovittatus Boulenger, 1901. Lake No, White Nile.

S. centralis Poll, 1971. Kunungu, Zaire.

S. clarias (Linnaeus, 1758). Americae, Africae fluviis.

S. congicus Poll, 1971. Gangala na Bodio, Dungu River, Zaire.

S. contractus Vinciguerra, 1928. Buta, Zaire.

S. courteti Pellegrin, 1906. Fort-Archamboult (Chari), Chad.

S. cuangoanus Poll, 1971. Cuango, Cafunfo, Zaire.

S. decorus Boulenger, 1899. Leopoldville, Congo.

S. depauwi Boulenger, 1899. Leopoldville, Congo.

S. dhonti Boulenger, 1917. Kilewa Bay, Lake Tanganyika.

S. dorsomaculatus Poll, 1971. Kadia, Kisale, Zaire.

S. eberneensis Daget, 1964. Lamto, Bandama, Ivory Coast.

S. eupterus Boulenger, 1901. Goz abu Gumah, White Nile.

S. fascipinna Nichols & La Monte, 1953. Birao, eastern French Equatorial Africa. (? = *nigrita*).

S. filamentosus Boulenger, 1901. Mouth of Lake No, White Nile.

S. flavitaeniatus Boulenger, 1919. Eala, Zaire basin.

S. frontosus Vaillant, 1895. White Nile, Sudan.

S. fuelleborni Hilgendorf & Pappenheim, 1903. Lake Rukwa.

S. gambiensis, Günther, 1864. Gambia.

S. geledensis Günther, 1896. Geledi on the Shebeli, Somalia.

S. gabroni Daget, 1954. Morti, Markala, Kona, Kolenze, Loa (Middle Niger).

S. granulosus Boulenger, 1900. North end of Lake Tanganyika.

S. greshoffi Schilthuis, 1891. Kinshasa, Stanley Pool.

S. guttatus Günther, 1865. Niger, East Africa.

S. haugi Pellegrin, 1906. Ngomo (Ogowe).

S. iturii Steindachner, 1911. Ituri River, Zaire.

S. katangae Poll, 1971. Lukonzolwa, Lake Moero (Mweru).

S. khartoumensis Abu Gideiri, 1967. Blue Nile, Khartoum.

S. koensis Pellegrin, 1933. Man, Ko River, Ivory Coast.

S. lacustricolus Poll, 1953. Karomo, Lake Tanganyika.

S. laessoei Norman, 1923. Kokema River (Angola).

S. leopardinus Pellegrin, 1914. Barotses (Upper Zambezi).

S. leopardus Pfeffer, 1894. Rufu by Korogwe.

S. longirostris Boulenger, 1902. Banzyville, Yembe River, Zaire.

S. longipinnis Pellegrin, 1930. Sangha, Zaire basin.

S. lufirae Poll, 1971. Koni Lake, Lufira, Zaire basin.

S. macrophthalmus Poll, 1971. Ampen, Lake Volta (Ghana).

S. macrops Greenwood, 1963. Aswa River (Teso District, Uganda).

S. macrostigma Boulenger, 1911. Ovovango River, Botswana.

S. maculipinna Norman, 1922. Rufigi River, Tanganyika Territory.

S. marmoratus Lönnberg, 1895. Bonge, Cameroon.

S. matthesi Poll, 1971. Mtera, Ruaha River, Tanzania.

S. melanopterus Boulenger, 1902. Oguta, Niger Delta.

S. multimaculatus Boulenger, 1902. Banzyville, Ubangi River.

S. multipunctatus Boulenger, 1898. Sumbu, Lake Tanganyika.

S. nebulosus Peters, 1852. Tette, Zambezi River, Mozambique.

S. nigrita Valenciennes, 1840. Senegal.

S. nigriventris David, 1936. Buta, Zaire.

S. nigromaculatus Boulenger, 1905. Lake Bangwelu.

S. njassae Keilhack, 1908. Lake Nyassa (Malawi).

S. notatus Vaillant, 1893. Oubangui at Bangui (Fr. Congo).

S. nummifer Boulenger, 1899. Leopoldville, Matadi (Congo).

S. obesus Boulenger, 1898. Opobo River (Old Calabar), Gabon.

S. ocellifer Boulenger, 1900. Konchow Creek, Gambia River.

S. omias Günther, 1864. Niger River, West Africa.

S. ornatipinnis Boulenger, 1899. Lake Tumba.

S. ornatissimus Gosse, 1982. Poko, Zaire basin (substitute name for *ornatus*).

S. pardalis Boulenger, 1908. Libi River (South Cameroon).

S. petricola Matthes, 1959. Lake Tanganyika.

S. pleurops Boulenger, 1897. Stanley Falls, Zaire.

S. polli Gosse, 1982. Lake Tanganyika (substitute name for *eurystomus*).

S. polyodon Vaillant, 1895. Adouma, Ogowe.

S. polystigma Boulenger, 1915. Luapula River, Lake Mweru.

S. pulcher Poll, 1971. Stanley Pool, Zaire.

S. punctifer Daget, 1964. Guiglo, Nzo River, Ivory Coast.

S. punctulatus Günther, 1889. Ruva River, Tanzania.

S. rebeli Holly, 1926. Sanaga River affluent,

Cameroon.

S. resupinatus Boulenger, 1904. Lokoja, Niger River, N. Nigeria.

S. robianus Smith, 1875. Ikorofiong, Old Calabar River, Nigeria.

S. robertsi Poll, 1974. Lukenia and Egombe Rivers, Central Zaire.

S. ruandae Matthes, 1959. Ragera to Rusumu, Ruanda.

S. rufigiensis Bailey, 1968. Lake Lugongwe, Rufigi basin.

S. schall (Bloch & Schneider, 1801). Nile River.

S. schoutedeni David, 1936. Kunungu, Zaire basin.

S. serpentis Whitehead, 1962. Atha River at Iilore, Kenya.

S. serratus Rüppell, 1829. Nile at Cairo.

S. smiti Boulenger, 1902. Banzyville (Ubangi).

S. soloni Boulenger, 1899. Zaire.

S. sorex Günther, 1864. Khartoum.

S. steindachneri Boulenger, 1913. Nyong River, S. Cameroon.

S. tessmanni Pappenheim, 1911. Akonangi aus dem Ntem basin, Kje River, Cameroon.

S. thysi Poll, 1971. Sierra Leone.

S. tourei Daget, 1962. Ballay, Bafing River, Lower Guinea.

S. unicolor Boulenger, 1915. Lake Mweru and Luapula River at Kasenga, Zaire.

?*S. vaillanti* Boulenger, 1897. Bangui, French Congo.

S. velifer Norman, 1935. Ejura; Afram River, Volta basin.

S. vermiculatus Daget, 1954. Koa, Kolenze, Upper Niger.

S. victoriae Boulenger, 1906. Entebbe and Baganga, Lake Victoria.

S. violaceus Pellegrin, 1919. Gribingi, Chad basin.

S. voltae Roman, 1975. Bougouriba, affluent of the Black Volta.

S. wamiensis Lohberger, 1930. Wami, Tanzania.

S. waterloti Daget, 1962. Konkoure basin, Lower Guinea.

S. woosmani Boulenger, 1911. Okovango River, Botswana.

S. xiphias Günther, 1864. Niger.

S. zambesensis Peters, 1852. Tette, Sana, Boror, Mozambique.

S. zanzibaricus Peters, 1868. Kenya (Mombasa?).

Acanthocleithron Nichols & Griscom, 1917. Type species *A. chapini* Nichols & Griscom.

Acanthocleithron chapini Nichols & Griscom, 1917. Avakubi, Ituri River, Zaire.

Microsynodontis Boulenger, 1903. Type species *M. batesii* Boulenger.

Microsynodontis batesii Boulenger, 1903. Mvile River, S. Cameroon.

M. lamberti Poll & Gosse, 1963. Lilanda River, Yangole.

M. polli Lambert, 1958. Gbin River, Guinee Forestiere.

Mochokiella Howes, 1980. Type species *M. paynei* Howes.

Mochokiella paynei Howes, 1980. Kassawe Forest Reserve, Sierra Leone.

Mochokus de Joannis, 1835. Type species *M. niloticus* de Joannis, 1835.

Mochokus brevis Boulenger, 1906. Fashoda and Lake No, White Nile.

M. niloticus de Joannis, 1835. Lower Nile to Bahr-el-Gebel.

Chiloglanis Peters, 1868. Type species *C. deckenii* Peters, 1868.

Chiloglanis angolensis Poll, 1967. South of Chiba, vicinity of Sa de Bandeira, Angola.

C. anoterus Crass, 1960. Upper Pivaan River (Pongola River system).

C. batesii Boulenger, 1904. Efulen and tributary streams of Lobe River, South Cameroon.

C. benuensis Daget & Stauch, 1963. Benoue a Lakdo, Niger system.

C. bifurcus Jubb & Le Roux, 1969. Crocodile River, Incomati River system.

C. brevibarbis Boulenger, 1902. Mathoiya River, Kenya District.

C. cameronesis Boulenger, 1904. Efulen, South Cameroon.

C. carnosus Roberts & Stewart, 1976. Rapids of the Lower Zaire River.

C. congicus Boulenger, 1920. Stanley Falls, Congo.

C. deckenii Peters, 1868. German East Africa.

C. disneyi Trewavas, 1974. Wowe River, Mungo system, West Cameroon.

C. elisabethianus Boulenger, 1915. Lubumbashi River at Elizabethville.
C. emarginatus Jubb & Le Roux, 1969. Lekkerloop River, tributary of the Komati River.
C. fasciatus Pellegrin, 1936. Cubango, Angola.
C. lamottei Daget, 1948. Guinee Fse: Mt. Nimba, Zie.
C. lufirae Poll, 1976. Muye (affluent of the Lufira).
C. lukugae Poll, 1944. Sange River, Angola.
C. macropterus Poll & Stewart, 1975. Luongo River, Zambia.
C. marlieri Poll, 1952. Ndakirwa at Meshe, affluent of the Luhoho.
C. micropogon Poll, 1952. Nzokwe River, Kabare Territory, Angola.
C. microps Matthes, 1965. Lurima River at Kiamakoto (Lufira).
C. modjensis Boulenger, 1903. Modjo River, southern Ethiopia.
C. neumanni Boulenger, 1911. Upper Bubu River, Masailand.
C. niloticus Boulenger, 1900. Isle of Arko, Soudan.
C. normani Pellegrin, 1933. Dunaue, Ivory Coast.
C. occidentalis Pellegrin, 1933. Doue koue and Man, Ivory Coast.
C. paratus Crass, 1960. Pongola River Barrage.
C. pojeri Poll, 1944. Mambwe region of Albertville, Lake Tanganyika.
C. polyodon Norman, 1932. Headwaters of Bagbwe River, Sierra Leone.
C. pretoriae Van der Horst, 1931. Crocodile River, Pretoria District, Transvaal.
C. sardinhai Ladiges & Voelker, 1961. Mujije River, Angola.
C. somereni Whitehead, 1958. Waroya River, Nyanza Prov., Kenya.
C. swierstrai van der Horst, 1931. Crocodile River, Pretoria District, Transvaal.
C. voltae Daget & Stauch, 1963. Bougouri Ba at pont de Nabere, Volta system.

Atopochilus Sauvage, 1878. Type species *A. savorgnani* Sauvage, 1879.
Atopochilus chabanaudi Pellegrin, 1938. Brazzaville, Zaire.
A. christyi Boulenger, 1920. Stanley Falls, Avakubi on the Ituri.
A. macrocephalus Boulenger, 1906. Kwango River, at Ft. Don Carlos.
A. mandevillei Poll, 1959. Stanley Pool, Zaire.
A. pachychilus Pellegrin, 1924. Kanda Kanda, in the Lubilonji, a tributary of the Kasai, affluent of the Congo.
A. savorgnani Sauvage, 1879. Ogoowe River, French Congo.
A. vogti Pellegrin, 1922. Wame River, Afr. Orientale.

Euchilichthys Boulenger, 1900. Type species *A. guentheri* Schilthuis, 1891.
Euchilichthys astatodon (Pellegrin, 1928). Luluaburg Saint Joseph, Kasai River, Zaire.
E. boulengeri Nichols & La Monte, 1934. Luluaburg, Kasai District, Belgian Congo.
E. dybowskii (Vaillant, 1892). Oubanghi.
E. guentheri (Schilthuis, 1891). Stanley Pool, Kinshasa.
E. royauxi Boulenger, 1902. Banzyville, Ubanghi.

Chapter 20

Family — Plates 95–103

DORADIDAE

(Talking Catfishes)

The family Doradidae is a family of South American freshwater catfishes most easily recognized by their possession of a single row or series of sometimes overlapping plates along their sides, each (at least the posterior ones) with a strong median backward projecting spine or hook, or other ornamentations, sometimes supplemented by smaller spines on the surface of the plate. Doradids are distributed from Buenos Aires throughout the Paraguay, Madeira, and Amazon River systems to the Guianas, and from the mouth of the Rio São Francisco and Para to an elevation of about 3,000 feet at the base of the Andes in Bolivia and Peru. They vary in size from the small *Physopyxis* species (about 50 mm) to the relatively enormous *Megalodoras* species (attaining several kilos in weight and a meter in length). Most species are crepuscular or nocturnal bottom-dwellers able to burrow into the substrate very quickly, often remaining there during the day. Doradids feed primarily on small invertebrates (insect larvae, worms, etc.) and are capable of making fairly loud noises, earning them the common name of "talking catfishes."

The body is generally robust, especially anteriorly. The bones of the skull are united by quite visible sutures (even in living fishes) into a solid shield or plate that is continuous with the predorsal plate. The upper surfaces of the head bones are granular or striated and covered with very thin skin. In broad-headed species the fontanel is small, oval between the anterior end of the frontals, and sometimes extending into the ethmoid (in extreme cases it is reduced and subcircular in shape and may be entirely occluded); in narrow-headed species it is more elongate. The nasal openings are generally remote from each other. The mouth is usually slightly subterminal. Three pairs of barbels are present, a maxillary pair and two mental or mandibular pairs (no nasal barbels), all moderately developed; in no species do the maxillary barbels extend much beyond the tip of the humeral process, and usually they are shorter. In many species the mental or mandibular barbels bear supplementary barbels or barblets. In these species the bases of the mental barbels, located close behind the lip, are frequently united by a broad basal membrane, and the barbels can be bent forward to form a screen or sieve over the mouth.

The dorsal fin is usually composed of a strong spine and 6 rays (but occasionally 4 or 5 rays instead of 6) and is situated well forward, immediately behind the nuchal shield. The dorsal fin spine may be either slender or large and heavy, and it may be serrated on both edges, on only the anterior edge, or without serrae (if without serrae, the dorsal fin spine is provided with longitudinal grooves and ridges). The anal fin generally has about 10 to 16 rays. The adipose fin is present and usually well defined and short, although in some of the larger, more heavily armored species it is prolonged forward as a heavy, low, poorly defined keel and in *Physopyxis* it is very small (Bailey and Baskin, 1976). The pectoral fin spines of some species are notably heavy and large while in others they may be long and slender, but they are always serrate on both margins and sometimes also on the dorsal surface. The pectoral fin spines as well as the dorsal fin spine can be locked in the erected position. The pectoral spines cannot be depressed forcibly when locked into position, but can be released by twisting, key fashion, the right one counter-clockwise, the left one clockwise (at least in *Pseudodoras niger*). Similarly, the dorsal fin spine can be released when the "latch" is raised. The articular surface and lock involves two interneurals, the one below the spine itself and the one below the "latch," the modified spine in front of it, and the modified first ray or spine that forms the latch. The caudal fin is rounded, truncate, emarginate, or deeply forked. Immediately above the humeral process the swim bladder is in contact with the skin to form a tympanum. Near the middle of the tympanum can be seen the beginning of the lateral series of characteristic scutes in the form of one to three small bony plates without hooks. Posterior to these are from 16 to 40 bony scutes provided with hooks, etc. The first one to three of these hook-bearing scutes are in contact with the predorsal plate and may or may not reach the humeral process. The posteriormost plate or scute is located about on the middle of the caudal base. The plates vary in form from species to species and are used to help distinguish between them (and commonly to distinguish between the genera as well). The plates may be minute, isolated, even embedded in the skin (as in *Hassar, Doras*), to very large and deep, nearly covering the entire sides (as in *Platydoras, Megalodoras, Acanthodoras*). In *Acanthodoras spinosissimus* the plates of the opposite sides of the body are so large they may meet along the middle of the back in the area between the dorsal and adipose fins. Occasionally plates are developed along the middle of the back between the dorsal and adipose fins, and in one species a large plate actually covers the anterior half of the adipose fin. Although unusual, dermal plates can develop at almost any point on the body's surface and in some very old individuals may fill in the bare spots to form a protective armor over the entire body. There are usually well-developed caudal fulcra extending anteriorly from the caudal fin on the caudal peduncle. The swim bladder is quite variable and has been divided into 5 general types by Eigenmann (1925): (1) the simplest and most primitive, being a simple subconical or subglobular bag partially divided internally into three sections (posterior two-thirds to three-quarters divided into right and left halves but still connecting with the anterior section); (2) two simple bladders connected with each other by a very short, thin canal, forming anterior and posterior sections that are similar but much smaller, elongate, and egg-shaped; (3) a modification of the second form in which the posterior bladder is double or split lengthwise, the two halves sometimes recurved; (4) a double swim bladder, with a third division behind the second; and (5) a swim bladder provided with a number of radiating tubes or ceca, the walls firm, not flexible, provided with internal ridges varying greatly in number and size. The pectoral girdle has two processes directed posteriorly, one above and one below the pectoral fin. The upper (humeral process) is long and narrow and quite noticeable.

According to Eigenmann (1925) there are two major groups of doradids: (1) broad-breasted, with a depressed head, broad mouth, a normal premaxillary provided with bands of teeth, and simple mental barbels; (2) narrow-breasted, with a compressed head and narrow and sometimes prolonged snout that is usually conical. In the first group the anterior nostril is near the lip; in the second group the anterior nostril is always a considerable distance from the lip. In the second group the premaxillary bone is subcircular with few or no teeth. The barbels in this second group are frequently feathery and can be folded forward and used as a screen over the small mouth.

Doradids are nocturnal or crepuscular fishes that spend most of the day hiding. In the wild they may be found beneath submerged logs along with trichomycterids and gymnotids in some areas. In captivity they prefer shade from rocky caves, driftwood, or heavy growths of plants and a dark substrate, usually of a soft material. They are bottom-dwellers that like to grub about the bottom for food when the lights go out. They are considered good scavengers for they are able to root out some food particles that become slightly buried. When frightened or when there is bright light (as during the daytime), doradids may burrow into the substrate (a feat they can accomplish with lightning rapidity) so that only their eyes are visible. Most of the species are feeders on small invertebrates (insect larvae, worms, etc.) although the larger representatives feed more on detritus, molluscs, and seeds. The smaller individuals may be found in association with floating plants, feeding on the associated fauna, while still others may be active midwater feeders (such as *Oxydoras*). In an aquarium, doradids are generally good feeders, accepting a wide variety of foods but preferring live foods such as different types of worms and insect larvae. They are generally slow growers. These are hardy fishes to which water conditions are not very important (although they apparently prefer slightly soft water) as long as extremes are avoided. A temperature range of 20° to 26°C is recommended, even though doradids are said to be quite resistant to sudden chilling.

Many of the species are able to produce audible noises commonly described as groaning, short chattering sounds, or even purring, especially when they are removed from the water. For this reason they are often called "talking" catfishes. They have another common name—thorny catfishes—referring of course to the thorns or hooks on the lateral scutes of almost all species. They also have strong dorsal and pectoral spines that can cause rather painful wounds to those who do not handle them carefully. These spines and thorns are also quite adept at getting tangled in nets. Some species are reported to emit a milky white liquid that has been said to cause skin irritations in some hobbyists. Reproduction of any of the species is not yet known, although there have been some reports that they may build nests of sorts.

There are approximately 36 genera now currently in use, a number that almost certainly will be reduced when the family is studied in more detail. The genera of Doradidae are often poorly defined and taxonomy of this family is in a state of flux, so problems may be encountered when attempting to identify genera. The genera can be distinguished by the following key:

1a. Maxillary and sometimes mental barbels fringed 2
1b. Barbels all simple 8
2a. Nuchal shields with a foramen on each side........ 3
2b. Nuchal shields without a foramen on each side........ 6
3a. A series of plates between dorsal and adipose fins and sometimes between the ventral and anal fins .... *Hemidoras*
3b. No series of plates between dorsal and adipose fins, nor between ventral and anal fins 4
4a. Origin of ventral fins nearer caudal than snout; adipose fin not continued forward as ridge or keel 5
4b. Origin of ventral fins nearer snout than caudal; adipose fin continued forward as a keel........ *Leptodoras*
5a. Eyes normal; spines of lateral plates present from humeral region.. *Opsodoras*
5b. Eyes elongate; spines of lateral plates only present posterior to vertical from origin of ventral fins........ *Hassar*
6a. Anterior lateral scutes small, not connecting with dorsal plate.... *Anduzedoras*
6b. Anterior lateral scutes moderate to large, connecting with dorsal plate..... 7
7a. Opercle, preopercle, and coracoid process granular; adipose continued forward as a keel .... *Trachydoras*
7b. Opercle, preopercle, and coracoid process covered with skin; adipose fin not continued forward as a keel .... *Doras*
8a. Caudal fin rounded to more or less truncate 9
8b. Caudal fin emarginate to strongly forked 15
9a. Dorsal fin spine serrate in front but not behind........ 10
9b. Dorsal fin spine grooved, without spines on sides, front, or back (except *Physopyxis*, whose spine is serrate on lower half of anterior margin only)........ 12
10a. Caudal peduncle lacking plates above and below........ 11
10b. Caudal peduncle with spiny plates above and below; caudal fin rounded.. *Agamyxis*
11a. Caudal fin rounded........ *Acanthodoras*
11b. Caudal fin truncate........ *Hildadoras*
12a. Adipose fin very small, easily overlooked .... *Physopyxis*
12b. Adipose fin normal........ 13
13a. A large plate covering anterior part of

adipose fin; caudal truncate; nasal bone serrate .... *Hypodoras*
13b. No plates present between dorsal and adipose fins 14
14a. Granulations of coracoid and clavicle confluent into a large buckler; nasal bone serrate .... *Amblydoras*
14b. Granulations of coracoid and clavicle not confluent, a space covered with skin between the granulations; nasal bone not serrate; adipose fin not elongate .... *Zathorax*
15a. Caudal fin emarginate 16
15b. Caudal fin distinctly forked............. 20
16a. Adipose fin continued forward as a low keel.................. *Megalodoras* (in part)
16b. Adipose fin not continued forward as a low keel..................................... 17
17a. Lateral plates relatively small............. .... *Autanodoras*
17b. Lateral plates moderate to quite large .. 18
18a. Dorsal spine serrate in front and behind 19
18b. Dorsal spine grooved, without spines on sides, front, or back .... *Anadoras*
19a. Nasal plate erect; width of head at clavicle greater than distance from snout to end of dorsal plate; posterior portion of swim bladder simple or forked .... *Astrodoras*
19b. Nasal bone procumbent; width at clavicle about 1.25 in distance between snout and end of dorsal plate; second swim bladder heart-shaped, with a simple cecum .... *Scorpiodoras*
20a. Caudal peduncle provided with plates above and below 21
20b. Caudal peduncle naked above and below 25
21a. Adipose fin continued forward as a long keel 22
21b. Adipose fin high or long and equal to anal fin base but not continued forward as a long keel (may continue forward as a slight keel in *Orinocodoras*) 24
22a. Head width at clavicle greater than head length (to end of bony opercle); mouth wide; scutes 28-34 .... *Platydoras*
22b. Head width at clavicle less than head length 23
23a. Jaws highly modified, strongly compressed, elongate, forceps-like in appearance and projecting ventrally. *Rhyncodoras*
23b. Jaws not as above; mouth relatively small; scutes 30 .... *Rhinodoras*
24a. Adipose fin high, longer than anal fin base but not continued forward as a keel; about 30 scutes....... *Franciscodoras*
24b. Adipose fin long, about equal to anal fin base and prolonged forward as a slight keel; scutes about 29 .... *Orinocodoras*
25a. Adipose fin not extending forward as a keel 26
25b. Adipose fin extending forward as a long keel 30
26a. Adipose fin shorter than the anal fin base 27
26b. Adipose fin equal to or longer than anal fin base 28
27a. Head width at clavicle greater than head length (to end of bony opercle); scutes about 16-20; mouth wide ...... *Lithodoras*
27b. Head width at clavicle less than head length; mouth relatively small; scutes 30-34(?) .... *Nemadoras*
28a. Spines of lateral plates only present posterior to a vertical from origin of the ventrals.............................. *Doraops*
28b. Spines of lateral plates present from humeral region 29
29a. Humeral process very short; barbels banded .... *Apuredoras*
29b. Humeral process long; barbels of uniform color....................... *Sachsdoras*
30a. Width of head at clavicle greater than length of head (to end of bony opercle). 32
30b. Width of head at clavicle less than head length 31
31a. Lateral scutes about 16-23; rows of tentacles present on roof of mouth.......... .... *Pseudodoras*
31b. Lateral scutes 34-40; no tentacles on roof of mouth .... *Oxydoras*
32a. Fewer than 21 lateral scutes............. 33
32b. More than 22 lateral scutes 35
33a. First four lateral plates very close, forming by their borders a sort of circle; lateral plates of anal region very deep, deeper than depth of caudal peduncle........... 34
33b. First four lateral plates not overlapping and with their borders not forming a circle; lateral plates of anal region very low, lower than minimum height of cau-

dal peduncle .... *Deltadoras*

34a. A second swim bladder or cecum; both depressed and fringed with numerous diverticula .... *Megalodoras* (in part)

34b. Only one swim bladder ....*Hoplodoras*

35a. Approximately 38-40 lateral scutes .... *Centrodoras*

35b. Approximately 22-30 lateral scutes....36

36a. About 20 thorns on posterior face of dorsal spine, of nearly of equal size with those covering opposite side or anterior face; lateral scutes 25-30 ....*Pterodoras*

36b. Posterior hooks of dorsal spines stronger than the anterior; lateral scutes 30....... .... *Centrochir*

The genus *Megalodoras* has less than 24 lateral plates and an adipose fin that is continued forward as a keel. The head is depressed, wider than long, and the snout is not conical. The dorsal fin spine is strong, the serrae of the posterior margin usually fewer and weaker than those of the anterior margin, and becoming obsolete with age. The eye is in the middle or near the middle of the head. The suborbital chain of bones consists of three

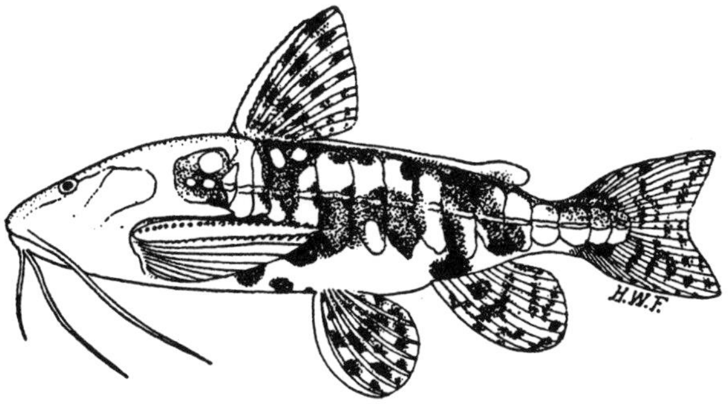

Megalodoras irwini. (From Fowler, 1951.)

bones, the anterior in contact with the lower surface of the preorbital, the second bordering about half of the eye and much wider than the posterior and with small spines at the upper border. Its anterior end is in contact with the first and with the preorbital. The preorbital is large, granular along its upper margin, and in contact with the premaxillary and maxillary in front. The occipital region is somewhat roof-shaped, with or without a median groove, but with a supraoccipital crest. The mouth is subterminal and provided with narrow bands of minute teeth. The barbels are simple. The caudal peduncle is naked along the median dorsal and ventral lines. The swim bladder is greatly depressed and divided into two parts, the anterior portion heart-shaped, with about a dozen tubular ceca or diverticula aligned in a row from the outer posterior angle around the sides to near the center in front.

Megalodoras irwini is one of the largest doradids, attaining a length of at least 60 cm. It is well protected by large lateral scutes and strong dorsal and pectoral fin spines. It feeds heavily on fruits and pulmonate snails in the flooded forests during the high water season. The native name is Key-way-mamma, which means "mother of the snails," referring to its diet of the large brown river snails. This species is a good agent for the dispersal of seeds since the fruits are swallowed whole and the seeds pass through the digestive system unharmed. The natives do not eat this species as they find the flesh too tough and it is not considered wholesome. The dorsal fin has a spine and 6 rays, while the anal fin has 12 or 13 rays. There are 2 + 15 to 17 scutes. The eye is small, about 8 in head. The skin of the back and sides is covered with papillae. The color is brown, often with black spots, especially on the stomach.

The monotypic genus *Centrodoras* has the plates more numerous, about 38-40, the anterior three in contact with the dorsal plate, the succeeding scutes increasing in size rapidly to about the sixth, then becoming more narrow. The bones of the head are striate, and the fontanel is not constricted and not continued as a groove. The eye is in the middle of the head. The dorsal fin spine has antrorse hooks on the anterior margin and straight to retrorse hooks on the posterior edge. The swim bladder is cardiform, depressed, and with numerous fimbriated or tufted diverticula. There is a narrower second bladder or cecum with very profusely tufted brittle lateral diverticula.

The type and only species of the genus, *C. brachiatus*, is described as having a flat head with the predorsal plate steeply roof-shaped and small eyes, about 8.5 in the head length. The humeral process is striate. The lateral scutes are low, except for those below the dor-

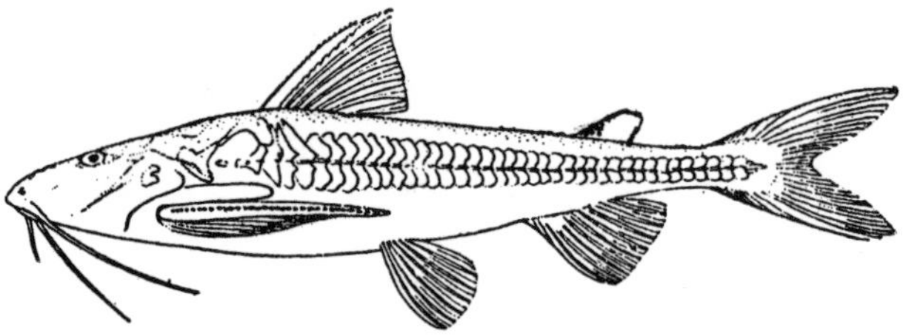

Centrodoras brachiatus. (From Fowler, 1945.)

sal fin that are quite deep. The dorsal surface between the dorsal and adipose fins is without plates, but the caudal peduncle has plates both above and below. The pectoral fin spines are flat, striate on the sides, and extend to the ventral fins. The dorsal fin has a spine and 6 rays, the anal fin has 11 rays, and the caudal fin is deeply forked. Cope reported that there is a yellow lateral band.

The genus *Hoplodoras* is a small genus of only two species. It is very similar to *Megalodoras* as far as the general appearance is concerned, but it differs from that genus by the form of the swim bladder. In *Hoplodoras* the swim bladder is single, broader than long, and has a single series of simple ceca or diverticula. As in *Megalodoras*, the adipose fin is

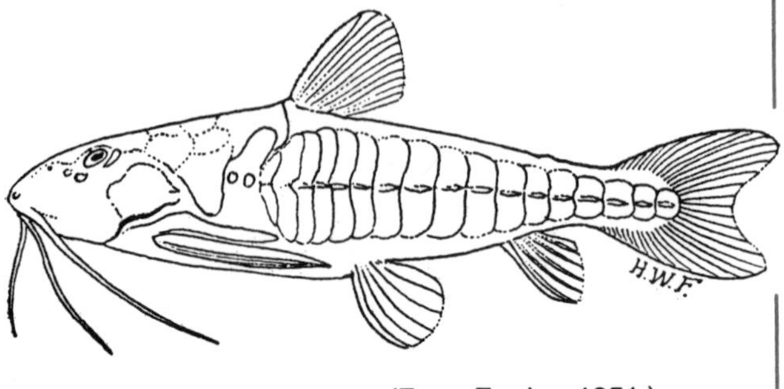

Hoplodoras uranoscopus. (From Fowler, 1951.)

prolonged forward as a keel and the lateral scutes are large and few in number, their spines present from the humeral region. The eyes are very small and located about in the middle third of the head. The nasal bone is well defined, as are the preopercle and opercle. The space between the dorsal fin and adipose fin is smooth and without plates, and the caudal peduncle is smooth, without fulcra. The dorsal fin spine is serrated on both edges, the caudal fin is forked, and the barbels are simple.

The type species of the genus, *H. uranoscopus*, has a rather heavy body that is depressed, although the caudal peduncle is rather slender. The top of the head to near the tip of the snout as well as the opercle, preopercle, suborbital, and prenasals are striate, although somewhat broken up into granules in places and becoming spine-like on the predorsal plate. The fontanel is elevated and does not extend to the posterior margin of the eye, and there is an elongate, diamond-shaped depression behind it. The small eyes look upward more than sideward. The snout is pointed, with the upper jaw projecting; the teeth in the jaws are villiform. The lateral scutes are deep, the third hook-bearing scute the deepest, then the scutes decrease in height until the last, but the median hooks increase in size until the caudal peduncle. The exposed surfaces of the plates in front of the caudal are covered with small spines. The accessory rays of the caudal fin are ossified, the anterior ones forming a small plate. The adipose fin is low and merges into the profile of the back anteriorly. The anal fin is high and rounded, and the caudal fin is emarginate.

The genus *Pterodoras* is a small genus of about two or three species. It is described as having very small eyes and simple barbels. The head is depressed and much wider than long, and the fontanel extends as a groove almost until the end of the occipital process. The lateral scutes are low, the deepest on the caudal peduncle with the rest decreasing in size anteriorly and posteriorly, 22 + 29 in number, and in line with those on the pseudotympanum. The space between the dorsal fin and the adipose fin is without plates, as is the caudal peduncle above and below. The adipose fin is prolonged forward as a keel, and the dorsal fin spine is strongly serrate on both edges. The caudal fin is forked, and the anal fin base is equal to or less than the adipose fin base (counting the keel). The teeth are villiform. The nasal bone is well defined, without armature, and the palatine is very small. The first suborbital is rudimentary; the second is small, attached for its entire length along the lower surface of the thick preorbital; and the preorbital is in con-

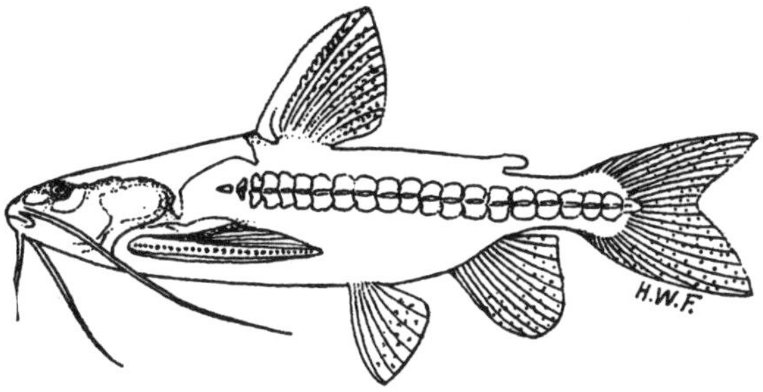

Pterodoras lentiginosus. (From Fowler, 1951.)

tact with the premaxillary and maxillary. There is no nuchal foramen. The anterior swim bladder is heart-shaped with a wide fringe of tubules along the sides; there is no posterior swim bladder.

Pterodoras is very similar to *Megalodoras* but differs from that genus by having narrower, more numerous lateral scutes, a very different swim bladder, and a bony stay from the epiotic behind the tympanum (toward the vertebrae). This is the only genus of the family having such a bony stay connecting the epiotic with the first spine-bearing scute. The type species of the genus, *P. granulosus*, attains a length of at least 60 cm. It is distributed in the Rio Madeira and its flood plain. Interestingly, it has never been caught in the clear-water tributaries. It does appear in relatively large schools at the beginning of the annual flooding. Many individuals that were captured had a large amount of fleshy fruits in their stomachs. They also feed on snails and aquatic macrophytes.

The genus *Centrochir* contains but a single species coming from the Magdalena and Amazon basins. The head is not depressed but is arched behind the fontanel, and the bones are finely granular. The snout is conical, depressed, and the mouth is narrow and terminal with well-developed teeth arranged in bands. The eyes are moderate in size, lateral, and located in the center or a little behind the center of the head. The fontanel may or may not continue as a groove, and the anterior nostril is near the lip. The lateral plates are numerous, the first two or three in contact with the dorsal plate, the remaining scutes gradually smaller to the last and each one with a simple central hook. The preorbital is overlying and in contact with the palatine but does not reach the maxillary and premaxillary in front, its free margin weakly but regularly notched. The first suborbital is under the preorbital; the second and third are of about equal width, entirely within the orbital border. The adipose fin is continued forward as

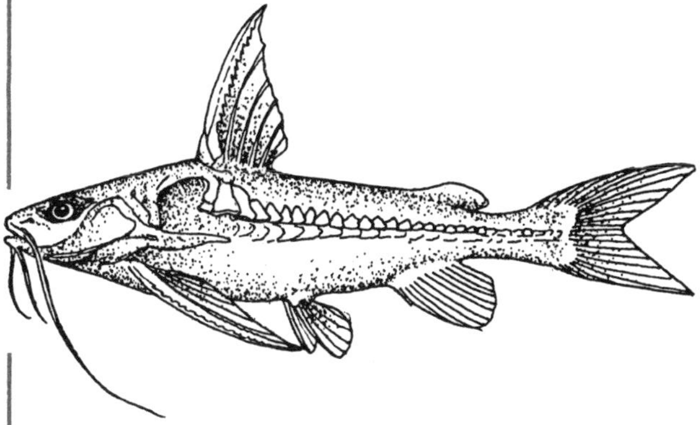

Centrochir crocodili. (After Eigenmann, 1925.)

a keel. The serrations on the posterior margin of the dorsal fin spine are stronger than those on the anterior margin. The swim bladder is deep, heart-shaped, and without diverticula; there is no second swim bladder.

The genus *Rhynchodoras* contains only two species. They have a large head that is longer than wide and somewhat conical in shape. The eyes are very small, ranging from about 12 to 24 times in the head length. The occipital process extends along the base of the dorsal fin, ending approximately at the base of the second to fourth dorsal fin rays. The barbels are simple, without feathery branchlets, and the two pairs of mental barbels are joined basally by a large membrane. The barbels do not extend as far as the origin of the pectoral fin. A frontal fontanel is present. The humeral process extends vertically from the pos-

Rhynchodoras xingui. (From Klausewitz & Rössel, 1961.)

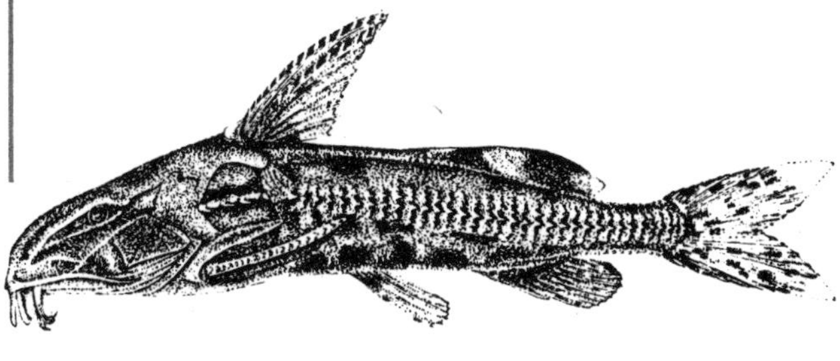

terior end of the lateral extension of the occipital process to the first plate of the main lateral series. The lateral scutes, 33-34 in number, have in addition two or three scutes in a line anterior to the humeral process and dorsal to the wedge-shaped cleithrum. On each of the plates there is a small spine, the tip of which overlaps the anterior base of the following plate. The dorsal and ventral surfaces of the caudal peduncle are provided with a single row of overlapping bony plates, somewhat rectangular in shape. The main feature that distinguishes this genus from all others in the family is the highly modified jaws, i.e., strongly compressed, elongate, forceps-like in appearance, and ventrally projecting. The teeth of both jaws are reduced to a small patch of minute villiform teeth anteriorly in each jaw, the ends extending backward along the sides of the jaws for half their length. The dorsal and pectoral fin spines are strong, the dorsal spine with the teeth along the anterior edge pointing toward the tip of the spine, those along the posterior edge recurved ventrally. The teeth of the pectoral spines are similarly arranged. The teeth of all three spines are larger on the posterior surface. The adipose fin extends forward as a keel and is longer than the anal fin base. The dorsal fin has a spine and 5 or 6 rays; the anal fin has about 12 to 14 rays.

The genus *Franciscodoras* is a small genus of but a single species from the Rio das Velhas. It has a high adipose fin whose base is longer than the anal fin base but is not continued forward for much more than a short distance, if at all, anteriorly. The caudal fin is deeply emarginate to deeply forked, and the dorsal fin spine is serrate on the anterior edge only. The scutes are large, heavy toward the end of the series, and the caudal peduncle is nearly completely covered above and below with modified fulcra that are not in contact with the lateral plates (which are not very deep). The eye is situated before the middle of the head. The fontanel is not continued as a groove beyond the middle of the head. In general appearance, in the nature of the skull, in the single swim bladder, and in the anterior scutes, among other characters, *Franciscodoras* resembles *Centrochir*.

Franciscodoras marmoratus. (From Fowler, 1951.)

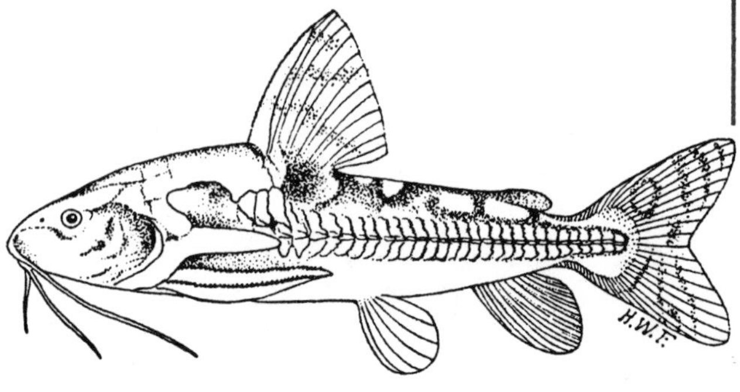

The genus *Lithodoras* is a small genus containing a single species from French Guiana. It is broader at the level of the clavicle than the length of the head. There are only a few narrow scutes, about 18-20 in number and each with a single hook or spine, the first two in contact with the dorsal plate. All of the naked parts of the body become more or less covered with bony plates with age. The snout is truncate and not depressed, with a terminal mouth provided with bands of well-developed teeth. The occiput is roof-shaped, and the fontanel is continued as a groove as far as the end of the nuchal plate. The eyes are large and lateral, situated about at the middle of the head or slightly in advance of this. The suborbital bone is large and reaches the premaxillary and maxillary bones in front and has divergent ridges ending in points along its free margin; the second suborbital is narrower than the third, the first appearing as a granular ridge below the preorbital. The preopercle is smooth. The adipose fin does not extend forward as a ridge. The serrae on the posterior margin of the dorsal fin spine are larger than those on the anterior margin. *L. dorsalis*, as the name implies (*litho* = stone), is the most heavily armored of the doradid species. Almost the entire body is covered with thick

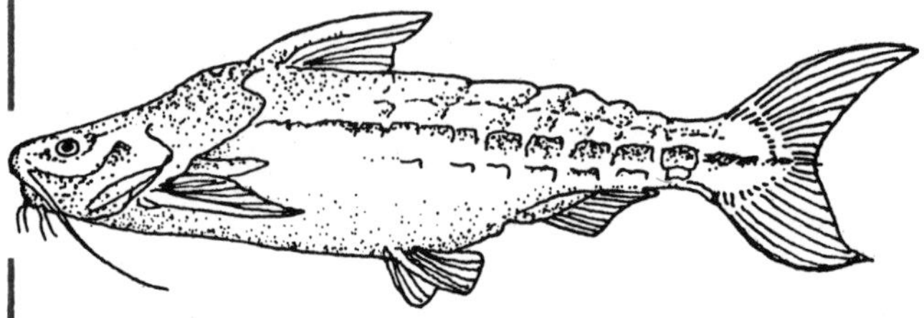

Lithodoras dorsalis. (After Goulding, 1981.)

bony plates (including the ventral area, which is usually naked in doradids). Attaining a length of about 90 cm and a weight of 12 kilos, *L. dorsalis* feeds on fruits when the forests are flooded and on the blades of macrophytes. This is another seed dispersal agent.

The genus *Acanthodoras* is unusual in that although it contains only three species, two of them have been imported for the aquarium

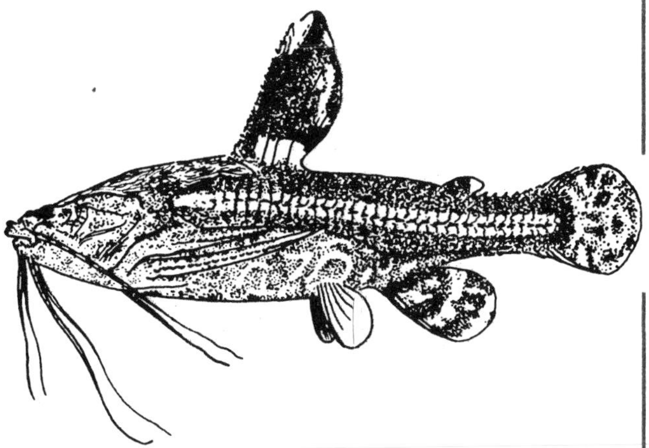

Acanthodoras spinosissimus. (From Fernandez-Yepez, 1968.)

trade. The width of the body at the clavicle is approximately 2.3 to 2.75 times in the length. The head is depressed, with the nuchal region only slightly arched; there is no nuchal foramen. The mouth is terminal, wider than the interorbital, with well-developed villiform teeth arranged in bands. The skull is finely granular (the granules along its edge are larger and sharper in *A. spinosissimus*) and the opercle is finely striate (*A. cataphractus*) to coarsely granular (*A. spinosissimus*). The fontanel is subcircular and not continued as a groove. The preopercle and interopercle are similar in sculpture to the opercle. The preorbital is short and in contact with the premaxillary in front, expanded and fan-like behind, with backward-directed serrae on the outer half of the expanded edge. The first suborbital is rather small and located along the lower surface of the well defined nasal bone; the second and third suborbitals are of about equal size and have sharp granules like those along the edge of the skull above the eye of *A. spinosissimus*. The coracoid is entirely covered with skin or its tip is finely granular. The eyes are very small, lateral, and situated well in advance of the middle of the head. The anterior nostrils are very close to the lip. The barbels are simple, without fringes. The lateral plates are numerous, high, cover more than half the sides, and have spines that start in the humeral region. There are no plates between the dorsal fin and the adipose fin nor are there any on the upper and lower surfaces of the caudal peduncle. The adipose fin is not continued forward as a keel, its base being shorter than the anal fin base. There are no serrae on the posterior margin of the dorsal spine. The caudal fin is rounded. The anterior swim bladder is short and heart-shaped; there is no trace of a second swim bladder.

Of the two species of *Acanthodoras* that are commonly seen in aquarium stores, *Acanthodoras spinosissimus* and *A. cataphractus*, the former is perhaps the most often available and better known, although the two are regularly confused and information reported for one of them might in reality be for the other. Fortunately, their needs and behavior are so similar it may not make that much difference anyway. Both are quite hardy and long-lived species that do not make many demands upon the aquarist. They are crepuscular catfishes that like to hide from the bright lights during the day. They will, if necessary, bury themselves in the substrate or dig under some flat rock where they will feel secure. In time some individuals may be a bit more active in very dim light. This means, of course, that a sufficient number of hiding places must be provided and that your specimens may not be seen very often in large well-planted and well-decorated aquaria. Additionally, while they are digging themselves in, plants may be uprooted or rocks may be undermined and come tumbling down, hopefully not on top of any of the fishes. Feeding is no great problem. They will accept most live foods, particularly worms. Some will even eventually accept prepared foods of various types. These fishes should be handled with care as their spines can inflict very nasty wounds. Many a surprised aquarist who has picked up a specimen with his fingers has found that the fish has clamped its pectoral spines down painfully on these fingers. Both these species are noted for their ability to produce sounds loud enough to be heard outside the aquarium. These are commonly made by rotation of the pectoral spines in their sockets, the sound being amplified by the swim bladder. Aquarists commonly call them talking catfishes for that reason as well as spiny catfishes. *A. spinosissimus* is said to attain a length of up to 15 cm in nature, although a length of about 10 cm is generally large for aquarium specimens. It has been stated that the female has a uniformly brown belly while that of the male has some white spots.

In *A. cataphractus* there has been an account of a spawning of individuals in captivity. The parents are said to prepare a nest by digging a depression in the substrate (in this case a fine gravel was used). The female deposited her eggs there and both parents proceeded to guard them. The eggs hatched in about four to five days but the fry were not raised.

The genus *Agamyxis* contains two species, one from Venezuela and the other from Ecuador. The eyes are moderate, located entirely in the anterior half of the head, and are surrounded by serrate ridges. There is no nuchal foramen, and the frontal fontanel is reduced. The barbels are simple. The teeth are villiform and arranged in bands. The lateral scutes are deep (less than four times in the predorsal length), covering the entire side of the caudal peduncle and more than the upper half of the area between the anal fin and the tip of the humeral process; spines are present starting from the humeral region. The space between the dorsal and adipose fins is without plates, but the caudal peduncle is provided

Agamyxis albomaculatus. (From Fernandez-Yepez, 1968.)

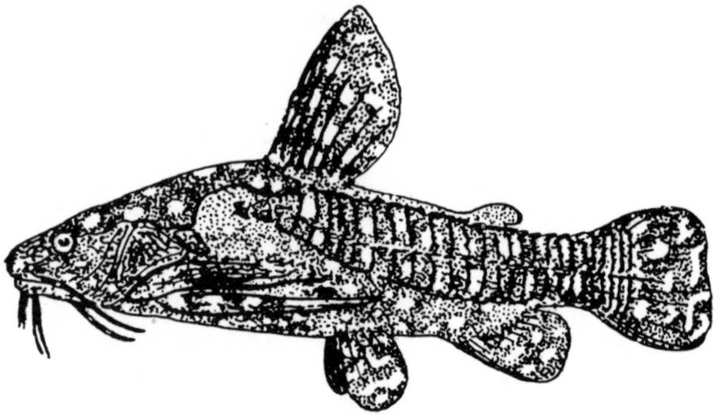

with spiniferous plates above and below. The adipose fin is not continued forward as a ridge, and the anal fin base is much longer than the base of the adipose fin. The dorsal fin spine is as long as the pectoral fin spines and is serrate in front and on the sides but smooth behind. The caudal fin is rounded. The nasal bone is defined, erect, and pectinate. The breast is covered with skin. This genus differs from *Acanthodoras* mostly by having the caudal peduncle with plates on the upper and lower surfaces.

The species most likely to be encountered by aquarists is *Agamyxis pectinifrons* from eastern Ecuador. It is a crepuscular species that is very hardy. The species attains a length of about 16 cm and prefers a diet of fairly large live foods of all kinds. It will eventually accept other meaty and dried foods.

The genus *Platydoras* is a small genus of less than a half dozen species. The body width at the level of the clavicle is greater than the head length. The head is somewhat depressed, arched over the occiput, with the nuchal bone defined but not armed, and there

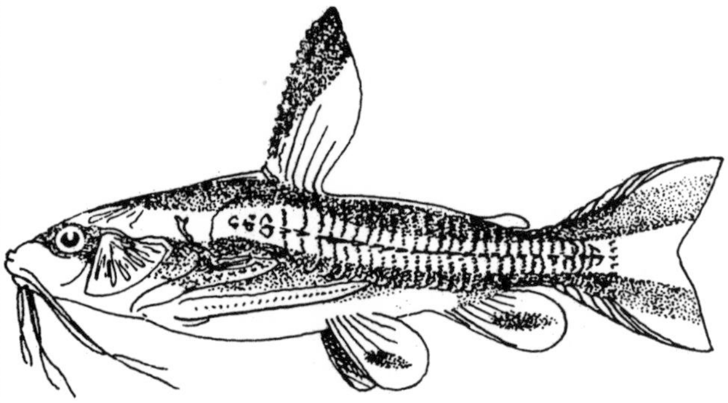

Platydoras armatulus. (From Fernandez-Yepez, 1968.)

is no nuchal foramen. The eyes are median and about a third of the way back from the tip of the snout. The snout is moderately depressed, with a subterminal mouth. The lower jaw is a bit shorter than the upper. The teeth are well developed and arranged in bands, those of the outer row enlarged in the young. The bones of the head, the opercles, nasals, and suborbitals are pitted-granular, and the opercle is striate. The anterior nostrils are close to the lips. The lateral scutes are numerous, very deep, and cover most of the sides, coming in contact with the modified caudal fulcra situated on the upper and lower surfaces of the caudal peduncle; the first three come in contact with the predorsal plate. The space between the dorsal fin and the adipose fin is smooth. The spines of the lateral plates are present from the humeral region back. The base of the anal fin is longer than that of the adipose fin (in *P. costatus*, however, there is a low preadipose keel). The dorsal fin spine is strong, the serrations on the posterior margin weaker than those on the anterior margin, and disappearing with age. The caudal fin is emarginate. The barbels are simple and there is no constriction in the fontanel. The swim bladder is double. The anterior portion is heart-shaped, with a median longitudinal groove, and there are no ceca; the posterior swim bladder is subconical, with a rounded base, without any constriction, and also without ceca.

The Raphael Catfish, *Platydoras costatus*, is one of the more common doradids imported for the aquarium trade. It is quite attractive because of the bright whitish band along the side of the body. These catfish are usually crepuscular, although in time they might come out during the day for food. It is still safer to feed them in dim light or just before the lights go out. They are not demanding and are relatively hardy. No known spawnings have been reported. At least one other species of this genus has also been sold as a Raphael Catfish.

The genus *Astrodoras* contains a single species from the Rio Guapore and Rio Negro that attains a length of about 10 to 12 cm. The body width at the clavicle is included approximately 2.6 times in the length. The head is depressed, with the nuchal region roof-shaped, while the skull bones are finely granular or striate. The fontanel is elongate and continued as an obscure, interrupted groove. The eyes are moderate and are positioned in the center or a little before the center of the head. The preorbital is short, its posterior edge expanded and with about ten spines; the suborbitals are narrow, of about equal width, and the middle one is granular. The anterior nostril is near the lip. The mouth is terminal, about equal to the interorbital width, and the teeth are arranged in bands. The lateral plates are numerous and spiny, covering half to more than half of the sides; plates are present on the upper and lower surfaces of the caudal peduncle. The dorsal spine has serrae only on the anterior margin and none on the sides or behind, in contrast to *Acanthodoras* and *Amblydoras*. The adipose fin is not continued forward as a keel, and the caudal fin is emarginate. The swim bladder is divided into two, the anterior heart- or kidney-shaped, and merging into the posterior without a constriction. The posterior bladder is forked to its base, the two "horns" turning laterally.

The single species is not often seen in aquaria. It is omnivorous and feeds well in captivity.

The genus *Scorpiodoras* contains a single species from the Rio Negro. The body is heavy anteriorly and tapers to a slender caudal peduncle. The head is short, depressed, and pointed, its width a little less than its length. The bones of the head are coarsely striate, becoming granular on the outer margins. A deeply pectinate nasal shield articulates with the somewhat granular or serrate suborbital bones. The fontanel is elongate triangular, the wider posterior end not attaining the posterior margin of the orbit. The eye is contained about five times in the head length and is well protected. The snout is narrow, the upper jaw longer than the lower; the teeth are well developed and arranged in moderate bands. The first two lateral scutes touch a process of the dorsal plate but do not extend below to the humeral process. In the region before the first lateral plate are two elongate dermal ossifications corresponding to the hooks of the lateral plate. The deepest plate (exclusive of the first two) is about equal to

Astrodoras asterifrons. (After Eigenmann, 1925.)

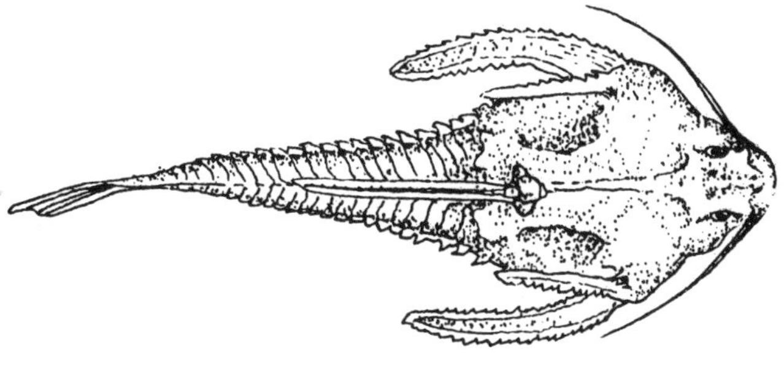

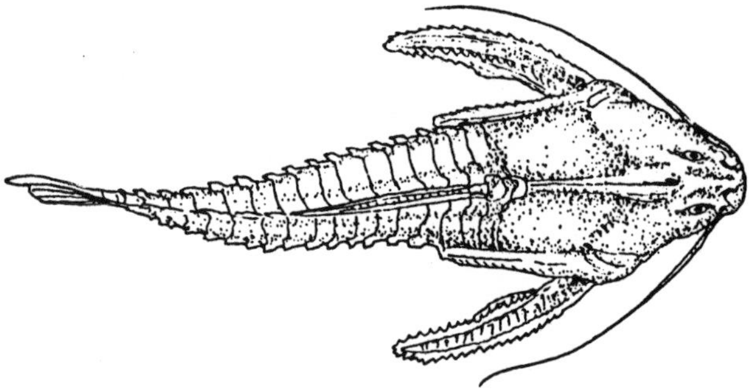

Scorpiodoras heckelii. (After Eigenmann, 1925.)

twice the eye diameter. There are no scutes or plates on the dorsal or ventral surfaces. The dorsal fin spine has the sides deeply furrowed, the anterior margin with serrae that are upturned, and the posterior margin broad, smooth, and with a median groove. The base of the adipose fin is about equal to that of the dorsal fin, and the anal fin is higher than long and is rounded. The pectoral spines are long and curved, the upper surface coarsely, the lower surface finely striate, and both margins with strong teeth. The caudal fin is emarginate, with conspicuous accessory rays. The genus *Scorpiodoras* is similar to the genus *Astrodoras*, but in *Scorpiodoras* the mouth is wider than the interorbital, the nasal bone is procumbent, the expanded edge is raised but little, there are more than 25 spines, the anterior swim bladder is large and kidney-shaped, the posterior swim bladder is banjo-shaped, and the body of the posterior swim bladder is heart-shaped, with a posterior horn longer than the main part and recurved like the tail of a scorpion.

The genus *Amblydoras* is a small genus of only one, possibly two, species from the Amazon basin and the Guianas. The body width at the clavicle is contained about three times in the length. The head is depressed, the skull arched, finely striate granular, and without a median groove. The fontanel is small and elongate-oval. The eye is about in the middle of the head, about equal to the interorbital space, and longer than the snout. The preorbitals are in contact with the premaxillaries in front, and its 15 spines are covered. The anterior nostrils are placed near the lip, and the prenasal bone is very dentate. The mouth is terminal, with well developed teeth arranged in narrow bands. The lateral scutes are very deep, covering almost all of the sides of the body and tail. The hind part of the caudal peduncle is shielded above and below by bony plates. The adipose fin is not continued forward as a keel, and there are no plates between the adipose fin and the dorsal fin. The dorsal fin spine is smooth on both margins, but it does have grooves and ridges on the sides and front. The caudal fin is rounded. The anterior swim bladder in *A. hancocki* is short, heart-shaped, and without ceca; there is no posterior swim bladder.

Amblydoras hancocki is a quiet, peaceful, undemanding catfish that is hardy and will live a long time in captivity. It is suitable for a community tank as long as the tankmates are not aggressive fishes. The tank should be heavily planted and provided with a number

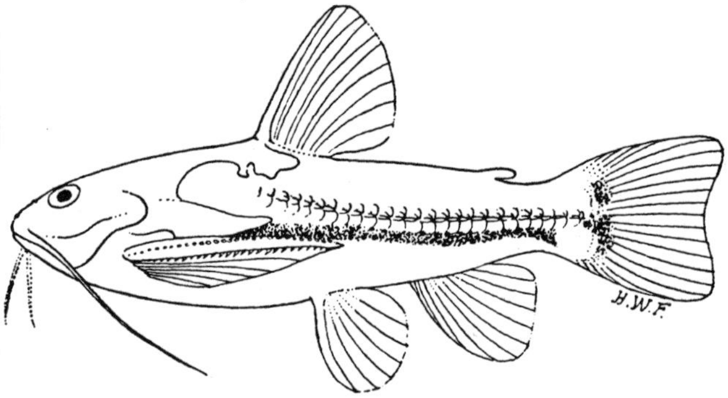

Amblydoras hancocki. (From Fowler, 1951.)

of hiding places. Driftwood is very good to use for decorations. The bottom material should be soft and preferably dark in color. The pH is not important, and the temperature is best around 22° to 24°C. Live foods such as tubificid worms and bloodworms are definitely preferred, but eventually almost any good nourishing food is accepted if it makes it to the bottom. Remember to feed shortly before lights-out because *A. hancocki* prefers to feed in deep shade or dim light. It is not a very active fish and will remain in one position, motionless, for hours, sometimes even if touched. But if you try and catch them they show an amazing speed and will dart to another section of the tank where they bury themselves in the gravel with lightning

The color of *Amblydoras hancocki* is quite variable although the pattern is fairly consistent. Photo by Gerhard Marcuse.

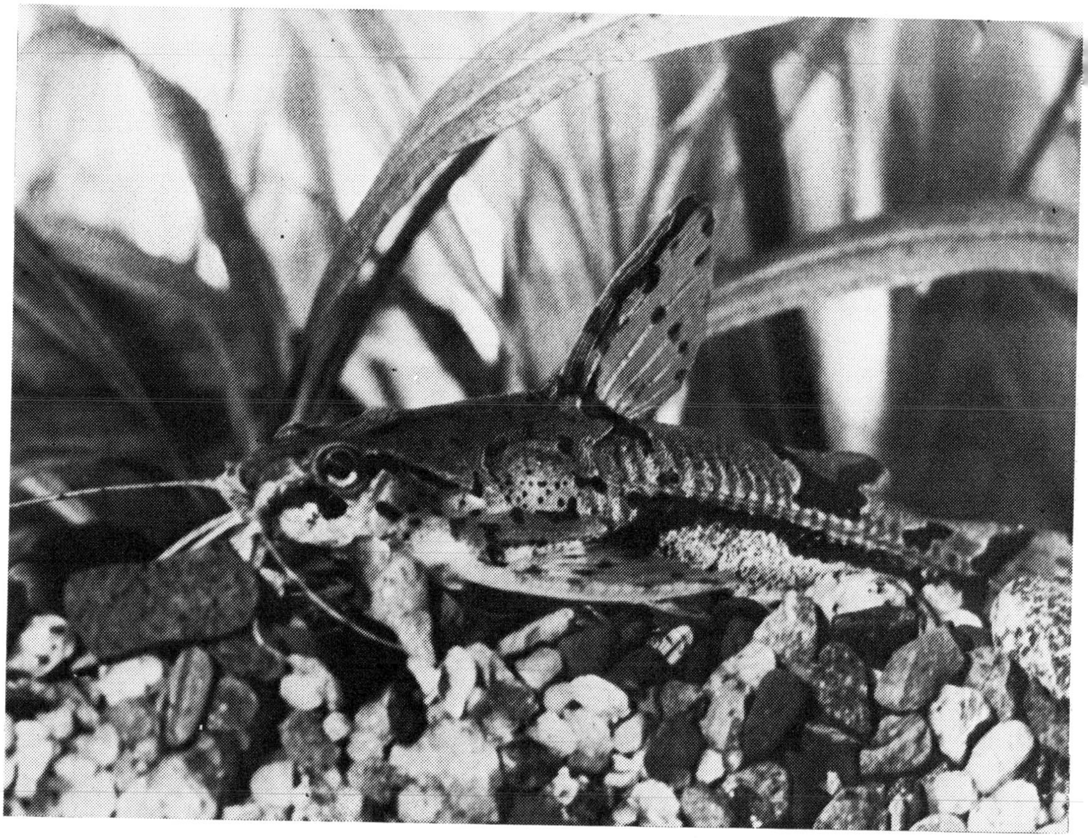

quickness or find a group of plants in which to hide. When buried, the eyes remain above the surface to keep watch for any sign of danger. This species is also said to make audible sounds and along with several other doradids is commonly referred to as the Talking Catfish.

The color is quite variable, generally a dark brown with violet-black patches and a white belly. The eyes are a bright gleaming blue, and there is an ivory or white stripe along the side. According to Meinken, the spines of the dorsal and pectoral fins in the male are more hooked than those of the female. The white stripe is also noticeably narrower in the female and the silvery dots on the sides are not as pronounced. The belly of the female is said to be much lighter, almost white, with brownish flecks toward the sides; the belly of the male is peppered with small round brown spots. *A. hancocki* is reported to construct a regular nest of leaves, plant stems, etc. The eggs are laid in a flattened cluster and carefully covered over. After that the parents guard the nest until the eggs hatch. Spawning apparently occurs in the rainy season. This species attains a length of about 15 cm in nature but only about 10 to 12 cm in captivity. In their natural habitat they are found in ponds that are seasonally flooded during the rainy season, as well as creeks that have a large amount of plant debris such as fallen branches.

The genus *Anadoras* contains about four species that are distributed in the Amazon basin. The width of the body between the clavicles is less than three in the length. The head is depressed and much wider than long, and the fontanel is oval and not continued as a groove. The head is minutely granular, and the snout is depressed. The mouth is terminal, with minute teeth arranged in bands. The eyes are entirely in the anterior part of the head, and the preorbital bone is inconspicuous. The granulations in the breast area are inconspicuous, narrow, or confined to the tip of the coracoid. The scutes are numerous, covering a fourth to a half of the sides. Modified fulcra are present and cover much of the upper and lower surfaces of the caudal peduncle. The adipose fin is short, its base shorter than that of the anal fin and not continued forward as a keel. The spine of the dorsal fin is without serrae but has longitudinal grooves

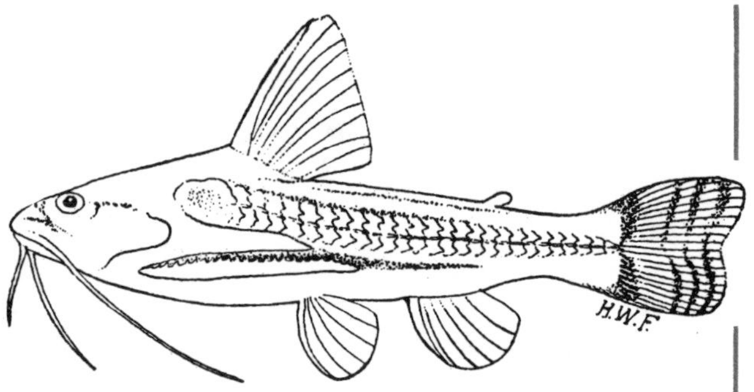

Anadoras insculptus. (From Fowler, 1951.)

on the anterior border. There are no plates in the area between the dorsal and adipose fins. The barbels are simple, without fringes. There are two swim bladders, the anterior heart-shaped, with a median longitudinal groove and without marginal prolongations. The second or posterior swim bladder is reduced to a minute tubule (in *A. weddellii*) or entirely suppressed (*A. regani, A. grypus*). Species of this genus are rarely seen for sale. Their care can be expected to follow that of the other doradids.

The genus *Hypodoras* contains a single species from Peru. The top of the head is granulose and the fontanel is not continued as a groove. The prenasal bone is deeply pectinate, as is the preorbital crest; the suborbital is granular. The humeral process is very strong and has a series of spines; the coracoid process is striate. The eyes are located immediately in front of the middle of the head and are contained about six times in the head length. The banded maxillary barbels extend to a point a little beyond the coracoid process. The teeth are minute and arranged in

Hypodoras forficulatus. (From Fowler, 1951.)

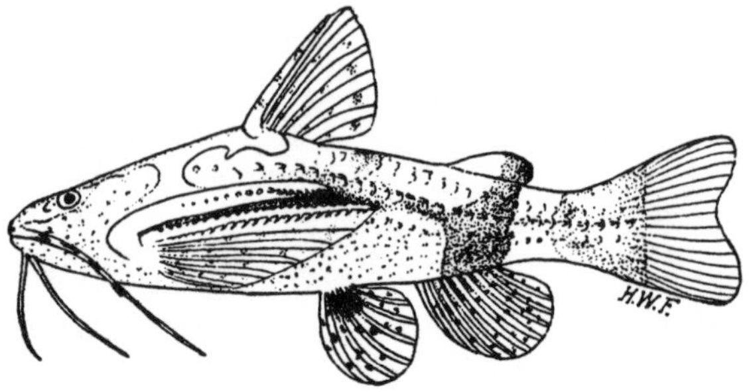

bands. The adipose fin is a little shorter than the anal fin base and its anterior two-thirds is covered by a rhomboidal plate that is keeled. The dorsal spine is striate in front and laterally, and there are no serrae. The dorsal and pectoral fins are lanceolate, while the ventrals are broad and rounded. The anal fin is rounded, and the caudal fin is truncate. The lateral scutes are very deep, covering the entire sides. They are crowded, and those of the caudal peduncle are in contact with the plates above and below and have a single hook; those in front of the caudal peduncle have two to five hooks above the median one and one or two below it. There are two or three scutes from the dorsal plate to the humeral process. The caudal peduncle is completely covered above and below with fulcra, and there is a single large plate between the adipose and these caudal fulcra. Anterior and posterior swim bladders are present, the anterior wider than long, kidney-shaped, and without marginal tentacles or ceca but with a marginal constriction directly continued into the posterior swim bladder, which, at the point of union, is about a third as wide as the anterior and is divided into two horns in its posterior three-fifths. The horns appear to be continuations of the lateral lobes of the anterior swim bladder. The genus *Hypodoras* differs from all other genera of the Doradidae by possessing a plate over the anterior part of the adipose fin and in the construction of the swim bladder.

The genus *Physopyxis* contains a single species from the Ambyiacu River. The snout is short and broadly truncated, and the dorsal plate is keeled, roof-shaped, its posterior process terminating behind the last dorsal fin rays. The humeral process is striate and extends to below the dorsal fin spine; the prenasal bones are pectinate, the postcoracoid process is striate, and the clavicles and coracoid are granular and are developed into a large shield extending forward to below the eyes. The eyes are small, about 4.2 in the length of the head, and located in the anterior half of the head. The teeth are minute and in several series. The dorsal fin spine is straight, grooved, and with spines on the lower portion of the anterior margin; it is smooth along the posterior edge. The pectoral spine is large,

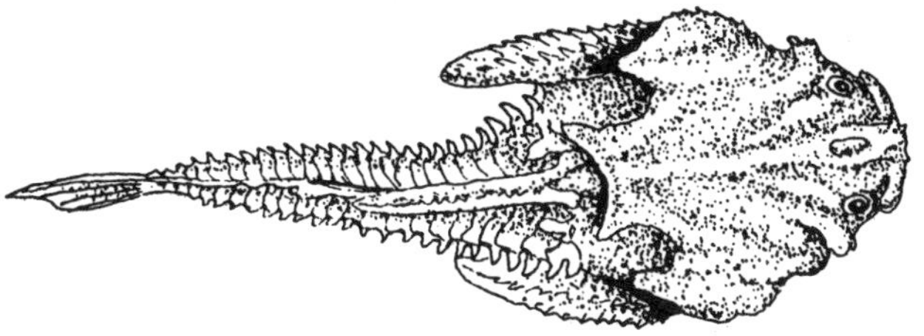

Physopyxis lyra. (After Eigenmann, 1925.)

curved, and extends beyond the origin of the anal fin. The caudal fin is truncate. The gill openings are much reduced. *P. lyra* is not likely to be seen in the aquarium hobby. Recently collected specimens from the Rio Iténez, Brazil, have a very small but well formed adipose fin. Although Cope described the holotype as lacking an adipose fin it seems likely he merely overlooked it (Bailey & Baskin, 1976).

The two genera *Oxydoras* and *Pseudodoras* are often confused and in some cases have even been combined into a single genus. The genus *Oxydoras* is distinguishable from *Pseudodoras* by having a higher number of lateral scutes (24-40 as opposed to 16-23 in *Pseudodoras*) and by lacking appendages in the mouth (*Pseudodoras* has fleshy tentacles in

Oxydoras sifontesi. (From Fernandez-Yepez, 1968.)

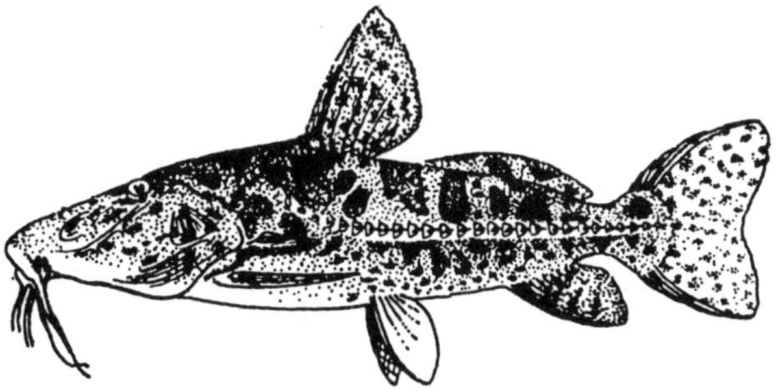

the roof of the mouth). There are two or three species in the genus *Oxydoras*. The two genera are otherwise so close that a more complete description is given only for *Pseudodoras*.

Oxydoras kneri is omnivorous, feeding mainly on insects, crustaceans, molluscs, other invertebrates, and some vegetable material. It attains a weight of 9 kilos in the Parana but only up to about 5 or 6 kilos in Uruguay. It has some economic importance. The eyes are very small, contained about ten times in the head length.

The genus *Pseudodoras* contains two or three species, the best known of which is *Pseudodoras niger*. The width of the body at the clavicles is less than the head length. The head is not depressed but is longer than wide; the occipital region is roof-shaped, granular or striate, and without a median groove or nuchal foramen. The fontanel is double. The opercle is striate, and in older individuals the suborbital is granular. The eyes are lateral and entirely behind the middle of the head.

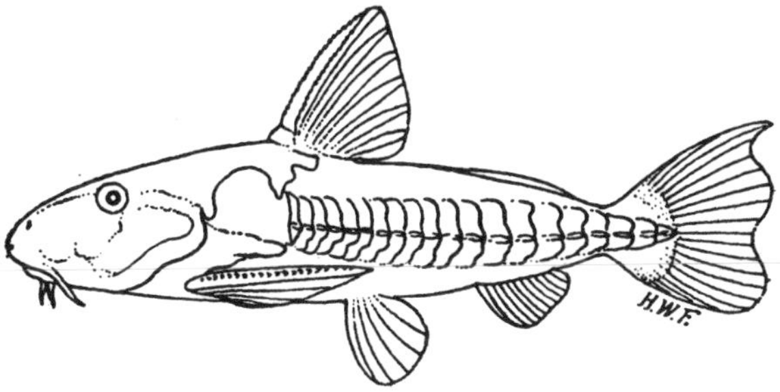

Pseudodoras niger. (From Fowler, 1951.)

The preorbital is comma-shaped, the front incurved, connected with the ethmoid; the first suborbital is in part located under the preorbital, while the second is large, only half of it forming part of the orbital border, and the third is slender. The snout is conical and the mouth is inferior, with rhomboidal premaxillaries. The teeth are feeble. There are several tentacles covered with taste buds on the roof of the mouth between the second and third pairs of gill arches and two rows of tentacles converging from in front of the first arch forward, ending in a ridge; smaller ones are present on the floor of the mouth. The barbels are simple and short. The anterior nostrils are remote from the lips; the nasal bone is not defined. The coracoid is covered with skin. The adipose fin is long and low, continued forward as a low keel. The dorsal fin spine has serrations on both edges, those on the posterior margin weaker than those on the anterior margin. The caudal fin is emarginate.

The lateral plates are few and narrow (about 3+18-23), and the scute spines start in the humeral region. There are no plates in the interdorsal area or on the caudal peduncle. The swim bladder of *P. niger* is double, both parts well developed and with marginal indications of lobules or the beginnings of ceca. The anterior swim bladder is elongate, heart-shaped; the posterior is elliptical and a little more than twice as long as wide, its length less than two times in the length of the anterior bladder. The vertical distribution of the genus is said to be from sea level to 3,000 feet.

Pseudodoras niger inhabits a wide variety of habitats in the wild, including floodplain lakes and flooded forests, and it may be captured commercially as it moves upstream in the Rio Madeira in schools. It attains a very large size and is probably the largest doradid, attaining a length of about 1.2 meters and a weight of some 20 kilos. The inferior mouth with weak or no teeth is used for vacuuming detritus or debris from the bottom. Analysis of the stomach contents revealed mud and decomposing leaves with insect larvae such as chironomid midges and mayflies (Ephemeroptera) and crustaceans such as shrimp. The tentacles in the mouth probably aid in the detection of the food among the detritus. Some reports also indicate that this species dines occasionally on flower buds and seeds. In captivity *P. niger* tends to be a shy fish that will spend most of the daylight hours in some secluded spot (under ledges, in caves, among dense plants, etc.). This spot is almost always the same one day after day, and it will maintain its presence often by sheer bulk, not to mention the lateral spines on the scutes. If too many other fishes decide to share this retreat, the *P. niger* may decide to shake itself a few times, usually clearing out its favorite spot in record time. Although mostly quiet, this species is capable of outbursts such as that just mentioned, but if it does dash about the tank it is likely to cause a bit of mayhem, including the dislodging of the power filter tubes.

This species is not as "flexible" as some of the other doradids and must therefore be housed in a fairly large aquarium with adequate swimming room. In addition to providing hiding places, it is recommended that the bottom material be soft and without sharp edges as this species will take up its sifting habits in the aquarium and sharp objects may damage the delicate gills. The size of the substrate particles can be increased as the fish grows. The water should be clear, clean and well-filtered, and good aeration is necessary. Regular water changes are beneficial. The hardness and pH are not important as long as extremes are avoided. *P. niger* is extremely tolerant of temperature fluctuations, but it will become more lethargic at higher temperatures. The maximum range is about 18° to 30°C, but 20° to 27°C is best. It is recommended that *P. niger* should not be moved often. Feeding is no problem as this fish will eat almost anything. A vegetable-based diet is good and could include such things as boiled oatmeal, spinach, trout or koi pellets, rabbit pellets, frozen peas, and even various flake foods. But it will also accept beef heart and liver, brine shrimp, tubificid worms, and earthworms. The food should be relatively small and must sink to the bottom. It should also be offered at night, for *P. niger* is very shy at feeding during the day, at least at first. Juveniles may be shy at first but may eventually become bold enough to cruise around the tank during the day.

This peaceful fish can be used in a community tank with other non-aggressive fishes of almost any size, though larger cichlids and catfishes that are aggressive should not be included. There is one major drawback—this species is prone to massive fungal and bacterial infections that are hard to cure. Because of its popularity, there have been many common names applied to this species, among which are Black Doradid, Blue Dolphin, Fork-snout Catfish, Terushuki, and Cuiu-cuiu. Braz Walker has affectionately referred to it as a "leather-tailed docile colossus."

The genus *Rhinodoras* contains a single species from Rio de la Plata. The head is about as long as wide or it is slightly longer than wide, subconical in shape, and the fontanel is continued as an obscure groove to the dorsal fin. The eyes are moderate and located in the middle of the head. The preorbital plates are obscure. The barbels are simple, the maxillaries not extending as far as the gill opening. The humeral process extends to the last one-fourth of the pectoral fin. The poste-

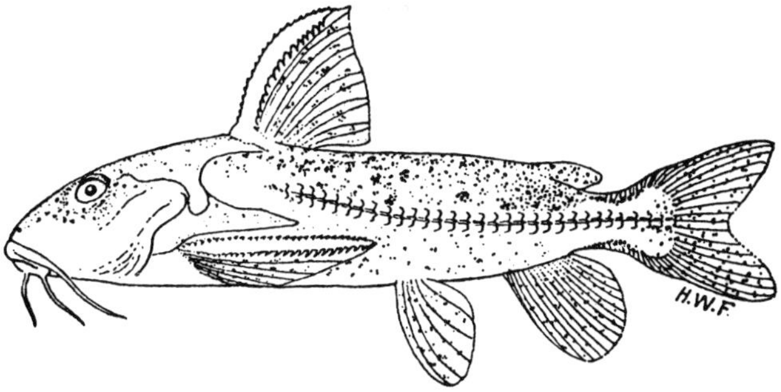

Rhinodoras dorbignyi. (From Fowler, 1951.)

rior nostrils are nearer the eyes than they are to the anterior nostrils, which are immediately behind the lip. Jaw teeth are present. The adipose fin is prolonged forward as a keel. The dorsal fin spine is strongly serrate, the serrae stronger on the posterior margin and directed downward. The lateral scutes, about 29 to 30 in number, are low, and the caudal peduncle is covered with modified fulcra above and below. The caudal fin is forked. The swim bladders are similar to those of *Pseudodoras niger*, but they have no indications of ceca and the anterior swim bladder is less depressed. According to Kner the dorsal and caudal fins have dark spots.

The genus *Trachydoras* is a small genus of about four species from the Paraguay and Amazon basins. The head is short and deep and the fontanel is not continued as a groove. There is no foramen in the dorsal buckler. The humeral process is long and narrow, more or less obliquely truncate. The short snout and the preopercle and opercle are granular; the coracoid process is partially or entirely granular. The anterior nostrils are equidistant from the tip of the snout and the posterior nostrils or closer to the former. The barbels are provided with barblets, the mental barbels are united by a membrane, and the maxillary barbels do not quite reach or just reach the gill openings. The mouth is very small, with feeble teeth, or the teeth are absent. One or more pectoral pores are present. The adipose fin is about half the length of the anal fin and is continued forward as a keel. The first lateral scute is very large, connecting with the humeral process and the descending process of the predorsal plate; the caudal peduncle is without scutes or plates above and below.

Trachydoras atripes. (From Fowler, 1951.)

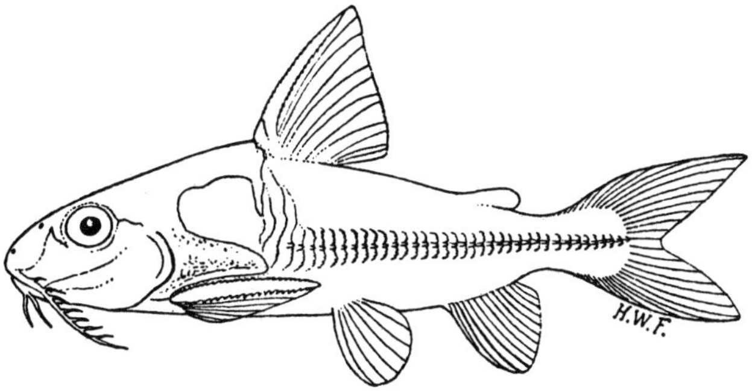

The genus *Doras* is a small genus of about five species. It has been confused in the literature, and the *Doras* of Lacépède (as described here) is generally not the same as the one of Valenciennes, Günther, and Eigenmann & Eigenmann, among others. The head is rather depressed, more or less as long as it is wide, and the nuchal buckler is intact, without a foramen or a median groove continued from the fontanel. The preopercle and interopercular area are covered with skin and are not granular; there is a bony stay from the epiotic to the lower end of the dorsal plate process and first scute, and the coracoid is not granular. The mandibular barbels are united by a basal membrane and may or may not possess small barblets; the maxillary barbels do have barblets. The lateral scutes are moderate in size, the first one connecting the dorsal plate, the first rib, and the humeral process. The interdorsal area is without scutes, and there are

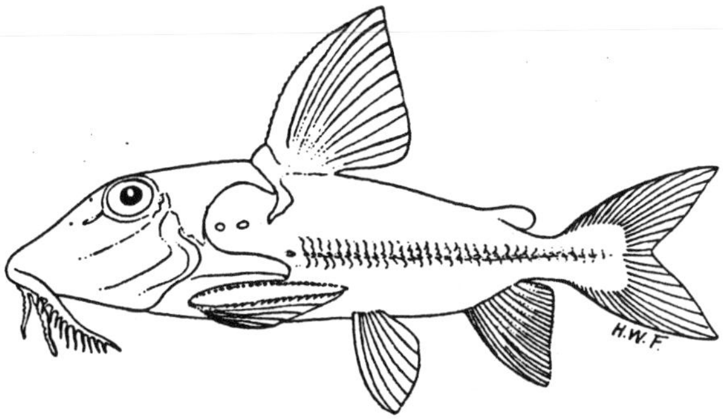

Doras carinatus. (From Fowler, 1951.)

none on the upper and lower surfaces of the caudal peduncle. The origin of the ventral fins is nearer the caudal than the snout. The adipose fin is short and not continued forward as a keel. The swim bladders of the species in this genus as currently accepted are of several types, which may or may not indicate that the genus should be restructured. In one type the swim bladder is simple and without diverticula, except that in old individuals a second, minute swim bladder is developed. In other species a second swim bladder is represented by two divergent, recurved tubes. In yet other species the swim bladder is heart-shaped and possesses numerous radial diverticula especially prominent in front.

The genus *Hemidoras* contains only two species. The depth of the body is usually more than 20% of the length. There is a long, smooth, subconical snout and a small mouth; the humeral process is longer than deep. A small foramen is present in the dorsal buckler

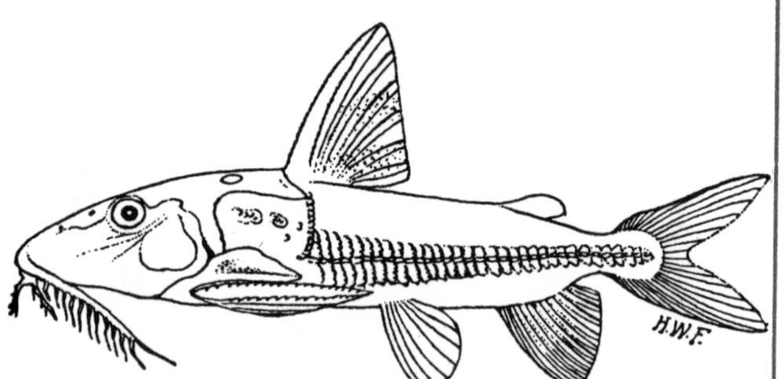

Hemidoras morrisi. (From Fowler, 1951.)

and the fontanel is continued as a groove. The maxillary barbels have many barblets and the mandibular (mental) barbels are united by a basal membrane and are fringed with a double row of barblets. The lateral plates are well-developed along the entire length, and there is a series of plates along the middle of the back between the adipose and dorsal fins and sometimes also on the ventral side between the anus and the anal fin. The ventral fins are placed behind the middle of the body. In the type species (*H. stenopeltis*) the mouth is inferior and without teeth or with small patches of minute teeth, the caudal peduncle has fulcra above and below, and the adipose fin is nearly as long as the anal fin. The swim bladder in *H. morrisi* is prolonged in a short diverticulum to a point; numerous branched tufts of diverticula can be seen along the entire margins.

The genus *Opsodoras* is perhaps the largest genus of the family with about 10 to 12 species that are distributed over the Amazon basin and the Guianas. The maxillary barbels are complicated and have many barblets, and the mandibular (mental) barbels have a double series of papillae or barblets. There is a well-defined foramen on each side of the nuchal shield, and the nasal bone is not defined.

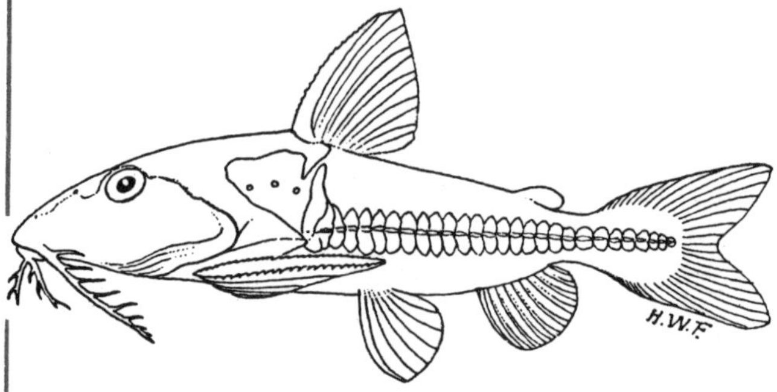

Opsodoras orthacanthus. (From Fowler, 1951.)

The lateral scutes are well-developed but not very high, and the successive scutes are in contact or the anterior ones are minute and not in contact; spines on the lateral scutes are present from the humeral area. There are no plates in the area between the dorsal fin and adipose fin, and they are absent from the upper and lower surfaces of the caudal peduncle. The dorsal fin spine has serrations on both the anterior and the posterior margins. The anal fin base is much longer than that of the adipose fin. The ventral fin origin is nearer the caudal than the snout, and the caudal fin is forked. The swim bladder is single, blunt or pointed posteriorly, and with fine, thread-like, branched diverticula (at least in *O. hemipeltis*, *O. parallelus*, *O. humeralis*, and *O. orthacanthus*). In *O. leporhinus*, of which only some young individuals have been examined, the swim bladder is without diverticula and ends in a blunt double point. In *O. orthacanthus*, type species of the genus, there are about 30 to 31 scutes, the eye is included 4.5 to 5 times in the head length, the snout is acutely pointed, and there are no teeth in the jaws. The base of the adipose fin is almost equal to the anal fin base and the dorsal fin spine is serrate in front and roughened behind.

Opsodoras leporhinus is one of the few species in the genus *Opsodoras* imported for the aquarium trade, but even it is seen only rarely. It is said to be a fairly delicate species in captivity, requiring a well-established tank with water that is clean, clear, and well-aerated. Moderately soft and slightly acid water is recommended. Like other members of the family, small live foods are preferred, although other aquarium foods will eventually be accepted.

The genus *Hassar* is another of the "larger" genera of doradids, with about nine species. The snout is decurved, extended, and pointed; the mouth is large, with a small patch of minute teeth on the lower jaw. The eyes are elongate, and the anterior nostril is equidistant between the tip of the snout and the eye or it is nearer the eye. There is a foramen on each side of the dorsal shield and there are many small pectoral pores; the nasal bone is not defined. The snout, preopercle, and interopercle are covered with skin. The barbels are slender, complex, with smaller branchlets, and there is a narrow connecting membrane. The lateral scutes are not very deep, and the anterior ones are very small. The spines of the lateral scutes begin only at the level of the ventral fin origin. The interdorsal space and the upper and lower surfaces of the caudal peduncle are without plates. The anal fin base is longer than that of the adipose fin, the ventral fins originate behind the middle of the length, and the pectoral spine barely reaches the ventrals or is shorter.

At least one species of *Hassar*, more often than not *H. orestis*, is somewhat regularly seen for sale. It is readily recognized by the elongate eyes and branched barbels, plus the large black spot on the first three rays of the dorsal

Many (if not most) species of *Hassar* exhibit some dark marking in the dorsal fin as seen here in what is probably *H. notospilus*. Photo by Dr. Herbert R. Axelrod.

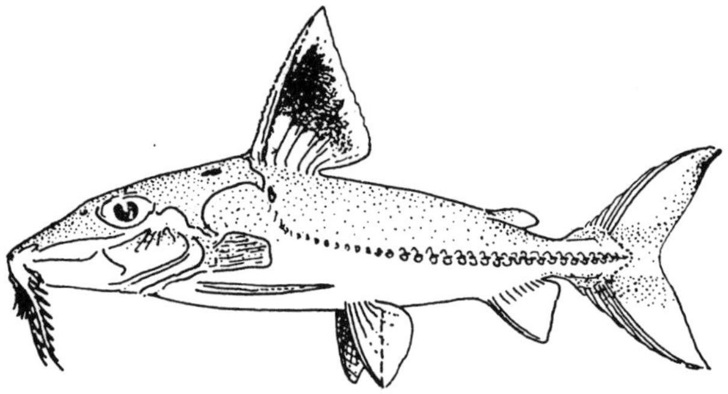

Hasser iheringi. (From Fernandez-Yepez, 1968.)

fin. It is distributed in the Amazon and its larger tributaries and is reported to attain a length of about 28 cm. Care is the same as that given for the majority of the doradids.

The genus *Leptodoras* is a small genus of about four species from the Amazon basin and the Guianas. The body is slender, the depth contained between five and nine times in the length. The snout is decurved, with smooth bones, and the snout, preopercle, and interopercle are covered with skin. The hu-

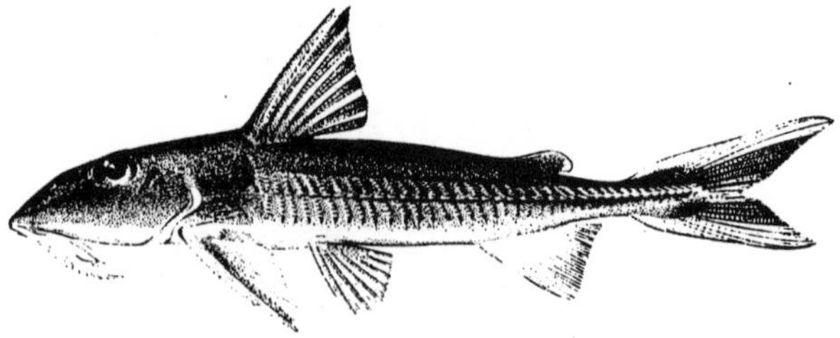

Leptodoras linnelli. (From Eigenmann, 1912.)

meral process is not half as long as the pectoral fin spine and is about as deep as long. The anterior nostril is nearer to the posterior nostril than to the snout. The mouth is large with no teeth. A small foramen is present in the dorsal shield or may be absent (?), and a narrow groove extending back from the fontanel has a tendency to disappear. There are about 36 to 44 lateral plates, the first extending down to the lower edge of the humeral process. The barbels are short, the maxillary barbels being divided beyond the bone into an outer lateral fimbriated part and an inner part coterminous with the mental barbels. The outer mental barbel is divided distally into two, and the bases of the mental barbels are connected by a membrane, the length of which is more than half their length. The adipose fin is sharply defined behind and continued as a low crest to near the tip of the depressed dorsal fin spine, and in all but *L. hasemani* the ventral fins are situated in front of the middle of the length. There is only one pectoral pore. The swim bladder is very short, its anterior end fitting into a cup-shaped downward process of the united anterior vertebrae. There are two diverticula at the posterior end and a pair at the outer anterior corners.

In the type species of the genus, *L. acipenserinus*, there are 4 + 42 scutes, the eye is contained 4.8 times in the head length, and the fontanel is continued as a narrow groove to the dorsal fin. The mouth is narrow, inferior, with the snout projecting. No teeth are present. The dorsal spine has serrae on the basal portion of the forward edge, the posterior margin being rough. The scutes are less than half the body depth and have a central spine and a serrated posterior edge.

The genus *Nemadoras* contains two species from the Rio Juruá. It is not well known but is said to have the same characteristics as the genus *Opsodoras* except that the maxillary barbels are simple. The fontanel is not contin-

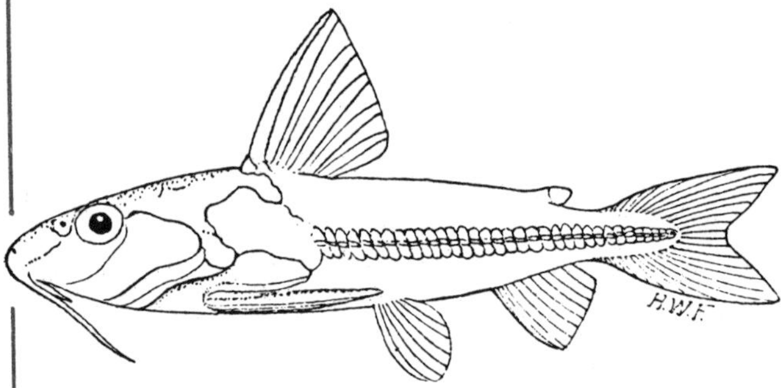

Nemadoras elongatus. (From Fowler, 1951.)

ued as a groove. In the type species, *N. elongatus*, there are about 33 scutes, the eye is contained 4.5 times in the head length, and the humeral process tapers to a point.

The genus *Doraops* contains a single species from the Lake Maracaibo basin in Venezuela. It has a depressed head and the eyes are located anterior to the middle of its length.

There is a wide median dorsal groove running anterior to the middle of the head and posteriorly to the fontanel between the rear of the orbits. The mouth is subterminal, the upper lip in front of the lower jaw, with a wide band of villiform teeth on the premaxillary bones and at the front of the dentary bones. The barbels are all simple, without barblets. The anterior pair of nostrils is tubular; the posterior nostrils have elevated rims. There are about 19 to 25 lateral scutes, each with a posteriorly directed spine, starting over the region of the anus and terminating at the base of the caudal fin rays. There are no scutes on the upper or lower surfaces of the caudal peduncle. There are three or four partially imbedded bony scutes at the front of the lateral line, the first two of which are each connected to the epiotic bone by a bony stay. The base of the adipose fin is longer than the anal fin base but it is not continued forward to form a keel. The pectoral fin spines are serrated both in front and behind; the dorsal fin spine is serrated in front and (in small individuals) behind. The spine becomes rough only in specimens of 30 cm standard length, and serrations become obsolete with age. The caudal fin is forked. The swim bladder is very large, with an anterior compartment separated from the posterior section by a constriction; the posterior section has long finger-like projections with numerous constrictions across them that extend to under the end of the body cavity posteriorly. The gill openings are restricted, extending to a little below the bases of the pectoral fin. The genus *Doraops* differs from the other genera of the Doradidae by having spiny scutes only posteriorly in the lateral series (the three or four bony scutes at the front of the lateral line are without spines). All other genera discussed by Eigenmann (1925) have the lateral series of spiny scutes continuous.

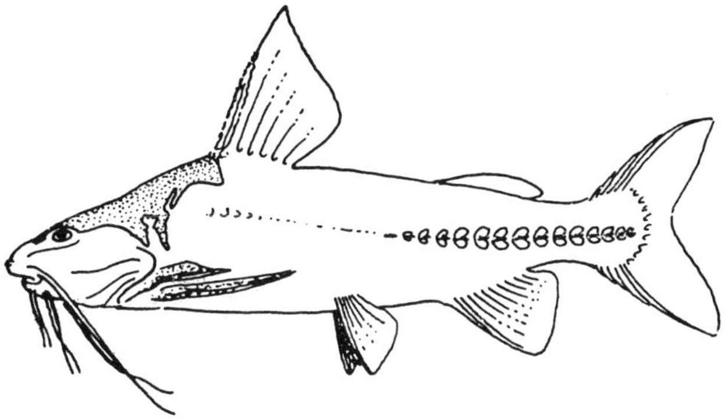

Doraops zuloagai. (From Fernandez-Yepez, 1968.)

The genus *Orinocodoras* contains a single species from Venezuela. The head is depressed, its width across the pectoral bases (cleithrum) greater than its length. The eyes are just anterior to the middle of the head, and the mouth is terminal. The preorbital bones are not serrate, and the nasal bones are not armed but they are defined. There is no nuchal foramen. The barbels are all simple. The lateral scutes are very narrow, about as wide as the eye or more than six times in the predorsal length, leaving much of the sides of the fish naked; one scute is in contact with the dorsal plate. The spines of the lateral plates start in the humeral region. The interdorsal area is smooth, without plates, but the caudal peduncle is covered entirely above and below by laminate plates. The dorsal fin spine is strongly serrate both in front and behind, the posterior serrae longer. The adipose fin is continued forward very slightly into a keel and is fairly high; without the keel it is about as long as the anal fin base. The caudal fin is forked. The swim bladder is double, without diverticula, the posterior part small and heart-shaped. *Orinocodoras* is allied to *Platydoras* and *Lithodoras*. It differs from *Lithodoras* by the armored peduncle and the more numerous scutes, and from *Platydoras* by the narrow scutes. Recent evidence indicates this genus may be synonymous with *Rhinodoras*.

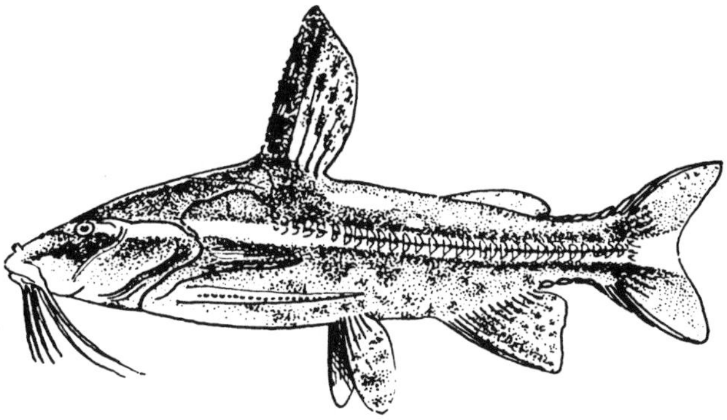

Orinocodoras eigenmanni. (From Fernandez-Yepez, 1968.)

The single species, *O. eigenmanni*, has, because of its elongate snout, been referred to as the "Long-nosed Raphael Catfish," and, in fact, may be imported with the Raphael Catfish (*Platydoras costatus*) from time to time. The color patterns are similar, but they can be distinguished by the scute size and the snout length without too much difficulty. *O. eigenmanni* inhabits the Orinoco River basin in Venezuela and is said to attain a length of about 17 or 18 cm. It is a nocturnal or crepuscular species and must have adequate hiding places where it can retire during the day or when the light levels are high. Eventually it may become adapted and wander about the tank in dim light. It is not particular about the water conditions as long as extremes are avoided, and it will accept a wide variety of foods. It is interesting to note that there are several species of doradid that are dark with a whitish lateral band, three species of which may be found in Venezuela. The other two have deep plates contained less than four times in the predorsal length (*Acanthodoras* spp.).

The genus *Anduzedoras* is a small genus of about three species. It was described by Fernandez-Yepez (1968) as having complicated, branched barbels, the nasal bone not being defined, and without a nuchal foramen. The dorsal fin spine is serrated on the anterior and posterior margins, the adipose fin base is

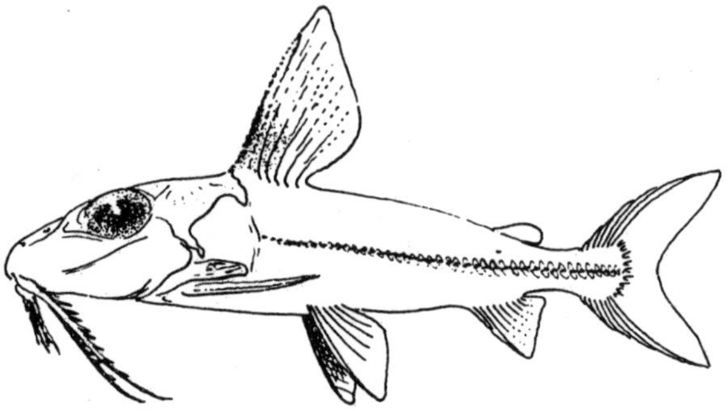

Anduzedoras arleoi. (From Fernandez-Yepez, 1968.)

shorter than the anal fin base, and the caudal fin is forked. The lateral scutes are not very deep and are contained more than six times in the predorsal length; the spines of the lateral plates are present from the humeral region. The interdorsal space is smooth, without plates, as are the upper and lower surfaces of the caudal peduncle. This genus may be synonymous with *Doras*.

The genus *Hildadoras* is another genus described by Fernandez-Yepez in the same publication. It contains only two species from the middle Orinoco River. The humeral process is armed with spines and the eyes are located in the central third of the head or a bit anterior to that position. The barbels are all simple. The dorsal fin spine is short and strong and is serrated in front and only weakly serrated on the posterior margin or not at all. The anal fin base is a little longer than the base of the adipose fin. The lateral plates are

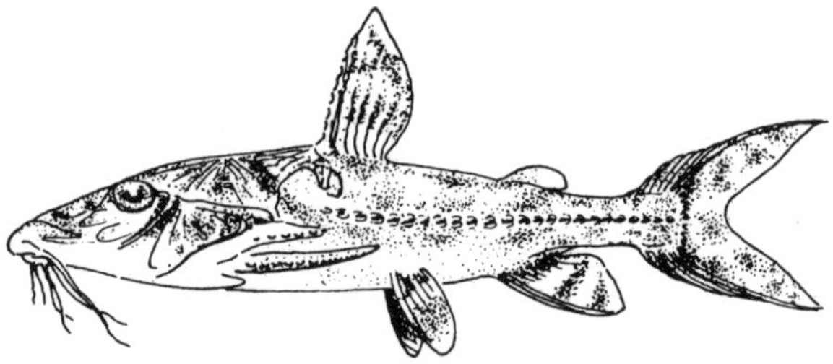

Hildadoras orinocensis. (From Fernandez-Yepez, 1968.)

not very deep, are contained more than six times in the predorsal distance, and spines are present from the humeral region. The interdorsal space is smooth, without bony plates, and the caudal peduncle is smooth above and below, without fulcra. *Hildadoras* is closely allied with *Autanodoras*, from which it differs in the presence of spines on the humeral process, the shape of the lateral plates, the length of the maxillary barbels, and the cephalic crest.

The genus *Apuredoras* contains a single species from the Apure River in Venezuela. It is another genus (and species) described by Fernandez-Yepez in the 1968 paper. The humeral process is short, equal to less than two eye diameters, and the eyes are located in the anterior third of the head. There is no nuchal foramen, and the nasal bone is defined but not serrated. The teeth are villiform, and the barbels are all simple. The dorsal fin spine is serrated on both anterior and posterior margins, the anal fin base is approximately equal to the base of the adipose fin, and the caudal fin is forked. The lateral plates are not very high, are contained more than six times in the pre-

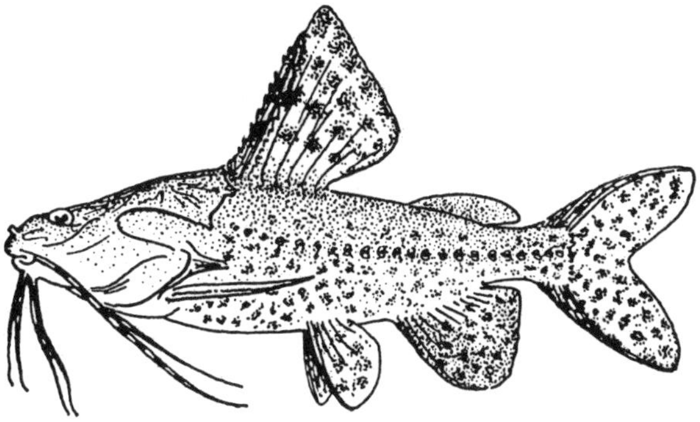

Apuredoras rivasi. (From Fernandez-Yepez, 1968.)

dorsal length, and have the spines starting from the humeral region. The interdorsal space is smooth and without bony plates, and the caudal peduncle is without fulcra on the upper and lower surfaces. This genus may be synonymous with *Pterodoras*.

The genus *Autanodoras* is another monotypic genus from the upper Orinoco River in Venezuela. The humeral process is longer than two eye diameters, the nasal bone is defined but not armed with spines, and there is no nuchal foramen. The eyes are located mostly in the anterior third of the head but extend into the middle third. The barbels are

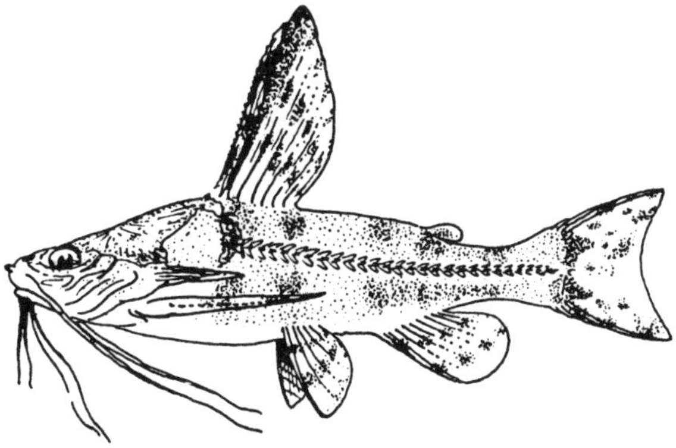

Autanodoras milesi. (From Fernandez-Yepez, 1968.)

long and are all simple. The dorsal fin spine is very long and is serrated in front only. The anal fin base is longer than the adipose fin base. The caudal fin is forked. The lateral plates are not very deep and are contained more than six times in the predorsal length; the spines of the lateral plates start from the humeral region. The interdorsal space is without plates, and the caudal peduncle is without laminated fulcra above and below.

The genus *Deltadoras* is yet another genus (and species) that was described by Fernandez-Yepez (1968), this one from the Orinoco delta. The nasal bone is well defined and

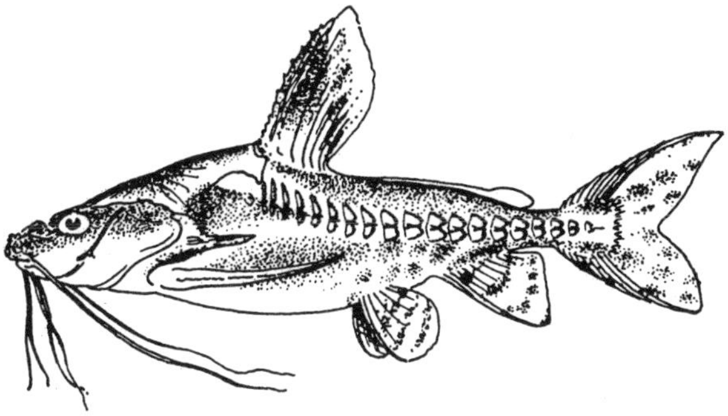

Deltadoras guayoensis. (From Fernandez-Yepez, 1968.)

there is no nuchal foramen. The maxillary barbels are simple. The dorsal fin spine is strong and serrated on both anterior and posterior edges. The anal fin base is longer than the adipose fin base if the anterior keel is not included; the caudal fin is forked. The keel of the adipose fin occupies about four-fifths of the interdorsal space and is an anterior prolongation of the adipose fin. The lateral plates are not very deep and are contained more than six times in the predorsal length; the spines of the lateral plates are present from the humeral region. The interdorsal space is without plates, and the caudal peduncle is without fulcra on the upper and lower surfaces. The lateral plates decrease in size posteriorly and are less than 25 in number. Deltadoras may be synonymous with *Megalodoras*.

The genus *Sachsdoras* is the final genus and species described by Fernandez-Yepez in his 1968 paper. The single species was discovered in the Rio Orinoco near the mouth of the Apure River. The humeral process is long, and the small eyes are situated in the anterior third of the head. The eye diameter is contained more than three times in the humeral process, the nasal bone is defined, and there is no nuchal foramen. The barbels are simple and long. The base of the anal fin is approximately equal to the adipose fin base, and the caudal fin is forked. The lateral plates are not very deep, the deepest located over the anal

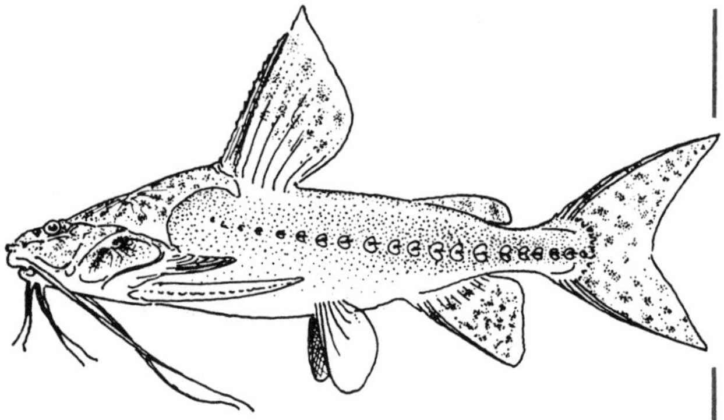

Sachsdoras apurensis. (From Fernandez-Yepez, 1968.)

fin base, the rest decreasing in size anteriorly and posteriorly as in *Pterodoras*; the spines of the lateral plates are present from the humeral region. The interdorsal space is without bony plates, and the upper and lower surfaces of the caudal peduncle are without fulcra. This genus is very closely related to *Pterodoras* and *Apuredoras*, and may even be synonymous with the former.

The genus *Zathorax* is a small genus of about three species. The nasal bone is defined, the frontal fontanel is reduced, and there is no nuchal foramen. The dorsal fin spine is without either anterior or posterior serrae. The anal fin base is equal to or longer than the adipose fin base. The caudal fin is truncate, not forked or rounded. The barbels are all simple. The lateral plates are high in front, decreasing in size posteriorly, the depth of the largest plate contained less than four times in the predorsal length; the spines of the lateral plates start at the humeral region.

Zathorax gonzalezi. (From Fernandez-Yepez, 1968.)

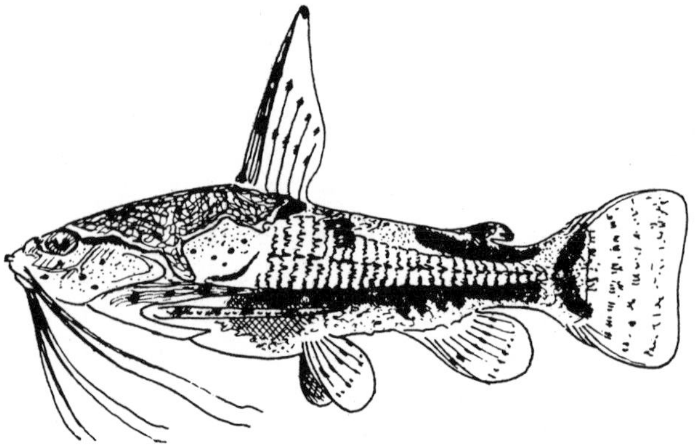

The interdorsal space and the upper and lower surfaces of the caudal peduncle are smooth. This genus may be synonymous with *Amblydoras*.

Checklist of the species of the family Doradidae and their type localities:

Hemidoras Bleeker, 1858. Type species *Doras (Oxydoras) stenopeltis* Kner, 1855.
- *Hemidoras morrisi* Eigenmann, 1925. Iquitos, Peru.
- *H. stenopeltis* (Kner, 1855). Rio Negro.

Leptodoras Boulenger, 1898. Type species *Oxydoras acipenserinus* Günther, 1868.
- *Leptodoras acipenserinus* (Günther, 1868). Keberos, Peru.
- *L. hasemani* (Steindachner, 1915). Rio Negro at its mouth; Rio Branco at Boa Vista and Serra Grande.
- *L. juruensis* Boulenger, 1898. Rio Juruá.
- *L. linnelli* Eigenmann, 1912. British Guiana at Tumatumari on the Potaro; Rockstone and Crab Falls on the Essequibo River. (Fernandez-Yepez places this species in *Opsodoras*.)

Opsodoras Eigenmann, 1925. Type species *O. orthacanthus* Eigenmann.
- *Opsodoras boulengeri* (Steindachner, 1915). Mouth of the Rio Negro.
- *O. hemipeltis* Eigenmann, 1925. Rio Ucayali at Cantamana, Peru.
- *O. humeralis* (Kner, 1855). Barra do Rio Negro.
- *O. leporhinus* (Eigenmann, 1910). British Guiana at Tumatumari, Potaro River, and Crab Falls, Essequibo River.
- *O. morei* (Steindachner, 1881). Rio Negro.
- *O. orthacanthus* Eigenmann, 1925. Iquitos, Peru.
- *O. parallelus* Eigenmann, 1925. Iquitos, Peru.
- *O. steindachneri* Eigenmann, 1925. Mouth of the Rio Negro.
- *O. stubelii* (Steindachner, 1882). Rio Huallaga, Peru.
- *O. ternetzi* Eigenmann, 1925. Tapajós at Santarém.
- *O. trimaculatus* (Boulenger, 1898). Rio Juruá.

Hassar Eigenmann & Eigenmann, 1888. Type species *Oxydoras orestis* Steindachner, 1875.
- *Hassar affinis* (Steindachner, 1882). Rio

Poti, trib. of the Parnahyba north of Therezina.

H. iheringi Fowler, 1941. Parnahyba, Terezina, Piaui.

H. lipophthalmus (Kner, 1855). Rio Negro.

H. notospilus (Eigenmann, 1912). Crab Falls, Essequibo River. (Fernandez-Yepez places this species in *Opsodoras*.)

H. orestis (Agassiz in Steindachner, 1875). Rio Xingu.

H. praelongus Myers & Weitzman, 1956. São Gabriel rapids of Rio Negro.

H. ucayalensis Fowler, 1939. Rio Ucayali, Cantamana, Peru.

H. wilderi (Kindle, 1894). Troceros on Rio Tocantins; Touceira.

H. woodi Fowler, 1941. Rio Parnahyba, Terezina, Piaui.

Anduzedoras Fernandez-Yepez, 1968. Type species *A. arleoi* Fernandez-Yepez. (=*Doras?*)

Anduzedoras arleoi Fernandez-Yepez, 1968. Rio Autana, to the east of Puerto Ayacucho, Terr. Fed. Amazonas.

A. copei Fernandez-Yepez, 1968. Lagoon beside Rio Capanapara.

A. microstomas (Eigenmann, 1912). Rockstone, British Guiana.

Trachydoras Eigenmann, 1925. Type species *T. atripes* Eigenmann.

Trachydoras atripes Eigenmann, 1925. Brook near Rio Itaya, above Iquitos, Peru.

T. nattereri (Steindachner, 1881). Teffé, Amazon River.

T. paraguayensis (Eigenmann & Ward, 1907). Corumbá.

T. trachyparia (Boulenger, 1898). Rio Juruá.

Doras Lacépède, 1803. Type species *Silurus carinatus* Linnaeus.

Doras brevis Heckel MS in Kner, 1853. Barro do Rio Negro.

D. carinatus (Linnaeus, 1766). Surinam.

D. eigenmanni (Boulenger, 1895). Descalvados, Mato Grosso.

D. fimbriatus Kner, 1855. Rio Guaporé.

D. micropoeus (Eigenmann, 1912). British Guiana at Lama stop-off and Wismar on the Demerara River.

Agamyxis Cope, 1878. Type species *Doras pectinifrons* Cope.

Agamyxis albomaculatus (Peters, 1877). Calobozo, Venezuela.

A. pectinifrons (Cope, 1870). Pebas, Ecuador.

Acanthodoras Bleeker, 1862. Type species *Silurus cataphractus* Linnaeus.

Acanthodoras calderonensis (Vaillant, 1880). Calderon.

A. cataphractus (Linnaeus, 1758). "America."

A. spinosissimus (Eigenmann & Eigenmann, 1888). Coarý.

Hildadoras Fernandez-Yepez, 1968. Type species *H. orinocensis* Fernandez-Yepez.

Hildadoras bolivarensis Fernandez-Yepez, 1968. The Qda. El Pilón. (to the east of the Rio Parguaza, affluent of the Rio Orinoco)

H. orinocensis Fernandez-Yepez, 1968. In front of the mouth of the cano San Juan. Terr. Delta Amacuro.

Physopyxis Cope, 1871. Type species *P. lyra* Cope.

Physopyxis lyra Cope, 1871. Ambyiacu River, Amazonas.

Hypodoras Eigenmann, 1925. Type species *H. forficulatus* Eigenmann.

Hypodoras forficulatus Eigenmann, 1925. Iquitos, Peru.

Amblydoras Bleeker, 1863. Type species *Doras affinis* Kner, 1855 (= *Amblydoras hancocki*).

Amblydoras hancocki (Valenciennes, 1840). Based on Hancock = Demerara.

Zathorax Cope, 1872. Type species *Z. monitor* Cope (? = *Amblydoras*).

Zathorax gonzalezi Fernandez-Yepez, 1968. Laguna "Punta Vista," at orillas of the Rio Caroní in Cachamay Park.

Z. monitor Cope, 1872. Rio Ambyiacu.

Z. nauticus Cope, 1874. Nauta, Peru.

Megalodoras Eigenmann, 1925. Type species *M. irwini* Eigenmann.

Megalodoras irwini Eigenmann, 1925. Kartabo, Bartica District, British Guiana.

M. laevigatulus (Berg, 1910). Dock Sur, in El Puerto de Buenos Aires.

M. libertatis (M. Ribeiro, 1912). Manaus.

M. paucisquamatus Stigchel, 1947. Brazil.

Autanodoras Fernandez-Yepez, 1950. Type species *A. milesi* Fernandez-Yepez.

Autanodoras milesi Fernandez-Yepez, 1950.

Rio Autana, Terr. Fed. Amazonas.

Anadoras Eigenmann, 1925. Type species *Doras grypus* Cope, 1871.

Anadoras grypus (Cope, 1871). Ambyiacu River.

A. insculptus (Miranda-Ribeiro, 1912). Manaus, Brazil.

A. regani (Steindachner, 1908). Pará.

A. weddellii (Castelnau, 1855). Chiquitos, Bolivia.

Astrodoras Bleeker, 1862. Type species *Doras asterifrons* Heckel in Kner.

Astrodoras asterifrons (Heckel MS in Kner, 1853). Barro do Rio Negro; Rio Guapore.

Scorpiodoras Eigenmann, 1925. Type species *Doras heckelii* Kner, 1855.

Scorpiodoras heckelii (Kner, 1855). Rio Negro.

Rhinodoras Bleeker, 1862. Type species *Doras (Oxydoras) dorbignyi* Kröyer in Kner, 1855.

Rhinodoras dorbignyi (Kröyer, 1855). Rio da Prata.

Platydoras Bleeker, 1863. Type species *Silurus costatus* Linnaeus, 1766.

Platydoras armatulus (Valenciennes, 1840). Rio Paraná.

P. costatus (Linnaeus, 1766). "In Indii" (= South America).

P. dentatus (Kner, 1855). Surinam.

P. helicophilus (Günther, 1868). Calobozo.

Franciscodoras Eigenmann, 1925. Type species *Doras marmoratus* Reinhardt, 1874.

Franciscodoras marmoratus (Reinhardt MS in Lütken, 1874). Rio das Velhas.

Orinocodoras Myers, 1927. Type species *O. eigenmanni* Myers. (= *Rhinodoras*?)

Orinocodoras eigenmanni Myers, 1927. Orinoco.

Lithodoras Bleeker, 1863. Type species *Doras lithogaster* Heckel (= *Doras dorsalis*).

Lithodoras dorsalis (Valenciennes, 1840). Cayenne, French Guiana.

Nemadoras Eigenmann, 1925. Type species *Oxydoras elongatus* Boulenger, 1898.

Nemadoras bachi (Boulenger, 1898). Rio Juruá.

N. elongatus (Boulenger, 1898). Rio Juruá.

Doraops Schultz, 1944. Type species *D. zuloagai* Schultz.

Doraops zuloagai Schultz, 1944. Maracaibo Basin, Venezuela.

Sachsdoras Fernandez-Yepez, 1968. Type species *S. apurensis* Fernandez-Yepez. (= *Pterodoras*?)

Sachsdoras apurensis Fernandez-Yepez, 1968. Rio Orinoco near the mouth of the Rio Apure.

Pseudodoras Bleeker, 1858. Type species *Doras niger* Valenciennes.

Pseudodoras holdeni (Fernandez-Yepez, 1968). Rio Apure.

P. huberi (Steindachner, 1911). Rio Tocantins at Cametá.

P. niger (Valenciennes 1817). "South America."

Oxydoras Kner, 1855. Type species *O. niger* Kner (= *O. kneri*).

Oxydoras kneri Bleeker, 1862. Cujaba, Brazil. (subst. name for *Doras niger* Kner, non Valenciennes).

O. sifontesi Fernandez-Yepez, 1968. Laguna rebalsera "El Medio," Ciudad Bolivar.

O. steindachneri Perugia, 1897. Rio Beni, Bolivia.

Deltadoras Fernandez-Yepez, 1968. Type species *D. guayoensis* Fernandez-Yepez. (= *Megalodoras*?)

Deltadoras guayoensis Fernandez-Yepez, 1968. Cano de Guayo, Terr. Delta Amacuro, Venezuela.

Hoplodoras Eigenmann, 1925. Type species *Doras uranoscopus* Eigenmann & Eigenmann, 1888.

Hoplodoras ramirezi Fernandez-Yepez, 1968. Lower Orinoco. (= *Megalodoras ramirezi*?)

H. uranoscopus (Eigenmann & Eigenmann, 1888). Lake Hyanuary.

Centrodoras Eigenmann, 1925. Type species *Doras brachiatus* Cope, 1872.

Centrodoras brachiatus (Cope, 1872). Somewhere between the mouth of the Rio Negro and the Rio Huallaga.

Pterodoras Bleeker, 1863. Type species *Doras granulosus* Valenciennes, 1833.

Pterodoras angeli Fernandez-Yepez, 1968. Rio Arauca.

P. granulosus (Valenciennes, 1833). "Amerique Equinoxiale."

P. lentiginosus (Eigenmann, 1917). Santárem; Manaus.

Centrochir Spix *in* Agassiz, 1829. Type species *Doras crocodili* Humboldt, 1811.

Centrochir crocodili (Humboldt, 1811). Magdalena basin.

Apuredoras Fernandez-Yepez, 1950. Type species *A. rivasi* Fernandez-Yepez. (= *Pterodoras*?)

Apuredoras rivasi Fernandez-Yepez, 1950. Rio Apure, Venezuela.

Rhyncodoras Klausewitz & Rössel, 1961. Type species *R. xingu* Klausewitz & Rössell.

Rhyncodoras woodsi Glodek, 1976. Upper Rio Xingu.

R. xingui Klausewitz & Rössel, 1961. Upper Rio Xingu.

Chapter 21

Family — Plates 104–115

AUCHENIPTERIDAE

(Driftwood Catfishes)

The Auchenipteridae is a moderate-sized family of naked catfishes inhabiting the fresh waters of South and Central America from Argentina to Panama. They are generally nocturnal catfishes commonly found beneath submerged logs and other debris with parasitic catfishes (Trichomycteridae) and gymnotids, although some species are active by day and live in schools, often being found with armored catfishes of the family Callichthyidae. At one time the Auchenipteridae was placed as a subfamily of the Doradidae (as in Gosline, 1945), while by some authors it has been divided into as many as four separate families, the Auchenipteridae, Trachycorystidae, Centromochlidae, and Asterophysidae (Miranda-Ribeiro, 1968). Mees (1974) believed that the auchenipterids (with the possible exception of some genera he had not yet studied) form a natural group. He did, however, draw attention to genus *Liosomadoras*, which appears to occupy an intermediate position between the Auchenipteridae and the Doradidae (thus prompting Gosline's position of uniting the two families) and is quite difficult to properly place. Rössell (1962) suggested that *Liosomadoras morrowi* (= *L. oncinus*) is not only an auchenipterid but that it may even be a synonym of a species of *Centro*mochlus (now *Tatia*). *Liosomadoras* differs from *Centromochlus* and *Tatia* by having a short body with a very broad, flat head, small eyes, a superior mouth, a very long and spiny humeral process, a large adipose fin, and a moderate anal fin (about 13 rays). In addition it differs from *Tatia* by having a well-developed caudal peduncle and long dorsal and pectoral fin spines. It differs also from *Centromochlus* by having strong teeth on both edges of the dorsal and pectoral fin spines. *Liosomadoras* is included in the Auchenipteridae in most recent publications. *Tetranematichthys* was regarded as a synonym of *Parauchenipterus* by Miranda-Ribeiro, but Britski, in a personal communication to Böhlke, relegated it to the vicinity of the genus *Ageneiosis* of the family Ageneiosidae.

The family Auchenipteridae can be characterized as follows. The nuchal bones extend as far as the dorsal fin spine and partly embrace it with a pair of processes or "horns"; the nuchal bones are exposed or covered with skin only. There is no free orbital margin even though the eyes of some species are large. There are usually three pairs of barbels present, a pair of maxillary barbels and two pairs of mandibular (mental) barbels, all well-developed but not long, the maxillary barbels longest but at most not reaching much beyond the middle of the body. The only exception is the genus *Gelanoglanis*, which has only a pair of maxillary barbels and a pair of mental barbels. The lateral line is generally a zigzag affair with short branches at each angle being present. The dorsal fin is short-based, usually with a strong, sharp, stout and occasionally elongate spine and about 3 to 6 rays, and is located anteriorly close to the head. The pectoral fins are provided with a strong spine, and a pectoral pore (*porus pectoralis*) is present though often not very conspicuous. The anal fin may be long (19 to 62 rays) or short (7 to 18 rays), and the anterior rays are frequently modified for sexual purposes. A small to moderate adipose fin is usually present, although in some genera it is completely lacking. The ventral fins are located posterior to the last ray of the dorsal fin. The caudal fin is emarginate or obliquely truncate. The teeth are arranged in bands in both jaws, and the vomer and palatines are toothless (except in *Asterophysus* and some larger individuals of *Tatia intermedia*). The gill openings are generally small and restricted, extending only to in front of the cleithrum, and the membranes are broadly attached to the isthmus (except in *Wertheimeria* and *Taunayia*, in which the gill openings extend forward along the isthmus). The swim bladder is well-developed and is not enclosed in a bony capsule. In many species there is some degree of sexual dimorphism present (usually in the anal fin).

There are about 64 species included in some 21 genera, the 19 genera accepted by Mees (1974) plus *Liosomadoras* and the recently described *Gelanoglanis*. They can be distinguished by the following key.

1a. Gill openings extending well forward along the isthmus.......................... 2
1b. Gill openings small, restricted, not extending much beyond front of cleithrum 3
2a. Anal fin rays 15-16 .... *Wertheimeria*
2b. Anal fin rays about 11........... *Taunayia*
3a. Adipose fin absent.......................... 4
3b. Adipose fin present........................ 7
4a. Anal fin rays less than 40................. 5
4b. Anal fin rays more than 50 6
5a. Ventral fins with 6 rays; eyes small, contained about 6 times in head.............. .... *Trachelyopterus*
5b. Ventrals with 10 rays; eyes larger, contained 4 times or less in head............ .... *Trachelyichthys*
6a. Ventral fins with 15-16 rays; dorsal fin I,4; anal fin with about 53 rays; teeth present in jaws .... *Trachelyopterichthys*
6b. Ventrals with 14 rays; dorsal fin I,3; anal fin with about 61 rays; teeth absent .... *Epapterus*
7a. Anal fin with 57-59 rays; ventral fins with 9-13 rays .... *Pseudepapterus*
7b. Anal fin with less than 50 rays; ventral fins with 6-15 rays 8
8a. Ventral fins with 12-15 rays; anal fin 37-49............................... *Auchenipterus*
8b. Ventral fins with 6-10 rays 9
9a. Ventral fins with less than 9 rays...... 12
9b. Ventral fin rays 9-10...................... 10
10a. Ventral fin rays 10; anal fin rays about 13 .... *Asterophysus*
10b. Ventral fin rays 9 or 10; anal fin rays 20-26 11
11a. Head strongly depressed, bones granular, exposed; eyes contained more than 6 times in head; fontanel small, round to oval............................ *Trachycorystes*
11b. Head not depressed, bones exposed or covered with thin skin; eye larger, contained less than 4 times in head length; fontanel elongate....... *Auchenipterichthys*
12a. Ventral rays 8; anal rays 17-25............ .... *Pseudauchenipterus*
12b. Ventral fins with less than 8 rays...... 13
13a. Ventral rays 7.............................. 14
13b. Ventral rays 6.............................. 16
14a. Adipose fin moderate, as long as anal fin base .... *Liosomadoras*
14b. Adipose fin very short, much shorter than anal fin base.......................... 15
15a. Anal fin 12; head depressed. *Tocantinsia*
15b. Anal fin 15-16; head not depressed...... .... *Pseudotatia*
16a. Anal fin rays more than 16.............. 17
16b. Anal fin rays less than 14................ 18
17a. Anal fin rays 18-21; maxillary barbels relatively long, extending as far as anal fin base; inner mandibular barbels reaching pectoral fin base; caudal fin forked, lobes pointed .... *Entomocorus*
17b. Anal fin rays 17-41 (usually 20-30); maxillary barbels shorter, reaching at most to level of dorsal fin; inner mandibular barbels not reaching pectoral fin base; caudal fin never forked, at most shallowly emarginate......... *Parauchenipterus*
18a. Pectoral fin rays I,7-12 .... *Centromochlus*
18b. Pectoral fin rays I,4-6 19
19a. One pair of mandibular barbels .... *Gelanoglanis*

19b. Two pairs of mandibular barbels......20

20a. Dorsal and pectoral fin spines with well developed teeth and hooks; upper surface of head and nuchal region covered with bony plates; pectoral fin I,4 or 5; anal fin 7-11............................ *Tatia*

20b. Dorsal and pectoral fin spines smooth or with small teeth; upper surface of head covered with thick skin; pectoral fin rays I,5 or 6; anal fin rays 10-13.......... .... *Glanidium*

The genus *Auchenipterus* is a small genus of three species from Uruguay, Paraguay, and Brazil. The body is slender and compressed (much deeper than wide), but the head is almost round in outline. The bones of the head are rather thick and are covered with skin, and the humeral process, although present, is also covered with skin. The occipital process extends to meet the dorsal plate; the fontanel is very long. The eyes are large and latero-inferior in position so that they are normally visible from below. The two pairs of mental

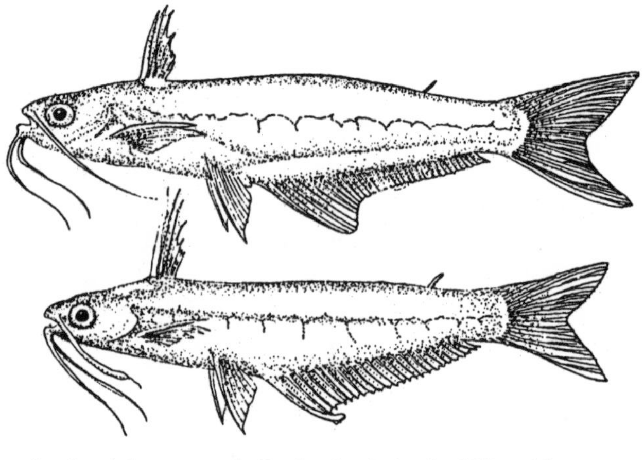

Auchenipterus nuchalis (male below). (After Mees, 1974.)

barbels are arranged in a straight line. The teeth are villiform in the jaws; the palate is edentulous. The dorsal and pectoral fin spines are thin and pungent, the pectoral spine with a smooth anterior border. The anal fin is long, with about 37-49 rays, and the caudal fin is emarginate. The ventral fins are situated posterior to the dorsal fin, have 12 to 15 rays, and are broadly united with the body. The adipose fin is very small. The lateral line is in the form of a zig-zag and has many dorsal and ventral branches. The pectoral pore is present over the middle of the pectoral fin base. The branchial openings are restricted, extending to below the level of the pectoral fins. At least one species exhibits sexual dimorphism in the anterior modification of the anal fin, the shape of the maxillary barbels, and the length of the dorsal fin spine. In general, the color is plain brownish to gray on the dorsal surface and very pale below. There may or may not be a silvery lateral band.

Mees doubts whether all five species usually listed for the genus are valid. *Auchenipterus brachyurus* and *A. fordicei* are known only from a single specimen each and are considered synonyms by him (pers. comm.). P. de Miranda-Ribeiro has suggested that there is only a single species, *A. nuchalis*. Mees suggests that in addition *A. paysanduanus* and *A. nigripinnis* may also be distinct.

Auchenipterus nuchalis occurs in the southern Amazon region and Paraguay, where it inhabits the lower courses of the larger rivers and may be considered common. It is a free-swimming species that normally may be found not too far below the water's surface. It attains a length of about 18 cm. The male is recognizable by his thick maxillary barbels that are ossified almost to their tips. The ossification restricts their vertical movements, although they can be moved sideways. The first few rays of the anal fin are modified and fused, supporting the urogenital tube running along the anterior border to the tip of the rays. Other sexual differences in the male include a more slender body and a longer dorsal fin spine.

The genus *Pseudauchenipterus* is a small genus of only about four species (possibily a single species) distributed in northern and eastern South America. The species are heavy-bodied, with the anterior part of the body roundish, the posterior part compressed. The head is roundish to oval, its depth equal to or slightly greater than its width, and covered with thick skin but leaving the bone structure clearly visible. The frontal bones are swollen and honeycomb-like, the nuchal bones are hard, and the occipital process is firmly joined to the dorsal plate. Small individuals, however, do not yet possess the spongy bone of the larger individuals. The eyes are moder-

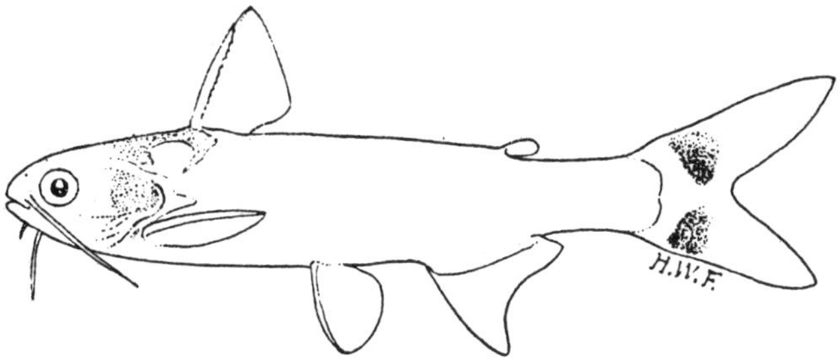

Pseudauchenipterus jequitinhonhae. (From Fowler, 1951.)

ate to large, lateral in position, and covered with skin. The teeth are villiform in the jaws, none being present on the vomer or palate. The barbels are well developed and relatively long, the inner mental barbels extending at least as far as the pectoral fin base (seen otherwise only in *Entomocorus*). The spines of the dorsal and pectoral fins are strong, pungent, and smooth or striate along their anterior edges but with serrae along the inner borders. The adipose fin is very short and the caudal fin is deeply forked. The ventral fins have 8 rays and are not attached to the body by a membrane. The anal fin is relatively long, with 20-24 rays. A pectoral pore is present well behind the pectoral fin base. The lateral line is complete and anteriorly slightly zigzagging, but straight posteriorly. Sexual dimorphism is evident in this genus. The anterior anal fin rays of the male are long, with the urogenital pore located at the end of a canal running along the anterior edge of the fin, the canal expanding into a vesicle toward the tip of the rays; the urogenital pore of the female is located in front of the anal fin origin on the belly, the anterior rays of the anal fin normal, not slightly elongate as in the male, whose anal fin is somewhat falcate in shape. Males also have their ventral fins slightly more pointed than the females, but this is not easy to see.

Mees (1974) cast doubt on the inclusion in *Pseudauchenipterus* of the other species placed in the genus with *P. nodosus* (the generic information above is based on *P. nodosus*) because of their lack of the honeycomb-like structure of the frontal bones (it was noted above, however, that small specimens lack this feature). The other species do have similar fin counts.

Pseudauchenipterus nodosus inhabits the lower courses and estuaries of the larger rivers of its range. It is therefore quite tolerant of brackish and perhaps even full salt water.

The genus *Trachycorystes* is a small genus of two (at most four) or perhaps only a single species from tropical South America. The precise geographical limits of the genus are not known, although there are records from the Essequibo River and the Mato Grosso. The head is broad and depressed, the width at the cleithra almost twice the depth. The posterior part of the body is comparatively slender, and the caudal peduncle is well developed. The bones of the head are entirely naked (without a covering skin) and fused, forming a solid, heavy, very rugose casque; there is a small oval fontanel. The eyes are rather small and lateral in position. The mouth is wide, horizontal, and the lower jaw

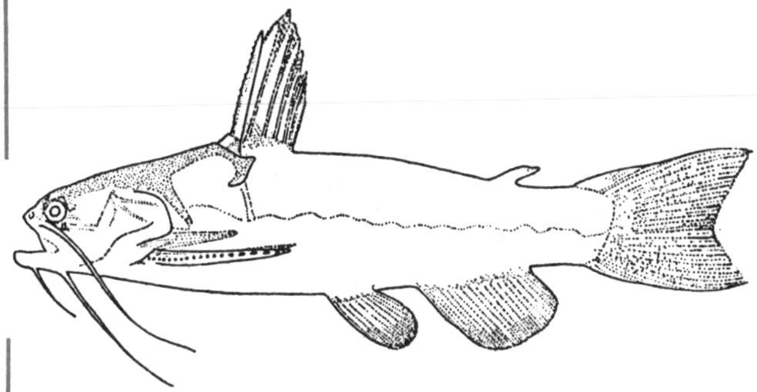

Trachycorystes trachycorystes. (From Mees, 1974.)

extends beyond the upper; a band of small teeth is present in each jaw, but there are none on the vomer or palatines. The dorsal and pectoral fin spines are strong, pungent, the dorsal fin spine with teeth along its anterior edge only, the longer, stronger pectoral fin spines with teeth along both edges. The adipose fin is very small, and the anal fin is of moderate length, with about 20 rays. The ventral fins have 9 or 10 rays, and the caudal fin is emarginate to slightly forked. The complete lateral line is somewhat wavy. So far there have been no reports of sexual dimorphism in this genus.

Before Mees's very important paper on the family, the genus *Trachycorystes* was considered to have almost two dozen species. However, Mees regarded the number of ventral fin rays, except in a few species that have many-rayed ventral fins (for example, species of *Auchenipterus* and *Pseudepapterus*), as a good generic character for the family. He took out of *Trachycorystes* all those species with only 6 ventral rays and placed them in the genus *Parauchenipterus* (this generic name was available in the synonymy of *Trachycorystes*), leaving only species with 9-10 ventral fin rays included in *Trachycorystes*. There is strong doubt that all these species are valid, and the genus may eventually wind up with a single species, *T. trachycorystes*. This species is widely distributed (but rare), presumably inhabiting the lower levels of large rivers.

The genus *Auchenipterichthys* is a small genus containing two quite similar species that are widely distributed in the Amazon basin. The body is moderately heavy and the caudal peduncle is not slender but is not so short and compact as in the genus *Parauchenipterus*. The head is wider than it is high, although it is not depressed; the bones of the head and nape are naked or covered with very thin

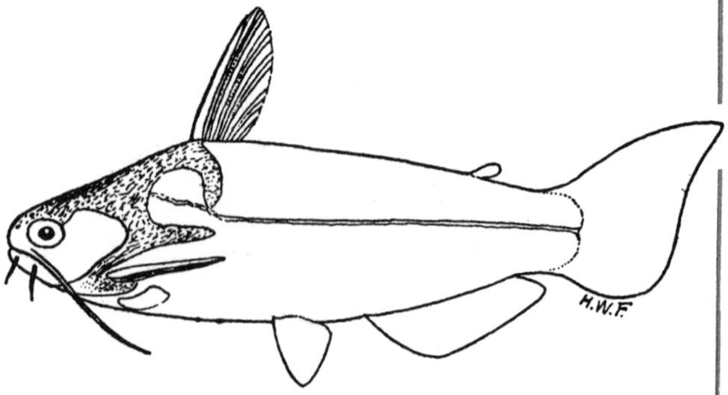

Auchenipterichthys thoracatus. (From Fowler, 1951.)

skin. The fontanel is large, elongate, and the occipital process is joined firmly to the dorsal plate. The eyes are large, lateral in position, and covered with skin. The mouth is moderately wide, with approximately equal jaws; a comparatively narrow band of villiform teeth is present in each jaw, and there are no teeth on the vomer or palatines. The dorsal fin has a spine and 6 rays; the adipose fin is very short. The pectoral fin spine is serrated on both margins. The ventrals have 9 or 10 rays and are not attached to the body by a membrane. The anal fin is of moderate length, with 20 to 25 rays, and the caudal fin is obliquely truncate or rounded. A pectoral pore is present on or a little behind a vertical through the posterior margin of the pectoral fin base. The wavy lateral line is complete and provided with short branches. Sexual dimorphism has been described for one of the two species, the anterior rays of the anal fin being elongate and bearing the urogenital organ in the male, and some differences were noted in the caudal fin. This genus is closely related to *Parauchenipterus*, but it differs in having a slightly more slender body, larger eyes, a larger fontanel, and 9 or 10 ventral fin rays.

Auchenipterichthys thoracatus (sometimes referred to as *Zamora cunchi*) is a nocturnal species and has received the common name Midnight Catfish. It attains a length of about 13.5 cm and tends to be predatory on small fishes. In an aquarium it can be fed chopped earthworms or other worm foods during the evening hours after the lights are turned off. When this fish is disturbed it makes a buzzing noise by rotating its pectoral spines in their sockets, the sound thus made being amplified by the swim bladder.

The genus *Parauchenipterus* contains about 11 species (with two subspecies) distributed in northern South America and Panama, including the area of South America east of the

Parauchenipterus fisheri (male above). (From Eigenmann, 1912.)

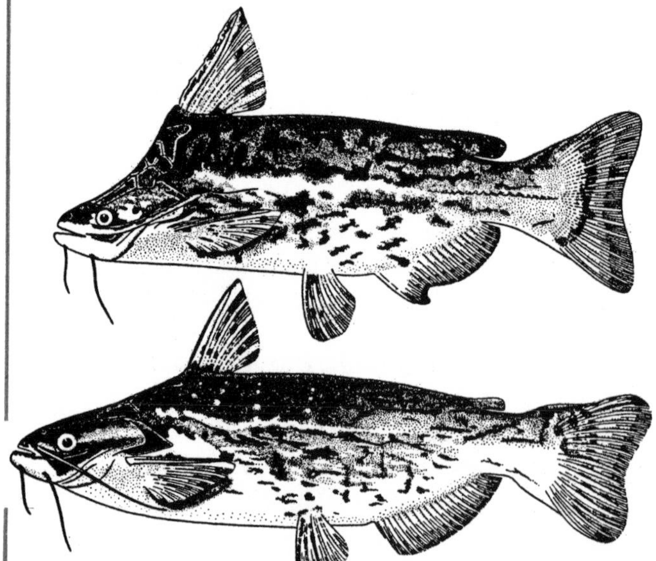

Andes and south to the Uruguay-Parana-La Plata basin. The body is short, heavy-built, and rounded; the head is only a little broader than deep, with the bones covered with skin that is thick and heavily pigmented in large individuals and thin and often transparent in the smaller specimens. The fontanel is small, oval, and behind the middle of the eyes. The eyes are small (but larger than the fontanel) and the lower jaw is slightly protruding. The anal fin is moderate to long, with 17-40 rays. The ventral fins have 6 rays. At the end of a short caudal peduncle the caudal fin is slightly emarginate to obliquely truncate or obliquely rounded. The pectoral pore is located above the middle of the pectoral fin base. Sexual dimorphism is evident in this genus in the shape of the head, the dorsal and anal fins, and the maxillary barbels.

Mees (1974) believes that the actual number of species in this genus will be something like four or five when it is studied more thoroughly, some of the current species being retained at the level of species while others would be considered simple synonyms.

The driftwood cats, as aquarium enthusiasts generally call members of the genus *Parauchenipterus*, are nocturnal and hide during the day in driftwood decorations, where they will remain motionless for hours and are difficult to detect. If driftwood is not available be sure to provide other hiding places constructed from rocks, plants, or whatever. When it becomes dark, the driftwood catfishes will wander about searching for food, often scraps that were overlooked by the daytime feeders as well as food placed in the tank after lights-out specifically for these nocturnal feeders. They are also likely to treat as food any small fishes they can find in the tank. Otherwise they are peaceful fishes and will do well in a community aquarium of species that are too large for them to swallow.

Spawning in some species of this genus has been investigated, and at least one has been spawned in captivity. Fertilization is internal as spermatozoa are introduced into the oviduct before the maturation of the ova. Actual fertilization takes place at the time of the deposition of the eggs, when the male may no longer be present. The male has the anterior rays of his anal fin thickened, stiff, and set close together to form an intromittent organ commonly called a pseudopenis. This modification is also seen in species of other genera such as *Asterophysis, Pseudauchenipterus, Tatia, Auchenipterichthys, Trachycorystes*, and *Auchenipterus*. It may also be found in other genera once they are better known. *Centromochlus* and *Glanidium* males have normal genital openings. In females the anal fin is not modified like that of the males, the rays remaining thin and flexible. The pseudopenis does not reach its full development until the fish are about 75% grown. The posterior part of the testis becomes modified also, producing a gelatinous substance instead of sperm. The sperm remain viable in this gelatinous fluid but become deformed when they come directly into contact with the water. The male will introduce the sperm in a gelatinous plug into the oviduct of the female, where it remains intact for about four months (this varies depending upon the species, however), when the actual egg-laying occurs.

One species of driftwood cat, tentatively identified as *Parauchenipterus insignis*, was bred in captivity by Hiroshi Azuma. The adults were kept in a 60 x 40 x 45 cm tank with a gravel substrate and some floating plants (water sprite). The pH was 6.0 to 7.0 and the temperature was 25° to 28°C. They were fed a wide variety of live foods and some dried foods. These catfish were, as expected, most active during the evening hours, preferring to seek shelter and remain hidden during the day. Initially, at about a size of 40-70 mm, there were only color differences, the male being a mottled color, the female plain. But at 80-95 mm the dorsal spine of the male became curved or "warped," the barbels of the upper jaw (maxillary barbels) changed from small, slender, soft structures to broader, stiffer, longer structures, and the anterior part of the anal fin became modified into the intromittent organ. At about one year of age, when the fish were 100-130 mm in total length, the catfish were ready to spawn. As the time for spawning approached, the maxillary barbels became stiffer and covered with minute tubercles. These spawning tubercles also covered the upper parts of the head and the anterior edge of the curved dorsal fin spine. The female did not change other than getting heavier as she filled with eggs.

After some preliminary courtship, which involved a lot of chasing around the aquarium, the male wrapped his body around that of the female so that his dorsal fin spine, enlarged maxillary barbels, and the tubercles aided him in holding this position while his intromittent organ was used to introduce the sperm plug into the female. His maxillary barbels were apparently clasped by the female's pectoral fins. The intromittent organ is quite small, only a few millimeters long, but is provided with a hooked, flexible tip. This flexibility is needed to locate the female opening. The insertion lasted only two to five seconds in the mating studied, although the embrace lasted about 10 to 20 seconds or so, after which the spawners broke apart. The embraces were repeated a few times a day, usually in late afternoon or early evening, after which the male was no longer needed and could be safely removed from the tank. Some two to four weeks later the female deposited 200 to 400 eggs, scattering them over the bottom gravel and some old leaves lying on the bottom. They were large (2.5-3.0 mm) but increased in size to about 4.5-6.0 mm in about a week, at which time they hatched.

The fry were 7 to 10 mm long and in two days were ready for newly hatched brine shrimp or similar sized foods. In 15 days after spawning (one week after hatching) the fry were about 15 mm long and could be offered a more balanced diet of chopped tubifex, daphnia, and whiteworms. One month after spawning, the young were about 30 mm long and grew fast on chopped earthworms, tubifex, and bloodworms, plus some dried food. At the end of 60 days the young catfish started to take on the coloration of the older fish. One behavioral note that was brought out by Azuma was that the 30-day-old young were active enough to accept food at any hour of the day or night. They congregated near the bottom during the daylight hours but moved higher in the water column when nighttime arrived. The adults were more strictly nocturnal, preferring to hide around the driftwood or rocks during the day. The parents had no inclination to guard or care for the eggs in any way, but they were not inclined to eat them either!

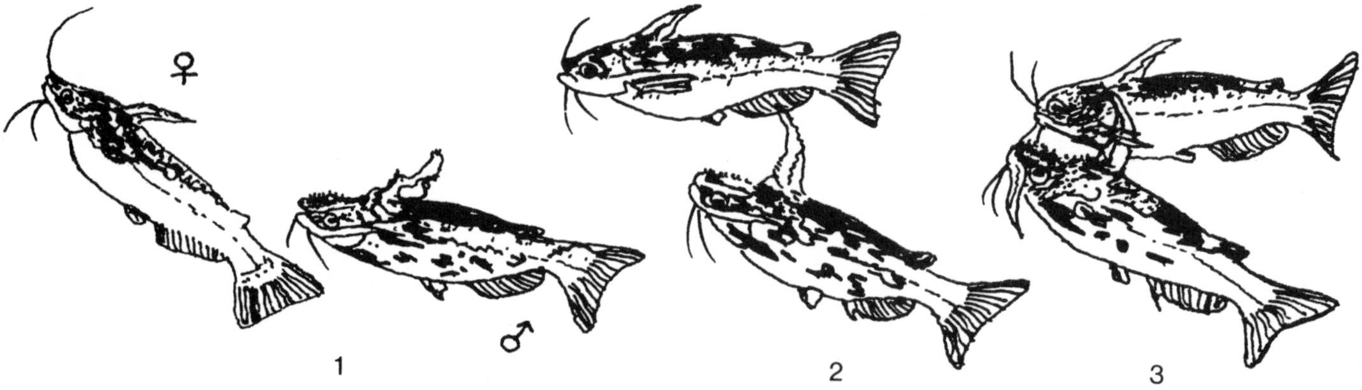

The spawning of the woodcat: Male approaches female (1) as his dorsal spine moves into position and makes contact with her (2 & 3). The pair wrap their bodies together as the sperm package is delivered to the female (4-7). Illustrations by Hiroshi Azuma.

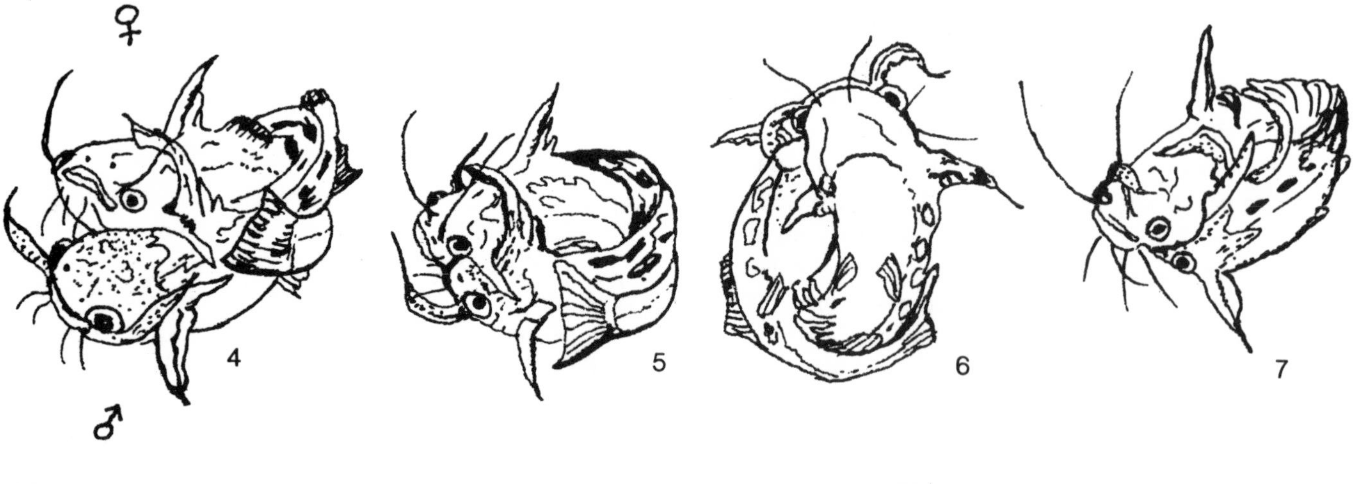

The genus *Centromochlus* is a small genus of only two, perhaps three, species widely distributed in Amazonia and the Orinoco basin. Other species formerly referred to this genus were placed in *Tatia* by Mees (1974). The body is slender, terete, tapers backward, and the caudal peduncle is quite distinct. The anterior portion of the body is relatively long, the predorsal distance included 2.7-3.25 times in the standard length. The head is subconical, with the surface of the bones granular and the horns of the nuchal plate curved inward and upward. The fontanels are situated in a depression extending posteriorly from the snout tip. The eyes are large to very large, and the mouth is narrow and inferior in position. The teeth, smaller than those of *Tatia*, are in a narrow band in each jaw, that of the upper jaw very narrow or even interrupted in the middle. The barbels are of variable

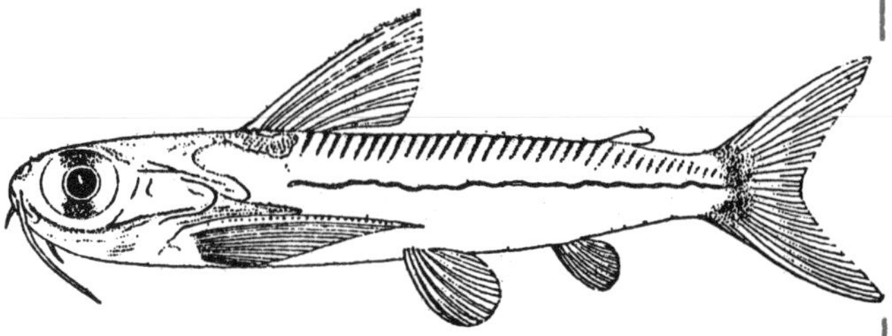

Centromochlus heckeli. (From Fowler, 1945.)

length, the maxillary pair longer or shorter than those of species of *Tatia*. The dorsal and pectoral fin spines are strong, pungent, and very long, the pectoral spines reaching or almost reaching to the ventral fins. The spines are without teeth and hooks, being only slightly rough, or the pectoral fin spines are serrated on the inner margin only. The pectoral pore is located over the pectoral fin base. The anal fin is normal (no sexual dimorphism) and the caudal fin is forked, the lobes with pointed tips. The ventrals are inserted posteriorly, from just behind the middle of the body to as far as two-thirds of the body length from the tip of the snout. The lateral line consists of small curves. The urogenital pore is situated against the origin of the anal fin in presumed males while in supposed females it is located well in advance of that position, about halfway between the anus and the origin of the anal fin. Although relatively close to the genus *Tatia, Centromochlus* can best be distinguished from that genus by the long, pungent spines and the distinct caudal peduncle.

Centromochlus heckeli occurs in the Amazon and the northern tributaries of the Paraná River. It attains a length of from 8 to 15 cm and is a fairly active species in the aquarium as long as the tank is relatively large and not too dark. This is an omnivorous species, but it particularly likes live foods, although other types are generally accepted.

The genus *Tatia* contains about 14 not very large species distributed throughout tropical South America east of the Andes from Venezuela and Colombia to southern Brazil. They are not, however, known from the Paraguay and La Plata systems, Paraguay, and in Bolivia they are known only from the Rio Guapore, which borders Brazil. The maximum size of species in this genus is less than 12 cm. The body is naked and the head is relatively short, the predorsal length contained about 3.25-3.7 times in the standard length. The surface of the head and the nuchal region (except the orbits and the interorbital fontanel) are covered with bony plates. The nuchal plate extends to and beyond the base of the dorsal fin spine, and the horns of the nuchal plate are curved downward and outward, never inward. The fontanel or fontanels form a deep, oval depression between the eyes without depressions in the skull anteriorly or posteriorly. The humeral process (spine) is normally well developed and variable in length. The eyes are moderately large and are covered with skin. The barbels are moderate in length, the longest reaching to or just past the dorsal fin origin. The mouth is terminal, not visible from below, and the teeth are moderate and arranged in a band in each jaw

Tatia intermedia. (From Mees, 1974.)

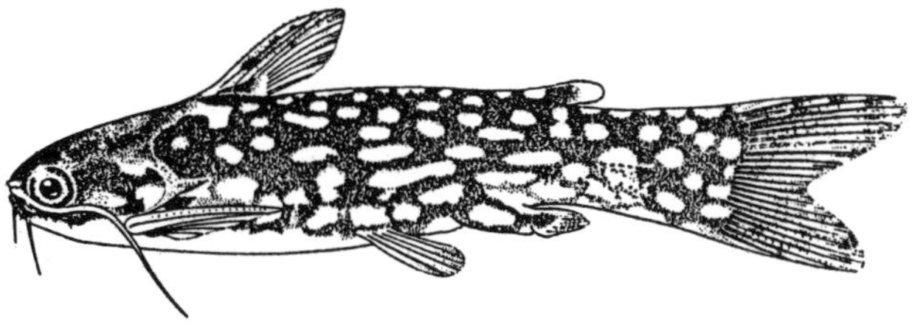

without any backward projections. The vomer and palatines are without teeth, except in some large *Tatia intermedia* that may have an irregular vomerine patch of teeth. The dorsal and pectoral fin spines are strong but comparatively short and nearly always have well-developed teeth and hooks. The pectoral spines are short, with a slight arc backward, and with some 18-26 outwardly directed teeth on the anterior edge and some 13-18 inwardly directed teeth on the posterior edge. The dorsal fin spine has teeth on its anterior edge only, the posterior margin being smooth. The anal fin is short and shows pronounced sexual dimorphism. The adipose fin is small. The ventral fins originate at about the middle of the body or slightly more posteriorly. The caudal fin is slightly to deeply forked, the tips of the lobes more or less rounded; it is also not clearly separated from the body. That is, there is no distinct caudal peduncle, but there are several rudimentary caudal rays in front of and above and below the caudal fin itself. The pectoral pore is located above the middle of the pectoral fin base. The lateral line is complete and more or less straight, but not very conspicuous. As for sexual dimorphism, females have a normal anal fin whereas the male's anal fin is modified into a copulatory organ. Its base is enveloped in skin, the outer portion forming a hard, somewhat leaf-shaped organ, the first or second ray being long and thickened and the posterior rays very fine. The genital opening is at the base of the visible part of the first ray, widely separated from the anal opening. Most species are distinctively patterned so that recognition of the various species is not too difficult. Both sexes are the same color and pattern as far as known. *Tatia intermedia* is perhaps the commonest and most widely distributed species of the genus.

Tatia perugiae inhabits larger rivers where the water is swift. The preferred areas are littoral zones adjacent to the shoreline over hard, sandy bottoms devoid of vegetation. Stomach contents included insect fragments, mostly ants, beetles, and mayflies (Saul, 1975).

The genus *Glanidium* is a small genus containing about five species widely distributed in eastern South America, particularly south-

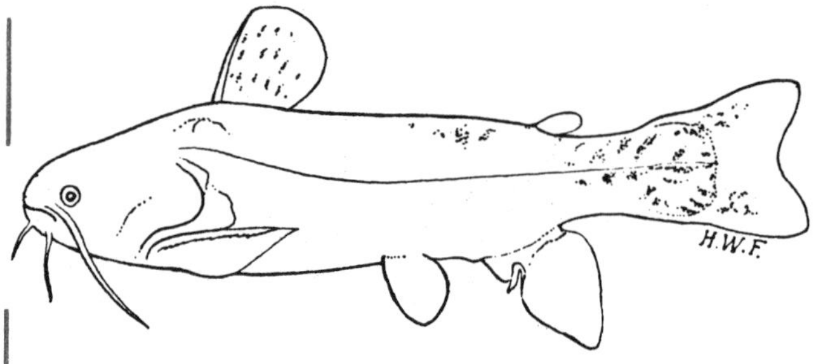

Glanidium albescens. (From Fowler, 1951.)

eastern Brazil. It is very close to *Tatia* (Eigenmann & Eigenmann considered it a subgenus of the genus *Centromochlus*, from which *Tatia* was split) and the differences are very slight, perhaps not enough to justify keeping the two separate. However, Mees (1974) retained the genus *Glanidium* as a separate entity, and this is what will be done in this book. Species of the genus *Glanidium* attain a distinctly larger size than those of *Tatia*, and the upper surface of the head and the humeral process are covered by thick skin. The horns of the nuchal plate are very slender. The anterior edges of the dorsal and pectoral fin spines are smooth or at most have some small teeth. The number of rays in the pectoral (I,5 or I,6) and anal (10-13) fins tends to be higher in *Glanidium* than in *Tatia*. The caudal fin is emarginate. The eyes are moderate in size, latero-posterior in position, and covered by skin. The fontanel is reduced. The lateral line is complete, although somewhat inconspicuous, with the pores in an almost straight line. The pectoral pore is similar to that of *Tatia*. Sexual dimorphism is also similar to that described for *Tatia*.

Although about seven species have been described for *Glanidium*, one (*G. cesarpintoi*) is doubtful, possibly being a synonym of *G. ribeiroi* or even a species of *Tatia*. Of the remaining six species, *G. catherinensis* may also be synonymized eventually. *G. piresi* is a *Tocantinsia* (Mees, pers. comm.).

The genus *Pseudotatia* contains only a single species known only from the type locality, the lower course of the Rio São Francisco on the border of Pernambuco and Bahia, Brazil. It is very close to *Tatia* and *Glanidium*, having the same body shape, but every fin with the exception of the caudal fin has a higher

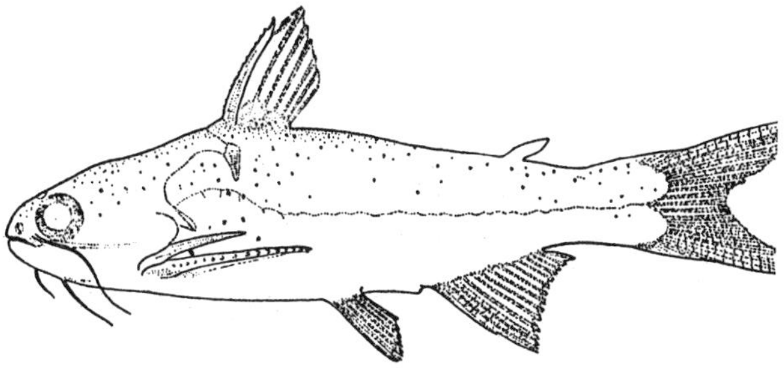

Pseudotatia parva. (From Mees, 1974.)

ray count. There is also a distinct, slender caudal peduncle, and the anal fin is emarginate. The males do not have a modified anal fin. The pectoral pore is distinct and located behind the pectoral fin base. In the group of genera to which *Pseudotatia* belongs the differences in the fin-ray counts as well as the presence or absence of a distinct caudal peduncle are in Mees's opinion clearly of generic value. To try and force the single species *P. parva* into *Tatia* would cause a disruption of that very uniform genus. Although there is no great sexual dimorphism in *Pseudotatia*, the supposed females do have the urogenital opening just before the origin of the anal fin; in the supposed males the urogenital opening is at the end of a tube that runs along the anterior edge of the anal fin.

The genus *Tocantinsia* has two species, one, *T. depressa*, known only from four specimens taken in the upper course of the Rio Tocantins. This is a relatively small species, the largest specimen being about 10 cm in standard length. The genus is similar to the other genera of the family, but the whole anterior part of the body is flattened and the head is broad and depressed, its width at the cleithra about twice its depth. The mouth is very wide, and the caudal peduncle is slender and deeper than wide. The dorsal fin has a spine and 6 rays, and the anal fin has 12 rays. The ventral fins have 7 rays, the pectoral fins a spine and 6 or 7 rays. The caudal fin is deeply forked with pointed tips. The pectoral pore is rather large and is located over the posterior half of the pectoral fin base.

Tocantinsia depressa; (b) dorsal view. (From Mees, 1974.)

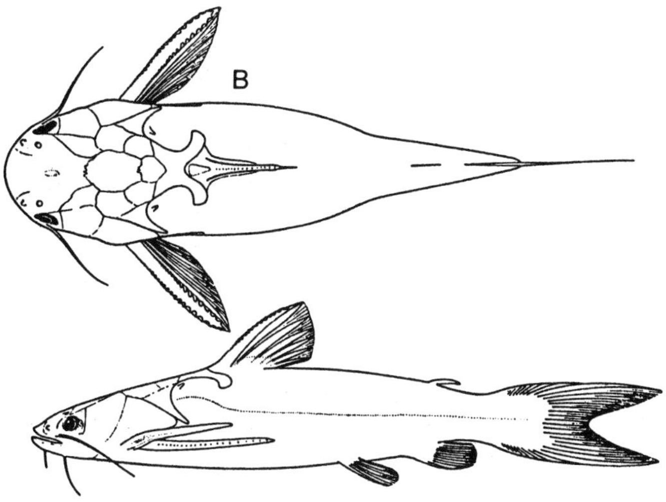

The genus *Trachelyichthys* is a small genus of only two species, one from the Rupununi River in Guyana and a second from Rio Mamón in Peru. In general appearance the species resemble *Trachelyopterus*, but differ from

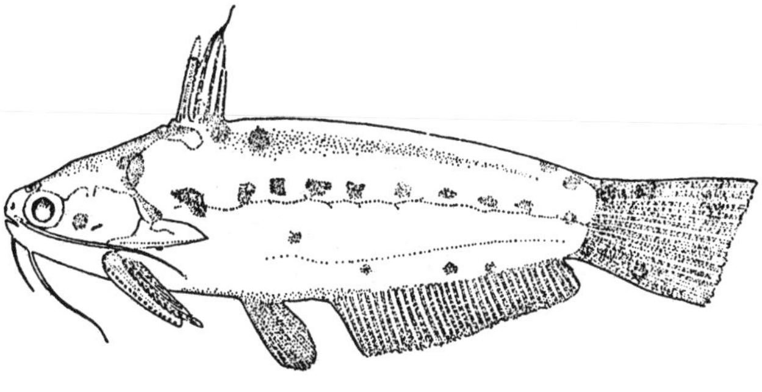

Trachelyichthys decaradiatus. (From Mees, 1974.)

the species in that genus by having 10 rays in the ventral fins, a caudal fin that is truncate, and much larger eyes. The body is compressed, the head is short, and the anal fin is long (about 35 rays). The pectoral pore is distinctly posterior to the pectoral fin base. There is no adipose fin.

There are not many species in the family Auchenipteridae that lack an adipose fin, but according to Mees (1974) those that do lack the fin do not form a natural grouping. He considers it likely, for instance, that *Epapterus*, which lacks an adipose fin, is more or less closely related to *Auchenipterus* and *Pseudepapterus*, both of which have an adipose fin but in both so small that they could justifiably be called rudimentary by some.

The genus *Trachelyopterus* contains only

two species, one from Porto do Moz, the second from Cayenne. The bones of the head are exposed and granular and the dorsal plate is fused with the occipital process. The fontanel is oval. The humeral process is present. The teeth are villiform in the jaws and there are no teeth on the vomer. The anal fin is of moderate length, the ventral fins have 6 rays, and there is no adipose fin. The gill membranes are confluent with the skin of the isthmus. In

Trachelyopterus coriaceus. (From Cuvier & Valenciennes, 1840.)

the type species of the genus, *T. coriaceus*, the body is short and compressed, the head is short with a steep profile and a truncate snout, and the eyes are small, contained about six times in the head length. The teeth are villiform and arranged in narrow bands. The dorsal fin spine is weak and terete; the anterior margin is smooth, the posterior margin has short teeth. The pectoral fin spines are smooth on the outer margin and have short teeth on the inner margin. The caudal fin is obliquely rounded.

The genus *Trachelyopterichthys* contains a single species from the Rio Guaporé. The body is elongate and compressed, while the head is short, its width greater than its length, its depth slightly less than its length, the bones exposed and granular. The dorsal plate is fused with the occipital process, the

Trachelyopterichthys taeniatus. (From Fowler, 1951.)

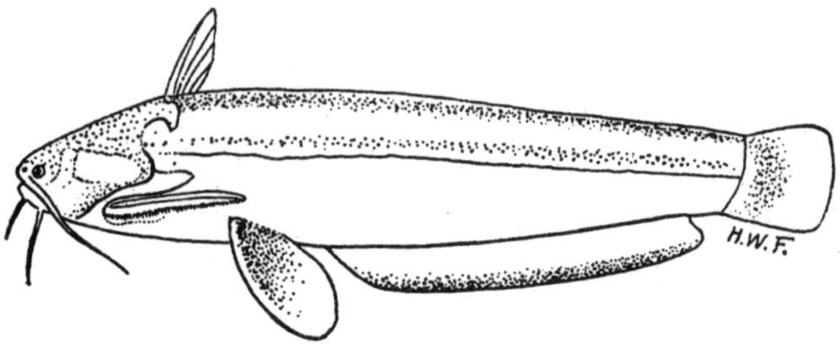

fontanel is elongate, and the humeral process extends beyond the middle of the pectoral fin. The eyes are small (about five in head length). The snout is short and rounded, with the jaws equal and the teeth all villiform in the jaws; no teeth are present on the vomer. The dorsal fin spine is sharply granular on the front margin, smooth posteriorly; the pectoral fin spines are serrated on both margins. The anal fin base is quite long, the caudal fin is obliquely rounded, and the ventral fins are very large, with 16 rays. There is no adipose fin. A pectoral pore is present.

The genus *Entomocorus* contains but two species, *E. benjamini* from Bolivia and *E. gameroi* from Venezuela. The top of the head is hard, reticulated or pitted, and the posterior margin of the occipital is bordered with a deep groove. The fontanel is about as long as the eye. The humeral process extends to about the level of the middle of the pectoral fin spine. The dorsal plate does not have the downward extending process behind. The snout is rounded, with the upper jaw sharp-

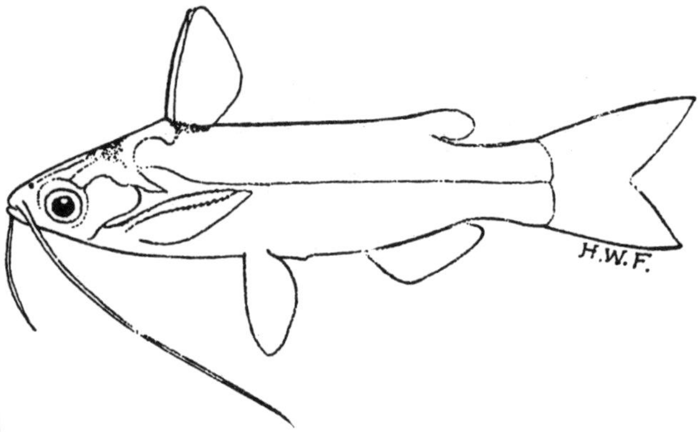

Entomocorus benjamini. (From Fowler, 1951.)

edged and bearing a single series of teeth along the edge, while the lower jaw has about two series of teeth in front and a single series on each side. The maxillary barbels are wiry at the base, fitted into a groove at the lower margin of the large eye, and extend to the tips of the ventral fins or to the origin of the anal fin. The dorsal fin spine has a smooth anterior margin while the posterior margin has minute hooks. The spine of the pectoral fin is strong, with about 15 curved thorns along its anterior margin and about the same number of shorter graduated teeth along the posterior margin. The anal fin is moderate, with 18-21 rays, its margin sloping, not emarginate. The adipose fin is short, its base equal to or shorter than the eye diameter. The ventral fins have 6 rays and are not adnate to the belly; the caudal fin is moderately forked. Secondary sexual dimorphism includes (in the male) pigmentation of the body and fins, modifications of the maxillary barbels and all fins except the caudal, as well as the development of a pseudopenis that probably serves as an intromittent organ.

Entomocorus gameroi spawns in July and August, which is the period of maximal annual flooding. The species is sexually dimorphic in several ways. The dorsal fin spine of the male becomes longer and curves anteriorly slightly in the middle and distal part. The serrations become irregular and new ones appear at the posterior edge. The pelvic spines of the male become excessively elongate, almost twice their former length, and become broader. In the anal fin of the male there is a reduction of the length of the base; the first seven rays become functionally associated, the first three fusing into a plate-like structure with strong surfaces for muscle attachment; and the margin of the fin becomes concave (changing from convex in normal males). The second ray of the male's left pectoral fin develops a kind of hook, and the second ray of the female's right pectoral fin develops some serrations. The bony part of the maxillary barbels of the male, normally almost half their length, become excessively enlarged. These barbels become transformed into two "cachos" giving the male a distinctive aspect. A pseudopenis is developed; it is short, made up of soft tissue, and positionally separated from the anal fin (not functionally). In other auchenipterids it can be very large (*Epapterus dispilurus*) or be fused to the anal fin (ex. *Auchenipterus*). Males develop increased dark pigment along the lateral line and broadening of the band in the upper lobe of the caudal fin. (Mago-Leccia, 1983.)

Entomocorus is related to the genera *Auchenipterus, Centromochlus*, and *Trachycorystes*.

The genus *Epapterus* contains three species from the Orinoco River basin, northern Argentina into Paraguay, and the Peruvian and

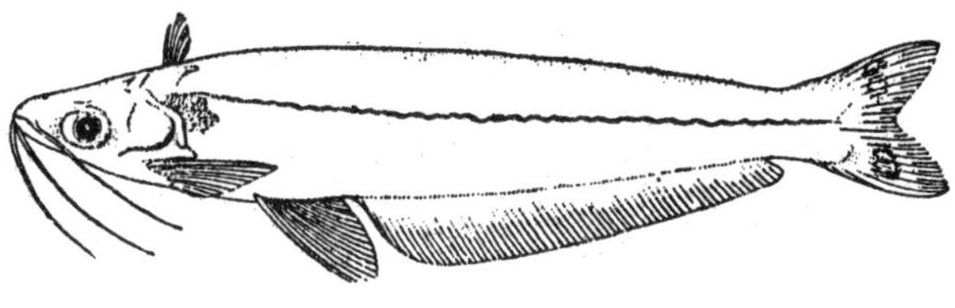

Eptapterus dispilurus. (From Fowler, 1945.)

central Amazon. They are elongate and strongly compressed, with the ventral outline gently curved to almost straight and the dorsal outline slightly arched. The short depressed head has the surface of the bones rough and covered with thin skin. The fontanel continues to the occipital, and the occipital process is more than twice as broad as long, rounded behind, and joined to the dorsal plate, which is widely forked posteriorly, the two sections of the fork longer than the rest of the plate and flanking the dorsal fin. The humeral process is present, and the postcoracoid process ends in a sharp point. The eyes are large and lateral in position, the orbital margin not free. The jaws are subequal and without teeth. The dorsal fin is rudimentary, with a short but pungent spine and two to three soft rays. The anal fin is very long, and the caudal fin is emarginate. The pectoral fins have a strong spine that may or may not reach the ventral fins and has serrae only on the inner margin, the other edges smooth. The ventral fins have 9-14 rays, are located far behind the dorsal fin, and their inner rays are connected by a membrane. There is no adipose fin. A pectoral pore is present. The lateral line follows a zig-zag course and has numerous branches (dendritic). Strong sexual dimorphism is reported in this genus. Males are less deep-bodied than females (of the same population) and have the dorsal spine twice as thick proximally and tapering only in the distal quarter (female dorsal fin spines taper from the base). Males have the maxillary barbel more extensively ossified (to the posterior third of the orbit). In males the first two anal fin rays are small while the third and fourth are greatly enlarged and have fused segments; female anal fins are normal.

E. blohmi occurs in a variety of aquatic habitats where there is poor visibility and the water is still or slow-flowing. It apparently feeds on filamentous algae and other plant material during the dry season.

The genus *Asterophysus* contains a single species from Marabitanos, Brazil. The mouth is terminal with the gape very wide, the cleft extending well past the level of the eye. The lower jaw is projecting for almost the entire width of the band of teeth. The bands of teeth in the jaws are interrupted in the middle, the premaxillary band of teeth twice as wide as the mandibular band and extending to the rictus; there are no teeth on the palate or vomer. The maxillary barbels extend to the gill opening; the anterior mental barbels are located near the symphysis while the postmental barbels reach to the base of the pectoral fins. The adipose fin is small. The dorsal fin originates over the gill opening; its spine granular in front. The ventral fins have 10 rays. The anal fin has 13 rays, the first anal ray of the male with the urogenital opening near its tip.

The genus *Wertheimeria* contains a single species from the Rio Jequitinhonha. The head is somewhat wider than long, the bones of the head granular. Granular plates are present on sides between the humeral processes, extending beyond the middle of the pectoral fin spine. The eyes are very small, contained 7 1/6 to 8 1/7 in the head length. The upper jaw is slightly projecting; the teeth are setiform with none on the palate. The maxillary barbels extend beyond the anterior third of the pectoral fins. The dorsal fin spine is shorter than the head and is serrated on its anterior margin. The pectoral fin spine is very long, much longer than the length of the head, and depressed. The adipose fin is unusual in being quite long, as long as the anal fin base.

Wertheimeria maculata. (From Fowler, 1951.)

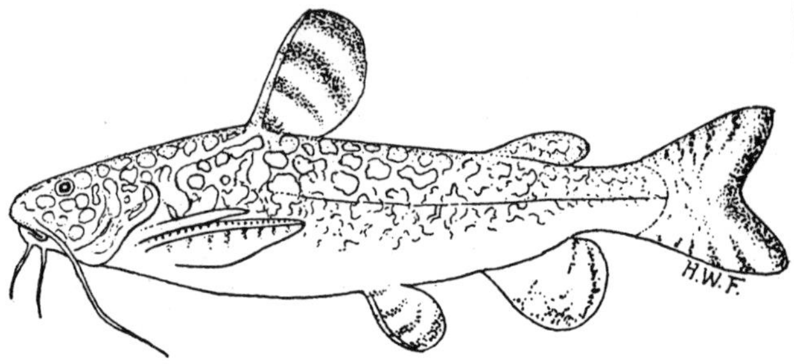

The anal fin has 15 to 16 rays, the pectoral fin has a spine and 9 rays, and the ventral fins each have about 5 to 7 rays. The caudal fin is emarginate. A pectoral pore is present. The gill openings are not restricted but continue well forward along the isthmus.

The genus *Taunayia* contains a single species from Piquete. It and *Wertheimeria* are the only genera of the family Auchenipteridae that have the gill openings not restricted but continuing well forward along the isthmus. Unlike *Wertheimeria*, which has 15 to 16 anal fin rays, *Taunayia* has 11 anal fin rays.

The genus *Pseudepapterus* contains only two species, one from Para, the other from Cucuhy on the Colombian border, Rio Negro. It

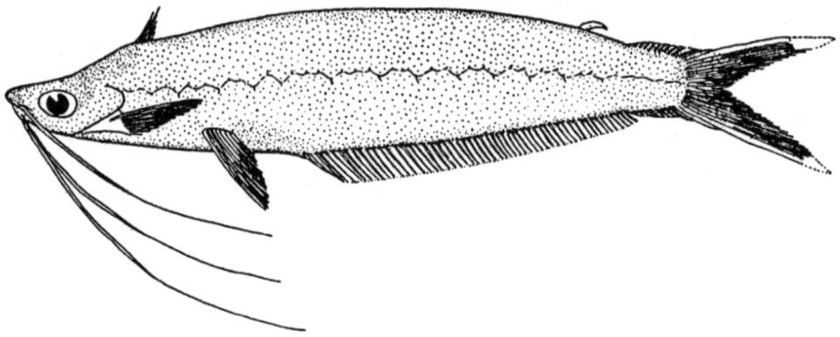

Pseudepapterus cucuhyensis. (From Böhlke, 1951.)

is one of the genera that does not possess an adipose fin. The ventral fin rays number 9 to 13, while the anal fin is very long, with 57 to 59 rays.

The genus *Liosomadoras* contains a single species from Brazil, Peru, and perhaps other countries in tropical South America. The body is rather short and robust, with a compressed caudal peduncle. The head is large and broad, its width at the clavicles greater than its length. The snout is short, broad, and obtuse, with a terminal mouth that is broad but with a short cleft, and the lower jaw protrudes slightly. The lips are thin and smooth and the teeth are villiform and arranged in bands in the jaws, there being no teeth on the palate. The surface of the head is rugose striate, and the frontal fontanel is broad and does not extend beyond the level of the eyes. The humeral extension has small spines. The barbels are thin and filamentous, without branches. The eyes are small and located in the anterior third of the profile of the head. The dorsal fin spine has the entire ante-

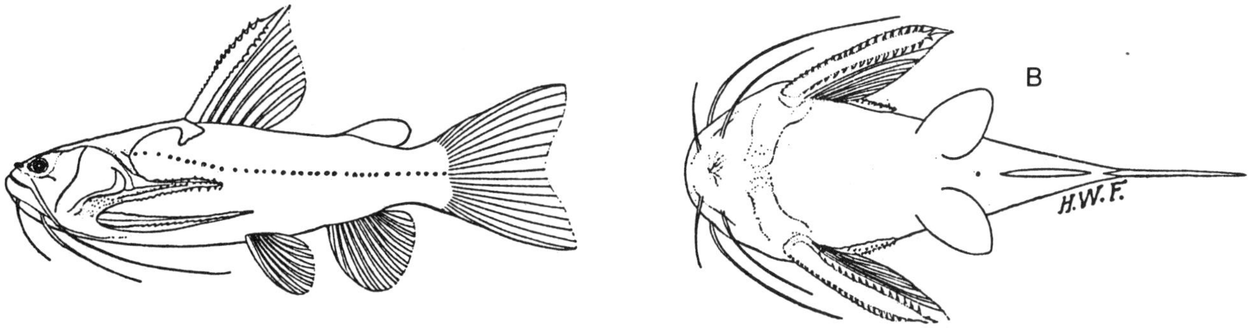

Liosomadoras oncinus; (b) ventral view. (From Fowler, 1951.)

rior margin and the terminal half of the posterior margin with a row of strong teeth; the pectoral spine has both the outer and inner margins strongly denticulated. The adipose fin is as long as the anal fin base, while the ventral fins are short, not very large, and positioned much closer to the anal than to the pectoral fin base. The caudal fin is large and slightly emarginate. The lateral line is complete and well marked. The gill openings are restricted.

There has been a lot of confusion with both the genus and species. It is one of those fishes for which the common name, Jaguar Catfish, has not changed at all, while the scientific name has been changed more than once. The history of these changes is well documented by Mees (1978), who established the correct name as being *Liosomadoras oncinus*. The Jaguar Catfish was originally described by Schomburgk in 1841 as *Arius oncinus*, the specific name taken from the scientific name of

The Jaguar Catfish was named after the real jaguar (*Panthera onca*) because of its spotted pattern. This fish has had a confused taxonomic history, even being placed in the family Doradidae for a time. Photo by Harald Schultz.

the jaguar, *Panthera onca*, apparently because of the similarity in color pattern. Günther (1864) even listed the species in a footnote under *Auchenipterus* but was unable to do much else with it. In 1940 Fowler described a new genus and species, *Liosomadoras morrowi*, and, because of the spiny humeral process, placed it erroneously in the family Doradidae, even though it did not have the lateral plates characteristic of that family. Gosline (1945) decided that *Liosomadoras* is a genus that is intermediate in characters between the two families and therefore placed the auchenipterids as a subfamily of the doradids. Mees finally investigated the problem after seeing an article by Brittan on the Jaguar Catfish in the *Tropical Fish Hobbyist* magazine using the name *Centromochlus* sp. Eventually Mees decided that *Arius oncinus, Liosomadoras morrowi*, and Brittan's Jaguar Catfish were all one and the same species. Since *oncinus* was the earliest name and of course it is not a species of *Arius*, the Jaguar Catfish had to assume the name *Liosomadoras oncinus*, and so it stands today.

The Jaguar Catfish is a retiring species in captivity and usually remains well hidden during the daylight hours. Its aquarium should therefore be provided with hiding places. The water in its natural habitat is a bit on the soft and acid side, so it probably will do somewhat better if these conditions are provided for the fish. Regular water changes are recommended. The Jaguar Catfish will eat a wide variety of foods including earthworms, tubificid worms, brine shrimp, and frozen and freeze-dried foods. Remember, however, that this species is more active after dark and its feeding schedule should be adjusted accordingly.

The genus *Gelanoglanis* contains a single species from the lowlands of eastern Colombia. The body is rather soft (gelatinous), thus prompting the generic name *Gelanoglanis*. The opening of the mouth is sinuous when viewed from the side, and the lower jaw is shorter than the upper and has three lobes when viewed from below, due mainly to a dorsally-directed fleshy flange on either side of the lower jaw; a free fleshy flange is present around the angle of the gape. The premaxillaries are lateral, broadly separated anteriorly, and each bear a patch of slender, pointed teeth. The dentary bears a patch of villiform teeth, and there are no vomerine or palatine teeth. There are only two pairs of barbels, a maxillary pair and a single mental pair, the maxillary pair ossified as far as or almost as far as the pectoral fin spine. The sides of the head bear grooves into which the maxillary barbels fit. The eyes are small, roundish, widely separated, and visible when viewed from above but not from below. The anterior nostrils are tubular, the posterior large and positioned directly in front of the eye. The dorsal, anal, and paired fins are short-based. The dorsal fin spine has hooks on the posterior margin only as do the pectoral fin spines. There is a very short second dorsal fin spine just anterior to the first that is involved with a locking mechanism. The adipose fin is slender and low, the posterior lobe free from the back; the caudal fin is forked and with rounded lobes, the lower lobe slightly longer than the upper. The first two rays of the anal fin are short, the total number 6 to 9. There are 6 ventral fin rays, 4 pectoral fin rays (plus a spine), and 5 dorsal fin rays (plus two spines). A small pectoral pore is present above the posterior end of the pectoral fin base. The gill openings are restricted laterally, and there are 5 branchiostegal rays. There is some sexual dimorphism in that the genital papilla of the female is closer to the anal opening than to the anal fin origin or about equidistant between the two; the genital papilla of the male is more elongated, has a pointed tip and is separated from the anterior margin of the anal fin by a notch. The color of the fish in life is rosy red.

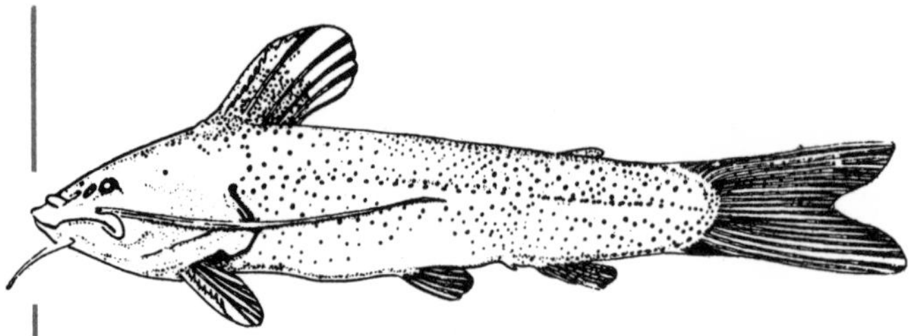

Gelanoglanis stroudi. (From Böhlke, 1980.)

Gelanoglanis stroudi was collected after dark on a shallow sandy bar along the inner edge of a bend in the Rio Metica. The current was moderately to fairly swift and the bottom was sand and gravel in the vicinity of capture. This species, according to Böhlke (1980), is not closely related to any other auchenipterid. It is similar in some respects to the Cetopsidae but has a different caudal fin structure and lacks vomerine teeth (Schultz, 1944, reported that all cetopsids have vomerine teeth), although some other auchenipterids also lack them, and possesses an adipose fin (cetopsids lack an adipose), although some other auchenipterids also lack an adipose fin. *Gelanoglanis* is also distinctive in the family Auchenipteridae in having only two pairs of barbels and in the position of the posterior nostrils. It is only some 25 mm long.

Checklist of the species of the family Auchenipteridae and their type localities:

Auchenipterus Valenciennes, 1840. Type species *Hypophthalmus nuchalis* Spix.
- *Auchenipterus nigripinnis* (Boulenger, 1895). Paraguay.
- *A. nuchalis* (Spix, 1829). Equatorial Brazil. (Incl. *osteomystax, ambyiacus, demerarae,* and *brevior*.)
- *A. paysanduanus* De Vicincenzi, 1933. Uruguay.

Pseudepapterus Steindachner, 1915. Type species *Auchenipterus (Pseudepapterus) hasemani* Steindachner.
- *Pseudepapterus cucuhyensis* Böhlke, 1951. Cucuhy on the Colombian border, Rio Negro.
- *P. hasemani* (Steindachner, 1915). Pará.

Epapterus Cope, 1878. Type species *Epapterus dispilurus* Cope.
- *Epapterus blohmi* Vari, Jewett, Taphorn & Gilbert, 1984. Laguna Los Guácimos, Guarico State, Orinoco Basin, Venezuela.
- *E. chaquensis* Risso & Risso, 1962. Chaco Province, Argentina.
- *E. dispilurus* Cope, 1878. Nauta, Peru.

Pseudauchenipterus Bleeker, 1862. Type species *Silurus nodosus* Bloch, 1794.
- *Pseudauchenipterus affinis* (Steindachner, 1876). Rio São Mateus; Rio Mucuri at "Porto Alegre."
- *P. flavescens* (Eigenmann & Eigenmann, 1888). Rio São Francisco.
- *P. jequitinhonhae* (Steindachner, 1876). Jequitinhonha River.
- *P. nodosus* (Bloch, 1794). "Tranquebar" (= tropical South America). (Incl. *P. guppyi*.)

Entomocorus Eigenmann, 1917. Type species *E. benjamini* Eigenmann.
- *Entomocorus benjamini* Eigenmann, 1917. San Joaquin, Bolivia; Rio Santa Rita.
- *E. gameroi* Mago-Leccia, 1983. Mouth of Rio Apurito in the Apure River, near San Fernando de Apure, Estado Guárico, Venezuela.

Auchenipterichthys Bleeker, 1862. Type species *Auchenipterus thoracatus* Kner.
- *Auchenipterichthys longimanus* (Günther, 1864). Rigo Capim, Pará.
- *A. thoracatus* (Kner, 1858). Rio Guaporé.

Gelanoglanis Böhlke, 1980. Type species *G. stroudi* Böhlke.
- *Gelanoglanis stroudi* Böhlke, 1980. Rio Metica, Dpto. Meta, Colombia.

Pseudotatia Mees, 1974. Type species *P. parva* Mees.
- *Pseudotatia parva* Mees, 1974. Joazeiro, Brazil.

Tocantinsia Mees, 1974. Type species *T. depressa* Mees.
- *Tocantinsia depressa* Mees, 1974. Tocantins near Piexa, Brazil.
- *T. piresi* A. Miranda-Ribeiro, 1920. Rio São Manoez.

Trachelyichthys Mees, 1974. Type species *T. decaradiatus* Mees.
- *Trachelyichthys exilis* Greenfield & Glodek, 1977. Rio Mamón, Peru.
- *T. decaradiatus* Mees, 1974. Rupununi, British Guiana.

Liosomadoras Fowler, 1940. Type species *L. morrowi* Fowler (= *L. oncinus*).
- *Liosomadoras oncinus* (Schomburgk, 1841). Rio Padauiri.

Glanidium Lütken, 1874. Type species *Glanidium albescens* Reinhardt in Lütken.
- *Glanidium albescens* Reinhardt in Lütken, 1874. Rio das Velhas, Brazil.
- *G. catherinensis* P. Miranda-Ribeiro, 1962. Rio do Braco do Norte, São Ludgero, State of Sta. Catarina.
- *G. leopardus* Hoedeman, 1961. Litany River, French Guiana.
- *G. melanopterum* Miranda-Ribeiro, 1918. Piquete, São Paulo.

G. ribeiroi Haseman, 1911. "Porto União da Vitória, Rio Iguassu, Paraná, Brazil." (Incl. *cesarpintoi*?)

Taunayia Miranda-Ribeiro, 1918. Type species *T. marginata* Miranda-Ribeiro.

Taunayia marginata A. Miranda-Ribeiro, 1918. Piquete, São Paulo.

Wertheimeria Steindachner, 1876. Type species *W. maculata* Steindachner.

Wertheimeria maculata Steindachner, 1876. Rio Jequitinhonha.

Trachelyopterus Valenciennes, 1840. Type species *T. coriaceus* Valenciennes.

Trachelyopterus coriaceus Valenciennes, 1840. Fresh waters of Cayenne, French Guiana.

T. maculosus Eigenmann & Eigenmann, 1888. Porto do Moz.

Trachelyopterichthys Bleeker, 1862. Type species *Trachelyopterus taeniatus* Kner, 1857.

Trachelyopterichthys taeniatus (Kner, 1857). Rio Guaporé.

Trachelyopterichthys anduzei, Ferraris & Fernandez, 1987. Laguna de Carida, Rio Orinoco, Venezuela.

Asterophysus Kner, 1857. Type species *A. batrachus* Kner.

Asterophysus batrachus Kner, 1857. Marabitanos, Brazil.

Tatia Miranda-Ribeiro, 1911. Type species *Centromochlus intermedius* Steindachner, 1876.

Tatia altae (Fowler, 1945). Morelia, Rio Caquetá Basin, Colombia. (Subsp. of *perugia*?)

T. aulopygia (Kner, 1957). Rio Guaporé.

T. brunnea Mees, 1974. Compagnia Creek, Surinam.

T. concolor Mees, 1974. Headwaters of Coppename River, Surinam.

T. creutzbergi (Boeseman, 1953). Djai Creek, Surinam.

T. galaxias Mees, 1974. L'Apure, Venezuela. (Subsp. of *aulopygia*?)

T. gyrina (Eigenmann & Allen, 1942). Brook near Rio Itaya, Iquitos.

T. intermedia (Steindachner, 1876). Marabitanos; Pará. (Incl. *T. dunni* Fowler, 1945.) (Subsp. of *aulopygia*?)

T. neivai (von Ihering, 1930). Piracicaba, Rio Piracicaba, Est. de São Paulo. (Subsp. of *aulopygia*?)

T. perugiae Steindachner, 1883. Canelos, Ecuador.

T. punctata Mees, 1974. Creeks between Kabel and Lombé, Surinam.

T. reticulata Mees, 1974. Karanambo, Rupununi, Br. Guiana.

T. schultzi (Rössel, 1962). Upper Rio Xingu, Brazil.

T. simplex Mees, 1974. Xaventina House Beach, Rio das Mortes, Mato Grosso.

Centromochlus Kner, 1858. Type species *C. megalops* Kner (= *C. heckelii*).

Centromochlus existimatus Mees, 1974. On *C. heckelii* in part.

C. heckelii (Filippi, 1853). Rio Napo. (Incl. *steindachneri*.)

C. sp. Mees, 1974.

Trachycorystes Bleeker, 1858. Type species *Auchenipterus trachycorystes* Valenciennes, 1840.

Trachycorystes cratensis Miranda-Ribeiro, 1937. Rio Granjeiro, Ceará, Brazil.

T. trachycorystes (Valenciennes, 1840). Brazil?.

Parauchenipterus Bleeker, 1862. Type species *P. galeatus* (Linnaeus, 1766).

Parauchenipterus albicrux (Berg, 1901). Rio de la Plata near the embo la dura of the Rio Santiago.

P. amblops (Meek & Hildebrand, 1913). Tuyra Basin, Panama.

P. analis (Eigenmann & Eigenmann, 1888). Arari?

P. brevibarbus (Cope, 1878). Pebas, Peru.

P. fisheri (Eigenmann, 1916). Atrato basin, Colombia. Rio Sucio.

P. insignis (Steindachner, 1878). Rio Magdelena.

P. galeatus (Linnaeus, 1766). "In America australi." Restricted to Surinam by Mees. (Incl. *jokeannae, striatulus*, & *glaber*.)

P. isacanthus (Cope, 1878). Pebas, Peru.

P. leopardinus (Borodin, 1927). Rio São Francisco, Minas Gerais Prov., Brazil.

P. magdalenae (Steindachner, 1878). Magdalena River.

P. striatulus (Steindachner, 1876). Rio Paraiba, em Campos; Rio Doce; Linhares; Rio Mucuri. (= *insignis*.)

P. teaguei (Devincenzi *in* Devincenzi & Teague, 1942). Rio Peguay affluent of middle Rio Uruguay.

Chapter 22

Family PIMELODIDAE (Antenna Catfishes)

Plates 116–145

The family Pimelodidae is a large and very diversified family of freshwater catfishes with over 300 species distributed among some 50 to 60 genera. Although the largest number of species inhabit South America (except its extreme southern tip), others are found northward through Central America into southern Mexico and still others occur on some of the larger Caribbean islands. The last systematic review was by Eigenmann and Eigenmann in 1890. At this time the family is too confused to be able to break it down into smaller units such as subfamilies (although some have tried without too much success) or to construct a workable key (presently available keys include well below half of the genera accepted as valid). Work on the pimelodids is continuing, and it is hoped that a more stable classification will be forthcoming before too long.

Generally, the body is elongate and covered with smooth, naked skin. The head may be covered with a thin skin leaving the bones of the upper part of the cranium clearly visible, or entirely covered by a thick skin concealing these bones; in some genera the head is extremely depressed. The anterior and posterior nostrils are far apart. The eyes may be large or small, with a free orbital rim or without one (especially the small-eyed species), and usually superior in position and not visible from a ventral view (except in *Sorubim* and *Parapimelodus*); the eyes are absent in some forms. There are three pairs of barbels; a maxillary pair, which in some species does not reach the pectoral fin base while in others extends well beyond the tip of the tail, and two mandibular or mental pairs. The mouth is terminal and provided with numerous small, comb-like (villiform) teeth arranged in bands in both jaws, or there are numerous incisor-like (flattened and rounded distally) teeth evenly spaced in a single row in each jaw; vomerine and palatine teeth may or may not be present. The occipital process may be present and extend to the dorsal plate, present and not reaching the dorsal plate, or absent; it never has "horns" that extend beyond the origin of the dorsal fin.

The dorsal fin is well developed and usually has a spine or simple ray and 5-7 branched rays. Dorsal and pectoral fin spines may be present or absent; if present, they may be strong or weak, strongly serrated or almost smooth. A well-developed adipose fin is present, often long and large. The ventral fins have 6 rays and are inserted below or a little behind the dorsal fin base. The anal fin is usually short, with as few as 8 rays, but there may also be more than 30 rays. The caudal fin is variable (usually forked), with about 14 to 16 branched rays. The lateral line is usually complete and there is a well-developed swim bladder. A pectoral pore is present or absent. The gill openings are large, the gill membranes free from the isthmus and from each other or only narrowly connected.

Most pimelodids are typical bottom-dwelling catfishes of fast rivers and creeks. According to Goulding (1981), in the area where his observations were made (Rio Madeira) only pimelodids and doradids were represented in the upstream migrations. These occurred between July and November during the period when the water was low. Most pimelodids are nocturnal or crepuscular and their extraordinarily sensitive barbels play an important function in their search for food. In many species these barbels are long and slender and are held stiffly forward like antennae, a habit that has earned them a common name of antennae catfishes. Several species are commonly imported for the aquarium trade, but they are not among the most popular of catfishes as they require a lot of space and their constant searching for food keeps the bottom badly stirred up. In a community tank, larger species will play havoc with the plants and will not hesitate to attack smaller fishes. Few species have as yet been spawned in captivity.

They are not difficult to keep. A typical aquarium should be large, with a bottom of mixed sand and gravel and a generous addition of round (not sharp) pebbles and perhaps some driftwood. Plants are optional for, as mentioned, there is the constant risk of their being uprooted. Subdued lighting is recommended. Feeding is no problem, as they will take large portions of meaty foods such as earthworms (whole or chopped depending upon the size of the fish to be fed), bloodworms, tubifex, and frozen brine shrimp.

The genus *Hemisorubim* contains only a single species usually confined to the deeper parts of large rivers of northern and eastern South America from the Orinoco to the La Plata basin. The head and body are strongly depressed, the width at the cleithra twice the depth, and the lower surface of the fish is flat from the snout to the anus. The postoccipital process is well developed, tapering, and its length is about twice its width at the base; this process is slightly shorter than the slender predorsal plate, which it reaches. The postorbital portion of the head is striate and granulose, and the skin of the sides of the head and snout is reticulate. The eyes are moderate to large, dorsally placed, and with a free orbital rim. The maxillary barbels extend as far as the adipose fin; the mental barbels are approximated and placed near the edge of the lip. The snout is long, broad, and strongly depressed; the mouth is wide, and the lower jaw projects beyond the tip of the snout, the upper jaw thin and truncate. The teeth are small and formed into a band in each jaw, the premaxillary band constricted at the middle and with a posteriorly directed process at each side; the vomerine tooth patch is large, deeper than the premaxillary band, and the two palatine patches are elongate-oval and very close to the vomerine patch. The dorsal and pectoral fin spines are well developed, the former with retrorse teeth on the posterior edge and the latter with strong teeth anteriorly and posteriorly. The adipose fin is well developed, longer than the anal, and the caudal fin has the lower lobe usually longer and broader than the upper. A pectoral pore is present above the insertion of the pectoral fin.

Hemisorubim platyrhynchos. (From Fowler, 1945.)

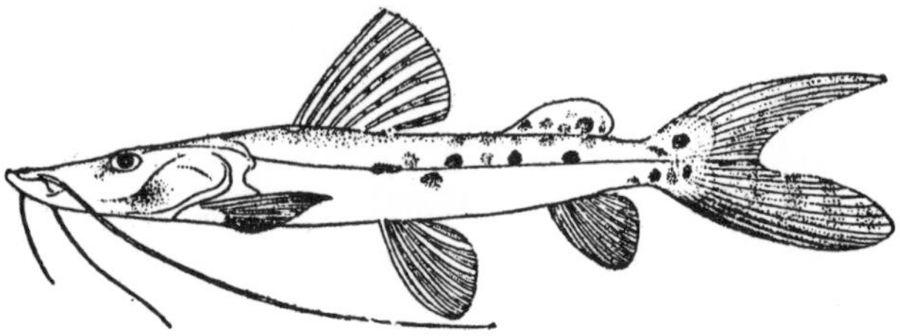

The single species, *Hemisorubim platyrhynchos*, is called the Porthole Shovelnose Catfish in the aquarium trade and attains a length of about 30 cm in captivity. It is relatively easy to care for, especially if it is given its favorite food, earthworms, on a regular basis along with other meaty foods.

The genus *Brachyplatystoma* includes rather large species occurring from Brazil, eastern Colombia, Venezuela, and the Guianas to Peru and Bolivia. Currently only six species are recognized. The head is broad, with a strongly depressed snout although the posterior portion of the head is deeper. The postoccipital process is long, almost twice as long as the predorsal plate, comparatively narrow and of equal width throughout, with a deeply forked end into which the slender tip of the predorsal fits but remains separate by a narrow gap. The head is covered with thin skin. The eyes are small, dorsolateral, contained more than 11 times in the head length, and with a free orbital rim. The maxillary barbels are very long, extending to or beyond

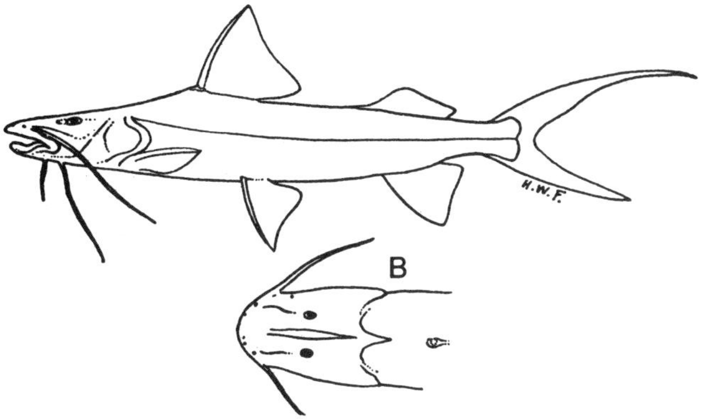

Brachyplatystoma flavicans; (b) dorsal view of head. (From Fowler, 1951.)

the caudal peduncle to twice the body length or more. The fontanel is elongate-elliptical. The snout is broadly rounded and the mouth wide, with the upper jaw protruding. The teeth are depressible and disposed in bands in the jaws, those of the upper jaw slightly larger than is usual in other members of the family and not contiguous with the band of smaller teeth covering the vomer and palatine bones. The dorsal and pectoral fin spines are not encased in skin; they are well developed but not very strong. The caudal fin is deeply forked, with the outermost rays long and filamentous. There is no pectoral pore. The adipose fin base is longer than the anal fin base. There are 11-12 branchiostegal rays. In general the color is plain, though sometimes there are dark spots or indistinct crossbars on the flanks. A few species are brightly colored and would be welcomed in the aquarium trade if they were ever imported.

Brachyplatstoma vaillanti, known commonly as the "Piramutaba," resembles *B. filamentosum* but can be recognized by its much larger adipose fin. It also does not get as large as *filamentosum*, attaining a length of about 80 cm FL (fork length) and a weight of 10 kilos. It is an important commercial fish in the Rio Madeira. According to Goulding (1981) fishermen report that schools appear at the Rio Madeira rapids every four to five years. These schools apparently originate in the Amazon estuaries and migrate upstream even as far as the Rio Solimoes.

B. filamentosum is referred to as the "Piraiba" or "Filhote," the latter name sometimes applied to other species as well. It is the largest catfish in the Amazon basin, attaining lengths of over 3 meters (second only to *Arapaima gigas*), although a length of 2 meters and a weight of 110 kilos is more likely to be seen. Most of the commercial fish are immature specimens (called "Filhotes") of about 100 cm FL and 5 to 15 kilos. *B. filamentosum* is not a sought-after food fish and in fact is said to be imbued with pathogenic properties, though this has yet to be proven. It is also said to have a toxic liver. Goulding reports two men who apparently had partaken of the liver and within a few hours contracted a high fever and severe skin inflammation over the entire body. In two or three days they shed their outer layer of skin, but within a couple of weeks they had recovered. Stomach contents of this catfish are said to include parts of monkeys, and Goulding quotes Roosevelt (1914) as saying, "our Brazilian friends told us that in the lower Madeira and part of the Amazon near the mouth, there is still a more gigantic catfish which in similar fashion occasionally makes prey of a man." This species also moves upstream, mostly during the period of low water.

B. flavicans is commonly called the "Dourada," or Gilded Catfish, because of its golden body. It is the most abundant catfish in the Rio Madeira and is usually confined to the deeper river channels although it may enter floodplain lakes. It is easily captured by drifting deep-water gillnets and forms an important commercial fishery. The vast majority caught are 70 to 100 cm in fork length and weigh 4 to 10 kilos. These are immature fish, as gonadal development apparently starts at a fork length of at least 1.2 meters. The fishermen of the Teotonio Rapids on the Madeira are sometimes referred to as "piscine miners" in reference to the golden color of their catch. *B. flavicans* is also migratory, possibly from the Amazon through the Rio Madeira to the Rio Beni or Rio Mamore in order to spawn in the flooded areas of eastern Bolivia. But spawning populations may also occur in the Amazon so more study is needed to be more certain. This fish will migrate during both high and low water and feeds mainly on fishes throughout the water column, particularly migratory characins. *B. flavicans* has the shortest barbels of any of the species in the genus.

B. juruense is called the "Dourada Zebra" or Golden Zebra because of its bright yellow body crossed by many black stripes. It would certainly make a striking aquarium inhabitant, although it does attain a length of about 60 cm FL.

The genus *Pseudoplatystoma* contains three species of very large size from northern and eastern South American fresh waters from east of the Andes and south to the Parana-La Plata basin. The large head is moderately to very depressed, the width at the cleithra about 1.3 times the depth at the same place. The occipital portion of the head is covered by thin skin and the postoccipital process is well developed, much longer than wide, and almost meeting or actually in contact with the predorsal plate. The fontanel extends from the middle of the snout to behind the eyes, where it continues as a groove to the occipital. The maxillary barbels are not long, extending to midway along the pectoral fins or as far as the anal fin origin. The eyes are relatively small, almost dorsal in position, and with a free orbital rim. The snout is long, depressed, the width of the mouth about equal to the maximum width of the head and less than half the head length. The upper jaw protrudes. The teeth are rather small and are arranged in bands in the jaws and patches on the palate (two patches on the vomer and two on the palatines, the latter in the form of a curved and elongate comma). The dorsal and

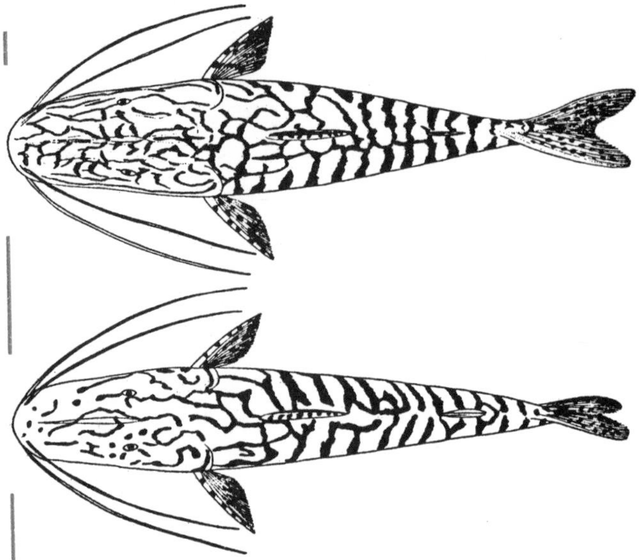

Pseudoplatystoma fasciatum. (From Fowler, 1951.)

Many of the large pimelodids have a flattened head and are called shovel-nosed catfishes. This is *Pseudoplatystoma fasciatum.* Photo by Gerhard Marcuse.

pectoral fin spines are well developed but inconspicuous as they are encased in a thick skin. The adipose fin base is shorter than the anal fin base or equal to it, and the caudal fin is scalloped to shallowly forked with rounded lobes (except in the very young). The gill rakers are short and few (about 4 plus some rudiments on the first arch); there are 14 or 15 branchiostegal rays. The pattern of the body usually involves crossbands or loops, earning them names such as Tiger Shovelnose Catfish.

Pseudoplatystoma tigrinum, the "Caparari" or Tiger Shovelnose Catfish, attains a length of 1.3 meters or more and a weight of 20 kilos in the wild and somewhat less (45-85 cm) in captivity. It is an attractive fish because of its tiger stripes (very variable) that prompted its common name. It is fairly common in a wide variety of habitats such as river channels, lakes, flooded forests, and floating meadows. It migrates upstream during the low water period. In captivity it needs a large tank, a 210-liter aquarium being a minimum size for a 45-cm individual. In addition, it is best to start with the largest tank possible even for a smaller specimen because it does not like changes. A newly moved Tiger Shovelnose is very fidgety and easily spooked, the dashing about the aquarium possibly leading to injury, especially of its "nose." Another possible reaction to a move is a hunger strike. It may be several weeks before normalcy is restored. Feeding usually is no problem as the Tiger Shovelnose will accept most foods up to and including live fishes. The only other thing this fish needs is a suitable hiding place such as a cave or dark recess among dense plants.

There have been workers in the group who have placed *P. tigrinum* as either a synonym of *P. fasciatum* or even a subspecies of *fasciatum*. More study is needed on this genus to resolve the situation. *P. fasciatum* is said to have thinner stripes that are more vertical than those of *tigrinum*, as well as a narrower snout. It also does not get as large, attaining a length of only about 90 cm FL. Both species are of economic importance. *P. fasciatum* also migrates upstream in the Rio Madeira during low water periods. In captivity it is also somewhat temperamental. It becomes unsettled if the tank is too confining and its barbels constantly come in contact with the tank sides. It is a voracious nocturnal feeder that in the wild (Rio Machado) includes small loricariids, cichlids, and characoids as well as freshwater crabs in its diet. In captivity it will accept a wide variety of foods, such as small fishes (therefore not recommended for a community tank), various worms, and meaty foods such as beef heart.

It was reported that *Pseudoplatystoma* carried young in its mouth and therefore was probably a mouthbrooder. Reinhardt (according to Eigenmann, 1918) offered a reward to any native who brought a specimen to him with the young still in the mouth. When one was brought he discovered that the fish in the mouth were not at all related to the "parent" fish and assumed the native was duping him for the reward. He finally realized that the small fishes living in the gill cavity were actually parasitic catfishes belonging to the family Trichomycteridae.

The genus *Sorubimichthys* currently has three species, but further study may reduce these to only a single species. The body is long and slender and the head is large and depressed, with a very projecting and very broad snout. The eyes are very small and superior in position, and the maxillary barbels are fleshy and extend as far as the anal fin. The width of the mouth is about half the head width, with the upper jaw much longer than the lower. The teeth are very small, those of the premaxillary in a very broad band, those on the vomer and palatines in two semicrescentic patches. The dorsal fin has a spine and 6 rays and is equidistant between the snout tip and the middle of the adipose fin. The ad-

Sorubimichthys planiceps. (From Fernandez-Yepez, 1949.)

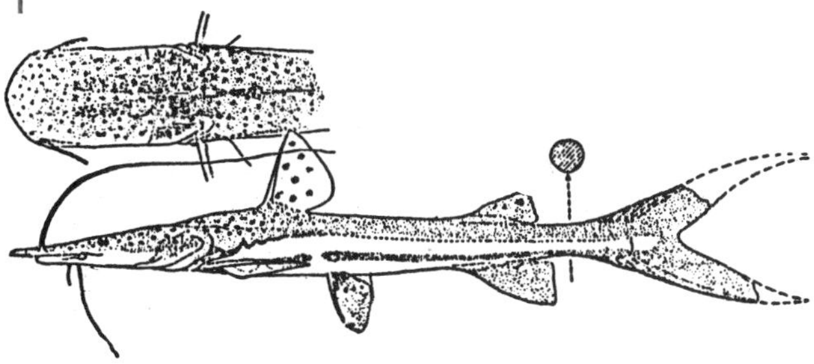

ipose fin base is shorter than or almost equal to the base of the anal fin. The pectoral fin spine is strong and is provided with teeth on the posterior edge and a few teeth on the tip of the anterior edge. The caudal fin is deeply forked, with pointed lobes. There is a large pectoral pore.

Sorubimichthys planiceps, the Roundhead Shovelnose Catfish or Firewood Catfish ("Peixe Lenha"), occurs in the Amazon and Orinoco basins. The true limits of this species's range are not clear because of the status of the other two species included in the genus. Actually, *S. planiceps* may be the only species in the genus; *S. spatula* and *S. gigas* were described on only one specimen each and the differences were stated as being very slight. This is another large catfish, with lengths of more than 2 meters (TL) reported. Most of the individuals imported for the aquarium trade are only 25 to 40 cm, making tanks of 210 liters or bigger a necessity. The Roundhead Shovelnose does fairly well in captivity but should have adequate filtration and aeration. Water conditions are otherwise not that important. This is an easily spooked fish, so adequate hiding places should be provided. It is also a strong jumper, thus sudden movements, tapping on the glass, turning the lights on suddenly, etc., are to be avoided. In addition, a cover weighted for more security should be used. The Roundhead Shovelnose Catfish is a predatory species that will dine on live fishes, so in a community situation its tankmates must be chosen carefully. Along with live fishes, you can feed things such as beef heart, frozen brine shrimp, frozen fish, and other meaty foods. Although quite attractive as smaller individuals, larger specimens tend to lose the spotting and banding to become a uniform grayish color.

This young individual of *Sorubimichthys planiceps* has the potential of growing to more than two meters in length. It is best to start it out in as large a tank as possible. Photo by Hilmar Hansen.

The genus *Sorubim* contains about three species. The body is elongate and the head is exceptionally flat. The eyes are lateral in position, visible equally from above and from below, and the barbels are fleshy. The upper jaw is longer than the lower jaw and the mouth is as wide as the broadest part of the head; most of the teeth on the front of the upper jaw are exposed by the prolongation of the upper jaw. The teeth of the upper jaw are arranged in a band that is wider than deep and slightly curved. Those of the vomer are in two patches (possibly confluent in large adults) that are oval-triangular in shape, and there is a very large elongate-oval patch of palatine teeth on each side. Some small plates may be present on the anterior portion of the lateral line. The dorsal fin is provided with a spine and is situated midway between the tip of the snout and the posterior end of the adipose fin. The adipose fin is shorter than the anal. The pectoral fin has a spine and about 8 rays; the ventral fin has 14 rays.

Sorubim lima, the Duckbeak Shovelnose Catfish ("Bico de Pato" or "Cucharon"), is occasionally seen in the hobby. It has a fairly

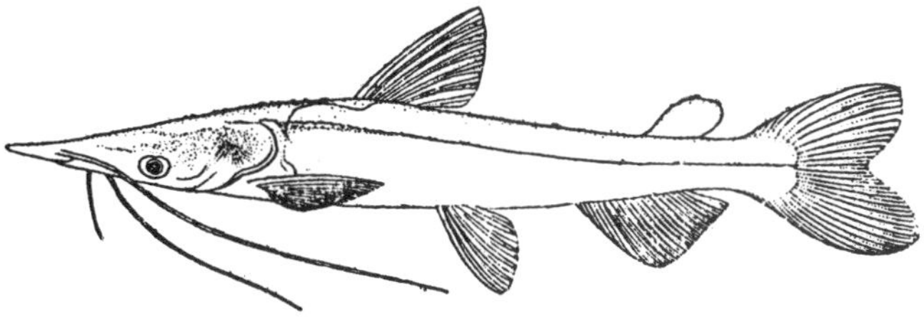

Sorubim lima. (From Fowler, 1945.)

broad range extending from the Amazon to the Rio de la Plata and including many of their affluents. It attains a length of at least 40 cm (FL) and may even get as large as 60 cm. It is a nocturnal or crepuscular fish that lies hidden among the debris of the river bed during the day and searches for food with the aid of its barbels during the evening hours. The barbels are said to have somewhat separate functions, the maxillary barbels being used for detecting obstacles and for the initial tasting of food items, while the mandibular barbels are primarily for the detection of the proximity of the food to the mouth. The barbels are brought into play as the fish moves four to five centimeters above the substrate. The main food items in nature are said to be small fishes and crustaceans.

Because of its size and activity the Duckbeak Shovelnose needs a large aquarium, one a meter long being sufficient for a couple of individuals. It is not fussy about water conditions, although slightly soft and acid water seems to be preferred. In nature the water tested was pH 6.5-6.9, carbonate hardness 3-10 THf, total hardness 5-15 THf, conductivity 150-250 μS/cm, and a temperature of 22-26°C. Good filtration and aeration are highly recommended, and there should be decorations providing adequate hiding places (driftwood, plants, rockwork, etc.). It is a good idea to provide some floating plants to cut down the light level. *Vallisneria* and *Echinodorus* may be used, as may be the floating *Salvinia* and *Limnobium*. Unfortunately, the flattened snout of this fish may be used to excavate the substrate, forcing the aquarist to replant the tank from time to time. If the fish

Sorubim lima is another popular shovelnosed catfish that also grows to a large size. The large snout may be used to dig up the tank substrate, making replanting necessary from time to time. Photo by Dr. Herbert R. Axelrod.

is startled or exposed to bright light it will most likely dash wildly about the tank, possibly injuring itself if it smashes its nose against the side of the tank, or it may leap out of an uncovered tank. It will eat a wide variety of foods including small fishes and crustaceans, assorted worms, frozen foods, and even dried foods; plants are not harmed directly. The Duckbeak Shovelnose is quite hardy and does not fall prey to many aquarium sicknesses. It has been reported to shed a mucous membrane in captivity if conditions become too intolerable. It is a good community tank fish as it does not seem to be an aggressive species, but smaller fishes, such as tetras 5 cm or less long will probably be eaten. Large *Leporinus, Abramites*, and *Anostomus* are okay.

Spawning in captivity is rare and no fry have been reported raised. In one instance the parents dug a shallow nest in the gravel beneath some driftwood. Eggs were laid and both parents guarded the nest. No fry were obtained. Sexual dimorphism was not reported.

Very young individuals are said to have a disproportionately long caudal fin, the lower lobe extended into a swordtail-like arrangement almost as long as the body of the fish itself. This tail, however, becomes proportionately more normal with growth, and by 15 cm the adult shape is attained.

When resting, this fish does not lie on the bottom but will seek shelter beneath an overhanging rock or piece of driftwood or even a leaf of a plant. If no suitable cover is available during the day, it may just hang in the corner. On one occasion an individual was seen hanging head-down next to a plant leaf. With its dark lateral stripe it blended in quite well and was difficult to see. This may possibly be a means for hunting unwary prey or perhaps just a unique way of hiding.

The genus *Paulicea* is a small genus of only two species. The head is quadrangular in shape and depressed. The postoccipital process does not extend as far as the predorsal plate; the postcleithral process is rugose; the fontanel is short and narrow. The barbels are short. The mouth is wide, about two-thirds the width of the head. The premaxillary teeth are arranged in the form of a broad band with the lateral portions projecting in a sharp angle; the vomerine and palatine teeth form a narrow band that, because of a pair of constrictions, is divided into three portions, one median vomerine and two lateral palatine, that may be united or partially separated. There is a strong pectoral fin spine that is toothed on the posterior edge and ends with a membranous point. The adipose and anal fins are about equal in length. There are 3-4 + 5-6 gill rakers on the first branchial arch.

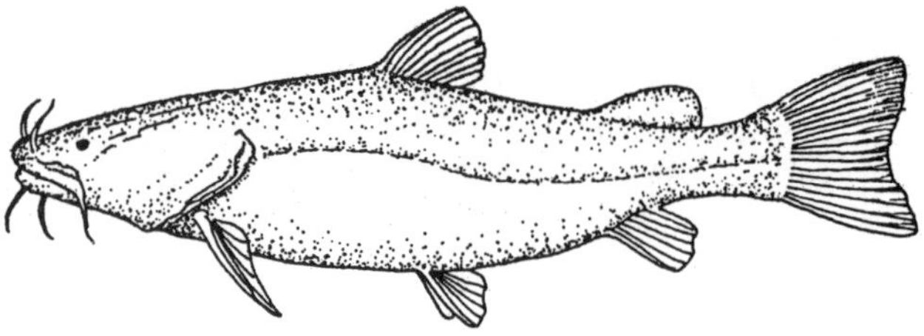

Paulicea lutkeni.

Paulicea luetkeni is known as the "Jáu" and occurs from the La Plata basin to the Amazon. It is a large catfish, attaining a length of 1.5 meters and a weight of 150 kilos. This heavy weight is due to the fact that it is the grossest Neotropical catfish in girth and has even been called blubbery. The adults are an olive-green, but the younger individuals may also have some dark spots dorsally. This is another catfish that has a reputation for causing problems when eaten. Among the problems attributed to the "Jaú" are all types of skin diseases, hemorrhoids, inflammations, and miscarriages. The larger individuals were observed at the Rio Madeira rapids feeding on medium-sized characins (20-40 cm) that conveniently are trapped below the crest of a cataract during low water. Goulding reports that more than the other catfishes it appears to actively chase these fishes in the turbulent waters caused by the cataract. Smaller individuals may feed on fleshy fruits as well when they enter the flooded plains.

The genus *Steindachneridion* is a small genus of only four species from southeastern Brazil. The head is large and depressed to greatly depressed, and the postoccipital process extends to or almost to the extended, triangular predorsal plate; the fontanel is moderate in length and narrow. The mouth is anterior and large, the premaxillary and man-

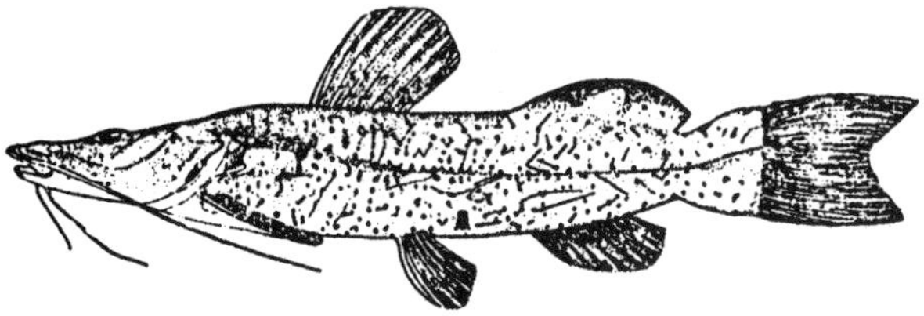

Steindachneridion scripta.

dibular teeth in bands with parallel sides and no prolongations or extensions. The vomerine teeth are disposed in a single large patch or in two separate oval patches; there are no palatine teeth. The eyes are supralateral in position. The dorsal fin is equidistant between the snout tip and the middle of the adipose fin. The dorsal and pectoral fin spines are weak and end in a membranous point. The adipose fin is longer than the anal fin. There are 8-10 branchiostegal rays.

The genus *Merodontotus* contains only a single species from the Rio Madeira. The body is elongate, subcylindrical, while the head is long and depressed, becoming narrower toward the front. The top of the cranium is

Merodontotus tigrinus. (From Britski, 1981.)

covered with thin skin so that the sculpture of the bones is visible through it; the supraoccipital process and predorsal plate are long, their tips almost in contact. The frontal fontanel is small and restricted to the interorbital area. The eyes are very small, about 5.5 times in the interorbital space; the barbels are terete. The teeth are small and depressible, those of the palate smaller than those of the premaxillary and dentaries. The band of premaxillary teeth is long, the ends extended posteriorly. The teeth of the palate are present only on the vomer and are in the form of two subtriangular patches separated in the middle by a narrow space. The first (spinous) ray of the dorsal and pectoral fins is weak and flexible, that of the pectoral with at least some fine teeth posteriorly. The dorsal has i+6 rays, the ventral i+5 rays. The ventral fins are situated behind the insertion of the dorsal fin. The adipose fin is much longer than the anal fin. The caudal fin is forked, the upper and lower lobes ending in filaments.

Merodontotus is most similar to *Brachyplatystoma* and *Goslinia*, having in common the general aspect of the body, the number of fin rays, the forked caudal fin, and the "rastros" is short and in the form of a spine. However, it differs from those two genera as follows: the ventral fins are posterior to the origin of the dorsal in *Merodontotus* but above the last rays of the dorsal in the other two; pterygoid teeth are present in *Merodontotus* but absent in *Goslinia* and *Brachyplatystoma*; vomerine teeth are separate in *Merodontotus*, united in *Goslinia* and *Brachyplatystoma*; and the posterior prolongation of the premaxillary tooth bands is present in *Merodontotus* but absent in the other two genera. In addition, the barbels are terete in *Merodontotus* and *Brachyplatystoma* but flattened in *Goslinia*; the skin of the upper portion of the cranium is thin in *Merodontotus* and *Brachyplatystoma vaillanti* but thick in *Goslinia* and other *Brachyplatystoma*; the supraoccipital process is almost touching the predorsal plate in *Merodontotus* and *B. vaillanti* but distant in *Goslinia* and the other *Brachyplatystoma* species; and finally, the adipose fin is long in *Merodontotus* and *B. vaillanti* but short in *Goslinia* and the other *Brachyplatystoma* species.

Merodontotus tigrinus has a very attractive color pattern that can be compared only with *Brachyplatystoma juruense*. They both have a yellow body with oblique black stripes, but the stripes of *M. tigrinus* are continuous when viewed laterally while those of *B. juruense* are broken or divided. This species appears at the Rio Madeira cataracts at low and rising water.

The genus *Goslinia* seems to be an intermediate form between the flat-headed members of the family and the typical heavier-bodied forms. It contains only a single species, *G. platynema*. The body is moderately elongate and the head depressed. The skin on the upper part of the cranium is thick, and the postoccipital process does not approach the predorsal plate. The eyes are very small and supralateral in position. The barbels are long

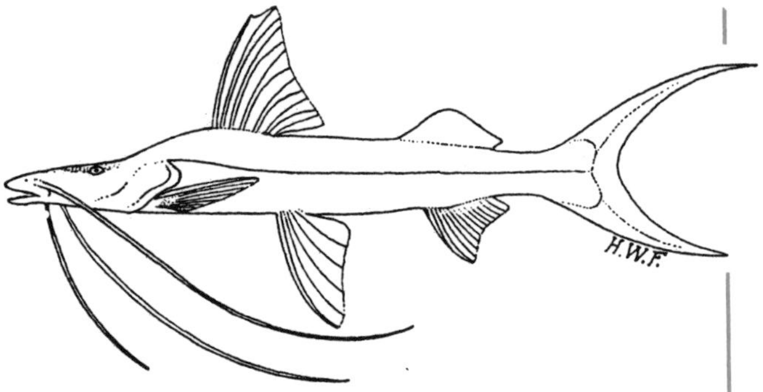

Goslinia platynema. (From Fowler, 1951.)

and flattened, the maxillary pair extending at least to the anal fin. The mouth is terminal and fairly large. There are no pterygoid teeth, and the vomerine teeth are disposed in a single, undivided patch. The premaxillary band of teeth is without the posterior prolongations on each side. The ventral fins are situated above the last rays of the dorsal fin. The adipose fin is approximately equal to and opposite the anal fin. The caudal fin is forked, with the upper lobe longest.

Goslinia platynema has been called the Slobberer or "Babão" because to the fishermen the wide, flattened, very long mandibular (mental) barbels look very much like mucus hanging from the mouth. It attains a length of about 80 cm (FL) and a weight of at least 5 kilos. It is not very colorful, being grayish to black dorsally fading to a dirty white ventrally, and would not be sought after by aquarists. It is not well known but does appear to migrate during the high water or flood season, perhaps the only species of large pimelodid to do so. It has been-suggested that the schools are moving toward spawning grounds that may be the swampy areas of the Rio Beni or Rio Mamore in eastern Bolivia. Nothing is known of its feeding habits (Goulding, 1981). It is caught commercially by means of gaffs and drifting deepwater gillnets, most of the catch being adult fish.

The genus *Luciopimelodus* contains only a single species from Parana, Rio de Prata; Corrientes; and Buenos Aires, Argentina. The head is more or less depressed, its top covered with skin. The frontal fontanel is prolonged until above the eyes, and there is a circular depression in the base of the postoccipital process. The postoccipital process does not extend to the predorsal plate. The upper portions of the cheek, nasal, and occipital surfaces are reticulated. The barbels are scarcely margined; the maxillary barbels are somewhat flattened and extend to beyond the origin of the anal fin, the mental barbels extending almost as far. The snout is broad, elongated, depressed to somewhat spatulate, and has a terminal mouth that is large and has the upper jaw projecting beyond the lower. The teeth are arranged in a band in each jaw, that of the premaxillary with a long extension posteriorly on each side; there are no teeth on the palate. The dorsal and anal fins are emarginate, the first rays of both fins slender, flexible, articulated in the upper half, but not branched or pungent. The first dorsal fin ray is longer than the succeeding rays, and the pectoral ray, which is similar, has some small teeth on the posterior margin. The adipose fin originates at the spot reached by the last rays of the folded dorsal fin, its base included about 3 times in the body length. The anal fin has 12 rays. The caudal fin is forked, with both lobes long and pointed. The swim bladder is reduced, divided anteriorly into two small lobes, and is separated from the skin by an adipose layer without forming a pseudotympanum.

Luciopimelodus pati is a riverine species that attains a length of about 41 cm. It is quite frequently caught on lines in the lower reaches of the rivers and is most common where the water is turbid and deep and there is a moderate current.

The genus *Megalonema* is a small genus containing about five or six species. The head is more or less depressed and the postoccipital process is narrow, not extending as far as the predorsal plate; there are no postcleithral or humeral processes. The occipital fontanel is absent or reduced to only a pore, while the postoccipital process is narrow and extends only to the middle of the distance to the dorsal fin. The eyes are without a free orbital rim, having a well-developed adipose eyelid, especially dorsally. The barbels are usually long, flattened and do not have a fringe; the anterior pair of mental barbels originates well in front of the base of the posterior pair. The premaxillary band of teeth does not have the

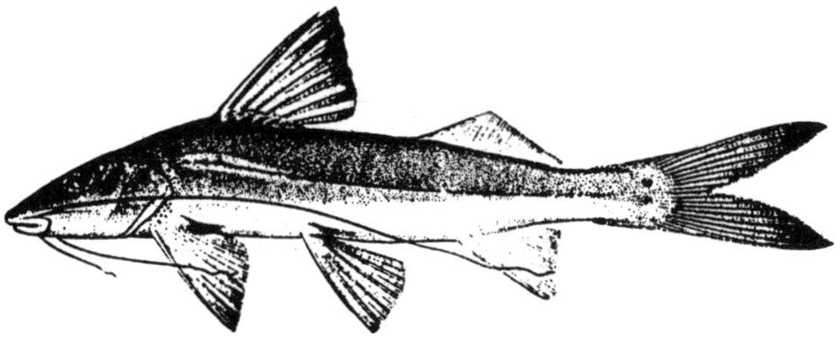

Megalonema platycephalum. (From Eigenmann, 1912.)

posteriorly directed lateral angles; there are no teeth on the palate. The first dorsal and pectoral fin rays are flexible, not pungent, and are prolonged into a filament. The pectoral fin has 12-14 branched rays. The swim bladder is reduced and divided anteriorly into two small lobes. It is separated from the skin by fatty tissue and no pseudotympanum is formed. The gill membranes are free from the isthmus.

M. platycephalum that was caught on a hook and line had beetle larvae, fish scales, and catfish spines in its stomach.

The genus *Perugia* contained only three species. The type species, *P. agassizi*, was found to be a synonym of *Pinirampus pirinampu*, the other two species, *P. argentina* and *P. xanthus*, were moved to genus *Megalonema* (Stewart, 1986).

The genus *Brachyglanis* is a genus of perhaps four or five species mostly from Guyana, although one species was discovered in the Rio Negro. The skull is covered with a thick layer of muscle tissue and has a median ridge to near the eye; the fontanel is short. The eyes are small, lack a free orbital notch, and are not strictly superior in position. The occipital process is very short. The premaxillary teeth are disposed in a band that does not have backwardly extending angles. The dorsal and pectoral fins have well-developed pungent spines. The adipose fin is not connected with the caudal fin, and the anal fin is short. The ventral fins are located under the posterior half of the dorsal fin. The caudal fin is forked, the lobes short and equal.

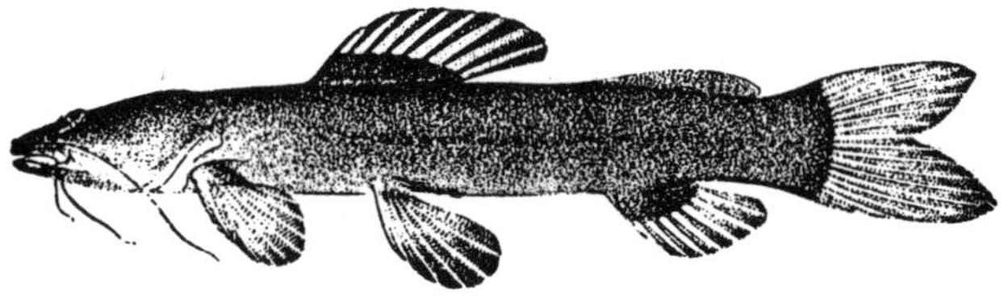

Brachyglanis melas. (From Eigenmann, 1912.)

The genus *Cetopsorhamdia* contains about nine species mostly from northern South America, especially Colombia and Venezuela. The head is subconical with a projecting snout. The frontal fontanel is small and far removed from the long parietal fontanel. The skull is covered with skin; it is not granular. The orbit is without a free margin and the occipital process is minute. The vomer and palate are toothless. The first dorsal and pectoral rays are not spinous. The adipose fin is three times as long as high and its base is longer than that of the anal fin. The anal fin is moderate. The origin of the ventral fins is below the dorsal fin. The caudal fin is forked, the lower caudal lobe the longer. (After Eigenmann & Fisher, 1916.)

The genus *Caecorhamdella* contains only a single species from São Paulo, Brazil. The body is long and slender and the head is rounded and somewhat depressed. The head is covered with skin and the fontanel is long

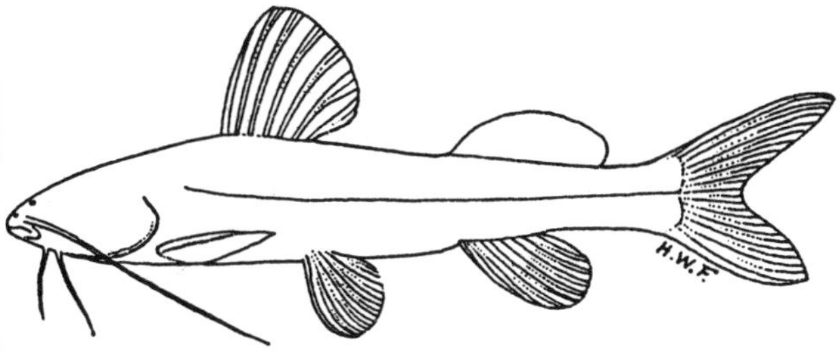

Caecorhamdella brasiliensis. (From Fowler, 1951.)

and slit-like, extending to the base of the occipital process. The occipital process is comparatively long and spear-shaped, but it does not extend as far as the predorsal plate, reaching only three-fourths of the distance to the plate. The eyes are entirely absent, with the orbit completely covered with skin. The maxillary barbels extend to or a little beyond the tips of the pectoral fins. The dorsal fin is short and high, with a spine (contained 1.25 times in the head length) and 6 rays. The adipose fin is short, included about 5 times in the standard length. The anal fin has 9 to 10 rays. The caudal fin is forked, with the upper lobe the longer. According to Borodin (1927), the only species of this genus is closely allied to *Rhamdella*, particularly *R. foina*, and he was inclined to designate it as merely a variety of that species. He eventually decided, however, that it was different enough to warrant its own genus. *Caecorhamdella* differs from *Rhamdella* not only by the absence of eyes (*Caecorhamdella* means blind *Rhamdella*), but in the form and length of the occipital process and in the length of the dorsal and adipose fins.

The genus *Cheirocerus* includes three species, one from Rio Mamore, one from Rio de los Pajaros, and the third from Rio Purus. It can be distinguished from all other pimelodids by the following features. The mouth is ventral and has relatively fleshy lips, the upper lip with a deep pocket on each side that extends mesially almost to the midline. The premaxilla is broad and thin, triangular in shape, and perforated with small holes. The swim bladder has crimped edges, some of which lie against the skin and can, in some individuals, be seen externally. The swim bladder also has slender, hollow tube extending anterolaterally on each side to just below the surface of the skin and terminating after some configurations with the free, closed end ventrolateral to the basioccipital. In addition to these diagnostic features other identifying characters include fleshy papillae on the gill arches; no teeth on the roof of the mouth or premaxilla (at least in adults); posterior cleithral process absent; pectoral fin spine serrate, without dorsal flange at the base; second dorsal fin ray (homologue of the dorsal spine) thin and flexible; relatively elongate adipose fin; and supraoccipital process relatively slender, articulating posteriorly with slender nuchal plate. (After Stewart & Pablik, 1985.)

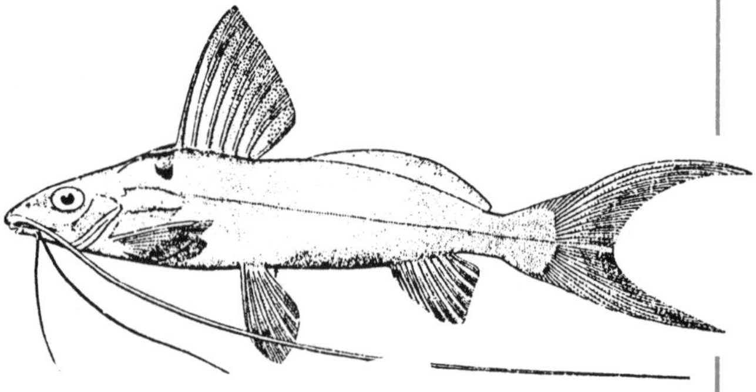

Cheirocerus eques. (From Eigenmann, 1917.)

Cheirocerus goeldii seems to be more typical of lowland big rivers in deeper, warmer waters, in contrast to *C. eques* which seems to prefer cooler, shallower waters of the Andean foothills. This latter species was captured by seining at night on sandy beaches in meter deep, swiftly flowing waters. Specimens of *C. goeldii* were taken by trawl in relatively deep water. All three species had a large midge larvae component in the stomach contents.

The genus *Sovichthys* was described for a single species from the Maracaibo Basin in Venezuela. The single species is *S. abuelo*. "Abuelo" is Spanish for "grandfather," a name applied to this fish possibly because of the extremely long maxillary barbels extending beyond the caudal fin. Because the unusual pouches of the upper lip, the structure of the premaxillaries and gill rakers, and the body form are very similar to *Cheirocerus eques*, *Sovichthys* has recently been synonymized with *Cheirocerus* (Stewart, 1982), an action that has not been challenged.

The genus *Perrunichthys* contains only a single species from the Maracaibo Basin in Venezuela. The head is greatly depressed anteriorly, the width included about 1.2 to 1.25 in the length. The supraoccipital process is longer than its base and extends as far as the predorsal plate. The interorbital space is a little concave, and the eyes, contained about 3.25 in the interorbital space, are superior (not visible from below) and have a free margin. The nostrils are widely separated and closer to the snout tip than to the eyes; the

Perrunichthys perruno. (After Schultz, 1944.)

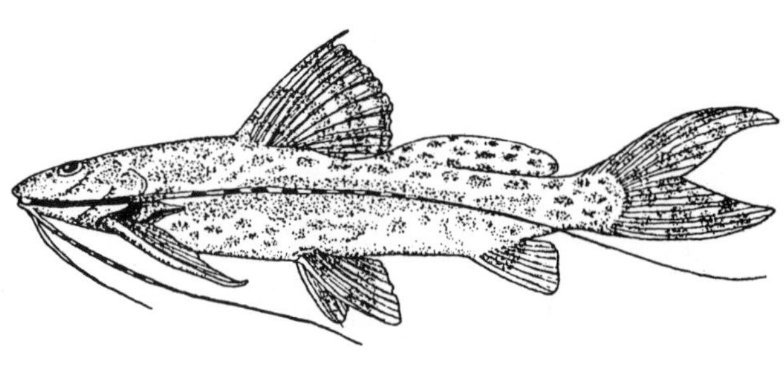

anterior nostril is tubular and the posterior nostril is covered with a flap. The maxillary barbels are thick at the base and gradually taper to a fine filament that extends in some specimens as far as the caudal fin. The mental barbels are remote from the tip of the chin. The band of premaxillary teeth does not have posteriorly projecting corners. There are very small patches of villiform teeth on the vomer and palatines, those of the vomer with their long axes running transversely, and the patches may or may not meet at the midline; the palatine patches are widely separated from the vomerine patches. The dentary also has a band of villiform teeth. There are groups of finger-like canals branching from the lateral line ventrally and ending in pores. The dorsal fin possesses a pungent spine that has a flexible produced tip extending beyond the branched rays. The adipose fin is very long, about twice the length of the anal fin base. The pectoral fin has a thick, broad spine with antrorse teeth on the anterior margin and strong retrorse teeth along the posterior margins. The rounded caudal peduncle supports a forked caudal fin. There is a sharply pointed triangular spiny projection a little longer than the eye diameter that extends posteriorly from the shoulder girdle above the pectoral fin axil. The gill membranes extend forward with the usual narrow free fold behind a pouch; the gill membranes are free from the isthmus. The gill rakers are stiff and about 15 or 16 in total number on the first arch (4 or 5 + 11). The swim bladder is large.

The single species, *Perrunichthys perruno*, has been kept in captivity. It is suggested that the tank be as large as possible and the water as clean as possible (good aeration and filtration) and the fish supplied with a varied diet. Among the food items can be chunks of meat

Perrunichthys perruno is one of the aquarist's favorite large pimelodids, largely because of its beautiful coloration. It bears a remarkable resemblance to one of the *Leiarius* species. Photo by Dr. Herbert R. Axelrod.

or fishes, small shrimp, and even dead and dying fishes. The species is capable of leaping out of the tank when disturbed, so a tight cover and no sudden movements when around the tank are highly recommended.

The genus *Platystomatichthys* contains only two species. The head is narrow and depressed anteriorly, with the snout somewhat produced, even spatulate, and with teeth covering its underside (mostly in front of the lower jaw). The inner edge of the operculum has one or two folds of skin (pouches). The eyes are small, superior (not visible from below), and have a free margin. The nostrils are widely separated, the posterior one always much closer to the anterior nasal opening than to the eye. The maxillary barbels are long, extending beyond the caudal fin, with the basal half ossified and the outer portion flexible; the bases of the mandibular barbels are far from the edge of the lower lip. The width of the mouth is contained about 1.5 times in the head length. The premaxillary and dentary teeth are arranged in bands, that of the premaxillary arrow-shaped. The vomer has a single patch of teeth; the palatines have elongate patches widely separated from the vomerine patch. The dorsal fin has a spine and 6 rays. The adipose fin is longer than the anal fin. The ventral fins are inserted approximately below the posterior end of the dorsal fin. The caudal fin is deeply forked, with pointed lobes. The gill membranes are not joined to one another but extend well forward before becoming attached to the isthmus; sometimes a narrow free fold is present.

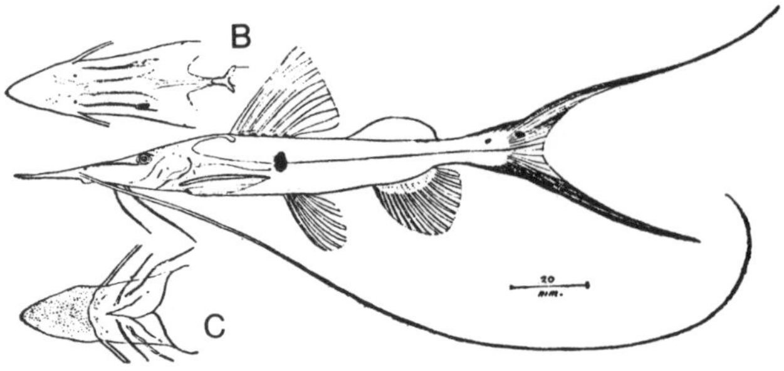

Platystomatichthys sturio; (b and c) dorsal and ventral views of head. (From Fowler, 1951.)

The type species, *P. sturio*, has roughened plates on the anterior portion of the lateral line and the dorsal fin spine is long, slender, and has recurved teeth on its posterior margin, as does the pectoral fin spine.

The genus *Duopalatinus* is a small genus of perhaps four species. The head is more or less conical and not greatly depressed anteriorly, the head width usually 1.5 to 1.7 times in its length. The snout is rather long and somewhat pointed, the upper jaw not greatly pro-

A young *Platystomatichthys sturio*. The flattened snout may turn up at the end as shown here. Photo by Hilmar Hansen.

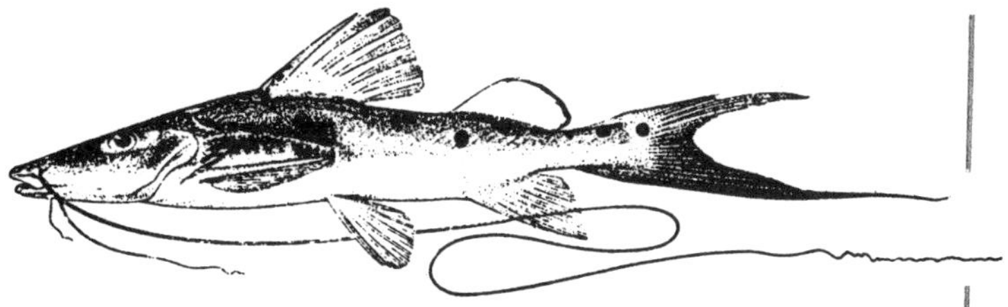

Duopalatinus goeldii.

longed and depressed but more normally shaped. The fontanel is continued behind the eyes as a deep groove that is continued as far as the predorsal plate; the occipital process is longer than wide and is firmly attached to the predorsal plate. The eyes are superior in position and have a free margin. The maxillary barbels are long, extending to beyond the tip of the caudal fin, and in some species ossified to almost half their length, the unossified portion flexible and ending in a long, hairlike filament. The bases of the mental barbels are remote from the edge of the upper lip. The nostrils are widely separated, the posterior one usually much closer to the anterior nasal opening than to the eye. The inner edge of the opercle has one or two folds of skin or "pouches." A bony process behind the upper angle of the gill opening ends in a couple of roughened plates situated on the anterior portion of the lateral line. The villiform teeth on the palate and the lower jaw are all uniform, those in the lower jaw in a band, those on the palate in patches. The vomerine and palatine patches are distant from each other and larger than the eye, the palatine patches oval, the vomerine patches confluent at the midline (*Duopalatinus*) or widely separated (*Platysilurus*, see below). The premaxillary band of teeth is broad and has backwardly projecting angles laterally. The dorsal fin has a spine and 6 or 7 soft rays. The adipose fin base is much longer than the anal fin base. The ventral fins are usually inserted under the rear base of the dorsal fin. The gill rakers number about 4 or 5 + 11-12. The gill membranes are not joined to one another but extend well forward before their attachment to the isthmus; sometimes a narrow free fold is present.

The genus *Platysilurus* is now considered a synonym of *Duopalatinus* since the single species of *Platysilurus*, *P. barbatus*, was found to be a synonym of *Duopalatinus goeldii*.

The genus *Platynematichthys* contains only two or three species. The head is broad and depressed anteriorly, the surface of the skull bones furrowed and granulate but covered with skin; the occipital process extends to the predorsal plate. The margins of the eyes are free. The nostrils are widely separated, the posterior nostril always much closer to the anterior nasal opening than to the eye. The inner edge of the operculum has one or two pouches. The maxillary barbels are broad, band-like, and extend as far as the middle of the pectoral fins; the mental barbels are distant from the edge of the lower lip. The upper and lower jaws are about equal and both are provided with a band of teeth. The vomer is provided with a patch of teeth that is broad at the sides; the palatines are edentulous. The dorsal fin has a long, flexible spine and 6 rays. The adipose fin base is shorter than that of the anal fin (which has about 16 rays). The pectoral fins have a spine (fine teeth on outer edge and strong teeth on the inner edge near the tip at least in *P. punctulatus*) and 9 rays. The ventral fins are usually inserted below the rear base of the dorsal fin. The caudal fin is forked. The gill membranes are separated from each other and extend well forward before their attachment to the isthmus.

Platynematichthys notatus is widespread and inhabits a wide variety of habitats. It is spotted dorsally and anteriorly and possesses a large black patch on the lower lobe of the caudal fin. It attains a length of about 80 cm.

The genus *Platypogon* is a monotypic genus containing only *P. coerulorostris* from Para The head is conical with the snout convex above and moderately rounded in front. The top of the head is covered by thick skin, forming a smooth surface with fine striations barely indicated. The eyes are large and round. The fontanel does not extend behind the eye, and a very short groove extends back and terminates abruptly. The occipital process tapers back to a narrow point where it barely comes in contact with the predorsal plate. The premaxillary teeth grow long posteriorly and lie flat, pointing straight backward. They are in broad bands, widest at the middle. The vomerine and palatine patches of

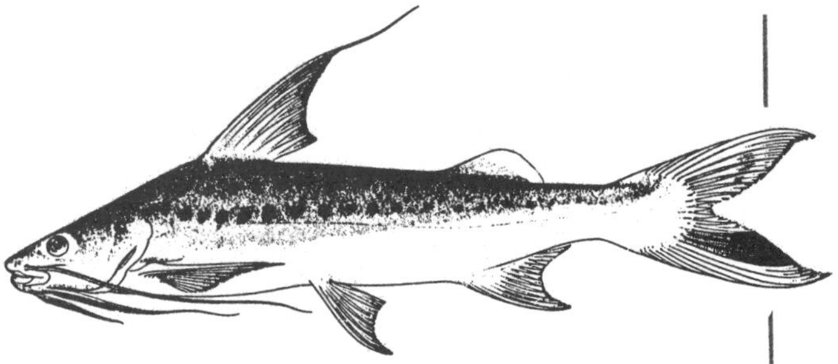

Platypogon coerulorostris. (From Starks, 1913.)

teeth form a continuous band, slightly narrower in the middle. All the teeth are freely movable. There are three pairs of barbels, a maxillary pair and two mental pairs. The maxillary pair extend as far as the base of the ventrals, the postmentals to a little beyond the middle of the pectoral fin, and the mentals to the base of the pectoral fins. The barbels have a membranous posterior margin, especially the mentals and postmentals where the membrane is as wide (or even a little wider) than the fleshy part of the barbels.

The dorsal fin has a filamentous spine reaching to the adipose fin, and 6 rays. Its base is contained 2 1/2 times in the space between it and the adipose fin. The adipose fin base is almost as long as the anal fin base and is situated opposite to it. The anal fin has 14 rays and is deeply emarginate. The caudal fin is widely forked, its lower lobe slightly longer.

Platypogon coerulorostris is doubtfully distinct from *Platynematichthys notatus*.

The genus *Phractocephalus* contains only a single species. The body is rather stout and tapers rapidly toward the caudal. The head is heavy, as broad as long, and the interorbital area is flattened; the upper portion of the head has vermiculate elevations, and the bones behind the eye are variously grooved and granulated. The occipital process is broadly rounded behind and does not quite reach as far as the predorsal plate, which is also rounded. The eyes are small, about 9 in the head length, and have free margins. The nostrils are far apart, the posterior much closer to the anterior nasal opening than to the eye. The inner edge of the operculum has one or two folds of skin (pouches). The maxillary barbels do not extend much beyond the

The very colorful *Phractocephalus hemioliopterus* does well in captivity feeding on a variety of items. In nature it attains a length of over a meter on a diet of fishes, crabs, and even fruit. Photo by Dr. Herbert R. Axelrod.

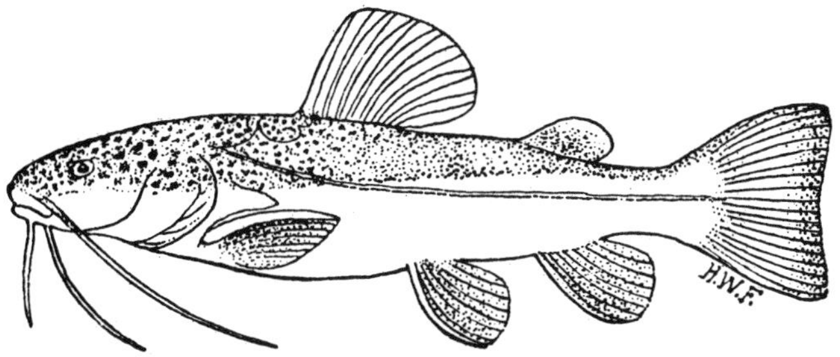

Phractocephalus hemioliopterus. (From Fowler, 1951.)

one always much closer to the anterior nostril than to the eye. The inner edge of the operculum has one or two folds of skin (pouches). The maxillary barbels are long, extending past the caudal fin and the bases of the mental barbels are far from the edge of the lower lip. The upper jaw is not greatly prolonged and is flattish but normal, the lower jaw only a little shorter than the upper jaw. The teeth in the jaws are all similar, those of the premaxillaries

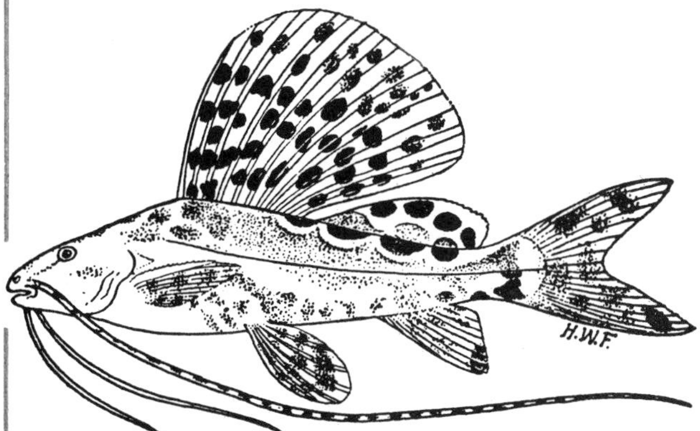

Leiarius pictus. (From Fowler, 1951.)

dorsal fin and are located on the edge of the lip opposite the anterior nostril; the bases of the mental barbels are remote from the edge of the lower lip. The lower jaw is included, and the teeth are all similar. The teeth of the premaxillaries and dentaries are arranged into bands, that of the premaxillaries broad and of equal width throughout. The vomerine teeth are arranged into a broad patch while those of the palatines are formed into narrower wedge-shaped patches contiguous with the vomerine patch. The dorsal fin has a spine and 7 rays, these rays as well as those of the broad, slightly emarginate caudal fin are thick, terete in cross-section, and branch only once or twice. The adipose fin is short, high, and with the distal portion generally transformed into rays; its base is longer than that of the anal fin. The pectoral fin spine is as thick as that of the dorsal fin and possesses broad lamellae in front and sharp, recurved teeth posteriorly. The gill membranes are separate from one another and extend well forward before their attachement to the isthmus. There are 4 + 15 gill rakers.

The single species, *Phractocephalus hemioliopterus*, is a large fish attaining a length of 1.3 meters and a weight of 80 kilos. It is quite colorful, with marked countershading and bright orange tips to the vertical fins (including the adipose fin). The underside may be a brilliant white. This species feeds on a variety of items including fishes, crabs, and even fruits.

The genus *Leiarius* contains only two species. The head is narrow and depressed, flattish above, and the fontanel is not continued beyond the frontal bones. The eyes are superior in position and have free margins. The nostrils are widely separated, the posterior

and dentaries in bands, those on the palate in patches. The small patches of palatine teeth are distant from those of the vomer and are transversely arranged. The dorsal fin has a spine and 9 or 10 rays. The adipose fin base is longer than that of the anal fin base. The ventral fins are inserted below the posterior part of the dorsal fin base. The caudal fin is deeply forked. The gill membranes are not joined to each other and are joined to the isthmus well forward.

Species of the genus *Leiarius* have occasionally been kept in captivity. They require large tanks and clean, clear water. The decorations should be smooth edged (no sharp rocks, etc.) for the barbels and fins are easily damaged (the barbels at least regenerate quickly). The diet should be varied. This is not difficult as the fishes will eat almost anything, but they prefer live fishes and worms. The tank should be well covered, for *L. pictus* (the species commonly kept) is said to be a bit nervous and will leap out of the tank easily when disturbed.

The genus *Rhamdiopsis* contains a single species from Rio Iguacu. The head is almost round and very little depressed, the posterior portion of the body somewhat compressed. The head is partially naked and granular and the fontanel extends to the occipital process but is weakly separated from it by a bridge behind the eye; the occipital process is not united with the predorsal plate. The humeral process is very small and pointed. The eyes are small and without free margins. The barbels are all flattened and band-like toward the

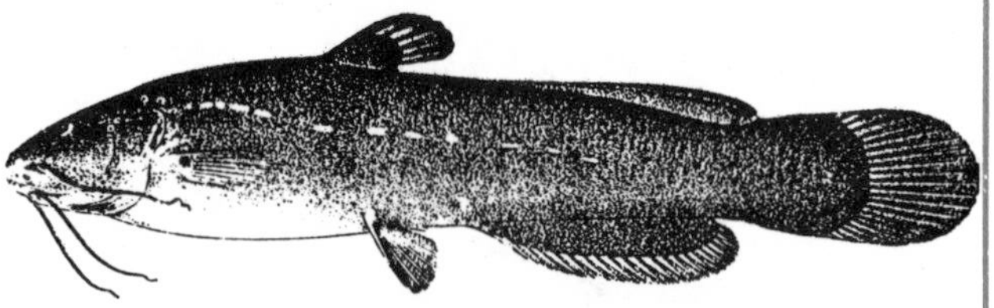

Rhamdiopsis moreirai. (From Haseman, 1911.)

tip, the margins on one side somewhat membranous. The jaws are weak and subequal, and the teeth are in narrow bands on the premaxillaries and dentaries. There are no teeth on the vomer. The distance between the dorsal and adipose fins is greater than the length of the dorsal fin base. There is a minute rudimentary spine at the base of the first dorsal fin ray. The dorsal fin has 7 rays and the anal fin has 21 rays. The anal and adipose fins are elongate, both more or less united to the rounded caudal fin but both separated from it by a notch in the membrane. The ventral fins have 7 rays and originate slightly behind the level of the dorsal. The pectorals are supplied with a weak, slender, soft-tipped spine. This genus, with the single species *R. moreirai*, is said to be closely related to *Heptapterus*. (After Haseman, 1911.)

The genus *Rhamdella* is a moderate-sized genus of about 12 species that has the general characters of *Rhamdia*. It differs from *Rhamdia* chiefly by having the frontal fontanel prolonged backward to the base of the postoccipital process; in *Rhamdia* it does not continue to the back of the eye. The head is covered with thick skin and is flattened; the snout is long and pointed. The postoccipital process does not touch the predorsal plate so that the bony bridge does not exist. The orbital margin is free. The premaxillaries have a visible

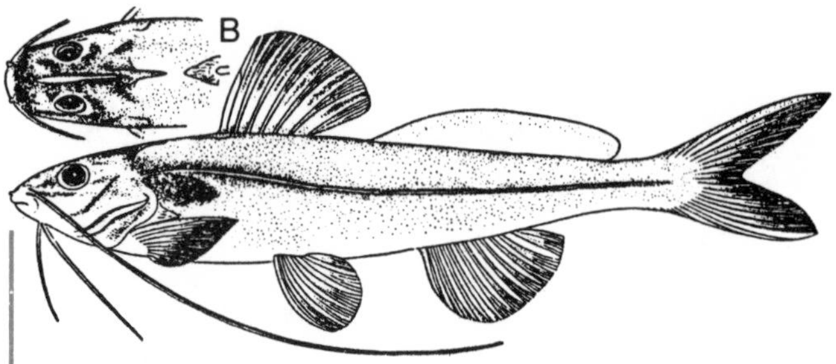

Rhamdella robinsoni; (b) dorsal view of head. (From Fowler, 1941.)

band of villiform teeth. The dorsal and pectoral fins are provided with strong spines. The adipose fin is long but separated from the forked caudal fin.

The type species, *R. eriarcha*, has an elongate, slender body and a long, pointed head. The eye is large. The maxillary barbels extend only to the edges of the opercles. The upper jaw is projecting and the lips are thick and strongly plicate. There are no teeth on the palate. The forked caudal fin has the upper lobe greatly produced.

The genus *Bagropsis* is very close to *Pimelodus*. The top of the head is striate and entirely covered with skin. There are two moderately large patches of teeth on the vomer and larger

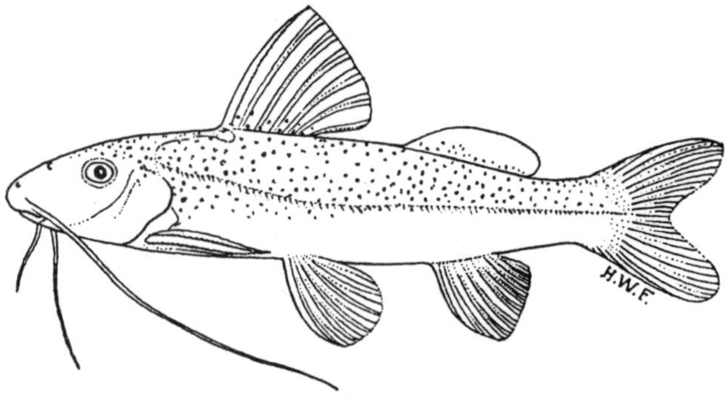

Bagropsis reinhardti. (From Fowler, 1951.)

patches on the posterior portion of the palate. The single species, *B. reinhardti* from Rio das Velhas, has a broad, depressed head with the fontanel between the eyes. The eyes are a little posterior to the center of the head. The upper jaw projects about half an eye diameter. The maxillary barbels extend to the anal fin. The dorsal fin has a strong spine that is serrated on the inner edge near the tip, while the pectoral fin spine is moderately broad, curved, and has strong teeth on the posterior margin.

The genus *Bergiaria* contains only two species, one from Rio das Velhas and the other from Rio da Prata. The type species, *B. westermanni*, has the head granulated and entirely naked above; the snout is long and subconical. The interorbital area is a little narrower

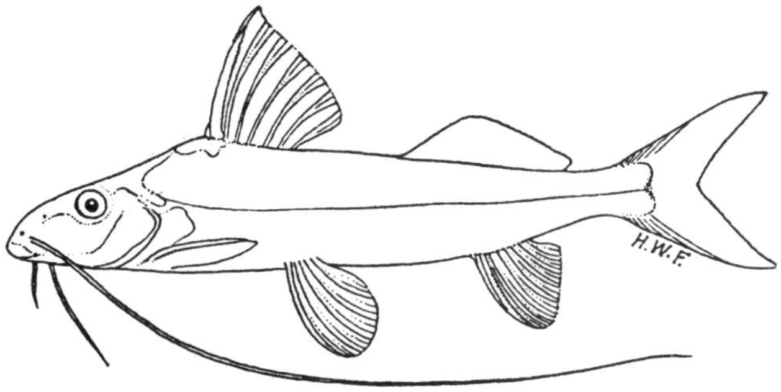

Bergiaria westermanni. (From Fowler, 1951.)

than the eye, which is contained about 5 times in the head length. The maxillary barbels are long, extending to the tip of the caudal fin. The mouth is small and the lips are broad; there are no premaxillary teeth. The dorsal fin contains a spine that is serrated posteriorly and 6 rays; and the pectoral fins possess spines. The adipose fin is long, about 4 in the body length, and the anal fin has 12 or 13 rays. The caudal fin rays are not produced.

The genus *Goeldiella* contains only a single species, *G. eques*, from Guyana. It is described as having a body that is not as wide as deep at the level of the pectoral fins and is compressed toward the caudal. The head is flattened or depressed, the whole upper portion striate or granulose, and the fontanel extends as a narrow groove to the occipital crest. The occipital crest is flat and emarginate, and it articulates with the shield-shaped predorsal plate. The eyes are large, being contained only about 5 times in the head length. There is a deep groove from the maxillary barbel to below the eye; the maxillary barbels are long, extending to beyond the tip of the caudal fin. The chin and snout are provided with numerous pores, and the jaws are subequal, the upper one a little longer than the

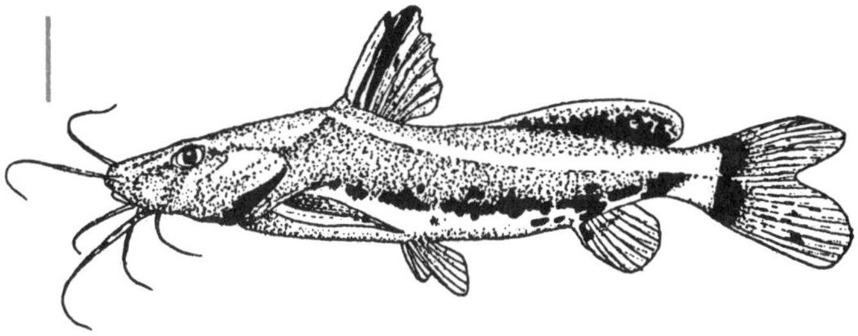

Goeldiella eques.

lower. Both lips are papillose. The teeth in the jaws are arranged in bands, that of the lower jaw broadly interrupted in the middle. The dorsal fin has a rather weak spine. The pectoral fin spine is very long and strong, with strong retrorse teeth on the posterior edge and extrorse teeth on the anterior edge. The anal fin is rounded. The adipose fin is long, about 3 to 3½ times in the length. The caudal fin is obliquely rounded, the lower portion longer.

The genus *Nemuroglanis* contains a single species, *N. lanceolatus*, from the Rio Jutay, a tributary of the middle Amazon. It is elongate and slender, with the head and body depressed and the tail compressed. The head is narrowed forward and its surface is covered with thin skin; there is no evident occipital process. There are no bucklers (basal plates) in front of the dorsal fin. The maxillary barbels reach beyond the origin of the dorsal fin, which is located above the ventral fins. The dorsal fin has no spine nor does the pectoral fin, which is long and lanceolate. The adipose fin is long and low and is joined to the caudal fin; the distance of the adipose from the dorsal is somewhat greater than the length of the dorsal fin itself. The anal fin is of about equal height throughout its length. The ventral fins are long and narrow. The caudal fin is lanceolate, the rays rapidly tapering from the middle ones, which are greatly prolonged. The color of the fish is a uniform yellow.

The genus *Conorhynchus* is a genus of perhaps two species from Brazil. The head is compressed and the snout (in the type species) is produced and pointed. The fontanel extends to near the occipital process but not to behind the eye; the occipital process extends to the predorsal plate. The humeral process is long and spine-like. The dentition

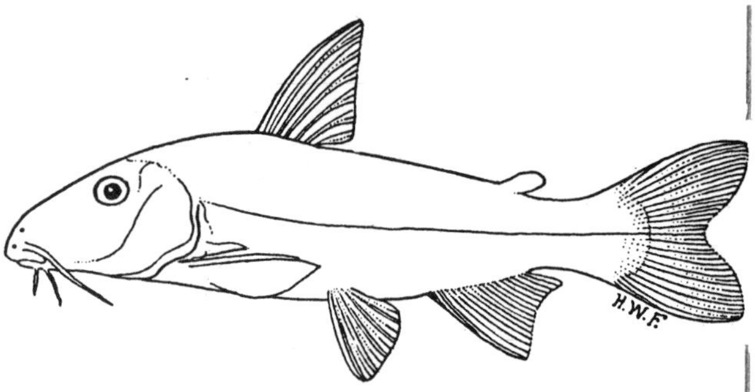

Conorhynchus glabrum. (From Fowler, 1951.)

is very weak and disappears with age; the teeth on the vomer, when present, are formed into minute patches. The adipose fin is higher than long. There are 18 to 20 anal fin rays. One of the species of the genus, *C. glaber* (not the type species), has a blunt snout with an inferior mouth. The eye is large, contained about three times in the head length. The dorsal fin has a spine and 6 rays, the spine with a few small teeth on the basal half of the posterior edge. The pectoral spine is about as long as the dorsal fin spine, and its anterior edge has hooks near the tip; its posterior edge has 7 large "thorns."

The genus *Rhamdia* is a large genus containing about 60 nominal species, although the number will probably become greatly reduced once the genus is revised. The head is depressed and longer than wide, the upper part not granulose but covered with skin. The fontanel is hidden and the parietal ends at the level of the eyes. The occipital process, although well developed in most species, does not extend to the predorsal plate, a character that distinguishes this genus from the very similar and closely related *Pimelodella*. The postcleithral process is short and has a wide base. The eye has a free orbital rim. The barbels are cylindrical or flat, with the bases of the mandibular and post-mental barbels almost in a straight line. The snout is depressed, not prolonged, and the vomer is edentulous or has only small teeth. The adipose fin is long. The caudal fin is forked, with more or less pointed lobes.

Rhamdia branneri. (From Eigenmann, 1917.)

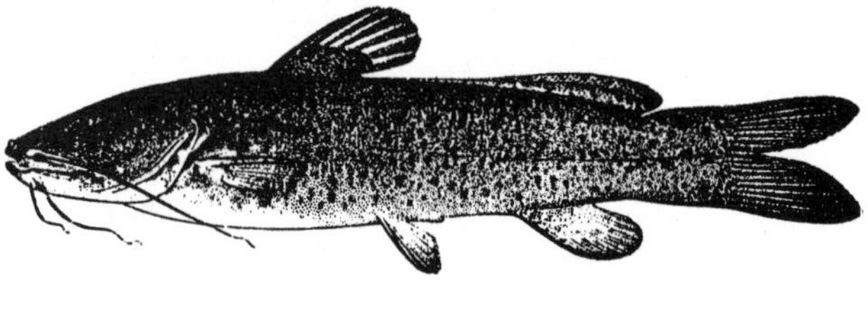

Rhamdia is widely distributed in Central and South America. In Central America it extends as far north as Mexico; in South America it is spread over much of the eastern and southern sections as far as Rio de La Plata. It extends westward to the Andes, and species have been found even in Lake Titicaca, but it seems to be absent in rivers that drain into the Pacific Ocean.

The genus *Caecorhamdia* is apparently a synonym of *Rhamdia*. The eyeless form described as *Caecorhamdia urichi* is, according to Norman (1926), almost identical to *Rhamdia*

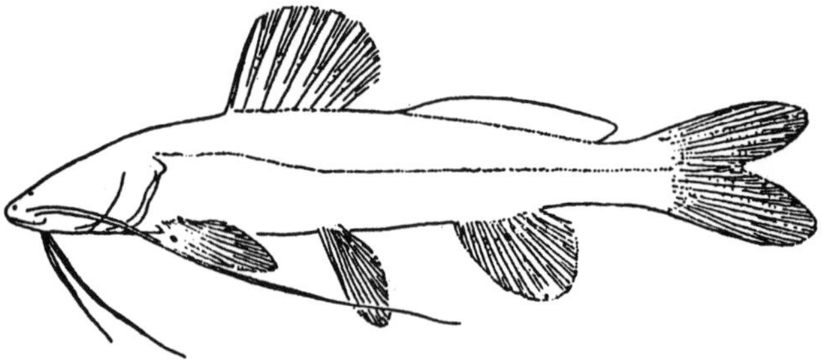

Rhamdia quelen urichi. (From Eigenmann, 1917.)

quelen except for the lack of eyes and the somewhat longer mandibular barbels. Norman admitted erecting the genus to draw attention to "this interesting fish" even though "were the eyes developed, the specimens from the Guacharo cave would probably be identified with the species *Rhamdia quelen*." As do most cave dwellers, *R. quelen urichi*, as it has now been called, lacks pigmentation, but according to Mees (1974) there is supposed to be a whole range of intermediates in the cave from eyeless and without pigment to fully eyed and normally pigmented.

R. quelen does well in captivity, growing rapidly if well-fed and kept at a temperature of about 20° to 25°C. The ground color of the juvenile is yellowish but this changes to a gray color with age, the speckling of the juveniles tending to become lost in the adult color. *R.*

quelen attains a length of about 35 cm.

Another species, *R. sapo*, inhabits both lakes and rivers of northern Argentina, Uruguay, and southeastern Brazil, but it seems to prefer rivers that have a very slight current. It grows to 41 cm and in some parts of its range has become a moderately important food fish.

R. sebae was collected in small streams, especially in debris-littered and mud-bottomed pools with occasional overhanging shoreline vegetation. It was best observed at night while foraging over the bottom. Stomach contents included insect material and plant debris. Ants and fly larvae were most abundant (Saul, 1975).

Rhamdia branneri is called the "bagre amarillo" because of its yellow coloration, although it also has dark brown spots and blotches and the fin tips are dark. The dorsal fin spine is small and weak while the pectoral fin spine is long and slender; the pectoral spine has teeth on both edges. The barbels are short and terete.

It has been discovered that some *Rhamdia* excavate burrows or subterranean chambers below the stream beds (Glodek, et al., 1978). This was found in *R. wagneri* in the tributaries of the Rio Palenque (Guayas drainage) in western Ecuador. *R. cinerascens* may also be involved in the actual construction of the chambers. The benefit to these fishes seems to be a cooler place to live and/or a place from which to escape some predators. Taking advantage of these ready-made burrows may be other catfishes (*Microglanis variegatus, Pimelodella modestus*, and some species of *Trichomycterus, T. taenium* and *T. laticeps*, for example) as well as non-catfishes (such as *Gymnotus* spp. and *Sternopygus macrurus*) on a permanent basis, although other species may occupy them when adverse conditions (drought, extreme temperatures, etc.) occur.

The genus *Imparfinis* (including *Nannorhamdia*) is a genus of some 14 or 15 species. The body is elongate and the head is much longer than its width across the pectorals. The posterior border of the skull is truncate, as if cut off straight, but there is a rudimentary postoccipital process; the predorsal plate does not reach the postoccipital process. The fontanel is a long slit that extends to the occiput. The eyes are superior in position and the orbital rim is free, although in small individuals the rim is poorly developed, especially above the eye. The maxillary barbels are short to moderate in length, extending in some species only to the pectoral fin base while in others they may reach as far as the end of the anal fin; the bases of the mental barbels usually are in a straight line. The posterior nostrils are nearer the eye than the anterior nasal openings. Bands of teeth are present on the premaxillaries and dentaries; there are no prominent or distinct teeth on the palate. The dorsal and pectoral fin spines are present but very inconspicuous and continued as soft, flexible rays that are longer than the bony part; the pectoral spines may, in some species, be weakly pungent. The dorsal fin has about 6 branched rays, sometimes 5. The ventral fins are normally inserted below the posterior base of the dorsal fin. The adipose fin is comparatively short. The caudal fin is forked. There is no pectoral pore. The gill membranes are not joined to each other but extend well forward before joining with the isthmus.

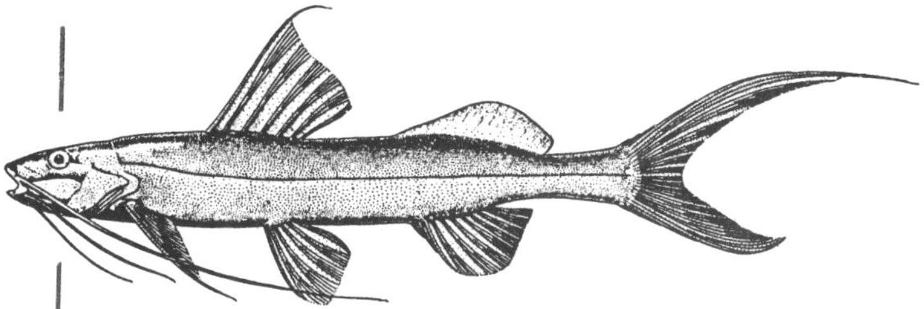

Imparfinis nemacheir. (From Eigenmann, 1922.)

The genus *Imparfinis* resembles *Rhamdella* and *Heptapterus* but differs principally in the non-development of the dorsal spine and the weakness or non-development of the pectoral spine. It also differs from *Heptapterus* by its possession of a free orbital rim, at least in older specimens (particularly noticeable in *I. piperatus* and least noticeable in *I. minutus*). The range of the genus is throughout tropical South America, both east and west of the Andes, and extending north into Central America at least as far as Costa Rica (Pacific drainage). The habitat, at least for some species, is said to be where small creeks run into a small water drop and pick up speed.

Imparfinis longicauda is unusual for the genus by having a long adipose fin and a long caudal fin. It is described as having about four conspicuous black bands and two black lines from the eyes to the tip of the snout as well as a black spot on the nape, all on a yellowish ground color. Two females about 6 cm long had insect remains in their stomachs.

I. lineata (formerly *Nannorhamdia lineata*) is taken in tributaries of the Rio Esquinas, Costa Rica. The streams are about 1-4 meters wide and have shallow rapids areas with small scattered pools; the bottom may be gravel or sand, and various grasses line the shore. The males are smaller than the females and have tubular papillae as opposed to the females' thicker, more conical papillae.

The genus *Pinirampus* contains only a single species. The husky body is elongate and compressed to a ridge above; the caudal peduncle is subcylindrical. The head is depressed, contained about 4.7 times in the length of the body, and covered with skin. The fontanel is not continued posterior to the eye, but a groove does extend to the occipital process; the occipital process is very narrow, and the postoccipital process extends to the predorsal plate. The eyes are small and superior in position. The barbels are band-like, margined with a broad membranous border, and extend to the anal fin. The snout tip is convex, and the upper jaw is a little longer than the lower one; the mouth is wide, the gape extending more than halfway to the eyes. The teeth of both jaws are minute, the ends of the premaxillary band rounded at all ages; there are no prominent or distinct patches of teeth on the palate. The first dorsal fin ray is not pungent but is continued as a filament, while the pectoral spine is flexible and flattened, with a roughened anterior edge and some straight teeth along its posterior margin. The adipose fin is long, the free margin of the anal fin is emarginate, and the caudal fin is lunate in small individuals and deeply forked in older individuals. The ventral fins are usually inserted below the posterior portion of the dorsal fin. The gill membranes are separate and are attached to the isthmus far forward. There are no rows of papillae at the base of the gill filaments.

Pinirampus pirinampu is sometimes referred to as the "Barba Chata," meaning flat whiskers, because of the flattened barbels. It is a large species attaining a length of at least 60 cm that is common along river banks or along the waterfronts of villages or even cities where it scavenges for whatever might be available. It is caught for food.

The genus *Iheringichthys* is a genus with only two species, one from Rio da Prata and the other from Rio Paraguay. The head is conical and the mouth is narrow, with fat lips. The eyes have free margins. There is no postcleithral or humeral process evident. The premaxillaries are without teeth in the adult, though in smaller individuals there are small inconspicuous teeth. There are no teeth on the palatines or vomer. The dorsal spine is pungent and has a locking mechanism that is well developed. This mechanism is unlocked by pulling out a short spine between the base of the predorsal plate and the base of the dor-

Pinirampus pirinampu. (From Fowler, 1951.)

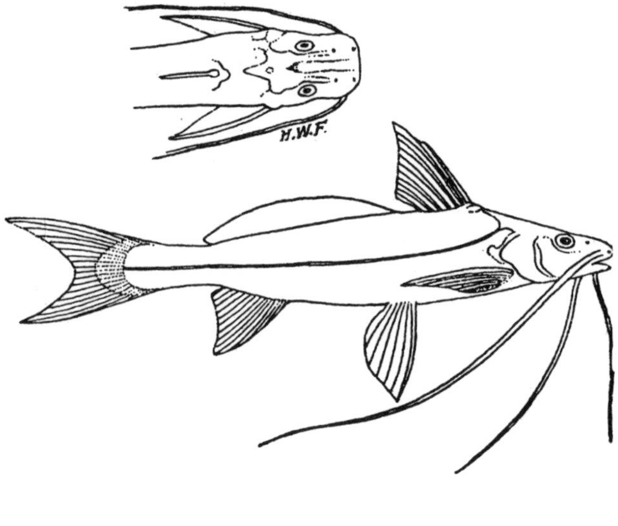

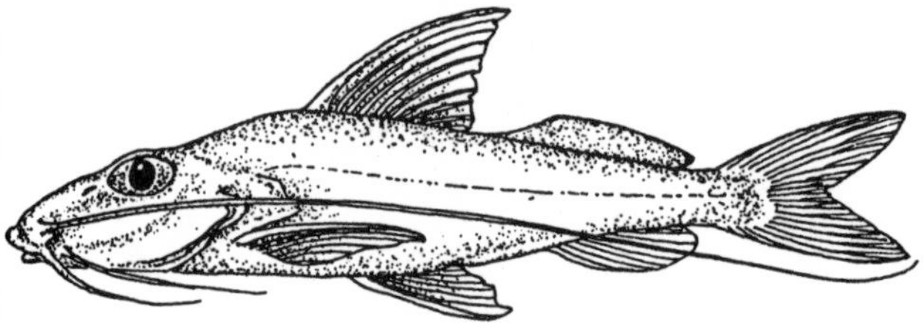

Iheringichthys sp.

sal fin spine. The pectoral fin spine is pungent, serrate on the anterior margin as well as on the posterior margin, and has a similar well-developed locking mechanism. The origin of the adipose fin is more than two eye diameters posterior to the dorsal fin base.

The genus *Myoglanis* contains only four species; *Leptoglanis* is a synonym. The cranium is covered by a thick layer of muscles. There is a frontal fontanel that barely extends beyond the eyes, and the skull behind the

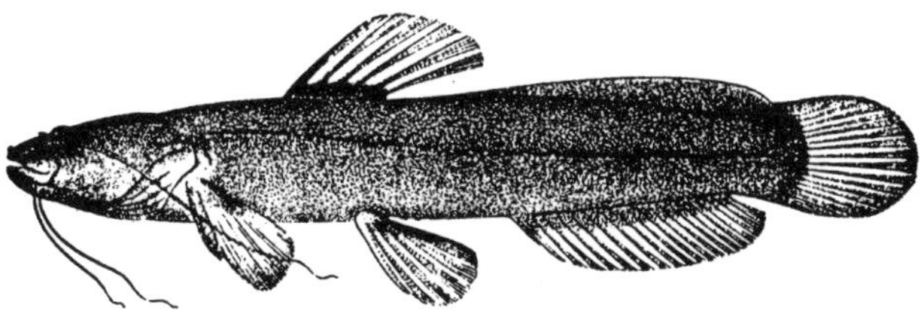

Myoglanis potaroensis. (From Eigenmann, 1912.)

fontanel is narrow and has a short occipital crest. The minute eyes are supralateral in position and are without free margins. The premaxillary teeth are arranged into two patches that form a crescent. The first ray of the dorsal fin is soft and flexible, but the pectoral fins have strong spines. The ventral fins are located below the posterior portion of the dorsal fin. The anal fin is long. The adipose fin is also long and low, continued toward the caudal fin with which it may or may not be united.

The genus *Parapimelodus* contains only a single species from the Rio de La Plata. The head is longer than it is wide but still anteriorly depressed. The upper surface of the head is exposed, the "bony" portion covered with thin skin. The postoccipital process extends backward to contact the predorsal plate, forming a bony bridge; the humeral or postcleithral process forms a triangular plate with a wide base. The eyes are lateral in position (visible both from above and below) and have free margins. The maxillary barbel is lodged in the supralabial groove that extends posteriorly to behind the eye. The premaxillary band of teeth is small and has rounded edges. The adipose fin is relatively short. The anal fin is a bit longer than that of species in the genus *Pimelodus*, its base longer than that of the adipose fin and having about 17 or 18 rays.

Parapimelodus valenciennis.

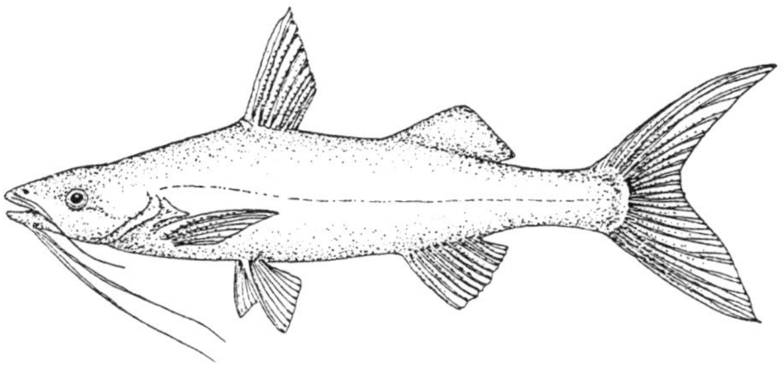

The genus *Piramutana* is a small genus containing but a single species, *P. piramuta*. It has the upper surface of the head and the occipital process granulated and covered with skin. The occipital process does not quite reach the predorsal plate. The maxillary barbels are flattened and band-like and extend beyond the base of the ventral fins. The teeth are cardiform, those of the vomer and palatines forming an uninterrupted band. The first ray of the dorsal fin is prolonged. The adipose fin originates half its length before the emarginate anal fin.

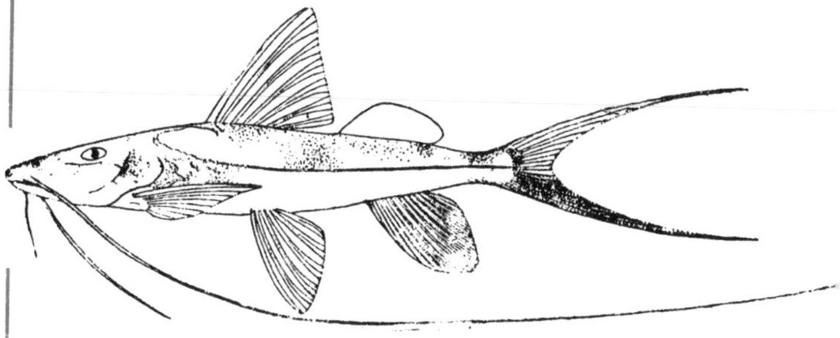

Piramutana piramuta. (From Fowler, 1945.)

The genus *Heptapterus* (including *Acentronichthys, Pariolius, Imparales*, and *Chasmocranus*) contains some two dozen species. The body is long and slender and the head is depressed. The head is entirely covered dorsally by a layer of thick skin. The occipital process is short and does not meet the predorsal plate, and the fontanel is narrow and usually extends to the occipital base, with or without

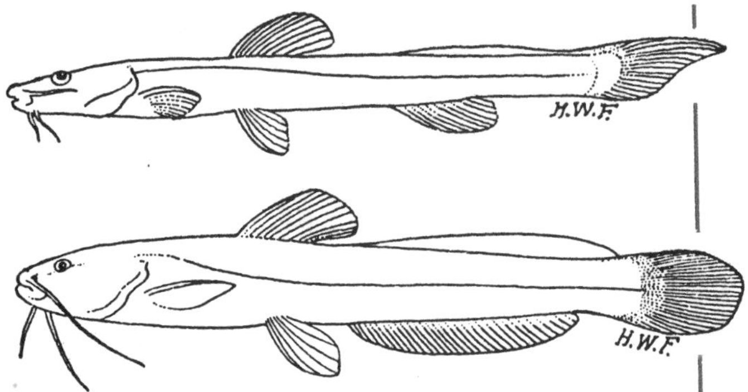

Heptapterus hollandi (above); *H. stewarti* (below). (From Fowler, 1951.)

an interruption behind the eyes. The eyes are small to minute, dorsal in position, and without free orbital margins. The barbels are short to moderate, extending in a few species as far as the base of the ventral fins. The teeth are arranged in bands in both jaws, and there may or may not be lateral posterior extensions to the premaxillary band; there are no teeth on the vomer or palatines. The dorsal and pectoral fins lack spines. The short dorsal (usually 7 rays) is located above the ventrals or a little in front or a little behind them; the ventrals are 6-rayed. The anal fin varies in length from short (with about 8 rays) to moderately long (with some 30 rays). The adipose fin is long and may be either broadly or narrowly connected to the caudal fin or entirely separate from it. The caudal fin is variable in shape, from pointed to rounded to forked. The gill membranes are separate at least to below the eye, and the swim bladder is free.

Most species are a brownish color, some with a few whitish markings and others with some weak dusky bars. They are distributed throughout tropical South America, as least as far south as Rio de la Plata, and barely extending into Central America (Panama).

Species of *Heptapterus* are not usually kept in aquaria. *H. leptos* is one of those that has been kept and is a crepuscular species requiring subdued lighting. The substrate should be relatively soft. Food is no problem, although live foods are preferred.

H. armillatus seems to prefer sand and gravel bottoms of creeks of relatively fast flowing water as well as sluggish waters of the same streams where aquatic vegetation is lacking. Trichoptera larvae were most abundant in stomach contents along with other insect debris and plant material (Saul, 1975).

The genus *Pseudopimelodus* (including *Zungaro* and *Cephalosilurus*) is a genus of perhaps a half dozen species and a few subspecies. The head is large and heavy, broadest between the opercles; the body tapers toward the tail and is covered with thick skin. The postoccipital process is well developed and extends to meet (or almost meet) the predorsal plate. The eyes are small, superior in position (directed upward), and without free orbital rims (covered with skin). The barbels are short to moderate in length, the maxillary pair extending to the pectoral base or as far as the second dorsal fin ray. The teeth are arranged in a band in each jaw, that of the premaxillaries with a backwardly projecting point on each side; there are no teeth on the vomer or palatines. The dorsal and pectoral

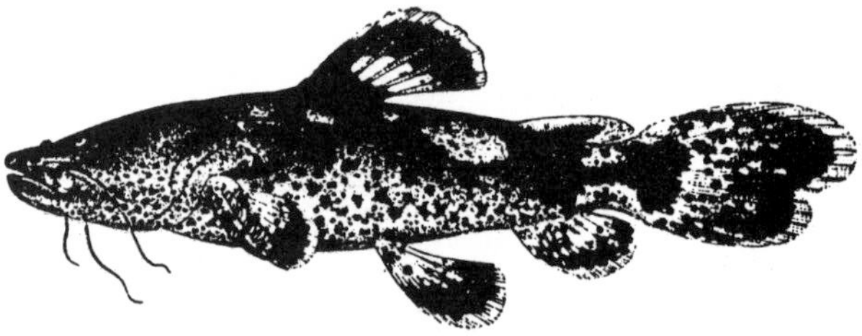

Pseudopimelodus albomarginatus. (From Eigenmann, 1912.)

fins have short spines; the dorsal spine may have teeth or be smooth, while the pectoral spine is longer and has well-developed teeth on both edges, although in rare instances on the posterior margin only. The adipose fin is short and rounded. The anal fin is short (only 7 to 9 rays). The caudal fin may be truncate, lanceolate, or even forked, with pointed or rounded lobes. A pectoral pore is present only in *P. zungaro*. The lateral line is complete but not conspicuous. Some species are not very colorful, being dark brown to blackish with paler markings (most noticeable in smaller individuals), while some may be very attractive with patterns of dark and light. The distribution includes tropical South America from Colombia to Uruguay, with at least one species inhabiting the Pacific side of the Andes from Colombia to Ecuador.

Probably the most popular species of

Pseudopimelodus in the hobby is *P. raninus*. This is one of the "bumblebee catfishes," a rather freely used common name involving not only another genus of the Pimelodidae (*Microglanis*) but also a genus in another family—*Leiocassis* of the family Bagridae. But since *Leiocassis* has a nasal barbel and the two genera of Pimelodidae under discussion do not, they are readily distinguished. Young *P. raninus* look like and are commonly confused with *Microglanis parahybae*, so much so that *P. raninus* entered in fish shows may win a prize for size when entered as *Microglanis parahybae*, for the former attains a length of over 15 cm while the latter reaces a size of only 6 cm. Although most species kept by aquarists are peaceful, as is *P. raninus*, some (such as *P. fowleri*) are very territorial and may not tolerate members of their own species in the same aquarium. Most species of the genus are easy to keep and grow well when fed with a variety of meaty foods. It has also been suggested (at least for *P. raninus*) that about 2 teaspoonsful of sea salt per 10 liters of water be added.

The genus *Lophiosilurus* is similar to *Pseudopimelodus* but its head is very large and very flattened. The occipital process meets the predorsal plate. The eyes are minute. The

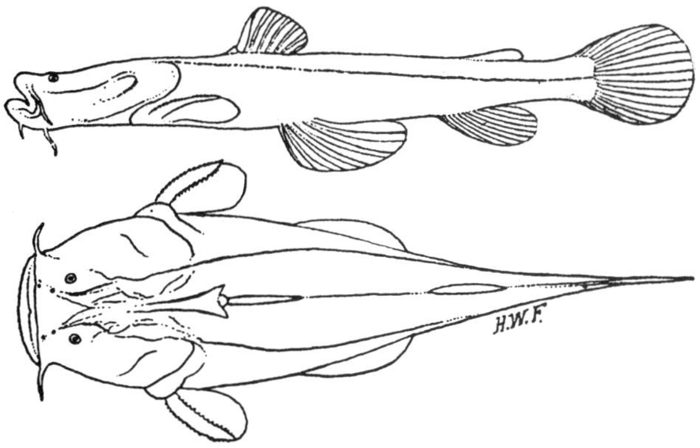

Lophiosilurus alexandri. (From Fowler, 1951.)

maxillary and postmental barbels extend only to the posterior margin of the orbit. The gape is oblique and the lower jaw projects. The premaxillary band of teeth is extended posteriorly at the outer edges. Both margins of the pectoral spines are serrated. The dorsal fin is short and the caudal fin is rounded. A single species from Brazil, *L. alexandri*, is included in this genus.

The genus *Microglanis* contains some eight species from tropical South America as far south as Rio de la Plata and extending west of the Andes in Ecuador. The head is large and heavy, about as wide as long, and flattened. The body tapers quickly to the tail. The cra-

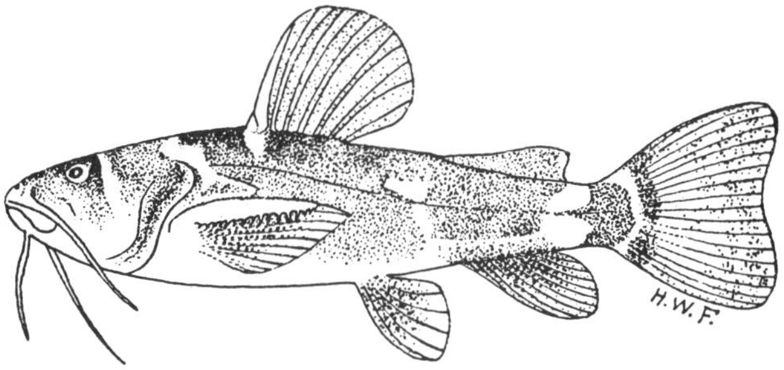

Microglanis parahybae. (From Fowler, 1951.)

nium is covered by skin. The frontal fontanel does not extend much, if any, beyond the eyes, and there may be a minute occipital fontanel; the occipital crest is small. The eyes are without free orbital margins, and the barbels extend to beyond the pectoral fin base, reaching at most a vertical through the origin of the dorsal fin. The band of premaxillary teeth does not have any backwardly projecting lateral edges as seen in the genus *Pseudopimelodus*. The dorsal and pectoral fin spines are well-developed, the dorsal spine with its posterior edge smooth, the pectoral spine with both edges serrate. The lateral line is complete, although there are no distinct pores on the posterior part of the body (*Pseudopimelodus* has the lateral line well developed and pores are evident through its entire length.) *Microglanis* is basically a miniature *Pseudopimelodus* differing chiefly in the shape of the band of premaxillary teeth, the reduction of the posterior portion of the lateral line, and its small size (Mees, 1976; 1978). As regards this last character, *Microglanis* does not get very large, its largest species, *M. parahybae*, reaching a maximum length of about 8 cm.

Microglanis is primarily nocturnal, usually hiding during the day in rocky caves, under driftwood, or even buried in the sand, and becoming more active at evening time or at night. The species are basically omnivorous and can be fed almost any of the normal aquarium live foods as well as some of the dry foods. A soft substrate is recommended, and the lighting should be subdued. Most species of the genus are peaceful enough for community tanks.

Microglanis poecilus from Surinam is a bottom-dweller inhabiting medium-sized forest creeks that have running water. They are usually found where the bottom is covered with decaying leaves in which they can seek shelter. *M. ater* from central Brazil is dark violet brown in color, the young, however, are lighter. *M. zonatus* has the distinction of being the only species of the genus with a rounded tail. *M. iheringi* is well marked and is considered one of the bumblebee catfishes. It prefers soft acidic (pH 6.9) water and is somewhat predatory in nature, feeding during the night.

M. parahybae, from the Rio Paraiba in southern Brazil, has a pleasing pattern and is often sold under the erroneous common names of bumblebee catfish or Siamese bumblebee catfish (actually *Leiocassis siamensis*). Its preferred common name is the Dwarf Marbled Catfish. It is rather peaceful, although it is not to be trusted with very small fishes as it has a large mouth for its size. It can also hold its own with many of the larger aggressive fishes, even some of the more territorial cichlids. It is not very demanding and can tolerate a wide range of conditions as long as extremes are avoided. Food is no problem as this omnivorous species will accept live as well as frozen and freeze-dried foods. Like the other *Microglanis*, this is an exclusively nocturnal fish and requires hiding places as well as subdued lighting.

M. iheringi prefers swift flowing waters over rock and gravel. The streams may be only a few centimeters deep and less than two meters wide. Insect debris (mostly ants) was found in the stomachs. (Saul, 1975.)

The genus *Pimelodina* contains a single species, *P. flavipinnis*, originally captured near Para, Brazil (Belem). The body is elongate and fusiform, with a compressed, trenchant back. The head is short, relatively slender, and covered with thick skin while the occipital process is long and narrow but does not reach to the predorsal plate. The eyes are small and slightly superior in position. Three pairs of barbels are present, a maxillary pair and two mental pairs arranged in a transverse line. The maxillary barbels extend at least to the end of the adipose fin in larger specimens and may reach past the caudal peduncle in specimens under 150mm. The snout is conical and produced well beyond the weak lower jaw. The dentition in both jaws is weak, consisting of narrow, transverse bands of loosely set conical teeth, yhose of the upper jaw in a wider band than the lower; no teeth are present on the vomer. The second ray of the dorsal fin (homologue of the dorsal fin spine) is articulated, long, and slender, scarcely spinous, and without serrations, extending, when depressed, well beyond the origin of the adipose fin. The first ray of the pectoral fin is also articulated and not pungent but has 30-40 slight serrations on the posterior margin. The anal fin is short with IV-VI,6-8 (total 11-14) rays, the pectoral with 12-13 rays, the dorsal with 1,6. The adipose fin is very long and the caudal fin is deeply forked. The lateral line is complete. There are a total of 20-29 gill rakers on the first arch. The branchiostegal membrane is free from the isthmus, overlapping slightly at the midline. The swim bladder is extremely reduced and mostly within a capsule. The non-capsulated portion is composed of two short, hollow, fingerlike structures. There is a short gizzard-like stomach with thick lateral muscle masses. (Stewart, 1986.)

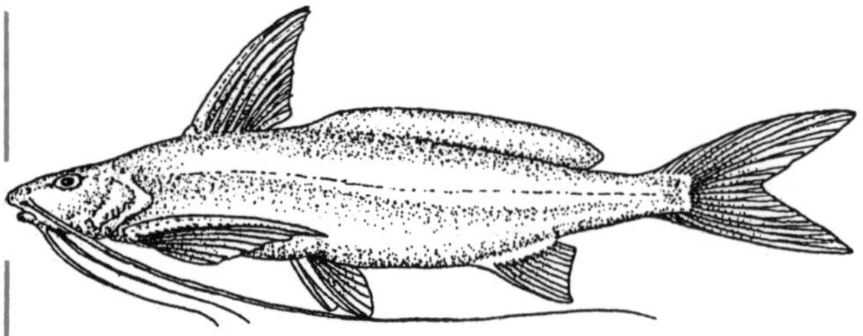

Pimelodina flavipinnis. (After Stewart, 1986.)

P. flavipinnis occurs in the Amazon River from Pucallpa, Peru to Belem, and has been recorded from Colombia and Venezuela as well. It is seen in lagoons where they are caught by commercial fishermen. Commercial fishermen also catch them as they migrate upstream in the Rio Amazonas together with *Semaprochilodus* in June. Their weak, ventral mouth probably means they are bottom suction feeders. Aquatic insects have been found among their stomach contents (Stewart, 1986).

Aguarunichthys is a monotypic genus, the single species, *A. torosus* from Aguaruna in the upper Rio Maranon region. The body is moderately elongate and the head broad and slightly depressed. There is a long, conical, fleshy snout above the distinctly subterminal mouth. The relatively small eyes are supralateral in position. The slender supraoccipital process extends posteriorly to the predorsal plate. The premaxillary teeth are in a broad band provided with posteriolateral extensions.

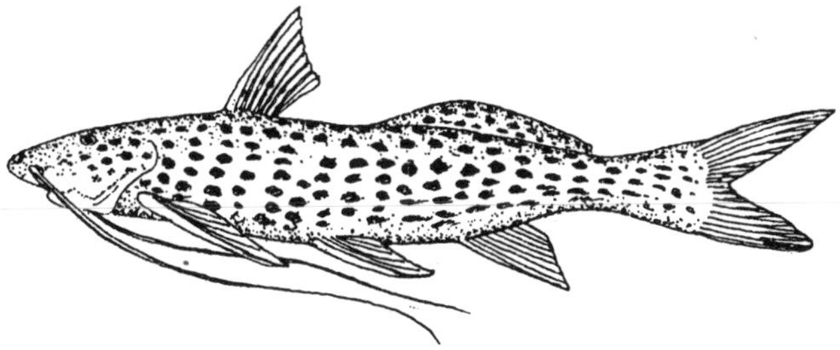

Aguarunichthys torosus. (After Stewart, 1986.)

A pair of maxillary barbels and two pairs of mandibular barbels present, the former extending posteriorly to just past the anal fin origin. The dorsal fin is short-based with a spine and 6 rays; the anal fin has 14 rays, the first five unbranched. The pectoral fin has a spine and 13 rays, the spine with fine serrations on its posterior edge. The adipose fin is moderately long but well separated from the dorsal and caudal fins. The caudal fin is forked with the upper lobe longer and more pointed than the lower.

Aguarunichthys has the swim bladder in which there are several fingerlike projections along its posterolateral margin and the anterior extension ending in a slightly expanded, pawlike distal tip lateral to the basioccipital. (Stewart, 1986).

The genus *Zungaropsis* contains a single species, *Z. multimaculatus*, from the Rio Xingu. This fairly compact fish (the body depth is contained slightly less than 4 times in the standard length) has a broad, depressed head. The eyes are not covered with skin and are free-bordered. The mouth opening is broad and the upper and lower jaws are about equal length. Palatine and vomerine teeth are present, forming a narrow band behind the broad band of jaw teeth which are about an eye diameter's width at the symphysis. The oval vomerine patches are separated from one another by a narrow gap. The nares are remote from each other. One pair of maxillary barbels and two pairs of mental barbels are present. The maxillary barbels extend as far as the tips of the ventrals. The skin is thick on the head, hiding the occipital process, and felt-like on the sides of the body. The occipital process appears to butt the predorsal plate. The dorsal and pectoral fin spines are well developed, the dorsal spine toothed posteriorly, the pectoral spine toothed on its inner edge. The dorsal fin has a spine and 6 rays and is 1 1/2 times higher than long; the anal fin, with 8 rays, is 2 times higher than long. The adipose fin originates at a vertical from the anal fin and ends behind it, its height about 1/3 its length. The upper lobe of the forked caudal fin is pointed, the lower rounded-oval. The body and fins are all covered with dark round spots, those on the head and nape smaller and more dense, those on the body increasing in size toward the caudal base, and those on the fins sometimes connected in vertical or oblique bands.

The genus *Typhlobagrus* contains a single blind cave-dwelling species from the area of São Paulo, Brazil. The body is robust and the head is depressed. The fontanel is very narrow and extends to the base of the occipital process, with a bridge across it above the posterior edge of the orbit, but is not easily detectable externally; the occipital process, also covered by skin, extends to the predorsal plate. The eyes are absent, two linear slits being the only indication of the position of the orbital region. The maxillary barbels are subterete and moderate in length, extending in the young to the bases of the ventral fins and in adults only to the tips of the pectoral fins. The snout is not produced, but the upper jaw is slightly projecting. The lips are very thin and adherent, while the teeth are arranged into bands of about equal width in each jaw such as found in *Rhamdia* or *Pimelodus*. The dorsal fin spine is well developed and about half the length of the head, but its tip is leathery, not pungent, and there are a few teeth present on the tip of the anterior edge; there are about 6 soft rays. The anal fin is relatively short, with 12-15 (usually 14) soft rays. The adipose fin is large. The pectoral fin is rounded, the spine moderate, with a smooth anterior margin and about 10 teeth along the posterior margin. The caudal fin is deeply forked, with the upper lobe longer than the lower lobe. The gill openings are wide, the membranes confluent with the isthmus under the orbital slits. The swim bladder is well developed.

Typhlobagrus kronei was found in Caverna das Areias (Sand Cave) of the subterranean course of Ribeiro das Areias, a tributary of the Rio Iporanga at São Paulo, Brazil. It is

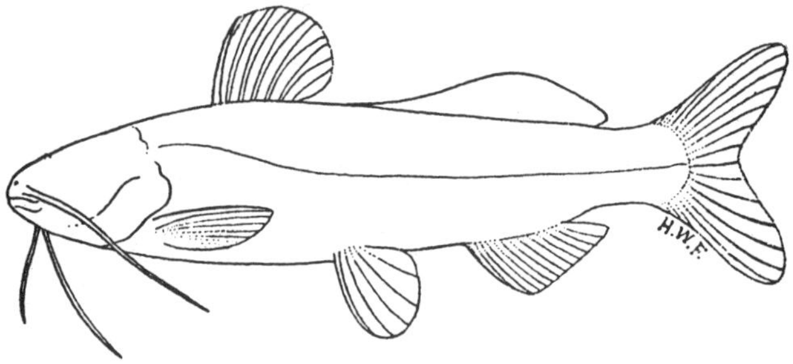

Typhlobagrus kronei. (After Fowler, 1951.)

very much like *Pimelodella lateristriga* but without eyes, and Haseman even suggested calling the species *Pimelodella lateristriga* var. *kronei*. In Iporanga they are called "ceguinho" by the natives who utilize them for food. Although eyeless, their other senses are very much developed (in almost all of them there are sensory pits beneath the head) and when touched they swim away rapidly. In aquaria they are omnivorous, eating a wide variety of items including earthworms, but they do not seem to feed well on insects or vegetable matter other than algae.

The genus *Pimelodus* contains about two dozen species and subspecies ranging from tropical South America into southern Central America (Panama). They are quite sturdy fishes of moderate to large size. The surface of the head is covered with thin skin, the

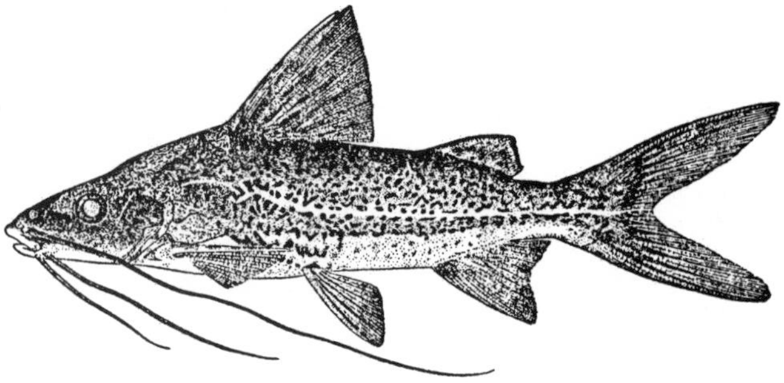

Pimelodus clarias. (After Schultz, 1944.)

bones beneath it having a granulose texture. The occipital process has a broad base then tapers posteriorly where it comes in contact with the predorsal plate. The frontal fontanel does not extend posteriorly beyond the level of the eyes. The eyes have free orbital rims. The barbels are long and cylindrical, the maxillary barbels extending at times to the base of the caudal fin or even beyond that point. The mouth is subterminal, with the teeth arranged into a band in each jaw; normally there are no teeth on the vomer and palatines (although a few species may have small patches on the vomer and pterygoids). The dorsal fin has a strong spine, almost always with teeth on the posterior margin, and 6 rays. The adipose fin is well developed but highly variable in length and height. The pectoral fin spine is strong, pungent, and serrated on both margins. The anal fin has about 10 to 14 rays and is rounded. The ventral fins have 6 rays. The caudal fin is large, deeply forked, the lobes sharply pointed. There may or may not be a pectoral pore.

The taxonomy of the genus *Pimelodus* (along with the genus *Pimelodella*) is very confused and much work is needed in this area to straighten things out. For example, *Pimelodus clarias* seems to have been a catch-all name for several species. Some "*clarias*" have turned out to be *P. blochii*, some *P. maculatus*, and some have been simply misidentified as totally different species as in the case of *P. albofasciatus*. To confuse the matter further for aquarists, the best way to distinguish *Pimelodus* from *Pimelodella* is by the shape of the postoccipital process, that of *Pimelodus* being more or less triangular, that of *Pimelo-*

della narrow and of equal width throughout, a character not readily investigated in living specimens.

Most species of *Pimelodus* are crepuscular and nocturnal to semi-nocturnal (a few species may be active during daylight hours), requiring tanks that have subdued lighting and many hiding places among the plants, rockwork, and driftwood decorations. The bottom material should be relatively soft and preferably dark in color. They are not demanding species but seem to be sensitive to very fresh, hard water. The temperature range should be in the neighborhood of 20° to 26°C. Most species are voracious feeders, staying hidden during the day, but as the light dims they become more active and start wandering about the tank in search of food. They require large amounts of food, especially live food. They especially like worms, with earthworms being an excellent food for the larger specimens. Insect larvae, bloodworms, and tubificid worms are eagerly accepted, and meaty foods of all kinds are taken. When well-fed these fishes grow rapidly and require larger and larger aquaria, therefore only the smaller individuals are generally suitable for most aquarists' tanks. These smaller fish are suitable for a community tank with fairly large tankmates; smaller surface-dwelling species may also be included. The larger individuals of *Pimelodus* are more aggressive and can only be kept with equal-sized, equally aggressive fishes, or they should be given their own tank. Like many other catfishes, their fin spines tend to catch in netting material (this has caused problems for fishermen who must spend hours removing them from their seines when they come upon a large school).

At this point discussions of individual species could be very misleading due to the confusion with the names. Besides the so-called *P. "clarias"* of aquarists (whatever it is), there is the Angelicus Pimelodella, often called *Pimelodella pictus*, a name that probably belongs in *Pimelodus* (several species are sold under this name, one of which seems to be a bagrid!), and the Four-lined Pimelodella of aquarists that may also be a species of *Pimelodus*.

Pimelodus ornatus is known to be a common inhabitant of rivers (though not creeks) of tropical South America from Colombia and

The genus *Pimelodus* is in great need of revision. The species are poorly understood, especially with regard to ontogenetic changes. This is probably *P. albofasciatus*. Photo by Dr. Herbert R. Axelrod.

Venezuela to Paraguay. It attains a length of about 25 cm and does fairly well with large cichlids and characins. Chopped earthworms along with small fishes and fat-free beef heart have been recommended for this species.

P. blochii is a species that also seems to prefer the larger bodies of water and keeps to the larger rivers and river mouths. *P. albofasciatus* occurs only in the upper course of the Sipaliwini River in Surinam.

The genus *Pimelodella* is one of the largest genera of the family, with more than 60 species currently recognized. They are distributed over tropical South America north to Panama. The species are generally slender in build and the head is not very large and is covered with thin skin. The postoccipital process is narrow, of equal width throughout, and extends to meet the predorsal plate. Frontal and parietal fontanels are present, the latter extending to meet the base of the postoccipital process. The humeral process is spine-like. The eyes are well developed and have free orbital rims. The nares are remote. The maxillary barbels are variable, extending to the end of the pectoral fin or even beyond the end of the caudal fin; the two pairs of mental barbels are sometimes arranged in a nearly straight line. The mouth is subterminal and the villiform teeth are arranged in a band in each jaw, the bands without any backwardly projecting angles at the end; there are no teeth on the vomer or palatines. The dorsal fin is essentially triangular in shape, the tip pointed or rounded off, and has a weak spine. The adipose fin is well-developed and usually very long, without a free portion at the posterior end (adnate). The anal fin is moderate in size, with 11 to 15 rays. The pectoral fins have strong pungent spines variously armed with teeth (usually on the posterior edge). The caudal fin is deeply forked, usually with one of its lobes longer or broader than the other. The gill membranes are free from the isthmus. There may be some form of sexual dimorphism present. The males of some species appear to have a filament on the dorsal fin that is absent in females and juveniles. Also, in *P. cristatus* there is a sexual difference in eye size (making some species described on the basis of eye size very dubious); individuals with eye diameters included less than 4 times in the head are males and those with eye diameters included more than 4 times in the head are females.

Pimelodella macturki is relatively small, of approximately 60 mm S.L., with ripe females of 50 mm S.L. being found (Mees, 1983).

P. hasemani was common over sand and mud bottoms free of vegetation, although they were found over rock and gravel bottoms as well. Stomach contents included insects and their larvae, fish scales, gastropods, and even small pebbles. Mayfly larvae and ants were most abundant (Saul, 1975.)

The genus *Brachyrhamdia* is considered by some authors (including G. S. Myers, who originally proposed it) a synonym of genus *Pimelodella*. The type species of that genus, now called *Pimelodella imitator*, was described as a naked catfish associated with *Corydoras melanistius* and having a color pattern almost identical to the *Corydoras* color pattern. It does not appear to school with the *Corydoras* nor actually with each other. Unlike the *Corydoras*, *P. imitator* is an aggressive feeder. Additional specimens of this or a similar species, but with a different color pattern (like a translucent *Corydoras* with a fairly distinct black area at the tip of the dorsal fin), were observed by Myers in captivity. They swam in mid-water like *Corydoras hastatus* but it could easily be seen that they had the very long maxillary barbels of the *Pimelodella* species. They were extremely nocturnal, preferring to hide among the upper portion of the plants during the day. Although they normally swam at a leisurely pace, they were capable of lightning-like dashes about the tank when disturbed. They accepted a wide variety of foods.

Pimelodella boliviana. (From Fowler, 1951.)

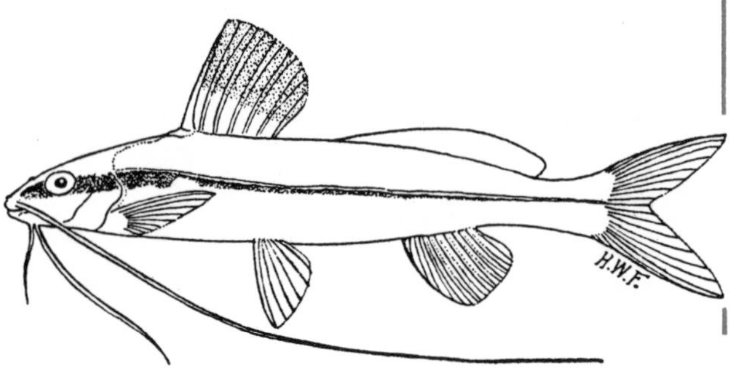

Pimelodella cristata is a bottom-dwelling species occurring in creeks as well as rivers. If it is synonymous with *P. gracilis*, the combined range would almost equal that of the entire genus. *Pimelodella "gracilis"* is a very confused species, at least in the aquarium field, where no less than three species are imported under that name. They are all long and slender with a dark stripe along the side, this stripe variously developed and usually becoming faded with age. They all seem to be similar in habits and are peaceful enough to be placed in a community tank that has subdued light. They are good scavengers and do not seem to get too large, the largest being about 17 cm when mature. The temperature of the tank should be in the range of 20° to 26°C. In one species the juveniles are grayish on the back shading to silvery white or silvery green on the sides and sporting the longitudinal black stripe from the gill cover to the caudal base. The adult males become more or less an overall blue-black with a strong metallic sheen. *Pimelodella lateristriga* attains a length of about 18 cm in captivity and is said to lay adhesive eggs. No further details of any spawning are available.

In general, most species of *Pimelodella* are relatively small, with the largest, *P. cristata*, reaching a length of about 34 cm. They require fairly large tanks with subdued lighting, as most species are nocturnal. A tank well-planted around the sides and back and with ample swimming space in front is recommended. They usually occupy the middle to lower reaches of the tank. Feeding is no problem as they accept a wide variety of foods, although meaty and live foods are preferred. Although they do well in community tank situations, do not place them with fishes that are too small or the small ones will start disappearing during the night when the *Pimelodella* species are most active.

Species of *Pimelodella* are all very similar. This one is possibly *P. hartwelli* or a similar species. Photo by Gerhard Marcuse.

These fishes are sometimes called "antenna" catfishes because of their elongate barbels. The barbels of some species grow disproportionately long as the fish grows, then slack off again as the fish gets larger. In some species the young may have rather short barbels, while in others the barbels vary not only with age but depending upon their geographic location. The pectoral fin spines, eye size, and color also vary with growth and sometimes geographically. It is no wonder that the species are in such turmoil systematically.

Phreatobius is a monotypic genus containing only *P. cisternarum*. The body is elongate and slightly compressed while the head is somewhat depressed. The eyes are rudimentary, located near the posterior nares. The mouth is terminal and wide, the lower jaw projecting. The teeth in the upper jaw are in about three series, those in the lower jaw in about two series. The inner teeth are larger and in very regular series. Three pairs of barbels are present, a maxillary pair and two mental pairs.

The short-based dorsal fin originates only slightly in front of the ventral fin origin, much nearer the snout than the caudal. The caudal fin is small, the accessory rays, however, large and numerous. The anal fin is long (its base more than one-third the length) and continuous with the lower accessory caudal rays while the upper accessory caudal rays begin about over the origin of the second third of the anal fin. There is no adipose fin. The

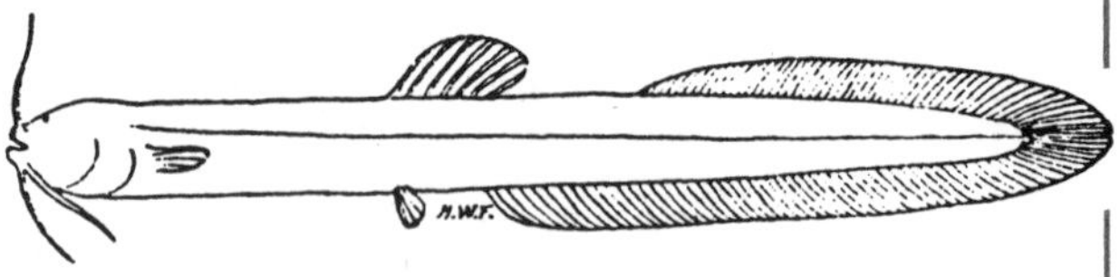

Phreatobius cisternarum. (From Fowler, 1954.)

pectoral fins are short and narrow, without a spine, and the ventral fins are a little shorter than the pectorals.

The gill membranes extend but little above the pectoral fin base and are narrowly joined to the isthmus.

The distinctive feature about this genus is the concomitant elongation of the caudal portion of the body, the anal fin, and the accessory portion of the caudal fin. (After Eigenmann, 1918.) Buckup (*Copeia*. 1988 (3)), has recently synonomized this genus with *Heptapterus*.

The genus *Calophysus* contains a single species, *C. macropterus*, from Brazil. The body is somewhat elongate and the head is rather

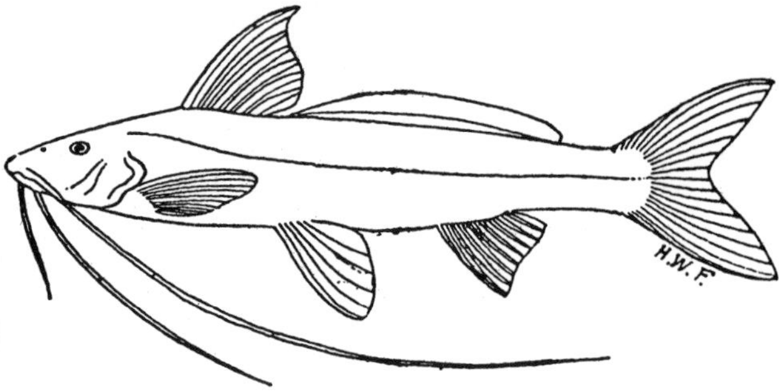

Calophysus macropterus. (From Fowler, 1954.)

broad, its surface entirely covered with skin. The occipital process does not meet or scarcely meets the predorsal plate; the occipital process is long and tapering, its base about twice as long as its tip. A wedge-shaped fontanel extends from about the posterior nasal openings to the posterior margins of the eyes and another circular one is present at the base of the occipital process. The eyes are superior in position. The barbels are all flattened, the maxillary pair long, extending at least to the end of the adipose fin and often extending beyond the end of the caudal fin. The upper jaw is a little longer than the lower. The teeth are in a single series in the lower jaw and two series in the upper. The inner series of teeth in the upper jaw is concealed or partly so, these teeth much smaller than those in the outer series, which are flattened, incisor-like, or semicuspid, and evenly spaced. The first dorsal fin ray is not spinous, although in some individuals the base is about half as "stiff" as some spines of other species and longer than the succeeding rays. The first ray of the pectoral fin is also soft and not spine-like. The ventral fins are inserted slightly behind the base of the dorsal fin. The adipose fin is long and the caudal fin is deeply emarginate. The gill membranes are joined to each other but extend well forward before becoming attached to the isthmus. (Eigenmann & Eigenmann, 1890.)

The genus *Calophysus* (often incorrectly spelled *Callophysus*) has at times been considered as belonging in its own family, the Calophysidae. Although it looks very much like a pimelodid externally, those who would like to place it separately believe so because the teeth are so different (single row versus bands), the positions of the fins are different, and above all, the swim bladder is reduced and encapsulated and provided with ceca. However, most modern workers have agreed that it is a pimelodid, though possibly meriting a separate subfamily.

The single species, *C. macropterus*, attains a length of about 50 cm. It is quite common along the river banks of the Rio Madeira according to Goulding (1981) and may be seen in large concentrations near populated areas such as villages or waterfront areas of larger cities, where it scavenges such items as offal and human excrement. The "Pintadinho" or "Piracatinga," as it is called locally, partially because of its spotted body, can be quite a voracious piscivore, armed as it is with incisor-like teeth. It is said to commonly attack the fishes caught in fishermen's nets and seines and even those hooked on trotlines or gaffed. It is not certain whether they also attack free-swimming fishes or just those already captured. It is possible that they cannot handle the free-swimming fishes and are normally just scavengers or feeders on fruits and seeds as they do in the flooded forests. When they do attack, however, they are voracious, ripping pieces out of the victim's body. They are often found with the trichomycterids and cetopsids that are well known for this type of action. At times they are so avid in their attack that they refuse to let go of their victim even though it has been removed from the water, and continue feeding as if still in the river.

The genera *Ginesia* and *Pteroglanis* are also included in this family, but insufficient information at the time of writing does not permit me to include a detailed discussion of them. The only described species of *Pteroglanis, P. manni*, appears to be endemic to the Rio Beni basin, Bolivia. The status of *Ginesia* and its type species is uncertain.

Pteroglanis manni. (From Fowler, 1951)

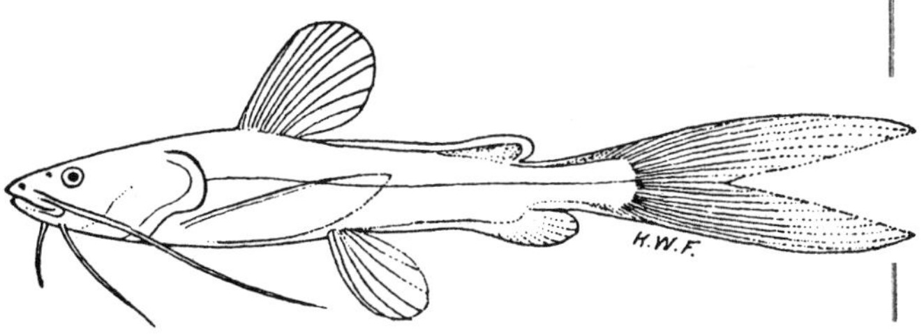

According to Chardon (1968) the pimelodids resemble the Bagridae but are commonly more slender fishes and have much longer barbels. They are also distinguished on the basis of cranial characters and by the distinctive structure of the envelope of the swim bladder and the muscles that are attached there. He believes that the Pimelodidae, Bagridae, and Ictaluridae are very closely related and suggests that the differences between these three families are scarcely greater than those between the Chrysichthinae and the Bagrinae, subfamilies of the family Bagridae.

Checklist of the species of the family Pimelodidae and their type localities:

Calophysus Müller & Troschel, 1843. Type species *Pimelodus macropterus* Lichtenstein, 1819.
- *Calophysus macropterus* (Lichtenstein, 1819). Brazil.

Luciopimelodus Eigenmann & Eigenmann, 1888. Type species *Pimelodus pati* Valenciennes, 1840.
- *Luciopimelodus pati* (Valenciennes, 1840). Parana, Rio de Prata; Corrientes; Buenos Aires, Argentina.

Megalonema Eigenmann, 1912. Type species *Megalonema platycephalum* Eigenmann.
- *Megalonema pauciradiatum* Eigenmann *in* Driver, 1919. Vila Rica, Paraguay.
- *M. argentina* MacDonagh, 1938. Argentina.
- *M. xanthus* (Eigenmann, 1912). Magdalena basin.
- *M. platanum* (Günther, 1880). Rio de la Plata; Rio Parana.
- *M. platycephalum* Eigenmann, 1912. Tumatumari, Guyana.
  - *p. psammium* Schultz, 1944. Maracaibo Basin, Venezuela.

Perugia Eigenmann & Norris, 1900. Type species *Pirinampus agassizi* Steindachner, 1875. (= *Pinirampus*.)
- *Perugia agassizi* (Steindachner, 1875). Para. (= *Pinirampus pirinampu*.)

Lophiosilurus Steindachner, 1876. Type species *L. alexandri* Steindachner.
- *Lophiosilurus alexandri* Steindachner, 1876. Brazil (probably Amazonas).

Pseudopimelodus Bleeker, 1858. Type species

Pimelodus raninus Valenciennes, 1840.
Pseudopimelodus albomarginatus Eigenmann, 1912. Guyana (Tukeit).
P. apurensis Mees, 1978. Rio Arichuna, Apure, Venezuela.
P. fowleri (Haseman, 1911). Cidade de Barra, Bahia, Rio São Francisco.
P. mathisoni (Fernandez-Yepez, 1972). Rio Yaracuy, Venezuela.
P. nigricaudus Mees, 1974. Sipaliwini, Surinam.
P. raninus (Valenciennes, 1840). La Mana. (Incl. *acanthochirus.*)
r. acanthochiroides Güntert, 1942. Santander, Colombia.
r. transmontanus Regan, 1913. Condoto, San Juan, Tamana, and Durango Rivers.
r. villosus Eigenmann, 1912. Potaro Landing, Guyana.
P. zungaro (Humboldt, 1833). Tomependa, on the banks of the Amazon. (Incl. *pulcher, variolosus.*)
z. bufonius (Valenciennes, 1840). Cayenne (but probably Surinam. (Incl. *charus.*)
z. mangurus (Valenciennes, 1834-1837), *in* d'Orbigny. No locality. (Incl. *roosevelti.*)
z. subsp. undetermined (see Mees, 1974, p. 204).
Microglanis Eigenmann, 1912. Type species *M. poecilus* Eigenmann.
Microglanis ater Ahl, 1936. Mid-Brazil.
M. iheringi Gomes, 1946. Rio Turmero near Turmero, Aragua, Venezuela.
M. parahybae (Steindachner, 1880). Rio Parahyba and Santa Cruz. (Incl. *cottoides.*)
M. pellopterygius Mees, 1978. Trib. streams of Rio Aguarico, Napo, Ecuador.
M. poecilus Eigenmann, 1912. Packeoo Falls, Guyana.
M. secundus Mees, 1974. Sipaliwini, Surinam.
M. variegatus Eigenmann & Henn, 1914. Forest pool near Vinces, Ecuador.
M. zonatus Eigenmann & Allen, 1942. Rio Morona (?).
Brachyglanis Eigenmann, 1912. Type species *B. frenata* Eigenmann.
Brachyglanis frenata Eigenmann, 1912. Guyana.
B. magoi Fernandez-Yepez, 1967. Venezuela.
B. melas Eigenmann, 1912. Guyana.
B. nocturnus Myers, 1928. Rio Negro (lagoas sobre as rochas das corredeiras de São Gabriel, no Rio Negro).
Myoglanis Eigenmann, 1912. Type species *M. potaroensis* Eigenmann.
Myoglanis collettii (Steindachner, 1882). Moldonado (or Rio de la Plata?).
M. essequibensis (Eigenmann, 1912). Guyana.
M. marmoratus (Myers, 1928). Rio Negro (lagoas sobre as rochas das corredeiras de São Gabriel, no Rio Negro).
M. potaroensis Eigenmann, 1912. Guyana.
Rhamdiopsis Haseman, 1911. Type species *R. moreirai* Haseman.
Rhamdiopsis moreirai Haseman, 1911. Serrinha Parana, Rio Iguaçu.
Heptapterus Bleeker, 1858. Type species *Pimelodus mustelinus* Valenciennes, 1847.
Heptapterus anisurus, Mees, 1987. Rio Guarapiche near Maturin, Monagas, Venezuela.
H. armillatus (Cope, 1871). Rio Ampiyacu.
H. bifasciatus (Eigenmann & Norris, 1900). São Paulo, Brazil.
H. bleekeri Boeseman, 1953. Marowini Basin, Nassau Mountains, Surinam.
H. bolivianus (Pearson, 1924). Beni basin, Bolivia. (Formerly in *Imparfinis.*)
H. brevior (Eigenmann, 1912). Waratuk, Guyana; Amatuk.
H. chimantanus (Inger, 1956). Rio Abacapa on the west side of Chimanta-tepui, Venezuela.
H. eigenmanni Steindachner, 1907. Moldonado, Uruguay. (= *mustelinus.*)
H. fasciatus (Boulenger, 1887). "sem determinar localidade" a leste do Ecuador.
H. fissipinnis Miranda-Ribeiro, 1911. Rio Estrella Basin, Rio Grande do Sul.
H. hollandi (Haseman, 1911). "Porto União da Victoria, Rio Iguaçu," Sta. Catarina.
H. leptos (Eigenmann & Eigenmann, 1889. São Mattheos, State of Espiritu Santo, Brazil.
H. longior (Eigenmann, 1912). Amatuk; Maripicru; Waratuk; Konawaratuk; Warraputa (Guyana).
H. mariai (Schultz, 1944). (Colombia.)

H. multiradiatus von Ihering, 1907. Alto da Serra, São Paulo, Brazil.

H. mustelinus (Valenciennes, 1847). Rio de la Plata basin; Buenos Aires; Surinam.

H. ornaticeps Ahl, 1936. Rio de Janeiro.

H. panamensis (Bussing, 1970). Panama; Veraguas Province, creek crossing road on south side of Santa Fe.

H. peruanas (Eigenmann & Pearson *in* Eigenmann & Allen, 1942). Puerto Melendez abaixo de Pongo de Manseriche.

H. quadrizonatus (Pearson, 1937). Tingo de Pauca; Pusic, upper Marañon.

H. rosae (Eigenmann, 1922). Rio Meta basin, Colombia.

H. somnians Mees, 1974. Sangadina, trib. of Rio das Mortes, Mato Grosso, Brazil.

H. stewarti Haseman, 1911. Serrinha Parana.

H. surinamensis Bleeker, 1862. Surinam.

H. sympterygium Buckup, 1988. Rio Grande do Sul, Brazil.

H. tapanahonensis Mees, 1974. Tapanahoni, Surinam.

H. tenebrosus (Schubart, 1964). Rio Mogi Guaçu.

H. tenuis Mees, 1987. Crique Cascade Moyen, Maroni, Fr. Guiana.

H. truncatorostris (Borodin, 1927). Colonia Hansa Joinvile, Santa Catarina Province.

Cetopsorhamdia Eigenmann & Fisher *in* Eigenmann, 1916. Type species *C. nasus* Eigenmann & Fisher.

Cetopsorhamdia boquillae Eigenmann, 1922. Cauca basin, Colombia.

C. insidiosus Steindachner, 1917. Rio Branco; Rio Surumu.

C. mirini (Haseman, 1911). Piracicaba, São Paulo.

C. molinae Miles, 1943. Upper Cauca, Colombia.

C. nasus Eigenmann & Fisher *in* Eigenmann, 1916. Honda, Colombia.

C. orinoco Schultz, 1944. Tariba, Orinoco system, Venezuela.

C. phantasia Stewart, 1985. Rio Napo Basin, Eastern Ecuador.

C. picklei Schultz, 1944. Maracaibo basin, Venezuela.

C. shermani Schultz, 1944. Orinoco system, Venezuela.

Nemuroglanis Eigenmann & Eigenmann, 1889. Type species *N. lanceolatus* Eigenmann & Eigenmann.

Nemuroglanis lanceolatus Eigenmann & Eigenmann, 1889. Rio Jutahy.

Imparfinis Eigenmann & Norris, 1900. Type species *I. piperatus* Eigenmann & Norris.

Imparfinis benedettii (Fernandez-Yepez & Martin, 1952). Quebrada Ojo de Agua, Baruta, Venezuela.

I. cochabambae (Fowler, 1940). Bolivia.

I. guttatus (Pearson, 1924). Rio Popoi, upper Beni basin, Bolivia.

I. hoehnei (Miranda-Ribeiro, 1914). Rio Taquary, Mato Grosso.

I. lineata (Bussing, 1970). Puntarenas Prov., Quebrada, Costa Rica.

I. longicauda (Borodin, 1927). Franca, Rio Grande, São Paulo

I. macrocephala (Miles, 1943). Upper Cauca, Colombia.

I. microps Eigenmann & Fisher *in* Eigenmann, 1916. Rio Negro at Villavicencio, Colombia.

I. minutus (Lütken, 1874). No locality (= Rio das Velhas).

I. nemacheir (Eigenmann & Fisher *in* Eigenmann, 1916). Magdalena and Maracaibo basins. "Gibardot, Colombia."

I. microcephala (Lütken, 1874). Rio das Velhas.

I. piperatus Eigenmann & Ward, 1900. São Paulo, Brazil.

I. rosae (Eigenmann, 1922). Rio Meta basin, Colombia.

I. schubarti (Gomes, 1956). Rio Mogi Guaçu, estado de São Paulo.

I. spurrelli (Regan, 1913). Rio Condoto, San Juan basin, Colombia.

I. stictonotus (Fowler, 1940). Todos os Santos, Rio Chapare, Bolivia.

Pteroglanis Eigenmann & Pearson *in* Pearson, 1924. Type species *P. manni* Pearson.

Pteroglanis manni Pearson, 1924. Rio Beni basin, Bolivia.

Pimelodina Steindachner, 1876. Type species *P. flavipinnis* Steindachner.

Pimelodina flavipinnis Steindachner, 1876. Rio Amazonas near Para.

Cheirocerus Eigenmann, 1917. Type species *C. eques* Eigenmann.

Cheirocerus abuelo (Schultz, 1944). Rio de los Pajaros, Maracaibo basin, Venezuela.

C. eques Eigenmann, 1917. Rio Mamore; Vila Bela; Santo Antonio.
C. goeldii (Steindachner, 1908). Rio Purus.
Zungaropsis Steindachner, 1908. Type species *Z. multimaculatus* Steindachner.
Zungaropsis multimaculatus Steindachner, 1908. Rio Xingu.
Pinirampus Bleeker, 1858. Type species *P. typus* Bleeker (= *Pimelodus pirinampu* Spix, 1829).
Pinirampus pirinampu (Spix, 1829). Brazil.
Caecorhamdella Borodin, 1927. Type species *C. brasiliensis* Borodin.
Caecorhamdella brasiliensis Borodin, 1927. São Paulo, Brazil.
Rhamdella Eigenmann & Eigenmann, 1888. Type species *Rhamdia eriarcha* Eigenmann & Eigenmann.
Rhamdella eriarcha (Eigenmann & Eigenmann, 1888). Rio Grande do Sul.
R. exsudans (Jenyns, 1842). Rio de Janeiro?
R. jenynsii (Günther, 1864). Rio de Janeiro.
R. ignobilis Steindachner, 1907. Rio Cubatao em Santa Catarina, Brazil.
R. leptosoma Fowler, 1914. Rio Rupununi.
R. longipinnis Borodin, 1927. São Paulo, Brazil.
R. montana Eigenmann, 1913. Tarma, Peru.
R. notata (Schomburgk, 1841). Fort San Joaquin, Rio Branco; Amazonas; Rio Negro.
R. papariae Fowler, 1941. Lago Papari, Rio Grande do Norte, Brazil.
R. robinsoni Fowler, 1941. São Jose do Egito, Pernambuco, Brazil.
R. rusbyi Pearson, 1924. Rio Beni basin. (Rio Colorado, Rio Bopi inferior, Bolivia.)
R. wolfi Fowler, 1941. Rio Choro, Ceara, Brazil.
Rhamdia Bleeker, 1858. Type species *Pimelodus sebae* Valenciennes, 1840.
Rhamdia alfaroi Fowler, 1932. Escobal, Costa Rica.
R. amatitlensis Fowler, 1936. Lake Amatitlan, Guatemala.
R. arekaima (Schomburgk, 1841). Upper Rio Essequibo; Rio Branco.
R. argentina (Humboldt, 1833). Rio Magdalena.
R. barbata Meek, 1907. Rio San Francisco, Nicaragua.
R. baronismuelleri (Troschel, 1865). Vertente Mexicana do Pacifico.
R. bathyurus Cope, 1878. Peruvian Amazon.
R. brachycephalus Regan, 1907. Guatemala (Rio Nacasil).
R. brachypterus (Cope, 1866). Mountain rapids "sul-centrais" de Vera Cruz. (Possibly is a *Rhamdella.*)
R. branneri Haseman, 1911. Creek of Rio Iguazu near Serrinha, Brazil.
b. voulezi Haseman, 1911. Rio Iguazu (Porto Uniao da Vitoria).
R. breviceps (Kner, 1857). Marabitanos.
R. cabrerae Meek, 1908. Lago Amatitlan, Guatemala.
R. cinerascens (Günther, 1860). Esmeraldas.
R. dorsalis (Gill, 1870). Maranon, and Rio Napo, upper Amazon.
R. duquei Eigenmann & Pearson *in* Eigenmann & Allen, 1942. Rio Urubamba, Santa Ana, Peru.
R. gilli (Starks, 1906). Rio Eten, Peru.
R. foina (Müller & Troschel, 1848). Takutu, Guyana.
R. godmani (Günther, 1864). Lago Nicaragua.
R. grunniens (Humboldt, 1833). Orinoco. (Possibly = *Phractocephalus hemiliopterus.*)
R. guairensis Eigenmann, 1920. Caracas, Venezuela.
R. guatemalensis (Günther, 1864). Guatemala.
g. decolor Hubbs, 1936. Yucatan.
g. depressa Barbour & Cole, 1906. Yucatan.
g. muriei Hubbs, 1935. Uaxactum, Guatemala.
g. oaxacae Meek, 1902. Rio Quiotepec, Cuicatlan, Oaxaca, Mexico.
g. sacrifici Barbour & Cole, 1906. Yucatan.
g. stygaea Hubbs, 1936. Yucatan.
R. heteracanthus Regan, 1906-1908. Costa Rica, Juan Viñas.
R. hilarii (Valenciennes, 1840). Rio São Francisco; Montevideo.
R. holomelas Günther, 1864. Essequibo.
h. rupununi Fowler, 1914. Rio Rupununi.
R. humilis (Günther, 1864). Venezuela.
R. hypselurus (Günther, 1864). Mexico.

R. laticauda (Heckel, 1867). Mexico.
?*R. laukidi* Bleeker, 1858. Demerara and Essequibo Rivers, Brazil.
R. longicauda (Boulenger, 1887). Canelos, eastern Ecuador.
R. managuensis (Günther, 1860). Lago Managua.
R. micayi Eigenmann *in* Pearson, 1924. Rio Popoi; Rio Colorado; Espia, Bolivia.
R. micropterus (Günther, 1864). Rio San Geronimo, Guatemala.
R. microps Eigenmann & Fisher, 1917. Uruguayana.
R. motageunsis (Günther, 1864). Rio Motagua.
R. mounseyi Regan, 1913. Rio Ucayali, Peru.
R. nasuta Meek, 1909. Buenos Aires de Terraba, Costa Rica.
R. nicaraguensis (Günther, 1864). Lago Nicaragua.
R. obesa Eigenmann & Eigenmann, 1888. Tefe, Brazil.
R. ortoni Fowler, 1915. Peruvian Amazon.
R. parryi Eigenmann & Eigenmann, 1888. Rio Zaneleneo, perto de Tonala, Mexico.
?*R. parvani* Boulenger, 1898. Rio Santiago, Ecuador.
R. parvus Boulenger, 1898. Rio Santiago, Rio Zamora, Rio Bombanaza.
R. pentlandi (Valenciennes, 1840). Tributary of Lake Titicaca, Peruvian Andes.
R. petenensis (Günther, 1864). Lago Peten & Chiapas, Mexico.
R. poeyi Eigenmann & Eigenmann, 1888. Goyaz.
R. policaulis (Günther, 1864). Rio San Geronimo, Guatemala.
R. pubescens Miranda-Ribiero, 1920. Mato Grosso (Urucum Corumba), Brazil.
R. quelen (Quoy & Gaimard, 1824). Brazil.
g. urichi (Norman, 1926). Trinidad. (Blind cave form.)
R. regani Meek, 1907. Turrialba, Costa Rica.
R. riojae Fowler, 1915. Rio Huallaga, Rioja, Peru.
R. rogersi Regan, 1907. Irazu, Costa Rica.
R. salvini (Günther, 1864). Rio San Geronimo, Guatemala.
R. sapo (Valenciennes, 1847). Buenos Aires.
R. sebae (Valenciennes, 1840). Surinam; Cayenne; Rio de Janeiro.
s. kneri (Steindachner, 1876). Marabitanos, Cujaba.
s. martyi Günther, 1942. Paraguay.
R. schomburgki Bleeker, 1858. Guyana; Rio Negro, Amazonas.
R. straminea Cope, 1894. Rio Grande do Sul; Rio Jacui.
R. tenella Eigenmann & Eigenmann, 1888. Cudajaz.
R. underwoodi Regan, 1907. Costa Rica, Juan Viñas.
R. velifer (Humboldt, 1805). Rio Magdalena.
R. wagneri (Günther, 1869). Tabasco, Mexico to Colombia.
R. wilsoni (Gill, 1858). Trinidad. (May = *R. quelen*.) (As *Pimelenotus Vilsoni*.)
R. wolfi (Fowler, 1941). Rio Choro, Ceara, Brazil.

Pimelodus Lacépède, 1803. Type species *Silurus clarias* Bloch, 1795.
Pimelodus albicans (Valenciennes, 1840). Buenos Aires.
P. albofasciatus Mees, 1974. Sipaliwini, Surinam.
P. altipinnis Steindachner, 1864. Demerara.
P. altissimus Eigenmann & Pearson *in* Eigenmann & Allen, 1942. Rio Ucayali, proximo de Orellana, Peru.
P. argenteus Perugia, 1891. Rio da Prata; Rio Parana; Colonia Resistencia.
P. blochii Valenciennes, 1840. Cayenne or Surinam.
P. brevis Marini, Nichols & La Monte, 1933. Rio da Prata.
P. clarias (Bloch, 1795). Rio da Prata to Panama.
c. punctatus (Meek & Hildebrand, 1913). Rio Tuyra basin, Panama.
c. coprophagus Schultz, 1944. Maracaibo basin, Venezuela.
P. fur (Reinhardt *in* Lütken, 1874). Rio das Velhas.
P. garciabarringi Dahl, 1961.
P. grosskopfii Steindachner, 1879. Magdalena basin (Cauca).
g. navarroi Schultz, 1944. Maracaibo basin, Venezuela.
P. heteropleurus Eigenmann, 1912. Guyana.
P. jivaro Eigenmann & Pearson *in* Eigen-

mann & Allen, 1942. Rio Morona, Peru.

P. maculatus Lacépède, 1803. "Le grand fleuve de la Plata"; Buenos Aires; Encenada.

P. ornatus Kner, 1857. Surinam: Rio Negro; Cujaba.

P. ortmanni Haseman, 1911. "Porto Uniao da Vitoria," Rio Iguaçu.

P. pictus Steindachner, 1876. Peruvian Amazon; Javari (Hyanuary).

P. platicirris Borodin, 1927. São Paulo (Salto de Pirassununga, Rio Mogi Guaçu).

P. quadrimaculatus (Bloch, 1794). America.

P. spegezzinii Perugia, 1891. Rio Durazno (Durango?), near Rio Parana.

Parapimelodus La Monte, 1933. Type species *Pimelodus valenciennis* Kröyer, 1874.

Parapimelodus valenciennis (Kröyer *in* Lütken, 1874). Rio de la Plata.

Iheringichthys Eigenmann & Norris, 1900. Type species *Pimelodus labrosus* Kröyer, 1874.

Iheringichthys labrosus (Kröyer *in* Lütken, 1874). Rio da Prata.

I. megalops Eigenmann & Ward *in* Eigenmann, MacAtee & Ward, 1907. Bahia Negra, Rio Paraguay.

Typhlobagrus Miranda-Ribeiro, 1907. Type species *T. kronei* Miranda-Ribeiro.

Typhlobagrus kronei Miranda-Ribeiro, 1907. Grutas de Santa Catarina, Rio Iporanga, São Paulo.

Pimelodella Eigenmann & Eigenmann, 1888. Type species *Pimelodus cristatus* Müller & Troschel, 1848.

P. avanhandavae Eigenmann, 1917. Rio Tiete at Salto Avanhandava.

P. boliviana Eigenmann, 1917. Santa Cruz de la Sierra, Bolivia.

P. boschmai van der Stigchel, 1964.

P. brasiliensis (Steindachner, 1876). Rio Paraiba (Parahyba).

P. buckleyi (Boulenger, 1887). Maranon basin (Canelos, eastern Ecuador).

P. chagresi (Steindachner, 1876). Rio Chagres and its trib. near Obispo.

c. odynea Schultz, 1944. Cucuta, Colombia and Maracaibo basin, Venezuela.

P. chaparae Fowler, 1940. Rio Chapare, Bolivia.

P. cochabambae Fowler, 1940. Rio Chapare, Cochabamba, Bolivia.

P. coguetaensis Ahl, 1923. Rio Coqueta, southeastern Colombia.

P. cristata (Müller & Troschel, 1848). Rio Takutu and Rio Mahu.

P. cruxenti Fernandez-Yepez, 1950.

P. cyanostigma (Cope, 1870). Pebas, Peru.

P. dorseyi Fowler, 1941. Rio Salgado, Icó, Ceara.

P. eigenmanni Boulenger, 1891. Macacos, Brazil; Rio Parahyba.

P. elongata (Günther, 1860). Esmeraldas, western Ecuador.

P. enochi Fowler, 1941. Acude Piloes, Rio Paraiba, Brazil.

P. eutaenia Regan, 1903. Rio San Juan, Colombia.

P. garbei Miranda-Ribeiro, 1918. Itaqui, Rio Grande do Sul; Rio Paraitinga, São Paulo; Rio Itanhaem.

P. geryi Hoedeman, 1961. French Guiana.

P. gracilis (Valenciennes, 1840). Buenos Aires; Rio Parana at Corrientes.

P. griffini Eigenmann, 1917. Near Sapucay, Paraguay.

P. grisea Regan, 1903. Northwestern Ecuador.

P. hartti Steindachner, 1876. Rio Parnahyba.

P. hartwelli Fowler, 1940. Contamina, Brazil (Rio Ucayali).

P. hasemani Eigenmann, 1917. Santo Antonio, no Rio Madeira; Ica; Obidos; Jutai.

P. howesi Fowler, 1940. Rio Chapare, Bolivia (Todos os Santos).

P. imitator (Myers, 1927). Cano de Quiribana, perto do Caicara, Venezuela. (*Brachyrhamdia.*)

P. itapicuruensis Eigenmann, 1917. Queimadas, Rio Itapicuru, Brazil.

P. lateristriga (Müller & Troschel, 1849). Brazil.

P. laticeps Eigenmann, 1917. Rio Sapucay, Paraguay.

l. australis Eigenmann, 1917. Uruguayana; Cacequi, Rio Ibicuhy, Rio Grande do Sul; Cachoeira, Rio Jacui; Porto Alegre.

P. laurenti Fowler, 1941. Rio São Francisco (Jatoba).

P. linami Schultz, 1944. Tariba, Orinoco system, Venezuela.

P. macturki Eigenmann, 1910. Creek in Mora Passage, trenches at Moronhanna, and Georgetown, Guyana.

P. marthae (Sands & Black, 1985). Peru. (*Brachyrhamdia*.)

P. martinezi Fernandez-Yepez, 19??.

P. meeki Eigenmann, 1910. Sao Paulo.

P. meesi (Sands & Black, 1985). Near Belem, Brazil. (*Brachyrhamdia*.)

P. megalops Eigenmann, 1910. Guyana.

P. megalura Miranda-Ribeiro, 1918. São Luiz de Caceres, Mato Grosso.

P. metae Eigenmann, 1917. Meta basin, Colombia.

P. modesta (Günther, 1860). Esmeraldas.

P. montana Allen *in* Eigenmann & Allen, 1942. Rio Huallaga, Huanuco, Peru.

P. mucosa Eigenmann & Ward *in* Eigenmann, MacAtee & Ward, 1907. Bahia Negra, Paraguay basin.

?*P. nigrofasciata* (Perugia, 1897). Rio Beni, Missioni Mosetenes.

P. notomelas Eigenmann, 1917. San Luiz de Caceres.

P. pappenheimi Ahl, 1923. Rio Pedro em Humboldt, Santa Catarina, Brazil.

P. parnahybae Fowler, 1941. Rio Parnahyba, Terezina, Piaui.

P. parva Günther, 1942. Riactis, Canawe, Deportamento de Ita, Paraguay.

P. pectinifera Eigenmann & Eigenmann, 1888. Paraiba basin (Campos).

P. peruensis Fowler, 1915. Peruvian Amazon.

P. peruana Eigenmann & Myers *in* Eigenmann & Allen, 1942. Rio Ucayali (Inhuaya).

P. procera Mees, 1983. Balaté Creek, trib. of Rio Moroni, Fr. Guiana.

P. rambarrani Axelrod & Burgess, 1987. Rio Unini (Trib. of Rio Negro) Amazonas, Brazil.

P. rendahli Ahl, 1923. Locality unknown (= South America).

P. roccae Eigenmann, 1917. Urubamba Valley, Peru.

P. rudolphi Miranda-Ribeiro, 1918. São Paulo (Sorocaba; Rio Tiete; Rio Feio; Rio Tamanduatei).

P. serrata Eigenmann, 1917. San Joaquin, Bolivia.

P. steindachneri Eigenmann, 1917. Para; Cudajas; Santarem; Rio Puty; Marajo, Rio Madeira.

P. taenioptera Miranda-Ribeiro, 1914. Tapirapoa, Rio Sepotuba.

P. tapatapae Eigenmann, 1920. Basin of Lake Valencia, Venezuela.

P. transitoria Miranda-Ribeiro, 1912. Iporanga, Rio Alambary.

P. vittata (Kröyer *in* Lütken, 1874). Rio das Velhas.

P. witmeri Fowler, 1941. Rio Jaguaribe, Oros, Ceara.

P. yuncensis Steindachner, 1912. Pacasmayo, Peru.

Goeldiella Eigenmann & Norris, 1900. Type species *Pimelodus eques* Müller & Troschel, 1848.

Goeldiella eques (Müller & Troschel, 1848). Guyana.

Bergiaria Eigenmann & Norris, 1901. Type species *Pimelodus westermanni* Reinhardt. (Substitute name for *Bergiella* Eigenmann & Norris, 1900, preoccupied.)

Bergiaria platana (Steindachner, 1908). Rio da Prata.

B. westermanni (Reinhardt *in* Lütken, 1874). Rio das Velhas.

Conorhynchus Bleeker, 1858. Type species *Pimelodus conirostris* Valenciennes.

Conorhynchus conirostris (Valenciennes, 1840). Rio São Francisco.

C. glaber Steindachner, 1876. Porto Seguro, eastern Brazil.

Bagropsis Lütken, 1874. Type species *B. reinhardtii* Lütken.

Bagropsis reinhardtii Lütken, 1874. Rio das Velhas.

Piramutana Bleeker, 1862. Type species *Bagrus piramuta* Kner, 1857.

Piramutana piramuta (Kner, 1857). Barra do Rio Negro; Borba; Rio Madeira. (Possibly = *Brachyplatystoma vaillanti*.)

Platynematichthys Bleeker, 1862. Type species *Bagrus punctulatus* Kner, 1857.

Platynematicthys araguayensis (Castelnau, 1855). Rio Araguaia. (The long adipose fin of this species makes its placement in *Platynematichthys* doubtful.)

P. notatus (Schomburgk, 1841). Fort St. Joaquim, Rio Branco; Rio Negro.

P. punctulatus (Kner, 1857). Forte do Principe, Rio Branco, and Rio Guapore.

Phractocephalus Agassiz, 1829. Type species *P. bicolor* Agassiz (= *P. hemioliopterus*).
Phractocephalus hemioliopterus (Schneider, 1801). "Flumine Maranham Brasiliae."

Leiarius Müller & Troschel. 1849. Type species *Bagrus (Sciades) pictus* Müller & Troschel.
Leiarius marmoratus Gill, 1870. Rio Maranon and Rio Napo, upper Amazon.
L. pictus (Müller & Troschel, 1849). Unknown.

Perrunichthys Schultz, 1944. Type species *P. perruno* Schultz.
Perrunichthys perruno Schultz, 1944. Maracaibo basin, Venezuela.

Goslinia Myers, 1941. Type species *Taenionema steerei* Eigenmann & Bean (= *G. platynema*). Subst. name for *Taenionema* Eigenmann & Bean, preoccupied).
Goslinia platynema (Boulenger, 1888). Para.

Platypogon Starks, 1913. Type species *P. coerulorostris* Starks.
Platypogon coerulorostris Starks, 1913. Para. (Doubtful species. ? = *Platynematichthys notatus*.)

Hemisorubim Bleeker, 1862. Type species *Platystoma platyrhynchos* Valenciennes, 1840.
Hemisorubim platyrhynchos (Valenciennes, 1840). No locality (= Brazil).

Brachyplatystoma Bleeker, 1862. Type species *Platystoma Vaillantii* Valenciennes.
Brachyplatystoma filamentosum (Lichtenstein, 1819). Südamerika (= Brazil).
B. flavicans (Castelnau, 1855). Amazonas.
B. juruense (Boulenger, 1898). Rio Jurua.
B. paraense Steindachner, 1909. Para.
B. parnahybae Steindachner, 1908. Rio Parnahyba.
B. vaillanti (Valenciennes, 1840). Cayenne; Surinam.

Pseudoplatystoma Bleeker, 1862. Type species *Silurus fasciatus* Bloch (= *Silurus fasciatus* Linnaeus).
Pseudoplatystoma coruscans (Agassiz, 1829). Rio São Francisco, central Brazil.
P. fasciatum (Linnaeus, 1766). Habitat in Brasilia (Surinam).
P. tigrinum (Valenciennes, 1840). Brazil (May = *fasciatum*).

Duopalatinus Eigenmann & Eigenmann, 1888. Type species *Platystoma emarginatum* Valenciennes, 1840.
Duopalatinus emarginatus (Valenciennes, 1840). Basin of Rio São Francisco.
D. goeldii Steindachner, 1908. Rio Purus.
D. malarmo (Schultz, 1944). Maracaibo basin, Venezuela.
D. puruanus Eigenmann & Allen, 1942. Rio Puinagua, mouth of the Rio Pacaya, Peru.

Paulicea von Ihering, 1898. Type species *P. jahu* von Ihering.
Paulicea jahu von Ihering, 1898. Rio Tiete, em São Paulo.
P. luetkeni (Steindachner, 1875). Middle Amazon.

Steindachneridion Eigenmann & Eigenmann, 1919. Type species *S. amblyura* Eigenmann & Eigenmann.
Steindachneridion amblyura (Eigenmann & Eigenmann, 1888). Rio Jequitinhonha.
S. doceana (Eigenmann & Eigenmann, 1889). Rio Doce.
S. parahybae (Steindachner, 1876). Rio Parnahyba near Juiz de Fora.
S. scripta (Miranda-Ribeiro, 1918). Rio Grande do Sul (Itaqui).

Sorubim Spix, 1829. Type species *Silurus lima* Schneider, 1801.
Sorubim latirostris Miranda-Ribeiro, 1920. Amazonas.
S. lima (Schneider, 1801). "Flumine Maranham Brasiliae."
S. trigonocephalus Miranda-Ribeiro, 1920. Porto Velho.

Sorubimichthys Bleeker, 1862. Type species *Sorubim jandia* Spix (= *S. spatula*).
Sorubim gigas (Günther, 1872). Rio Huallaga, Peru.
S. planiceps (Agassiz, 1829). Amazonas; Solimoes; Rio Negro.
S. spatula (Agassiz, 1829). Rivers of Equatorial Brazil.

Platystomatichthys Bleeker, 1862. Type species *Platystoma sturio* Kner, 1857.
Platystomatichthys mucosus Vaillant, 1879. Calderon, upper Amazon.
P. sturio (Kner, 1857). Rio Branco.

Merodontotus Britski, 1981. Type species *M. tigrinus* Britski.
Merodontotus tigrinus Britski, 1981. Cachoeira do Teotonio, Rio Madeira, Terr. de Rondonia.

Phreatobius Goeldi, 1904. Type species *P. cist-*

ernarum Goeldi. (= *Heptapterus*.)
Phreatobius cisternarum Goeldi, 1904. Ilha de Marajo. (Blind form.)
Aguarunichthys Stewart, 1986. Type species *A. torosus* Stewart.
Aguarunichthys torosus Stewart, 1986. Rio Cenepa, Departamento Amazonas, Peru.
Incerta sedis:
Ginesia cunaguaro Fernandez-Yepez, 1951.

Chapter 23

Family — Plates 109, 146–147

AGENEIOSIDAE

(Slopehead Catfishes)

The ageneiosids are pelagic catfishes of the fresh waters of South America. They mostly inhabit the northeastern sections of the continent but extend as far south as Argentina. The body is relatively streamlined for their midwater existence, and their heads are very flattened anteriorly and deep posteriorly. The eyes are large and lateral, and they do not have free margins. The body is naked, without scales, bony plates, or scutes. The teeth are villiform and in the jaws only. There is a small pair of maxillary barbels only, or a small pair of mandibular barbels only. The dorsal fin is placed anteriorly (near the head) and the adipose fin is small. The ventral fins are also placed anteriorly. The anal and caudal fins are long. There is a strong spine in the dorsal fin and one in each of the pectoral fins. The gill membranes are joined to the isthmus, with the gill opening restricted, not extending forward. The swim bladder is much reduced and is enclosed in a partially membranous capsule that involves the processes of the anterior vertebrae.

There has been a constant rearrangement of three apparently related families, the Doradidae, Auchenipteridae, and Ageneiosidae. These three families were accepted as such by Berg (1940), Stigchel (1947), and Greenwood, et al. (1966). Gosline (1945), placing the auchenipterids as a subfamily of the Doradidae, wound up with two families, the Doradidae and the Ageneiosidae. Some earlier workers, such as Jordan (1923) and Regan (1911) considered that there was only a single family, the Doradidae. Among the reasons for the close association of these families by catfish workers are, according to Chardon (1968), that the anterior branch of the fourth parapophysis is free from the posttemporal bone and is distinct from its base of the posterior branch. This last attachment has a posterior process of the epiotic. There is a large confluence of the supraoccipital and of the bucklers, but without an intercalar scale. Finally, the transformator is narrow and in the form of a plate. There are, however, many differences between the ageneiosids and these other two families. The formation of the capsule is different, there is a reduction of the swim bladder in the ageneiosids, the form of the attachment of the posttemporal is different, the attachment of the fifth parapophysis to the fourth is different, and the ageneiosids have a long line of contact between the sphenotic and the supraoccipital.

With the transfer of the genus *Tetranematichthys* to this family from the Auchenipteridae, the three genera can be distinguished by the following key:

1a. Maxillary barbels only.................... 2
1b. Mandibular barbels only.................... .... *Tetranematichthys*
2a. Swim bladder projecting into the abdominal cavity, naked laterally, the skin over it forming a large pseudotympanum; snout short, about equal to eye ... . *Tympanopleura*
2b. Swim bladder minute, concealed under peritoneum and largely covered with bone; no pseudotympanum; snout much longer than eye .... *Ageneiosus*

The genus *Ageneiosus* is the largest genus of the family, containing approximately two dozen species. The bones of the head are thin and covered with thin skin; the occipital process is firmly joined to the dorsal plate. There is no humeral process visible. There are only maxillary barbels. The teeth are villiform, none on the palate. The dorsal fin has a weak spine and 6 or 7 rays. The adipose fin is very short, and the anal fin is long. The ventral fins are placed behind the dorsal fin and each has 7 or 8 rays, the innermost ray joined to the belly by a membrane for about half its length. The lateral line zigzags and has many branches.

Species of this genus are said to be voracious predators that pursue prey in midwater,

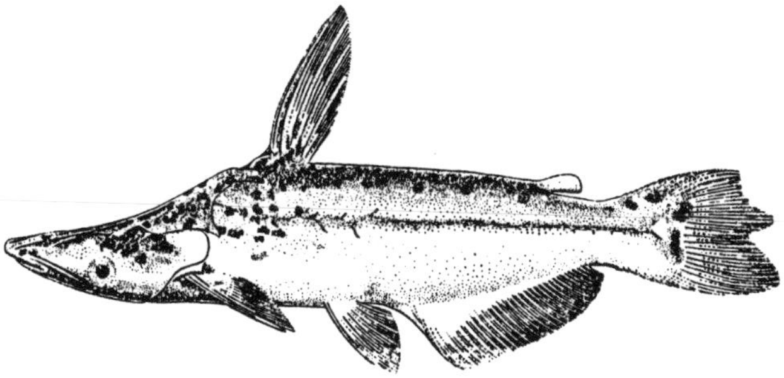

Ageneiosus madeirensis. (From Eigenmann, 1917.)

near the surface, or at the bottom. Most feed on other fishes. In an aquarium they will dine on fishes and lean meat. Because of their predatory nature they are definitely not good community tank fishes. Some species are reported to have an attractive color when young. The species grow to lengths of about 20 cm for the smaller ones and up to 100 cm for the largest. They have some commercial value as food.

Ageneiosus brevifilis is one of the moderate-sized species, attaining a length of about 55 cm and a weight of over 2 kilos. In its natural habitat it prefers rivers in overgrown backwaters where the current is not too great. Its natural diet consists of fishes and crustaceans, and its flesh is esteemed for its very fine flavor. In an aquarium they do very well. They are entirely piscivorous but can be weaned onto other meaty foods like chunks of meat. They have been called Gulper Catfish because of their feeding habits. They will lunge at their prey holding their mouth agape to gulp down the whole fish. They should be fed when light levels are low, for these are reported to be nocturnal catfishes. Males have shorter barbels than females and the dorsal fin spine is also shorter; males also lack the prolonged anterior anal fin lobe of the female.

The genus *Tympanopleura* is a small genus of only about three species. They also have only a short pair of maxillary barbels. The snout is relatively short and the anterior profile is concave. The dorsal and pectoral fin spines are pungent. The origin of the anal fin

Tympanopleura alta. (From Fowler, 1951.)

is about equally distant from the rictus as from the middle caudal fin rays. The swim bladder is large, projecting into the abdominal cavity and laterally forming a pseudotympanum. The male has maxillary barbels with an osseus base extending to below the anterior margin of the eye, the non-osseus portion extending but little further. The maxillary barbels of the female are fleshy, minute, and extend only as far as the rictus.

The third genus, *Tetranematichthys*, contains a single species. It is very much like the

Tetranematichthys quadrifilis. (From Fowler, 1951.)

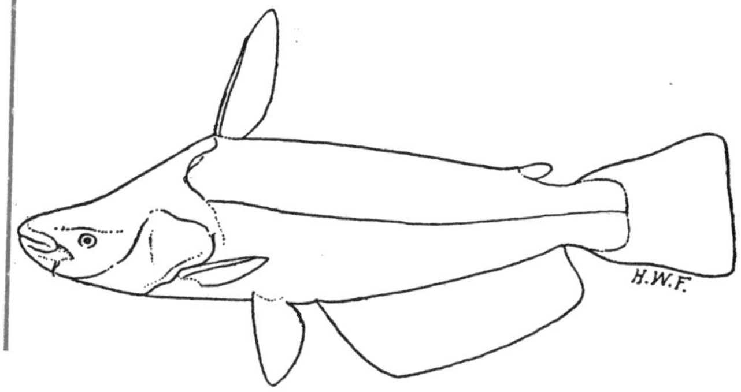

other genera except that it possesses a single pair of small mandibular barbels. The top of the head is granular, without a covering, and the swim bladder lacks the bony capsule. Although this genus was originally placed in the family Auchenipteridae, and in fact was considered a synonym of *Parauchenipterus* Bleeker (1862) by Miranda-Ribeiro (1968), it was apparently misplaced according to Britski and should be added to the family Ageneiosidae. The type species selected by Bleeker for his new genus was even a member of the genus *Ageneiosus*.

Checklist of the species of the family Ageneiosidae and their type localities:

Tympanopleura Eigenmann, 1912. Type species *T. piperata* Eigenmann.
- *Tympanopleura alta* Eigenmann & Myers, 1928. Iquitos; Rio Marañon, Peru.
- *T. nigricollis* Eigenmann & Allen, 1943. Iquitos; Orcellana, Peru.
- *T. piperata* Eigenmann, 1912. Crab Falls.

Tetranematichthys Bleeker, 1862. Type species *Ageneiosus quadrifilis* Kner.
- *Tetranematichthys quadrifilis* (Kner, 1857). Rio Guaporé.

Ageneiosus Lacépède, 1805. Type species *Ageneiosus armatus* Lacépède.
- *Ageneiosus armatus* Lacépède, 1805. Surinam.
- *A. atronasus* Eigenmann & Eigenmann, 1888. Unknown. (Brazil?)
- *A. axillaris* Günther, 1864. Surinam.
- *A. brevifilis* Valenciennes, 1840. Cayenne, Fr. Guiana.
- *A. brevis* Steindachner, 1882. Coari Javari (Amazon).
- *A. caucanus* Steindachner, 1879. Rio Cauca.
- *A. dawalla* Schomburgk, 1849. Guiana.
- *A. dentatus* Kner, 1857. Surinam.
- *A. freiei* Schultz, 1944. Rio Agua Caliente, 2-3 km above Lake Maracaibo. (Possible synonym of *A. caucanus*.)
- *A. guianensis* Eigenmann, 1912. Wismar.
- *A. inermis* (Linnaeus, 1758). Surinam.
- *A. madeirensis* Fisher, 1917. San Joaquin, Bolivia.
- *A. marmoratus* Eigenmann, 1912. Creek below Potaro landing.
- *A. melanopogon* Miranda-Ribeiro, 1917. Solimões.
- *A. ogilviei* Fowler, 1914. Rupununi River.
- *A. parnaguensis* Steindachner, 1910. Lago Parnaguá near Piauı.
- *A. polystictus* Steindachner, 1917. Mouth of the Rio Negro.
- *A. porphyreus* Cope, 1867. Surinam.
- *A. rondoni* Miranda-Ribeiro, 1914. Rio Negro, Manaus.
- *A. therezine* Steindachner, 1909. Rio Parnahyba; Rio Poti at Terezina.
- *A. ucayalensis* Castelnau, 1855. Rio Ucayali, Peru.
- *A. uruguayensis* Devincenzi, 1933. Rio Uruguay before Paysando, Uruguay.
- *A. valenciennesi* Bleeker, 1864. Based on Valenciennes, no locality given.
- *A. vittatus* Steindachner, 1908. Rio Purus.

Chapter 24

Family — Plate 148

HELOGENIDAE

(Marbled Catfishes)

The family Helogenidae is a small family of freshwater catfishes distributed in the Amazon basin and to the north of the Amazon. They appear to be midwater swimmers, possibly feeding on insect larvae and planktonic invertebrates. Although some specimens are seen in the aquarium trade from time to time, they are not generally imported in any quantities. A single genus, *Helogenes*, with four species is currently included in the family. *Leyvaichthys* is a synonym.

Members of this family are small, naked, and have a moderately elongate body that is compressed, especially at the caudal peduncle. The head is bullet-shaped, and there are three pairs of moderately long barbels, the maxillary barbels fitting into a groove below the eyes. The very small eyes are superior (directed upward and outward), are covered with skin, and are reported to shine in the dark—the helogenids are reported to be nocturnal in habit. The dorsal fin is small and without a spine or is even absent, and when present it is located behind the middle of the body. The adipose fin is present or absent, when present it is very small to minute; there is a long anal fin. The pectoral fins lack spines. The caudal fin is forked, the lower lobe somewhat longer.

The species of *Helogenes* are small, free-swimming catfishes with a small or no dorsal fin in the middle of the body. The eyes are small, covered with skin, and are positioned above the angle of the mouth; the eyes lack free orbital margins. The barbels are not margined; the two mental barbels are remote from one another and are located below the angle of the mouth. The fontanel extends to the base of the occipital process. They have the mouth of a predator, similar in shape to certain members of the Siluridae such as *Wallago*. The upper jaw is heavy, the lower jaw included. The upper jaw has two series of teeth, the inner row obscure, while the lower jaw has a narrow band of teeth, some of the outer teeth distinctly larger; the vomerine teeth are in two separate patches. The ventral fins are 6-rayed.

The gill membranes overlap but are free from the isthmus. The gill rakers are very short, and there are about 12 to 13 branchiostegal rays. The swim bladder is reduced to an anterior chamber that is incompletely divided into two vesicles that are not enclosed by bone. The posttemporal bone is loosely attached to the cranium and the coalesced vertebrae have a broad lateral process.

Helogenes marmoratus attains a length of about 8 to 10 cm and has a range extending from Guyana and Surinam throughout northeastern South America. It is nocturnal and will most probably be encountered in heavily overgrown river backwaters and pools among the tangles of roots and fallen trees. In spite of its predatory appearance it is not an aggressive fish. In an aquarium it is active at night, so it is best to provide many hiding places and subdued lighting conditions for the daylight hours. A dark substrate is recommended. *H. marmoratus* is omnivorous and will accept a wide variety of food material, but worms and insect larvae are preferred. Although a temperature range of 23° to 28°C is acceptable, 24°C is about right. Breeding habits are not yet known. This species has been reported to lie still on one side to rest for long periods of time; this is seemingly a natural posture and not attributable to any distress. The first aquarium specimens were imported from Surinam about 1956.

The Helogeneidae resembles the Siluridae and the Schilbeidae by their general shape, apparently an adaptation to pelagic life. The articulations of the first vertebra and the posttemporal are free, however. As in the Siluridae, the lateral edges of the pterotic and the sphenotic are rudimentary (Chardon, 1968). The distinctions of the fourth and fifth vertebrae and the independence of their neural arches are very important archaic characters and can only be found otherwise in the Diplomystidae. The flattening of the cranium, the considerable enlargement of the posttemporal in the dorsal plate, and the lateral attachment of the two edges of the groove of the cleithrum make one think of the family Trichomycteridae, but the characters of the cranium and the vertebrae are quite different and oppose such an association.

Checklist of the species of the family Helogenidae and their type localities:

Helogenes Günther, 1863. Type species *H. marmoratus* Günther.

- *H. castaneus* (Dahl, 1960). Tributaries of the Rio Orinoco.
- *H. gouldingi* Vari & Ortega, 1986. Rio Madeira, Brazil.
- *H. marmoratus* Günther, 1863. Rio Essiquibo, Guyana.
- *H. uruyensis* Fernandez-Yepez, 1967. Guayana, Rio Uruyen near Auyantepui, Venezuela.

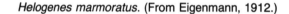

Helogenes marmoratus. (From Eigenmann, 1912.)

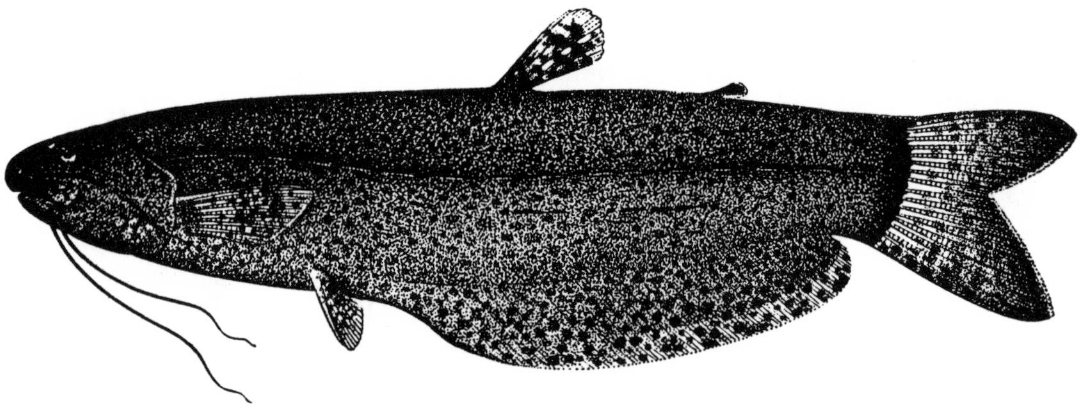

Chapter 25

Family CETOPSIDAE (Whale Catfishes)

Plates 148, 154–157

The family Cetopsidae is a fairly small family of small to moderate-sized freshwater catfishes distributed over much of South America. They are immediately recognizable by their regularly oval form that they owe to the muscular collar that encases the entire body, most particularly the anterior region. Cetopsids are naked catfishes with the skin smooth and lacking any bony plates or scutes. The body is streamlined and cylindrical in shape, while the head is somewhat compressed. The opercles are unarmed. The jaw teeth are conical or incisor-like and arranged in series or in a band; the vomer also has teeth. The small eyes are almost entirely concealed under the skin, the margins fused. The ectopterygoids are lacking. There are three pairs of barbels, a maxillary pair and two mandibular pairs. The anterior and posterior nares are quite distant, the anterior pair almost labial in position. The dorsal fin is small, triangular in shape, and located well forward in front of the ventral fins. There is no strong dorsal fin spine; there is no adipose fin. The anal fin is moderate in size with about 20-29 rays.

The gill membranes are broadly attached to the isthmus, and the gill openings are restricted to in front of the pectoral fin base. The swim bladder is reduced to two separate vesicles that are enclosed in bony capsules that open only laterally.

The Cetopsidae has often been considered as only a subfamily of the Trichomycteridae. They share a number of common characters, such as the cranium being covered with muscle, the lack of an adipose fin, the loss of the claustrum of the intercalare and of the transformer of the tripus, the reduction of the lower arm of the posttemporal bone, and the swim bladder being divided into two vesicles enclosed in capsules formed by the parapophysis of the fourth vertebra (Chardon, 1968). Weitzman & Myers (1966), however, raised them to a full family. The cetopsids differ from the trichomycterids by having a compressed head with an occipital crest (depressed and without a crest in the Trichomycteridae); by having a (weak) spine in the dorsal fin preceded by a "buckler" (not preceded by a buckler in the Trichomycteridae); by having the posttemporal flexibly articulated with the cranium and quite distinct from it, not forming a horizontal plate and not participating in the sealing of the capsule (assimilated and fused with the cranium and the capsule in the Trichomycteridae); by having a normal articulation of the cleithrum with the posttemporal (the articulation is in a bony collar in the trichomycterids); by having a different form of the labyrinth; by having the first vertebra distinct (not so in the Trichomycteridae); by having the vesicles of the swim bladder slightly more reduced (more complete capsules that are fused to the cranium in the Trichomycteridae); by the tripus having a very different form; and by other osteological characters.

The family Cetopsidae contains four genera and only about a dozen species. The genera can be distinguished by the following key.

1a. Premaxillary teeth quadrangular and in

a single series.................. *Hemicetopsis*
1b. Premaxillary teeth minute and arranged in patches 2
2a. Ventral fins joined to the body by a membrane from the last ray... *Pseudocetopsis*
2b. Ventral fins not joined to body by a membrane.................................... 3
3a. Ventral fins situated just below dorsal fin base; vomerine teeth arranged in patches .... *Cetopsogiton*
3b. Ventral fins situated just behind a vertical through last dorsal fin ray; vomerine teeth quadrangular in form, arranged in a single series........................ *Cetopsis*

According to Goulding (1980) the whale catfishes, most particularly members of the genera *Cetopsis* and *Hemicetopsis*, are predatory and a nuisance to fishermen. Attaining lengths of between 15 and 25 cm, their smooth, streamlined bodies enable them to penetrate wounds or ripped or torn flesh, becoming wedged in as they continuously chew away at the flesh of the fish. It is a regular occurrence that when a fisherman catches one of the large catfishes (usually a pimelodid) and hauls it in he will find several of these voracious whale catfishes actually inside the body cavity. The cetopsids are still alive and still feeding on their prey even though it is out of the water. In some instances a combination of the cetopsids and trichomycterids can destroy a gaffed catfish. Schools of these predators can literally eat the larger fish in less than a minute, perhaps rivaling the piranhas with such a feat. One species of *Cetopsis* was even captured as it attempted to rasp the skin off the leg of one of the collectors.

The genus *Cetopsis* is a small genus of only two species from Brazil. The body is relatively heavy, little compressed, and tapers rapidly to the caudal peduncle. The head is compressed and bluntly conical, the bones covered with a thick layer of muscle. The eyes are small, almost rudimentary, and are covered with skin. The maxillary barbel can be almost entirely concealed in a slit-like groove on the side of the head, and the mental barbels are also receivable into shallow grooves. The mouth is inferior in position. The premaxillaries have minute conical teeth

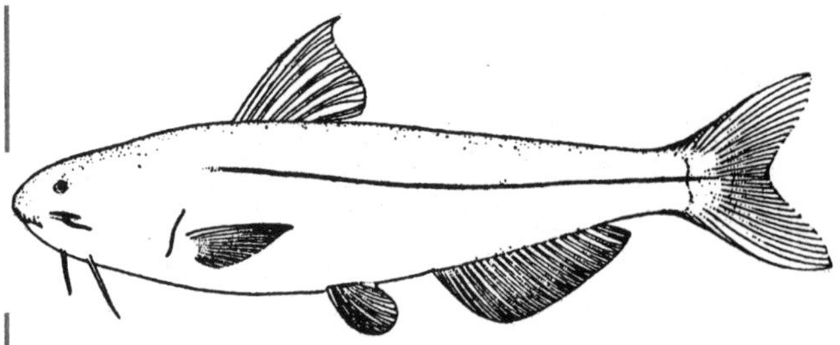

Cetopsis coecutiens. (From Fowler, 1945.)

arranged in several series; the dentaries and vomer have a single series of firm incisiform teeth. The dorsal is short and triangular. The anal fin rays decrease in height posteriorly. The ventral fins are short, the inner ray united to the belly by a membrane for about half its length. The caudal fin is deeply emarginate. The gill opening is a small slit located just before the pectoral fin base.

The genus *Hemicetopsis* is the largest genus of the family, with about seven species. The body is subterete and little compressed. It does not taper posteriorly as in *Cetopsis*. The

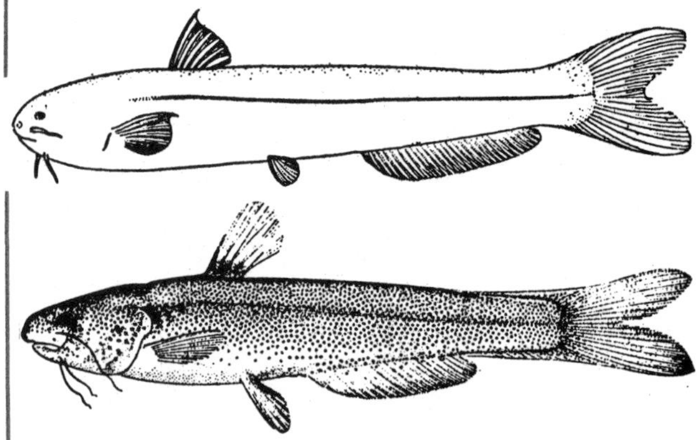

Hemicetopsis candiru (above); *H. minutus* (below). (From Fowler, 1945, and Eigenmann, 1912.)

head is short and heavy, the surface bones covered with a thick layer of muscle. The eyes are small and inconspicuous. The barbels are rather thick and short, and they are at least partially received in grooves at their bases. The mouth is terminal, with the upper jaw slightly projecting. The teeth are simple, somewhat compressed, and arranged in a single series on the premaxillaries, dentaries, and vomer. The ventral fins are short, and the inner rays are not united to the belly by a membrane. A pectoral pore is present. The gill openings are very small, entirely restricted to below the first pectoral fin ray.

Hemicetopsis candiru is perhaps the best known and most commonly seen species of this genus. It is easily captured because of its voracious predatory tendencies. A few chunks of raw fish placed on a string in areas where fishes are butchered and there is much blood and offal in the water is all that is needed to attract it. Very little is known about the other species of the genus.

Fernandez-Yepez (1971) supplied some information on a few of the species. *H. minutus* was collected near the Amatuk Cataract (waterfall) in clear, slightly alkaline water. The temperature was 27°C and the fish were 30 to 40 mm long. *H. macilentus* is common in the Rio Aguaro basin in clear, slightly alkaline waters (pH 7.0-7.4) where the temperature was about 27°C. They seem to prefer areas where embankments, crevices, and dead trees are prevalent. Fernandez-Yepez and Dr. Herbert R. Axelrod collected some 75 mm specimens burrowed into rock crevices and cracks of submerged roots and dead trees. *H. morenoi* was also collected in the Aguaro River in Venezuela in clear, slow-moving, slightly alkaline (pH 7.0-8.2) waters with a temperature also around 27°C. The small (42 mm) specimens are probably nocturnal. In fact all three species were found swimming in midwater at sunrise and sunset.

The genus *Pseudocetopsis* is a small genus of about three species from Brazil and eastern Ecuador. The genus is very similar to the others in general aspect but it does differ in some ways, particularly in the arrangement of the teeth. The teeth on the premaxillaries and dentaries are arranged in several rows (2-4), while those on the vomer are more irregular but generally uniserial and not interrupted in the middle. The dorsal and pectoral fins each have a produced filament. The anal fin rays usually number around 22. The ventral fins are united to the belly for almost their entire length. The eyes are more or less conspicuous. The gill openings are about as long above as below the base of the pectoral fin.

Pseudocetopsis gobioides. (From Fowler, 1954.)

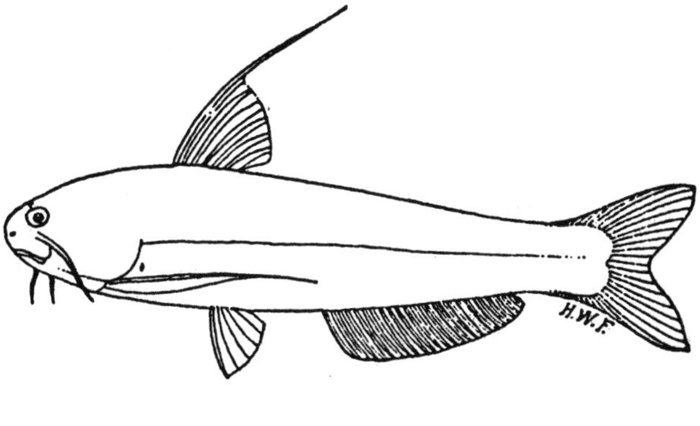

The type species of the genus, *Pseudocetopsis gobioides*, is a small (to 15 cm), little known species from the upper Amazon, Brazil, the Rio Paraguay, and parts of Argentina.

The last genus, *Cetopsogiton*, contains only a single species from the rivers around Guayaquil. This genus was originally called *Paracetopsis* until it was discovered that the name was preoccupied and the name *Cetopsogiton* was substituted for it. *Cetopsogiton* is similar to *Pseudocetopsis* but the ventral fins are not joined to the belly by a membrane and the teeth are arranged in many rows on the premaxillaries, dentaries, and vomer, those on the vomer in a transverse band that is interrupted in the middle. The eyes are conspicuous and the anal fin has about 30 rays.

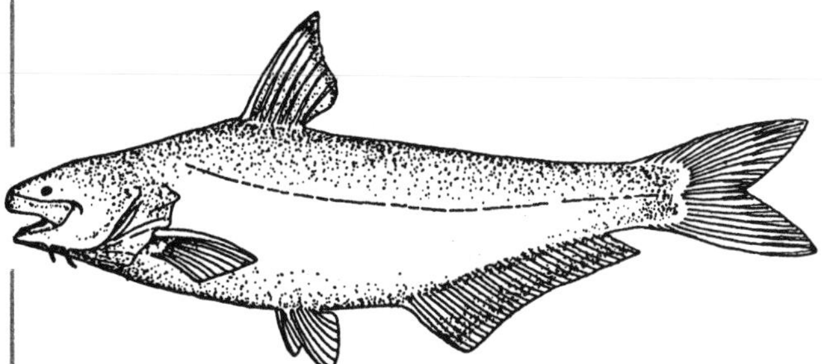

Cetopsogiton occidentalis. (After Eigenmann & Bean, 1907.)

Checklist of the species of the family Cetopsidae and their type localities:

Pseudocetopsis Bleeker, 1862. Type species *Cetopsis gobioides* Kner, 1857.

- *Pseudocetopsis gobioides* (Kner, 1857). Irisanga (Brazil).
- *P. macropteronema* (Boulenger, 1898). Rio Zamora, eastern Ecuador.

P. ventralis (Gill,, 1870). Rio Marañon and Rio Napo (upper Amazon).

Cetopsogiton Eigenmann, 1910. Substitute name for *Paracetopsis* Eigenmann & Bean, 1907, the name preoccupied. Type species *Cetopsis occidentalis* Steindachner, 1880.

Cetopsogiton occidentalis (Steindachner, 1880). Rivers near Guayaquil.

Cetopsis Agassiz, 1829. Type species *Silurus coecutiens* Lichtenstein, 1829.

Cetopsis chalmersi Norman, 1926. Rio das Velhas, probably east of the state of São Paulo.

C. coecutiens (Lichtenstein, 1829). Brazil.

Hemicetopsis Bleeker, 1862. Type species *Silurus candiru* Spix, 1829.

Hemicetopsis amphiloxus Eigenmann, Henn & Wilson, 1914. Basins of Patia, San Juan, and Atrato Rivers.

H. candiru (Spix *in* Agassiz, 1829). "Habitat in Brasiliae aequatorialis fluviis." (Ric Cupai at Rio Huallaga.)

H. macilentus Eigenmann, 1912. Guyana.

H. minutus Eigenmann, 1912. Guyana.

H. morenoi Fernandez-Yepez, 1971. Aguaro River, west of Santa Rita, Venezuela.

H. othonops Eigenmann, 1912. Basins of the Magdalena and Cauca Rivers.

H. plumbeus Steindachner, 1883. Canelos, Ecuador.

p. orinoco (Schultz, 1944). Rio Torbes, Orinoco system, Venezuela.

p. motatanensis (Schultz, 1944). Maracaibo basin, Venezuela. (Rio Motatan.)

Chapter 26

Family HYPOPHTHALMIDAE (Lookdown Catfishes)

Plate 148

The family Hypophthalmidae is a small family of South American freshwater catfishes with but a single genus and only about three species. The range, however, is quite large, extending from the Guianas to Argentina. The species are not very large (to about 46 cm) and are naked, lacking scutes or other body armor. The body is compressed and the head is more or less broad and depressed anteriorly but higher posteriorly. The eyes are small and ventrolaterally placed, but they are visible from both above and below; they are located behind and slightly below the angle of the mouth. The jaws are toothless and there are no teeth on the palate.

There are three pairs of barbels, a maxillary pair and two mandibular pairs. The dorsal fin is short-based and inserted slightly behind the level of the ventral fins; the dorsal and pectoral fin spines are weak or only slightly ossified and do not have any denticles. The adipose fin is small or reduced. The ventral fins are small and 6-rayed. The anal fin originates slightly behind the level of the dorsal and immediately behind the ventral fins and is very long (with about 63-68 rays). The caudal peduncle is moderately long, and the caudal fin is slightly emarginate to forked, with the outer rays prolonged.

The gill rakers are numerous, long, and fine, forming a filtering apparatus apparently used for feeding on plankton, for these fishes seem to have become adapted to a pelagic life style. The gill membranes are free from each other and from the isthmus. The gill openings are very wide, extending almost as far as the mandibular symphysis. There are 13 or 14 branchiostegal rays. The swim bladder is much reduced, being enclosed by the processes of the anterior vertebrae, by the scapular, and by other occipital-scapular bones.

Hypophthalmus edentatus, as the specific name suggests, has no teeth in its jaws but it does have many long gill rakers that are used as a sieve for feeding on crustacean zooplankton. It is said to be a generally silvery fish, slate gray dorsally with darker spots and silvery on the sides and belly. The fins are dark-margined. According to Eigenmann & Eigenmann (1890), *H. edentatus* (probably also including *H. perporosus*) has a much compressed body, the eyes included 9-13 times in the head length, the upper jaw thin and papery, and all the barbels flattened and with their posterior margins membranous, especially in younger individuals. The lateral line is well-marked and has branches running downward and backward to below the level of the pectoral fins and other branches running upward and backward, forming a network along each side of the lateral line.

H. oremaculatus is occasionally caught commercially as schools migrate upstream in the Rio Madeira. It attains a length of about 36 cm and is blue-violet dorsally, the sides and belly a rosy violet with a yellowish tint; the barbels and fin edges are black. *H. perporosus* is very much like *H. edentatus* and is even considered by some workers to be a synonym of that species. It is also a planktivore.

According to Chardon (1968), the hypophthalmids resemble the families Loricarii-

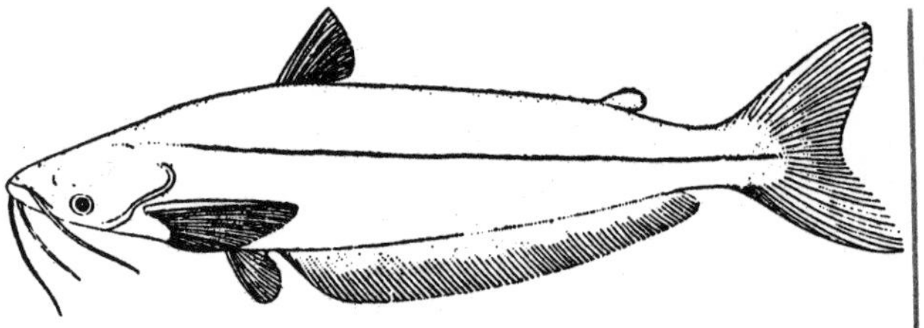

Hypophthalmus edentatus. (From Fowler, 1945.)

dae, Callichthyidae, and Trichomycteridae in several internal characters, including the disappearance of the boundaries of the first vertebra, the fusion of the capsules to the skull, and especially the simplification of the chain of ossicles. The hypophthalmids also resemble the family Helogenidae, from which it differs by lacking teeth in the jaws and on the palate; the species of the family Helogenidae have both jaw and vomerine teeth.

Checklist of the species of the family Hypophthalmidae and their type localities:

Hypophthalmus Spix *in* Agassiz, 1829. Type species *H. edentatus* Spix.

- *Hypophthalmus edentatus* Spix *in* Agassiz, 1829. Rivers of Equatorial Brazil.
- *H. marginatus* Valenciennes, 1840. Cayenne.
- *H. oremaculatus* Nani & Foster Plaza, 1947. Puerto Gaboto in the Rio Paraná.
- *H. perporosus* Cope, 1878. Nauta, Peru. (Possible synonym of *H. edentatus*).

Chapter 27

Family — Plates 149–153

ASPREDINIDAE

(Banjo Catfishes)

The family Aspredinidae is a small family of small to medium-sized catfishes confined to South America. They inhabit fresh waters, brackish estuaries, and even littoral marine waters. The anterior part of the body and the head are broad and flattened and the tail is long and slender. This combination gives them a rather unique appearance and has prompted such common names as frying pan catfishes and banjo catfishes. The head is protected by a strong bony shield that is more or less visible through the skin and gives them the appearance of being at least partially armored. The head and body are sometimes bumpy or have knobs, and in some species there are series of platelets along the lateral line and the base of the dorsal and anal fins. The opercle is reduced and without spines. The eyes are small to minute. The anterior nares are remote from the posterior nares, neither possessing a barbel. There is always a large pair of maxillary barbels and two pairs of mental barbels, although there may be in addition numerous postmental barbels covering the breast and the anterior part of the head. The mouth is terminal or subterminal, never truly inferior, and is set with villiform teeth arranged in bands; the vomer is without teeth. The dorsal fin is short, situated over the ventral fins, and often spineless or with only a weak, flexible spine. There is no adipose fin. The pectoral fins are low and provided with a strong, serrated spine that can be locked in the erect position. The anal fin is variable. The gill membranes are joined to the isthmus, and the gill opening is reduced to a narrow slit in front of the pectoral fin. The swim bladder is large and well-developed, free in the abdominal cavity, and touching in the area bounded by the humeral process and the lateral processes of the anterior vertebrae. The anterior vertebrae are coalesced, with broad lateral processes that curve downward posteriorly, their posterior margins reinforced and prolonged outward, touching the skin. The neural spines of the anterior vertebrae also form a crest from the occipital region to the dorsal fin and are in contact with the skin; the caudal vertebrae are compressed. The digestive tract is short. (Eigenmann & Eigenmann, 1890.)

Most species of the family are nocturnal, hiding during the day under dead leaves or aquatic vegetation, where they blend in quite well. Some living individuals were seen all but encapsulated with sheets of algae that must have taken some time to form. At night they may be seen swimming actively over the bottom searching for food. They enjoy an aquarium provided with subdued lighting and sufficient bottom material in which they can burrow or hide. They are good eaters, some gorging themselves almost to the bursting point on live worms and worm-like foods such as tubifex, bloodworms, and earthworms. Some species can make audible noises, apparently by using their pectoral spines and swim bladder.

The banjo catfishes are not of any great economic importance. Some of the larger euryhaline members of the subfamily Aspredininae that may attain lengths of up to 50 cm are utilized as food. A few species, notably of the genera *Bunocephalus* and occasionally *Agmus* of the subfamily Bunocephalinae and *Aspredo* of the subfamily Aspredininae, are imported as aquarium fishes.

As just noted, the family Aspredinidae is generally subdivided into two subfamilies, Aspredininae and Bunocephalinae. These subfamilies are distinct both in their anatomy and distribution, and there is still a lingering doubt as to whether they should be regarded as separate families. They are readily distinguished (even living specimens in an aquarium) by the length of the anal fin. In the subfamily Bunocephalinae it is short, having 18 or fewer rays; in the Aspredininae it is low but quite elongate, having 50 or more rays. Members of the subfamily Bunocephalinae are found in inland waters throughout tropical South America east of the Andes from Venezuela to northern Argentina. The Aspredininae, on the other hand, are lowland catfishes distributed along the coasts of the Guianas and Amazonia. They occur in brackish, muddy waters (even in the sea) of estuaries and the tidal portions of rivers. They are not found anywhere inland beyond the lower Amazon delta area where the influence of tides is felt.

The majority of species in the subfamily Bunocephalinae inhabit low altitude streams of many (if not most) of the tropical major river systems of South America east of the Andes. They are normally found in shaded forest brooks, igarapes, and caños in or near areas where some current occurs, such as riffles or rapids. They are considered primary freshwater fishes, and no species are known to even enter the estuaries or other brackish waters. Eight genera are usually included in this subfamily, which can be distinguished by the following key (after Myers, 1960, and Stewart, 1985).

1a. Body with 6 longitudinal rows of bony plates, the lateral line series formed of smaller plates than the paired dorsal (from dorsal fin origin to caudal fin base) and ventral (from anal fin origin to caudal fin base) series; D. 7; ventral fins originating anterior to dorsal fin (tribe Hoplomyzontini)................... 6

1b. Body without prominent longitudinal series of bony scutes or plates; D. 2-5 (tribe Bunocephalini)....................... 2

2a. Anterior and posterior edges of pectoral fin spines relatively smooth, without strong teeth 3

2b. Anterior and posterior edges of pectoral fin spines with stout teeth; D. 5; caudal peduncle relatively slender............... 4

3a. Dorsal fin very small, with only 2 rays; head rugose, broad, and depressed, its greatest depth less than depth of the very deep caudal peduncle; lower lip not fringed .... *Amaralia*

3b. Dorsal fin with 5 rays; head relatively smooth; caudal peduncle slender; lower lip with a fringe of fine barbels directed forward .... *Xyliphius*

4a. Head extremely depressed, smooth; anal fin rays 16 to 18.................... *Petacara*

4b. Head depressed or deep, rugose; anal fin rays fewer than 12 5

5a. Head depressed, rugose, its greatest depth equal to about half its greatest width .... *Bunocephalus*

5b. Head deep, excessively rugose, its greatest depth equal or nearly equal to its greatest width .... *Agmus*

6a. Upper lip provided with 4-5 fleshy papillae; 11 plates preceding anal fin, with 4 sets of paired elements; pectoral spine length less than 25% S.L.; 47-51 lateral line scutes .... *Hoplomyzon*

6b. Upper lip lacking fleshy papillae; 5-9 plates preceding anal fin, with 1-3 sets of paired elements.......................... 7

7a. 5-6 teeth on posterior edge of pectoral fin spine; pectoral fin spine not strongly recurved, only slightly longer than first branched pectoral ray; 5 plates preceding anal fin, with 1 set of paired elements; 33-39 lateral line scutes.. *Dupouyichthys*

7b. 10-18 teeth on posterior edge of pectoral fin spine; pectoral fin spine strongly recurved and distinctly longer than first branched pectoral fin ray; 7-9 plates preceding anal fin, with 2-3 sets of paired elements; 42-64 lateral line scutes .... *Ernstichthys*

The genus *Hoplomyzon* is a genus of only two species, *H. atrizona* from Venezuela and *H. papillatus* from Ecuador. Both species are relatively tiny, neither exceeding 25 mm in length. These and the other fishes of the tribe Hoplomyzontini are generally confined to swift streams, where they have become adapted to the moving waters in much the

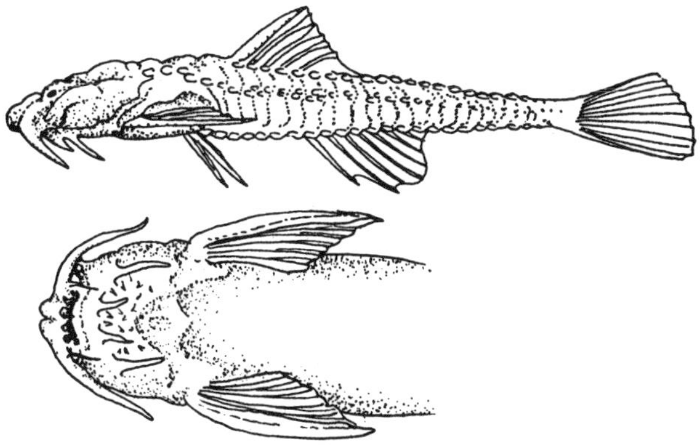

Hoplomyzon papillosus. (After Stewart, 1985.)

same way as the hill-stream catfishes. The lower surfaces of the head and body have become flattened and the enlarged pectoral and ventral fins are set more horizontally than usual; the head and maxillary barbels are also modified for this type of existence. The body is quadrangular anteriorly (in region of the dorsal fin) and hexagonal posteriorly; the caudal peduncle is slender.

In *Hoplomyzon* there are three pairs of longitudinal series of plates, the dorsal and ventral paired series large and strong, the lateral line series (composed of 47-51 plates) small and weak. The individual plates of the dorsal and ventral series are set close together, even closer posteriorly, the series of the right and left sides coming together behind the dorsal and anal fins to form a flattened, bony armor above and below the tail. There are 11 plates preceding the anal fin, with 4 sets of paired elements. The dorsal and ventral series of plates form the major angles of the body cross-section; posteriorly these plates plus the lateral series combine to form the hexagonal cross-section. All plates are covered by thick skin. The skin is faintly villiform on the head and between the dorso-ventral armor and the small plates of the lateral line.

The head is depressed, with the humeral process very short or absent. The coracoid process is even shorter, strongly curved inward, and with its tip immediately in front of and lateral to the origin of the ventral fin. The head is covered with the usual rugosities, all reduced save the median dorsal series. The snout is broadly rounded and has a median indentation. The eyes are very small. The mouth is narrow, about equal to the interorbital width, and the upper lip bears 4 or 5 stout, fleshy papillae; the lower lip is thin and has neither papillae nor a fringe. There are three pairs of barbels, a maxillary pair and two mental pairs (very small). The maxillary barbels extend to beyond the middle of the coracoid process, each barbel connected to the side of the head by a broad membranous web that extends to below the eye. The undersides of the head and body form a flattened surface, and the vent is much nearer the tip of the snout than the caudal base.

The dorsal fin is short based, with 6 to 7 rays, and the anal fin is short, of only 6 rays, and originates under the posterior portion of the dorsal fin. The ventral fins originate well in advance of the dorsal fin, and the spine is curved, the outer (anterior) margin smooth and the inner (posterior) margin with 6 large retrorse teeth or spines; the fin is provided with a membrane like that of *Exostoma* or *Glyptosternon*. The pectoral and ventral fins are arranged horizontally, in a plane with the flat undersurface of the body. The length of the pectoral fin spine is less than 25% of the standard length. The caudal fin is truncate. The gill openings are small and inferiorly placed, such as that seen in the genus *Xyliphius*.

The genus *Dupouyichthys* is monotypic, containing only *D. sapito* from Rio Guasare at El Paso, Venezuela. This is a small species of less than 25 mm standard length. *Dupouyichthys* is very much like *Hoplomyzon* and *Ernstichthys*, the other members of the tribe Hoplomyzontini, except that it has a relatively deeper body and fewer lateral line scutes (33-39, compared with 47-51 in *Hoplomyzon* and 43-64 in *Ernstichthys*). There are 5 plates preceding the anal fin, with only one set of paired elements. It also can be distinguished from *Hoplomyzon* by the absence of

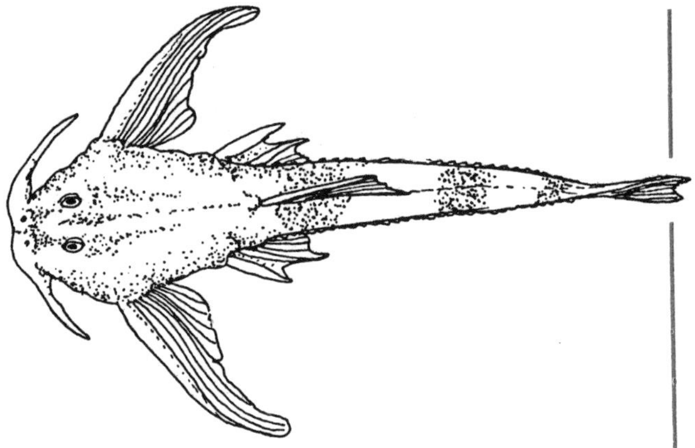

Dupuoyichthys sapito. (After Schultz, 1944.)

papillae on the upper lip, the longer posterior coracoid and cleithral processes, and the longer pectoral fin spine (28.2% of standard length). From *Ernstichthys* it can be told by the shorter pectoral spine (33-41% of standard length) with only 5-6 teeth on the posterior margin (10-18 in *Ernstichthys*), relatively larger eye (3.3% of S.L. compared with 1.8-2.3% in *Ernstichthys*), and greater interorbital width (7.6% of S.L. compared with 4.5-6.3 in *Ernstichthys*).

The genus *Ernstichthys* contains only three species, *E. anduzei* from Venezuela and *E. megistus* and *E. intonsus* from Ecuador. This genus is also similar to *Hoplomyzon* and *Dupouyichthys* (in fact, the three genera of the tribe sometimes are synonymized into *Hoplomyzon*) but differs from them by having 7-9 plates preceding the anal fin, with 2-3 sets of

Ernstichthys intonsus. (After Stewart, 1985.)

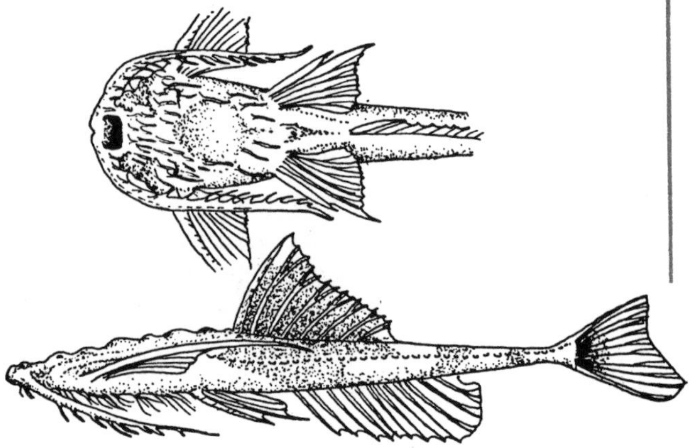

paired elements. It is further distinguished by the pectoral fin spine being strongly recurved, having 10-18 teeth on the anterior edge, and being noticeably longer than the first branched ray. The interorbital space is narrower than in the other two genera, there is less space between the nostrils, and the caudal peduncle is shallower. It is distinguishable from *Hoplomyzon* by the lack of the fleshy papillae of the upper lip and the longer posterior cleithral and coracoid processes; it is distinguishable from *Dupouyichthys* by having more than 40 plates in the lateral line.

The genus *Agmus* is mostly characterized by a deeper body than *Bunocephalus*, and in profile it actually looks hunchbacked. The shape and rugosity of the head, as noted in the key, are different. There are only two species of *Agmus*, *A. scabriceps* from the Brazilian Amazon and *A. lyriformis* from Guyana.

Agmus lyriformis attains a length of about 12 cm, has a very rugose body, and is brown-black in color with some small grayish spots on its upper sides. It was collected by Eigenmann in small streams of an island in the Es-

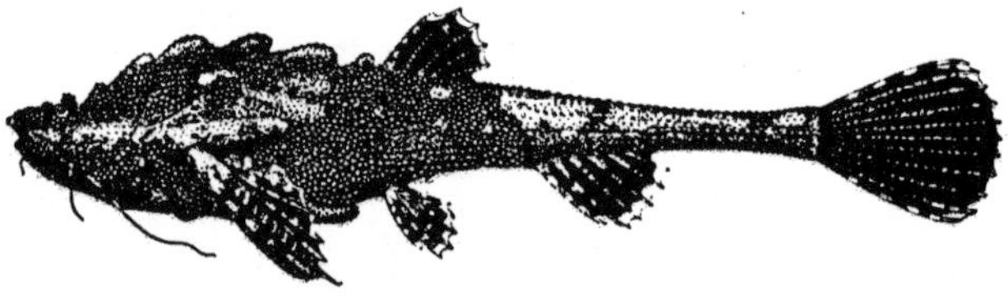

Agmus lyriformis. (From Eigenmann, 1912.)

siquibo River not far from where it joins the Rupununi. This species has been imported on occasion for the aquarium trade and it may be seen more and more with time. It is strictly nocturnal, living on the bottom and pretending (quite successfully) to be a piece of wood or other inanimate object. As it rests motionless among the debris or in the plant thickets it is very difficult to spot, and many an aquarist has feared for his prize, which to all intents and purposes appeared dead. At night, however, the fish may move about searching the bottom for bits of food. In captivity they do well on tubifex, bloodworms, chopped earthworms, and small gammarids; and in a pinch it is even said to accept pieces of squid. A temperature of 23-25°C seems to suit them fine. The swimming motion is said to be rather awkward and slow, the movement provided mainly by a thrust of the caudal fin. When disturbed, an individual resting on the bottom will fold its tail toward its head (usually toward the left side), the movement being slow and the position being held for some minutes. On one occasion an individual was seen sitting in a bunch of Java fern.

The genus *Amaralia* has a body that lacks prominent longitudinal series of bony scutes or plates. Its head is broad and depressed, the greatest depth less than the depth of the relatively deep, compressed caudal peduncle. The dorsal surface of the head is rugose and covered with bony protuberances usually in two curved series. The lower lip is not fringed. The caudal peduncle is compressed and deeper than broad. The dorsal fin is very small, with only 2 rays, and the anal fin is relatively short. The paired fins are strong, the pectorals each provided with a strong spine with a smooth outer edge. The caudal fin is rounded. The single species, *A. hypsiurus*, is known only from the Rio Branco of the Rio Negro, Brazil. Aquarists who are familiar with that river know its waters to be quite acidic.

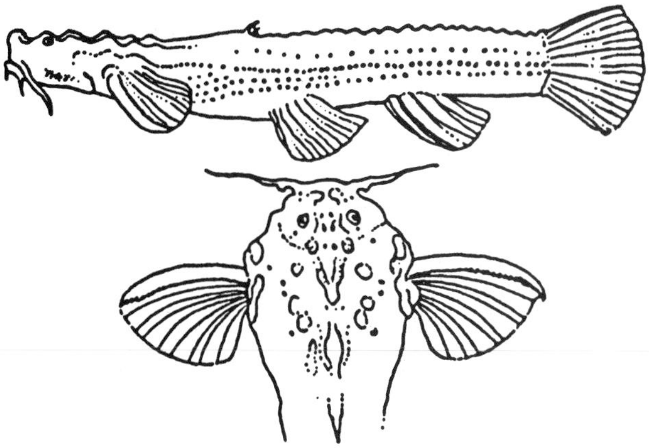

Amaralia hypsiurus. (From Fowler, 1954.)

The genus *Xyliphius* is a genus of only two species, the second one described as recently as 1962. The genus (based only on characters given in a redescription of the type species in 1942) has the depth about equal to the width at the level of the vent and about half the width at the pectoral origin. The head is about as wide as long, has several ridges, and is depressed. The eyes are minute, their distance from the snout about equal to the interorbital space. The anterior nares are not completely margined. The mouth is broad, subterminal, the lower lip with a series of tapering papillae screening the mouth opening. The lower lip is also attached to the maxillary barbels at the rictus by a membrane; the maxillary barbels extend to or just past the pectoral fin origin. There are two pairs of mental barbels. The pectoral spine is produced into a short filament, the spine itself being strong with several hooks on the posterior margin; the anterior margin is smooth. The caudal fin is obliquely truncate, and the caudal peduncle is subcylindrical to compressed. The gill membranes are attached to the isthmus and the gill opening is short, remote, and entirely inferior in position (not easily seen). *X. magdalenae* is reported to reach a length of about 15 cm.

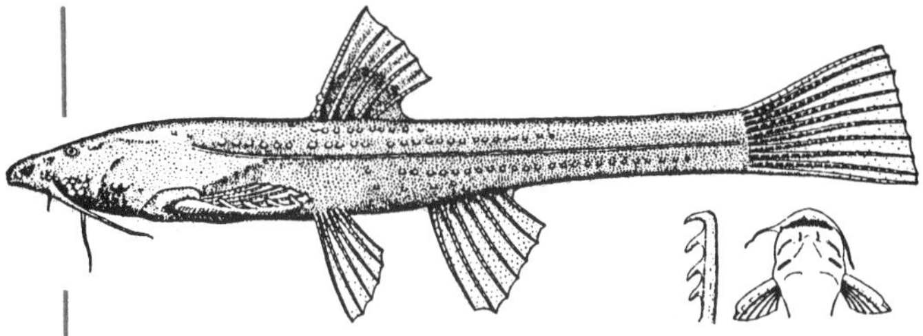

Xyliphius magdalenae. (From Eigenmann, 1922.)

The genus *Petacara* is a monotypic genus containing only *P. dolichurus* from the Rio Trombetas near Obidos. This species had been included in *Bunocephalus*, to which *Petacara* is most closely related, until Böhlke (1959) placed it in its own genus on the basis of a combination of characters, the most obvious of which is the number of anal fin rays. In this species there are 16 to 18 anal fin rays compared with fewer than 12 (normally 6 to 11) in the other members of this subfamily. This still falls far short of the 50 or more found in the Aspredininae. The body and head are depressed, the head excessively so (only 8.3% of the standard length), and relatively smooth (without the knobs or ridges so common in these fishes). The tail is rather elongated, and there are 5 longitudinal rows of papillae along either side of the body. The midlateral row is provided with a series of small ossified platelets or ring-like segments. The eyes are minute, the snout is incised medially, and the mouth is small, the lower jaw included. The mandibles contain small teeth in bands, while the upper jaw is toothless or has extremely reduced teeth. The dorsal fin is composed of 5 rays, the base of the last ray situated well in advance of the first anal fin ray. The pectoral fins have a strong spine serrated on both edges and 5 rays. The ventrals have 6 rays, the caudal fin has 10, and the anal fin, as mentioned, has 16 to 18 rays. Three pairs of barbels are present, a maxillary pair extending back well beyond the pectoral fin bases and two pairs of mental barbels that are arranged more or less in a semicircle.

The last genus in the subfamily Bunocephalinae is the one best known to aquarists—*Bunocephalus*. This genus includes about 20 species, more than half the known species of the entire family. They are generally small in size, none exceeding a length of about 150 mm. Their preferred habitat appears to be smaller streams shaded by the rainforest cover, where they are difficult to detect among the aquatic vegetation and dead leaves. The body is very depressed, and the caudal peduncle is cylindrical or quadrangular in cross-section and compressed posteriorly. The head is depressed, granular, with more or less prominent bony crests, its greatest depth approximately equal to half its width. The skin of the body and head is covered by papillae or bumps. The mouth is small, anterior, and provided with patches of villiform teeth in each jaw. The eyes are small in size and superior in position. The dorsal fin is well developed, with about 5 rays, the last of which is adnate to the body. The pectoral fin spine is very strong, both edges with strong recurved serrations or teeth, the largest near the tip. The maxillary barbels usually do not extend beyond the middle of the pectoral fin. The gill openings are very small.

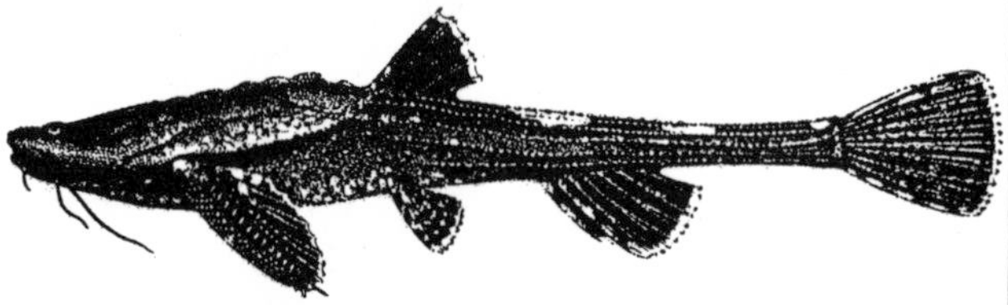

Bunocephalus amaurus. (From Eigenmann, 1912.)

Several species of *Bunocephalus* have been imported for the aquarium trade, and at least one of them is said to have spawned in captivity. The species in general are inactive, crepuscular, bottom-dwellers that lie motionless for hours buried in the substrate or secreted into small holes or crevices in the driftwood or rockwork. When they do swim they do so awkwardly and usually take frequent rests. They are said to also propel themselves in a jerky motion at times by jetting water out from the gill slits. For keeping these fishes a large tank with a relatively soft bottom material and numerous hiding places (such as driftwood, rockwork, plants) is recommended. They are said to prefer soft water but also seem to do as well in medium to medium hard water. The temperature range that suits them best appears to be from 20°C to 25°C. They are omnivorous and will accept a variety of foods.

Bunocephalus coracoideus, sometimes referred to as the "Guitarrita" (= little guitar) in some areas in South America, is the species probably most commonly kept by aquarists—at least that is the name the fish is sold under. It attains a length of about 10 cm and hails from the Amazon to Uruguay.

It is this species that has been reported as spawning in captivity. Spawning is more likely to occur in the spring after several months of conditioning. The male usually selects the spawning site, where he will fan out a hollow or depression. With large spawns the nests were quite large. This depression may be out in the open away from any rocks or plants or it may be in a sheltered area such as below a rock or plant. During the actual spawning attempts the plants may become uprooted. The eggs are deposited in the depression by the female and they are guarded by the male. In two spawnings the yield was in the neighborhood of 4,000 to 5,000 fry. The fry can be started on rotifers and microworms, although one report indicated that the fry would eat only a particular species of rotifer (*Brachionus rubins*). At about 12-13 mm the fry can graduate to chopped tubificid worms. Once the proper food is provided the fry grow rapidly. There are no obvious external sexual differences that the aquarist can rely on to sex his banjo catfishes.

The adults are omnivorous and do very well on a diet of tubifex worms and a variety of other worms and worm-like foods. Newly imported banjos are said to be difficult to start on an aquarium diet. A tank of about 130 liters capacity is recommended (especially if spawning is attempted) filled with about 35 cm of water, some bottom sand, rocks, and plants. The pH can be around 7.3 to 7.9 and the temperature about 20°C to 25°C. The banjo can be seen gliding along the bottom when the lights are very low, seemingly without effort as it moves its tail back and forth sinuously. If no cover plants are used the fish will remain on or near the bottom, but if there are plenty of bushy plants they will venture into the upper layers and lie among the leaves, coming down to the bottom only to feed.

B. knerii from northeastern South America has a body covered with a thick, leathery skin, and the head and sides are covered with little bumps or warts. Their color and shape make them extremely difficult to spot even in the aquarium if it is properly decorated with driftwood, rocks, and perhaps plants. This species is also nocturnal and extremely shy when the lights are on. It usually will dig itself into the substrate for security, so make sure the bottom material is relatively soft. At night some of the shyness disappears and there is more activity as it searches about the aquarium for food. There is no problem as far as diet is concerned, and almost all aquarium foods are accepted. A temperature range of 21°C to 26°C is recommended for at higher temperatures there is a tendency for the fish to become somewhat sluggish. *B. knerii* makes a good community tank occupant, but it should be kept only with non-aggressive fishes of approximately the same size (it attains a length of about 20 cm).

B. aleuropsis occurs in shaded waters over sand, clay, and bedrock areas below riffles. Its stomach contents included insect and plant debris (Saul, 1975).

The members of the subfamily Aspredininae inhabit what is generally known as the Guiana Mangrove Province. This is a relatively unbroken line of low-lying, muddy, mangrove-fringed coastline extending over 2,400 km from the Orinoco delta to the Brazilian state of Maranhao. This province may even be said to be defined by the presence of this subfamily along with some species of ariid catfishes that occupy the same habitat. It should be emphasized here that the aspredinine catfishes are euryhaline forms, in contrast to the strictly freshwater bunocephaline catfishes, and enter fresh water only in estuaries and where there is a tidal influence. Coinhabiting the province with the aspredinines are the well-known *Anableps anableps* and *A. microlepis*, as well as *Tomeurus gracilis*. Two genera are included in this subfamily and can be distinguished by the following key.

1a. Usually 7 or more pairs of mental and postmental barbels or small tentacles covering ventral surface from corners of mouth to anterior portion of abdomen; maxillary barbels free from head throughout their length..*Aspredinichthys*

1b. Only two pairs of mental barbels; large pair of maxillary barbels adnate, joined to head by basal membrane.............2

2a. Two pairs of maxillary barbels; no ridges on sides of body except for lateral line; usually plain coloration.............. ....*Aspredo (Aspredo)*

2b. One pair of maxillary barbels; 3 or 4 longitudinal ridges along sides of body; usually mottled....*Aspredo (Platystacus)*

When Myers reviewed the subfamily in 1960, he also recognized three genera, but he accepted the genus *Chamaigenes* for the single species *C. filamentosus*. *Aspredinichthys* was thus left with the single species *A. tibicen*, and *Aspredo* had two species, *A. aspredo* and *A. cotylephorus*. Taylor's 1978 classification included the same four species, but *Chamaigenes filamentosus* became *Aspredinichthys filamentosus* and *Aspredo cotylephorus* became *Platystacus cotylephorus*, the remaining species not changing. Mees (1987) recognized only two genera, *Apredo* and *Aspredinichthys*, *Platystacus cotylephorus* becoming *Aspredo cotylephorus*. So, although the species of the subfamily are few and have remained relatively stable in recent years, the generic lines have shifted quite a bit.

Aspredinichthys tibicen is known from the Guyanan and Brazilian coasts. Eigenmann (1912) reported it as the most common banjo catfish in the Georgetown fish market. Specimens over 200 mm in length were recorded by him. The head is somewhat elongate and subconical, with the snout little projecting. The mouth is narrow, and the teeth are long

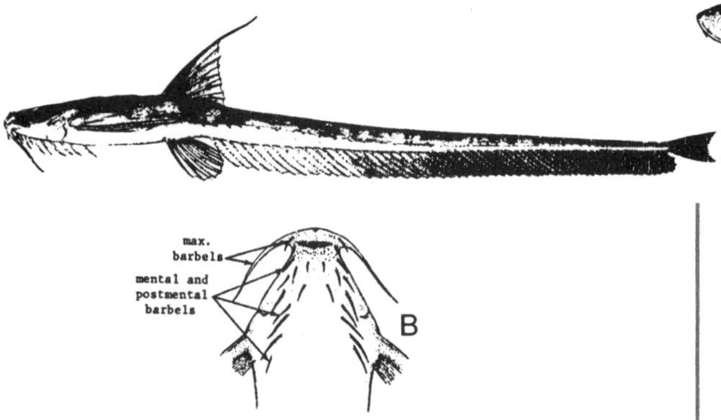

Aspredinichthys tibicen; (b) ventral view of head. (From Fischer, 1978.)

and fine, those in the upper jaw in a continuous band. The main maxillary barbel reaches about to the gill opening, and there is an accessory barbel on the anterior margin of its bony base. The snout has four broad, hooked spines. There are about 10 pairs of mental and postmental barbels. The first dorsal fin ray and the outer caudal fin rays are somewhat produced. The pectoral fin spine is flattened, the posterior margin with a series of teeth becoming longer and stronger nearer the tip, and the anterior margin with somewhat weaker teeth. The breeding of this species, and perhaps the entire subfamily, is quite unusual. The female apparently develops spongy tentacles on her belly during the breeding season. She will incubate her eggs by carrying them about attached to these tentacles.

Aspredinichthys filamentosus also attains lengths of over 20 cm and it too is a common market fish along the Guyana coast. It is caught in coastal traps of stakes driven into the tidal mud (Chinese fish traps). According to Puyo (1949), it "lives only in salt water strongly charged with alluvium." *A. filamentosus* is similar to *A. tibicen* but differs by having the tip of the snout smooth, without hooks, and by having only about 7 pairs of mental and postmental barbels. The first dorsal fin ray is very elongate, filamentous, and the outer caudal rays are somewhat extended.

Aspredo aspredo reaches a fairly large size of 40 cm. The head is greatly depressed and spatulate, and the mouth is broad, the snout

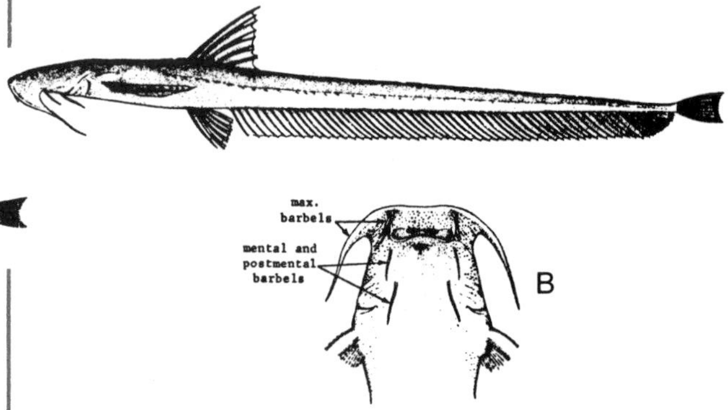

Aspredo aspredo; (b) ventral view of head. (From Fischer, 1978.)

projecting almost its entire length. Each jaw possesses two patches of small teeth. The main maxillary barbel extends to the pectoral fin base, and there is an accessory barbel anterior to it. The mental barbels are placed near the lip, exterior to the postmental pair. A minute pectoral pore is present. The first dorsal fin ray and the outer caudal fin rays are slightly produced. The pectoral fin spine is similar to that of *Aspredinichthys tibicen*. There are about 50-55 anal fin rays.

Aspredo cotylephorus has a greatly depressed head that becomes narrow anteriorly. The snout projects about half its length. The upper jaw is provided with two rhomboidal patches of villiform teeth and the lower jaw with broader patches of similar teeth. The single pair of maxillary barbels extends to the gill openings. There are 3 or 4 longitudinal ridges along the sides of the body. The first dorsal fin ray is scarcely produced, although the out-

Aspredo cotylephorus. (From Fischer, 1978.)

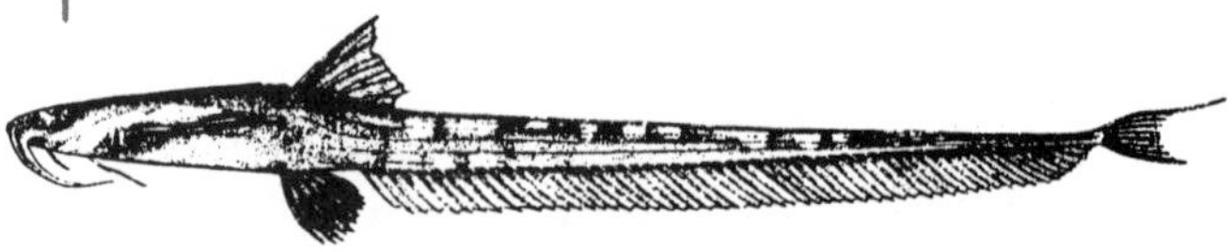

ermost caudal fin rays are somewhat extended. There are about 53 to 57 anal fin rays. *A. cotylephorus* is generally mottled, with the variation in pattern quite remarkable. The background color can vary considerably from light tan or purplish to a dark chocolate brown. This is usually overlaid with a number of cream to white spots, patches, or even bands.

Aspredo has females that carry their eggs and young attached to the ventral surface of the body. The skin is said to have differentiated so that each egg rests in a cup-like hollow provided with a spongy tentacle or short peduncle. It has been theorized that the females lay their eggs on the bottom and then lie on them, at which time the eggs become attached. An excavated depression in the substrate serves as the spawning site. *A. cotylephorus* is reported to have spawned in captivity. The few fry that were retrieved (they were about 2 mm long) were raised on microworms and newly hatched brine shrimp. They were said to be identical in shape to their parents. According to Sands, these fish migrate against the current of the estuary into fresh water in nature, although the actual spawning apparently took place in brackish water. He believes the fry developed in fresh water. The specialization of the female carrying her eggs attached to the underside of the body seems to lend credence to a possibility of migration or movement by the female. Possibly the attachment is necessary in running water, or even as an adaptation to particular predation pressure. It appears that *Aspredo* is a much better swimmer than the smaller and more clumsy bunocephalines that have been observed in captivity. (Sands, 1986.)

Checklist of the species of the Family Aspredinidae and their type localities:

Subfamily Bunocephalinae

Agmus Eigenmann, 1910. Type species *Bunocephalus scabriceps* Eigenmann & Eigenmann.
- *Agmus lyriformis* Eigenmann, 1912. British Guiana.
- *A. scabriceps* (Eigenmann & Eigenmann, 1889). Rio Jutai.

Amaralia Fowler, 1954. Type species *Bunocephalus hypsiurus* Kner.
- *Amaralia hypsiurus* (Kner, 1855). Rio Branco.

Bunocephalus Kner, 1855. Type species *Platystacus verrucosus* Bloch.
- *Bunocephalus albofasciatus* Fowler, 1943. Todos os Santos, Bolivia. (As *Pterobunocephalus albofasciatus* in Fowler, 1943.)
- *B. aleuropsis* Cope, 1870. Pebas, Ecuador. (Gosline, 1945 includes *B. melas* as a synonym, Fowler does not.)
- *B. amaurus* Eigenmann, 1912. British Guiana.
  - *a. aloikae* Hoedeman, 1961. French Guiana.
  - *a. sipaliwini* Hoedeman, 1961. French Guiana.
- *B. bifidus* Eigenmann *in* Eigenmann & Allen, 1942. Yurima Guas, Peru and Lake Rogoagua, Bolivia.
- *B. carvalhoi* Miranda-Ribeiro, 1944. Mage, State of Rio de Janeiro.
- *B. chamaizelus* Eigenmann, 1912. British Guiana.
- *B. colombianus* Eigenmann, 1912. Bacia do Atrato, Colombia.
- *B. coracoideus* (Cope, 1874). Nauta, Peru. (Includes *B. bicolor*.)
- *B. depressus* Haseman, 1911. Rio Machupo near San Joaquin, Bolivia.
- *B. doriae* Boulenger, 1902. Rio Coxipo, Mato Grosso, Paraguay.
- *B. gronovii* (Bleeker, 1858). Embocaduras do Rio Negro do Demerara.
- *B. iheringi* Boulenger, 1891. Rio Grande do Sul, Paraguay.
- *B. knerii* Steindachner, 1883. Canelos, eastern Ecuador.
- *B. larai* von Ihering, 1930. Rio Piracicaba, Sao Paulo.
- *B. minutus* H. Günther, 1942. Paraguay.
- *B. retropinnis* Eigenmann *in* Eigenmann & Allen, 1942. Uruguaiana, Brazil.
- *B. rugosus* Eigenmann & Kennedy, 1903. Laguna, port of Arroyo Chagalalina, Paraguay.
- *B. salathei* Myers, 1927. Rio de Janeiro.
- *B. verrucosus* (Bloch, 1794). No locality indicated.

Xyliphius Eigenmann, 1912. Type species *X. magdalenae* Eigenmann.
- *Xyliphius barbatus* Arambourg & Aram-

bourg, 1962. Rio Parana (en) Rosario, Santa Fe.

X. magdalenae Eigenmann, 1912. Magdalena Basin.

Petacara Böhlke, 1959. Type species *Bunocephalus dolichurus* Delsman, 1941.

Petacara dolichurus (Delsman, 1941). Rio Trombetas near Obidos.

Hoplomyzon Myers, 1942. Type species *H. atrizona* Myers.

Hoplomyzon atrizona Myers, 1942. Tributary of the Rio Zulia, Estado Tachira, Venezuela.

a. petroleus Schultz, 1944. Rio Motatan, Maracaibo basin, Venezuela.

H. papillatus Stewart, 1985. Rio Agarico, Napo Prov., Ecuador.

Dupuoyichthys Schultz, 1944. Type species *D. sapito* Schultz.

Dupuoyichthys sapito Schultz, 1944. Rio Guasare at El Paso, Estado Zulia, Venezuela.

Ernstichthys Fernandez-Yepez, 1953. Type species *E. anduzei* Fernandez-Yepez.

Ernstichthys anduzei Fernandez-Yepez, 1953. Rio Bocono at La Veguita, Estado Barinas, Venezuela.

E. intonsus Stewart, 1985. Rio Napo at Anangu, Napo Province, Ecuador.

E. megistus (Orces, 1961). Lower Rio Bobonaza at Chicherota, Ecuador.

Subfamily Aspredininae

Aspredinichthys Bleeker, 1858. Type species *Aspredo tibicen* Temminck.

Aspredinichthys filamentosus (Valenciennes, 1840). Guianas.

A. tibicen (Temminck, 1840). Surinam.

Aspredo Scopoli, 1777. Type species *A. batrachus* Gronow (= *Silurus aspredo* Linnaeus). (Because of nomenclatural problems, this genus is often credited to Bleeker, 1858.)

Aspredo aspredo (Linnaeus, 1758). "In Americae fluviis."

A. cotylephorus Bloch, 1794. Type locality not indicated.

Chapter 28

Family TRICHOMYCTERIDAE (Parasitic Catfishes)

Plates 148, 154–157

The family Trichomycteridae is a rather large family of small to very small slender-bodied freshwater catfishes that have been described as almost loach-like or worm-like in appearance. This appearance has prompted some dealers to sell them as "coolie catfishes." The family is distributed from Panama and Colombia in the north to Chile and Argentina in the south. In many references they have been referred to as family Pygidiidae, but it has been determined that the name Trichomycteridae has priority.

It is this family that contains the infamous candiru (actually this name is applied to several species in several different genera) that is reported as being urinophilus ("lovers of urine"), for they are said to be attracted to a stream of urine (perhaps because the current may be similar to the current that might lead them to a fish's gill chamber—their natural prey) and may become lodged in the urinary tracts of animals, including man. Local Indians even wear protective clothing and other devices because of these fishes. More will be said about this habit under the genus *Vandellia*.

Not as well known, but perhaps just as dangerous to their intended victims, are the scale-eaters and the parasitic species. Among the latter are small species of no more than 50 mm that are said to live as parasites in the gill chambers of larger fishes, including larger catfishes, eating the gill filaments and drinking the blood and body juices of the host. Some of these are quite voracious, attacking pimelodids that become concentrated in certain areas during their migrations. These "candiru" are a nuisance to fishermen, destroying some of the catch before they can even be landed. Schools of these fishes in company with some cetopsids of similar habits can reduce a living fish to merely a head and skeleton in a matter of minutes. In the Trichomycteridae, members of the genera *Pseudostegophilus* and *Pareiodon* are involved. These fishes have inferior mouths provided with teeth that are well suited for biting or rasping out small pieces of flesh. Devincenzi (1942) was of the opinion that some trichomycterids, such as *Homodiaetus*, inflict wounds by means of the erectile spines on the gill covers. Trichomycterids not only attack larger fishes but will attach themselves to other animals as well, including man. By means of suction, provided by their well adapted mouths, they adhere to their victim and go to work. Their bite or rasping is apparently relatively painless, and they often are able to gorge themselves on the blood without any objection from the victim. Wounds seen on fishes in the markets are often attributable to these little fishes.

Most of the trichomycterids are free-living in streams and undeserving of the reputation that some of the other family members have brought upon the whole family. Most of the species are crepuscular or nocturnal, burrowing into the mud or sand bottom, into the banks of streams, or hiding in the leaf litter and fallen tree branches. They obtain their food from the soft substrate. In a creek called Igarape Irura, Haseman (1911) collected 400 specimens of a species of *Stegophilus* that were buried in the sand. They were very small but were present by the millions in areas where the water was too shallow for any larger fishes. He stated that fishes of the genus *Vandellia*, as well as other trichomycterids that were buried in the sand bars, when disturbed rose quickly out of the sand but disappeared into it again in an instant, leaving only a small hole or depression where the fish reentered.

Some trichomycterids inhabit mountain streams, often above waterfalls that should have proved an effective barrier to their ascent. It is said, however, that they are able to climb the rock faces a centimeter at a time by surging and then gripping the rocks with their specialized gill cover spines, even against the flow of the falling water.

In contrast to the mountain streams species that live in highly oxygenated waters, some trichomycterids do not seem to be bothered by polluted waters and may actually be attracted by wastes, human or otherwise. At least some species are able to utilize atmospheric air (including both parasitic and non-parasitic species).

Although generally considered unsuitable for home aquaria, at least a few species can be maintained in captivity quite well. Since the free-living species are generally bottom-fishes that like to burrow into the substrate, the bottom material must be selected carefully. Material that is soft is preferred, and it should be of a dark color. For the non-burrowers, the tank should be provided with hiding places, such as those formed using driftwood, plants, or even rock caves. Most of the species imported for the aquarium trade are peaceful and crepuscular, although there are a few that are active during the daylight hours. They are omnivorous, with a preference for small worms. The recommended temperature range is 20 to 25°C. Most of the aquarium species are quite small, although some trichomycterids may grow to a length of 30 cm or more.

The body is completely naked and generally elongated, even eel-like or loach-like, terete or subterete in cross-section, with the caudal peduncle compressed and deep. The head is depressed and the cranium is covered with muscles. The eyes are small, superior in position, and without free orbital margins. The interopercle has numerous retrorse spines in various series, those of the outermost series larger; the opercle often has similar spines. A nasal barbel is present on the posterior border of the anterior nares and there are two maxillary barbels at the angle of the mouth, the upper in connection with the rudimentary maxilla; mandibular barbels may be present or absent. The nares are remote from each other. The mouth is of moderate size, terminal or subterminal, usually with bands of two or more series of incisiform or caniniform teeth; there are no labial or vomerine teeth. The dorsal fin is short-based and rounded, without a spine, and positioned posteriorly, its origin over or in advance of the origin of the anal fin; there are 6 to 11 developed rays, or up to 14 counting the anterior short or hidden rays. The anal fin is rounded and short-based, with a variable number of accessory rays. The pectoral fins are usually without spines. The ventral fins are small. An adipose fin is normally absent (rarely present).

The gill membranes are attached to the isthmus, with or without a free fold across it. There are 10-12 branchiostegal rays. The swim bladder is much reduced, the two vesicles enclosed in a bony capsule formed by the lateral processes of the coalescent anterior vertebrae.

There are about 30 or so genera included in the family Trichomycteridae, most of which can be distinguished by the following key.

1a. Body compact, little elongated; adipose fin present; upper jaw without teeth; conspicuous sac-like, fat-filled adipose organ present laterally immediately above pectoral fins . . . (subfamily Sarcoglanidinae)................................ 2

1b. Body elongate, terete to subterete; adipose fin absent; upper jaw with teeth; no adipose organ immediately above pectoral fin.................................. 3

2a. Thick, conspicuous, free-edged, discoid flap extending upward from maxillary present .... *Malacoglanis*

2b. Thick, conspicuous, free-edged, discoid flap extending upward from maxillary absent .... *Sarcoglanis*

3a. Opercular or interopercular spine pat-

ches absent 4
3b. Patch of spines present on the interoperculum and usually on the operculum.. 7
4a. Pectoral fin with spine; mental and nasal barbels present; dorsal fin inserted over ventral fins . . . (subfamily Nematogenyinae) .... *Nematogenys*
4b. Pectoral fin without spine or entirely absent; dorsal fin absent; nasal, rostral, and maxillary barbels present; no mental barbels; anal fin (if present) and caudal fin not confluent . . . (subfamily Glanapteryginae) 5
5a. Anal fin present; eyes rudimentary; caudal fin well developed but small 6
5b. Anal fin absent; eyes functional; caudal fin degenerated into a fringe; eel-shaped .... *Glanapteryx*
6a. No externally visible vestige of eyes; snout shovel-shaped; pectoral fin present; form compact, compressed .... *Pygidianops*
6b. Vestigial eyes present; snout trowel-shaped; no pectoral fins; body very elongate, subterete .... *Typhlobelus*
7a. Mouth terminal, not sucker-like 8
7b. Mouth inferior, sucker-like 14
8a. Gill membranes free from or narrowly connected with isthmus; caudal fin rounded to emarginate; head flattened; nasal barbel present . . . (subfamily Trichomycterinae) 9
8b. Gill membranes confluent with isthmus; caudal deeply forked; head rather deep; nasal barbel absent . . . (subfamily Stegophilinae, in part) .... *Pareiodon*
9a. Opercle with long dermal flap; maxillary bone larger than its barbel ... *Scleronema*
9b. Opercle without dermal flap; maxillary very small 10
10a. Dorsal fin long; caudal peduncle rounded or compressed 11
10b. Dorsal fin shorter; caudal peduncle compressed 12
11a. Caudal peduncle cylindrical and narrow; dorsal fin origin approximately in middle of total length; number of caudal fin rays less than 32 .... *Bullockia*
11b. Caudal peduncle narrow, strongly compressed; dorsal fin origin behind middle of total length; caudal fin rays more than 32 .... *Trichomycterus* (part)

[species formerly in *Hatcheria*]
12a. Ventral fins absent .... *Eremophilus*
12b. Ventral fins present 13
13a. Anal fin long, more than 30 rays .... *Trichogenes*
13b. Anal fin shorter, less than 30 rays .... *Trichomycterus* (part)
14a. Anal fin short, 7 to 11 rays, its origin behind or rarely below dorsal fin base..... 15
14b. Anal fin long, 15-25 rays, its origin in front of that of dorsal fin . . . (subfamily Tridentinae) 28
15a. Rami of mandibles meeting anteriorly; mouth wide; teeth numerous and fine, in bands or rows . . . (subfamily Stegophilinae) 16
15b. Rami of mandibles separated anteriorly; mouth narrow; teeth few but large . . . (subfamily Vandelliinae) 23
16a. Lips wide and extrusible, when extruded extending backward in points behind corners of mouth, normally folded into mouth; opercular spines absent .... *Apomatoceros*
16b. No backwardly extending extrusible lips; opercular spines present 17
17a. Eyes lateral, set wide apart and staring; head very flattened and depressed; interorbital nearly as wide as head and almost perfectly flat (as in *Tridens*) .. *Haemomaster*
17b. Eyes superior, set close together and usually partially hidden by cheeks when viewed from the side; interorbital narrow, usually concave 18
18a. Gill membranes united, free from isthmus .... *Acanthopoma*
18b. Gill membranes confluent with the isthmus 19
19a. Caudal fin deeply forked, lobes rather long and pointed; head and body rather deep and compact, the caudal peduncle slender; body with wide, dark, vertical bands .... *Pseudostegophilus*
19b. Caudal fin emarginate, truncate, or rounded; body rather slender; head depressed; body spotted or plain 20
20a. Accessory procurrent caudal rays numerous and conspicuous; tail tadpole-like, but not sharply pointed .... *Ochmacanthus*
20b. Accessory procurrent caudal rays few and relatively inconspicuous; caudal not

tadpole-like 21
21a. Operculum with only 2 spines............ .... *Stegophilus* (part) [species formerly in *Henonemus*, now a synonym]
21b. Operculum with 4 or more spines.....22
22a. Origin of ventral fins almost equidistant from snout tip and caudal origin......... .... *Homodiaetus*
22b. Ventral fin origin 1.5-2.0 times as far from snout tip as from base of caudal fin .... *Stegophilus*
23a. Gill membranes united, free from isthmus; teeth present in lower jaw; rami of mandibles rather close together.......... .... *Paracanthopoma*
23b. Gill membranes confluent with isthmus 24
24a. Large claw-like tooth at end of each maxillary bone (scarcely visible without dissection); 2 series of depressible teeth in middle of upper jaw flanked laterally by single series of much smaller teeth; 2 short series of teeth on ends of mandibular rami; caudal subtruncate...*Branchioica*
24b. No claw-like tooth at end of each maxillary bone (not verified in *Paravandellia*) 25
25a. A few depressible teeth in single series in middle of upper jaw; caudal rounded or emarginate...............................26
25b. Several series of depressible teeth in middle of upper jaw flanked by single series of smaller teeth at each side....27
26a. Mandibles devoid of teeth...... *Vandellia*
26b. A patch of minute teeth on each mandibular ramus .... *Plectrochilus*
27a. A small series of teeth at extremities of mandibular rami; caudal emarginate..... .... *Branchioica* (part) [species usually included in *Parabranchioica*, now a synonym]
27b. Mandible devoid of teeth; caudal with upper lobe elongated ...... *Paravandellia*
28a. Opercular and interopercular patches of spines confluent with each other; gill membranes confluent with isthmus...... .... *Miuroglanis*
28b. Opercular and interopercular spine patches distinct from each other; gill membranes united, free from isthmus; eyes lateral, set far apart; interorbital wide and flat 29
29a. Body not greatly elongate, depth 4 to 8 times in standard length; head 5 to 6.5 in SL; interopercular spines 4 to 8 in number..30
29b. Body greatly elongate, depth 13 times in SL; head about 9 times in SL; interopercular spines reduced in number to 3 or 4 .... *Tridens*
30a. Opercular spines 10; 2 maxillary barbels present; nasal barbels present .... *Tridentopsis*
30b. Opercular spines 6; one maxillary barbel; nasal barbel absent..... *Tridensimilis*

The genera *Parastegophilus, Pleurophysus,* and *Schultzichthys* have not been included in the key because of lack of sufficient information on their characters.

The subfamily Sarcoglanidinae, described by Myers & Weitzman in 1966, was based on a few small specimens less than 20 mm in length. The first specimen was collected in early 1925 by Dr. Ternetz in rock pools below the rapids of São Gabriel on the Rio Negro. The species was named *Sarcoglanis simplex.* Two additional specimens were collected at Tres Esquinas in a small caño of the Rio Orteguaza, Caqueta Province, Colombia. This species was named *Malacoglanis gelatinosus.* Living individuals of only this latter species were seen. They were described as being of a soft, gelatinous consistency and of a pale, translucent, reddish brown color without any pattern. In fact, at the collecting site they were almost overlooked because of their small size, their soft, gelatinous nature, and their translucent color. In the habitats of both species there was a sandy to muddy bottom into which these fishes apparently burrow, perhaps to help keep them from being swept away in the current when the waters are higher or as protection from predators.

The subfamily is distinct by virtue of the following features: The body is compact and not much elongated, with the head quite large and relatively deep. The eyes are tiny but apparently functional. A long adipose fin extends from the posterior dorsal fin base to or almost to the caudal fin base (but not involving any procurrent supporting elements of the caudal fin). The pectoral fins are extremely large and broad, longer than the head, and the tips of the non-filamentous rays project far beyond the membrane. The ventral fins are inserted below or only slightly anterior to the dorsal fin origin. The caudal fin is well developed and emarginate to slightly forked. There are no spines present in any of the fins. There are a pair of nasal barbels, a pair of maxillary barbels, and a pair of rictal barbels; there are no mandibular or mental barbels. The opercular and interopercular spines are very inconspicuous, the latter absent in one species. The upper jaw is toothless, while the lower jaw includes teeth that are long, cylindrical, conical, hooked inward at the tip, and arranged uniserially. The maxillary bone is of greater length than its associated barbel. There is a conspicuous sac-like, fat-filled, adipose organ on each side immediately above the pectoral fins, while a broad band of fatty tissue extends ventrally from each of these organs around the entire ventral thoracic region. Conspicuous fatty organs are also found on the head. There are 6 branchiostegal rays. So far only the two genera, each with a single species, have been discovered. (Myers & Weitzman, 1966.)

The genus *Sarcoglanis* has a broad, deep body that becomes more and more compressed posteriorly and a globose, blunt, not noticeably depressed head. All fins are present and lack spines. The dorsal fin is short-based, high, and pointed, with 4 rays. The caudal fin is emarginate to slightly forked. There is a conspicuous, high, thin adipose fin extending from the dorsal fin to the caudal fin, the higher portion closer to the dorsal than to the caudal. The opercular spines are reduced and not conspicuous; the interopercular spines are apparently absent. There is a large fatty sac below the eye attached below to the base of the maxillary barbel; the suprapectoral organ is rounded. A broad corselet or band of fatty tissue extends downward from each suprapectoral adipose organ around the entire ventral thoracic region. The gill membranes are free from the isthmus, excised far forward, and therefore united for only a short distance. There is no free fold of skin over the opercular apparatus. There are 6 branchiostegal rays. (Myers & Weitzman, 1966).

Sarcoglanis simplex. (From Myers & Weitzman, 1966.)

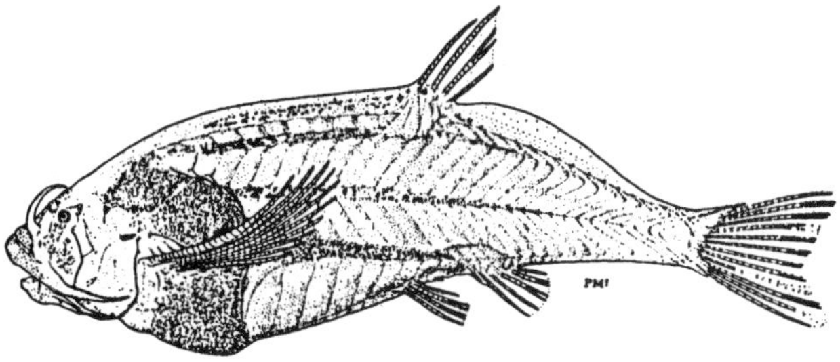

Malacoglanis has a more slender body than *Sarcoglanis*, while the head is also blunt and moderately depressed. There are three pairs of barbels, nasal, maxillary, and rictal, plus a small close-set pair of barbels underneath the head (one on each side of the midline). All fins are present and without spines. The dorsal fin is more like other trichomycterids than that of *Sarcoglanis*, with ii,7 or iii,6 rays. A fold-like adipose fin extends from the dorsal fin to the caudal fin but is considerably lower and less conspicuous than that of *Sarcoglanis*; there is no predorsal fold. The caudal fin is emarginate to slightly forked. The opercular and interopercular spines are present but much reduced, the latter contained in an opercular skin flap. The suprapectoral organ is present but much more horizontally elongated than that of *Sarcoglanis*, while the thoracic adipose corselet is less conspicuous and less well developed than in *Sarcoglanis*. The head has a raised area around the eye that is not continuous with a fat-filled sac on the cheek; however, it is not continuous anteriorly with a ridge of skin that attaches to the mid-anterior base of the maxillary bone. A thick, conspicuous, partially discoidal flap of skin extending upward from the maxillary is

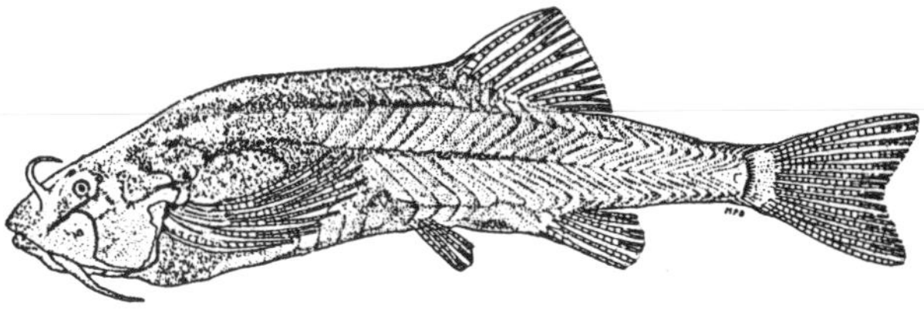

Malacoglanis gelatinosus. (From Myers & Weitzman, 1966.)

present, but it is not attached to or confluent with the cheek. There is a free fold of skin over most of the opercular apparatus (slightly anterior to the edge of the opercle). The gill membranes are deeply incised, almost completely free from each other and from the isthmus. (Myers & Weitzman, 1966.)

The subfamily Nematogenyinae contains a single genus, *Nematogenys*, which in turn contains only a single species, *N. inermis*. *Nematogenys* is the most unspecialized member of the family and there is considerable doubt whether it should remain in this family. Baskin (pers. comm.) suggests that it should be set apart as a family of its own (Nematogenyidae). The body is elongate, with a strongly compressed caudal peduncle. The head is covered with soft skin, the occipital crest is small, and the fontanel extends to the base of the occipital process and is interrupted above the posterior margin of the orbit. The opercle is not armed. The eyes are very small. Three pairs of barbels are present: nasal, mental, and maxillary. The dorsal fin is short-based, located in the middle of the body length above the ventral fins, and has no spine. The pectoral fin is provided with a spine. There is no adipose fin, and the caudal fin is short and rounded. The teeth are villiform, forming a band in each jaw; the palate is edentulous. The gill openings are rather wide and subcontinuous at the isthmus. The swim bladder is enclosed by a bony complex. The genus is endemic to some rivers in Chile.

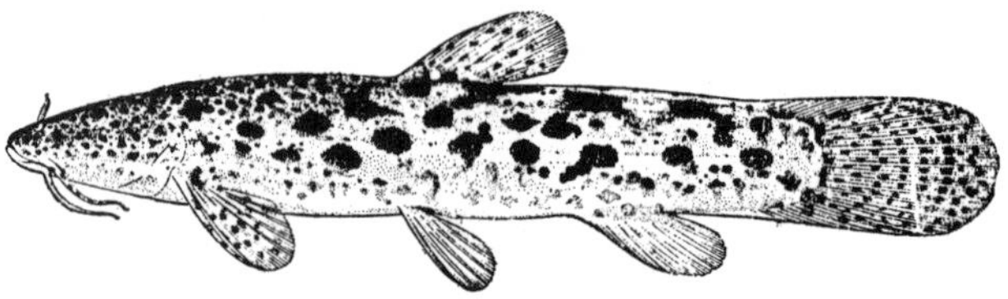

Nematogenys inermis. (From Eigenmann, 1927.)

The subfamily Glanapteryginae is a small subfamily that contains only three genera, each apparently containing a single species. The subfamily is defined by Myers (1944) as having no dorsal fin, and there may or may not be an anal fin. The pectoral and ventral fins are reduced or absent. There are three pairs of barbels present: a pair of nasal barbels, a pair of maxillary barbels, and a pair of rostral barbels; there are no mental barbels. The eyes are quite small and functional, vestigial, or may even be absent. The mouth is small, not sucker-shaped, and with little or no lateral gape. The teeth are conical and in a single series in each jaw. The cheeks are without spines. The three known species are quite small (less than 40 mm in standard length) and are all known only from the vicinity of the Rio São Gabriel rapids, Rio Negro, Brazil.

The genus *Pygidianops* as described by Myers (1944) has a rather compact and laterally compressed body, while the snout is flattened, shovel-shaped, and merges at the sides into the connective membrane of the rostral and maxillary barbels. The three pairs of barbels, nasal, rostral, and maxillary, all have a stiff core and a fringing wing of membrane. The eyes are apparently completely absent, Myers being unable to find a vestige of their presence visible externally. The mouth is a transverse slit, narrow, inferior, slightly posterior to the insertion of the rostral barbel, and without a complicated lip structure or sucking disc. The teeth are comparatively large, apparently conical, and in a single close-set series in each jaw. The dorsal fin is absent, but in its stead there is a narrow rayless membrane (not an adipose fin) from the nape to the caudal; a similar membrane extends from the anal fin to the caudal. An anal fin is present. There is a vestigial pectoral fin of a single ray with fringing web (much like the

Pygidianops eigenmanni; (b-d) ventral, dorsal, and lateral views of head. (From Myers, 1944.)

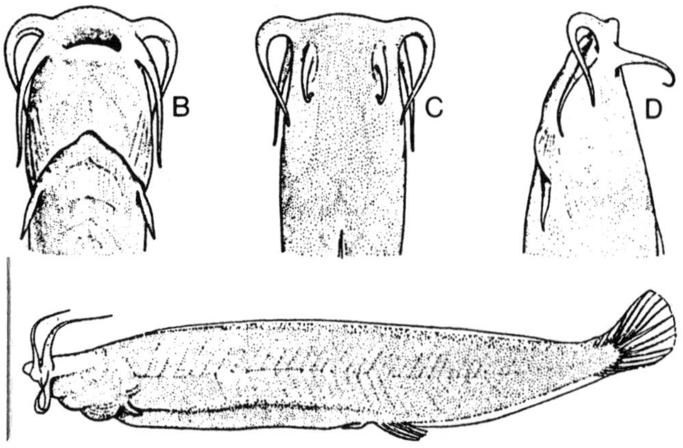

barbels). The ventral fins are absent, but the caudal fin is well developed. There is a constriction across the lower surface of the head behind the insertion of the maxillary barbel. The gill openings are restricted to the lower part of the sides, below the level of the pectoral fin; the gill membranes form a free fold across the isthmus and are attached to the latter at a single median line. The myomeres are very conspicuous.

There is a single species, *Pygidianops eigenmanni*, the largest specimen being a mere 23 mm in standard length. This blind fish was first collected in 1925 by Dr. Ternetz.

The second genus, *Typhlobelus*, is similar to *Pygidianops* but differs in the following characters according to Myers (1944): The eyes are present, though vestigial and visible only as minute black dots. The body is greatly elongated and subterete in cross-section. The snout is elongate, trowel-shaped, and does not merge into the membranous wings of the barbels; the occiput is bulbous behind. The mouth is a little anterior to the insertion of the rostral barbels, and the teeth are widely spaced in the jaws. There is no vestige of the pectoral fins, and the caudal fin is reduced. The gill membranes are as in *Pygidianops*.

There is only a single known species, *T. ternetzi*, the largest specimen of which was only

Typhlobelus ternetzi; (b-d) ventral, dorsal, and lateral views of head. (From Myers, 1944.)

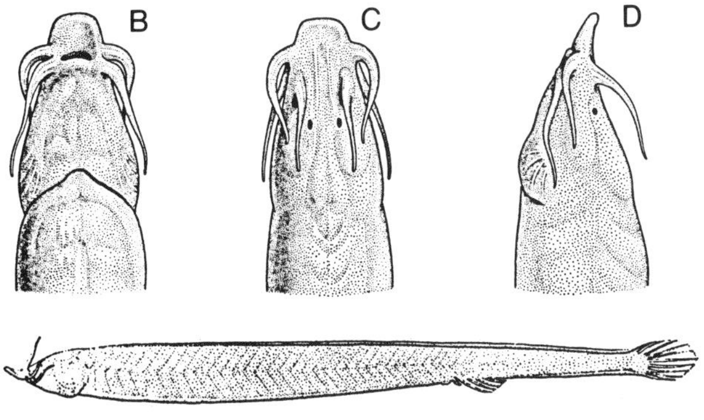

33.5 mm standard length. This fish was named by Dr. Myers for Dr. Ternetz, "whose valiant labors, while collecting these fishes in a little known and fever-laden region, were the ultimate cause of his death."

The third and last genus of the family Glanapteryginae is *Glanapteryx*. The body is eel-like, cylindrical anteriorly but compressed and slightly deeper posteriorly (in the caudal region). The head is small and flattened. The cheeks are without spines, and the teeth in

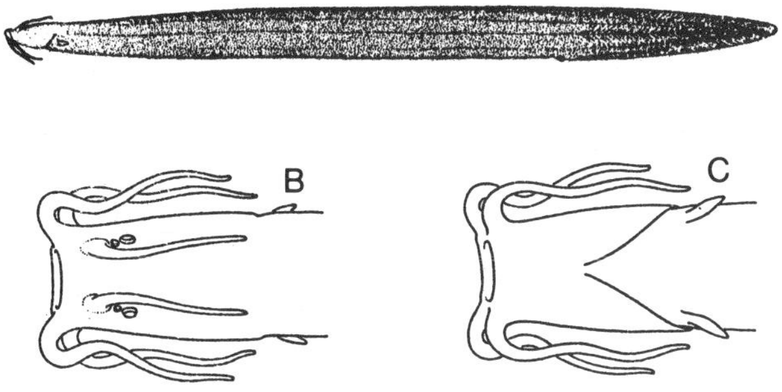

Glanapteryx anguilla; (b) dorsal view of head; (c) ventral view of head. (From Myers, 1944.)

the jaws are small and apparently conical. There are no mental barbels, but nasal, rostral, and maxillary barbels are present; the barbels are not stiff or fringed. The eyes are small and imbedded in the skin, but they are functional. The dorsal and anal fins are absent but there are rudimentary pectoral and ventral fin flaps. The caudal fin, which is well formed in the other two genera, is reduced to a narrow fringe around the caudal end of the body, its tip rounded-acuminate. The two blind genera are white or colorless (undoubtedly of a glassy translucency in life according to Myers), but this one is dark brown. The only species, *G. anguilla*, is known from a single specimen discovered mixed in with a jar of young *Synbranchus*. Its barbels gave it away. This species probably spends much of its time burrowing in the sand, like *Trichomycterus*, and is not parasitic as indicated by its tiny mouth and weak, unspecialized dentition (Myers, 1944).

The subfamily Trichomycterinae contains about five genera at present, one of which, *Trichomycterus* (formerly *Pygidium*), contains the bulk of the species in the family. All members of this subfamily are free-living forms that are native to clear, cold, running waters, but the species are most numerous in the Patagonian subregion. They are sometimes called torrent catfishes, eel catfishes, or "bagres serranos." They are elongate fishes with strongly compressed or cylindrical caudal peduncles. There is no occipital crest. Three pairs of barbels are present: a nasal pair and two maxillary pairs; there are no mental barbels. Both opercle and interopercle have variable numbers of teeth or denticles. The mandible is of considerable length antero-posteriorly and is armed with strong teeth that occupy less than half its total length. The anal fin is short and the caudal fin is truncated, slightly rounded, or emarginate. The bony complex that encloses the swim bladder includes one visible vertebra.

The most speciose genus of the family is *Trichomycterus*, with possibly more than 75 species. These are widely distributed in South America from the shores of the Atlantic to the shores of the Pacific and in the Andes to an elevation of about 4500 meters. The naked body is elongated and subterete, but the caudal peduncle is strongly compressed and

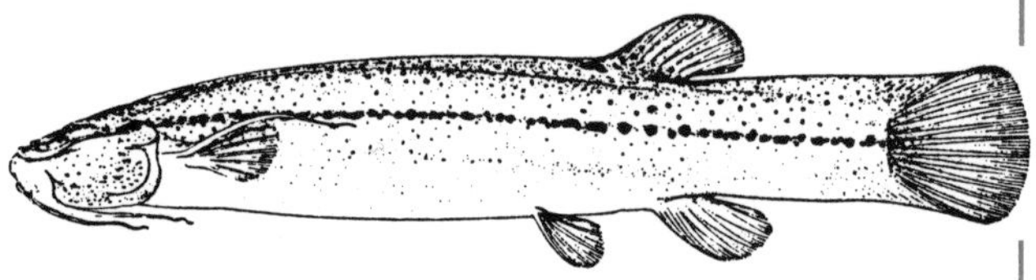

Trichomycterus stellatum. (From Eigenmann, 1918.)

deep. The head is depressed and covered with soft skin. The supraorbital is short and of variable shape, and the orbitosphenoid is short. The interopercle has numerous spines in various series, those of the outer series larger; the opercle has similar spines. The eyes are small and without a free orbital margin. The mouth is of moderate size, terminal or subterminal in position, with two or more series of incisiform or caniniform teeth arranged in bands; there are no labial or vomerine teeth. There are three pairs of barbels: a nasal pair on the posterior border of the anterior nares and two barbels at the angle of the mouth, the upper in connection with the rudimentary maxilla; there are no mental barbels. The fins are without spines. The dorsal is short-based and in the middle or behind the middle of the total length. It has 6 to 11 developed rays (up to 14 counting some anterior undeveloped shorter rays). There is no adipose fin, but a series of rudimentary caudal rays extends forward toward the dorsal and anal fins and in well-fed individuals is covered with fat. The anal fin is short, of 7-11 rays, and located totally or partially posterior to the dorsal fin. The ventrals are small, the pectoral fins have or do not have a filament, and the ventral fins are small. The caudal fin is short, truncate, slightly rounded to rounded, and has a variable number of accessory rays and 6+7 principal rays. The gill membranes are united at the isthmus and form a free fold across it.

The species of the genus *Trichomycterus* are smallish fishes usually inhabiting mountain streams from central Chile to Panama. *T. itatiayae* is a small (to 15 cm), dull-colored fish that is crepuscular and likes to stay hidden during the day by burrowing into the mulm or remaining buried under leaves and other bottom material. They have been kept successfully in home aquaria and have proved to be quite hardy. They are omnivorous and accept a wide variety of foods but prefer small worms. Since they hide during the day, their aquarium should be provided with a dark, soft substrate and plenty of hiding places. After a while they may even be brave enough to venture out during daylight hours. The recommended temperature range is 20-25°C. They are peaceful. The females are said to be more robust than the males.

T. laticeps and *T. taenium* are burrowers that may in times of drought survive (providing some water remains in the burrow) until the next rains.

T. metae occurs in mountainous regions in a variety of habitats from very small streams to quite large lakes. They may be found under rocks or burrowing in the mud of the bottom or of the banks of rivers. In an aquarium they are considered good scavengers that root out food from hard to get at places. They feed heavily on a variety of foods, but worms seems to be preferred. Although feeding should be at night for *T. metae*, you might see some individuals hungry enough during the day to make a quick dart or two to grab a morsel of food. These fish attain a length of over 7.5 cm and are considered suitable in a community tank situation, although it is reported that they are sensitive to chill.

The genus *Hatcheria* previously has been

considered a close relative of *Trichomycterus* but recently has been reduced in status to a synonym of that genus (Baskin, pers. comm.). The species of *Hatcheria* supposedly differ from *Trichomycterus* by being slightly larger and having a longer dorsal fin (of more than 17 rays) than in typical *Trichomycterus*.

The genus *Bullockia* contains a single species from Chile. At first there were thought to be two species, *H. bullocki* and *H. moldonadoi* being removed from the genus *Hatcheria* (= *Trichomycterus*) to form the genus *Bullockia*,

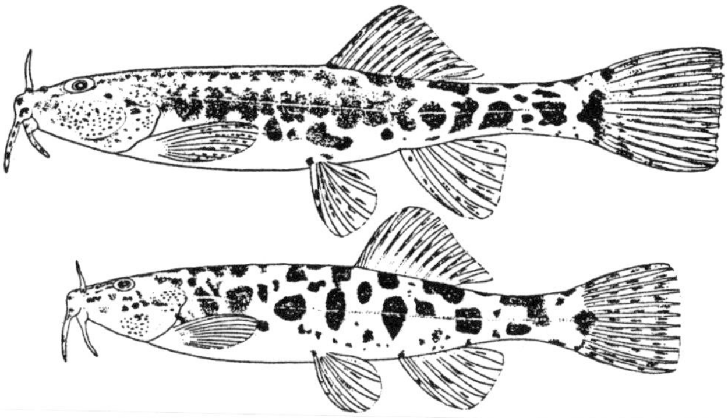

Bullockia moldonadoi. (From Fowler, 1940.)

but *bullocki* was later considered a synonym of *moldonadoi*. The body is elongated, with a cylindrical and narrow caudal peduncle. The dorsal fin is long, with the superior border rounded to straight or slightly concave; its origin is approximately in the middle of the total length. The anal fin is entirely or partially below the dorsal fin. The caudal fin has less than 32 rays and is truncated to slightly rounded.

The genus *Eremophilus* is a small genus of only a couple of species. It is very close to *Trichomycterus* but is distinguished from that genus mainly by not possessing any ventral fins. The head is covered with soft skin, and the operculum and interoperculum are armed with patches of small prickles. The eyes are small. The teeth are villiform, forming bands in the jaws; the palate is toothless. There are three pairs of barbels—a pair of nasal barbels and two pairs of maxillary barbels. The dorsal fin is short-based and has no spine, its origin behind the middle of the body. The anal fin is short and the caudal fin is truncate. There are no adipose and ventral fins. This

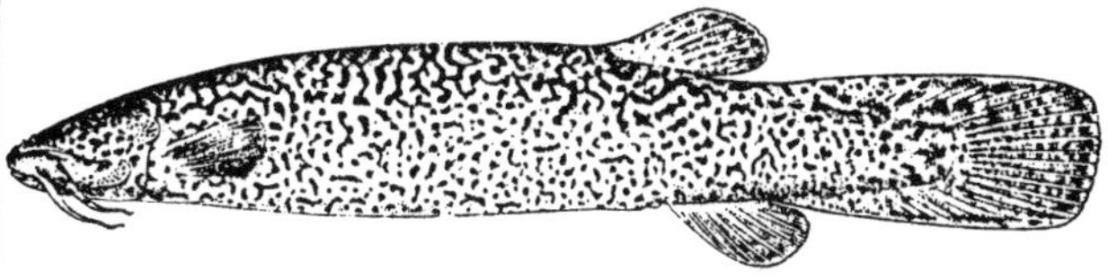

Eremophilus mutisii. (From Eigenmann, 1918.)

lack of ventral fins as a distinguishing character from the genus *Trichomycterus* is very weak, for some species of *Trichomycterus* have individuals without ventral fins.

The genus *Scleronema* contains only a single species from the Uruguay basin. It has a subterminal mouth that is not sucker-like. There

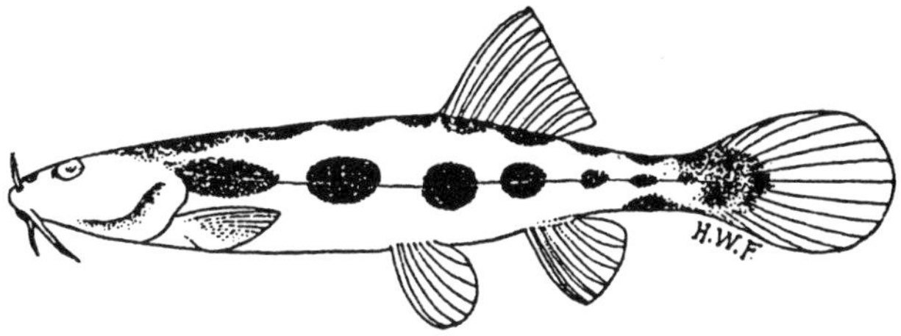

Scleronema minutum. (From Fowler, 1954.)

is a patch of spines on the interoperculum and usually also on the operculum. It is distinguishable from the genera *Trichomycterus* and *Eremophilus* by having a long dermal flap on the opercle and by having a maxillary bone that is larger than its associated barbel.

The subfamily Stegophilinae contains about ten genera and is diagnosed as trichomycterids that lack nasal and mental barbels but have a pair of maxillary barbels and another small inferior pair, both at the angle of the mouth. The mouth is wide and inferior, with numerous teeth arranged in various regular rows along the entire margin. The dentaries are in contact, and the opercle and interopercle are spinous. This subfamily includes small fishes that live a parasitic life on other fishes by drinking their blood.

The genus *Homodiaetus* is a small genus of about three or four species. The head is depressed, the eyes are superior and directed upward, while the mouth is wide and inferior. There are no nasal or mental barbels but there are two pairs of maxillary barbels, a long one and a short one on each side. The

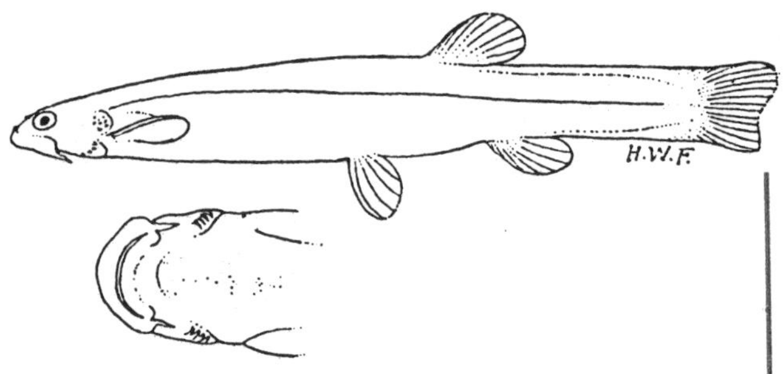

Homodiaetus anisitsi. (From Fowler, 1954.)

opercle is provided with about 4 to 7 spines; the interopercle is provided with about 6 to 12 spines. The upper jaw and lips have some 6 to 8 widely separated series of teeth that are narrow and more or less spatuliform or spoon-shaped, those of the inner series slightly larger. The labial teeth are fine, hair-like, and very movable, those of the jaw more firmly attached. The lower lip is without teeth; the lower jaw has 3 to 6 series of teeth, those of the innermost series larger and forming a compact series. All the teeth are more or less angularly bent backward near their tips. There are no vomerine teeth. The dorsal fin is located behind the ventral fins, while the anal fin, of about 7 to 11 rays, is behind the dorsal or below its anterior quarter. The caudal fin is emarginate to truncate, the accessory caudal rays few and not conspicuous. A large glandular swelling is present behind each pectoral fin. The gill membranes are united with each other and with the isthmus so that the gill openings are reduced to a narrow slit in front of the pectoral fins.

The genus *Homodiaetus* is very weakly differentiated from *Stegophilus*, differing in having the ventral fins almost equidistant between the snout and caudal fin (nearer caudal fin in *Stegophilus*). It differs from *Miuroglanis*, which it resembles (although in different subfamilies), by having an emarginate instead of rounded caudal fin and by having several series of labial teeth, which *Miuroglanis* lacks. The genus *Parastegophilus* was erected in 1946 by Miranda-Ribeiro for the single species *P. maculatus* (? = *Homodiaetus maculatus*).

Homodiaetus maculatus attains a length of about 10 cm and occurs in the rivers of Argentina, especially in the Rio de La Plata, the Rio Paraguay, and the Upper and Middle Parana Rivers. It may be found free in the more weedy parts of the rivers but is actually parasitic and will attach to the back or sides of other kinds of fishes, including catfishes such as the large pati catfish (*Luciopimelodus pati*) that may be found in the same habitat. It probably enters the gill chambers of the host, where it feeds on the blood of the gills. It is said that this species needs a great deal of oxygen, so plenty of aeration is recommended.

The genus *Haemomaster* is a monotypic genus from the Orinoco River of Venezuela. It is diagnosed as having large, staring eyes set far apart and lateral in position, not superior and close together as in related genera. The head is very flat and depressed, with the interorbital almost as wide as the head and almost perfectly flat. The opercle has about 5 or 6 spines, the interopercle about 5. The maxillary barbel at the angle of the mouth is minute; there are no nasal or mental barbels. The mouth is wide, inferior, with the teeth of the upper jaw imbedded in soft flesh and therefore difficult to see. The teeth are very fine and arranged in many even series, the outer series along the lip; in the middle there is a patch of enlarged retrorse teeth. The teeth of the mandible are similar but less numerous than those of the upper jaw, and there is no enlarged central patch of retrorse teeth. The dorsal fin is inserted above the middle of the adpressed ventral fins; the anal fin, of about 7 to 11 rays, is positioned behind, rarely below, the dorsal fin origin. The ventral fins are inserted nearly twice as far from the tip of the snout as from the caudal fin base. The caudal fin is very slightly emarginate and has fairly numerous accessory rays, although they are not very conspicuous. The gill membranes are united to each other and are confluent with the isthmus, the opening being reduced to a slit in front of the pectoral fin. The single species is colorless except for a caudal stripe.

The genus *Ochmacanthus* has about five species. It is characterized by having a flattened head with the eyes superior in position, set close together, and usually partially hidden by the cheeks when viewed from the side. The interorbital is narrow, usually concave. The body is rather slender. Both interopercu-

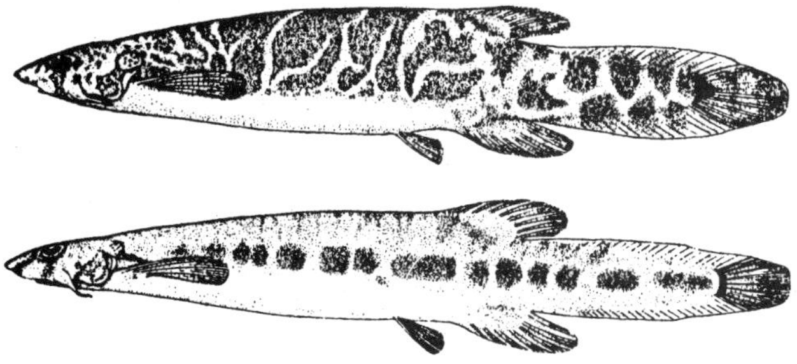

Ochmacanthus alternus (above); *O. orinoco* (below). (From Myers, 1944.)

lar and opercular spines are present. Only maxillary barbels are present, the lower barbels shorter, with a membranous flap below. The mouth is wide and wholly inferior in position. There are no backwardly extending extrusible lips. The teeth are small, numerous, in several regular series; there are no hair-like teeth on the upper lip. The dorsal fin is positioned over the anal fin, which is short (of 7 to 11 rays). The caudal fin is emarginate, truncate, or rounded, the fully developed caudal rays much diverging from a narrow base. The tadpole-like tail is not sharply pointed. The caudal fulcra are greatly developed, and the accessory procurrent caudal rays are numerous and quite conspicuous.

O. reinhardti, like *Plectrochilus* spp., secrete copious amounts of mucus around themselves, possibly acting as a lubricant for penetrating small openings (Saul, 1975).

The genus *Stegophilus* contains fewer than ten species (including those formerly in the genus *Henonemus*). The body is elongate and slender, and the head is depressed and covered with soft skin. The eyes are rather large, superior, set close together, and usually are partially hidden by the cheeks when viewed from the side; there is no free orbital margin. The interorbital is narrow, usually concave. The operculum has 4 or more spines, and the interopercle has sharp hooks in series. No nasal or mental barbels are present, but there is a pair of maxillary barbels on each side, the lower barbel minute and with an attached membranous flap below. The mouth is wide and inferior, with no backwardly extending extrusible lips. Each jaw has numerous fine teeth arranged in several series, and the upper lip has two or more series of elongate, freely movable teeth. Vomerine teeth are present, forming a patch that is confluent with the intermaxillary band and situated well in front of the jaw. The dorsal fin short, without a pungent spine, and situated behind the origin of the ventrals. The anal fin is short, of 7 to 11 rays, with its origin usually behind, but rarely under, the dorsal fin origin. The ventrals are inserted behind the middle of the body but in front of the dorsal fin origin. The caudal fin is emarginate, truncate, or rounded, the accessory procurrent caudal rays few and relatively inconspicuous; the caudal is not tadpole-shaped. The gill membranes are united with each other and with the isthmus so that the gill openings are narrow, restricted, and separated by a broad isthmus.

Stegophilus septentrionalis (above); *S. insidiosus* (below). (From Myers, 1944, and Fowler, 1954.)

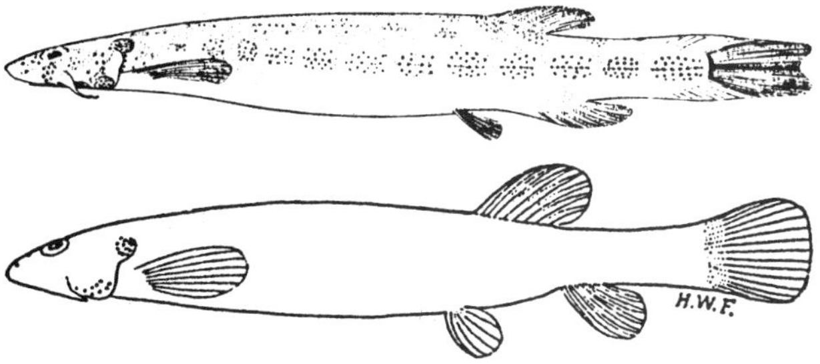

Stegophilus insidiosus is a true parasite living in the gill chambers of larger fishes, including catfishes such as *Sorubim lima*. It uses its strong teeth to bite into the gill filaments to suck the blood.

S. punctatus burrows in soft mud bottoms where there is a sluggish current.

In the monotypic genus *Apomatoceros* from the Peruvian Amazon, the lips are wide and extrusible. When extruded they extend backward in points behind the corners of the mouth, but normally they are folded into the mouth. Opercular spines are present.

The genus *Pseudostegophilus* is a genus of only one or two species. The body is comparatively short and thick, and the head is short, as broad as long, and with a broadly rounded snout. The eyes are superior, close together, contained about 4 times in the head, and usually partially hidden by the cheeks when viewed from the side; the interorbital region is narrow and usually concave. The opercle

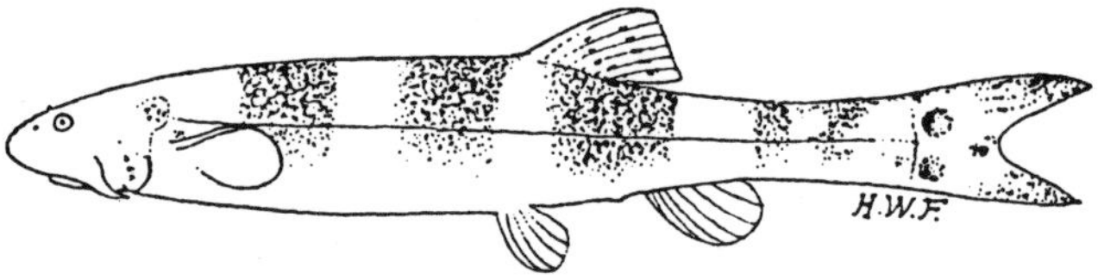

Pseudostegophilus nemurus. (From Fowler, 1954.)

has a group of about 8 spines; the preopercle has similar spines. The mouth is broad and inferior, and the lips do not extend posteriorly and are not extrusible. Each jaw has a series of fine teeth, and there are several series of fine, movable teeth on the upper lip, those of the inner series longer; there are no teeth on the vomer. The dorsal originates about midway between the tip of the snout and the tip of the middle caudal rays; the anal fin is entirely behind the dorsal fin. The ventral fins originate midway between the base of the caudal fin and the tip of the snout. The caudal peduncle is slender, and the caudal fin is deeply forked, the lobes rather long and pointed. There is a small pectoral pore. The gill membranes are confluent with the isthmus.

P. nemurus from the Rio Mamore has broad dark vertical bands on the body. *P. scarificator* is probably a synonym of *Homodiaetus maculatus* and is said to become attached to the gills, anal region, and fins of dead, dying, or disabled fishes. It is also said to attach itself to the legs of children who are in the water.

The genus *Acanthopoma* contains only two species. The eyes are superior in position, set close together, and usually partially hidden by the cheeks when viewed from the side; the interorbital area is narrow and usually concave. Opercular and interopercular spines are present. The mouth is wide, and there are no backwardly extending extrusible lips. The teeth are numerous, fine, and disposed in

Acanthopoma annectens. (From Fowler, 1954.)

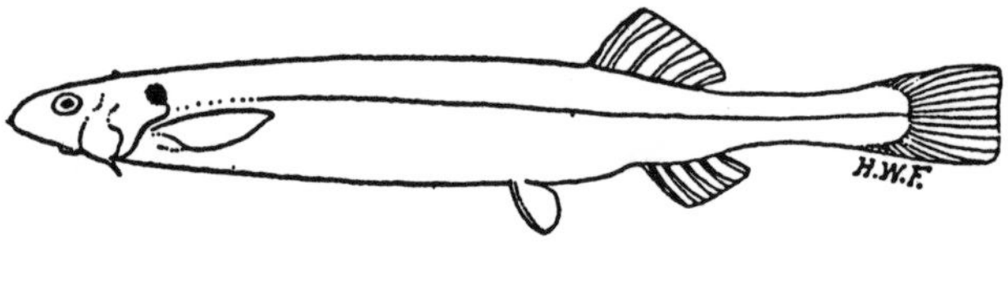

bands or rows; the upper lip has fine, hair-like, movable teeth. The dorsal fin is located behind the ventral fins; the anal fin is short, of about 7 to 11 rays, its origin usually behind the dorsal fin origin. The accessory caudal rays are few and not very conspicuous. The gill membranes are united with each other but free from the isthmus.

Acanthopoma annectens is one of those fishes that have the name "candiru," and of course it has the familiar candiru habits. It attacks like a leech and produces wounds all over the fish. It spreads a bundle of opercular and interopercular spines into the wound and remains there, being very difficult to remove. They also invade the "private parts" of wading or swimming animals but apparently exist in these passages only a short time, as they quickly die from a lack of oxygen. *A. annectens* is of a dark color and has indistinct blotches.

The genus *Pareiodon* is a monotypic genus from the Amazon basin that was once considered distinct enough to merit its own subfamily, the Pareiodontinae. However, Baskin (pers. comm.) prefers to include it with the Stegophilinae. *Pareiodon* has a terete body. The head is covered with soft skin, the eyes

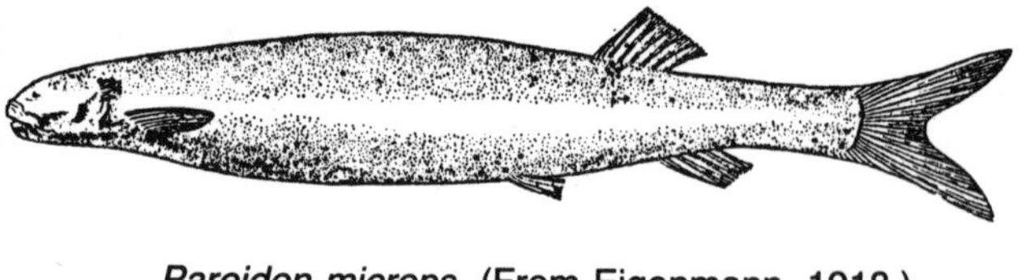

Pareidon microps. (From Eigenmann, 1918.)

are very small, and the opercle and interopercle are armed with a strip of small bony prickles or spines. The only barbels are a pair of maxillary barbels on each side. The cleft of the mouth is rather narrow, and the lips are thickly papillose. The jaws are provided with a single series of flat, truncated, incisor-like teeth; the palate is toothless. The dorsal fin is short, without a pungent spine, and usually is located behind the middle of the body and above or behind the ventral fins. The anal fin is short. The ventral fins are inserted far behind the middle of the body. The caudal fin is forked. There is no adipose fin. The gill membrane is united with the isthmus, and the gill openings are rather narrow, reduced to a slit in front of the pectoral fin.

The remaining genera of the subfamily cannot be characterized at this time due to lack of pertinent papers. The genus *Pleurophysus* was noted by Myers (1944) as *incerta sedis*, possibly synonymous with *Paracanthopoma* of the subfamily Vandelliinae. Gosline (1945), however, listed it under the subfamily Stegophilinae, a move that Baskin (pers. comm.) seems to agree with. I have not been able to obtain any information on *Schultzichthys*, the final genus of this subfamily.

The subfamily Vandelliinae contains about five genera. These are trichomycterids without mental or nasal barbels, much as the condition in the Stegophilinae. The mouth is wide and is provided with small depressible teeth that are fine and pointed. The teeth of the upper jaw are in two groups or discontinuous series. The dentary bones are not in contact. The fishes of this subfamily are small and are parasitic in nature, attacking the gills of larger fishes and feeding on their blood. It has been well documented that the "candiru" or "carnero" (species of *Vandellia*) of the Amazon region penetrate the natural orifices of human bathers (ears, nose, anus, urethra, and vulva). In order to extract them it is necessary to undergo a surgical procedure.

The genus *Branchioica* is a genus of perhaps five species, including those formerly placed in the genus *Parabranchioica*. The genus is without nasal or mental barbels but there are two maxillary barbels at each buccal angle, the lower one the smaller. The mouth is inferior, with two or three series of teeth in the upper jaw and a single lateral series of smaller teeth; there are two series of teeth in the mandibles opposite the lateral series of the upper jaw. The caudal fin is truncate. The gill openings are small, and the membranes are united to the isthmus.

Branchioica bertonii. (From Eigenmann, 1918.)

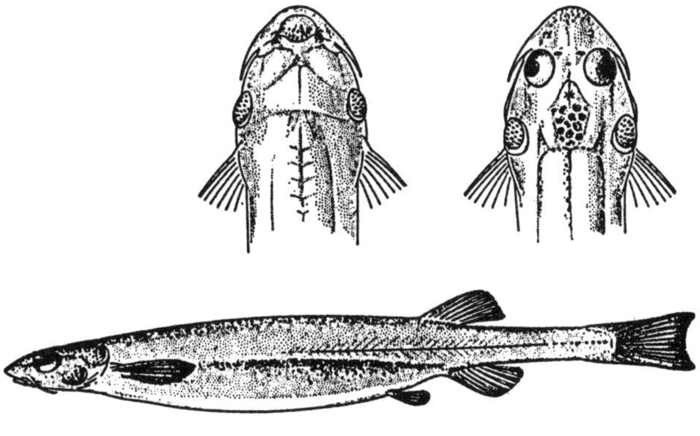

Branchioica bertonii has been collected in the gill chambers of large fishes such as *Colossoma brachypomum*. *Branchioica teaguei* was described on the basis of eight specimens, seven of which were attached to the gills of a species of characin, the other on a catfish.

The genus *Plectrochilus* (including as a synonym the genus *Urinophilus*) contains only about three species. There is a maxillary barbel and a lower rudimentary barbel. The interopercle has a single greatly enlarged spine

Plectrochilus sanguineus. (From Eigenmann, 1918.)

and a very few tiny complimentary ones; the opercular spines are rudimentary, hidden beneath the skin. There is no claw-like tooth at the end of the maxillary, but there are a few depressible teeth in a single series in the middle of the upper jaw; there is a patch of minute teeth on each ramus of the mandible. The caudal fin is rounded or emarginate. The gill membranes are confluent with the isthmus. This genus will probably eventually be merged with *Vandellia*. The presence or absence of a patch of minute teeth on each ramus of the mandible depends on the condition of the museum specimens, as well as there being intermediates between the two genera. Specimens of *P. machadoi* were found partially buried in the belly of a specimen of *Pseudoplatystoma* where it apparently had burrowed through the body wall. The *machadoi* were distended with blood.

The genus *Paravandellia* is a monotypic genus from the Paraguay River. It lacks the claw-like tooth at the end of the maxillary (not verified), and there are several series of depressible teeth in the middle of the upper jaw that are flanked by a single series of smaller teeth on each side; the mandible is devoid of teeth. The caudal fin has an elongated upper lobe. The gill membranes are confluent with the isthmus. *P. oxyptera* was collected from under the scales of a characin, and one specimen of *Paravandellia* was collected from an electric eel.

The genus *Paracanthopoma* is a monotypic genus from the upper Catrimani River in Brazil. It is readily distinguishable from the other genera by having the gill membranes united

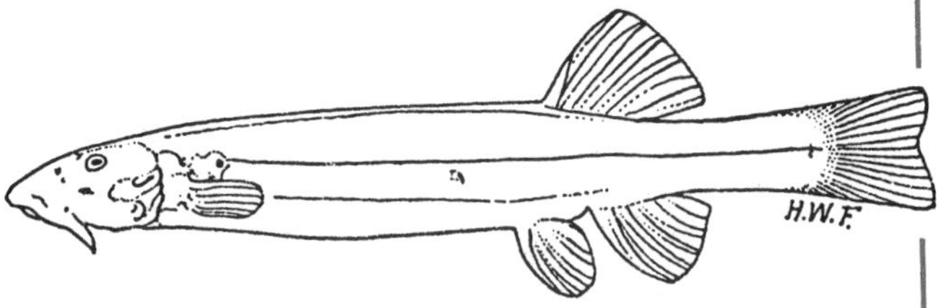

Paracanthopoma parva. (From Fowler, 1954.)

but free from the isthmus. Teeth are present in the lower jaw, and the rami of the mandibles are rather close.

Finally, the genus *Vandellia* contains about six or seven species. The body is greatly elongate, slender, and terete in cross-section. The opercle and interopercle are armed with spines. The eyes are superior and without free margins. There are no mental or nasal barbels, and the maxillary barbels have the lower barbel at the angle of the mouth minute. The mouth is inferior, narrow, with no claw-like tooth at the end of the maxillary. The teeth are few and depressible, in a single series in the middle of the upper jaw; the mandibles are without teeth or with a few very minute teeth on the ends of the rami. There is no adipose fin. The dorsal fin is short, without a

Vandellia plazaii (above); *V. hasemani* (below). (From Eigenmann, 1918.)

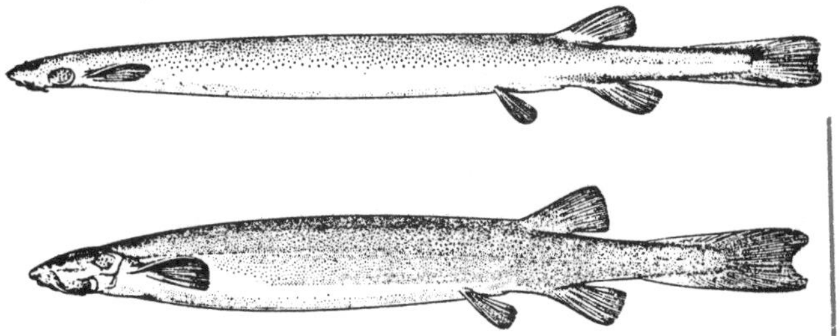

pungent spine, and situated posterior to the ventral fins; the ventrals are inserted behind the middle of the body. The anal fin is short, with 7 to 11 rays, its origin usually posterior to the origin of the dorsal fin. The caudal fin is rounded to emarginate. The gill membranes are broadly united to the isthmus, and the gill openings are reduced to short slits in front of the pectoral fins. The species of *Vandellia* are approximately 2.5 to 6.0 cm long and up to 3.5 mm thick.

Although other fishes have similar habits and may be included in the collective term "candiru," *Vandellia cirrhosa* is probably the species most commonly meant when referring to the candiru. This is a small, almost transparent (it may have a yellowish tinge) catfish that appears somewhat specialized for a parasitic existence—the fins are small and rounded and set far back on the body, the mouth is small, the eyes are large, and the gill covers have distinct spines for lodging in their host's body. The body is quite slender but capable of considerable distension as it gorges itself with the blood of its host and then drops off and burrows into the sandy bottom. This delicate species is also said to enter the gill chambers of larger fishes and to feed on the blood from their gills. They can easily be caught by the use of a bloody cow lung as bait. Perhaps the most notoriety that the candiru has received is by its habit of at times entering the urogenital openings of mammals, including human bathers, especially if they happen to urinate while in the water. Natives are known to protect themselves from this fish by wearing tight-fitting clothing or even coconut shell guards over their private parts. The fish is said to possibly follow the flow of urine as it would the flow of water from the exhalent gill chambers of a fish. After penetrating as far as the slender but powerful fish can manage, it locks its opercular and interopercular spines into position, resulting in excruciating pain for the victim, possible massive hemorrhage, probable infection, and commonly the need for surgical procedures for removal of the offending fish. This tiny fish is often referred to as the only vertebrate parasite of man.

Observations were made on some specimens of candiru that were kept in the Cleve-

Vandellia are able to feed on the blood of live goldfish. When sated they drop off to the bottom where they remain quietly for a while. Photo by Richard M. Segedi.

land Aquarium for about six months. They refused a wide variety of aquarium foods as well as minced smelt gills, freshly killed goldfish, and goldfish blood offered by way of a plastic tube and eyedropper. However, when live black moor goldfish were placed in with them they initiated searching movements directed toward the head end of the goldfish, and three of them were soon able to extract blood from the gills. The candiru did not force their way into the gill chamber but swam around the head often parallel to the goldfish and were able to enter the gill chamber from that position due to the breathing movements of the goldfish. As soon as the anterior part of the candiru disappeared into the gill chamber the body began to swell with the blood of its host. Although the entry might take only about 30 seconds, the feeding might last as long as three to four minutes. When satisfied, the candiru would drop off the fish and remain on the bottom quietly for a time. Normally they would swim about the tank with eel-like movements or rest on the bottom. The goldfish did not react very much to the attentions of the candiru, although the smaller goldfish might settle to the bottom when being fed upon. Damage to the gills was evident as bits and pieces of gill tissue were observed at the gill opening. Although the larger goldfish survived several attacks by the candiru, the smaller ones sometimes perished after a single attack.

Other species of *Vandellia* have also been found to exhibit this parasitic trait. *V. hematophaga*, for example, was collected in the gill cavities of larger fishes (possibly characins), while *V. plazaii* was taken from a wound on a crocodile. Referring to this latter species, Dahl (1960) "permitted specimens which had just been collected in a cast net to fasten to his hand for a short while during which time it succeeded in drawing blood, apparently using its mouth as a sucking apparatus and rasping with the long teeth in the middle part of its upper jaw. It seemed to be utterly avid for a meal of blood and had to be forcibly removed."

The final subfamily, the Tridentinae, contains four genera. It is readily distinguishable by the long anal fin of 15 to 25 rays, the origin of which is in front of that of the dorsal fin. Some specimens were kept in aquaria for about a year, after which time they still were only about 25 mm in length. They were glass-clear but with a light amber coloration. They would normally stay hidden on natural sand bottoms where they were extremely difficult to detect, but on darker sand they were more active.

The genus *Tridens* contains a single species (*T. melanops*) from Icá, on the border of Brazil and Peru. The body is greatly elongate, its depth contained about 13 times in its standard length; the head is greatly depressed and con-

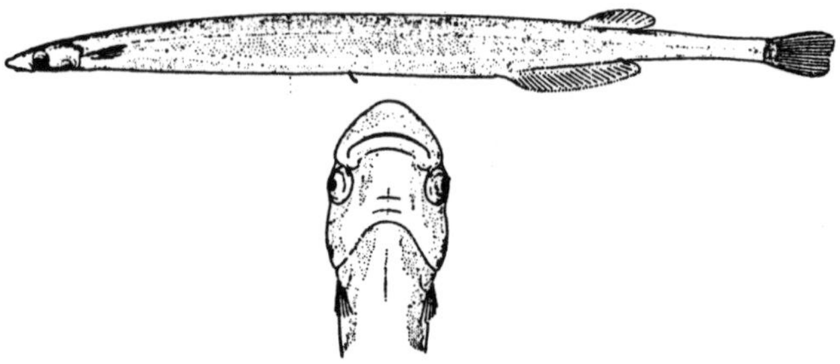

Tridens melanops. (From Eigenmann, 1918.)

tained about 9 times in the standard length; the interorbital area is broad and flat. The eyes are lateral, set far apart, and infringe on the upper and lower surfaces of the head. Both the opercular and interopercular areas are armed, the former with about 10 curved spines, the latter with 3 or 4 smaller but similar spines. The maxillary barbels are minute, scarcely evident. The anal fin is long, inserted in front of the dorsal fin, and the anal rays decrease rapidly in height posteriorly, the last ray positioned under the last ray of the dorsal fin. The ventral fins are small to minute, originating nearer the tip of the snout than the base of the caudal. The caudal fin is rounded and without accessory rays. There is a series of fine labial teeth and there are stronger teeth in the jaws. The gill membranes are united, forming a broad, free fold across the isthmus.

The genus *Tridentopsis* contains only two species. It differs from *Tridens* by having a much more compact form, by the greater number of opercular (10 strong, recurved) and interopercular (a bunch of about 8 slightly weaker, recurved) spines, by possessing nasal barbels (absent in *Tridens*), and in the much greater development of the maxillary barbels. The body is not excessively elongate (depth 4 to 8 times in the standard length). The head is contained 5 to 5.6 times in the standard length and is depressed, flat. The nares are widely separated. There are two maxillary barbels present, the exterior the longer, and a nasal barbel. The eyes are lateral, far apart, and the interorbital is broad and flat. The opercular and interopercular spine patches are distinct from one another as in *Tridens*. The premaxillary teeth are rather long and recurved, conical, and arranged in slightly irregular, posteriorly directed rows. The dorsal fin is short-based, with 7 to 10 rays; the anal fin is longer, with 17 to 21 rays. The ventral fins are well developed. The caudal fin is deeply emarginate, lobed, with the upper lobe slightly longer. The gill membranes are united and free from the isthmus. There are no gill rakers.

The genus *Miuroglanis* is similar to the above but is readily distinguishable by having the opercular and interopercular patches of spines confluent with each other. There are two maxillary barbels. The mouth is inferior, and each jaw has several series of strong teeth. The caudal fin is rounded. The gill membranes are broadly united with the isthmus, without a free margin.

The single species, *Miuroglanis platycephalus*, has a short, compressed and rather deep body, and the head is greatly depressed. The eyes are large, lateral, and placed behind the angle of the mouth. There are no nasal or mental barbels, and the maxillary barbel scarcely extends to the gill opening. The origin of the dorsal fin is slightly behind that of the anal fin; the dorsal has 10 rays, the anal 15.

Finally, the two species of the genus *Tridensimilis* are distinguishable from the other genera of the subfamily by the following combination of characters (according to Schultz, 1944): 6 opercular spines and 4 to 6 interoper-

Tridensimilis venezuelae. (After Schultz, 1944.)

cular spines present, these patches distinctly separated and separately movable; the gill membranes are joined across the isthmus with a broad free fold; the eyes are lateral; the body depth is contained 6 to 8 times and the head 5 to 6.5 times in the standard length; the teeth are small, curved, and conical, in three separate rows above; the dorsal fin rays number 9-11 and the anal fin rays number 15-25; there are 5 branchiostegal rays; and the nasal barbel is absent.

It is possible that this genus will be included with *Tridentopsis* eventually. The only certain and well-marked character that differentiates them seems to be the number of opercular spines (6 versus 10).

Recently a new genus was described as belonging to the family Trichomycteridae (Britski and Ortega, 1983). This genus, *Trichogenes*, was described from specimens collected from small litoranean rivers of southeastern Brazil. The genus, placed in the subfamily Trichomycterinae, was characterized by the authors as follows: opercle bearing two patches of spines and interopercle bearing spines as well; nasal barbel present, mental barbels absent, and two barbels (maxillary) present at the angle of the mouth; the orbit has a free margin; the gill membranes are free from the isthmus; the first ray of the pectoral fin is not pungent; the dorsal fin is short, with 9 rays; and nearer the caudal fin base than the tip of the snout; ventral fins originate in front of the middle of the body; the anal fin is long (more than 30 rays) and originates in front of the dorsal fin base; the infraorbital canal is complete, formed by the lachrymal plus 6 tube-shaped infraorbitals; and the swim bladder capsule is separated from the posterior part of the skull.

Trichogenes longipinnis. (From Britski & Ortega, 1983.)

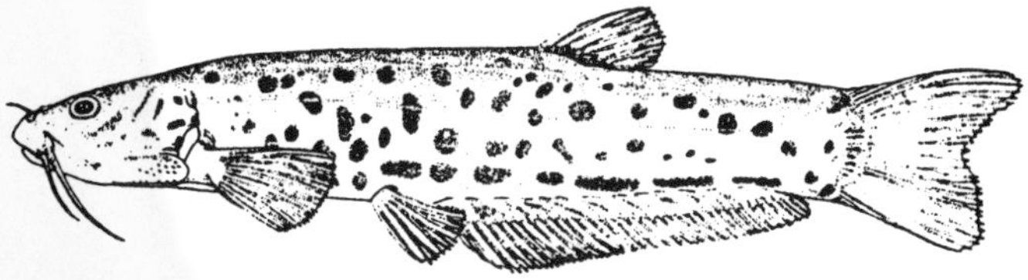

Checklist of the species of the family Trichomycteridae and their type localities:

Subfamily (or family) Nematogenyinae

Nematogenys Girard, 1854. Type species *Trichomycterus inermis* Guichenot.
- *Nematogenys inermis* (Guichenot *in* Gray, 1848). Chile.

Subfamily Trichomycterinae

Scleronema Eigenmann, 1917. Type species *S. operculatum* Eigenmann.
- *Scleronema operculatum* Eigenmann, 1917. Cacequi, Uruguay basin.

Trichomycterus Valenciennes *in* Humboldt, 1833. Type species *Thrycomycterus nigricans* Valenciennes (genus described without an included species).
- *Trichomycterus alternatum* (Eigenmann, 1917). Rio Doce.
- *T. alternum* (Marini, Nichols, & La Monte, 1933). La Rioja, Argentina. (Rio de Los Sauces).
- *T. amazonicum* Steindachner, 1883. Codajaz.
- *T. angustirostris* (Devincenzi & Teague, 1942). Rio Uruguay. (Placed by some in *Scleronema*.)
- *T. areolatum* (Valenciennes, 1846). Sul de Chile ("la riviere de San-Jago").
- *T. arleoi* (Fernandez-Yepez, 1972). Rio Yaracey, Venezuela.
- *T. banneaui* Eigenmann, 1912. Correntes perto de Honda, Colombia.
  - *b. maracaiboensis* Schultz, 1944. Maracaibo basin, Venezuela.
- *T. barbouri* (Eigenmann, 1910). Rio Beni, east of Bolivia.
- *T. bogotense* (Eigenmann, 1912). Planalto de Bogota e para o norte.
- *T. borellii* Boulenger, 1897. Chaco boliviano; Argentina (mission d'Aguairenda, Tala, Lesser).
- *T. boylei* Nichols, 1956. Tilcara (Jujuy).
- *T. brasiliensis* Reinhardt, 1873. Rio das Velhas and Rio Doce a Ribeira do Iguape.

T. burmeisteri Berg, 1895). Province of Mendoza, Rio Mendoza, Argentina.
T. caliense (Eigenmann, 1912). Calima.
T. chapmani (Eigenmann, 1912). Upper valley of the Cauca, Boquia.
T. chiltoni Eigenmann, 1927. Centro do sul do Chile.
T. chungaraensis Arratia F., 1983. Streams of Vertiente de Mal Paso, Chungara Lake, northern Chile.
T. conradi (Eigenmann, 1912). Baixo rio Potaro, Guyana.
T. davisi (Haseman, 1911). São Paulo, Serrinha, Est do Parana.
T. dispar Tschudi, 1845. Altos Andes do leste e oeste do Peru (incl. *T. cordovensis* Weyenberg).
T. dorsostriatum (Eigenmann, 1918). Villavicencio, Colombia.
T. eichorniarum Miranda-Ribeiro, 1912. Calares, upper Paraguay, Mato Grosso.
T. eigenmanni (Boulenger, 1898). Cumbaca.
T. emanueli Schultz, 1944. Rio Chama at Estanques, Maracaibo basin, Venezuela.
e. motatanensis Schultz, 1944. Motatan system, Maracaibo basin, Venezuela.
T. fassli (Steindachner, 1915). Rio Songo, north of Yungas, Bolivia.
T. florense (Miranda-Ribeiro, 1943). Rio das Flores, near Ipaibas, Estado do Rio de Janeiro.
T. fuscum (Meyen, 1835). Peru.
T. gabrieli (Myers, 1926). Corredeiras de São Gabriel, Rio Negro, Brazil.
T. goeldii Boulenger, 1896. Vicinity of Rio de Janeiro (about 2,600 feet altitude).
T. gracilior (Eigenmann, 1912). Rio Potaro basin, Guyana.
T. guianense (Eigenmann, 1909). Upper Rio Potaro, Guyana.
T. hasemani (Eigenmann, 1914). Santarem. San Joaquim, Bolivia.
T. herberti (Miranda-Ribeiro, 1940). Rio Bodoquena, Mato Grosso, Brazil.
T. heterodontum (Eigenmann, 1918). Rio Mendoza, Palmira, Argentina.
T. iheringi (Eigenmann, 1917). São Paulo and Prata basin. (Sapina).
T. immaculatum (Eigenmann & Eigenmann, 1889). Paraiba and Doce Rivers; Goiaz (Juiz de Flora, São Mateus).
T. itatiayae Miranda-Ribeiro, 1906. Itatiaia, Serra da Mantiqueira. (Possible synonym of *immaculatum*.)
T. johnsoni (Fowler, 1932). Descalvados, Mato Grosso.
T. knerii Steindachner, 1882. Canelos and Rio Zamora, Ecuador.
T. laticeps Kner & Steindachner, 1864. Vertente de oeste dos Andes do Ecuador.
T. latidens (Eigenmann, 1918). Rio Calima.
T. latistriatum (Eigenmann, 1918). Santander, Colombia.
T. laucaensis Arratia F. 1983. Systems of Laula River, Parinacota, 4,390 meters above sea level, northern Chile.
T. macraei (Girard, 1855). Vertientes de leste de Andes (Uspallata).
T. maculatum (Valenciennes, 1846). Santiago, Chile.
T. meridae Regan, 1903. Cordillera de Merida, Rio Albireggas, Venezuela.
T. metae (Eigenmann, 1918). Barrigona.
T. minutum Boulenger, 1891. San Lorenzo district, south of Rio Grande do Sul, Brazil. (Placed in *Scleronema* by Fowler.)
T. mondolfi (Schultz, 1945). Quebrado Chacaito, Rio Tay system, near Caracas, Venezuela.
T. nigricans Valenciennes, 1846. Santa Catarina, Brazil.
T. nigromaculatum Boulenger, 1887. Andes da Colombia.
T. paolence (Eigenmann, 1917). Rio Tiete, São Paulo. (A synonym of *proops* in Fowler.)
T. paquequerense (Miranda-Ribeiro, 1943). Rio Paquequer Grande, Estado de Rio de Janeiro.
T. parkoi (Miranda-Ribeiro, 1944). Rio Iticoai, que desagua no Javari, affluente do Amazonas.
T. patagoniensis (Eigenmann, 1909). Rio Blanco (Andes).
T. pique (MacDonagh, 1938). Fortin Mercedes, Pedro Luro, on the Rio Colorado (Buenos Aires).
T. poeyanum Cope, 1877. Arequipa, Peru. (Synonym of *rivulatum*.)
T. proops Miranda-Ribeiro, 1908. Rio Paraiba basin; São Paulo.
T. punctatissimum Castelnau, 1855. Rio Araguaia.
T. punctulatum Valenciennes, 1840. Rio Re-

mac, Peru. (A variety of *dispar* according to Miranda-Ribeiro.)

p. piurae Eigenmann, 1922. Piura, northern Peru.

T. regani (Eigenmann, 1918). San Juan Basin, Colombia.

T. reinhardti (Eigenmann, 1917). Rio das Velhas basin (Rio Itabira).

T. retropinne Regan, 1903. Cabeceiras do Rio Magdalena.

T. riojanum Berg, 1897. Northern Argentina (arroyo de la Cordillera de la Rioja).

T. rivulatum Valenciennes, 1846. Guasacona, upper Andes of Peru. (Incl. *poeyanum, oroyae, quechuorum,* & *eigenmanni.*)

T. romeroi Fowler, 1941. Honda, Colombia.

T. santaeritae (Eigenmann, 1918). Santa Rita, Rio Preto, Estado da Bahia.

T. septentrionale Behre, 1928. Baixios do Rio Chiriqui del Tire, Panama.

T. spegazzinii (Berg, 1897). Rio de Cachi, Salta, Argentina.

T. spilosoma (Regan, 1913). Cordova, sobre o Rio Dagua, Colombia.

T. stellatum (Eigenmann, 1918). Quebrada Sarjento.

T. stramineum (Eigenmann, 1918). Santander, Colombia.

T. striatum Meek & Hildebrand, 1913. Rio Cana, Tuyra basin, Panama.

T. taczanowskii Steindachner, 1883. North and central Peru, in the Andes. Rio Huambo; Rio Totara em Chiricimoto.

T. taenium Kner, 1863. Vertente do oeste dos Andes do Ecuador e do sul da Colombia.

t. transandianum Steindachner, 1917. Rio Combeima, central Colombia.

T. tenuis Weyenbergh, 1879. Rio Primero, Cordoba, Argentina. (Fowler replaced name with *taeniatus, tenue* preocc.)

T. titcombi (Eigenmann, 1918). Vertentes in the eastern Andes.

T. totae Miles, 1942. Tota Lake, Boyaca, Cordillera Orientale, Colombia.

T. triguttatum (Eigenmann, 1918). Jacarei, Rio Paraiba, Brazil.

T. unicolor (Regan, 1913). San Juan Basin, Colombia.

T. venulosum (Steindachner, 1915). Andes de l'este da Colombia.

T. vermiculatum (Eigenmann, 1917). Rio Paraiba. (Juiz de Fora.)

T. vittatum Regan, 1903. Vale Marcapata, eastern Peru.

T. zonatum (Eigenmann, 1918). Rio Cubatao, Agua Quinto, perto de Santos, São Paulo.

Eremophilus Humboldt, 1811. Type species *Eremophilus mutisii* Humboldt.

Eremophilus candidus Miranda-Ribeiro, 1949. Espirito Santo, affluent of the Rio Claro and east of Sapucai, Brazil.

E. mutisii Humboldt, 1811. Planalto de Bogota.

Bullockia Arratia, Chang, Menu-Marque, & Rojas, 1978. Type species *Hatcheria moldonadoi* Eigenmann.

Bullockia moldonadoi (Eigenmann, 1927). Centro do sul do Chile. (Incl. *Hatcheria bullocki.*)

Trichogenes Britski & Ortega, 1983. Type species *T. longipinnis* Britski & Ortega.

Trichogenes longipinnis Britski & Ortega, 1983. Cachoeira do Amor, southeastern Brazil.

Subfamily Stegophilinae

Pareiodon Kner, 1855. Type species *P. microps* Kner.

Pareiodon microps Kner, 1855. Amazon basin: Araguay Borba, a margem do Madeira cerca de 4 dias de sua embocadura.

Stegophilus Reinhardt, 1858. Type species *S. insidiosus* Reinhardt.

Stegophilus insidiosus Reinhardt, 1858. São Francisco, Rio das Velhas.

S. intermedius Eigenmann & Eigenmann, 1889. Cabeceiras do Araguaia, Goias.

S. macrops Steindachner, 1883. Lake Manacapuru.

S. panzeri (Ahl, 1931). Baixo Amazonas.

S. passarellii Miranda-Ribeiro, 1944. Bacia da baia de Guanabara, Estado do Rio de Janeiro.

S. punctatus Boulenger, 1887. Canelos, Ecuador.

S. septentrionalis Myers, 1927. Santa Barbara, Orinoco, Venezuela.

S. taxistigmus (Fowler, 1914). Rio Rupununi, Guyana.

Pseudostegophilus Eigenmann & Eigenmann, 1889. Type species *Stegophilus, nemurus* Günther, 1868.

Pseudostegophilus nemurus (Günther, 1868)

Upper Amazon; Rio Mamore.

?*P. paulensis* (Miranda-Ribeiro, 1918). Avanhandava, Rio Tiete.

?*P. scarificator* Ihering, 1930. Emas, Pirassununga, Rio Mogi-Guacu. (Gosline placed this species as synonym of *Homodiaetus maculatum*.)

?*Parastegophilus* Miranda-Ribeiro, 1946. Type species *Stegophilus maculatus* Steindachner. (May actually be a synonym of *Homodiaetus* and is treated as such in text.)

Parastegophilus maculatus (Steindachner, 1879). São Paulo, bacio do Prata, La Plata.

Schultzichthys (no information available).

Homodiaetus Eigenmann & Ward *in* Eigenmann, MacAtee, & Ward, 1907. Type species *H. anisitsi* Eigenmann & Ward.

Homodiaetus anisitsi Eigenmann & Ward *in* Eigenmann, MacAtee, & Ward, 1907. Villa Rica, Paraguay.

H. haemomyzon Myers, 1942. Rio Guarico, Venezuela.

H. vazferreirai Devincenzi *in* Devincenzi & Le Grand, 1936. Rio Uruguay.

Pleurophysus Miranda-Ribeiro, 1918. Type species *P. hydrostaticus* Miranda-Ribeiro.

Pleurophysus hydrostaticus Miranda-Ribeiro, 1918. Rio Claro, Brazil.

Haemomaster Myers, 1927. Type species *H. venezuelae* Myers.

Haemomaster venezuelae Myers, 1927. Santa Barbara, Orinoco, Venezuela.

Apomatoceros Eigenmann, 1922. Type species *A. alleni* Eigenmann.

Apomatoceros alleni Eigenmann, 1922. Rio Morona, Peruvian Amazon.

Acanthopoma Lütken, 1891. Type species *A. annectens* Lütken.

Acanthopoma annectens Lütken, 1891. Rio Huallaga.

A. bondi Myers, 1942. Rio Apure at San Fernando de Apure, Venezuela.

Ochmacanthus Eigenmann, 1912. Type species *O. flabelliferus* Eigenmann.

Ochmacanthus alternus Myers, 1927. Cano do Quiribana, Venezuela.

O. batrachostoma (Miranda-Ribeiro, 1912). Upper Rio Paraguay around São Luiz de Caceres.

O. flabelliferus Eigenmann, 1912. Essiquibo basin at Konawaruk.

O. orinoco Myers, 1927. Playa Matepalma, Orinoco, Venezuela.

O. reinhardti (Steindachner, 1883). Iça, Monte Alegre, and Manacapuru, Amazonas.

Subfamily Vandelliinae

Vandellia Valenciennes, 1846. Type species *V. cirrhosa* Valenciennes.

Vandellia balzanii Perugia, 1897. Mission Mosetenes, Rio Beni.

V. beccarii de Caporiacco, 1935. Rio Essequibo.

V. cirrhosa Valenciennes, 1846. Not cited. Probably bacios do Amazonas e do Orinoco.

V. hasemani Eigenmann, 1918. Rio Mamore.

V. hematophaga Guimaraes, 1935. Rio Tiete.

V. plazaii Castelnau, 1855. Amazon basin; Rio Ucayali (Peru), Sarayaco.

V. wieneri Pellegrin, 1909. Rio Napo, Ecuador.

Plectrochilus Miranda-Ribeiro, 1917. Type species *P. machadoi* Miranda-Ribeiro.

Plectrochilus erythrurus (Eigenmann, 1922). Rios Morona (Gosulimacocha), Ucayali (perto do Orellana), and Paranapura.

P. machadoi Miranda-Ribeiro, 1917. Rio Solimoes.

P. sanguineus (Eigenmann, 1918). Santo Antonio do Rio Madeiro.

Paravandellia Miranda-Ribeiro, 1912. Type species *P. oxyptera* Miranda-Ribeiro.

Paravandellia oxyptera Miranda-Ribeiro, 1912. Rio Paraguay perto de São Luiz de Caceres.

Paracanthopoma Giltay, 1935. Type species *P. parva* Giltay.

Paracanthopoma parva Giltay, 1935. Upper Rio Catrimani, Brazil.

Branchioica Eigenmann, 1918. Type species *B. bertonii* Eigenmann.

Branchioica bertonii Eigenmann, 1918. Asuncion, Paraguay basin.

B. magdalenae Miles, 1943. Rio Magdalena, Colombia.

B. phanreonema Miles, 1943. Upper Cuaca, Colombia.

B. teaguei (Devincenzi & Vaz-Ferreira, 1939). Rio Uruguay.

Subfamily Tridentinae

Tridens Eigenmann & Eigenmann, 1889. Type species *T. melanops* Eigenmann & Eigenmann.

Tridens melanops Eigenmann & Eigenmann, 1889. Ica, perto da fronteira do Brazil com o Peru.

Tridentopsis Myers, 1925. Type species *T. pearsoni* Myers.

Tridentopsis pearsoni Myers, 1925. Lagoons at Lago Rogoagua, Bolivia.

T. tocantinsi La Monte, 1939. Rio Tocantins, northern Brazil.

Tridensimilis Schultz, 1944. Type species *T. venezuelae* Schultz.

Tridensimilis brevis (Eigenmann & Eigenmann, 1889). Tabatinga, Amazonas.

T. venezuelae Schultz, 1944. Maracaibo basin, Venezuela.

Miuroglanis Eigenmann & Eigenmann, 1889. Type species *M. platycephalus* Eigenmann & Eigenmann.

Miuroglanis platycephalus Eigenmann & Eigenmann, 1889. Rio Jutai.

Subfamily Glanapteryginae

Glanapteryx Myers, 1927. Type species *G. anguilla* Myers.

Glanapteryx anguilla Myers, 1927. Corredeiras de São Gabriel, Rio Negro. (Lagos de rochas a jusante da Corredeiras de São Gabriel.)

Pygidianops Myers, 1944. Type species *P. eigenmanni* Myers.

Pygidianops eigenmanni Myers, 1944. Rock pools below São Gabriel rapids, Rio Negro, Brazil.

Typhlobelus Myers, 1944. Type species *T. ternetzi* Myers.

Typhlobelus ternetzi Myers, 1944. Rock pools below São Gabriel rapids, Rio Negro, Brazil.

Subfamily Sarcoglanidinae

Sarcoglanis Myers & Weitzman, 1966. Type species *S. simplex* Myers & Weitzman.

Sarcoglanis simplex Myers & Weitzman, 1966. Rock pools below São Gabriel rapids of the Rio Negro (below the town of Uaupes).

Malacoglanis Myers & Weitzman, 1966. Type species *M. gelatinosus* Myers & Weitzman.

Malacoglanis gelatinosus Myers & Weitzman, 1966. Small cano of the Rio Orteguaza, Caqueta Province, Colombia.

Chapter 29

Family — Plates 158–223

CALLICHTHYIDAE

(Armored Catfishes)

The family Callichthyidae is a large family of relatively small, heavily armored freshwater catfishes from South America and Trinidad. Most are bottom-dwelling fishes, and they occur in a variety of habitats from slow-flowing streams and drainage ditches to ponds and even flooded areas. Some are able to live in swampy or muddy areas where the oxygen has become depleted. They can do this by virtue of their ability to take atmospheric air into the mouth and pass it on to their intestines where the oxygen is extracted. In humid areas or during rains many species are able to travel out of the water over land obstacles such as sand banks or mud flats to find food or better conditions. Most of the species live in large schools (often composed of mixed species) in sandy or weedy areas or as smaller groups in the slow-flowing streams. The natural diet of most species consists of worms and insect larvae that they root out with the use of their barbels in the soft sandy or muddy bottom material. Although relatively small, the larger, more abundant species are utilized as food by man. These are roasted in their armor and when done broken apart to obtain the flesh. Although this is easily accomplished with the *Corydoras* species, with *Callichthys* the use of a stone or other implement is needed to break through the armor.

In aquaria callichthyids are adaptable to a wide variety of conditions and as such are probably the most used of any of the catfish families in a community tank. They are peaceful and their armor enables them to survive attacks by all but the most aggressive fishes (usually cichlids). This armor also helps prevent parasitic attacks and, if accidents should happen where the catfish is out of water for a time (jumping out of a broken tank), prevents them from drying out very quickly. The tank size can vary considerably depending upon the size and activity of the species. For the large bubblenest builders a 20-gallon tank or larger is necessary; for some of the dwarf corys even a 5-gallon tank will suffice if not too crowded. The bottom material has been argued about for many years. Some aquarists believe no bottom material should be used. Others say only soft material can be used because of the erosive effects of large, sharp gravel pieces on the delicate barbels. Actually, almost any bottom material can be used except those that do have very sharp edges (even this might be all right, but why take any chances). Normal planting and rockwork should be added, the lighting can be normal (these fishes are mostly diurnal), and the water should be close to neutral or slightly on the alkaline side (this varies with the species) and soft. Some aquarists advocate up to three tablespoons of salt per four gallons of water, but this is not necessary and not recommended unless other inhabitants of the community tank need it. Although callichthyids can in general withstand a temperature range of about 8° to 36°C (also dependent upon the species), they should be kept within the range of 18° to 32°C. Normal filtration and some aeration (especially for the bubblenest builders) should be used. The diet should be varied and sufficient. All too often these catfishes are placed in a tank solely to clean up after the *real* fishes and may not get enough food. They will accept almost anything, although live foods such as tubificid worms and other live foods that will sink to the bottom are best. Flake foods and other slow-sinking materials should be added in sufficient quantity to reach the bottom if there are fast-swimming mid- or upper-layer feeders in the tank. More specific information, including breeding techniques, will be given under the individual species.

Callichthyids have their entire flanks covered by only two lateral rows of bony dermal scutes. These are arranged so that they overlap along the rows as well as between the rows, giving full protection but at the same time allowing a certain amount of freedom of movement. Anteriorly these scutes connect with the solid bones of the head, and the head itself may be covered with bony plates. The upper row of lateral scutes may either meet on the back or there may be a narrow bare area that may or may not be filled in with small oval or roundish bony platelets. The body is usually rather deep and the upper profile of the head is steep. The eyes are usually large and movable, a condition that has caused some aquarists to swear that these little catfishes were actually winking at them. Actually the winking that they see is only an illusion caused by the movement of the eyes. There are up to two pairs of well-developed barbels and a pair of thread-like processes on the upper jaw, and a pair of fleshy flaps or one or two pairs of fleshy flaps or a pair of "barbels" on the underlip. The simplest arrangement of barbels is in *Hoplosternum* and *Callichthys*, with two pairs of well-developed barbels and a pair of thread-like processes on the upper jaw and a pair of fleshy flaps on the lower. In *Dianema* and *Cataphractops* the arrangement is similar but the lower lip has two pairs of fleshy barbel-like flaps. In *Aspidoras*, *Corydoras*, and *Brochis* the lower lip flaps are more developed and barbel-like and there are no thread-like appendages on the upper lip. The mouth is small and inferior. The large dorsal fin has a strong spine, as do the pectoral fins, both of which can be locked into a fully extended position. An adipose fin is present and consists of a stout, movable spine followed by a flap of skin. The swim bladder is short and two-chambered and is encased in bone. Some of the scutes or bony plates and fin spines may be covered with hair-like denticles; these are more developed on the head and fin spines of some males of some genera.

Seven genera are currently accepted as valid (*Cascadura* is said to be a young form of *Hoplosternum*) and can be distinguished by the following key (after Gosline, 1940):

1a. Snout depressed; interorbital width greater than or equal to head depth at anterior margin of orbit .... Subfamily Callichthyinae...2
1b. Snout compressed or rounded; interorbital width considerably less than head depth at anterior margin of orbit; rictal barbels short, not reaching much beyond gill opening; lower lip reverted to form single pair of short barbels................. .... Subfamily Corydoradinae...5
2a. Eyes more or less superior, the diameter contained two or more times in their distance from lower end of bony opercle... 3
2b. Eyes lateral, the diameter contained 1.3 times or less in distance from lower end of bony opercle.............................. 4
3a. Coracoids expanded on abdominal surface between pectoral fin bases; suborbital bones not covered with flesh............... ....*Hoplosternum*
3b. Abdomen between pectoral fin bases completely covered with flesh; suborbitals covered with flesh........... *Callichthys*
4a. Nuchal scutes not meeting dorsally........ .... *Cataphractops*
4b. Nuchal scutes fused across midline between occipital and dorsal....... *Dianema*
5a. Nuchal scutes not meeting above; coracoids more or less expanded; frontal fontanel elongate; no supraoccipital fontanel 6
5b. Nuchal scutes meeting or not along midline between occipital and dorsal; abdomen between pectoral fin bases entirely covered with flesh; two cranial fontanels present, a supraoccipital fontanel and a small roundish or elongate frontal fontanel ....*Aspidoras*
6a. D. I,7-9 .... *Corydoras*
6b. D. I,10-18 ....*Brochis*

The family Callichthyidae is generally divided into two subfamilies, Callichthyinae and Corydoradinae, that can be distinguished by the characters given in the above key. The subfamily Callichthyinae is said to be the more primitive of the two and includes the genera *Hoplosternum, Callichthys, Dianema,* and *Cataphractops.* Hoedeman prefers to further divide the subfamily into two tribes, with *Dianema* and *Cataphractops* in the Dianemini, and *Hoplosternum* and *Callichthys* in the Callichthyini. The genus *Cascadura* was found to be only a young *Hoplosternum* in which the body scutes were not yet fully developed. (*Callichthys* has been separated into its own subfamily by Miranda-Ribeiro (1959), the other genera *(Hoplosternum, Cataphractops,* and *Dianema)* being placed by him in the subfamily Hoplosterninae.)

Callichthys and *Hoplosternum* are normally found on the muddy bottoms of slow-flowing rivers, pools, drainage ditches, and swampy areas. In these latter areas they are capable of utilizing atmospheric air by taking in a gulp of air at the surface of the water and passing it back to the hind gut. The walls of the gut are lined with a mesh of tiny blood vessels into which the oxygen from the air can pass much as in true lungs. The number of trips a particular individual makes to the surface appears to be dependent upon the amount of oxygen in the water: less oxygen means more trips to the surface. The remaining gases pass out through the anus. When there is a severe drought the air breathers are, of course, the last to die, although when things get too bad these catfishes are able to traverse short stretches of land seeking better conditions. One *Hoplosternum* was observed to travel about 90 meters in the course of two hours. Both genera are commonly found in large schools and are easily netted, although removing them from a net is often a very long and arduous task for the spines catch in the meshwork and are difficult to disentangle. In some cases these fishes can be caught by hand, making things a bit easier. These catfishes are also capable of making sounds, both grunts and squeaks.

Spawning has been accomplished for both genera in aquaria. Both build bubblenests constructed from plant parts, some bottom material, and bubbles (formed by a mouth secretion and air). Additional bubbles are blown into the bottom portion of the nest until an almost solid mass about 20 cm in diameter and up to 10 cm high is formed. In most cases the male is the one that builds the nest. He is said to utilize his toothed pectoral spines in cutting off bits of plants and his barbels for setting them into the proper position. During the construction of the nest the female is either completely ignored or actively chased away. When the nest construction is finished the male will finally accept the female. The female will expel several eggs into a basket formed by the folding together of her ventral fins. These are carried to the nest, and as she flips over on her back she deposits them among the bubbles. The male follows her and secures the eggs in place by adding more bubbles. There may eventually be several hundred eggs released by the female at one spawning. The male or the pair will keep watch over the nest for about four weeks. At that time the young catfish, about 2.5 cm long, will come out of the nest. They are still vulnerable at that time for their armor is not yet fully hardened.

Feeding the fry and adults poses no problem. They will accept all normal aquarium foods. A substantial portion of vegetable matter should, however, be included.

The genus *Cataphractops* contains a single species from Peru and possibly Para. The body is compressed but the snout is depressed. The supraoccipital forms a short posterior projection that does not contact the azygous predorsal plate. The fontanel is elongate, and the nuchal plates do not fuse along the midline between the supraoccipital and the dorsal; the suborbital is naked. The coracoids are somewhat exposed on the abdomen between the pectoral fin bases. The eyes are large and lateral, visible as much from above as from below. The rictal barbels are long, extending as far as the end of the ventral fins or beyond that. The dorsal fin has a spine and 7 rays, its base shorter than the distance between it and the adipose fin. The caudal fin is emarginate.

The genus *Dianema* contains only two species from the Amazon. The head is somewhat depressed, its width much less than the depth

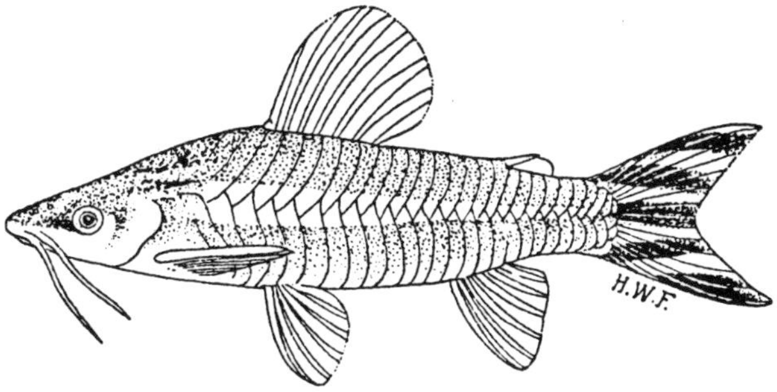

Dianema urostriata. (From Fowler, 1954.)

of the body. The fontanel is elongate, and the supraoccipital does not form a backward projection. The suborbital is very narrow and naked, and the nuchal plates fuse along the midline between the supraoccipital and the dorsal. The abdomen between the pectoral fin bases is usually completely covered by the expansion of the coracoids. There is no azygous predorsal plate. The eyes are large and lateral in position. The lower lip has two to four pairs of short barbel-like flaps in addition to the rictal barbels; the rictal barbels extend to the pectoral fin origin or beyond. The dorsal fin has a spine and 7 or 8 soft rays, its base length contained one to one and a half times in its distance from the adipose fin. The caudal fin is forked.

Species of the genus *Dianema* are commonly kept in home aquaria. A pair will do fairly well in a 10-gallon tank, but it is recommended that they be kept in small schools of about a dozen individuals, in which case a 20- to 30-gallon long tank is the smallest tank that should be considered. Filtration and aeration should be present and the tank should be well planted and some floating plants should be present. Sharp stones and sharp pieces of gravel should be avoided, and the tank itself must be covered. These fishes often swim in the middle parts of the tank and when startled (they are nervous fishes) are capable of easily leaping out of the tank. Luckily, they have the capability of aerial respiration and can survive for some time out of water in a wet or damp atmosphere. In fact, in their natural habitat they are reported to retreat into the mud and debris that is found along the bottom and sides of streams that have dried up, only to reappear during the next rainy season. Food is no problem as the list of foods accepted is very long and includes such items as worms of all types, insects and insect larvae, brine shrimp, daphnia, beefheart, frozen foods, and even flake foods. The optimum temperature range is 23° to 26°C.

According to various sources, sexes may be distinguished in several ways. The female, of course, is generally heavier than the male. The soft portion of the pectoral fin of the male thickens into a creamy opaque pad; the female's pectoral membrane is transparent. A bubblenest is built, and the male's behavior is similar to that of the other bubblenest-building members of the subfamily. According to Langhammer, his pair built a huge bubblenest beneath a mat of water sprite. Another observer reported prespawning behavior in which the pair swam side by side as the female's belly took on a rosy hue and they investigated every centimeter of the tank. Unfortunately, there was no actual spawning.

Dianema longibarbis, the Porthole Catfish, is active and peaceful in aquaria. It stays in midwater most of the time, as does *D. urostriatum,* and may rest in an inclined position, head up, in the water column or against some support such as a plant leaf. This species attains a length of about 10 cm and is called the porthole catfish by virtue of a row of black dots along each side, although this is highly variable. The second species, *D. urostriatum,* is called the flagtail port because of the banded caudal fin, although this pattern may break up into a spotted pattern in older fish.

The genus *Callichthys* contains a single species, *C. callichthys*. The head is broad and depressed, its width greater than the depth of the body; the body is compressed posteriorly. The fontanel is small, nearly circular, and the supraoccipital does not form a posterior extension. There is no azygous predorsal plate. The suborbital is covered with flesh and the nuchal plates fuse along the midline between the supraoccipital and the origin of the dorsal. The abdomen between the pectoral fins is completely covered with flesh. The eyes are small and superior in position while the nares are less than or equal to an orbit's diameter apart, the posterior one a diameter or less from the eye. The terminal mouth has the lower lip reverted to form a pair of fleshy flaps, and the premaxillary is rudimentary and without teeth; the lower jaw has an elongate patch of brown-tipped teeth on each side. The rictal barbels extend to midway between the pectoral and ventral fin bases. The dorsal fin has a flat spine and 7 or 8 rays, its base contained two or more times in its distance from the adipose fin. The anal fin is short and rounded and the caudal fin is broad and rounded. The ventral fins are rounded and inserted below the posterior half of the dorsal. The pectoral fin spine is short and thick, serrated on the inner margin in the young. The sides of the unpaired fins and the lower surface of the paired fins are thickly covered with short bristles; the opercle has a marginal group of short, slender bristles; and the posterior margins of the lateral plates have fine bristles. The gill openings are rather wide. Young individuals have a narrow band of teeth along the entire lower jaw, and the fontanel extends to the occipital and is divided near its middle. The lateral plates are not very deep and do not cover the entire sides. The nuchal plates are rudimentary.

Callichthys callichthys is very wide ranging, extending from Trinidad to Buenos Aires, and including the upper Amazon and Paraguay systems. They mostly inhabit fairly shallow still to slow-flowing waters of sluggish creeks or swamps with a muddy or fine material bottom and a dense growth of vegetation along the banks. At night when a light was shone on them individuals would dart from place to place and eventually burrow into the soft bottom. They were caught by kicking mud and debris into the seine. Stomach contents included sand, plant debris, diatoms, and insect debris (including chironomids). They attain a length of about 20 cm in the wild but usually only about 14 cm in captivity. *Callichthys callichthys* is a peaceful and relatively undemanding species, usually active in dim light or at night but hiding when the light is bright. It is an excellent jumper and its tank should be well covered. They need a large aquarium (at least a 20-gallon tank) although the water should be fairly shallow (about 13 cm or less), especially for breeding.

Callichthys callichthys inhabits still to slow-flowing waters where the bottom is mostly soft and there is a dense growth of vegetation along the banks. Photo courtesy of the New York Zoological Society.

Part of the reason for this is their habit of taking gulps of air from the surface from time to time which is eventually expelled at the anus. The bottom material should be fine and dark in color. Plants should be strong and well rooted; fine-leaved plants are not recommended as the bottom is constantly being stirred up and the fine leaves only seem to contribute to the mess. Surface plants, however, may be used for keeping the light level down and for breeding these catfish. A temperature range of 24° to 26°C is adequate although for brief periods temperatures as low as 18°C can be tolerated. The water chemistry is not critical but the water should be kept clean. With such fishes that stir up the bottom, this demands an efficient filtration system. *Callichthys callichthys* is easy to feed. It is what is known as an indiscriminate omnivore, meaning that it will accept almost anything, both animal and vegetable. This is an active and greedy feeder that prefers live foods but takes whiteworms, chopped earthworms, tubificid worms, bloodworms, frozen brine shrimp, beefheart mix, various salad items, etc. Although it is primarily a bottom forager, if it is not well fed it will include small fishes in its diet, probably taking them by surprise at night while they sleep. Being good scavengers they are accepted as community tank fishes even though they are shy and stir up the bottom regularly.

Spawning has been reported many times and, in fact, this species is being bred commercially, albeit not in large quantities. The females are larger and more robust, while the males are brighter in color, exhibiting a delicate blue or violet sheen laterally; the female is a rather dull olive-green. The males also have a more well developed and longer pectoral fin spine that is reddish brown and edged with orange or reddish orange. The plates cover the abdomen of the male fully but do not in the female; this gap is probably due to the expansion of the area as the female fills with eggs. For spawning this catfish, a large bare tank is commonly used, say about 20 gallons capacity. It is filled to about 25% capacity (no more than about 13 cm deep). Some aquarists prefer to add some rocks or plants for hiding purposes. Floating on the surface should be a piece of styrofoam (or similar object) about 12 to 15 cm to a side or, for those who like the "natural" method, some floating plants such as water hyacinth. The water should be soft and warm (about 24°C) although some aquarists believe that 20°C is sufficient. The prospective parents should be conditioned with live foods and chopped earthworms and should be at least 10 cm in length. The pair (some aquarists prefer two or three males per female) can be added to the spawning tank in the evening with the expectation that the male will start construction of a bubblenest the following day. The males are aggressive at this time and when courting can be heard making quite audible grunts. If the action is a bit slow to start, the pair can be separated and further conditioned or a new combination tried. One spawner suggests that fluctuations in temperature may be an inducement for the onset of spawning.

If all goes well the male will start his bubblenest. In the wild this nest is constructed using clumps of overhanging grass, twigs, or floating plants; in the aquarium the floating plants or styrofoam square will be utilized, or even a broad leaf of a bottom plant that has grown to the surface. The male will take in air from the surface in an inverted position and move to the undersurface of the nest site where he emits mucus-covered bubbles from his gill openings. This continues until a substantial bubblenest is completed (one was measured at 15 cm in diameter and some 6 cm in height). During nest construction the female is not allowed near the site although the male may nudge her abdomen from time to time between his bubble-making sessions.

Upon completion of the nest spawning will commence, usually in the morning. The female will form a pouch or basket by clamping her ventral fins together and deposit about 15 to 20 eggs in it. The male will then "flip" her over on her back and with their ventral surfaces opposed he fertilizes the eggs. The female then swims to the bubblenest and deposits the eggs therein. The male may add more bubbles from time to time. This action is repeated again and again over the course of about two hours, when anywhere from 150 to 400 eggs are in the nest. The female is best removed after her eggs are depleted for both her protection (from the male) and the protection of the eggs (she may eat them). The male assumes the duty of guarding the nest full of eggs and does so with vigor. During this time he emits grunting noises, possibly as a warning. The fairly large (about 2 mm diameter) eggs are a transparent pink and should hatch in about four to five days. The fry apparently absorb the nourishment in the yolk sac during the incubation period and are free-swimming as soon as they hatch. The male can now be removed.

Within 24 hours the fry should receive rotifers, cyclops, enchytreae, microworms, newly hatched brine shrimp, or even chopped tubificid worms. For best results feed at least three times a day. The fry and young grow rapidly at first but the growth rate slows down after a while. In a couple of months the young *Callichthys* should be at least 25 mm in length. The fry are a tan color sprinkled with black spots.

Although this species has been in the hobby for many, many years it has not attained the popularity of other species in the subfamily.

The genus *Hoplosternum* contains only three or four species (the fourth is still in question). *H. shirui* Fowler (1940) has recently been

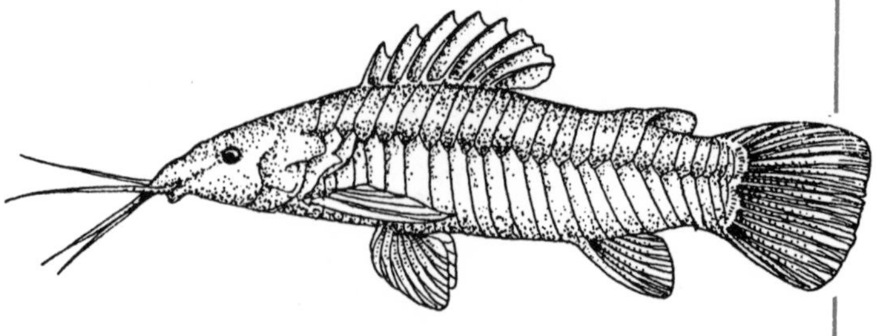

Hoplosternum thoracatum.

listed as a valid species (Ortega & Vari, 1986). It previously was included as a synonym of *H. littorale*. The head is depressed, its width equal to or less than the width of the body. The fontanel is rounded or elongate and the suborbital is naked. The supraoccipital does not form a posterior extension and there is no azygous predorsal plate. The nuchal plates fuse along the midline between the supraoccipital and the dorsal and the abdomen between the pectoral fins is totally or mostly enclosed by the expanded coracoids. The eyes are somewhat superiorly placed, being more visible from above than from below. The lower lip is reverted and forms a pair of fleshy flaps; the rictal barbels extend as far as midway between the pectoral and ventral fin bases or a bit farther. The dorsal fin has a spine and 7 or 8 rays, its base contained slightly more than one time in its distance from the adipose fin. The caudal fin may be rounded or emarginate.

Hoplosternum littorale is distributed from Trinidad through Venezuela and the Guianas to the La Plata region. It is the largest of the *Hoplosternum* and *Callichthys* species, attaining a length of about 20 cm. It is common in marshes, swamps, and larger rivers where it feeds to a great extent on aquatic plants. In some areas it is fished for on a commercial basis as a food fish. It is not brightly colored, being a drab gray to grayish brown and only rarely with a few fine black spots. The caudal fin is emarginate. Aquarium care for this species is essentially the same as that for *Callichthys,* but it should have a temperature of about 24°C. Although not strictly nocturnal, *H. littorale* prefers subdued lighting. The smaller individuals are said to hide more than the larger ones. A large tank is recommended (20 gallons or more) suitably furnished with sand, rocks (without sharp edges), and coarse-leaved plants that are well rooted. Some floating plants for protection from the light and for possible spawning action should be added. The water conditions are not critical but good filtration is a must. Water changes are beneficial, especially when combined with a siphoning of any bottom material that would be stirred up by these bottom dwellers. Food is also no problem as the hoplos will accept a wide variety of foods from live foods (which they prefer) to flake foods. They will even eat from the surface if sufficiently motivated by hunger.

The males have an enlarged, thickened pectoral fin spine that at maturity turns up at the end like a ski and with the onset of the spawning season takes on a maroon to blood-red coloration; in *H. thoracatum* the pectoral spine also becomes thickened but there are no reports of it turning up at the end and the color most quoted for it is orange, not dark red. Male *H. littorale* also have thickened and fused pectoral rays (the females less so) and

Courting behavior in *Hoplosternum* species involves nest construction and physical contact between the male and female. Photo by B. Biegner.

the females usually have a gap in the pectoral region between the coracoids as they fill up with eggs. Like the other hoplos, this species is a bubblenest builder. As the temperature is raised slowly to about 26° or 27°C and possibly with the water change, the male will begin to construct his bubblenest and courtship begins. Surface material should be provided in the form of floating plants or a floating object such as a piece of styrofoam such as that used for *Callichthys*. If nothing is available the male will improvise by removing pieces of the rooted plants (possibly through use of his serrated pectoral fin spines by clamping them against the body with the leaf trapped inside) or by actually uprooting the plants themselves. The nest is fairly large, the diameter often exceeding 30 cm and the thickness 8 cm. The aeration should be kept at a low level so as not to disturb the nest.

After a complicated courtship ritual (unfortunately this was not described) about 200 to 300 (some report up to 500) amber eggs about 1 mm in diameter are placed in the nest. These are stuck together with a secretion similar to that which holds the nest bubbles together and another layer of bubbles is blown by the male under the eggs to hold them in the nest. The male stands guard over the nest after chasing the female from the vicinity. In about three to four days the fry hatch out and have already absorbed their yolk sac. They can be seen sticking to the plants and glass sides of the tank and are ready for food within 24 hours. Microworms and crushed flake food or similar fare can be used for the first few days and then larger food such as newly hatched brine shrimp should be added. The male can be removed once the eggs hatch. The fry grow quickly and before long are a dark gray with darker markings. However, they do not assume the bottom-dwelling habits of the adults until after about a couple of weeks. They develop their armor at a size of about 1.2 cm. In a year's time they should have grown to about 12.5 cm. Most of the spawnings reported for this species have occurred in the springtime, apparently coinciding with the onset of the rainy season in their natural habitat. It is suggested that the breeders not be spawned continuously but be allowed rest periods from time to time.

The female will sometimes help to build the nest but this is the exception, not the rule. Photo by B. Biegner.

Often one or both spawners will invert themselves to care for the nest or deposit eggs in it. Photo by B. Biegner.

The male *Hoplosternum thoracatum* (note the approximated coracoids) utilizes some floating object, natural (leaves) or artificial (styrofoam), to receive the bubbles forming his nest. Photo by B. Biegner.

The female ready to spawn (note the swollen abdominal area) takes an interest in the proceedings but often will not participate in the nest building at this point. Photo by B. Biegner.

Spawning continues until 200 to 300 eggs are deposited in the nest. The female here is nudging the male to continue spawning as she still carries a number of eggs yet to be laid. Photo by B. Biegner.

The male will add eggs to the nest and tend to its care even during the spawning. The female will probably be driven away when she is finished spawning and the male will guard the nest by himself. Photo by B. Biegner.

Hoplosternum thoracatum is a wide ranging species said to occur from southern Panama to Paraguay in a variety of different habitats. The color is quite variable, not only within a population but from one locality to another, but normally it is lighter than *Callichthys callichthys* and *H. littorale,* often being a rich reddish brown with dark spots (sometimes a few, sometimes numerous) on the upper part of the body and whitish spotted with black ventrally. The caudal fin is truncate and in both sexes the caudal base is crossed by a pale transverse band. The aquarium care is as given for *Callichthys.*

Of the larger callichthyids, *H. thoracatum* is said to be the easiest to spawn. The male's pectoral spine is thick and flattened and with the start of the spawning season turns a bright orange to orange-red. This species is ready to spawn at about a year old when it has attained a size of 9 cm (fully grown it is 15-16 cm long), and spawns best in the springtime (April or May). Although not an aggressive species, spawning ready males may become combative and actual damage can be done. Therefore only a single male should be used for spawning. A bubblenest is constructed by the male as in the other species, utilizing plant material if it is available. The water level should be relatively low, also similar to that for the other species. Courtship commences and eventually the male swims alongside the female. After some vibrations a "T" is formed, possibly with the male hanging vertically below the bubblenest. A batch of 10 to 30 eggs is deposited into the female's ventral basket and she swims upside down below the nest and deposits the eggs safely therein. She may at times sink to the bottom and rest between egg-laying bouts. There is a controversy as to when the eggs are fertilized by the male. Some say they are fertilized as soon as they are laid into the basket and while still in the "T" position; others say the eggs are deposited in the bubblenest and the male follows her there immediately to fertilize the eggs; still others report that the female takes sperm into her mouth while in the "T" position and, after sinking to the bottom and resting, she swims to the nest to deposit the eggs and fertilizes them herself with the sperm she has collected beforehand. The first two sound much more plausible than the last mainly because of the time involved before the eggs are fertilized in the last method. In any event the process continues until somewhat over 500 eggs are safely ensconced in the nest. The male drives off the female and guards the eggs.

The eggs hatch in four to five days but the fry may remain in the nest for several days afterward, apparently sheltering there until they are able to swim freely. Since the yolk in the yolk sac is virtually depleted upon hatching, the fry will be ready for food within 24 hours. Microworms and other similar sized live foods should be fed. Crushed flake food has also been given along with other foods with satisfactory results. Newly hatched brine shrimp can be added to the menu in a few days. When the young do become free-swimming they move to the bottom where they dig in and are very difficult to spot. They are dark in color and look like miniature adults. At this time they are very active and feedings should be sufficient and often.

Hoplosternum magdalenae is the questionable species. It is brownish gray with light yellowish white vertical barring of sorts along the sides. Some say this is one and the same with the "dwarf hoplo," a small species that is in the hobby but whose identity has (dubiously) been determined as *H. pectorale.* The dwarf hoplo, as the name implies, is smaller than the other species, with a maximum length of some 12 cm. It is yellowish brown and covered with numerous small black spots. The caudal fin is emarginate and the tips are slightly rounded. This small active species can be housed in a smaller tank than the other two common hoplos, a 15-gallon aquarium being okay for a half dozen or so individuals. Success has been achieved with a pH of 7.4, a temperature range of 22° to 26°C, and weekly partial water changes. As with the other hoplos, this fish is a good feeder and will accept a wide variety of aquarium foods, including even flake foods, but with live foods favored.

Sexes are distinguished by the relatively heavier pectoral spine of the male (the distinction is not so great as in the other hoplos). In addition, the dwarf hoplo has an opaque cream-colored nuptial pad in the soft rays of

Male *Hoplosternum* species can be recognized by the closeness (even contact) of the coracoids (above), while in females there is a distinct space between them (especially when she is filled with eggs)(below). Photos by B. Teichfischer.

the pectoral fin of the male; the female's pectoral fin ray membranes remain transparent. The larger females also show some smooth white skin between the coracoids as they fill up with eggs. Spawning has been accomplished in a 7-gallon tank filled with about 5 gallons of water. There was no gravel, but a sponge filter, some floating plants, and a floating plastic lid were added. The temperature was 20-22°C. A pair was added and the male built a bubblenest. A single male was used because competition for space and material develops with more than one male in a tank, and there are numerous encounters between the males. The male, when his nest is ready, will vigorously court the female, performing what has been referred to as a frenzied dance. The female extrudes some eggs and moves to the bubblenest to place them there; the male follows immediately and fertilizes them. After this act is repeated over a period of about 2½ hours the female has exhausted her egg supply and is driven from the scene. She should be removed at this time.

Hatching at this temperature occurred in about a week and an additional three days were needed before the fry became free-swimming. Feeding should commence at this time. Several feedings per day are urged for best growth. Microworms, newly hatched brine shrimp, etc., are the most commonly used starter foods. Small water changes are recommended on a daily basis for two weeks, then twice a week. At about six weeks the young hoplos can take chopped tubificid worms, chopped whiteworms, small daphnia, and still the baby brine. Crushed flake food may also be added.

It is interesting to note that reports on the other hoplos maintain that the fry are free-swimming immediately upon hatching; in this species it is said that they remain in the nest for several days before becoming free-swimming. It could be possible that in the other species the actual hatching time was missed and that the time the fry left the nest was interpreted as hatching time.

The subfamily Corydoradinae is said to be derived from *Hoplosternum*-like ancestors. It consists of three genera, *Aspidoras, Brochis,* and *Corydoras,* although the differences are not so great as to preclude some lumpers from considering them all in a single genus. Their biotope is similar to that of the Callichthyinae. All three genera have representatives in the aquarium hobby, but it is *Corydoras* that has gained the affection of almost every hobbyist and it is a rare sight to see a community tank without a few individuals scurrying about on the bottom searching for food. Most species are easy to care for, having no special demands as far as water chemistry is concerned as long as extremes are avoided. Since most species are bottom feeders and may stir the bottom up almost continuously, adequate filtration is required. Food type is no problem as almost anything edible is accepted. However, the aquarist must ensure that enough food reaches the bottom for the catfishes — not just leftovers but a well rounded diet. Live foods of all kinds, especially worms, are recommended. A temperature range of about

18° to 26°C is generally adequate although some species have less of a range tolerance and need higher (or lower for cool water species) temperatures. In the wild many of the species inhabit slowly moving waters where they can be found in small groups to many hundreds in a single aggregation. The species may often be intermingled. They will investigate the bottom for food as well as the mud and sand banks or even leaves of aquatic or bog plants that can be reached. In an aquarium, members of some *Corydoras* species have been observed feeding upside down off the surface, so they do seem to be quite adaptable. Those species that live in swampy areas or places where their water supply might dwindle to next to nothing in the dry season are able to utilize their gut respiration mechanism to survive. It has been reported that thousands were found together, partly covered with wet mud, just surviving until the next rains. At the onset of the rains, they come to life and many start courting. Spawning in captivity has been achieved for members of all three genera. The various techniques are discussed under the appropriate genera and species.

The genus *Aspidoras* is a moderately sized genus consisting of 14 species from Brazil. They are all small, the largest not surpassing 5 cm in length. The head is compressed and the supraoccipital forms a broad but short triangle posteriorly. There are two cranial fontanels. The anterior fontanel is small, roundish to elongate, its length equal to about half the eye diameter; the posterior or supraoccipital fontanel is closed in adult specimens, leaving only a small roundish shallow pit. The suborbital is naked and the nuchal plates barely meet along the midline between the supraoccipital and the azygous predorsal plate. The eyes are small and superior in position, and the abdomen between the pectoral fins is completely covered with flesh. The lower lip is reverted to form a single pair of barbels besides the rictal barbels, these latter extending as far as the gill opening. The dorsal has a spine and 7 rays, the dorsal fin base being somewhat shorter than its distance from the adipose fin; both dorsal and pectoral fin spines are short. The caudal fin is forked.

Aspidoras. Photo by Harald Schultz.

The character that serves to distinguish this genus from the others of the family is the number and shape of the cranial fontanels. Previous accounts relied on the position of the nuchal plates (meeting or not meeting) to distinguish between *Aspidoras* and *Corydoras*. However, this has proven to be inadequate, for in some species of *Aspidoras* they are separated along the midline by the supraoccipital process as in most (but not all) species of *Corydoras*. It was found that *Aspidoras* possessed two cranial fontanels, a supraoccipital fontanel and a small, roundish or oval to elongate frontal fontanel. In *Corydoras, Brochis,* and *Dianema* there is a single, open fontanel, albeit much larger and more elongate than that of *Aspidoras,* with a commisural bar anteriorly. *Callichthys* and *Hoplosternum* possess a rounded frontal fontanel with foramens both

Aspidoras. Photo by Harald Schultz.

anterior and posterior to the commisural bar. In addition, except for *Aspidoras poecilus,* all species of *Aspidoras* have a rounded transverse head shape as opposed to a triangularly depressed one.

Aspidoras do fairly well in aquaria under similar conditions as for most *Corydoras.* The water conditions that seem best are a pH of 6.8-7.0 and a temperature of about 22° to 26°C. The only species that seems to regularly appear in dealers' tanks is *Aspidoras pauciradiatus.* This little species has caused a bit of a stir as two separate populations are known, living contentedly a considerable distance apart, one in the Rio Negro and the other in the Rio Araguaia. The newer population was discovered nearly 3,000 river kilometers beyond the previously known range of the genus. The differences in the two populations (which will not be discussed here) are not clear enough to establish whether we are dealing with separate subspecies, separate species, or just normal variation for the species. Eggs were found in some of the female specimens of 16-23 mm SL (standard length). In five male paratypes of *A. virgulatus* enlarged odontodes (bristles) such as are found in *Corydoras barbatus, C. macropterus, C. bondi coppenamensis,* and many species of Loricariidae were seen.

Several species of *Aspidoras* have been spawned by aquarists. *A. menezesi,* a species that attains a length of only about 5 cm, is one of them. The males are a little smaller and slimmer than the females. One account of a successful spawning related that four pairs were placed in an 11-gallon breeding tank that was provided with an inside box filter, fine gravel, a clump of Java moss, and some Java fern. The spawners were conditioned on live foods (mostly tubificid worms and microworms). Spawning was not actually observed but fry were soon found searching for food. The fish repeated their spawnings as eggs were found in the Java moss. Some of the eggs were well in the middle of the moss, the female having to drive well into it to place them there. About 50 to 60 eggs were found in groups of two to four, stuck together, and were just under 2 mm in diameter. The parents should be removed immediately after spawning since, like *A. pauciradiatus,* they are avid egg eaters. If the eggs are removed to a separate hatching tank they should be separated and provided with sufficient aeration to move them about but not enough to damage them. The water should be from the spawning tank and of the same temperature (25°C). After about four days hatching occurs. The fry are about 5 mm long and are provided with a small yolk sac which is absorbed in another day. Microworms or similar food should be given twice a day. Daily water changes should be made. In about five days (after hatching) the fry have doubled their size, and after three weeks they have assumed the adult color pattern. At this time the fins are also forming — the dorsal has separated, the caudal is formed, and the adipose is prominent but still will become reduced in size with the growth of the fish. Subsequent spawns were placed on the Java moss, the Java fern, and even the glass sides of the tank. The spawners seemed to be prompted by a water change every time. Egg numbers varied with a high of more than 200 late in the spawning season, which seemed to last from early December to late February. It was noted that this species has a habit of burying themselves in the sand so that at times only the top of the dorsal fin shows.

Aspidoras pauciradiatus has been spawned in captivity as well. This is one of the smaller species, adults being usually less than 25 mm in standard length. The males are generally trimmer, the females quite plump when ripe with eggs. Also in the ripe females there is a large white area when viewed from the side. The breeding tank is set up at this time. No special water conditions are necessary, except more water circulation than for other species is preferred. More males than females are used. Eggs are deposited on the glass or plants. They hatch in about four days. Once the yolk sac is absorbed normal first foods (microworms, etc.) are recommended.

The genus *Brochis* contains only three species, the most recent described in 1983. The body and head are compressed. The supraoccipital forms a projection extending along the midline to the azygous predorsal plate; the fontanel is elongate. The nuchal plates never meet along the mid-dorsal line and the coracoids are exposed ventrally between the pec-

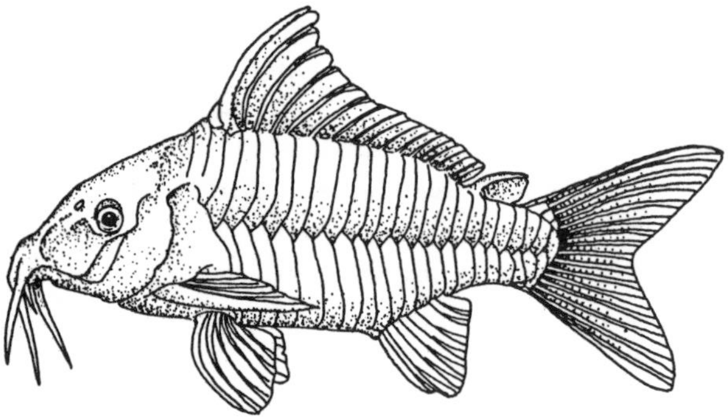

Brochis britskii.

toral fin bases. The eyes are more or less superior in position and the lower lip forms a single pair of short barbels in addition to the rictal barbels (a condition similar to that of the genus *Corydoras,* the unusual formations described by Cope due most likely to decay of the flesh behind the lips, as it was found to be in *Dianema*); the rictal barbels never extend much beyond the level of the gill openings. The dorsal fin has a spine and 10 to 18 rays, its base being much longer than its distance from the adipose fin; the caudal fin is forked.

Brochis is very similar to *Corydoras* but differs mainly in the deeper body and the higher number of dorsal fin rays, a character that can be used with confidence by aquarists. At first glance *Brochis* species appear like large *Corydoras aeneus* and, indeed, have many times been sold under that name. In fact, the behavior that both groups show is very much alike. *Brochis* are peaceful and hardy fishes that live in schools on the bottom. They are undemanding aquarium fishes that attain a length of about 8 cm.

Probably the most widely available species of *Brochis* in the aquarium trade is *B. splendens.* This species was once commonly called *B. coeruleus.* Gosline (1940) was the first to suspect the synonymy of *coeruleus* and *splendens,* but it was actually Nijssen & Isbrücker (1970) who combined the two, giving sufficient reasons for doing so. *B. splendens* occurs in the upper reaches of the Amazon, Rio Ucayali to Pucallpa, Rio Ambiyacu, and the environs about Iquitos, where it is seen mostly in sluggish waters with dense vegetation along the banks. This species, which attains a length of between 7 and 9 cm, is called the emerald catfish or the emerald brochis because, depending upon the angle of the lighting, the body reflects a metallic green, a blue-green, or even a bluish color. The ventral area is yellow-ochre with the pectoral, ventral, and anal fins yellowish and the dorsal, caudal, and adipose fins a translucent brownish. This peaceful species is not very demanding and can be maintained under the same conditions as most *Corydoras* species. They are shy and easily frightened when kept as individuals so it is best to keep small groups (at least half a dozen or more). The tank (not under 80 liters) should have only soft, fine bottom material or if coarser material is desired it should be relegated to those parts of the tank where feeding does not occur. The aquarium should be thickly planted and decorated with driftwood, etc., so that sufficient hiding places are available. The water itself should be neutral (pH 7.0) and slightly hard with a temperature between 23° and 25°C. Strong filtration and a partial water change (preferably from the bottom) are essential. Feeding is not difficult. In the wild these bottom feeders dine on insect larvae, worms, and small crustaceans; in the aquarium almost anything is accepted although worms, especially tubificid worms, are preferred. *B. splendens* does well in a community tank and does not tear up the plants.

Spawning has been accomplished for this species. Spawning, it has been suggested, is possibly a group affair, and success has been achieved with two females and three males on at least two occasions. It has also been suggested that it occurs on an annual basis, perhaps with the onset of the rainy season, for on one occasion the spawning took place as the barometer fell. The females are larger and more robust than the males and have a more pinkish belly as opposed to the more yellowish one of the male. The spawning tank is best without a substrate but supplied with a number of floating plants. The water should be soft (to 8° DH), slightly acid, and extremely clean. The temperature should be about 24° or 25°C. With the addition of three males and two females, all well conditioned on live foods, spawning should commence.

Essentially the spawning agreed very well

with that of many *Corydoras* species, but differs as regards the details. First of all, *B. splendens* does not spawn in open water but on the substrate. The female drops about ten eggs into her ventral fin basket and they are fertilized after some preliminary chasing. The eggs are then placed about the tank one by one until about 300 eggs are scattered over the entire tank but with the floating surface plants (*Riccia fluitans* has been used) receiving the greatest share. The eggs, which are slightly larger than most cory eggs, are not bothered by the parents according to the reports.

The eggs hatch in approximately four days. After about two days the yolk sac is about depleted and newly hatched brine shrimp can be fed. After a few more days give finely chopped tubificid worms and microworms, grindal worms, and finely chopped enchytrae. The bottom should be siphoned frequently and daily water changes are strongly suggested starting with the feeding. At an age of about ten days the first color in the form of a darkish spot develops in the middle of the body. At two to three weeks of age the dorsal fin starts to become larger and is of a dark color. The emerald green color starts to develop at a size of about 35 mm when the young are some six weeks old. This starts as a number of spots that eventually coalesce. What is very striking is the development of the dorsal fin. In young individuals the dorsal fin is proportionally very large and it is very colorful, being orange with a variable pattern of dark markings. At an age of six months the young fish should be almost 5 cm in length.

Brochis multiradiatus has about 17 dorsal fin rays as compared with the 11 or 12 commonly seen in *B. splendens.* The snout is obviously longer than that of *splendens,* and for this reason the common name most usually applied to this species is Hog-nosed brochis. This species has either been quite rare in the hobby or has not been recognized—any many-rayed dorsal-finned cory-like catfish would naturally be referred to as *B. splendens,* especially since *multiradiatus* was at first known from a single specimen that was thought to be an aberrant *splendens.* The aquarium care is essentially the same as that for the emerald catfish.

The third species, *B. britskii,* also has a high number of dorsal fin rays (15-18). It has a shorter snout, a larger eye, grows to a larger size, and (uniquely in the family) has its head covered ventrally by a large shield extending beyond the tip of the mental barbels. It is not known if the young of this species have the large orange and black dorsal fin of the other two species.

The genus *Corydoras* is one of the two most important genera of catfishes as far as aquarists are concerned, the second being of course *Hypostomus* of the family Loricariidae. *Corydoras* is a very large genus with approximately 100 species, give or take a dozen depending upon the amount of variability allowed. They are almost all small forms ranging in size from 2.5 to about 12 cm with the majority in the range of 5 to 7 cm. The head and body are compressed, with the supraoccipital forming a process posteriorly that may or may not meet the azygous predorsal plate. The fontanel is elongate and the suborbital is naked. The sides of the body are covered by approximately 22 to 26 dorsolateral and 19 to 24 ventrolateral scutes. The number of azygous preadipose scutes and the number and position of small scutes on the caudal peduncle are variable, and the nuchal plates never meet along the mid-dorsal line. The area between the coracoid processes may or may not be covered by a mosaic of plates. The eyes are more or less superior in position. The lower lip has a single pair of short barbels in addition to the rictal barbels, these latter never reaching very much beyond the level of the gill openings. The dorsal fin has a spine and 7 (occasionally 8) rays, its base being equivalent to its distance from the adipose fin. The anal fin usually has i,6 and the ventral fin i,5 rays, whereas the pectoral fin has a spine and 8 rays. The number of pectoral fin rays and lateral body scutes may be higher in the so-called long-snouted species. The caudal fin is forked.

Nijssen (1970) attempted to break the large genus *Corydoras* down into species groups, a move that was again attempted in conjunction with Isbrücker in 1980. Although the first groups were somewhat defined on the basis of color pattern, snout length, etc., the second set of groups were only listed. The second set (of species described up til 1980) includes: the **punctatus-group,** with *C. punctatus, C. armatus, C. ambiacus, C. trilineatus, C. amphibelus, C. agassizii, C. julii, C. multimaculatus, C. polystictus, C. melanistius melanistius, C. m. brevirostris, C. leopardus, C. reticulatus, C. leucomelas, C. sychri, C. concolor, C. caudimaculatus, C. haraldschultzi, C. sterbai, C. schwartzi, C. evelynae, C. bicolor, C. surinamensis, C. atropersonatus, C. orphnopterus, C. acrensis, C. bifasciatus, C. ephippifer, C. xinguensis, C. pulcher, C. ornatus,* and *C. robustus;* the **barbatus-group,** with *C. barbatus, C. paleatus, C. nattereri, C. erhardti, C. flaveolus, C. garbei, C. micracanthus, C. macropterus, C. cochui, C. steindachneri,* and *C. prionotos;* the **aeneus-group,** with *C. aeneus, C. eques, C. melanotaenia, C. metae, C. potaroensis, C. melini, C. arcuatus, C. bondi bondi, C. b. coppenamensis, C. griseus, C. rabauti, C. zygatus, C. osteocarus, C. reynoldsi, C. habrosus, C. axelrodi, C. boesemani, C. sanchesi, C. baderi, C. guianensis, C. heteromorphus, C. panda, C. weitzmani, C. gossei, C. oiapoquensis,* and *C. condiscipulus;* the **elegans-group,** with *C. elegans, C. hastatus, C. undulatus, C. latus, C. guapore, C. pygmaeus, C. nanus,* and *C. gracilis;* and the **acutus-group,** with *C. acutus, C. aurofrenatus, C. treitlii, C. spilurus, C. septentrionalis, C. ellisae, C. fowleri, C. cervinus, C. pastazensis pastazensis, C. p. orcesi, C. semiaquilus, C. oxyrhynchus, C. octocirrus, C. saramaccensis, C. simulatus, C. maculifer, C. blochi blochi, C. b. vittatus, C. amapaensis, C. ourastigma,* and *C. narcissus.*

Members of the genus *Corydoras* are distributed over South America from southeastern Brazil, Uruguay, and northern Argentina to the Guianas, Venezuela, and Colombia, and Trinidad. They seem to prefer slowly moving almost still (but seldom stagnant) streams and small rivers where the water is shallow (only to 2 meters in Surinam according to Nijssen) and very clear. The preferred bottom seems to be sand, but this may vary with species and area and the bottom may be pure sand or sand mixed with mud, and it may be covered with detritus and dead leaves. The banks and sides of the streams are covered with a luxuriant growth of plants, and this is where the corys are found. The temperature range depends of course upon the individual species and their respective ranges and altitudes, with the minimums for the temperate and high altitude species about 10° to 12°C and the maximum for the more tropical species to 32°C. With such a widespread distribution both horizontally and vertically (they are found to altitudes of over 3,000 meters), the corys inhabit a wide variety of water types but generally seem to prefer soft, neutral to slightly acidic or slightly alkaline pH (in Surinam, Nijssen reports they are found in slightly acidic waters of pH 5.3-6.7, not in the very acid tea-colored creeks with a pH of 4.6 or lower), and a hardness of 5-10°DH. They have a limited tolerance to salt (though most species can tolerate normal amounts used in aquaria) and are absent from the lowland coastal areas that are subject to tidal influences. Many species are commonly seen in schools or aggregations of hundreds to even thousands of individuals including males, females, and juveniles. Although they prefer their own company and the schools are mostly of a single species, other species can sometimes be seen mixed in.

The corys usually will be milling about the bottom (a few species such as *C. hastatus* spend more of their time in mid-water) searching for food, stirring up the bottom as they do. Their main food is bottom-dwelling insects and insect larvae and various worms, but at least some vegetable matter is also necessary. Although no corys are piscivorous, they will eat flesh from dead fishes. Their feeding method is to search the bottom with their sensory barbels and pick up food items with their mouth, often burying their snout up to their eyes. Long-snouted forms are better suited for this manner of feeding and perhaps can reach a different food supply than the short-snouted forms that are relegated to the upper surface layers. *Corydoras* are not restricted to this type of feeding and many, as well as some from other families, will feed from the surface layers by inverting themselves like the upside-down catfishes of the family Mochokidae. Others will feed on animals that live on the surface of the plant leaves. Corys seem to find their food by means of chemical "odors," for although food may be dropped literally in front of their noses they may ignore it completely until they

Corydoras melanistius is a member of the punctatus-group.

Corydoras pygmaeus is one of the dwarf species of the elegans-group.

Corydoras garbei belongs to the barbatus-group.

The elegans-group is named after this species, *C. elegans*.

Corydoras rabauti is a member of the aeneus-group.

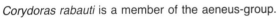

Corydoras septentrionalis belongs to the acutus-group.

can follow the scent right to the food.

Most of the callichthyids are able to survive in less than ideal conditions (polluted waters, low oxygen waters, or even when the shallow waters that they live in dry up) by their ability to utilize atmospheric air. As corys dart about on the bottom searching for food, they will suddenly stop and dash upward to the water's surface and quickly return to the bottom. This may be done in a quick straight dash or the fish may rise partway in the water, hover for a moment, and then finish the trip. Even the downward movements may be rapid or at a more leisurely pace. Air is taken into the mouth at the surface and released through the anus on the downward trip. The movement may be by an individual fish, by a group of fish that break the surface, or by the original fish only breaking the surface, its followers just along for the ride so to speak and never reaching the surface. If the oxygen dissolved in the water is very low, preventing the catfish from reaching the surface can cause its death by suffocation. If the oxygen level is sufficient, however, preventing the catfish from reaching the surface will do it no harm as its branchial breathing is quite sufficient for sustaining life. In fact, this could be a good barometer in assessing the pollution in your aquarium. If the corys start to depend more and more on aerial respiration, it is evidence that an immediate water change be made and a search for the reason(s) for this pollution must be started. It has also been found that aerial respiration is probably more important to the shallow water corys; this makes sense when one thinks about the energy that must be expended in reaching the surface from the greater depths as well as the longer time the fish is exposed to possible predation in the more open mid- and upper-water layers.

Although the corys do not seem to be able to traverse "dry" land as well as the callichthyins, they are quite able to make shorter overland journeys when their water hole dries up.

Corys generally spawn right after the dry season (April or May in Surinam according to Nijssen), for with the rise in water level many more suitable spawning sites become available and there is an abundance of food for the fry that is washed down into the creeks from the land.

Finally, the intensity of colors of many of the species varies depending upon the type and the color of the bottom they are presently over. This is in addition to the high degree of variability of the color pattern in some of the species. It is quite possible that because of these variations many of the so-called "species" may turn out to be merely variants of one or another of the older species. So far only two species, *C. aeneus* and *C. paleatus*, are known to have albino forms commonly available.

It is generally accepted that the first exportation of a *Corydoras* species was as early as 1880, when *C. paleatus* was shipped from the La Plata region to Europe; it arrived in North America at a later date, around 1915. Most of the *Corydoras* species are hardy and highly adaptable to most aquarium conditions and are almost always sought out to be members of a community tank because of their reputation for helping to keep the tank clean. Whether one calls them scavengers or bottom cleaners, the fact remains that they do eat food items that reach the bottom and are quite adept at finding small food items that fall between the gravel particles and that are otherwise lost in nooks and crannies of the decorations. They do not eat droppings of other fishes. These must be siphoned out or if the volume is extremely small can be left in the tank to provide fertilizer for the plants. What is not used by the plants must be then broken down by the biological filter. The problem is usually to get enough food past the faster and heavier feeders of the upper layers. If corys are left to feed on only the "leftovers" of other fishes (providing there are any) they may find this diet inadequate and become listless and hollow-bellied. It is best to have a particular section of the tank where the corys can be hand-fed. The diet should be as varied as possible, preferably a good meaty food base with some vegetable matter. Live foods are very much preferred, with tubificid worms heading the list, but frozen and freeze-dried foods and even a good flake food are suitable. Remember, when they are very hungry they do not hesitate to come up to the surface and feed inverted on anything floating there.

Any size aquarium can be used for housing these droll little catfishes, but a minimum size of five gallons for a single pair of one of the smaller species is recommended. In very cramped quarters they tend to become somewhat sluggish. For the pygmy species (*C. pygmaeus, C. hastatus,* etc.) a 2½-gallon tank is sufficient. A shallow tank is preferred to a deeper tank since they will come to the surface occasionally for a gulp of air. The bottom material should not be extremely coarse and sharp edges should be avoided (quartz and marble clips usually have sharp edges and should not be used). The substrate should not be too fine (silica sand is bad because it packs too tightly) or too coarse. A coarse grade of builder's sand (#6) or #4 red flint river gravel has been suggested as good substrates. Good filtration is highly recommended, the choice being up to the individual tastes. Driftwood pieces are often used with good results, and the tank should be heavily planted, leaving an open area for feeding and for swimming. Smooth-edged rocks can also be used. Among the suggested plants for corys are those that are native to their natural habitat. Those suggested include bunch plants such as *Elodea, Cabomba, Myriophyllum, Bacopa,* and *Ceratophyllum,* and rooted plants such as the swordplants, *Vallisneria, Sagittaria,* etc. Everything should be placed so that the effect is pleasing to the eye while it also provides hiding places for the shy species. When frightened, some corys will hide in small spaces and spread their sharp pectoral and dorsal spines locking themselves in.

The water itself can vary widely in its chemistry, but a pH of 6-8 is best as is a temperature of 21° to 26°C and a hardness of about 100 ppm. Weekly partial water changes are strongly recommended. It has been reported that corys will go into shock when placed into unaged tap water with no regard to temperature differences. They will go into a faint and actually keel over, but with luck they will start to wiggle a bit after a while and eventually recover completely. Otherwise they are quite hardy and very disease resistant, possibly in part due to their armor plating.

Certain types of fungus do attack them when they are housed under adverse conditions such as poor diet, excessive detritus, stress, water too acid, etc. Fungus may also appear as a secondary infection if a cory has been attacked by a larger, aggressive species and damage has been done. Another problem is characterized by pressure of petechiae under the belly plates and is called "blood spots" by aquarists. There is no known cure. Although the corys may not manifest any sign of a particular disease that is occurring in one of their tanks, do not move them to a healthy tank, for they are known to be carriers.

Caution should be exercised when handling corys. Like many other catfishes with strong spines, they can damage each other when too crowded in a shipment or puncture the plastic bag so that all the water leaks out. They also cause problems when they are netted. If the spines get stuck in your net your first attempt to free them should be to invert the net in the aquarium and let them try to extricate themselves; this frequently works. If you must free them by hand be very careful, even cutting the net away if you have to.

These little catfishes are commonly very shy and will frequently hide among your plants and other decorations. It is highly recommended that they be kept in groups of at least a half dozen individuals. Even when the species are mixed they will aggregate when foraging or resting. In general, some corys will spend most of the day foraging for food while others will remain in seclusion, usually in an area of subdued light such as under the broad leaf of a plant. Corys should not be placed in a community tank that contains large, aggressive fishes such as cichlids and large barbs, but with smaller non-aggressive species such as small characins, livebearers, and possibly rasboras.

In addition to all their good points corys have also been said to destroy unwanted planaria and to clean up the blue-green algae infesting a tank, neither of which I have been able to confirm. But they are one of the most popular of the catfishes for not only are they peaceful, harmless, of an excellent size for aquaria, hardy, and spawnable, but they also "wink" at their owners from time to time. Actually it is not a true wink, but the rapid movement when the eyes are rotated (the eyes can be moved independently) in their socket. Their hardiness borders on legend, for there are reports of one species known to survive temperatures up to 40°C and another (possibly *C. paleatus*) whose eggs hatched out at a very chilly 7°C. Longevity records are also amazing, for *C. aeneus* is said to have lived 27 years in captivity and 20 years is not too uncommon.

Most corys are currently still being shipped in from South America even though there are export restrictions on some species by several countries. Be wary of some of the imports, for improper conditions at the holding stations in some areas (usually overcrowding with some fouling of the water) cause stress and this may lead to hemorrhaging; if there are any disease organisms or parasites infecting the fishes they may become more dangerous to the weakened fishes. One more item—since corys are able to utilize atmospheric air they should not be shipped in bags loaded with pure oxygen (this is also true of the labyrinthfishes such as gouramis) lest it cause damage to the fish's delicate air breathing apparatus.

Of all the *Corydoras* species, *C. aeneus* and *C. paleatus* are the most common. Indeed, the latter species has the distinction of having been discovered by none other than Charles Darwin on his famous voyage of the *Beagle* over 150 years ago. Both of these species are bred commercially by the hundreds of thousands, *C. aeneus* mostly in the United States, *C. paleatus* in Europe. Albinos of both species have been successfully bred and in some cases are more popular than the original pigmented fishes. In addition to the two just mentioned, hobbyists have bred a large percentage of the species of *Corydoras* (at least 40%) in home aquaria. A partial list of these species includes *aeneus, paleatus, hastatus, "schultzei" (aeneus), arcuatus, undulatus, melanistius, metae, elegans, cochui, panda, adolfoi, reticulatus, rabauti, barbatus, axelrodi, pygmaeus, schwartzi, bondi, habrosus, melanotaenia, nattereri, ornatus, amapaensis, eques, macropterus, agassizii, leucomelas, caudimaculatus, haraldschultzi, trilineatus, boesemani,* and *sterbai.* They were spawned under a variety of conditions, and accounts will be discussed under the individual species when known. In general, however, there are some similarities or generalities that can be reported here. Although some corys are thought to be relatively easy to spawn and others relatively hard, depending of course upon the individual aquarist's skill and luck, it is not as easy to spawn corys as some of the beginner's fishes that will spawn almost anywhere anytime, like white clouds or zebra danios. It does take some care and preparation and a lot of patience to spawn corys, but once they have started they seem to do so on a regular basis. One aquarist even reports that once started they are hard to turn off. The general consensus is that one must use two males for every female in the spawning tank. Some say three males per female should be used and others just state that the more males per female the better, so the 2:1 ratio might be regarded as a minimum with additional males added when possible.

Sexing corys is not too difficult with mature fish. If a number of them are placed together and viewed from above it can be seen that the females are distinctly heavier across the body at the level of the pectoral fins; if viewed from the side they appear to have a deeper body and may bulge in the ventral surface area if they are ripe with eggs (in some cases, especially albinos, the eggs may be visible through the skin). The males may also have longer and more pointed ventral fins and slightly longer dorsal and pectoral fin spines or higher dorsal fins. In a few species the males are larger, in others they have bristles on their cheeks, and in still others there may be a color difference between the two sexes. If you are not sure you can always use the tried and true method of starting with at least a half dozen individuals and letting them sort things out for themselves. Of course the male to female ratio may not be ideal using this method.

The tank size does not seem to be very important as success has been achieved with a trio (two males and one female) in a five-gallon tank. Larger species of course would necessarily require larger tanks. The tank should be shallow and have a dark bottom — either bare slate or a layer of dark-colored sand or gravel. Provide hiding places, usually in the form of plants, such as broad-leaved Amazon sword plants and/or some bunch plants. Filtration and aeration are necessary. In fact, some aquarists believe that added aeration will help bring the fish into a spawning mood more quickly. Weekly water changes are also advised. Beyond these suggestions for inducement of spawning there have been several "sure-fire" methods that are advocated by one aquarist or another. These include things like sudden drops or sudden changes both up and down (a fluctuation) of the water temperature and sprinkling the surface with water using a watering can to simulate the onset of the rainy season. This last is most likely involved with observations that some spawnings have occurred during periods of major changes in atmospheric pressure. The temperature changes, when and if made, should be gradual enough so that the fish are not stressed. One aquarist advocates simply unplugging the heater and letting the water cool to room temperature naturally over several days' time. The temperature differences should be no more than 3° to 8°C. None of the above methods are surefire. Under reasonable conditions with healthy breeders they will go ahead and spawn, especially if they are domestically bred, even in a community tank, although chances are that under such conditions the spawning is rarely observed and the eggs are quickly disposed of by the other fishes. One thing that must be done is to properly condition the potential spawners. This means a high protein diet of live foods, preferably tubificid worms. Chopped earthworms and a good flake food can be added for variety. Feed small amounts several times a day. The length of the conditioning period varies depending upon the species being spawned, their health at the time of the start of conditioning, and the type of food fed, and may last for as little as two to three days to as much as a month or more. All this providing, of course, that the corys are fully mature and able to spawn.

The first indication that something is about to happen is an increased activity, for the actual spawning is usually preceded by a rather long courtship period. These normally slow, albeit nervous, fishes suddenly become quite frisky, dashing about back and forth and up and down. The females are usually in front and the males behind. Although this has often been described as a chase by the males, one aquarist has noted that in his courting corys the males were hard put to keep up with the females. This procession proceeds all over the tank as the males do some little dances in front of the females. The females, as they become more and more interested in the actions of the males and hence in spawning, will pay attention to prospective spawning sites. These may be on leaves, rocks, driftwood, filters, heaters, glass tank sides, or anything solid that attracts them. Cleaning now starts. This may be accomplished solely by the females or in some instances the males take part and help clean. Most species prefer a site off the bottom but well below the surface of the water; however, other species prefer higher or lower localities. Specific preferences will be noted under the species accounts when known. Regardless of the substrate or level selected, an area near an airstone is commonly preferred. In addition to the interruptions for cleaning of the spawning sites, both males and females will make short dashes to the surface for air with a frequency somewhat greater than their normal habit. Sites that were cleaned may be revisited for some "touching up."

After all of this lively dashing about things become more serious. The males seem to pay particular attention to an area behind the female's head as they swim over her back. As they swim in this position there is an occasional contact with the barbels on the suprascapular region of the female. This was described by one aquarist as a "kiss" of sorts. The males also nudge or butt the females on the sides and head as the female swims among them with her barbels feeling about. Actual spawning then commences.

The early morning hours are the most popular spawning time for many species, but some have been seen to spawn even during late evening hours. When the female is "satisfied" that everything is in readiness she may turn around and start chasing the males. It is at this time that the famous "T" position is assumed. In all the chasing and moving about the excited female will sometimes, but not always, position herself so that she will be nudging or pushing at the side of the male near his vent with her head, her barbels very

Several males usually are involved in the courting of a single female as seen here in these *Corydoras aeneus*. Photo by R. Zukal.

active. Although it is usually the female that initiates this action, in some cases it is the male who will place himself in front of the female, soliciting her attention. Occasionally the males of some species will, in their excited state, use their mouth to attach themselves to almost any part of the female. In the "T" position, however, the male may become "paralyzed with ecstasy" and roll over slightly as the female nudges him and clasps her barbels to his side with his strong pectoral spines. Locked in this position the partners quiver a bit as the eggs and sperm are released. The "T" position then acts as a stimulus for the simultaneous release of the sexual products. The close proximity of the pair, along with the movements of the fish, their gill movements, their fin movements, and the amount of sperm released (a cloud surrounding the two fishes is usual), serves to ensure that the eggs are properly fertilized. Other theories involving sperm passing into the mouth of the female and out the gills to the eggs, sperm taken into the female's mouth for later fertilization of the eggs as they are deposited on the cleaned sites, and sperm smeared on the female's barbels for later fertilization at the site of egg-laying all seem to be less plausible. In fact, in some instances the "T" position is not assumed and egg laying and fertilization are accomplished just as well while the pair are parallel to each other or belly to belly as they both roll on their sides.

The "T" position (or other spawning position) lasts approximately 10 to 20 seconds, during which time it is difficult to disturb them. The female ejects anywhere from one to many eggs into a special pouch formed by the juxtaposition of her ventral fins, and with the cloud of sperm surrounding the pair they are immediately fertilized. As this is happening the other male or males are swimming about excitedly and may even approach the spawners and touch them with their barbels. Actually only a single male is involved in the fertilization of a batch of eggs, but the next spawning bout may involve one of the other males. With the eggs safely ensconced in the ventral fin pouch, the female frees herself from the male and may rest a moment or may immediately start off looking for a place where her eggs may be deposited. She may carry the eggs about for several minutes until finally settling on the "proper" spot for her eggs. This is usually one of the previously cleaned sites, but she may also decide to clean a new one for that particular batch of eggs. The site chosen varies widely with the species. Some prefer midwater sites, some like the area near the surface, some like stones, others glass, others leaves of plants, and still others seem to scatter them all over the tank. Actually "scatter" is not the proper word for these fishes nor is substrate spawner; perhaps they should best be called egg depositors. Some species might deposit all eggs of the entire spawn at one site; others place small batches at different sites throughout the aquarium, whether carefully selected or purely at random.

The small batches usually number from a single egg to as many as 30 or so depending upon the particular species involved. The eggs are pushed onto the substrate that is finally selected by the female as she glides over the spot, belly to the surface. The adhesive eggs stick tightly in place. It is interesting to speculate as to why the eggs stick so well to the smooth glass walls of the aquarium but not to the fins that envelop them. Perhaps the mucous coating of the female's fins prevents this or perhaps a special fluid is secreted to prevent their sticking to the fins. The eggs vary in size from 1.2 to 2.0 mm and are generally opaque (whitish or light colored but becoming dark as development proceeds).

As the female is placing the eggs, the males are usually following her about ready for the next spawning bout. Spawning times and activity vary depending on the species, perhaps lasting a few hours, perhaps lasting intermittently over a whole week. The bouts ("T" position) are repeated over and over again (one aquarist estimated 30-50 times) until the fe-

The now famous "T" position is assumed. The male is positioned in front of the female with her barbels clasped by his pectoral spine. Photo by R. Zukal.

The extruded eggs are held in a pocket formed by the female's ventral fins until she is able to find a suitable site where she can deposit them. Photo by R. Zukal.

The substrate chosen depends on the species. Some will accept any flat surface, including the glass of the aquarium. Several batches of eggs have already been deposited on the glass in this spawning. Photo by R. Zukal.

A broad leaf is also accepted as seen here. Other species may not spawn unless suitable plants are available for the deposition of the eggs. Photo by R. Zukal.

male is depleted of eggs. If several males are involved they probably all will have taken their turns to fertilize the female's eggs. Some spawners are deceptive in that they may spawn a few eggs on one day and then rest, seemingly finished with spawning. The next day the bulk of the eggs may be laid or another short spawning bout may occur, the big spawning held off until the third day. Many unknowing aquarists, observing the spawning on the first day, may assume spawning has been completed and most of the eggs eaten and remove the spawners before the real spawning has gotten underway. Check the female to see if she looks depleted. If she is still rotund and appears full of eggs, have patience. When the corys are at their spawning peak they will be spawning every 2 to 3 minutes, with very few rest periods in between. When several hundred eggs have been deposited, the females appear empty of eggs, and both sexes seem to lose interest in each other and begin their food searching, rooting about in the bottom material, spawning is most likely finished.

Depending upon species and the level of hunger in the spawners, the parents may eat the eggs or may not. Although many well fed corys will not eat their eggs, some will, or they may ignore the eggs but finish off the fry. Since this behavior varies not only with the species involved but also with individuals, it might be best to separate spawners from the spawn. The eggs are fairly tough and may be scraped from their place of attachment without damage or, easier still, the adult fishes may be removed and the eggs hatched in the tank where they were spawned. This may be preferable especially when the eggs are spawned on rocks or other places from which they are difficult to remove. The eggs can be placed in gallon jars or relatively small aquaria to hatch. The addition of some acriflavine or methylene blue helps control fungus and an airstone is suggested. The number of eggs deposited varies with the species and the size and health of the spawners. Some species lay only about 30 eggs, others as many as 800, with 200 to 300 being average. It has been suggested that the eggs be kept protected from bright lights. Depending upon species and the temperature, the eggs will hatch in anywhere from two or three to eight to ten days. Just prior to hatching the fry can be seen moving about within the egg. There is no parental care of eggs or fry.

At the time of hatching the fry, by vigorous wriggling, break through the egg membrane and fall to the bottom. The newly hatched fry appear as tiny slivers with all the fins connected like those of a tadpole. If gravel is present in their hatching tank they will be very hard to see for a couple of days. The yolk sac is absorbed in about two or three days, at which time food should be offered. Actually, during the first couple of days after hatching a few drops of liquid fry food can be added to promote a growth of infusoria. After this, microworms, newly hatched brine shrimp, and powdered flake food that has been wetted down to male it sink are fed on a regular schedule. Growth is fairly rapid under proper conditions and they soon will have to be moved to larger quarters. Growth is also augmented if there is a fine coating of filamentous green algae on the glass sides of the tank that the fry can feed from. These active fry do consume a lot of food for their size and sufficient food must be available for them at all times, yet not so much food that the tank becomes foul. Too small a raising tank becomes foul quickly, too large a tank means that the fry have to search further afield for the food and may even starve in the process. A 10-gallon tank has been suggested as ideal for this purpose. A sponge filter will help keep pollution under control as will the addition of a few freshwater snails such as *Pomacea* once the fry are mobile enough. Once the yolk has been absorbed the fry will be seen skipping or hopping over the bottom, but they soon become more proficient swimmers.

Remember, catfish babies feed from the bottom and brine shrimp may wind up throughout the water column. This can be rectified by placing a small light (not too bright) near the bottom to attract the baby brine to the vicinity of the hungry catfish fry. It has been reported that catfish fry die from too much salt being added with the brine shrimp if they are not thoroughly rinsed before being fed. This has been disputed, the deaths being attributed to velvet possibly introduced with the brine shrimp or due to uneaten food decaying in the tank.

Since the fry are very susceptible to fouled water. (as are adults) periodic water changes are highly recommended. Some suggest daily water changes, some weekly, but in either case the water should be aged at least 24 hours under aeration before use. In a short time the fry are ready for chopped tubificid worms. Other recommendations include a low light level and some hiding places. The water in the raising tank should be relatively shallow at first. One can actually start with a 15- or 20-gallon tank with a small portion of it filled with water. As the fry get larger the water level can be raised accordingly, thus making it unnecessary to move them to larger quarters — they are already there! The critical period is the first three weeks. The water level can be raised about 2 cm every time the water is changed, ideally every third day or so. As the fry grow it is natural that some will do better than others. The aquarist must keep a wary eye on them and start sorting them early. With growth the catfish's menu can grow also, both in size and variety. Although most adult corys will accept baby brine, microworms, etc., they can also receive live tubificid worms, adult brine shrimp, whiteworms, and even flake food.

Meanwhile, the parents are probably ready to spawn again and the whole process can be repeated. Most adults spawn regularly over a period of several months and then should be rested. The spawning bouts are a week to ten days apart and there may be several spawning periods within a year.

Corydoras aeneus and *C. paleatus* are by far the most common species in the hobby today. They are both easily bred and are produced in commercial quantities in the United States, Europe, and Singapore. Most of the available fish are therefore domestic strains. Any wild imports are reported to be less easy to breed.

Corydoras aeneus was first discovered in clear streams in Trinidad, the original home of the guppy, but appears to be a fairly wide-

Corydoras aeneus is one of the most common of aquarium catfishes. It is easy to care for and easy to breed. Several *aeneus* look-a-likes are now commonly available. Photo by Klaus Paysan

spread and complex species covering much of tropical South America. This species is easy to keep and is commonly kept in community tanks as a scavenger. It requires no specific conditions, but very acid water should be avoided. It does best in a temperature range of 18° to 26°C and on a diet of mostly live foods, particularly tubificid worms, enchytrae, and chironomid larvae. *C. aeneus* also does best when kept in small groups of its own kind.

Spawning follows the above routine fairly closely (much of the general discussion was based on *aeneus* and *paleatus* behavior) with the actual spawning precipitated by a drop in water temperature, a large water change, or the fish starting to spawn spontaneously. For those who advocated a temperature drop, usually about 5°C, the best method was to unplug the heater and let the water cool slowly and naturally. Some made a water change but the new water was purposefully about 5° cooler than the aquarium water. Others moved the spawners to a new tank. Although those advocating the more drastic methods say no harm came to their fish, it is still a risky proposition. With healthy, mature, well-conditioned adults a normal water change should be enough of a stimulus.

C. aeneus seems to prefer spawning on a flat surface, commonly utilizing the glass sides of the aquarium or the plastic filter box if an inside filter is used (a sponge filter would be better). As many as 500 to 600 eggs have been reported spawned in a group spawning situation, but the average is closer to 200 to 300 eggs for a normal spawn. Anywhere from 5-15 eggs are dropped each time a "T" position is assumed. Many aquarists leave the parents in with the eggs and fry as this species is less inclined than other species to eat either. However, it has been known to happen and the aquarist must decide for himself. The hatching period depends upon the temperature and may take anywhere from three to four days to a week; the hatching at three days was at a temperature of 28°C, the longer periods at about 20°C. The fry when first hatched will drop to the bottom of the tank and burrow into the gravel so that they are very difficult to see. In a few days they are moving about searching for food and can be fed microworms and newly hatched brine shrimp. The fry are said to be somewhat sensitive to temperature and water changes.

The albino *C. aeneus,* as expected, differ very little if at all in their behavior from the normally colored individuals. Some say the fry are a little slower to develop than the regular *aeneus,* others say the albinos are practically blind and the males sometimes sterile. This might be caused by inbreeding too extensively and does not apply to all the albinos in the hobby but perhaps only to a small portion of them. As the female albinos fill with eggs the belly starts to take on a pinkish or rosy hue due to the blood vessels that are more visible with the expanded body walls.

Many aquarists advise getting young *aeneus* (about six months old or so) and raising them to maturity (about 2-2½ years old) for best spawning results.

Corydoras aeneus seems to have a number of lookalikes that use its name in the hobby whether deliberately or by simple misidentification. *Brochis* species are often called giant *aeneus;* and the green-gold *aeneus* from Colombia has turned out to be a different species, *C. melanotaenia.* It is hoped that at some early date this complex species will be studied in earnest and its mysteries revealed.

Corydoras paleatus originates from the slow-moving waters of southern Brazil and northern Argentina. The female is slightly larger than the male, attaining a length of about 7 cm to the male's 5 cm. The fish in the hobby are virtually all commercially bred and wild-caught individuals are no longer seen, though it is reported that they are more colorful than the aquarium strains, most of which now come from Singapore. There is an albino *C. paleatus,* but this is not seen very often. It is easily distinguishable from the *aeneus* albino because the pattern of *paleatus* is still present while the *aeneus* albino is very plain.

Spawning has been accomplished in captivity for this species for over a century. The behavior follows the above procedures fairly closely as this species was, along with *C. aeneus,* used as a model. There are no specific conditions needed by *C. paleatus* for keeping or breeding, and it does well in a community tank. Some aquarists suggest a 50% water change a week, others more, and still others less. The proper temperature range is 18° to 20°C but it will live at lower temperatures (to 15°C) and at higher temperatures (to 23°C), but at the higher temperatures there are many more trips to the surface for air and usually it will not breed. The spawning tank should have some natural gravel (no black gravel please) and be planted (perhaps with *Aponogeton* and/or *Hygrophila)* or bare. Some indirect sunlight is permissible. The potential spawners should be conditioned for at least two weeks on a high-protein diet. As the female fills with eggs her belly can be seen changing to a pinkish or salmon color. It has been suggested that the sexes should be conditioned separately for best results. Since the temperature drops during the rainy season (which is the spawning season for these fish), a stimulus for spawning is a drop in water temperature (as noted above) or a large water change, or both. A six to eight degree change is sufficient. Two or more males (these are smaller and with higher and more pointed dorsal fins) are used for each female.

Spawning usually takes place over several days, with the largest batch deposited on the second or third day. The initial batches of eggs will probably be eaten. Since most of the spawning activity occurs in the morning hours an evening feeding has been suggested. A feeding during the spawning might disrupt the spawners. The "T" position is generally assumed, but the female will also attach herself to the male's side or belly with her mouth at times. About four to six eggs are released into the fin pouch, although some estimates run as high as 20 or as low as one egg. In one report the female was said to move backward over the bottom to scoop up the eggs that were dropped. The eggs are deposited in the higher levels of the tank, usually at some distance from the bottom. If plants are present eggs may also be deposited on the leaves (it should be noted that the corys will not place eggs on unhealthy plants), again in the upper levels. The number of eggs spawned seems to

Corydoras paleatus is another common aquarium inhabitant. It is often chosen over *C. aeneus* because of its pleasing pattern. This is a wild specimen from Porto Alegre, Brazil. Photo by Harald Schultz.

The "T" position is clearly seen in this photo of *C. paleatus* spawning. The pectoral spine holding the female's barbels is also quite evident. Photo by Ruda Zukal.

average about 250 to 300 (one aquarist reported 372 eggs deposited in 3½ hours!). Infertile eggs turn a bluish white in methleyne blue treated water after a few hours while the healthy eggs remain a creamy white. Hatching time varied from a low of two days to a high of 14 days, but the majority of reports claim four to seven days as average, depending upon temperature.

Feeding the fry is as above. The newly hatched fry are a light brown in color and with the continuous fins look like tiny tadpoles. They are light-sensitive and burrow into the gravel or seek out the darkest spots in the aquarium. After about a week, however, with the yolk all used up and the search for food beginning, they take on a dark, almost black, color. In about five weeks they start to become lighter in color again except for some darker patches over the body. At this time they should be at least 12 mm in length. Daily water changes in the fry tank (about 15% or so) are recommended, and gentle aeration is beneficial to keep the surface as clean as possible for the time (about six to eight weeks) when the young catfishes first start to take air from the surface. For this reason the water depth should not be too great, at least for the first couple of months. The parents may be allowed to spawn again in about three weeks. Because of the high temperatures, summertime spawning attempts are not likely to be successful.

Corydoras hastatus is a small (to about 35 mm) species from the Amazon basin to adjacent areas of Boliva and Paraguay. It differs from most *Corydoras* species by preferring the midwater areas, spending most of its time well off the bottom among the plants. When it does rest it does so on the available plant leaves still high above the bottom and is not adverse to inverting itself belly-up against the bottom of a leaf. All plants are utilized whether they are fine-leaved, as hornwort, or with broader leaves, as Amazon sword plants or *Sagittaria,* although the latter seem to be preferred, as is a position where they can remain horizontal to the bottom. They maintain themselves while swimming in the open water by rapid fin movements, principally of the pectoral fins. Its movements, combined with a high breathing rate, give the impression of a very nervous fish ceaselessly active, reminiscent of the well known hummingbirds. *C. hastatus* should only be kept in small groups, which immediately form into schools. In one instance there were only three *hastatus* in a tank. When two tetras that had patterns similar to those of the *hastatus* were added, the five were soon swimming around the tank together, although the *Corydoras* would dash to the surface for a gulp of air from time to time. *C. hastatus* will feed both in midwater and on a substrate whether it is one of the plant leaves or actually on the bottom like other *Corydoras* species. There is no particular food preference other than live foods, but most frozen, freeze-dried, and flake foods are accepted. The aquarium need not be very large, a 5-gallon tank being quite sufficient for a small school of *C. hastatus.* The tank should be clean and well aerated and the water slightly alkaline (pH about 7.6) within a temperature range of 25° to 29°C. These peaceful, inoffensive little fish (aquarium specimens rarely exceed 25 mm total length) are good community tank fish and good scavengers for fry tanks.

Spawning has been accomplished with this species, and the behavior follows that already outlined fairly closely. The spawning tank can be as small as 2½ gallons but at least a 5-gallon tank is recommended. A small sponge filter and some plants should be added. No special water is needed other than its being aged. Since *hastatus* may spawn as a school the whole group can be conditioned for spawning. Be sure there are at least two males for every female. The males are more slender and have a more pointed dorsal fin. Condition with the usual tubificids and whiteworms and you will soon see the females getting quite plump. Cleaning of sites includes the plant leaves, and after the usual courtship the "T" position is seen along with trembling of both sexes on the bottom of the tank. In contrast to the other species, however, only a single egg is extruded and fertilized. The female, carrying the egg in the ventral pouch, swims toward the surface and deposits the adhesive egg on one of the plant leaves that was previously cleaned. The act is repeated about every three minutes for from one to two hours with 10- to 15-minute rests between the egg

Although sitting on the bottom in this photo, *Corydoras hastatus* is usually seen in the upper layers of an aquarium. Photo by G. J. M. Timmerman.

releases. Never is there more than a single egg released. About seven to ten eggs are spawned in a day (usually between 7 a.m. and 2 p.m.), and spawning occurs on three to four consecutive days. Very little food is accepted over the spawning period, but after they are finished the spawners start looking for something to eat. A total of anywhere from 30 to 60 or more eggs may be spawned by a single female, but when a group spawns the total number may reach 300 or more depending upon how many females are present. If not enough suitable plants are available, the aquarium glass may be used as an egg deposition site (one aquarist reported eggs were placed anywhere and everywhere).

Eggs hatch in three to nine days (most report a hatch time of three to four days). The eggs start as tiny translucent spheres with a tiny dark spot in the center. As they develop they turn a light amber in color. The fry are about 6 mm long at hatching, mostly translucent but also with a dark spot or spotting. They are ready to accept newly hatched brine shrimp as well as microworms soon after they hatch. For a couple of weeks the fry are a dark olive with black blotches all over the body, but they then start to look more and more like their parents. In two months they are about 18 mm long. They mature in six to eight months. The parents will be ready to spawn again in a couple of weeks. The parents remain very translucent, much like the glass cats of the genus *Kryptopterus* but with a large black marking on the caudal base. Myers (1953) erected the subgeneric name *Microcorydoras* for this species.

Corydoras pygmaeus is another dwarf species and attains a length of only about 3 cm. It is fairly widespread in South America but was originally discovered in the Rio Madeira system. Like *C. hastatus, C. pygmaeus* is more of a midwater species than a bottom-dwelling one. They swim out in the open by the rapid movements of their pectoral and caudal fins with the barbels held against the body. In this manner they can also remain in one spot, hovering so to speak, for as much as 30 seconds at a time. In their swimming back and forth in the aquarium, they will occasionally come to rest on a leaf and have been likened to hummingbirds flitting from flower to flower. Single individuals do not do very well. A small group of at least half a dozen specimens is recommended, and because of its small size a dozen fish in a tank is not unheard of. The tank should be at least 5 gallons capacity and provided with a sand or gravel substrate and be well planted. A few rocks (no sharp edges) and some driftwood can complete the decora-

Another midwater species is this *Corydoras pygmaeus*. It also is a dwarf species attaining a length of only 3 cm. Photo by G. J. M. Timmerman.

tions. If the tank is to be a community tank, perhaps some *Nannostomus* or small hatchetfishes, neons, or small *Rasbora* species can be added. A sponge filter and regular water changes help to keep the tank quite clean and well aerated. The water should then be glass-clear, have a German hardness of 2 to 8°, and a temperature of 24° to 26°C.

Some elements of their feeding behavior are quite different from the normal *Corydoras* feeding behavior. As they swim through the water they make sudden stops on one or another of the plant leaves and move about on the leaf as if "sniffing" at it. Actually they are searching for various microorganisms that they would normally find on the leaves in their normal habitat. Not only do they search the upper side of the leaves, but they will move to the underside of the leaf and give it a good going over as well. Since there will not be enough natural food in the aquarium, they will need supplementary feedings of daphnia (they can catch these animals in midwater), baby brine shrimp, grindal worms, chironomid larvae, and tubificid worms, as well as some frozen, freeze-dried, and even flake foods. A lettuce leaf should be added from time to time. One report mentioned that when a ball of tubificid worms was fed and the *C. pygmaeus* first came into contact with it, the catfish darted around the tank as if frightened, but after several minutes they quieted down and started to feed. There was no explanation for this unusual behavior.

Of several spawning accounts recorded, the actual spawning behavior was not witnessed, but it was assumed to parallel quite closely that of *C. hastatus*. Water changes with cooler water are suggested in order to trigger the spawning, making sure of course that the temperature does not drop too low. The sexes should also be in a ratio of two males for each female. According to one account the best time of the year to spawn *C. pygmaeus* is from autumn to spring. Success for this aquarist was never achieved out of this time period. *C. pygmaeus* may have a specific spawning period or it may be that the summer temperatures are too high for it to spawn. Like *C. hastatus*, the eggs were deposited singly on plants throughout the aquarium; unlike *C. hastatus*, which would utilize the glass walls of the aquarium along with other objects, *C. pygmaeus* seems to accept only the plant leaves. *Hygrophila polysperma* appears to be preferred over other fine-leaved plants. Some 20 to 40 eggs were spawned, the eggs being about 2 mm and grayish with a brown luster. They are quite adhesive and can be removed and reattached in a more suitable place by the aquarist for about the first 24 hours. With time the adhesiveness decreases.

At 25°C the eggs hatch in 50 to 72 hours. They become darker and the egg membrane becomes clear enough so that the embryo can be seen prior to hatching. It sports a blackish zone immediately behind the small head. Upon hatching a large yolk sac is still evident and the pectoral fins are large and transparent. As the yolk is absorbed the black spot spreads out so that after 36 hours the yolk sac is much smaller and the black spot has spread out to form a band between the eyes. The body exhibits several (three?) vertical bars. After 72 hours feeding must start as the yolk sac is depleted. With the water level quite low (to concentrate the food) microworms and baby brine shrimp can be introduced. Water changes and siphoning will help to keep the water clean. After a few weeks the young are colored much like the parents.

Corydoras metae is a small (to 6 cm) catfish from the Rio Meta system of Colombia. It is strikingly patterned and as such is usually in demand by aquarists. The body color may vary from a grayish to a tan depending upon their mood, and females commonly exhibit a golden pink tone over the entire body while the abdomen becomes rosy. The tank should be set up with the usual sand bottom, driftwood, rocks, etc., and should be well planted. For spawning, *Microsorium pteropus* (Java fern) and *Ceratopteris thalicroides* (water sprite) seem to be the favorites when they are allowed to float at the surface. The diet and conditioning foods are the same as recommended for *C. aeneus* and *C. paleatus*. The pH should be slightly on the acid side (one spawning was reported at 5.2), and the DH 4 or 5; the temperature range should be 23° to 26°C. Water changes of about 20 to 30% per week are recommended.

Spawning is similar to that of *C. aeneus*, with the chasing about the tank eventually

A very young *Corydoras metae*. This species hails from the Rio Meta system in Colombia. Photo by Dr. Herbert R. Axelrod.

ending in a "T" position. This is held for about five seconds and the pair then lie motionless for another 25 to 30 seconds or so. *Corydoras metae* will apparently release a single egg (about 2 mm) each time. If the tank is bare the glass walls of the tank are the recipients of the eggs. However, if the "preferred" plants are available 90% of the eggs will be deposited on them. The undersides of the plant leaves as well as the fine rootlets are utilized, and the eggs may be clustered in several spots, the eggs being placed there one at a time. Areas where the aeration is higher also seem to be preferred. The eggs can be transferred to a small (2½-gallon) tank with a sponge filter (this is done with many species of *Corydoras* for initial raising). Anywhere from 30 to more than 100 large yellowish eggs may be laid by two pairs of spawners. They hatch in about four or five days at 24° to 25°C. The fry can be raised easily with a starting food of microworms and newly hatched brine shrimp as soon as the yolk sac disappears. The newly hatched fry are tan with some speckling and the beginnings of a mask through the eyes. After about three weeks the dorsal fin starts to become darker and at five weeks the dark band on the back makes its appearance. By the time the young reach a length of 2 cm or so most of the speckling disappears and they look like their parents. The spawning itself lasts a few hours at a time but may be continued over a period of a couple of days. They may be ready to spawn again in about two weeks if they are properly conditioned.

Corydoras elegans comes from sluggish creeks with clear, alkaline water of the middle Amazon. It attains a length of about 6 cm. Although not a midwater species like *C. hastatus* and *C. pygmaeus*, *elegans* can frequently be seen off the bottom browsing on plants (both the upper and lower sides of the leaves). In a well planted aquarium that had some flowerpots added, *C. elegans* exhibited some territorial behavior by taking possession of the pots and became somewhat aggressive. Battles between males were of greater and greater violence as a female filled up with eggs. Males were said to clean the undersides of some of the leaves. When the female started to similarly clean, the males became very active in trying to force their attentions on her and crowd out the other males. Eventually spawning occurred and continued about every fourth day over a seven-week period. Although most reports of this species's spawning say it agrees with the basic behavior of the *Corydoras* spawning (including the "T" position), one aquarist said his *elegans* never did assume the "T" position. The actual spawning occurred a short distance above the bottom and the spawners slowly sank to the bottom, after which the female left to deposit the eggs she laid. The eggs are fairly small, about 1.2 mm in diameter, and yellowish in color, although they turn darker as they develop. They are placed mainly on the underside of plant leaves (*Cryptocoryne* were used in one report), but also were found on the glass sides of the aquarium and on the plant roots. At about 26°C the fry hatch out in three or four days. Some 8 to 25 eggs were spawned during each bout, and a total per spawning of more than 350 eggs was counted. The newly hatched fry look like the fry of *C. hastatus*, but at about 12 mm a dark horizontal stripe makes its appearance along with a spot in the dorsal fin. The stripe disappears later and a series of bands appears. Early foods should be microworms and newly hatched brine shrimp along with cultured rotifers if available. With good feeding the *elegans* can reach sexual maturity in about ten months.

Corydoras cochui was originally collected in the Rio Araguaia, Goiaz, Brazil. It is a small species of less than 4 cm and as such requires smaller food particles than those fed to the larger *Corydoras* species. It is largely transparent but with dark spots in a row on the side and some small dark spots on the head and back. The dorsal and caudal also have dark spots. A golden sheen is seen when the body is lighted in a certain way, making it an attractive species. Spawning is standard, with the eggs being placed mostly on leaves of plants, in one instance *Sagittaria* being the preferred spot. The eggs hatched in about four days, with the fry burrowing into the bottom gravel as they dropped to the bottom.

Corydoras undulatus comes from northern Argentina and southeastern Brazil. It attains a length of about 5.5 cm. It spawns in a method similar to that of *C. aeneus,* possibly precipitated by a water change with water slightly cooler than that removed. The small, clear eggs are usually deposited on the underside of plant leaves, usually in clusters of 25 to 50 eggs per leaf.

Corydoras habrosus is a small (less than 4 cm) species from Venezuela. It tends to school somewhat more than *C. aeneus* or *C. paleatus.* It is easy to spawn, and the spawning behavior resembles that of *C. aeneus.* Spawning usually occurs in the morning hours, resulting in a number of egg clusters made up of about 25 to 40 eggs adhering to the glass, filter boxes and stems, or whatever is available. These are ignored (usually) by the parents and hatch in about five to seven days. The fry drop to the bottom and immediately hide. On about the second day the fry can be fed microworms and baby brine shrimp. The fry are said to be sensitive to water conditions, so a little extra care in keeping the water clean and in making water changes must be exercised.

Corydoras adolfoi is a moderate-sized *Corydoras* from the upper Rio Negro attaining a length of about 6 cm. This species breeds very much like *C. aeneus.* A successful spawning has been initiated by a water change using water two to three degrees cooler than that which had been removed, in concordance with a greater turbulence of the water created by a power filter. The males (in about a 2 to 1 ratio to females) began their courtship by a frenzied chasing of the females. The males

Corydoras adolfoi is a recently described species but already spawned by many aquarists. The larger individual was subsequently described as another species, *C. imitator*, but it eludes me as to why two *Corydoras* species should inhabit the same area with one imitating the other. Until this is resolved I cannot accept this second species. Photo by Dr. Herbert R. Axelrod.

were usually above and behind and to one side or the other, and would touch the female on the top of the head. Although most of the males would join in the chasing of the females, only one or two would be the main "suitors." The usual "T" position was assumed for five to ten seconds, after which there was a short 10 to 12 second rest. The female would clean the spot just before the deposition of the eggs after some two to eight minutes elapsed while she searched for just the right one. Most of the time this would be in the upper 12 mm of the water, the rest rarely below about 5 cm from the water's surface. Only a single egg at a time was deposited (actually on rare occasions two eggs might be laid at one time). The eggs, about 25% smaller than those of *C. aeneus,* were a milky white or pearly white with a dark spot; infertile eggs became a dead white and were readily attacked by fungus. Once the eggs were placed there was a resting period of a couple of minutes' duration, after which the males suddenly (by some signal?) took interest in her again. Over a period of four to eight hours 22-46 eggs were laid. The parents took no notice of the eggs once spawning was completed, perhaps because they were at such a high level. By the third day the eyes were visible in the eggs, and by the fifth day they started to hatch. The last of the eggs hatched more than 24 hours later. It took about three days for the yolk to be absorbed and the raising could proceed like that of *C. aeneus.*

Corydoras panda is a moderately small (4.5-5 cm) species from the Rio Ucayali system. It was recently collected live from Rio Lullapichis, a tributary of Rio Pachitea, in a clear mountain stream with a rocky bottom. In the area where *C. panda* was taken the trees closed in overhead to form a canopy so that the sun could shine only in scattered places and only for a short time. The water itself had a temperature range of about 22° to 23.5°C although it could vary between 21° and 28°C. The carbonate hardness (total) was 3.1° and the pH 7.7. No water plants and no mulm were present except in small still-water pockets. The water moved freely in the dry season when the specimens were captured but was expected to be a torrential stream in the rainy season, a rather unusual habitat for *Corydoras.* The individuals captured were about 3.5 to 4 cm long, sand colored, and had black markings across the eyes, in the dorsal fin, and at the caudal peduncle.

In captivity *C. panda* was spawned in a 30-liter tank with no bottom cover but with an inside filter, Java moss, and some hiding places formed from clay bowls or flowerpots. On a diet that included daphnia, tubificid worms, chironomid larvae, and even frozen foods, they grew to nearly 5 cm. There was a water change of 33% every two days. The water had a total hardness of 10°, a carbonate hardness of 13°, and the temperature was 22° to 24°C. *C. panda* seems to propagate better in small groups during a particular season. They would spawn mainly from December to April, which coincided with the rainy season in their natural habitat. The sexes are difficult to distinguish outside the spawning season as the female does not get very robust. Spawning proceeded in normal *Corydoras* fashion. The eggs were about 1.5 mm in diameter, clear, and with a yellow-gold color. They became light brown after three days and dark brown after four days when the eyes became visible. About 12 hours later the eggs hatched. The fry were 7.5 mm in length and possessed a yolk sac that was absorbed in another day and a half. At that time they accepted baby brine shrimp and microworms. In another ten days the fry grew to 11 mm and were given in addition to the other food some chopped grindal worms.

The color pattern started as pigmentation in the area of the forehead, nape, and behind the gill covers. A few days after hatching these areas became darker and at one week the dorsal and caudal fins began to differentiate from the embryonic fin membranes. By two weeks the dark pigment around the eyes was distinctly darker and dark markings seen at the front and back of the dorsal fin and on the caudal peduncle intensified. By the end of four weeks the fry were 2 cm long and resembled the adults; the dark pigment behind the gill covers was almost gone at this time.

After about a month the adults spawned again, and this continued at intervals of four to 24 days over the breeding season. The number of eggs fluctuated from a low of 18 to a high of over 60 in the dozen spawnings obtained. The eggs were rarely attached to the glass sides of the tank but most usually to the Java moss with some of them scattered on the bottom. The newly hatched pandas seem to be sensitive to disturbances.

Corydoras barbatus is a relatively large species attaining a length of over 10 cm. It is quite different in many ways from other *Corydoras* species and, as such, had been given the subgeneric name *Scleromystax* by Günther. It is quite common in almost all bodies of water along the São Paulo coast from Santos to Rio de Janeiro, but more likely to be found in soft and quite acid (pH 5 or lower) tea-colored (black-water) streams where the water is clear and flowing briskly over sand or sand with pebbles and scattered rock slabs bottoms. These areas are subject to winter flooding. The temperatures are relatively cool, not rising much above 20°C in the summertime and dropping to perhaps 10° to 12°C in the wintertime for short periods. *C. barbatus* has been found together with *C. nattereri* and *C. macropterus*. *C. barbatus* is a bottom-dweller commonly found in groups of up to 50 or more along the sides of the rivers or creeks, where they can quickly disappear under the dense shrubbery. It has the ability to change the pattern somewhat depending upon the bottom type, and it has been said that the Rio populations differ somewhat from those collected about Santos. The slightly larger females were also captured among some flooded channels away from the creek during flood tide; few adult males were present.

Sexes are easily distinguishable. They not only differ in color (the males being much more colorful), but the males have their cheeks covered by bristles (these are weak or absent in females) and their pectoral spines are more developed. In addition, the first two rays of the dorsal fin are more elongate in the male. At a length of about 7 cm the males were readily identifiable, even though their cheek bristles had not yet made their appearance.

Suggested tank setups include a layer of fine sand (*barbatus* are said to like to burrow,

Corydoras barbatus is a very colorful and unusual species. It had at one time been placed in a separate genus (*Scleromystax*). I am tempted to resurrect this situation due to the uniqueness of this species. Photo by Harald Schultz.

sometimes becoming almost completely covered), some driftwood, and some rocks. Plants are optional, and one breeder added spawning mops for receiving the eggs. A variety of live and dried foods were sufficient to keep the fish in good condition. The temperature range should be from about 20° to 25°C, although this species is reported to have spawned at 18° C in the wild. Apparently the parents will spawn under a variety of water conditions — up to pH 7.2 and a temperature of 26°C — but in their natural habitat the pH is less than 5 and the temperature is closer to 18° so these conditions should be approached if a successful spawn is desired. It has been reported that the acid condition is a prerequisite for a good hatch. An inside filter with peat moss has been suggested for bringing the pH down to proper levels. In addition, the spawners should have as much peace and quiet as possible. With heavy feedings of tubificid worms and other live foods, spawning should occur.

When things get going the female seems to be the aggressor; sometimes when nudging the male on his side she will push him all the way across the tank and pin him against the glass wall of the tank. The "T" position is held for several seconds and may occur both in midwater and on the bottom. About three to six eggs are laid, and as the male rests on the bottom the female searches for a place to put the eggs. There does not seem to be a pattern in the distribution of the eggs, but they are usually near the surface. About half a dozen are in a cluster and as many as 130 have been reported for a single spawn. Spawning lasts for half an hour to an hour. The eggs are approximately 1.7 mm in diameter and hatch out in about three or four days. After another two days the fry have absorbed the yolk sac and will accept microworms and newly hatched brine shrimp. At this time they are about 3 mm long. The fry grow quickly if properly fed, and in a month and a half they are about 18 mm long. Spawnings occurred at about weekly intervals. If the pH rose considerably the percentage of eggs that hatched decreased significantly.

Corydoras macropterus is from the same area but does not attain the large size of *C. barbatus,* the average size being about 6 cm. It is not encountered in the usual coastal waters but prefers small brooks or creeks that are shaded by overhanging trees. The water is tea-colored and the bottom covered with decaying leaves; the banks are muddy. Underwater plants are scarce but fallen branches and twigs are plentiful. The *C. macropterus* are seen more often lying on a horizontal branch or leaf in midwater like *C. hastatus.* Like *C. barbatus, C. macropterus* males have bristles on the cheek. They have extremely elongate dorsal and pectoral fin spines as well, more developed than in any other *Corydoras* species. The two sexes are about the same size. *C. macropterus* is considered a peaceful species that will accept the usual foods that it grubs from the bottom substrate in the normal fashion.

Very little need be said about other species that are commonly imported from South America, as they act and breed much like the species already discussed, especially *C. aeneus* and *C. paleatus. C. arcuatus* is reported to be a little harder to spawn (try softer water); *C. rabauti* may yield as many as 800 eggs per spawn that hatch in five to eight days; *C. garbei* spawns no more than about 20 large (2.5 mm in diameter) eggs; *C. undulatus* is said to be sexually dichromatic; *C. zygatus* has eggs that are 1.5 mm in diameter but the female can lay up to 400 eggs per spawning; *C. melanistius brevirostris* is said to be sensitive to fresh tap water; and *C. nattereri,* a lover of cooler water, shows symptoms of distress at temperatures above 24°C. *Corydoras rabauti* prefers the upper range of temperatures (24°-28°C) and cannot tolerate low temperatures. It is actually sensitive to temperature fluctuations as well. Spawning reports (sometimes as *C. myersi,* a synonym) indicate the young are quite distinctly colored at first. Up to a length of about 12 mm the front half of the body is green and the back half a reddish color. *C. reticulatus* has an unusual history. Fraser-Brunner's specimens were aquarium fish (a pair) that were loaned to a German aquarist for breeding purposes and were not preserved. Fraser-Brunner redescribed the species (1947) based on a specimen from "Monte Alegre, River Amazon" that Weitzman (1960) designated as a neotype while re-redescribing the species. Incidentally, when keeping this species fresh tap water and highly acid water should be avoided.

The resemblance of the Callichthyidae to the Loricariidae is quite basic and includes such things as the armor, the structure of the cranium and of the labyrinth system, and the structure of the vertebrae. They do differ, however, by the participation of the skull in the anterior closure of the capsule (Chardon, 1968). The Callichthyidae also seem to be allied to the Astroblepidae, the Trichomycteridae, and the Aspredinidae (Chardon, 1968). These five families have in common the following characters: the unpaired sinus is not separated from the medulla oblongata by any processes of the exoccipital; the anterior points of the sacculae are vestigial or missing; and the lagenas are abnormally dorsal (Chardon, 1968). They of course share other characters that are also shared by other catfish families.

Checklist of species of the family Callichthyidae, with their type localities:

Callichthys Scopoli, 1777. Type species *Silurus callichthys* Linnaeus, 1758.
- *Callichthys callichthys* (Linnaeus, 1758). "In America rivulis."
  - *c. bolteni* Hoedeman, 1952. Surinam.
  - *c. demararae* Hoedeman, 1952. Guyana.

Cataphractops Fowler, 1915. Type species *Callichthys melampterus* Cope, 1872.
- *Cataphractops melampterus* (Cope, 1872). Rio Ambiyacu, Peru. (includes *C. verissimi* (Miranda-Ribeiro)).

Dianema Cope, 1870. Type species *Dianema longibarbis* Cope.
- *Dianema longibarbis* Cope, 1870. Rio Ambiyacu, Peru.
- *D. urostriatum* (Miranda-Ribeiro, 1912). Manaus, Brazil.

Hoplosternum Gill, 1858. Type species *Callichthys laevigatus* Valenciennes (= *H. littorale*).
- *Hoplosternum littorale* (Hancock, 1828). Demarara, Guyana.
  - *l. daillyi* Hoedeman, 1952. Surinam (near Paramaribo).
- *H. thoracatum* (Valenciennes, 1840). Mana, Fr. Guiana; Martinique (probably erroneous).
  - *t. cayenne* Hoedeman, 1961. Fr. Guiana.
  - *t. surinamensis* Hoedeman, 1952. Surinam.
- *H. magdalenae* (Eigenmann *in* Ellis, 1913). Soplaviento and Calamar Cienega, Colombia (status doubtful).
- *H. pectorale* (Boulenger, 1895). Monte Sociedad, Paraguay.

Brochis Cope, 1871. Type species *Brochis coeruleus* Cope (= *B. splendens).*
- *Brochis britskii* Nijssen & Isbrücker, 1983. Upper Paraguay system, Mato Grosso, Brazil.
- *B. multiradiatus* (Orcés-Villagomez, 1960). Western affluent of the Rio Lagartococha, upper Napo system, Ecuador.
- *B. splendens* (Castelnau, 1855). "Rio Tocantins," Brazil.

Aspidoras von Ihering, 1907. Type species *A. rochai* von Ihering.
- *Aspidoras albater* Nijssen & Isbrücker, 1976. Rio Tocantinzinha near São Joao da Alianca, Est. Goiás, Brazil.
- *A. brunneus* Nijssen & Isbrücker, 1976. Serra do Roncador, Mato Grosso, Brazil.
- *A. carvalhoi* Nijssen & Isbrücker, 1976. Acude Canabrava, Guaramiranga, Est. Ceara, Brazil.
- *A. eurycephalus* Nijssen & Isbrücker, 1976. Corrego Vermelho into Rio das Almas, trib. of Rio Maranho, Est. Goias, Brazil.
- *A. fuscoguttatus* Nijssen & Isbrücker, 1976. Corrego Corguinho, Estradas da Tres Lagoas, Est. Mato Grosso, Brazil.
- *A. lakoi* Miranda-Ribeiro, 1949. Pequeño corrego na floresta na Grotâo, Fazenda da Cachoeira, Est. Minas Gerais.
- *A. maculosus* Nijssen & Isbrücker, 1976. Rio Paiaia, into headwaters of Rio Itapicuru, Est. Bahia, Brazil.
- *A. menezesi* Nijssen & Isbrücker, 1976. Rio Granjeiro at Crato, Est. Ceara, Brazil.
- *A. pauciradiatus* (Weitzman & Nijssen, 1970). Rio Araguaia, near Aruana, Est. Goias, Brazil.
- *A. poecilus* Nijssen & Isbrücker, 1976. Upper Xingu, Est. Goias, Brazil.
- *A.* sp. affin. *poecilus.* Rio Palmas, Est. Goias, Brazil.
- *A. raimundi* (Steindachner, 1907). "In dem Bächchen, welches bei Victoria in den Rio Parnahyba mündet."

A. rochai von Ihering, 1907. Fortaleza, capital of the state of Ceara.
A. spilotus Nijssen & Isbrücker, 1976. Riacho dos Macacos, Est. Ceara, Brazil.
A. virgulatus Nijssen & Isbrücker, 1980. Espirito Santo, Brazil.

Corydoras Lacepède, 1803. Type species *C. geoffroyi* Lacepède (= *C. punctatus*).
Corydoras acrensis Nijssen, 1972. Furo do Lago São Francisco, Brazil-Acre.
C. acutus Cope, 1872. Rio Ampiyacu, Shansho Cano, Loreto, Peru.
C. adolfoi Burgess, 1982. Upper Rio Negro, near São Gabriel da Cachoeira, Brazil.
C. aeneus (Gill, 1858). Trinidad.
C. agassizii Steindachner, 1877. Rio Amazonas near Tabatinga, Amazonas, Brazil.
C. amapaensis Nijssen, 1972. Cachoeira Creek at right bank of Rio Amapari, Amapa, Brazil.
C. ambiacus Cope, 1872. Rio Ampiyacu, Loreto, Peru.
C. amphibelus Cope, 1872. Rio Ampiyacu near Pebas, Loreto, Peru.
C. approuaguensis Nijssen & Isbrücker, 1983. Rio Approuague, Fr. Guiana.
C. arcuatus Elwin, 1939. Aquarium specimen, said to be from "?Teffe, Amazon," Brazil.
C. armatus (Günther, 1868). Rio Huallaga, Peru.
C. atropersonatus Weitzman & Nijssen, 1970. Rio Conambo at mouth of Rio Shione, Pastaza, Ecuador.
C. aurofrenatus Eigenmann & Kennedy, 1903. Aguada, near Arroyo Trementina, Paraguay.
C. axelrodi Rössel, 1962. Either Vichada, Meta, Arauca and/or Boyaca, Rio Meta, Colombia.
Corydoras baderi Geisler, 1969. Rio Paru do Oeste, Para, Brazil.
C. barbatus (Quoy & Gaimard, 1824). Fazenda da Japuhyba near Angra dos Reis, Rio de Janeiro, Brazil.
C. bicolor Nijssen & Isbrücker, 1967. Corantijn River system, Sipaliwini River, Nickerie, Surinam.
C. bifasciatus Nijssen, 1972. Creek at left bank of Rio Cururu, trib. of upper Rio Tapajos, Para, Brazil.
C. blochi Nijssen, 1971. Moco Moco Creek near Lethem, Essequibo, Guyana.
b. vittatus Nijssen, 1971. Trib. of Rio Itapicuru at Caxias, Maranhao, Brazil.
C. boehlkei Nijssen & Isbrücker, 1982. Rio Caura system, Venezuela.
C. boesemani Nijssen & Isbrücker, 1967. Suriname River system, Brokopondo, Surinam.
C. bolivianus Nijssen & Isbrücker, 1983. Rio Mamore basin, Beni Province, Bolivia.
C. bondi Gosline, 1940. Rio Yuruari, Bolivar, Venezuela.
b. coppenamensis Nijssen, 1970. Creek at left bank of Coppename River, Saramacca, Surinam.
C. burgessi Axelrod, 1987. Rio Unini, trib. of the Rio Negro, Amazonas, Brazil.
C. carlae Nijssen & Isbrücker, 1983. Petit Arroyo, Parana basin, Misiones Province, Argentina.
C. caudimaculatus Rössel, 1961. Main stream of upper Rio Guapore, Rondonia, Brazil.
C. cervinus Rössel, 1962. Main stream of upper Rio Guapore, Rondonia, Brazil.
C. cochui Myers & Weitzman, 1954. Rio Araguaia, Goiaz, Brazil.
C. concolor Weitzman, 1961. Las Mangas, in a trib. of the Rio Parguaza, western part of Bolivar, Venezuela.
C. condiscipulus Nijssen & Isbrücker, 1980. Cumuri Creek at left bank of Oyapock River, Fr. Guiana.
C. copei Nijssen & Isbrücker, 1986. Loreto, lower course of Rio Huytoyacu, affluent of Rio Pastaza, Peru.
C. delphax Nijssen & Isbrücker, 1983. Guainia, Rio Inirida system, Colombia.
C. ehrhardti Steindachner, 1910. Affluents from Jaragua mountains near Joinville, Santa Catarina, Brazil.
C. elegans Steindachner, 1877. Rio Amazonas at Teffe.
C. ellisae Gosline, 1940. Sapucay, Arroyo Pona, Paraguay.
C. ephippifer Nijssen, 1972. Cachoeira Creek at right bank of Rio Amapari, Amapa, Brazil.
C. eques Steindachner, 1877. Rio Amazonas at Codajas, Amazonas, Brazil.

C. evelynae Rössel, 1963. Upper Rio Solimoes, Amazonas, Brazil.
C. filamentosus Nijssen & Isbrücker, 1983. Corantijn basin, Nickerie District, Surinam.
C. flaveolus R. von Ihering, 1911. Trib. of Rio Piracicaba above Salto, São Paulo, Brazil.
C. fowleri Böhlke, 1950. Cano del Chancho near Pebas, Loreto, Peru.
C. garbei R. von Ihering, 1911. Rio São Francisco, Bahia, Brazil.
C. geryi Nijssen & Isbrücker, 1983. Rio Mamore basin, Beni Province, Bolivia.
C. gossei Nijssen, 1972. Creek near Guajara Mirim, Rondonia, Brazil.
C. gracilis Nijssen & Isbrücker, 1976. Rio Juana (= Rio Juma) at Transamazonica Highway, Amazonas, Brazil.
C. griseus Holly, 1940. Aquarium specimen, said to be from Guyana.
C. guapore Knaack, 1961. Main stream of upper Rio Guapore, Rondonia, Brazil.
C. guianensis Nijssen, 1970. Creek at right bank of Nickerie River, Nickeria, Surinam.
C. habrosus Weitzman, 1960. Rio Salinas, trib. of Rio Pao Viejo, El Baul, Cojedas, Venezuela.
C. haraldschultzi Knaack, 1962. Brazil.
C. hastatus Eigenmann & Eigenmann, 1888. Villa Bella (= Parintins), Amazonas, Brazil.
C. heteromorphus Nijssen, 1970. Creek at right bank of Coppename River, Saramacca, Surinam.
?*C. imitator* Nijssen & Isbrücker, 1983. Amazonas, Brazil. (= *adolfoi*)
C. julii Steindachner, 1906. Creek into Rio Paranaiba near Alto Parnaiba (= Victoria), Maranhao, Brazil.
C. lamberti Nijssen & Isbrücker, 1986. Loreto, lower course of the Rio Huytoyacu, affluent of Rio Pastaza, Peru.
C. latus Pearson, 1924. Lago Logoagua, Rio Beni basin, Beni, Bolivia.
C. leopardus Myers, 1933. Aquarium specimen, said to be from "one of the Brazilian coastal rivers south of the Amazon."
C. leucomelas Eigenmann & Allen, 1942. Yarinacocha, cutoff lake at right bank of Rio Pacaya, Loreto, Peru.
C. loretoensis Nijssen & Isbrücker, 1986. Loreto, Prov. Maynas, Rio Nanay, Peru.
C. loxozonus Nijssen & Isbrücker, 1983. Meta, Lomalinda near Rio Ariari, Colombia.
C. macropterus Regan, 1913. Paranagua, Parana, Brazil.
C. maculifer Nijssen & Isbrücker, 1971. Sangadina stream, Mato Grosso, Brazil.
C. melanistius Regan, 1912. Essequibo, Guyana.
m. brevirostris Fraser-Brunner, 1947. Orinoco, Venezuela (aquarium specimen).
C. melanotaenia Regan, 1912. Honda, Rio Magdalena basin, Tolima, Colombia.
C. melini Lönnberg & Rendahl, 1930. Iuarete, Amazonas, Brazil.
C. metae Eigenmann, 1914. Barrigon, Rio Meta, Colombia.
C. micracanthus Regan, 1912. Salta, Salta, Argentina.
C. multimaculatus Steindachner, 1907. Trib. of Rio Preta, Bahia, Brazil.
Corydoras nanus Nijssen & Isbrücker, 1967. Surinam River system, Brokopondo, Surinam.
C. napoensis Nijssen & Isbrücker, 1986. Loreto, Prov. Maynas, Morona Cocha, Iquitos, Peru.
C. narcissus Nijssen & Isbrücker, 1980. Rio Purus system, Amazonas, Brazil.
C. nattereri Steindachner, 1877. Affluent of Rio Parahyba, Rio de Janeiro, Brazil.
C. octocirrus Nijssen, 1970. Marechal Creek, Surinam River system, Brokopondo, Surinam.
C. oiapoquensis Nijssen, 1972. Cumuri Creek at left bank of Oyapock River (= Rio Oiapoque, Amapa, Brazil), Inini, Fr. Guiana.
C. ornatus Nijssen & Isbrücker, 1976. Rio Tapajos, Para, Brazil.
C. orphnopterus Weitzman & Nijssen, 1970. Lower Rio Bobonaza, Pastaza, Ecuador.
C. osteocarus Böhlke, 1951. San Fernando de Atabapo, Amazonas, Venezuela.
C. ourastigma Nijssen, 1972. Rio Iquiri (= Rio Ituxi), Acre, Brazil.
C. oxyrhynchus Nijssen & Isbrücker, 1967. Gojo Creek, trib. of the Saramacca River, Brokopondo, Surinam.
C. paleatus (Jenyns, 1842). Rio Parana at

San Pedro, Buenos Aires, Argentina.

C. panda Nijssen & Isbrücker, 1971. Aquas Amarillas, Rio Ucayali system, Huanuco, Peru.

C. pastazensis Weitzman, 1963. Chicherota, Pastaza, Ecuador.

p. orcesi Weitzman & Nijssen, 1970. Rio Conambo, Pastaza, Ecuador.

C. polystictus Regan, 1912. Descalvados, Mato Grosso, Brazil.

C. potaroensis Myers, 1927. Potaro River, Essequibo, Guyana.

C. prionotos Nijssen & Isbrücker, 1980. Linhares, Lagoa Juparana, Espirito Santo, Brazil.

C. pulcher Isbrücker & Nijssen, 1973. Rio Purus, Amazonas, Brazil.

C. punctatus (Bloch, 1794). Surinam.

C. pygmaeus Knaack, 1966. Surroundings of Calama, Rondonia, Brazil.

C. rabauti La Monte, 1941. Trib. of Amazon River, Amazonas, Brazil.

C. reticulatus Fraser-Brunner, 1938. Rio Amazonas at Monte Alegre, Para, Brazil.

†*C. revelatus* Cockerell, 1925. Sunchal, Jujuy, Argentina. (Fossil.)

C. reynoldsi Myers & Weitzman, 1960. Caqueta, Colombia.

C. robineae Burgess, 1983. Rio Aiuana, middle Rio Negro, Amazonas, Brazil.

C. robustus Nijssen & Isbrücker, 1980. Rio Purus system, Amazonas, Brazil.

C. sanchesi Nijssen & Isbrücker, 1967. Gojo Creek, Brokopondo, Surinam.

C. saramaccensis Nijssen, 1970. Saramacca River system, Brokopondo, Surinam.

C. schwartzi Rössel, 1963. Mouth of Rio Purus, Amazonas, Brazil.

C. semiaquilus Weitzman, 1964. Igarape Preto, Amazonas, Brazil.

C. septentrionalis Gosline, 1940. Rio Pina, Monagas, Venezuela.

C. simulatus Weitzman & Nijssen, 1970. Rio Ocoa, Meta, Colombia.

C. sodalis Nijssen & Isbrücker, 1986. Loreto, Rio Yavari, Caño de Guavariba in Lake Matamata, Peru.

C. solox Nijssen & Isbrücker, 1983. Rio Oiapoque, Amapa Territory, Brazil.

C. spilurus Norman, 1926. Iponcin Creek into Approuage River, Inini, French Guiana.

C. steindachneri Isbrücker & Nijssen, 1973. Paranagua, Parana, Brazil.

C. stenocephalus Eigenmann & Allen, 1942. Loreto, Yarinococha, Rio Ucayali system, Peru.

C. sterbai Knaack, 1962. Brazil.

C. surinamensis Nijssen, 1970. Creek at right bank of Coppename River, Saramacca, Surinam.

C. sychri Weitzman, 1961. Mangas, western part of Bolivar, Venezuela.

C. treitlii Steindachner, 1906. Creek into Rio Parnaiba near Alto Parnaiba (= Victoria), Maranhao, Brazil.

C. trilineatus Cope, 1872. Rio Ampiyacu, Loreto, Peru.

C. undulatus Regan, 1912. La Plata, Buenos Aires, Argentina.

C. weitzmani Nijssen, 1971. Aquarium specimens. (Rio Vilcanota system at Cizco, Peru?)

C. xinguensis Nijssen, 1972. Suia Missu Creek, trib. of upper Xingu, Mato Grosso, Brazil.

C. zygatus Eigenmann & Allen, 1942. Rio Huallaga system, Loreto, Peru.

Chapter 30

Family — Plates 224–285

LORICARIIDAE

(Suckermouth Catfishes)

The Loricariidae is a very large family of catfishes distributed from Panama to Uruguay. Almost all of the species are primary freshwater fishes; that is, they have almost no tolerance for salt water. Although a few species have vast distributions over much of tropical South America, most are restricted to small geographical areas, and many are known only from the original site from which they were first discovered. Most of the exceptions to the strictly freshwater distributions occur in *Ancistrus* and *Hypostomus*, these genera being found at times in slightly brackish waters of riverine estuaries. Common names for this family include suckermouth catfishes, armored catfishes (causing confusion with the callichthyids), spiny armored catfishes, and in some areas of South America "armadillo del rio," meaning river armadillo. Several of the scientific names are known to aquarists, including among which are *Hypostomus* (formerly *Plecostomus*, a name still occasionally used by aquarists), *Loricaria, Ancistrus, Xenocara* (which is now a synonym of *Ancistrus*), *Farlowella*, and *Otocinclus*.

Loricariids occur in a wide variety of habitats ranging from stagnant pools and marshes (often with very soft acid water) to swiftly flowing mountain streams or creeks barren of any vegetation and with rocky beds up to 3,000 meters altitude. They may be found in jungle streams with a great deal of vegetation. In large streams they are usually found along the banks where the current is not as strong. Most live in smaller bodies of water where it is clear and the bottom material is sandy or rocky. They like to hide in crevices or small cavities in the rocks or, over sandy areas, will bury themselves in the sand. Most of the species are nocturnal and feed only at night, while others are crepuscular (only active at dawn and at dusk), while still others are diurnal, being active during the daylight hours. These catfishes are bottom-dwellers living on the substrate, which may take the form of submerged tree trunks, rocks, pebbles, sand, or even muddy bottoms of still waters. Most loricariids are poor swimmers, but in their own inimitable fashion can often move better than strong-swimming fishes in swiftly moving waters thanks to a high degree of specialization to these type waters.

Modifications include the general form of the head and body (ventral area quite flattened), the structure of the fins (particularly the paired fins, which have their edges roughened), the presence of odontodes (particularly salient on the sides of the snout and the fin spines), and a suctorial mouth. The mouth in many species forms, along with the lips, a roughly circular sucking disc that is augmented by adhesive tubercles and papillae. By means of this sucking disc these fishes are able to attach themselves so tightly to the substrate that they sometimes cannot be pulled free without doing damage. Movement is then by short "hops" between which they attach themselves to the substrate so that the strong current cannot pull them free as they rest. Of course breathing becomes a problem when they are so attached, but they can compensate by taking water into the gill chamber and expelling it only by means of the gill openings. As expected, the fish breathe twice as fast as when they use the ordinary means of taking water in through the mouth. This suctorial mouth arrangement, along with a set of rasping teeth, provides the means by which they are able to feed on algae, detritus, small crustaceans, insect larvae, and perhaps even rotting flesh. These catfishes are said to cut a path through a bed of algae without missing a single strand. Often the detritus ingested contains such items as chironomid larvae. While thick, the lips are also sensitive. Usually loricariids are in contact with the bottom or some other surface most of the time and may remain in a single spot for several hours between bursts of activity.

The body is flattened, especially the broad chest and belly, and is almost entirely covered by a complex of thick, solid bony scutes, with normally only small areas left clear, such as the nostrils, eyes, sensory pores, and fin insertions. The belly is often naked but may be covered with plates that may be very tiny or fairly large and may extend forward almost to or extend under the margin of the lower lip. Those provided with belly plates usually lack an adipose fin. The body plates are arranged in more than two (usually three to five) longitudinal rows or series, in contrast to the callichthyids, which have only two rows. The individual scutes are each set with a number of little toothlike pointed formations called odontodes. These cover all dermal ossifications, including the fin spines, so that when the body is touched (especially if one's hand is drawn across the body from tail toward head) it has a roughened feeling. At the caudal peduncle, which is slightly elongate to elongate and usually compressed, there may be some extra plates on the back and belly between the lateral scutes. In spite of the solid cuirass covering the body, loricariids are flexible enough to maneuver with apparent ease without exposing any of the bare body.

The head shields are constructed differently and help distinguish between different subfamilies. There are no frontal or occipital fontanels and the nares are usually close together. The eyes are usually provided with a papillary iris flap for the control of light, the flap expanding in strong light and contracting with less light. This is said to be analogus to a similar flap in flatfishes and resembles that of squatinids and rays. The mouth is wholly inferior and not protrusible. In most species the lips are in the form of a sucker or disc, the upper lip being relatively narrow to quite broad. The outer surface of the lips is covered with papillae in most species, while in some specialized forms numerous cirri are present. All species possess a pair of commisural barbels (which may be very small or extremely long) connecting the upper and lower lips. The premaxillaries and the dentaries are very often separate so that each half jaw can be moved independently of the other. The teeth vary considerably and are even lacking in the upper jaw of some species. They may be simple, bilobed, trifid (rare), spoon-shaped, or hooked, but usually they are bilobed with a main lobe and a small lateral lobe on the outside. The active teeth are usually in a single series, the number varying from 3 to about 150 on one side of a jaw; there are no teeth on the palate. There are no mental or nasal barbels; the rictal barbels are sensitive to touch, vibrations, and possibly even smell. In some species there are numerous long and slender cirri on the snout that in some forms may be branched (males of *Ancistrus*).

The dorsal fin is usually well developed and has a short base. The dorsal, pectoral, and ventral fins have the first ray developed as a non-pungent spine, with the remaining rays branched. This branching may be dichotomous or with all of the accessory branchlets inserted on the same side of the principal ray. The dorsal and pectoral fin spines can be locked into position. The anal fin is short-based. The caudal fin has about 10 to 14 rays. The adipose fin may be absent or, when present, have a spine (derived from a mid-dorsal scutelet) and a fatty fold covered by skin and ending in a thin membrane.

The caudal vertebrae are compressed, with more or less expanded neural and haemal spines. The swim bladder is reduced to two small capsules lying beneath the supracleithral plates, with the exception of *Pogonopomoides*, which has a large, well-developed, and functional posterior section. The intestine is long, slender, and spirally coiled. The gill membranes are united to the isthmus, with the gill openings being restricted to the sides.

Keeping most of the available loricariids in home aquaria is not difficult once they have become acclimated. The size of the tank depends upon the species being kept, for there are species of *Otocinclus* less than 5 cm long as well as species of *Hypostomus* that will attain a length of over 40 cm. For the larger species a tank of 76 liters or more is recommended. The water chemistry is not important, although extremes are to be avoided, as well as fresh tap water. A neutral to slightly acid pH has been suggested as standard. Since many of the species come from highly oxygenated mountain streams, clean, well-oxygenated water is recommended. Good aeration and good filtration will do very well, especially if some water turbulence is created. Water changes on the order of 30% to 40% on a weekly basis are sufficient. Since many species come from cool mountain streams, temperatures for these species can be lower than for those from lower altitude, warmer areas. The former can stand water temperatures of 19°C, while the latter are said to breed at about 27°C. The bottom material should be sand or gravel fine enough to allow burrowing without fear of damage to the fishes. The tank should be heavily planted and supplied with irregularly shaped pieces of driftwood or petrified wood, rock work, or flower pots and hollow tubes for the tube spawners. These should supply the fishes with dark and obscure hiding places as well as definable territories that can be easily defended by territorial species such as some ancistrines and hypostomines. Subdued lighting is recommended. A fairly large open sandy region should be left, especially for members of the Loricariinae.

Feeding is not difficult. For most species the diet should consist principally, but not exclusively, of vegetable matter. Initially this can consist of the layer of green algae that has built up on most surfaces of a well lighted tank, but they will dispose of this in a very short time and start looking for additional material. This can be almost anything, for aquarists have been resourceful in finding different greens for their fishes. Included in some menus are lettuce (boiled or scalded), boiled spinach, peas, endives, zucchini, and Italian squash. Meaty material (which should be fed in moderation because it is reported to cause constipation in some of these fishes) includes finely chopped earthworms, other small worms, tubificid worms, beefheart, and daphnia. Dried foods are accepted, but those rich in cereal and flake foods with a high vegetable content are the best choices. Boiled oatmeal and rabbit pellets are acceptable. For the nocturnal species, feed in the evening when the lights are low or turned off. It is reported that the ingestion of sand grains, plant debris, and small fragments that become detached when these catfishes rasp driftwood is important to aid digestion.

Most species of loricariids are harmless and peaceful and do little active swimming. They are commonly found resting or working over some area of the tank for tidbits of food. If there is a heavy growth of algae you will probably see much more activity as they go about cleaning it up. Some species are shy and secretive and will spend much of their time hidden away someplace. If hiding places are not available some species, especially of *Hypostomus* and *Ancistrus*, may burrow into the sand, rearranging the tank as they do so. Several specimens of a given species in a tank are usually a good idea, for the fish seem to feel more at ease and will spend more time out in the open than when a single individual inhabits a tank. If there are too many for the tank (that is, if they are crowded) there may be battles for the available spaces. Some species, regardless of the space available, may fight over a particularly attractive area. Species of *Hypostomus* and *Panaque* have been cited as doing this. Others may be peaceful most of the time, but as spawning time nears they suddenly become territorial and aggressive. Males are generally the ones battling for a territory, using undulatory movements and trying to bring their spines into play. It has also been reported that isolated individuals of some *Hypostomus* species become rogue killers, but this is only on rare occasions. Most loricariids are reasonably tolerant of other fishes, and many will not even bother other fishes' fry. If they are placed in a community tank they should be housed with fishes that are not aggressive and will not compete with them for the algae or vegetable-based foods. For a good start, place the loricariids in a tank heavily overgrown with algae. Best for algal control in large tanks are the *Hypostomus* species; best for smaller community tanks are *Otocinclus* species, *Farlowella* species, and species of *Rineloricaria*.

When captured in a net, they will often get themselves all tangled up in the meshes, for they will spread and lock their fins. The best way to free them is to invert the net in the water and let them work themselves free. If they are taken from the water they are capable of emitting relatively loud buzzing noises.

Armored catfishes are generally resistant to diseases but may become infected with ich. Many harbor an amazing number of parasites, including such things as flukes, roundworms, and protozoans. When diseases do strike, some species will often become blotchy in appearance, the discoloration of the skin appearing as patches over the body. Epizoic commensal chironomid larvae were found on species of *Ancistrus, Chaetostoma, Hemiancistrus*, and *Hypostomus*. These larvae gain by such an attachment in having more access to food and protection from predators. There are a couple of favorite attachment sites, the first being among the bristles of the interopercular area, the second near the base of one of the fins (including the adipose fin). Other sites may be selected, but usually not the open areas of the body. Those species without bristles usually are also without the chironomid larvae. This type of commensalism is quite rare (as far as known) for it requires a unique combination of sedentary habits of the fishes, anatomy allowing such an attachment on the fishes, and matching ecologies of both fishes and invertebrate. It is probable that the larvae crawl onto their hosts by chance and then first become attached by the anal prolegs. This is a rather simple and not very secure attachment and they are likely to get knocked off easily if on an open part of the body. They then secrete holdfast material from their salivary glands. In the tuft area they are not only more securely fastened, but they obtain more food there in the currents.

Very few observations of breeding suckermouth catfishes have been made in the wild, and even then they were on the large, more easily observable species. The observations occurred mostly at the end of the dry season or the onset of the rainy season when the water levels were at their lowest. Commercial breeding of some species of *Hypostomus* has been accomplished in large ponds where the fishes can dig burrows into the soft banks. Species of *Ancistrus* (sometimes recorded as *Xenocara*), *Otocinclus, Farlowella, Rineloricaria* (usually under the name *Loricaria*), *Sturisoma*, and some others have been spawned in home aquaria. Many show some form of sexual dimorphism aside from the usual more rounded belly of the spawning-ready female. This usually takes the form of head bristles and/or appendages in the male. In some species, however, sexual dimorphism is only exhibited during the spawning season then disappears again until the next time. Conditioning of the spawners usually involves a diet with a high (up to 100%) vegetable content. Some breeders also recommend a drop in temperature similar to that used in the Callichthyidae to help induce spawning. The eggs may be deposited on some substrate in the open or in a secluded place such as the interior of a hollow tube placed in the aquarium for just that purpose. The potential sites are thoroughly scrubbed by the male or both the male and female. The male fertilizes the eggs as soon as they are laid and in many species takes over the duty of cleaning and guarding them, sometimes even covering them with his body. Males of some species develop an enlarged lower lip and carry the eggs in a clutch covered by the lower lip until they hatch. Whether this is strictly for protection or involves moving them from a "dangerous" site to a more "safe" site is not known. The incubation period varies depending upon the species involved and the temperature, ranging from about four to nearly 20 days, but generally lasts a week to ten days.

Some three or four days after hatching the

fry have absorbed their yolk and are ready to be fed. The first foods most often recommended by breeders are algae, green water, and infusoria promoted by the addition of young, fresh lettuce leaves. Newly hatched brine shrimp is also recommended, but some breeders warn that too heavy a proportion of live foods can cause constipation in the young catfishes. As the young grow, some show a distinct "metamorphosis," with changes in color and pattern as well as fin size and shape. Young *Hypostomus* may have the dorsal fin proportionately larger than that of the adults, or the opposite may be true in that the dorsal fin becomes proportionately larger with age, as in *Pterygoplichthys* and some members of the Loricariinae. The pectoral fins also continue to grow as long as the fish lives according to some reports, while the length of the barbels varies according to the age and the species involved. The color pattern and the armor or dermal bone develop completely in about a week to ten days after the fry have started feeding. Many young have up to a half dozen dark crossbars that disappear with growth. The growths on the head make their appearance only after the fishes mature and vary widely depending upon the species, the sex, the age, and whether it is during the spawning season or not. These appendages may range from short, simple spines to rather large, branched, antler-like formations. These may be used for defensive purposes and/or may be involved with the senses of taste, smell, and touch, some being reported able to detect and measure the speed and strength of the water currents flowing past them. The species that have been spawned in home aquaria are necessarily the smaller species of the family, the larger ones requiring aquaria of at least 570 liters for any chance of success.

Some loricariids are fished for commercially, being captured by the use of cast nets during the times of low water when the fishes become concentrated by the drying up of floodplain lakes and lagoons. Live suckermouths are most easily captured by means of fish anesthetics.

The more than 600 species and 70+ genera are divided into six subfamilies: Hypostominae, Ancistrinae, Lithogeneinae, Neoplecostominae, Hypoptopomatinae, and Loricariinae. Some authors have also included the Astroblepidae as a subfamily of the Loricariidae, but most recent workers have regarded them as a separate family. The same is true of the Scoloplacidae. The subfamilies of the family Loricariidae can be distinguished by the following key (after Gosline, 1945).

1a. Pectoral fin rays I,8; anal fin placed well back, well behind tip of last, depressed dorsal fin ray; body with a few rudimentary scutes; teeth in a single series in each jaw; caudal fin bilobed, the two outermost rays not the longest; a series of enlarged papillae on lower lip just behind the mandibular teeth.. Lithogeneinae

1b. Pectoral fin rays I,6, sometimes I,5; sides of body usually completely covered with bony scutes; anal fin placed nearly under or anterior to tip of last, depressed dorsal fin ray.................. 2

2a. Anus often separated from anal fin origin by single azygous preanal plate, but never by a pair of ventrolateral plates that meet along midline just behind anus; belly never enclosed and shielded by series of smooth, interlocking plates; lower, transverse portion of pectoral girdle never exposed as a bony ridge across front of chest; caudal peduncle roundish or compressed.............................. 3

2b. At least one pair of ventrolateral plates meeting along midline between anus and anal fin origin........................ 4

3a. Interopercular area normally developed, never specialized as a group of fused platelets that are automatically forced outward and forward when outer border of opercle is raised 5

3b. Platelets in interopercular region fused, usually bearing hooks and articulating with opercle in such a way that raising of outer opercular border forces interopercular area outward and forward..................................... Ancistrinae

4a. Lower transverse portion of pectoral girdle exposed as a bony bridge across front of chest; caudal peduncle compressed or rounded.. Hypoptopomatinae

4b. Lower transverse portion of pectoral girdle not exposed, this area usually covered with small platelets; caudal peduncle strongly depressed.. Loricariinae

5a. Anal rays I,4; supracleithral plate bordered posteroventrally by the exposed cleithrum; cheeks never with bristles; predorsal plate V-shaped, closely appressed to the dorsal spine, with the prongs of the V extending anteroventrally; normally three rather symmetrical azygous scutes between supraoccipital and predorsal plate.. Hypostominae (part)

5b. Anal rays usually I,5 to I,6 (possibly I,4 in *Corymbophanes andersoni*); supracleithral (supratemporal) plate bordered posteroventrally at least in part by a naked area or by a few to several small platelets.. 6

6a. Lateral scutes 27-32; predorsal plate minute or absent, never closely attached to the dorsal spine; four or more scutes, exclusive of the predorsal scute, on the midline between supraoccipital and dorsal origin....................................... 7

6b. Lateral scutes 22-26; cleithrum extending backward over base of pectoral spine .... *Hypostominae* (part)

7a. Tooth row of lower jaw not followed by one or more distinct series of enlarged papillae; abdomen without an isolated, regularly six-sided shield of platelets.... .... Hypostominae (part)

7b. Tooth row of lower jaw followed by one to several series of distinct, enlarged papillae; abdomen with a rather regular six-sided shield of small, prickly platelets, bordered on all sides by a naked area .... Neoplecostominae

Four of the six subfamilies (Loricariinae, Ancistrinae, Lithogeneinae, and Hypoptopomatinae) are readily distinguishable one from the other and from the other two. These last two are, however, problematical in that the dividing line can be placed in one of several positions. Gosline (1947) considered the subfamily Neoplecostominae to contain 12 genera, although he stated that other lines could be drawn just as well. Isbrücker (1980), on the other hand, regards *Neoplecostomus* as the sole genus of the Neoplecostominae, all the other genera that Gosline included in the subfamily being placed in the Hypostominae. Isbrücker also makes the observation that the line between subfamilies could have been drawn in several other places and that further study will be needed in order to determine the proper division.

The subfamily Lithogeneinae seems to occupy an intermediate position between the Astroblepidae (which is sometimes considered a subfamily of the Loricariidae) and the Neoplecostominae. It contains the single genus *Lithogenes* with only one species (*L. villosus*) from Guyana. The body is naked except for a double series of plates dorsally from either side of the adipose fin spine to the caudal and another double series ventrally on the caudal peduncle from the end of the anal fin. About 14 platelets extend along the middle of the sides from above the anal fin origin to the base of the middle caudal rays. These platelets are widest above the tip of the anal, where they are slightly wider than the eye diameter. The eye is moderately small, contained about 8 times in the head length. The oral disc is large and margined by a series of incisions. There is a bunch of about 25 villi immediately associated with the dentary; the dentary has only 2 bicuspid teeth. The premaxillary has 8 bicuspid teeth, the inner cusp of each much longer than the outer cusp. A narrow, free membrane from the barbel margins the lip exterior to the incised inner margin from the barbel to a point behind the angle of the mouth; the free part of the barbel is equal to the eye diameter. The dorsal fin has 8 rays, the first of which is not spinous. The pectoral fin has a spine and 8 rays, the spine being not much larger than adjacent rays. The ventral fins have a spine and only 4 rays. The adipose fin spine has a base much wider than the rest of the fin. The pectoral spine, the adipose fin spine, and some of the caudal rays are provided with prickles or small spinelets. The interopercular area is spineless and not evertible. The caudal peduncle is roundish.

The subfamily Neoplecostominae contains only a single genus, *Neoplecostomus*, which includes only two species, both apparently found in the area around Rio de Janeiro. The head is broad and flattened, with the upper surface granular and the lateral borders without bristles. The snout is granular. The eyes

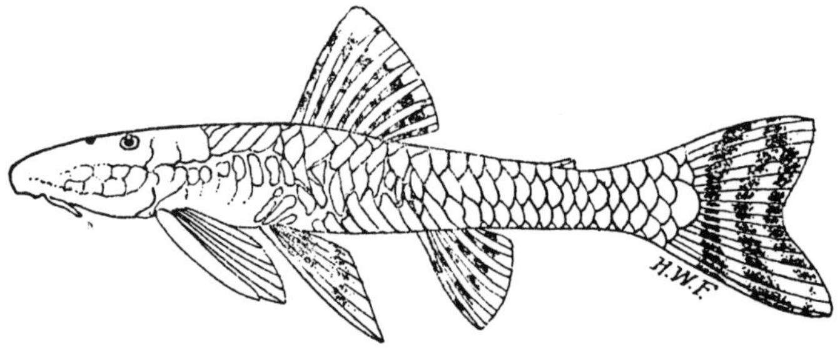

Neoplecostomus granosus. (From Fowler, 1954.)

are small, superior, with the interorbital space approximately equal to the width of the cheek. There are about 29 scutes in the lateral series that are in part fused along the middorsal line between the dorsal and adipose fins. Five or 6 irregular scutes are present between the supraoccipital and the dorsal fin, and the chest has a rather regular 6-sided shield composed of small plates, each of which has 4-8 posteriorly projecting spicules. This shield develops at an early stage and is considerably developed in individuals 50 mm in total length. There are about 20 teeth on the side of each jaw, each tooth bicuspid with a well-developed lateral lobe. The teeth of the lower jaw are followed by 1 to 3 rows of enlarged papillae. The cleithrum does not extend backward over the base of the pectoral fin spine. The anus is somewhat nearer the origin of the anal fin than the base of the spine of the ventral fin. The dorsal fin has a spine and 7 rays, its base included nearly 2 times in its distance from the adipose fin. The anal fin has a spine and 5 to 6 rays, its origin slightly behind the tip of the last, depressed dorsal fin ray. The ventral fin has a spine and 5 rays and is inserted somewhat ahead of the dorsal fin insertion. The caudal lobes are rounded and unequal, the lower lobe slightly longer than the upper. The caudal peduncle is roundish in cross-section. The interopercular area is not evertible. The swim bladder is generally without a posterior division. The intestine is relatively short, with less than a dozen convolutions.

The subfamily Hypostominae contains some 18 genera and approximately 175 species, most of which belong to the genus *Hypostomus*. They are distinguishable from the Ancistrinae mainly by having the interopercular area not evertible. The scutes are usually present on both sides and back and there normally are 3 symmetrical scutes on the middorsal line between the supraoccipital and the predorsal plate. The predorsal plate is well developed, V-shaped, and forms a part of the locking mechanism of the dorsal fin spine. The teeth are simple or bicuspid, in a single row in each jaw; the pharyngeals are toothless. The anus is located close to the anal region, and the anal fin originates about under the last, depressed dorsal fin ray. The anal fin has a spine and 4 or 5 rays, the ventral fins have a spine and 5 rays, and the pectoral fins have a spine and 6 rays. The caudal peduncle is compressed. The gill rakers resemble the gill filaments in structure. There is no posterior division of the swim bladder.

The following key helps distinguish between the genera of the Hypostominae (modified from Gosline, 1947):

1a. Anal fin rays usually I,5 (I,4 in *Corymbophanes andersoni*?); supratemporal (supracleithral) plate bordered posteroventrally at least in part by a naked area or by a few to several small platelets 2

1b. Anal fin rays I,4 (sometimes I,5 in *Monistiancistrus*); supratemporal plate bordered posteroventrally by the exposed cleithrum; predorsal plate V-shaped, closely appressed to the dorsal fin spine, with the prongs of the V extending anteroventrally; normally 3 rather symmetrical azygous scutes between supraoccipital and predorsal plate 12

2a. Lateral scutes 27-32; predorsal plate minute or absent, never closely attached to the dorsal spine; 4 or more scutes (exclusive of the predorsal scute) on midline between supraoccipital and dorsal origin 3

2b. Lateral scutes 22-26; cleithrum extending backward over base of pectoral spine 7

3a. Each tooth with two approximately equal lobes; lateral scutes failing to meet anywhere along the middorsal line between dorsal and adipose fins, leaving naked middorsal band nearly equal in width to eye diameter .... *Upsilodus*

3b. Each tooth either simple or with a single

small lateral lobe; lateral scutes meeting along middorsal line at least for part of the distance between dorsal and adipose fins.. 4

4a. Head length (to end of supraoccipital) included 3.4 or fewer times in standard length; head broad and flattened, distance from lower rim of eye to outer border of cheek about equal to or greater than interorbital width.......... 5

4b. Head short and comparatively narrow, more or less quadrangular in shape; head length (to end of supraoccipital) included about 3.67 times in standard length; greatest width of cheek contained about twice in interorbital width; adipose fin present; abdomen naked; cheeks without bristles....... *Kronichthys*

5a. Adipose fin present; caudal peduncle comparatively short, rounded or ovate, its depth included 3.2 or fewer times in its length....................................... 6

5b. Adipose fin absent; back behind dorsal fin sharply flattened so that whole of caudal peduncle is rather rectagonal; anal fin set far forward; depth of caudal peduncle included 3.7 or more times in its length .... *Pareiorhina*

6a. Abdomen nearly naked; adults with straight bristles on cheek that become greatly elongate spines in adult males... ....*Hemipsilichthys*

6b. Abdomen with scattered embedded platelets; cheek with minute bristles in specimens 80 mm in total length......... ....*Pareiorhaphis*

7a. Caudal peduncle flattened below, somewhat triangular in cross-section; abdomen entirely naked; supratemporal (supracleithral) plate bordered posteroventrally by a naked area; anal fin low, its longest ray about one-third length of ventral fin 8

7b. Caudal peduncle rounded below; abdomen in adult with platelets at least along bases of lateral scutes; supracleithral plate bordered posteriorly by a few to numerous small platelets; anal fin rays at least half as long as ventral fin...... 9

8a. Dorsal fin rays I,9 or I,10 .... *Delturus*

8b. Dorsal fin rays I,7 .... *Corymbophanes*

9a. Belly almost entirely covered with small platelets in the adult; interorbital space very broad, the frontals not reaching the supraorbital rim.......................... 10

9b. Belly in adult largely naked, but with well developed transversely elongate platelets at the bases of the lowermost lateral scutes; frontals forming part of the supraoccipital border................ 11

10a. Cheek region with well-developed bristles....................... *Pseudorinelepis*

10b. Cheek region without well-developed bristles .... *Rhinelepis*

11a. Adipose fin present; bristles present on cheek; 22 lateral scutes...... *Pogonopoma*

11b. Adipose fin absent; no bristles on cheek; 25-26 lateral scutes....... *Pogonopomoides*

12a. Teeth numerous, filiform, with bifid crown that curves abruptly toward interior of buccal cavity...................... 13

12b. Tooth number reduced; teeth with short, solid, thick stem, the crown in form of a spoon; teeth not curved....... .... *Cochliodon*

13a. Dorsal fin with a spine and 7 rays..... 14

13b. Doral fin with a spine and 10-13 rays.... .... *Pterygoplichthys*

14a. Adipose fin absent; well-developed odontodes present on head and body, forming very visible and pronounced ridges; anal fin large, with 4 (last ray split to base) or 5 branched rays; 9 or 10 relatively large thoracic scutes between base of last branched pectoral fin ray and base of ventral fin spine.............. .... *Monistiancistrus*

14b. Character combination not as above (an adipose fin may be absent in a few species of *Hypostomus*)....................... 15

15a. Caudal peduncle long and slender, almost rounded in cross-section; sexual dimorphism very strong, the females with well-developed odontodes, those of the males excessively long.............. *Isorineloricaria*

15b. Caudal peduncle not long and slender or round in cross-section; sexual dimorphism not as pronounced............... 16

16a. Numerous conspicuous papillae of irregular form and size present in buccal cavity between base of teeth and buccal valvate membrane .... *Aphanotorulus*

16b. No conspicuous papillae of irregular form and size present in buccal cavity......... 17

17a. Width of ramus of lower jaw contained fewer than 1.5 times in interorbital space, the two usually being nearly equal in length and width.............*Pseudancistrus*

17b. Width of ramus of lower jaw contained more than 1.75 times in interorbital space, usually 2 to 5 times ..*Hypostomus*

The genus *Upsilodus* contains a single species, *U. victori*, from the vicinity of Rio de Janeiro. It has a broad, flattened head, the top of which is granular forward almost to the tip of the snout (which is naked). The supraoccipital is short, and the lateral borders of the head are provided with a few short, backwardly hooked spines. The eyes are small and superior, and the interorbital width is about equal to the distance from the eye to the border of the cheek. The barbel is free, its length

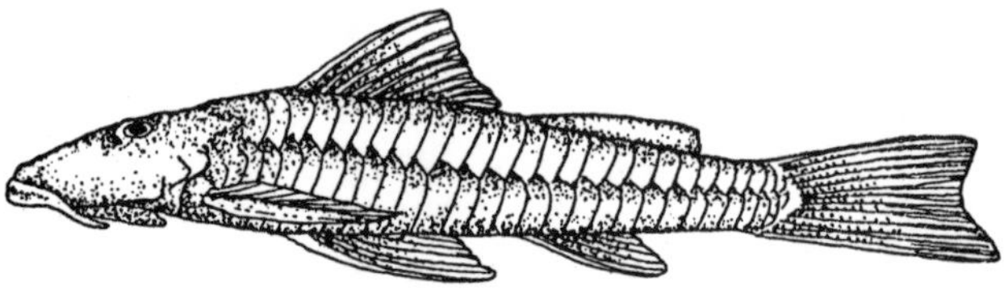

Upsilodus victori.

about equal to the diameter of the eye. The lateral scutes number about 30, the four lower series incomplete anteriorly. About 6 irregular plates are present between the supraoccipital and the dorsal origin. The scutes do not meet along the surface or under the skin between the dorsal and adipose fins; the abdomen is entirely naked. The mandibular ramus is contained about 1.25 times in the interorbital width. About 20 teeth are present on either side of each jaw, each tooth with two approximately equally developed, deeply divided lobes (as in *Lithogenes*). The cleithrum does not extend backward over the top of the pectoral fin spine, this spine being free to rotate in an arc of more than 30°. About 6 keeled, azygous preadipose scutes are present, the anterior ones lying free in the naked mid-dorsal ridge, the posterior ones adjoining the lateral scutes. The dorsal fin has a spine and 7 rays, and its base is contained about 1.7 times in its distance from the adipose fin. The anal fin has a spine and 5 rays and originates only slightly behind the tip of the last, depressed dorsal fin ray. The ventral fins are inserted about under the dorsal fin spine. The caudal fin is concave posteriorly, the lowermost ray somewhat longer than the uppermost. The anus is posteriorly located, its distance from the anal fin contained about 4 times in its distance from the base of the ventral spine.

The genus *Hemipsilichthys* includes about a half dozen species. The head is broad and depressed, with the posterior border of the supraoccipital poorly defined. The snout is broadly rounded, its tip granular in the young but with prickles in older individuals. The eyes are small and superior, the interorbital width approximately equal to the distance from the eye to the edge of the cheek. There are 27 to 29 lateral scutes and about 5 azygous preadipose plates, the dividing line between these and the lateral plates being poorly defined. Four or more irregular plates are present between the supraoccipital and predorsal plate, while the abdomen is entirely naked. The dorsal fin base is bordered by a fleshy area covering the scutes that extends a short distance behind the dorsal fin base along the midline. The dorsal fin has a spine and 7 rays; its base is contained about 1.3 times in its distance from the base of the adipose fin in the type species. The anal fin has a spine and 5 rays and is inserted before the tip of the last, depressed dorsal fin ray. The ventral fins are inserted about under the dorsal fin spine.

Hemipsilichthys gobio; (b) dorsal view of head. (From Fowler, 1954.)

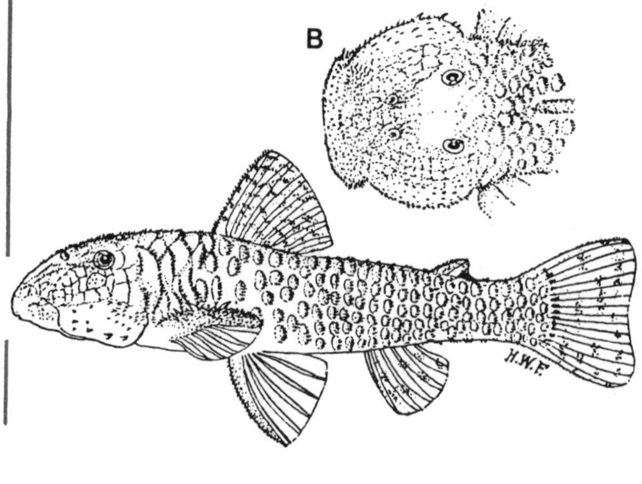

The cleithrum does not extend backward over the top of the pectoral fin spine, so the base of the spine is free to rotate in an arc of about 30°. The buccal disc may or may not have free barbels opposite the corners of the mouth. The mandibular ramus is contained about 1.3 to 1.75 times in the interorbital width. There are about 55 teeth on one side of each jaw, the teeth with a minute lateral cusp or lacking one. The anus is situated about half as far from the anal origin as from the base of the ventral fin spine. Sexual dimorphism is quite apparent, for the males are richly provided with long, straight spines extending out horizontally from the cheek. These spines are able to puncture plastic fish shipping bags, making nuptial males of the species of this genus difficult to ship.

The genus *Pareiorhaphis* contains only two species from southeastern Brazil (São Paulo and Parana). The back is rounded between the dorsal and caudal fins and the head is broad and depressed, its top granular to its margin except for a small naked area at the snout tip. The supraoccipital is short. The lateral borders of the head have minute bristles, the bristly area extending forward to the naked area at the tip of the snout. The eyes are small and superior, the interorbital width approximately equal to the width of the cheek. The barbel is an adnate flap. There are about 30 scutes in the lateral series and 6 or 7 irregular plates between the supraoccipital and the dorsal fin origin, some of the lateral pairs of scutes meeting, but not fusing, along the midline of the back between the dorsal and adipose fins; there is 1 azygous preadipose plate. The abdomen is provided with small platelets from which backwardly projecting spicules arise (as in *Neoplecostomus*, but the plates not nearly so well developed). The mandibular ramus is contained 1.5 to 2 times in the interorbital width. There are about 25 to 35 teeth on one side of either jaw, each simple or with a small lateral cusp. The cleithrum does not extend backward over the base of the pectoral fin spine. The dorsal fin has a spine and 7 rays, its base included about 1.5 times in its distance from the adipose fin. The anal fin has a spine and 5 rays and originates only slightly behind the tip of the last, depressed dorsal fin ray. The ventral fins are inserted somewhat ahead of the insertion of the dorsal fin. The anus is anterior in position, only slightly nearer the anal fin origin than the base of the ventral fin spine.

The genus *Pareiorhina* includes only a single species, *P. rudolphi*, from the state of São Paulo in Brazil. The head is broad and depressed, its top granular to its margin except for a small naked area at the tip of the snout. The lateral borders of the head are granular, but without developed bristles. The caudal peduncle is distinctly flattened above between the dorsal and caudal fins. The eyes are small and superior, and the interorbital width is more or less equal to the width of the cheek. The barbel is very short. There are about 27 to 30 scutes in a lateral series, with 4 to 6 ir-

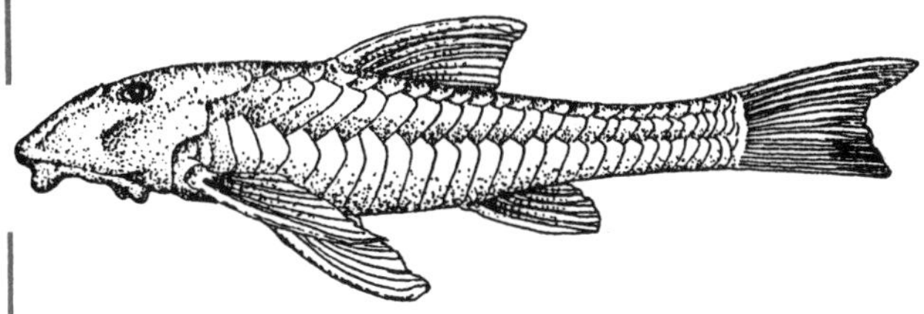

Pareiorhina rudolphi.

regular scutes between the supraoccipital and the dorsal fin. The lateral scutes are fused along the middorsal line between the dorsal and caudal fins. The abdomen possesses scattered embedded platelets. The mandibular ramus is contained about 1.2 to 1.5 times in the interorbital width. There are about 25 to 40 simple teeth on one side of either jaw. The dorsal fin has a spine and 7 rays. The anal fin has an unbranched ray and 5 branched rays and originates approximately under the tip of the last, depressed dorsal fin ray. The adipose fin is lacking. The ventral fin insertion is somewhat anterior to the dorsal fin insertion. The caudal fin is concave, the lower half only slightly longer. The cleithrum does not extend posteriorly over the pectoral fin spine. The anus is nearly twice as far from the base of the ventral fin spine as from the anal fin origin. This genus is very close to *Pareiorhaphis* but differs by lacking and adipose fin.

The genus *Kronichthys* contains only two species, both from southeastern Brazil (São Paulo). The body is more or less cylindrical and the head is comparatively deep and narrow. The snout is granular almost, but not quite, to its border. The eyes are small and supralateral, and the depth of the cheek is contained almost twice in the interorbital width. The barbel is short or absent. There are 30 to 32 lateral scutes and a small predorsal scute plus 4 or 5 irregular scutes between the supraoccipital and dorsal fin origin; there is a single azygous preadipose scute. The abdomen is entirely naked and the fleshy area at the base of the dorsal fin is small. The dorsal fin has a spine and 7 rays, its base contained more than 1.5 times in its distance from the adipose fin. The anal fin has a spine and 5 rays, and it originates under the last, depressed dorsal fin ray. The ventral insertion is slightly posterior to the dorsal insertion. The caudal peduncle is somewhat flattened above and below; the caudal fin is slightly emarginate, its longest, lowermost ray being considerably shorter than the length of the head. The cleithrum extends backward over the base of the pectoral fin spine. The anus is slightly nearer the anal fin origin than the base of the ventral fin spine.

The genus *Corymbophanes* contains two species apparently well separated geographically, one from Guyana, the other from Bahia, Brazil. The head is depressed, its surface granular almost to the tip of the snout, which remains naked. There is no externally visible supraoccipital crest. The lateral borders of the head have short marginal bristles. The eyes are moderately small, superior, their diameter contained about 2.3 to 3 times in the interorbital width; the width of the cheek is somewhat less than the interorbital width. The barbel is short but free. The mandibular ramus is contained about 1.5 to 2 times in the interorbital width. About 30 to 40 teeth are present on one side of either jaw, each tooth having a small lateral cusp. There are 24 to 26 scutes in the lateral series and about 4 irregular scutes plus a minute predorsal plate between the supraoccipital and the origin of the dorsal fin. The lateral scutes behind the dorsal fin are fused along the middorsal line. There are 1 or 2 azygous preadipose plates, and the abdomen is entirely naked. The dorsal fin has a spine and 7 rays, its base contained about 1.2 times in its distance from the adipose fin area. The adipose fin is generally absent but may be replaced by a low median ridge. The anal fin has a spine and 4 or 5 rays. The ventral fins are inserted slightly behind the origin of the dorsal fin. The caudal peduncle is decidedly flattened below while the caudal fin is obliquely concave to emarginate. The cleithrum has a broad flange extending posteriorly over the base of the pectoral fin spine. The anus is about twice as far from the ventral spine base as from the anal fin origin, the anus to anal fin origin area more or less encroached upon by the lowermost lateral plates.

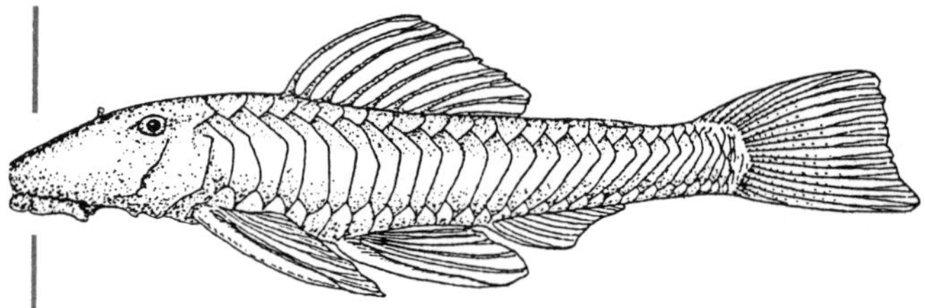

Corymbophanes bahianus.

The genus *Rhinelepis* contains three species from eastern Brazil and Paraguay. The head is broad and depressed, its upper surface granular to its margin and with no naked area at the tip of the snout. The lateral borders of the head lack bristles, and the supraorbital is short. The eyes are small and the interorbital width is almost half the width of the cheek. The barbel is short. The mandibular ramus is contained about 4 times in the interorbital. The upper lip is granular to, or almost to, the base of the barbel. There are about 35 teeth on one side of either jaw; the teeth simple or

Rhinelepis aspera. (From Fowler, 1954.)

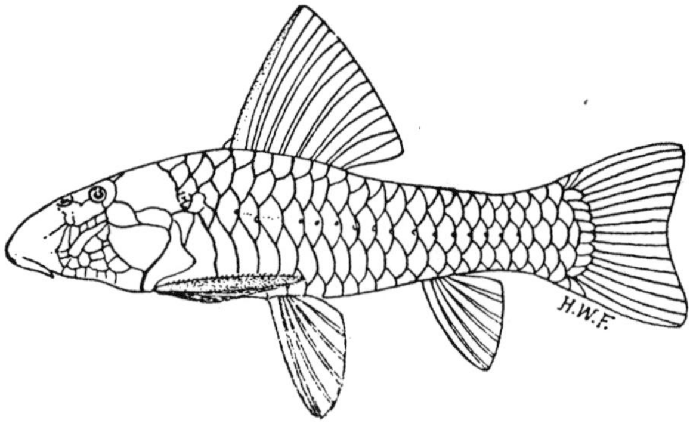

with a small lateral cusp. There are about 24 or 25 scutes in a lateral series, with 3 plates between the supraoccipital and the predorsal plate on the middorsal line. The supracleithral plate is bordered posteroventrally by small plates, and the lower surfaces of the head and belly are almost completely covered by plates in adults. The dorsal fin has a spine and 7 rays, while the anal fin has a spine and 5 rays and originates under the last, depressed dorsal fin ray. The adipose fin is absent, but its position is marked by 1 or 2 poorly defined azygous scutes; otherwise the back is rather flattish behind the dorsal. The insertion of the ventral fins is slightly posterior to the dorsal origin. The caudal peduncle is compressed, about equally rounded above and below, and the caudal fin is short, not very deeply incised. The cleithrum extends posteriorly over the pectoral spine base, and the anus is close to the anal origin. The gill openings extend well in toward the isthmus on the undersurface of the head, the distance between the gill openings contained about 3 times in the width of the head.

The genus *Pseudorinelepis* contains three species from the Amazon drainage in Brazil. It is very close to the genus *Rhinelepis*, differing chiefly by the presence of bristles on the opercular region. Although this by itself usually is not considered of enough importance

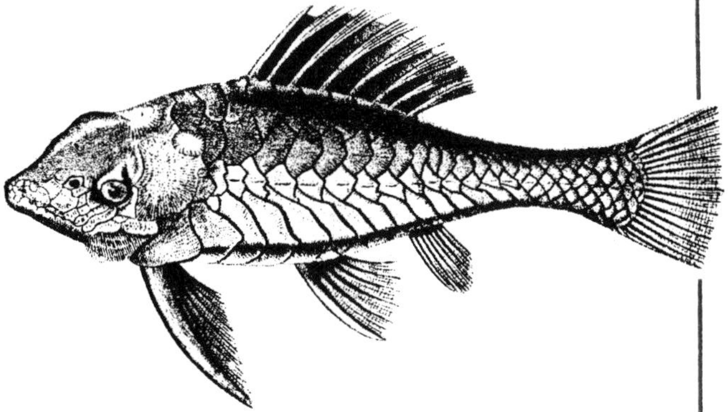

Pseudorinelepis genibarbis. (From Cuvier & Valenciennes, 1840.)

to warrant separate generic status, it has been maintained as such by Isbrücker (1980), perhaps on the basis of additional characters. *Canthopomus* is a synonym.

The genus *Pogonopoma* contains a single species from Brazil. The head is not particularly depressed, its upper surface is granular to its margin, and the snout is broad and rounded, its tip naked. There is a large patch of bristles on the side of the head (larger and more numerous in the adult male). The supraoccipital is short and blunt; the eyes are moderate, contained about 7 or so in the head length. The barbel is well developed, about equal in length to the eye diameter. The mandibular ramus is contained about twice in the interorbital. There are over 100 teeth on one side of either jaw, each tooth with a small lateral cusp. The upper lip is granular, but the granulations do not nearly reach the base of the barbel. There are 22 scutes in a lateral series. A series of three enlarged plates is present between the eye and the tip of the snout, and the supraoccipital is followed by 3 azygous plates as well as a well-developed predorsal plate. The supracleithral plate is bordered posteroventrally by a few small platelets and is apparently in contact with the upper anterior edge of the exposed cleithrum. The belly has one or more series of well developed transversely elongate plates lying along the base of the lateral scutes between the ventral and pectoral fin bases, leaving the central belly area naked. Some smaller platelets are present at the front of the chest and behind the ventral fin base. The dorsal fin has a spine and 7 rays and is little higher (if any) than long. The anal fin is large and has a spine and 5 rays and originates under the last, depressed dorsal fin ray. An adipose fin is present with

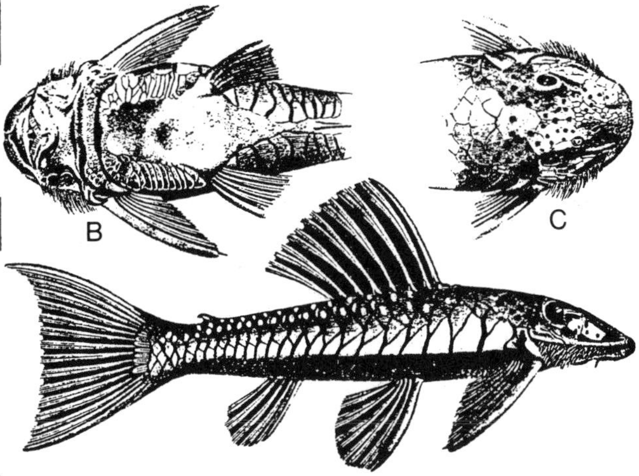

Pogonopoma wertheimeri; (b) ventral view; (c) dorsal view of head. (From Steindachner, 1867.)

no more than 1 azygous plate before the spine. The insertion of the ventral fins is somewhat posterior to the dorsal insertion. The caudal fin is moderate, lunate, with the upper ray produced. The cleithrum extends posteriorly over the base of the pectoral fin spine. The gill openings are restricted as in *Hypostomus*.

The genus *Pogonopomoides* contains a single species, *P. parahybae*, from the Parahyba River. The head is very much like that of *Pogonopoma* except that there is no small naked area on the snout and there are no cheek bristles. The supraoccipital also tapers posteriorly to a sharp, elongate point. The mandibular ramus is contained about 2 times in the interorbital width. There are about 70 teeth on one side of either jaw, each tooth with a small lateral cusp. There are about 25 or 26 scutes in the lateral series. The posterior section of the swim bladder is well developed, and the intestine has over 30 coils. The predorsal plate, gill openings, barbel, granulations of the upper lip, cleithrum, ventral fin insertion, plating of the belly, anal fin, and caudal fin all are as in *Pogonopoma*. In fact, these two genera cannot be readily distinguished by any single character that is strong enough to merit generic separation. There are a number of characters, however, that when combined seem to make the generic separation plausible. A small adipose fin is present in *Pogonopoma*, for instance, and absent in *Pogonopomoides*; cheek bristles are present in *Pogonopoma* but absent in *Pogonopomoides*; *Pogonopoma* has 22 scutes in a lateral series compared to about 26 in *Pogonopomoides*; and the supracleithral plate in *Pogonopoma* appears to be bordered posteroventrally by 4 small platelets as well as partly by the first lateral scute, while in *Pogonopomoides* it is bordered posteroventrally by numerous platelets and is nowhere in contact with the first lateral scute.

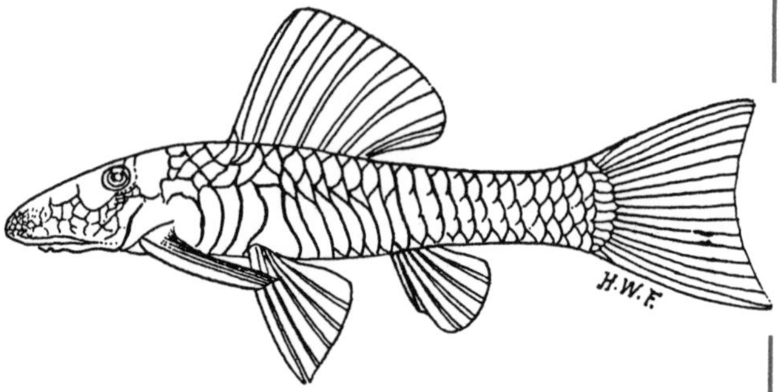

Pogonopomoides parahybae. (From Fowler, 1954.)

The genus *Delturus* contains three species from Brazil. The head is rather deep, its upper surface granular to the snout tip. Bristles are present on the lateral borders of the head and at the base of the pectoral fin in adult males. The eyes are comparatively large, included about 2 times in the interorbital width. The barbel is free, about half an eye diameter in length. The mandibular ramus is about 1.3 times in the interorbital width. There are about 20+ bicuspid (the cusps are about equal) teeth on one side of either jaw. There are about 25 scutes in a lateral series that, in part, meet along the midline between the dorsal and adipose fins. Four more or less regular azygous plates and a small predorsal plate are present between the supraoccipital and the dorsal fin; there are 3 or 4 sharply keeled azygous preadipose scutes. The abdomen is entirely naked. The dorsal fin has a spine and 9 or 10 rays, the last ray attached to the 3 scutes following it by a membrane; the dorsal fin base is longer than its distance from the adipose fin. The anal fin has a spine and 5 rays and originates about below the base of the last dorsal fin ray. The ventral fin insertion is somewhat behind the origin of the dorsal fin. The caudal peduncle is flattened below, the caudal fin obliquely concave with the lowermost ray the longest. The cleithrum extends posteriorly over the top of the pectoral fin spine base and limits its movement strictly to a backward and forward plane of

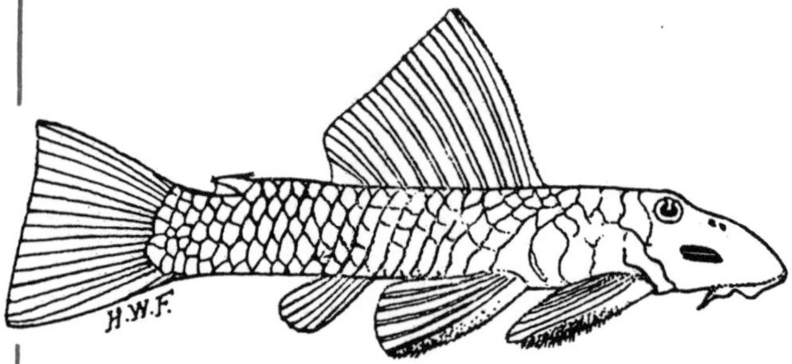

Delturus angulicauda. (From Fowler, 1954.)

motion. The anus is located immediately before the anal fin.

The genus *Isorineloricaria* contains two species from Ecuador. This is one of the newer genera of the subfamily Hypostominae being erected by Isbrücker (1980) to accommodate *Isorineloricaria spinosissimus* and *I. festae* (formerly of the genus *Hypostomus*). *I. festae* is re-

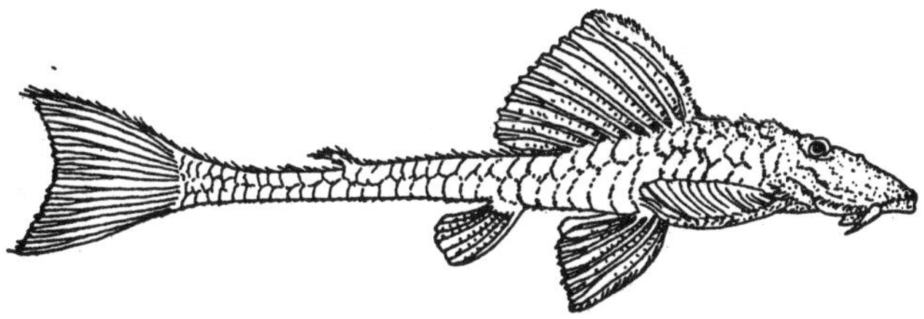

Isorineloricaria spinosissimus.

garded as only tentatively valid by Isbrücker until, as he states, "there is evidence to the contrary." These species are distinct by their long and slender caudal peduncle, almost round in cross section, and their unusual and very prominent sexual dimorphism. The males have several odontodes extremely elongated, while even the females are somewhat more rugose than the average *Hypostomus* species. *Isorineloricaria* is similar to *Rineloricaria* in general body shape as well as in the presence of the well-developed odontodes, and specifically in their secondary sexual dimorphism. In this respect it also resembles *Harttia*. The caudal peduncle is quite different, however, being rounded in *Isorineloricaria*, strongly compressed in *Hypostomus*, and strongly depressed in *Harttia* and *Rineloricaria*. These last two genera are, of course, contained in the subfamily Loricariinae and differ from the other two genera by the characters that set that subfamily apart from the Hypostominae.

Isorineloricaria spinosissimus has the head somewhat elongated, the occipital plate ending in a pointed occipital crest. The head also bears three distinct ridges. The snout is pointed, its tip granular. The posthumeral ridge is strongest anteriorly, and the back has a median depression. The eye is small, contained about 9.4 times in the head length. There are about 32 lateral plates in a series, the free margins covered with long spines. The belly is completely covered with small granular plates. The upper and lower edges of the caudal are similar.

The genus *Monistiancistrus* includes but a single species, *M. carachama*, from the Ucayali River basin in Peru. This genus had been placed in the subfamily Ancistrinae until recently when Isbrücker and Nijssen (1983) moved it to the subfamily Hypostominae and, in fact, included it among the genera that they consider to comprise the *Hypostomus*-group. The body is comparatively long, quite depressed, convex above, and flattened below. The head is broad, with a snout much wider than long. The caudal peduncle is long and compressed. The eyes are set high, near the pectoral origin in the vertical; the interorbital space is broad. The mouth is large, as is the mandibular ramus. There is a broad buccal disc. The teeth are bifid, very fine and

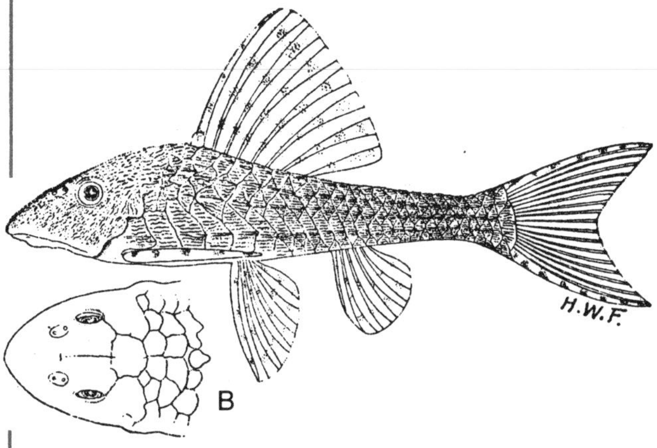

Monistiancistrus carachama; (b) dorsal view of head. (From Fowler, 1954.)

slender, close set, and the ends are curved. The scutes are quite rough and spinescent and form longitudinal spinescent ridges on the upper slope of the body. The scutes on the undersurfaces are distinct but small, with the median undersurface of the head naked. The dorsal fin insertion is well premedian. The anal fin is small. The pectoral fins are placed low, extending little beyond the origin of the ventral fins. There is no adipose fin. The ventral fins are inserted beneath the anterior third of the dorsal fin. The caudal fin is long, with pointed lobes. The gill openings are restricted, about twice the eye diameter. (Fowler, 1940).

The genus *Aphanotorulus* is based on a single species, *A. frankei*, from the Ucayali basin in Peru. It is very closely related to *Hypostomus*, from which it differs by the presence of numerous conspicuous papillae in the buccal cavity between the bases of the teeth and the buccal valvate membrane. These papillae are quite unique in the subfamily. The body is flattened between the level of the dorsal spine and the level of the anal spine, as is the caudal peduncle behind the anal fin spine. There are 31 lateral scutes and 4 predorsal scutes between the supraoccipital process and the dorsal fin origin. Nine scutes are present between the base of the last branched ray of the dorsal fin and the base of the adipose spine and 14 between the last branched ray of the anal fin and the caudal. There are 9 to 13 small and inconspicuous thoracic scutelets. The abdomen anterior to the anal fin origin is almost completely covered by minute polygonal dermal ossifications as far as the posterior margin of the lower lip. The lower lip is narrow; the outer surface of the upper lip is almost completely covered by small irregular dermal ossifications that bear the minute odontodes. The posterior and internal margins of the upper lip have papillae. There are about 16 fusiform, bicuspid (inner cusp longer) teeth on each side of the upper jaw and 16 to 19 similar teeth on each side of the lower jaw. The dorsal fin has a slender spine or unbranched ray) and 6 (last ray split to the base) or 7 branched rays. The anal fin has a weak spine or unbranched ray and 3 (last ray split to the base) or 4 branched rays. The pectoral fin has a solid spine and 6 branched rays. The ventral spine is weak but thickset, and there are 5 branched ventral fin rays. The base of the adipose fin membrane has three scutes and the pectoral spine has an outer series of short spiniform odontodes as well as some odontodes that are a little less salient along the interior dorsal edge. The caudal fin is less forked than that of *Hypostomus plecostomus*. This recently described genus belongs to the *Hypostomus*-group of genera along with *Cochliodon, Pterygoplichthys, Monistiancistrus*, and *Isorineloricaria* (Isbrücker & Nijssen, 1982).

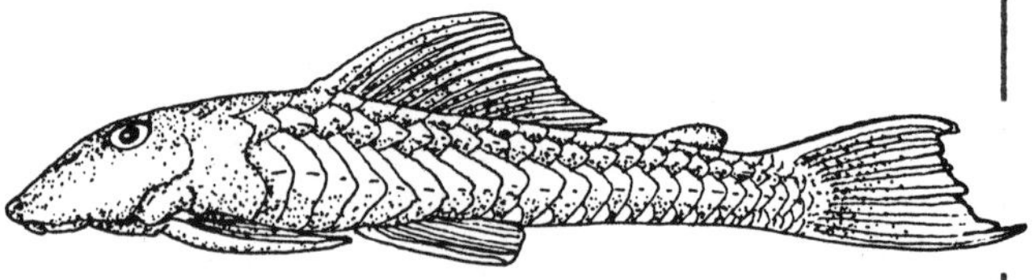

Aphanotorulus frankei.

The genus *Pseudancistrus* contains about a half dozen species, most of which are distributed in northeastern South America. The snout is bony to its tip and the caudal peduncle is not greatly depressed or elongate. The eyes are superior in position and not visible from below. The ramus of the lower jaw has its width contained fewer than 1.5 times in the interorbital space (usually they are about equal). There are about 100 to 150 bilobed teeth on each ramus of the jaw. The dorsal fin has a spine and 7 to 9 rays and originates a little anterior to the insertion of the ventral fins. In *P. barbatus* both sexes possess elongate odontodes along the margin of the head. These are in the form of pin-like bristles and are slightly longer in the males than in the females. These bristles can be extremely long in certain males of a population, possibly an exhibition of dominance or perhaps only a temporary condition when the fish is ready to spawn.

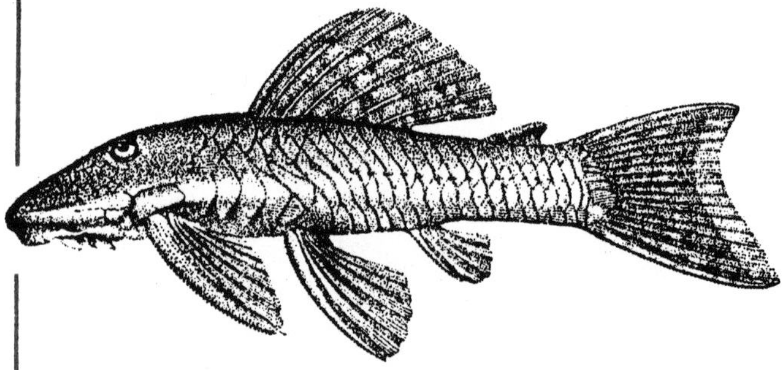

Pseudancistrus nigrescens. (From Eigenmann, 1912.)

Pseudancistrus possesses characteristics of both the subfamily Hypostominae and the subfamily Ancistrinae, and its position is still uncertain. I have followed the checklist of Isbrücker (1980), where it is placed in the subfamily Hypostominae, even though a year earlier (Isbrücker, 1979) he had indicated that he was leaning toward placing this genus in the

Ancistrinae.

The genus *Hypostomus* is one of the largest genera of the family, having approximately 116 species distributed from Panama to Uruguay. The body is relatively short and robust, and the caudal peduncle is not depressed. The upper parts of the head and body are encased in longitudinal rows of scutes, while the lower surface of the head and the abdomen are naked or possess only small granular plates. The snout is covered with granular plates until its margin. The first plate of the lower lateral series is completely separated

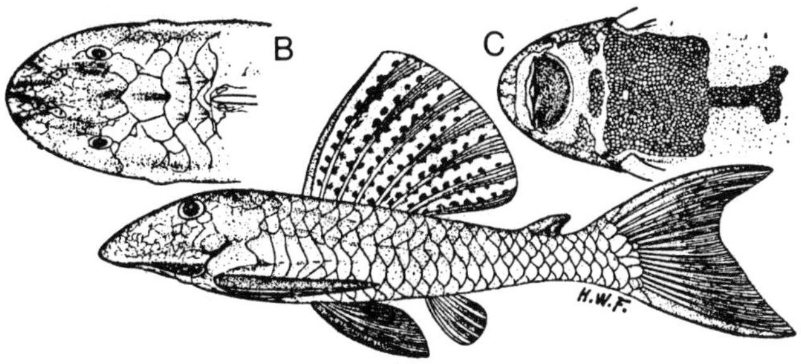

Hypostomus plecostomus; (b) dorsal view of head; (c) ventral view. (From Fowler, 1954.)

from the clavicle and the temporal plate of the second scute of the same series. The opercle and interopercle are firmly connected and immovable. The premaxilla and dentary are of approximately equal length. The teeth are numerous, slender, bicuspid, and arranged in an almost straight line in each jaw; the palate is toothless. The dorsal fin has a spine and 7 rays and is located in front of the ventral fins and separated from the supraoccipital by 2 to 4 (usually 3) scutes. The anal fin has a spine and 3 to 5 rays, while the adipose fin is represented by a spine and a small membrane. The pectoral fin has a large, toothed spine and 6 rays. The ventral fins each have a spine and 5 rays. The gill opening is very narrow.

Boeseman, in his paper on the genus *Hypostomus* and its Surinam representatives (1968), discusses the situation regarding the use of the name *Hypostomus* in preference to the name *Plecostomus*. The name *Plecostomus*, it appears, was used several times previous to the proposal of the name *Hypostomus*, which normally would indicate that it should take priority. But the uses, such as in Gronovius (1754, 1763), Meuschen (1778), and Walbaum (1792), have for one reason or another been rejected by the International Commission on Zoological Nomenclature or are pre-Linnaean. *Hypostomus*, erected in the year 1803 by Lacépède, was the first valid proposal of a generic name for the genus. The name *Plecostomus* is still with us, however, for although just about all the scientific literature is now using the name *Hypostomus*, hobbyists still cling to the name as a common name for all *Hypostomus* species, shortening it to "plecos" for added convenience. The species name *Hypostomus plecostomus* certainly has contributed to the perpetuation of the common name plecostomus. Those aquarists who are not as familiar with the loricariids as catfish enthusiasts also tend to refer to species of other genera (such as *Ancistrus* and *Pterygoplichthys*) as plecos. Boeseman (1968) found he could separate the Surinam species of *Hypostomus* into two groups ecologically, one coastal and one interior. The interior species usually occurred only in or near the clear, well oxygenated water of cataracts or rapids. In the Surinam River basin he also noted that smaller individuals were occasionally found in the forest tributaries where the temperatures ranged from 24° to 25°C and the pH was 5.0 to 6.1, while the larger individuals were in the main rivers where the temperature was higher (to about 30°C) and the pH about neutral. He believed that the adults might have even lost the ability to pass through the slowly moving waters of the rivers, although possibly only in an upstream direction. This would tend to restrict the different species to small ranges, such as a single river system or only a few river systems. The coastal species inhabit areas where there are no cataracts or rapids and, in fact, the waters are slowly flowing, sometimes muddy, and, occasionally in estuarine situations, quite brackish. This division of the habitats seems to occur throughout the range.

Baked *Hypostomus* seems to be a favorite food of some of the South American Indians. Fishermen in some areas will catch them by sliding a hand beneath a submerged rock or log until a pleco is encountered and grabbed. Needless to say this is a very hazardous operation considering the number of dangerous animals that might be in residence under the log or stone at the time. A net may be held downstream in case the pleco makes a run for it.

Hypostomus species feed mainly on algae and other vegetable matter as well as animal life (small crustaceans, worms, etc.) that may live on the surface of submerged objects. In some specimens from Panama it was found that the intestines were jammed with soft, flocculent material (mud, algae, etc.) scraped from the submerged rocks.

Hypostomus species range in size from about 14 to perhaps over 50 cm. They are usually difficult to identify in an aquarium, the main character being their color pattern. According to Boeseman (1968) in some species the spots tend to remain about the same size during growth but become more numerous; in others the pattern of juveniles is markedly different from that of the adults. Even when patterns of the same size individuals of the same species are compared it is seen that there may be a pronounced difference in intensity. As with many of the aquarium fishes, the largest tank is the best, keeping in mind that the most common species imported, the so-called *H. plecostomus*, may grow to a length of 40 to 50 cm. The gravel should be of a grain size that will permit burrowing without causing any damage to the fish. Heavy plantings of broad-leaved plants are recommended, and hiding places should be provided through rockwork caves and/or a few flowerpots. The water chemistry is not critical, as *Hypostomus* species are very tolerant of pH and temperature as long as extremes are avoided. Neutral to slightly acid water at a temperature of 20° to 26°C is reasonable. The lighting should be subdued or at least there should be spots where the plecos can hide from the brightness. Floating plants help in this respect. The water should be well aerated as the oxygen requirements are generally high for the swift-water species. The water should also be very clean—good filtration that causes turbulence is best.

Their diet should be properly balanced. Being mostly vegetarian means providing them with food high in vegetable content such as boiled and raw spinach, lettuce, celery tops, green beans, and even zucchini. Boiled oatmeal, rabbit pellets, and good grade flake foods with a high vegetable content are also good. The best food, of course, is naturally growing algae. However, these enthusiastic algae-eaters will quickly eat all of the available algae in a "green" tank in a very short time. They will scour the leaves of aquarium plants, usually without damage to the plants themselves. Feeding is best accomplished when the lights are low in the evening. Do not rely on leftovers from other fishes, for plecos consume a great deal. Although plecos make fairly good community tank fishes, usually one to a tank is enough for the territorial species. If started together at a very young age, two or more can be safely kept in the same tank. If an adult is added to a tank where there is an already established adult, fights generally occur. The large and powerful toothed pectoral fin spines may be used by males in combat, possibly resulting in some damage to loser and winner both. As the fights progress, the tank usually becomes a disaster area. Since plecos that are territorial generally select a particular cave or corner and remain there much of the time, they become quite upset when the tank decorations are rearranged and their favorite spots no longer exist. They might dash around the tank creating havoc. Two more items in regard to plecos: never select a pleco that is hollow-bellied; and the addition of a teaspoon of salt for each 10 liters for the coastal species helps them adjust to tank life more quickly.

Although *Hypostomus* species are hardy and relatively disease-free in aquaria, they do on occasion (for example, when placed under poor aquarium conditions) become subject to attack by bacteria. A myxobacterium, possibly *Chondrococcus columnaris*, has been reported to cause a discoloration of the skin, forming patches over the entire body as well as sloughing of the surface layer of the skin, cottonmouth appearance, and damage to the gills. More prevalent, perhaps, are infestations of parasites, including such pests as *Vorticella* (which may initially settle on a weakened fish as epibionts), gyrodactylid flukes on the gills, intestinal nematodes, *Costia* (which causes the raising of the scutes to give a "ruffled" appearance), blood trypanosomes, and of course the ever-present ich (*Ichthyophthirius multifiliis*) and its allies.

The most common species of *Hypostomus* in aquaria (as far as can be determined) is often

A wild caught *Hypostomus plecostomus*. There are certainly several species that go under this name in the aquarium trade. This confusion will last at least until there is a comprehensive revision of the genus (or even longer?). Photo by Harald Schultz.

called *Hypostomus plecostomus*, although it is almost certain that other species have been masquerading under that name for years. It grows to a length of about 50 cm in the wild, but in most cases reaches only half that in captivity. In Surinam it is found in more or less brackish coastal waters, while the smaller individuals tend to be located more upstream in the main rivers or their tributaries (Boeseman, 1968). None were collected in the cataract areas. In nature they have been observed feeding in beds of algae and aquatic plants, scraping away the algae or small crustaceans that they find there.

This species is found outside its normal range, having been introduced for algae control or simply released by aquarists who have seen specimens grow too large for their tanks. At one point the *Hypostomus* population of the United States was estimated at some 7 million, a figure that is probably much larger by now. Specimens introduced into the San Antonio River, Texas, averaged about 14 cm in length and grew to 50 cm. Since they found the area to their liking, feeding on algae, worms, crustaceans, and even small fishes, they eventually spawned. The eggs were apparently deposited on smooth rocks and guarded by one or both parents for a period of about two weeks. Small individuals (15 mm to 40 mm) were captured by scraping a hand net along the underside of the leaves of the submerged plants, while larger ones were taken by dragging a net over the stones that littered the bottom.

A different story is reported by the fish farmers who raise these fish in dirt ponds. There the plecos construct burrows in the dirt sides of the ponds. (This type substrate was not available to the Texas fish, possibly explaining the difference in spawning methods.) The burrow usually has a single opening, but this branches out into several tunnels, all horizontal, and ending some 120 to 150 cm deep. Eggs are deposited at the back of the tunnels and may number over 500. They were found clustered into a sticky ball, attached to each other by some connective tissue (mucous secretions). They can stand relatively cool water temperatures but cannot live through some of the colder Florida winters and therefore must be taken indoors until the spring. Trouble seems to start developing below 10° to 15°C. A large tank is recommended (190 liters or more) if the fish is expected to grow to its full potential.

H. watwata was also found in the lower reaches of rivers, in the outlets, or even along the shore in Surinam according to Boeseman (1968). It is better adapted than *H. plecostomus* to the semi-marine environment on sandy or muddy bottoms where there may be silty conditions. This species is probably also in the hobby.

The spotted pleco, *Hypostomus punctatus*, from the Rio de Janeiro area, occurs regularly in the hobby and has been reported as spawning in captivity. A pair in a rather large tank (490 liters) suddenly changed their behavior from aggression by the smaller male to mutual chasing about the tank and spending more and more time around a particular piece of driftwood that had a hole in it. Both fish cleaned the hole for about five days before spawning in it, leaving a clump of dark brownish eggs just inside the entrance. The male took over the fanning and guarding duties. In about a week the eggs hatched and the fry were next seen under the root but still in the protection of the male. In about ten days the fry were 2 cm long and swimming about picking algae off the glass sides of the tank. Since this fish comes from clean, clear, well-aerated streams, the aquarium should have good filtration and aeration as well.

In a spawning of an undetermined species of *Hypostomus*, the male was about 18.5 cm in length, the female 19.5 cm. The male proceeded to clean a PVC tube positioned beneath a stone. About a week before spawning commenced the pair began to quarrel. The male would tremble with the dorsal fin fully erect and would move the lateral parts of his body convulsively. Actual damage to the fish occurred in the form of torn fins and an eye scratched by one of the pectoral fin spines. The aquarium suffered as well, as large quantities of gravel were moved and plants were broken and uprooted. The male finally succeeded in pushing the female to the vicinity of the PVC tube. After a few days she briefly entered the tube. During the next four or five days she paid many more visits to the tube and eventually remained in the tube for a time as the male sucked at her anal region and fluttered his fins and body. The female responded by depositing a shapeless clump of eggs loose in the tube. It was estimated that there were about 260 of the yellowish 4-mm eggs. The male alone guarded the eggs, fanning them and rolling them about with his mouth until they hatched after some five days. The fry at that time were about 1 cm in length. The yolk was absorbed in approximately nine days, when the fry had attained a length of close to 2 cm. In about 12 days they were 2.5 cm long and the first coloring started to appear; after about two months they were 4.5 cm long.

Hypostomus commersonii is very common in the La Plata region, occurring as much in the estuarine waters as in the arroyos and lagunas. Here they reproduce in the spring, as one encounters individuals as small as 10 mm between November and February in the ponds and small lagoons. At about one year of age they are some 7 cm in length, but the growth rate from then on depends to a great extent on the available food supply. They feed on the organic material of the bottom mud. Small examples are kept in aquaria, where they do very well. They prefer water temperatures greater than 20°C and can survive water temperatures to a maximum of 34°C. At higher temperatures they frequently take air from the surface to use in their intestinal respiration. Brazilian researchers have discovered that *H. plecostomus* has a dilation of the rectum where the urogenital ducts empty. The air taken into the gut is discharged through the anus.

The genus *Pterygoplichthys* contains about 20 species coming mostly from Paraguay, Brazil, and Peru. It is very similar to *Hypostomus* but can easily be distinguished (even in the aquarium) by the 10 or more dorsal fin rays. The snout has a granular margin, and the articulation of the interopercle with the opercle is movable. The interopercle is armed with fine, hooked, needle-like spines that are capable of being everted. The mouth is provided with numerous bifid teeth. The last ray of the dorsal fin is connected at its base to the following scute by an inconspicuous membrane.

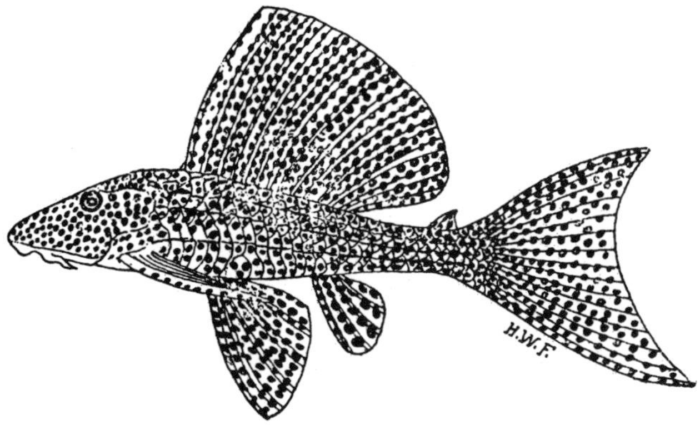

Pterygoplichthys gibbiceps. (From Fowler, 1954.)

The anal fin has a spine and 4 to 5 rays.

Members of the genus *Pterygoplichthys* are commonly imported for the aquarium trade. *P. anisitsi*, otherwise known as the Snow King because of its gray-white background color covered by black reticulations, has an unusually high number of dorsal fin rays (14) and grows to a considerable size (75 cm). In Argentina it is said to come up to the surface for air at regular intervals in areas where the oxygen supply is low. This aerial respiration apparently begins just about as soon as the young catfish leave their nest. The nest is a burrow or hole in the soft banks or bottom, usually among the aquatic vegetation. This has also been observed by commercial fish farmers who have successfully bred the Snow King. The standard method is quite simple. Just add a well-conditioned pair to a large pond, and tunnels are soon constructed in which the eggs are laid. After the fry have hatched and the yolk has been absorbed, they leave the nest and become scattered throughout the pond searching for food. They must be supplied with algae if they are to survive. This is accomplished by placing some greenhouse cloth a few inches below the surface of the water, where the sunlight causes a rapid growth of algae. Harvesting the young is either by seine (not very efficient, for the young can easily burrow into the soft bottom to avoid the net) or by placing some palmetto fronds strategically along the sides of the pond and periodically removing them and vigorously shaking them out over a net.

Pterygoplichthys gibbiceps, the other most common species of the genus in our tanks, is relatively common in the central Amazon, where it attains a length of over 40 cm and is a prized catch for the fishermen. It has been reported that importers consider this species as harder to acclimate than *Hypostomus* species, suffering a higher mortality rate. The aquarium should be well oxygenated and not too warm. The food should contain a high proportion of vegetable matter. Two specimens introduced into a tank full of algae practically cleaned it all out within two days. This is a territorial species. Combats may occur, but usually injuries or fin damage is minor and heals within a few days. Aside from the usual undulations with spines erect, the fish may attach themselves to their opponents by their sucker mouths. Spawning has been accomplished with this species also. A drop in temperature might help initiate the spawning.

The genus *Cochliodon* is a relatively small genus of about a half dozen species mostly from Brazil, Colombia, and Venezuela that attain lengths of between 100 and 250 mm. It is very similar to *Hypostomus* but is easily distin-

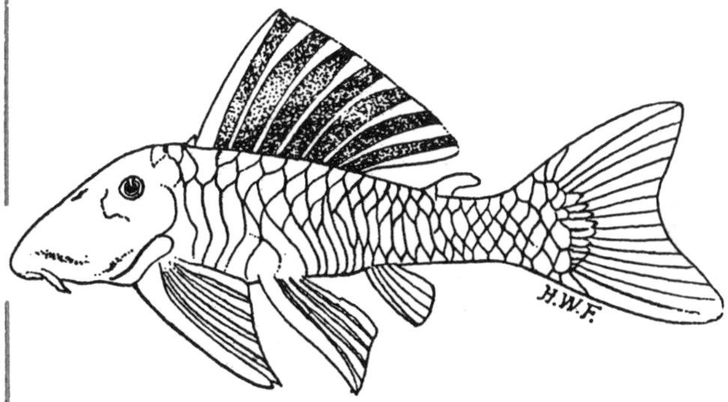

Cochliodon pyrineusi. (From Fowler, 1954.)

guishable (even by aquarists) from that genus by its spoon-shaped teeth. Only one or two species have been imported for the aquarium trade. *C. plecostomoides* is easily cared for but must be supplied with a fair amount of greens in its diet. Along with the other items mentioned for other species, cooked oatmeal that has been allowed to cool and alfalfa (rabbit) pellets have been fed with good results. As with other suckermouth catfishes, beware of hollow-bellied individuals.

The subfamily Ancistrinae contains 18 genera with more than 175 species, the largest genus being *Ancistrus*. They are most closely related to the subfamily Hypostominae and at times have been included with them. The distinguishing feature is an evertible interopercular area that usually bears hooks. Like *Cochliodon* of the Hypostominae, one of the genera (*Panaque*) has spoon-shaped teeth. The adipose fin is usually, but not always, present, and the anal fin is lacking in two genera. The snout or sides of the head are commonly provided with some sort of ornamentation (spines, tentacles, etc.) that is most noticeable in the males. Otherwise the external characters are as in subfamily Hypostominae.

The following key will help to distinguish the genera of the subfamily Ancistrinae:

1a. Adipose fin absent.......................... 2
1b. Adipose fin present........................ 5
2a. Anal fin absent.............................. 4
2b. Anal fin present 3
3a. Caudal fin with long, filamentous upper and lower lobes .... *Acanthicus*
3b. Caudal fin without long, filamentous upper and lower lobes....*Lithoxus* (part)
4a. Originating from Panama and Colombia .... *Leptoancistrus*
4b. Originating only from South America.. .... *Lipopterichthys*
5a. Last dorsal fin ray attached by a membrane to the adipose fin......*Parancistrus*
5b. Last dorsal fin ray not attached to adipose fin or near its base by a membrane 6
6a. Teeth small, numerous, more than 20 on each ramus 10
6b. Teeth larger, fewer, less than 20 on each ramus 7
7a. Teeth spoon-shaped, 6-8 in ramus of each jaw; belly covered with small platelets ....*Panaque*
7b. Teeth not spoon-shaped; belly naked.. 8
8a. Several filamentous barbels, in addition to the commisural barbels, present on the margin of the upper and lower lips. .... *Exastilithoxus*
8b. No such barbels present in addition to the commisural barbels 9
9a. Odontodes well developed; body deep, with very spinous dermal ossifications; attains fairly large body size.............. ....*Pseudacanthicus*
9b. Head and dermal ossifications without very conspicuous odontodes; small species with a flat body......*Lithoxus* (part)
10a. Dorsal fin rays 10..........*Megalancistrus*
10b. Dorsal fin rays 8 or fewer 11
11a. Width or ramus of lower jaw contained fewer than 1.5 times in interorbital space, the two commonly being nearly equal in length and width; belly naked; at least 25% of anterior dorsal surface of snout naked and without barbels; interopercle with short, evertible spines, sometimes with curved or hooked tips.. .... *Chaetostoma*
11b. Width of ramus of lower jaw contained more than 1.75 times in interorbital space (usually 2-5 times); belly naked or with small platelets (granular scales); snout various 12
12a. Anterior ¼ or more of upper snout surface naked and with well developed barbels, at least in the males; opercle and interopercle separately movable, latter with graduated evertible spines having hooked tips; belly naked........*Ancistrus*
12b. Anterior dorsal surface of snout bony, except for a few species that have roundish naked patch not much larger (sometimes smaller) than orbit................ 13
13a. Spines and bristles on interoperculum, if present, not arranged in rosette pattern; interopercle and opercle separately (but only moderately) movable, former with evertible spines; belly with granular scales or platelets (except in young)... 14
13b. Interopercle with a rosette pattern of graduated spines with hooked tips and long, slender bristles on outer margin of spines; interopercle and opercle separately movable; belly naked............ 15
14a. Posterior lateral body scutes distinctly rugose; color pattern distinctive (commonly with black bands); usually of a small size .... *Peckoltia*
14b. Posterior lateral body scutes not distinctly rugose; color plain; moderately large size.......................*Hemiancistrus*
15a. Three plates present from dorsal fin base to origin of adipose fin; head about as wide as long................ *Cordylancistrus*
15b. Five to six plates from dorsal fin base to

adipose origin 16
16a. Head wide, almost as wide as long; some very long interopercular odontodes extending much beyond head in adult males .... *Dolichancistrus*
16b. Head width only about 75% of its length; very long odontodes not present .... *Lasiancistrus*

The genus *Hypocolpterus* is a monotypic genus containing only *H. analis* from Rio Orteguasa in Colombia. It has a moderately long body with a rather short, deep caudal peduncle. The head is large and depressed, greatly wider than long. The broad snout is covered with smooth, though finely wrinkled to papillate, soft skin around a wide border. The eyes are moderate, being contained about 5½ times in the snout, and closer to the dorsal than the tip of the snout. The broad, inferior mouth is provided with broadly papillate lips

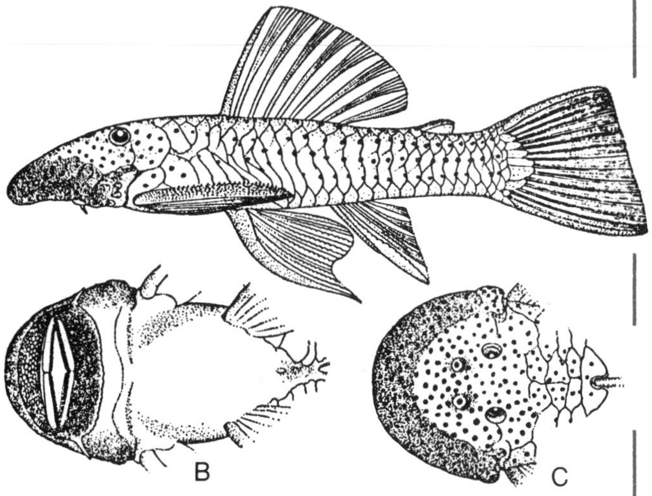

Hypocolpterus analis; (b) ventral view; (c) dorsal view of head. (From Fowler, 1954.)

with a cirrus on each side. The teeth are very fine, slender, hooked and bifid, numbering about 60 on each side in the upper jaw and 75 on each side of the lower jaw. The interopercle is retractile with 5 large hooked spines largely concealed in the thick tegument. The body scutes are large, finely asperous or denticulate, and number 26 + 1 in the lateral line. There are 3 predorsal scutes bordered behind with 4 more. The belly and chest are naked.

The dorsal fin has a flexible spine and 8 rays. The anal fin is as long as the dorsal fin is high. It has a spine and 5 rays, the spine and first ray each with an expanded cutaneous flange. An adipose fin composed of a spine and fleshy flap is present. The long pectoral fins have 6 rays and a broad, compressed, rigid spine that is denticulated on its outer edge. The ventral fins are long, reaching beyond the anal fin base. They each have 5 rays and a flexible pointed spine with a cutaneous flange along the outer edge. The rays have similar though shorter flanges. The caudal fin is obliquely truncate, the lower edge the longer. The gill openings are lateral, located largely below the hind part of the eye. (Fowler, 1943.)

Hypcolpterus is very similar to *Chaetostoma* and *Ancistrus* but differs from them by the enlarged paired and anal fins, and the cutaneous flanges on the ventral and anal spines and rays. The broad naked snout border is similar to that of *Chaetostomus*.

The genus *Leptoancistrus* contains two species from small mountain streams in Colombia and from near Cana in the upper Tuyra basin in Panama. The body is broad and low anteriorly, nearly twice as wide as deep, and the caudal peduncle is posteriorly compressed. The head is broad and low, the snout granular to its margin and bearing short bristles. The interopercle is freely movable and bears spines that cannot be retracted beneath the opercle. The eye is small and the mouth wide, with the lips expanded. The mandibular ramus is almost equal to the interorbital width. The teeth are slender, bifid, and curved inward near the tips. The head and body are without prominent ridges or carinations, although the body scutes are spinulose. The ventral surfaces of the head and abdomen are naked, and the median line posteriorly is crossed by only a single scute.

Leptoancistrus canensis.

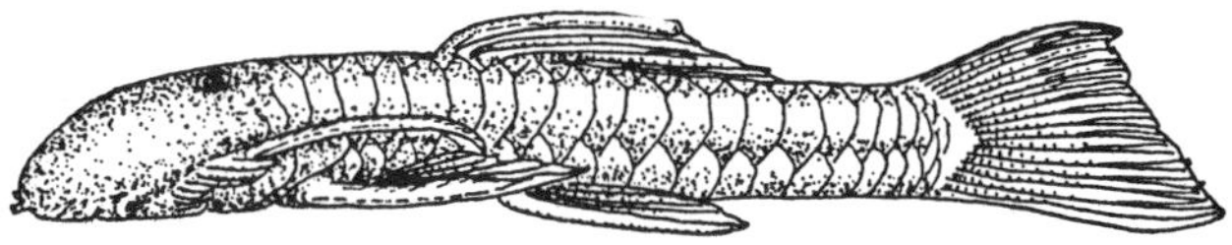

Three scutes are present in front of the dorsal, and the occipital is bordered by two scutes. The adipose and anal fins are absent. The dorsal fin has a spine and 8 rays. The ventral fins are only moderately developed, but the pectoral fins are large. The caudal fin is obliquely truncate, the lower rays longest, and the caudal peduncle is provided with a low keel above.

The genus *Lasiancistrus* contains about 24 species from northern South America, Panama, and Trinidad. The body is broad anteriorly while the caudal peduncle is posteriorly compressed. The head is low and wide, and the snout margin is granular and has bristles. The mandibular ramus is much shorter than the interorbital width, and the teeth are small and bifid. The preopercle is armed with strong spines and is more or less freely movable. The plates are not carinate and the head does not have prominent ridges. The scutes of the back, however, do have spinules. The lower surfaces of the head and abdomen are naked. The dorsal fin has a spine and 7 rays, the last of which is connected to the scute following it by an inconspicuous basal membrane. There is a well-developed adipose fin. *Lasiancistrus* was originally proposed as a subgenus of *Ancistrus* by Regan (1904).

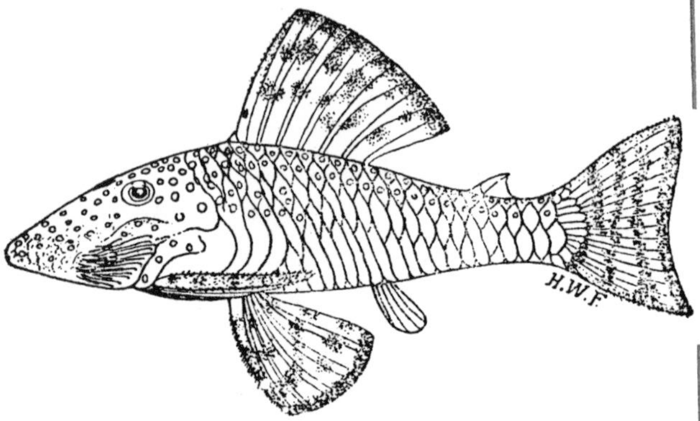

Lasiancistrus pictus. (From Fowler, 1954.)

L. nationi is said to be quite efficient in algae removal and control. In the aquarium substitutes may include wilted spinach, lettuce, or a flake food with a high algal content.

The genus *Neblinichthys* is a monotypic genus containing only *N. pilosus* from the Rio Baria system. It belongs to the tribe Ancistrini, subfamily Ancistrinae according to Isbrucker's definition (1980), but to subfamily Chaetostominae *sensu* Howes (1983), displaying a unique sexual dimorphism. The adult males possess a series of elongate, anteriorly directed bristles on the snout. It is said to be related to *Hemiancistrus* with similar opercle shape, articulation to the hyomandibula, evertible cheek spines and certain cheek plates. *Hemiancistrus* does not exhibit secondary sexual dimorphism. Female and juvenile *Neblinichthys* are somewhat similar to some species of *Lasiancistrus* in which nuptial males develop enlarged odontodes along the snout margin. These are, however, not reminiscent of the bristles in mature males of *Neblinichthys*.

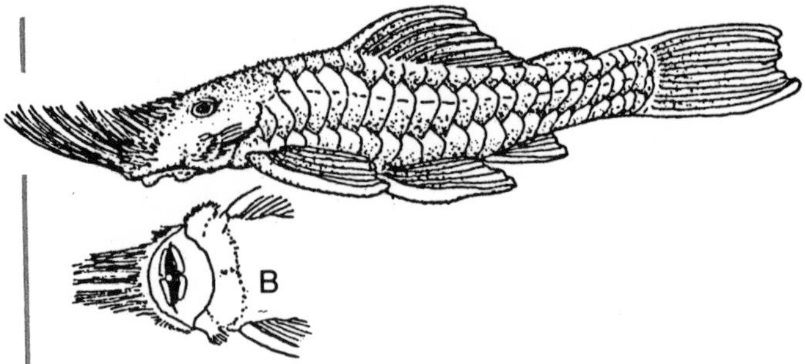

Neblinichthys pilosus; (b) ventral view of head.

The genus *Dolichancistrus* is a small genus of only three species from Colombia and Venezuela. The head and body are broad and depressed, with the caudal peduncle compressed posteriorly. There is a small naked area near the tip of the snout, and there are some very long interopercular odontodes that project well beyond the head in the adult male. The

Dolichancistrus pediculatus. (From Eigenmann, 1917.)

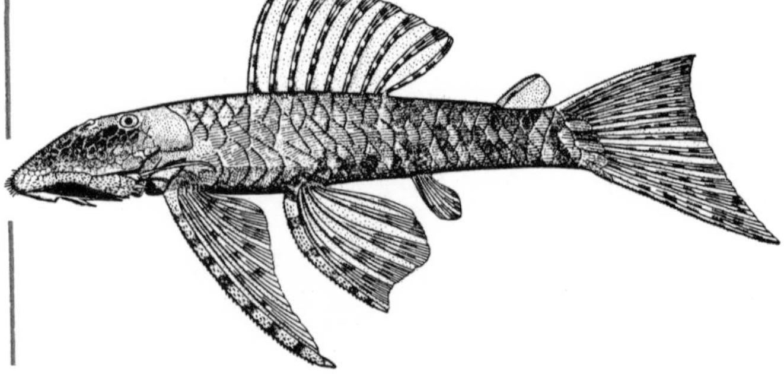

lips are papillate, with the posterior margin of the lower lip with lappets. The teeth on the jaws are bifid, slender, and quite numerous. About 24 or 25 scutes are in a lateral series, and 5 to 6 plates are present between the dorsal and the origin of the adipose fin; 4 plates precede the dorsal fin. The dorsal fin has a spine and about 8 or 9 rays. The anal fin is small, with a spine and 4 rays. A well-developed adipose fin is present. The pectoral fin rays of the males are greatly elongated, extending at times to the tips of the ventral fin rays; in juveniles and females they reach only to the middle third of the ventral fins.

No description of *Lipopterichthys* was available.

The genus *Cordylancistrus* is based on a single species (*C. torbesensis*) from the Orinoco system of Venezuela. It is greatly depressed anteriorly, with a very wide head whose width almost equals its length. The bristles on the head completely cover the snout. There are usually 24 plates in a lateral series and only 3 plates from the dorsal to the origin of the adipose fin; 3 plates precede the dorsal fin. The caudal peduncle is triangular in shape, the lower part flat with 11 plates present between the anal fin and the base of the caudal. The dorsal fin has a spine and 8 rays. The anal fin is small and has a weak spine that lacks prickles and 5 rays. There is a well-developed adipose fin. The pectoral fin spines of mature males have strong spines on the upper surface. Along the upper surface of each ray in fully mature males there is an elongate dermal flap, that of the ventral spine widest, a little greater than the diameter of the eye. The original specimens came from swiftly running water among boulders, rubble to coarse gravel (Schultz, 1944).

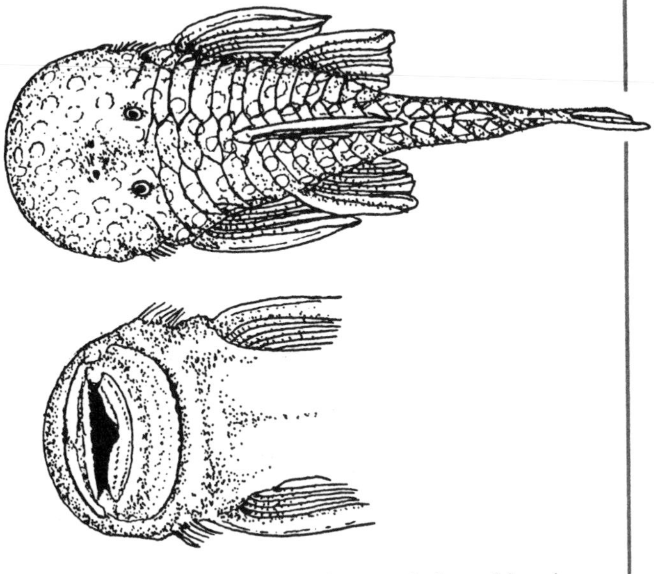

Cordylancistrus torbesensis; (b) ventral view of head. (After Schultz, 1944.)

The genus *Acanthicus* also contains a single species (*A. hystrix*), this one from the Amazon and possibly Guyana. The head is broad and depressed, nearly flat above, and the entire margin of the snout has numerous short spines or bristles. The temporal plates are greatly developed, extending posteriorly well beyond the clavicles; both supraoccipital and temporal plates have radiating spinate (short, conical spines) lines. The eyes are small and contained about 16 times in the head. The interopercle is armed with numerous slender erectile spines that are flattened and curved at the tips. The barbels are long, reaching almost to the gill opening. The lateral scutes, about 25 in number, are isolated and have strong spiny keels; the smallest scutes are located below the base of the dorsal fin, the largest on the dorsal and ventral surfaces of the tail. The scutes of the nuchal region are small, numerous, and isolated, while the lower surface of the head has isolated granules and the abdomen is completely covered with small granular scales. The region behind the dorsal fin is covered with some rather large scutes. The first 2 or 3 scutes of the lower lateral series are located below the temporal plate and in contact with it superiorly. The

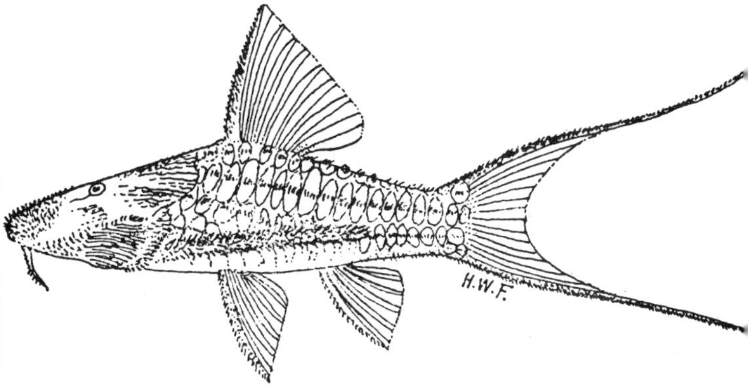

Acanthicus hystrix. (From Fowler, 1984.)

dorsal fin originates over the ventral fins and has a spine and 7 or 8 rays. The dorsal fin spine is about as long as the head, and its anterior surface is covered with short, stout spines. There is no adipose fin. The anal fin has a spine and 5 rays. The caudal fin is emarginate to lunate, with the outer rays produced into filaments that are longer than the dorsal fin spine. The pectoral fin spine is long and strong, extending to past the middle of the ventral fins, and its entire surface is covered with short, stout spines. The single species attains a length of about 45 cm.

The genus *Pseudacanthicus* contains about five species from Surinam, Guyana, and Brazil. It includes as a synonym the genus *Stoneiella*, a name familiar to many hobbyists. The body is relatively deep and the head, body, and fins are rough, covered with spinous dermal ossifications; the odontodes are well developed. The supraoccipital lacks a distinct ridge and the supraorbital ridges are only slightly raised. There is no smooth space behind the temporal plate. The snout is totally granular or covered by small bony plates until the edge. The interopercle is armed with some strong spines. The premaxillae are shorter than the dentaries and are very firmly united. The teeth of the premaxillaries form an undivided series, with fewer than 20 teeth on each intermaxillary arm (there are more teeth in the dentary arm). About 24 to 26 scutes are present in a lateral series, each scute with a median series of 2-6 strong spines, increasing in length to the last. The lower surfaces of the head and abdomen is naked. The dorsal fin has a spine and 8 rays, the last dorsal ray free (without a membranous connection to the back). The anal fin has a spine and 5 rays. An adipose fin is present. The ventral and anal spines are normal, without fleshy extensions at the posterior border.

There is difficulty in handling members of this genus as well as those of *Acanthicus*. Besides the possibility of the strong spines puncturing plastic bags while they are being shipped, their spiny nature makes them difficult to remove from nets when they are captured. *P. histrix*, for example, has long, brushlike spines extending outward from the anterior edge of the pectoral fin spine. *P. leopardus* (formerly *Stoneiella leoparda*) occasionally is available in the aquarium trade. It attains a length of about 14 cm, has a high dorsal fin, and is said to be suitable for a community tank.

The genus *Lithoxus* contains about five species from the Guianas, where they are apparently restricted to stony rivulets. Although they can reach a length of about 9 cm, they are usually smaller. The head and body are considerably to strongly depressed and broad anteriorly. The plates on the snout extend to the margins. The interopercles have a distinct bunch of variously developed spines that are curved near the tips. The mouth is small and surrounded by a nearly circular papillose oral disc. The premaxillaries are short, not con-

Pseudacanthicus histrix. (From Fowler, 1954.)

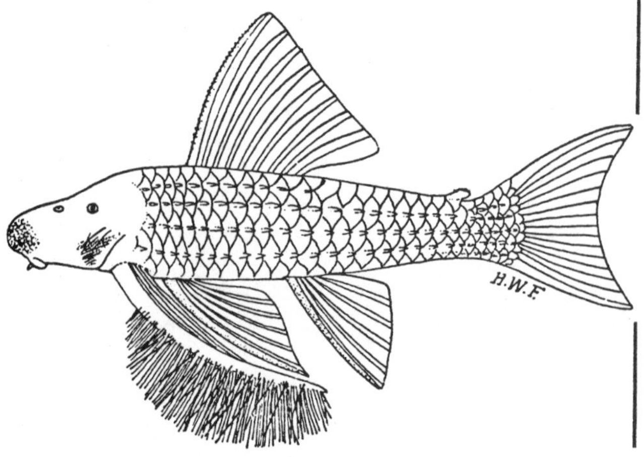

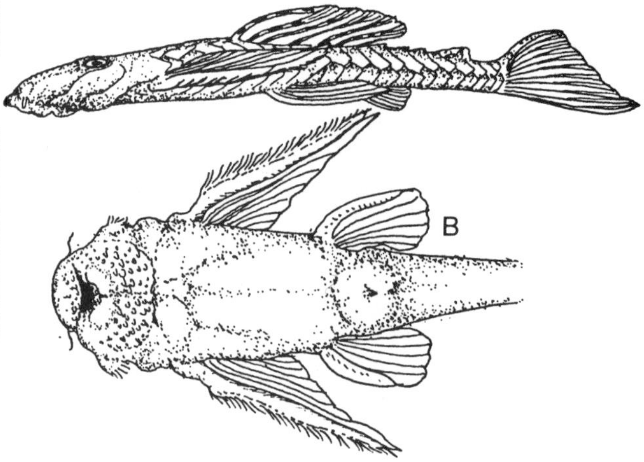

Lithoxus lithoides; (b) ventral view. (After Boeseman, 1982.)

nected, and each bears 2-5 slender, bilobed teeth in a transverse series. The mandibular ramus is considerably larger and each has 4-12 bilobed teeth that are often minute or hidden and also in a transverse series. All scutes are rather rough, having rows of spinules angled obliquely backward, forming about 5 to 10 longitudinal series on the body scutes. There are about 23 to 25 scutes in a lateral series, 10 to 11 posterior to the anal fin, usually 3 + 1 between the occipital and the dorsal fin, and 3 bordering the occipital. The ventral surface is naked but papillose. The dorsal fin has a spine and 7 rays. The anal fin has a spine and 5 rays. The pectoral fins of adult males often have long bristles on their upper and outer surfaces. All spines and rays are themselves spinulous. The adipose is present in some species, absent in others.

Isbrücker & Nijssen (1985) indicated that *Paralithoxus*, which was established as a subgenus of *Lithoxus* by Boeseman (1982), deserves full generic status. As such it would include the species here listed under *Lithoxus* other than *lithoides*.

The genus *Exastilithoxus* was erected for the single species *E. fimbriatus* by Isbrücker & Nijssen (1979). They found it unique among the Ancistrinae in having several filamentous

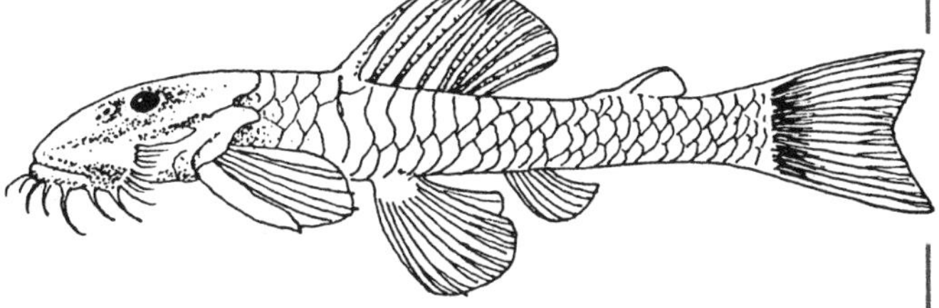

Exastilithoxus fimbriatus. (After Isbrücker & Nijssen, 1985.)

barbels in addition to the commisural barbels on the margins of the upper and lower lips. In 1985 these two authors added another species, *E. hoedemani*, to the genus.

The genus *Hemiancistrus* contains about 14 species, mostly from Colombia, Ecuador, and the Guianas, but also from Panama. The body is robust and the head is as broad as long or a little longer than broad. The supraoccipital may or may not have a median elevation or ridge, and the temporal plates may be carinate (in both cases these ridges become less

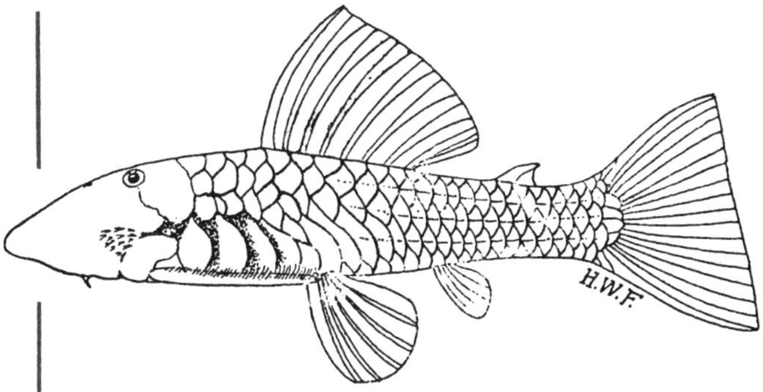

Hemiancistrus platycephalus. (From Fowler, 1954.)

obvious with age); the supraorbital edges are raised. The interopercle and opercle are not so freely movable as in some closely related genera, and the interopercle may be armed with a few to more than 30 spines, the longer ones usually curved at their tips. The mandibular ramus is included from 1.75 to more than 3 times in the interorbital width. The teeth are small, numerous, and bifid. The scutes are usually strongly spinulose and sometimes carinate (the keels also tend to decrease in size with age). There are about 24 to 27 scutes in a lateral series, with 6 to 8 between the dorsal fin and the adipose and 12 or 13 between the anal and caudal fins. The supraoccipital is bordered posteriorly by a single scute or a median scute and 2 lateral scutes. The lower surfaces of the head and abdomen are covered with granular scales. The dorsal fin has a spine and 7 rays and is not connected to the back by a membrane. The anal fin has a spine and 4 rays. There is a well-developed adipose fin present. The pectoral fin spine extends beyond the base of the ventral fins, sometimes as far as the middle of the ventral fin spine. The caudal fin is obliquely emarginate to truncate.

The genus *Megalancistrus* consists of only three species, two from Paraguay and a third from the Rio São Francisco in Brazil. The species are quite large, the largest being approximately 53 cm in length. The head is about 1.2 times as long as broad, and the snout is broad and rounded. The occipital and interorbital regions are flat and the supraorbital edges are not raised. The interopercle is armed with numerous slender spines that have curved tips. The eyes are small. The

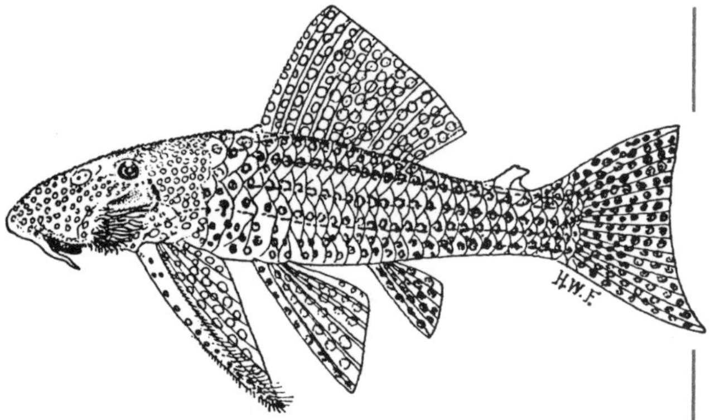

Pterygoplichthys aculeatus. (From Fowler, 1954.)

mandibular ramus is contained about 3.7 times in the interorbital width. The scutes are strongly spinulose and are all carinate. There are about 25 in a lateral series, 5 between the dorsal and adipose fins, and 11 between the anal and caudal fins. The supraoccipital is bordered posteriorly by a single scute. The lower surfaces of the head and abdomen are completely covered with small granular scales. The dorsal fin has a spine and 10 rays. The anal fin has a spine and 5 rays. The pectoral fin spine is long, extending to the middle of the ventral fins. The caudal fin is truncate. This genus is readily distinguishable by its large size and the high number of dorsal fin rays. For this reason members of this genus previously have been placed in the genus *Pterygoplichthys* (for example, by Fowler, 1954) but are separable from that genus on the basis of the subfamilial characters.

Peckoltia contains about 19 species from Brazil, Venezuela, Colombia, and Peru. They are generally of a smallish size but usually have a distinct and very attractive color pattern, making them very welcome by aquarists. The body is usually short and heavy anteriorly, the depth 4.3-6.7 in the length. The head is short and high, with a steep profile, and a little longer than broad. The snout narrows anteriorly, its margin granular except at the tip. The interopercle has a few to 15 or more erectile spines, while the opercle is fixed. The supraorbital margins are raised only slightly or not at all, and the supraoccipital has a low median ridge or none at all; the temporal plates are not carinate. The eyes are moderate, about 4.5 to 7.5 in the head. The mandibular ramus is 2.3 to 3.8 in the interorbital width; the teeth are small, slender, bifid, and numerous. The posterolateral body scutes are distinctly rugose but usually are not carinate. There are about 25 to 27 in a lateral series, 7 to 8 between the dorsal and adipose fins, and 12 to 13 between the anal and caudal fins. The supraoccipital has a median scute and one on each side. The lower surfaces of the head and abdomen are completely covered with small granular scales (these areas may be naked in juveniles except for a granular strip between the pectoral fins). The dorsal fin has a spine and 7 rays, the last not attached to the back by a membrane. A well-

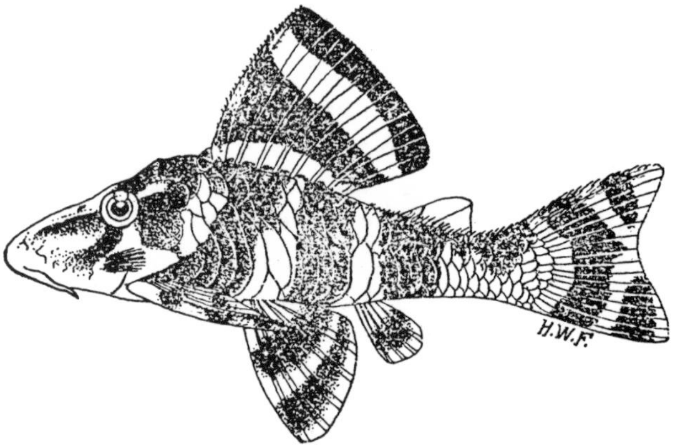

Peckoltia vittatus. (From Fowler, 1954.)

developed adipose fin is present. The anal fin has a spine and 4 (sometimes 5?) rays. The pectoral spine is long, reaching to the middle of the ventral fin. The caudal fin is obliquely truncate or semilunar in shape.

Although the species of *Peckoltia* have commonly been included within the genus *Hemiancistrus*, Isbrücker (1980) believes that they merit generic status. They are small and colorful species that aquarists have dubbed clown plecos. The most commonly imported species (if the identification is correct) is *P. vittata*. It makes an ideal community tank fish although it is territorial and does become aggressive toward its own kind. Other fishes, even smaller ones, are generally left alone. They do well in water that is neutral to slightly acid and soft to medium hard with a temperature of 21° to 25°C. The light can be medium to strong as long as there are sufficient hiding places. Algae must constitute a large portion of the diet. Since these are fishes from running water, good aeration and filtration are necessary.

The genus *Parancistrus* includes about half a dozen species from the Amazon system. The body is fairly stocky, its depth 4.5 to 5 in its length. The head, as broad as or broader than long, is granular on the sides (without bristles), and the rounded to obtuse snout has its sides also granular but with a broad naked area at the tip. The supraorbital edges are not to only slightly raised, and the supraoccipital is flat; the temporal plates are not carinate. The interoperculum has slender spines (sometimes numerous) with hooked tips that can be everted and completely retracted beneath the operculum. The eyes are moderately small, being contained 6 to 8 times in the head length. The mandibular ramus is contained 1.75 to 3.75 times in the interorbital width; the teeth are small, slender, and bicuspid. The scutes are spinulose but not carinate, and there are 22 to 24 in a longitudinal series.

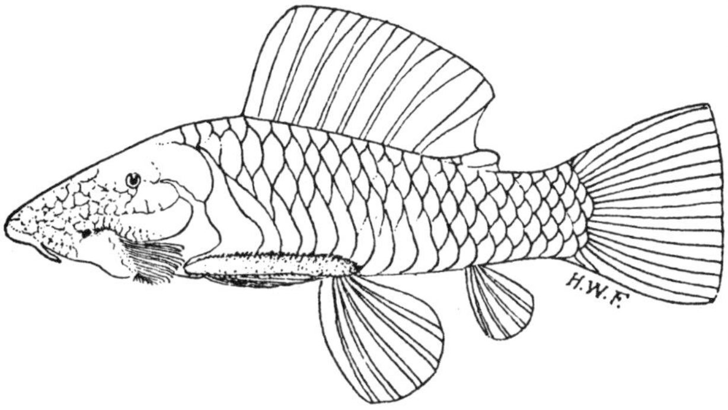

Parancistrus aurantiacus. (From Fowler, 1954.)

There are 5 to 6 scutes between the dorsal and adipose fins and 9 to 13 scutes between the anal and caudal fins. The supraoccipital is bordered posteriorly by a single scute or by a single median scute and one on each side. The lower surfaces of the head and abdomen are naked. The dorsal fin has a spine and 7 rays, the last ray being connected by a well-developed membrane either to the 3 or 4 scutes of the back following it or to the spine of the adipose fin. The anal fin has a spine and 4 rays and the stout pectoral fin spine extends to the base of the ventral fins (usually juveniles) or to the middle of that fin (usually adults). The caudal fin is obliquely truncate or obliquely or weakly marginate.

The genus *Chaetostoma* is a relatively large genus with about 40 species from Brazil, Ecuador, Peru, Colombia, Venezuela, and Panama. The highest concentration of species seems to be in Colombia and Venezuela. They are commonly found in mountain streams with swiftly running water over gravel and rubble bottoms to altitudes as high as 3,500 meters. The body is generally short and stocky, its depth 4.5 to 6 in its total length. The head is approximately as broad as long, perhaps a bit broader in some species. The interopercle and opercle are separately movable. The eye size varies with species, being anywhere from 5 to 12 times in the head length. At least 25% of the anterior dorsal surface of the snout is naked and without bristles, but the interopercle may have from one to 10-15 short spines depending upon the species. The mandibular ramus is approximately equal to, a little bit more, or a little bit less than the interorbital width (but always less than 1.5 times), and there are numerous (100 or more on each ramus) bifid teeth. There are 23 to 26 scutes in a lateral series, 4-8 between the dorsal and adipose fins, and 9-13 between the anal and caudal fins. The lower surfaces of the head and abdomen are naked. The dorsal fin has a spine and 7 or 8 (occasionally 9) rays. The anal fin has a spine and 3-5 (rarely 2) rays. The pectoral fin spine is strong and extends as far as the middle of the ventral fins in some species. The adipose fin is generally well developed, but in at least one species it can be weak or even absent and may be pre-

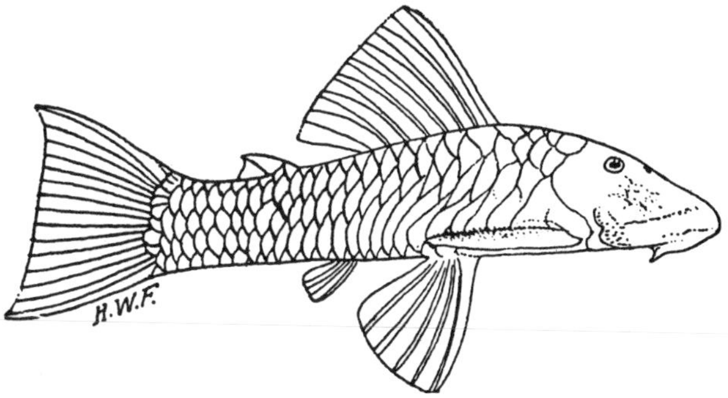

Chaetostoma brevis. (From Fowler, 1954.)

ceded or replaced by three or four scutes forming a keel. The caudal fin is slightly to obliquely emarginate to deeply concave.

The genus *Panaque* consists of about half a dozen species from northern South America. The body is generally short and heavy, its depth 3.5 to 5 in the total length. The head is a little bit longer than broad, the profile before the eyes strongly sloping. The snout narrows anteriorly, its anterior dorsal surface bony with no naked area at the tip. The supraoccipital is nearly flat or has a median ridge; the temporal plates are obscurely carinate or not carinate at all. The eye is contained from 5 to 9 times in the length of the head, and the supraorbital is moderately raised to quite elevated. The interopercle and opercle are separately movable, and the interopercle is provided with graduated, elongate, evertible spines (except in the young), some of which have hooked tips. The mandibular ramus is contained more than 1.75 times in the interorbital width (but usually less than 5 times); about 4 to 9 spoon-shaped teeth are on the ramus of each jaw. The scutes are spinulose and may be carinate or not. There are 24 to 27 scutes in a lateral series, 5 to 8 between the dorsal and adipose fins, and 12 to 15 between the anal and caudal fins. The lower surfaces of the head and abdomen are covered with rough platelets (except in the young). The supraoccipital is entirely bordered posteriorly by a single scute or there is one posterior scute and one on each side. The dorsal fin has a spine and 7 rays, the anal a spine and 4 rays. The pectoral fin spine is long (extending beyond the origin of the ventral fins), heavy, and with numerous spines on its dorsal surface posteriorly. The caudal fin is obliquely truncate or emarginate to strongly emarginate.

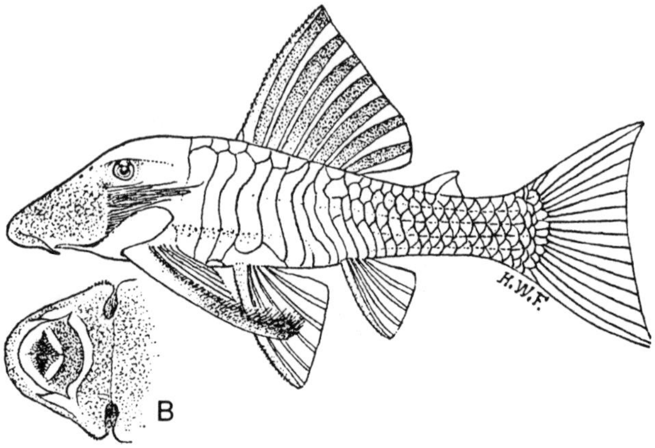

Panaque cochliodon; (b) ventral view of head. (From Fowler, 1954.)

Two species of *Panaque* are currently imported for the aquarium trade often enough to have been given common names. The most popular one is the Royal Panaque (sometimes also called the Emperor Pleco), *P. nigrolineatus*. The second one is the Blue-eyed Pleco, *P. suttoni*. The Royal Panaque attains a length of about 30 cm or more. When small it is quite attractive, with a pattern of spots and lines that changes to all lines, but with growth the pattern fades into a uniform gray color. The tank should be clean, well aerated, and well filtered, particularly when introducing new individuals to captivity. They seem to be somewhat sensitive to excessive nitrates. The temperature should be around 23° to 26°C, and a slightly acid pH is preferred. Feeding is no problem as the Royal Panaque eats almost anything, including flake food, but its diet should contain a high vegetable content; supplements of spinach, lettuce, peas, and other greens are recommended. Even the flake food should be high in greens. It is best to feed this shy fish in a dim light. The Royal Panaque has a good reputation for algae control. It also has a reputation for being territorial, especially with members of its own kind. They use their opercular spines and pectoral fin spines to show their aggressiveness, and the resulting battles may prove quite destructive to the tank decor. Plants are uprooted, driftwood is displaced, and the sand is often piled up in one corner. Even so, by itself it can be considered a reasonable inhabitant for a community tank of larger fishes.

The Blue-eyed Pleco has, as its name implies, blue eyes. Otherwise it is not very colorful. Like its cousin, it needs a large amount of vegetable matter in its diet, but both species will accept tubificid worms, bloodworms, earthworms, non-fatty beef heart, and frozen brine shrimp. Also like the Royal Panaque, it can be placed in a community tank with larger fishes. It is quite territorial with members of its own species, however, with resulting tank destruction as described above. Although quite disease resistant, there was one report of a case of ich on a Blue-eyed Pleco. The cure was to raise the temperature to 30°C in an isolation tank provided with only a flowerpot. The water was changed in an amount equal to 20% every other day, and a few teaspoons of non-iodized salt were added. This apparently did the trick.

The genus *Ancistrus* is a moderately large genus of just over 50 species from South America and Panama; some species are found at fairly high altitudes. The body is broad and depressed, approximately 5 to 6 times as long as deep. The depressed head is about as broad as long or a little bit longer than broad and usually twice as long as deep. The broad snout has a bare border (without plates), narrow in the female and broader in the male, and may be provided with a variable number of cutaneous tentacles, small in some females and quite large and bifurcate in some males. The head is without crests. The eye is variable, contained from 5 to 10 times in the head length depending upon the species. The articulation of the interopercle and opercle is movable, the interopercle possessing from 8-16 spines (sometimes with hooked tips) that can be everted. The mandibular ramus is contained 2.0 to 3.5 times in the interorbital width; the teeth are small, numerous, and bifid. The scutes are spinulose but not carinate. There are 23 to 26 scutes in a lateral series, 5

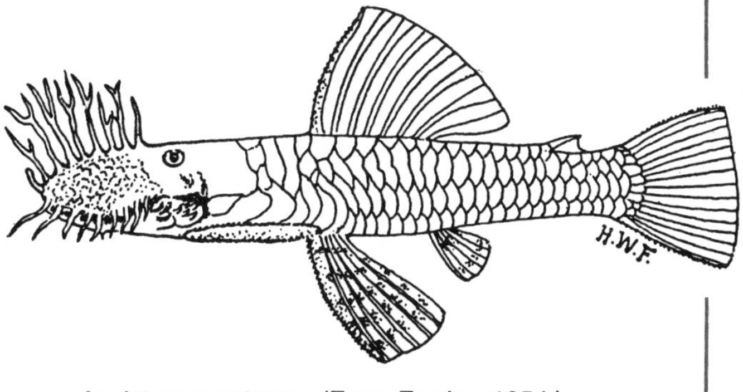

Ancistrus montanus. (From Fowler, 1954.)

to 7 between the dorsal and adipose fins, and 10 to 13 between the anal and caudal fins. The supraoccipital is bordered posteriorly by 1 or 2 median scutes and 1 on each side. The lower surfaces of the head and abdomen are naked. The dorsal fin has a spine and 7 to 9 rays. The anal fin has a spine and 3 or 4 rays. The pectoral fin spine is relatively short, usually barely reaching the origin of the ventral fins. The caudal fin is obliquely truncate.

Members of the genus *Ancistrus* are generally not very large, attaining lengths of only up to about 15 cm. They inhabit fresh to brackish waters where they are bottom-living, generally clinging to rocks, logs, or other objects by their sucker mouths. They are shy fishes hiding in caves or other secluded spots much of the time, but eventually they will be seen out in the open during the day or night if there are a sufficient number of hiding places to which they can scoot off if frightened. They are normally harmless, although some displaying or mild combats can be seen between males because of territoriality or if one of them is brooding eggs or fry. During these fights the interopercular and pectoral fin spines are used both for attack and defense. Although success has been achieved with tanks as small as 38 liters, a 76-liter tank or larger is recommended. The water chemistry is not critical, but neutral to slightly alkaline and slightly hard water seems to suit many species better than soft, acid water. In any event, partial water changes on a regular basis are generally necessary. These not only help keep the parents in a healthy state (and may even initiate spawning), but are usually necessary to ensure a high survival of fry in the rearing tank. A temperature range of 20° to 27°C is sufficient (spawning has been reported even at the lower end of this range for some species). Gravel is optional; some aquarists recommended dark gravel, but this is usually for the very shy or nocturnal species where dark, secluded conditions are needed. Plants are also optional. They are not eaten but are scoured by the suckermouths for anything that might be growing on them, especially algae. Driftwood or other soft wood is highly recommended as these fishes will rasp away at the wood, ingesting the cellulose; the lignin is essential in aiding the digestion. Rockwork forming caves is also essential, everything being arranged to provide many hiding places.

Like many other suckermouth catfishes, *Ancistrus* species are efficient algae-eaters. Un-

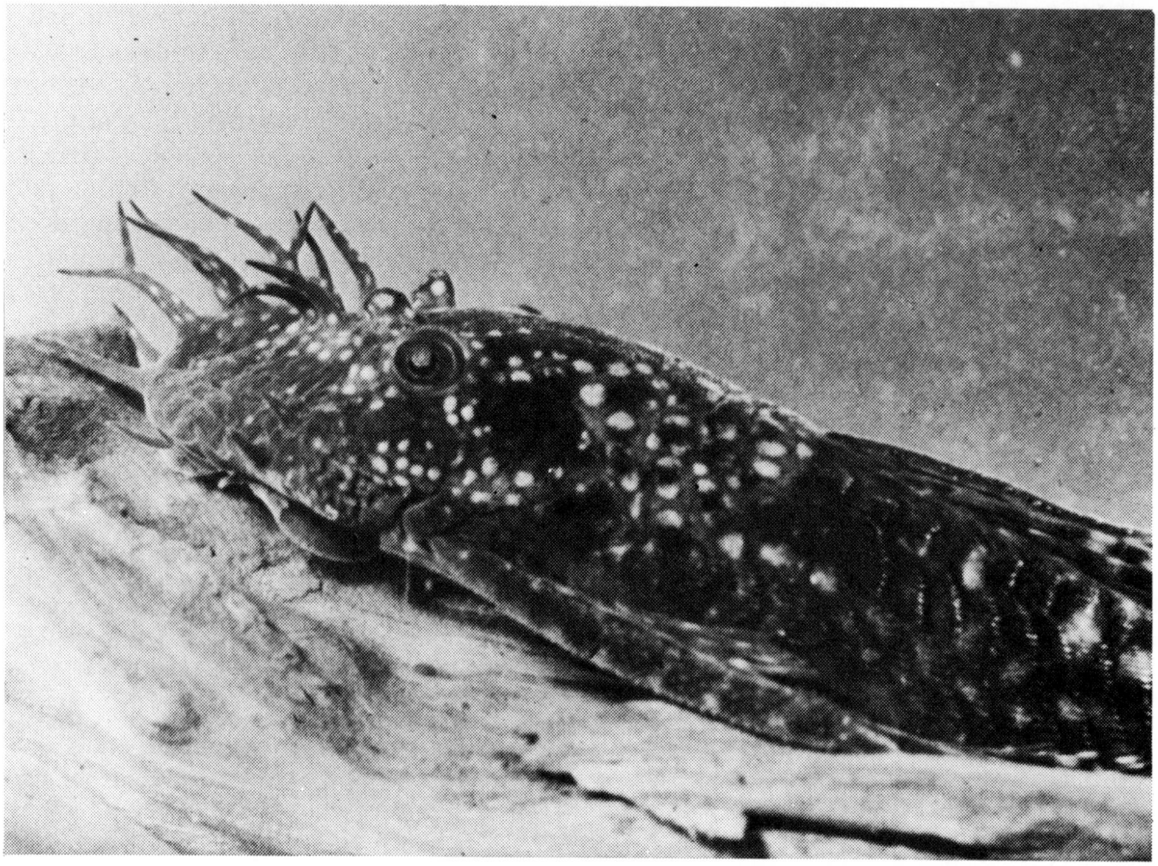

Species of *Ancistrus* are readily recognized by the often branched bristles on their snout. Although both sexes may bear them they are larger and more prevalent in the males. Photo by Dr. Herbert R. Axelrod.

fortunately, they are so good that they often clean up a tank overgrown with algae in a matter of a couple of days, and the aquarist then must provide a diet with a high proportion of vegetable matter. Boiled lettuce leaves, spinach, cabbage, and kale are usually substituted for the algae, as are peas, green beans, and even zucchini. Rounding out the diet can be various types of worms, mosquito larvae, and chironomid larvae.

The *Ancistrus* species are usually distinguished by aquarists from the other members of the family by being referred to as bristle-nosed catfishes or bushy-faced catfishes (or even bristle-nosed plecos) because of their characteristic of possessing to varying degrees tentacles on their snouts. Although these might be present in both sexes, they are commonly more developed in the males, often growing quite large and branching one or more times. They generally become noticeable on individuals that have reached a length of 4 to 6 cm. In some females they develop into a row of small fleshy tentacles on the margin of the snout and another row between the eyes; in the males they grow larger, with two rows between the eyes forming into a "Y". Other species of course vary, some having very small tentacles that may even be absent in the females. In still others the tentacles may grow larger during the spawning season and decrease in size again after the season is over. The use of such tentacles is theorized by some to have to do with sensing the speed and direction of the currents and perhaps even detecting odors. As spawning approaches, the male will seek out a dark corner of the tank, such as under a piece of driftwood, in a rock cave, under a flowerpot, or in a bamboo tube, or will even hollow out a piece of wood by using its teeth and pectoral spines. This he guards against intruders, especially if they happen to be males of his own species. Courtship may last a few hours or several days as the male becomes more active and starts to clean the site he has chosen with his mouth. In some species the male is said to chase the female around the tank for several hours until she finally follows him back to his home base. One report has the male inverting himself so that his tail is just out of the water, and he then vigorously slaps the surface with it, causing a great deal of noise and turbulance. (This also occurs when the fish is hungry [Nijssen, pers. comm.] and may not be sexual in nature.) As the female approaches he stops, but if she departs he resumes this activity, trying to attract her back again. In deeper water he is said to attach himself to the spawning site and vibrate his body.

Once the female remains there is a great deal of contact between the two. Incidentally, the female can be checked in the aquarium to see if she is ready to spawn by waiting until she attaches herself to one of the glass sides of the tank and then examing her abdomen (with a flashlight if necessary), for the yellowish eggs are clearly visible through the abdominal wall when fully developed. The male occasionally arches his body over that of the female. If she leaves the site the male will often follow her a short distance trying to entice her back. Both spawners will take food during the courtship. When the female decides to lay the eggs in the nest the male constantly prods her with his snout. Anywhere from 50 to 200 eggs will be deposited on the ceiling, sides, and even the bottom of a cave or piece of tubing. The eggs, about 2 to 3 mm in diameter, are usually yellowish white to yellowish orange in color and laid in a clump.

The female leaves (or is forcibly evicted)

A male *Ancistrus* sp. guarding his eggs. Normally these species will spawn in caves or other sheltered locations. Photo by Dr. W. Foersch.

and generally takes no more interest in eggs or fry. The male, on the other hand, stands guard over the eggs and eventually the fry, chasing off any potential enemies. If another male intrudes there is a vigorous fight, the two standing parallel to one another, head to tail, while the interopercular area (with all the spines) is everted. The two males may circle each other, directing their lightning speed attacks at the head of the opponent. The dorsal and pectoral fins are held erect. The thrashing about may uproot some plants and cause other mayhem in the aquarium, but when the intruder withdraws all returns to a semblance of normal. For about five to ten days the male will stand guard using his fins and mouth to clean and aerate the eggs. In some cases the male does not eat during this period, but in others he will dash out for a bit of food and return quickly to his chores. Eventually the eggs hatch, a process that might last for two to six hours, and the fry emerge with large yellow yolk sacs. Although natural brooding is relatively safe, if the male is frightened he may dash about and dislodge the sticky eggs. Chances are good that if they fall on the gravel at the bottom of the tank they will not survive. The aquarist can hatch them artificially by means of a gentle air stream and some methylene blue. The male remains at the site even after hatching and may guard the fry for another week to ten days. The empty eggshells may be pushed from the nest.

The fry usually drop to the bottom of the nest at first, and the male will fend off any intruders, even covering the young catfish with his body and fins if necessary. In from two to four days the yolk sac has been absorbed and the fry start moving about looking for food. They can cling to any surface with their sucker mouths and are hard to remove from the tank because of this. The body is generally a mottled grayish green or tan, and some are darker than the others. The fry are relatively easy to raise. Some suggest preparing a green water tank with a heavy coating of algae for the young fry as soon as eggs are spotted. Others give a wide variety of foods with a proportionately high vegetable content. It has been reported that meatier foods, if fed in high concentrations, will cause constipation and possibly death. Add only enough food so that the fry can consume it in about a half hour. This helps avoid pollution of the tank. The fry must also be fed often, perhaps five times a day, for best results. Driftwood should be available. In about six weeks the fry are similar to the parents. Adulthood can be attained in about a year's time, with the sexes becoming distinguishable (by the growth of the snout appendages) after eight to ten months.

The number of eggs produced depends upon the age, size, and condition of the female, and may range from about a dozen to somewhat over 200. The female may be ready to spawn again in five to six weeks. In the wild the male is said to spawn with several females over a short period of time.

Ancistrus cirrhosus is a moderate size species of the genus attaining a length of about 14 cm. It inhabits running waters (sometimes brackish water rivers) of the eastern Amazon basin, the Guianas, Paraguay, and Trinidad. It therefore requires clean water with good aeration and rather frequent water changes. It often remains hidden during the day and comes out looking for food at night. The female is said to have a slightly more pointed head and smaller tentacles than the male. This species is a good algae-eater, but wood must also be available. The eggs are creamy orange, 1.5-2.0 mm in diameter, and laid in clusters. They hatch in about a week. Bristles started to appear in eight months, and spawning was accomplished in a year. Eventually 50 to 60 eggs were obtained.

Ancistrus triradiatus is called the Branched Bristle-nose Catfish as the male has about a dozen large snout appendages that branch more than once; those of the female are very small and do not branch. Spawning was accomplished with a pair about a year and a half old, the male being 10 cm at the time and the female slightly smaller. A rather small 38-liter tank was used; it was planted and provided with driftwood and rock caves. The pH was neutral to slightly alkaline. One third of the water was changed weekly, the lighting was subdued, and the temperature was 21° to 25°C. A high proportion vegetable diet was provided. The female soon became quite rounded as she filled up with eggs. The eggs were yellowish to orange and hatched in four to seven days as the male guarded. The fry were about 6 mm long and varied between 50 and 150 in number. They attained their natural color in about a week to ten days and started wandering about. In two months they were about 50 to 60 mm. At this time the parents are ready to spawn again.

Ancistrus multispinis is a fairly hardy species and, like the others, a good algae-eater. Foods accepted readily include the usual lettuce and spinach leaves, but other vegetable matter may be offered such as peas, beans, and dandelion leaves. Trout pellets may also be fed. Meaty foods taken include tubificid worms, earthworms, beef heart, and frozen brine shrimp. For spawning, live foods and vegetable matter are recommended. The tank should be set up with heavy plant growth (*Echinodorus* has been suggested), driftwood, and rocks forming many hiding places and leaving the bottom area dimly lit. The water chemistry is not too important, for spawning has been achieved with pH readings from 6.0 to 7.5. Water changes about every two weeks are highly recommended. The temperature should be between 22° and 26°C.

The male will usually select a secluded spot and chase other fishes away, even females of his own species. However, upon onset of the breeding season this will change. Females allowed to approach will usually inspect the spawning site carefully, commonly moving about the outside a while before entering the cave or hole that the male has selected. Actual spawning occurs mostly in the early hours of the morning (one report indicated the barometric pressure was low) when the female enters the nest and deposits a cluster of eggs in a dark spot (most likely on the ceiling). The male follows to fertilize them, and the act is repeated again and again until the female is depleted. In some instances another female will also spawn in the nest. One report had the male spawning with several females. The female usually will leave after spawning. The male stands guard over the eggs, although there has been at least one case in which the male completely ignored the eggs and they had to be hatched by artificial means. The male will periodically inspect the eggs, removing infertile ones. He will fan them with his pectoral fins and guard them from all intruders.

Clutches vary between 50 and 100 large (about 3 mm) yellowish eggs that adhere to the walls and roof of the cave. They hatch in four to six days, the newly born fry being about 6 to 9 mm in length and sporting a large yellow yolk sac. One report said the fry were milky white, another that they were black. This possibly means that two different species were involved as misidentifications are not unusual in this family. In most cases it does not matter as the closely related species that are available will spawn in a very similar manner. If an aquarist uses a little common sense he can adjust to any differences noted between the different species. In a few days the yolk sac is absorbed and the fry must be fed food of appropriate size. In a week they are starting to wander about the tank, and in less than two weeks they look like miniature adults. Growth is rapid, and many attain a length of 3 cm in a couple of months when well fed. As an added note of interest, S. Frank said that these fish secrete substances that would be noxious to certain species of characoids.

The most commonly available species of *Ancistrus* is called *A. dolichopterus* (commonly referred to as *Xenocara dolichoptera*). It is often sold as a pleco, but even in young fish the snout bristles can be seen. It matures at about 8 to 10 cm in captivity but may grow to 13 cm. It does well under the general conditions outlined above. Since it does occur in brackish water in some areas, hard water with a little bit of salt added will not harm it. It is quite shy in a community tank, appearing only when the lights are low or if it becomes very hungry. It is very peaceful and highly resistant to disease, characteristics that have increased its popularity considerably. Two males of this species will fight with each other, especially over a preferred female. The upper portions of the body are dark with a bluish cast and many white spots; the undersides are sooty with fewer light spots. Under bright light or other adverse conditions the colors may fade so that the spots are not easily discernible. The fins are dark, with white spots and pale margins (in the young the colors are more intense and the spots and fin edges are more brilliant white). The snout bristles of the male are heavier and larger than those of the female and are often forked; those of the female are in a single row on the edge of the snout (which is more pointed than that of the male), are shorter, thinner, and darker in color. Spawning has been accomplished on a regular basis with few problems. Although selected pairs will spawn it is best if they can be allowed to pair naturally and then transferred to a separate spawning tank. Males tend to be territorial and aggressive toward one another when spawning time approaches.

Like the other species, *A. dolichopterus* is a secretive cave-spawner. If no appropriate site is available, the male may take it upon himself to construct one by fanning out the sand from under a piece of slate or driftwood until a cave is formed; hollow tubes are also used. The male cleans the nest site and then starts to chase females about the tank, apparently trying to drive one back to the nest. When one obliges she may do her own cleaning, chasing out any other fishes and rearranging any sand in the vicinity. The pair may enter the cave at night and spawn early the next morning, after which the female leaves and the male starts his vigil. The eggs are 2-3 mm in diameter, pale yellowish to bright orange (possibly more than one species involved ?) in color, and adhesive. Anywhere from 20 to 120 eggs may be deposited, although older, well-conditioned females may lay up to 200 eggs on a good day. The fry hatch out in four to seven days depending upon the temperature and have absorbed the yolk sac and become free-swimming after another three or four days. During this time the male will remain on guard and may or may not leave to grab a bite of food. Early foods that can be offered the fry include algae-covered lettuce leaves, microworms, baby brine shrimp, and finely ground flake food, perhaps mixed with vegetable-based baby food. Later chopped tubifex and whiteworms can be fed along with the vegetable matter. The fry remain hidden and attach themselves to the ceiling and walls of the cave at first but eventually start moving about. They grow fast and at a month are 12 to 13 mm long; by ten weeks they have grown to 2.5 to 3 cm; and at a year and a half they may be 7 cm in length (females) to 8 cm (males). The fry need very clean water, necessitating frequent water changes. The catfish may spawn after about two years, when they are about 8 cm in length. The original spawners may give a repeat performance after two and a half to three weeks. They may do this for several months straight, then rest for six months or so.

The subfamily Hypoptopomatinae consists of about a half dozen genera containing some 56 species, most of which are included in *Parotocinclus*, *Otocinclus*, and *Hypoptopoma*. *Hypoptopoma*, the most distinctive genus of the subfamily, is distributed in the Orinoco, Amazon, and Paraguay basins. The other genera (except *Otocinclus*) are more or less confined to southeastern Brazil. All of the species are relatively small (less than 15 cm) and occur mostly in the smaller streams. The metapterygoid is large and articulates both with the skull and with the palatine, and the supracleithral plate is followed directly (posteroventrally) by the exposed cleithrum. The cleithra and hypocoracoids interlock on the midventral line and are exposed where they cross the chest. The interopercular area is not evertible. The body armor is unusually developed with enlarged plates normally encasing the snout and chest along with the rest of the body. There are usually 3 scutes between the supraoccipital plate and predorsal plate (which is small or even absent). The teeth are bifid and arranged in a single series in each jaw; the pharyngeal teeth are minute and villiform.

The anal fin has a spine and 5 rays and originates approximately under the last depressed dorsal fin ray; there is a median plate and one or more pairs of lateral plates between the anal fin and the anus. The pectoral fin has a spine and 5 or 6 rays, and the ventral fin has a spine and 5 rays. The gill rakers resemble the gill filaments in structure, the intestine is short and has relatively few coils, and the swim bladder is without a posterior division (after Gosline, 1947).

The genus *Hypoptopoma* is distinguishable from the other genera of the subfamily by having the posttemporals imperforate. Isbrücker (1980) even separated the subfamily into two tribes, the Hypoptopomatini, with only the genus *Hypoptopoma*, and Otocinclini, which includes the other genera. Of the Otocinclini, *Parotocinclus* is distinguishable from *Otocinclus* and *Otothyris* by its having an adipose fin and the abdomen covered by large plates. *Otothyris* and *Otocinclus* do not possess an adipose fin, and the abdomen may be naked, covered with a number of small plates, or covered by 3 series of plates. These two genera can be distinguished (according to Myers, 1927) by *Otothyris* having the cranium sculptured "in a most remarkable manner," and lacking the "projecting tongue of the iris to the center of the pupil." Three other genera, *Pseudotocinclus, Schizolecis,* and *Pseudotothyris* are distinguishable by having the snout tip covered by small platelets as opposed to fewer, larger plates. Finally, *Microlepidogaster* is very close to *Otocinclus* but has numerous platelets irregularly disposed over the abdomen, whereas in *Otocinclus* there are three series of plates. The eight genera can be distinguished by the following key.

1a. Posttemporals imperforate (Hypoptopomatini) .... *Hypoptopoma*
1b. Posttemporals not imperforate (Otocinclini) 2
2a. Adipose fin present .... *Parotocinclus*
2b. Adipose fin absent 3
3a. Snout tip covered with small platelets. 4
3b. Snout tip covered by larger plates 6
4a. Abdomen covered with numerous platelets .... *Pseudotocinclus*
4b. Abdomen naked or with scattered platelets 5
5a. Two preorbital plates; orbit almost superior .... *Schizolecis*
5b. One preorbital plate; orbit almost lateral .... *Pseudotothyris*
6a. Head rugose and much keeled; abdomen naked except for rudimentary small platelets .... *Otothyris*
6b. Head smooth, with only medial keel; abdomen covered with plates or platelets 7
7a. Three series of plates on abdomen .... *Otocinclus*
7b. Numerous platelets irregularly disposed on abdomen .... *Microlepidogaster*

The genus *Pseudotocinclus* contains a single species, *P. tietensis,* from the Upper Rio Tietê, São Paulo State. It has a moderately long, low body and a depressed head. The tip

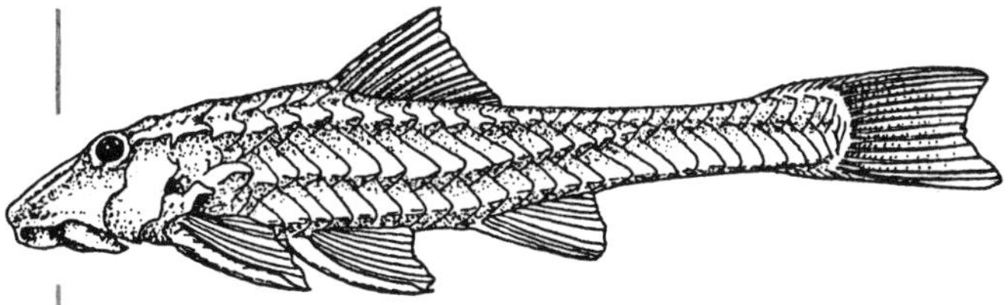

Pseudotocinclus tietensis.

of the snout is formed by small platelets which sometimes leave relatively large naked areas. The orbit is almost superior and there are two preorbital plates. The abdomen is entirely covered with numerous platelets, without the lateral series of wide plates between the scapular bridge and the pelvic fin. There are 29-32 perforated plates on the lateral line. The adipose fin is absent. The swin bladder capsule is well developed. Males have a urogenital papilla. (Britski & Garavello, 1984.)

The genus *Schizolecis* is also monotypic, the single species, *S. guntheri*, being found in the coastal rivers of southeastern Brazil. It has a relatively short, depressed body. The head is depressed, its snout tip formed by a series of small platelets bearing small spines, similar to those of the head. The orbit is almost supe-

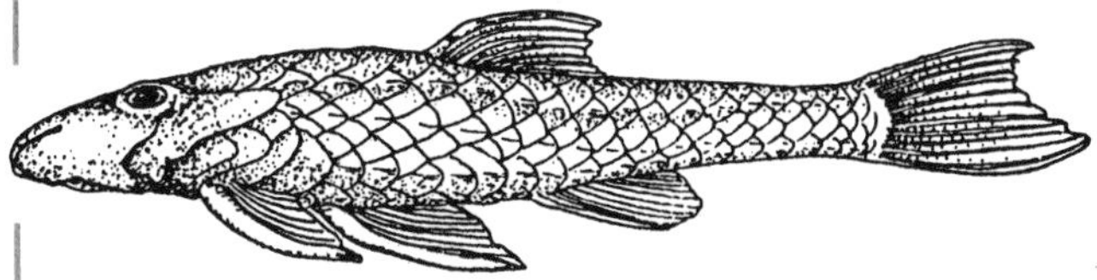

Schizolecis guntheri.

rior, and there are two preorbital plates. The abdomen is naked except for a few scattered platelets. There are 23 to 26 perforated plates along the lateral line. There is no adipose fin. The swim bladder is well developed. Males have a urogenital papilla. (Britski & Garavello, 1984.)

The genus *Pseudotothyris* contains two species, *P. obtusa* from coastal rivers from São Paulo to Santa Catarina States, and *P. janeirensis* from Rio de Janeiro State. The body is relatively short. The tip of the snout is formed by small platelets that bear small spines on the surface smaller than those of the head. The orbit is almost lateral, and there is

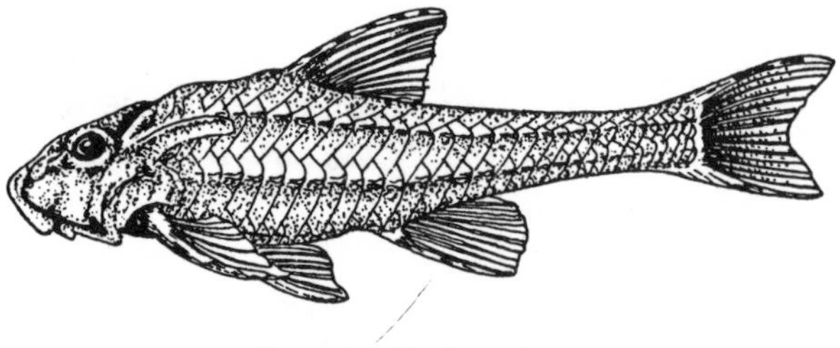

Pseudotothyris obtusa.

a single preorbital plate. The abdomen is naked or partially covered with small and scattered plates. There are 22 to 24 perforated plates on the lateral line. There is no adipose fin. The swim bladder capsule is usually well developed. Males have urogenital papillae. (Britski & Garavello, 1984.)

Pseudotocinclus, *Schizolecis*, and *Pseudothyris* have the tip of the snout formed by small platelets, covered by weak spines, identical to those on the head. The other genera of the subfamily have the tip of the snout covered by large plates bearing strong, recurved spines (Britski & Garavalla, 1984). *Pseudotocinclus* and *Schizolecis* have the orbit almost superior and two preorbital plates; *Pseudotothyris* has the orbit almost lateral and a single preorbital plate. *Pseudotocinclus* has the abdomen entirely covered with numerous platelets and 29 to 32 perforated plates on the lateral line; *Schizolecis* has a naked abdomen except for a few scattered platelets and 23 to 26 perforated plates on the lateral line.

The genus *Parotocinclus* contains 14 species distributed in coastal streams from Santa Catarina to Ceara, and in the Rio Solimões and the Coppename River, Surinam, but they are missing from the São Francisco, Jequitinhonha, Mucuri, and other large rivers flowing into the Atlantic Ocean, as well as the Parana-Paraguay basin. They generally are found attached to vegetation along the banks of the streams that they inhabit. These are small species with the body only about 5 cm in standard length. The head is slightly depressed, and the preopercle emerges at the surface of the head as an elongated bony plate. The posttemporal perforations are variable in size and never on the entire surface of the bony plate. The opening of the swim bladder capsule is immediately below the posttemporal plate but is covered by skin. The eyes are small and slightly superior in position. There are about 13-32 premaxillary teeth and 11-29 dentary teeth; the pharyngeal teeth are small. Small plates cover the body, and the denticles on the plates are irregularly distributed. About 21 to 25 perforated scutes are in a lateral series. The rostral margin of the head is composed of regular bony scutes bearing variously sized reverted denticles. There are two pairs of bony plates just behind the supraoccipital followed by a large plate in front of the dorsal insertion; posterior to the dorsal are 15 to 16 plates, with an unpaired

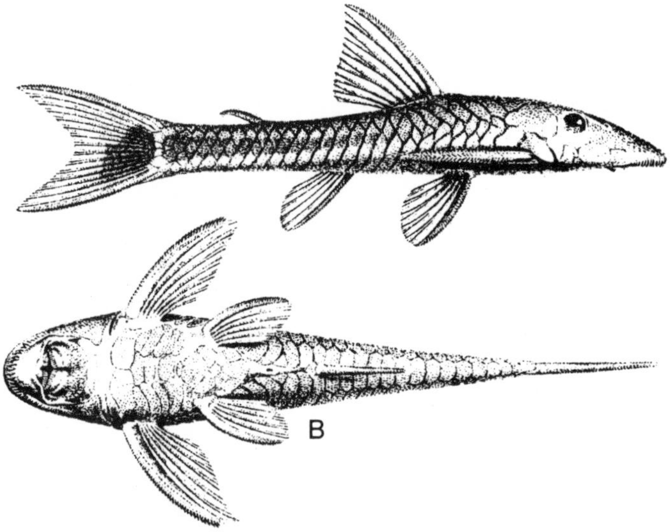

Parotocinclus maculicauda; (b) ventral view. (From Steindachner, 1877.)

platelet just before the adipose fin. The abdomen is entirely covered with large plates or platelets that may or may not be regularly distributed. The dorsal fin has a spine and 7 rays, the anal a spine and 5 rays, the pectoral a spine and 6 rays, and the ventrals a spine and 5 rays. Males have a genital papilla. (After Garavello, 1977.)

The genus *Otothyris* contains a single species from the hills in the vicinity of Rio de Janeiro. The head is rugose and much keeled, and the posttemporals are perforate. The eyes are set high on the head and lack the projecting tongue of the iris extending to the center of the pupil. The lower transverse areas of the clavicles and coracoids are exposed and rough. There are 21 lateral scutes in a series and 3 large plates on the preventral area, one on each side anteriorly and one posteriorly between the ventral fins; the rest of the breast is naked except for an occasional rudimentary plate or two. The dorsal fin has a spine and 4 rays, the anal fin a spine and 5 rays. The pectoral fin spine extends nearly as far as the end of the ventral fin. The single species, *O. canaliferus*, has a conspicuous rounded dark spot in the center of the caudal fin. (After Myers, 1927.)

The genus *Otocinclus* contains about 20 species, many of which come from the Rio Grande do Sul and La Plata regions. The

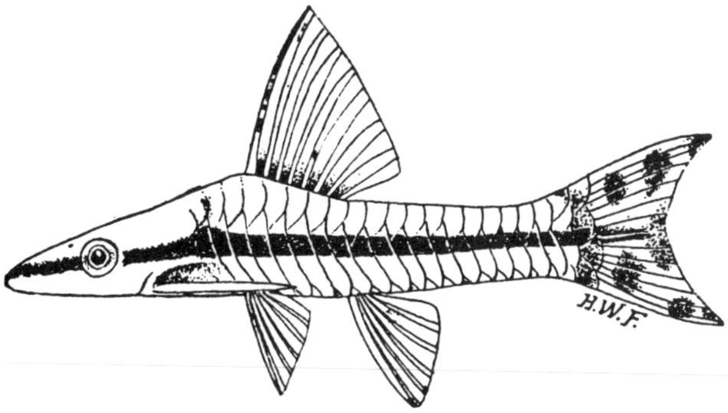

Otocinclus vittata. (From Fowler, 1954.)

body depth is contained from 4 to 6.5 times in its length. The supraoccipital may or may not have a median ridge. The eyes, supralateral in position, are contained from 3.7 to 8.5 times in the head length. The scutes are spinulose, carinate or not, and number 21 to 27 in a lateral series. The lower surface of the head has a naked area in front of the clavicles, and the abdomen is covered by 3 series of plates. The dorsal fin has a spine and 7 rays and the anal fin a spine and 5 rays. There is no adipose fin. The caudal fin is emarginate.

Otocinclus species are peaceful and harmless fishes that usually do not grow larger than 6 cm. They can be kept healthy for years in a well-planted community tank, but without live plants they seem to do poorly. The water chemistry is not critical, but partial water changes are strongly recommended. *Otocinclus* species are strongly herbivorous, feeding mostly on algae when available. In fact, they are said to do quite well for their size in keeping the algae under control even in large community tanks, grazing the algal film from stones, leaves, and the aquarium glass. The plants (even delicate ones) usually are not damaged, although if no other vegetable material is available they may start on the fine-leaved plants that are present. They will take the usual lettuce and spinach leaves along with vegetable-based foods in lieu of algae; meatier foods such as brine shrimp, worms of all types, and even flake food also will be accepted. Like other loricariids they rasp at their food in contrast to fishes like *Corydoras* species that sift for their food through the substrate material. The temperature range should be between 22° and 29°C. Most *Otocinclus* species are crepuscular, usually remaining on plant leaves during the day with very little activity shown. Even small ones prefer to hang vertically from the leaves or glass of the aquarium by their sucker mouths. Some individuals were seen to attach themselves to other fishes, including *Corydoras* species, but are easily shaken off and not further molested. For their well-being most *Otocinclus* species should not be kept singly but as small groups of perhaps a half dozen.

Spawning has been accomplished with several species of *Otocinclus*. Courtship or prespawning behavior may include mad chases through the tank with an ultimate stop on the broad leaves of the plants for actual deposition of eggs. This is repeated, with another batch of eggs being deposited in another part of the tank. With insufficient plants or perhaps because of species preferences, some batches of eggs may be placed on stones, filters, or even the sides of the tank. One species was observed spawning in a head-to-tail position, with the body of the slimmer male wrapped around that of the female as well as in a head-to-head (parallel) position as they were vibrating. Others spawned like *Corydoras* species, forming a "T", the female pushing her snout at the male's vent area. In the leaf-spawning species the male would touch the female on the nape soon after deposition of a batch of 4-12 eggs and the chase would start again. A half dozen such batches or more were deposited. In the other species the eggs were spawned into a ventral pouch and were placed on a previously cleaned surface (like *Corydoras*). The eggs are small (in one case 1.0-1.2 mm in diameter), transparent or pale cream colored, and adhesive. Some 40 to more than 100 eggs per spawn may be laid. Hatching in all cases took only about two to three days.

A batch laid on the middle of plant leaves was raised artificially and started hatching after 40 hours. By 22 hours the eyes were visible, and after 32 hours some movement could be discerned and the color had changed from transparent to amber. All the fry were able to attach themselves immediately to a substrate with their sucker mouths. The yolk sac was absorbed in another two to three days. Among the fry foods recommended by successful breeders were chopped tubifex, rotifers, microworms, powdered egg yolk, and powdered flake food of high quality. With good food, growth is rapid. However, growth may slow down if the aeration is poor or regular water changes are neglected. There is no brood care by either parent. In the pair that spawned on leaves, additional eggs were laid after a couple more days, indicating that rest periods such as seen in some species of *Corydoras* occur. Suggestions for stimulation of spawning include high quality conditioning diets, large water changes, and increased aeration (many species are found in rapidly flowing streams with a high oxygen content).

Among the more commonly imported species of *Otocinclus* is *O. vestitus* from southeastern Brazil, which attains a length of about 6 cm. They inhabit swiftly flowing rivers, where they move about with the aid of their sucking mouth. In an aquarium the species is not as shy as some other species and will be out in the open even in fairly brightly lit tanks. It is relatively quiet when the lights are out. It prefers high oxygen content water, but even when the oxygen is low it does not make much use of its intestinal respiration. It does well in cooler water (about 15°-25°C) that can hold a higher proportion of oxygen than warmer waters. The sexes are hard to distinguish, though the females are larger and heavier-bodied than males. They breed like *Corydoras* species.

Another species, *O. affinis*, is very shy during the daytime, feeding at dusk and during the evening hours. This species is ideal for small aquaria (it grows to 5 cm) as long as there is sufficient aeration (since the species inhabits swiftly flowing streams) and is not crowded. Although territorial, this species is nevertheless quite harmless. With ample vegetation and a temperature of 20° to 23°C they do quite well. They spawn like *Corydoras*, but the eggs are laid individually on plants, tank sides, and other flat substrates. First food can be the smallest nauplii of crustaceans, finely powdered egg yolk, or microworms.

O. flexilis is only occasionally available to aquarists. It schools with *Corydoras paleatus* and even resembles them in color and pattern very closely. However, in aquaria they often pale out a bit, losing the intensity of color of the freshly caught individuals.

O. vittatus and *O. arnoldi* may also appear for sale. *O. notatus* from Santa Cruz in southeastern Brazil is a smaller species attaining a length of only about 4 cm. It is peaceful and, like the other species, does best when kept in a small group. More males than females are usually available, which makes spawning easier. About 20-25 eggs are deposited per clutch. The young are similar to *O. vittatus* in color albeit paler and seem to develop at a significantly slower rate than that species.

Microlepidogaster is most closely related to *Otocinclus* and shares most of the features of that genus including the larger plates on the snout tip. It differs from *Otocinclus* mainly by

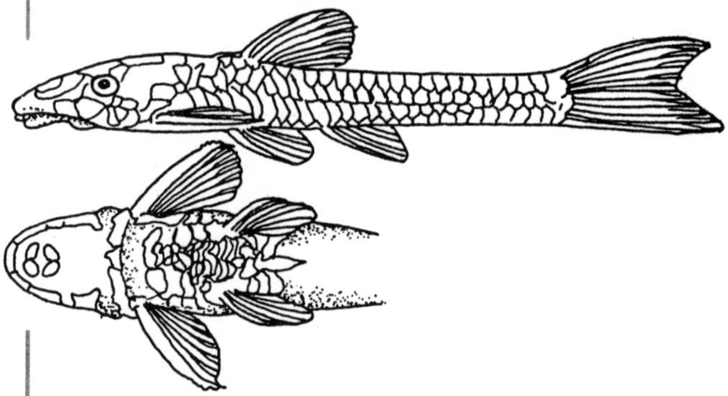

Microlepidogaster taimensis. (After Buckup).

having the abdominal area naked or composed of numerous irregulary disposed plates; *Otocinclus* has basically three longitudinal series of plates. There are approximately eight species in the genus from southeastern Brazil.

The genus *Hypoptopoma* contains a dozen species, most of which are distributed in the

Amazon basin with at least one from a waterfall area and another from a lake. The body is moderately elongate, its depth normally around 5.0-5.5 in its length, but it may be as much as 7.5. The head may be flattened, and the occipital has a median ridge. The snout is margined with recurved spines. The interoperculum is a plate on the lower surface of the head; the temporal plate is not perforate. The eyes, about 5.0 to 6.0 in the head length, are placed very low, being as equally visible from above as from below. The jaw teeth are numerous, slender, and bifid. The scutes are spinulose and not carinate or those of the middle lateral series have a keel; 22-25 scutes are present in a lateral series. The lower surface of the head has a naked area in front of the clavicles or there is a transverse series of 4 small plates or a single plate in front of the clavicles. The abdomen is covered by 3 longitudinal series of plates or only 2, the third

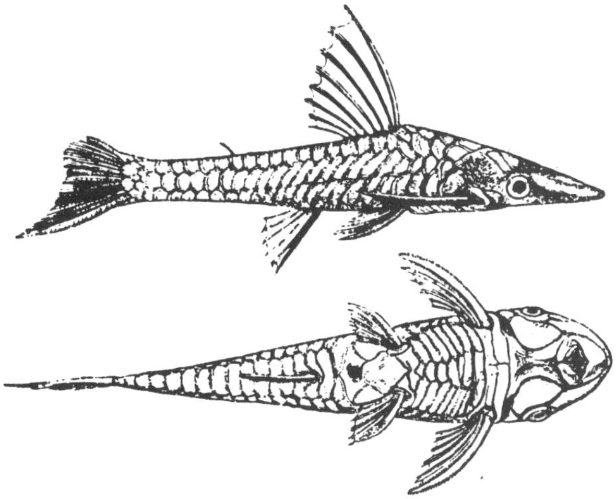

Hypoptopoma thoracatum. (From Günther, 1880.)

Species of *Hypoptopoma* can generally be recognized by the longish snout and the straight, flat head profile. This wild caught specimen is probably *H. guentheri* from the Mato Grosso. Photo by Harald Schultz.

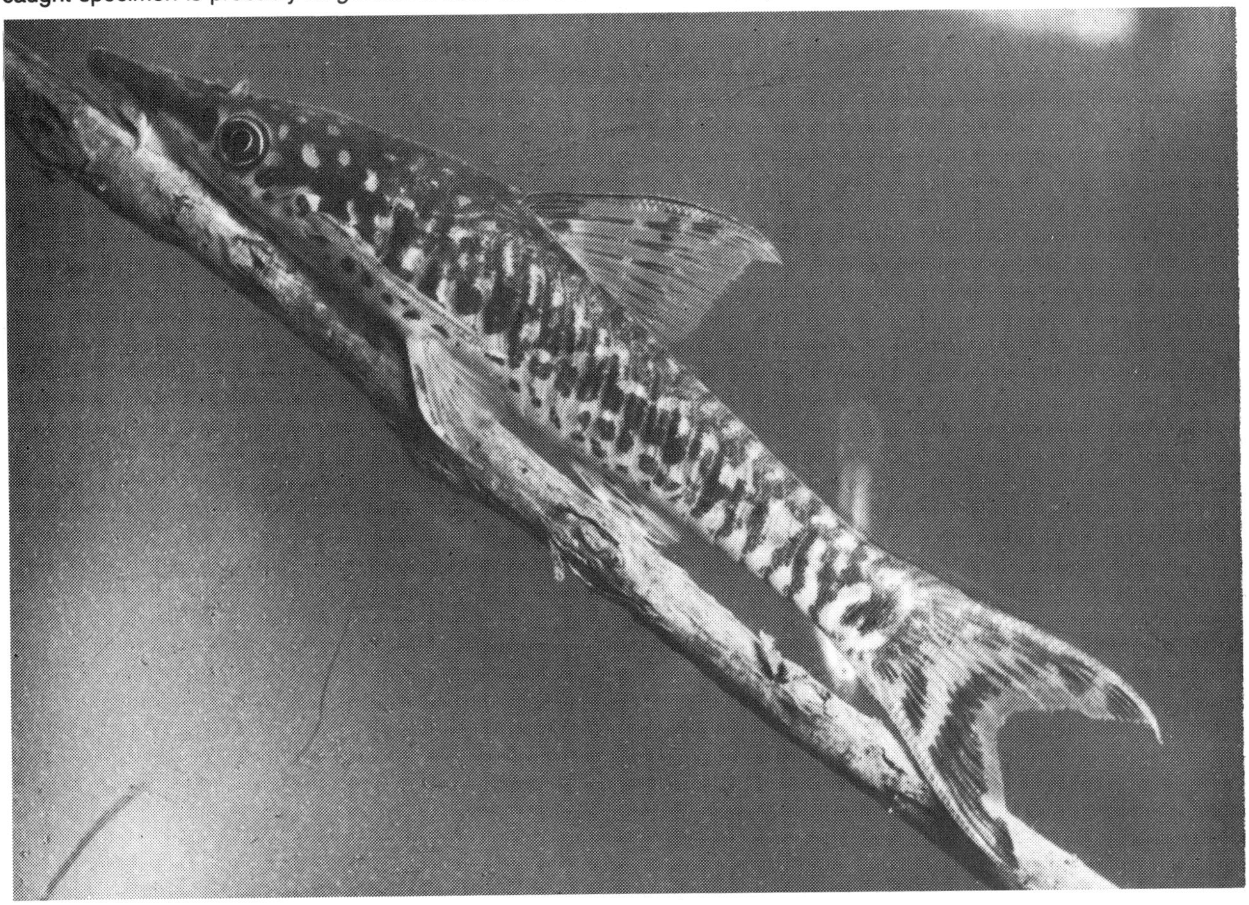

represented by a single anterior median plate. The dorsal fin, with a spine and 7 rays, is located above or a little behind the ventrals. The anal fin has a spine and 5 rays, the pectorals a spine and 6 rays, and the ventrals a spine and 5 rays. The adipose fin, if present, is represented by a weak spine. The caudal fin is usually emarginate.

The subfamily Loricariinae is quite large, with about 30 genera and some 185 species. Members of this subfamily have a general tendency for the head and body to become flattened (especially the caudal peduncle) and for the relative elongation of all parts (such as the caudal peduncle, snout, and upper and lower caudal rays). The interopercle is not evertible. The teeth may be bifid, unicuspid (spoon-shaped), or possibly even trifid (although this last type has yet to be documented), in a single series in each jaw (in certain groups the teeth may be rudimentary or even absent in the upper jaw). The lower pharyngeals and the fourth pair of upper plates have villiform or peculiarly shaped molariform teeth. The armature generally extends onto the ventral surface. The caudal peduncle is covered dorsally and ventrally by a median row of unpaired scutes. Generally there are 3 (in elongate forms there may be more) scutes between the supraoccipital and predorsal plates; the predorsal plate is usually small and may be absent. The anus is separated from the anal fin by a median azygous plate and one or more pairs of lateral plates that touch along the median ventral line. The dorsal fin usually has a spine and 6 rays (rarely 5), the anal fin a spine and 4 rays (rarely 5); the anal fin usually originates somewhere under the last depressed dorsal fin ray. The pectoral fin has a spine and 6 rays, and the ventral fin has a spine and 5 (exceptionally 4) rays. The gill rakers are little developed, normal, or resemble the gill filaments in structure. The intestine is comparatively short, with few convolutions, and the swim bladder does not have a posterior division.

Sexual dimorphism is evident in several of the genera. For example, *Hemiodontichthys*, *Loricariichthys*, and *Pseudoloricaria* have males that develop longer and larger lower lips than the females in order to accommodate the eggs. Males of *Farlowella* develop bristles on the extended snout and those of *Sturisoma* develop them on their cheeks as well, while those of *Rineloricaria* develop them on the head, cheeks, and pectoral fins. Bristles that are present may increase in size with the onset of the breeding season.

In at least *Farlowella, Sturisoma*, and *Rineloricaria* it has been recommended that the eggs or fry be removed to another tank for rearing. Once the yolk sac has been absorbed they can be fed the usual fry fare. More specific breeding information will be given under the individual species accounts.

The subfamily Loricariinae has been divided into four tribes by Isbrücker (1979). They can be identified by the following key:

1a. Origin of dorsal approximately opposite origin of ventral fins....................... 2
1b. Origin of dorsal approximately opposite origin of anal fin.......................... 3
2a. Caudal fin with 10 branched rays; postorbital groove generally present, sometimes absent..................... Loricariini
2b. Caudal fin with 12 (rarely 11) branched rays; never a postorbital notch; usually little diversity in teeth and lip structure; odontodes of males strongly elongated, developing along border of snout and sometimes on dorsal surface of spine and rays of pectoral fins........ Harttiini
3a. Odontodes usually small, never very visible except in mature males; teeth numerous, filiform; coracoid completely covered ventrally by some dermal ossifications; head and body extremely thin, the rostrum being almost always strongly elongate............. Farlowellini
3b. Odontodes very visible, disposed in wavy lines; teeth in moderate number; coracoid completely exposed ventrally, not covered by dermal ossifications; head and body similar to Farlowellini, rostrum even more strongly elongate and provided with a small terminal expansion .... Acestridiini

The tribe Acestridiini contains but a single genus (*Acestridium*), which itself contains only a single species (*A. discus*) from a grassy, cool, shady, swampy creek near Manaos, Brazil. The tip of the elongated snout is expanded, disc-like, and provided with spines. The caudal peduncle is elongate, posteriorly depressed, and provided with a single series of plates on the sides. All of the scutes are provided with many series of delicate spiny ridges and depressions. There are 25-27 scutes in a lateral series, 5 between the supraoccipital and the dorsal plate, and the abdomen does not have a median series of plates. The dorsal fin has a spine and 6 rays and the anal a spine and 4 rays; the dorsal fin is inserted approximately above the anal fin. There is no adipose fin, and the caudal fin is rounded. Otherwise in general aspect it is similar to the genus *Farlowella*.

The tribe Farlowellini contains two genera, *Farlowella* and *Aposturisoma*; the former genus is quite large (about 37 species) while the latter has only a single species. The head and body are extremely slender, with the snout almost always very elongate (but without a terminal expansion). The teeth are numerous and filiform, usually with strongly curved, bilobate crowns. The coracoid is completely covered ventrally by dermal ossifications. The dorsal fin origin is approximately opposite the origin of the anal fin. The odontodes are ordinarily very small and inconspicuous, but in the case of mature males a zone of bristles of moderate length develops, especially along the elongate rostrum. In one species of *Farlowella* with a shorter snout (*Farlowella curtirostra*) these are restricted to the lateral border of the head and snout. The two genera can be distinguished by the following key:

1a. Lateral coalescent scutes 22-26; teeth numerous (about 125), arranged on the premaxillary in a rectilinear transverse line and on the dentaries in an almost straight transverse line with a little notch at the level of the symphysis...... .... *Aposturisoma*

1b. Lateral coalescent scutes 10-20; teeth fewer (about 20), arranged in the shape of a "V" on both premaxillaries and mandible .... *Farlowella*

The genus *Farlowella* is a moderately large one with approximately 37 species from northern South America. The body is notably slender and the head is elongated with a well-developed elongate bony rostrum; the caudal peduncle is elongate, strongly depressed. The

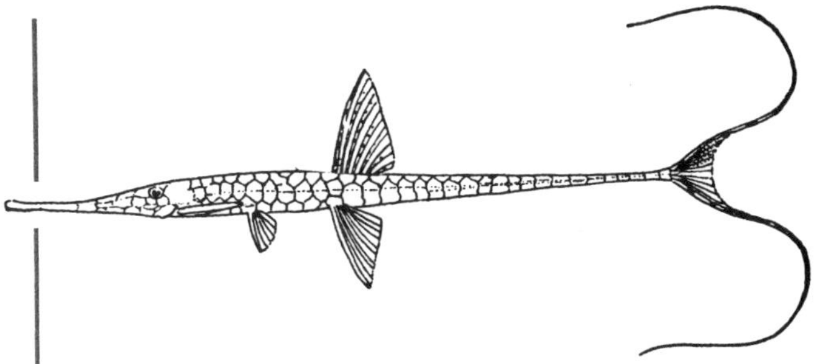

Farlowella gladia. (From Fowler, 1954.)

interopercle and opercle are not separately movable. The side of the head may have bristles in mature males. The head length is approximately 3.0-4.5 in the total length. The eyes, contained 12-20 times in the head length, are without an orbital groove. The teeth are setiform, about 20 on each ramus, and disposed in the shape of a "V" in both jaws. In a lateral series there are 33-34 scutes; there are 7-10 plates between the supraoccipital and the predorsal plate and 10-20 lateral coalescent scutes. The abdomen is covered with scutes, either with a median series between the lateral series or with only one or two anteriorly. The region between the mouth and the pectoral fins may be covered with small irregular plates. The dorsal fin, with a slender spine and 5 (rarely 6) rays, is located opposite the anal fin, which has a slender spine and 4 rays. The pectoral fins have a spine and 6 rays, the ventral fins a spine and 4 or 5 rays. The outer caudal fin rays are often strongly produced, filamentous.

Species of *Farlowella* are peaceful bottom dwellers usually inhabiting rapidly flowing streams where they can be found attached to rocks, logs, and plant leaves, grazing on the algal cover with their sucker-like mouth and scraping teeth. In an aquarium the same habit prevails, and although they may be quiescent during the day as they hang motionless from rocks or leaves of aquatic plants, they will scour almost every inch of surface where algae can grow during the hours of darkness. These nocturnal algae-eaters must, therefore, receive vegetable matter as the largest portion of their diet. Clean water is beneficial, even necessary, especially if you are planning to spawn them. These twig or stick catfishes (so-called because of their slender, "woody" appearance) are good indicators of the oxygen content of the water in the tank, for when the oxygen levels drop the twig catfishes will move to the upper levels of the tank. In extreme oxygen depletion the snouts may even be stuck out of the water. Soft, well-aged water seems to be preferred, and the tank should be supplied with plenty of hiding places in the form of rocks, logs (driftwood), and heavy plant growth. The encouragement of algal growth is recommended. A good current provided by the aeration and filtration systems is also recommended. Once established, these catfishes do not take well to being moved, and such shifts in housing should be avoided or at least kept to a minimum. Movement is usually minimal. Swimming is accomplished by body undulations and propulsion with the caudal fin. The color may vary from a lighter tan or yellowish brown to very dark, almost black, depending upon the color of the background.

At least one or more species of *Farlowella* have been spawned in home tanks. Although spawning in captivity can be accomplished at any time of the year given proper conditions, in the wild it occurs principally between November and March. The male is usually territorial and will not even allow females near unless they are in spawning condition. If extra stimulation is needed to precipitate spawning, try adding cool fresh water, causing a slight temperature decrease. The nest site is selected and cleaned by the male (one report indicated that both parents cleaned). It is normally a smooth surface in a quiet, dark area (dim light) and always off the bottom, never on it. Male and female are sometimes seen side by side, even entwined, when spawning; the female will lay three to seven eggs that are immediately fertilized by the male. This is repeated until anywhere from 50 to 120 eggs have been deposited. Once a female has depleted her supply of eggs she departs or is forcibly ejected from the area by the male. Other females will be allowed to add to the eggs as long as they appear a few days after the first spawning. The eggs are about 2 mm in diameter, translucent, and very adhesive. As the embryo develops the eggs become very dark. The male guards the eggs, fanning them with his fins and mouthing them from time to time. During this time he usually will accept food. In about a week to ten days the fry hatch out. They are 6-7 mm in length and remain attached to the substrate where they were born. After the eggs hatch the male seems to lose all interest in the brood. Fry food should include a great deal of vegetable matter including, if possible, naturally growing algae. However, crushed algal flakes, finely chopped spinach leaves, and similar items can be substituted. Sexual dimorphism appears in the form of bristles along the outside edge of the elongated snout in the males; these are absent in the females. The actual identity of the species imported is not surely known, although it appears that *F. acus* and *F. gracilis* may be among those seen.

The genus *Aposturisoma* contains only a single species, *A. myriodon*, from the Rio Aguaytia basin, Peru. It is most similar to *Farlowella* and *Sturisoma*, sharing with the former genus such characters as the position of the dorsal fin opposite the anal fin; the 5 branched rays of the dorsal fin; the higher number of predorsal scutes when compared with the Harttiini and Loricariini; the 11 branched caudal fin rays in addition to the simple outer rays; the elongate rostrum; the latero-external side of the soft part of the mouth independent (for the most part) from the internal bony wall of the mouth; the short fins; and even the similar color pattern in many species. *Aposturisoma* shares with *Sturisoma* the elongate body and head and the long bony rostrum. *Aposturisoma* differs from both *Farlowella* and *Sturisoma* primarily by its more elongate lip, the more numerous teeth,

Aposturisoma myriodon; (b) ventral view of head. (After Isbrücker, Britski, Nijssen, & Ortega, 1983.)

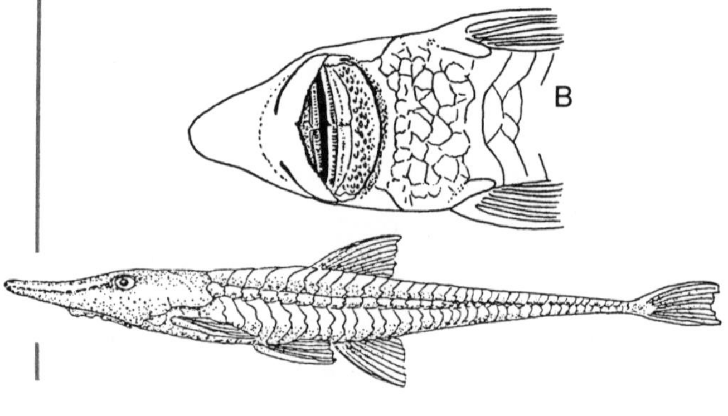

and the more numerous coalescing body scutes. Also, the premaxillary teeth of *Aposturisoma* are arranged in a rectilinear transverse line and those of the dentary are in almost a straight line with a small indentation at the symphysis, whereas those of the genus *Sturisoma* are in a weakly curved line on the premaxillary and in a "V" on the dentary; the teeth of *Farlowella* are in the form of a "V" on both premaxillary and dentary. Although compared to both of these genera, it must be remembered that *Aposturisoma* is more closely related to *Farlowella*, *Sturisoma* being relegated to a different tribe by virtue of the characters indicated in the key to the tribes.

The tribe Loricariini contains approximately 20 genera with somewhere in the neighborhood of 110 species. These are generally slender, elongate catfishes with the following combination of characters: 10 branched rays in the caudal fin; 6 branched rays in the dorsal fin; the dorsal fin origin located approximately opposite the origin of the ventral fins; no more (and often considerably less) than 18 teeth in each side of each upper jaw (premaxilla) in adult specimens; and great differentiation in dentition and lip shapes and structures. The orbital rim is provided, with few exceptions, with a fairly obvious notch posteriorly. The upper unbranched ray of the caudal fin is often greatly elongated into a filament that is fragile and may break off with rough handling; a similar filament on the lower edge of the caudal fin is seen only in some of the members of the tribe Rineloricariina (*Ixinandria, Rineloricaria, Dasyloricaria*, and *Spatuloricaria*). The fin rays are usually dichotomously branched and the naked surface of the upper lip is devoid of dermal ossifications. The anal fin usually has 4 branched rays, the pectoral fin I,6, and the ventral fins I,5. Several species of this tribe grow to a fairly large size (over 30 cm SL), larger than other members of the subfamily. Numerous slender, filiform teeth, so common in the Hypostominae, Hypoptopomatinae, Ancistrinae, all Harttiini, and Farlowellini, are not seen in the Loricariini. Sexual dimorphism occurs as: extensive odontode growth on head, dorsum of body, before dorsal fin or on pectoral fins; change in shape of teeth; development of large lower lip; or change in shape of certain odontodes such as on the spines of the ventral and anal fins. Additional differences will probably be found when more of the species are better known. The following key will help distinguish 20 of the 21 currently accepted genera (the genus *Furcodontichthys* is omitted due to the lack of the original description).

1a. Teeth in upper jaw reduced in size and number or even completely absent..... 2
1b. Teeth in upper jaw well developed.... 10
2a. Snout (rostrum) elongate; lower lip broad, without barbels; orbital notch conspicuous.................................. 3
2b. Snout short, acute or rounded; upper and lower lips provided with numerous, often long, barbels; orbital notch absent to well developed.......................... 4
3a. Rostrum often expanded at its tip; abdomen covered with large, well-developed plates; dermal denticles well developed. ....*Hemiodonticthys*
3b. Rostrum not expanded at its tip; abdomen covered with small, mosaic-like dermal platelets (fully developed only in adults); dermal denticles weakly developed .... *Reganella*
4a. Orbital notch absent or only weakly developed; snout rounded; teeth present in lower jaw only; 40 scutes in lateral series, 19 to 20 coalescing....*Planiloricaria*
4b. Orbital notch conspicuous; 31-34 lateral body scutes in series, 13-21 coalescing.. 5
5a. Dermal ossifications (small scutelets) present on barbels...............*Dentectus*
5b. No dermal ossifications present on barbels....................................... 6
6a. Abdomen naked except for single median strip of small, roundish scutelets (except *C. rhami*) ....*Crossoloricaria*
6b. Abdomen naked or covered with different patterns of scutelets, not, however, arranged into a single median strip.... 7
7a. Sides of head and snout more or less triangular in shape when viewed from above; caudal peduncle depth 12.3-17.3 in head length.............................. 8
7b. Sides of head tapering, sides of snout narrow and somewhat concave when viewed from above; depth of caudal peduncle 9.7 in head length............... 9
8a. Ventral flap covering branchiostegal membrane; 29-30 lateral body scutes;

pectoral fins large, broad ...*Pyxiloricaria*

8b. No fleshy flap covering branchiostegal membrane; 31-40 lateral body scutes; pectoral fins normal .... *Pseudohemiodon*

9a. Iris circular, relatively narrow, without the dorsal expansion covering the lens; prolongation of the dorsal "spine" in largest specimen 2.2-2.5 in standard length.......................... *Apistoloricaria*

9b. Dorsal expansion covering the lens present; dorsal spine not as long, 4.8-6.0 in standard length .... *Rhadinoloricaria*

10a. Large number of barbels present 11

10b. Barbels absent or only rictal barbels present 14

11a. Upper jaw with 6 or more teeth on each side..12

11b. Upper jaw with 5 or less teeth on each side 13

12a. Upper jaw with up to 9 teeth on each side; maxillary (rictal) barbels with subbarbels that are not subdivided into minute branches .... *Paraloricaria*

12b. Upper jaw with up to 15 teeth on each side; maxillary barbels with subbarbels that are subdivided into minute branches ....*Ricola*

13a. Teeth in upper jaw long, about twice length of teeth in lower jaw.... *Loricaria*

13b. Teeth in upper jaw about ⅓ longer than those of lower jaw; teeth of lower jaw about as long as upper jaw teeth of *Loricaria* ....*Brochiloricaria*

14a. Sexual dimorphism in mature males in the form of greatly enlarged lower lip....... 15

14b. Sexual dimorphism in mature males not in the form of greatly enlarged lower lip but as head bristles 17

15a. Upper lip narrow, with series of pointed barbel-like flaps; up to 13 teeth on each side of upper jaw, up to 15 on each side of lower jaw 16

15b. Upper lip narrow, without barbel-like flaps; teeth weakly developed, up to 17 on each side of upper jaw, up to 34 on each side of lower jaw.....*Loricariichthys*

16a. Normally 34-36 scutes in lateral series, 23-27 coalescing; 9-27 small scutes bordering preanal scute anteriorly........... ....*Pseudoloricaria*

16b. Lateral scutes 31-32, 18-22 coalescing; 3-5 small scutes bordering preanal scute anteriorly.....................*Limatulichthys*

17a. Abdomen naked.................*Ixinandria*

17b. Abdomen variously covered with scutes or scutelets 18

18a. Usually 4 or 5 (sometimes 6) teeth on each side of both jaws ..... *Spatuloricaria*

18b. Usually 8-10 (sometimes as few as 6) teeth on each side of each jaw..........19

19a. Abdomen with 3-6 rows of plates between lateral series; lateral series of scutes 28-31 ....*Rineloricaria*

19b. Abdomen with 2 or 3 median rows of scutes between lateral series; 30-32 scutes in lateral series ...... *Dasyloricaria*

The genus *Ricola* is a small genus containing but a single species, *R. macrops*, from the Rio de la Plata and the upper reaches of the Rio Parana in Uruguay and Argentina. It is quite similar to species of *Loricaria* with the exception of the structure of the barbels and the shape and number of the teeth. The upper lip is narrow and provided with a number of barbels that are branched, with small barblets coming off in a linear series from the main barbel. The lower lip is also narrow, the anterior portion provided with papillae, the posterior portion with a number of barbels, also branched in a manner similar to the barbels of the upper lip. The teeth are somewhat similar to those found in *Rineloricaria*. There are up to 15 teeth on each premaxilla and up to 14 on each dentary, the former being twice as long as the latter. The teeth are bilobed, the outer lobe the smaller. As in many other species of the subfamily, the lobes of mature males are somewhat broader and less pointed at the tip than those of the females and juveniles. Sexual dimorphism is also manifested in

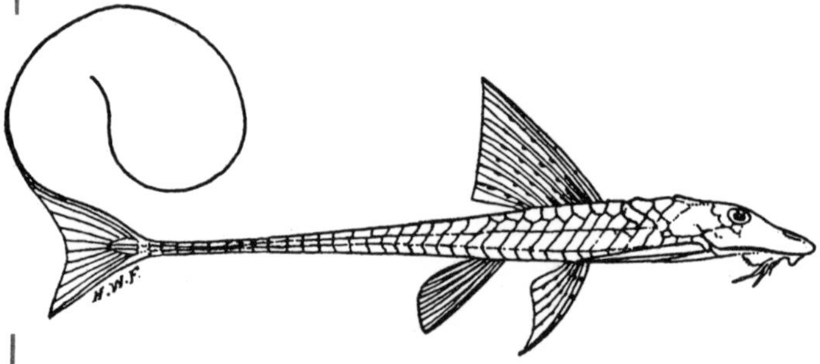

Ricola macrops. (From Fowler, 1954.)

the thickness of the pectoral fin spine, that of the male being thicker than that of the female. The number of body scutes is on the high side (37-39) when compared to closely related genera such as *Loricaria, Paraloricaria*, and *Brochiloricaria*, which make up Nijssen's (1983) subtribe Loricariina.

The Loricariina consisted of the genera *Loricaria, Pseudohemiodon, Rhadinoloricaria, Ricola, Brochiloricaria, Crossoloricaria*, and *Paraloricaria* (Isbrücker, 1977), but in the last few years Isbrücker, et al. modified this scheme considerably, erecting a new subtribe for *Ricola* and moving *Crossoloricaria, Pseudohemiodon*, and *Rhadinoloricaria* into the subtribe Planiloricariina along with *Planiloricaria* and *Dentectus* (Martin Salazar, Isbrücker, and Nijssen, 1982). The Loricariina (referred to as the *Loricaria*-group by Isbrücker in his 1981 paper) was postulated to perhaps be derived from a Rineloricariina (*Ixinandria, Rineloricaria, Dasyloricaria*, and *Spatuloricaria*) that developed a tendency toward having fewer teeth, slightly larger lips, more and better developed papillae that turned into filaments, more lateral body scutes that tended to coalesce more posteriorly, and a gradual diminishing of the odontode development in sexually mature males. These three genera (*Paraloricaria, Loricaria*, and *Brochiloricaria*) are distinguished from the Planiloricariina by having their teeth firm and quite long in one or both jaws.

The genus *Loricaria* is a moderate-sized genus of about eleven species from tropical South America. The body is relatively elongate and slender, the head with a rounded to slightly pointed snout. A conspicuous orbital notch is usually present. The upper lip is short, and around its edges are numerous slender barbels that may be simple or bifid (rarely trifid) and subbarbels or long papillae. Cirri are present on the ventral surface of the upper lip, around the base of the teeth, in the buccal cavity, and on the surface of the maxillary barbel. The lower lip is also well developed and possesses a more or less deep median notch. Posterior to the dentary, the lip surface is provided with a pad or cushion bearing low papillae; posterior to this there are numerous long filaments. There are usually 3 or 4 teeth on each premaxilla (occasionally 5) and up to 11 on each dentary. The teeth of the premaxillae are about twice as long as those of the dentary. All are simple or bilobed, the outer lobe the smaller, and those of the females and juveniles have a large, oblong crown with a more or less rounded tip. There are about 32 to 37 lateral body scutes, of which the posterior 17-26 coalesce. The abdomen is naked to partially or entirely covered with small scutelets that develop with age. The scutelets may develop at different rates in different species. The upper unbranched ray of the caudal fin is commonly developed into a long filament that may be as long as the body itself. Sexual dimorphism may be shown in some species (males and females of all species have not been studied) by the mature males having hypertrophied pectoral fin spines, more blunt odontodes on the ventral and anal fin spines, and shorter, more rounded tooth lobes. At least one species, *Loricaria clavipinna*, is said to have the lower lip enlarged in a manner suggestive of *Dasyloricaria, Limatulichthys, Pseudoloricaria, Loricariichthys*, and *Hemiodontichthys*. Although the largest species in the genus grows to a length of over 35 cm, the smallest mature male is a little over 10 cm.

Although the aquarium literature contains a number of references to caring for and breeding species of *Loricaria*, because of the extreme splitting of the group it is very probable that few (if any) of these references are actually to species now regarded as in this genus. *"Loricaria" parva* is now *Rineloricaria parva*, for example, and *"Loricaria" filamentosa* of aquarists may not be the real *Loricaria filamentosa*. The same may be true of *L. cataphracta* of aquarists, although this is a com-

Loricaria clavipinna; (b) dorsal view of head; (c) ventral view. (From Fowler, 1954.)

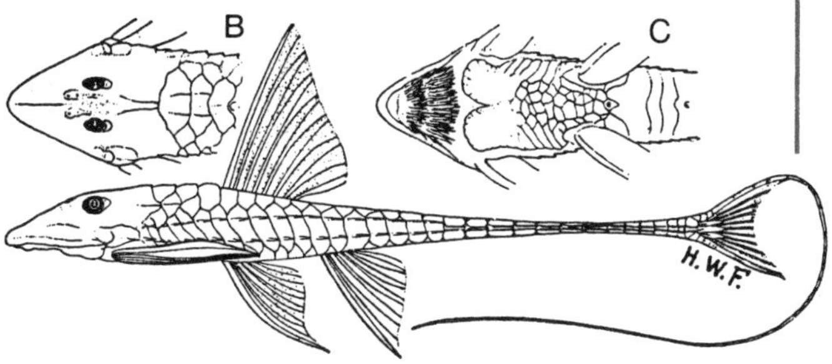

mon species and may have entered the aquarium trade.

Loricaria simillima, a species from (among many other localities) a large, shallow lake (Lago Ypacarai) in Paraguay, was mostly collected over hard, sandy bottoms. The males were slightly smaller (mean length of males = 22.5 cm; mean length of females = 23.3 cm) than females, and the females had dense concentrations of tentacles on the ventral surface of the lower lip in adults whereas these were considerably reduced or even lacking in breeding males. The ovaries of the females as they filled with eggs became greatly enlarged, distending the abdomen considerably regardless of the confining effects of the body armor. The spawned egg mass is described as an elongate, flattened sheet approximately 2 to 4 eggs thick that is attached to the male's lower lip along the posterior margin, leaving the remainder of the egg mass to trail along the abdomen. All the eggs, usually between 150 and 350 in number, were found to be in similar states of development, indicating that they were the result of a single spawn. The bright yellow eggs each had a diameter of about 2.6 mm.

Ribeiro (1912) described what he considered as *L. cataphracta* as carrying the eggs attached to the ventral surface of the male; Azevedo (1938) reported the same thing for *L. piracicabae*. It would be interesting if these observations could be confirmed, indicating slightly different modes of carrying the eggs.

The genus *Brochiloricaria* contains only two species, *B. chauliodon* from Argentina and *B. macrodon* from the Cuiaba River in Brazil. The genus agrees in almost every character with *Loricaria* but differs from that genus by the tooth structure. In *Brochiloricaria* the teeth in both jaws are excessively long, the lower jaw teeth at least twice as long as those of species of *Loricaria*.

Brochiloricaria macrodon. (From Fowler, 1954.)

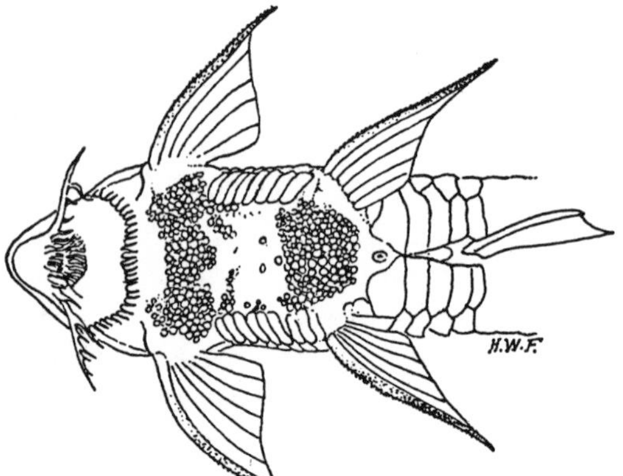

The third genus of the subtribe Loricariina is *Paraloricaria. Paraloricaria* contains three species, one from Paraguay (*P. agastor*), one from the Rio Uruguay (*P. commersonoides*), and one from the vicinity of Buenos Aires (*P. vetula*). This genus also closely resembles *Loricaria* but similarly differs from that genus by the teeth. In *Paraloricaria* the teeth of the two jaws are much shorter than those of species of *Loricaria* (about half as long) and the number of teeth in the upper jaw is a bit higher than those of *Loricaria* (6 versus 4-5).

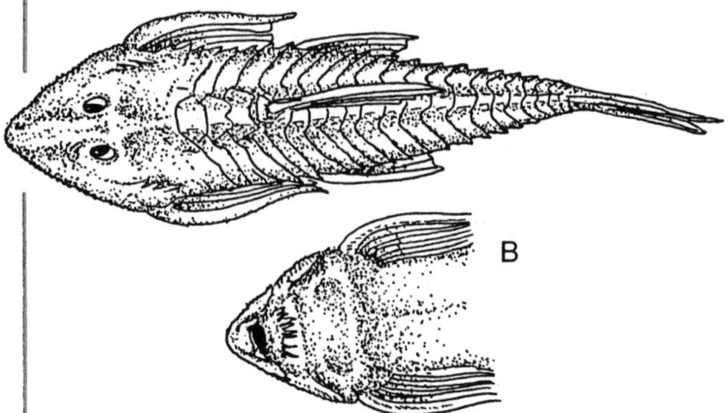

Paraloricaria agastor, (b) ventral view. (After Isbrücker, 1979.)

The genus *Rineloricaria* belongs to Isbrücker's subtribe Rineloricariina along with *Ixinandria, Dasyloricaria,* and *Spatuloricaria.* It is the largest genus of the group, with more than 40 species. They are comparatively small, the largest species attaining a length of about 23 cm, but most not reaching that size. The body is quite slender, and the head does not have a prolonged rostrum. A conspicuous postorbital notch is present. All dermal ossifications (including scutes, fin spines and rays) are covered with odontodes (minute, acute dermal denticles), the body ridges being covered by somewhat more prominent odontodes. The abdomen is covered with a few scutes in front of the anal opening, covered with numerous scutes on the posterior half, or

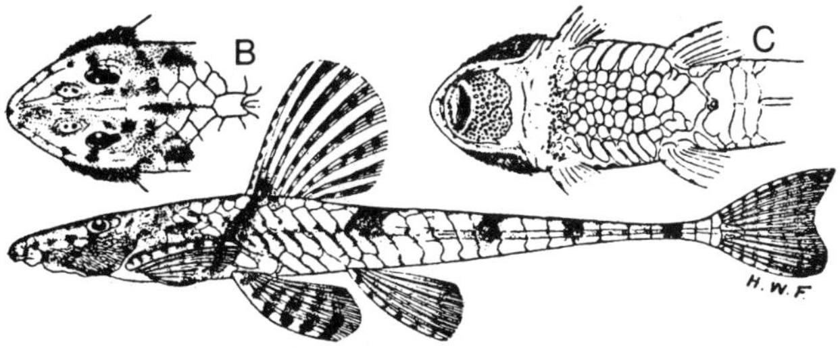

Rineloricaria pareiacantha; (b) dorsal view of head; (c) ventral view. (From Fowler, 1954.)

completely covered with several series of small platelets. The upper lip is narrow, the edge with short, rounded papillae, and dorsally naked; the lower lip is covered ventrally with numerous isolated papillae. A short rictal barbel is present. The strongly bifid teeth are present in both jaws, those of the upper jaw smaller than those in the lower. The dorsal fin is located opposite or nearly opposite the origin of the ventral fins and has a spine and 6 (rarely 5) rays. The anal fin has a spine and 4 rays, the pectoral fins a spine and 6 rays, and the ventral fins a spine and 5 rays. Sexual dimorphism is present in the form of bristle-like structures along the sides of the snout, usually on the dorsum of the pectoral fin spine and rays, and often on the dorsum of the head and postoccipital and predorsal scutes in mature males.

Most of the spawning reports of whiptail catfishes, regardless of what generic and specific names are given to them by the aquarist, involve species of *Rineloricaria*. These are normally peaceful, slow, bottom-living species that are more active during twilight hours or when the light level is low. When fed (this should be in the evenings) they criss-cross the bottom in zigzag movements searching for the food. When algae are present they will browse on it, scraping it from the rocks, glass, or even plant leaves. The mouth is also used for holding fast in strong currents. If an aquarium individual is disturbed when so attached it may hold fast or may dart around the tank to another, more protected, spot and reattach itself. The tanks housing whiptails should not be smaller than 38 to 76 liters capacity. A bottom substrate should be provided and many hiding places formed by rockwork, driftwood, and plants (*Aponogeton* and *Echinodorus* have been mentioned). Good aeration and filtration are usually beneficial and often necessary when dealing with fish from fast-flowing streams that require a high oxygen content. Although spawnings have occurred in both hard and soft water, almost all accounts refer to a pH of 6.4 to 6.8. The temperature range seems to be best between 18° and 27°C. At higher temperatures problems may occur. Minimal water changes are recommended (approximately 10% per week). Whiptails will accept a varied diet including most live and prepared foods available for aquarium fishes. Vegetable matter should be well represented.

For spawning, a darkened cave or similar area must be provided (these fishes are said to spawn in hollow logs in nature). The favorite with aquarists seems to be PVC tubing. Glass and bamboo tubes can also be used, but the glass may prove too slippery for the adhesive eggs to properly attach to the sides. The PVC tube should be open at both ends and roughened on the inside to provide a better attachment site for the eggs. The tube should then be placed in a darkened area where there is free access to both openings by the fish. The diameter of the tube should be a quarter to a half time larger than the diameter across the male's pectoral fins. Larger tubes are commonly shunned. At least one account tells how for four weeks there was no spawning action in the breeding tank, yet when a proper size PVC tube was added, spawning started within 45 minutes. Other accounts related that their whiptails would spawn on any suitable substrate as long as it was in a secluded place, and this even included plant leaves and the aquarium glass. This variation may be due to the intensity of the sex drive (high = will spawn in wide variety of places; low = will only spawn in tight, secluded place) or to the spawning of a variety of different species with different habits. Sexual dimorphism is easily observed in mature fishes for the males develop bristles on the sides (and sometimes the top) of the head and on the pectoral spines (and fins in some). The size of these bristles may vary with the season, sexually active males possessing the better developed "whiskers." Additionally, the head of the female is more pointed than that of the male when viewed from above and the pectoral fin of the male is more powerfully developed. In ripe females the eggs can also be seen through the abdominal wall with proper lighting.

Although spawning is relatively easily accomplished in the community tank, when several males are present there seems to be less spawning activity and more combat between the territorial males. Most of the fights are ritual in nature and actual physical contact is not made, the combatants being satisfied by threats alone. However, more serious fights do occur, especially in sexually active males. These will sit side by side and engage in tail-beating in a head to tail position or orient themselves head to head in which case the bristles may actually become entangled for a few moments. In a set up spawning tank the action can be more controlled. In fact, one aquarist advocates separate conditioning for the sexes and indicates that, when the fish are placed in the freshly aged cooler water of the spawning tank, spawning should occur within 24 hours. In most instances the male will take over one of the PVC tubes and guard his residence (territory) from all intruders. Again, depending either upon whether there is individual variation or more than one species involved, the male will clean the nest site or he will allow a female to enter his domain and both will clean it for one to three days. In many cases the spawning cannot be observed, the best indication of spawning being a pair of tails sticking out of one end of the PVC tube. But one account reports that the female deposits 2-5 eggs at a time that adhere to the substrate. The male pushes her away and fertilizes them. The action is repeated over and over until the female is depleted. This could mean anywhere between 40 and 200 or more eggs, depending on the condition of the spawners and the species involved, and takes several hours. The male guards the eggs from

The plate arrangement on the ventral surface of many loricariids is systematically important, often defining genera. Fortunately for aquarists loricariids, like this *Rineloricaria* sp. (?cf *nigricauda*), will exhibit their ventral surface as seen here. Photo by Chvojka Milan.

this point as the female departs and takes no more notice of them. The male will ignore the female, in contrast to species of *Sturisoma* where the female is not tolerated in the same tank with the male. *Sturisoma* males are also said to sometimes eat during the incubation period, sometimes leaving the eggs to seek out food. *Rineloricaria* males do not eat during the incubation period. The male, if pushed away from the eggs, will even frantically try to get back to them and will cover them with his body on his return. The male will fan and clean the eggs for a period of anywhere from one to three weeks.

The eggs, initially amber, yellow, green, or gray (different species ?), turn darker as they develop. They are 2-3 mm in diameter and adhesive. Hatching takes anywhere from three to 16 days (different species ?) but usually ten to 12 days. The length of hatching time is also dependent upon the temperature. Hatching of a spawn will extend over a 36-hour period, with the resulting fry 6-10 mm in length. There is a green yolk sac in those fry that hatch from the green eggs, yellow yolk sac from yellow eggs. The sucker mouth is said to be functional from hatching, one account relating how the fry "rock" back and forth on their yolk sacs until their mouth contacts the substrate, whereupon they "stick." After about three days the yolk is about used up and feeding should begin. At this time they may be scattered about the aquarium, hanging onto the plants, rocks, and sides of the tank. The fry have good appetites and should be fed several (five or six) times a day on a variety of foods. Natural algae should be fed if available. Microworms, chopped Grindal worms, and brine shrimp have been used with success, with supplements of lettuce and spinach in the absence of algae. The fry grow rapidly for the first month or so, then the growth rate slows. After about two weeks the fry look like miniature adults (some say they are perfect miniatures from hatching). Spawning of tank-bred individuals is said to have been accomplished after seven months. Spawnings are usually accomplished in the early evening hours, and at least one pair is said to have spawned every ten days for several spawnings.

Rineloricaria uracantha from Panama breeds all year in the wild but peaks during the height of the rainy season (October), then there is a lull at the end of the dry season (April). *R. fallax* is reported to spawn 200 or more eggs in one season; larger species like *R. latirostris* spawn about the same number, smaller species about 120. Little else is known about specific species.

One more thing. Identification of the whiptails in aquaria is usually based on whether the caudal fin has only an upper or both an upper and a lower filament. It should be noted that these filaments are quite fragile and break off easily in aquaria, making them very unreliable characters. It is hoped that with further study the species commonly kept and bred by aquarists can be identified and that characters that will enable the aquarists themselves to recognize them will be put forth.

The genus *Ixinandria* is a small genus containing two species from Bolivia and Argentina, *I. montebelloi* and *I. steinbachi*. It resembles *Rineloricaria* in most of its characteristics but differs by having a completely naked abdomen. It must be remembered, however, that certain species of *Rineloricaria* (the *R. lima* complex) have an abdomen incompletely covered with derman ossifications. In addition, the development of the bristles in mature males is strikingly different in *Ixinandria* from all the other genera.

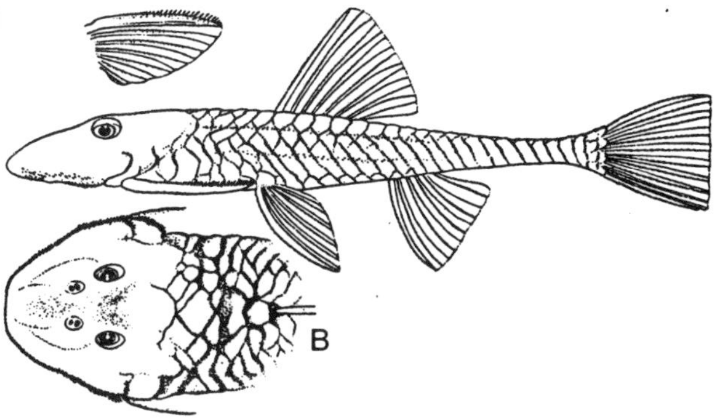

Ixinandria montebelloi; (b) dorsal view of head. (From Fowler, 1940.)

The genus *Dasyloricaria* is another small genus. It consists of only about five species from Panama and Colombia that resemble *Spatuloricaria* in general appearance as well as

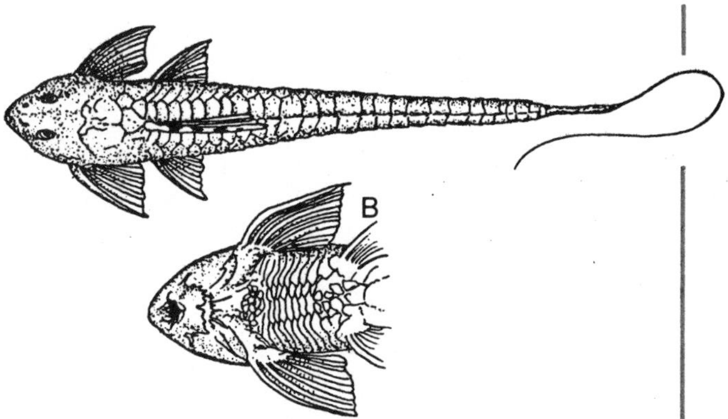

Dasyloricaria filamentosa; (b) ventral view.

in the structure of the lips, but it differs by the peculiar and complete covering of the abdomen by salient scutes. The mature males possess thin, rather short bristles along the side of the head like a brush, not much different from those seen in many species of *Rineloricaria*. Males carry the eggs around on their enlarged lower lip.

The genus *Spatuloricaria* contains about 11 species mostly from Colombia, but also from Venezuela, Brazil, and Peru. The snout is bony, without a naked area near its tip, and the supraoccipital terminates posteriorly in an elevated spiny keel. The sides of the head in mature males are provided with numerous stiff bristles. A postorbital notch is present. The lips are papillate, the lower lip margined with barbels or dermal lappets and the upper with a series of barbels along the anterior margin but disposed in a double row in front of the gape. The teeth are slender, expanded at their tips into bilobed spoon-shaped lobes, the inner lobe much larger than the outer. Schultz (1944) took this as a major distinguishing character, but it was subsequently found (Isbrücker, 1973) that these teeth are not that unique and can be found at least in some species of *Crossolòricaria*. Thus Schultz' statement that *Spatuloricaria* is a *Loricaria* with spoon-shaped teeth must be taken with this in mind. All the lateral scutes have serrated keels. On the side of the supraoccipital keel is a pair of small, keeled plates followed by two median plates with a pair of keels and a predorsal plate with a single keel. The abdomen is covered by numerous small platelets in adults; young individuals may have naked bellies. The upper surface of the pectoral fin is spiny, the ventral fin spine is produced a bit beyond the soft rays, and the spine of the anal is about equal to the next branched ray. The posterior margin of the dorsal fin is concave, its first rays longest; the anal fin is rounded. The caudal fin has its upper ray elongate; the lower ray is also elongate but not nearly as long as the upper.

Spatuloricaria caquetae; (b) top view; (c) ventral view. (From Fowler, 1954.)

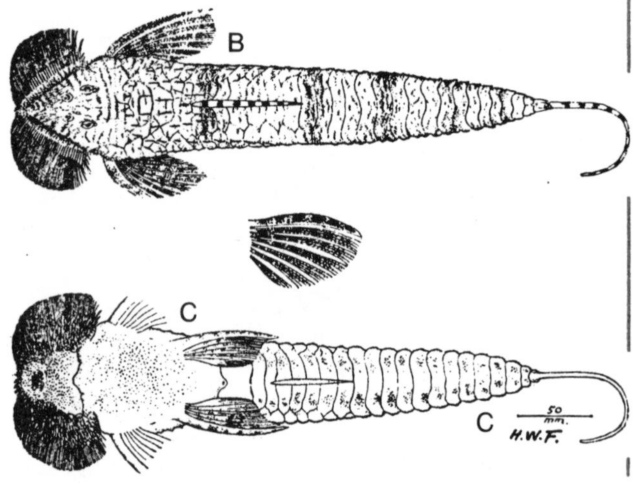

Isbrücker's subtribe Planiloricariina as late as 1981 included only the genus *Planiloricaria*. In 1982, however, was described (Martin Salazar, Isbrücker, & Nijssen, 1982) the genus *Dentectus*, which was placed in this subtribe along with the entire *Pseudohemiodon*-group (*Pseudohemiodon, Rhadinoloricaria, Crossoloricaria*), bringing the total genera of the subtribe to five. *Pyxiloricaria* was added in 1984 and *Apistoloricaria* in 1986, increasing the total to seven. This subtribe is diagnosed as having small jaws with reduced dentition (not only small teeth but also few teeth) and numerous long barbels along the upper and lower lips as well as in the buccal cavity. The Loricariina have larger and fewer premaxillary teeth and the dentary teeth are more robust. The filaments present along the posterior edge and on the surface of the lower lip are longer, smooth, and may be bifid or trifid in the subtribe Loricariina, but they are almost absent on the surface and sometimes reduced to small elongate papillae, and the long filaments along the lower lip are not smooth but have papillae (sometimes elongate) in Planiloricariina. Finally, the snout may be produced in some members of Planiloricariina but not produced in any of the Loricariina.

The genus *Planiloricaria* contains only a single species, *P. cryptodon*, from the Rio Ucayali in Peru. The head is greatly depressed and broad, with a rounded snout. The eyes are small and without a flap, and the orbital notch is absent or only slightly evident. The lower lip is narrow and possesses numerous long, fringed barbels. The rictal barbels are long and have about 20 subbarbels. Upper jaw teeth are absent, while in the lower jaw there are only three small, simple, spoon-shaped teeth on each side. The dorsal surface of the head is without prominent ridges of denticles. The dorsal fin has a spine and 6 rays and has a long dorsal filament. The anal fin has a spine and 4 rays, the pectoral fin a spine and 6 rays, and the ventral fin a spine and 5 rays. The caudal fin has a long filament in the upper part. There are 40 lateral body scutes. The abdomen is almost completely covered with minute scutelets. Secondary sexual dimorphism is not known.

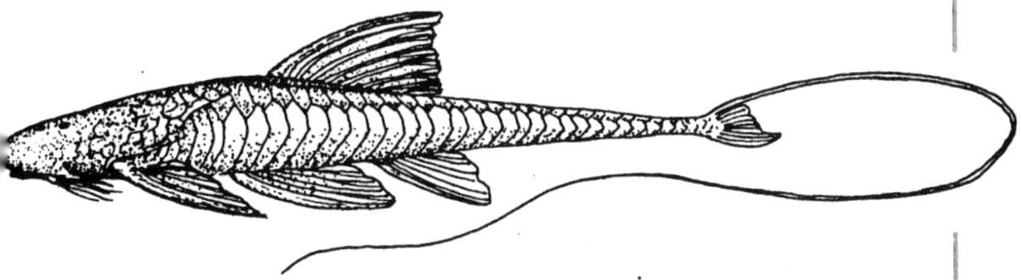

Planiloricaria cryptodon.

The genus *Pseudohemiodon* contains some seven species from Brazil, Uruguay, Ecuador, and Paraguay. The head and body are depressed, the head about as long as broad and with a triangular or rounded snout. The supraorbitals have a pair of weak keels, the eyes are small and have a dorsal flap, and there is a shallow, sometimes quite inconspicuous orbital notch. The lower lip is narrow and usually possesses short and rounded papillae. The teeth in the jaws are spoon-shaped and simple or with only a slight notch on one side that may indicate a tendency toward a second lobe. The upper jaw has 4 to 7 teeth on each side, the lower jaw 5-10. The lateral body scutes usually number about 32 to 34, with 13-21 that are coalescing. The abdomen may have a few large plates in a single series, a median row of half a dozen transverse scutes between the pectoral and ventral fins surrounded anteriorly and posteriorly by small and irregular scutelets, or may be completely covered with small, irregular scutelets. The dorsal fin has a spine and 6 rays, the anal fin a spine and 4 rays, the pectoral fin a spine and 6 rays, and the ventral fin a spine and 5 rays. The caudal fin usually has long filaments.

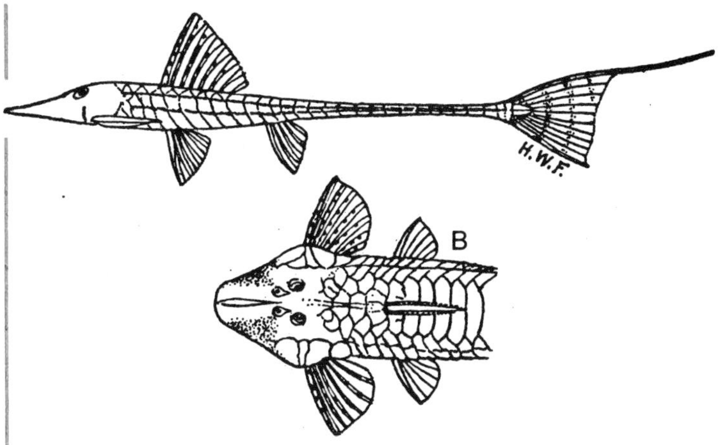

Pseudohemiodon platycephala; (b) dorsal view. (From Fowler, 1954.)

Members of this genus are rarely seen imported for the aquarium trade. It is probable that *P. laticeps* has been brought in among other miscellaneous similar-looking species. An almost strict vegetable diet has been recommended for this species.

The genus *Pyxiloricaria* was described in 1984 by Isbrücker & Nijssen on the basis of a single species, *P. menezesi*, from Rio Miranda and Rio Cuiaba, Mato Grosso, Brazil. The body is long and slender, the head triangular and depressed. The eyes are moderate, oval, and have a small anterior notch and a larger posterior notch. The teeth are small, simple, and have a broad, rounded crown. The upper lip is narrow and possesses at either side six or seven simple barbels along or near the edge. The premaxilla is surrounded by three series of slender, simple barbels, a longitudinal trifid barbel at the jaw's symphysis, and a series of three barbels at each side. The maxillary barbel has six barblets, is free from the margin of the snout, and is embedded in a groove. The lower lip possesses short, smooth, simple barbels (a few bifid and trifid barbels in front of these) that decrease in length toward the posterior margin. The mandibulae are surrounded by few, slender barbels and by a wide naked area. The snout tip is covered with odontodes. A large, fleshy, transverse flap covers about half of the branchiostegal membrane. The ventral surface of the head is naked except for marginal series of dermal osssifications. A preanal plate is ab-

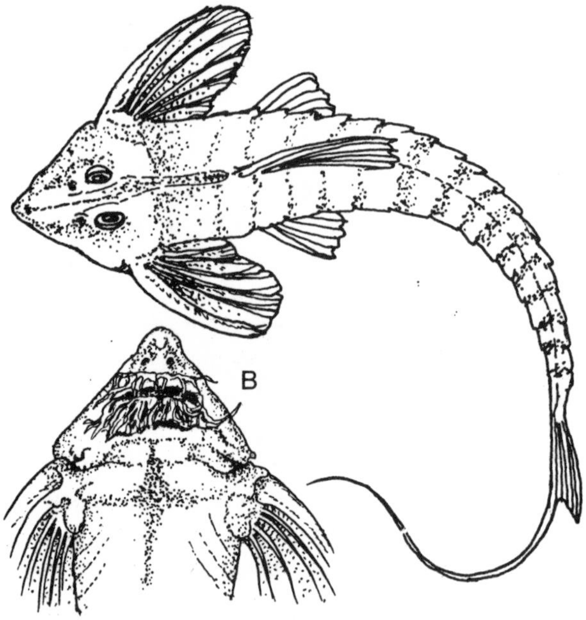

Pyxiloricaria menezesi; (b) ventral view of head.

sent. The abdomen is partially covered with scutelets, with naked areas between them and the thoracic scutelets. There are 29 to 30 lateral scutes along the body.

The dorsal fin has a spine and 6 + i rays, the anal with a spine and 4 + i rays. The pelvic fins have a spine and 5 rays and the pectoral fin has a rather large and broad, flattened spine and 6 proximally flattened rays. (Isbrücker & Nijssen, 1984.)

The genus *Crossoloricaria* contains only four species, *C. cephalaspis* from the Rio Magdalena in Colombia, *C. rhami* from Peru, *C. variegata* from Panama, and *C. venezuelae* from Venezuela. The genus agrees very well with *Pseudohemiodon* but differs by the structure of the lower lip, which in *Pseudohemiodon* bears

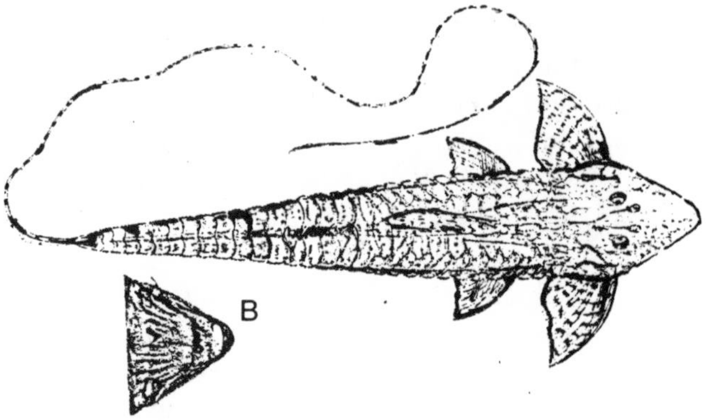

Crossoloricaria variegata; (b) view of mouth. (From Schultz, 1944.)

short and rounded papillae whereas that of *Crossoloricaria* is covered by numerous filamentous barbels. In addition, *Crossoloricaria* is unique in the subfamily by possessing an abdomen that has only a single series of longitudinal plates in the middle, leaving a naked space between it and the lateral scutes of the body. An exception is *C. rhami* where the abdomen resembles that of *Pseudohemiodon*.

The genus *Dentectus* contains a single species, *D. barbarmatus*, from Venezuela. The head and body are strongly depressed, and the caudal peduncle is long and slender. There is a pair of ridges on the supraoccipital, and the snout is rounded. There is an anterior orbital notch and a shallow, less prominent posterior orbital notch. The premaxillaries are very small and are widely separated from both each other and the maxillaries; the dentaries are also widely separated from each other. Both lips are narrow and have numerous long, filamentous barbels arranged in sev-

Dentectus barbarmatus. (From Fernandez-Yepez, ?)

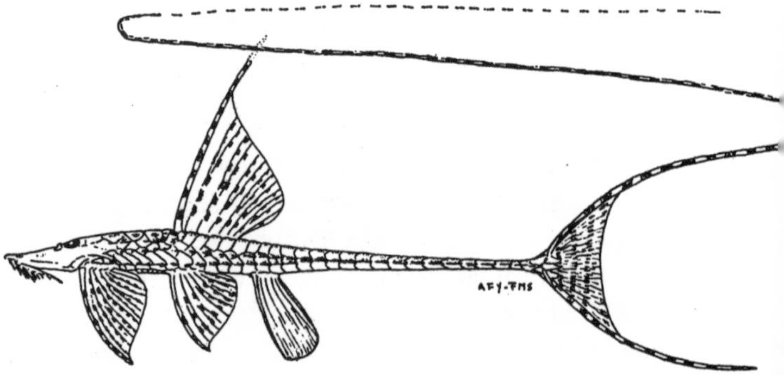

eral somewhat irregular rows. The externolateral bases of the filaments of the upper lip and most of the margins of the maxillary barbels are provided with odontode-bearing dermal ossifications. The barbels of the margin of the lower lip possess enlarged papillae laterally while the other barbels, with the exception of the maxillary barbel, are usually smooth. Three small elongate teeth with expanded tips are present on each premaxillary and, similarly, up to three similar teeth are present on each dentary. There are 31-33 lateral body scutes, 16-18 coalescing. The abdominal and thoracic areas have an irregular pattern of small scutelets, but the ventral surface of the head is naked. The dorsal fin has a filamentous spine and 6 rays, the pectoral fin a spine and 6 rays, the ventral fin a spine and 5 rays, and the anal fin a spine and 4 or 5 rays. The upper and lower unbranched rays of the caudal fin are produced into filaments, the upper filament about 2½ times longer than the standard length of the fish, the lower filament much shorter.

The presence of dermal ossifications on the barbels along with the structure of the lips, jaws, and teeth are not seen in any other member of the family.

The genus *Rhadinoloricaria* contains a single species, *R. macromystax*, from the Peruvian Amazon. The head and body are depressed and the snout is quite acute, the sides of the snout being concave. The eye is moderate in size, and an orbital notch is present. The lips possess numerous long, fringed barbels; the upper lip is quite narrow. The teeth are slender and spoon-shaped with no outer lobe or only a minute one, and are present in both jaws. There are 33 lateral body scutes, 17 or 18 coalescing, and the abdomen is covered with small scutes from the anus to the posterior margin of the gill openings with only a median notch anteriorly that is left naked. There are long rictal barbels. The dorsal and pectoral fins have a spine and 6 rays, the ventral a spine and 5 rays, and the anal a spine and 4 rays. The caudal fin has an upper filament.

Rhadinoloricaria macromystax; (b) ventral view. (From Fowler, 1954.)

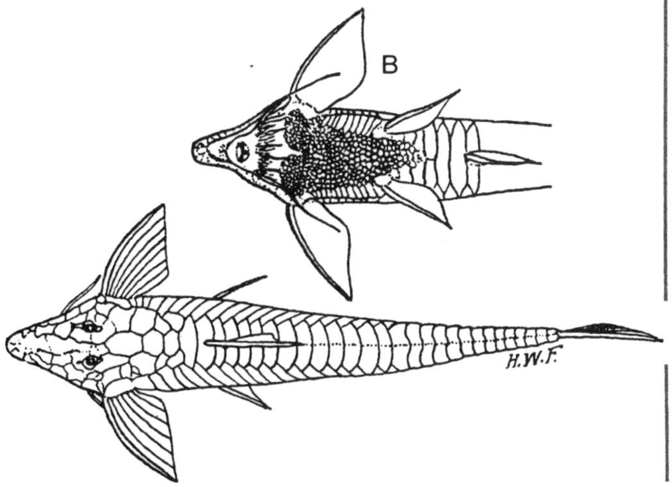

Rhadinoloricaria is closely related to *Pseudohemiodon* but differs from that genus by the acute snout and the long rictal barbels. It also resembles *Sturisoma* but differs in the structure of the lips and the dentition.

The genus *Apistoloricaria* is a monotypic genus containing only *A. condei* from Rio Tiputini and Rio Aguarico, tributaries of the Rio Napo in Ecuador. It belongs to the subtribe Planiloricariina along with *Planiloricaria, Rhadinoloricaria, Dentectus, Pyxiloricaria, Pseudohemiodon,* and *Crossoloricaria. Apistoloricaria* appears closest to *Rhadinoloricaria* and was contrasted with that genus by Isbrücker & Nijssen (1986) as follows. *Apistoloricaria* has a circular iris which is relatively narrow and without the dorsal expansion covering the lens; *Rhadinoloricaria* has the expansion. *Apistoloricaria* has filamentous prolongations to the "spines" (simple rays) of the dorsal and pectoral fins; these are not present in *Rhadinoloricaria. Apistoloricaria* lacks the ventrorostral prolongation of the ventral edge of the snout that is present in *Rhadinoloricaria.* In addition, *Apistoloricaria* has a smaller but deeper head, shorter predorsal area, bigger inferior lip, larger outer barbel on the edge of the lower lip, shorter thorax, deeper body, and longer caudal peduncle than *Rhadinoloricaria*. It also has 14 barbels along the edge of the lower lip compared to 12 in *Rhadinoloricaria*.

Most of the specimens were collected in dark, turbid water with a slow to rapid current. The depth varied between 2 and 10 meters, and no aquatic vegetation was present. The bottom consisted of sand, mud, dead leaves, twigs, branches, and small logs. The banks were forested. Of importance to aquarists were temperatures of 25.5-26.5°C and a pH of 6.8 (Isbrücker & Nijssen, 1986).

The genus *Hemiodontichthys* is the only member of the subtribe Hemiodontichthyina. It contains the single species *H. aciperserinus* from the Rio Guapore, Mato Grosso, Brazil, and many other localities. The body is elongate and depressed but fairly sturdy, not especially slender and sticklike. The snout is elongated and usually possesses an expansion at its tip that is provided with distinct recurved

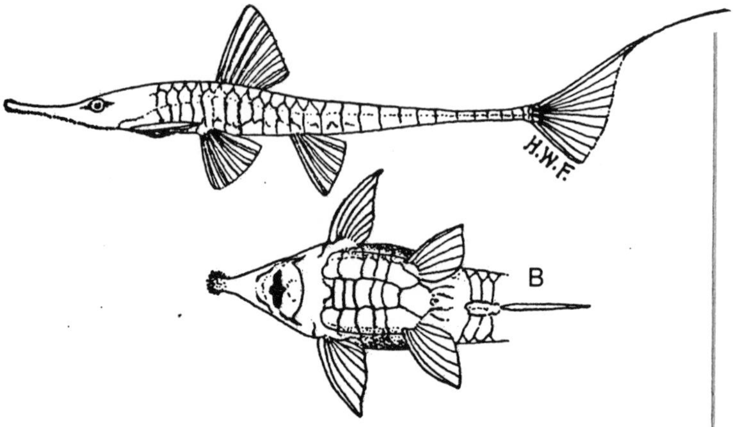

Hemiodontichthys acipenserinus; (b) ventral view. (From Fowler, 1954.)

dermal denticles. The snout tip has a narrow naked area, and the supraoccipital process has a broad tip. The eyes are moderate, the orbit with a fairly large posterior notch. Dermal denticles are present on the dorsal surface of the head and body and on both sides of the rostrum; these denticles are arranged in strongly wavy lines. Dermal denticles also form distinct ridges along the longitudinal lateral body scutes. The edges of both upper and lower lips have small, irregular flaps; the upper lip has a deep median notch and the lower lip also is notched in the middle. Both lips are covered dorsally and ventrally by numerous small papillae, these papillae more strongly evident in nuptial males. There are about 10 to 16 small teeth in each of the lower jaws; the upper jaw is toothless. Pharyngeal teeth are present. About 27 to 29 lateral body scutes are present, 11 to 14 coalescing. The chest and abdomen are covered by large squarish scutes arranged in three median rows. Anterior to these may be two or more small triangular to irregular scutes. The dorsal fin has a spine and 6 rays, the anal fin a spine and 4 rays, the pectoral fin a spine and 6 rays, and the ventral fin a spine and 5 rays. The upper caudal fin ray may be prolonged into a filament. Nuptial males develop large, broad upper and lower lips, and the teeth of the two sexes differ slightly. (Isbrücker & Nijssen, 1974.)

Although *Hemiodontichthys acipenserinus* has been imported for the aquarium trade, it apparently has not become a favorite and presently appears only occasionally.

The genus *Reganella* has also been placed in its own subtribe, Reganellina. It contains a single species, *R. depressa*, from the Rio Negro and Marabitanos in Brazil. It is very similar in general aspect to *Hemiodontichthys*. It has an elongated snout that is slightly concave laterally but without a terminal expansion. The tip has a very narrow naked area. The dermal denticles on the external ossifications are not well developed but do form ridges along the lateral scutes. The eyes are moderate, and the orbit has a posterior notch. The upper lips are narrow, the outer edge possessing small papillae. The lower lip is moderate and deeply to moderately notched medially; the outer edge has as many as 4 somewhat prolonged papillae or small flaps, and the ventral surface has numerous tiny papilla. Up to 18 teeth are present on each side of the lower jaw; the upper jaw is toothless. About 29 or 30 lateral body scutes are present, 14 or 15 coalescing. The throat, chest, and abdo-

Reganella depressa; (b) ventral view. (From Fowler, 1954.)

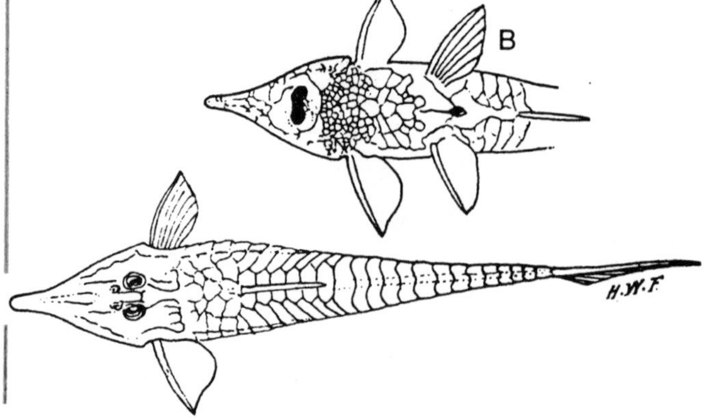

men are covered with small, irregular scutelets that become smaller anteriorly and extend almost as far as the margin of the lower lip. The dorsal and pectoral fins have a spine and 6 rays, the anal fin a spine and 4 rays, and the ventral fin a spine and 5 rays. The caudal fin may have the upper ray elongated into a filament. *Reganella* does not seem to develop enlarged lips in order to protect the eggs as does *Hemiodontichthys, Dasyloricaria, Limatulichthys, Pseudoloricaria*, and *Loricariichthys*. (Isbrücker & Nijssen, 1974.)

Since *Reganella* and *Hemiodontichthys* are quite similar, Isbrücker & Nijssen (1974) prepared a table listing several distinguishing characters. Among these were: opercle reaching lower margin of head in *Hemiodontichthys* but not in *Reganella*; interorbital broad anteriorly in *Hemiodontichthys*, narrow in *Reganella*; head more slender than body in *Hemiodontichthys*, broader than body in *Reganella*; upper lip well developed and fused with ventral margin of head in *Hemiodontichthys* but narrow, weakly developed, and not fused with ventral margin of head in *Reganella*; and area surrounding anal papilla almost completely ossified in *Hemiodontichthys*, naked in *Reganella*.

The genus *Loricariichthys* is the only genus of its subtribe (Loricariichthyina). It contains about 15 species from northern South America and as far south as Rio de Janeiro. The body is elongate, depressed, and the snout is rounded or pointed (but not elongated). The supraoccipital may or may not have a pair of keels. The eyes may be moderate to small, and there is a postorbital notch. The upper lip has the edges of the right and left sides separated from each other, while the lower lip, which is smooth or with small papillae, may be moderate or, in nuptial males, quite large and cover the entire naked surface of the head. There is a somewhat smooth-edged flap in front of the outer sides of the upper jaws that extends as acute small "flaps." Posterior to these flaps may be seen small barbel-like papillae. The teeth are weakly developed, with up to 17 on each of the upper jaws and up to 34 on each of the lower jaws. The tips of these teeth are rather acute in females and more rounded in males. There are about 30-36 body scutes in a longitudinal line, the lateral keels being sharp and separate. The lower surface of the head is naked, and the abdomen is provided with 2 to 5 median series of scutes in *L. stuebeli*, etc., and one or 2 series in species like *L. nudirostris*. An anal plate is present, bordered anteriorly by 2 or 3 scutes. The dorsal fin has a spine and 6 rays, the anal fin a spine and 4 rays, each pectoral fin a spine and 6 rays, and each ventral fin a spine and 5 rays. The caudal fin is generally emarginate, with the upper lobe the longer and the upper caudal ray elongate.

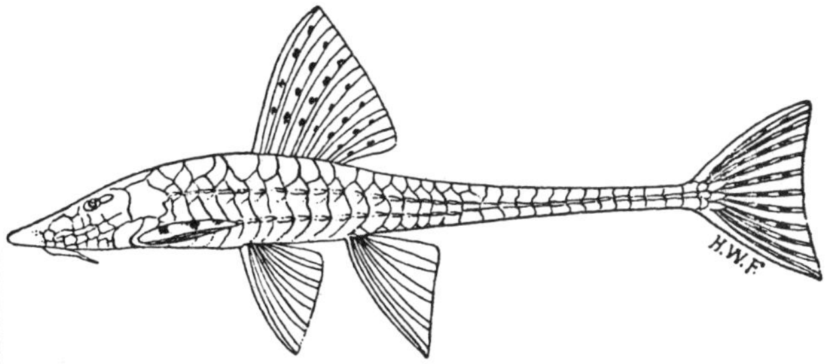

Loricariichthys maculatus. (From Fowler, 1954.)

One of the most interesting and unusual aspects of this genus (which is shared by other genera as already noted) is the development of the lower lip of males and the use to which it is put. The lower lip of brooding males is enlarged posteriorly as a sheet-like membrane over the lower part of the head and in some instances even extends beyond the pectoral fin bases. Adult females have much shorter and thicker lower lips, and males that are not yet sexually mature have lips similar to those of the females and are virtually indistinguishable from them. It was apparently Agassiz who first discovered that some of the loricariine species carried their eggs by using these expanded lips. Steindachner seems to have misinterpreted the use of the male's lip, reporting for *L. spixii* that the eggs were held between the lip and the underside of the head. Regan later cleared up this erroneous conclusion—the eggs are carried on the lower lip.

In Lake Ypacarai, Paraguay, *L. platymetopon* and *L. labialis* females were observed with their abdomens greatly distended with ripe eggs, body armor or no body armor. The eggs were yellow to yellowish orange in color. Observations on other species seem to agree, although one described the eggs as lime green. The eggs deposited have been described as forming large globular pads. The eggs are said to be spherical and without a yolk plug or embryonal streak when first spawned, with a mean diameter of about 2.1 mm. More advanced eggs are reported to be larger, between 2.5 and 4.0 mm. The egg pad was measured in one case at roughly 25-45 mm for a clutch of about 92 eggs (Allison & Rojas, 1975); they reported the newly hatched fry to be about 8.5 mm, which agrees with other observations. However, clutch sizes of up to 1,000 (192-1,005 with a mean of 508) eggs were observed. *Loricariichthys* species are usually collected over soft, muddy substrates.

In 1981, Isbrücker erected the subtribe Pseudoloricariina for *Pseudoloricaria* and *Limatulichthys*. The former genus was considered by Isbrücker and Nijssen in 1976 to include two species, but the second species was later placed in its own genus (*Limatulichthys*) by Isbrücker & Nijssen (in Isbrücker, 1979). The subtribe is characterized by having a narrow upper lip that has numerous minute papillae extending anteriorly into a series of short, broad, separated, pointed, barbel-like flaps. The largest flaps are located anterior to each of the upper jaws, and they decrease posteriorly along the outer sides of the rictal barbels; the largest flaps may be bifid or trifid and deeply notched. The mouth is cup-like, the teeth longer and heavier than those of Loricariichthyina. There are up to 13 teeth on each side of the upper jaw and up to 15 on each side of the lower jaw. The postorbital notch is not as well developed as in some species of the Loricariichthyina, and there are generally more abdominal scutes than in that subtribe. *Pseudoloricaria* and *Limatulichthys* are probably descendents of a lineage involving *Rineloricaria* and *Dasyloricaria* that lost the ability to develop enlarged odontodes in the males, replacing it instead with the ability to develop the enlarged lower lip.

The genus *Pseudoloricaria* contains a single species, *P. laeviuscula*, from the state of Para, Brazil, and other localities. The head and body are depressed, the depth of the head contained about twice in its width. The occipital ends in a triangular process bordered by a pair of obscurely bicarinate nuchal plates. The head does not have distinct ridges or keels. The orbit has a shallow posterior notch, and the eyes are moderate, contained 5 to 7 times in the head length. The snout is pointed, with the sides and tip granular. The barbels are fringed, and the upper lip has a fringe of long cirri. The lower lip is covered with larger and smaller papillae, it is narrow in the female but covers the entire underside of the head in the male. The teeth are well developed and numerous in both jaws. The lower surface of the snout and head are naked, and the middle portion of the belly is entirely covered with small scutes in the adult and naked in the young. The anal plate in adults is bordered anteriorly and laterally by a series of small plates that are larger in the male than they are in the female. The caudal fin is emarginate.

The genus *Limatulichthys* contains a single species, *L. punctatus*, from the Amazon. It is very much like *Pseudoloricaria* but differs from that species by the disposition of the scutelets of the abdomen. In *Pseudoloricaria*

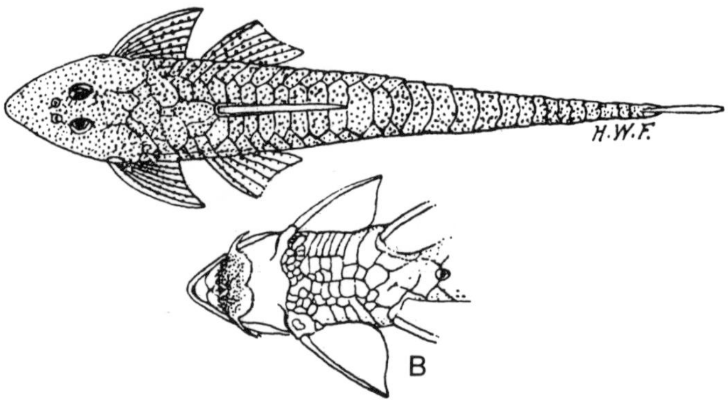

Limatulichthys punctatus; (b) ventral view. (From Fowler, 1954.)

they are nearer to those seen in several species of the genus *Loricaria*, while in *Limatulichthys* they are arranged more like those of species of the *Rineloricaria platyura*-complex. Also, there are 34 to 36 lateral scutes in *Pseudoloricaria*, 23 to 27 coalescing, while in *Limatulichthys* there are 31 or 32 lateral scutes, 18 to 22 coalescing.

The final group to be dealt with in this family is the Harttiini. This was originally proposed as a subfamily by Boeseman (1971) but was considered by Isbrücker & Nijssen (1978) as representing only a tribe. As defined, the Harttiini includes the *Harttia*-group (*Harttia, Harttiella*, and *Cteniloricaria*), the *Sturisoma*-group (*Sturisoma, Lamontichthys, Pterosturisoma*, and *Sturisomatichthys*), and the Metaloricariina (*Metaloricaria*), the first two groups comprising the subtribe Harttiina. The Harttiini is diagnosed as having the origin of the dorsal fin approximately opposite the origin of the ventral fins; the caudal fin with 12 (rarely 11) branched rays; never a postorbital notch; numerous teeth (15-125, apparently increasing in number with age) that are bilobed and form a comb (with the exception of *Metaloricaria*); little developed gill rakers (filamentous); small, villiform (possibly even absent) pharyngeal teeth; and a usually strongly depressed body that from the dorsal aspect may be broad to quite slender. Usually there is little diversity in the tooth and lip structure. Secondary sexual dimorphism is seen in the strongly elongated odontodes of mature males along the edge of the snout sometimes extending onto the dorsal surface of the spine and rays of the pectoral fins. The two subtribes are diagnosed as follows: Harttiina—numerous filiform teeth present in the jaws; the lips rather narrow and with a short commisural barbel located on each side. Metaloricariina—like the Harttiina, but with less numerous teeth that are much larger than those of the Harttiina and with a lower lip that is distinctly wider, more or less horseshoe-shaped when compared to that of the Harttiina, where it is narrow and semicircular or semioval.

The genus *Metaloricaria*, the only genus in the subtribe Metaloricariina, contains only a single species, *M. paucidens*, which is further divided into two subspecies, one from Surinam and one from French Guiana. The species is the largest of the tribe, with specimens attaining a standard length of up to 29.5 cm. *Cteniloricaria*, the next largest, reaches only 19 cm. The body is elongate and depressed but not stick-like; the head is triangular in shape. The eyes are rather large and are provided with a narrow dorsal fleshy skin flap that has scattered minute odontodes in some specimens; there is no postorbital notch. There is a large gap between the premaxillaries at the symphysis, and the premaxillaries and dentaries are considerably shorter in

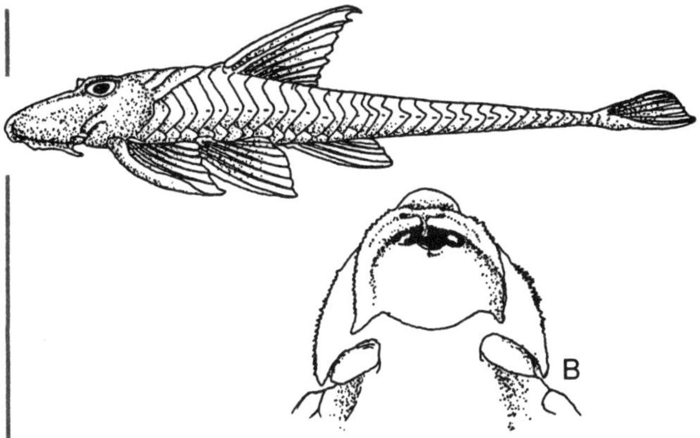

Metaloricaria paucidens; (b) ventral view.

transverse view than those of the Harttiina. The anterior and lateroventral sides of the upper lip are papillose, the upper lip itself being broad and conspicuous when compared to that of the Harttiina. The lower lip is also longer and broader and the maxillary barbel longer than those of the Harttiina. The posterior margin of the lower lip is convex medially and concave at either side toward the maxillary barbel. The upper and lower lips, with the maxillary barbels included, form a horseshoe-shaped pattern that is unique in the family Loricariidae. A prominent fleshy papillose flap is present on the surface of the lip inside the buccal cavity. The teeth have bilobate crowns with a small outer lobe and a larger inner lobe, the outer lobe originating much lower on the tooth than in the Harttiina; the teeth are also less bent at the crown than those of the Harttiina. There are a maximum of 26 teeth (on each side of each jaw), the number increasing with the size of the fish from 4 in specimens of 5.7 cm to 26 in the largest specimens. There are 33 to 36 scutes in the lateral series, 20 to 25 coalescing. Two postoccipital scutes are present as well as three pairs of scutes between the anus and the origin of the anal fin. Four to eight oblong scutes are present on the thorax between the last pectoral fin ray and the ventral fin spine. In specimens larger than about 15 cm S.L. the interthoracic area is completely covered with small, irregular polygonal plates or scutes. The dorsal and pectoral fins each have a spine and 6 rays, the anal fin a spine and 4 rays, and each ventral fin a spine and 5 rays. The caudal fin in smaller individuals is forked, with the lower lobe slightly to distinctly larger than the upper. In larger individuals the caudal fin is frequently damaged in life, making the exact shape difficult to determine (especially when there is already some signs of regeneration), although it is probable that the upper and lower rays do not form filamentous extensions. There is no pectoral pore.

The males do show some form of sexual dimorphism in that they develop odontodes along the side of the head and on the dorsal surface of the pectoral fin. In addition, the pectoral fin spine is thicker than that of the female. Males also exhibit enlarged short odontodes on the ventral side of the ventral fin spine that are more blunt (slender but with thick, rounded tips) than those of females. The inner lobe of each tooth is somewhat shorter and more rounded than the corresponding tooth lobe of females.

The subtribe Harttiina differs from the Metaloricariina as noted above—the teeth of the Harttiina are filiform and very numerous and the lips are much narrower and with a short commisural barbel on each side. A key to the genera is not attempted at this time due to lack of complete descriptive information on some of the genera included.

The genus *Harttia* contains some five species, four from Brazil and one from Surinam. The head and body are strongly depressed, and the head is about as broad as long or slightly longer than it is wide. The snout is rounded to triangular. The eyes are moderate, about 6.5 to 7.5 in the head length; there is no orbital notch. The anterior margin of the snout and the lower surface of the head are naked; the margin of the head has very fine movable bristles. The very papillose lips are narrow and formed into a semicircle. The teeth are fine and numerous (at least 40 in each jaw) with bifurcate crowns, both lobes of the crown being about equal. Scutes in the lateral series are about 29 to 31, none distinctly carinate. There are 2 to 3 plates bordering the occipital. A pair of large anal plates sometimes with a few small plates in front of them are present, otherwise the belly is naked. The caudal fin is slightly emarginate with the outer rays thickened. The first dorsal fin ray (spine) is thickened and flexible.

Harttia loricariformis. (From Fowler, 1954.)

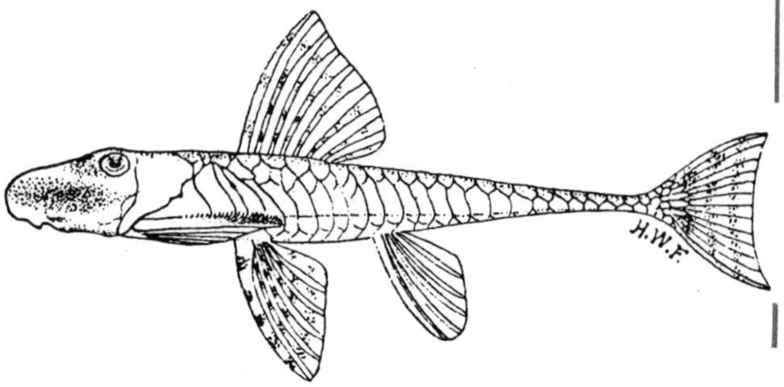

The genus *Harttiella* contains a single species, *H. crassicauda*, from Surinam. It is moderately depressed and broad with the head about as broad as long. The snout when viewed from above is broad and rounded, not projecting. There are about 27 or 28 lateral series body scutes and 3 predorsal scutes. The carinae are rounded and indistinct, even those along the sides of the caudal peduncle. The belly is naked. Otherwise this catfish is similar to *Harttia*.

The genus *Cteniloricaria* contains three species, one from French Guiana and two from Surinam. It resembles *Harttia* in most characters but differs from that genus by its more elongated body and by having its abdomen completely covered by more salient scutes. The caudal fin, moreover, is deeply notched compared to that of *Harttia*, which is only slightly notched.

The genus *Lamontichthys* contains two species, *L. filamentosus* from the Brazilian Amazon and *L. stibaros* from the Ecuadorian Amazon. Based on a description of the type species (*filamentosus*), the head is approximately twice as long as deep. The eyes are moderate, about 7 in the head length; there is no orbital notch. The barbel is minute and the teeth are setiform. There are about 33 scutes in a lateral series, with no keel in front of the dorsal fin. Posterior to the dorsal there is a series of plate-like scutes that are quite smooth except for a small spinulose patch on the lateral edges and a posterior denticulate margin. A second series of scutes below the dorsal origin is weakly bicarinate over about 7 scutes. These plus the lateral series are carinate from the shoulder to the tail. The belly

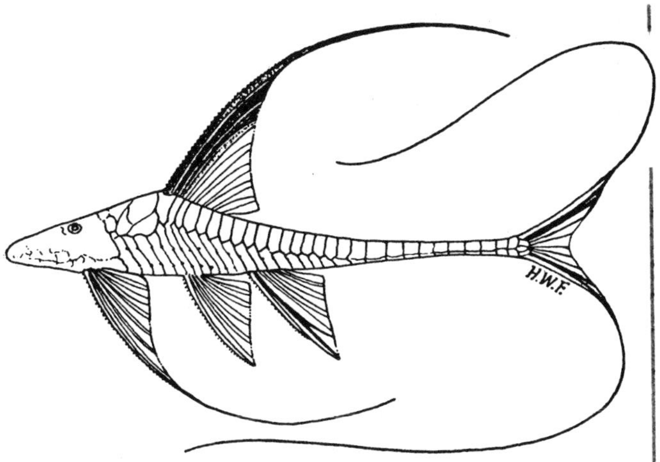

Lamontichthys filamentosus. (From Fowler, 1954.)

is covered with spinulose scutes that extend on the chest and lower surface of the head to the margin of the lower lip. The dorsal, pectoral, and caudal fins are provided with long filaments.

Lamontichthys stibaros is similar to *L. filamentosus* but differs in several characters. It has no filamentous extensions as in *filamentosus*, it shows more conspicuous fusion lines on some of the more prominent scutes, it has the lower lip in a semi-oval (not semicircular) shape, and the interorbital is narrower than that of *filamentosus*. (Isbrucker & Nijssen, 1978.)

The genus *Pterosturisoma* resembles *Lamontichthys* in general body and head shape and the form of the pectoral fin spine and fila-

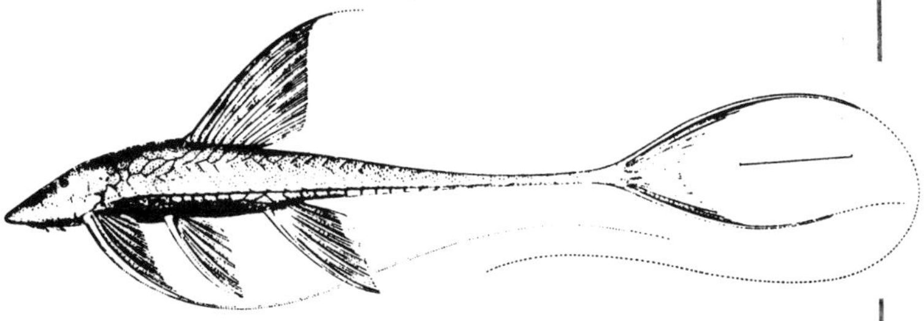

Pterosturisoma microps. (From Eigenmann & Allen, 1942.)

ments. The dorsal fin lacks the filaments, however. *Pterosturisoma* has 6 branched pectoral fin rays. *Lamontichthys* has seven. It contains a single species, *P. microps*, from the vicinity of Iquitos, Peru (Isbrücker & Nijssen, 1978).

The genus *Sturisoma* is the largest genus of this tribe, with approximately 15 species mostly from northern South America and Panama. The body is relatively slender for the tribe, and the caudal peduncle is elongate and stick-like. The head width is contained about 1.4 to 1.8 times in its length, and the snout is generally projecting (less so in *S. brevirostre*). The head has no distinct ridges or prominences, and the sides of the male's snout are provided with bristles. The eyes are moderate to small and are contained between 7 and 11 times in the head length; there is no orbital notch. The lips are papillose, the lower lip rounded and with short marginal fringes; the barbel is short. The teeth are very numerous and setiform. There are between 31 and 37 scutes in a lateral series, the lateral keels being distinct and sharp to weak and obsolete

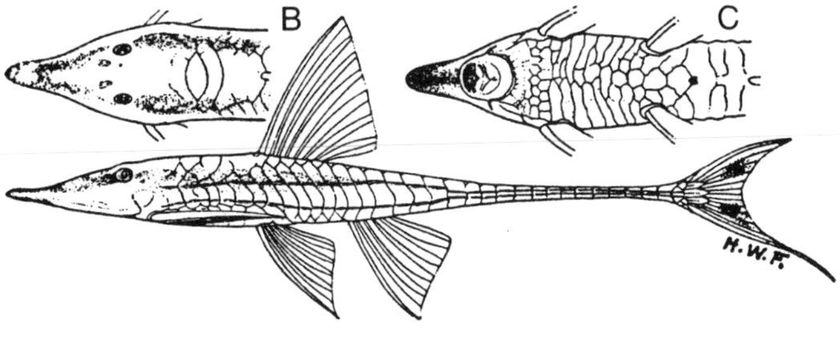

Sturisoma nigrirostrum; (b) dorsal view of head; (c) ventral view. (From Fowler, 1954.)

(at least anteriorly). There are 3 to 4 predorsal scutes and an anal plate bordered anteriorly by 3 scutes that are again bordered by 3 to 5 scutes. The lower surface of the head is covered by small plates except for an area below and behind the lower lip; the abdomen is provided with 2 to 3 series of plates between the lateral series. The caudal fin is emarginate, the outer rays produced.

At least one species of *Sturisoma* is commonly imported for the aquarium trade. Most reports refer to this species as *S. nigrirostrum*, which comes from the Ucayali River basin in Peru, or *S. panamense*, which of course comes from Panama. There is another report that *Sturisoma* is shipped from a point in Colombia, which could indicate that perhaps another species entirely is involved. Hobbyists have dubbed *Sturisoma* species as royal whiptails, hi-fin whiptails, or even sturgeon catfish. They grow fairly large, attaining a length of up to 25 cm, although being quite slender there is not much bulk involved.

The natural habitat of *S. nigrirostrum* has been described as mostly soft water backwaters in which there are no water plants although the banks are overgrown with *Pistia* and/or *Eichhornia*. Branches extending below the surface and driftwood on the bottom serve as surfaces that the fish can scour for "aufwuchs," and they actually scrape off some of the wood itself as an aid in digestion. The surface temperature at one locality was 21°C, the pH 6.9-7.0, the hardness 38°dH, and the conductivity 42 microSiemens. However, the same species has been found in various other water types, possibly due in some cases to seasonal flooding, from 0.2-4.5°dH, pH 5.5-6.5, and 30-100 microSiemens, to hard white water of 9-11°dH, pH 6.9, and 600-650 microSiemens. So it is not very difficult to find a proper water chemistry for this type of catfish as long as extremes and sudden changes are avoided.

Although the whiptail is not so demanding when it comes to oxygen as, for example, species of *Chaetostoma*, it does need clean water. If the dirt in the tank starts to accumulate the whiptail will show its displeasure by increased respiratory movements and will seek out higher oxygen areas such as filter outlets. Periodic water changes, therefore, are highly recommended. One German aquarist replaces a third to a half of the water twice weekly. A 76-liter or larger tank is sufficient, depending upon the size of the individual whiptail. The bottom can be bare or have a moderate grain gravel; fine sand is to be discouraged. A surface cover of water sprite helps cut down the light level, and there should be some rocks or stones along with pieces of driftwood. The driftwood is recommended not only as a source of lignin for the whiptail's digestion, but because they seem to seek out the highest point on which to rest and this usually is the driftwood. A whiptail will often "sit" on one of the higher points and wave its tail back and forth. Caves and PVC tubes are not only not utilized but are actually avoided by the whiptails. These are peaceful and lethargic to moderately active catfishes that do well in a community tank as long as very active fishes are not included. Tankmates such as *Farlowella*, *Peckoltia*, *Rineloricaria*, and *Chaetostoma* have been recommended. During the day the whiptails will be in their resting position, but at twilight they start to become more active and begin to hunt for food. The food is no problem as the usual aquarium fare is accepted, even to flake food. Vegetable matter such as scalded lettuce leaves, spinach, peas, beans, and natural algae is a must. Frozen brine shrimp, chopped or whole tubifex, and bloodworms can round out the diet.

Spawning has been accomplished on a regular basis in captivity. The sexes are readily distinguished by the male's thick growth of head bristles and the female's noticeably heavier body when she fills up with eggs. The adults will usually sit in different parts of the tank until they are ready to spawn. At this time they can be seen together most of the time, side by side. One of the parents cleans a number of areas, possibly including pieces of slate, stones, a flowerpot, or (commonly) the sides of the aquarium. Even the bare tank bottom has been cleaned by one pair. It is interesting to note that in some reports the male is said to do this cleaning and in others the female. Given the sexual dimorphism of the whiptails it is probable that mistaken identity is not involved and both parents may participate. As spawning preparations progress the male will butt the female with its snout and caress her vigorously with his bristles; caudal movements are also increased and vigorous at this time. Eventually the female will choose a site and deposit 3 to 4 eggs in a relatively straight line as the male follows to fertilize them. This continues for a while, with the male nudging the female from time to time to keep her mind on the job. The eggs are about 2 mm in diameter and quite clear. In *S. nigrirostrum* in the wild, spawning is said to occur between June and October. About 80-150 eggs are deposited and are guarded by the male alone. After about three days the eggs become spotted, and after some six days they are quite dark, almost black. By the eighth day the eggs start to hatch, although the time depends upon the temperature of the water. The male loses interest once the fry hatch out. They are about 6 mm long and equipped with a yolk sac. This is absorbed in a couple of days, and the first foods must then be offered. These can be such things as infusoria, natural algae grown in the rearing tank, powdered fry food, and pureed greens.

A second (unnamed) species was also spawned, this one yielding smaller eggs of a pale greenish color, some 200 in number. These parents spawned at intervals of about three weeks. The fry hatched out in five or six days; the actual hatching took up to two days and was often aided by the male mouthing the eggs. The yolk sacs were absorbed over a period of five to six days.

The genus *Sturisomatichthys* contains about four species, three from Colombia and one from Panama. It is very similar to *Sturisoma* but has a triangular snout, not one so prolonged as in *Sturisoma*.

List of species of the family Loricariidae (adapted from Isbrücker, 1980, with additions of subsequently described taxa):

Subfamily Lithogeneinae

Lithogenes Eigenmann, 1909. Type species *L. villosus* Eigenmann.

Lithogenes villosus Eigenmann, 1909. Br. Guiana, Aruataima Falls, Upper Potaro.

Subfamily Neoplecostominae

Neoplecostomus Eigenmann & Eigenmann, 1888. Type species *Plecostomus (Neoplecostomus) microps* = *Plecostomus microps* Steindachner, 1876.

Neoplecostomus granosus (Valenciennes, 1840.) Syntype localities Cayenne & Brazil, Rio de Janeiro.

N. microps (Steindachner, 1876). Der Umbegung von Rio de Janeiro, Rio Parahyba ?.

Subfamily Hypostominae

Rhinelepis von Spix, 1829. Type species *R. aspera*.

Rhinelepis aspera von Spix, in von Spix & Agassiz, 1829. In flumine São Francisco, Lusitanis Roncador.

R. paraguensis Borodin, 1927. Paraguay.

R. strigosa Valenciennes, 1840. Le Parana et d'autres rivers of Corrientes Province.

Pseudorinelepis Bleeker, 1862. Type species *P. genibarbis* = *Rinelepis genibarbis* Valenciennes, 1840.

Pseudorinelepis agassizii (Steindachner, 1877). Manacapouru and the Amazon river "ohne nähere Angabe des Fundortes."

P. genibarbis (Valenciennes, 1840). Probably Brazil.

P. pellegrini (Regan, 1904). Upper Amazon.

Monistiancistrus Fowler, 1940. Type species *M. carachama* Fowler.

Monistiancistrus carachama Fowler, 1940. Ucayali River basin, Contamana, Peru.

Delturus Eigenmann & Eigenmann, 1889. Type species *D. parahybae* Eigenmann & Eigenmann.

Delturus angulicauda (Steindachner, 1876). Rio Mucuri bei Santa Clara, and Rio Parahyba.

D. carinotus (La Monte, 1933). Rio Doce, State of Espirito Santo, Eastern Brazil.

D. parahybae Eigenmann & Eigenmann, 1889. Parahyba.

Pogonopoma Regan, 1904. Type species *Plecostomus (Pogonopoma) wertheimeri* = *Plecostomus Wertheimeri* Steindachner.

Pogonopoma wertheimeri (Steindachner, 1867). Dem Flusse Mucuri im gleichnamigen Districte bei Santa Clara in Brazil.

Pseudancistrus Bleeker, 1862. Type species *Hypostomus barbatus* Valenciennes, 1840.

Pseudancistrus barbatus (Valenciennes, 1840). La Mana, ? Surinam.

P. coquenani (Steindachner, 1915). Coquenan river, a "Nebenflusse" of the Caroni in Venezuela.

P. depressus (Günther, 1868). Probably Surinam.

P. guentheri (Regan, 1904). Br. Guiana.

P. luderwaldti Miranda Ribeiro, 1918. Hansa, às margens do rio Itajati, puerto de blumenau, Estado de Santa Catarina.

P. nigrescens Eigenmann, 1912. Br. Guiana, Amatuk.

Hemipsilichthys Eigenmann & Eigenmann, 1889. Type species *Xenomystus gobio* Lütken. (Incl. *Xenomystus* preoccupied.)

Hemipsilichthys cameroni (Steindachner, 1907). Cabatão River in State of Santa Catherina, Brazil.

H. cerosus Miranda Ribeiro, 1951. Not known (= ? Rio de Janeiro).

H. garbei von Ihering, 1911. No curso superior, montanha acima, do Rio Macahe, no Est. do Rio de Janeiro = State of Rio Janeiro, im Oberlaufe, d.h. am Gebirgsrande.

H. gobio (Lütken, 1874). Not known (? northern South America).

H. regani Giltay, 1936. Rio Curi Curiay, au S. of Rio Negro.

H. steindachneri Miranda Ribeiro, 1918. Flum. Itapucu, Sta. Catarina.

Pareiorhaphis Miranda Ribeiro, 1918. Type species *Hemipsilichthys duseni* Miranda Ribeiro, 1907.

Pareiorhaphis alipionis Gosline, 1947. Ribeirão do Monjolinho, in the Iporanga basis of São Paulo. Label reads: Rio Bethary, São Paulo.

P. duseni (Miranda Ribeiro, 1907). Paraná, and Ribeirão do Monjolinho at 300 m above sea level.

Kronichthys Miranda Ribeiro, 1908. Type species *K. subteres* Ribeiro.

Kronichthys heylandi (Boulenger, 1900). Mountain stream 400 feet above sea level near Santos, southern Brazil.

K. subteres Miranda Ribeiro, 1908. Rios Bethary, Pardo, & Iporanga.

Corymbophanes Eigenmann, 1909. Type species *C. andersoni* Eigenmann.

Corymbophanes andersoni Eigenmann, 1909. Br. Guiana, Aruataima Falls, Upper Potaro.

C. bahianus Gosline, 1947. Fazenda Almada, Ilheus, Bahia.

Upsilodus Miranda Ribeiro, 1924. Type species *U. victori* Ribeiro, 1924.

Upsilodus victori Miranda Ribeiro, 1924. Paqueqer ad Therezopolis, Rio de Janeiro.

Pareiorhina Gosline, 1947. Type species *Rhinelepis rudolphi* Miranda Ribeiro.

Pareiorhina rudolphi (Miranda Ribeiro, 1911). Piquete (Lorena), State of São Paulo.

Pogonopomoides Gosline, 1947. Type species *Rhinelepis parahybae* Steindachner.

Pogonopomoides parahybae (Steindachner, 1877). Parahyba.

Isorineloricaria Isbrücker, 1980. Type species *Plecostomus spinosissimus* Steindachner.

Isorineloricaria festae (Boulenger, 1898). Rios Vinces and Peripa, Ecuador.

I. spinosissimus (Steindachner, 1880). Flüssen um Guayaquil, Ecuador.

Aphanotorulus Isbrücker & Nijssen, 1982. Type species *A. frankei* Isbrücker & Nijssen.

Aphanotorulus frankei Isbrücker & Nijssen, 1982. Peru, Dept. Ucayali, Prov. Corona Porpillo, syst. of Rio Aguaytia, Rio Neshua (about 8°36′S, 74°50′W).

Hypostomus Lacépède, 1803. Type species *Hypostomus guacari* Lacépède, 1803 = *Acipenser plecostomus* Linnaeus, 1758.

Hypostomus affinis (Steindachner, 1876). Rio Mucury near Santa Clara, and Rio Parahyba and "dessen Nebenflusse Muriahe, im Rio Mucury and S. Antonia" near San Antonia de Ferres.

H. agna (Miranda Ribeiro, 1907). Rio de Ribeira, affluent of the Iporanga, São Paulo.

H. alatus de Castelnau, 1855. Rio Sabara, in Minas Geraes Province.

H. albopunctatus (Regan, 1908). Rio Piracicaba, São Paulo, Brazil.

H. ancistroides (von Ihering, 1911). Rio Tatuhy, affluent do lado esquerdo do Rio Sorocaba, Rio Piracicaba, Est. de São Paulo = Rio Tatuhy, linker Nebenzufluss des Rio Sorocaba, São Paulo State, Rio Piracicaba.

H. angipinnatus (Leege, 1922). Mato Grosso?

H. annae (Steindachner, 1882). Para.

H. argus (Fowler, 1943). Villavicencio, Rio Meta basin, Colombia.

H. asperatus de Castelnau, 1855. l'Araguay.

H. aspilogaster (Cope, 1894). Jacuhy, Rio Grande do Sul.

H. atropinnis (Eigenmann & Eigenmann, 1890). Goyaz.

H. auroguttatus Natterer & Heckel, 1954. No locality.

H. biseriatus (Cope, 1872). The Amazon.

H. bolivianus (Pearson, 1924). Popoi River, Upper Beni, Bolivia.

H. borellii (Boulenger, 1897). Bolivia.

H. boulengeri (Eigenmann & Kennedy, 1903). Mato Grosso or Asuncion.

H. brevicauda (Günther, 1864). Bahia, Brazil.

H. brevis (Nichols, 1919). State of São Paulo.

H. butantanis (von Ihering, 1911). Rio Pinheiros perto de São Paulo = Rio Pinheiros, Nebenfluss des Tiete, nahe der Haupstadt São Paulo.

H. carinatus (Steindachner, 1882). Amazon River ohne nähere Angabe des Fundortes; das MCZ besitzt Examplare von Jatuarana, Ueranduba, und aus dem See Saraca.
H. carvalhoi (Miranda Ribeiro, 1937). Rio Graneiro, Crato, Ceara.
H. chapare (Fowler, 1940). Boco Chapare, Rio Chimore, Cochabamba, Bolivia.
H. commersonii Valenciennes, 1840. Saint-Francois River, Brazil, and le fleuve la Plata et ses affluens.
H. commersonoides (Marini, NIchols, & La Monte, 1933). Darsena Norte, Buenos Aires, Argentina.
H. coppenamensis Boeseman, 1969. Left tributary of Left Coppename River 3°54′ N, 56°46′ W, Surinam.
H. corantijni Boeseman, 1968. Sipaliwini River, Surinam.
H. cordovae (Günther, 1880). Cordova, Rio de La Plata.
H. crassicauda Boeseman, 1968. Sipaliwini River, Surinam.
H. derbyi (Haseman, 1911). Porto União da Victoria, Rio Iguassu.
H. emarginatus Valenciennes, 1840. Probably Brazil.
H. fluviatilis (Schubart, 1964). Corrego da Lazica, perto de Ouro Fino (MG); Cachoeira do Espraiado, no alto Mogi Guacu, acima do Soledad, Ouro Fino (MG); and Alto Mogi Guacu, 5 km a jusante de Inconfidentes (Mun. Ouro Fino, MG).
H. francisci (Lütken, 1874). Rio São Francisco.
H. garmani (Regan, 1904). Rio das Velhas, eastern Brazil.
H. gomesi (Fowler, 1942). Ceara.
H. goyazensis (Regan, 1908). Goyaz.
H. gymnorhynchus (Norman, 1926). Iponcin Creek, into Approuage River, French Guiana.
H. hemiurus (Eigenmann, 1912). Amatuk, Br. Guiana.
H. hermanni (von Ihering, 1905). Rio Piracicaba, São Paulo.
H. horridus Heckel, 1854. Forte de Principe am Rio Guapore.
H. iheringii (Regan, 1908). Rio Piracicaba, São Paulo, Brazil.
H. interruptus (Miranda Ribeiro, 1918). Rio Juquia.
H. jaguribensis (Fowler, 1915). Rio Jaguribe at Barro Alto, Brazil.
H. johnii (Steindachner, 1876). Rio Puty and Rio Preto.
H. lacerta (Nichols, 1919). Poco Grande, State of São Paulo, Rio Juquia.
H. laplatae (Eigenmann, 1907). Buenos Aires.
H. latirostris (Regan, 1904). Rio Jungada, Mato Grosso, and Goyaz (latter material became *H. goyazensis* in 1908).
H. levis (Pearson, 1924). Huachi, Bolivia.
H. lexi (von Ihering, 1911). Rio Pardo, perto de Barretos (State São Paulo), quasi na foz do rio, que e affluente do Rio Grande, por sua vez tributario do lado esquerdo do Rio Parana = Barretos, im Western des Staates São Paulo, dem Rio Pardo-flusse, einem Nebenflusse des Rio Grande, welcher seinerseits in den Rio Parana vom La Plata system mündet.
H. lima (Reinhardt, 1874). Ribeirao do Mato, og andre smaa Bifloder til Rio d. Velhas = in rivulis flumini Rio das Velhas affluentibus.
H. limosus (Eigenmann & Eigenmann, 1888). Rio Grande do Sul.
H. longiradiatus (Holly, 1929). Rio Guana, vermutlich einem Nebenflusse des Madeira, der selbst ein Nebenfluss des Amazon R. ist.
H. luetkeni (Steindachner, 1877). Küstenflusse des südöstlichen Brazil, Rio Parahyba, Rio Mucuri, Rio San Antonio, Rio Quenda, Rio de Pedra.
H. luteomaculatus Devincenzi & Teague, 1942. Rio Uruguay.
H. macrophthalmus Boeseman, 1868. Sipaliwini River, near air strip, Surinam.
H. macrops (Eigenmann & Eigenmann, 1888). Rio das Velhas.
H. madeirae (Fowler, 1913). Madeira River about 200 miles E of W Long. 63°54′, Brazil.
H. margaritifer (Regan, 1908). Rio Piracicaba, São Paulo, Brazil.
H. meleagris (Marini, Nichols, & La Monte, 1933). Southeastern Brazil.
H. micromaculatus Boeseman, 1968. Mamadam Falls, Surinam.
H. micropunctatus (La Monte, 1935). Rio

Purus, in vicinity of mouth of Rio Macauhan, a trib. of Rio Yaco, which in turn is trib. of Rio Purus, 69°W 9°20′S.

H. myersi (Gosline, 1947). Rio Iguacu at Porto Uniao, State of Parana.

H. nematopterus Isbrücker & Nijssen, 1984. Left bank trib. to Camopi River, Oyapok River System, French Guiana.

H. niceforoi (Fowler, 1943). Florencia, Rio Orteguasa, Colombia.

H. nickeriensis Boeseman, 1969. Stondansie Falls, Nickerie River, Surinam.

H. niger (Marini, Nichols, & La Monte, 1933). SE Brazil.

H. nigromaculatus (Schubart, 1964). Rio Mogi Guacu, Cachoeira de Emas, na regiao da corredeira (Topava), Mun. Pirassununga, State of São Paulo.

H. nudiventris (Fowler, 1941). Rio Choro, Ceara, near Fortaleza.

H. obtusirostris (Steindachner, 1907). Dem flusse Cubatao, State Santa Catherina bei Theresopolis.

H. occidentalis Boeseman, 1968. Surinam River near Brokopondo.

H. panamensis (Eigenmann, 1922). Rio Gatun, at Monte Lira and at Gatun.

H. pantherinus (Kner, 1854). Rio Guapore, ohne nähere Angaben.

H. papariae (Fowler, 1941). Lago Papary, Rio Grande do Norte.

H. paranensis Weyenberg, 1877. ? Not known.

H. paucimaculatus Boeseman, 1968. Surinam River near Brokopondo.

H. paulinus (von Ihering, 1905). Rio Piracicaba, São Paulo, Brazil.

H. phrixosoma (Fowler, 1940). Ucayali River basin, Contamana, Peru.

H. plecostomus (Linnaeus, 1758). India = Surinam, probably in neighborhood of Paramaribo.

H. popoi (Pearson, 1924). Popoi River, Upper Beni, Bolivia.

H. pseudohemiurus Boeseman, 1968. Kabalebo River Corantijn River basin, Surinam.

H. punctatus Valenciennes, 1840. Rio Janeiro.

H. pusarum (Starks, 1913). Little disconnected ponds and muddy stream at Ceara Mirim.

H. rachovii (Regan, 1913). Near Rio de Janeiro.

H. regani (von Ihering, 1905). Rio Piracicaba, São Paulo, Brazil.

H. robinii Valenciennes, 1840. La Trinite and affluents de La Plata.

H. rondoni (Miranda Ribeiro, 1912). San Manoel, Rio Tapajoz.

H. saramaccensis Boeseman, 1968. Feddipratti (rapids), middle Saramacca River, Surinam.

H. scabriceps (Eigenmann & Eigenmann, 1888). São Matheus.

H. scaphyceps (Nichols, 1919). Cerqueira Cezar, State of São Paulo.

H. scopularius (Cope, 1871). Amazon above mouth of Rio Negro.

H. seminudus (Eigenmann & Eigenmann, 1888). Brazil?

H. sipaliwinii Boeseman, 1968. Sipaliwini River, upper Corantijn River basin, Surinam.

H. spiniger (Hensel, 1870). Rio Cadea.

H. squalinus Schomburgk, 1841. Rios Branco, Negro, and Essequibo.

H. strigaticeps (Regan, 1908). Rio Piracicaba, São Paulo.

H. subcarinatus de Castelnau, 1855. Rivers of the Province des Mines.

H. surinamensis Boeseman, 1968. Surinam River near Brokopondo.

H. taeniatus (Regan, 1908). Rio de La Plata.

H. tapanahoniensis Boeseman, 1969. Tapanahoni River, Surinam.

H. tenuicauda (Steindachner, 1878). Der Grossen, seeartig ausgebreiteten Cienega, welche der Magdalenen-Strom mit einem seiner östlich gelegenen Hauptarme kurz vor seiner Mündung in das Meer bildet.

H. tenuis Boeseman, 1968. Near Paramaribo, Surinam.

H. ternetzi (Boulenger, 1895). Paraguay.

H. tietensis (von Ihering, 1905). Rio Tiete, São Paulo, Brazil.

H. topavae (de Godoy, 1969). Mogi Guassu River, São Paulo.

H. unae (Steindachner, 1878). Rio Una, südlich von Bahia.

H. unicolor (Steindachner, 1908). Rio Purus.

H. vaillanti (Steindachner, 1877). Rio

Preto.

H. variipictus (von Ihering, 1911). Rio Pardo de Barretos, Est. de S. Paulo, quasi em sua foz no Rio Grande, trib. do lado esquerdo de Rio Parana = dem Rio Pardo, nahe bei Barretos, Staat S. Paulo; o, beinahe an seiner Mündung in den Rio Grande, einem linken Nebenflusse des R. Parana.

H. varimaculosus (Fowler, 1945). Morelia, Rio Caqueta drainage, Colombia.

H. variostictus (Miranda Ribeiro, 1912). Coxim, M. Grosso.

H. ventromaculatus Boeseman, 1968. Surinam River between Afobaka and Brokopondo, Surinam.

H. vermicularis (Eigenmann & Eigenmann, 1888). Rio Parahyba, R. Janeiro, Mendez, Macacos, Goyaz.

H. verres Valenciennes, 1840. Cayenne.

H. villarsi (Lütken, 1874). Carracas?, Venezuela.

H. virescens (Cope, 1874). Upper Amazon.

H. watwata Hancock, 1828. Demerara, on the sea-shores.

H. winzi (Fowler, 1945). Honda, Colombia.

H. wuchereri (Günther, 1864). Bahia, Brazil.

Cochliodon Heckel, 1854. Type species *Hypostomus cochliodon* Kner.

Cochliodon cochliodon (Kner, 1854). Rio Cujaba.

C. hondae (Regan, 1912). Honda, Colombia.

C. oculeus (Fowler, 1943). Florencia, Rio Orteguasa, Colombia.

C. plecostomoides Eigenmann, 1922. Quebrada Cramalote, Villavicencio.

C. pospisili Schultz, 1944. Rio Palmar near Totuma, about 100 km southwest of Maracaibo, Venezuela.

C. pyrineusi Miranda Ribeiro, 1920. Probably Jamari.

Pterygoplichthys Gill, 1858. Type species *Hypostomus duodecimalis* Valenciennes = *Pterygoplichthys duodecimalis* sensu Gill.

Pterygoplichthys alternans (Regan, 1904). Paraguay and southern Bolivia.

P. altipinnis (Günther, 1864). River Cupai.

P. ambrosettii (Holmberg, 1893). Rio Paraguay, al pie de Formosa.

P. anisitsi Eigenmann & Kennedy, 1903. Laguna of the Rio Paraguay at Asuncion.

P. barbatus (Steindachner, 1911). Rio Tapajos at Vila Braga.

P. brevitentaculatus (Ranzani, 1842). Ref. only in Eigenmann & Eigenmann.

P. duodecimalis (Cuvier & Valenciennes, 1840). Sainte Francois River, Brazil.

P. etentaculatus (von Spix, 1829). In Brasiliae septentrionalis fluviis.

P. gibbiceps (Kner, 1854). Rio Negro bei Marabitanos.

P. jeanesianus (Cope, 1874). Nauta, Peru.

P. juvens Eigenmann & Kennedy, 1903. Asuncion, Rio Paraguay.

P. lituratus (Kner, 1854). Rio Guapore bei Cidade do Matogrosso.

P. longimanus (Kner, 1854). Unknown.

P. multiradiatus (Hancock, 1828). Demerara.

P. paranaus Peters, 1881. ? Para.

P. pardalis (de Castelnau, 1855). Amazon.

P. punctatus (Natterer, 1854). S. vicente . . . aus einer Lache.

P. scrophus (Cope, 1874). Nauta, Peru.

P. undecimalis (Steindachner, 1878). Der grossen, seeartig ausgebreiteten Cienega, welche der Magdalenen-Strom mit einem seiner östlich gelegenen Hauptarme kurz vor seiner Mündung in des Meer bildet.

P. varius (Cope, 1872). Ambyiacu River, and between the mouth of the Rio Negro and the Peruvian Amazon or Ucayali River.

Subfamily Ancistrinae

Lasiancistrus Regan, 1904. Type species *Ancistrus (Lasiancistrus) heteracanthus* = *Chaetostoma heteracanthus* Günther, 1869.

Lasiancistrus brevispinis Heitmans, Nijssen & Isbrücker, 1983. Surinam, district Nickerie, Nickerie River system, Fallawatra River, rapid 5 km S.W. of Stondansie Fall.

L. carnegiei (Eigenmann, 1916). Rio San Gil, Santander, Rio Magdalena system.

L. caucanus Eigenmann, 1912. Cartago, Rio Cauca system.

L. daguae (Eigenmann, 1912). Caldas, a div. of Colombia.

L. fuessi (Steindachner, 1911). Sosomoco, eastern Colombia.

L. genisetiger (Fowler, 1941). Rio Jaguaribe,

Oros, Ceara.

L. guacharote (Valenciennes, 1840). Fw. of Puerto Rico?

L. heteracanthus (Günther, 1869). Upper Amazon; Peruvian Amazon.

L. longispinis Heitmans, Nijssen & Isbrücker, 1983. French Guiana, Oyapock River system, Camopi River at Pauwé Jean-Jean, upstream of Saut Mauvais (03°11'N, 52°22'W).

L. maracaiboensis Schultz, 1944. Rio Socuy.

L. mayoloi (Eigenmann, 1912). Istmina, 5°11'N, 76°39'W, along the Rio San Juan.

L. multispinis (Holly, 1929). Mercado Blein, Brazil.

L. mystacinus (Kner, 1854). Carracas.

L. nationi Fernandez-Yepez, 1976. Station #140 of the Complejo Hidrografico (4), Venezuela, Rio Yaracuy.

L. niger (Norman, 1926). Oyapock River at Sant Cafoseca, Fr. Guiana.

L. papariae (Fowler, 1941). Lago Papary, Rio Grande do Norte.

L. pictus (de Castelnau, 1855). Ucayali.

L. planiceps (Meek & Hildebrand, 1913). Rio Tuyra, Boca de Cupe, Panama.

L. schomburgkii (Günther, 1864). Br. Guiana, probably Essequibo River.

L. scolymus Nijssen & Isbrücker, 1985. Humboldt, Rio Aripuaña (Rio Madeira system) Estado Mato Grosso do Sul, Brazil (10°10'S, 59°27'W).

L. setosus (Boulenger, 1887). Colombia.

L. snethlageae (Steindachner, 1911). Rio Tapajoz bei Villa Braga und Goyana.

L. trinitatis (Günther, 1864). Trinidad.

L. volcanensis Dahl, 1941. Rio Volcan near its junction to Rio San Bartolome.

Dolichancistrus Isbrücker, 1980. Type species *Pseudancistrus pediculatus* Eigenmann, 1917.

Dolichancistrus atratoensis (Dahl, 1960). Western Colombia, Quebrada La Noche, trib. to the Upper Atrato, about 550m above sea level.

D. cobrensis (Schultz, 1944). Rio Cobre, trib. to Rio Quinta, latter trib. to Rio La Grita, below La Grita, Catatumbo system, Maracaibo Basin, Venezuela.

D. pediculatus (Eigenmann, 1917). Rio Negro, Villavicencio, Rio Meta system.

Cordylancistrus Isbrücker, 1980. Type species *Pseudancistrus torbesensis* Schultz, 1944.

Cordylancistrus torbesensis (Schultz, 1944). 1 km above Tariba, 7°48'N, 72°10'W, in the Rio Torbes, Orinoco system, Venezuela.

Hemiancistrus Bleeker, 1862. Type species *Ancistrus medians* Kner, 1854.

Hemiancistrus annectens (Regan, 1904). NW Ecuador, St. Javier and Rio Durango.

H. aspidolepis (Günther, 1866). Veragua, Pacific slope, NE Panama.

H. braueri Eigenmann, 1912. Takutu?, Br. Guiana.

H. fugleri Ovchynnyk, 1971. Ecuador, Province Esmeraldas, Rio Bogota, Parroquia Cadondelet, 78°45'W, 1°6'N.

H. hammarlundi Rendahl, 1937. Ecuador, Rio de Clementina system, NW of Babahoyo.

H. holostictus Regan, 1913. The Condoto, a trib. of San Juan, a river of Pacific slope in SW Colombia.

H. itacua (Valenciennes, 1840). Des affluens de La Plata.

H. landoni Eigenmann, 1916. Naranjito, Ecuador.

H. macrops (Lütken, 1874). Surinam.

H. maracaiboensis Schultz, 1944. Venez., near mouth of Rio Concha in Lago Maracaibo.

H. medians (Kner, 1854). No locality (possibly Surinam?).

H. megacephalus (Günther, 1868). Surinam.

H. platycephalus (Boulenger, 1898). Rio Bomboize, eastern Ecuador.

H. wilsoni Eigenmann, 1916. Truando.

Megalancistrus Isbrücker, 1980. Type species *Chaetostomus gigas* Boulenger, 1895.

Megalancistrus aculeatus (Perugia, 1891). Asuncion, Rio Paraguay.

M. barrae (Steindachner, 1910). Rio San Francisco bei Barra.

M. gigas (Boulenger, 1895). Paraguay.

Peckoltia Miranda Ribeiro, 1912. Type species *Chaetostomus vittata* Steindachner.

Peckoltia albocincta (Ahl, 1936). Umgebung von Rio de Janeiro.

P. arenaria (Eigenmann & Allen, 1942). Peru, Yurimaguas at Rio Huallage, 5°54'S, 76°7'W.

P. bachi (Boulenger, 1898). Rio Jurua, Brazil.

P. brachyura (Kner, 1854). Barra do Rio Negro.
P. brevis (La Monte, 1935). Rio Purus, coll. in vicinity of mouth of Rio Macauhan, a trib. of Rio Yacu, which, in turn, is trib. of Rio Purus, 69°W, 9°20′S.
P. caquetae (Fowler, 1945). Morelia, Rio Caqueta drainage, Colombia.
P. filicaudata (Miranda Ribeiro, 1917). Fluvio Solimoes.
P. kuhlmanni (Miranda Ribeiro, 1920). Tapajoz.
P. niveata (La Monte, 1929). Cano Pescado, about 5 miles N of Esmeralda, at an elevation of 325 feet, upper Orinoco drainage, neighborhood of Mt. Duida, Venezuela.
P. oligospila (Günther, 1864). Rio Capin.
P. picta (Kner, 1854). Barra do Rio Negro.
P. platyrhyncha (Fowler, 1943). Florencia, 1°37′N, 75°37′W, Rio Orteguaza, Rio Caqueta system.
P. pulcher (Steindachner, 1915). Rio Negro bei Moura, 1°32′S, 61°38′W.
P. salgadae (Fowler, 1941). Rio Salgade, Ico, 6°25′S, 38°50′W.
P. scaphyrhyncha (Kner, 1854). Barra do Rio Negro.
P. ucayalensis (Fowler, 1940). Ucayali River, Cantamana.
P. vermiculata (Steindachner, 1908). Dem mittleren Laufe des Amazon River, and/or the waters around Para.
P. vittata (Steindachner, 1882). Amazon River, Tajapouru, Xingu bei Porto do Moz, Rio Madeira.
P. yaravi (Steindachner, 1915). Dem Rio Coquenan, Venezuela.

Parancistrus Bleeker, 1862. Type species *Hypostomus aurantiacus* de Castelnau, 1855.
Parancistrus aurantiacus (de Castelnau, 1855). Ucayali.
P. longipinnis (Kindle, 1895). Trocera on Tocantins.
P. nigricans (de Castelnau, 1855). Amazon.
P. niveatus (de Castelnau, 1855). Rio Araguay, de la province de Goyaz.
P. punctatissimus (Steindachner, 1882). Amazon River, ohne nähere Angabe des Fundortes.
P. vicinus (de Castelnau, 1855). Ucayale.

Hypocolpterus Fowler, 1943. Type species *H. analis* Fowler.
Hypocolpterus analis Fowler, 1943. Florencia, Rio Orteguasa, Colombia.

Chaetostoma von Tschudi, 1845. Type species *C. loborhynchos* von Tschudi.
Chaetostoma aequinoctiale Pellegrin, 1909. Rio Pove, Santo Domingo de los Colorados, 560 m, Equator, 00°13′S, 79°09′W.
C. alternifasciatum Fowler, 1945. Morelia, Rio Caqueta drainage, Colombia.
C. anomalum Regan, 1903. Merida, Venezuela, alt. 1500 m, and the Albirregas and Milla Rivers, above Merida, alt. 3500 m.
C. branickii Steindachner, 1882. Callacate, Peru.
C. brevilabiatum Dahl, 1942. Rio Volcan, near its junction to Rio San Bartolome, trib. to Rio Magdalena on left side, between Rios Nare and Ite, municipio of Remedios, depart. of Antioquia, Republic of Colombia.
C. breve Regan, 1904. Bomboiza and Zamore Rivers, E Ecuador.
C. dermorhynchum Boulenger, 1887. Canelos, Eastern Ecuador.
C. dorsale Eigenmann, 1922. Quebrada Cramalote, Villavicencio.
C. dupouii Fernandez-Yepez, 1945. Rio Encantado into Rio Grande of Rio Tuy system, Venezuela.
C. eptingi Fowler, 1941. Fortaleza, Ceara.
C. fischeri Steindachner, 1879. Mamoni-Fluss, Panama.
C. furcatum Fowler, 1940. Ucayali River basin, Cantamana, Peru.
C. guairense Steindachner, 1882. Dem Guaire bei Caracas.
C. lepturum Regan, 1912. Rio Tamana, Rio San Juan, Choco, SW Colombia.
C. leucomelas Eigenmann, 1917. Rio Patia. halway between Rios Magui and Telembi.
C. lineopunctatum Eigenmann & Allen, 1942. Rio Azupizu.
C. loborhynchos von Tschudi, 1845. Dem Rio Tullumayo in der Montana de Vitoc, am Ostabhang der Anden.
C. machiquense Fernandez-Yepez & Martin Salazar, 1953. Rio Negro, a 16 km oeste de Machiques.

C. maculatum Regan, 1904. Rozmaiu, Upper Peru.
C. marcapatae Regan, 1904. Marcapata Valley.
C. marginatum Regan, 1904. Salidero, NW Ecuador.
C. marmorescens Eigenmann & Allen, 1942. Huancachupa Creek near Huanuco, elevation 6000 feet.
C. microps Günther, 1864. Andes of western Ecuador.
C. milesi Fowler, 1941. Honda, Colombia; Orinoco River system, Venezuela.
C. mollinasum Pearson, 1937. Balsas, 3500 ft., and Cajamarca, 9843 ft., Peru.
C. niveum Fowler, 1944. Clear water of Rio Jurubida, Nuqui, northwestern Colombia.
C. nudirostre Lütken, 1874. Valencia, Venezuela.
C. palmeri Regan, 1912. Rio Tamana, Rio San Juan, Choco, SW Colombia.
C. patiae Fowler, 1945. Rio Patia, at 3000 ft., Pacific slope of SW Colombia.
C. paucispinis Regan, 1912. Tado, Rio San Juan, Choco, Colombia.
C. pearsei Eigenmann, 1920. Venezuela, Rio Castano at Maracay, under rocks.
C. sericeum Cope, 1872. Ambyiacu R. = Ambiyacu or Ampiyacu River.
C. sovichthys Schultz, 1944. Venezuela, near bridge over Rio San Pedro, trib. of Rio Motatan, SE of Mene Grande, in Maracaibo basin.
C. stannii (Kröyer in Lütken, 1874). Puerto Cabello, Venezuela.
C. taczanowskii Steindachner, 1883. Rio de Tortora.
C. tachiraense Schultz, 1944. Rio Tachira 7 km N of San Antonio, Estado de Tachira, Venezuela.
C. thomsoni Regan, 1904. Villeta, Colombia.
C. trifasciatum Steindachner, 1902. Unknown.
C. vagum Fowler, 1943. Florencia, Rio Orteguasa, Colombia.
C. venezuelae Schultz, 1944. Rio Caripe, Caripito, Venezuela.

Leptoancistrus Meek & Hildebrand, 1916. Type species *Acanthicus canensis* Meek & Hildebrand, 1913.
Leptoancistrus canensis (Meek & Hildebrand, 1913). Rio Cana, Cana, Panama.
L. cordobensis Dahl, 1964. Colombia, Rio Batatal, Alto Rio Uré.

Lipopterichthys Norman, 1935. Type species *L. carrioni* Norman.
Lipopterichthys carrioni Norman, 1935. Rio Zamora, Loja, Ecuador.

Lithoxancistrus Isbrücker, Nijssen, & Cala, 1988. Type species *L. orinoco* Isbrücker, Nijssen, & Cala.
Lithoxancistrus orinoco Isbrücker, Nijssen, & Cala, 1988. Rio Orinoco, Prov. Vichada, Columbia.

Neblinichthys Ferraris, Isbrücker, & Nijssen, 1986. Type species *N. pilosus* Ferraris, Isbrücker, & Nijssen.
Neblinichthys pilosus Ferraris, Isbrücker, & Nijssen, 1986. Rio Mawarinuma trib., Rio Baria drainage, Territorio Federal Amazonas, Venezuela.

Ancistrus Kner, 1854. Type species *Hypostomus cirrhosus* Valenciennes, 1840.
Ancistrus alga (Cope, 1872). Ambyiacu = Ambiyacu or Ampiyacu River.
A. baudensis Fowler, 1945. Alto Rio Baudo, Pacific slope at 3000 ft.
A. bodenhameri Schultz, 1944. Rio San Pedro at the bridge S of Mene Grande, Motatan system, Venezuela.
A. bolivianus (Steindachner, 1915). Rio Songo, Nord Yungas, Bolivia.
A. brevifilis Eigenmann, 1920. Venezuela, El Concejo, Rio Tiquirito.
A. brevipinnis (Regan, 1904). Rio Grande do Sul.
A. bufonius (Valenciennes, 1840). Rio Apurimac, which descends from the mountains du haut Perou, a environ 2000m of height.
A. calamita (Valenciennes, 1840). In the mountains of haut Perou, in the Rio Apurimac.
A. caucanus Fowler, 1943. Sonson, Cauca R. basin, Colombia.
A. centrolepis Regan, 1913. Colombia, Choco, Rio San Juan.
A. chagresi Eigenmann & Eigenmann, 1889. Panama Canal Zone, Rio Chagres.
A. cirrhosus (Valenciennes, 1840). Aux Missions; Buenos Aires; pres de Rio Janeiro.
A. clementinae Rendahl, 1937. Rio de Clem-

entina, NW of Babahoyo.

A. cryptophthalmus Reis, 1987. Rio São Vicente System, Tocantins Drainage, Brazil.

A. damasceni (Steindachner, 1907). Dem Parnahyba bei Victoria and Santa Filomena.

A. dolichopterus Kner, 1854. Barra do Rio Negro.

A. dubius Eigenmann & Eigenmann, 1889. Gurupa.

A. erinaceus (Valenciennes, 1840). Chili.

A. eustictus (Fowler, 1945). Alto Rio Baudo, Pacific Slope at 3000 ft.

A. fulvus (Holly, 1929). Alto Rio Acara, Brazil.

A. gymnorhynchus Kner, 1854. Puerto Cabello.

A. heterorhynchus (Regan, 1912). Uruhuasi, Peru, 4000 ft.

A. hoplogenys (Günther, 1864). Para, River Capin.

A. jelskii (Steindachner, 1876). Den Gebirgsbächen der hohen Anden in Peru, Amable Maria, Monterico.

A. latifrons (Günther, 1869). Upper Amazon, Peruvian Amazon.

A. leucostictus (Günther, 1864). Essequibo.

A. lineolatus Fowler, 1943. Florencia, Rio Orteguasa, Colombia.

A. lithurgicus Eigenmann, 1912. Br. Guiana, Crab Falls.

A. macrophthalmus (Pellegrin, 1912). Orenoque.

A. maculatus (Steindachner, 1882). Cudajas, Obidos, dem Rio Tajapouru, dem Rio Chagres.

A. malacops (Cope, 1872). Ambyiacu River.

A. maracasse Fowler, 1946. Maracas River, Trinidad.

A. martini Schultz, 1944. Rio Tachira, 7 km N of San Antonio, Catatumbo system, Venezuela.

A. mattogrossensis Miranda Ribeiro, 1912. Mato Grosso.

A. megalostomus Pearson, 1924. Huachi, at junction of Bopi and Cochabamba Rivers, alt. 2235 ft.

A. melas Eigenmann, 1916. Condoto.

A. montanus (Regan, 1904). Tumupara, Andes of Bolivia, 1500 ft.

A. multispinis (Regan, 1912). Humboldt and Novo Rivers, Sta. Catherina, SE Brazil.

A. nudiceps (Müller & Troschel, 1848). Dem Takutu, Guyana.

A. occidentalis (Regan, 1904). Canelos, E Ecuador.

A. occloi Eigenmann, 1928. Ollantaytambo, Rio Urubamba, Peru, 9000 ft.

A. punctatus (Steindachner, 1882). Dem Rio Branco and Guapore in Matogrosso, Coary and Tabatinga.

A. rothschildi (Regan, 1905). San Esteban, near Porto Cabello, Venezuela.

A. sp. (*Hypostoma punctatum* Schomburgk, 1841). Rio Branco.

A. spinosus Meek & Hildebrand, 1916. Rio Calobre, trib. of Rio Bayano, Panama.

A. stigmaticus Eigenmann & Eigenmann, 1889. São Matheos and Goyaz.

A. tamboensis Fowler, 1945. Satipo a 600 meters alt., na bacia do alto Tambo, bacia do Ucayali, Peru.

A. taunayi Miranda-Ribeiro, 1918. Itaqui, Rio Lageado, Rio Grande do Sul.

A. tectirostris (Cope, 1872). Ampyiacu River.

A. temmincki (Valenciennes, 1840). Cayenne.

A. triradiatus Eigenmann, 1917. Andes E of Bogota, Quebrada Cramalote, Villavicencio.

A. variolus (Cope, 1872). Ampyiacu River.

Panaque Eigenmann & Eigenmann, 1889. Type species *Chaetostomus nigrolineatus* Peters, 1877.

Panaque albomaculatus Kanazawa, 1958. Ecuador, trib. of Rio Suno, upper Napo River, 0°47′S lat., 77°16′W long., Rio Pucuno.

P. cochliodon (Steindachner, 1879). Dem Cauca.

P. dentex (Günther, 1868). Xeberos.

P. nigrolineatus (Peters, 1877). Calabozo, Venezuela.

P. purusiensis La Monte, 1935. Rio Purus, coll. in vicinity of mouth of Rio Macauhan, a trib. of Rio Yacu, which in turn is trib. of Rio Purus, 60°W, 9°20′S.

P. suttoni Schultz, 1944. Rio Negro below mouth of Rio Yasa, Maracaibo basin, Venezuela.

Acanthicus von Spix, 1829. Type species *A. hystrix* von Spix.

Acanthicus hystrix von Spix, in von Spix & Agassiz, 1829. In flumine Amazonum.

Pseudacanthicus Bleeker, 1862. Type species *Hypostomus serratus* Valenciennes, 1840.

Pseudacanthicus fordii (Günther, 1868). Surinam.

P. histrix (Valenciennes, 1840). No locality.

P. leopardus (Fowler, 1914). Rupununi R., Br. Guiana.

P. serratus (Valenciennes, 1840). Surinam.

P. spinosus (de Castelnau, 1855). La river des Amazones.

Lithoxus Eigenmann, 1910. Type species *L. lithoides* Eigenmann.

Lithoxus bovallii (Regan, 1906). Kaat River, trib. to Treng River, Upper Potaro, Br. Guiana, in a rapid on underside of stones.

L. lithoides Eigenmann, 1910. Cataracts of Br. Guiana.

L. pallidimaculatus Boeseman, 1982. Kwamabaolo Creek, right trib. of Sara Creek above dam, Surinam River system, Surinam.

L. planquettei Boeseman, 1982. Boulenger Creek, Compté system, Fr. Guyana.

L. surinameusis Boeseman, 1982. Near Awaradam Gran Rio, upper Surinam River system, Surinam.

Exastilithoxus Isbrücker & Nijssen, 1979. Type species *Pseudacanthicus (Lithoxus) fimbriatus* Steindachner, 1915.

Exastilithoxus fimbriatus (Steindachner, 1915). Coquenanfluss.

E. hoedemani Isbrücker & Nijssen, 1985. Rio Maurauiá, est. Amazonas, Brazil.

Subfamily Hypoptopomatinae

Parotocinclus Eigenmann & Eigenmann, 1889. Type species *Hisonotus (Parotocinclus) maculicauda* Steindachner, 1877.

Parotocinclus amazonensis Garavello, 1977. Ilha Sorubim, Rio Solimoes, Amazonas, Brazil.

P. bahiensis (Miranda Ribeiro, 1918). Villa Nova, E da Bahia.

P. britskii Boeseman, 1974. Left trib. of the Coppenname R., 3°51′N, 56°55′W, Surinam.

P. cearensis Garavello, 1977. Cachoeira do Gusmao, Ipu, Ceara, Brazil.

P. cesarpintoi Miranda Ribeiro, 1939. Rio Paraiba que atravessa a Vila de Quebrangulo, no Estado de Alagoas, NE Brazil.

P. collinsae Schmidt & Ferraris, 1985. Trib. to Takuto R., Essequibo Province, Guyana.

P. cristatus Garavello, 1977. Fazenda Almada, Ilheus, Bahia, Brazil.

P. doceanus (A. de Miranda Ribeiro, 1918). Rio Doce, E. Santo.

P. jimi Garavello, 1977. Rio do Peixe, small trib. of Rio de Contas, Fazenda Pedra Branca, Itagiba, Bahia, Brazil.

P. maculicauda (Steindachner, 1877). Südöstlichen, Brazil.

P. minutus Garavello, 1977. Rio Vasa Barris, Canudos, Bahia, Brazil.

P. polyochrus Schaefer, 1988. Rio Mawarinuma trib., Rio Baria System, Venezuela.

P. spilosoma (Fowler, 1941). Campina Grande, Parahyba.

P. spilurus (Fowler, 1941). Rio Salgade, Ico, Ceara.

Otocinclus Cope, 1871. Type species *O. vestitus* Cope.

Otocinclus affinis Steindachner, 1877. Flüssen bei S. Crux in der Umgebung von Rio Janeiro.

O. arnoldi Regan, 1909. The La Plata.

O. cephalacanthus Miranda Ribeiro, 1911. Brazil.

O. depressicauda Miranda Ribeiro, 1911. Brazil.

O. fimbriatus Cope, 1894. Rio Jacuhy, Rio Grande do Sul.

O. flexilis Cope, 1894. Rio Jacuhy, Rio Grande do Sul.

O. francirochai von Ihering, 1928. Creeks by Pirangy, headwaters of the Rio Turvo, into Rio Grande of the Parana-La Plata.

O. gibbosus Miranda Ribeiro, 1908. Rio Bethari.

O. hasemani Steindachner, 1915. Engenho da Agua im Flussgebiete des Paranahyba im Staate Maranhao.

O. hoppei Miranda Ribeiro, 1939. Belem, Para, Brazil-Norte.

O. laevior (Cope, 1894). Rio Jacuhy, Rio Grande do Sul.

O. leucofrenatus Miranda Ribeiro, 1908. Rio das Pedras.

O. macrospilus Eigenmann & Allen, 1942.

Rio Morona.

O. maculipinnis Regan, 1912. La Plata.

O. mariae Fowler, 1940. Boca Chapare, Rio Chimore, Cochabamba, Bolivia.

O. notatus (Eigenmann & Eigenmann, 1889). Santa Cruz and Juiz de Fora.

O. paulinus Regan, 1908. Rio Piracicaba, São Paulo, Brazil.

O. spectabilis Eigenmann, 1914. Quebrada Cramalote, Villavicencio, Rio Meta Basin of eastern Colombia.

O. vestitus Cope, 1872. Tributaries of Ampiyacu.

O. vittatus Regan, 1904. Descalvados, Mato Grosso, Paraguay system.

Microlepidogaster Eigenmann & Eigenmann, 1889. Type species *M. perforatus* Eigenmann & Eigenmann.

Microlepidogaster bourguyi (Miranda Ribeiro, 1911). Brazil.

M. depressinotus Miranda-Ribiero, 1918. Piracicaba, Sao Paulo, Brazil

M. doceanus Miranda-Ribeiro, 1918. Rio Doce, Estado do Espirito Santo.

M. leptochilus (Cope, 1894). Rio Grande do Sul.

M. lophophanes (Eigenmann & Eigenmann, 1889). Santa Cruz, Brazil.

M. nigricauda Boulenger, 1891. Province Rio Grande do Sul, Brazil.

M. perforatus (Eigenmann & Eigenmann, 1889). Rio Carandahy, Brazil.

M. taimensis Buckup, 1981. Banhado do Taim, Municípios de Rio Grande e Santa Vitória do Palmar, Rio Grande do Sul, Brasil.

Otothyris Myers, 1927. Type species *O. canaliferus* Myers.

Otothyris canaliferus Myers, 1927. Brazil, hills vicinity Rio de Janeiro.

Pseudotocinclus Nichols, 1919. Type species *P. intermedius* Nichols (= *Otocinclus tietensis* von Ihering, 1907).

Pseudotocinclus tietensis (von Ihering, 1907). Rio Tiete, São Paulo.

Schizolecis Britski & Garavello, 1984. Type species *Microlepidogaster guntheri* Miranda Ribeiro, 1918.

Schizolecis guntheri (Miranda Ribeiro, 1918). Praia do Piraíque, Ilha da São Sebastião, São Paulo.

Pseudotothyris Britski & Garavello, 1984. Type species *Otocinclus obtusus* Miranda Ribeiro, 1911.

Pseudotothyris janeirensis Britski & Garavello, 1984. Rio dos Macacos, Represa Engenho da Serra, Paulo de Frontin.

P. obtusa (Miranda Ribeiro, 1911). Brasil.

Hypoptopoma Günther, 1868. Type species *H. thoracatum* Günther.

Hypoptopoma acutirostre (Miranda Ribeiro, 1951). Paricachoeira, Rio Taquie, afl. do Vaupes que e afl. do Negro, Amazonas.

H. bilobatum Cope, 1870. Pebas, Peru.

H. carinatum Steindachner, 1879. Einem Nebenflusse des Amazonenstromes an der peruanische Grenze.

H. guentheri Boulenger, 1895. Descalvados, Mato Grosso.

H. guianense Boeseman, 1974. Left trib. of Nickerie River, a few km upstream from Stondansie Falls, Surinam.

H. gulare Cope, 1878. Pebas, Peru.

H. inexspectatum (Holmberg, 1893). Rio Paraguay, al pie de Formosa.

H. joberti (Vaillant, 1880). Calderon, Brazil.

H. psilogaster Fowler, 1915. Peruvian Amazon.

H. steindachneri Boulenger, 1895. Amazon near outlet of Rio Negro.

H. thoracatum Günther, 1868. Xeberos.

H. wrightianum (Eigenmann & Eigenmann, 1889). Lake Hyanuary.

Subfamily Loricariinae

Harttiella Boeseman, 1971. Type species *Harttia crassicauda* Boeseman.

Harttiella crassicauda (Boeseman, 1953). Surinam, Nassau Mountains, in creek.

Harttia Steindachner, 1876. Type species *Harttia loricariformis* Steindachner.

Harttia carvalhoi Miranda Ribeiro, 1939. Rio Paquequer, Estado Rio de Janeiro.

H. kronei Miranda Ribeiro, 1908. Rio Bethary.

H. loricariformis Steindachner, 1876. Oberer Lauf des Rio Parahyba und dessen Nebenflusse, SE Brazil (lectotype from Rio Paraiba).

H. rhombocephala Miranda Ribeiro, 1939. Rio Farias.

H. surinamensis Boeseman, 1971. Grandam, Gran Rio, upper Surinam River, Surinam.

Ctenilorlcaria Isbrücker & Nijssen, 1979.

Type species *Loricaria platystoma* Günther, 1868.
Ctenilorcaria fowleri (Pellegrin, 1908). Riviere Camopi, Guyana francaise.
C. maculata (Boeseman, 1971). Sipaliwini, near airstrip, upper Corantijn River basin, Surinam.
C. platystoma (Günther, 1868). Surinam.
Lamontichthys Miranda Ribeiro, 1939. Type species *Harttia filamentosa* La Monte, 1935.
Lamontichthys filamentosus (La Monte, 1935). Brazilian Amazon, Rio Jurua, in vicinity of mouth of Rio Embira, a trib. of Rio Tarauaca, which, in turn, is trib. of Rio Jurua, 70°15'W, 7°30'S.
L. stibaros Isbrücker & Nijssen, 1978. Ecuador, Prov. Pastaza, Rio Amazon system, Rio Bobonaza at Chicherota, 2°25'S, 76°38'W, alt. approx. 260-280 meters, upper Rio Pastaza.
Pterosturisoma Isbrücker & Nijssen, 1978. Type species *Harttia microps* Eigenmann & Allen, 1942.
Pterosturisoma microps (Eigenmann & Allen, 1942). Iquitos, Peru.
Sturisomatichthys Isbrücker & Nijssen, 1979. Type species *Oxyloricaria leightoni* Regan, 1912.
Sturisomatichthys caquetae (Fowler, 1945). Morelia, Rio Caqueta drainage, Colombia.
S. citrensis (Meek & Hildebrand, 1913). Rio Cupe, Cituro, Panama, Tuyra River basin.
S. leightoni (Regan, 1912). Honda, Colombia.
S. tamanae (Regan, 1912). Rio Tamana, Rio San Juan, Choco, SW Colombia, 200 feet.
Sturisoma Swainson, 1838. Type species *Loricaria rostrata* von Spix, 1829.
Sturisoma aureum (Steindachner, 1900). Bodega central, Rio Magdalena.
S. barbatum (Kner, 1854). Cujaba-Fluss.
S. brevirostre (Eigenmann & Eigenmann, 1889). Ica. (Holotypes: Brazil, Est. Amazonas, Rio Amazonas sys., Rio Ica, trib. of Rio Solimoes.)
S. dariense (Meek & Hildebrand, 1913). Rio Tuyra, Boca de Cupe, Panama.
S. festivum Myers, 1942. Rio Monay, 35 km N of Trujillo, Motatan system, Maracaibo basin, Venezuela.
S. frenatum (Boulenger, 1902). NW Ecuador, St. Javier (60'), Salidero (350'), and Rio Durango (350'). Lectotype from Salidero.
S. guentheri (Regan, 1904). Xeberos, Upper Amazon.
S. kneri (de Filippi, 1940). Lago di Maracaibo, Venezuela.
S. lyra (Regan, 1904). Rio Jurua.
S. monopelte Fowler, 1914. Rupununi River, Br. Guiana.
S. nigrirostrum Fowler, 1940. Ucayali River basin, Contamana, Peru.
S. panamense Eigenmann & Eigenmann, 1889. Panama.
S. robustum (Regan, 1904). Rio Paraguay.
S. rostratum (von Spix, in von Spix & Agassiz, 1829). Rivers of Brazil.
S. tenuirostre (Steindachner, 1910). Dem Rio Meta in Venezuela.
Aposturisoma Isbrücker, Britski, Nijssen, & Ortega, 1983. Type species *A. myriodon* Isbrücker, Britski, Nijssen, & Ortega.
A. myriodon Isbrücker, Britski, Nijssen, & Ortega, 1983. Rio Huacamayo, Rio Aguaytia Drainage, Departmento de Ucayali, Peru.
Metaloricaria Isbrücker, 1975. Type species *M. paucidens* Isbrücker.
Metaloricaria paucidens Isbrücker, 1975. Fr. Guiana, creek at right bank of Ouaqui River, upstream of Saut Bali, Maroni River system.
p. nijsseni (Boeseman, 1976). Sipaliwini River, SW Surinam.
Farlowella Eigenmann & Eigenmann, 1889. Type species *Acestra acus* Kner.
Farlowella acestrichthys Pearson, 1924. Rurrenabaque, Rio Beni Basin, Bolivia.
F. acus (Kner, 1854). Caracas.
F. agustini Martin Salazar, 1964. Venezuela, en una quebrada limite entre los Estados Cojedes Y Carabobo, carretera Campo Carabobo Taguanes, afluente del rio Chirgua que a su vez lo es del rio Pao.
F. amazona (Günther, 1864). Santarem, River Amazonas.
F. angosturae Martin Salazar, 1964. Venezuela, Cano Largo al oeste de Cuidad Bolivar, Edo. Bolivar.
F. azygia Eigenmann & Vance, 1917.

Santarem.

F. boliviana Steindachner, 1910. Kolumbien.

F. carinata Garman, 1889. Santarem, Teffé, Gurupa, Obidos, Jutahy, Tabatinga. (Lectotype from Para, Brazil, Gurupa (01°25′S, 51°36′W.)

F. curtirostra Myers, 1942. Quebrada Tabor, trib. of Rio Motatan system, 30 km N of Trujillo, Maracaibo basin, Venezuela.

F. gladiolus (Günther, 1864). Rio Cupai.

F. gladius (Boulenger, 1898). Rio Jurua.

F. gracilis Regan, 1904. Rio Caqueta, Cauca Valley, S. Colombia.

F. guaricensis Martin Salazar, 1964. Rio Guarico, en el puente de Uverito, carretera San Juan de Loa Morros a Ortiz, Guarico, Venezuela.

F. hahni Meinken, 1937. Mittleren Paranagebiete.

F. hargreavesi Eigenmann, 1912. Br. Guiana.

F. hasemani Eigenmann & Vance, 1917. Para.

F. henrique Miranda Ribeiro, 1918. Rio Vermelho, affl. do Araguaya, Sta. Rita das Antas.

F. jauruensis Eigenmann & Vance, 1917. Jaura.

F. kneri (Steindachner, 1883). Canelos, Ecuador.

F. latisoma Miranda Ribeiro, 1939. Oriximina, Amazonas.

F. mariaelenae Martin Salazar, 1964. Venezuela, Rio Salinas, brazo del rio Pao Viejo al noreste de El Baul, afluente del rio Portuguesa, Edo. Cojedes.

F. martini Fernandez-Yepez, 1972. Rio or Quebrada Guarataro, trib. of Rio Aroa, Rio Magdalena basin, Venezuela.

F. nattereri Steindachner, 1910. Dem mittleren Amazonas-gebiete ohne nähere Angabe des Fundortes, wahrscheinlich aus dem Rio Negro.

F. oliveirae Miranda Ribeiro, 1939. Para.

F. oxyryncha (Kner, 1854). Rio Mamore, Cachoeira de Bananeira.

F. paranaensis Meinken, 1937. Mittleren Parana-gebiete.

F. parvicarinata Boeseman, 1971. Right trib. of Nickerie River, 12 km WSW of Stondansie Falls, Surinam.

F. pleurotaenia Miranda Ribeiro, 1939. Para.

F. pseudogladiolus Steindachner, 1910. Dem mittleren Gebiete des Amazonenstromes ohne nähere Angabe des Fundortes, wahrscheinlich aus dem Rio Negro.

F. reticulata Boeseman, 1971. Maka Creek, left trib. of Lawa River, 10 km S of Stoelmanseiland, Marowijne River basin, Surinam.

F. roncallii Martin Salazar, 1964. Venezuela, en la quebrada El Ahorcado Aguirre, affl. del rio Tirgua, Carabobo.

F. rugosa Boeseman, 1971. Kamaloea or Saloea Creek, right trib. of Marowijne River, 9 km SE of outlet of Gran Creek, Fr. Guyane.

F. schreitmuelleri Ahl, 1937. Santarem.

F. scolopacina (de Filippi, 1853). In rivis prov. Venezuelae, Caracas.

F. smithi Fowler, 1913. Madeira River, about 200 miles E of W long. 62°20′, Brazil.

F. venezuelensis Martin Salazar, 1964. Venezuela, rio Colorado, de la Hoya del rio Guarapiche en San Antonio de Maturin, Monagas.

F. vittata Myers, 1942. Trib. of Rio Uribanto, from San Cristobal to the llanos, Venezuela.

Acestridium Haseman, 1911. Type species *A. discus* Haseman.

Acestridium discus Haseman, 1911. Igarape de Cachoeira Grande, near Manaos, Brazil.

Furcodontichthys Rapp Py-Daniel, 1981. Type species *F. novaesi* Rapp Py-Daniel.

Furcodontichthys novaesi Rapp Py-Daniel, 1981.

Ixinandria Isbrücker & Nijssen, 1979. Type species *Loricaria steinbachi* Regan, 1906.

Ixinandria montebelloi (Fowler, 1940). Monte Bello, Tarija, Bolivia.

I. steinbachi (Regan, 1906). Salto, Argentina.

Rineloricaria Bleeker, 1862. Type species *Loricaria lima* Kner, 1854.

Rineloricaria altipinnis (Breder, 1925). Rio Chico, Rio Chucunaque drainage, Darien, Panama.

R. beni (Pearson, 1924). Lagoons, Lake

Rogoagua, Rio Beni basin, Bolivia.

R. cacerensis (Miranda Ribeiro, 1912). Caceres, Mato Grosso, Aguas do Paraguay.

R. cadeae (Hensel, 1868). Southern Brazil, in the kleinen steinigen Bächen, die in den Rio Cadea münden.

R. caracasensis (Bleeker, 1862). Caracas.

R. castroi Isbrücker & Nijssen, 1984. Rio Trombetas, Est. Para, Brazil.

R. catamarcensis (Berg, 1895). Argentina, Arroyo del Tala, en la Provincia de Catamarca.

R. cubataonis (Steindachner, 1907). Dem Flusse Cubatao im State Santa Catharina bei Theresopolis, Brazil.

R. eigenmanni (Pellegrin, 1908). Sarare, Venezuela.

R. fallax (Steindachner, 1915). Brazil, Est. Roraima, Igarape, de Carauna (= Sa. Grande, 02°35′N, 60°45′W) near Boa Vista (2°51′N, 60°43′W), alt. 200 m above sea level, Rio Branco drainage, Rio Amazonas basin. Lectotype: Roraima State, Brazil, Igarapé de Carauná, 2°35′N, 60°45′W.

R. felipponei (Fowler, 1943). Uruguay.

R. formosa Isbrücker & Nijssen, 1979. Colombia, lagoon about 1 km upriver from Puerto Inirida, Rio Inirida/Rio Orinoco drainage.

R. hasemani Isbrücker & Nijssen, 1979. Brazil, Est. Para, Maguary near Belem, along Braganca railroad, in forest streams that empty into Rio Guama.

R. henselii (Steindachner, 1907). Dem flusse Cubatao im Staate Santa Catharina bei Theresopolis, Brazil.

R. heteroptera Isbrücker & Nijssen, 1976. Brazil, Est. Amazonas, creek in reserve Ducke near Manas, 3°06′N, 60°00′W, a trib. of Rio Preto da Eva, 10 km NE of Manaus, forest creek.

R. hoehnei (Miranda Ribeiro, 1912). Coxim, no Rio Paraguay.

R. jaraguensis (Steindachner, 1909). Dem Jaragua und dessen Nebenflussen im Brazilian State Sta. Catharina.

R. jubata (Boulenger, 1902). NW Ecuador, St. Javier (60 feet) and Río Durango (350′). (Lectotype Rio Durango.)

R. konopickyi (Steindachner, 1879). Dem mittleren Laufe des Amazonenstromes.

R. kronei (Miranda Ribeiro, 1911). Rio Iporanga, São Paulo.

R. lanceolata (Günther, 1868). Xeberos.

R. latirostris (Boulenger, 1900). Southern Brazil, Province São Paulo, Mogy-guassu River, about 250 miles inland of Santos.

R. lima (Kner, 1854). Brazil.

R. longicauda Reis, 1983. Banhado do Taim, em Rio Grando, Santa Vitoria do Palmar e Arroio Grande, Rio Grande do Sul.

R. magdalenae (Steindachner, 1878). Aus der grossen, seeartig ausgebreiteten Cienega, welche der Magdalenen-Strom mit einem seiner östlich gelegenen Hauptarme kurz von seiner Mündung in das Meer bildet.

R. melini (Schindler, 1959). Rio Solimoes beim Ort Manacapuru, nahe der Mündung des Rio Negro.

R. microlepidogaster (Regan, 1904). Rio Grande do Sul.

R. microlepidota (Steindachner, 1907). Dem Jurua.

R. morrowi Fowler, 1940. Ucayali River basin, Cantamana, Peru.

R. nigricauda (Regan, 1904). Porto Real, Province Rio Janeiro.

R. pareiacantha (Fowler, 1943). Rio Santa Lucia, Canelones, Uruguay.

R. parva (Boulenger, 1895). Descalvados, Mato Grosso, Brazil.

R. phoxocephala (Eigenmann & Eigenmann, 1889). Coary.

R. platyura (Müler & Troschel, 1848). Rupununi, Br. Guiana.

R. quadrensis Reis, 1983. Lagoa dos Quadros e curso inferior de sus afluentes, em Osório, Rio Grande do Sul.

R. rupestre (Schultz, 1944). Venezuela, in Rio San Pedro at the bridge S of Mene Grande, Motatan system, Maracaibo basin.

R. sneiderni (Fowler, 1944). NW Colombia, Rio Jurubida, Nuqui, in brook, at 3000 ft. elevation.

R. steindachneri (Regan, 1904). E Brazil, from Rio Preto to Rio Parahyba.

R. stewarti (Eigenmann, 1909). Br. Guiana, Chipoo Creek, a trib. of the Ireng.

R. strigilata (Hensel, 1868). Southern Brazil, in einem steinigen Bache bei Santa

Cruz.

R. teffeana (Steindachner, 1879). Teffe, Amazon River.

R. thrissoceps (Fowler, 1943). Rio Santa Lucia, Canelones, Uruguay.

R. uracantha (Kner & Steindachner, 1863). Rio Chagres, Nordseite von Panama.

R. wolfei Fowler, 1940. Ucayali River basin, Cantamana, Peru.

Dasyloricaria Isbrücker & Nijssen, 1979. Type species *Loricaria filamentosa* Steindachner.

Dasyloricaria capetensis (Meek & Hildebrand, 1913). Rio Capeti, Panama, Tuyra River basin.

D. filamentosa (Steindachner, 1878). Magdalenen-Strom.

D. latiura (Eigenmann & Vance, 1912). Colombia, Boca de Certegal.

D. seminuda (Eigenmann & Vance, 1912). Colombia, Girardot.

D. tuyrensis (Meek & Hildebrand, 1913). Rio Tuyra, Boca de Cupe, Panama.

Spatuloricaria Schultz, 1944. Type species *S. phelpsi* Schultz.

Spatuloricaria atratoensis Schultz, 1944. Rio Truando, a trib. of Rio Atrato, Colombia.

S. caquetae (Fowler, 1943). Florencia, Rio Orteguasa, Colombia.

S. curvispina (Dahl, 1941). Rio Batatal, trib. to Rio San Jorge, which is next to Rio Cauca, the largest trib. to Rio Magdalena, Dept. of Bolivar, Colombia.

S. euacanthagenys Isbrücker, 1979. Morelia, Rio Caqueta drainage, Colombia.

S. evansii (Boulenger, 1892). Jangada, Brazil, Province of Mato Grosso.

S. fimbriata (Eigenmann & Vance, 1912). Colombia, Boca de Certegai.

S. gymnogaster (Eigenmann & Vance, 1912). Colombia, Apulo.

S. lagoichthys (Schultz, 1944). Venezuela, the Rio Palmar near Totuma, about 100 km SW of Maracaibo.

S. nudiventris (Valenciennes, 1840). River de Sainte-Francois au Brazil.

S. phelpsi Schultz, 1944. Rio Socuy 3 km above its mouth, Maracaibo basin, Venezuela.

S. puganensis (Pearson, 1937). Pusoc, Rio Maranon, Peru.

Ricola Isbrücker & Nijssen, 1978. Type species *Loricaria (Loricaria) macrops* Regan, 1904.

Ricola macrops (Regan, 1904). Rio de La Plata.

Paraloricaria Isbrücker, 1979. Type species *Loricaria vetula* Valenciennes, 1840.

Paraloricaria agastor Isbrücker, 1979. Paraguay, Rio Paraguay.

P. commersonoides (Devincenzi, 1943). El Rio Uruguay, frente a la ciudad de Paysandu.

P. vetula (Valenciennes, 1840). Des environs de Buenos Aires.

Loricaria Linnaeus, 1758. Type species *Loricaria cataphracta* Linnaeus.

Loricaria apeltogaster Boulenger, 1895. Paraguay, Rio Paraguay.

L. cataphracta Linnaeus, 1758. America meridionali. (Type loc. restricted to Surinam, Marowijne district, mouth of Marowijne River near Galibi [5°45′N, 54°00′W].)

L. clavipinna Fowler, 1940. Ucayali River basin, Cantamana, Peru.

L. lata Eigenmann & Eigenmann, 1889. Goyaz. (Brazil, Goiaz State, Rio Araguaia drainage [15°57′S, 50°07′W].)

L. lentiginosa Isbrücker, 1979. Brazil, Est. São Paulo, haut bassin du Rio Parana, Represa de Volta Grande, Rio Grande.

L. nickeriensis Isbrücker, 1979. Surinam, district Nickerie, rapide dans la riviere Fallawatra, 5 km SSW des chutes Stondansie, largeur 60 cm, fond de sable, pierres.

L. parnahybae Steindachner, 1907. Rio Parnahyba an der Mündung eines Baches bei Victoria (now Alto Parnaiba).

L. piracicabae von Ihering, 1907. Piracicaba, Piracicabe River, State of São Paulo.

L. prolixa Isbrücker & Nijssen, 1978. Brazil, Est. São Paulo, Rio Piracicaba, through Rio Tiete, Rio Parana system, Piracicaba, 22°45′S, 47°40′W.

L. simillima Regan, 1904. Canelos, E Ecuador.

L. tucumanensis Isbrücker, 1979. Argentina, Prov. Tucuman (San Miguel de —), Tucuman, 26°47′S, 65°15′W.

Brochiloricaria Isbrücker & Nijssen, 1979. Type species *B. chauliodon* Isbrücker.

Brochiloricaria chauliodon Isbrücker, 1979. Argentina, Prov. Entre Rios, Isla El Dorado, Parana Guaza.
B. macrodon (Kner, 1854). Cujabaflusse.
Crossoloricaria Isbrücker, 1979. Type species *Loricaria variegata* Steindachner, 1879.
Crossoloricaria cephalaspis Isbrücker, 1979. Colombia, Rio Magdalena, soit —a) Prov. Atlantico, Barranquilla, 11°00′N, 74°50′W, —b) Prov. Antioquia, Puerto Berrio, 6°28′N, 74°28′W, ou —c) Prov. Tolima, Honda, 5°15′N, 74°50′W.
C. rhami Isbrücker & Nijssen, 1983. Peru, Dept. Ucayali, Prov. Coronel Portillo, Rio Aguaytia basin, Rio Huacamayo (9°00′S, 75°29′W).
C. variegata (Steindachner, 1879). Panama, dem Mamoni-Flusse bei Chepo (also indicated as: dem Mamoni-Flusse, welcher ungefahr 15 englischen Meilen oberhalb der Mündung des Bayano (in den Stillen Ocean) in letzteren Fällt.
C. venezuelae (Schultz, 1944). Venezuela, in the Rio Palmar at the bridge about 70 km SW of Maracaibo.
Dentectus Salazar, Isbrücker & Nijssen, 1982. Type *D. barbarmatus* Salazar, Isbrücker, & Nijssen.
Dentectus barbarmatus Salazar, Isbrücker & Nijssen, 1982. Venezuela, Estado Cojedes, Rio Salinas, trib. upper Pao Viejo (09°13′N, 68°07′W).
Pseudohemiodon Bleeker, 1862. Type species *Hemiodon platycephalus* Kner.
Pseudohemiodon amazonus (Delsman, 1941). Trombetas River near Obidos.
P. apithanos Isbrücker & Nijssen, 1978. Ecuador, Prov. Napo, Rio Conejo, a trib. of Rio San Miguel, vicinity of Santa Cecilia, 00°06′N, 76°51′W, upper Rio Amazonas system.
P. devincenzii (Soriano Senorans, 1950). Sobre fondo de arena fangosa con red de playa, a 200 meters agua abajo de la desembocadura del arroyo Espinillar de Salto.
P. lamina (Günther, 1868). Xeberos.
P. laticeps (Regan, 1904). Paraguay.
P. platycephalus (Kner, 1854). Rio Cujaba.
P. thorectes Isbrücker, 1975. Bolivia, Est. Santa Cruz, Buena Vista, 17°28′S, 63°37′W, west of Rio Palacios, trib. of Rio Mamore, which is trib. of Rio Madeira, Rio Amazonas system.
Pyxiloricaria Isbrücker & Nijssen, 1984. Type species *P. menezesi* Isbrücker & Nijssen.
Pyxiloricaria menezesi Isbrücker & Nijssen, 1984. "Lagoas marginais da rodovia Transpantaneira, município de Miranda," Est. Mato Grasso do Sul, Brazil.
Apistoloricaria Isbrücker & Nijssen, 1986. Type species *A. condei* Isbrücker & Nijssen.
Apistoloricaria condei Isbrücker & Nijssen, 1986. Rio Napo basin (upper Amazon), Napo Prov., Ecuador.
Rhadinoloricaria Isbrücker & Nijssen, 1974. Type species *Loricaria macromystax* Günther, 1869.
Rhadinoloricaria macromystax (Günther, 1869). Peruvian Amazon.
Planiloricaria Isbrücker, 1971. Type species *Pseudohemiodon (Planiloricaria) cryptodon* Isbrücker.
Planiloricaria cryptodon (Isbrücker, 1971). Peru, Rio Ucayali near Pucallpa.
Reganella Eigenmann, 1905. Type species *Hemiodon depressus* Kner. (Subst. name for *Hemiodon* Kner, preocc.)
Reganella depressa (Kner, 1854). Rio Negro und Marabitanos. (Lectotype: Brazil, Amazonas, Marabitanas, 00°57′N, 66°55′W, upper Rio Negro.)
Limatulichthys Isbrücker & Nijssen, 1979. Type species *Loricaria (Pseudoloricaria) punctata* Regan, 1904.
Limatulichthys punctatus (Regan, 1904). Manaos, Rio Negro, Middle Amazon. Brazil, Est. Amazonas, Rio Amazonas at Manaus, 3°06′S, 60°00′W.
Pseudoloricaria Bleeker, 1862. Type species *Loricaria laeviuscula* Valenciennes, 1840.
Pseudoloricaria laeviuscula (Valenciennes, 1840). L'ancien Cabinet. (Brazil, Est. Pará, north of Rio Tapajós into Rio Amazonas at Santarem, 2°26′S, 54°41′W.)
Loricariichthys Bleeker, 1862. Type species *Loricaria maculata* Bloch, 1794.
Loricariichthys acutus (Valenciennes, 1840). On peut croire qu'il venait du Brazil.
L. anus (Valenciennes, 1840). Sur les bords de la riviere de la Prata pres de Buenos Aires.
L. brunneus (Hancock, 1828). Venezuela,

branches and lakes of the Orinoco.

L. cashibo (Eigenmann & Allen, 1942). Lago Cashiboya.

L. castaneus (de Castelnau, 1855). Donne a Rio de Janeiro comme venant des rivieres du voisinage.

L. chanjoo (Fowler, 1940). Ucayali River basin, Contamana, Peru.

L. derbyi Fowler, 1915. Rio Jaguribe at Barro Alto, Brazil.

L. hauxwelli Fowler, 1915. Ambyiacu River, Ecuador.

L. labialis (Boulenger, 1895). Paraguay.

L. maculatus (Bloch, 1794). No locality. (Surinam, district Surinam, ditches at Cultuurtuin at Paramaribo West, 5°50′N, 55°10′W.)

L. microdon (Eigenmann, 1909). Rupununi, Br. Guiana.

L. nudirostris (Kner, 1854). Barra do Rio Negro.

L. platymetopon Isbrücker & Nijssen, 1979. Paraguay, Lago Ypacarai, San Bernardino, 25°16′S, 57°16′W, Rio Paraguay system.

L. spixii (Steindachner, 1881). Rio Parahyba.

L. stuebelii (Steindachner, 1883). Huallaga.

L. ucayalensis Regan, 1913. River Ucayali, Peru.

Hemiodontichthys Bleeker, 1862. Type species *Hemiodon acipenserinus* Kner.

Hemiodontichthys acipenserinus (Kner, 1854). Brazil, Est. Rondônia = Est. Guaporé, Rio Amazonas system, Rio Madeira drainage, Rio Guaporé.

Addenda:

Spectracanthus Nijssen & Isbrücker, 1986. Type species *S. murinus* Nijssen & Isbrücker.

Spectracanthus murinus Nijssen & Isbrücker, 1986. Rio Tapajos system, Est. Para, Brazil.

Acanthicus adonis Isbrücker & Nijssen, 1988. Rio Tocantins near Cametá, Est. Pará, Brazil.

Chapter 31

Family — Plate 285

ASTROBLEPIDAE

(South American Hillstream Catfishes)

The family Astroblepidae is a moderate to small family of catfishes inhabiting the fresh waters of mountainous regions of South America, often in rather fast-flowing torrents. Most species are of small size, the largest, *Astroblepus grixalvii*, attaining a length of about 30 cm. The head and body are depressed, flattened and not covered by an armor of dermal scutes. Two pairs of barbels are present, one maxillary and one nasal. The teeth in the jaws are flattened and bicuspid or mixed bicuspid and conical and lie in a narrow band in each jaw. There is a short dorsal fin of 6 to 7 rays that is provided with a stout spine. An adipose fin is present or absent, when present it is often long and low and frequently also provided with a stout spine. The gill slits are separated into inhalent and exhalent orifices, and the gill rakers are rudimentary or absent on the first gill arch although on subsequent arches they may be well developed. Males have an elongate urogenital papilla that apparently functions as an intromittent organ.

The family is composed of a single genus, *Astroblepus*, that contains a total of approximately 35-40 species. It can be defined as follows. The body is naked, without scutes, and the entire head is covered with muscle. The mouth is inferior, with the lips expanded and forming a sucker. The teeth are simple or bifid and not aligned in a single row in either jaw but in a narrow band of three to four distinct rows. The pharyngeals have teeth on their entire surface, those on the upper pharyngeal conical, those on the lower rather pavement-like. The metapterygoid is small and does not extend as far as the skull and does not articulate with the palatines. The interopercular area is without spines. The dorsal fin is composed of a spine and 6 to 7 rays. The anal fin has a count of i,4-i,6, the pectoral i,9-i,12, and the ventral fins i,3-i,4. The gill rakers are either absent or rudimentary on the first gill arch but present and often well developed on subsequent arches. The gill membranes are broadly joined to the isthmus. The posterior division of the air bladder is absent.

Astroblepus is limited to the Andean region of South America, where it is one of the limited number of genera found at high altitudes in the mountain torrents. Eigenmann described members of this genus as occurring in the torrential streams up to an elevation of 13,400 feet, although they are also present at various intervals down to an altitude of a few hundred feet above sea level. Many of the species are therefore adapted to life in fast-flowing, even torrential, waters of the mountain regions and are able to cling to the rocks, even on a vertical surface. Under usual stream conditions they are said to be clumsy and awkard swimmers, wriggling through the water in a manner like that of a tadpole. Yet, moving against a strong current they are able to shuffle along and climb better than almost any other fishes known. To do this so efficiently, they have a small mouth surrounded by a broad flap that is thin and flexible at the edges, forming a sucker like that of the loricariids. The ventral area is flattened. The anterior ventral fin rays are broad and flattened and their surfaces are thickly studded with small, sharp, backwardly directed denticles.

Muscles attached to the pelvic girdle make them remarkably maneuverable and are able to make the fins move forward where a new purchase on the surface can be made. The sucker-like mouth along with this ventral fin - pelvic girdle apparatus serves as the means of locomotion for these fishes. By means of the alternate action of the mouth and this apparatus the fish can hitch its way slowly forward, even against a current of great force. They are thus perfectly adapted so that they have little difficulty in attaching themselves to rock surfaces or any other convenient object.

While the sucker mouth is attached to the substrate, the ability to take in water for breathing purposes is thereby removed. Since the gills must be supplied with this essential flow of oxygen-bearing water, the gill openings have become modified so that there are inhalent and exhalent orifices present. Water that is drawn into the gill chamber when it is expanded by muscular action passes over the gills and is then pumped out through the exhalent orifice, the direction of the water controlled by various valves. The fish can therefore breathe normally while the mouth is primarily occupied with keeping the fish in place in the current.

Observations on a Colombian species called *Arges marmoratus* (= *Astroblepus chotae*) by a mining engineer, a Mr. R. D. O. Johnson, gave firsthand evidence of the remarkable ability of this fish to climb. He described the fish in the following manner: "In external appearance the skin is smooth and scaleless, the color is a dark mottled gray shading into a yellowish tint on the posterior parts. They rarely appear to grow beyond 12 inches and are considered excellent food by the natives who refer to them as 'capitan'." Johnson discovered these fish while diverting a stream to examine a deep pothole in the stream bed some 22 feet deep. When the water level had dropped to a few feet from the bottom the *Astroblepus* came into view. A small trickle of water still ran down one side of the pothole. The catfish started to climb up this side of the pothole in the trickle, the water keeping the body of the fish wet, at least from the mouth backward, perhaps necessary to keep a sufficient suction with the surface or as a possible guide to better conditions. They "hitched" themselves up for a foot or more before stopping for a brief period, apparently to rest. After a few minutes they resumed their journey. By this method they were able to escape. Johnson, intrigued by the feat of these small catfish, examined the pothole more closely. The total ascent he determined was 18 feet, with the walls vertical or even with an inward incline of some 30° to the vertical. In addition, the path they took was covered with algae. Not only were the fish well adapted to living in such an environment, but they apparently were able to breed there as well. Johnson, in examining the deepest potholes of the stream bed, observed eggs deposited there that were attached individually to the underside of large rocks.

Astroblepus grixalvii. (From Fowler, 1954.)

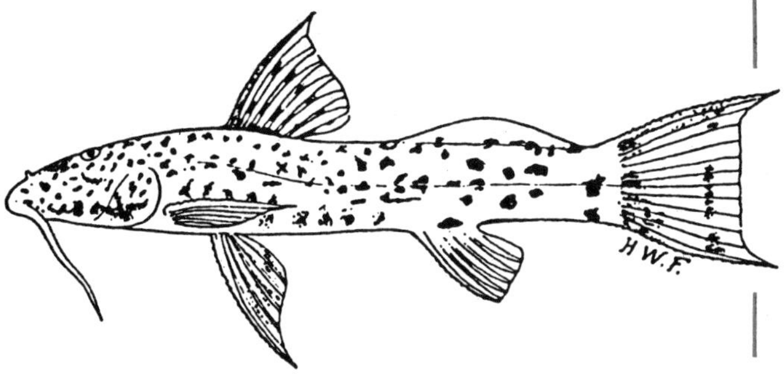

A more recently discovered species, *Astroblepus pholeter*, was found in a cave in eastern Ecuador. What is so unusual about this species is that it is a true cave form, complete with minute eyes and lack of pigment. It also has long, filamentous tips on the leading or outer elements of the dorsal, pectoral, and caudal fins. It has a long maxillary barbel extending to the pectoral fin base, an elongate barbel on the nasal flap, and a well-developed spine at the anterior end of the adipose fin. This species resembles another species, *A. longifilis*, which has long dorsal and anal fin filaments and a nasal flap barbel, but differs from it by its tiny eyes, lack of pigment, longer nasal barbel, longer pectoral fin filament, well-developed adipose fin spine, and lack of an adipose ridge. *A. pholeter* was found only in the perpetually dark regions of the cave some 300 meters to 2 kilometers from its mouth. These catfish were very timid, hiding in holes in the rocks, and therefore were extremely difficult to capture. They were usually found in an area where detritus had been washed down into the cave or near bat guano. This latter material commonly contains large numbers of invertebrate larvae. Examination of the stomach contents of a male specimen revealed three mayfly nymphs. The water in the cave was cool, about 15°C, and notably calcareous.

An interesting association has been discovered between midge larvae and catfishes of the families Loricariidae and Astroblepidae. The larvae were found attached at various sites on members of these two families and apparently had arrived there by chance. The favored sites on the naked astroblepids seemed to be the leading elements of the fins, particularly the denticles of the ventral fins. The ventral fin site would be one where the chironomid larvae would come most into contact with detritus, which constitutes their food. Other preferred sites are the gill chambers and barbels. Since these fishes are very sedentary, the larvae have every opportunity to find their host and make a firm attachment. They gain some protection from their hosts, although if they attach in an open region of the body they may be lost or eaten (freshwater cleaners?). The association also aids the larvae in obtaining food, for the catfish remain very close to the bottom to scrape algae and other organic matter from rock and plant surfaces, to feed on the bottom detritus, or even to feed on insect larvae and other small organisms. The chironomid larvae may further gain by having a means to prevent them from being carried downstream in the strong current, perhaps to less favorable conditions.

Astroblepus grixalvii is the largest member of the family, with a maximum length of about 30 cm. It occurs in the fast-running rivers of the Central and Eastern Cordillera in Colombia. It has well-developed, thick barbels and well-developed fins with strong dorsal and pectoral spines. The adipose fin is long and large, but it is without a spine. This species, referred to as "Pez Negro," has some economic importance as a food fish. Unfortunately, its range and abundance have declined greatly in recent years.

The astroblepids strongly resemble the loricariids and, in fact, were at one time considered a subfamily of the Loricariidae, i.e. the Astroblepinae (Argiinae of Regan). They are similar to the loricariids particularly in the sucker-like mouth, in the asperous fin spines, in the morphology of the cranium, in the attachment of the ribs, and in the labyrinths not being covered by the occipital bones. The principal distinguishing characters are the naked skin, the separation of the gill slits into exhalent and inhalent pores, and the muscles that cover the cranium. Other differences, consisting of the number of rays and vertebrae, scarcely exceed the levels between the subfamilies of the Loricariidae. The question is then raised as to whether, as Regan believes, the Astroblepidae is an ultraspecialized loricariid adapted to life in the torrents and rapids by having lost the armor (along with many internal structural changes due to this loss), or whether it is a descendant of naked forms from which are also descended the loricariids. The answer is still not known. The lack of armor in the astroblepids could just as well be accounted for by the lack of major predators in the mountain streams.

Astroblepids have never been known to have been imported for the aquarium trade, at least in quantity. These torrent-loving catfishes would certainly prove a challenge to any aquarists wishing to provide them with a situation as close to their natural environment as possible. The tank must have moving, highly oxygenated water and must be well-covered for obvious reasons.

Checklist of the species of the family Astroblepidae and their type localities:

Astroblepus Humboldt, 1805. Type species *Astroblepus grixalvii* Humboldt.

- *Astroblepus boulengeri* (Regan, 1904). Canelos, Ecuador.
- *A. caquetae* Fowler, 1943. Florencia, Rio Orteguasá, Colombia.
- *A. chapmani* Eigenmann, 1912. Central Andes of Colombia.
- *A. chotae* (Regan, 1904). Chota Valley, northern Ecuador.
- *A. cyclopus* (Humboldt, 1805). Subterranean waters of the Andes near Quitos, Ecuador.

A. festae (Boulenger, 1898). Vale de Gualaquiza, east of Ecuador (upper Amazon).

A. fissidens (Regan, 1904). Andes of Ecuador.

?*A. formosus* Fowler, 1945.

A. frenatus Eigenmann, 1917. Santander, Colombia.

A. grixalvii Humboldt, 1805. Popayan, southwest Colombia.

A. guentheri (Boulenger, 1887). Colombia.

A. heterodon (Regan, 1904). Western part of Colombia.

A. homodon (Regan, 1904). Colombia.

A. labialis Pearson, 1937. Balsas, Peru.

A. latidens Eigenmann, 1917. Eastern part of the Colombian Andes.

A. longiceps Pearson, 1924. Rio Colorado, Laixo Bopi, Bolivia; Rio Yanahuana, Peru.

A. longifilis (Steindachner, 1883). Rio Huambo; Rio Totora near Chirimoto, Peru.

A. mancoi Eigenmann *in* Myers, 1928. Rio Comberciato, Urubamba, Peru.

A. mariae Fowler, 1919. Colombia.

A. micrescens Eigenmann, 1917. Andes around Bogota, Colombia.

A. mindoense (Regan, 1904). Mindo, western part of Ecuador.

A. nicefori Myers, 1932. Sonson, Antiquia, Colombia.

A. orientalis (Boulenger, 1903). Rios Albireggas and Milla, Venezuela.

A. peruanus (Steindachner, 1875). Amable Maria, Peru.

A. phelpsi Schultz, 1944. Maracaibo basin, Venezuela.

A. pholeter Collette, 1962.

?*A. pirrense* Meek & Hildebrand, 1913. Rio Cana, Cana, Panama.

A. praeliorum Allen *in* Eigenmann & Allen, 1942. Tarma, Palca, Huancayo, Oroya, Huancachupa Creek, Peru.

A. retropinnis (Regan, 1904). Rio Dagua, Colombia.

A. rosei Eigenmann, 1922. Rio Jequetepeque, Llallan, Peru.

A. sabalo (Valenciennes, 1840). Mission Santa Ana, Lago Titicaca.

A. simonsii (Regan, 1904). Huaras, Peru.

A. stubeli Wandolleck, 1916. Lago Titicaca.

A. supramollis Pearson, 1937. Balsas, Peru; Rio Marañon.

A. taczanowskii (Boulenger, 1890). Amable Maria, Peruvian Andes.

A. trifasciatum Eigenmann, 1912. Rio Dagua, Colombia.

A. theresiae (Steindachner, 1907). Cayendelet, Andes.

A. ubidiai (Pellegrin, 1931). Lago St. Paul, Olavalo, Imbabura Province, Ecuador.

A. unifasciatus Eigenmann, 1912. Caldas, Colombia.

A. vanceae (Eigenmann, 1913). Tarma, Peru.

Chapter 32

Family SCOLOPLACIDAE (Spiny Dwarf Catfishes)

The family Scoloplacidae contains a single genus, *Scoloplax*, which in turn contains a single species, *S. dicra*, from Bolivia. It has caused some discussion as to its proper placement in relation to other catfish families. Because of its general appearance, it was first thought to be an aspredinid, but more detailed examination placed it more with the loricarioid families (Loricariidae, Callichthyidae, Trichomycteridae, and Astroblepidae). It was initially regarded as a subfamily of the Loricariidae (Bailey & Baskin, 1976) but was later elevated to family status by Isbrücker (1980).

The head is greatly depressed and the body is flattened; the caudal peduncle is quadrangular in cross-section. There is no bony bridge between the supraoccipital and the supraneural plate. The eyes are without free orbital rims. There are a number of integumentary teeth that are widespread on the head and fins as well as on the body plates. Large teeth are present at the front of the snout and smaller teeth may be seen along the posterior part of the dorsal rim of the orbit, the lateral edge of the sphenotic, laterally on the compound pterotic-supracleithrum, and on the opercle. The interopercular area is without spines and not eversible. The mouth is subterminal and the lips are normal, i.e., not expanded into a sucking disc. The teeth are bifid, arranged in a single row in each jaw, that of the lower jaw in a continuous, gently curving row; there are about 14 teeth in the upper jaw and about 10 in the lower jaw. The maxillary barbel is forked and extends to beyond the insertion of the pectoral fin. Two pairs of mental barbels are present, the outer near the corner of the mouth and lateral to the inner pair; there are no nasal barbels.

The body is partially covered by five series of toothed plates. There are two series of dorsolateral postdorsal plates each containing 17 or 18 plates, two series of ventrolateral plates from the anal fin to the caudal fin base containing 8 or 9 plates per series, and a midventral series of 5-7 plates between the anus and the anal fin. All plates are separate, but supported internally. A movable, densely toothed, shield-shaped rostral plate is present. A pair of toothed plates lies under the pelvic girdle, and there is a striking clump of teeth on a lateral plate at midside below the dorsal spine. The partly enclosed belly area is naked to the base of the ventral fins.

The dorsal fin has a spine and 4 rays, the spine with teeth distally. The pectoral fins each have a spine and 5 to 7 rays, the spine with 4 to 7 series of teeth along the dorsal, anterior, and ventral surfaces. Both the dorsal and pectoral spines have a locking mechanism. There is no adipose fin. The anal fin is located well behind the dorsal fin and has an unbranched ray with a few teeth followed by 4 or 5 branched rays. The ventral fins each have an unbranched ray and 4 branched rays,

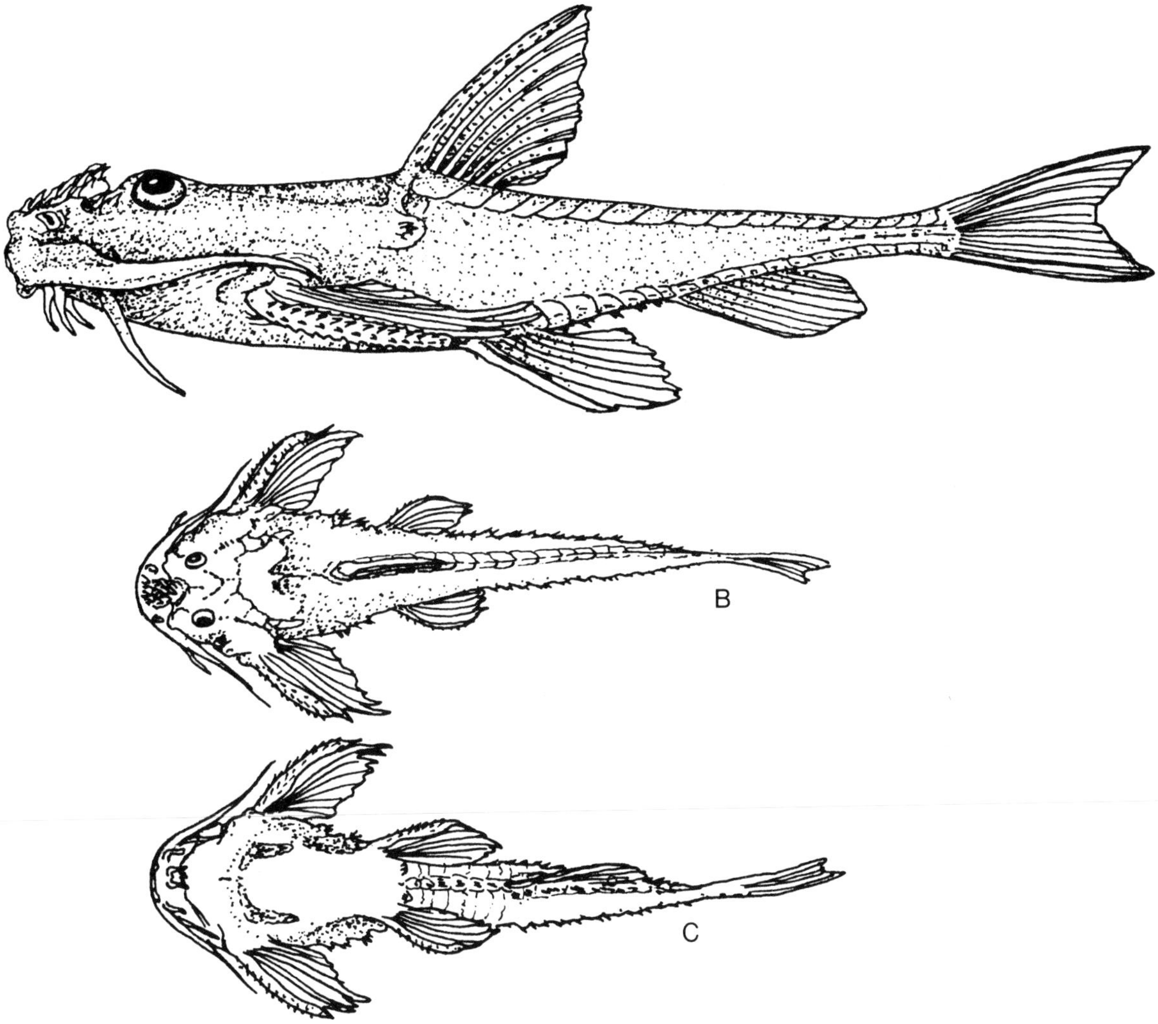

Scoloplax dicra; (b) dorsal view; (c) ventral view. (After Bailey & Baskin, 1976.)

the first ray with a few teeth. The caudal fin has 10 or 11 rays, the upper and lower with some teeth.

The gill opening is lateral in position and moderately restricted. The short gill rakers are few in number. The swimbladder vesicles are encapsulated by a pair of lateral bony spheres, each with a sharp lateral projection that lies below a lateral foramen. (Bailey & Baskin, 1976.)

This tiny catfish, the largest known specimen only 13.8 mm in standard length, was seined in water less than a meter deep. It was found at two localities in ox-bow lagoons that were stagnant and had the bottom covered with leaf debris and other organic litter. These lagoons were heavily shaded by lowland forest. A third locality was a small cutoff pond where the water was murky and the bottom was of mixed sand and silt with some organic debris. There were thick mats of aquatic vegetation, and the pond itself was bordered by forest but partially exposed. The temperature of the water at the first localities was 25° and 26.6°C while that of this last site was 30°C.

Checklist of the species of the family Scoloplacidae and its type locality:

Scoloplax Bailey and Baskin, 1976. Type species *Scoloplax dicra* Bailey and Baskin.

Scoloplax dicra Bailey and Baskin, 1976. Rio Itenez, Costa Marques, Beni, Bolivia.

BIBLIOGRAPHY

Agrawal, V. P. & R. S. Sharma, 1965. Sound producing organs of an Indian catfish, *Heteropneustes fossilis*. *Ann. Mag. Nat. Hist., ser. 13*, 8: 339-344.

Ahmad, Naseer-ud-Din & M. R. Mirza, 1963. Hill streams fishes of Kaghan and Swat. *The Scientist*, 6: 153-161.

Alfred, Eric, 1966. A new catfish of the genus *Akysis* from Malaya. *Copeia*, 1966, no. 3, pp. 467-470.

Allen, G. R. 1982. *A field guide to Inland Fishes of Western Australia*. Western Australian Museum. 86pp, pls.

Allen, G. R. 1985. Description of two new species of freshwater catfishes (Plotosidae) from Papua New Guinea. *Rec. West. Aust. Mus.*, 12(3): 247-256.

Allen, G. R. 1989. *The Freshwater Fishes of Australia*. T. F. H. Publications, Inc.

Allen, G. R. & M. Boeseman, 1982. A collection of freshwater fishes from Western New Guinea with descriptions of two new species (Gobiidae and Eleotridae). *Rec. West. Aust. Mus.*, 10(2): 67-103.

Arratia F., G. 1983. Preferencias de habitat de peces siluriformes de aguas continentales de Chila (Fam. Diplomystidae y Trichomycteridae). *Studies on Neotrop. Fauna & Environ.*, 18(4): 217-237.

Arratia F., G. 1983. *Trichomycterus chungaraensis* n. sp. and *Trichomycterus laucaensis* n. sp. (Pisces, Siluriformes, Trichomycteridae) from the High Andean Range. *Studies on Neotrop. Fauna & Environ.*, 18: 65-87.

Arratia F., G., A. Chang-G., S. Menu-Marque, & G. Rojas M. 1978. About *Bullockia* gen. nov., *Trichomycterus mendozensis* n. sp. and revision of the family Trichomycteridae (Pisces, Siluriformes). *Studies on Neotrop. Fauna & Environ.*, 13: 157-194.

Axelrod, H. R. 1987. Two new species of catfishes (Siluriformes, Callichthyidae and Pimelodidae) from the Rio Unini, Amazonas, Brazil. *Trop. Fish Hobbyist Mag.* 35(12):22-25.

Bailey, R. G , S. Churchfield, T. Petr, & R. Pimm, 1978. The ecology of the fishes in Nyumba ya Mungu reservoir, Tanzania. *Biol. Journ. Linn. Soc.*, 10: 109-137.

Bailey, R. M. & W. R. Taylor, 1950. *Schilbeodes hildebrandi*, a new ameiurid catfish from Mississippi. *Copeia*, 1950, no. 1, pp. 31-38.

Bailey, R. M. & J. N. Baskin, 1976. *Scoloplax dicra*, a new armored catfish from the Bolivian Amazon. *Occas. Pap. Mus. Zool., Univ. of Mich., #674*, 14 pp.

Bailey, R. M. & D. J. Stewart, 1984. Bagrid catfishes from Lake Tanganyika, with a key and descriptions of new taxa. *Misc. Publ. Mus. Zool., Univ. of Mich., #168*, 41 pp.

Balon, E. K. 1974. *Fishes of Lake Kariba, Africa*. T. F. H. Publ., Inc., Neptune, 144pp.

Balon, E. K. & A. G. Coche, 1974. *Lake Kariba: A man-made tropical ecosystem in central Africa*. Dr. W. Junk Publ., The Hague, 767pp.

Balon, E. K. & D. J. Stewart, 1983. Fish assemblages in a river with unusual gradient (Luongo, Africa — Zaire system), reflections on river zonation, and description of another new species. *Environ. Biol. Fishes*, 9(3/4): 225-252.

Barnard, K. H. 1927. 8. Report on a collection of fishes from the Okovongo River, with notes on Zambesi fishes. *Ann. S. Afr. Mus.*, 17: 407-458.

Barnard, K. H. 1942. A note on *Amphilius natalensis* Blgr. (Siluroidea, Amphiliidae). *Ann. Natal Mus.*, 10(2): 257-259.

Baskin, J. N., T. M. Zaret, & F. Mago-Leccia, 1980. Feeding of reportedly parasitic catfishes (Trichomycteridae and Cetopsidae) in the Rio Portuguesa Basin, Venezuela. *Biotropica*, 12(3): 182-186.

Behre, E. H. 1928. V. A list of the fresh water fishes of western Panama between long. 81°45′ and 83°15′W. *Ann. Carnegie Mus.*, 18(2): 305-328.

Berg, C. 1897. Contribuciones al conocimiento de los Peces Sudamericanos especialmente de los de la Republica Argentina. *Anales Mus. Nac. de Buenos Aires*, 5: 263-302.

Bernacsek, G. M. 1980. *Introduction to the Freshwater Fishes of Tanzania*. Univ. Dar Es Salaam, Dept. Zool., 78pp.

Berra, T. M., R. Moore, & L. F. Reynolds, 1975. The freshwater fishes of the Laloki River system of New Guinea. *Copeia*, 1975, no. 2, pp. 316-326.

Birkhead, W. S., 1972. Toxicity of stings of ariid and ictalurid catfishes. *Copeia*, 1972, no. 4, pp. 790-807.

Blache, J. 1964. *Les poissons du bassin du Tchad et du bassin adjacent du Mayo Kebbi*. O. R. S. T. O. M., Paris, 483pp.

Blanc, M., P. Banarescu, J.-L. Gaudet, & J.-C. Hureau. 1971. *European Inland Water Fish: A multilingual catalogue*. Fishing News (Books) Ltd., London, (F. A. O.), 165pp.

Blumer, L. S. 1979. Male parental care in the bony fishes. *Quart. Rev. Biol.*, 54: 149-161.

Boeseman, M. 1954. On *Sciadeichthys (Selanaspis) walrechti*, a new South American catfish. *Zool. Meded.*, 33(9): 59-62.

Boeseman, M. 1957. On a collection of East Indian fishes. *Zool. Meded.*, 35(7): 69-78.

Boeseman, M. 1957. On a collection of fishes from Stanley Pool (Belgian Congo). *Zool. Meded.*, 35(11): 139-151.

Boeseman, M. 1960. The fresh-water fishes of the island of Trinidad. *Stud. Fauna Curacao*, 10(#48): 72-153.

Boeseman, M. 1966. A new sisorid catfish from Java, *Sundagagata robusta* gen. et spec. nov. *Proc. Koninkl. Nederl. Akad. Weten., ser. C*, 69(2): 242-247.

Boeseman, M. 1968. The genus *Hypostomus* Lacepede, 1803, and its Surinam representatives (Siluriformes, Loricariidae). *Zool. Verhand. no. 99*, 89pp., pls.

Boeseman, M. 1971. The "comb-toothed" Loricariinae of Surinam, with reflections on the phylogenetic tendencies within the family Loricariidae (Siluriformes, Siluroidei). *Zool. Verh., no. 116*, 56pp.

Boeseman, M. 1972. Notes on South American catfishes, including remarks on Valenciennes and Bleeker types in the Leiden Museum. *Zool. Meded.*, 47(23): 293-320.

Boeseman, M. 1974. On two Surinam species of Hypoptopomatinae, both new to science (Loricariidae, Siluriformes, Ostariophysi). *Proc. Konink. Nederl. Akad. van Wetens. Amst., ser. C*, 77(3): 257-271.

Boeseman, M. 1976. A short review of the Surinam Loricariinae: with additional information on Surinam Harttiinae, including the description of a new species (Loricariidae, Siluriformes). *Zool. Meded.*, 50(11): 153-177.

Boeseman, M. 1982. The South American mailed catfish genus *Lithoxus* Eigenmann, 1910, with the description of three new species from Surinam and French Guyana and records of related species (Siluriformes, Loricariidae). *Proc. Konink. Nederl. Akad. Wetens., ser. C*, 85(1): 41-58.

Boeseman, M. 1983. Some remarks on the South American pimelodid catfish usually known by the name of *Phractocephalus hemiliopterus* (Bloch & Schneider) (Pimelodidae, Siluriformes). *Zool. Meded.*, 57(12): 105-114.

Böhlke, J. E. 1951. Description of a new auchenipterid catfish of the genus *Pseudepapterus* from the Amazon basin. *Stan. Ichthyol. Bull.*, 4(1): 38-40.

Böhlke, J. E. 1951. A new miniature catfish of the genus *Corydoras* from the Rio Orinoco in Venezuela. *Ann. Mag. nat. Hist., ser. 12*, 4: 824-827.

Böhlke, J. E. 1953. A catalogue of the type specimens of recent fishes in the natural history museum of Stanford University. *Stan. Ichthy. Bull.*, 5: 1-168.

Böhlke, J. E. 1959. Results of the Catherwood Foundation Peruvian Amazon Expedition: *Petacara*, a new genus for the bunocephalid catfish, *Bunocephalus dolichurus* Delsman. *Not. Nat. #318*, 6pp.

Böhlke, J. E. A new species of the doradid catfish genus *Leptodoras*, with comments on related forms. *Proc. Calif. Acad. Sci., 4th ser.*, 38(3): 53-62.

Böhlke, J. E. 1980. *Gelanoglanis stroudi*: A new catfish from the Rio Meta system in Colombia (Siluriformes, Doradidae, Auchenipterinae). *Proc. Acad. Nat. Sci. Phila.* 132: 150-155.

Borodin, N. A. 1927. A new blind catfish from Brazil. *Amer. Mus. Novitates #263*,

5pp.

Borodin, N. A. 1927. Some new catfishes from Brazil. *Amer. Mus. Novitates #266*, 7pp.

Borodin, N. A. 1927. *Pimelodus platicirris*, new species, and other notes on Brazilian catfishes. *Amer. Mus. Novitates #271*, 4pp.

Borodin, N. A. 1934. *Netuma hassleriana*, a new catfish from Panama. *Copeia*, 1934, no. 1, pp. 33-34.

Boulenger, G. A. 1898. X. On a collection of fishes from the Rio Jurua, Brazil. *Trans. Zool. Soc. London*, 14(7): 421-428, pls.

Boulenger, G. A. 1901. IV. Third contribution to the ichthyology of Lake Tanganyika. —Report on the collection of fishes made by Mr. J. E. S. Moore in Lakes Tanganyika and Kivu during his second expedition, 1899-1900. *Trans. Zool. Soc. London*, 16(3): 137-178.

Boulenger, G. A. 1907. A revision of the African silurid fishes of the subfamily Clariinae. *Proc. Zool. Soc. London, 1907*, pp. 1062-1097.

Boulenger, G. A. 1908. Note on *Clarias capensis* C. & V. *Ann. Natal Mus.*, 1(3): 237-239.

Boulenger, G. A. 1911. V. On a collection of fishes from the Lake Ngami Basin, Bechuanaland. *Trans. Zool. Soc. London*, 18(5): 399-432.

Boulenger, G. A. 1911. *Catalogue of the freshwater fishes of Africa in the British Museum (Natural History). Vol. II*. Brit. Mus. (Nat. Hist.), London, 529pp.

Boulenger, G. A. 1912. Poissons recueillis dans la region du Bas-Congo par M. le Dr. W. J. Ansorge. *Ann. Mus. Congo Belge, Zool., ser. 1*, 2(3): 1-28.

Boulenger, G. A. 1917. XX.- Description of a new silurid fish from Natal. *Ann. Natal Mus.*, 1(4): 432.

Boulenger, G. A. 1920. Poissons recueillis au Congo Belge par l'Expedition du Dr. C. Christy. *Ann. Mus. Congo Belge: Zool., ser. 1*, 2(4): 1-38.

Breder, C. M. 1925. New loricariate characin and poeciliid fishes from the Rio Chucunaque, Panama. *Amer. Mus. Novitates #180*, 9pp.

Breder, C. M. 1927. The fishes of the Rio Chucunaque Drainage, Eastern Panama. *Amer. Mus. Nat. Hist.* 57(3): 91-176.

Breder, C. M. & D. E. Rosen, 1966. *Modes of reproduction in fishes*. Amer. Mus. Nat. Hist., 941pp.

Brichard, P. 1978. *Fishes of Lake Tanganyika*. T. F. H. Publ., Inc., Neptune, 448pp.

Brichard, P. 1978. Un cas d'isolement de substrats rocheux au milieu de fonds de sable dans le nord du Lac Tanganyka. *Rev. Zool. afr.*, 92(2): 518-524.

Brichard, P. 1978. Notes sur le comportement nocturne de certaines especes de poissons petricoles du Lac Tanganyika. *Rev. Zool. afr.*, 92(1): 187-190.

Britski, H. A. 1981. Sobre um novo genero e especie de Sorubiminae da Amazonia (Pisces, Siluriformes). *Papeis Avulsos de Zool., Sao Paulo*, 34(7): 109-114.

Britski, H. A. & H. Ortega, 1983. *Trichogenes longipinnis*, novo genero e especie de Trichomycterinae do sudeste do Brasil (Pisces, Siluriformes). *Rev. bras. Zool., Sao Paulo*, 1(3): 211-216.

Britski, H. A., Y. Sato, & A. B. S. Rosa, 1984. *Manual de identificacao de peixes da regiao de Tres Marias*. Camara dos Deputados CODEVASF, 143pp.

Britski, H. A. & J. C. Garavello, 1984. Two new southeastern Brazilian genera of Hypoptopomatinae and a redescription of *Pseudotocinclus* Nichols, 1919 (Ostariophysi, Loricariidae). *Papeis Avulsos de Zool., Sao Paulo*, 35(21): 225-241.

Browman, M. W. & D. L. Kramer, 1985. *Pangasius sutchi* (Pangasiidae), an air-breathing catfish that uses the swimbladder as an accessory respiratory organ. *Copeia, 1985, no. 4*, pp. 994-998.

Brown, B. E. & J. S. Dendy, 1961. Observations on the food habits of the flathead and blue catfish in Alabama. *Proc. 15th Annual Conf., Southeastern Assoc. of Game & Fish Commissioners, Oct. 22-25*, pp. 219-222.

Buckup, P. A. 1981. *Microlepidogaster taimensis* sp. n., novo Hypoptopomatinae da Estacao Ecologica do Taim, Rio Grande do Sul, Brasil (Ostariophysi, Loricariidae). *Iheringia, ser. zool., Porto Alegre*, 60: 19-31.

Buckup, P. A. & L. R. Malabarba, 1983. A list of the fishes of the Taim ecological station, Rio Grande do Sul, Brazil. *Iheringia*, 63: 103-113.

Burgess, W. E. 1982. *Corydoras adolfoi*, a new species of catfish (Siluriformes, Callichthyidae) from the Upper Rio Negro, Brazil, near Sao Gabriel da Cachoeira. *Trop. Fish Hobby. Mag.* 30(7):15-16

Burgess, W. E. 1983. *Corydoras robinae*, a new species of callichthyid catfish from Brazil. *Trop. Fish. Hobby. Mag.* 31(9):42-43.

Burkhead, N. M., R. E. Jenkins, & E. G. Maurakis, 1980. New records, distribution and diagnostic characters of Virginia ictalurid catfishes with an adnexed adipose fin. *Brimleyana, no. 4*, pp. 75-93.

Bussing, W. A. 1967. New species and new records of Costa Rican freshwater fishes with a tentative list of species. *Rev. Biol. Trop.* 14(2): 205-249.

Bussing, W. A. 1970. Two new species of catfishes of the genera *Nannorhamdia* and *Imparales* (family Pimelodidae) from Central America. *Contrib. Sci., Los Angeles County Mus. #196.*

Bussing, W. A. 1985. Patterns of distribution of the Central American ichthyofauna. Chapt. 17 of *The Great American Biotic Interchange, F. G. Stehli & S. D. Webb (eds.)*, pp. 453-473.

Carr, A. F. Jr. & L. Giovannoli. 1950. The fishes of the Choluteca drainage of southern Honduras. *Occas. Pap. Mus. Zool., U. Mich., #523*, 38pp.

Carr, M. G. & J. E. Carr, 1985. Individual recognition in the juvenile brown bullhead (*Ictalurus nebulosus*). *Copeia, 1985, no. 4*, pp. 1060-1062.

Carr, M. G. & J. E. Carr, 1986. Characterization of an aggression suppressing pheromone in the juvenile brown bullhead (*Ictalurus nebulosus*). *Copeia, 1986, no. 2*, pp. 540-544.

Castelnau, F. L. 1878. Essays on the ichthyology of Port Jackson. *Proc. Linn. Soc. N. S. W.*, 3: 347-402.

Castro-Aguirre, J. L. 1978. Catologo sistematico de los peces marinos que penetran a las aguas continentales de Mexico con aspectos zoogeograficos y ecologicos. *Dept. de Pesca, Ser. cientifica, no. 19*, 298pp.

Chardon, M. 1968. Anatomie compare de l'appareil de Weber et des structure connexes chez les Siluriformes. *Ann. Mus. Roy. Afr. Centr., ser. 8, Sci. Zool. #169*, 277pp.

Cheetham, J. L., C. T. Garten, Jr., C. L. King, and M. M. Smith. 1976. Temperature tolerance and preference of immature channel catfish (*Ictalurus punctatus*). *Copeia, 1976, no. 3*, pp. 609-612.

Chevey, P. 1932. Poissons des campagnes du "de Lanessan" (1925-1929). *Trav. Inst. Ocean. Indochine, 4th mem.*, pp. 1-155, pls.

Chirichigno F., N. 1963. Estudio de la fauna ictiologica de los esteros y parte baja de los rios del Departamento de Tombes (Peru). *Minist. Agric., ser. de divulgacion cientifica, servicio de Pesqueria Peru, #22*, 87pp.

Chitray, B. B. 1965. Functional anatomy of the digestive organs of a freshwater fish of Uttar Pradesh: *Bagarius bagarius* (Ham.) (Siluroidea: Sisoridae). Part I. Morphology. *Journ. Zool. Soc. India*, 17(1/2): 18-31.

Clay, D. 1979. Sexual maturity and fecundity of the African catfish (*Clarias gariepinus*) with an observation on the spawning behaviour of the Nile catfish (*Clarias lazera*). *Zool. Journ. Linn. Soc.*, 65: 351-365.

Clay, W. M. 1975. The Fishes of Kentucky. *Kentucky Dept. Fish & Wildlife Resources, Frankfurt, Kent.*, 416pp.

Collette, B. B. 1962. *Astroblepus pholeter*, a new species of cave-dwelling catfish from Eastern Ecuador. *Proc. Biol. Soc. Wash.*, 75: 311-314.

Cope, E. D. 1894. On the fishes obtained by the Naturalist Expedition in Rio Grande do Sul. *Proc. Amer. Phil. Soc.*, 33: 84-108, pls.

Costa, W. J. E. M. 1987. Feeding habits of a fish community in a tropical coastal stream, Rio Mato Grosso, Brazil. *Studies Neotrop. Fauna & Environ.*, 22(3): 145-153.

Crass, R. S. 1960. Notes on the freshwater fishes of Natal with descriptions of four new species. *Ann. Natal Mus.*, 14(3): 405-458.

Cuvier, G. & A. Valenciennes, 1839. *Histoire Naturelle des Poissons. Vol. XIV.* Paris, 464pp, pls.

Cuvier, G. & A. Valenciennes, 1840. *Histoire Naturelle des Poissons. Vol. XV.* Paris, 540pp., pls.

Daget, J. 1954. Les poissons du Niger Superieur. *Mem. I. F. A. N. no. 36*, 391pp.

Daget, J. 1978. Description de *Platyglanis depierrei* n. gen., n. sp. (Pisces, Bagridae) du

Sanaga (Sud Cameroun). *Bull. Mus. natn. Hist. nat., Paris, 4 ser., 1, sect. A, no. 3*, pp. 821-825.

Daget, J., J.-P. Gosse, & D. F. E. Thys van den Audenaerde, 1986. Check-list of the freshwater fishes of Africa. CLOFFA 2. *ISBN, Bruxelles; MRAC, Tervuren; ORSTOM, Paris*, 520pp.

David, A. 1961. Notes on the embryonic and larval development of the "Goonch" — *Bagarius bagarius* (Hamilton). *Journ. Zool. Soc. India*, 13(2): 194-205.

David, L. & M. Poll, 1937. Contribution a la faune ichthyologique du Congo Belge collections du Dr. H. Schouteden (1924-1926) et d'autres recolteurs. *Ann. Mus. Congo Belge*, 3(ser. 1): 189-294.

Day, F. 1876. On some fishes of the Deccan.

Day, F. 1877. On amphibius and migratory fishes of Asia.

Day, F. 1878. *The Fishes of India being a natural history of the fishes known to inhabit the seas and fresh waters of India, Burma, and Ceylon*. Reprinted by William Dawson & Sons, Ltd., London (1958). 778pp.

Day, F. 1889. *The Fauna of India including Ceylon and Burma. Fishes (vol. 1)*. Taylor & Francis, Calcutta, 548pp.

de Hassan, C. Pignalberi, & E. Cordiviola de Yuan, 1985. Fish populations in the Parana River. I. Temporary water bodies of Santa Fe and Corrientes areas, 1970-1971 (Argentine Rep.). *Stud. Neotrop. Fauna & Environ.*, 20(1): 15-26.

de Vos, L. 1981. Description of *Eutropius nyongensis* spec. nov. from the Cameroons. *Rev. Zool. afr.*, 95(4): 968-974.

Douglas, N. H. 1972. *Noturus taylori*, a new species of madtom (Pisces, Ictaluridae) from the Caddo River, Southwest Arkansas. *Copeia, 1972, no. 4*, pp. 785-789.

Douglas, N. H. 1974. *Freshwater fishes of Louisiana*. Claitor's Publ. Div., Baton Rouge, 443pp.

Duncker, G. 1904. Die Fische der malayischen Halbinsel. *Mitt. Naturh. Mus. Hamburg*, 21:135-207, pls.

Eaton, T. H. 1935. The teeth of *Plecostomus*, an armored catfish. *Copeia, 1935, no. 4*, pp. 161-162.

Eigenmann, C. H. 1905. The mailed catfishes of South America. *Science, N. S.*, 21(#542): 792-795.

Eigenmann, C. H. 1909. 1. Reports on the expedition to British Guiana of the Indiana University and the Carnegie Museum, 1908. Report no. 1. Some new genera and species of fishes from British Guiana. *Ann. Carnegie Mus.*, 4: 1-54.

Eigenmann, C. H. 1911. X. Description of a new species of *Pygidium*. *Ann. Carnegie Mus.*, 7(2): 1p, 1pl.

Eigenmann, C. H. 1912. The Freshwater Fishes of British Guiana, including a study of the ecological grouping of species and the relation of the fauna of the plateau to that of the lowlands. *Mem. Carnegie Mus.*, 5: 1-578, pls.

Eigenmann, C. H. 1913. XVI. On two new species of fishes collected by Miss Lola Vance in Peru. *Ann. Carnegie Mus.*, 8(16): 421-422.

Eigenmann, C. H. 1913. 18. Some results from an ichthyological reconnaissance of Colombia, South America, Part II. *Indiana Univ. Studies, no. 131*, 32pp.

Eigenmann, 1916. VI. New and rare fishes from South American rivers. *Ann. Carnegie Mus.*, 10(6): 77-86.

Eigenmann, C. H. 1917. *Pimelodella* and *Typhlobagrus*. *Mem. Carnegie Mus.*, 7(4): 229-258.

Eigenmann, C. H. New and rare species of South American Siluridae in the Carnegie Museum. *Ann. Carnegie Mus.*, 11(3/4): 398-404.

Eigenmann, C. H. 1918. The Pygidiidae, a family of South American catfishes. *Mem. Carnegie Mus.*, 7(5): 259-373.

Eigenmann, C. H. 1918. The Pygidiidae. *Proc. Indiana Acad. Sci. 1917*, pp. 59-66.

Eigenmann, C. H. 1920. The fishes of Lake Valencia, Caracas, and of the Rio Tuy at El Concejo, Venezuela. *Indiana Univ. Studies, no. 44*, 7: 1-16.

Eigenmann, C. H. 1921. The nature and origin of the fishes of the Pacific slope of Ecuador, Peru and Chili. *Proc. Amer. Phil. Soc.*, 60:503-523.

Eigenmann, C. H. 1922. The Fishes of Western South America, Part I. The fresh-water fishes of northwestern South America, including Colombia, Panama, and the Pacific slopes of Ecuador and Peru, together with an appendix upon the fishes of the Rio Meta in Colombia. *Mem Carnegie Mus.*, 9(1): 1-346, pls.

Eigenmann, C. H. 1924. The fresh-water fishes of Chile. *Mem. Natl. Acad. Sci.*, 22: 1-80.

Eigenmann, C. H. 1925. A review of the Doradidae, a family of South American Nematognathi, or catfishes. *Trans. Amer. Phil. Soc., N. S.*, 22: 280-365.

Eigenmann, C. H. & R. S. Eigenmann, 1890. A revision of the South American Nematognathi or cat-fishes. *Occas. Pap. Calif. Acad. Sci.*, 508pp.

Eigenmann, C. H. & R. S. Eigenmann, 1891. A catalogue of the fresh-water fishes of South America. *Proc. U. S. N. M. (1891)*, 14(#842): 1-81.

Eigenmann, C. H. & B. A. Bean, 1907. An account of Amazon River fishes collected by J. B. Steere; with a note on *Pimelodus clarias*. *Proc. U. S. N. M.*, 31(#1503): 659-668.

Eigenmann, C. H., W. L. McAtee, & D. P. Ward, 1907. On further collections of fishes from Paraguay. *Ann. Carnegie Mus.*, 4: 110-157.

Eigenmann, C. H., A. Henn, & C. Wilson, 1914. 19. New fishes from western Colombia, Ecuador, and Peru. *Indiana Univ. Studies, no. 133*, 15pp.

Eigenmann, C. H. & L. Vance, 1917. Some species of *Farlowella*. *Ann. Carnegie Mus.*, 11(1/2): 297-303.

Eigenmann, C. H. & H. G. Fisher, 1917. On some species of *Rhamdia*, a genus of South American Siluridae, in the Carnegie Museum. *Ann. Carnegie Mus.*, 11(3/4): 394-397.

Eigenmann, C. H. & W. R. Allen, 1942. *Fishes of Western South America. I. The Intercordilleran and Amazonian lowlands of Peru. II. The high pampas of Peru, and northern Chile*. Univ. Kentucky, Lexington, 429pp., pls.

Ellis, M. D. 1913. The plated Nematognaths. *Ann. Carnegie Mus.*, 8(3/4): 384-413.

Evermann, B. W. & E. L. Goldsborough, 1902. A report on fishes collected in Mexico and Central America with notes and descriptions of five new species. *Bull. U. S. Fish. Comm. For 1901*, pp.137-159.

Evermann, B. W. & W. C. Kendall, 1905. An interesting species of fish from the high Andes of Central Ecuador. *Proc. Biol. Soc. Wash.*, 18: 91-106.

Evermann, B. W. & W. C. Kendall, 1906. Notes on a collection of fishes from Argentina, South America, with descriptions of three new species. *Proc. U. S. N. M.*, 32 (#1482): 67-108.

Evermann, B. W. & L. Radcliffe, 1917. Fishes of the west coast of Peru and the Titicaca basin. *U. S. N. M., Bull. #95*, 157pp, pls.

Evermann, B, W, & T.-H. Shaw, 1927. IV. Fishes of eastern China, with descriptions of new species. *Proc. Calif. Acad. Sci.*, 16(4): 97-122.

Fernandez-Yepez, A. 1949. La Doncella (*Sorubimichthys planiceps*). *Evincias, no. 8*, 2pp.

Fernandez-Yepez, A. 1951. Algunas notas sobre peces de la familia "Doradidae". *Mem. Soc. Ciencias Nat. La Salle*, 11(29): 181-182.

Fernandez-Yepez, A. 1953. Algunas notas sobre los peces Asprediformes con descripcion de *Ernstichthys anduzei*, nuovo e interesante Bunocephalido. *Novidades Cientificas, Contrib. Occas. del Mus. Hist. Nat. La Salle, Zool. #11*, 6pp.

Fernandez-Yepez, A. 1968. Contribucion al conocimiento de la familia Doradidae en Venezuela. *Bol. Inst. Ocean., Univ. Oriente*, 7(1): 7-72.

Fernandez-Yepez, A. 1969. Venezuela y sus peces. Album Ictiologico, Primera entrega. *Rep. de Venezuela, Minist. de Agric. y Cria, Oficina Nac. de Pesca. Bol. Tec. del MAC, no. 1*, 62pp.

Fernandez-Yepez, A. 1971. *Pseudacanthicus histrix* nuevo genero y nueva especie, de pez, para Venezuela. *Evencias, #27*, 6pp.

Fernandez-Yepez, A. & F. Martin Salazar, 1952. Notas sobre la fauna ictiologica de la region Baruta-El, Hatillo. *Mem. Soc. Ciencias Nat., La Salle*, 12(31): 31-35.

Ferraris, C. J. Jr., I. J. H. Isbrücker, & H. Nijssen, 1986. *Neblinichthys pilosus*, a new genus and species of mailed catfish from the Rio Baria system, southern Venezuela (Pisces, Siluriformes, Loricariidae). *Rev. fr. aquar. herp.*, 13(3): 69-72.

Ferraris, C. J. Jr. & J. Fernandez, 1987. *Tra-*

chelyopterichthys anduzei, a new species of auchenipterid catfish from the Upper Rio Orinoco of Venezuela with notes on *T. taeniatus* (Kner). *Proc. Biol. Soc. Wash.*, 100 (2): 257-261.

Fink, W. L. & S. V. Fink, 1979. Central Amazonia and its fishes. *Comp. Biochem. Physiol.*, 62A: 13-29.

Fischer, W. (ed.), 1974. *FAO Species Identification Sheets for Fishery Purposes — Eastern Indian Ocean and Western Central Pacific.* Food & Agric. Org. of the U. N.

Fischer, W. (ed.), 1978. *FAO Species Identification Sheets for Fishery Purposes — Western Central Atlantic.* Food & Agric. Org. of the U. N.

Fischer, W., G. Bianchi, & W. B. Scott (eds.), 1981. *FAO Species Identification Sheets for Fishery Purposes — Eastern Central Atlantic.* Food & Agric. Org. of the U. N.

Fischer, W. & G. Bianchi (eds.), 1984. *FAO Species Identification Sheets for Fishery Purposes — Western Indian Ocean.* Food & Agric. Org. of the U. N.

Fisher, H. G. 1917. A list of the Hypophthalmidae, the Diplomystidae, and of some unrecorded species of Siluridae in the collections of the Carnegie Museum. *Ann. Carnegie Mus.*, 11(3/4): 405-427.

Fontaine, P. A. 1944. Notes on the spawning of the shovelhead catfish, *Pilodictis olivaris* (Rafinesque). *Copeia, 1944, no. 1*, pp. 50-51.

Fowler, H. W. 1904. A collection of fishes from Sumatra. *Journ. Acad. Nat. Sci. Phila.*, 12 (ser. 2, part 4): 495-560.

Fowler, H. W. 1917. Some notes on the breeding habits of local catfishes. *Copeia, 1917, no. 42*, 32-36.

Fowler, H. W. 1924. Some fishes collected by the Third Asiatic Expedition in China. *Bull. Amer. Mus. Nat. Hist.*, 50(7): 373-405.

Fowler, H. W. 1930. The fresh-water fishes obtained by the Gray African Expedition — 1929. With notes on other species in the Academy collection. *Proc. Acad. Nat. Sci. Phila.*, 82: 27-83.

Fowler, H. W. 1934. Zoological results of the Third de Schuaensee Siamese Expedition. Part I. Fishes. *Proc. Acad. Nat. Sci. Phila.*, 86: 67-163.

Fowler, H. W. 1934. Zoological results of the Third de Schuaensee Siamese Expedition, Part V. Additional Fishes. *Proc. Acad. Nat. Sci. Phila.*, 86: 335-352.

Fowler, H. W. 1934. Natal fishes obtained by Mr. H. W. Bell-Marley. *Ann. Natal Mus.*, 7(3): 403-433.

Fowler, H. W. 1938. A list of fishes known from Malaya. *Fish. Bull. #1, Singapore*, 268pp.

Fowler, H. W. 1939. Zoological results of the Third de Schuaensee Siamese Expedition. Part IX. — Additional fishes obtained in 1936. *Proc. Acad. Nat. Sci. Phila.*, 91: 36-76.

Fowler, H. W. 1939. A small collection of fishes from Saigon, French Indo-China. *Not. Nat. #8*, 6pp.

Fowler, H. W. 1940. Fishes obtained in Chile by Mr. D. S. Bullock. *Proc. Acad. Nat. Sci. Phila.*, 92: 171-190.

Fowler, H. w. 1940. A collection of fishes obtained by Mr. William C. Morrow in the Ucalayi River Basin, Peru. *Proc. Acad. Nat. Sci. Phila.*, 91: 219-289.

Fowler, H. W. 1940. Zoological results of the Second Bolivian Expedition for the Academy of Natural Sciences of Philadelphia, 1936-1937. Part. I. The Fishes. *Proc. Acad. Nat. Sci. Phila.*, 92: 43-103.

Fowler, H. W. 1941. Contributions to the Biology of the Philippine Archipelago and Adjacent Regions.: The fishes of the groups Elasmobranchii, Holocephali, Isospondyli, and Ostariophysi obtained by the United States Bureau of Fisheries Steamer "Albatross" in 1907 to 1910, chiefly in the Philippine Islands and adjacent seas. *U. S. N. M. Bull. #100*, 13: 1-879.

Fowler, H. W. 1941. A collection of fresh-water fishes obtained in eastern Brazil by Dr. Rodolpho von Ihering. *Proc. Acad. Nat. Sci. Phila.*, 93: 123-199.

Fowler, H. W. 1945. Los peces del Peru: Catalogo sistematico de los peces que habitan en aquas Peruanas. *Mus. Hist. Nat. "Javier Prado", Univ. Nac. de San Marcos, Lima*, 298pp.

Fowler, H. W. 1949. Results of the two Carpenter African Expeditions, 1946-1948. Part II.— The Fishes. *Proc. Acad. Nat. Sci.*

Phila., 101: 233-275.
Fowler, H. W. 1951. Os Peixes de Agua Doce do Brasil. *Arquivos de Zool. do Estado de Sao Paulo*, 6: 405-628.
Fowler, H. W. 1954. Os Peixes de Agua Doce do Brasil. *Arquivos de Zool. do Estado de Sao Paulo*, 9: 1-390.
Fowler, H. W. & B. A. Bean, 1920. The fishes of the U. S. Eclipse Expedition to West Africa. *Proc. U. S. N. M.*, 56: 195-292.
Freihofer, W. C. & E. H. Neil, 1967. Commensalism between midge larvae (Diptera: Chironomidae) and catfishes of the families Astroblepidae and Loricariidae. *Copeia, 1967, no. 1*, pp. 39-45.
Fryer, G. 1959. The trophic interrelationships and ecology of some littoral communities of Lake Nyasa with special reference to the fishes, and a discussion of the evolution of a group of rock-frequenting Cichlidae. *Proc. Zool. Soc. London*, 132(2): 153-281.
Ganguly, D. N., N. C. Datta, & S. Sen, 1972. Two new catfishes of the genus *Glyptothorax* Blyth (Family: Sisoridae) from Subarnarekha River, Bihar, India. *Copeia, 1972, no. 2*, pp. 340-344.
Garavello, J. C. 1977. Systematics and geographical distribution of the genus *Parotocinclus* Eigenmann & Eigenmann, 1889 (Ostariophysi, Loricariidae). *Arquivos de Zool.*, 28(4): 1-37.
Gauba, R. K. 1966. Studies on the osteology of Indian sisorid catfishes. II. The skull of *Glyptothorax cavia*. *Copeia, 1966, no. 4*, pp. 802-810.
Geisler, R. 1969. *Corydoras baderi*, ein neuer Panzerwels, und sein Lebensraum im Grenzgebeit Brasilien-Surinam (Pisces, Teleostei, Callichthyidae). *Senck. biol.*, 50(5/6): 353-357.
Ghiot, F. & N. Bouchez, 1980. The central rod of the barbels of a South American catfish, *Pimelodus clarias*. *Copeia, 1980, no. 4*, pp. 908-909.
Gilbert, C. H. & E. C. Starks, 1904. The fishes of Panama Bay. Contrib. Biol., Hopkins Seaside Lab.; *Mem. Calif. Acad. Sci.*, 4: 1-304, pls.
Gilbert, C. R. (ed.), 1978. Fishes. Vol. 4 of *Rare and Endangered Biota of Florida*, Univ. Presses of Florida.
Gill, T. 1858. Synopsis of the fresh water fishes of the western portion of the island of Trinidad, W. I. *Ann. Lyceum Nat. Hist., N. Y.*, 6:1-70.
Gill, T. 1870. On some new species of fishes obtained by Prof. Orton from the Maranon, or upper Amazon, and Napo Rivers. *Proc. Acad. Nat. Sci. Phila. for 1870*, pp. 92-96.
Gill, T. 1890. Note on the genus *Felichthys* of Swainson. *Proc. U. S. N. M.*, 13(#832): 353-354.
Gill, T. 1891. Note on the Aspredinidae. *Proc. U. S. N. M*, 13(#831): 347-352.
Gill, T. 1903. The use of the name *Torpedo* for the electric catfish. *Proc. U. S. N. M.*, 26(#1329): 697-698.
Gill, T. 1905. Parental care among the freshwater fishes. *Smithsonian Inst. Rept.*, (#1688): 403-581.
Glodek, G. S. 1976. *Rhynchodoras woodsi*, a new catfish from eastern Ecuador (Siluriformes: Doradidae) with a redefinition of *Rhynchodoras*. *Copeia, 1976, no. 1*, pp. 43-46.
Glodek, G. S. 1978. The importance of catfish burrows in maintaining fish populations of tropical freshwater streams in Western Ecuador. *Fieldiana, Zool.*, 73(1): 1-8.
Glodek, G. S. & H. J. Carter, 1978. A new helogeneid catfish from eastern Ecuador (Pisces, Siluriformes, Helogeneidae). *Fieldiana, Zool.*, 72(6): 75-82.
Godinho, H. M. & H. A. Britski, 1965. Peixes de agua doce. *Hist. Nat. Organismos Aquaticos do Brasil*: 317-342.
Goel, H. C. 1966. Sound production in *Clarias batrachus* (Linn.). *Copeia, 1966, no. 3*, pp. 622-624.
Gomon, J. R. & W. R. Taylor, 1982. *Plotosus nkunga*, a new species of catfish from South Africa, with a redescription of *Plotosus limbatus* Valenciennes and key to the species of *Plotosus* (Siluriformes: Plotosidae). *J. L. B. Smith Inst. Ichthy. Spec. Publ. #22*, 16pp.
Gosline, W. A. 1940. Rediscovery and redescription of *Pariolius armillatus*, a genus and species of pimelodid catfishes described by E. D. Cope from the Peruvian Amazon in 1872. *Copeia, 1940, no. 2*, pp. 78-80.
Gosline, W. A. 1940. A revision of the Neo-

tropical catfishes of the family Callichthyidae. *Stan. Ichthy. Bull.*, 2(1): 1-29.

Gosline, W. A. 1941. Synopsis of the genera of pimelodid catfishes without a free orbital rim. *Stan. Ichthy. Bull.*, 2(3): 83-88.

Gosline, W. A. 1942. Studies on South American catfishes (Nematognathi). *Diss. Absts. Stan. Univ.*, 17(49): 10-11.

Gosline, W. A. 1942. Notes on South American catfishes (Nematognathi). *Copeia, 1942, no. 1*, pp. 39-41.

Gosline, W. A. 1944. The problem of the derivation of the South American and African fresh-water fish faunas. *Anales Acad. Brasil Cienc.*, 16(3): 211-223.

Gosline, W. A. 1945. Catalogo dos Nematognatos de agua-doce da America do Sul e Central. *Bol. Mus. Nac. Zool. Ser. (Rio de Janeiro)*, 33: 1-138.

Gosline, W. A. 1947. Contributions to the classification of the loricariid catfishes. *Arquivos do Mus. Nac.*, 41: 79-134.

Gosline, W. A. 1975. The palatine-maxillary mechanism in catfishes with comments on the evolution and zoogeography of modern siluroids. *Occas. Pap. Calif. Acad. Sci. #120*, 31pp.

Gosse, J.-P. 1963. Le milieu aquatique et l'ecologie des poissons dans la region de Yangambi. *Ann. Mus.-Roy. l'Afr. Centr. —ser. IN-8 — Sci. Zool. #116*, pp. 113-270, pls.

Gosse, J.-P. 1966. Poissons d'eau douce du versant Pacifique du Costa Rica et de Panama recoltes par sa Majeste le Roi Leopold de Belgique. *Bull. Inst. roy. Sci. nat. Belg.*, 42(28): 1-24.

Gosse, J.-P. 1968. Les poissons du bassin de l'Ubangi. *Mus. Roy. l'Afr. Centr., Doc. Zool. #13*, 56pp.

Goulding, M. 1981. Man and Fisheries on an Amazon Frontier. *Dev. in Hydrobiol. 4*. Dr. W. Junk Publ., The Hague, 137pp.

Grant, E. M. 1978. *Guide to Fishes*. Dept. Harbours & Marine, Brisbane, 768pp, 440 col. pls., 256 b & w pls.

Greenfield, D. W. & G. S. Glodek, 1977. *Trachelyichthys exilis*, a new species of catfish (Pisces: Auchenipteridae) from Peru. *Fieldiana, Zool.*, 73(3): 47-58.

Greenfield, D. W., T. A. Greenfield, & R. L. Woods, 1982. A new subspecies of cave-dwelling pimelodid catfish, *Rhamdia laticauda typhla* from Belize, Central America. *Brenesia*, 19/20: 563-576.

Greenwood, P. H., D. E. Rosen, S. H. Weitzman, & G. S. Myers, 1966. Phyletic studies of Teleostean fishes, with a provisional classification of living forms. *Bull. Amer. Mus. Nat. Hist.*, 131(4): 339-456.

Gregory, W. K. 1959. *Fish Skulls*. Eric Lundberg, Laurel, Fla., 481pp.

Gudger, E. W. 1916. The gaff-topsail *Felichthys felis*, a sea catfish that carries its eggs in its mouth. *Zoologica*, 2(5): 123-158.

Gudger, E. W. 1918. Oral gestation in the gaff-topsail catfish, *Felichthys felis*. *Pap. Dept. Mar. Biol. Carnegie Inst. Wash.*, 12: 25-52.

Gudger, E. W. 1930. On the alleged penetration of the human urethra by an Amazonian catfish called Candiru, with a review of the allied habits of other members of the family, Pygidiidae. *Amer. Journ. Surg., n. s.*, 8: 171-188, 443-457.

Gunter, G. 1947. Observations on breeding of the marine catfish, *Galeichthys felis* (Linnaeus). *Copeia, 1947, no. 4*, pp. 217-223.

Günther, A. 1864. *Catalogue of the fishes of the British Museum*, vol. 5, British Museum (Natural History), 455pp.

Haig, J. 1950. Studies on the classification of the catfishes of the Oriental and Palearctic family Siluridae. *Rec. Indian Mus.* 48: 59-116.

Halstead, B. W. 1970. *Poisonous and venomous marine animals of the world*. vol. 3. 1006pp. U. S. Gov't Printing Office.

Halstead, B. W. & R. L. Smith, 1954. Presence of an axillary venom gland in the Oriental catfish *Plotosus lineatus*. *Copeia, 1954, no. 2*, pp. 153-154.

Hamilton-Buchanan, F. 1822. *An account of the fishes found in The River Ganges and its Branches*. Archibald Constable & Co., Edinburgh, 405pp., pls.

Harry, R. R. 1953. A contribution to the classification of the African catfishes of the family Amphiliidae, with descriptions of collections from Cameroon. *Rev. Zool. Bot. Afr.*, 47(3/4): 177-232.

Haseman, J. D. 1911. Descriptions of some new species of fishes and miscellaneous notes on others obtained on the expedition to central South America. *Ann. Carnegie*

Mus., 7: 315-328, pls.

Haseman, J. D. 1911. XIX. Some new species of fishes from the Rio Iguassu. *Ann. Carnegie Mus.*, 7: 374-387.

Hassur, R. L. 1970. Rediscovery of the loricariid catfish, *Acestridium discus* Haseman, near Manaus, Brazil. *Proc. Calif. Acad. Sci., 4th ser.*, 38(9): 157-161.

Henn, A. W. 1928. IV. List of types of recent fishes, in the collection of the Carnegie Museum on September 1, 1928. *Ann. Carnegie Mus.*, 19: 51(41)-99(89).

Herre, A. W. C. T. 1924. Distribution of true fresh-water fishes in the Philippines. II. The Philippine Labyrinthici, Clariidae, and Siluridae. *Phil. Journ. Sci.*, 24(6): 683-709.

Herre, A. W. C. T. 1926. A summary of the Philippine catfishes, order Nematognathi. *Phil. Journ. Sci.*, 31(3): 385-413.

Herre, A. W. C. T. 1940. New species of fishes from the Malay Peninsula and Borneo. *Bull. Raffles Mus., Singapore, no. 16*, 26pp.

Herre, A. W. C. T. 1942. *Glyptothorax housei*, a new sisorid catfish from South India. *Stan. Ichthy. Bull.* 2(4): 117-119.

Herre, A. W. C. T. 1949. A case of poisoning by a stinging catfish in the Philippines. *Copeia, 1949, no. 3*, p.222.

Hildebrand, S. F. 1925. Fishes of the Republic of El Salvador, Central America. *Bull Bur. Fish.*, 41(Doc. 985): 237-287.

Hildebrand, S. F. 1930. Notes on a collection of fishes from Costa Rica. *Copeia, 1930, no. 1*, pp. 1-9.

Hildebrand, S. F. 1938. A new catalogue of the fresh-water fishes of Panama. *Field Mus. Nat. Hist., Zool. ser., Publ. #425*, 22(4): 219-359.

Hildebrand, S. F. 1946. A descriptive catalog of the shore fishes of Peru. *U. S. N. M. Bull. 189*, 530pp.

Hoedeman, J. J. 1952. Notes on the ichthyology of Surinam (Dutch Guiana). The catfish genera *Hoplosternum* and *Callichthys*, with a key to the genera and groups of the family Callichthyidae. *Beaufortia, no. 12*, 12pp.

Hoedeman, J. J. 1957. Notes on the ichthyology of Surinam (Dutch Guiana). 4. Additional records of Siluriform fishes (1). *Beaufortia no. 71*, 6: 147-160.

Hoedeman, J. J. 1960. Studies on callichthyid fishes. 3. Notes on the development of *Callichthys* (1) (Pisces, Siluriformes). *Bull. Aquatic Biol.*, 1(9): 53-72.

Hoedeman, J. J. 1960. Studies on callichthyid fishes. 4. Development of the skull of *Callichthys* and *Hoplosternum* (1) (Pisces, Siluriformes). *Bull. Aquatic. Biol.*, 1(10): 73-84.

Hoedeman, J. J. 1960. Studies on callichthyid fishes. 5. Development of the skull of *Callichthys* and *Hoplosternum* (2) (Pisces, Siluriformes). *Bull. Aquatic. Biol.*, 2(13): 21-36.

Hoedeman, J. J. 1960. Studies on callichthyid fishes. 6. The axial skeleton of *Callichthys* and *Hoplosternum*. *Bull. Aquatic. Biol.*, 2(14): 37-44.

Hoedeman, J. J. 1961. Notes on the ichthyology of Surinam and other Guianas. 8. Additional records of siluriform fishes (2). *Bull. Aquatic. Biol.*, 2(23): 129-139.

Hoedeman, J. J. 1974. *Naturalist's Guide to Fresh-water Aquarium Fish.* Sterling Publishing Co., 1152pp.

Hoese, H. D. 1966. Ectoparasitism by juvenile sea catfish, *Galeichthys felis*. *Copeia, 1966, no. 4*, pp. 880-881.

Hogue, J. J. Jr., R. Wallus, & L. K. Kay, 1976. A preliminary guide to the identification of larval fishes in the Tennessee River. *Tenn. Valley Authority, Div. of Forestry, Fisheries, and Wildlife Dev.: Tech. Note B19*, 66pp.

Hora, S. L. 1936. Siluroid fishes of India, Burma, and Ceylon. II. Fishes of the genus *Akysis* Bleeker. *Rec. Indian Mus.*, 38: 199-209.

Hora, S. L. 1936. Siluroid fishes of India, Burma, and Ceylon. VI. Fishes of the genus *Clarias* Gronovius. *Rec. Indian Mus.*, 38: 347-361.

Hora, S. L. & J. C. Gupta, 1941. Notes on Malayan fishes in the collection of the Raffles Museum, Singapore. *Bull. Raffles Mus.*, 17: 12-43.

Hora, S. L. & N. C. Law, 1941. Siluroid fishes of India, Burma, and Ceylon. IX. Fishes of the genera *Gagata* Bleeker and *Nangra* Day. *Rec. Indian Mus.*, 43(1): 9-27.

Hora, S. L. & N. C. Law, 1941. Siluroid fishes of India, Burma, and Ceylon. X. Fishes of the genus *Batasio* Blyth. *Rec. Indian Mus.*, 43(1): 28-42.

Hora, S. L. & E. G. Silas, 1951. XLVII. Revision of the glyptosternoid fishes of the family Sisoridae, with descriptions of new genera and species. *Rec. Indian Mus.*, 49: 5-29.

Hora, S. L. & E. G. Silas, 1952. Evolution and distribution of glyptosternoid fishes of the family Sisoridae (Order: Siluroidea). *Proc. nat. Inst. Sci. India*, 18(4): 309-322.

Howes, G. J. 1980. A new catfish from Sierra Leone. *Bull. Br. Mus. (Nat. Hist.), zool.*, 38(3): 165-170.

Howes, G. J. 1983. Problems in catfish anatomy and phylogeny exemplified by the Neotropical Hypophthalmidae (Teleostei: Siluridei). *Bull. Br. Mus. (Nat. Hist.), zool. ser.*, 45(1): 1-39.

Howes, G. J. 1983. The cranial muscles of loricarioid catfishes, their homologies and value as taxonomic characters (Teleostei: Siluroidei). *Bull. Br. Mus. (Nat. Hist.), zool. ser.*, 45(6): 309-345.

Hubbs, C. L. Fresh-water fishes collected in British Honduras and Guatemala. *Misc. Publ., Univ. Mich. Mus. Zool., #28*, 22pp.

Hubbs, C. L. 1936. XVII. Fishes of the Yucatan Peninsula. *Publ. Carnegie Inst., Wash., no. 457*, 17: 157-287.

Hubbs, C. L. 1938. XXI. Fishes from the caves of Yucatan. *Publ. Carnegie Inst. Wash., no. 491*, 21: 261-295.

Hubbs, C. L. 1953. Geographic and systematic status of the fishes described by Kner and Steindachner in 1863 and 1865 from fresh waters in Panama and Ecuador. *Copeia, 1953, no. 3*, pp. 141-148.

Hubbs, C. L. & E. C. Raney, 1944. Systematic notes on North American silurid fishes of the genus *Schilbeodes*. Occas Pap. Mus. Zool., Univ. Mich., no. 487, 36pp.

Hubbs, C. L. & K. F. Lagler, 1947. Fishes of the Great Lakes region. *Cranbrook Inst. Sci., Bull. #26*, 186pp.

Hubbs, C. L. & R. M. Bailey, 1947. Blind catfishes from Artesian waters of Texas. *Occas. Pap. Mus. Zool., Univ. Mich., #499*, 15pp.

Hubbs, C. L. & R. R. Miller, 1960. *Potamarius*, a new genus of ariid catfishes from the fresh waters of Middle America. *Copeia, 1960, no. 2*, 101-112.

Hutchins, B. & M. Thompson, 1983. *The marine and estuarine fishes of southwestern Australia: A field guide for anglers and divers.* Western Aust. Mus., 103pp.

Ihering, R. von, 1937. Oviducal fertilization in the South American catfish, *Trachycorystes*. *Copeia, 1937, no. 4*, pp. 201-205.

Inger, R. F. 1955. Ecological notes on the fish fauna of a coastal drainage of North Borneo. *Fieldiana: zool.*, 37: 47-90.

Inger, R. F. 1956. Notes on a collection of fishes from southeastern Venezuela. *Fieldiana: zool.*, 34(37): 425-440.

Inger, R. F. & C. P. Kong, 1959. New species of fresh-water catfishes from North Borneo. *Fieldiana: zool.*, 39(27): 279-296.

Inger, R. F. & C. P. Kong, 1962. The freshwater fishes of North Borneo. *Fieldiana: zool.*, 45: 1-268.

Isbrücker, I. J. H. (1970)1971. *Pseudohemiodon (Planiloricaria) cryptodon* a new species and subgenus from Peru (Pisces, Siluriformes, Loricariidae). *Bonn. zool. Beitr.*, 21: 274-283.

Isbrücker, I. J. H. 1971. A redescription of the South American catfish *Loricariichthys maculatus* (Bloch, 1794), with designation of the lectotype and restriction of its type locality (Pisces, Siluriformes, Loricariidae. *Bijdr. Dierk.*, 41(1): 10-18.

Isbrücker, I. J. H. 1972. The identity of the South American catfish *Loricaria cataphracta* Linnaeus, 1758, with redescriptions of the original type specimens of four other nominal *Loricaria* species (Pisces, Siluriformes, Loricariidae). *Beaufortia #325*, 19: 163-191.

Isbrücker, I. J. H. 1973. Status of the primary homonymous South American catfish *Loricaria cirrhosa* Perugia, 1897, with remarks on some other loricariids (Pisces, Siluriformes, Loricariidae). *Ann. Mus. Civico Storia Nat. Genova*, 79: 172-191.

Isbrücker, I. J. H. 1973. Redescription and figures of the South American mailed catfish *Rineloricaria lanceolata* (Günther, 1868)(Pisces, Siluriformes, Loricariidae). *Beaufortia #278*, 21: 75-89.

Isbrücker, I. J. H. 1973. Zes recent beschreven *Corydoras*-soorten van Brazilie, Peru, Guyana en Venezuela. *Het Aquarium*, 43(8): 183-186.

Isbrücker, I. J. H. 1974. *Metaloricaria pauci-*

dens, a new species and genus of mailed catfish from French Guiana (Pisces, Siluriformes, Loricariidae). *Bull. Inst. roy. Sci. nat. Belg.*, 50(4): 1-9.

Isbrücker, I. J. H. 1975. *Pseudohemiodon thorectes*, a new species of mailed catfish from the Rio Mamore system, Bolivia (Pisces, Siluriformes, Loricariidae). *Beaufortia #300*, 23: 85-92.

Isbrücker, I. J. H. 1978. Descriptions preliminaires de nouveaux taxa de la famille des Loricariidae. *Rev. fr. Aquariol. Herp.*, 5(4): 86-116.

Isbrücker, I. J. H. 1979. Les poissons de la famille des Loricariides ou Poissons-Chats cuirasses. *Rev. fr. Aquariol. Herp.*, 6(4): 109-124.

Isbrücker, I. J. H. 1980. Classification and catalogue of the mailed Loricariidae (Pisces, Siluriformes). *Versl. Techn. Gegevens., no. 22*, 181pp.

Isbrücker, I. J. H. 1981. Revision of *Loricaria* Linnaeus, 1758 (Pisces, Siluriformes, Loricariidae). *Beaufortia*, 31(3): 51-96.

Isbrücker, I. J. H. & H. Nijssen, 1973. Two new species of the callichthyid catfish genus *Corydoras* from Brazil (Pisces, Siluriformes, Callichthyidae). *Beaufortia #272*, 21: 1-7.

Isbrücker, I. J. H. & H. Nijssen, 1974. On *Hemiodontichthys acipenserinus* and *Reganella depressa*, two remarkable mailed catfishes from South America (Pisces, Siluriformes, Loricariidae). *Beaufortia #294*, 22: 193-222.

Isbrücker, I. J. H. & H. Nijssen, 1974. *Rhadinoloricaria* gen. nov. and *Planiloricaria*, two genera of South American mailed catfishes (Pisces, Siluriformes, Loricariidae). *Beaufortia #290*, 22: 67-81.

Isbrücker, I. J. H. & H. Nijssen, 1976. The South American mailed catfishes of the genus *Pseudoloricaria* Bleeker, 1862 (Pisces, Siluriformes, Loricariidae). *Beaufortia #325*, 25: 107-129.

Isbrücker, I. J. H. & H. Nijssen, 1976. *Rineloricaria heteroptera*, a new species of mailed catfish from Rio Amazonas near Manaus, Brazil (Pisces, Siluriformes, Loricariidae). *Zool. Anz.*, 196(1/2): 109-124.

Isbrücker, I. J. H. & H. Nijssen, 1978. Two species and a new genus of Neotropical mailed catfishes of the subfamily Loricariinae Swainson, 1838 (Pisces, Siluriformes, Loricariidae). *Beaufortia #339*, 27: 177-206.

Isbrücker, I. J. H. & H. Nijssen, 1978. The Neotropical mailed catfishes of the genera *Lamontichthys* P. de Miranda Ribeiro, 1939 and *Pterosturisoma* n. gen., including the description of *Lamontichthys stibaros* n. sp. from Ecuador (Pisces, Siluriformes, Loricariidae). *Bijdr. Dierk.*, 48(1): 57-80.

Isbrücker, I. J. H. & H. Nijssen, 1979. Three new South American mailed catfishes of the genera *Rineloricaria* and *Loricariichthys* (Pisces, Siluriformes, Loricariidae). *Bijdr. Dierk.*, 48(2): 191-211.

Isbrücker, I. J. H. & H. Nijssen, 1982. New data on *Metaloricaria paucidens* from French Guiana and Surinam (Pisces, Siluriformes, Loricariidae). *Bijdr. Dierk.*, 52(2): 155-168.

Isbrücker, I. J. H. & H. Nijssen, 1982. *Aphanotorulus frankei*, une espece et un genre nouveaux de Poissons-chats cuirasses du Bassin du Rio Ucayali au Perou (Pisces, Siluriformes, Loricariidae). *Rev. fr. Aquariol. Herp.*, 9(4): 105-110.

Isbrücker, I. J. H., H. A. Britski, H. Nijssen, & H. Ortega, 1983. *Aposturisoma myriodon*, une espece et un genre nouveaux de Poisson-chat cuirasse, tribu Farlowellini Fowler, 1958 du Bassin du Rio Ucayali, Perou (Pisces, Siluriformes, Loricariidae). *Rev. fr. Aquariol. Herp.*, 10(2): 33-42.

Isbrücker, I. J. H. & H. Nijssen, 1983. *Crossoloricaria rhami* n. sp., un nouveau Poisson-chat cuirasse du Rio Huacamayo, Perou (Pisces, Siluriformes, Loricariidae). *Rev. fr. Aquariol. Herp.*, 10(1): 9-12.

Isbrücker, I. J. H. & H. Nijssen, 1984. *Pyxiloricaria menezesi*, a new genus and species of mailed catfish from Rio Miranda and Rio Cuiaba, Brazil (Pisces, Siluriformes, Loricariidae). *Bijdr. Dierk.*, 54(2): 163-168.

Isbrücker, I. J. H. & H. Nijssen, 1984. *Rineloricaria castroi*, a new species of mailed catfish from Rio Trombetas, Brazil (Pisces, Siluriformes, Loricariidae). *Beaufortia*, 34(3): 93-99.

Isbrücker, I. J. H. & H. Nijssen, 1984. *Hypostomus nematopterus*, a new species of mailed catfish from the Oyapok River system, French Guiana (Pisces, Siluriformes, Loricariidae). *Bull Zool. Mus., Amst.*, 10(2): 9-

14.

Isbrücker, I. J. H. & H. Nijssen, 1985. *Exastilithoxus hoedemani*, a new species of mailed catfish from Rio Marauia, Est. Amazonas, Brazil. *Spixiana*, 8(3): 221-229.

Isbrücker, I. J. H. & H. Nijssen, 1985. *Apistoloricaria condei*, nouveau genre et nouvelle espece de Poisson-chat cuirasse, tribu Loricariini Bonaparte, 1831, du bassin du Rio Napo, haute Amazone, Equateur (Pisces, Siluriformes, Loricariidae). *Rev. fr. Aquariol. Herp.*, 12(4): 103-108.

Isbrücker, I. J. H., H. Nijssen, & P. Cala, 1988. *Lithoxancistrus orinoco*, nouveau genre et espece de Poisson-chat cuirasse de Rio Orinoco en Colombie (Pisces, Siluriformes, Loricariidae). *Rev. fr. Aquariol. Herp.* 15(1): 13-16.

Isbrücker, I. J. H. & H. Nijssen, 1988. *Acanthicus adonis*, ein neuer Harnischwels aus dem Rio Tocantins, Brasilien (Pisces, Siluriformes, Loricariidae). *D. A. T. Z.*, 41(6): 164-167.

Iwai, T. 1963. Taste buds on the gill rakers and gill arches of the sea catfish, *Plotosus anguillaris* (Lacepede). *Copeia, 1963, no. 2*, pp. 271-274.

Jackson, P. B. N. 1959. revision of the clariid catfishes of Nyasaland, with a description of a new genus and seven new species. *Proc. Zool. Soc. London*, 132(2): 109-128.

Jackson, P. B. N. 1975. Common and scientific names of the fishes of southern Africa. Part II. Freshwater fishes. *J. L. B. Smith Instit. of Ichthyol., Spec. Publ. No. 14*, pp. 179-214.

Jayaram, K. C. 1956. Nomenclatural status of the names *Bagre* Cuvier (Oken), *Bagrus* Valenciennes and *Porcus* Geoffroy St. Hilaire. *Copeia, 1956, no. 4*, pp. 248-249.

Jayaram, K. C. 1956. Taxonomic status of the Chinese catfish family Cranoglanididae Myers, 1931. *Proc. nat. Inst. Sci. India*, 21B(6): 256-263.

Jayaram, K. C. 1960. Racial analysis of *Rita chrysea* Day inhabiting the Mahanadi River. *Journ. Zool. Soc. India*, 12(1): 85-103.

Jayaram, K. C. 1960. The proper generic names for some common Indian fishes of commercial importance. *Journ. Zool. Soc. India*, 12(2): 239-242.

Jayaram, K. C. 1962. Systematic status of *Ailichthys punctata* Day and its relationship with *Ailia coila* (Hamilton) (Siluroidea: Schilbeidae). *Journ. Zool. Soc. India*, 14(1/2): 244-248.

Jayaram, K. C. 1963. A new species of sisorid fish from the Kameng Frontier Division, Nefa. *Journ. Zool. Soc. India*, 15(1): 85-87.

Jayaram, K. C. 1966. Contributions to the study of the fishes of the family Bagridae. 2. A systematic account of the African genera with a new classification of the family. *Bull. I. F. A. N.*, 28(ser. a, #3): 1064-1139.

Jayaram, K. C. 1968. Contributions to the study of bagrid fishes (Siluroidea: Bagridae). 3. A systematic account of the Japanese, Chinese, Malayan and Indonesian genera. *Treubia*, 27(2/3): 287-386.

Jayaram, K. C. 1969. Siluroid fishes of India, Burma and Ceylon. 17. Nomenclatural status of *Plotosus anguillaris* Bloch, 1794. *Journ. Zool. Soc. India*, 21(1): 129-131.

Jayaram, K. C. 1970. Contribution to the study of bagrid fishes. 6. The skeleton of *Rita gogra* (Sykes). *Journ. Zool. Soc. India*, 22(2): 117-146.

Jayaram, K. C. 1971. Contributions to the study of bagrid fishes. 7. First record of *Pimelodus chandramara* Hamilton (Siluroidea: Bagridae). *Journ. Zool. Soc. India*, 23(2): 131-133.

Jayaram, K. C. 1971. Contributions to the study of bagrid catfishes. 9. Generic status of *Aorichthys* Wu (Siluroidea: Bagridae). *Proc. Zool. Soc. Calcutta*, 24: 149-156.

Jayaram, K. C. 1971. Siluroid fishes of India, Burma and Ceylon. 18. Resurrection of the genus *Nangra* Day and its systematic position (Sisoridae). *Journ. Zool. Soc. India*, 23(2): 171-174.

Jayaram, K. C. 1978. Contributions to the study of bagrid fishes. 14. The systematic position of the species of *Mystus* Scopoli known from China. *Proc. Indian Acad. Sci.*, B 87(9): 221-228.

Jayaram, K. C. 1981. *The Freshwater Fishes of India ....a handbook*. Zool. Survey of India, Calcutta, 475 pp., pls. I-XIII.

John, M. A. 1951. Pelagic fish eggs and larvae of the Madras coast. *Journ. Zool. Soc. India*, 3(1): 41-69.

Johnsen, P. 1963. Notes on fishes along the

River Kwae Noi in western Thailand. *Nat. Hist. Bull. Siam Soc.*, 20(3): 143-154.

Jones, P. W., F. D. Martin, & J. D. Hardy. 1978. *Development of fishes of the Mid-Atlantic Bight: An atlas of egg, larval and juvenile stages. Vol. I: Acipenseridae through Ictaluridae.* U. S. Fish & Wildlife Serv., FW-S/OBS-78/12, 366pp.

Jordan, D. S. 1885. A list of fishes known from the Pacific coast of Tropical America, from the Tropic of Cancer to Panama. *Proc. U. S. N. M., 1885*, pp. 361-394.

Jordan, D. S. 1895. The fishes of Sinaloa. *Contrib. Biol. from the Hopkins Lab. of Biol. I. Leland Stanford Jr. Univ. Publ.*, pp. 377-514, pls. 27-55.

Jordan, D. S. 7 B. W. Evermann, 1898. The fishes of North and Middle America. *Bull U. S. N. M.*, 47(2): 1241-2183.

Jordan, D. S. & J. O. Snyder, 1900. Notes on a collection of fishes from the rivers of Mexico. *U. S. Fish. Comm. Bull. for 1899*, pp. 115-147.

Jordan, D. S. & H. W. Fowler, 1903. A review of the siluroid fishes or catfishes of Japan. *Proc. U. S. N. M.*, 26(#1338): 897-911.

Jordan, D. S. & W. R. Thompson, 1913. Record of the fishes collected in Japan in 1911. *Mem. Carnegie Mus.*, 6(4): 205-313.

Jordan, D. S. & B. W. Evermann, 1934. *American Food and Game Fishes.* Doubleday, Doran & Co., N. Y., 574 pp. (Reprint of 1907 Ed.)

Jubb, R. A. 1965. A new species of *Clariallabes* (Pisces, Clariidae) from the Upper Zambezi River. *Ann. Mag. Nat. Hist.*, ser. 13, 7: 393-395.

Jubb, R. A. 1967. *Freshwater fishes of Southern Africa.* A. A. Balkema, Cape Town, 248 pp, pls.

Kailola, P. & B. Pierce, 1988. A new freshwater catfish (Pisces: Ariidae) from northern Australia. *Rec. Western Aust. Mus.*

Kanazawa, R. H. 1958. A new species of catfish, family Loricariidae, from Ecuador. *Copeia, 1958, no. 4*, pp. 327-328.

Kapoor, B. G. 1953. The anatomy and histology of the alimentary canal in relation to its feeding habits of a siluroid fish, *Wallago attu. Journ. Zool. Soc. India*, 5(2): 191-210.

Karamchandani, S. J. & M. P. Motwani. 1955. Early life history, bionomics and breeding of *Rita rita. Journ. Zool. Soc. India*, 7(2): 115-126.

Karamchandani, S. J. & M. P. Motwani, 1956. On the larval development of four species of freshwater cat fishes from the River Ganga. *Journ. Zool. Soc. India*, 8(1): 19-34.

Karamchandani, S. J. & V. R. Desai, 1964. On the early larval development of two freshwater catfishes from River Narbada. *Journ. Zool. Soc. India*, 16(1/2): 21-37.

Kelley, W. E. 1964. A pygidiid catfish that can suck blood from goldfish. *Copeia, 1964, no. 4*, pp. 702-704.

Kesteven, H. L. 1925. Contributions to the cranial osteology of the fishes. No. 1. *Tandanus tandanus* Mitchell. *Rec. Aust. Mus.*, 14(4): 271-288.

Khalaf, K. T. 1961. *The marine and fresh water fishes of Iraq.* Univ. of Baghdad, 164 p.

Khanna, S. S. & M. C. Pant, 1967. Seasonal changes in the ovary of a sisorid catfish, *Glyptosternum pectinopterum. Copeia, 1967, no. 1*, pp. 83-88.

Kindle, E. M. 1894. IX. The South American cat-fishes belonging to Cornell University. *Contrib Zool. Lab. Indiana Univ., No. IV*, pp.249-256.

Klausewitz, W. & F. Rössel, 1961. *Rhyncodoras xingui*, ein bemerkenswerter neuer wels aus Brasilien (Pisces, Siluroidea, Doradidae). *Senck. biol.*, 42(1/2): 45-48.

Kner, R. & F. Steindachner, 1864. Neue gattungen und arten von fischen aus Central-Amerika (gesammelt von Prof. Moritz Wagner). *Abhand. k. bayer. Akad. der W. II. CL. X. Bd. I. Abth.*, pp. 1-61, pls.

Kner, R. & F. Steindachner, 1867. Neue Fische aus dem Museum der Herran Joh. C. Godeffroy and Sohn in Hamburg. *Sitzber. Akad. Wiss. Wien*, 54: 356-395, pls.

Knoppel, H.-A., 1970. Food of central Amazonian fishes: Contribution to the nutrient-ecology of Amazonian rain-forest-streams. *Amazoniana*, 2(3): 257-352.

Kong, C. P. 197-. Chapt. 12. *Fresh-water fishes of Kinabalu National Park and its vicinities.*

Kottelat, M. 1982. A small collection of fresh-water fishes from Kalimantan, Borneo, with descriptions of one new genus and three new species of Cyprinidae. *Rev. Suisse Zool.*, 89(2): 419-437.

Kottelat, M. 1983. A new species of *Erethistes* Müller & Troschel from Thailand and Burma (Osteichthys: Siluriformes: Sisoridae). *Hydrobiol.*, 107: 71-74.

Kowarsky, J. 1976. Clarification of the name and distribution of the plotosid catfish *Cnidoglanis macrocephalus*. *Copeia, 1976, no. 3*, pp. 593-594.

Kramer, D. L. & J. B. Graham. 1976. Synchronous air breathing, a social component in respiration in fishes. *Copeia, 1976, no. 4*, pp. 696-697.

Kramer, D. L. & M. McClure, 1980. Aerial respiration in the catfish, *Corydoras aeneus* (Callichthyidae). *Canad. Journ. Zool.*, 58(11): 1984-1991.

Kramer, D. L. & M. McClure. 1981. The transit cost of aerial respiration in the catfish *Corydoras aeneus* (Callichthyidae). *Physiol. Zool.*, 54(2): 189-194.

Lagler, K. F., J. E. Bardach, & R. R. Miller. 1962. *Ichthyology*. John Wiley & Sons, 545 pp.

Lake, J. S. 1978. *Australian freshwater fishes*. Nelson Field Guides, Thomas Nelson Australia Pty., Ltd., 160 pp.

LaMonte, F. R. 1929. Two new fishes from Mt. Duida, Venezuela. *Amer. Mus. Novitates #373*, 4pp.

LaMonte, F. R. 1933. *Pimelodus valenciennis* Kr. the type of a new genus. *Copeia, 1933, no. 4*, p. 226.

LaMonte, F. R. 1933. A new subgenus of *Plecostomus* from Brazil. *Amer. Mus. Novitates #591*, 2pp.

LaMonte, F. R. 1935. Fishes from the Rio Jurua and Rio Purus, Brazilian Amazonas. *Amer. Mus. Novitates #784*, 8pp.

LaMonte, F. R. 1939. *Tridentopsis tocantinsi*, a new pygidiid fish from Brazil. *Amer. Mus. Novitates #1024*, 2pp.

LaMonte, F. R. 1941. 2. A new *Corydoras* from Brazil. *Zoologica, N. Y.*, 26(1): 5-6.

Lee, D. S., C. R. Gilbert, C. H. Hocutt, R. E. Jenkins, D. E. McAllister, & J. R. Stauffer, Jr., 1980. *Atlas of North American freshwater fishes*. North Carolina State Mus. of Nat. Hist., Raleigh, N. C., 854 pp.

Lee, G. 1937. Oral gestation in the marine catfish, *Galeichthys felis*. *Copeia, 1937, no. 1*, pp. 49-56.

LeGrande, W. H. 1981. Chromosomal evolution in North American catfishes (Siluriformes: Ictaluridae) with particular emphasis on the madtoms, *Noturus*. *Copeia, 1981, no. 1*, pp. 33-52.

Lehri, G. K. 1966. The pituitary gland of a catfish, *Clarias batrachus*. *Copeia, 1966, no. 4*, pp. 810-818.

Leveque, C. & P. Herbinet. 1982. Caracteres meristiques et biologie d'*Eutropius mentalis* dans les rivieres de Cote d'Ivoire (Pisces, Schilbeidae). *Rev. Zool. afr.*, 96(2): 366-398.

Loftus, W. F. 1979. Synchronous aerial respiration by the walking catfish in Florida. *Copeia, 1979, no. 1*, pp. 156-158.

Lönnberg, E. & H. Rendahl. 1920. On some freshwater fishes from Lower Congo. *Ann. Mag. nat. Hist.*, (ser. 9), 6: 167-176.

Lopez, H. L., R. C. Menni, & A. M. Miquelarena. 1987. Lista de los peces de agua dulce de la Argentina. *Biol. Acuatica no. 12*, 50 pp.

Lopez, M. I. & W. A. Bussing. 1982. Lista provisional de los peces marinos de la Costa Pacifica de Costa Rica. *Rev. Biol. Trop.*, 30(1): 5-26.

Luengo, J. A. 1963. La fauna ictiologica del lago de Valencia (Venezuela) y algunas consideraciones sobre las demas hoyas del pais y Trinidad. *Acta Biol. Venezuelica*, 3(22): 319-339.

Lundberg, J. G. 1975. Homologies of the upper shoulder girdle and temporal region bones in catfishes (order Siluriformes), with comments on the skull of the Helogeneidae). *Copeia, 1975, no. 1*, pp. 66-74.

Lundberg, J. G. 1982. The comparative anatomy of the toothless blindcat, *Trogloglanis pattersoni* Eigenmann, with a phylogenetic analysis of the ictalurid catfishes. *Misc. Publ. Mus. Zool., U. Mich. no. 163*, 85 pp.

Lundberg, J. G. & J. N. Baskin, 1969. The caudal skeleton of the catfishes, order Siluriformes. *Amer. Mus. Novitates #2398*, 49 pp.

Lundberg, J. G. & L. A. McDade. 1986. On the South American catfish *Brachyrhamdia imitator* Myers (Siluriformes, Pimelodidae), with phylogenetic evidence for a large intrafamilial lineage. *Notulae Naturae #463*,

24pp.

Mago-Leccia, F. 1970. Lista de los peces de Venezuela. *Ministerio de Agricultura y Cria, Caracas*, 283pp.

Mago-Leccia, F. 1978. *Los peces de agua dulce de Venezuela*. Cuadernos Lagoven. 35pp.

Mago-Leccia, F. 1983. *Entomocorus gameroi*, una nueva especie de bagre auquenipterido (Teleostei, Siluriformes) de Venezuela, incluyendo la descripcion de su dimorfismo sexual secundario. *Acta Biol. Venezolana*, 11(4): 215-236.

Mahajan, C. L. —. Fish fauna of Muzaffarnagar District, Uttar Pradesh. *Journ. Bombay Nat. Hist. Soc.*, 62(3): 440-454.

Mahy, G. J. D. 1974. Osteologie descriptive et comparee de la famille des Malapteruridae (Pisces: Ostariophysi). *Ann. Mus. Roy. Afr. Centr. - ser. In-8 Sci. Zool. #209*, 52pp.

Majumdar, N. N. 1951. Notes on Delhi fishes. *Journ. Zool. Soc. India*, 3(2): 243-247.

Marini, T. L., J. T. Nichols, & F. R. LaMonte, 1933. Six new eastern South American fishes examined in the American Museum of Natural History. *Amer. Mus. Novitates, no. 618*, 7pp.

Marshall, T. C. 1965. *Fishes of the Great Barrier Reef and coastal waters of Queensland.* Angus & Robertson, Ltd., 566 pp.

Masuda, H., K. Amaoka, C. Araga, T. Uyeno, & T. Yoshino (eds.), 1984. *The fishes of the Japanese Archipelago*, Tokai Univ. Press, vols I & II, 437 text pages.

Matthes, H. 1962. Poissons nouveaux ou interessants du Lac Tanganika et du Ruanda. *Ann. Mus. Roy. l'Afr. Cent. - ser. In-8 - Sci. Zool. #111*, pp. 27-88, pls.

Matthes, H. 1964. Les poissons du Lac Tumba et de la region d'Ikela: etude systematique et ecologique. *Ann. Mus. Roy. Afr. Cent. - ser. IN-8 - Sci. Zool. #126*, 204 pp., pls.

Matthes, H. 1964. List of the types of African fishes in the Amsterdam Zoological Museum, with notes on their synonymy. *Beaufortia #122*, 10: 177-182.

Matthes, H. 1973. *A bibliography of African freshwater fish.* FAO, 299pp.

McDowall, R. M. (ed.), 1980. *Freshwater fishes of South-eastern Australia (New South Wales, Victoria and Tasmania)*. A. H. & A. W. Reed Pty., Ltd., 208pp.

Meek, S. E. 1904. The fresh-water fishes of Mexico north of the Isthmus of Tehuantepec. *Field Columbian Mus. Publ. #93, Zool. Ser.*, 5:1-252.

Meek, S. E. 1906. Description of three new species of fishes from Middle America. *Field Columbian Mus., Publ. #116 Zool. Ser.*, 7: 93-95.

Meek, S. E. 1907. Synopsis of the fishes of the Great Lakes of Nicaragua. *Field Columbian Mus., Publ. #121, Zool. Ser.*, 7(4): 97-132.

Meek, S. E. 1907. Notes on fresh-water fishes from Mexico and Central America. *Field Columbian Mus., Publ. #124, Zool. Ser.*, 7(5): 133-157.

Meek, S. E. 1908. The zoology of Lakes Amatitlan and Atitlan, Guatemala, with special reference to ichthyology. *Field Columbian Mus., Publ. #127, Zool. Ser.* 7(6): 159-206.

Meek, S. E. 1909. New species of fishes from Tropical America. *Field Columbian Mus., Publ. #132, Zool. Ser.* 7(7): 207-211.

Meek, S. E. 1914. An annotated list of fishes known to occur in the fresh waters of Costa Rica. *Field Mus. Nat. Hist., Publ. #174*, 10(10): 101-134.

Meek, S. E. & S. F. Hildebrand, 1916. The fishes of the fresh waters of Panama. *Field Mus. Nat. Hist., Publ. #191, Zool. Ser.*, 10(15): 217-374.

Mees, G. F. 1974. The Auchenipteridae and Pimelodidae of Suriname (Pisces, Nematognathi). *Zool. Verhand., No. 132*, 256 pp.

Mees, G. F. 1978. On the identity of *Arius oncinus* R. H. Schomburgk (Pisces, Nematognathi, Auchenipteridae). *Zool. Meded.*, 52(23): 267-276.

Mees, G. F. 1978. Two new species of Pimelodidae from Northwestern South America (Pisces, Nematognathi). *Zool. Meded.*, 53(23): 253-261.

Mees, G. F. 1983. Naked catfishes from French Guiana (Pisces, Nematognathi). *Zool. Meded.*, 57(5): 43-58.

Mees, G. F. 1986. Records of Auchenipteridae and Pimelodidae from French Guiana (Pisces, Nematognathi). *Proc. Konink. Nederl. Akad. Wetens., ser. C*, 89(3): 311-325.

Mees, G. F. 1987. The members of the subfamily Aspredininae, family Aspredinidae in Suriname (Pisces, Nematognathi). *Proc. Konink. Nederl. Akad. Wetens., Ser. C*, 90(2): 173-192.

Mees, G. F. 1987. A new species of *Heptapterus* from Venezuela (Pisces, Nematognathi, Pimelodidae). *Proc. Konink. Nederl. Akad. Wetens., Ser. C*, 90(4): 451-456.

Meinken, H. 1957. XXIV. Über zwei der Liebhaberei bislang unbekannte *Corydoras*-Neuheiten (Callichthyidae-Ostariophysi). *D. A. T. Z.*, 10(1): 4-7.

Menon, A. G. K. 1951. On certain features in the anatomy of *Horaglanis* Menon. *Journ. Zool. Soc. India*, 3(2): 249-253.

Menon, A. G. K. 1974. A check-list of fishes of the Himalayan and the Indo-Gangetic Plains. *Spec. Publ. No. 1, Inland Fisheries Soc., India*. 136pp.

Merrick, J. R. & G. E. Schmida, 1984. *Australian freshwater fishes - biology and management*. Griffen Press Ltd., Netley, South Australia, 409pp.

Miles, C. 1942. Rediscovery of the bunocephalid catfish *Xyliphius* in the Rio Magdalena, Colombia. *Stanford Ichthy. Bull.* 2(4): 115-117.

Miles, C. 1947. *Los peces del Rio Magdalena*. Rep. Colombia, Minist. de Econ. Nac. sect. Piscic., pesca y Caza, 214pp.

Miller, R. R. 1966. Geographical distribution of Central American freshwater fishes. *Copeia, 1966, no. 4*, pp. 773-802.

Miller, R. R. 1976. An evaluation of Seth E. Meek's contributions to Mexican ichthyology. *Fieldiana, Zool.* 69(1): 1-31.

Miranda-Ribeiro, A. 1908. On fishes from the Iporanga River, S. Paulo-Brazil. *Arkiv. för Zoologi*, 4(19): 1-3, pl.

Miranda-Ribeiro, A. 1917. Consideracoes sobre os generos *Brachyplatystoma* e *Platystomatichthys* de Bleeker. *Nota lida na Soc. Brasiliera de Sciences*.

Miranda-Ribeiro, A. 1918. Tres generos e dezesete especies novas de peixes brasileiros determinados nas colleccoes do Museu Paulista. *Sao Paulo Typ. do "Diario Official"*.

Miranda-Ribeiro, P. 1943. Dos novos pigidideos Brasilieros (Pisces - Pygidiidae). *Bol. Mus. Nac. (new ser.), Zool. 9*, 3pp.

Miranda-Ribeiro, P. 1944. Uma nova especie para o genero *Bunocephalus* Kner, 1855 (Pisces - Aspredinidae). *Bol. Mus. Nac., Zool. #13*, 3pp.

Miranda-Ribeiro, P. 1944. Um pigidideo do alto Amazonas (Pisces - Pygidiidae). *Bol. do Mus. Nac., Zool. #19*, 3pp.

Miranda-Ribeiro, P. 1944. Nova especie para o genero *Stegophilus* Reinhardt, 1858 (Pisces - Pygidiidae - Stegophilinae). *Bol. do Mus. Nac., Zool. #20*, 3pp.

Miranda-Ribeiro, P. 1946. Notas para o estudo dos Pygidiidae Brasileiros (Pisces - Pygidiidae - Stegophilinae). *Bol. do Mus. Nac., Zool. #58*, 20pp. pl.

Miranda-Ribeiro, P. 1947. Notas para o estudo dos Pygidiidae Brasileiros (Pisces - Pygidiidae - Vandelliinae) -II. *Bol. do Mus. Nac., Zool. #78*, pp. 1-8.

Miranda-Ribeiro, P. 1949. Notas para o estudo dos Pygidiidae Brasileiros (Pisces, Pygidiidae, Pygidiinae) -III. *Bol. do Mus. Nac., Zool. #88*, 3pp.

Miranda-Ribeiro, P. 1954. Cat. dos peixes do Museo Nacional. I. Pygidiidae Eigenmann & Eigenmann, 1888. *Publ. Avulsas do Mus. Nac. #15*, 17pp.

Miranda-Ribeiro, P. 1959. Consideracoes sobre Callichthyidae Gill, 1872 (Nematognathi). *Bol. do Mus. Nac., N. S., Rio de Janeiro, Zool. #206*, 9pp.

Miranda-Ribeiro, P. 1959. Sobre a determinacao de uma peca de ceramica representando um Pygidiidae. *Bol. Mus. Nac., Zool. #211*, 5pp.

Miranda-Ribeiro, P. 1959. Catalogo dos peixes do Museu Nacional. III. Callichthyidae Gill, 1872. *Publ. Avulsas do Museu Nacional*.

Mirza, M. R. 1970. A contribution to the fishes of Lahore including revision of classification and addition of new records. *Biologia*, 16(2): 71-118.

Mirza, M. R. 1972. Freshwater fishes of Baluchistan Province, Pakistan. *Biologia*, 18(2): 153-190.

Mirza, M. R. 1974. Freshwater fishes and ichthyogeography of Baluchistan and adjoining areas of the Indus Plain, Pakistan. *Biologia*, 20(1): 67-82.

Mirza, M. R. 1975. Freshwater fishes and zoogeography of Pakistan. *Bidj. Dierk.*, 45(2): 143-180.

Mirza, M. R. 1976. Fish and fisheries of the northern Montane and Submontane regions of Pakistan. *Biologia*, 22(1): 107-120.

Mirza, M. R. & M. I. Awan, 1973. Two new catfishes (Pisces, Siluriformes) from Pakistan. *Biologia*, 19(1): 145-159.

Mirza, M. R. & K. M. Kashmiri, 1973. Fishes of the River Soan in Rawalpindi District, Pakistan. *Biologia*, 19(1/2): 161-182.

Mirza, M. R. & H. Nijssen, 1978. *Glyptothorax stocki*, a new sisorid catfish from Pakistan and Azad Kashmir (Siluriformes, Sisoridae). *Bull. Zool. Mus., Amst.*, 6(11): 79-82.

Misra, K. S. 1976. *The Fauna of India and the adjacent countries. Pisces. (second ed.). Vol. III. Teleostomi: Cypriniformes; Siluri.* Proc. Zool. Soc. India, 367pp, pls.

Mithel, M. 1964. The cranial nerves of the sisorid catfish *Bagarius bagarius*. *Copeia, 1964, no. 4*, pp. 673-678.

Munro, I. S. R. 1955. *The marine and fresh water fishes of Ceylon.* Dept. Ext. Affairs, Canberra, 351pp., pls.

Munro, I. S. R. 1967. *The fishes of New Guinea.* Gov't Printing Office, Dept. Agric., Stock & Fisheries, Port Moresby, New Guinea, 651pp, pls.

Myers, G. S. 1925. Description of a new catfish from Abyssinia, *Clarias depressus*. *Copeia #139*, pp. 12-13.

Myers, G. S. 1925. *Tridentopsis pearsoni* a new pygidiid catfish from Bolivia. *Copeia #148*, pp. 83-86.

Myers, G. S. 1926. Descriptions of a new characin fish and a new pygidiid catfish from the Amazon basin. *Copeia #156*, pp. 150-152.

Myers, G. S. 1927. Descriptions of new South American fresh-water fishes collected by Dr. Carl Ternetz. *Bull. Mus. Comp. Zool., Harvard*, 68(3): 107-135.

Myers, G. S. 1931. On the fishes described by Koller from Hainan in 1926 and 1927. *Lignan Sci. Journ.*, 10(2/3): 255-262.

Myers, G. S. 1936. Report on the fishes collected by H. C. Raven in Lake Tanganyika in 1920. *Proc. U. S. N. M.*, 84(#2998): 1-15.

Myers, G. S. 1938. Notes on *Ansorgia, Clarisilurus, Wallago*, and *Ceratoglanis*, four genera of African and Indo-Malayan catfishes. *Copeia, 1938, no. 2*, p. 98.

Myers, G. S. 1941. A new name for *Taenionema*, a genus of Amazonian siluroid fishes. *Stan. Ichthy. Bull.*, 2(3): 88.

Myers, G. S. 1942. Studies on South American freshwater fishes I. *Stan. Ichthy. Bull.*, 2(4): 89-114.

Myers, G. S. 1944. Two extraordinary new blind Nematognath fishes from the Rio Negro, representing a new subfamily of Pygidiidae, with a rearrangement of the genera of the family, and illustrations of some previously described genera and species from Venezuela and Brazil. *Proc. Calif. Acad. Sci., 4 ser.* 23(40): 591-602.

Myers, G. S. 1948. Note on two generic names of Indo-Malayan silurid fishes, *Wallago* and *Wallagonia*. *Proc. Calif. Zool. Club*, 1(4): 19-20.

Myers, G. S. 1953. A note on the habits and classification of *Corydoras hastatus*. *Aquar. Journ.*, 24(11): 268-270.

Myers, G. S. 1960. The names of the South American catfish genera *Conorhynchos* and *Diplomystes*. *Stan. Ichthy. Bull.*, 7(4): 246-248.

Myers, G. S. 1960. The genera and ecological geography of the South American banjo catfishes, family Aspredinidae. *Stan. Ichthy. Bull.*, 7(4): 132-139.

Myers, G. S. 1966. Derivation of the freshwater fish fauna of Central America. *Copeia, 1966, no. 4*, pp. 766-773.

Myers, G. S. & S. H. Weitzman, 1954. Another new *Corydoras* from Brazil. *Aquar. Journ.*, 25(4): 93.

Myers, G. S. & S. H. Weitzman, 1956. Two new Brazilian fresh-water fishes. *Stan. Ichthy. Bull.*, 7(1): 1-4.

Myers, G. S. & S. H. Weitzman, 1960. Two new fishes collected by General Thomas D. White in eastern Colombia. *Stan. Ichthy. Bull.*, 7(4): 98-109.

Myers, G. S. & S. H. Weitzman, 1966. Two remarkable new trichomycterid catfishes from the Amazon basin in Brazil and Colombia. *Journ. Zool., London*, 149: 277-287.

Nawar, G. & E. G. Yoakim, 1964. A study on the fecundity of the Nile Schilbeidae, *Schilbe mystus* (Linnaeus 1762). *Ann. Mag. nat. Hist., (ser. 13)*, 7: 1-3.

Nelson, J. S. 1984. *Fishes of the World. Sec-*

ond edition. Wiley Interscience Publ., John Wiley & Sons, New York, 523pp.

Nichols, J. T. 1919. A new genus of loricariid catfishes. *Revista do Museu Paulista* 11: 2-10.

Nichols, J. T. 1925. Some Chinese fresh-water fishes. X. Subgenera of bagrin catfishes. *Amer. Mus. Novitates #185*, 7pp.

Nichols, J. T. 1926. Some Chinese fresh-water fishes. XV. Two apparently undescribed catfishes from Fukien. *Amer. Mus. Novitates #214*,, 7pp.

Nichols, J. T. 1926. Some Chinese fresh-water fishes. XVIII. New species in recent and earlier Fukien collections. *Amer. Mus. Novitates #224*, 7pp.

Nichols, J. T. 1928. Chinese fresh-water fishes in the American Museum of Natural History collections. *Bull. Amer. Mus. Nat. Hist*. 58(1): 1-62.

Nichols, J. T. 1930. Some new Chinese fresh-water fishes. XXVI.-Two new species of *Pseudogobio*. XXVII.-A new catfish from northeastern Kiangsi. *Amer. Mus. Novitates #440*, 5pp.

Nichols, J. T. 1931. Some Chinese fresh-water fishes. XXIX.-A new goby from Hohou, Kiangsi. XXX.-Six type specimens figured. *Amer. Mus. Novitates #499*, 5pp.

Nichols, J. T. 1940. Results of the Archibald Expedition. No. 30. New catfishes from northern New Guinea. *Amer. Mus. Novitates #1093*, 3pp.

Nichols, J. T. 1941. Four new fishes from western China. *Amer. Mus. Novitates #1107*, 3pp.

Nichols, J. T. 1943. *Natural history of Central Asia: vol. 9. The fresh-water fishes of China. Central Asiatic Expeditions*. Amer. Mus. Nat. Hist., New York, 322pp.

Nichols, J. T. 1956. A new pygidiin catfish from Argentina. *Amer. Mus. Novitates #1760*, 2pp.

Nichols, J. T. & L. Griscom, 1917. Fresh-water fishes from the Congo Basin obtained by the American Museum Congo Expedition, 1909-1915. *Bull. Amer. Mus. Nat. Hist.*, 37(25): 653-756.

Nichols, J. T. & C. H. Pope, 1927. The fishes of Hainan. *Bull. Amer. Mus. Nat. Hist.* 54(2): 321-394.

Nichols, J. T. & F. R. LaMonte, 1933. A new catfish, *Amphilius pictus*, and a discussion of a small Liberian collection of fishes. *Amer. Mus. Novitates #626*, 3pp.

Nichols, J. T. & F. R. LaMonte, 1933. New fishes from the Kasai district of the Belgian Congo. *Amer. Mus. Novitates #656*, 6pp.

Nichols, J. T. & F. R. LaMonte, 1934. More new fishes from the Kasai district of the Belgian Congo. *Amer. Mus. Novitates #723*, 6pp.

Nichols, J. T. & F. R. LaMonte, 1953. Two new African catfishes from eastern French Equatorial Africa. *Amer. Mus. Novitates #1648*, 4pp.

Nijssen, H. 1970. Revision of the Surinam catfishes of the genus *Corydoras* Lacepede, 1803 (Pisces, Siluriformes, Callichthyidae). *Beaufortia, no. 230*, 18: 1-75.

Nijssen, H. 1971. Two new species and one new subspecies of the South American catfish genus *Corydoras* (Pisces, Siluriformes, Callichthyidae). *Beaufortia #250*, 19: 89-98.

Nijssen, H. 1972. Records of the catfish genus *Corydoras* from Brazil and French Guiana with descriptions of eight new species (Pisces, Siluriformes, Callichthyidae). *Neth. Journ. Zool.*, 21(4): 412-433.

Nijssen, H. & I. J. H. Isbrücker, 1967. Notes on the Guiana species of *Corydoras* Lacepede, 1803, with descriptions of seven new species and designation of a neotype for *Corydoras punctatus* (Bloch, 1794) - (Pisces, Cypriniformes, Callichthyidae). *Zool. Meded.*, 42(5): 21-50.

Nijssen, H. & I. J. H. Isbrücker, 1970. The South American catfish genus *Brochis* Cope, 1872 (Pisces, Siluriformes, Callichthyidae). *Beaufortia, no. 236*, 18: 151-168.

Nijssen, H. & I. J. H. Isbrücker, 1971. Two new species of the catfish genus *Corydoras* from Brazil and Peru (Pisces, Siluriformes, Callichthyidae). *Beaufortia, no. 239*, 18: 183-189.

Nijssen, H. & I. J. H. Isbrücker, 1975. *Cataphractus punctatus* Bloch, 1794 (Pisces, Siluriformes, Callichthyidae): Request for invalidation of neotype and validation of a rediscovered syntype as lectotype. Z. N. (S.). *Bull. Zool. Nomen.*, 32(1): 63-64.

Nijssen, H. & I. J. H. Isbrücker, 1976. The South American plated catfish genus *Aspidoras* R. von Ihering, 1907, with descriptions of nine new species from Brazil (Pisces, Siluriformes, Callichthyidae). *Bijd. Dierk.*, 46(1): 107-131.

Nijssen, H. & I. J. H. Isbrücker, 1976. *Corydoras ornatus*, a new species of callichthyid catfish from the Rio Tapajos drainage, Brazil (Pisces, Siluriformes, Callichthyidae). *Bull. Zool. Mus. Amst.*, 5(15): 125-129.

Nijssen, H. & I. J. H. Isbrücker, 1979. Chronological enumeration of nominal species and subspecies of *Corydoras* (Pisces, Siluriformes, Callichthyidae). *Bull. Zool. Mus.*, 6(17): 129-135.

Nijssen, H. I. J. H. Isbrücker, 1980. *Aspidoras virgulatus* n. sp., a plated catfish from Espirito Santo, Brazil (Pisces, Siluriformes, Callichthyidae). *Bull. Zool. Mus. Amst.*, 7(13): 133-139.

Nijssen, H. & I. J. H. Isbrücker, 1980. Three new *Corydoras* species from French Guiana and Brazil (Pisces, Siluriformes, Callichthyidae). *Neth. Journ. Zool.*, 30(3): 494-503.

Nijssen, H. & I. J. H. Isbrücker, 1980. A review of the genus *Corydoras* Lacepede, 1803 (Pisces, Siluriformes, Callichthyidae). *Bijd. Dierk.*, 50(1): 190-220.

Nijssen, H. & I. J. H. Isbrücker, 1980. On the identity of *Corydoras nattereri* Steindachner, 1877 with the description of a new species, *Corydoras prionotus* (Pisces, Siluriformes, Callichthyidae). *Beaufortia*, 30(1): 1-9.

Nijssen, H. & I. J. H. Isbrücker, 1982. *Corydoras boehlkei*, a new catfish from the Rio Caura system in Venezuela (Pisces, Siluriformes, Callichthyidae). *Proc. Acad. Nat. Sci. Phila.*, 134: 139-142.

Nijssen, H. & I. J. H. Isbrücker, 1983. *Brochis britskii*, a new species of plated catfish from the upper Rio Paraguai system, Brazil (Pisces, Siluriformes, Callichthyidae). *Bull. Zool. Mus. Amst.*, 9(20): 177-186.

Nijssen, H. & I. J. H. Isbrücker, 1983. Review of the genus *Corydoras* from Colombia, with descriptions of two new species (Pisces, Siluriformes, Callichthyidae). *Beaufortia*, 33(5): 53-71.

Nijssen, H. & I. J. H. Isbrücker, 1983. Sept especes nouvelles de Poissons-Chats cuirasses du genre *Corydoras* Lacepede, 1803, de Guyane francaise, de Bolive, d'Argentine, du Surinam et du Bresil (Pisces, Siluriformes, Callichthyidae). *Rev. fr. Aquariol.*, 10(3): 73-82.

Nijssen, H. & I. J. H. Isbrücker, 1985. *Lasiancistrus scolymus*, a new species of mailed catfish from Rio Aripuana, Est. Mato Grosso do Sul, Brazil (Pisces, Siluriformes, Loricariidae). *Bijd. Dierk.*, 55(2): 242-248.

Nijssen, H. & I. J. H. Isbrücker, 1985. Cinq especes nouvelles de Poissons-Chats cuirasses du genre *Corydoras* Lacepede, 1803, du Perou et de l'Equateur (Pisces, Siluriformes, Callichthyidae). *Rev. fr. Aquariol.*, 12(3): 65-76.

Nijssen, H. & I. J. H. Isbrücker, 1986. Review of the genus *Corydoras* from Peru and Ecuador (Pisces, Siluriformes, Callichthyidae). *Stud. Neotrop. Fauna & Environ.*, 21(1/2): 1-68.

Nijssen, H. & I. J. H. Isbrücker, 1986. *Spectracanthus murinus*, nouveaux genre et espece de Poisson-Chat cuirasse du Rio Tapajos, Est. Para, Bresil, avec des remarques sur d'autres genres de Loricariides (Pisces, Siluriformes, Loricariidae). *Rev. fr. Aquariol.*, 13(4): 93-98.

Novak, J. 1983. On albinotic *Clarias batrachus* (Pisces, Clariidae). *Vest. cs. Spolec. zool.*, 47: 48-50, pls.

Ogilby, J. D. 1899. Contribution to Australian ichthyology. *Proc. Linn. Soc. N. S. W.* 1899, part 1.

Omer, T. & M. R. Mirza, 1975. A checklist of the fishes of Hazara District, Pakistan, with the description of a new subspecies. *Biologia*, 21(2): 199-209.

Ortega, H. & R. P. Vari, 1986. Annotated checklist of the freshwater fishes of Peru. *Smith. Contrib. Zool. #437*, 25pp.

Oshima, M. 1919. Contributions to the study of the fresh water fishes of the island of Formosa. *Ann. Carnegie Mus.*, 12(2-4): 169-328.

Parameswaran, S., C. Selvaraj, & S. Radhakrishnan, 1967. A review of the Indian freshwater fishes of the genus *Ompok* Lacepede. *Journ. Zool. Soc. India*, 19(1/2): 89-98.

Parameswaran, S., C. Selvaraj, & S. Radhakrishnan, 1971. Notes on the life history and biology of the catfish *Ompok pabda* (Hamilton). *Journ. Zool. Soc. India*, 23(2): 137-150.

Parameswaran, S., S. Radhakrishnan, & C. Selvaraj, 1971. Notes on the life-history and biology of the catfish, *Mystus tengara* (Hamilton). *Journ. Zool. Soc. India*, 23(2): 151-162.

Pearson, N. E. 1937. The fishes of the Atlantic and Pacific slopes near Cajamarca, Peru. *Proc. Calif. Acad. Sci., 4 ser.*, 23(7): 87-98.

Pellegrin, J. 1908. Les poissons d'eau douce de Madagascar. *La Rev. Coloniale*, 14pp.

Pellegrin, J. 1910. *Notice sur les titres et travaux scientifiques de M. Jacques Pellegrin.* Paris, Libraires de l'Academie de Medecine, 104pp.

Pellegrin, J. 1911. Poissons de l'equateur recueillis par M. Le Dr. Rivet. *Arc de Meridien Equatorial*, 9(2): 1-15.

Pellegrin, J. 1914. Description d'un siluride nouveau recolte au Congo Belge. *Rev. Zool. Afr.*, 12(4): 487-489.

Pellegrin, J. 1919. Poissons nouveaux du Mozambique. *Bull. Soc. Zool. France*, 44: 397-401.

Pellegrin, J. 1922. Poissons de l'Oubanghi-Chari recueillis par M. Baudon. Description d'un genre, de cinq especes et d'une variete. *Bull. Soc. Zool. France*, 47: 64-76.

Pellegrin, J. 1925. Poissons du nord du Gabon et de la Sangha recueillis par M. Baudon. Description de deux especes et d'un variete nouvelles. *Bull. Soc. zool. France*, 50: 97-106.

Pellegrin, J. 1928. Poissons du Chiloango et du Congo recueillis par l'expedition du Dr Schouteden (1920-1922). *Ann. Mus. Congo Belge. Zool. Ser. I. Materiaux pour la Faune du Congo*, 3(1): 1-50.

Pellegrin, J. 1933. Les poissons des eaux douces de Madagascar (et des iles voisines (Comores, Seychelles, Mascareignes)). *Mem. Acad. Malgache*, 14: 1-222.

Pellegrin, J. 1934. Sur une collection de poissons du Moyen-Congo recueillis par Madame Petit-Renaud. *Ann. Soc. Sci. Nat. Charente-inferieure*, 1(7): 121-127.

Pellegrin, J. & P. W. Fang, 1939. Poissons de Chine de M. Ho, description de deux especes nouvelles. *Bull. Soc. Zool. France*, 64: 338-343,

Pellegrin, J. & P. W. Fang, 1940. Poissons du Laos recueillis par MM. Delacour, Greenway, ed Blanc. Description d'une genre, de cinq especies et d'une variete. *Bull. Soc. Zool. France*, 65: 111-123.

Pfeiffer, W. & J. F. Eisenberg, 1965. Die lauterzeugung der dornwelse (Doradidae) und der fiederbartwelse (Mochokidae). *Z. Morph. Ökol. Tiere*, 54: 669-679.

Pienaar, U. de V. 1978. *The freshwater fishes of the Kruger National Park.* National Parks Bd. South Africa, 91pp.

Pillai, R. S. & G. M. Yazdani, 1971. First record of the catfish, *Olyra horae* Prashad and Mukherji (Siluriformes: Olyridae) from India with a brief redescription of the species. *Journ. Zool. Soc. India*, 23(2): 135-136.

Poll, M. 1933. Contribution a la faune ichthyologique du Katanga. *Ann. Mus. Congo Belge: C.-Zool. Ser. I -Tome III - Fasc. 3*, pp. 101-152.

Poll, M. 1939. Les poissons du Stanley-Pool. *Ann. Mus. Congo Belge, ser. I*, 4(1): 1-60.

Poll, M. 1942. Description d'un genre nouveau de Bagridae du Lac Tanganika. *Rev. Zool. Bot. Afr.*, 35(3): 318-322.

Poll, M. 1943. Descriptions de poissons nouveaux du Lac Tanganika, appartenant aux familles des Clariidae et Cichlidae. *Rev. Zool. Bot. Afr.*, 37(3/4): 305-318.

Poll, M. 1943. Description du *Tanganikallabes mortiauxi*, gen. nov., sp. n. de la famille des Clariidae. *Rev. Zool. Bot. Afr.*, 37(1/2): 126-133.

Poll, M. 1946. Revision de la faune ichthyologique du Lac Tanganyika. *Ann. Mus. Congo Belge*, 4(3): 141-364.

Poll, M. 1952. Poissons de riviers de la region des lacs Tanganika et Kivu recueillis par G. Marlier. *Rev. Zool. Bot. Afr.*, 46(3/4): 221-236.

Poll, M. 1953. Exploration hydrobiologique du Lac Tanganika (1946-1947). Resultats scientifiques. Poissons non Cichlidae. Vol. 3, part 5A, pp. 1-251, pls.

Poll, M. 1956. Les poissons du Congo Belge et l'aquariophilie. *Notre Aquarium, Dec. 1955 et Jan. 1956.*

Poll, M. 1957. Les genres des poissons d'eau douce de l'Afrique. *Ann. Mus. Congo Belge, Tervuren, - ser. IN-8 -, Sci. Zool.*, 54: 1-191.

Poll, M. 1957. Redescription du *Gymnallabes tihoni* Poll, 1944, Clariidae microphthalme du Stanley-Pool (Congo Belge). *Rev. Zool. Bot. Afr.*, 55(3/4): 237-248.

Poll, M. 1959. Recherches sur la faune ichthyologique de la region de Stanley Pool. *Ann. Mus. Roy. Congo Belge - ser. IN-8 - Sci. Zool. 71*, pp. 75-174, pls.

Poll, M. 1966. Genre et espece nouveaux de Bagridae du fleuve Congo en region de Leopoldville. *Rev. Zool. Bot. Afr.*, 74(3/4): 425-428.

Poll, M. 1967. Contribution a la faune ichthyologique de l'Angola. *Mus. do Dundo, Diamang, Publ. Cult. No. 75*, 381pp.

Poll, M. 1971. Revision des *Synodontis* africains (famille Mochokidae). *Ann. Mus. Roy. Afr. Cent. - ser. IN-8 - Sci Zool. #191*, 497pp., pls.

Poll, M. 1973. Nombre et distribution geographique des poissons d'eau douce africains. *Bull. Mus. natn. Hist. Nat., ser. 3, no. 150*.

Poll, M. 1976. Poissons. *Exploration du Parc National de l'Upemba*. Fondation pour Favoriser les Recherches Scientifiques en Afrique, fasc 73, 127pp., pls.

Poll, M. 1977. Les genres nouveaux *Platyallabes* et *Platyclarias* compares au genre *Gymnallabes* Gthr. Synopsis nouveau des genres de Clariidae. *Bull. Classe Sci., Acad. Roy. Belgique, ser. 5*, 63: 122-149.

Poll, M. & J.-P. Gosse, 1963. Contribution a l'etude systematique de la faune ichthyologique du Congo Centrale. *Ann. Mus. Roy. Afr. Cent. - ser. IN-8 - Sci. Zool. #116*, pp. 43-110, pls.

Poll, M. & J.-P. Gosse, 1969. Revision des Malapteruridae (Pisces, Siluriformes) et description d'une deuxieme espece de silure electrique: *Malapterurus microstoma* sp. n. *Bull. Inst. Roy. Sci. Nat. Belg.*, 45(38): 1-12.

Poll, M. & J. Lambert, 1958. Un cyprinodontide et un Clariidae nouveaux de la grande foret Congolaise. *Rev. Zool. Bot. Afr.*, 58(3/4): 328-339.

Poll, M., B. Lanza, & A. R. Sassi, 1972. Genre nouveau extraordinaire de Bagridae du fleuve Juba: *Pardiglanis tarabinii* gen. n. sp. n. (Pisces, Siluriformes). *Monitore Zool. Italiano #15*, pp. 327-345.

Poll, M. & T. Roberts, 1968. Description d'une espece nouvelle de *Synodontis* du Bassin du Congo. *Rev. Zool. Bot. Afr.*, 77(3/4): 296-302.

Poll, M. & B. Roman, 1967. Poissons nouveau de la Haute Comoe. *Rev. Zool. Bot. Afr.*, 75(1/2): 179-187.

Poll, M. & D. Stewart, 1975. Un Mochocidae et un Kneriidae nouveaux de la reviere Luongo (Zambia), affluent du bassin du Congo. *Rev. Zool. Afr.*, 89(1): 151-158.

Pucke, J. P. & B. L. Umminger, 1979. Histiophysiology of the cells and dendritic organ of the marine catfish, *Plotosus lineatus*, in relation to osmoregulation. *Copeia, 1979, no. 2*, pp. 357-360.

Puyo, J. 1949. Poissons de la Guyane Francaise. *Faune de l'Empire Francaise, O. R. S. T. O. M.*, 12: 1-280.

Rajan, S. 1965. Notes on the food of some cat fishes of the Chikla Lake. *Journ. Zool. Soc. India*, 17(1/2): 97-107.

Raney, E. C. 1950. Freshwater fishes (of the James River Basin, Virginia). *The James River Basin - Past, Present and Future*, pp. 151-194.

Raney, E. C. & D. A. Webster, 1940. The food and growth of the young of the common bullhead, *Ameiurus nebulosus* (LeSueur), in Cayuga Lake, New York. *Trans. Amer. Fish. Soc.*, 69: 205-209.

Reed, H. D. 1924. The morphology of the dermal glands in Nematognathous fishes. *Zeit. Morphol. Anthrop.* 24: 227-264.

Regan, C. T. 1904. III. A monograph of the fishes of the family Loricariidae. *Trans. Zool. Soc. London*, 17(3): 191-326.

Regan, C. T. 1906-1908. *Biologia Centrali-Americana. Pisces*. Antiquariat Junk, Lochem, Netherlands. (Reprint, 1972.)

Regan, C. T. 1913. The fishes of the San Juan River, Colombia. *Ann. Mag. Nat. Hist., (ser. 8)*, 12: 462-473.

Regan, C. T. 1923. Note on the siluroid fishes of the genera *Glyptosternum* and *Exostoma*. *Ann. Mag. Nat. Hist., (ser. 9)*, 11: 608-610.

Reis, R. E. 1983. *Rineloricaria longicauda* e *Rineloricaria quadrensis*, duas novas especes de Loricariinae do sul do Brasil (Pisces, Siluriformes, Loricariidae). *Iheringia, ser. Zool., Porto Alegre*, 62: 61-80.

Reis, R. E. 1987. *Ancistrus cryptophthalmus* sp. n. a blind mailed catfish from the Tocantins River basin, Brazil (Pisces, Siluriformes, Loricariidae). *Rev. fr. Aquariol.*, 14(3): 81-84.

Rendahl, H. 1928. Beitrage zur Kenntnis der Chinesischen Süsswasserfische. I. Systematischer Teil. *Arkiv. Zool. K. Svenska Vetens.*, 20A(1): 1-194.

Risch, L. 1981. The systematic status of *Gephyroglanis longipinnis* Boulenger 1899, *Chrysichthys magnus* Pellegrin 1922 and *Gephyroglanis gigas* Pellegrin 1922 (Pisces, Bagridae). *Rev. Zool. Afr.*, 95(3): 508-524.

Roberts, T. R. 1967 (1968). *Rheoglanis dendrophorus* and *Zairichthys zonatus*, bagrid catfishes from the lower rapids of the Congo River. *Ichthyologica*, 39(3/4): 119-131.

Roberts, T. R. 1972. Ecology of fishes in the Amazon and Congo basins. *Bull. Mus. Comp. Zool., Harvard*, 143(2): 117-147.

Roberts, T. R. 1978. An ichthyological survey of the Fly River in Papua New Guinea with descriptions of new species. *Smiths. Contrib. Zool. #281*, 72pp.

Roberts, T. R. 1982. Systematics and geographical distribution of the Asian silurid catfish genus *Wallago*, with a key to the species. *Copeia, 1982, no. 4*, pp. 890-894.

Roberts, T. R. 1982. A revision of the South and Southeast Asian angler-catfishes (Chacidae). *Copeia, 1982, no. 4*, pp. 895-901.

Roberts, T. R. 1982. Unculi (horny projections arising from single cells), an adaptive feature of the epidermis of Ostariophysan fishes. *Zool. Scripta*, 11(1): 55-76.

Roberts, T. R. 1983. Revision of the South and Southeast Asian sisorid catfish genus *Bagarius*, with description of a new species from the Mekong. *Copeia, 1983, no. 2*, pp. 435-445.

Roberts, T. R. & D. J. Stewart, 1976. An ecological and systematic survey of fishes in the rapids of the lower Zaire or Congo River. *Bull. Mus. Comp. Zool.*, 147(6): 239-317.

Robinson, H. W. & G. L. Harp, 1985. Distribution, habitat and food of the Ouachita madtom, *Noturus lachneri*, a Ouachita River drainage endemic. *Copeia, 1985, no. 1*, pp. 216-220.

Roman, B. 1966. Les poissons des Hauts-Bassins de la Volta. *Ann. Mus. Roy. Afr. Centr. - Ser. IN-8 - Sci. Zool. #150*, 191pp., pls.

Roman, B. 1971. *Peces de Rio Muni. Guinea Ecuatorial (Aguas dulces y solobres).* Fundacion La Salle de Ciebcias Naturales, 295pp.

Rössel, F. 1961. *Corydoras caudimaculatus*, ein neuer Panzerwels aus Brasilien (Pisces, Teleostei, Callichthyidae). *Senck. biol.*, 42(1/2): 49-50.

Rössel, F. 1962. *Centromochlus schultzi*, ein neuer Wels aus Brasilien (Pisces, Teleostei, Auchenipteridae). *Senck. biol.*, 43(1): 27-30.

Rössel, F. 1962. *Corydoras cervinus*, ein neuer Panzerwels aus Brasilien (pisces, Teleostei, Callichthyidae). *Senck. biol.*, 43(1): 31-33.

Rössel, F. 1966. Two newcomers and a rarity: New and unusual *Corydoras* species from Brazil. *Ichthyologica*, 37(1): 7-12.

Salazar, F. J. Martin-, 1964. Las especies del genero *Farlowella* de Venezuela (Pisces-Nematognathi-Loricariidae) con descripcion de 5 especes y 1 sub-especie nuevas. *Mem. Soc. Ciencias Nat. La Salle #69*, 25: 242-260.

Salazar, F. J. Martin-, I. J. H. Isbrücker & H. Nijssen. 1982. *Dentectus barbarmatus*, a new genus and species of mailed catfish from the Orinoco Basin of Venezuela (Pisces, Siluriformes, Loricariidae). *Beaufortia*, 32(8): 125-137.

Sandon, H. 1956. An abnormal specimen of *Synodontis membranaceus* (Teleostei, Siluroidea), with a discussion on the evolutionary history of the adipose fin in fish. *Proc. Zool. Soc. London*, 127(4): 453-460.

Sands, D. D. & B. K. Black. 1985. Two new species of *Brachyrhamdia*, Myers, 1927, from Brazil and Peru, together with a redefinition of the genus. Pisces, Siluriformes, Pimelodidae. *Catfishes of the World, Suppl.*

Saul, W. G. 1975. An ecological study of fishes at a site in upper Amazonian Ecuador. *Proc. Acad. Nat. Sci. Phila*, 127(12): 93-134.

Saxena, D. B. 1960. On the asphyxiation and influence of CO_2 on respiration of air-breathing fish, *Heteropneustes fossilis* Bloch and *Clarias batrachus* (Linn.). *Journ. Zool. Soc. India*, 12(1): 114-124.

Saxena, D. B. 1964. Studies on the physiology of respiration in fishes. VI. Comparative study of the gill area in some freshwater catfishes of India. *Journ. Zool. Soc. India*, 1(1/2): 38-47.

Saxena, S. C. 1962. On the pelvic girdle and fin of a hill stream sisorid fish, *Pseudecheneis sulcatus*. *Copeia, 1962, no. 3*, pp. 656-657.

Schaeffer, S. A. 1984. Mechanical strength of the pectoral spine girdle complex in *Pterygoplichthys* (Loricariidae; Siluroidei). *Copeia, 1984, no. 4*, pp. 1005-1008.

Schaeffer, S. A. 1988. A new species of the loricariid genus *Parotocinclus* from southern Venezuela (Pisces: Siluroidei). *Copeia, 1988, no. 1*, pp. 182-188.

Schifter, H. 1965. Beobachtungen am grossmaulwels *Chaca chaca*. *Natur. und Museum*, 95(11): 465-472.

Schmidt, R. E. 1985. New distribution records and complementary description of *Haemomaster venezuelae* (Siluriformes: Trichomycteridae), a rare and poorly known fish from northern South America. *Stud. Neotrop. Fauna & Environ.*, 20(2): 93-96.

Schmidt, R. E. 1987. Redescription of *Vandellia beccarii* (Siluriformes: Trichomycteridae) from Guyana. *Copeia, 1987, no. 1*, pp. 234-237.

Schmidt, R. E. & C. J. Ferraris, 1985. A new species of *Parotocinclus* (Pisces: Loricariidae) from Guyana. *Proc. Biol. Soc. Wash.*, 98(2): 341-346.

Schultz, L. P. 1942. The fresh-water fishes of Liberia. *Proc. U. S. N. M. #3152*, 92: 301-348, pls.

Schultz, L. P. 1944. A new loricariid catfish from the Rio Truando, Colombia. *Copeia, 1944, no. 3*, pp. 155-156.

Schultz, L. P. 1944. The catfishes of Venezuela, with descriptions of thirty-eight new forms. *Proc. U. S. N. M. #3172*, 94: 173-338, ols.

Schultz, L. P. 1945. Ichthyology.- *Pygidium mondolfi*, a new catfish from Venezuela. Journ. Wash. Acad. Sci., 35(1): 29-31.

Scott, T. D., C. J. M. Glover, & R. V. Southcott, 1980. *The marine and freshwater fishes of South Australia*. Handbook of the Flora and Fauna of South Australia. D. J. Woolman, Gov't Printer, second edition. 392pp.

Scott, W. B. & E. J. Crossman, 1969. Checklist of Canadian freshwater fishes with keys for identification. *Roy. Ont. Mus., Life Sci., Misc. Publ.*, 104pp.

Scott, W. B. & E. J. Crossman, 1975. Freshwater fishes of Canada. *Fish. Res. Bd. Can., Bull. #184*, 966pp.

Skelton, P. H. 1981. The description and osteology of a new species of *Gephyroglanis* (Siluriformes, Bagridae) from the Olifants River, South West Cape, South Africa. *Ann. Cape Prov. Mus. (Nat. Hist.)*, 13(15): 217-250.

Skelton, P. H. 1984. A systematic revision of species of the catfish genus *Amphilius* (Siluroidei, Amphiliidae) from east and southern Africa. *Ann. Cape Prov. Mus. (Nat. Hist.)*, 16(3): 41-71.

Skelton, P. H. 1985 (1986). Two new *Amphilius* (Pisces, Siluroidei, Amphiliidae) from the Zaire River system, Africa. *Rev. Zool. Afr.*, 99: 263-291.

Skelton, P. H., L. Risch, & L. de Vos, 1984. On the generic identity of the *Gephyroglanis* catfishes from southern Africa (Pisces, Siluroidei, Bagridae). *Rev. Zool. Afr.* 98(2): 337-372.

Smith, H. M. 1931. Notes on Siamese fishes. *Journ. Siam Soc., Nat. Hist., Suppl.*, 8(3): 177-190.

Smith, H. M. 1931. Descriptions of new genera and species of Siamese fishes. *Proc. U. S. N. M.*, (79(7): 1-48.

Smith, H. M. 1939. A new genus of clariid catfishes. *Copeia, 1939, no. 4*, p. 236.

Smith, H. M. 1945. The fresh-water fishes of Siam, or Thailand. *Bull. U. S. N. M. #188*, 622pp.

Smith, H. M. & L. G. Harron, 1903. Breeding habits of the yellow catfish. *Bull. U. S. Fish. Comm.*, 22: 149-154.

Smith, H. M. & A. Seale, 1906. Notes on a collection of fishes from the island of Mindanao, Philippine Archipelago, with descriptions of new genera and species. *Proc. Biol. Soc. Wash.*, 19: 73-82.

Smith-Vaniz, W. F. 1968. *Freshwater fishes of Alabama*. Auburn Univ. Agric. Exper. Sta., 211pp.

Sneed, K. E. & H. P. Clemens. 1963. The morphology of the testes and accessory reproductive glands of the catfishes (Ictaluridae). *Copeia, 1963, no. 4*, pp. 606-611.

Sowerby, A. de C. 1921. On a new silurid fish from the Yalu River, South Manchuria. *Proc. U. S. N. M. #2408*, 60(13): 1-2.

Starks, E. C. 1906. On a collection of fishes made by P. O. Simons in Ecuador and Peru. *Proc. U. S. N. M. #1468*, 30: 761-800.

Starks, E. C. 1913. The fishes of the Stanford Expedition to Brazil. *Publ. Stan. Univ., Univ. ser. no. 12*, pp. 1-77, pls.

Steindachner, F. 1867. Ichthyologische Notizen (V). I. Über eine neue *Plecostomus*-Art aus Brasilien. *Sitz. Akad. Wiss.*, 55: 1-5.

Steindachner, F. 1867. Ichthyologische Notizen (IV). V. Über zwei *Glyptosternum*-Arten aus Simla. *Sitz. Akad. Wiss.*, 55: 16-18, pl.

Steindachner, F. 1869. Zur fischfauna des Senegal. Part. 2. *Sitz. Akad. Wiss.*, 60: 1-51.

Steindachner, F. 1870. Zur fischfauna des Senegal. Part. 3. *Sitz. Akad. Wiss.*, 61: 1-51, pls.

Steindachner, F. 1877. Die Süsswasserfische des südöstlichen Brasilien. (IV). *Sitz. Kais. Akad. Wiss.*, 76: 1-14, pls.

Steindachner, F. 1882. Betrage zur Kenntnis der Flussfische Südamerika's. IV. Über einige Siluroided un Characinen von Canelos (Ecuador) und aus dem Amazonen-Strome. *Denks. Math.-Natur. Classe Kais. Akad. Wiss.*, 46: 26-31

Steindachner, F. 1883. Ichthyologische Beitrage (XIII). III. *Macrones chinensis*, n. sp. *Sitz. Kais. Akad. Wiss.*, 88(1): 47-48.

Steindachner, F. 1896. Bericht über die wahrend der Reise Sr. Maj. Schiff "Aurora" von Dr. C. Ritter v. Mieroszewski in den Jahren 1895 und 1896 gesammelten Fische. *Ann. K. K. Natur. Hofmus.*, 11(2): 197-230, pl.

Steindachner, F. 1906. Sitzung der mathematisch-naturwissenschaftlichen Klasse vom 13. Dezember 1906. *Kais. Akad. Wiss. Wien, Anz. #27*, 3pp.

Steindachner, F. 1907. Sitzung der mathematisch-naturwissenschaftlichen Klasse vom 4 Juli 1907. *Kais. Akad. Wiss. Wien, Anz. #17*, 4pp.

Syeindachner, F. 1907. Über einige Fischarten aus dem Flusse Cubatao im Staate Santa Catherina bei Theresopolis. *Sitz. Kais. Akad. Wiss. Wien.* 116(1): 475-492.

Steindachner, F. 1907. Sitzung der mathematisch-naturwissenschaftlichen Klasse vom 25 April 1907. *Kais. Akad. Wiss. Wien, Anz. #10*, 4pp.

Steindachner, F. 1907. Sitzung der mathematisch-naturwissenschaftlichen Klasse vom 28 Februar 1907. *Kais. Akad. Wiss. Wien, Anz. #6*, 4pp.

Steindachner, F. 1908. Sitzung der mathematisch-naturwissenschaftlichen Klasse vom 13 Februar 1908. *Kais. Akad. Wiss. Wien, Anz. #6*, 8pp.

Steindachner, F. 1908. Sitzung der mathematisch-naturwissenschaftlichen Klasse vom 20 Februar 1908. *Kais. Akad. Wiss. Wien, Anz. #7*, 4pp.

Steindachner, F. 1908. Sitzung der mathematisch-naturwissenschaftlichen Klasse vom 5 Marz 1908. *Kais. Akad. Wiss. Wien, Anz. #8*, 4pp.

Steindachner, F. 1908. Sitzung der mathematisch-naturwissenschaftlichen Klasse vom 11 Marz 1908. *Kais. Akad. Wiss. Wien, Anz. #9*, 5pp.

Steindachner, F. 1908. Sitzung der mathematisch-naturwissenschaftlichen Klasse vom 2 April 1908. *Kais. Akad. Wiss. Wien, Anz. #11*, 6pp.

Steindachner, F. 1909. Sitzung der mathematisch-naturwissenschaftlichen Klasse vom 13 Mai 1909. *Kais. Akad. Wiss. Wien, Anz. #12*, 3pp.

Steindachner, F. 1909. Sitzung der mathematisch-naturwissenschaftlichen Klasse vom 21 Oktober 1909. *Kais. Akad. Wiss. Wien, Anz. #20*, 2pp.

Steindachner, F. 1910. Über einige *Ageneiosus-* und *Farlowella*-Arten. *Ann. K. K. Naturhist. Hofmus., Wien*, 24: 399-408.

Steindachner, F. 1910. Die Fische des Itapocu und seiner Zuflüsse im Staate Sa. Catherina (Brasilien). *Ann. K. K. Naturhist. Hofmus., Wien*, 24: 419-433, pl.

Steindachner, F. 1910. Sitzung der mathematisch-naturwissenschaftlichen Klasse vom 10 Marz 1910. *Kais. Akad. Wiss. Wien, Anz. #8*, 6pp.

Steindachner, F. 1910. Sitzung der mathematisch-naturwissenschaftlichen Klasse vom 1 Dezember 1910. *Kais. Akad. Wiss. Wien, Anz. #25*, 2pp.

Steindachner, F. 1911. Sitzung der mathematisch-naturwissenschaftlichen Klasse vom 21 Dezember 1911. *Kais. Akad. Wiss. Wien,*

Anz. #27, 5pp.

Steindachner, F. 1911. Beitrage zur Kenntnis der Fischfauna des Tanganyikasees und des Kongogebeites. *Sitz. Kais. Akad. Wiss., Wien.*, 129(1): 1-16, pls.

Steindachner, F. 1912. Sitzung der mathematisch-naturwissenschaftlichen Klasse vom 14 November 1912. *Kais. Akad. Wiss. Wien, Anz.#23*, 6pp.

Steindachner, F. 1913. Zur fischfauna des Dscha, eines sekundären nebenflusses des Kongo, im Bezirke Molundu, Kamerun. *Denk. Natur. Kais. Akad. Wiss.*, 89: 1-64, pls.

Steindachner, F. 1915. Sitzung der mathematisch-naturwissenschaftlichen Klasse vom 1 Juli 1915. *Kais. Akad. Wiss. Wien, Anz. #17*, 4pp.

Steindachner, F. 1915. Ichthyologische Beitrage (XVIII). *Sitz. Kais. Akad. Wiss. Wien*, 124 (8-10): 507-591, pls.

Steindachner, F. 1915. Berichte über die ichthyologischen aufsammlungen der brüder Adolf und Albin Horn während einer im sommer 1913 ausgeführten reise nach Deutsch-Ostafrika. *Denk. Kais. Akad. Wiss. Wien*, 92: 1-28, pls.

Steindachner, F. 1915. Beiträge zur kenntnis der flussfische Süamerikas. V. *Denk. Kais. Akad. Wiss., Wien*, 93(2): 1-92, pls.

Stewart, D. J. 1985. A review of the South American catfish Tripe Hoplomyzontini (Pisces, Aspredinidae), with descriptions of new species from Ecuador. *Fieldiana, Zool. new ser. #25, Publ. #1360*, 19pp.

Stewart, D. J. 1985. A new species of *Cetopsorhamdia* (Pisces: Pimelodidae) from the Rio Napo basin of eastern Ecuador. *Copeia, 1985, no. 2*, pp. 339-344.

Stewart, D. J. 1986. Revision of *Pimelodina* and description of a new genus and species from the Peruvian Amazon. *Copeia, 1986, no. 3*, pp. 653-672.

Stewart, D. J. & M. J. Pavlik, 1985. Revision of *Cheirocerus* (Pisces: Pimelodidae) from tropical freshwaters of South America. *Copeia, 1985, no. 2*, pp. 356-367.

Strauss, R. E. 1985. Evolutionary allometry and variation in body form in the South American catfish genus *Corydoras* (Callichthyidae). *Syst. Zool.*, 34(4): 381-396.

Sundararaj, B. I. 1958. The seminal vesicles and their seasonal changes in the Indian catfish, *Heteropneustes*. *Copeia, 1958, no. 4*, pp. 289-297.

Suttkus, R. D. 1955. Biological study of estuarine and marine waters of Louisiana. Ictaluridae and Ariidae. *Rept. to Louisiana Wildlife & Fish Comm., Progress Rept. #12*, 19pp.

Suttkus, R. D. & W. R. Taylor, 1965. *Noturus munitus*, a new species of madtom, family Ictaluridae, from southern United States. *Proc. Biol. Soc. Wash.* 78: 169-178.

Suvatti, C. 1950. *Fauna of Thailand*. pp. 180-446.

Sydenham, D. H. J. 1978. Redescriptions of the type specimens of six clariid species (Pisces) from West Africa. *Zool. Journ. Linn. Soc.*, 64: 347-371.

Taverne, L. & A. Aloulou-Triki, 1974. Etude anatomique, myologique et osteologique du genre *Synodontis* Cuvier (Pisces: Siluriformes, Mochokidae). *Ann. Mus. Roy. Afr. Cent. - ser. IN-8 - Sci. Zool. #210*, 69pp, pls.

Taylor, J. N. 1983. Field observations on the reproductive ecology of three species of armored catfishes (Loricariidae: Loricariinae) in Paraguay. *Copeia, 1983, no. 1*, pp. 257-259.

Taylor, W. R. 1964. Fishes of Arnhem Land. *Rec. Amer.-Austral. Sci. Exp. to Arnhem Land*, 4: 45-308.

Taylor, W. R. 1969. A revision of the catfish genus *Noturus* Rafinesque with an analysis of higher groups in the Ictaluridae. *Bull. U. S. N. M. #282*, 315pp.

Taylor, W. R., R. E. Jenkins, & E. A. Lachner, 1971. Rediscovery and description of the ictalurid catfish, *Noturus flavipinnis*. *Proc. Biol. Soc. Wash.*, 83(41): 469-476.

Teugels, G. G. 1982. A systematic outline of the African species of the genus *Clarias* (Pisces; Clariidae), with an annotated bibliography. *Mus. Roy. Afr. Cent. - ser. IN-8 - Sci. Zool. #236*, 249pp.

Teugels, G. G. 1982. Preliminary data of a systematic outline of the African species of the genus *Clarias*. *Rev. Zool. Afr.*, 96(4): 731-748.

Teugels, G. G. 1982. On the rehabilitation of *Clarias gabonensis* Günther 1867 with a redescription and notes on the systematical status (Pisces, Clariidae). *Rev. Zool. Afr.*, 96(1): 45-60.

Teugels, G. G. 1986. A systematic revision of the African species of the genus *Clarias* (Pisces; Clariidae). *Mus. Roy. Afr. Cent., Zool. Wetens. Ann., Sci Zool.*, 247: 1-199.

Teugels, G. G., H. Skelton, & G. Leveque, 1987. A new species of *Amphilius* (Pisces, Amphiliidae) from the Konkoure Basin, Guinea, West Africa. *Cybium, 1987*, 11(1): 93-101.

Thorson, T. B. (ed.), 1976. *Investigations of the ichthyofauna of Nicaraguan lakes*. School of Life Sciences, Univ. Nebraska, Lincoln. 663pp.

Thys van den Audenaerde, D. F. E. & L. D. G. de Vos, 1982. Description of *Eutropius djeremi* spec. nov. from the Cameroons (Pisces, Schilbeidae). *Rev. Zool. Afr.*, 96(1): 179-184.

Tilak, R. 1963. Studies on the nematognathine pectoral girdle in relation to taxonomy. *Ann. Mag. nat. Hist., ser. 13*, 6: 145-155.

Tilak, R. 1963. The osteocranium and the Weberian apparatus of the fishes of the family Schilbeidae (Pisces: Siluroidea). *Proc. Zool. Soc. London*, pp. 15-24.

Tilak, R. 1963. Relationships between the osteocranium and Weberian apparatus in two Indian catfishes of the genus *Clarias* (Siluridae). *Copeia, 1963, no. 4*, pp. 623-629.

Tilak, R. 1967. Studies on the osteology of the Nematognathine girdle in relation to taxonomy. *Journ. Zool. Soc. India*, 19(1/2): 101-110.

Trautman, M. B. 1948. A natural hybrid catfish, *Schilbeodes miurus* X *Schilbeodes mollis*. *Copeia, 1948, no. 3*, pp. 166-174.

Trewavas, E. 1962. Fishes of the Crater Lakes of the northwestern Cameroons. *Bonner Zoologische Beitrage*, 1/3: 146-192.

Trewavas, E., J. Green, & S. A. Corbet, 1972. Ecological studies on crater lakes in West Cameroon - Fishes of Barombi Mbo. *Journ. Zool. London*, 167: 41-95.

Tripathy, N. K. & C. C. Das, 1980. Chromosomes in three species of Asian catfishes. *Copeia, 1980, no. 4*, pp. 916-917.

Tweedie, M. W. F. 1950. Notes on Malayan fresh water fishes. *Bull. Raffles Mus. #21*, pp. 97-105.

Tweedie, M. W. F. 1952. Notes on Malayan fresh-water fishes. *Bull. Raffles Mus. #24*, pp. 63-95.

Tweedie, M. W. F. 1956. Notes on Malayan fresh-water fishes. Nos. 6-8. *Bull., Raffles Mus. #27*, pp. 56-64.

Vari, R. P., S. L. Jewett, D. C. Taphorn, & C. R. Gilbert, 1984. A new catfish of the genus *Epapterus* (Siluriformes: Auchenipteridae) from the Orinoco River basin. *Proc. Biol. Soc. Wash.* 97(2): 462-472.

Vari, R. P. & H. Ortega, 1986. The catfishes of the Neotropical family Helogenidae (Ostariophysi: Siluroidei). *Smiths. Contrib. Zool. #442*, 20pp.

Wallace, C. R. 1967. Observations on the reproductive behavior of the black bullhead (*Ictalurus melas*). *Copeia, 1967, no. 4*, 852-853.

Wang, J. C. S. 1979. *Fishes of the Delaware estuaries. A guide to the early life histories*. EA Communications, 410pp.

Ward, J. W. 1957. The reproduction and early development of the sea catfish, *Galeichthys felis*, in the Biloxi, (Miss.) Bay. *Copeia, 1957, no. 4*, pp. 295-298.

Watson, D. J. & E. K. Balon, 1983. Structure and production of fish communities in tropical rain forest streams of northern Borneo. *Canad. Journ. Zool.*, 62: 927-940.

Weber, M. & L. F. de Beaufort, 1913. *The fishes of the Indo-Australian Archipelago. Vol. II. Malacopterygii, Myctophoidea, Ostariophysi: I Siluroidea*, E. J. Brill, Ltd., Leiden, 404pp.

Weibezahn, F. H. 1951. Un nuevo pez para la fauna ictiologica Venoezolana. *Mem. Soc. Ciencias Nat. La Salle*, 11(29): 179-180.

Weitzman, S. H. 1955. Redescription and relationships of *Corydoras triseriatus* von Ihering from the Rio Doce, Brazil. *Wasmann Journ. Biol.*, 13(1): 101-106.

Weitzman, S. H. 1956. A description, supplementary notes and a figure of *Corydoras cochui* Myers and Weitzman, a Brazilian catfish. *Stan. Ichthyol. Bull.*, 7(2): 14-18.

Weitzman, S. H. 1960. Figures and descriptions of four South American catfishes of the genus *Corydoras*, including two new species. *Stan. Ichthyol. Bull.*, 7(4): 140-154.

Weitzman, S. H. 1960. Figures and description of a South American catfish, *Corydoras reticulatus* Fraser-Brunner. *Stan. Ichthyol. Bull.*, 7(4): 155-161.

Weitzman, S. H. 1961. A new catfish, *Corydoras concolor* (Callichthyidae) from Venezuela. *Proc. Biol. Soc. Wash.*, 74: 105-110.

Weitzman, S. H. 1963. A new catfish, *Corydoras pastazensis* (Callichthyidae) from Ecuador. *Proc. Biol. Soc. Wash.*, 76: 59-64.

Weitzman, S. H. 1964. One new species and two redescriptions of catfishes of the South American callichthyid genus *Corydoras*. *Proc. U. S. N. M. #3498*, 116: 115-126.

Weitzman, S. H. & H. Nijssen, 1970. Four new species and one new subspecies of the catfish genus *Corydoras* from Ecuador, Colombia and Brazil (Pisces, Siluriformes, Callichthyidae). *Beaufortia #233*, 18: 119-132.

Wheeler, A. 1969. *The fishes of the British Isles and Northwest Europe*. Mich. State Univ. Press, East Lansing, 613pp.

Whitley, G. P. 1933. Studies in ichthyology. No. 7. *Rec. Aust. Mus.*, 19(1): 60-112.

Whitley, G. P. 1938. Descriptions of some New Guinea fishes. *Rec. Aust. Mus.*, 20(3): 223-233.

Whitley, G. P. 1956. Fishes from inland New Guinea. *Rec. Aust. Mus.*, 24(3): 23-30.

Whitley, G. P. 1956. A new catfish from New Guinea. *Proc. Roy. Zool. Soc. N. S. W. for 1954-55*.

Whitley, G. P. 1957. The freshwater fishes of Australia. *Aqualife, June, 1957*, pp. 6-10.

Wu, H. W. & K. F. Wang, 1931. On a collection of fishes from the Upper Yangtze Valley. *Contrib. Biol. Lab. Sci. Soc. of China, Zool. ser.*, 7(6): 221-237.

Yanez-Arancibia, A. 1978. Taxonomy, ecology and structure of fish communities in coastal lagoons with ephemeral inlets on the Pacific Coast of Mexico. *Publ. Espec. Centro Ciencias Mar y Limnologia #2*, 306pp.

Yates, T. L., M. A. Lewis, & M. D. Hatch, 1984. Biochemical systematics of three species of catfish (genus *Ictalurus*) in New Mexico. *Copeia, 1984, no. 1*, pp. 97-101.

Yerger, R. W. & K. Relyea, 1968. The flat-headed bullheads (Pisces: Ictaluridae) of the southeastern United States, and a new species of *Ictalurus* from the Gulf Coast. *Copeia, 1968. no. 2*, pp. 361-384.

Ziesler, R. 1979. Bibliography of Latin American freshwater fish. *FAO COPESCAL Tech. Pap. #2*, 187pp.

Diplomystes papillosus. Valdivia, Chile.

Ictalurus melas. (North America.)

Ictalurus nebulosus. (North America.)

Ictalurus catus. (North America.)

Ictalurus natalis. (North America.)

Ictalurus punctatus (albino). (North America.)

Ictalurus punctatus. (North America.)

PLATE 2

Nesting habitat of *Noturus exilis*.

Noturus miurus. (North America.)

Noturus elegans. Smoky Mountains, Tennessee.

Noturus exilis. (North America.)

Noturus insignis. Roanoke River, Roanoke Co., Virginia.

Noturus flavater. White River, Ozark Co., Missouri.

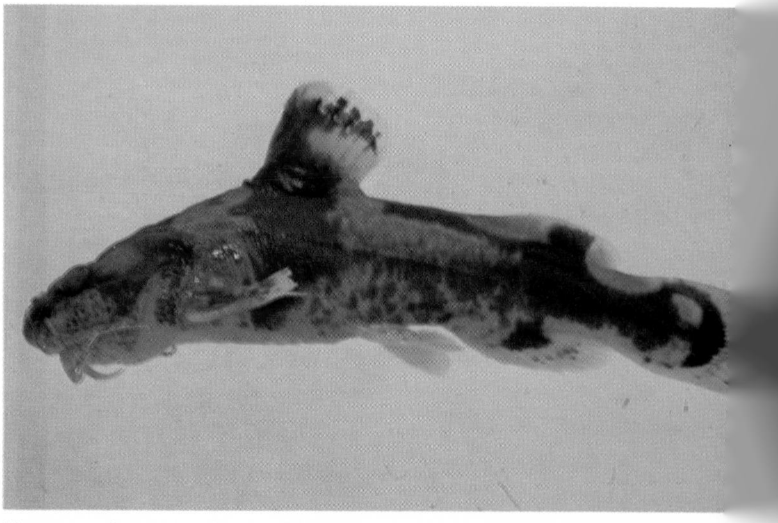

Noturus stigmosus. (North America.)

Phyllonemus typus. Lake Tanganyika.

Phyllonemus typus. Lake Tanganyika.

Bagrus ubangensis. Zaire River system.

Lophiobagrus cyclurus. Lake Tanganyika.

Lophiobagrus cyclurus. Lake Tanganyika.

PLATE 4

Heterobagrus bocourti. (Thailand.)

Heterobagrus bocourti. (Thailand.)

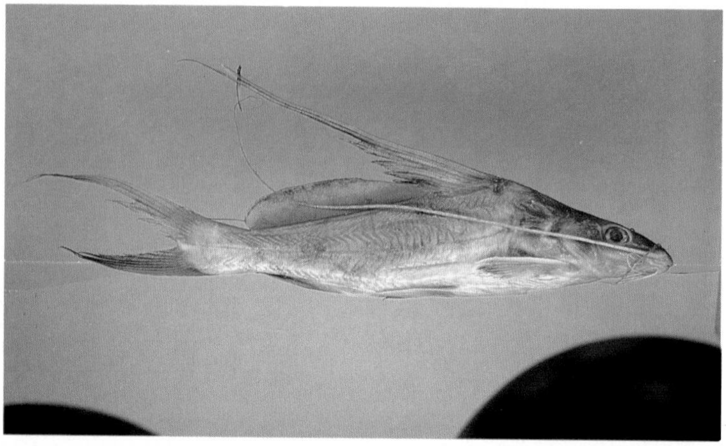

Heterobagrus bocourti, 143 mm. (Thailand.)

Bagrichthys hypselopterus. (Sumatra; Borneo.)

Auchenoglanis ngamensis. Upper Zambezi River system.

Bagrichthys hypselopterus. (Sumatra; Borneo.)

Parauchenoglanis guttatus. (Equatorial Africa.)

Parauchenoglanis sp. (Africa.)

Liauchenoglanis maculatus. (Sierra Leone.)

Parauchenoglanis macrostoma. (Cameroon; Gabon; Zaire.)

Leptoglanis n. sp. Off Cape Maclear, Lake Malawi.

Parauchenoglanis macrostoma. (Cameroon; Gabon; Zaire.)

Auchenoglanis ngamensis. (Upper Zambezi River system.)

Auchenoglanis ngamensis. (Upper Zambezi River system.)

Auchenoglanis occidentalis (juv.). (Tropical Africa.)

Auchenoglanis occidentalis. (Tropical Africa.)

PLATE 6

Auchenoglanis occidentalis has a wide distribution. It occurs in the Nile, Lake Chad, West Africa, Zaire-Lualaba River system, East African lakes, Omo River, and the Giuba River.

This young *Auchenoglanis occidentalis* resembles the adult shown above. On close inspection, however, subtle differences may be seen such as head size, shape of tail, etc.

Auchenoglanis occidentalis. (Tropical Africa.)

Auchenoglanis occidentalis (juv.). (Tropical Africa.)

Auchenoglanis occidentalis. Niger.

Auchenoglanis biscutatus? Niger.

Auchenoglanis pantherinus. (Ntem River.)

Auchenoglanis sp. cf. *occidentalis*. Rio Muni.

Pelteobagrus nudiceps. Biwa-ko, Japan.

Pelteobagrus ornatus. (Malay Peninsula.)

PLATE 8

Pseudobagrus fulvidraco. (Amur Basin.)

Pelteobagrus brashnikowi. (Amur Basin.)

Pseudobagrus fulvidraco. (Amur Basin.)

Pelteobagrus brashnikowi. (Amur Basin.)

Rita rita. (Pakistan across northern India and Nepal to Burma.)

Chandramara chandramara. (North Bengal: Assam.)

Chandramara chandramara. (North Bengal; Assam.)

Leicassis sp. cf. *leiacanthus*, 75 mm. (Sumatra.)

Leiocassis siamensis (juv.). (Thailand.)

Leiocassis siamensis. (Thailand.)

Leiocassis stenomus. (Java, Borneo, Sumatra, Malaya, Thailand.)

Leiocassis poecilopterus. (Sumatra, Borneo, Java.)

Leiocassis siamensis. (Thailand.)

Leiocassis ussuriensis. (Amur Basin.)

Unknown bagrid.

PLATE 10

Chrysichthys brevibarbis. (Zaire River system below Stanley Falls.)

Chrysichthys ornatus. (Zaire River system below Stanley Falls.)

Clarotes laticeps. (East Africa, Nile, Niger, & Senegal Rivers, Lake Chad.)

Chrysichthys sianenna. (Lake Tanganyika.)

Bagrichthys hypselopterus. (Sumatra; Borneo.)

Bagrichthys macropterus. (Sumatra to Thailand.)

Leiocassis siamensis (juv.). (Thailand.)

Leiocassis siamensis. (Thailand.)

Chrysichthys brachynema. Lake Tanganyika.

Chrysichthys stappersi. Lake Tanganyika.

Gnathobagrus depressus. "Boma."

Chrysichthys ornatus. (Zaire River system below Stanley Falls.)

Chrysichthys ornatus (var.). (Zaire River system below Stanley Falls.

Chrysichthys walkeri. Rio Muni.

Leptoglanis rotundiceps. Lupa River.

Leptoglanis dorae. Zambezi River.

PLATE 12

These two photos depict actual courtship between a pair of Big-eyed African Catfish (*Chrysichthys* sp. cf. *furcatus*), with the male assuming a position close to or actually covering the female. These fish were spawned by Hiroshi Azuma.

Newly laid eggs of the Big-eyed African Catfish.

The eggs blend in quite well with the gravel.

The fry hatch out in about 60 to 70 hours.

The fry are about 15 mm long in 18 days.

At 22 days they are some 18 mm long.

With proper feeding the fry soon grow into replicas of the parents. These are about 50 mm long.

PLATE 14

Chrysichthys sp. cf. *furcatus*. (Tropical Africa.)

Chrysichthys sp. cf. *furcatus*. (Tropical Africa.)

Chrysichthys longipinnis. (Zaire-Lualaba system.)

Chrysichthys velifer. (Ivory Coast and Ghana.)

Pseudobagrus aurantiacus. (Japan.)

Bagrus sp. cf. *orientalis*. (Tropical Africa.)

Mystus bleekeri? (Pakistan; Nepal; India; Bangladesh.)

Mystus vittatus. (Pakistan to Malaya.)

Mystus wyckii. (Sumatra and Java to Thailand.)

Mystus vittatus (left) and *M. tengara* (right).

Mystus gulio. (India to Borneo.)

Leiocassis stenomus. (Java; Borneo; Sumatra; Malaya; Thailand.)

Mystus sp. cf. *montanus*. (India.)

Mystus vittatus. (Pakistan to Malaya.)

Mystus micracanthus. (Malaysia; Thailand.)

Mystus bleekeri. (Pakistan; Nepal; India; Bangladesh; Burma.)

PLATE 16

Mystus nemurus. (East Indies; Malaya; Indo-China; Thailand.)

Mystus nemurus. (East Indies; Malaya; Indo-China; Thailand.)

Mystus wyckii. (Sumatra and Java to Thailand.)

Mystus wyckii. (Sumatra and Java to Thailand.)

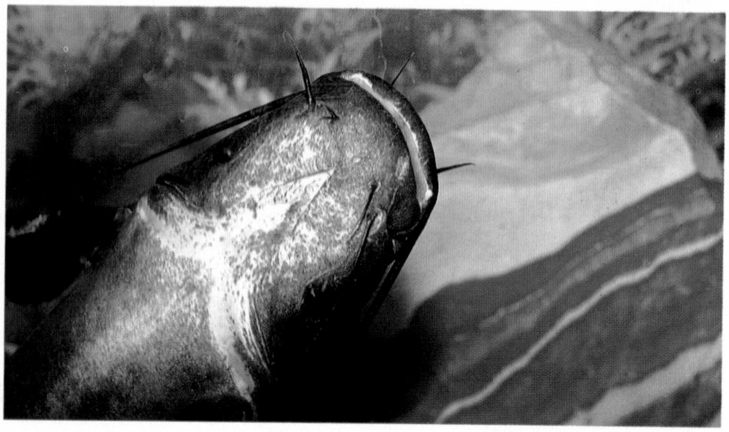

Mystus sp. (Unknown.)

Mystus nemurus, 81.3 mm. (East Indies; Malaya; Indo-China; Thailand.)

Mystus vittatus, 83.1 mm. (Pakistan to Malaya.)

Mystus sp. cf. *micracanthus*, 39.9 mm. (Malaysia; Thailand.)

Mystus micracanthus. (Malaysia; Thailand.)

Mystus bleekeri, 67.6 and 66.4 mm. (Pakistan; India; Nepal; Bangladesh; Burma.)

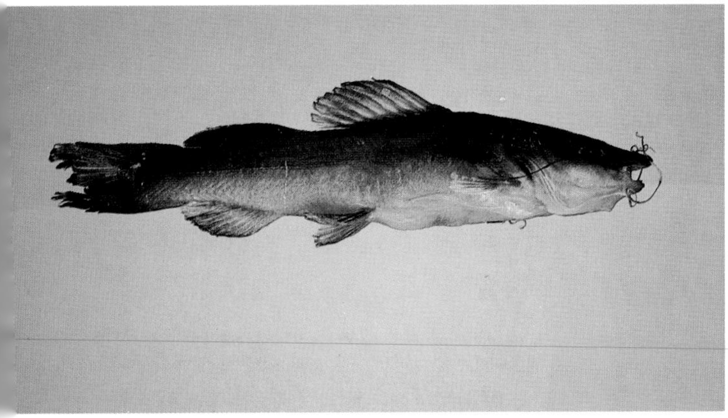

Mystus wolfii, 89.5 mm. (Sumatra and Java to Thailand.)

Mystus sabanus, 97.4 mm. (North Borneo.)

Mystus nigriceps. (Borneo to Thailand.)

Mystus cavasius, 85 mm. (Pakistan to Borneo.)

Mystus pulcher, 63 mm. Rangoon.

Mystus bleekeri, 87.1 mm. (Pakistan; Nepal: India; Bangladesh; Burma.)

PLATE 18

Bagrus ubangensis from the Zaire River system attains a length of about 30 cm. The dark body spots are common in species of *Bagrus*.

Bagroides melapterus ranges from Sumatra and Borneo to Thailand. It has a magnificant pattern that should please almost any aquarist. According to Weber & de Beaufort (1913) it should reach a length of about 34 cm.

Bagrus orientalis(?) attains a length of about 35 cm. This specimen is about half that size. It was captured in Lake Malawi.

Kryptopterus bicirrhis. (Java, Sumatra, and Borneo to Thailand.)

Kryptopterus macrocephalus. (Sumatra: Borneo.)

Ompok eugeneiatus. (Sumatra; Borneo.)

Kryptopterus bicirrhis. (Java, Sumatra, and Borneo to Thailand.)

Kryptopterus bicirrhis. (Java, Sumatra, and Borneo to Thailand.)

Kryptopterus cryptopterus. (Borneo and Sumatra to Thailand.)

Ompok eugeneiatus. (Sumatra: Borneo.)

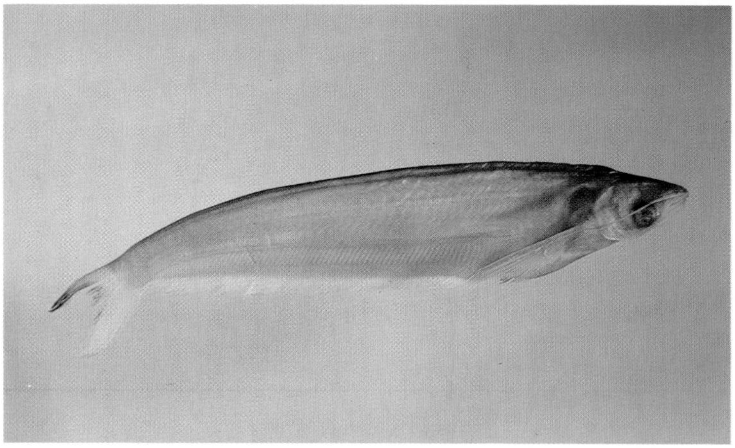

Kryptopterus cryptopterus, 104.9 mm. (Borneo and Sumatra to Thailand.)

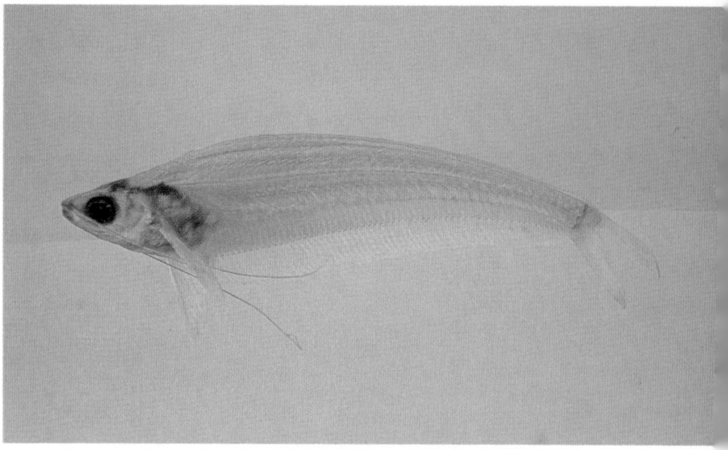

Kryptopterus lais, 71.0 mm. (Borneo.)

Kryptopterus bicirrhis, 120.0 mm. (Java, Sumatra, and Borneo to Thailand.)

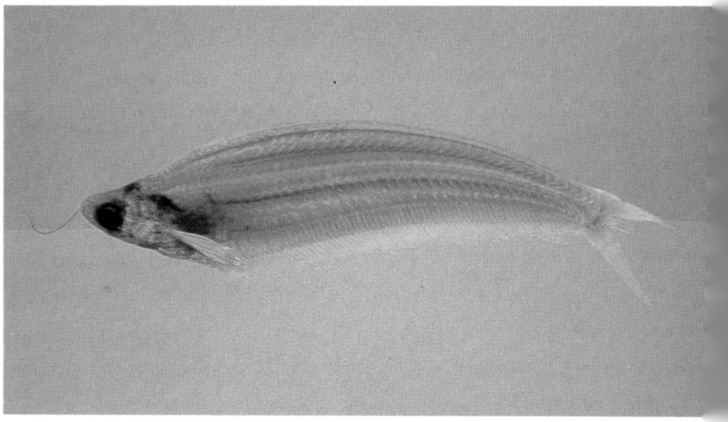

Kryptopterus schilbeides, 56.6 mm. (Sumatra; Borneo.)

Kryptopterus macrocephalus, 41.2 mm. (Sumatra; Borneo.)

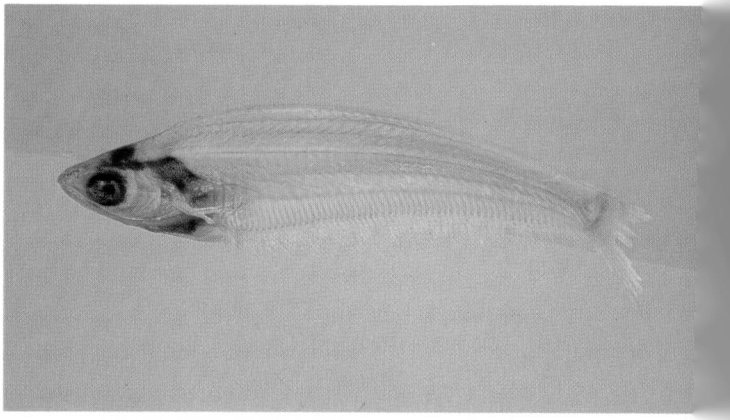

Kryptopterus sp. cf. *bicirrhis*, 56.6 mm. (Unknown.)

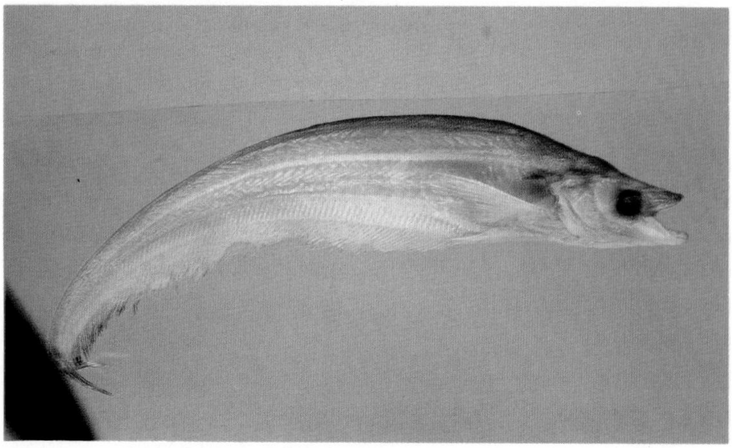

Kryptopterus micronema, 140.0 mm. (Borneo to Thailand.)

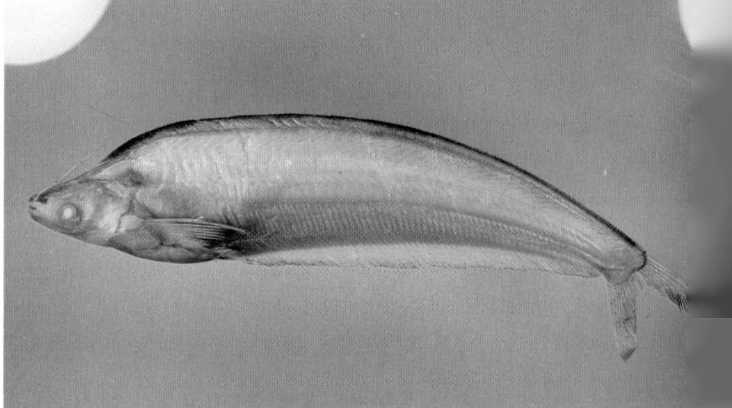

Kryptopterus cheveyi. (Cambodia.)

Kryptopterus macrocephalus. (Sumatra; Borneo.)

Kryptopterus bicirrhis. (Java, Sumatra, and Borneo to Thailand.)

Schilbe marmoratus. (Zaire basin.)

Kryptopterus lais. (Borneo.)

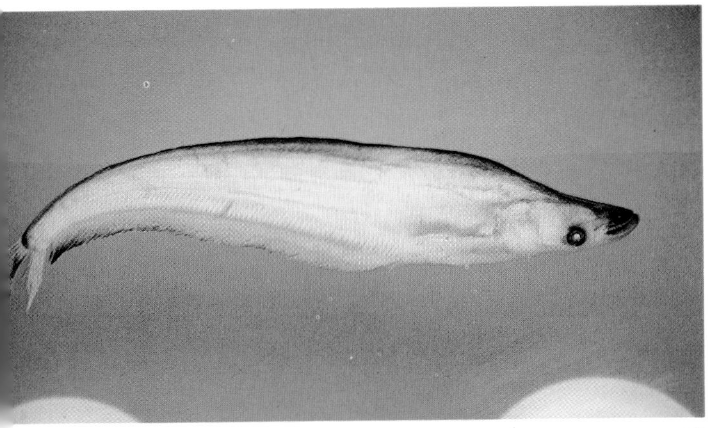

Kryptopterus bleekeri. (Indo-China; Thailand.)

Kryptopterus cryptopterus. (Borneo and Sumatra to Thailand.)

Kryptopterus apogon. (Sumatra and Borneo to Thailand.)

Kryptopterus apogon. (Sumatra and Borneo to Thailand.)

PLATE 22

Silurichthys phaiosoma. (Sumatra; Borneo; Malaya.)

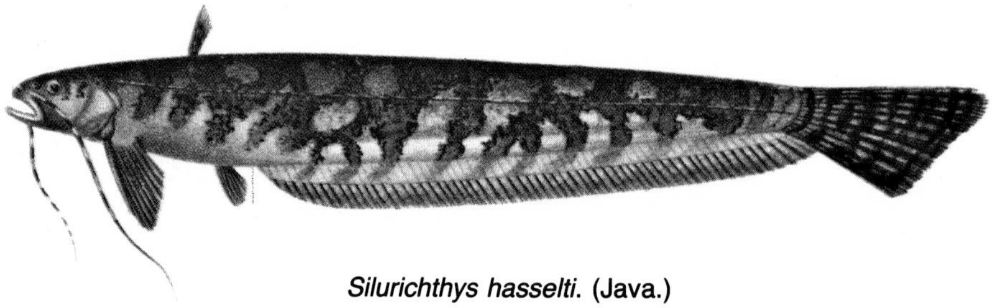

Silurichthys hasselti. (Java.)

Ceratoglanis scleronema. (Java; Borneo; Sumatra.)

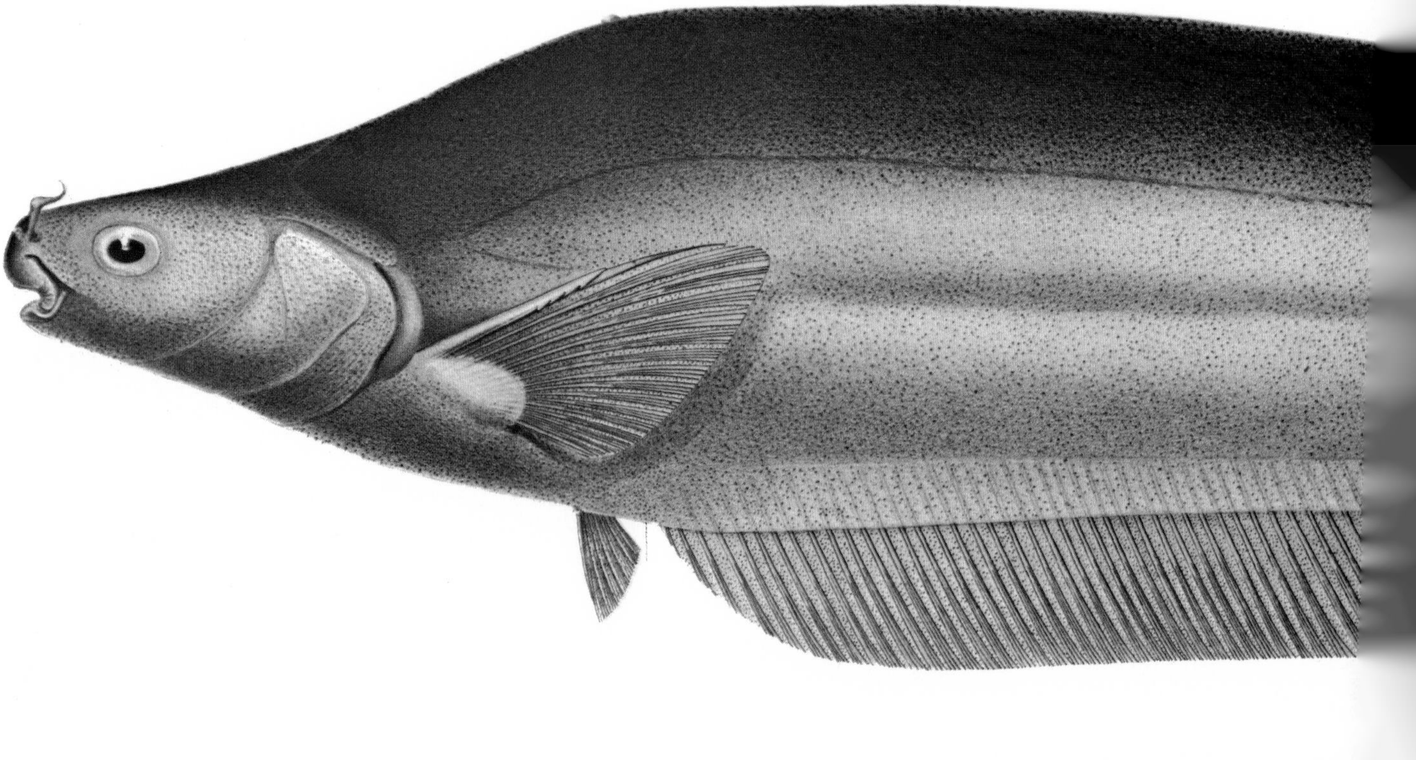

Silurus glanis. (Eastern and northern Europe and Asia Minor.)

Wallago leeri. (Sumatra; Borneo.)

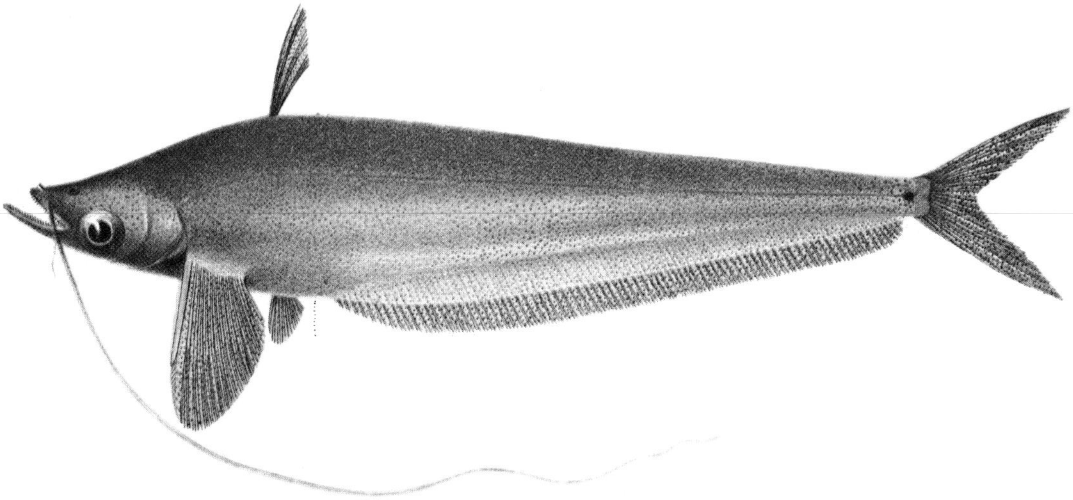

Ompok hypophthalmus. (Java; Sumatra; Borneo.)

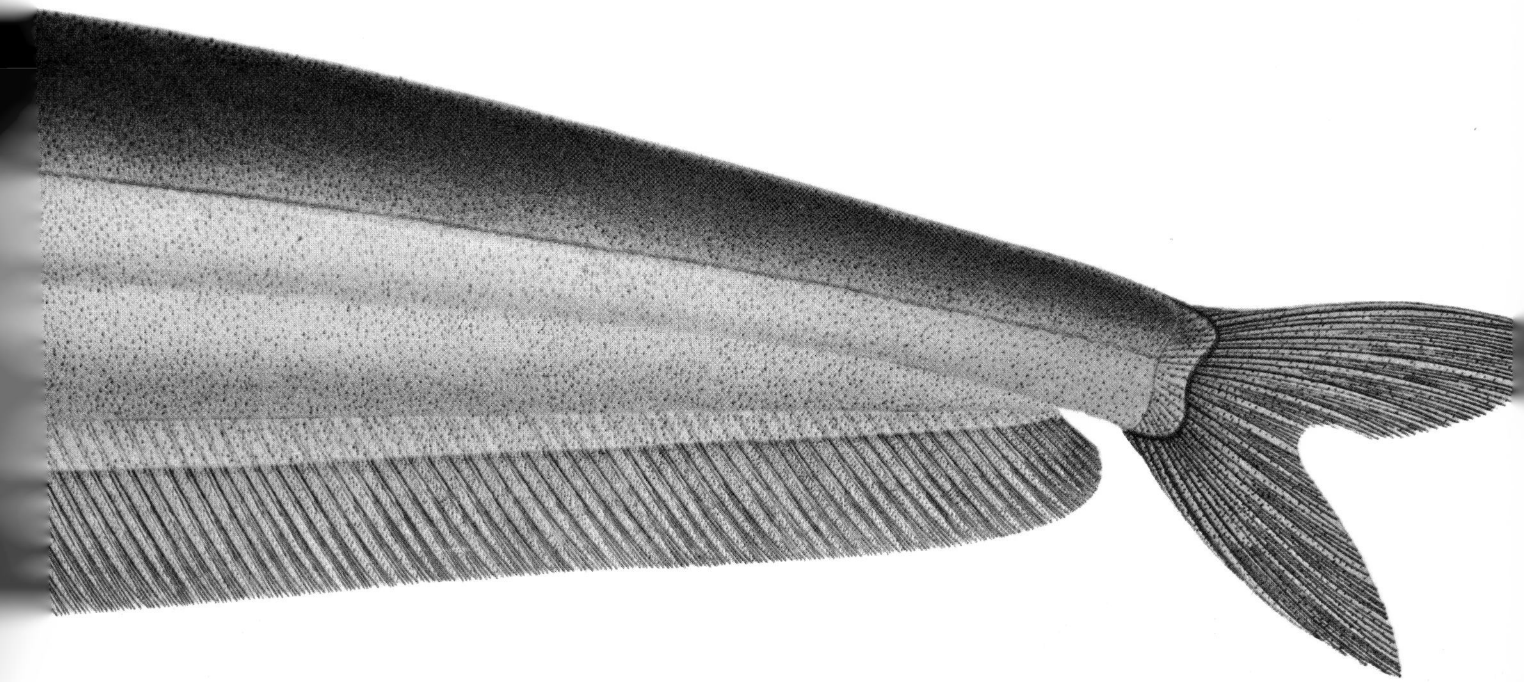

PLATE 23

Wallago leeri. (Sumatra; Borneo; Malaysia.)

Wallago attu. (India to Java and Sumatra.)

Ompok sp. (Unknown.)

Ompok bimaculatus. (Borneo to India.)

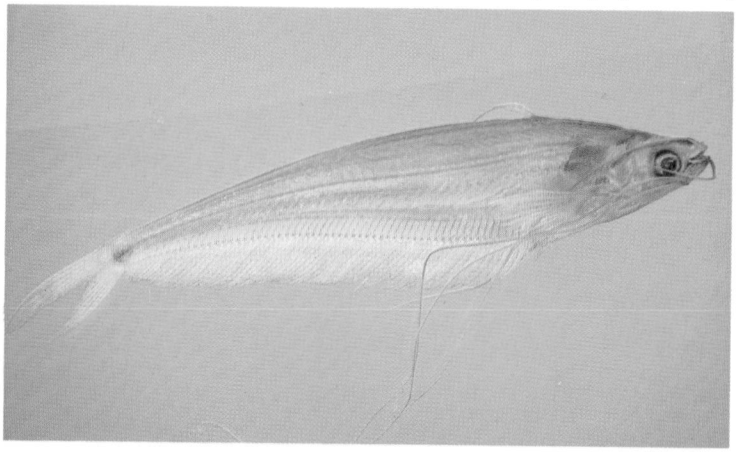

Ompok eugeneiatus. (Sumatra; Borneo.)

Ompok hypophthalmus. (Java; Sumatra; Borneo.)

Ompok leiacanthus. (Sumatra; Borneo.)

Ompok eugeneiatus. (Sumatra; Borneo.)

Belodontichthys dinema. (Borneo to Thailand.)

Silurus (Parasilurus) asotus. (Asia.)

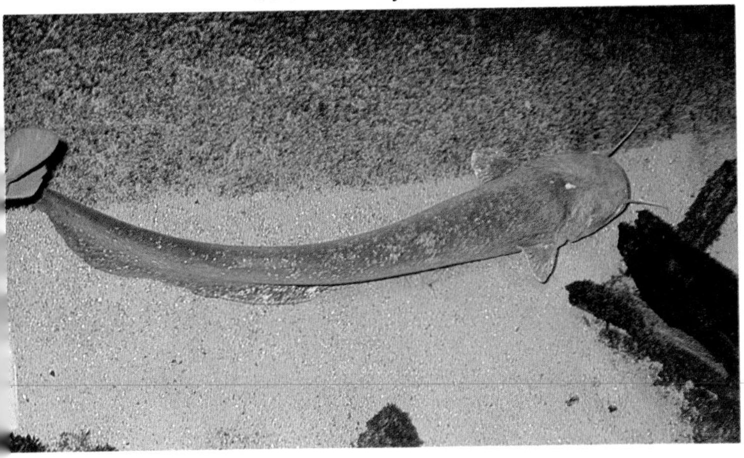

Silurus glanis. (Eastern and northern Europe and Asia Minor.)

Silurus glanis. (Eastern and northern Europe and Asia Minor.)

Silurus cochinchinensis, 101.1 mm. (Southeast Asia.)

Silurus lithophilus. (Unknown.)

Silurichthys hasselti, 75.7 mm. (Java.)

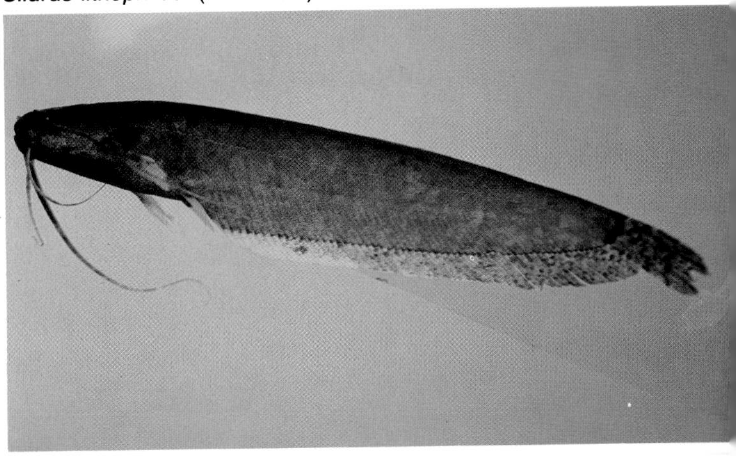

Silurichthys sp. (possibly *phaiosoma*). (Southeast Asia.)

PLATE 25

Siluranodon auritus. Niger.

Platytropius siamensis. (Thailand.)

Parailia congica. (Zaire; Niger.)

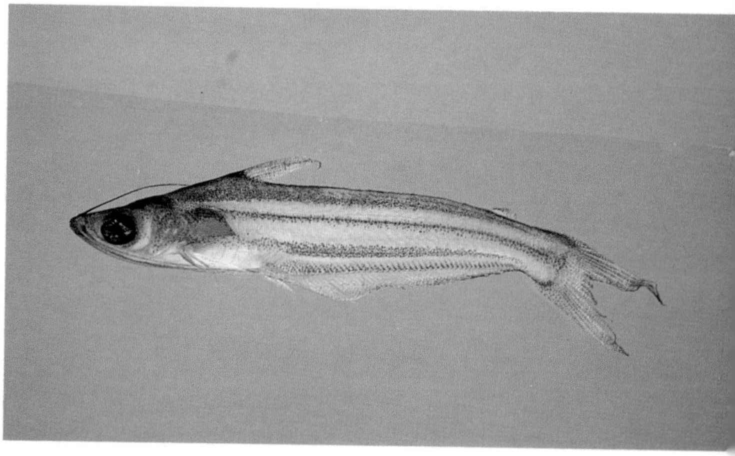

Pseudeutropius moolenburghae, 61.5 mm. (Sumatra.)

Pseudeutropius moolenburghae, 82.5 mm. (Sumatra.)

Pseudeutropius brachypopterus, 82.5 mm. (Sumatra; Borneo.)

Eutropiellus buffei. (Lower course of the Oueme, the Ogun, and Niger.)

Eutropiellus buffei. (Lower course of the Oueme, the Ogun, and Niger.

Eutropiellus debauwi. (Zaire system; Chiloango River; Ogowe River.)

Parailia congica. (Zaire; Niger.)

Eutropiellus debauwi. (Zaire system; Chiloango River; Ogowe River.)

Eutropiellus debauwi. (Zaire system; Chiloango River; Ogowe River.)

Parailia cf. *congica*. (Tropical Africa.)

Schilbe mystus. (Widespread in tropical Africa.)

Parailia occidentalis. (Ogowe; Zaire; Quanza; Luculla; Chiloango.)

Parailia pellucida. (Upper Nile; West Africa.)

PLATE 27

Schilbe mystus. (Unknown.)

Clupisoma garua. (India; Pakistan; Nepal; Bangladesh.)

Platytropius siamensis. (Thailand.)

Pseudeutropius brachypopterus. (Sumatra; Borneo.)

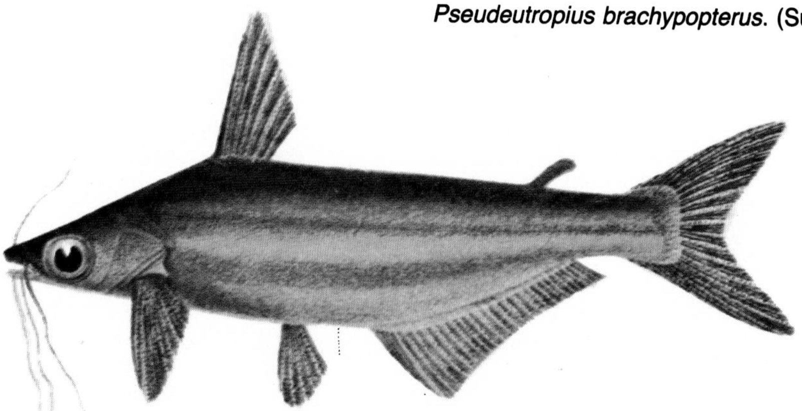

Schilbe marmoratus. (Zaire basin.)

Schilbe marmoratus. (Zaire basin.)

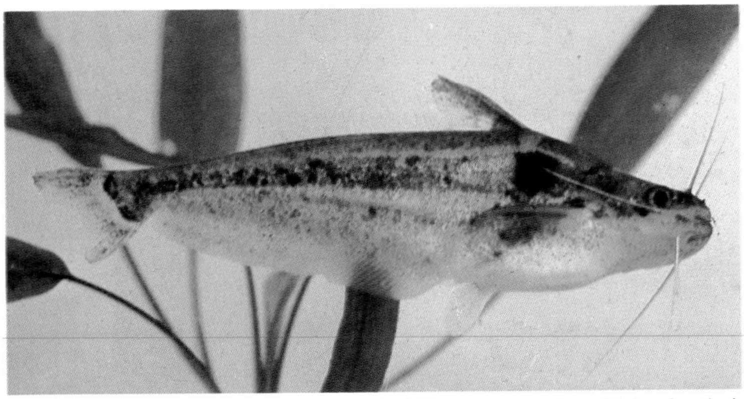

Schilbe marmoratus. (Zaire basin.)

Schilbe uranoscopus. (Nile, Niger, Chad, Cross, Turkana system.)

Schilbe mystus. Kutu, Zaire.

Schilbe mystus. (Widespread in tropical Africa.)

Schilbe mystus. (Widespread in tropical Africa.)

Schilbe mystus. (Widespread in tropical Africa.)

Pangasianodon gigas. (Mekong River.)

Pangasianodon gigas (juv.), 80.0 mm. (Mekong River.)

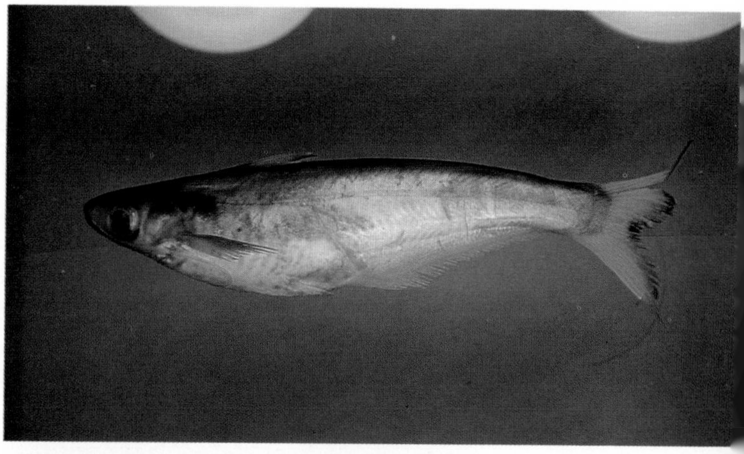

Pteropangasius cultratus, 145 mm. (Thailand.)

?*Helicophagus waandersi*. (Sumatra.)

?*Laides hexanema*. (Unknown.)

Pangasius sutchi. (Thailand.)

Pangasius sutchi. (Thailand.)

Pangasius sutchi. (Thailand.)

Pangasius pangasius. (Pakistan to Java.)

Pangasius sp. (*micronemus*?). (Unknown.)

Pangasius larnaudi. (Southeast Asia.)

Pangasius sanitswongi. (Thailand.)

Pangasius sanitswongi. (Thailand.)

PLATE 31

One of the most popular pangasiids in the aquarium trade is *Pangasius sutchi*. It is called the Iridescent Shark by aquarists.

PLATE 32

Pangasius sp. (Unknown.) *Pangasianodon gigas*. (Mekong River.)

Laides hexanema. (Java; Sumatra; Borneo.)

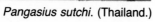

Pangasius sutchi. (Thailand.)

Amblyceps mangois. (India to Thailand.)

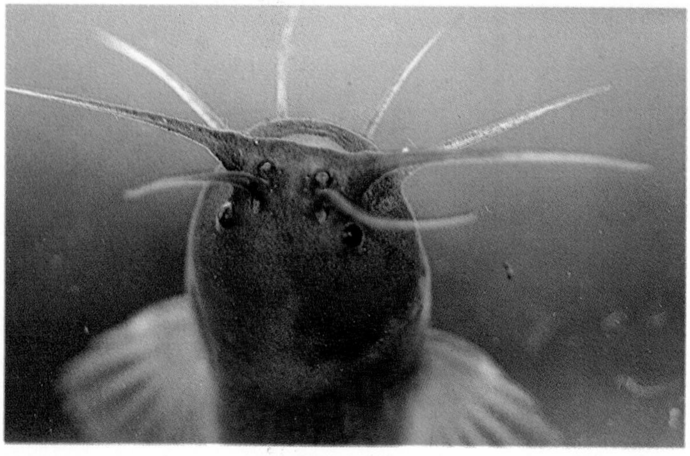

Amblyceps mangois. (India to Thailand.)

Amblyceps mangois. (India to Thailand.)

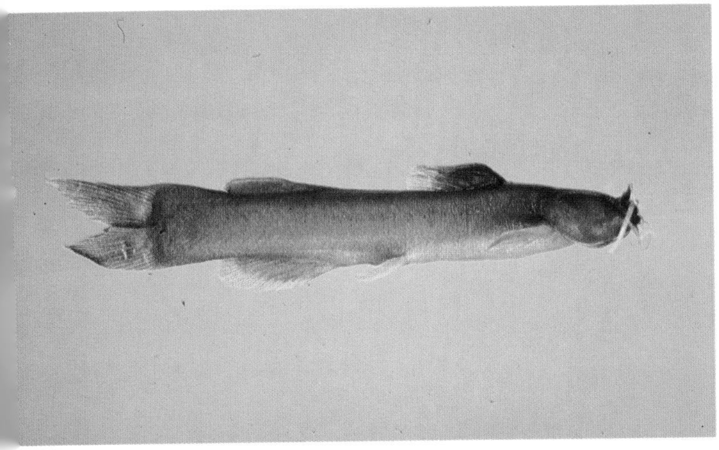

Amblyceps mangois. (India to Thailand.)

Leiobagrus reini. (Japan.)

?*Amphilius* sp. (Africa.)

Amphilius sp. Sio River, Kenya.

Amphilius grandis. Upper Athi River, Kenya.

Amphilius grandis. Upper Athi River, Kenya.

Phractura sp. cf. *intermedia*. (Tropical Africa.)

Amphilius longirostris. Rio Muni.

PLATE 34

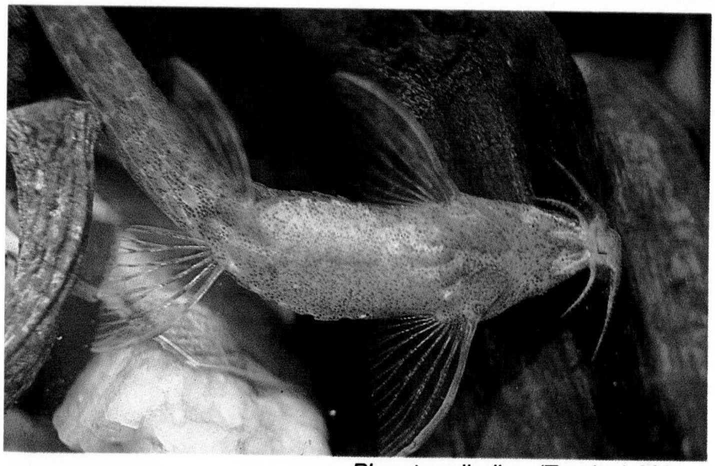
Phractura lindica. (Tropical Africa.)

Phractura lindica. (Tropical Africa.)

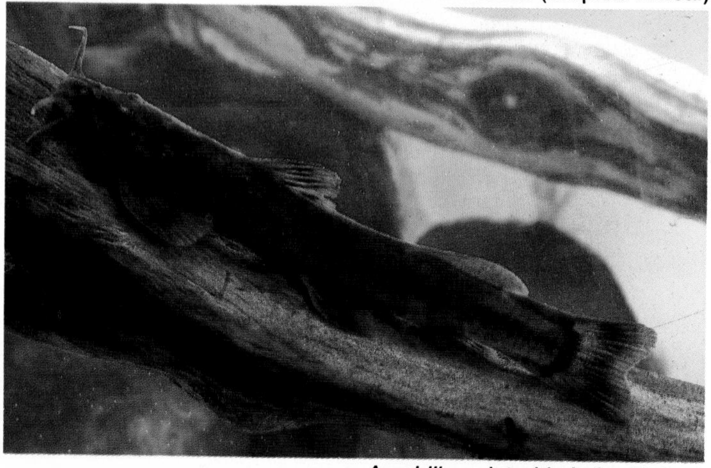
Amphilius platychir. Lake Malawi.

Amphilius atesuensis. (Guinea and Sierra Leone to Ghana.)

Amphilius platychir. Lake Malawi.

Phractura ansorgii. (Lower Niger.)

Phractura ansorgii. (Lower Niger.)

Phractura ansorgii (fry). (Lower Niger).

Phractura clauseni. Camoe River, Upper Volta.

Trachyglanis minutus. (Zaire River system.)

Phractura lindica? (Africa.)

Phractura lindica? (Africa.)

Phractura intermedia. Rio Muni.

Phractura longicauda. Rio Muni.

Belonoglanis tenuis. (Zaire system.)

Belonoglanis tenuis. (Zaire system.)

Doumea typica. (Zaire River system and coastal rivers from Cameroon to Congo.)

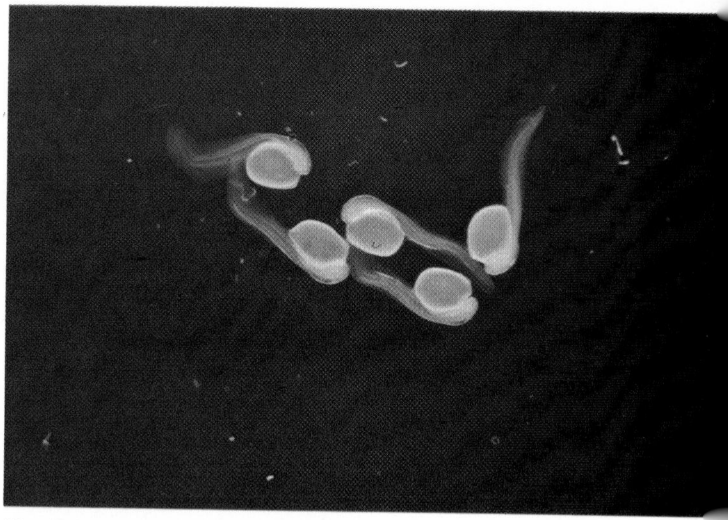

Newly hatched *Phractura ansorgii*.

Phractura sp. (Africa.)

Akysis variegatus, 30.8 mm. (Java.)

Akysis brachybarba, 34.5 mm. (Unknown.)

Akysis hendricksoni. (Malaya.)

Akysis leucorhynchus. (Thailand.)

Akysis prashadi? (Upper Burma.)

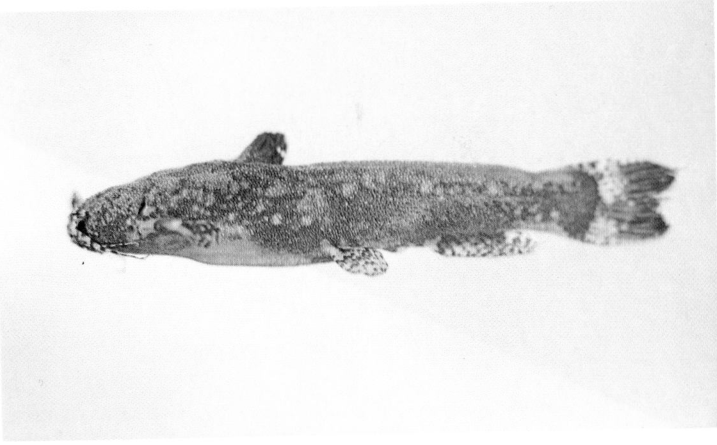

Parakysis verrucosus, 56.3 mm. (Johore.)

?*Glyptothorax telchitta*. (Unknown.)

Breitensteinia insignis, 75.3 mm. (Borneo, Sumatra.)

PLATE 38

Acrochordonichthys sp., 104.0 mm. (Sumatra, Java.)

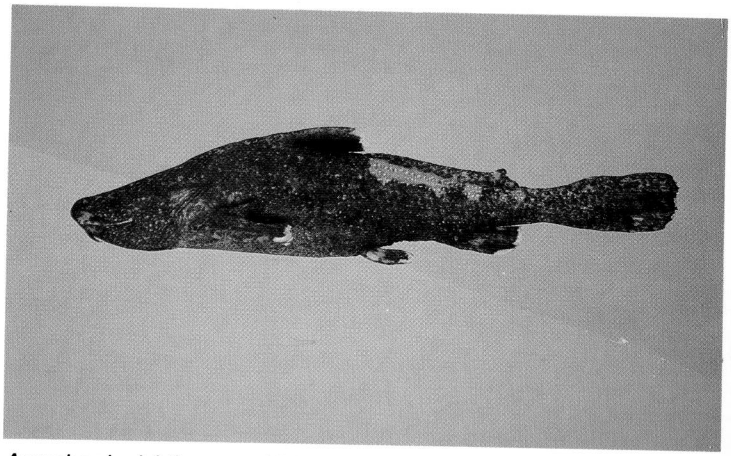

Acrochordonichthys sp., 104.0 mm. (Sumatra, Java.)

Acrochordonichthys rugosus. (Sumatra, Java.)

Acrochordonichthys rugosus. (Sumatra, Java.)

Gagata schmidti. (Sumatra.)

Gagata cenia, 88.0 mm. (India; Burma; Nepal; Pakistan; Bangladesh.)

Glyptosternon reticulatum. (Afghanistan.)

Gagata schmidti. (Sumatra.)

Hara hara. (Nepal.)

Hara hara. (Nepal.)

Conta conta (male). (Northeastern Bengal.)

Conta conta (female). (Northeastern Bengal.)

Bagarius bagarius. (Pakistan to Thailand.)

Bagarius bagarius. (Pakistan to Thailand.)

Glyptothorax trilineatus. (India; Burma; Nepal; Thailand; Laos.)

Glyptothorax telchitta. (India; Nepal; Bangladesh.)

PLATE 40

Hara hara, 47.4 mm. (Nepal.)

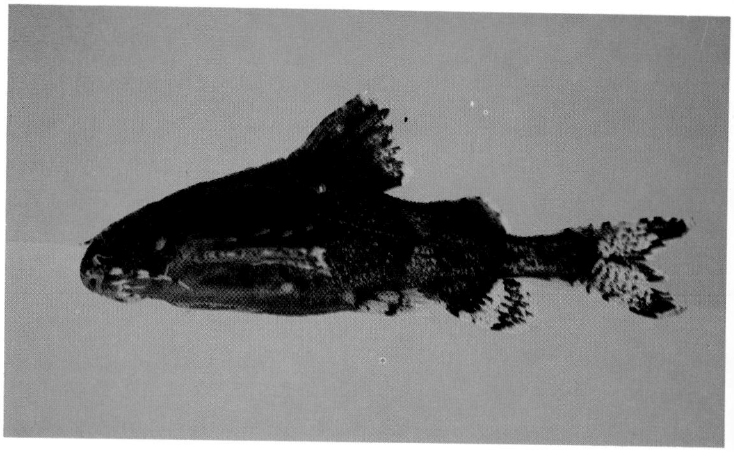

Hara hara, 47.4 mm. (Nepal.)

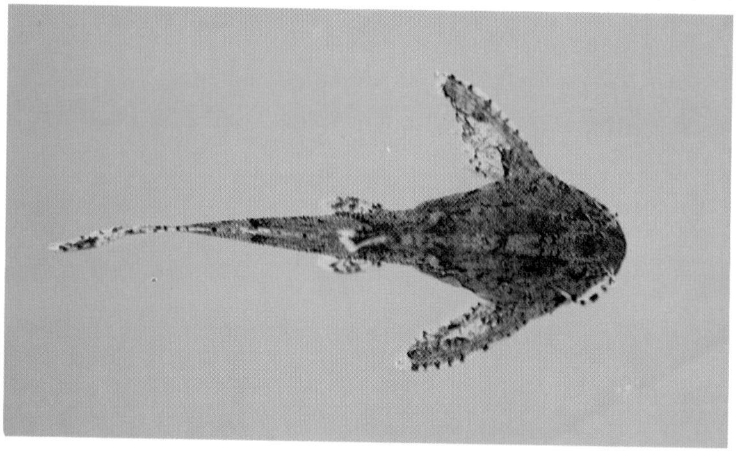

Hara hara (juv.), 27.5 mm. (Nepal.)

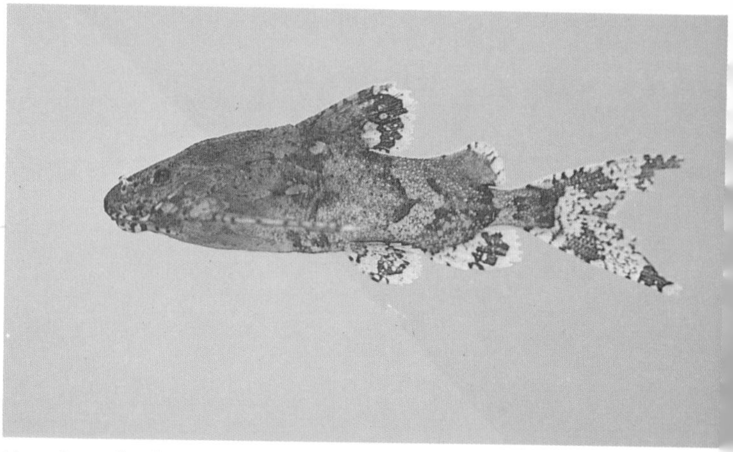

Hara hara (juv.), 27.5 mm. (Nepal.)

Exostoma berdmorei, 65.4 mm. (Burma.)

Exostoma berdmorei, 65.4 mm. (Burma.)

Erethistes maesotensis. (Thai-Burmese border river.)

Erethistes maesotensis. (Thai-Burmese border river.)

Oreoglanis siamensis, 79.5 and 90.5 mm. (Thailand.)

Pseudecheneis sulcatus, 85.0 mm. (India; Burma; Nepal.)

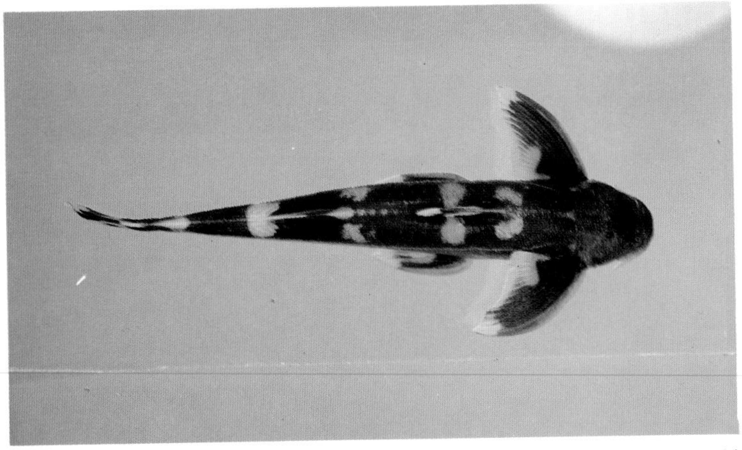

Pseudecheneis sulcatus, 85.0 mm. (India; Burma; Nepal.)

Pseudecheneis sulcatus, 85.0 mm. (India; Burma; Nepal.)

Euchiloglanis longicauda, 129.0 mm. (Unknown-Southeast Asia.)

Euchiloglanis longicauda, 129.0 mm. (Unknown-Southeast Asia.)

Euchiloglanis kamengensis. (India.)

Euchiloglanis kamengensis. (India.)

PLATE 42

Bagarius bagarius. (Pakistan to Thailand.)

Bagarius bagarius. (Pakistan to Thailand.)

Bagarius bagarius. (Pakistan to Thailand.)

Bagarius bagarius. (Pakistan to Thailand.)

Bagarius suchus. (Thailand.)

Bagarius suchus. (Thailand.)

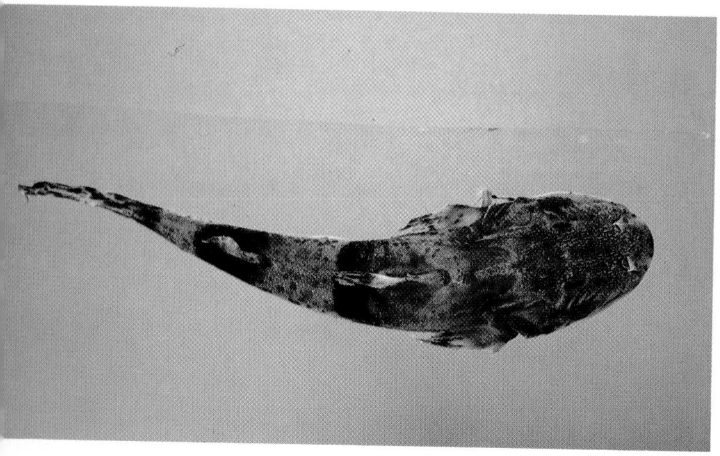

Bagarius yarrelli, 97.0 mm. (India.)

Bagarius yarrelli, 97.0 mm. (India.)

Glyptothorax telchitta. (India; Nepal; Bangladesh.)

Glyptothorax telchitta. (India; Nepal; Bangladesh.)

Glyptothorax trilineatus. (India; Burma; Nepal; Thailand; Laos.)

Glyptothorax sp. (India?)

Glyptothorax trilineatus. (India; Burma; Nepal: Thailand; Laos.)

Glyptothorax sp. (India?)

Glyptothorax platypogonides, 74.0 and 73.7 mm. (Sumatra.)

Glyptothorax platypogon. (Java.)

PLATE 44

Glyptothorax minimaculatus, 61.2 mm. (Unknown.)

Glyptothorax minimaculatus, 61.2 mm. (Unknown.)

Glyptothorax zainaensis, 78.0 mm. Yangbi River, China.

Glyptothorax zainaensis, 78.0 mm. Yangbi River, China.

Glyptothorax macromaculatus. (Unknown.)

Glyptothorax macromaculatus. (Unknown.)

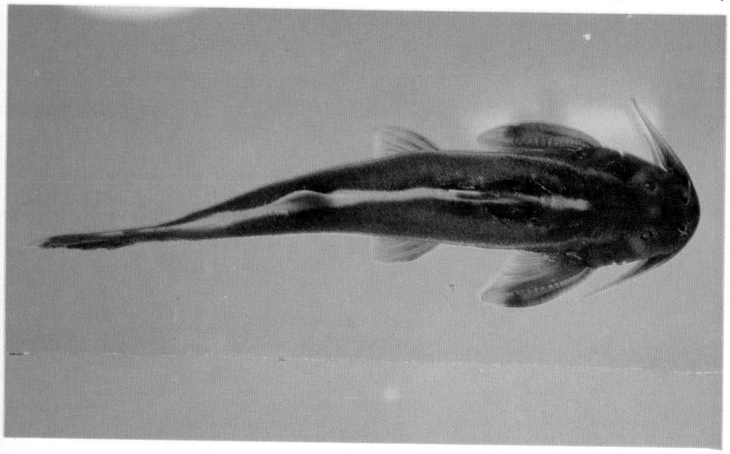

Glyptothorax laoensis, 85.2 mm. Yangbi River, China.

Glyptothorax laoensis, 85.2 mm. Yangbi River, China.

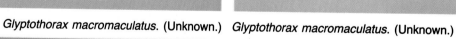

Glyptothorax cavia, 69.3 mm. (India; Nepal; Burma.) *Glyptothorax cavia*, 69.3 mm. (India; Nepal; Burma.)

Glyptothorax lampris, 57.4 mm. (Thailand.) *Glyptothorax lampris*, 57.4 mm. (Thailand.)

Glyptothorax sp., 71.0 mm. (Unknown.) *Glyptothorax* sp., 71.0 mm. (Unknown.)

Glyptothorax major, 78.0 mm. (Borneo.) *Glyptothorax major*, 78.0 mm. (Borneo.)

PLATE 46

Clarias angolensis. (Lower and Central Zaire system.)

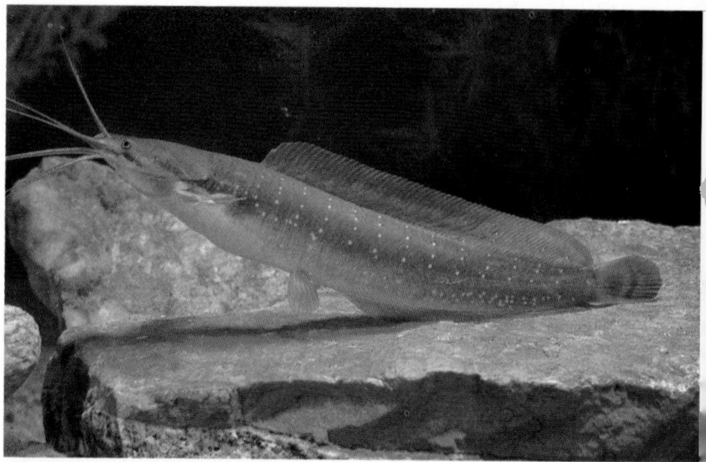

Clarias angolensis. (Lower and Central Zaire system.)

Channallabes apus. (Zaire system.)

Gymnallabes typus. (Niger River to Cameroon.)

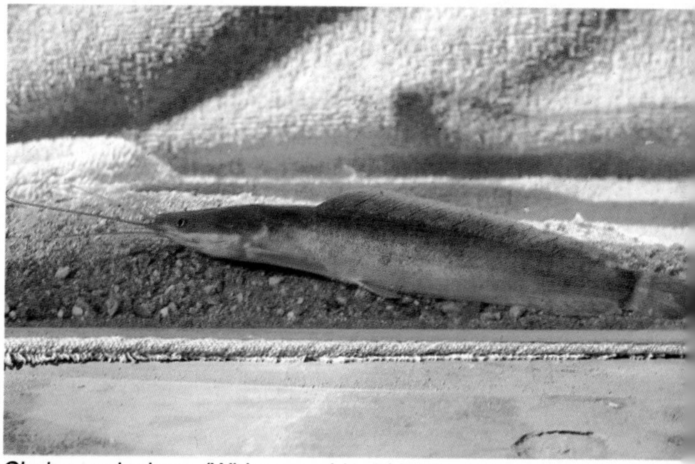

Clarias gariepinus. (Widespread in Africa.)

Gymnallabes typus. (Niger River to Cameroon.)

Gymnallabes typus. (Niger River to Cameroon.)

Clarias camerunensis. Rio Muni.

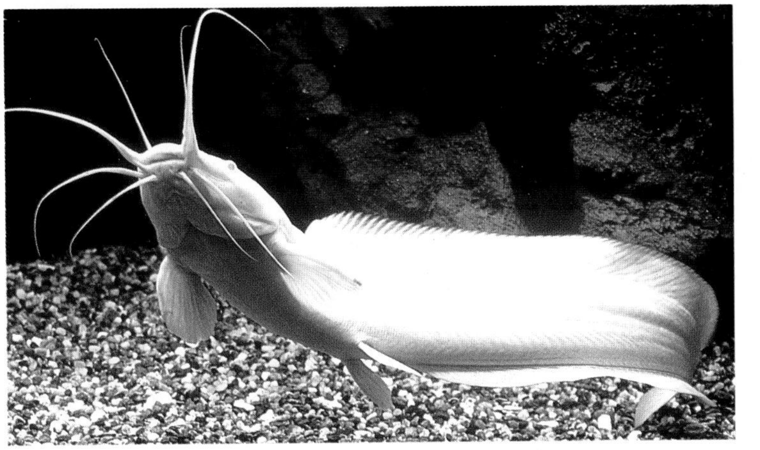

Clarias batrachus (albino). (Southeast Asia.)

Clarias gariepinus. (Widespread in Africa.)

Clarias gariepinus. (Widespread in Africa.)

Clarias sp. Lake Mineru Wantipa, Zambia.

Clarias sp. (Unknown.)

Clarias buthupogon. Rio Muni.

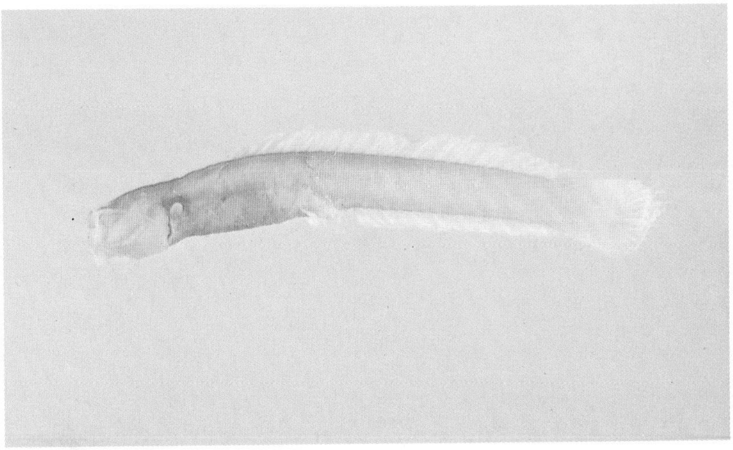

Horaglanis krishnai. (India.)

PLATE 48

Clarias sp. (Unknown.) *Clarias* sp. (Unknown.)

Heterobranchus longifilis. Ghana.

Heterobranchus longifilis. (Nile, Niger, Senegal, Zaire system, upper and middle Zambezi.)

Chaca bankanensis. (Sumatra; Borneo.)

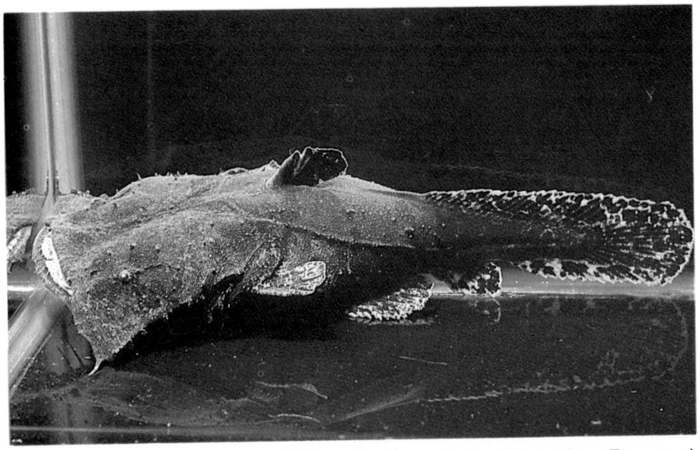

Chaca bankanensis. (Sumatra; Borneo.)

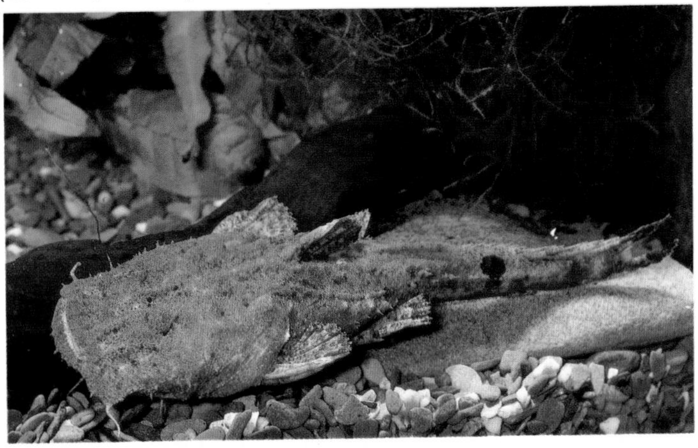

Chaca chaca. (India.)

Chaca bankanensis. (Sumatra; Borneo.)

Chaca bankanensis. (Sumatra; Borneo.)

PLATE 50

Heteropneustes fossilis. (Southeast Asia.)

Heteropneustes fossilis. (Southeast Asia.)

Chaca bankanensis. (Sumatra: Borneo.)

Chaca bankanensis. (Sumatra; Borneo.)

Malapterurus electricus (albino). (Tropical Africa.)

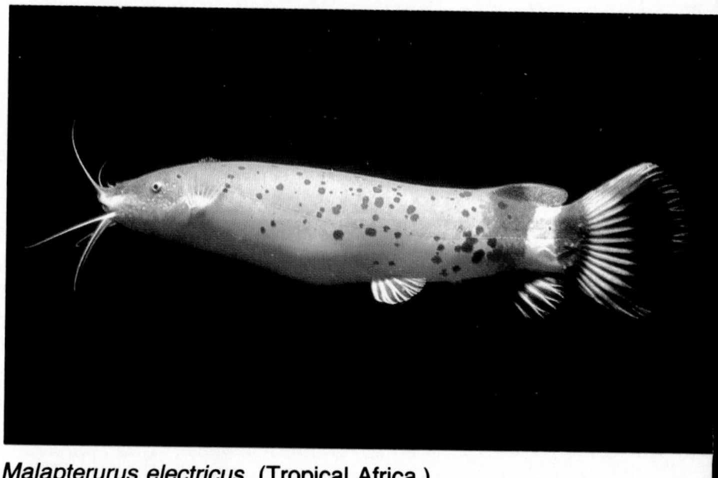

Malapterurus electricus. (Tropical Africa.)

Malapterurus electricus. (Tropical Africa.)

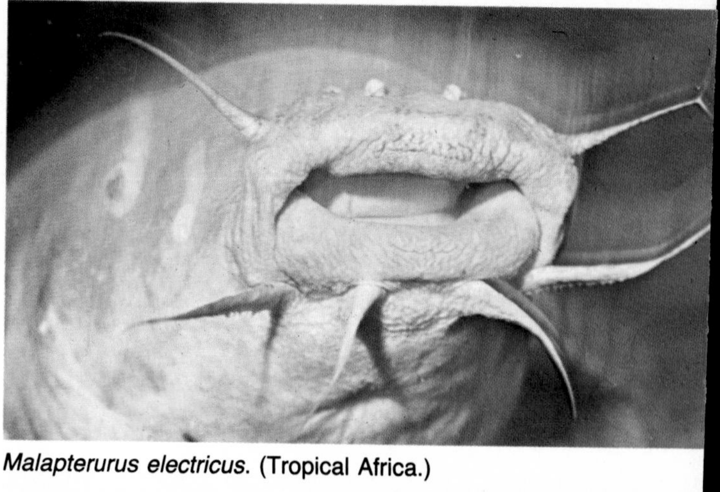

Malapterurus electricus. (Tropical Africa.)

Arius leptaspis. (Southwestern New Guinea.)

Arius bernayi. (Northern Australia; southern New Guinea.)

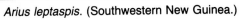

Arius graeffei. Prince Regent River, Australia.

PLATE 52

Arius graeffei. (Australia.)

Arius bernayi. (Northern Australia; southern New Guinea.)

Arius sp. Cape York, Australia.

Arius sp. (Australia.)

Arius jordani?. (Tropical East Pacific.)

Arius sp. (Unknown.)

Hemipimelodus borneensis. (Borneo.)

Arius felis. (Tropical Western Atlantic.)

Hemipimelodus papillifer. (Sepik River, New Guinea.)

Arius "leptaspis". (Australia.)

Arius sp. (Australia.)

Arius sp. (Australia.)

Arius nox. (Sepik River, New Guinea.)

Hemipimelodus velutinus. (New Guinea.)

Arius solidus. (Sepik River, New Guinea.)

Arius stirlingi. (Australia.)

PLATE 54

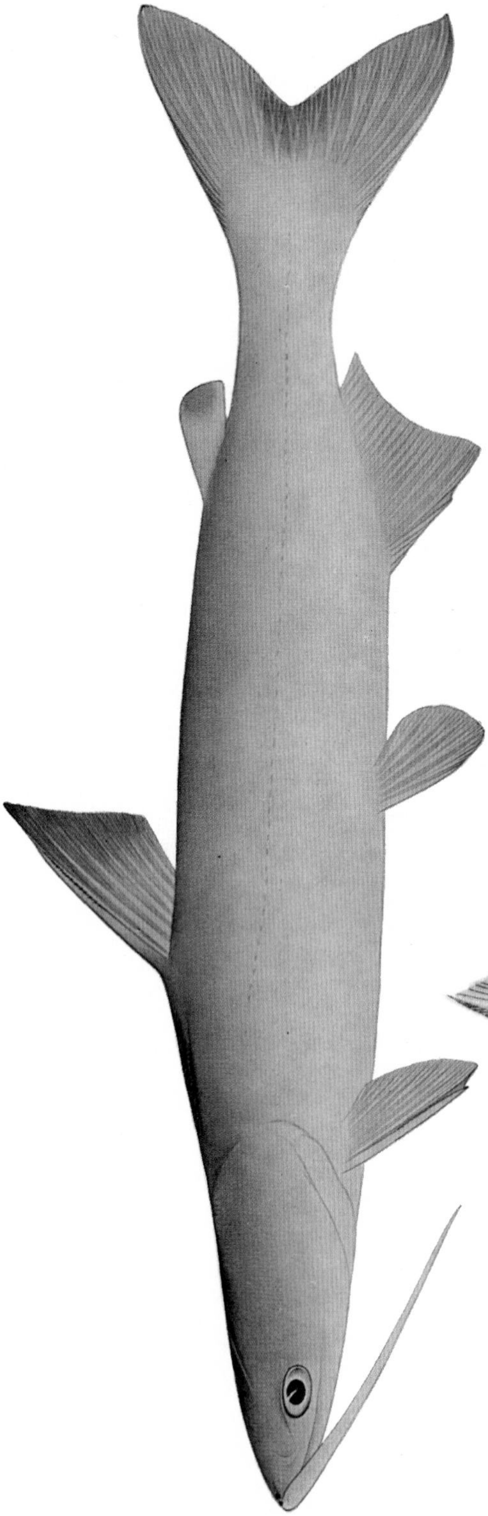

Osteogeneiosus militaris. (Southeast Asia.)

Arius leptonotacanthus. Madura Sea near Surabaya.

Arius jordani juveniles are commonly imported for the aquarium trade.

PLATE 56

Arius leptaspis. (Southwestern New Guinea.)

Batrachocephalus mino. (Java, Sumatra, Borneo, to India.)

Tandanus (Neosilurus) hyrtlii. (Australia.)

Porochilus obbesi. (New Guinea.)

Tandanus tandanus. (Australia.)

Tandanus (Neosilurus) ater. (Australia and southern New Guinea.)

Tandanus (Neosilurus) ater. (Australia and southern New Guinea.)

Tandanus (Neosilurus) sp. aff. *ater*. (Australia.)

PLATE 58

Tandanus (Neosilurus) ater. (Northern Australia and New Guinea.)

Tandanus (Neosilurus) ater. (Northern Australia and New Guinea.)

Tandanus (Neosilurus) hyrtlii. (Queensland, Australia.)

Tandanus (Neosilurus) hyrtlii. (Queensland, Australia.)

Tandanus (Neosilurus) hyrtlii. (Queensland, Australia.)

Porochilus rendahli. (Australia.)

Tandanus bostocki. (Southwestern Australia.)

Tandanus tandanus. (Australia.)

Anodontoglanis dahli. (Northern Australia.)

Tandanus (Neosilurus) brevidorsalis. (Southern New Guinea.)

Tandanus (Neosilurus) ater. (Northern Australia and New Guinea.)

Tandanus (Neosilurus) hyrtlii. (Queensland, Australia.)

Tandanus (Neosilurus) argenteus. (Australia.)

Anodontoglanis dahli. (Northern Australia.)

Anodontoglanis dahli. (Northern Australia.)

Anodontoglanis dahli. (Northern Australia.)

Tandanus (Neosilurus) sp. (Australia.)

Tandanus (Neosilurus) sp. (Australia.)

Tandanus bostocki. (Southwestern Australia.)

Anodontoglanis dahli. (Australia.)

Porochilus rendahli. (Northern Australia.)

Anodontoglanis dahli. (Australia.)

Tandanus (Neosilurus) sp. Innesfail area, Queensland.

Tandanus (Neosilurus) sp. (Australia.)

Tandanus (Neosilurus) glencoensis. Scott's Creek, Northern Territory.

Tandanus (Neosilurus) sp. (Australia.)

Tandanus tandanus, 12 cm. Mulgrave River, Queensland.

Tandanus bostocki, 15 cm. Moon River, Western Australia.

PLATE 62

Oloplotosus luteus. (Fly River, New Guinea.)

Tandanus (Neosilurus) novaeguineae (female). (Irian Jaya.)

Tandanus (Neosilurus) sp. (New Guinea.)

Tandanus (Neosilurus) sp. (New Guinea.)

Tandanus (Neosilurus) brevidorsalis. Southern New Guinea.)

Porochilus obbesi. (New Guinea.)

Oloplotosus toboro. Lake Kutubu, New Guinea.

Tandanus sp. (Australia.)

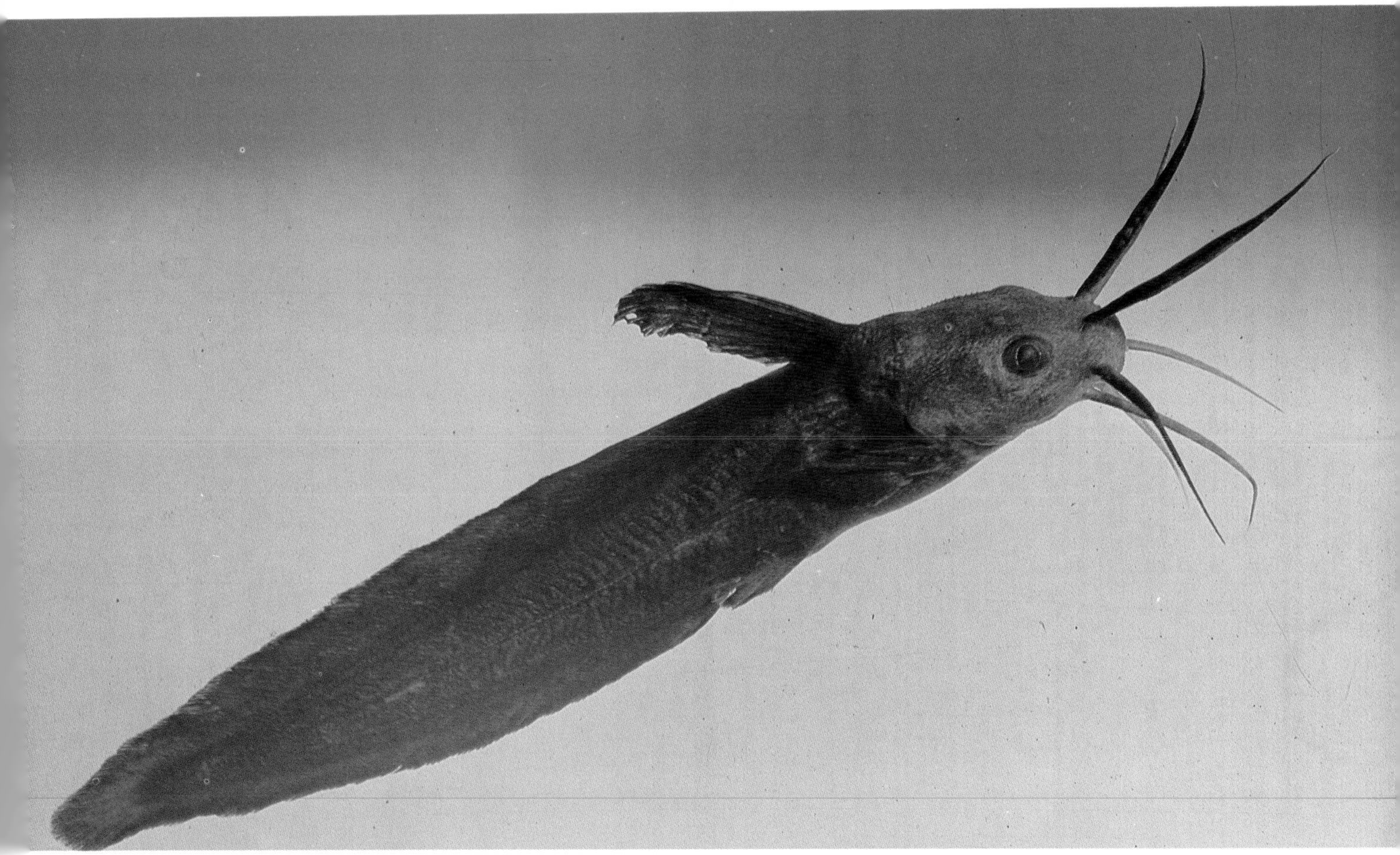

This Black Sailfin Catfish, *Paraplotosus* sp., was captured at North West Cape, Western Australia, at a depth of about three meters. It is 11 cm total length.

This is the White-lipped Catfish, *Paraplotosus albilabrus*. It is about 12 cm total length and was taken at Lady Nora Island, Dampier Archipelago, also at a depth of three meters.

PLATE 64

The barbel arrangement of *Plotosus lineatus.* Note the bronzy color of the stripes.

This is the normal behavior of young plotosids. This school of yellow-lined *Plotosus lineatus* will move over the reef floor stopping occasionally to feed.

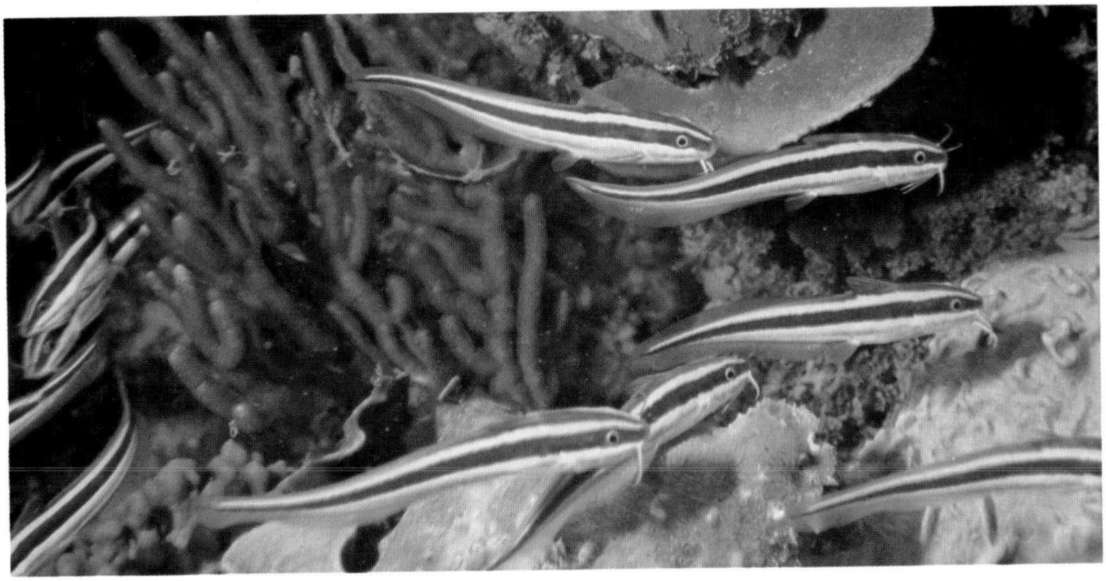

A white-lined form of *Plotosus lineatus* can also be found. The lines seem to be broader than those of the yellow ones.

Schools of *Plotosus lineatus* should be treated with respect as their dorsal and pectoral spines can cause painful wounds. They grow to almost a meter in length.

PLATE 66

Euristhmus lepturus. (Coastal Queensland and New South Wales.)

?Paraplotosus sp. (Australia.)

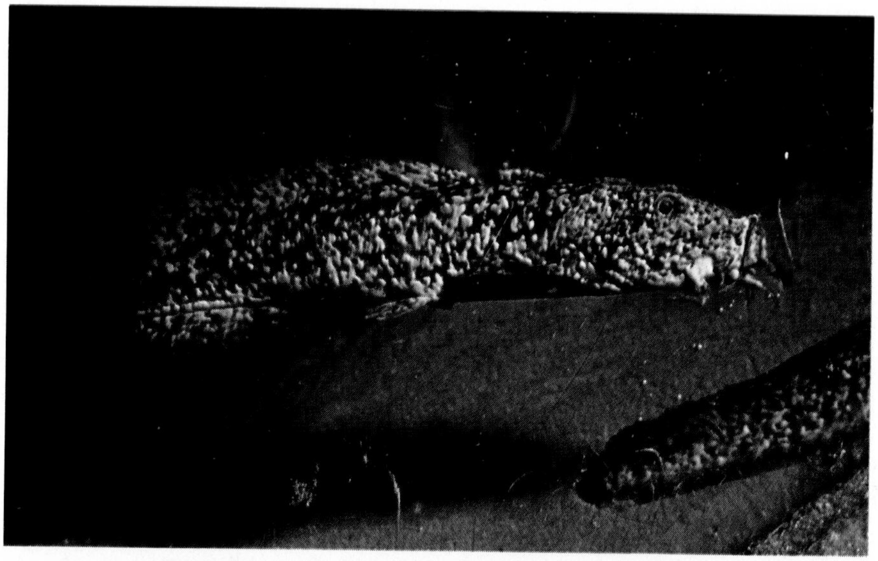

Cnidoglanis macrocephalus. (Australia; New Guinea.)

Cnidoglanis macrocephalus. Point Peron, Western Australia.

Chiloglanis deckeni?. (Kenya; Tanzania.)

Chiloglanis deckeni?. (Kenya; Tanzania.)

Chiloglanis paratus. (Southern Africa.)

Atopochilus macrocephalus. (Zaire Basin.)

Chiloglanis neumanni. (Tropical Africa.)

Atopochilus savorgnani. (Upper Ogowe, Rio Muni, southern Cameroon.)

PLATE 68

?*Euchilichthys* sp. (Zaire?)

?*Euchilichthys* sp. (Zaire?)

?*Euchilichthys* sp. (Zaire?)

Chiloglanis lukugae. (Luapula basin.)

Mochokiella paynei. (Sierra Leone.)

Mochokiella paynei. (Sierra Leone.)

Chiloglanis sp. Lupa River (Lake Rukwa).

Chiloglanis sp. Lupa River (Lake Rukwa).

Chiloglanis sp. Athi River, Athi, Kenya.

Chiloglanis sp. Athi River, Athi, Kenya.

Chiloglanis cameronensis. Rio Mami affluent, Rio Muni.

Chiloglanis neumanni. Wami River, Tanzania.

PLATE 70

Atopochilus savorgnani. Rio Muni.

Microsynodontis batesi. Rio Muni.

Synodontis pleurops. (Zaire basin.)

Synodontis sp. (Tropical Africa.)

Synodontis schoutedeni. (Central Zaire.)

Synodontis camelopardalis. (Central Zaire basin.)

Synodontis sp. cf. *macrostigma*. (Tropical Africa.)

Synodontis sp. (Tropical Africa.)

Synodontis nebulosus. (Zambezi basin.)

Synodontis soloni. (Zaire basin.)

Synodontis velifer. (Sassandra, Bandama, and Volta basins.)

Mochokiella paynei. (Sierra Leone.)

Mochokiella paynei. (Sierra Leone.)

Hemisynodontis membranaceus. (Nile, Chad, Niger, Senegal, Gambia, and Volta basins.)

Hemisynodontis membranaceus. (Nile, Chad, Niger, Senegal, Gambia, and Volta basins.)

PLATE 72

Synodontis brichardi is named for one of the foremost collectors of tropical fishes in Africa Pierre Brichard.

One of the distinguishing characters of *Synodontis* is their branched barbels. These can clearly be seen in this *S. schoutedeni*.

This wild-caught *Synodontis schoutedeni* exhibits a great deal of yellow. Other individuals of this species may not show any yellow at all.

PLATE 74

Synodontis multipunctatus. Lake Tanganyika.

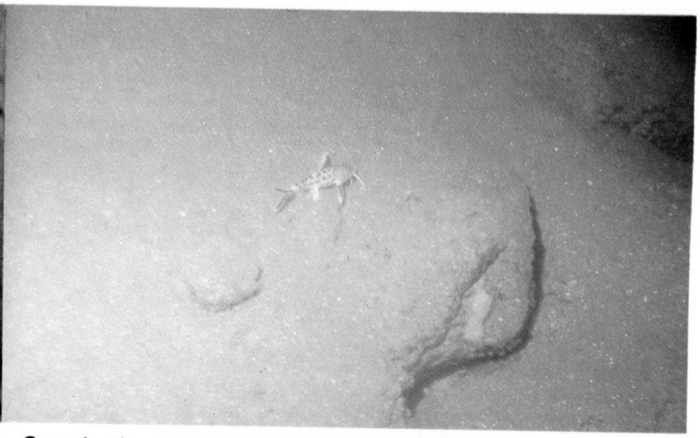

Synodontis multipunctatus. Lake Tanganyika.

Synodontis multipunctatus. (Lake Tanganyika.)

Synodontis petricola. (Lake Tanganyika.)

Synodontis polli. (Lake Tanganyika.)

Synodontis marmoratus. (Cameroon.)

Synodontis greshoffi. (Zaire basin.)

Synodontis nigrita. (Tropical Africa.)

Synodontis pleurops. (Zaire basin.)

Synodontis pleurops. (Zaire basin.)

Synodontis decorus. (Zaire basin.)

Synodontis flavitaeniatus. (Central Zaire.)

Synodontis caudovittatus? (Nile basin.)

Synodontis notatus. (Zaire basin.)

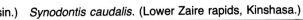

Synodontis contractus. (Zaire basin.)

Synodontis caudalis. (Lower Zaire rapids, Kinshasa.)

PLATE 76

Synodontis congicus. (Zaire basin.)

Synodontis cuangoanus. (Zaire basin.)

Synodontis centralis. (Central Zaire basin.)

Synodontis eburneensis. (Ivory Coast.)

Synodontis eupterus. (White Nile, Chad basin, Niger and Volta.)

Synodontis koensis. (Ivory Coast.)

Synodontis macrops. Uganda.)

Brachysynodontis batensoda. (Nile, Chad, Niger, Senegal, and Gambia basins.)

Synodontis petricola var. (Lake Tanganyika.)

Synodontis petricola. South Tanzania.

Synodontis polli. (Lake Tanganyika.)

Synodontis polli var. (Lake Tanganyika.)

Synodontis polli. Lake Tanganyika.

Hemisynodontis membranaceus. (Nile, Chad, Niger, Senegal, Gambia, and Volta basins.)

Brachysynodontis batensoda. (Nile, Chad, Niger, Senegal, and Gambia basins.)

Brachysynodontis batensoda. (Nile, Chad, Niger, Senegal, and Gambia basins.)

Synodontis multipunctatus. (Lake Tanganyika.)

Synodontis multipunctatus. (Lake Tanganyika.)

Synodontis petricola. (Lake Tanganyika.)

Synodontis polli. (Lake Tanganyika.)

Synodontis acanthomias. (Zaire basin.)

Synodontis nigromaculatus. (Tropical Africa.)

Synodontis nigromaculatus. (Tropical Africa.)

Synodontis robbianus. (Lower Niger and Cross River.)

Synodontis ornatipinnis (juv.). (Zaire system.)

Synodontis ornatipinnis. (Zaire system.)

Synodontis brichardi. (Lower Zaire rapids.)

Synodontis flavitaeniatus. (Central Zaire.)

Synodontis pleurops. (Zaire basin.)

Synodontis pleurops. (Zaire basin.)

Synodontis pleurops. (Zaire basin.)

Synodontis pleurops. (Zaire basin.)

PLATE 80

Synodontis angelicus. (Zaire basin.)

Synodontis angelicus. (Zaire basin.)

Synodontis angelicus. (Zaire basin.)

Synodontis angelicus. (Zaire basin.)

Synodontis brichardi. (Lower Zaire rapids.)

Synodontis brichardi. (Lower Zaire rapids.)

Synodontis brichardi. (Lower Zaire rapids.)

Synodontis ornatipinnis. (Zaire River system.)

Synodontis angelicus. (Zaire basin.)

Synodontis angelicus. (Zaire basin.)

Synodontis angelicus. (Zaire basin.)

Synodontis angelicus. (Zaire basin.)

Synodontis angelicus. (Zaire basin.)

Synodontis schoutedeni. (Central Zaire.)

Synodontis decorus. (Zaire basin.)

Synodontis ornatipinnis. (Zaire River system.)

PLATE 82

Synodontis eupterus. (White Nile, Chad basin, Niger and Volta.)

Synodontis robertsi. (Central Zaire.)

Synodontis longirostris. (Zaire basin.)

Synodontis longirostris. (Zaire basin.)

Synodontis longirostris. (Zaire basin.)

Synodontis nigromaculatus. Lake Tanganyika.

Synodontis njassae. (Lake Malawi.)

Synodontis nigromaculatus. Lake Tanganyika.

Synodontis nigromaculatus? (Tropical Africa.)

Synodontis omias. (Niger basin.)

Synodontis ocellifer. Nigeria.

Synodontis ocellifer. (West Africa, various river basins from Senegal to Chad.)

Synodontis filamentosus. (Nile, Chad, Niger and Volta basins.)

Synodontis polystigma. (Zaire, Luapula-Mwero basin.)

Synodontis robbianus. (Lower Niger and Cross River.)

Synodontis sp. cf. *schall*. (Tropical Africa.)

Synodontis acanthomias. (Zaire basin.)

Synodontis afrofischeri. Nile basin to Lake Victoria.)

Synodontis sp. cf. *schall*. (Tropical Africa.)

Synodontis sp. cf. *schall*. (Tropical Africa.)

Synodontis aterrimus. (Central Zaire basin.)

Synodontis caudalis. (Lower Zaire raoids, Kinshasa.)

Synodontis camelopardalis (juv.). (Central Zaire basin.)

Synodontis camelopardalis (juv.). (Central Zaire basin.)

Synodontis petricola. (Lake Tanganyika.)

Synodontis multipunctatus. (Lake Tanganyika.)

Synodontis longirostris. (Zaire basin.)

Synodontis sp. (Tropical Africa.)

Synodontis sp. (Tropical Africa.)

Synodontis sp. (Tropical Africa.)

Synodontis longirostris. (Zaire basin.)

Synodontis sp. (Tropical Africa.)

PLATE 86

Synodontis caudovittatus? (Nile basin.)

Synodontis resupinatus. (Niger basin.)

Synodontis notatus (var.). (Zaire basin.)

Synodontis notatus. (Zaire basin.)

Synodontis ocellifer. (West Africa, various river basins from Senegal to Chad.)

Synodontis batesii. Rio Kie, Rio Muni.

Synodontis victoriae. (Lake Victoria basin.)

Synodontis sp.. (Tropical Africa.)

Synodontis brichardi. (Lower Zaire rapids.)

Synodontis brichardi (juv.). (Lower Zaire rapids.)

Synodontis decorus. (Zaire basin.)

Synodontis angelicus. (Zaire basin.)

Synodontis angelicus. (Zaire basin.)

Synodontis angelicus. (Zaire basin.)

Synodontis sp. Miyombo River (Wami).

Synodontis sp. Miyombo River (Wami).

PLATE 88

Synodontis sp. (Tropical Africa.)

Synodontis greshoffi? (juv.). (Zaire basin.)

Synodontis sp. (tropical Africa.)

Synodontis greshoffi. (Zaire basin.)

Synodontis njassae. (Lake Malawi.)

Synodontis sp. (Tropical Africa.)

Synodontis sp. (Tropical Africa.)

Synodontis sp. (Tropical Africa.)

Synodontis nigriventris. (Central Zaire basin.)

Synodontis contractus. (Zaire basin.)

Synodontis robbianus. (Lower Niger and Cross River.)

Synodontis robbianus. (Lower Niger and Cross River.)

Synodontis nigrita. (Tropical Africa.)

Synodontis sp. (Tropical Africa.)

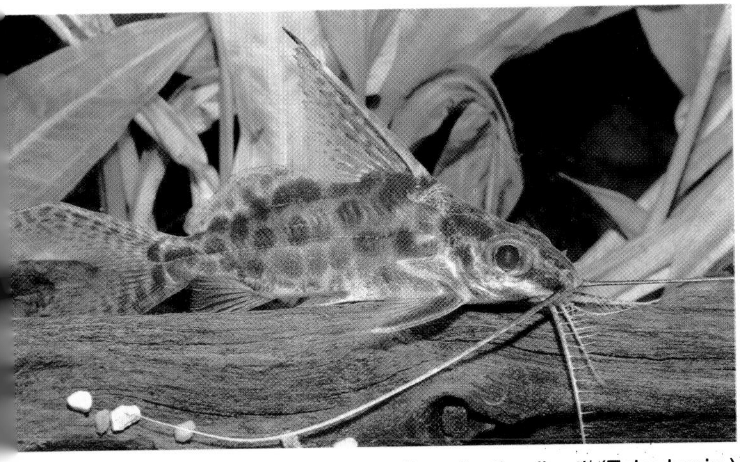

Synodontis alberti. (Zaire basin.)

Synodontis alberti. (Zaire basin.)

PLATE 90

Synodontis sp. cf. *obesus*. (Tropical Africa.)

Synodontis nigrita? Fada N'Gorma, Niger.

Synodontis sp. cf. *velifer*. Niandam, Guinea.

Synodontis greshoffi. (Zaire basin.)

Synodontis sp. cf. *gambiensis*. Niandam, Guinea.

Synodontis bastiani. (Ivory Coast.)

Synodontis voltae. Bougouriba, affl. Volta Noire.

Synodontis voltae (juv.). Bougouriba, affl. Volta Noire.

Synodontis alberti. (Zaire basin.)

Synodontis alberti. (Zaire basin.)

Synodontis sp. cf. *pardalis*. (Tropical Africa.)

Synodontis sp. cf. *robertsi*. (Tropical Africa.)

Synodontis schoutedeni. (Central Zaire.)

Synodontis schoutedeni. (Central Zaire.)

Synodontis nigriventris. (Central Zaire basin.)

Synodontis nigriventris. (Central Zaire basin.)

PLATE 92

Synodontis schoutedeni. (Central Zaire.)

Synodontis schoutedeni. (Central Zaire.)

Synodontis notatus. (Zaire basin.)

Synodontis notatus. (Zaire basin.)

Synodontis congicus. (Zaire basin.)

Synodontis decorus. (Zaire basin.)

Synodontis zambezensis. (Tropical Africa.)

Synodontis contractus. (Zaire basin.)

Synodontis greshoffi. (Zaire basin.)

Synodontis nigriventris. (Central Zaire basin.)

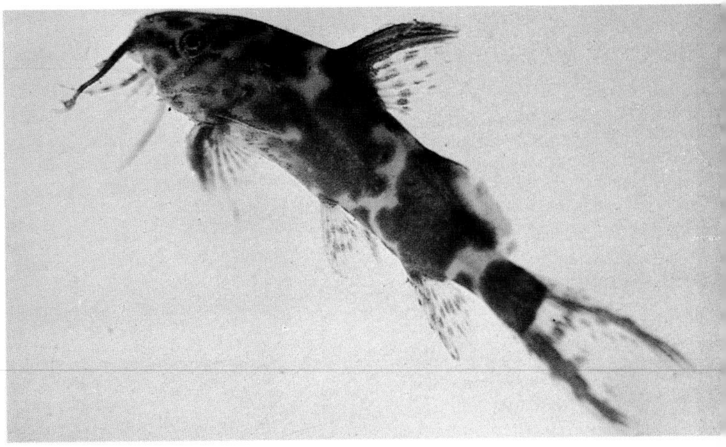

Synodontis nigriventris. (Central Zaire basin.)

Synodontis angelicus. (Zaire basin.)

Synodontis angelicus. (Zaire basin.)

Synodontis alberti. (Zaire basin.)

Synodontis alberti. (Zaire basin.)

PLATE 94

Synodontis granulosus. (Lake Tanganyika.)

Synodontis nigromaculatus. (Tropical Africa.)

Synodontis nigromaculatus. (Tropical Africa.)

Synodontis polli. (Lake Tanganyika.)

Synodontis multipunctatus (sport). (Lake Tanganyika.)

Synodontis haugi. (Ogowe basin.)

Synodontis budgetti. (Niger and Oueme Rivers, Lake Nokoue.

Synodontis frontosus. (Nile basin to Chad basin.)

Hassar iheringi. (Brazil.)

Anduzedoras microstomas. (Guyana.)

Trachydoras paraguayensis. (Paraguay and Amazon basins.)

Trachydoras paraguayensis. (Paraguay and Amazon basins.)

Pseudodoras niger. (Tropical South America.)

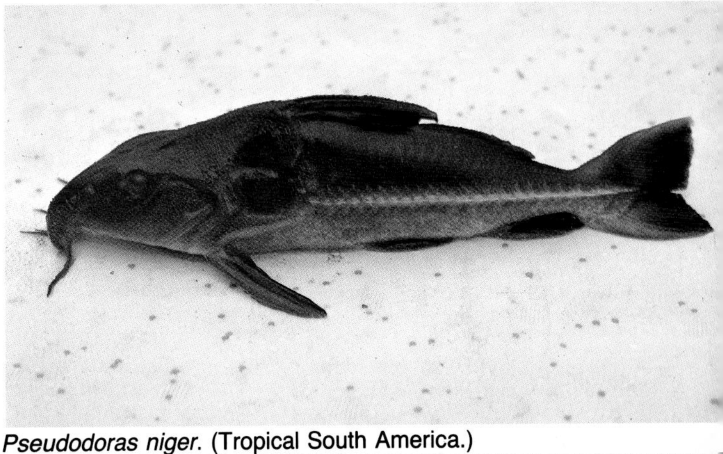

Pseudodoras niger. (Tropical South America.)

Pseudodoras holdeni. (Rio Apure.)

Anadoras grypus. (Amazonia, Peru.)

PLATE 96

Hassar notospilus. (Guyana.)

Opsodoras leporhinus. (Central Amazon, Bolivia, and Peru.)

Liosomadoras oncinus. (Peru, Brazil.)

Doras sp. (Tropical South America.)

Opsodoras stubeli? (Rio Maranon, Brazil.)

Doras sp. (Tropical South America.)

Platydoras costatus. (Tropical South America.)

Pseudodoras niger. (Tropical South America.)

Agamyxis pectinifrons, ventral view.

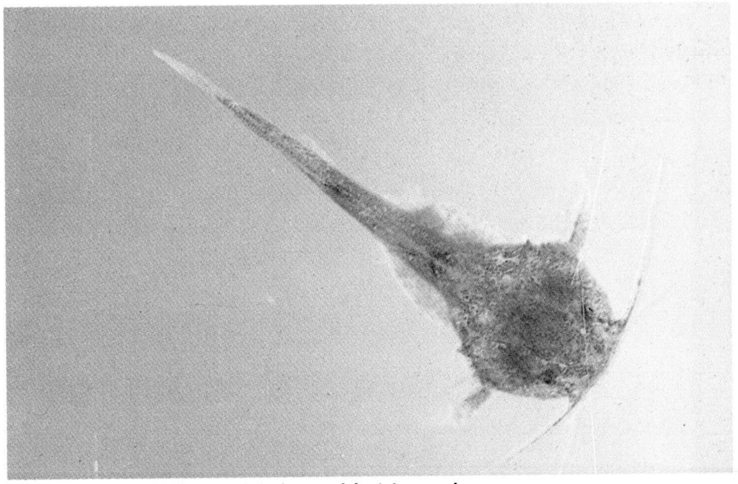

Agamyxis pectinifrons, 15 days old, 14 mm long.

Agamyxis pectinifrons, 17-20 mm long.

Agamyxis pectinifrons, 26-30 mm long.

Agamyxis pectinifrons, 48 days old.

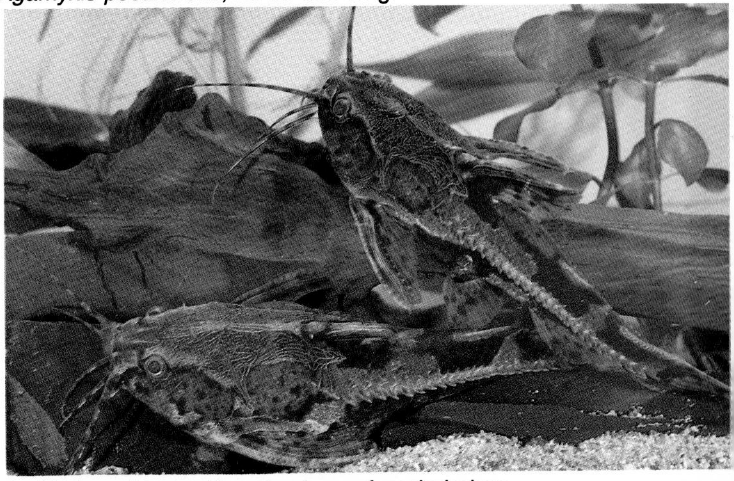

Amblydoras hancocki, male above, female below.

Amblydoras hancocki, 20-22 mm long.

Platydoras costatus, about 35 mm long.

PLATE 98

Agamyxis pectinifrons. (Upper Amazon; Peru.)

Acanthodoras spinosissimus. (Amazon system.)

Acanthodoras cataphractus. (Amazon system; Guianas.)

Orinocodoras eigenmanni. (Amazonia; Bolivia; Paraguay.)

Acanthodoras cataphractus? (Amazon system; Guianas.)

Hassar notospilus. (Guyana.)

Hassar sp. cf. *iheringi.* (Tropical South America.)

Hassar sp. cf. *notospilus.* (Tropical South America.)

Opsodoras humeralis. (Amazonia; Peru; Bolivia.)

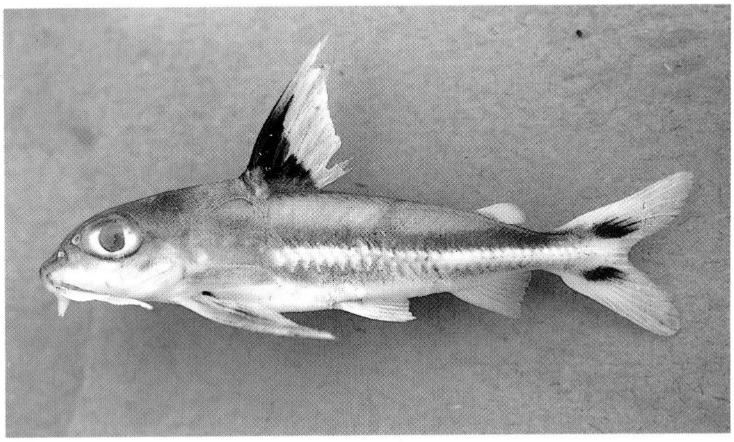

Opsodoras leporhinus. (Central Amazon; Bolivia; Peru.)

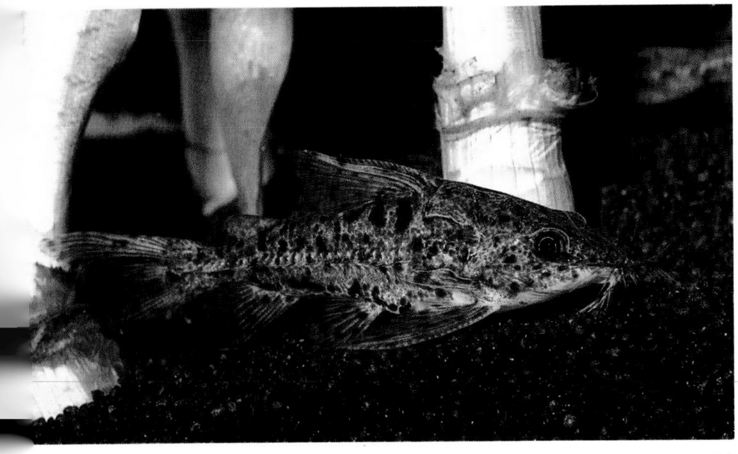

Opsodoras stubeli. (Rio Maranon, Brazil.)

Doras cariu. (Tropical South America.)

Unknown doradid.

Doras micropoeus (Guyana.)

Pseudodoras sp. cf. *niger*. (Tropical South America.)

Pseudodoras sp. cf. *niger* (juv.). (Tropical South America.)

Anadoras grypus. (Amazonia; Peru.)

Anadoras grypus. (Amazonia; Peru.)

Astrodoras asterifrons. (Bolivia; Amazonia.)

Amblydoras hancocki. (Tropical South America.)

Doras eigenmanni sp. (Amazonia; Bolivia; Paraguay.)

Pterodoras granulosus. (Tropical South America.)

Rhinodoras dorbignyi? (Southeastern Brazil; Paraguay.)

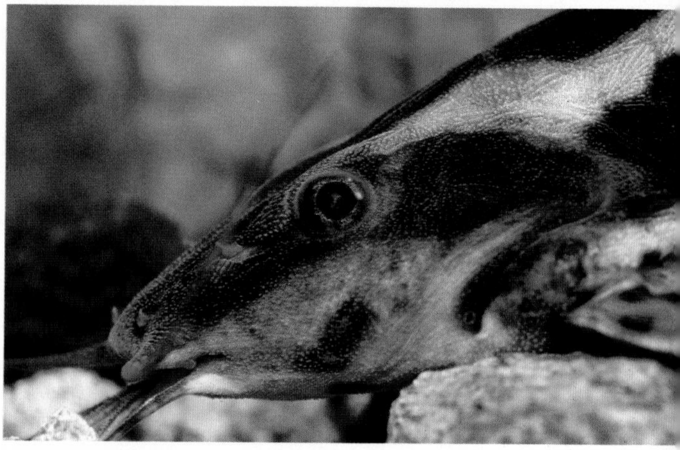

Megalodoras irwini. (Brazil; Peru; Guianas.)

Platydoras armatulus. (Upper Amazon; Paraguay; Rio Parana.)

Platydoras armatulus. (Upper Amazon; Paraguay; Rio Parana.)

Platydoras costatus. (Tropical South America.)

Platydoras costatus. (Tropical South America.)

Platydoras costatus. (Tropical South America.)

Acanthodoras cataphractus. (Amazonas; Guyana.)

Acanthodoras cataphractus. (Amazonas; Guyana.)

Acanthodoras cataphractus. (Amazonas; Guyana.)

PLATE 102

Doras eigenmanni. (Amazonia; Bolivia; Paraguay.)

Doras eigenmanni. (Amazonia; Bolivia; Paraguay.)

Amblydoras hancocki. (Amazonia; Bolivia; Peru; Guyana.)

Amblydoras hancocki. (Amazonia; Bolivia; Peru; Guyana.)

Autanadoras milesi. (Amazonas.)

Amblydoras hancocki. (Amazonia; Bolivia; Peru; Guyana.)

Agamyxis pectinifrons. (Upper Amazon; Peru.)

Agamyxis pectinifrons. (Upper Amazon; Peru.)

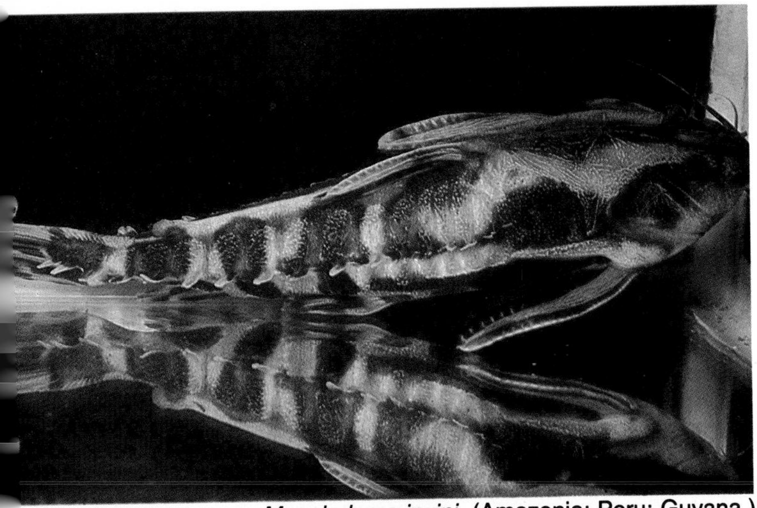

Megalodoras irwini. (Amazonia; Peru; Guyana.)

Pterodoras granulosus. (Tropical South America.)

Rhinodoras dorbignyi. (Southeastern Brazil; Paraguay.)

Astrodoras asterifrons. (Middle Amazon and Bolivia.)

Megalodoras sp. (Tropical South America.)

Megalodoras sp. (Tropical South America.)

Amblydoras hancocki. (Amazonia; Bolivia; Peru; Guyana.)

?*Franciscodoras marmoratus*. (Rio das Velhas.)

The fully mature male Woodcat (*Parauchenipterus fisheri*) that has undergone modifications in preparation for spawning.

The female Woodcat lacks the color as well as the specializations of the male.

An adult male not yet ready for spawning. There are no head tubercles and the maxillary barbels are soft and flexible.

A close-up of the intromittent organ in front of the anal fin of the male.

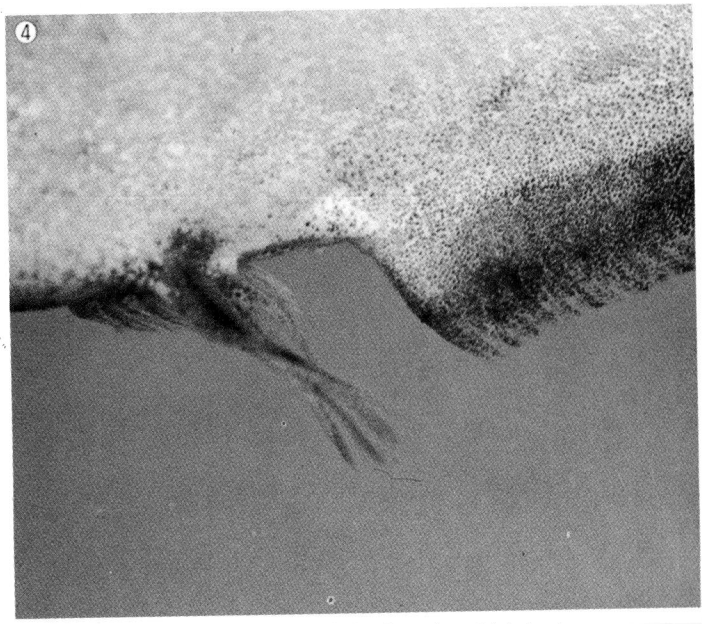

A close-up of the same area of the female which lacks such an organ.

PLATE 106

1. A pair of Woodcats, the male with the curved dorsal spine. 2. This curved spine fits against the curvature of the female's body. 3. Courting. 4. An early attempt at a spawning embrace.

5. A spawning embrace with the male wrapping his body around that of the female. 6. After a considerable delay the eggs are scattered over the substrate. 7. Stages in development: (a) A 10-hour-old egg. (b) Developing embryo after 30 hours. (c) Five days after spawning — about ready to hatch. (d) Hatched fry hiding near some driftwood.

PLATE 108

Parauchenipterus galeatus. (Surinam.)

Trachelyichthys decaradiatus. (Guyana.)

Trachelyichthys exilis. (Peru.)

Trachelyichthys exilis. (Peru.)

Auchenipterichthys longimanus. (Peru; Brazil.)

Auchenipterichthys longimanus. (Peru; Brazil.)

Epapterus chaquensis. (Argentina.)

Tatia neivai. (Southern Brazil.)

Parauchenipterus galeatus. (Surinam.)

Parauchenipterus galeatus. (Surinam.)

Entomocorus benjamini. (Bolivia.)

Auchenipterichthys thoracatus. (Rio Guapore.)

Parauchenipterus fisheri. (Colombia.)

Parauchenipterus sp. (Tropical South America.)

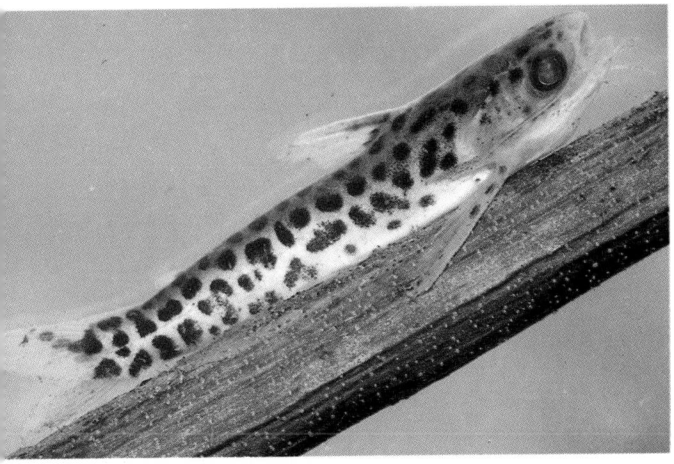

Tatia perugiae. (Upper Amazon; Ecuador.)

Tetranematichthys quadrifilis. (Rio Guapore.)

Parauchenipterus sp. (Tropical South America.)

Parauchenipterus sp. (Tropical South America.)

Parauchenipterus fisheri. (Colombia.)

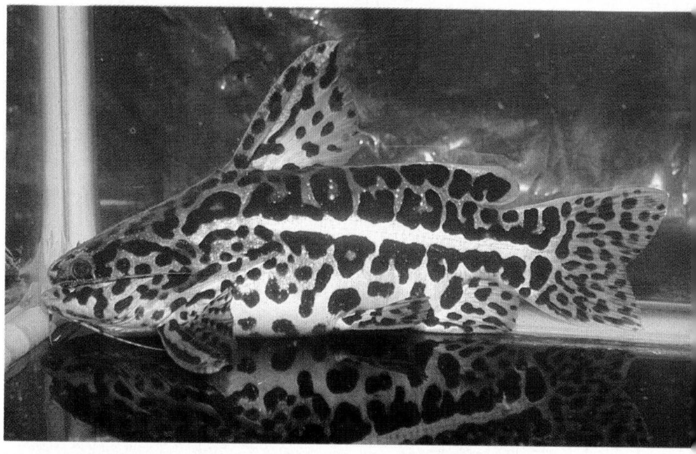

Liosomadoras oncinus. (Upper Amazon; Peru.)

Pseudauchenipterus nodosus. (Tropical South America.)

Pseudauchenipterus nodosus. (Tropical South America.)

Trachelyichthys sp. (Tropical South America.)

Trachelyichthys sp. (Tropical South America.)

Liosomadoras oncinus. (Upper Amazon; Peru.)

Trachelyichthys exilis. (Peru.)

Auchenipterichthys thoracatus. (Rio Guapore.)

Auchenipterichthys thoracatus. (Rio Guapore.)

Auchenipterichthys longimanus. (Peru; Brazil.)

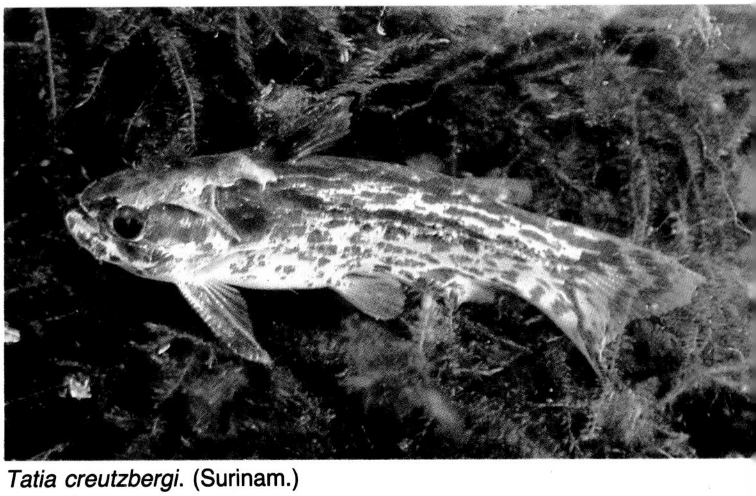

Tatia creutzbergi. (Surinam.)

Parauchenipterus galeatus. (Surinam.)

Parauchenipterus fisheri. (Colombia.)

Trachycorystes trachycorystes is one of the lesser known members of this family. It was recently imported, the photographs from various angles and magnifications being shown here.

Tatia aulopygia. (Northeastern South America.)

Tatia sp. cf. *brunnea*. (Tropical South America.)

Tatia intermedia. (Amazon system and Guianas.)

Tatia sp. Rio Jamal Ariquenos.

Trachelyopterichthys taeniatus. (Amazonas.)

Epapterus chaquensis. (Argentina.)

Entomocorus benjamini. (Bolivia.)

Entomocorus benjamini. (Bolivia.)

PLATE 114

Tatia creutzbergi. (Surinam.)

Tatia aulopygia. (Northeastern South America.)

Tatia aulopygia. (Northeastern South America.)

Pseudepapterus hasemani. (Para; Upper Amazon; Venezuela.)

Trachelyopterichthys taeniatus. (Amazonas.)

Trachelyopterichthys taeniatus. (Amazonas.)

Auchenipterus nuchalis. (Tropical South America.)

Auchenipterus nuchalis. (Tropical South America.)

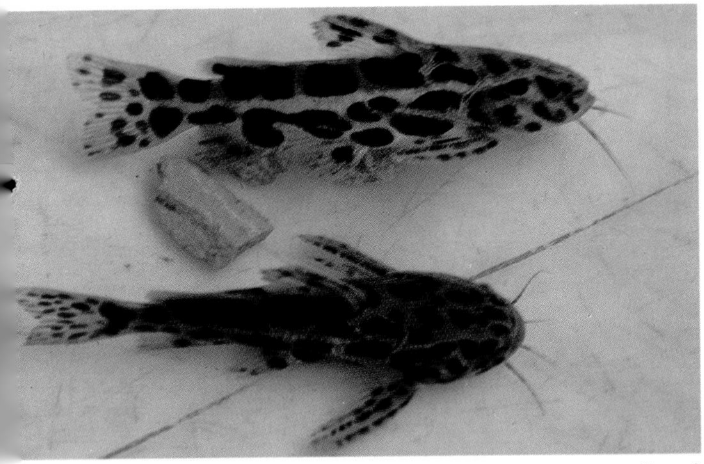

Liosomadoras oncinus. (Upper Amazon; Peru.)

Liosomadoras oncinus. (Upper Amazon; Peru.)

Liosomadoras oncinus. (Upper Amazon; Peru.)

Liosomadoras oncinus. (Upper Amazon; Peru.)

Centromochlus heckelii. (Amazonia; Bolivia; Peru; Venezuela.)

Pseudauchenipterus nodosus. (Tropical South America.)

Parauchenipterus fisheri. (Colombia.)

Parauchenipterus sp. (Tropical South America.)

PLATE 116

Brachyplatystoma juruense (above) and *Merodontotus tigrinus* (below) have recently taken the aquarium world by storm. They are spectacular in appearance as well as price. Only small individuals can be kept as both species grow quite large.

Activities along the Teotonio rapids showing fishing methods. This is where many large pimelodids, including *Merodontotus tigrinus*, are captured.

PLATE 118

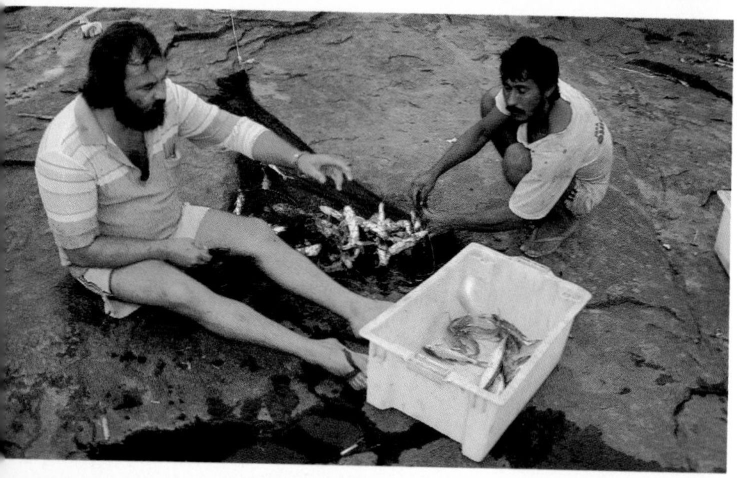

It is difficult to imagine how fishing could be accomplished in such turbulent waters. Both small and large fishes are taken.

a

b

c

d

Above: (a) Dr. Howard Groder with a *Brachyplatystoma filamentosum*. (b) Pole fishing in the rapids. (c) A quiet backwater area where boats can be brought. (d) Teotonio sign. **Below:** Three specimens of *Merodontotus tigrinus* showing variations in their pattern.

A young *Merodontotus tigrinus* with a more vertical pattern. It is not hard to see how the pattern on the previous page could evolve.

Pseudoplatystoma fasciatum is another large pimelodid that has found its way into aquarists' tanks as juveniles.

Brachyplatystoma filamentosum. (Northern South America.)

Brachyplatystoma flavicans. (Amazonas.)

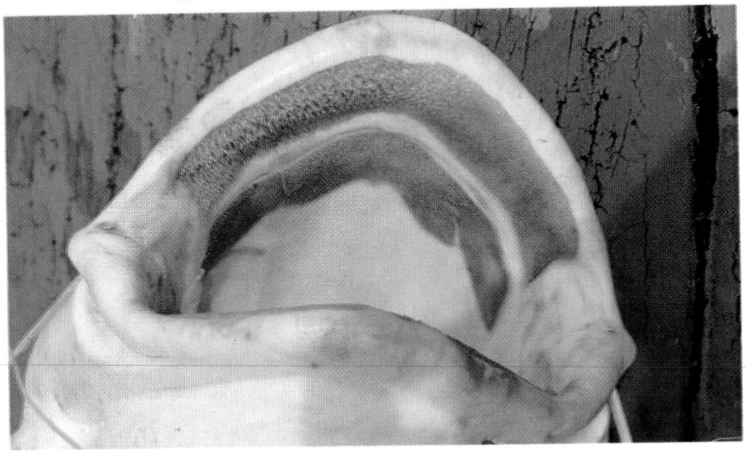

Brachyplatystoma filamentosum. (Northern South America.)

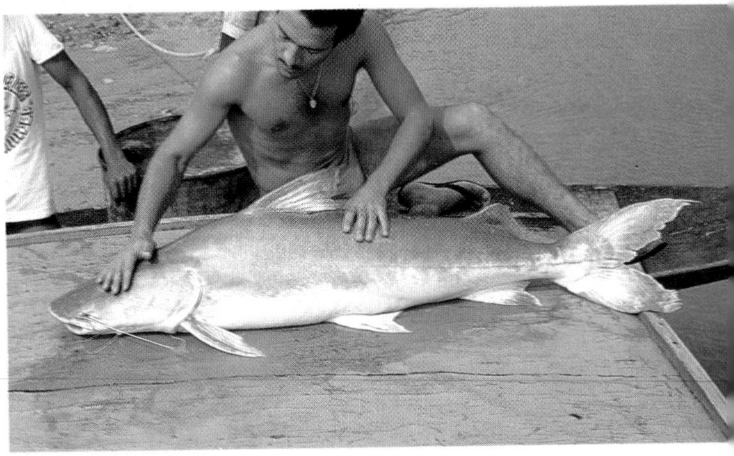

Brachyplatystoma filamentosum. (Northern South America.)

Brachyplatystoma filamentosum (juv.) (Northern South America.)

Unidentified *pimelodid,* possibly *Bagropsis reinhardti.*

Unknown pimelodid. (Tropical South America.)

Unknown pimelodid. (Tropical South America.)

PLATE 122

Pseudoplatystoma sp. (Tropical South America.)

Pseudoplatystoma sp. (Tropical South America.)

Brachyplatystoma juruense. (Amazonia; Peru.)

Merodontotus tigrinus. (Amazonas; Peru.)

Brachyplatystoma juruense. Apure, Cuna Guaro, Manta Negro.

?*Paulicea* sp. Tropical South America.

?*Paulicea* sp. Tropical South America.

?*Paulicea* sp. Tropical South America.

Pseudoplatystoma fasciatum (var.). (Tropical South America.)

Pseudoplatystoma tigrinum. Venezuela?

Pseudoplatystoma fasciatum. (Tropical South America.)

Pseudoplatystoma fasciatum. (Tropical South America.)

Unknown ariid. (Tropical South America.)

Goslinia platynema. (Amazonas.)

Paulicea lutkeni. (Amazonas; Rio Parana; Paraguay.)

Paulicea lutkeni. (Amazonas; Rio Parana; Paraguay.)

PLATE 124

Sorubim lima. (Tropical South America to Argentina.)

Sorubim lima. (Tropical South America to Argentina.)

Hemisorubim platyrhynchus. (São Paulo to Venezuela ; Peru.)

Duopalatinus sp. (Tropical South America.)

Platystomatichthys sturio. (Upper Amazon; Peru.)

Pseudoplatystoma coruscans. (Amazon system.)

Sorubimichthys planiceps. (Widespread in South America.)

Sorubimichthys planiceps. (Widespread in South America.)

Pseudoplatystoma fasciatum usually has thinner, more vertical stripes than its close relative *P. tigrinum*. It also is a smaller species reaching about 90 cm in fork length in the Rio Madeira.

Juvenile *Pseudoplatystoma coruscans* have a distinctive pattern as seen here. This species has also entered the aquarium trade.

Sorubim lima is commonly known as the Bico de Pato, or duck's beak, because of its elongated snout. It only attains a length of about 40 cm fork length. Schools appear at the Teotonio rapids toward the end of the low water season.

PLATE 126

Sorubimichthys planiceps. (Widespread in South America.)

Sorubimichthys planiceps (var.). Venezuela.

Sorubim lima. (Tropical South America to Argentina.)

Sorubim lima. (Tropical South America to Argentina.)

Platynematichthys notatus. Amazon.

Platystomatichthys sturio. (Upper Amazon; Peru.)

?*Pimelodella* sp., 40 mm, possibly cave form. (Tropical South America.)

Brachyplatystoma sp. cf. *vaillantii*. Amazon.

Brachyplatystoma filamentosum is not very colorful and therefore is not often seen in the aquarium trade.

Sorubim lima in a typical vertical pose.

Sorubim lima. (Tropical South America to Argentina.)

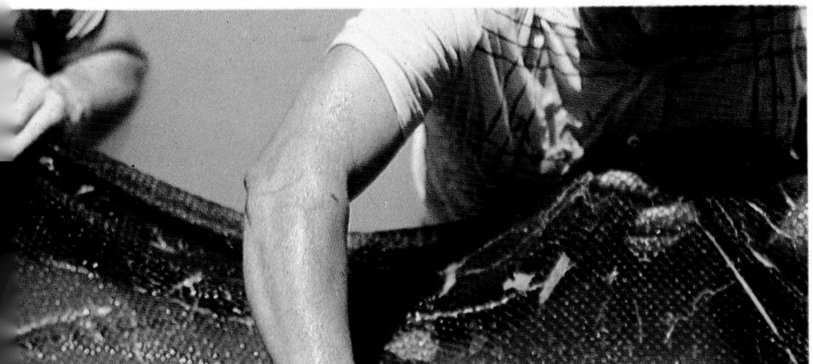

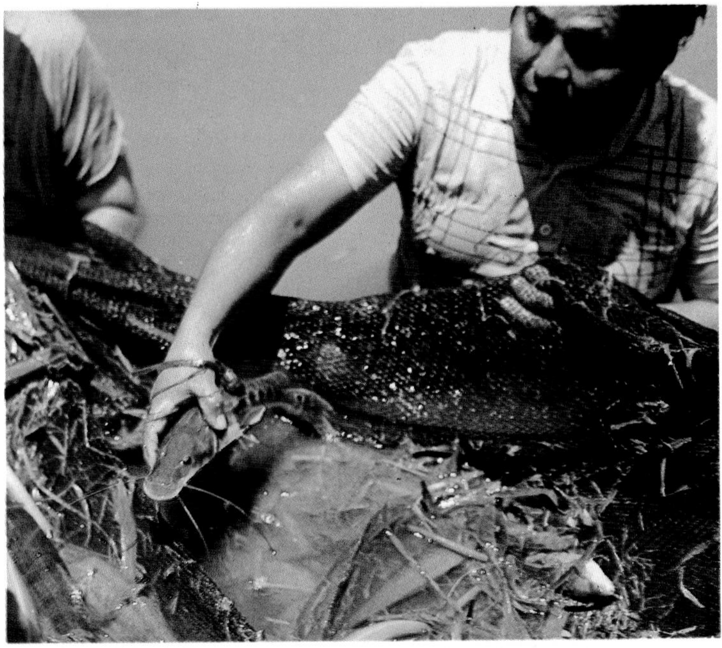

Perrunichthys perruno (left) and *Hemisorubim platyrhynchos* (right) are carefully removed from a seine haul. These fishes were collected in Peru in 1984.

Goeldiella eques. (Amazonia; Peru; Guyana.)

Hemisorubim platyrhynchos (var.). Peru.

Hemisorubim platyrhynchos. Apure.

Hemisorubim platyrhynchos. Apure.

Hemisorubim platyrhynchos. (São Paulo to Venezuela; Peru.)

Hemisorubim platyrhynchos? (juv.). (São Paulo to Venezuela; Peru.)

"Duopalatinus" sp. Rio Palmar.

"Duopalatinus" malarmo. (Venezuela).

Phractocephalus hemioliopterus (albino). (Amazon system.)

Phractocephalus hemioliopterus (juv.). (Amazon system.)

Phractocephalus hemioliopterus (young). (Amazon system.)

Phractocephalus hemioliopterus (adult). (Amazon system.)

Phractocephalus hemioliopterus (var.). (Amazon system.)

Phractocephalus hemioliopterus (var.). (Amazon system.)

Leiarius pictus. (Amazonas; Paraguay.)

Leiarius pictus. (Amazonas; Paraguay.)

PLATE 130

Perrunichthys perruno. (Venezuela.)

Perrunichthys perruno. (Venezuela.)

Leiarius marmoratus. (Amazonia; Peru; Colombia.)

Leiarius marmoratus. (Amazonia; Peru; Colombia.)

Perrunichthys perruno. (Venezuela.)

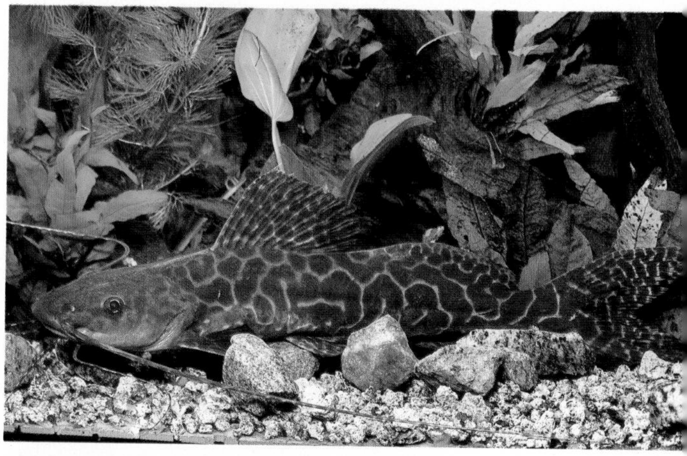

Perrunichthys perruno. (Venezuela.)

Leiarius marmoratus. (Amazonia; Peru; Colombia.)

Leiarius marmoratus. (Amazonia; Peru; Colombia.)

Calophysus macropterus (var.). (Northern South America.)

Calophysus macropterus (var.). (Northern South America.)

Calophysus macropterus. (Northern South America.)

Calophysus macropterus (var.). (Northern South America.)

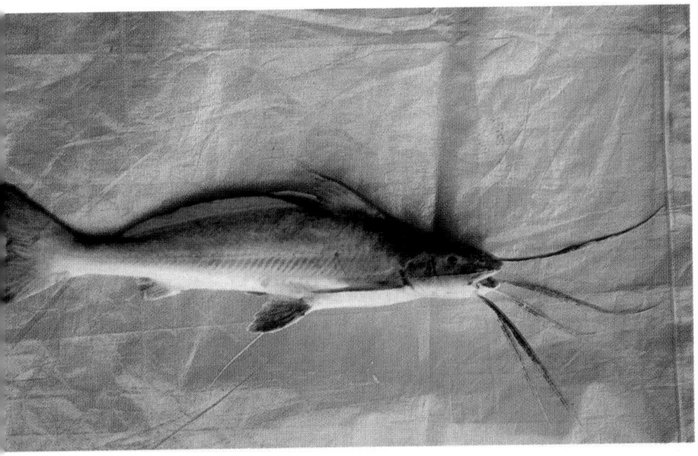

Pinirampus pirinampu. (Paraguay to Venezuela.)

Platynematichthys notatus. (Rio BRanco: Rio Negro.)

Iheringichthys sp. (Tropical South America.)

Iheringichthys sp. (Tropical South America.)

PLATE 132

Pinirampus pirinampu. (Paraguay to Venezuela.)

Pinirampus pirinampu. (Paraguay to Venezuela.)

Calophysus macropterus (var.). (Northern South America.)

Calophysus macropterus (var.). (Northern South America.)

Pimelodella gracilis. (Argentina to Venezuela.)

Pimelodella gracilis. (Argentina to Venezuela.)

Pimelodella linami. (Venezuela.)

Pimelodella laticeps. (Paraguay to Bolivia.)

Pimelodella rambarrani. (Rio Unini, Amazonas, Brazil.)

Pimelodella marthae. (Peru.)

Pimelodella meesi. (Near Belem, Brazil.)

Pimelodella imitator. (Venezuela.)

PLATE 134

Pimelodella cristata. (Tropical South America.)

Goeldiella eques. (Amazonia; Peru; Guyana.)

Pimelodella chagresi. (Panama.)

Imparfinis minutus. Cana, Panama.

Heptapterus stewarti?. (Unknown.)

Heptapterus stewarti?. (Unknown.)

Pimelodella gracilis. (Argentina to Venezuela.)

Pimelodella sp. cf. *gracilis*. (Unknown.)

Pimelodella meesi. (Near Belem, Brazil.)

Pimelodella imitator. (Venezuela.)

Pimelodella marthae. (Peru.)

Pimelodella marthae? (Peru?.)

Pimelodella sp. (Unknown.)

Pimelodella rambarrani. Rio Unini, Amazonas, Brazil.

? *Rhamdia* sp. (Unknown.)

Imparfinis or *Nannorhamdia* sp. (Unknown.)

PLATE 136

Pimelodella gracilis. (Argentina to Venezuela.)

Pimelodella sp. (Unknown.)

Pimelodella sp. (Unknown.)

Pimelodella sp. cf. *gracilis*. (Unknown.)

Pimelodella sp. (Unknown.)

?*Rhamdia* sp. (Tropical South America.)

Pimelodus pictus?. (Unknown.)

Pimelodus pictus. (Amazonia; Peru; Venezuela.)

Rhamdia quelan. (Tropical South America.)

Rhamdia sp. (Unknown.)

Rhamdia wagneri. Rio Oritruo.

Rhamdia laticauda. (Mexico.)

Heptapterus sp. (Unknown.)

Heptapterus sp. (Unknown.)

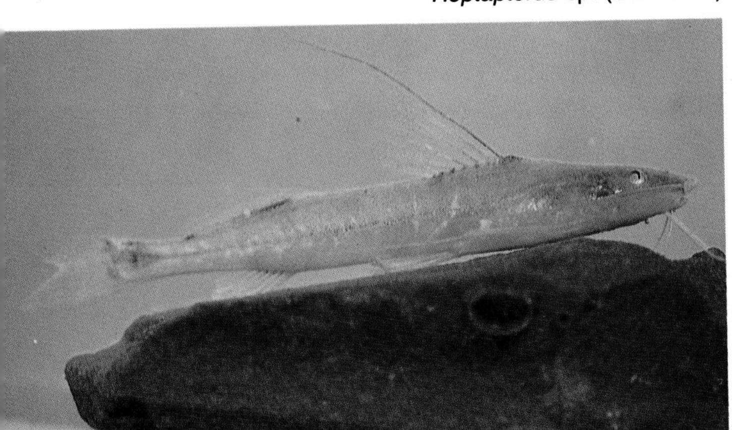

? *Imparfinis* or *Nannorhamdia* sp. (Unknown.)

? *Imparfinis* or *Nannorhamdia* sp. (Unknown.)

PLATE 138

Pimelodella parnahybae. (Rio Parnaiba.)

Pimelodella dorseyi. (Ceara.)

Pimelodus. sp. (Upper Amazon; Peru.)

Pimelodus. sp. (Upper Amazon; Peru.)

Pimelodus of the *altissimus*—group. (Tropical South America.)

Duopalatinus malarmo. (Venezuela.)

Goeldiella eques. (Amazonia; Peru: Guyana.)

Heptapterus mustelinus. (Surinam to Uruguay.)

Pimelodella sp cf. *gracilis*. (Unknown.)

Pimelodus pictus. (Amazonia; Peru; Venezuela.)

Pimelodus ornatus. (Amazonia: Peru.)

Pimelodus albofasciatus. (Surinam.)

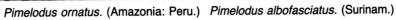

Pimelodus blochii. (Surinam.)

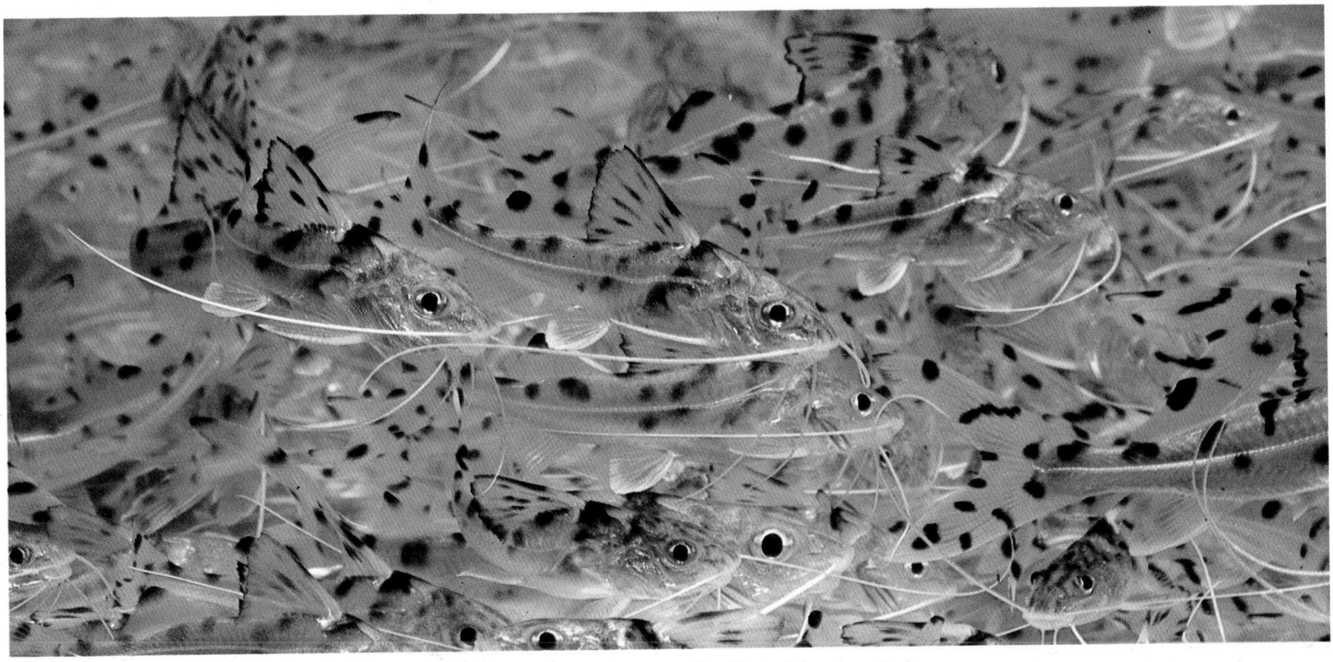

Pimelodus pictus. (Amazonia; Peru; Venezuela.)

PLATE 140

Pimelodus ornatus. (Amazonia; Peru.)

Pimelodus ornatus. (Amazonia; Peru.)

Pimelodus of the *blochii/rigidus*-group. (Tropical South America.)

Pimelodus ornatus. (Amazonia; Peru.)

Pimelodus of the *blochii/rigidus*-group. (Tropical South America.)

Pimelodus of the *blochii/rigidus*-group. (Tropical South America.)

Pimelodus pictus. Peru.

Pimelodus sp. cf. *pictus*. Venezuela.

Pimelodus blochii. (Surinam.)

Pimelodus ornatus. (Amazonia; Peru.)

Pimelodus maculatus (juv.). (Brazil.)

Pimelodus sp. (blochii?). (Unknown.)

Pimelodus maculatus. (Brazil.)

Pimelodus pictus. (Amazonia; Peru; Venezuela.)

Pimelodus of the *blochii/rigidus*-group. Rio Trombetas, Brazil.

Pimelodus pictus. (Amazonia; Peru; Venezuela.)

PLATE 142

Pimelodus of the *blochii/rigidus*-group. (Tropical South America.)

Pimelodus of the *blochii/rigidus*-group. Venezuela.

Pimelodus of the *blochii/rigidus*-group. (Tropical South America.)

Pimelodus of the *blochii/rigidus*-group. (Tropical South America.)

Pimelodus sp. Rio Jamari (Ariquenos).

Pimelodus sp. *(blochii?).* (Unknown.)

Pimelodus maculatus. (Brazil.)

Pimelodus maculatus. (Brazil.)

Pseudopimelodus nigricauda. (Surinam.)

Pseudopimelodus nigricauda. (Surinam.)

Pseudopimelodus fowleri. (Southern Brazil.)

Pseudopimelodus raninus. (Northern South America.)

Pseudopimelodus sp. (Unknown.)

Pseudopimelodus raninus (Northern South America.)

Pseudopimelodus raninus acanthochiroides. (Colombia.)

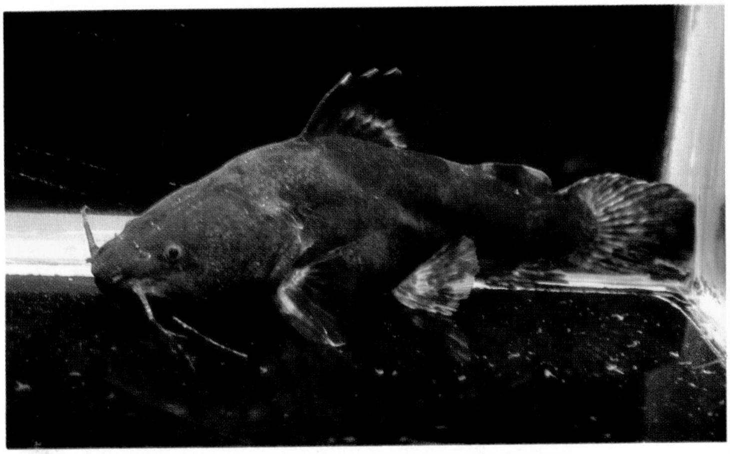

Pseudopimelodus raninus acanthochiroides. (Colombia.)

Pseudopimelodus raninus. (Northern South America.)

Pseudopimelodus sp. (albino). (Unknown.)

Pseudopimelodus albomarginatus? (Guyana.)

Pseudopimelodus nigricauda. (Surinam.)

Microglanis poecilus. (Guyana.)

Microglanis poecilus. (Guyana.)

Pseudopimelodus zungaro bufonius. (Surinam.)

Microglanis iheringi. (Venezuela.)

Microglanis poecilus. (Guyana.)

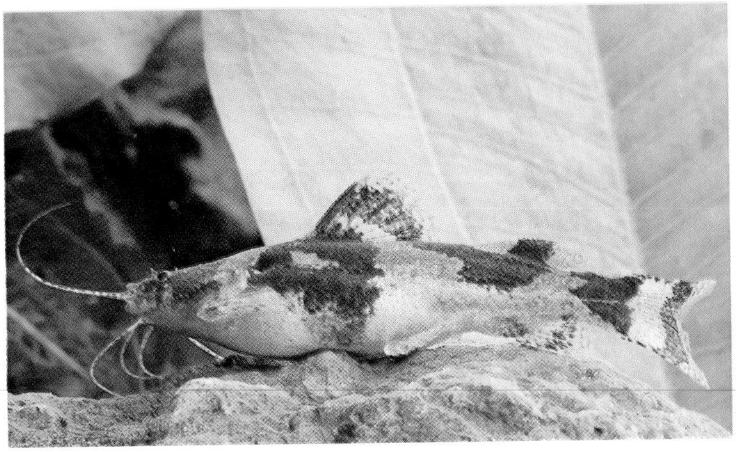

Microglanis sp. cf. *iheringi*. (Unknown.)

Microglanis parahybae. (Southern Brazil; Paraguay.)

Microglanis parahybae. (Southern Brazil; Paraguay.)

Pseudopimelodus raninus (juv.). (Northern South America.)

Pseudopimelodus raninus. (Northern South America.)

PLATE 146

Ageneiosus sp. cf. *marmoratus*. (Unknown.)

Ageneiosus sp. cf. *marmoratus*. (Unknown.)

Ageneiosus sp. cf. *marmoratus* (female). (Unknown.)

Ageneiosus sp. cf. *marmoratus* (male). (Unknown.)

Ageneiosus caucanus, 220 mm. Rio Guapore.

Ageneiosus sp. Apure.

Ageneiosus sp. Rio Grande do Sul.

Ageneiosus sp. cf. *brevifilis*. Rio Guapore.

Ageneiosus caucanus. (Rio Cauca.)

Ageneiosus sp. cf. *guianensis*. (Tropical South America.)

Ageneiosus caucanus. (Rio Cauca.)

Ageneiosus sp. cf. *madeirensis*. Yaviza, Panama.

Ageneiosus vittatus. Rio Tefe, Brazil.

PLATE 148

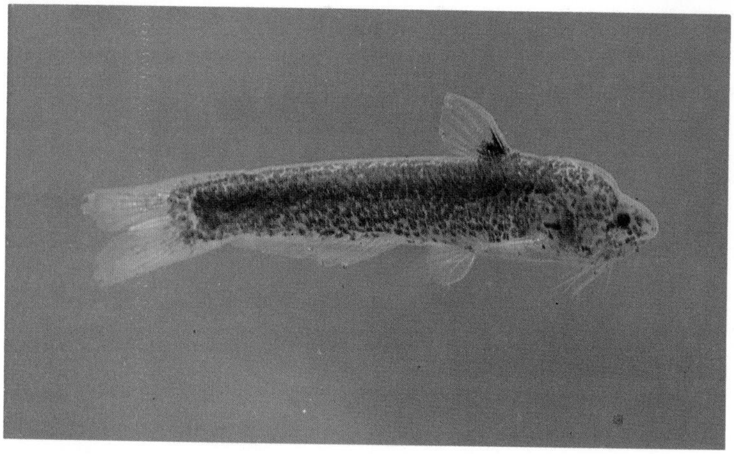

Hemicetopsis morenoi. Aguaro River, Venezuela.

Pseudocetopsis sp. (Unknown.)

Hemicetopsis macilentus. (Guyana.)

Hemicetopsis minutus. (Guyana.)

Ochmacanthus flabelliferus. (Essequibo basin.)

?*Cetopsis* sp. (Unknown.)

Helogenes marmoratus. (Guyana.)

Hypophthalmus edentatus. Rio Trombetas.

Platystacus cotylephorus. (Amazonas; Guianas.)

Agmus lyriformis. (Guyana.)

Agmus lyriformis. (Guyana.)

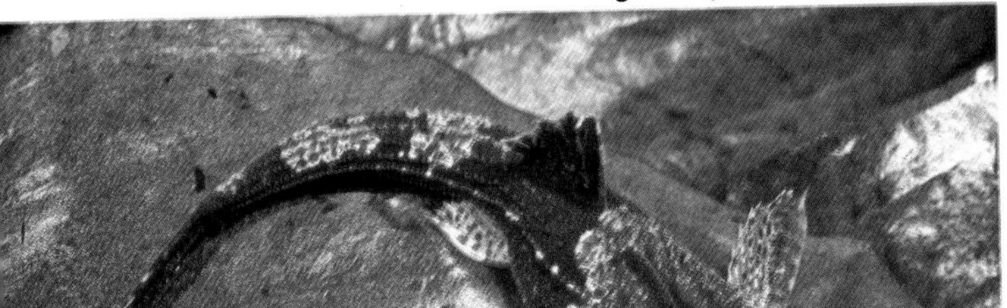

Bunocephalus sp. cf. *coracoideus*. (Amazonas; Uruguay; Peru.)

Bunocephalus sp. cf. *retropinnis*. (Tropical South America.)

PLATE 150

Bunocephalus sp. cf. *coracoideus*. (Tropical South America.)

Bunocephalus coracoideus. (Amazonas; Uruguay; Peru.)

Bunocephalus sp. (Unknown.)

Platystacus cotylephorus. (Amazonas; Guianas.)

Agmus lyriformis. (Guyana.)

Platystacus cotylephorus. (Amazonas; Guianas.)

Platystacus cotylephorus. (Amazonas; Guianas.)

Bunocephalus amaurus. (Guyana.)

Agmus sp. (Tropical South America.)

Bunocephalus knerii? (Tropical South America.)

Agmus lyriformis. (Guyana.)

Agmus scabriceps. (Rio Jutai.)

Bunocephalus aleuropsis? (Ecuador.)

Agmus lyriformis. (Guyana.)

Amaralia hypsiurus. (Rio Branco.)

Amaralia hypsiurus. (Rio Branco.)

PLATE 152

Platystacus cotylephorus. (Amazonas; Guianas.)

Aspredo aspredo. (Brazil; Guianas.)

Platystacus cotylephorus. (Amazonas; Guianas.)

Bunocephalus amaurus. (Guyana.)

Bunocephalus sp. cf. *coracoideus*. (Tropical South America.)

Agmus lyriformis. (Guyana.)

Bunocephalus coracoideus. (Amazonas; Uruguay; Peru.)

Bunocephalus coracoideus. (Amazonas; Uruguay; Peru.)

A breeding pair of *Bunocephalus* sp. cf. coracoideus (formerly *B. bicolor*) with the smaller male on the left.

A group of nine-month-old *Bunocephalus coracoideus* juveniles. They are very much like the adults by this time.

A ripe female *Bunocephalus coracoideus* visibly distended with her eggs.

Ventral view of an adult male *Bunocephalus coracoideus*.

PLATE 154

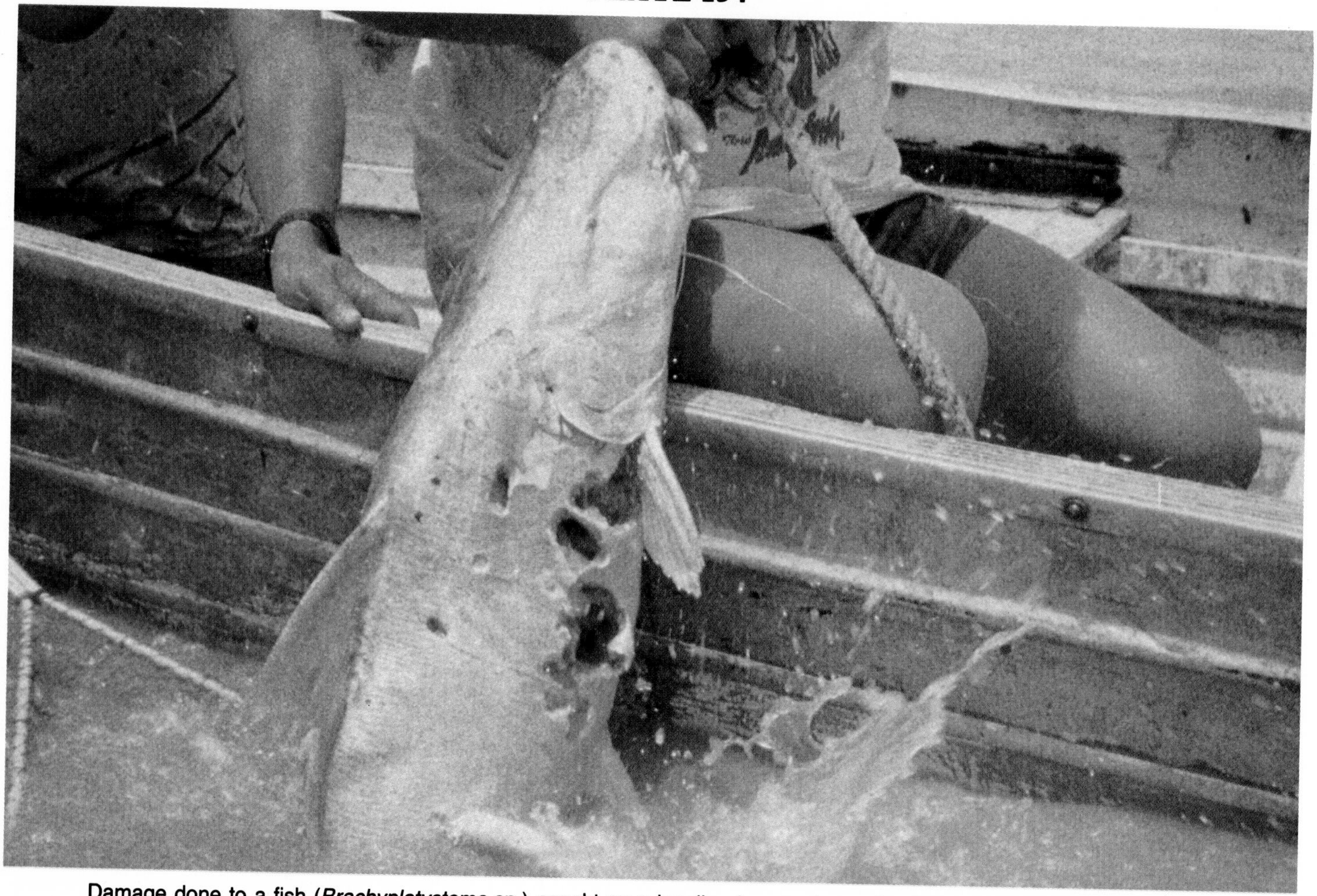

Damage done to a fish (*Brachyplatystoma* sp.) caught on a longline by members of at least two other catfish families. Involved are *Pseudostegophilus* and *Pareiodon* (Trichomycteridae) and *Cetopsis* and *Hemicetopsis* (Cetopsidae) as well as *Calophysus* (Pimelodidae).

A species of *Vandellia* searching for prey.

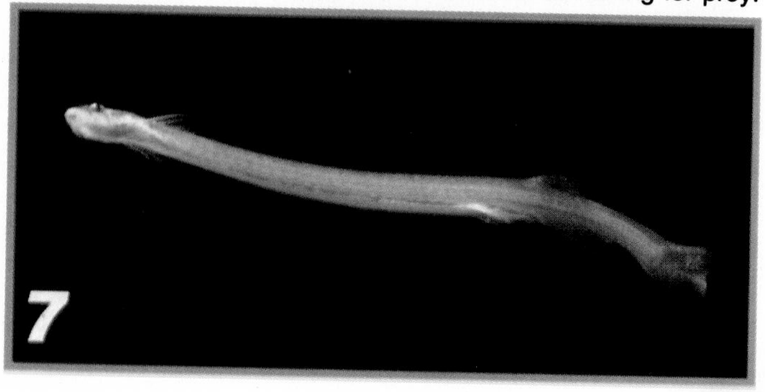

An unknown cetopsid sitting on a net.

Eremophilus mutisii is without ventral fins.

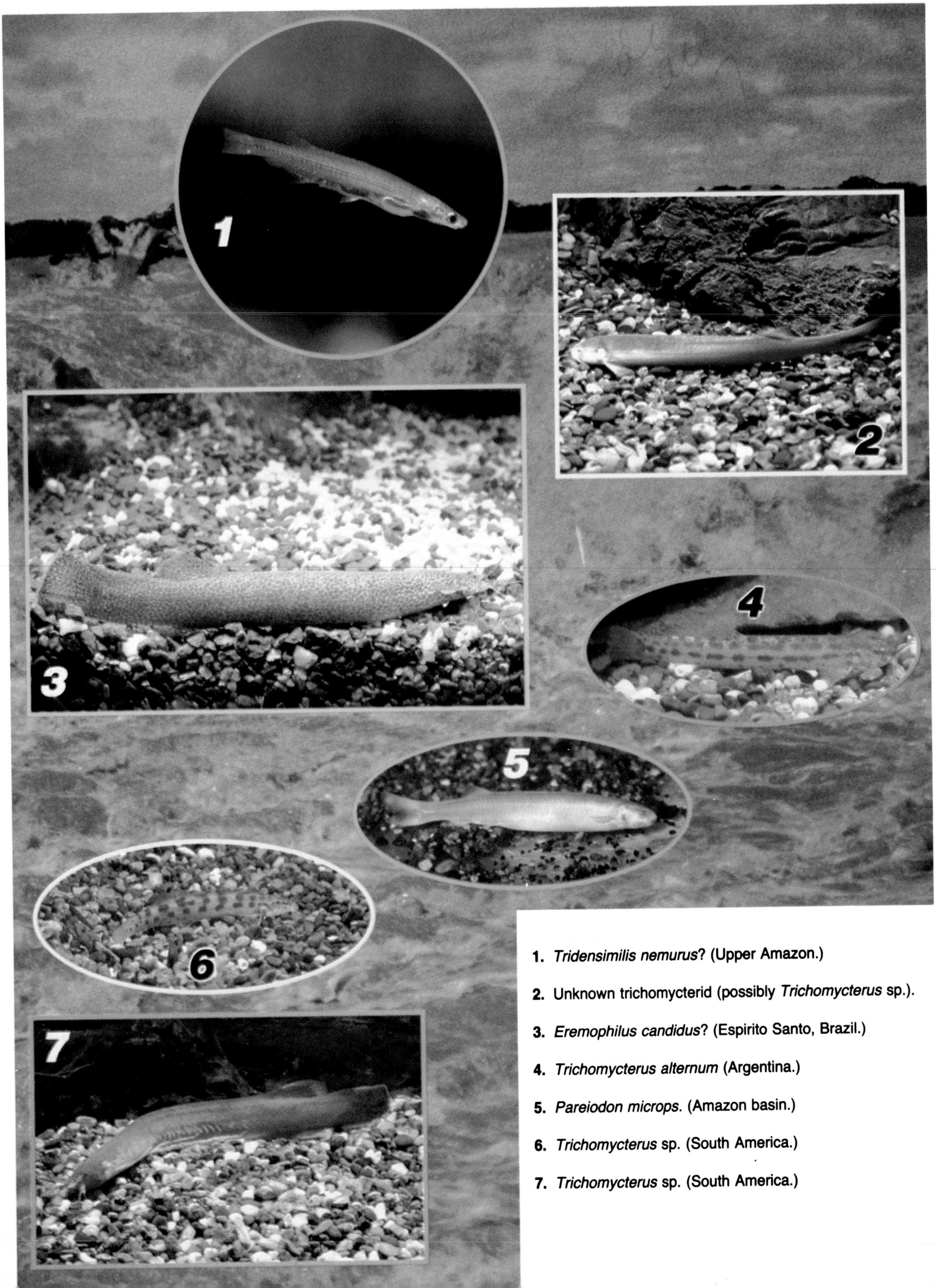

1. *Tridensimilis nemurus*? (Upper Amazon.)

2. Unknown trichomycterid (possibly *Trichomycterus* sp.).

3. *Eremophilus candidus*? (Espirito Santo, Brazil.)

4. *Trichomycterus alternum* (Argentina.)

5. *Pareiodon microps*. (Amazon basin.)

6. *Trichomycterus* sp. (South America.)

7. *Trichomycterus* sp. (South America.)

PLATE 156

Plectrochilus erythrurus. (Ucayali system, Peru.)

Tridensimilis venezuelae. (Venezuela.)

Bullockia moldonadoi? (Chile.)

Pseudostegophilus nemurus? (Upper Amazon.)

Cetopsis sp. (Brazil.)

Eremophilus mutisii. (Colombia.)

Eremophilus mutisii. (Colombia.)

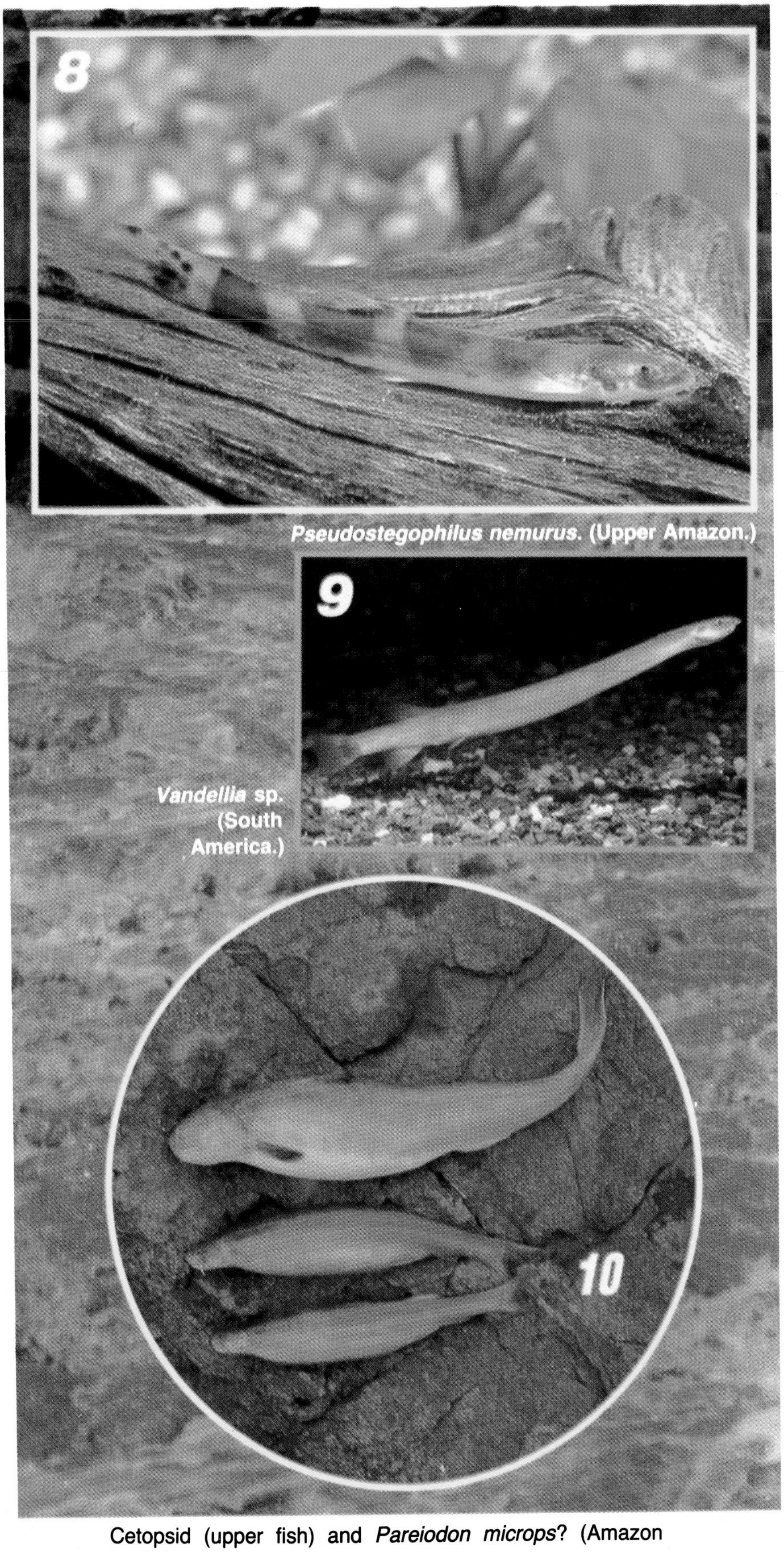

Pseudostegophilus nemurus. (Upper Amazon.)

Vandellia sp. (South America.)

Cetopsid (upper fish) and *Pareiodon microps*? (Amazon basin.)

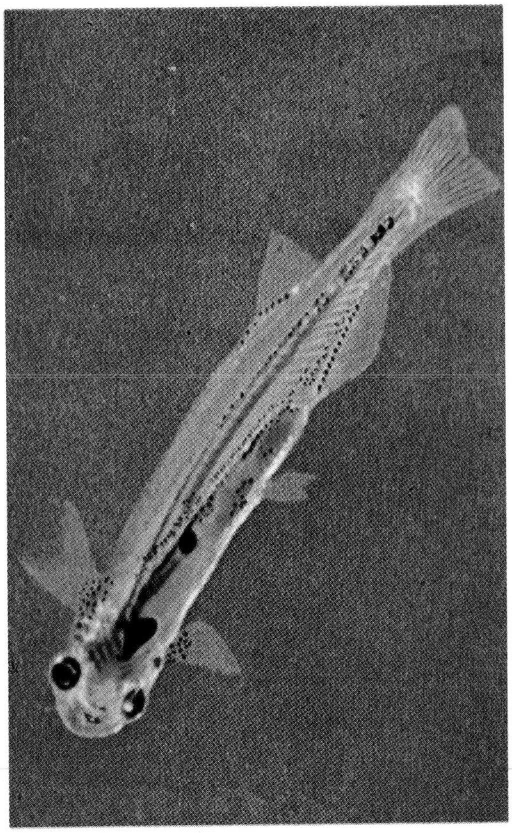

Tridensimilis sp. (South America.)

Branchioica bertoni on gills of *Pseudoplatystoma*.

The Porthole Catfish, *Dianema longibarbis* is so named because of the row of black spots along its sides.

Hoplosternum thoracatum grows to about 18 cm. It prefers small live foods and is one of the bubblenest builders.

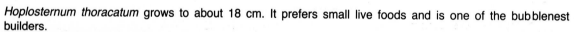

Callichthys callichthys. (Guianas.)

Dianema urostriatum. (Amazonas.)

?*Callichthys callichthys*. (Guianas.)

Hoplosternum pectorale. (Paraguay.)

Hoplosternum thoracatum. (Northern South America.)

Hoplosternum magdalenae. (Colombia.)

Hoplosternum thoracatum crossing dry stretch.

Hoplosternum. sp. (Unknown.)

PLATE 160

An *Aspidoras pauciradiatus* male is generally more slender than the female.

The female *Aspidoras pauciradiatus*. This was one of the early importation of the genus. Now several different species are available.

One of the newer imports is this *Aspidoras menezesi*. It did not take long for aquarists to spawn this species. This is a male.

PLATE 167

A female *Aspidoras menezesi* not in spawning condition. When she is ready she will be swollen with eggs.

A five-week-old *Aspidoras menezesi*.

Some eggs deposited on a Java fern.

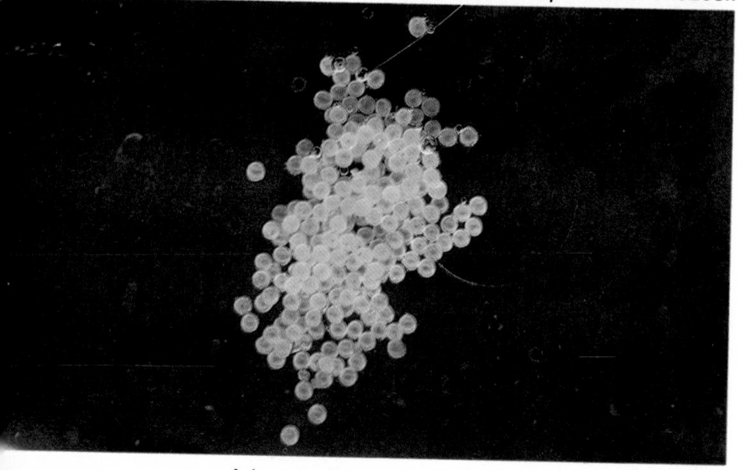

A larger cluster of eggs laid on the top of a filter.

A juvenile *Aspidoras pauciradiatus*.

Top: The magnificent male *Corydoras barbatus*. This species is difficult to spawn and commands a high price. **Left:** A head-on view of *Corydoras barbatus* showing the yellow predorsal stripe. **Bottom left:** At times *Corydoras barbatus* will assume a blotchy pattern as seen here. **Bottom right:** The snout of *Corydoras barbatus* is rather elongate, especially when seen from this angle.

PLATE 169

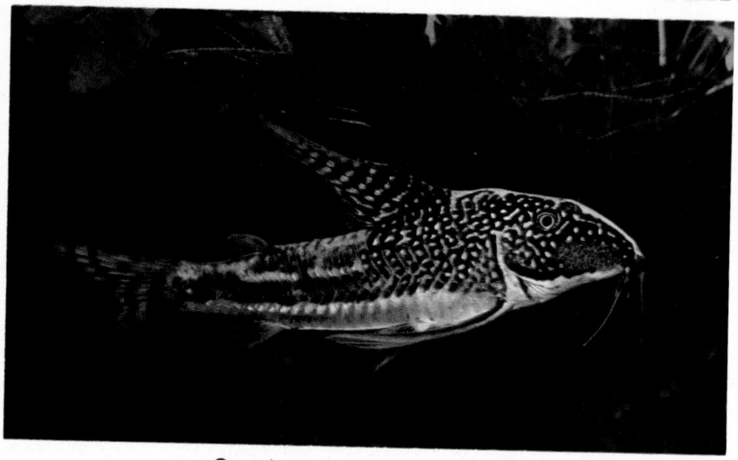

Corydoras barbatus (male). (Southeastern Brazil.)

Corydoras barbatus (male). (Southeastern Brazil.)

Corydoras barbatus (male). (Southeastern Brazil.)

Corydoras barbatus (male). (Southeastern Brazil.)

Corydoras barbatus. (Southeastern Brazil.)

Corydoras barbatus. (Southeastern Brazil.)

Corydoras macropterus (female). (Southeastern Brazil.)

Corydoras macropterus (male). Santos Shore, Brazil.

Corydoras panda (var.). (Rio Ucayali system, Peru.)

Corydoras panda (var.). (Rio Ucayali system, Peru.)

Corydoras panda. (Rio Ucayali system, Peru.)

Corydoras panda. (Rio Ucayali system, Peru.)

Corydoras guapore. (Rio Guapore, Brazil.)

Corydoras caudimaculatus. (Rio Guapore, Brazil.)

Corydoras metae (var. *davidsandsi*).

Corydoras metae. (Colombia.)

PLATE 171

Corydoras guapore. (Rio Guapore, Brazil.)

Corydoras caudimaculatus. (Rio Guapore, Brazil.)

Corydoras panda. (Rio Ucayali system, Brazil.)

Corydoras melini. (Amazonas, Brazil.)

Corydoras metae (var.). Rio Magdalena, Colombia.

Corydoras metae. (Colombia.)

Corydoras arcuatus (juv.). Humaita, Brazil.

Corydoras arcuatus. (Amazonas, Brazil.)

Corydoras narcissus. (Rio Purus system, Brazil.)

Corydoras arcuatus. (Amazonas, Brazil.)

Corydoras narcissus. (Rio Purus system, Brazil.)

Corydoras arcuatus. (Amazonas, Brazil.)

Corydoras axelrodi (var.). (Rio Meta, Colombia.)

Corydoras axelrodi (var.). (Rio Meta, Colombia.)

Corydoras sp. cf. *axelrodi*. (Unknown.)

Corydoras evelynae. (Rio Solimoes, Brazil.)

PLATE 173

Corydoras rabauti. (Amazon system.)

Corydoras zygatus. (Peru.)

Corydoras rabauti fry of six weeks.

Corydoras zygatus fry at four weeks.

Corydoras rabauti of six months.

Corydoras zygatus at three months.

Mature young of both species, *C. rabauti* on the left with the deeper, more robust profile.

A sequence of photos showing aspects of the courtship and spawning of *Corydoras adolfoi*. The female in the last photo is depositing some of her eggs.

PLATE 177

Corydoras simulatus. (Colombia.)

Corydoras metae. (Colombia.)

Corydoras bondi. (Venezuela; Surinam.)

Corydoras sp. cf *arcuatus*. (Unknown.)

Corydoras arcuatus. (Amazonas, Brazil.)

Corydoras rabauti. (Amazon system.)

Corydoras melini (var.). (Amazonas, Brazil.)

Corydoras axelrodi. (Rio Meta, Colombia.)

Corydoras loxozonus. (Colombia.)

Corydoras melini. (Amazonas, Brazil.)

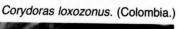

Corydoras loxozonus. (Colombia.)

Corydoras melini. Tabatinga.

Corydoras rabauti. (Amazon system.)

Corydoras burgessi. (Rio Unini, Amazonas, Brazil.)

Corydoras burgessi. (Rio Unini, Amazonas, Brazil.)

Corydoras burgessi. (Rio Unini, Amazonas, Brazil.)

Corydoras adolfoi. (Sao Gabriel da Cachoeira.)

Corydoras adolfoi "imitator". (Sao Gabriel da Cachoeira.)

PLATE 179

Corydoras approuaguensis (female) (Holotype). Rio Approuague, Fr. Guiana.

Corydoras approuaguensis (male) (Paratype). Rio Approuague, Fr. Guiana.

Corydoras orphnopterus. (Ecuador.)

Corydoras stenocephalus. (Rio Ucayali system, Peru.)

Corydoras bolivianus (female) (Holotype). Rio Mamore basin, Bolivia.

Corydoras bolivianus. (male) (Paratype). Rio Mamore basin, Bolivia.

Corydoras copei (Holotype). Rio Huytoyacu, Loreto, Peru.

Corydoras fowleri. Leticia.

Corydoras weitzmani (Paratype). Rio Vilcanota system, Peru.

PLATE 181

Corydoras filamentosus (Holotype). Corantijn basin, Nickerie District, Surinam.

Corydoras solox (Holotype). Rio Oiapoque, Amapa Territory, Brazil.

Corydoras carlae (Holotype). Petit Arroyo, Parana basin, Misiones Province, Argentina.

Corydoras geryi (Holotype). Rio Mamore basin, Beni Province, Bolivia.

Corydoras aeneus (var.). (Tropical South America.)

Corydoras aeneus (var.). (Tropical South America.)

Corydoras aeneus (var.). (Tropical South America.)

Corydoras aeneus (var.). (Tropical South America.)

Corydoras aeneus (var.). (Tropical South America.)

Corydoras aeneus (albino). (Tropical South America.)

Corydoras sp. cf. *aeneus*. (Unknown.)

Corydoras aeneus (var.). (Tropical South America.)

Corydoras aeneus (var.). (Tropical South America.)

Corydoras aeneus (var.). (Tropical South America.)

Corydoras aeneus (var.). (Tropical South America.)

Corydoras aeneus (var.). (Tropical South America.)

Corydoras aeneus (albino). (Tropical South America.)

Corydoras latus. Humaita, Brazil.

Corydoras sp. cf. *aeneus*. (Unknown.)

PLATE 185

Corydoras melanotaenia. (Colombia.)

Corydoras melanotaenia?. (Colombia.)

Corydoras aeneus. (Tropical South America.)

Corydoras sp. cf. *aeneus*. Paraguay.

Corydoras aeneus (var.). (Tropical South America.)

Corydoras latus. (Upper Amazon; Bolivia.)

Corydoras melanotaenia. (Colombia.)

Corydoras amapaensis. (Brazil.)

Corydoras garbei. (Southeastern Brazil.)

Corydoras treitlei. (Brazil.)

Corydoras semiaquilus. (Amazonas, Brazil.)

Corydoras semiaquilus. (Amazonas, Brazil.)

Corydoras melanotaenia. (Colombia.)

Corydoras melanotaenia (juv.). (Colombia.)

Corydoras zygatus. (Peru.)

Corydoras sp. cf. *eques*. (Tropical South America.)

PLATE 187

Corydoras sp. cf. *septentrionalis*. (Tropical South America.)

Corydoras simulatus. (Tropical South America.)

Corydoras simulatus. (Tropical South America.)

Corydoras simulatus. (Tropical South America.)

Corydoras sp. cf. *simulatus*. (Tropical South America.)

Corydoras sp. cf. *septentrionalis*. Transamazonica.

Corydoras blochi blochi. (Guyana.)

Corydoras blochi blochi. (Guyana.)

A breeding pair of *Corydoras habrosus*. The male is the slimmer fish (in front of the female).

Corydoras habrosus in the typical "T" position.

Female *C. habrosus* carrying single egg.

Female *C. habrosus* cleaning egg deposition site.

The male of the spawning pair.

PLATE 189

This juvenile male *Corydoras habrosus* appears quite normal from this side.

Looking at it from the other side reveals that one eye is missing, apparently a birth defect.

Corydoras habrosus fry at 2-3 weeks of age.

Corydoras habrosus fry at 6 weeks of age.

Corydoras habrosus fry at ten weeks of age. The adult pattern is beginning to surface.

Corydoras habrosus (var.). (Venezuela.)

Corydoras habrosus. (Venezuela.)

Corydoras hastatus. (Upper Amazon; Rio Paraguay.).

Corydoras pastazensis (juv.). Rio Napo, Ecuador.

Corydoras nanus. (Surinam.)

Corydoras elegans. (Amazonas; Peru.)

Corydoras pygmaeus. (Brazil.)

Corydoras hastatus. (Upper Amazon; Rio Paraguay.)

A pair of *Corydoras pygmaeus* preparing to assume the "T" position. The male is crossed in front of the female.

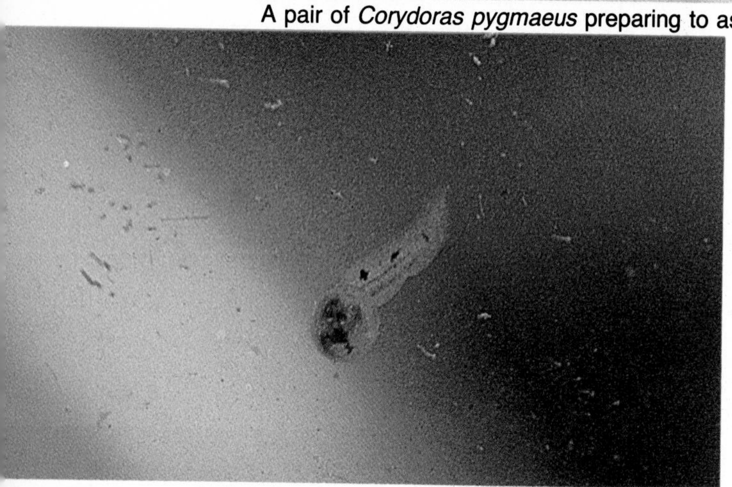

A *Corydoras pygmaeus* fry emerging from the egg.

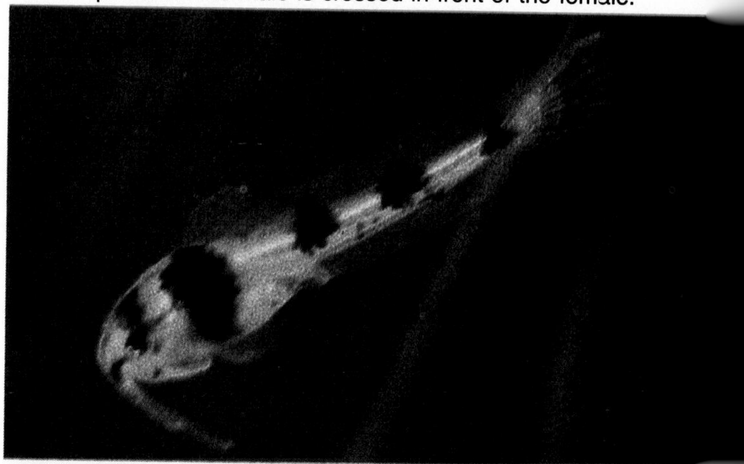

At 3-4 weeks *C. pygmaeus* fry with blotched pattern.

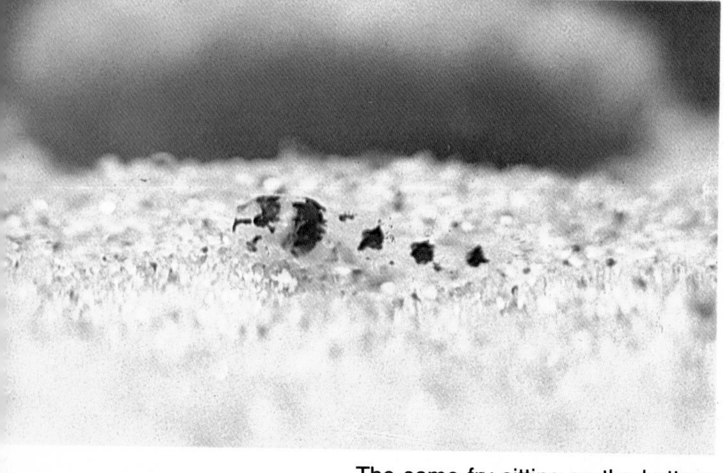

The same fry sitting on the bottom.

At 8-9 weeks the adult pattern starts to emerge.

Corydoras axelrodi (var.). (Rio Meta, Colombia.)

Corydoras axelrodi. (Rio Meta, Colombia.)

Corydoras habrosus. (Venezuela.)

Corydoras gracilis. Transamazonica, Brazil.

Corydoras paleatus (juv.). (Southeastern Brazil; Paraguay; Uruguay.)

Corydoras pastazensis. (Ecuador.)

Corydoras aeneus (var.). (Tropical South America.)

Corydoras septentrionalis. (Venezuela.)

PLATE 193

Corydoras ehrhardti. (Santa Catarina, Brazil.)

Corydoras ehrhardti. (Santa Catarina, Brazil.)

Corydoras septentrionalis (var.). (Venezuela.)

Corydoras sp. cf. *septentrionalis*. (Tropical South America.)

Corydoras sp. cf. *septentrionalis*. (Tropical South America.)

Corydoras sp. cf. *septentrionalis*. (Tropical South America.)

Corydoras sp. (Tropical South America.)

Corydoras sp. (juv.). (Tropical South America.)

Corydoras aeneus (var.). (Tropical South America.)

Corydoras ehrhardti. (Santa Catarina, Brazil.)

Corydoras hastatus. (Upper Amazon; Rio Paraguay.)

Corydoras sp. cf. *latus*. (Tropical South America.)

Corydoras melanotaenia. (Colombia.)

Corydoras simulatus. (Colombia.)

Corydoras paleatus. (Southeastern Brazil; Paraguay; Uruguay.)

Corydoras paleatus. (Southeastern Brazil; Paraguay; Uruguay.)

PLATE 195

Corydoras paleatus (var.) (female). (Southeastern Brazil; Paraguay; Uruguay.)

Corydoras paleatus (var.) (male). (Southeastern Brazil; Paraguay; Uruguay.)

Corydoras ehrhardti (juv.). (Southeastern Brazil.)

Corydoras paleatus (wild caught). Rio Grande do Sul.

Corydoras sp. cf. *macropterus*. (Tropical South America.)

Corydoras macropterus (male). (Southeastern Brazil.)

Corydoras garbei. (Brazil.)

Corydoras garbei. (Brazil.)

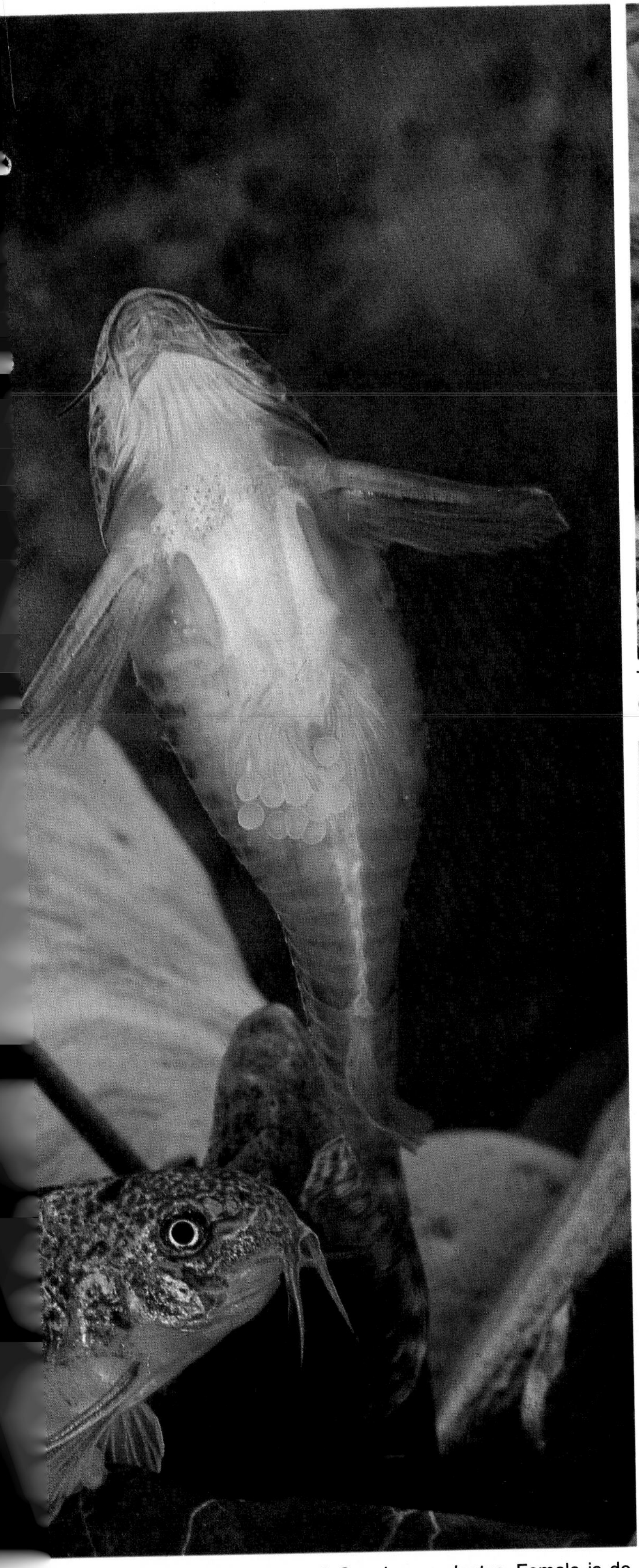

The "T" position which is common to many species of *Corydoras*.

Spawning sequence of *Corydoras paleatus*. Female is depositing eggs on the side glass of an aquarium.

Further courtship and spawning occurs over a period of several hours until all the eggs are deposited.

PLATE 197

Corydoras sp cf. *schwartzi*. (Brazil.)

Corydoras sp cf. *schwartzi*. (Brazil.)

Corydoras schwartzi. (Amazonas, Brazil.)

Corydoras schwartzi. (Amazonas, Brazil.)

Corydoras haraldschultzi. (Brazil.)

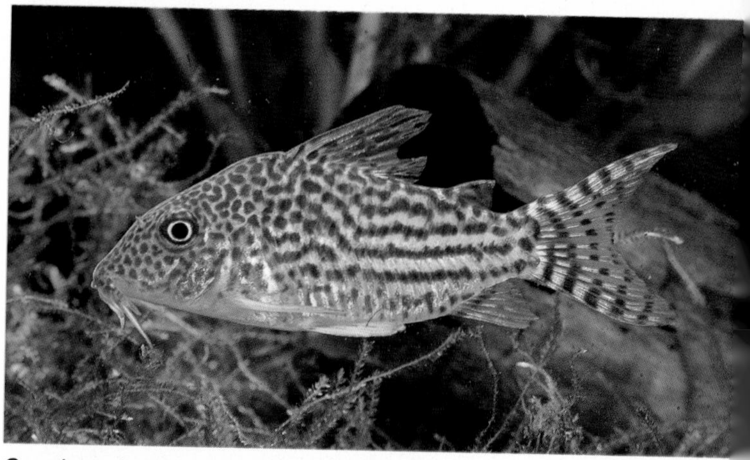

Corydoras haraldschultzi (var.). (Brazil.)

Corydoras sp. cf. *haraldschultzi*. (Brazil.)

Corydoras sp. cf. *sterbai*. (Brazil.)

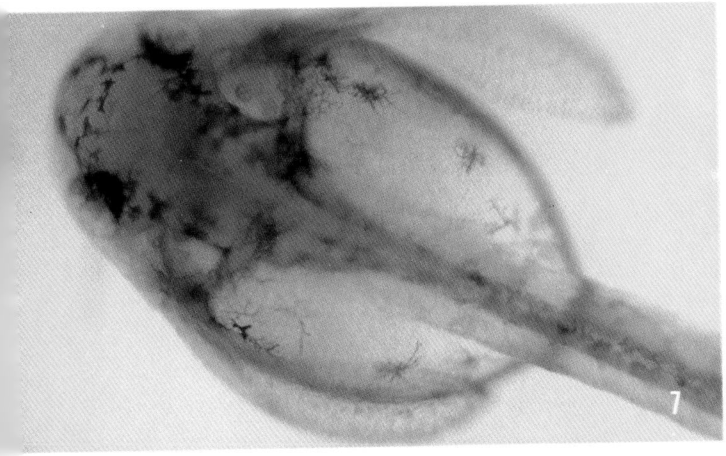

Spawning results in *Corydoras haraldschultzi*. 1. A male *Corydoras haraldschultzi*. 2. *C. haraldschultzi* prefer to deposit their eggs on leaves. 3. *Corydoras haraldschultzi*. 4. Fry a day or two after absorbing yolk. 5. An individual about two weeks old. 6. A young *C. haraldschultzi* about a month old. 7. A newly hatched *Corydoras* fry, probably *C. aeneus*.

PLATE 199

Corydoras ornatus. (Brazil.)

Corydoras schwartzi. (Amazonas, Brazil.)

Corydoras evelynae. (Amazonas, Brazil.)

Corydoras leucomelas. (Upper Amazon; Peru.)

Corydoras haraldschultzi. (Brazil.)

Corydoras sterbai. (Brazil.)

Corydoras reticulatus. (Brazil.)

Corydoras reticulatus. (Brazil.)

Corydoras sodalis. (Peru.)

Corydoras sodalis. (Peru.)

Corydoras reticulatus. Humaita, Brazil.

Corydoras reticulatus. Humaita, Brazil.

Corydoras sodalis. (Peru.)

Corydoras napoensis. (Peru.)

Corydoras napoensis. (Peru.)

Corydoras napoensis. (Peru.)

PLATE 201

Corydoras sodalis. (Peru.)

Corydoras reticulatus. (Brazil.)

Corydoras sodalis (Holotype). Lake Matamata, Loreto, Peru.

Corydoras sodalis. (Peru.)

Corydoras napoensis. (Peru.)

Corydoras nanus. (Surinam.)

Corydoras acutus? (Upper Amazon; Peru.)

Corydoras sychri. (Venezuela.)

Corydoras melanistius melanistius. (Venezuela.)

Corydoras leucomelas. (Upper Amazon; Peru.)

Corydoras melanistius brevirostris. (Venezuela.)

Corydoras sp. cf. *orphnopterus.* (Tropical South America.)

Corydoras sodalis. (Peru.)

Corydoras sodalis. (Peru.)

Corydoras loretoensis (Holotype). Rio Nanay, Loreto, Peru.

Corydoras loretoensis. (Peru.)

Corydoras atropersonatus. (Ecuador.)

Corydoras sychri. Rio Nanay system, Peru.

Corydoras napoensis (Holotype). Morona Cocha, Iquitos, Peru.

Corydoras armatus. Rio Yavari, Peru.

Corydoras lamberti (Holotype). Rio Huytoyacu, Loreto, Peru.

Corydoras leopardus. (Tropical South America.)

Corydoras acutus. (Upper Amazon; Peru.)

Corydoras pastazensis. (Ecuador.)

Corydoras sp. (Tropical South America.)

PLATE 205

Corydoras ambiacus. (Peru.)

Corydoras elegans. (Amazon River.)

Corydoras agassizi. (Amazonas, Brazil.)

Corydoras leucomelas. (Upper Amazon; Peru.)

Corydoras agassizi. (Amazonas, Brazil.)

Corydoras evelynae. (Amazonas, Brazil.)

Corydoras sychri (var.). (Venezuela.)

Corydoras sychri. (Venezuela.)

Corydoras sychri (var.). (Venezuela.)

Corydoras armatus? (Peru.)

Corydoras sp. (Tropical South America.)

Corydoras armatus. (Peru.)

Corydoras sp. cf. *trilineatus*. (Tropical South America.)

Corydoras sp. cf. *trilineatus*. (Tropical South America.)

Corydoras sp. cf. *trilineatus*. (Tropical South America.)

Corydoras melanistius brevirostris. Venezuela.

Corydoras leucomelas. Transamazonica.

Corydoras ambiacus. (Peru.)

Corydoras leucomelas. (Upper Amazon; Peru.)

Corydoras delphax. (Colombia.)

Corydoras delphax. (Colombia.)

Corydoras delphax. (Colombia.)

Corydoras ambiacus? (Peru.)

Corydoras ambiacus. (Peru.)

Corydoras ambiacus. (Peru.)

Corydoras ambiacus. (Peru.)

Corydoras sp. cf. *ambiacus*. (Tropical South America.)

Corydoras reticulatus. (Brazil.)

Corydoras trilineatus. (Peru.)

Corydoras trilineatus. (Peru.)

Corydoras trilineatus. (Peru.)

Corydoras bondi bondi. (Venezuela.)

Corydoras bondi coppenamensis. (Surinam.)

Corydoras trilineatus. (Peru.)

Corydoras trilineatus. (Peru.)

Corydoras sp. Humaita, Brazil.

Corydoras punctatus? (Surinam.)

Corydoras sp. cf. *trilineatus.* (Tropical South America.)

Corydoras ambiacus. Humaita, Brazil.

Corydoras atropersonatus? (Ecuador.)

Corydoras sp. cf. *sychri*.

Corydoras sp. Rio Xeruini, Brazil.

Corydoras sychri. (Venezuela.)

Corydoras sp. cf. *latus*. Humaita, Brazil.

Corydoras sp. Villa Bella, Rio Guapore.

Corydoras delphax. (Colombia.)

Corydoras armatus? Lower Xingu River.

PLATE 211

Corydoras sp. Rio Meta, Colombia.

Corydoras osteocarus. (Venezuela.)

Corydoras sp.cf. *pulcher*. (Tropical South America.)

Corydoras ornatus. (Brazil.)

Corydoras blochii. (Guyana.)

Corydoras leopardus. (Brazil.)

Corydoras sp. (Tropical South America.)

Corydoras condiscipulus. (French Guiana.)

Corydoras robinae. (Middle Rio Negro, Brazil.)

Corydoras robinae. (Middle Rio Negro, Brazil.)

Corydoras concolor. (Venezuela.)

Corydoras concolor. (Venezuela.)

Corydoras geryi. (Bolivia.)

Corydoras ornatus. (Brazil.)

Corydoras sp. (Tropical South America.)

Corydoras sp. (Tropical South America.)

PLATE 213

Corydoras undulatus (var.). (Southeastern Brazil; northern Argentina.)

Corydoras undulatus. (Southeastern Brazil; northern Argentina.)

Corydoras elegans. (Rio Amazonas.)

Corydoras elegans (var.). (Rio Amazonas.)

Corydoras elegans. (Rio Amazonas.)

Corydoras sp. cf. *elegans*. (Tropical South America.)

Corydoras elegans (male). Amazonas, Brazil.

Corydoras elegans (female). Amazonas, Brazil.

Corydoras sp. cf. *xinguensis*. (Tropical South America.)

Corydoras xinguensis. Rio Guapore.

Corydoras sp. cf. *xinguensis*. Rio Guapore.

Corydoras sp. Rio Meta.

Corydoras sp. cf. *nattereri*. (Tropical South America.)

Corydoras sp. cf. *septentrionalis*. (Tropical South America.)

Corydoras prionotus. Rio Sao Paulo, Brazil.

Corydoras nattereri? (Southeastern Brazil.)

PLATE 215

Corydoras acutus. (Peru.)

Corydoras osteocarus. (Venezuela.)

Corydoras amapaensis (juv.). (Brazil.)

Corydoras ambiacus. (Peru.)

Corydoras blochi blochi. (Guyana.)

Corydoras barbatus. (Southeastern Brazil.)

Corydoras delphax. (Colombia.)

Corydoras ehrhardti. (Santa Catarina, Brazil.)

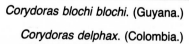

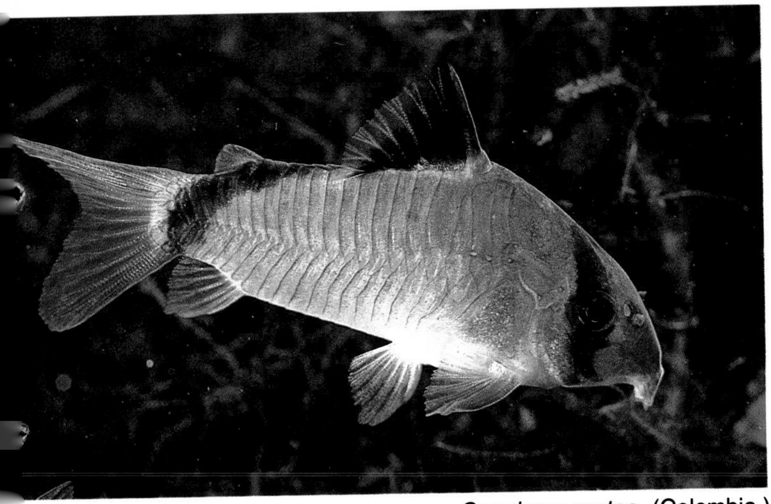

Corydoras metae. (Colombia.)

Corydoras haraldschultzi. (Brazil.)

Corydoras elegans. (Rio Amazonas.)

Corydoras bondi bondi. (Venezuela.)

Corydoras griseus. (Guyana.)

Corydoras griseus. (Guyana.)

Corydoras evelynae. (Amazonas, Brazil.)

Corydoras melanistius brevirostris. (Venezuela.)

PLATE 217

Corydoras robinae. (Middle Rio Negro, Brazil.)

Corydoras ambiacus (var.). (Peru.)

Corydoras sp. cf. *acutus*. (Tropical South America.)

Corydoras bondi. (Venezuela; Surinam.)

Corydoras bondi. (Venezuela; Surinam.)

Corydoras bondi. (Venezuela; Surinam.)

Corydoras sp. cf. *nanus*. (Tropical South America.)

Corydoras nanus. (Surinam.)

Corydoras nattereri. (Southeastern Brazil.)

Corydoras nattereri. (Southeastern Brazil.)

Corydoras xinguensis. (Brazil.)

Corydoras polystictus. (Brazil.)

Corydoras sanchesi. (Surinam.)

Corydoras polystictus. (Brazil.)

Corydoras atropersonatus. (Ecuador.)

Corydoras osteocarus. (Venezuela.)

Corydoras sp. Between Corrientes and Rosario, Argentina.

Corydoras sp. cf. *nanus*. (Tropical South America.)

Corydoras undulatus (var.). (Southeastern Brazil; northern Argentina.)

Corydoras sp. cf. *napoensis*. (Tropical South America.)

Corydoras paleatus (male). (Southeastern Brazil; Paraguay; Uruguay.)

Corydoras paleatus (female). (Southeastern Brazil; Paraguay; Uruguay.)

Corydoras ehrhardti. (Santa Catarina, Brazil.)

Corydoras paleatus (albino). (Southeastern Brazil; Paraguay; Uruguay.)

Corydoras ornatus. (Brazil.)

Corydoras sp. cf. *xinguensis*. (Tropical South America.)

Corydoras melanistius melanistius. (Guyana.)

Corydoras melanistius brevirostris. (Venezuela.)

Corydoras paleatus. (Southeastern Brazil; Paraguay; Uruguay.)

Corydoras garbei. (Brazil.)

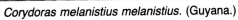

Corydoras ellisae. (Paraguay.)

Corydoras treitlii. (Brazil.)

PLATE 221

Corydoras punctatus. (Amazonas; Guianas.)

Corydoras julii. (Brazil.)

Corydoras sychri. (Venezuela.)

Corydoras leopardus. (Brazil.)

Corydoras orphnopterus (juv.). (Ecuador.)

Corydoras orphnopterus (adult). (Ecuador.)

Corydoras bondi coppenamensis. (Surinam.)

Corydoras osteocarus. (Venezuela.)

Corydoras loretoensis? (juv.). (Peru.)

Aspidoras sp. (Tropical South America.)

Corydoras bondi bondi? (Venezuela.)

Corydoras blochi vittatus. (Maranhao, Brazil.)

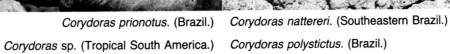

Corydoras prionotus. (Brazil.)

Corydoras nattereri. (Southeastern Brazil.)

Corydoras sp. (Tropical South America.)

Corydoras polystictus. (Brazil.)

Corydoras acutus. (Peru.)

Corydoras ellisae. (Paraguay.)

Corydoras septentrionalis. (Venezuela.)

Corydoras treitlii. (Brazil.)

Corydoras sp. cf. *acutus*. (Tropical South America.)

Corydoras simulatus. (Colombia.)

PLATE 224

Ancistrus lineolatus. Rio Aguaro.

Ancistrus sp. (dorsal view). (Tropical South America.)

Ancistrus sp. (ventral view). (Tropical South America.)

Ancistrus temmincki. (Guianas.)

Ancistrus sp. snout appendages.

PLATE 225

Head of a male *Ancistrus* sp. showing development of appendages.

Male *Ancistrus* sp. on glass of an aquarium. The sucker mouth holds it there easily.

Head of a female *Ancistrus* sp. showing lack of development of appendages.

A close-up photo of the spawn of this pair of *Ancistrus*.

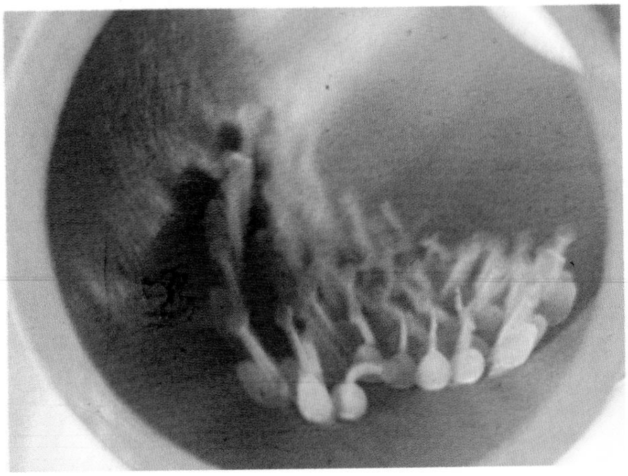

Above: *Ancistrus* sp. male guarding a group of eggs. Left: Five-day-old fry still with considerable yolk to be absorbed. Below: Male *Ancistrus* guarding his progeny. The young are starting to resemble him in shape and coloration.

PLATE 227

Ancistrus dolichopterus. (Northern South America.)

Pseudorinelepis carachama. (Peru.)

Ancistrus dolichopterus. (Northern South America.)

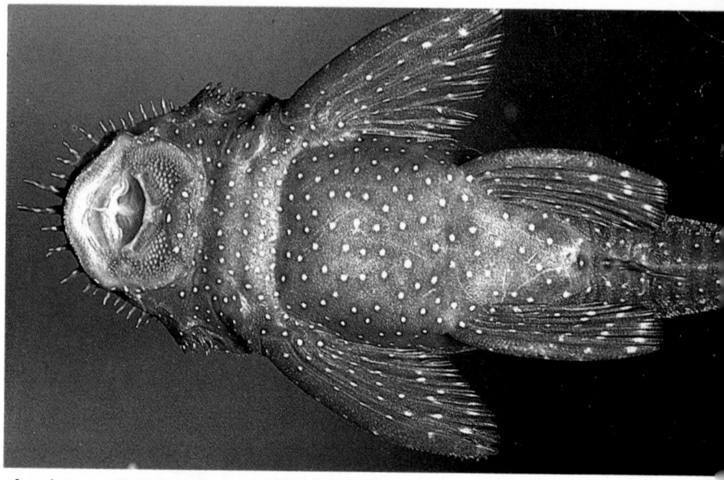

Ancistrus dolichopterus. (Northern South America.)

Ancistrus sp. (Tropical South America.)

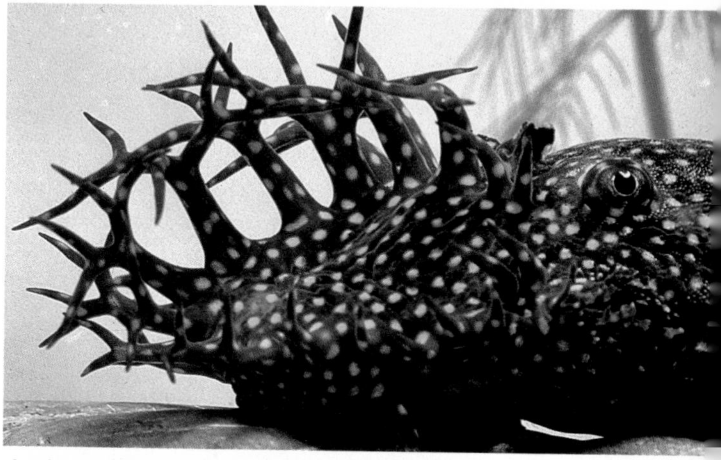

Ancistrus temmincki. (Brazil; Peru; Guianas.)

Ancistrus sp. (Tropical South America.)

Ancistrus sp. (Tropical South America.)

Ancistrus dolichopterus? (Northern South America.)

Ancistrus dolichopterus? (Northern South America.)

Ancistrus sp. (Tropical South America.)

Ancistrus sp. (Tropical South America.)

Ancistrus temmincki. (Brazil; Peru; Guianas.)

Ancistrus temmincki. (Brazil; Peru; Guianas.)

Ancistrus triradiatus? (Colombia.)

Ancistrus triradiatus? (Colombia.)

PLATE 229

Ancistrus temmincki. (Brazil; Peru; Guianas.)

Ancistrus temmincki. (Brazil; Peru; Guianas.)

Ancistrus sp. (Tropical South America.)

Ancistrus sp. (Tropical South America.)

Panaque nigrolineatus. (Venezuela.)

Panaque nigrolineatus. (Venezuela.)

Panaque suttoni. (Venezuela.)

Panaque suttoni. (Venezuela.)

Pseudacanthicus sp. cf. *leopardus* (juv.). (Tropical South America.)

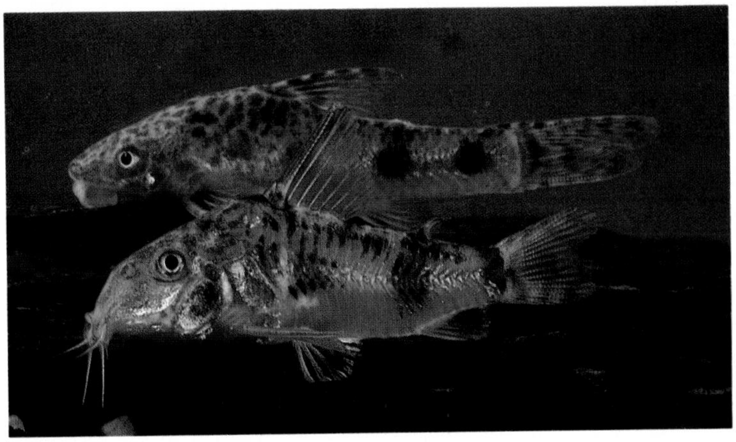

Otocinclus flexilis (above); *Corydoras ehrhardti* (foreground). Rio Grande do Sul.

Panaque sp. cf. *nigrolineatus*. (Tropical South America.)

Peckoltia. sp. (Tropical South America.)

Panaque nigrolineatus. (Venezuela.)

Panaque nigrolineatus. (Venezuela.)

Lithoxus sp. (Tropical South America.)

Lithoxus sp. (Tropical South America.)

Pterygoplichthys sp. (Tropical South America.)

Pterygoplichthys sp. (Tropical South America.)

Pterygoplichthys sp. (Tropical South America.)

Pterygoplichthys sp. (Tropical South America.)

Pterygoplichthys sp. (Tropical South America.)

Pterygoplichthys anisitsi. (Rio Paraguay system.)

Pterygoplichthys sp. (Tropical South America.)

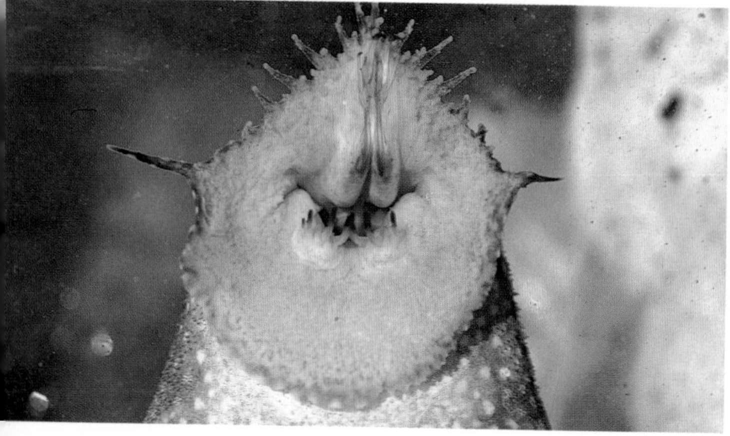

Pterygoplichthys sp. (Tropical South America.)

A river where specimens of *Pterygoplichthys* have been captured. They seem to like this oxygen-rich habitat.

PLATE 233

A very beautiful *Pterygoplichthys* sp. cf. *gibbiceps*. Note the shape of the dorsal and caudal fins.

This *Pterygoplichthys* sp. has ridged scutes making its armor more invulnerable.

Another very attractive species of *Pterygoplichthys*. Again look at the shape of the dorsal and caudal fins.

Pterygoplichthys species are sought after for food. This young boy probably speared this large individual for supper.

PLATE 235

This species is probably related to *Pterygoplichthys multiradiatus.* It has a low, rather straight dorsal fin compared with some of the others.

Snow King Pleco *(Pterygoplichthys anisitsi),* ventral view. Belly pattern and mouth structures are helpful in identification.

A ventral view of another species showing a very different pattern. The teeth appear to be different as well.

Cochliodon hondae. (Colombia.)

Cochliodon hondae. (Colombia.)

Cochliodon hondae (juv.). (Colombia.)

Pterygoplichthys sp. cf. gibbiceps. (Tropical South America.)

Pterygoplichthys gibbiceps. (Brazil.)

Pterygoplichthys gibbiceps. (Brazil.)

Pseudorinelepis carachama. (Peru.)

Pseudorinelepis carachama. (Peru.)

PLATE 237

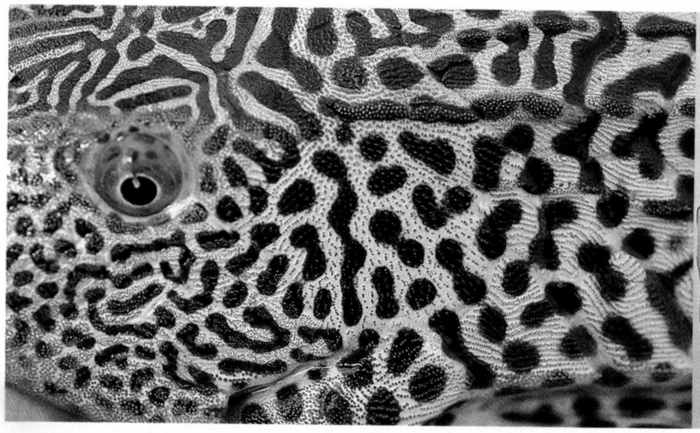

Pterygoplichthys anisitsi. (Paraguay.)

Pterygoplichthys anisitsi. (Paraguay.)

Pterygoplichthys anisitsi. (Paraguay.)

Pterygoplichthys anisitsi (juv.). (Paraguay.)

Pterygoplichthys sp. cf. *gibbiceps*. (Tropical South America.)

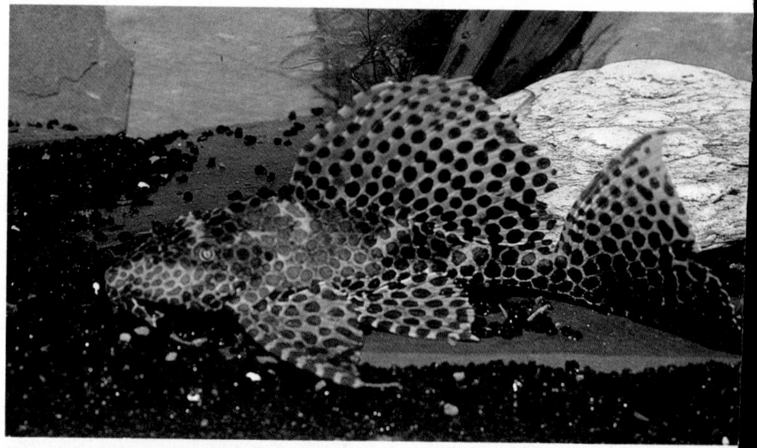

Pterygoplichthys gibbiceps. (Brazil.)

Pterygoplichthys gibbiceps. (Brazil.)

Pterygoplichthys gibbiceps. (Brazil.)

Peckoltia pulcher. (Rio Negro, Brazil.)

Peckoltia pulcher. (Rio Negro, Brazil.)

Hypostomus sp. (Tropical South America.)

Hypostomus sp. (Tropical South America.)

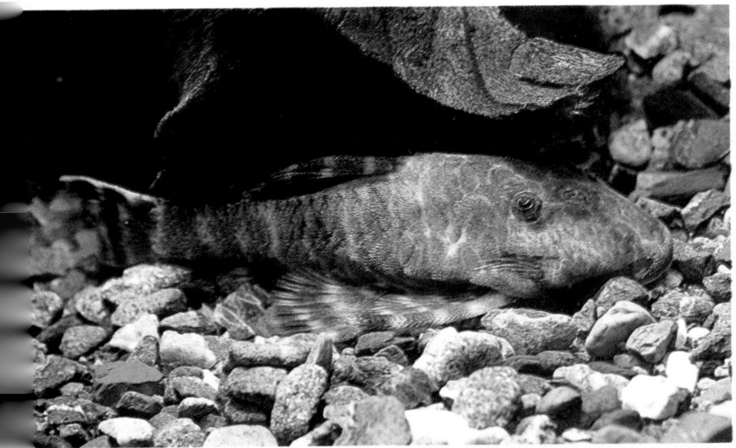

Parancistrus aurantiacus. (Ucayali system.)

Hypostomus sp. (Tropical South America.)

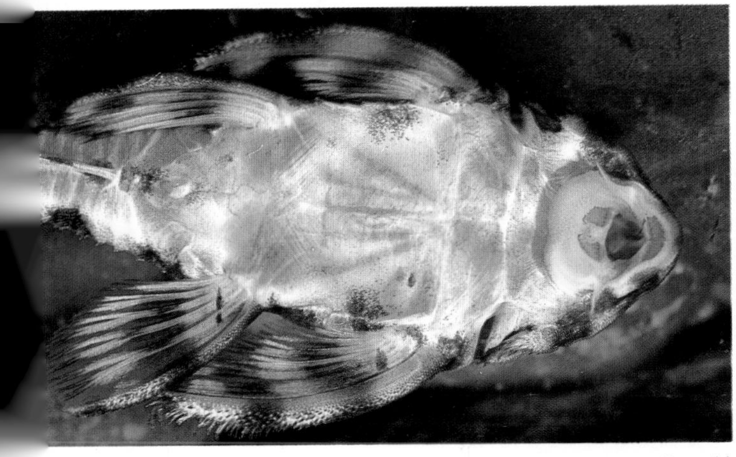

Peckoltia pulcher. (Rio Negro, Brazil.)

Peckoltia pulcher. (Rio Negro, Brazil.)

PLATE 239

Peckoltia sp. (*brevis*?). (Tropical South America.)

Peckoltia sp. (*platyrhyncha*?). (Tropical South America.)

Peckoltia sp. cf. *vittata*. (Tropical South America.)

Peckoltia sp. cf. *pulcher*. (Tropical South America.)

Peckoltia sp. cf. *pulcher*. (Brazil.)

Peckoltia sp. cf. *pulcher*. (Brazil.)

Peckoltia vittata. (Amazon River.)

Peckoltia vittata. (Amazon River.)

Peckoltia vittata. (Amazon River.)

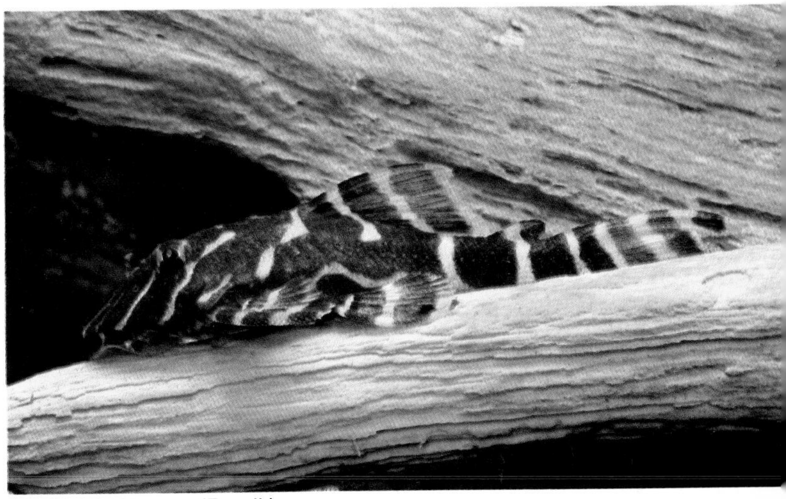

Peckoltia pulcher. (Brazil.)

Peckoltia sp. (*gibbiceps*?). (Tropical South America.)

Panaque sp. (Tropical South America.)

Peckoltia brevis. (Brazil.)

Peckoltia arenaria. (Peru.)

Unknown loricariid. Rio Madeira.

Unknown loricariid. Rio Madeira.

PLATE 241

One of the many species of attractively patterned *Peckoltia* species. These species do not grow large and are favorites of aquarists.

An ocellated pattern is unusual among catfishes. This is probably a species of *Pseudacanthicus*, possibly *P. leopardus* from Guyana.

The yellow trim to the fins of this species sets off the darker colors nicely. This is probably a species of *Hypostomus*.

Pterygoplichthys sp. (aberrant). (Tropical South America.)

Parancistrus punctatissimus. (Amazon River.)

Chaetostoma sp. (Tropical South America.)

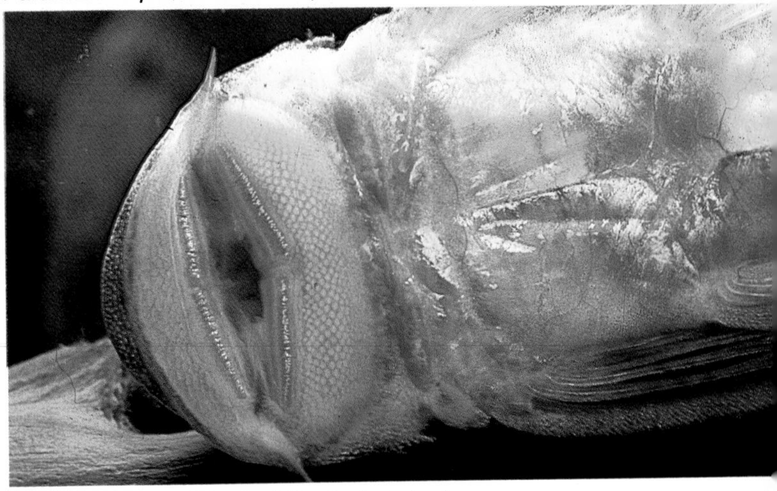

Chaetostoma sp. (Tropical South America.)

Panaque sp. (Tropical South America.)

Panaque sp. (Tropical South America.)

Peckoltia arenaria. (Peru.)

Peckoltia arenaria. (Peru.)

PLATE 243

After the first specimen of this *Peckoltia* appeared the race was on to supply the immediate demand it generated. It has as yet not been identified to species.

Very similar in general appearance to *Hypostomus* species, this *Pseudacanthicus spinosus* has anatomical features to separate it from them (see text).

Parancistrus sp. (Tropical South America.)

Parancistrus sp. (Tropical South America.)

Pterygoplichthys sp. (Tropical South America.)

Pterygoplichthys sp. (Tropical South America.)

Pseudacanthicus spinosus. (Amazon River.)

Pseudacanthicus spinosus. (Amazon River.)

Pseudacanthicus spinosus. (Amazon River.)

Pseudacanthicus spinosus. (Amazon River.)

PLATE 245

Chaetostoma sp. (Tropical South America.)

Chaetostoma sp. (Tropical South America.)

Parancistrus aurantiacus. (Ucayali River)

Parancistrus aurantiacus. (Ucayali River)

Parancistrus aurantiacus. (Ucayali River)

Parancistrus aurantiacus (odontodes). (Ucayali River)

Pseudacanthicus sp. (Tropical South America.)

Unknown loricariid. (Tropical South America.)

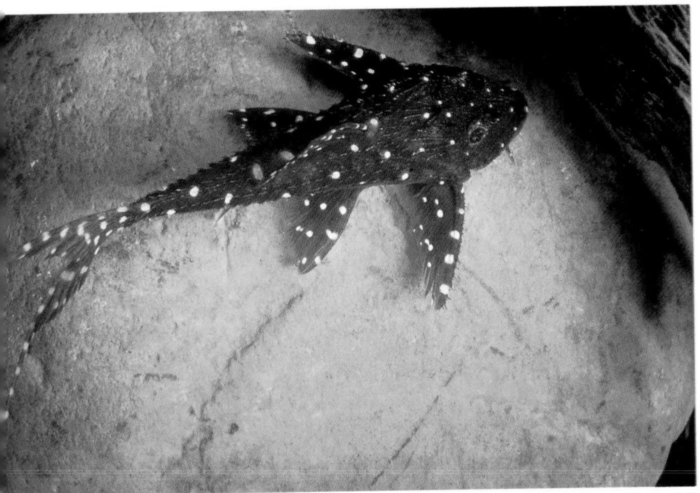

Acanthicus adonis (juv.). (Rio Tocantins, Brazil.)

Pseudacanthicus spinosus. (Amazon River.)

Pseudacanthicus histrix. (Tropical South America.)

Pseudacanthicus histrix. (Tropical South America.)

Pseudacanthicus histrix. (Tropical South America.)

Lithoxus lithoides. (Guyana.)

Lithoxus lithoides. (Guyana.)

Lithoxus lithoides. (Guyana.)

PLATE 247

Acanthicus adonis. (Rio Tocantins, Brazil.)

Acanthicus adonis (adult). (Rio Tocantins, Brazil.)

Acanthicus sp. cf. *hystrix*. (Brazil.)

Acanthicus adonis (juv.). (Rio Tocantins, Brazil.)

Peckoltia oligospila. (Tropical South America.)

Acanthicus sp. (Tropical South America.)

Pseudacanthicus histrix? (Tropical South America.)

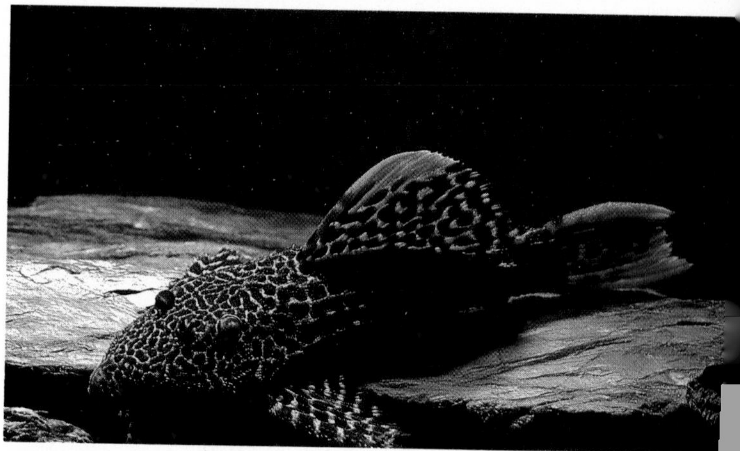

Pseudacanthicus leopardus? (Guyana.)

Ancistrus sp. (*lineolatus*?). (Tropical South America.)

Ancistrus hoplogenys. (Peru and Bolivia to the Guianas.)

Peckoltia platyrhyncha. (Colombia.)

Ancistrus hoplogenys. (Peru and Bolivia to the Guianas.)

Ancistrus hoplogenys. (Peru and Bolivia to the Guianas.)

Pseudacanthicus leopardus. (Guyana.)

Hypostomus sp. (Tropical South America.)

Pterygoplichthys sp. (Tropical South America.)

PLATE 249

Hypostomus sp. (Tropical South America.)

Hypostomus sp. Rio Guapore.

Hypostomus sp. (Tropical South America.)

Ancistrus sp. (Tropical South America.)

Hypostomus sp. (Tropical South America.)

Hypostomus sp. (Tropical South America.)

Ancistrus sp. (Tropical South America.)

Hypostomus sp. (Tropical South America.)

Hypostomus sp. (?*watwata*). (Tropical South America.)

Hypostomus sp. (?*punctatus*). (Tropical South America.)

Hypostomus sp. (Tropical South America.)

Hypostomus sp. (?*varimaculosus*). (Tropical South America.)

Hypostomus sp. (?*jaguribensis*). (Tropical South America.)

Hypostomus sp. (?*niceforoi*). (Tropical South America.)

Hypostomus sp. (?*micromaculatus*). (Tropical South America.)

Hypostomus sp. (?*micropunctatus*). (Tropical South America.)

PLATE 251

Hypostomus sp. (Tropical South America.)

Hypostomus or *Pterygoplichthys* sp. (Tropical South America.)

Lasiancistrus niger. (French Guiana.)

Hypostomus sp. (Tropical South America.)

Hypostomus sp. (Tropical South America.)

Hypostomus sp. (Tropical South America.)

Hypostomus sp. (Tropical South America.)

Hypostomus sp. (Tropical South America.)

Hyp Hypostomus plecostomus. (Tropical South America.)

Hypostomus plecostomus. (Tropical South America.)

Hypostomus plecostomus (var.). (Tropical South America.)

Hypostomus plecostomus (var.). (Tropical South America.)

Hypostomus plecostomus (albino). (Tropical South America.)

Hypostomus plecostomus. (Tropical South America.)

Hypostomus plecostomus (juv.). (Tropical South America.)

Hypostomus plecostomus (juv.). (Tropical South America.)

PLATE 253

Hypostomus sp. (Tropical South America.)

Hypostomus sp. (Tropical South America.)

Hypostomus jaguribensis. (Brazil.)

Unknown loricariid. (Tropical South America.)

Pterygoplichthys etentaculatus. (Brazil.)

Hypostomus sp. (Tropical South America.)

Hypostomus sp. (Tropical South America.)

Hypostomus micropunctatus. (Rio Purus system.)

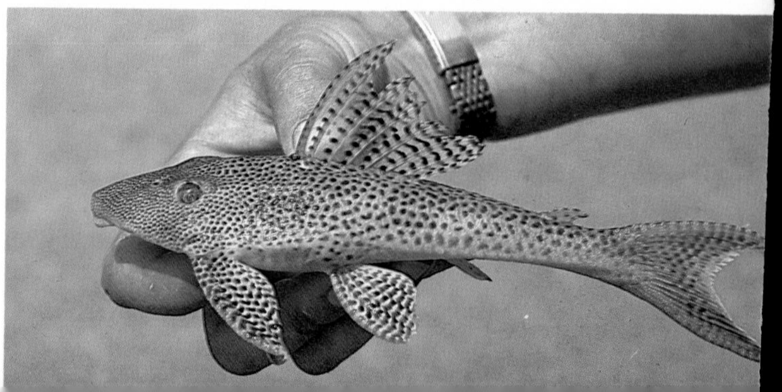

With the net set collectors remove dead branches wherever possible.

Some fishes are scooped out with smaller nets.

The large net is finally brought into shore to harvest the rest of the catch.

One of the fishes collected was this *Hypostomus* sp.

Other collectors use small nets along the shore.

This, also, proves successful as can be seen by the *Hypostomus* species captured.

Ancistrus sp. cf. *hoplogenys*. (Tropical South America.)

Ancistrus sp. cf. *hoplogenys*. (Tropical South America.)

Ancistrus sp. Alto Xingu, Mato Grosso.

Ancistrus sp. cf. *lineolatus*. (Tropical South America.)

Acanthicus sp. cf. *hystrix*. (Tropical South America.)

Ancistrus or *Peckoltia* sp. (Tropical South America.)

? *Pterygoplichthys* sp. (Tropical South America.)

Unknown *Hypostomus* species.

Close-up of mouth of a Hypostomus sp.

Hypostomus species will prop themselves up on their ventral fins.

Hypostomus species from Rio Trombetas, Brazil.

Above and below: Courting and prespawning behavior in a pair of *Hypostomus* species. The female is often approached by the male from above with contact on the female's predorsal area. **Right:** A clutch of *Hypostomus* eggs from a different spawning. The eggs are usually guarded by the male.

Aphanotorulus frankei holotype in lateral and ventral views. This species was discovered in the Rio Ucayali basin in Peru.

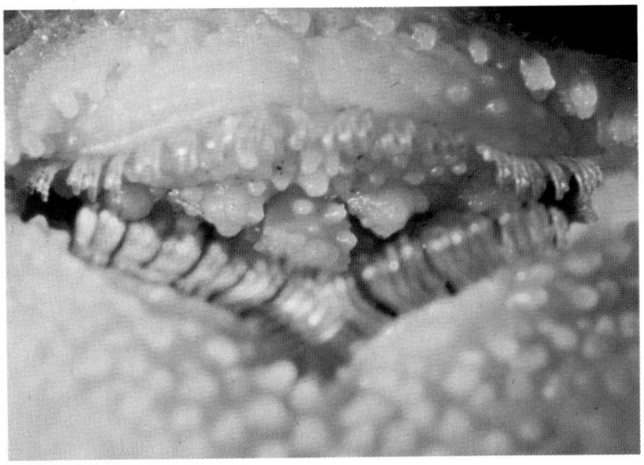

Detail photo of the mouth of *Aphanotorulus frankei*.

Detail of the mouth of *Hypostomus plecostomus*.

Hypostomus plecostomus collected at Mama Creek, Surinam.

PLATE 259

Ventral view of the holotype of *Spectranthus murinus*. This species is from the Rio Tapajos, Est. Para, Brazil.

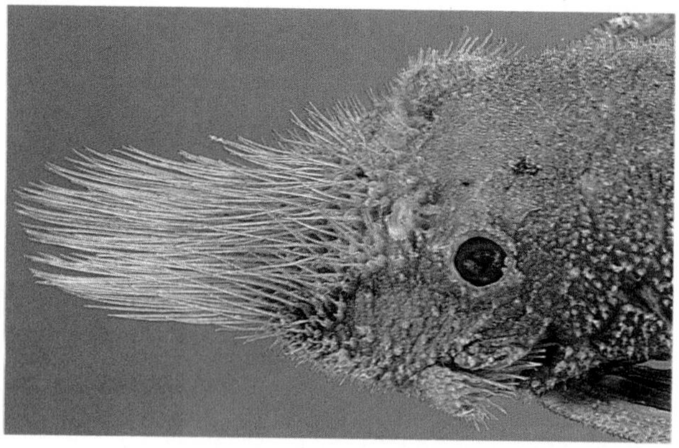

Detail of the head of *Neblinichthys pilosus*.

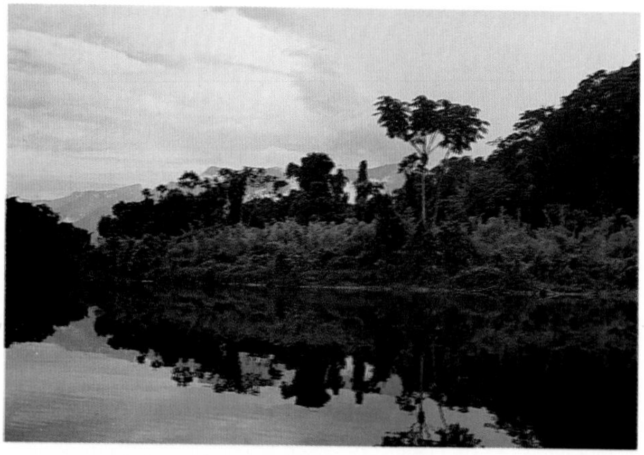

This is where *Neblinichthys pilosus* was collected.

Dorsal, ventral, and lateral views of the holotype of *Neblinichthys pilosus*. This species is from the Rio Baria system in southern Venezuela.

Otocinclus flexilis. (Southeastern Brazil.)

Otocinclus flexilis. (Southeastern Brazil.)

Otocinclus vittatus. (Mato Grosso, Paraguay system.)

Otocinclus sp. (*vestitus*?). (Southeastern Brazil.)

Otocinclus vittatus. (Mato Grosso, Paraguay system.)

Otocinclus sp. (Southeastern Brazil.)

Hypoptopoma inexpectatum? (Rio Paraguay.)

Hypoptopoma inexpectatum? (Rio Paraguay.)

PLATE 261

Otocinclus vestitus. (Upper Amazon; Peru.)

Otocinclus vestitus. (Upper Amazon; Peru.)

Otocinclus sp. cf. *affinis*. (Southeastern Brazil.)

Hypoptopoma sp. (Tropical South America.)

Otocinclus mariae? (Bolivia.)

Otocinclus mariae? (Bolivia.)

Otocinclus flexilis. (Southeastern Brazil.)

Otocinclus flexilis. (Southeastern Brazil.)

Oxyropsis sp. (Amazon system.)

Hypoptopoma sp. Belen, Brazil.

Hypoptopoma guentheri. (Mato Grosso, Brazil.)

Oxyropsis sp. (Amazon system.)

Microlepidogaster sp. (Southeastern Brazil.)

Parotocinclus maculicauda. São Paulo, Brazil.

Otocinclus paulinus. (Southeastern Brazil.)

Otocinclus sp. cf. *affinis*. (Southeastern Brazil.)

PLATE 263

Otocinclus affinis. (Southeastern Brazil.)

Hypoptopoma sp. (Tropical South America.)

Otocinclus vestitus. (Upper Amazon; Peru.)

Otocinclus sp. cf. *affinis.* (Sourtheastern Brazil.)

Panaque nigrolineatus. (Venezuela.)

Panaque suttoni. (Venezuela.)

Otocinclus vestitus. (Upper Amazon; Peru.)

Parotocinclus maculicauda. (Southeastern Brazil.)

Farlowella acus. (Venezuela.)

Pterygoplichthys multiradiatus. (Guyana.)

PLATE 265

Otocinclus affinis. (Southeastern Brazil.)

Sturisoma aureum. (Colombia.)

Unknown loricariid. (Tropical South America.)

Pseudorinelepis pellegrini. (Upper Amazon.)

Peckoltia sp. (*brevis*?). (Tropical South America.)

Ancistrus temmincki? Transamazonica Highway.

Ancistrus dolichopterus? Transamazonica Highway.

Ancistrus leucostictus. (Guyana.)

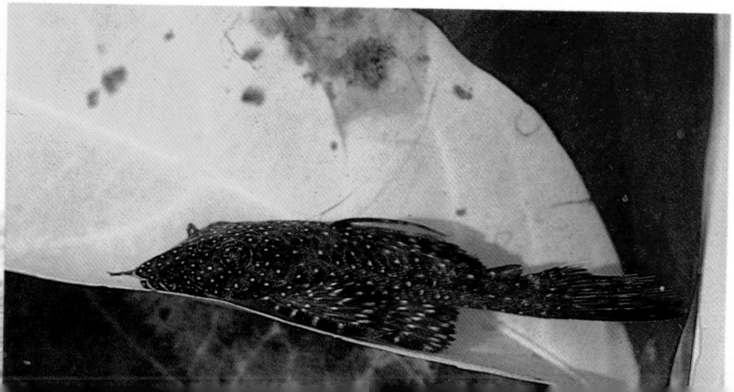

Sturisoma sp. (Tropical South America.)

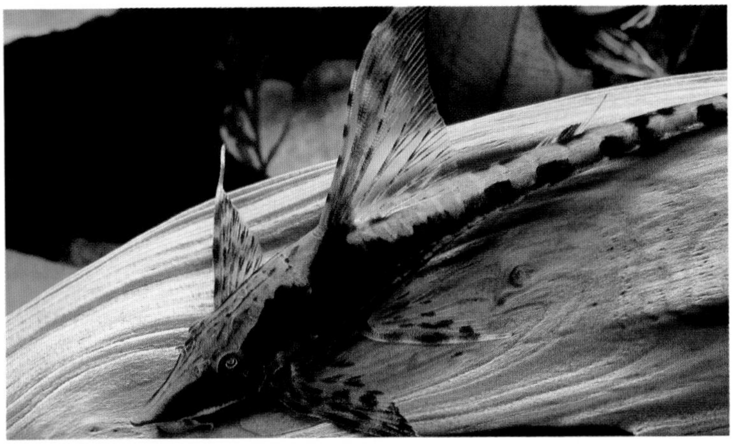
Sturisoma sp. (Tropical South America.)

Sturisoma aureum. (Colombia.)

Sturisoma panamense. (Panama.)

Sturisoma barbatum. (Mato Grosso, Brazil.)

Sturisoma sp. (Tropical South America.)

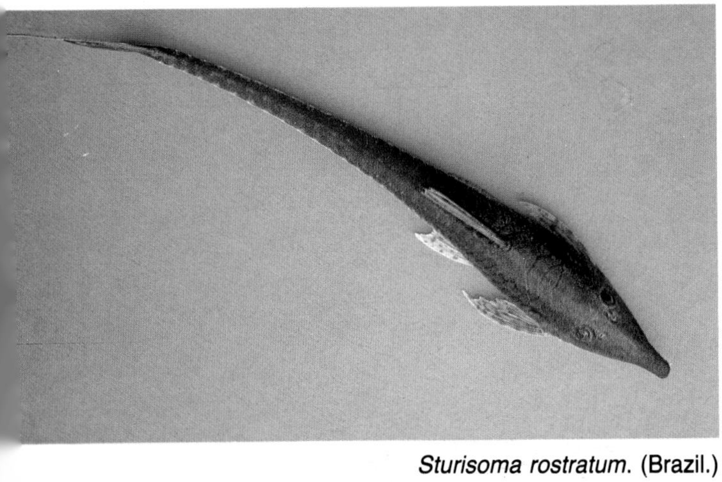
Sturisoma rostratum. (Brazil.)

Lamontichthys sp. (Venezuela).

Sturisoma nigrirostrum. (Ucayali basin, Peru.)

Sturisoma aureum. (Colombia.)

Farlowella sp. (Tropical South America.)

Sturisoma barbatum. (Mato Grosso, Brazil.)

Sturisomatichthys leightoni. (Colombia.)

Sturisomatichthys leightoni. (Colombia.)

Farlowella sp. cf. *gracilis*. (Colombia.)

Farlowella sp. (Tropical South America.)

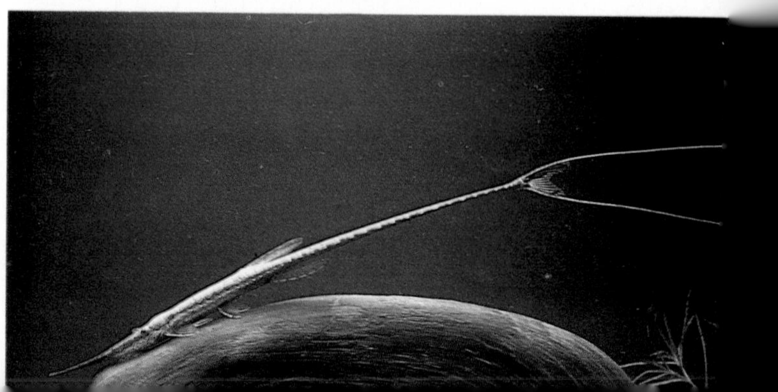

A male *Sturisoma panamense* caring for a clutch of eggs. He will drive off egg predators as well as fan them with his fins.

Six-week-old fry feeding on chopped precooked stringbeans.

Fry this size are hard to detect on the bottom of the tank. They resemble their parents with a high dorsal fin and forked caudal.

PLATE 269

Pseudohemiodon laticeps. (Paraguay.)

Pseudohemiodon laticeps. (Paraguay.)

Rineloricaria heteroptera. (Amazonas, Brazil.)

Rineloricaria hasemani (Brazil.)

Sturisoma aureum. (Colombia.)

Sturisoma aureum (var.). (Colombia.)

Sturisoma aureum. (Colombia.)

Sturisoma aureum. (Colombia.)

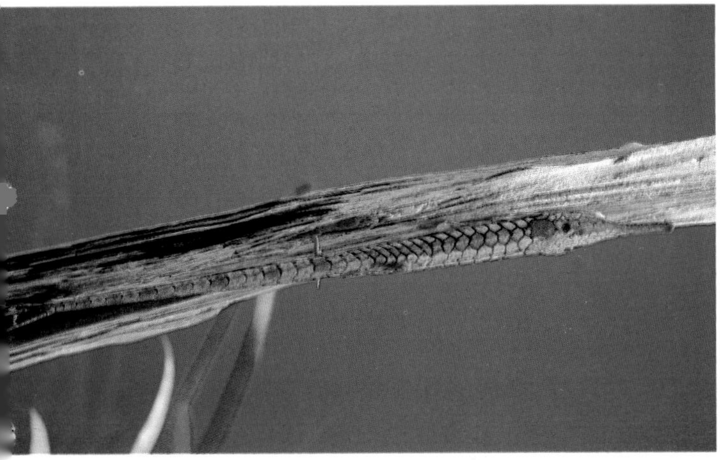
Farlowella knerii. (Ecuador.)

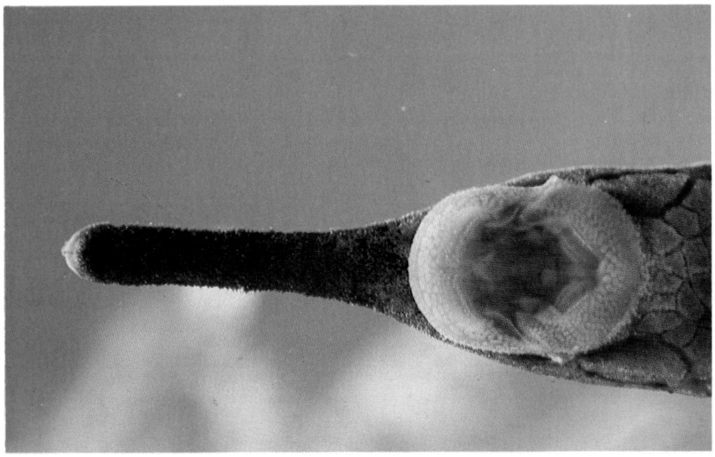
Farlowella knerii. (Ecuador.)

Farlowella acus. (Venezuela.)

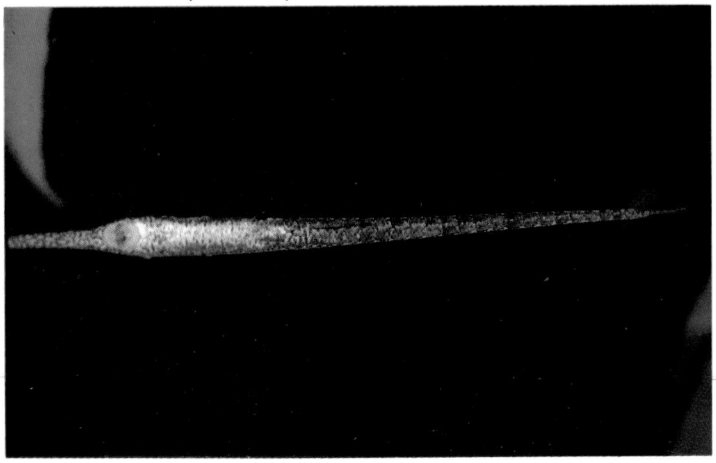
Faclowella gracilis (Colombia.)

Hemiodontichthys acipenserinus. (Rondonia, Brazil.)

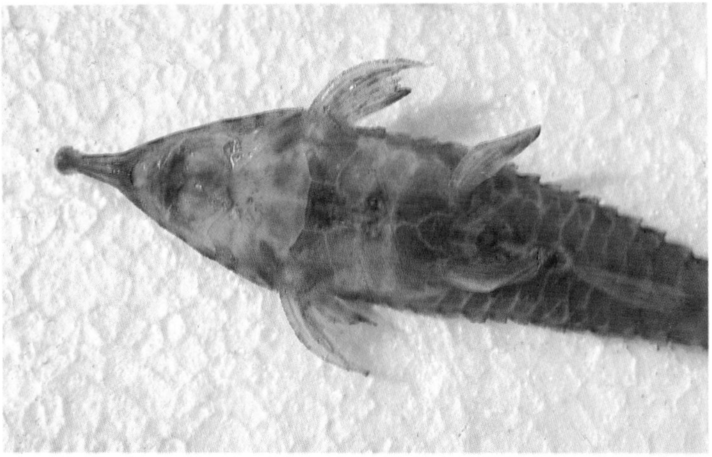
Hemiodontichthys acipenserinus. (Rondonia, Brazil.)

Sturisoma sp. (Tropical South America.)

Sturisoma barbatum. (Mato Grosso, Brazil.)

PLATE 271

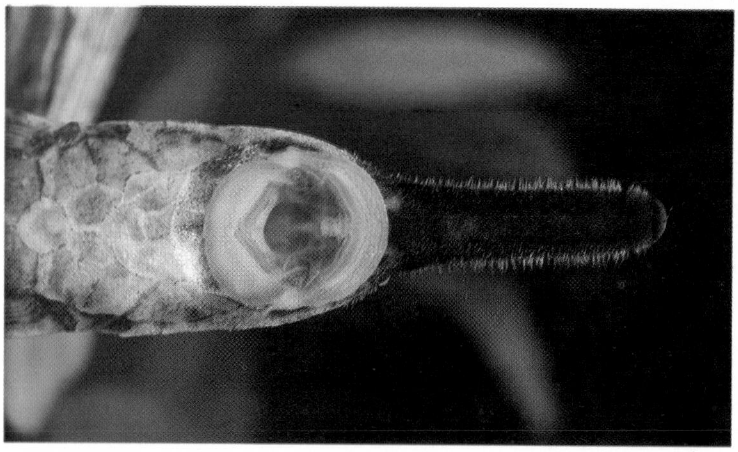

Farlowella sp. (Tropical South America.)

Rineloricaria lanceolata. (Upper Amazon; Peru; Bolivia; Ecuador.)

Farlowella sp. (Tropical South America.)

Farlowella sp. (Tropical South America.)

Loricaria simillima (Ecuador.)

Loricaria simillima (Ecuador.)

Cteniloricaria fowleri. Oyapok River.

Cteniloricaria fowleri. Oyapok River.

Aposturisoma myriodon (Holotype). Rio Huacamayo, Peru.

Aposturisoma myriodon (Holotype, ventral view). Rio Huacamayo, Peru.

Rio Huacamayo, place of capture of *A. myriodon*.

Crossoloricaria rhami (Paratype, dorsal and lateral views). Rio Huacamayo, Peru.

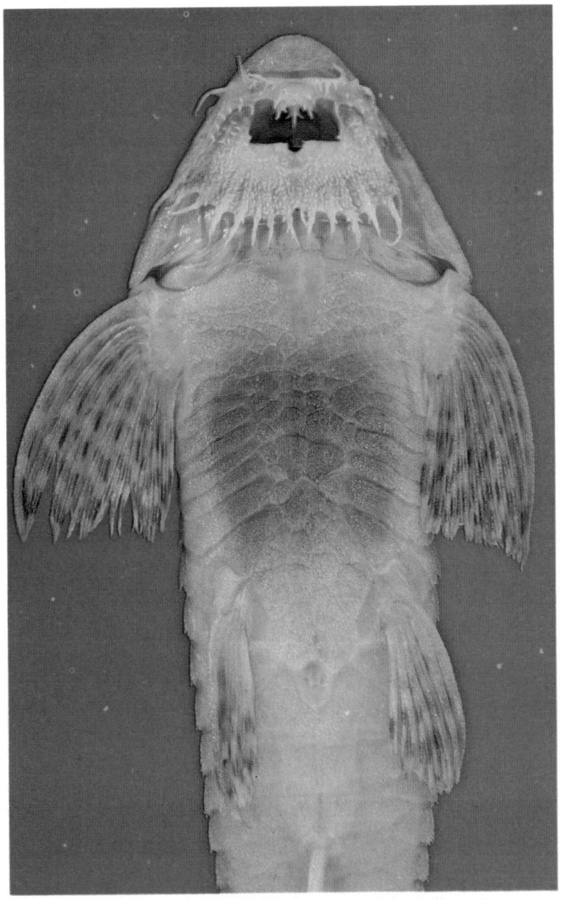

Crossoloricaria rhami (ventral view of Holotype). Rio Huacamayo, Peru.

Crossoloricaria cephalaspis (specimen from type series). Rio Magdalena, Colombia.

Loricaria tucumanensis (dorsal view of male Holotype). Tucuman Prov., Argentina.

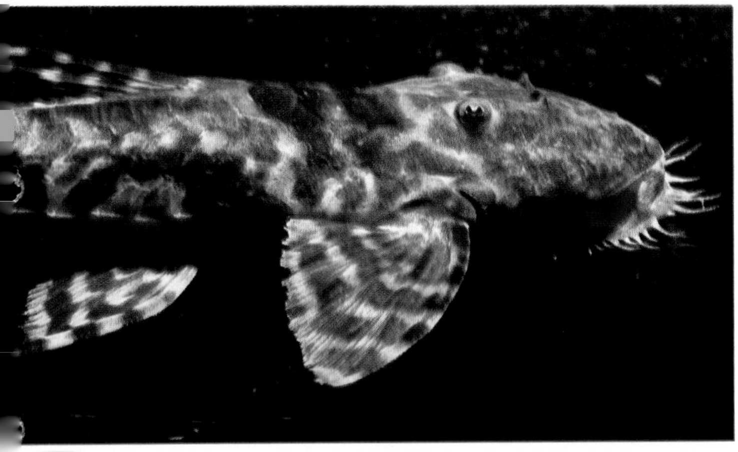

Loricaria sp. (Tropical South America.)

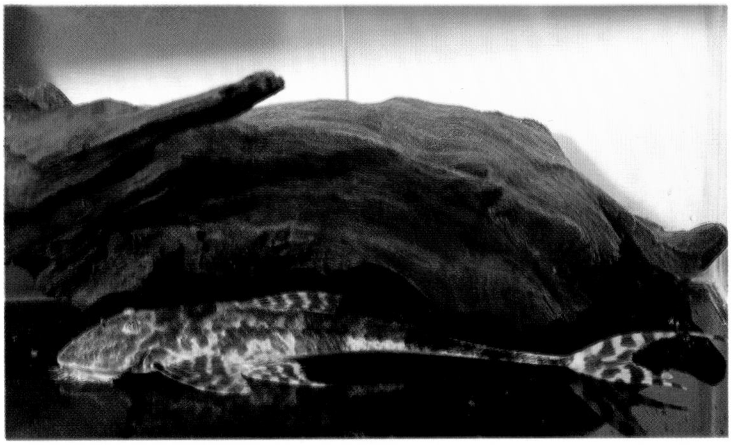

Loricaria sp. (Tropical South America.)

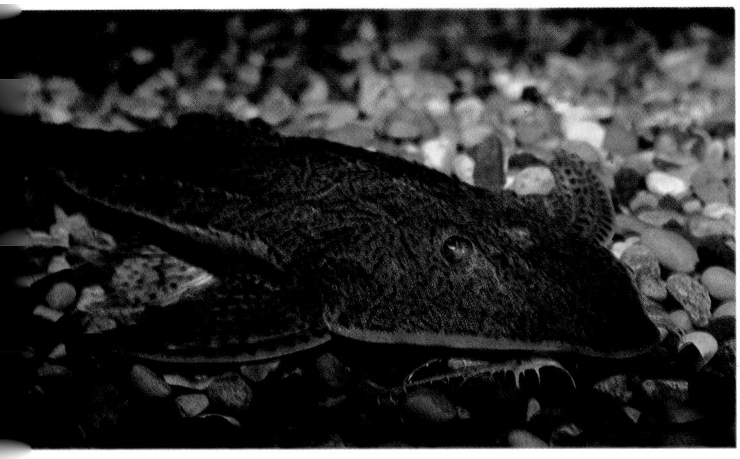

Pseudohemiodon laticeps. (Paraguay.)

Loricaria simillima. (Ecuador.)

Pseudohemiodon sp. cf. *amazonas*. Rio Aruaua.

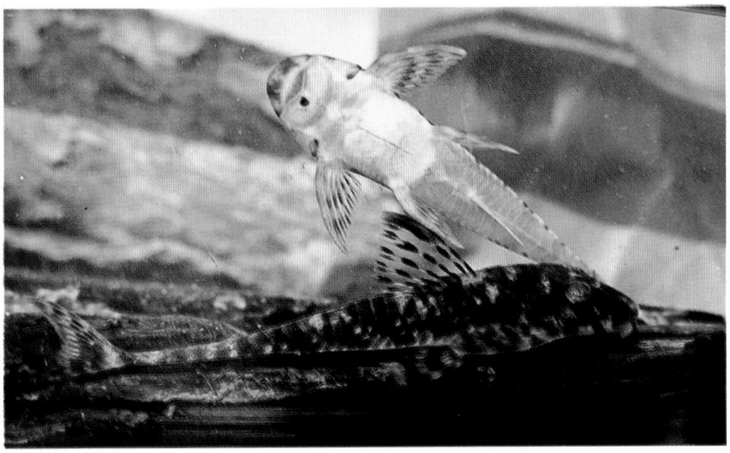

Cteniloricaria sp. cf. *maculata*. (Tropical South America.)

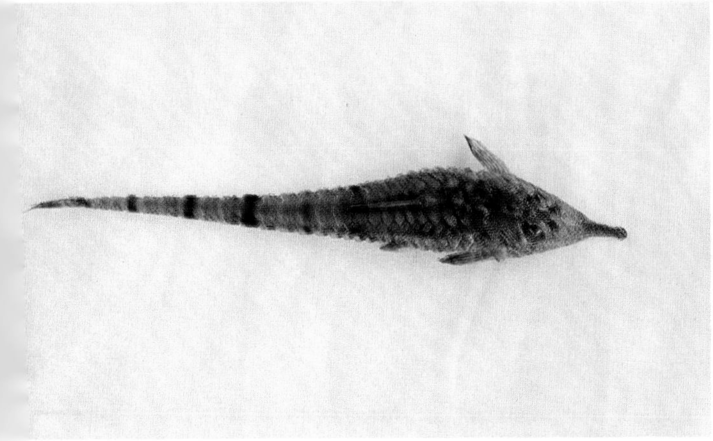

Hemiodontichthys acipenserinus. Tocantins.

Hemiodontichthys acipenserinus. (Mato Grosso, Brazil.)

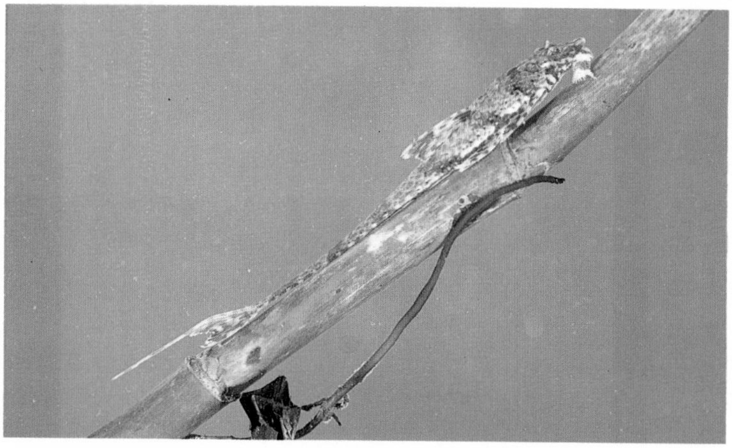

Rineloricaria sp. (Tropical South America.)

Rineloricaria sp. (Tropical South America.)

Rineloricaria sp. Guyane.

Loricaria simillima. (Ecuador.)

Ctenioloricaria maculata. (Surinam.)

Rineloricaria sp. (Tropical South America.)

Loricariichthys sp. Rio Tunapire (Guarico).

Loricariichthys platymetopon. El Baiil.

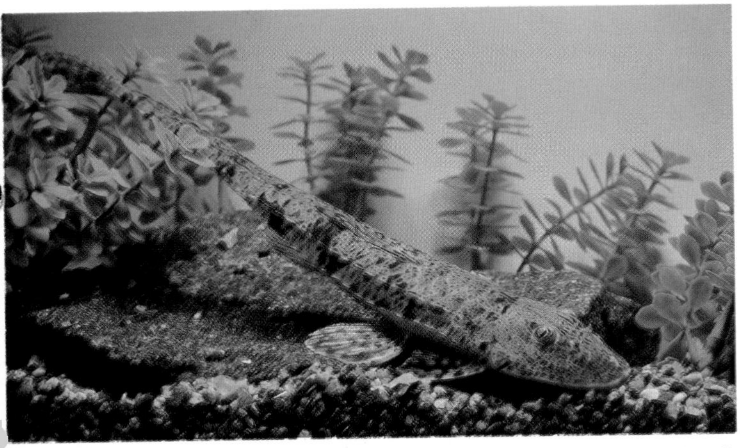

Loricariichthys ucayalensis. Rio Negro, Brazil.

Rineloricaria sp. cf. *phoxocephala*. (Tropical South America.)

Rineloricaria lanceolata (male). (Colombia.)

Rineloricaria lanceolata (male). (Colombia.)

Rineloricaria sp. (Tropical South America.)

Rineloricaria sp. Colombia.

Rineloricaria sp. Colombia.

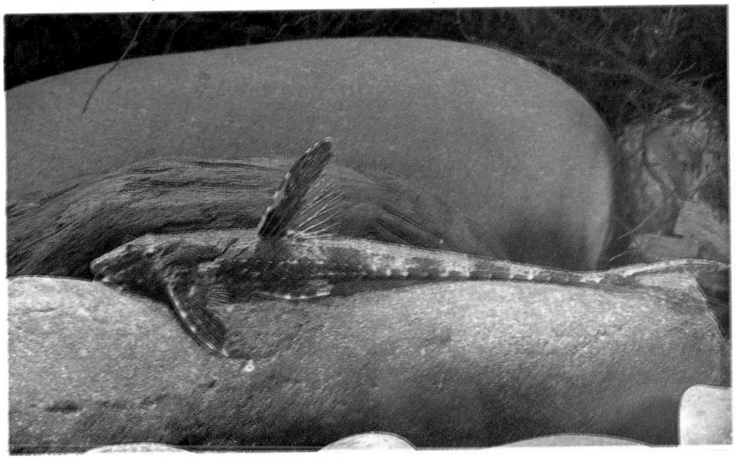

Rineloricaria lanceolata. Colombia.

Rineloricaria castroi. (Est. Para, Brazil.)

Rineloricaria microlepidogaster. (Rio Grande do Sul.)

Rineloricaria microlepidogaster. (Rio Grande do Sul.)

Rineloricaria lanceolata. (Upper Amazon; Peru; Bolivia; Ecuador.)

Rineloricaria lanceolata. (Upper Amazon; Peru; Bolivia; Ecuador.)

Rineloricaria lanceolata. (Upper Amazon; Peru; Bolivia; Ecuador.)

Hypoptopoma gulare. (Peru.)

Hypoptopoma gulare. (Peru.)

Rineloricaria castroi. (Est. Para, Brazil.)

Rineloricaria microlepidogaster. (Rio Grande do Sul.)

Rineloricaria hasemani. (Brazil.)

Rineloricaria hasemani. (Brazil.)

Ctenilоricaria sp. (Tropical South America.)

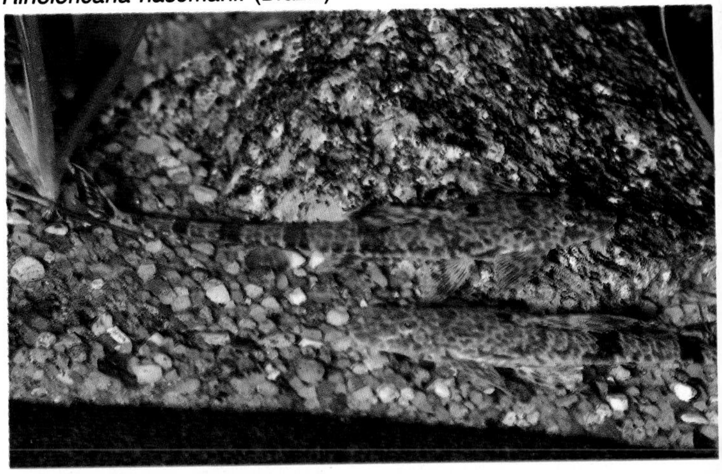

Rineloricaria fallax. (Brazil.)

PLATE 279

Rineloricaria lima. (Brazil.)

Rineloricaria fallax (female). (Brazil.)

Rineloricaria fallax (male). (Brazil.)

Rineloricaria fallax. (Brazil.)

Rineloricaria hasemani. (Brazil.)

Rineloricaria hasemani. (Brazil.)

Rineloricaria castroi. (Est. Para, Brazil.)

Rineloricaria morrowi. (Ucayali basin, Peru.)

Rineloricaria teffeana. (Amazon system near Tefe.)

Rineloricaria teffeana. (Amazon system near Tefe.)

Rineloricaria hasemani. (Brazil.)

Rineloricaria nigricauda. (Rio de Janeiro, Brazil.)

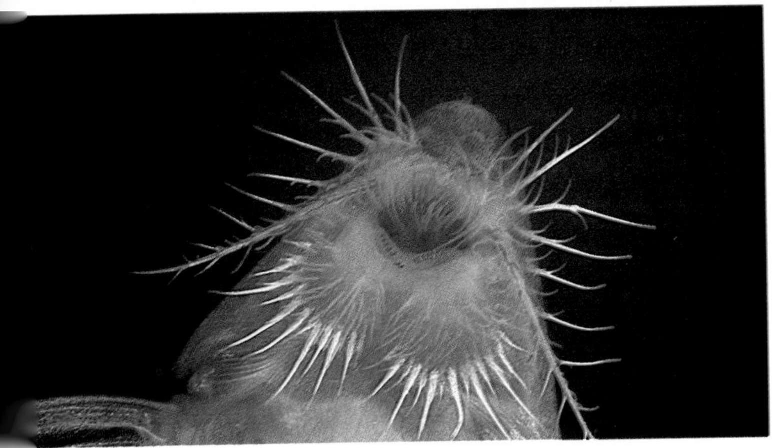

Loricaria nickeriensis. (Surinam.)

Loricaria nickeriensis. (Surinam.)

Rineloricaria sp. cf. *lima* (male). (Tropical South America.)

Loricariichthys maculatus. (Northern Brazil; Surinam.)

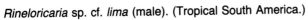

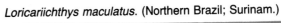

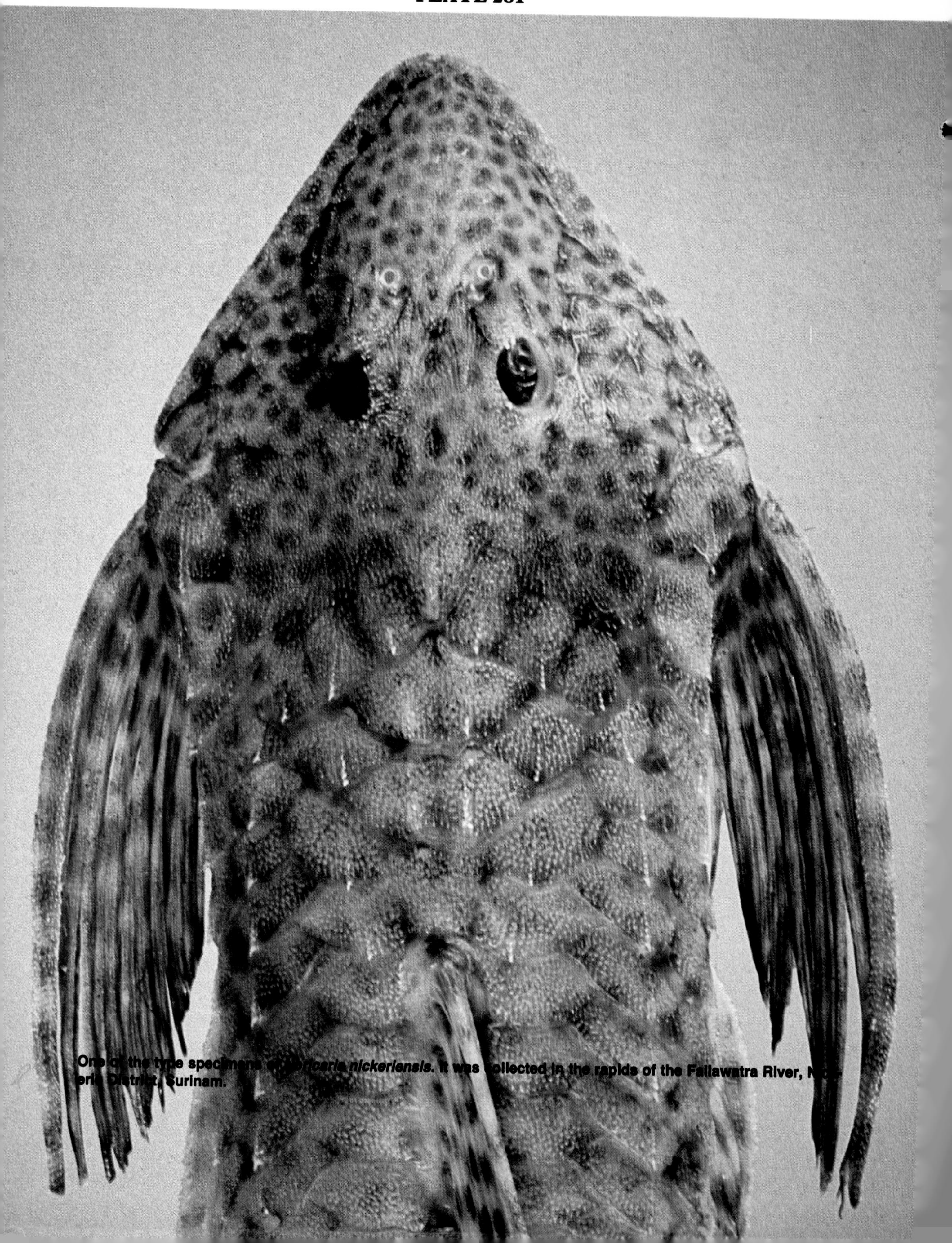

One of the type specimens of *Loricaria nickeriensis.* It was collected in the rapids of the Fallawatra River, Nickerie District, Surinam.

Originally described as a subspecies of *Loricaria prolixa*, *L. lentiginosa* is now considered a full species. This is one of the type specimens collected Represa de Volta Grande, Rio Grande, Est. Sao Paulo, Brazil.

PLATE 283

Rineloricaria castroi male carefully tending eggs that were laid on the leaf of an aquarium plant.

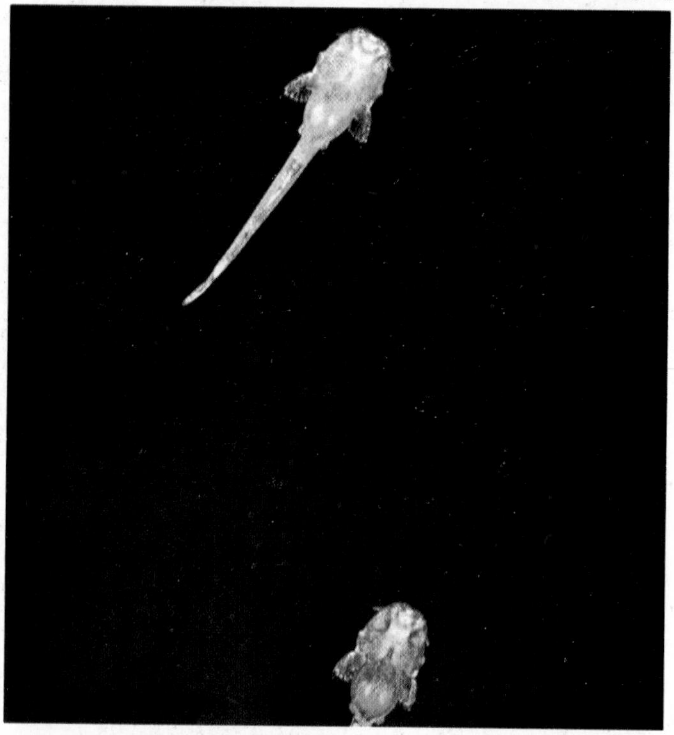

Fry from a hatching of *Rineloricaria castroi*.

Fry from a hatching of *Rineloricaria latirostris*.

Unusual view of *Rineloricaria magdalenae* male showing bristles on head and fins.

Rineloricaria lanceolata resting on an aquarium plant leaf.

A ventral view may be just as valuable in identifying a genus or species as a dorsal or lateral view. Visible in this position are the ventral plates and the tooth arrangement, both diagnostic characters. This is *Rineloricaria lima*.

PLATE 285

Rineloricaria sp. exhibiting the slender caudal peduncle of the group.

Species of *Rineloricaria* will cling to rocks, leaves, or whatever in a current to maintain their position.

Rineloricaria sp. guarding eggs by actually resting on them. Note the "cheek" bristles and the construction of the eye.

Astroblepus sp. (Peru; Colombia; Ecuador.)

INDEX TO SCIENTIFIC NAMES

This index is set up to provide the reader with the information needed to direct him to the section of the book desired. The page numbers in **BOLD TYPE** refer to a discussion of the taxon listed; those in *ITALIC TYPE* refer to an illustration of the taxon (line drawing or photograph); those in Roman type are from the checklists at the end of each family chapter. A separate index is provided for species depicted in color photographs.

I

K

L

M

N

O

COLOR ILLUSTRATIONS INDEX

ACKNOWLEDGMENTS

A book of this size and scope could not be accomplished without the help of numerous individuals. Unfortunately space does not permit the singling out of many of these persons, so I must simply say thank you to all of you who have in one way or another contributed to the completion of this book.

I have received a great deal of help from my colleagues in the scientific community, particularly Drs. John Lundberg, Donald J. Stewart, G. F. Mees, Jonathan Baskin, Isaac Isbrücker, and Han Nijssen, who have read sections of the book, have identified photographs, or have helped in other ways. Hopefully, additional workers who had agreed to read other sections but due to other commitments were unable to do so, will have completed their task in time for the next edition. Dr. Gerald R. Allen has helped in many aspects of the work, even supplying reprints dealing with catfishes that he came across and that I did not have. Thanks are due also to those persons who have provided reprints upon my request and who have kept me on their mailing list as new taxa were published.

Many people have gone out of their way to inform me of unusual catfishes that are being imported so that photographs could be made of the living specimens. Several importers/exporters have helped, in particular Mr. Adolf Schwartz, by earmarking unusual specimens for me in shipments to New Jersey.

Mr. Aaron Norman has not only supplied photos of catfishes but has also traveled to places in the area to photograph them specifically for this book. Dr. Guido Dingerkus also went out of his way to seek out catfishes for photographing.

Many of the excellent illustrations were done by Mr. John R. Quinn, who often created a decent drawing from a poor xerographic copy or photograph where features were not readily visible.

Thanks are also due to the staff of T. F. H. Publications who contributed to the completion of this book and who have had to put up with my various moods (particularly my bad ones when things were not going smoothly). Mr. Jerry G. Walls had the onerous task of reading the manuscript and, again, the text layout, making corrections and suggestions throughout. Artwork (pasting up and design) was accomplished by Ms. Lisa Marie O'Connell and Sheri Urban of our art department. Of course thanks are always due to Dr. Herbert R. Axelrod for publishing this book and being supportive in many ways while it was being put together.

Special thanks are due my wife Lourdes for her support throughout this project.

WARREN E. BURGESS

PHOTO CREDITS: Akiyama, H.; Allen, Dr. G. R.; Allison, D.; Armstrong, N.; Attwood, K.; Axelrod, G. S.; Axelrod, Dr. H. R.; Azuma, Dr. H.; Bitter; Bleher, H.; Brichard, P.; Burgess, Dr. W. E.; Burr, B.; Busse, Dr. K.; Cole, K.; Coleman, N.; Deas, W.; Dingerkus, Dr. G.; Elek, V.; Fernandez-Yepez, Dr. A.; Foersch, W.; Géry, Dr. J.; Horsthemke,; Ikeda; Kahl, B.; Kochetov, A.; Konings, A.; Köpke; Kottelat, Dr. M.; Linke, H.; Lucas, K.; Mahnert, V.; Marine Planning (*Aqua Life Magazine*); Mayden, R.; Mayland, H.; Meola, G.; Meyer, M.; Midori Shobo (*Fish Magazine*); Mori; Nieuwenhuizen, A.; Norman, A.; Page, Dr. L.; Paysan, K.; Purvis, G.; Richter, H.-J.; Roman, Dr.; Roth, A.; Sandford, M.; Sasaki; Schmida, G.; Schultz, H.; Seegers, L.; Steene, R.; Taylor, E. C.; Uchiyama,; Ziehn, D.

Colored illustrations are from P. Bleeker's *Atlas Ichthylogique* or made by the Japanese artists Arita or Tomita.

ERRATA

p. 9, col. 1, line 8: Citation should read Greenwood, Rosen, Weitzman and Myers (1966)

p. 10: Adipose and anal fins of illustration of Malapteruridae were inadvertently removed. Correct illustration is on p. 156.

p. 30, col. 2: Caption should read: *Trogloglanis pattersoni*; (b) ventral view of head. (After Lundberg, 1982.)

p. 31, col. 2. Caption should read: *Noturus flavus*. (From Jordan & Evermann, 1902.)

p. 76, col. 1, line 36: Change *bi cirrhis* to *bicirrhis*.

p. 86: *O. miostoma* should be placed after *O. malabaricus* in list.

p. 98, col. 2, line 37: Change *Euthropiichthys* to *Eutropiichthys*.

p. 124, col. 2: Caption should read: *Laguvia asperus*; (b) ventral view of mouth. (After Misra, 1976; (b) After Jayaram, 1977.)

p. 128, col. 2, line 33: Change *Glyptosternon pectinopterum* to *Glyptothorax pectinopterum*.

p. 137, col. 1, lines 35 and 36: Add: (ventral fins may be absent)...

p. 144, col. 1, last line: Change logitudinally to longitudinally.

p. 165, col. 2: *Catharops* should read *Cathorops*.

p. 170, **Addenda**: Change *Arius midgley;* to *Arius midgleyi*.

p. 183, col. 1, line 11: A row of dots should precede generic name. ....*Acanthocleithron*

p. 197, col. 2, line 43: Change *cameronesis* to *cameronensis*.

p. 204, col. 1, line 11: Should read: only one or two species.

p. 220, col. 2, line 21: Should read: allied to or synonymous with *Autanodoras*,

p. 221, col. 2, lines 23 and 24: change Deltadoras to *Deltadoras*.

p. 223, col. 2, line 18: Add: (*Autanodoras bolivarensis*?).

p. 223, col. 2, line 21: Add: (?)

p. 226, col. 1, line 30: Should read: *Centromochlus*

p. 254, col. 1, line 28: Tube should be tubes.

p. 262, col. 1, upper caption: *glabrum* should read *glaber*.

p. 265, col. 1, line 8: Should read: *Leptoglanis* of Eigenmann is a synonym.

p. 268, col. 2, line 12: Should read: set conical teeth, those of the upper jaw in a

p. 297, caption: Change *papillosus* to *papillatus*.

p. 338, col. 1, caption: *Aspidoras* sp. Photo by Harald Schultz.

p. 338, col. 2, caption: *Aspidoras poecilus*. Photo by Harald Schultz.

p. 373, col. 1, line 27: Hypostominae should not be italicized.

p. 389, col. 2, line 23: Change *Chaetostomus* to *Chaetostoma*.

p. 394: Caption names should read *Megalancistrus aculeatus* and *Peckoltia vittata*.

p. 395: caption name should be *Chaetostoma breve*.

p. 402, col. 2, line 19: Should read: mostly in the smaller streams. The metaptery-

p. 404, col. 1, line 8: Should read: *Pseudotocinclus*, *Schizolecis*, and *Pseudotothyris*

p. 406, col. 2: Caption should read *Microlepidogaster taimensis*. (After Buckup, 1981.)

p. 438, col. 1, line 27: Should read: *L. surinamensis* Boeseman, 1982. Near

p. 454, col. 2, line 42: Böhlke, J. E. 1970.

p. 457, col. 2, line 31: Eigenmann, C. H. 1917.

p. 459, col. 2, line 23: Fowler, H. W.

p. 582, photo no. 5: Delete sp. after *Doras eigenmanni*.

p. 742: Genus name should read *Spectracanthus*.